W9-CEC-751

The World Book Encyclopedia

C-Ch Volume 3

World Book, Inc.
a Scott Fetzer company
Chicago London Sydney Toronto

The World Book Encyclopedia

Printed in the United States of America

ISBN 0-7166-0085-4

Library of Congress Catalog Card Number 84-50815

Cc

C is the third letter of our alphabet. It was also the third letter in the alphabet used by the Semites, who once lived in Syria and Palestine. *C* comes from the same letter as our *G* or *g*. The Semites named it *gimel*, their word for a throwing stick. The sign is possibly adapted from an Egyptian *hieroglyphic*, or picture symbol, for a boomerang. The Romans gave it its capital C form, and used it to indicate two sounds, that of *g* and that of *k*. The Romans finally made two letters by adding a vertical stroke to the C to make G. See ALPHABET.

Uses. *C* or *c* is about the 13th most frequently used letter in books, newspapers, and other printed material in English. As a grade, *C* means average on a school report card. In Roman numerals, *C* means *100;* in chemistry, the element *carbon*. Used with other letters, *C* may represent a number of words, such as *CBC*, for *Canadian Broadcasting Corporation; C.O.D.* for *cash on delivery;* and *L.C.* for *Library of Congress*. It is also used for *cent;* for *capacity* in electricity; for *Celsius* in temperature; and in Latin, for *circa*, meaning *about*.

Pronunciation. In English, C is pronounced two ways, like *s* as in *city* and *face*, and like *k* as in *camp*. For the *s* sound, a person places the tongue against the edges of the lower front teeth and forces breath through open lips. For the *k* sound, a person places the tongue back, with its sides touching the velum, or soft palate. The velum is closed, and the vocal cords do not vibrate. *C* is silent in such words as *indict* and *fascinate*. See PRONUNCIATION.

MARIANNE COOLEY

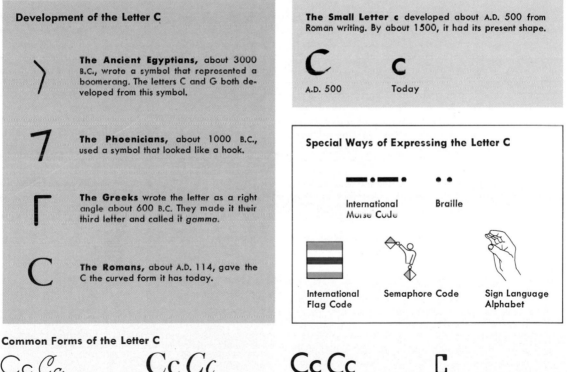

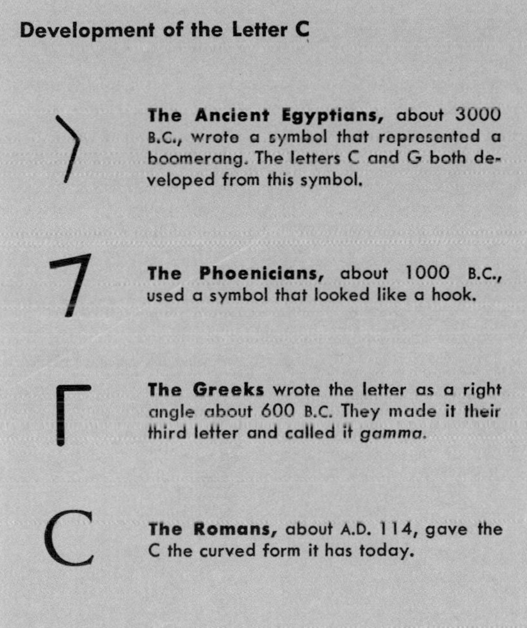

Development of the Letter C
The Ancient Egyptians, about 3000 B.C., wrote a symbol that represented a boomerang. The letters C and G both developed from this symbol.
The Phoenicians, about 1000 B.C., used a symbol that looked like a hook.
The Greeks wrote the letter as a right angle about 600 B.C. They made it their third letter and called it gamma.
C
The Romans, about A.D. 114, gave the C the curved form it has today.

The Small Letter c developed about A.D. 500 from Roman writing. By about 1500, it had its present shape.

c — A.D. 500

c — Today

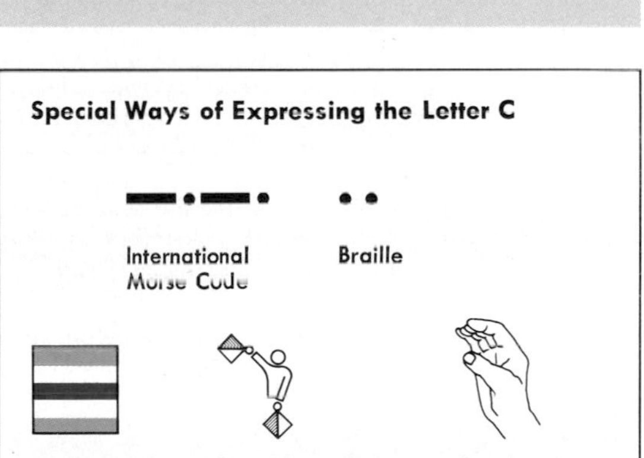

Special Ways of Expressing the Letter C
International Morse Code
Braille
International Flag Code
Semaphore Code
Sign Language Alphabet

Common Forms of the Letter C

Cc *Cc*

Handwritten Letters vary from person to person. *Manuscript* (printed) letters, *left*, have simple curves and straight lines. Cursive letters, *right*, have flowing lines.

Cc *Cc*

Roman Letters have small finishing strokes called *serifs* that extend from the main strokes. The type face shown above is Baskerville. The italic form appears at the right.

Cc *Cc*

Sans-Serif Letters are also called *gothic letters*. They have no serifs. The type face shown above is called Futura. The italic form of Futura appears at the right.

C

Computer Letters have special shapes. Computers can "read" these letters either optically or by means of the magnetic ink with which the letters may be printed.

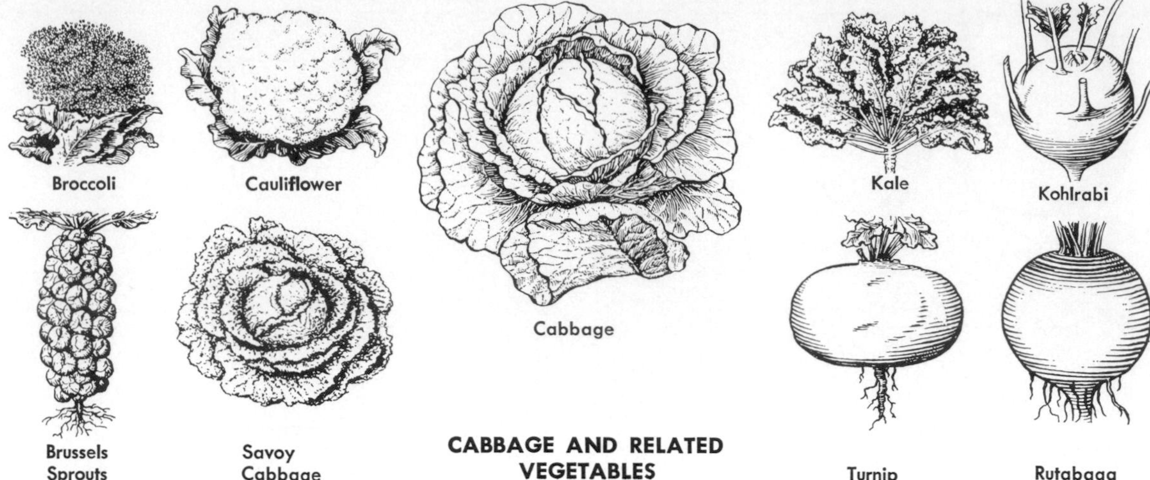

CABBAGE AND RELATED VEGETABLES

CAABA. See KAABA.

CAB. See PEDICAB; TAXICAB.

CABAL, *kuh BAL,* is a close-knit group of persons who work privately or secretly to carry out their own plans. The word has become a term of reproach, and implies plotting, scheming, and conspiring to overthrow legitimate authority.

The term *cabal* is frequently associated with five members of the Privy Council under King Charles II of England. These men had widely differing points of view, but they united their efforts to carry out certain of the king's more unpopular projects. By chance, the initials of their names—Clifford, Ashley, Buckingham, Arlington, and Lauderdale—spelled *cabal.*

The *Conway cabal* was a famous group of American army officers and Congressmen who plotted to remove George Washington from his post as commander-in-chief in 1777-1778. The cabal was named after Major General Thomas Conway. When the plot was made public, it aroused unfavorable reaction and strengthened Washington's position. W. M. SOUTHGATE

CABALA, *KAB uh luh,* or *kuh BAH luh,* was a mystical movement in Judaism that flourished throughout the Jewish communities of Europe during the Middle Ages. Cabalists sought hidden symbolic meanings in every word and letter of the Hebrew Bible. The *Zohar* contains the fundamental teachings of the Cabala.

See also HEBREW LANGUAGE AND LITERATURE (Medieval Works).

CABBAGE, *KAB ihj,* is a common vegetable native to England and northwestern France, but grown throughout Europe, Asia, and America. Other leafy vegetables closely related to the cabbage include cauliflower, Brussels sprouts, broccoli, and turnips.

Kinds of Cabbage. There are three kinds of cabbage, *white, red,* and *savoy.* The leaves of the plant grow close together to form a hard, round head. The leaves of the white and red cabbage are usually quite smooth, but have rather prominent veins. Those of the savoy appear wrinkled or blistered. White cabbage, which has pale green leaves, is the most popular type in the United States. People eat it raw in salads, cooked as a hot vegetable, or pickled as sauerkraut. Red cabbage, with its reddish-purple leaves, is not so popular as the white, but can be eaten raw or cooked. The savoy type perhaps has the best flavor. *Chinese,* or *celery, cabbage* is not a true cabbage. Its long, thin leaves form stalks similar to celery.

Cultivation. Cabbage grown commercially under normal conditions is a biennial. Farmers grow the plants one year and leave them in the ground during winter. In the spring the plants produce seed. Sometimes cabbage plants that have been subjected to cool weather (50° to 55° F., or 10° to 13° C), produce seeds rather than marketable heads. Many biennial plants show this response to cold weather. In warmer weather, about 60° to 70° F. (16° to 21° C), cabbage plants produce heads.

Cabbage seeds are small and look almost exactly like those of cauliflower, broccoli, or other similar plants. In regions with a mild climate, most farmers prefer to plant the seed directly in the field. They sow the seed in rows about 3 feet (91 centimeters) apart. When the young plants grow, workers thin the rows to allow a space of about 18 to 24 inches (46 to 61 centimeters) between the plants. In regions with short growing seasons, farmers may start the seeds in a greenhouse or hotbed. They plant the seeds in small, shallow boxes called *flats.* Shortly after the plants sprout, workers transplant them to larger flats, spacing them 2 inches (5 centimeters) apart. The plants grow for another 8 to 10 weeks, then workers transplant them to the field. How-

Cabbage Pests include cabbage butterflies, *top,* which develop from caterpillars, *lower left.* Another pest that injures cabbage plants is the harlequin cabbage bug, *lower right.*

USDA

ever, each plant must re-establish itself every time it is transplanted, so growth is retarded. Therefore, most farmers, particularly those in mild climates, seed cabbage directly in the field. But home gardeners often prefer to buy the small plants.

Insects and Diseases. Cabbage plants are attacked by aphids, cabbage loopers, maggots, cabbage worms, and other insects. Some insects eat the leaves, destroying the shape of the head. Insecticides can control insects.

Diseases that affect cabbages include blackleg, club root, mildew, mosaic, root rot, and yellows. Club root and yellows are soil-borne diseases. Scientists have developed cabbage varieties that are resistant to yellows.

Scientific Classification. Cabbage belongs to the mustard family, *Cruciferae*. It is genus *Brassica*, species *B. oleracea*, variety *capitata*. Chinese cabbage is classified as *B. pekinensis*. JOHN H. MACGILLIVRAY

Related Articles in WORLD BOOK include:

Broccoli	Chinese Cabbage	Mustard
Brussels Sprouts	Kale	Turnip
Cauliflower	Kohlrabi	

CABBAGE PALM is the name given to several kinds of palm trees whose young leaf buds can be eaten. The name is sometimes used to mean only a palm of the West Indies, a relative of the royal palm. Its bud is said to have the flavor of young cabbage. The palmetto palm of the Southeastern United States is sometimes called a cabbage palm. It has fan-shaped leaves and may grow from 30 to 50 feet (9 to 15 meters) or higher. The graceful cabbage palm of the West Indies may grow over 100 feet (30 meters) tall. The bud is formed of new leaves that are developing in the center of the leaf cluster and have not yet opened. The bud may be roasted, boiled, or eaten raw. The buds are not often eaten, because the trees are killed when the buds are removed. But many people consider them a delicacy. Canned buds of South American palms are imported.

Scientific Classification. The cabbage palms belong to the palm family, *Palmae*. The West Indian palm is genus *Roystonea*, species *R. oleracea*. The common palmetto is *Sabal palmetto*. HAROLD E. MOORE, JR.

See also PALM; PALMETTO.

CABELL, *CAB'l,* **JAMES BRANCH** (1879-1958), was an American author. His fame depended largely on unsuccessful attempts to suppress his novel *Jurgen* (1919). *Jurgen* is one of a series of novels written between 1904 and 1929, which deal with a romanticized place called *Poictesme*. Cabell was deeply interested in genealogy and aristocratic ideals of the conservative South. Some of his works include *The Eagle's Shadow* (1904); *Cream of the Jest* (1917); *Beyond Life* (1919); *The Way of Ecben* (1929); *Hamlet Had an Uncle* (1940); and *The St. Johns* (1943), written with A. J. Hanna. After he finished the Poictesme novels, he announced that James Branch Cabell would write no more. All his books after that time were signed "Branch Cabell." Cabell was born in Richmond, Va. ARTHUR MIZENER

CABEZA DE VACA, *kah VAY thah thay VAH kah,* **ÁLVAR NÚÑEZ** (1490?-1557?), was a Spanish explorer in both North and South America. In 1528, as a member of an expedition attempting to colonize Florida, he was shipwrecked on an island off the Texas coast. He and a few companions were prisoners of the Indians for several years. They finally reached Mexico on foot. His reports that great wealth lay north of Mexico led to the expedition of Marcos de Niza into what is now Arizona and New Mexico, and to those of Francisco Coronado and Hernando de Soto.

In 1540, Cabeza was appointed governor of Paraguay. On the way to Paraguay, he discovered the Iguaçu Falls in Brazil. He was a failure as governor and the colonists later deposed him. RICHARD A. BARTLETT

CABINDA is a district of Angola and a major oil-producing area. It is separated from the rest of Angola by the Congo River and the western end of Zaire (see ANGOLA [map]). Cabinda covers 2,807 square miles (7,270 kilometers) and has a population of about 81,000. The district's capital and largest city, also called Cabinda, is an important seaport. Cabinda produces most of Angola's oil, the nation's chief export. Cabinda also produces coffee, palm oil, and timber.

Black Africans inhabited the Cabinda area more than 2,000 years ago. During the 1500's, Portuguese settlers claimed possession of Cabinda and other parts of Angola. In the 1960's, the discovery of oil off Cabinda's coast and on the mainland gave the area new economic importance. Angola—including Cabinda—was controlled by Portugal until 1975, when it gained independence. Members of a nationalist movement in Cabinda tried to gain independence from Angola. However, Angolan forces, supported by Cuban troops, defeated most of these rebels. Zaire has also claimed Cabinda. L. H. GANN

See also ANGOLA (History).

CABINET consists of a group of advisers who help the head of a government establish policies and make decisions. It is nearly always composed of the officials who supervise the executive or administrative operations of a government. These officials usually have the title of *minister*, or *secretary*, of a department or office. The term *cabinet* is also used to describe a system of government in which officials who direct the executive work of the government are directly responsible to the parliament or legislature.

Cabinet of the United States

Development of the Cabinet. The Constitution of the United States makes no mention of a Cabinet. In describing the powers of the President, it states that "he may require the opinion, in writing, of the principal officer in each of the executive departments, upon any subject relating to the duties of their respective offices . . ." In 1789, Congress established three departments—State, War, and Treasury—and the office of the attorney general. President George Washington frequently consulted with the department heads and the attorney general. The first recorded meeting of this group, held in 1791, included the three secretaries and the Vice-President. Later, the attorney general and the secretary of the navy also attended the meetings.

By the early 1800's, the Cabinet was commonly regarded as consisting of the heads of the existing executive offices. But not until 1907 did a federal statute first use the term *cabinet*. Some Presidents discontinued Cabinet meetings. Andrew Jackson, for example, had a group of personal advisers known as the *kitchen cabinet*.

Membership in the Cabinet is determined by the President. Today, most people refer to the heads of

The President's Cabinet usually meets with the Chief Executive about once a week in the Cabinet Room of the White House. The Cabinet includes the heads of the executive departments. The Vice President usually attends Cabinet meetings, and sometimes other officials of the executive branch are invited to these sessions to advise the President on important government matters.

The White House

the 13 executive departments as "the Cabinet." These heads are the secretaries of agriculture; commerce; defense; education; energy; health and human services; housing and urban development; the interior; labor; state; transportation; and the treasury; and the attorney general.

Various Presidents have asked other officials in the executive branch of government to take part in Cabinet meetings regularly. In 1961, for example, President John F. Kennedy began the custom of having the U.S. ambassador to the United Nations attend Cabinet meetings. The President calls Cabinet meetings, usually once a week, in the Cabinet Room of the White House.

As department heads, Cabinet members are legal officers of the federal government. The President appoints them with the advice and consent of the Senate, and may dismiss them at any time. They are responsible for administering their department and carrying out government policies. Each Cabinet member receives a salary of $82,900 as the head of an executive department. By custom, Cabinet members resign when a new President takes office. This procedure enables the new chief executive to select his or her own Cabinet.

Policymaking Role of the Cabinet has varied with different Presidents. That role diminished in the 1960's and early 1970's. During those years, the Executive Office and the White House staff grew in size and importance. The President relied increasingly on smaller advisory groups in making important foreign and domestic policy decisions. In the early 1970's, for example, national economic policy was largely determined by four persons. Of this group, only the secretary of the treasury belonged to the Cabinet. The others were the chief of the Council of Economic Advisers, the director of the Office of Management and Budget, and the head of the Federal Reserve Board. In matters of foreign policy and defense, the National Security Council played a more important part than the Cabinet.

See the separate articles on each executive department, such as STATE, DEPARTMENT OF. For the order in which Cabinet members succeed to the presidency, see PRESIDENTIAL SUCCESSION. For the flags of the Cabinet members, see FLAG (color pictures: Flags of the United States Government). For lists of Cabinet members, see the tables with the biographies of Presidents of the United States. For example, see NIXON, RICHARD M. (table: Vice Presidents and Cabinet).

The Cabinet System of Government

The cabinet system of government is often called the *parliamentary system of government*. The officers who direct the executive work of the government are directly responsible to the *parliament* (legislature). In some countries with cabinet systems, the cabinet officials are members of the parliament.

The official head of the government, such as a king, queen, or president, selects the *prime minister*, or *premier*, from the parliament. The prime minister has executive authority in the government (see PRIME MINISTER). Advisers to the prime minister help form the ministry (see MINISTRY). If one party has a majority in the parliament, the leader of that party usually becomes prime minister. The prime minister selects members of his or her party to head the departments of the government. If no party has a majority, the monarch or president picks a person who can gain the support of a *coalition*, or combination of parties (see COALITION). In such a cabinet, the prime minister divides the cabinet posts among members of the supporting parties so that the cabinet will have the support of a majority in parliament.

A cabinet resigns if it no longer has the support of the parliament. For example, the parliament may refuse to approve a program that the prime minister considers basic. Or it may vote "no confidence" in the cabinet. In each case, the cabinet resigns. The prime minister or his or her successor forms a new cabinet that has the support of parliament. In Great Britain, a prime minister who believes that the people support his or her program can dissolve Parliament instead of resigning. The people are then asked to elect a new one. Even with the support of Parliament, a British Cabinet cannot stay in power indefinitely. A prime minister must call a general election after five years in office. Canada and most Commonwealth and European nations have the cabinet system of government. CHARLES E. JACOB

See also the Government section of articles on countries that have the cabinet system of government, such as GREAT BRITAIN (Government).

CABINETMAKER is a skilled woodworker who makes or finishes woodwork, including the furniture, fixtures, and built-in parts of a home, office, store, or laboratory. A cabinetmaker must know how to design, shape, assemble, and repair all these features. The cabinetmaker's skills include inlaying, doweling, carving, and finishing. Much of the work is not concerned with cabinets. For example, a cabinetmaker may have to design, construct, and install a built-in ironing board, or some other type of built-in fixture. PETER E. TERZICK

See also CARPENTRY.

CABLE is a unit of nautical measurement. It is commonly called a *cable's length*, because it was once the approximate length of a ship's *cable*, or anchor chain. The length varies. The British cable is 608 feet (185 meters). A U.S. cable is 720 feet (219 meters). See also WEIGHTS AND MEASURES (Length and Distance).

A.T. & T. Co.

An Undersea Cable is pulled from the C.S. *Long Lines, above,* which can carry and lay 2,000 miles (3,200 kilometers) of cable.

A.T. & T. Co.

A Land Cable is placed underground to provide a constant temperature and to protect the cable from weather damage.

CABLE, in communications, is one or more protected *conductors* (wires or tubes) that carry messages in the form of electrical signals. Cables carry telegraph and telephone messages. They also transmit radio and television programs, pictures, maps, and handwritten, printed, or coded materials.

Cables make quick communication possible over long distances. A single telephone cable can carry 4,200 conversations across the Atlantic Ocean at one time. A land cable can carry up to 132,000 telephone messages at a time. Telegraph messages travel over cables at the rate of 2,500 words a minute.

The chief intercontinental cable routes run under the north Atlantic Ocean. Eight transatlantic cable systems link North America and Europe. Cables also link North America with Asia, Australia, Central America, and South America. Messages may travel much farther by connection with land cables.

Most communications cables consist of several parts. These are electrical conductors; a strengthening or supporting material, such as armor wire; insulation to protect the conductors; and an outer covering, usually of *jute* (a fiber) or plastic. Messages travel along the conductors in the form of electrical signals. At the destination, special receiving equipment changes the signals back into audio or visual form.

Kinds of Cables

Undersea Cables lie on the ocean floor. Almost all long-distance undersea cables in use today are *coaxial*

The contributors of this article are Lowell Broomall, Senior Executive Vice-President, Western Union International; and C. C. Duncan, former Vice-President for Overseas Operations, American Telephone and Telegraph Company.

UNDERSEA TELEPHONE CABLES

This map shows the places connected by undersea telephone cables. These cables also provide telegraph and teleprinter service. Many older undersea telegraph cables still exist, but these are being abandoned in favor of the new telephone cables.

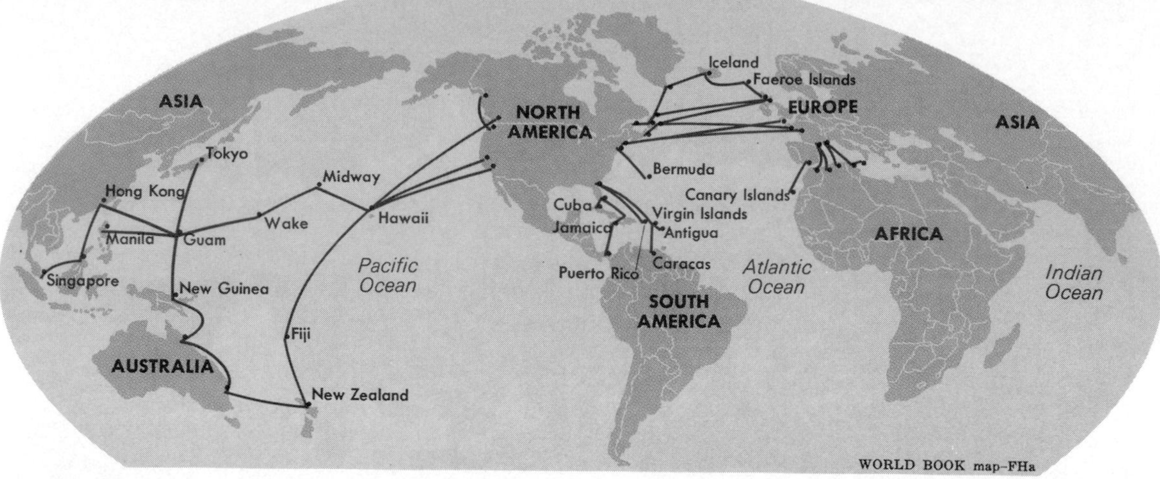

cables. Undersea coaxial cables have two copper conductors, which carry electricity. The smaller one runs through the center of the larger one. These together form one *coaxial*. They are so named because both conductors have the same *axis* (center). An insulating material called a *dielectric* separates the two conductors. Steel wires in the center strengthen the cable. A protective jute or plastic jacket forms the cable's outer layer. Undersea coaxial cables have only one coaxial.

Coaxial cables with special equipment called *repeaters*, or *amplifiers*, can transmit both telegraph and telephone messages, as well as various other forms of information. The newest undersea cables in service are equipped with two-way repeaters spaced about 5 miles (9.5 kilometers) apart. Two-way repeaters make it possible for one cable to carry messages in both directions. Repeaters greatly increase the number of frequencies that can be received over the cable and also strengthen the electrical current in the cable.

Land Cables carry local and long-distance telephone conversations, and television and radio programs. They are also used to transmit pictures, maps, charts, and coded, typed, and handwritten messages (see FACSIMILE; TELETYPEWRITER). Some cables in cities have over 4,000 conductors to carry local telephone calls.

Coaxial cables are often used to speed communication over long distances. A single cable may have as many as 22 coaxial tubes. The coaxial tubes work in pairs. One carries voices in one direction, while another carries the voice from the opposite direction. If voice signals are to be clear, they must be kept at a constant level. Signals are affected by temperature changes. Most coaxial cables are placed underground to provide a stable temperature and reduce weather damage.

Development of Land Cables

Thousands of telephones came into use in the late 1800's. Poles and housetops could no longer hold all

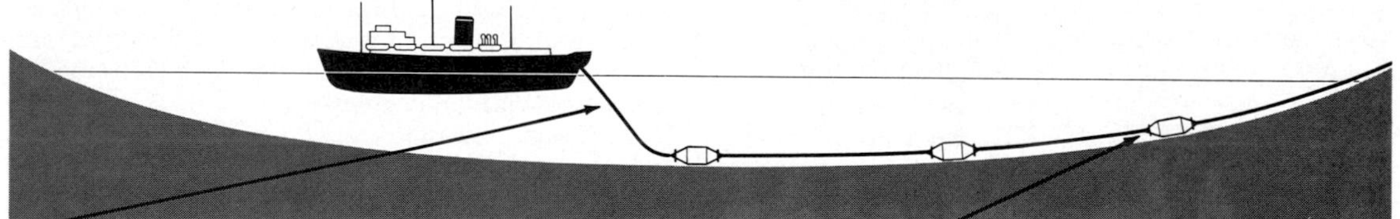

Undersea Cables have two copper tubes that serve as electrical conductors. Steel wires in the center strengthen the cable.

Repeaters increase the number of frequencies that can be received over an undersea cable and strengthen its electrical current.

Cutaway drawings courtesy of A.T.& T. Co.

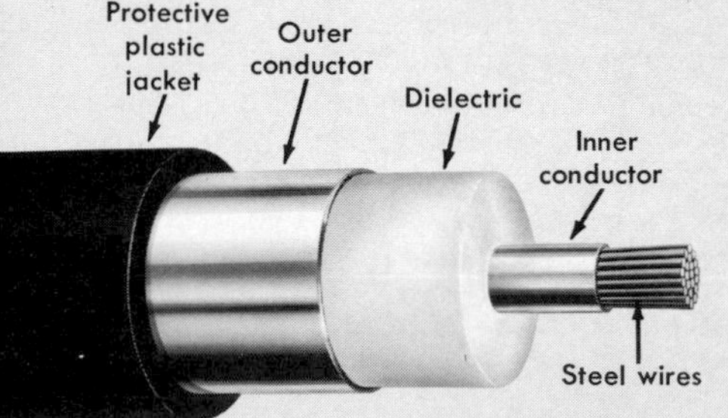

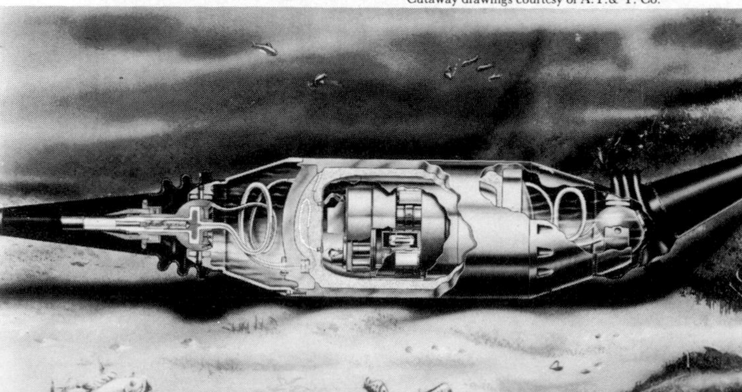

the single telephone lines, and a way had to be found to group the wires in some sort of bundle. Overhead cables were first used to carry telephone wires in the late 1880's. An underground cable was first used between New York City and Newark, N.J., in 1902.

A coaxial cable was first used commercially in 1941. It provided telephone service between Stevens Point, Wis., and Minneapolis, Minn. The cable had only four coaxial tubes and provided 480 two-way telephone circuits. Since then, the size and message capacity of coaxial cables have greatly increased. In the mid-1960's, repeaters equipped with small electronic devices called *transistors* were tested, and proved effective. A 22-tube cable with transistorized repeaters can provide up to 132,000 telephone circuits. See TRANSISTOR.

Development of Undersea Cables

Early Cables. During the 1840's, many attempts were made to lay cables under water. All attempts were unsuccessful until cable makers began using a rubber-like substance called *gutta-percha* as insulation (see GUTTA-PERCHA). Two English brothers, Jacob and John Brett, laid a gutta-percha cable under the English Channel in 1851. Cyrus W. Field, an American businessman, headed a company that laid an undersea cable in 1856. It ran across Cabot Strait, from Cape Ray, Nfld., to Cape Breton Island, N.S.

The Atlantic Telegraph Cable. In the early 1850's, Matthew Fontaine Maury and other U.S. Navy engineers discovered that the ocean floor between Newfoundland and Ireland is fairly level and is made up of soft mud. This part of the ocean was therefore an ideal route for a transatlantic cable.

In 1856, Field organized the Atlantic Telegraph Company and began the plans to lay a cable from Newfoundland to Ireland. He worked nine years to complete this project. His first two cables broke. In 1858, the U.S. warship *Niagara* and the British warship *Agamemnon* laid a cable for Field that did not break. But it failed after only four weeks of service. Signals sent over this cable became extremely weak and distorted by the time they reached the receiving end. But they could be read with the aid of a receiving device called a *mirror*, or *reflecting, galvanometer*. This instrument, invented by Lord Kelvin, operated on the same principles as the D'Arsonval galvanometer that is used today (see GALVANOMETER [The D'Arsonval Galvanometer]).

In 1865, Field made his fourth attempt to lay a cable under the Atlantic. He rented the British steamship *Great Eastern*, then the largest ship afloat. The cable broke and sank when the project was almost completed. Success came finally, on July 27, 1866. Crewmen aboard the *Great Eastern* laid a cable that stretched from Valentia, Ireland, to Heart's Content, Nfld. Signals traveled clearly over the cable. About six weeks later, the cable that had been lost in 1865 was recovered from the floor of the ocean. It was repaired and put in working order. This cable also was laid between Valentia and Heart's Content.

The Atlantic cables marked the beginning of fast communication across the seas. They made it possible to send a message and receive an answer in only a few hours. By 1900, 15 cables had been laid across the Atlantic. By the 1930's, improved sending and receiving techniques and better cables made it possible to send up to 400 words a minute. Messages could be sent over cables at 2,500 words a minute by the mid-1960's.

Undersea Telephone Cables. Early undersea cables could transmit telegraph signals, but they could not carry the wide frequency of vibrations that make up speech. Coaxial cables with built-in repeaters made long-distance telephoning by cable possible.

The first transatlantic telephone cable was laid in 1956. It stretched 2,250 miles (3,621 kilometers), from Clarenville, Nfld., to Oban, Scotland. Other cables were laid in the next few years. Since 1959, channels on most coaxial cables have also been made available to international telegraph companies.

Transatlantic telephone cables laid before the 1960's can carry messages in only one direction. These early systems consist of two cables laid side by side. Steel wires are wrapped around the cables to strengthen and protect them. The cables have flexible one-way repeaters spaced about 40 miles (64 kilometers) apart.

At first, these cable systems carried 36 telephone calls at one time. But improved terminal equipment later permitted 48 calls. By 1960, almost 100 calls could be made over the same cable at one time. This increase resulted from terminal equipment of new design and a complex switching system known as TASI. When a person pauses in conversation, TASI places this momentarily unused conversational path at the disposal of someone who at that very instant is starting to speak. TASI switches voice signals from channel to channel wherever it finds one idle.

In 1963, a single two-way cable was developed to provide 138 telephone circuits across the Atlantic Ocean. This single-cable system is effective at distances up to 3,500 miles (5,630 kilometers). A special cable-laying ship, the C.S. *Long Lines*, was built to lay these cables. The single-cable system is described in the *Undersea Cables* section of this article.

In the mid-1960's, Bell Telephone Laboratories developed a transistorized two-way repeater for the single-cable system. This system can provide up to 845 telephone circuits over a distance of 4,000 miles (6,400 kilometers). A system providing 4,200 telephone circuits over a transatlantic route was developed in the mid-1970's.

LOWELL BROOMALL and C. C. DUNCAN

Related Articles in WORLD BOOK include:

Coaxial Cable
Field (Cyrus West)
Kelvin, Lord
Maury, Matthew F.
Telegraph
Telephone

CABLE, GEORGE WASHINGTON (1844-1925), an American author, became known for his books about old French New Orleans. His works include the collection of short stories *Old Creole Days* (1879), the novelette *Madame Delphine* (1881), and the novels *The Grandissimes* (1880) and *The Cavalier* (1901). Cable was born in New Orleans, La., and fought for the Confederacy during the Civil War. But he later moved to Massachusetts, where he did much humanitarian work, particularly for blacks.

EDWARD WAGENKNECHT

CABLE CAR is a vehicle that is pulled by a cable, and carries passengers or freight. It provides a fast, safe way to carry a load up and down a steep grade.

Andrew S. Hallidie invented the cable car in 1873 to be used on the steep hills of San Francisco. The cable cars of San Francisco have since become a landmark and tourist attraction. They run on rails and are pulled by an endless steel cable moving in a slot beneath the street surface. Another type of cable car runs on cables suspended between towers. Many ski lifts are of this type. The world's longest cable-car line transports ore 60 miles (97 kilometers) from a Swedish mine.

See also PACIFIC ISLANDS (picture: The Spectacular Scenery of the Pacific Islands).

CABLE TELEVISION. See TELEVISION (Cable Television Systems).

CABOT, *KAB uht,* is the family name of two navigators, father and son, who made important explorations in the Western Hemisphere.

John Cabot (1450?-1498?) made the first English voyage to North America. His voyage, in 1497, gave England a claim to the mainland of North America and led to the founding of the English colonies in America.

Cabot was born in Genoa, Italy. His name in Italian was Giovanni Caboto. As a boy, Cabot moved to Venice, Italy, with his parents. He grew up there and became a mapmaker and a trader. He sailed the Mediterranean Sea between Venice and Egypt, trading Italian goods for spices from the Far East. Cabot married and had three sons. The family moved to Bristol, England, in the 1480's, and was living there when Christopher Columbus made his historic voyage to America for Spain in 1492.

People assumed that Columbus had reached the Indies (now called the East Indies) in Asia. Cabot believed there was a shorter route than Columbus had taken. He dreamed of crossing the Atlantic Ocean farther north and bringing spices and jewels from Asia.

Cabot asked King John II of Portugal and King Ferdinand of Spain to finance a voyage, but both refused to help him. In 1496, King Henry VII of England gave Cabot permission to sail in the service of England. Cabot agreed to give the king a fifth of the profit from any discoveries. Bristol businessmen helped Cabot pay for the voyage.

Oil painting (1906) by Ernest Board; City Art Gallery, Bristol, England

John and Sebastian Cabot sailed from Bristol, England, in May 1497, on the first English voyage to North America. They returned in August 1497.

In May 1497, Cabot sailed west from Bristol in a small ship, the *Matthew*, with a crew of 18 men. He sighted land on June 24. Cabot had probably reached either the island of Newfoundland or Cape Breton Island, which is now part of Nova Scotia. He claimed the land for England. Cabot believed he had reached Asia. Although he did not find the riches he had hoped for, he did find the important fishing area now called the Grand Banks. The fish there were so plentiful that they could be caught by lowering a basket into the sea.

Cabot returned to England in August 1497, and announced that he had reached Asia. He was called "The Great Admiral," and the king paid him a reward and gave him an annual pension.

In 1498, the king and several merchants paid for a second voyage. Cabot sailed from Bristol with five ships, intending to explore southward from the place where he had landed. Storms forced one ship back to England. No one knows what happened to Cabot and the other four vessels. Most historians believe he was lost at sea. Some think he explored part of the eastern coast of what is now the United States and returned to England.

Additional Resources

MORISON, SAMUEL E. *The European Discovery of America: The Northern Voyages,* A.D. *500-1600.* Oxford, 1971. Includes a chapter on Cabot's voyages.

WILLIAMSON, JAMES A. *The Cabot Voyages and Bristol Discoveries Under Henry VII.* Cambridge, 1962.

Sebastian Cabot (1484?-1557), the second son of John Cabot, sailed to North America and explored its eastern coastline. He also made a voyage of exploration to South America.

Cabot was born in Venice and grew up in Bristol, England. He became a navigator and mapmaker and may have accompanied his father on his first North American voyage in 1497. About 1508, Cabot sailed to North America in command of two English ships. He sought a Northwest Passage—that is, a route to Asia through the Arctic Ocean. He reached the mouth of Hudson Bay in what is now Canada and thought he had found the Northwest Passage. But his crew refused to sail farther west. Cabot sailed south along the coast of America and then returned to England.

In 1526, Cabot sailed from Spain with four ships. Spanish business people paid for the voyage hoping that he would bring riches from the Spice Islands, in what is now Indonesia. But Cabot explored the eastern coast of South America and inland, hoping to find gold. After finding none, he returned to Spain in 1530. LESLIE HARRIS

CABRAL, *kuh BRAHL,* **PEDRO ÁLVARES,** *PAY throo AHL vuh reesh* (1467?-1528?), was a Portuguese navigator who sailed to Brazil in 1500 and claimed it for Portugal. His voyage helped Portugal develop a large overseas empire in the 1500's.

Cabral was born near Covilhã, Portugal. He was educated at the royal court and became a member of the King's Council. In 1499, King Manuel I appointed him commander of a fleet to carry on the work of Portuguese explorer Vasco da Gama (see DA GAMA, VASCO). Cabral probably had never sailed a ship before.

Cabral and his fleet of 13 ships sailed from Belem, near Lisbon, on March 9, 1500. He headed for India and planned to follow the route taken by Da Gama.

The fleet sailed southwest and passed the Canary and Cape Verde islands. The sailors hoped for winds that would carry them around the Cape of Good Hope at the bottom of the African continent. But for some reason, probably the weather, the fleet sailed off course.

On April 22, the men sighted what is now southeastern Brazil. Cabral claimed the area for Portugal. The land lay within Portuguese territory as determined by the Treaty of Tordesillas in 1494 (see LINE OF DEMARCATION). Cabral had lost one ship, and another returned to Portugal with news of the landing. The remaining ships stayed in Brazil for eight days and then continued the voyage to India.

On May 24, a storm scattered the fleet. Four of the vessels were lost, but one reached Madagascar. The other six ships met at Mozambique and followed the African coast northward. The fleet crossed the Indian Ocean and arrived in Calicut, India, on September 13. There, many crew members were killed in a battle with a band of Arab merchants. Cabral's fleet then sailed to the Indian towns of Cochin and Cannanore, where the ships were loaded with spices.

The fleet returned to Lisbon on June 23, 1501. Manuel I considered Cabral for command of another expedition to India but chose Da Gama instead. Cabral then retired from royal service. JOHN PARKER

CABRILLO, *kah BREE yoh,* **JUAN RODRÍGUEZ,** *hwahn roh THREE gayth* (? -1543), led the first European expedition to explore the coast of what is now California. His explorations aided the Spanish in the settling of California.

Cabrillo was born in Portugal. Scholars know little about his early life. He came to Cuba about 1520 and joined the Spanish army there. Cabrillo participated in the Spanish conquest of what is now Mexico in 1521 and of present-day Guatemala in 1523 and 1524.

In 1541, Antonio de Mendoza, the Spanish ruler of Mexico, ordered Cabrillo to explore the Pacific coast north of Mexico. Cabrillo commanded two ships, the *San Salvador* and the *Victoria.* The expedition set out from Navidad, Mexico, near Manzanillo, in June 1542. Three months later, the explorers reached San Diego Bay. They then continued to sail northward along the coast and met Indians from several villages. Some of the Indians gave Cabrillo fish and other supplies.

In November 1542, a storm blew Cabrillo's ships past the Golden Gate, the entrance to San Francisco Bay. Soon afterward, the expedition turned south. The explorers anchored at San Miguel Island, about 50 miles (80 kilometers) west of Santa Barbara. Cabrillo died on San Miguel Island. JOHN PARKER

See also CALIFORNIA (Spanish and English Exploration).

CABRILLO NATIONAL MONUMENT, *kuh BRIHL oh,* in San Diego, Calif., honors the Portuguese explorer Juan Rodríguez Cabrillo, who sailed into San Diego Bay on Sept. 28, 1542, while serving Spain. The monument was established in 1913. For area, see NATIONAL PARK SYSTEM (table: National Monuments).

CABRINI, *kuh BREE nee,* **SAINT FRANCES XAVIER,** *ZAY vih ur* (1850-1917), was the first United States citizen to be made a saint by the Roman Catholic Church. She was *canonized* (declared a saint) in 1946. In 1950, Pope Pius XII named her patron saint of emigrants.

She was born Maria Francesca Cabrini in Lombardy, Italy, the 13th and youngest child of a farmer. Her family was seriously religious, and early in her life she wanted to be a missionary in China. She was trained to be a schoolteacher. When she was 30, she established the Missionary Sisters of the Sacred Heart, an order originally formed for the instruction of poor children.

Cabrini League
Saint Frances Cabrini

In 1889, the nun came to the United States, where she immediately displayed the courage, hope, vision, and endurance of a pioneer. She lived in New York City and Chicago, and traveled in Latin America. She and her followers opened several charitable institutions, including orphanages, schools, and free clinics. She founded Columbus Hospital in New York City in 1892 and Columbus Hospital in Chicago in 1905. In 1909, she became a U.S. citizen.

Four miracles were credited to her from the time she died until she was canonized. Her feast day is December 22. Her body is in Saint Frances Xavier Cabrini High School in New York City.

MATTHEW A. FITZSIMONS and FULTON J. SHEEN

CACAO, *kuh KAY oh,* is an evergreen tree whose seeds, or beans, are used to make chocolate and cocoa. It may grow 25 feet (7.6 meters) high. Its fruit is a melonlike pod that may be 12 inches (30 centimeters) long. The cacao seeds, imbedded in the pod, are about the size of lima beans. They range from light brown to purple. Cacao trees are cultivated in Central and South America, the East and West Indies, and West Africa. The beans supply not only chocolate and cocoa, but also cocoa butter, used in candies and medicines. The

Hershey Foods Corp.
The Cacao Tree bears seed pods on short stems close to the trunk. The pods contain the beans used to make chocolate and cocoa.

Allan D. Cruickshank, NAS

The Barrel Cactus has tough, curved spines that Indians once used as fishhooks. The plant's juicy pulp has saved the life of many thirsty travelers in the desert.

David Muench

The Organ-Pipe Cactus has stems that resemble the pipes of an organ. It may grow 25 feet (7.6 meters) high. Some people enclose their property with rows of these cactuses.

Norman Myers, Bruce Coleman Inc.

The Old Man Cactus has a shaggy coat of white hair that shields it from the sun. This thornless cactus is a popular house plant.

E. S. Ross

The Prickly Pear has thorny, leaflike stems. This cactus grows in dry or rocky ground in many parts of North America. The plant bears pear-shaped fruit that is good to eat.

Alan Pitcairn from Grant Heilman

The Jumping Cholla has a false reputation for leaping at passers-by. Its thorny branches break off easily and cling to people and animals. The spines may cause painful wounds.

people of Mexico and Central America once used cacao beans as money.

See also CHOCOLATE.

Scientific Classification. Cacao trees belong to the sterculia family, Sterculiaceae. They are classified as genus *Theobroma*, species *T. cacao*. WILSON POPENOE

CACHALOT. See SPERM WHALE.

CACKLING GOOSE. See CANADA GOOSE.

CACOMISTLE. See RINGTAIL.

CACTUS is any one of a family of plants, most of which live in North America. Many of the more than 1,000 different kinds of known cactus grow in Mexico. In the United States, cactuses are found in greatest abundance in the Southwest.

Most cactuses live in dry regions. They are well suited to places with little rainfall. In most other plants, the food for the plant is made in the leaves, and the leaves also give off water. In the cactus, most of the leaves have disappeared so that the plant may better hold its moisture. Cactus stems have taken over the task of making food for the plant. These stems can store water. *Barrel cactuses* are examples of plants able to store water. If the top of a barrel cactus is sliced off and the pulp inside is mashed, several quarts of juice can be obtained from the plant.

Most cactus plants are protected by sharp bristles and spines. The spines of the cactus help protect it against animals that live in the desert. Were it not for these spines, the cactus plants would be eaten and die out. Cactus spines grow from parts of the plant called *areoles*, which look like tiny cushions. The areoles are arranged in definite patterns over the surface of the plants. The new branches and beautiful flowers of the cactus also grow, like the spines, from the areoles of the plant.

The roots of the cactus plant are covered with a corklike bark and lie close to the surface. They spread far out so they can catch the water from light rains and quick floods that may take place in desert areas. A cactus plant only 3 feet (0.9 meter) tall may have roots over 10 feet (3 meters) long.

Kinds of Cactuses. Cactuses differ greatly in shape and size. Some are low, weak bushes. Others grow like vines with roots that are exposed to the air. Some are

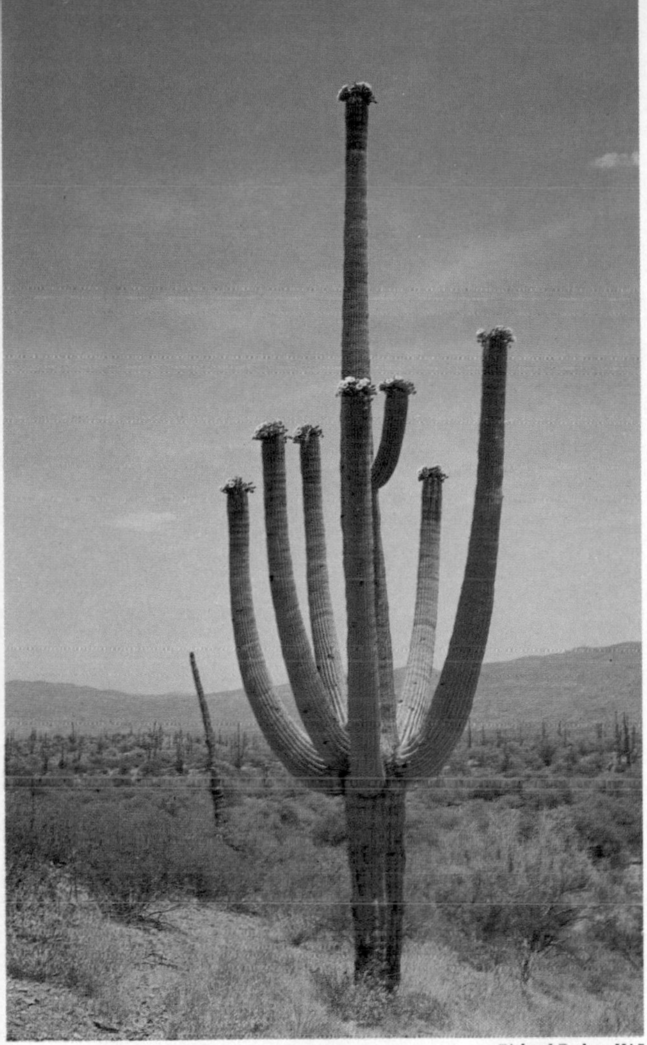

Richard Parker, NAS

The Saguaro, or Giant Cactus, may reach a height of 50 feet (15 meters) and a diameter of 2½ feet (76 centimeters). In spring, flowers bloom on the tips of its branches and stem.

straight or bushy, while others grow as large as trees.

The *saguaro*, or giant cactus, ranks as the largest cactus in the United States. It grows in forests or scattered groups in the lands that drain into the Gulf of California. Indians of Arizona use the dried woody ribs of the saguaro stems for fuel and for making frames for their houses. The fruits of this cactus ripen in June and July. The Indians eat these fruits fresh or as preserves.

Many beautiful smaller plants are members of the *Cereus* group. These include the night-blooming cereus, whose large fragrant flowers open only at night.

A kind of cactus called the *old man* cactus is covered with long white hairs. It is often grown indoors.

A small cactus called *peyote* grows in northern Mexico and southern Texas. This cactus contains a powerful drug used by certain Indians in religious rites.

The people of Mexico find uses for the many kinds of cactuses that grow in their country. The joints of a flat-leaved cactus called *opuntia* are eaten boiled or fried. The flowers can be made into salads. The juicy fruits of this kind of cactus are eaten raw or cooked. The seeds of many different kinds of cactuses are ground up into a meal and made into cakes. The people grow the bushy cactuses in hedges around their houses.

Several kinds of opuntia, called *chollas*, grow in the southwestern United States. Their joints have barbed spines. These spines break off easily and cause great pain when they work into human or animal flesh.

Luther Burbank, the plant breeder, developed a spineless cactus that proved to be a useful source of food for both human beings and animals.

Cactuses as House Plants. Small kinds of cactuses are popular house plants, because they can live in dry, artificial heat better than most other plants. Cactuses grown indoors should be potted in light, sandy soil with good drainage.

Scientific Classification. Cactus plants belong to the cactus family, *Cactaceae*. The peyote is genus *Lophophora*, species *L. williamsii*.

EDMUND C. JAEGER

Related Articles in WORLD BOOK include:

Arizona (Natural Resources; color picture: Giant Saguaro Cactus)
Bud (picture)
Mescaline
Organ Pipe Cactus National Monument
Plant (Water Storage; pictures)
Prickly Pear
Saguaro
Saguaro National Monument

CADDIS FLY. See TRICHOPTERA.

CADDO INDIANS, *KAD oh,* formed a group of allied tribes that once lived in Louisiana, Arkansas, and Texas. Caddo is an abbreviation of the native name *Kadohadacho*, meaning *real chiefs*.

The Caddo lived in large houses of post framework covered with grass. Each house held several families. The Caddo cultivated fields of corn, beans, and pumpkins, and collected wild grapes and berries. They also hunted deer, bear, wild fowl, and buffalo. The men cut and traded the wood of the Osage orange, the favorite bowwood among tribes of the Western plains. The women made excellent pottery. Caddo chiefs were highly respected, and rode from place to place on litters or on the shoulders of their subjects.

Early Spanish explorers learned to respect the Caddo warriors, who bravely hurled fire-hardened lances at the invading soldiers. But explorers who came from Mexico about a hundred years later, in the middle 1600's, knew these Indians as *Texas* or *Tejas*, meaning *friends*. When French explorers met the Caddo in the 1680's, they found these Indians riding swift Spanish horses. During the 1700's, warfare between the Spanish and French in Caddo territory killed many of these Indians, and most of the remainder moved to Texas.

In 1855, the U.S. government assigned the Caddo a reservation on the Brazos River in Texas. They were moved in 1859 to southwestern Oklahoma, where their descendants still live.

JOHN C. EWERS

See also TEXAS (Indian Days).

CADENCE is rhythm of sound or motion. In music, it is the closing air or tune of a song, or of a phrase or movement within the composition. In present-day music, a *perfect cadence* is the progression of the dominant chord to the tonic.

CADET, *kuh DEHT,* is a student in officer's training at the United States Military and Air Force academies. Students in the United States Navy and Air Force flying schools are also called cadets. Until 1902, students at the United States Naval Academy were called *naval cadets*. English and Canadian military academies also use the term. Some private military schools call their students cadets. *Cadet* is a French word meaning *younger son*. CHARLES B. MACDONALD

See also UNITED STATES AIR FORCE ACADEMY; UNITED STATES MILITARY ACADEMY.

CADILLAC, *KAD uh LAK*, **ANTOINE DE LA MOTHE,** *ahn TWAN duh la MAWT* (1656?-1730), a French colonist, founded Detroit, Mich. He also served as governor of French Louisiana.

Cadillac was born in Gascony, France. After army service, he went to America in 1683, and lived in Nova Scotia and in Maine. In 1694, he received command of Mackinac (Mich.), then the most important fur-trading post in the west. The French abandoned their western posts in 1697, and Cadillac returned to France. He obtained a grant for the Detroit area, and took a large number of colonists there in 1701.

In 1711, King Louis XIV appointed him governor of Louisiana. Cadillac early became unpopular and failed to establish a prosperous settlement. In 1716, he returned to France and retired. WILLIAM P. BRANDON

CÁDIZ, *kuh DIHZ* or *KAY dihz* (pop. 142,242), is a great Spanish port. It lies on the Atlantic Ocean, 60 miles (97 kilometers) northwest of Gibraltar. Cádiz has long been Spain's chief naval station, and ships of many nations use its harbor. See SPAIN (political map).

The Phoenicians founded Cádiz in 1130 B.C., and many experts believe it to be the oldest city in Europe. The settlement prospered and became one of the great outposts of Phoenician power. About 550 B.C., Cádiz found itself threatened by local Iberian tribes, and called on Carthage for help. Carthage sent forces to help Cádiz, but the Carthaginians captured the city. The Romans seized Cádiz from the Carthaginians in 205 B.C. Hundreds of years later, the city became a Moorish stronghold. In 1262, King Alfonso X of Castile drove the Moors out of Cádiz. Christopher Columbus sailed from Cádiz in 1493 on his second voyage to America. During the next 300 years, when Spain had a world-wide empire, the riches of the American colonies poured into the city, and Cádiz became wealthy. Cádiz is the capital of Cádiz province. STANLEY G. PAYNE

CADMIUM, *KAD mee uhm*, is a soft, silvery-white metallic element used for alloys and plating. Friedrich Stromeyer of Germany discovered it in 1817. For every ten million parts of the earth's crust, only about five parts are cadmium. The metal occurs with zinc minerals and is obtained as a by-product of zinc refining.

Cadmium is poisonous. People have become seriously ill or have died soon after breathing cadmium dust or fumes of cadmium oxide. Small amounts of cadmium entering the body over long periods may also damage the kidneys and deform bones. As people became concerned about environmental pollution, they feared that hazardous amounts of cadmium were reaching the environment from widespread industrial use of the metal.

Industry uses cadmium in alloys for high-speed bearings, and as a protective coating for other metals. Cadmium is often used instead of zinc for galvanizing iron and steel. It provides poorer long-term protection than zinc. But it keeps a brighter color for longer periods. Cadmium rods are used in nuclear reactors to control nuclear reactions. Nickel-cadmium storage batteries have advantages over small-sized lead-acid batteries.

Cadmium has the symbol Cd. Its atomic number is 48 and its atomic weight is 112.41. Its density is 8.65 grams per cubic centimeter at 20° C. Cadmium melts at 320.9° C and boils at 765° C. J. GORDON PARR

See also BATTERY (Nickel-Cadmium Storage Batteries).

CADMUS, *KAD muhs*, in Greek mythology, was the son of Agenor, the king of Tyre, a city in Phoenicia. He set out to find his sister Europa, whom Zeus had stolen. But an oracle told him his search was useless, and directed him instead to follow a cow. Cadmus was to build a city where the cow lay down. A dragon was guarding the spot. Cadmus killed the dragon and sowed its teeth in the ground. At once, armed men sprang up and fought with each other until only five were left. These five helped Cadmus build the city of Thebes in Boeotia (see THEBES). From Phoenicia, it is said, he brought the alphabet into Greece. H. L. STOW

CADUCEUS. See MERCURY (mythology).

CAECILIAN. See AMPHIBIAN.

CAEDMON, *KAD muhn*, was an English poet who lived in England in the late 600's. An uneducated herdsman, Caedmon entered the monastery of Whitby late in life. The Venerable Bede reported in his *Ecclesiastical History* that Caedmon dreamed he was commanded to sing the praises of God (see BEDE). To the monks' surprise, Caedmon sang what is now known as Caedmon's *Hymn*. This song, the only authentic poem Caedmon left, praised God in the heroic tradition of Anglo-Saxon poetry (see ENGLISH LITERATURE [Old English Literature]). The monks believed that they had witnessed a miracle.

The *Hymn* influenced much later Anglo-Saxon poetry. Critics once credited paraphrases of the books of Genesis, Exodus, and part of Daniel to Caedmon, but they now believe these paraphrases confirm Caedmon's influence, not his authorship. GEORGE F. SENSABAUGH

CAESAR, *SEE zuhr*, was a title which came from the family name of Julius Caesar, who ruled Rome as a monarch without a crown from 49 to 44 B.C. Octavian, Caesar's nephew and adopted son, took his uncle's name and also the title of Augustus. The next four Roman emperors all had some claim, by family or adoption, to the name of Caesar, which became so closely associated with the idea of the emperor that it was a kind of title. In choosing the person to follow him as supreme ruler, the emperor would confer upon his heir the title *Caesar*. In the days of the Byzantine Empire, anyone chosen as ruler of a country under the Empire might be called Caesar. In the Russian language the title became *czar*. In German, Caesar was changed to *kaiser*. See also CZAR; KAISER. FRANK C. BOURNE

CAESAR, *SEE zuhr*, **JULIUS** (100?-44 B.C.), a Roman general and statesman, was one of the greatest men in the history of the world. He became a brilliant military leader and helped make Rome the center of an empire that stretched across Europe. Caesar also won fame as an orator, politician, and writer. Caesar's many skills helped him become dictator of the Roman world. But his power frightened many of his political opponents, and a group of them assassinated him.

Early Life. Gaius Julius Caesar was born in Rome of an aristocratic family. At the age of 17, he married

Cornelia, the daughter of Lucius Cornelius Cinna. Cinna led the *Marian group*, followers of Gaius Marius, a great popular leader. Lucius Sulla, the aristocratic dictator of Rome, ordered Caesar to divorce Cornelia. But Caesar refused to do so. He then went to Greece to study philosophy and oratory. Sulla later pardoned Caesar, and he returned to Rome. Caesar and Cornelia had a daughter, Julia. Cornelia died about 68 B.C.

Caesar became increasingly interested in public affairs, and tried always to gain the favor of the people. In 65 B.C., he was elected to direct public works and games. He won favor because he spent much money to provide recreation for the people, although he went heavily into debt to do so. In 62 B.C., he became *praetor*, the office next in rank to consul (see PRAETOR).

Alliance with Pompey. Catiline, a dissatisfied Roman politician, plotted a revolt. In breaking up this plot, leading aristocrats sought to disgrace the entire group of popular leaders, including Caesar (see CATILINE). But they failed to hurt his political prospects.

In 60 B.C., Caesar allied himself with Marcus Licinius Crassus and Gnaeus Pompey in the *First Triumvirate*, an alliance that ruled Rome. Crassus was a man of enormous wealth and political ambition. Pompey had returned from Asia Minor in 62 B.C. as a great military leader and the idol of the people. The three took power when, through violence and bribery, Caesar was elected a consul in 59 B.C. He used force to push through the triumvirate's program, and won the hatred of the conservatives. He took the post of proconsul of several provinces north of Italy. In 59 B.C., Caesar married Calpurnia, daughter of Lucius Piso of Rome. Also that year, Pompey married Caesar's daughter, Julia.

Campaigns in Gaul. By training, Caesar was a politician rather than a soldier. But he knew he needed military fame and a loyal army to gain more power. In 58 B.C., Caesar began a campaign to conquer Gaul (France). It soon became clear that he was a military genius. During his nine years in Gaul, Caesar lost only two battles in which he personally took part. He conquered all territory east to the Rhine River, drove the Germans out of Gaul, and crossed the Rhine to show them the might of Rome. He also invaded Britain twice, in 55 and 54 B.C.

Civil War. Although great public thanksgiving celebrations were held in Rome for his victories, not everyone rejoiced over Caesar's conquests. Pompey became alarmed at Caesar's success. Pompey's growing jealousy threw him into an alliance with the conservatives, who ordered Caesar to give up his army in 49 B.C.

Caesar had no intention of surrendering his army and leaving himself defenseless. He led 5,000 soldiers across the Rubicon, a stream that separated his provinces from Italy. After this hostile act, there was no turning back. Caesar had provoked a civil war, his greatest step toward grasping supreme power. As Caesar dashed south, he met little opposition. Pompey's troops surrendered, forcing Pompey to flee to the Balkans. The conservatives who had ordered Caesar to give up his army fled with Pompey.

Within 60 days, Caesar became master of Italy. But it took him nearly five years to complete his conquest of the rest of the empire. In 49 B.C., Caesar had himself appointed dictator and consul, as well as tribune for life. He met Pompey's army in Greece where, at Pharsalus in 48 B.C., he defeated the man who had dared oppose him. He then followed Pompey to Egypt and found that his enemy had been murdered. There, Caesar met and fell in love with Cleopatra.

Last Victories. Before returning to Rome, Caesar won the war he fought to make Cleopatra ruler of Egypt. He later brought her to Rome. Caesar won his next victory in 47 B.C., over Pharnaces II, King of Pontus. *Veni, vidi, vici* ("I came, I saw, I conquered") was Caesar's brief but meaningful dispatch to the Roman Senate, reporting this victory at Zela in what is now northwestern Turkey.

Pompey's forces reorganized after the death of their leader. But, in 46 B.C., at Thapsus in northern Africa, Caesar defeated them decisively. Cato the Younger, one of Pompey's supporters, killed himself when he heard of the defeat. In 45 B.C. at Munda, Caesar defeated the two sons of Pompey. This was his last battle.

Caesar had now become undisputed master of the Roman world. He pardoned the followers of Pompey. The people honored Caesar for his leadership and triumphs by granting him the powers of dictator for 10 years. Later, he was made dictator for life. At a public festival, Mark Antony tested popular feeling by offering Caesar the crown of a king. Because the Romans hated kings, Caesar refused the crown.

Assassination. Even though Caesar refused the crown, the conservatives suspected that he intended to

Julius Caesar was one of the great military leaders of all time. This statue shows Caesar in the uniform of a Roman general.

Marble statue carved between 99 B.C., and 1 B.C. by an unknown Roman sculptor; Museo Capitolino, Rome (Oscar Savio)

make himself king someday. Marcus Junius Brutus and Gaius Cassius, both of whom Caesar had pardoned after the battle of Pharsalus, led a group of aristocrats in a plot to kill the dictator. On March 15 (the Ides of March), 44 B.C., they stabbed Caesar to death as he entered a Senate meeting. He received more than 20 wounds from men who had accepted his favors and who he had believed were his friends. In Shakespeare's play *Julius Caesar*, Mark Antony says at the funeral of Caesar:

> You all did see that on the Lupercal
> I thrice presented him a kingly crown,
> Which he did thrice refuse: was this ambition?
> Yet Brutus says he was ambitious;
> And, sure, he is an honorable man.
> I speak not to disprove what Brutus spoke,
> But here I am to speak what I do know.

His Reforms. Caesar used wisely the power he had won, and made many important reforms. He stopped dishonest practices in the Roman and provincial governments. He improved the calendar, clearing up confusion that had existed for hundreds of years in computing time. He established a plan for reorganizing city government in Italy. He tried to reconcile his opponents by appointing them to public office. He replaced dishonest governors with honest ones, and granted Roman citizenship to many persons who lived in the provinces.

Caesar encouraged poor people in Rome to improve their way of living by establishing colonies, notably at Carthage and Corinth. He continued to distribute free grain, but gave it only to those who were in need. He is said to have planned many other reforms, such as the founding of public libraries, the draining of marshes, and the construction of a canal across the Isthmus of Corinth.

Caesar had proved he was capable of governing Rome and its vast possessions. Yet many of Caesar's actions offended Roman pride. Caesar treated the Senate as a mere advisory council, and the Romans resented this disrespect. He also did not try to disguise the fact that he was a dictator. In addition, the Romans considered themselves conquerors of the world, and objected to measures that gave full citizenship to peoples they regarded as their subjects.

Other Talents. As an orator, Caesar ranked second only to Cicero, the great Roman statesman and philosopher. Caesar is also famous as a writer. His *Commentaries on the Gallic War* describes his conquests in Gaul. The clear, direct style of this work makes it a model of historical writing. CHESTER G. STARR

Related Articles in WORLD BOOK include:

Antony, Mark	Cleopatra
Augustus	Crassus, Marcus Licinius
Brutus, Marcus Junius	Pompey the Great
Cassius Longinus, Gaius	Sulla, Lucius Cornelius

See also *Caesar, Julius*, in the RESEARCH GUIDE/INDEX, Volume 22, for a *Reading and Study Guide*.

Additional Resources

DURANT, WILL. *Caesar and Christ: A History of Roman Civilization and of Christianity from Their Beginnings to A.D. 325.* Simon & Schuster, 1944.

GRANT, MICHAEL. *Caesar.* Follett, 1975.

MCDONALD, A. H. *Republican Rome.* Praeger, 1966. An account of the society of the time.

SUETONIUS, TRANQUILLUS C. *The Twelve Caesars.* An ancient biographical work. Available in various eds.

CAESAREAN SECTION. See CHILDBIRTH (The Birth Process); SURGERY (Gynecology and Obstetrics).

CAFETERIA. See RESTAURANT.

CAFFEINE, *KAF een* or *KAF ee ihn* (chemical formula, $C_8H_{10}N_4O_2 \cdot H_2O$), is an odorless, slightly bitter solid. It is a stimulant, and is found in small amounts in coffee, tea, and colas. Caffeine dissolves in water and alcohol, and has crystals that look like needles. When taken in small amounts, caffeine increases the circulation, and it is considered harmless for most people. When taken in large amounts, however, it causes nervousness and loss of sleep. The use of caffeine also may cause headaches and digestive disturbances. Caffeine has been linked to the development of birth defects in laboratory animals, and many physicians advise pregnant women to avoid excessive caffeine consumption.

Caffeine was produced from plants in the pure form in 1820. It can now be made in the laboratory. Caffeine is used as a stimulant of the heart and nervous system in certain disorders. It is also a remedy for poisoning by alcohol, opium, and other drugs that *depress* (slow down) the nervous system. A. KEITH REYNOLDS

See also ALKALOID; COFFEE; MATÉ; TEA.

CAGE, JOHN (1912-), is perhaps the most original and controversial modern American composer. He is best known for his experiments with *aleatoric* (random or chance) music. For example, his *Imaginary Landscape No. 4.* (1951) was written for 12 radios, 24 musicians, and a conductor. As the piece progresses, each radio is tuned to a different station and the volume is changed. Thus, the sound of the composition cannot be predicted, and it varies with each performance.

Cage was born in Los Angeles. Since 1938, he has written music for *prepared piano.* This music calls for various objects—bolts, screws, or strips of rubber, for example—to be inserted between some of the piano strings. When the performer hits the keys for these strings, unusual sounds are produced.

Some music critics doubt Cage's seriousness and sincerity. His supporters credit him with questioning the values and ideas of traditional music while seeking new approaches and sounds. REINHARD G. PAULY

See also ALEATORY MUSIC.

CAGLIARI, PAOLO. See VERONESE, PAOLO.

CAGNEY, JAMES (1899-), an American motion-picture actor, became famous for his roles as a cocky tough guy. Cagney also was an accomplished dancer. He won an Academy Award as best actor for his performance in *Yankee Doodle Dandy* (1942). This motion picture portrayed the life of the Broadway showman George M. Cohan.

Warner Bros.

James Cagney

Cagney appeared in more than 60 motion pictures, of which the first was *Sinner's Holiday* (1930). His performance as a gangster in *The Public Enemy* (1931) established him as a star. Cagney made several other gangster films, including *G-Men* (1935), *Angels with Dirty Faces* (1938), *The Roaring Twenties* (1939), and *White Heat* (1949). Cagney's other films included *Footlight Parade* (1933), *Mister Roberts* (1955), *Love Me or Leave Me* (1955), *Man of a Thousand Faces* (1957), and *One, Two, Three* (1961).

James Francis Cagney, Jr., was born in New York City. During the 1920's, he performed in vaudeville and on Broadway in New York City. ROGER EBERT

CAHOW, *kuh HOW*, is a rare sea bird. The cahow is in the petrel family, and the bird is sometimes called the *Bermuda petrel* because it nests only in the Bermuda Islands in the Atlantic Ocean. There are only about 100 cahows alive. Their total nesting area consists of less than 5 acres (2 hectares). The name *cahow* comes from the sound of the bird's call.

Cahows are black on the top of the head and grayish-black on the back and wings. The underside of the body is white. Cahows measure about 15 inches (38 centimeters) long and have a wingspread of up to 35 inches (89 centimeters). The females lay a single egg in a hole dug in the ground.

WORLD BOOK illustration by John Rignall, Linden Artists Ltd.

The Cahow Is a Rare Sea Bird Found Only in Bermuda.

In 1615, British colonists in the Bermuda Islands saved themselves from starvation by eating cahows. A few years later, the birds disappeared and were not seen again until 1906. In 1951, their nests were found on a few small islands off Bermuda.

Scientific Classification. Cahows belong to the family Procellariidae. They are *Pterodroma cahow*. JAMES J. DINSMORE

CAIN was the eldest son of Adam and Eve. He was the first person in the Bible to commit a murder (Gen. 4). According to the story in Genesis, Cain became angry when the Lord liked his brother Abel's sacrifice of sheep better than Cain's sacrifice of the "fruit of the ground." He killed Abel. When the Lord asked Cain where Abel was, Cain made the famous remark: "I know not: am I my brother's keeper?" (Gen. 4: 9).

To punish Cain, the Lord sent him away to be a wanderer. Cain feared he would be killed, so the Lord placed a mark on him and commanded that no one should harm him. MERRILL F. UNGER

See also ABEL.

CAIRN TERRIER is a breed of dog that originated in the highlands and island regions of Scotland. It received its name because of its ability to dig under *cairns* (heaps of stones) to hunt rats and other animals. The terrier's broad, short head looks more like that of a cat than that of a dog. Its ears are wide apart, and the dog holds them erect. The cairn has a hard wiry topcoat and an undercoat of soft fur. Its coat may be any color but white. It weighs from 13 to 14 pounds (5.9 to 6.4 kilograms). See also DOG (picture: Terriers). JOSEPHINE Z. RINE

CAIRO, *KY roh* (pop. 6,133,000), is the capital of Egypt. It has more people than any other city in Africa. Cairo covers about 83 square miles (215 square kilometers) on the east bank of the Nile River in northeastern Egypt. For the location of Cairo, see EGYPT (political map).

Cairo is part of the Nile Valley and Delta, one of the few parts of Egypt that has fertile soil and plentiful water. Huge deserts lie east and west of the city. Some famous reminders of ancient Egypt—pyramids and the Great Sphinx—stand at Giza in the desert west of Cairo (see PYRAMIDS; SPHINX).

Description. Cairo is a mixture of the new and the old. In general, the western part of the city is modern, and the eastern part is old.

Western Cairo borders the Nile River. Bridges connect this section with the islands of Gezira and Roda in the river, and with the suburbs of Giza and Imbabah west of the Nile. Most of Cairo's government buildings, foreign embassies, hotels, museums, and universities are in the western section, on the islands, or in the suburbs.

Many buildings of western Cairo were constructed in the 1900's. Their design is modern, in the style of present-day American and European architecture (see EGYPT [color picture: Modern Buildings of Cairo]). Western Cairo has many gardens, parks, public squares, and wide boulevards. These features make western Cairo less crowded and more orderly than the eastern part of the city.

Eastern Cairo offers a sharp contrast with the western section. The eastern section is famous for its *old quarters*—areas of narrow, winding streets, and buildings that are hundreds of years old. *Bazaars* (outdoor shopping areas) fill almost all the available space in some streets. In many of the buildings of the eastern section, open-front shops occupy the ground floor. Small apartments take up the upper floors.

Eastern Cairo is also known for its more than 250 *mosques* (Muslim houses of worship). *Minarets* (tall, slender towers) are important features of the mosques. Muslim officials called *muezzins* announce prayer time from atop the minarets five times a day. Eastern Cairo has so many mosques that at least one minaret can be seen from almost any place in the area.

Many of Cairo's mosques are outstanding examples of Muslim architecture. Some of the most famous mosques and their construction dates are Ahmed Ibn Tulun (A.D. 870's), Al-Azhar (about 970), Sultan Hassan (mid-

Morroe Berger, the critical reviewer of this article, is Professor of Sociology and former Director of the Program in Near Eastern Studies at Princeton University.

O. Bessim, Shostal

Cairo, the Capital of Egypt, lies on the Nile River. Gezira, *foreground,* an island in the Nile, has many homes and parks. The Cairo Tower, *left,* is a city landmark.

1300's), Kayit Bey (about 1475), and Muhammad Ali (early 1800's). The mosque of Al-Azhar is also a university, and the Muhammad Ali mosque is part of a walled fortress called the *Citadel.*

Cairo's museums house many priceless treasures from ancient tombs. The treasures in the city's Egyptian Museum include the mummy of Ramses II and the gold mask and other belongings of King Tutankhamen. For a picture of this mask, see EGYPT, ANCIENT.

People. The people of Cairo are called *Cairenes.* Many of them are poor, unskilled factory workers who live in crowded apartments in the old quarters. Most of the poor people wear long, flowing robes, the traditional Arab garment. Most middle-class and wealthy Cairenes live in western Cairo, on the islands, or in the suburbs. These people include doctors, factory managers, government officials, lawyers, and teachers. They dress like Americans and Europeans.

Most Cairenes are Arabs and Muslims. The Copts form the largest Christian group in Cairo. They trace their origin back to the Christians who lived in Egypt before the Arabs came. Many Europeans and some Jews live in Cairo, but their numbers have decreased greatly since the mid-1900's. At that time, the government took over most businesses and adopted policies that promoted the economic opportunities of Egyptian Muslims. These policies limited the opportunities of minority groups and foreigners.

Schools. Most of Egypt's schools of higher learning are in or near Cairo. They include the University of Cairo, in nearby Giza, the largest university in the country. The University of Al-Azhar in Cairo is a major center for the study of Islam, the religion of Muslims. This university was founded about 970 and ranks among the world's oldest.

Climate. Cairo has hot summers and mild winters. In July, the average daily high temperature is 96° F. (36° C) and the average low is 70° F. (21° C). The average daily high in January is 65° F. (18° C) and the average low is 47° F. (8° C). During the summer, many families leave the city and go to seaside resorts to escape the heat. Others live on boats on the Nile. Cairo's mild winters attract many tourists from colder places.

Cairo receives only about 1 inch (2.5 centimeters) of rain a year. The sun shines almost every day. For more details on Cairo's climate, see EGYPT (Climate).

Economy. The Cairo area is an important manufacturing center. A factory at Hulwan, south of the city, makes iron and steel. Cotton mills operate at Al Mahallah al Kubra, north of Cairo. Other industries in and near Cairo process sugar and manufacture chemicals, paper, textiles, and other products. Many companies and individuals make such small items as jewelry and statues that are sold to tourists as souvenirs. During the mid-1900's, the government took over all but the smallest industries. Since the mid-1970's, many industries have been returned to private ownership. But the government still owns the majority of them.

Tourism is a key part of Cairo's economy. Each year, thousands of visitors come to see the mosques, museums, old quarters, pyramids, sphinx, and other attractions.

History. In the A.D. 630's, Egypt was a province of the Byzantine, or East Roman, Empire. Its people were Christians and were descendants of the ancient Egyptians who founded a great civilization along the Nile about 3100 B.C. Arabs from east of Egypt conquered the province in the A.D. 640's. In 640, the Arabs established a military camp in the area that is now southern Cairo. They later built houses, mosques, and palaces, and the camp became a permanent settlement.

The *Fatimites* (Arabs from North Africa) conquered Egypt in 969 and made Cairo their capital. They built up the area north of the first Arab settlement, and Cairo soon became one of the most important cities of the Arab world. The Fatimites founded the University of Al-Azhar, which attracted students of Islam from many countries. The Fatimites called their city *Al Qahirah* because the planet Mars (*Al Qahir* in Arabic) was rising in the sky when they began building. The name *Cairo* comes from *Al Qahirah.*

Saladin, the founder of Egypt's Ayyubid *dynasty* (family of rulers), expanded the city's boundaries and built the Citadel in the late 1100's. The Mamelukes, who had served the Ayyubids as bodyguards, ruled the country from 1250 to 1517. They built many of Cairo's finest mosques and extended the city to its present boundaries. The Ottoman Turks controlled Egypt from 1517 to 1882. They allowed the Egyptians a large degree of self-government.

Many of the treasures of ancient Egypt were discovered in the early 1800's. Exhibitions and lectures about Egypt's past aroused great interest among people in the United States during the 1800's. Thousands visited Cairo to see the wonders they had heard about.

Many people from Europe settled in Cairo during the 1800's, when European nations became increasingly involved in Egypt's affairs. A program to modernize Cairo began about 1865. This program continued during the British rule of Egypt from 1882 to 1922 and during the Egyptian monarchy from 1922 to 1953.

Egypt became a republic in 1953. The government

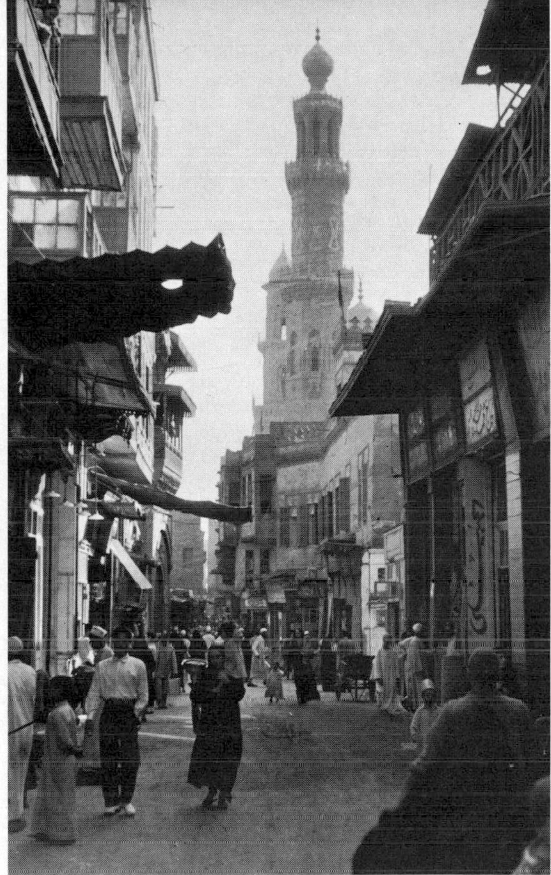

Henri Cartier-Bresson, Magnum

The Old Sections of Cairo have narrow, crowded streets and many Muslim houses of worship called *mosques, background.*

Traditional Egyptian Dress, including the *galabiyah,* a long robe, is worn by many Cairenes. Others wear Western clothing.

H. Fristedt, Carl Östman

has done much to modernize Cairo, but extreme poverty still exists in many parts of the city.

Cairo's rapidly growing population contributes to the poverty problem. The city's population increased from about 375,000 in 1882 to more than 3½ million in the 1960's and over 6 million in the 1970's. This growth resulted from three causes—(1) a high birth rate, (2) thousands of Egyptian families moving from rural areas to Cairo, and (3) refugees who moved from Ismailia, Port Said, and Suez. These cities were heavily damaged in fighting between Egyptian and Israeli forces along the Suez Canal in the late 1960's and early 1970's.

Critically reviewed by MORROE BERGER

See also GIZA.

CAISSON. See ARTILLERY.

CAISSON, *KAY sahn,* in building, is a box or casing that is lowered through water or into the ground to provide a shell for a foundation which is built inside the caisson. Caissons are constructed of metal, concrete, or wood.

Caissons are used to make foundations for buildings and for bridge piers. Sometimes large buildings are built on many small caissons. When the caisson for a bridge foundation rests on the river bottom, or on piles, no excavation is necessary to place it. The caisson is a box with a bottom and an open top. It is called a *box caisson.* This type of caisson is floated to position and sunk. Some caissons are sunk into the earth below the water. They are called *open caissons* because they are open at both top and bottom. They consist simply of walls with openings between them known as *wells.* The bottom edges are constructed so they will cut into the earth. The earth is taken out through the wells by hoisting devices.

Where it is necessary to lower a caisson under difficult conditions, a *pneumatic caisson* may be used. The lower section, where the workers are, has cutting edges and a roof. The section above is open at the top. The foundation is built in the upper section, and its weight helps to drive the lower section into the ground. Compressed air is forced into the lower section until the water inside is forced out. Then, workers go into the lower section and dig out the earth until the caisson has sunk to the right level. High air pressure is maintained while the work is being done, to keep the water from seeping back into the lower section.

United Press Int.

Caisson to be used in building a new tunnel is moved into place by two tugboats. This view shows four tubes leading to the compressed air chamber. Mud and rock dug out of the river bottom will be removed through these tubes.

Before entering the working chamber, the workers sit in *air locks.* The air pressure in the air lock is gradually increased until it is equal to the pressure in the working chamber. This saves the workers from sudden pressure changes which might be fatal. When they leave the chamber they pass through the air lock again, and the pressure is gradually reduced to normal.

Air pressure is also used in digging tunnels under rivers. The railway tunnels under the Detroit River in Detroit, and those under the Hudson River in New York, were dug with pneumatic shells. ROBERT G. HENNES

See also AIR LOCK; BENDS; COFFERDAM.

CAISSON DISEASE. See BENDS.

CAJUNS, *KAY juhnz,* are a group of people in southern Louisiana and Texas who are descendants of French settlers called Acadians. The Acadians came from the Acadia region of Canada, which included New Brunswick and Nova Scotia (see ACADIA). The word *Cajuns* comes from *Acadians.*

During the 1750's, British troops drove the Acadians from Canada. At that time, the British and French were fighting the French and Indian War, a struggle for control of eastern North America. Many Acadians eventually settled in southern Louisiana, where swamps and slow-moving streams called *bayous* cover much of the land. The American poet Henry Wadsworth Longfellow described their journey in his poem *Evangeline.* The Cajuns lived in relative isolation in the bayou area. They continued to regard themselves as a separate people and maintained a unique culture that had many Acadian French characteristics.

Today, most Cajuns speak both English and a French dialect that includes many words no longer used by other French-speaking peoples. The majority of the people are Roman Catholics. Many Cajun families live by fishing and trapping. Others raise cattle or such crops as rice, sugar, and sweet potatoes. Cajun cooking is spicy and includes much seafood. Favorite foods include a thick soup called *gumbo* and a rice dish called *jambalaya.* Traditional Cajun music is played by a band consisting of a fiddle, accordion, and triangle.

Since the mid-1900's, better communication and transportation have put the Cajuns into closer contact with other people. A boom in the area's oil industry has brought prosperity to many families, who now live much like their non-Cajun neighbors. Many young Cajuns do not speak French or follow Cajun customs. Some Cajuns worry about losing their cultural heritage and have led a movement to preserve it. For example, Louisiana schools once discouraged Cajun children from speaking French. Today, most pupils study the language in elementary school. JAMES H. DORMON

CALABASH, *KAL uh bash,* is a gourd that grows on a climbing vine in the tropics. It looks like a squash or a pumpkin, and is cultivated like a squash.

The *calabash tree* is an evergreen tree of tropical America. It bears a gourdlike fruit, much like that of the vine calabash. The hard, tough outer shells can be used as cooking pots. Calabash smoking pipes are made from the curved ends of this gourd.

Scientific Classification. The vine calabash belongs to the gourd family, Cucurbitaceae. It is *Lagenaria siceraria.* The calabash tree belongs to the bignonia family, Bignoniaceae. It is *Crescentia cujete.* Arthur J. Pratt

See also Gourd.

Field Museum of Natural History

Calabash Gourd

CALADIUM, *kuh LAY dee uhm,* is a group of foliage plants that grow in tropical America. They have huge, arrow-shaped leaves beautifully marked in various colors and patterns. Thousands of varieties of caladiums are grown commercially in Florida. They are shipped to florists early in spring for potting. Caladiums grow well in shady, protected sites such as window boxes.

Scientific Classification. Caladiums belong to the arum family, Araceae. Marcus Maxon

Paul E. Genereux

Caladium

CALAIS, *KAL ay* (pop. 78,820), a seaport in northern France, is closer to England than any other city in mainland Europe. It lies on the English Channel coast at the Strait of Dover, 26 miles (42 kilometers) southeast of Dover, England (see France [political map]). Calais is a leading shipping center for trade between mainland Europe and England. It is also a major port for travel between the mainland and England.

Calais is divided into a section centering on the port and a section devoted to industrial activity. Its industries include food processing and the manufacture of chemicals, electric appliances, plastics, paper, and textiles—especially lace. The city is France's largest lace-manufacturing center.

Calais' founding date is unknown. Originally a fishing village, it became a major port during the Middle Ages. Modern port facilities were installed in the 1800's. Calais suffered heavy damage during World War I (1914-1918) and World War II (1939-1945) but was rebuilt afterward. Mark Kesselman

CALAMITY JANE (1852?-1903), was the nickname of Martha Jane Canary, a famous American frontierswoman. There are many stories of how she got her nickname. According to one, she used to warn men that to offend her was to court calamity.

Martha Jane was born near the town of Princeton, in northern Missouri. In 1864, she moved with her parents to Virginia City, Mont. They separated, and Martha Jane was raised there and in other mining camps in Wyoming and Utah. She learned to be a skilled horsewoman and an expert with a rifle and revolver. Because of the roughness of the life she led, she usually dressed in men's clothes.

She became associated with the 7th Cavalry of the United States Army near Rawlins, Wyo. Some writers believe that because of her knowledge of the frontier territory she served as a scout for General George Custer. She spent some time at Fort Bridger and Fort Russell in Wyoming, and also lived in Denver, Colo.

In 1875, Martha Jane went to the Black Hills of South Dakota. She lived in the town of Deadwood at the time of the gold rush, and became a heroine for helping treat victims of a smallpox outbreak there in 1878. Later, she was married to a man named Burke, and moved to El Paso, Tex.

In 1903, she returned to Deadwood. The citizens supported her, and took up a collection to send her daughter east to school. She died in 1903, and is buried near the grave of Wild Bill Hickok. Thomas D. Clark

CALCIMINE, *KAL suh myn,* also spelled *Kalsomine,* is a water-thinned paint. It was the forerunner of present-day latex paints. Calcimine consists of glue, whiting (carbonate of lime), pigments, and water. It is rarely used today because it rubs off easily and cannot support additional coatings. Edward W. Stewart

CALCINATION, *KAL suh NAY shuhn,* is the process of heating a substance to a high temperature but below its melting point. One of the most common uses of calcination is in the production of lime from limestone. Heating drives off carbon dioxide (CO_2) from the limestone ($CaCO_3$) to produce lime (CaO). Calcination is also used to produce plaster of Paris. Walter J. Moore

CALCITE, *KAL syt,* is one of the most common minerals in the earth. It is the most stable form of calcium carbonate. Its chemical formula is $CaCO_3$. Pure calcite is colorless or white. But calcite may occur in various other colors due to the presence of mineral impurities or small

Culver

Calamity Jane Was an Expert with a Horse and Rifle.

amounts of cobalt, iron, magnesium, or manganese. Calcite crystals belong to the *hexagonal system* (see CRYSTAL). They can be split to form perfect *rhombohedrons*, six-sided objects in which the opposite sides are parallel.

Calcite crystals occur in many kinds of rocks. Chalk, limestone, and marble contain large amounts of calcite. Such rock formations as stalactites and stalagmites found in caves consist of a type of calcite called *travertine*. In addition, calcite acts as a cementing material to combine different minerals in coarse-grained *sedimentary rocks* (see SEDIMENTARY ROCK).

Calcite is the world's chief source of *lime*, a substance used in manufacturing many items including glass and steel (see LIME). Calcite is mixed with clayey materials to produce portland cement and with sand to form mortar. An extremely pure form of calcite called *Iceland spar* is used in such optical instruments as polarizing microscopes. ROBERT W. CHARLES

See also CALCIUM CARBONATE; CHALK; LIMESTONE; MARBLE; TRAVERTINE.

CALCIUM, *KAL see uhm*, is a soft, silvery-white metallic element found most widely in such rocks as chalk, limestone, and marble. It is one of the most abundant metals and makes up about $3\frac{1}{2}$ per cent of the earth's crust. It reacts readily with both oxygen and water. In nature, it occurs only in compounds—chiefly as calcium carbonate, calcium fluoride, and calcium sulfate.

Calcium has an atomic number of 20 and an atomic weight of 40.08. Its chemical symbol is Ca. It belongs to the group of elements called *alkaline earth metals* (see ELEMENT, CHEMICAL [Periodic Table of the Elements]). Calcium melts at 839° C and boils at 1484° C. It has a density of 1.55 grams per cubic centimeter at 20° C (see DENSITY).

Calcium and its compounds have many industrial uses. Pure calcium metal, used in certain kinds of alloys, is obtained from molten calcium chloride through a process called *electrolysis*. Various industrial processes, such as leather tanning and petroleum refining, involve calcium oxide. This compound is prepared by heating calcium carbonate in furnaces called *kilns*. Calcium fluoride and calcium sulfate are used in making cement and plaster for construction work. Manufacturers use other calcium compounds in a wide variety of products ranging from fertilizer to paint.

Calcium is essential to all living things, especially human beings and other animals. It is vital for the growth and maintenance of the bones and teeth, and it helps the blood to clot and the muscles to contract. A daily diet that includes green vegetables, milk, and milk products supplies enough calcium for the human body's normal needs.

Sir Humphry Davy, an English chemist, first isolated calcium as a pure metal in 1808. However, the ancient Egyptians, Greeks, and Romans knew about calcium compounds and used them to make mortar. IAIN C. PAUL

See also CALCITE; CALCIUM CARBIDE; CALCIUM CARBONATE; LIME; LIMESTONE; NUTRITION (tables).

CALCIUM BLOCKER is any of a group of drugs used to treat various disorders of the heart and blood vessels. These drugs are also called *calcium channel blockers* or *calcium entry blockers*. Calcium blockers increase blood flow to the heart and reduce blood pressure. They play an important role in the treatment of *angina pectoris*—chest pains caused by inadequate oxygen supply to the heart. Calcium blockers are also effective in treating high blood pressure.

Calcium blockers include the drugs diltiazem, nifedipine, and verapamil. They act by preventing the entry of calcium into the muscle cells of the heart and blood vessels. Calcium must enter muscle cells for the muscles to contract (see MUSCLE [How Muscles Are Stimulated]). By interfering with the contraction of blood vessels, calcium blockers cause blood vessels to *dilate* (expand). Many cases of angina pectoris result from spasms of the coronary arteries. Such spasms keep blood—and the oxygen it carries—from reaching the heart. Calcium blockers help prevent spasms by dilating—and thus relaxing—coronary blood vessels. In addition, by dilating other blood vessels in the body, calcium blockers reduce blood pressure. The reduction in pressure lessens the heart's workload and so lessens its need for oxygen.

All the calcium blockers do not act in exactly the same way. Therefore, although all of them relieve angina pectoris, only some are effective against certain other disorders. For example, diltiazem and verapamil are useful in combating *arrhythmia* (abnormal heartbeat), but nifedipine is not. Calcium blockers rarely cause side effects. EUGENE M. JOHNSON, JR.

CALCIUM CARBIDE, *KAL see uhm KAHR byd*, is a hard, brittle, crystalline compound made of calcium and carbon. Its chemical formula is CaC_2. Calcium carbide is used in industry to make acetylene, a gas used in welding or cutting metal. It also serves as the source of calcium cyanamide, which is used in the manufacture of fertilizer.

Calcium carbide is produced by heating lime and coke in an electric furnace at a temperature of 2800° C. This method was discovered in 1892 by T. L. Willson, an American chemist. HARRIET V. TAYLOR

See also ACETYLENE.

CALCIUM CARBONATE, *KAL see uhm KAHR buh nayt*, is a white, crystalline mineral. It is widely distributed in nature and is the main ingredient in limestone, marble, coral, calcite, and chalk. In caves, ground waters deposit calcium carbonate over time to form stalactites and stalagmites. Calcium carbonate is an ingredient of some toothpastes and toothpowders. It is also used in some medicines to reduce acidity in the stomach.

Calcium carbonate dissolves only slightly in pure water but forms calcium bicarbonate if carbon dioxide is present. The chemical formula of calcium carbonate is $CaCO_3$. ROBERT J. OUELLETTE

See also CALCITE; CHALK; SALT, CHEMICAL.

CALCULATOR is a device that adds, subtracts, multiplies, and divides with accuracy and speed. Businesses use calculators for keeping accounts and figuring taxes. Engineers and scientists rely on them to solve complicated mathematical problems. Statisticians compute averages and find percentages with calculators. Other people, including homemakers and students, use calculators for various tasks involving arithmetic.

The most widely used calculators are *electronic calculators*. They perform calculations automatically by the use of miniature electronic circuits. Besides adding, subtracting, multiplying, and dividing, many of them perform more complicated functions, such as extracting square roots and cube roots. Some

Texas Instruments Incorporated

A Desk-Top Calculator is used in many offices and homes to perform a variety of mathematical operations.

models have a *memory*, a device that stores for future use numbers or instructions for solving certain problems.

Manufacturers produce both large, desk-top electronic calculators and handheld models. The handheld model, or *pocket calculator*, has become popular with traveling business people and with the general public because of its convenience. This calculator is not only portable, but it can also do all the calculations for such tasks as schoolwork and balancing checkbooks. Some pocket calculators can solve advanced engineering and scientific problems.

Electronic calculators have different ways of recording and presenting information. Some models, called *display calculators*, show entries and results instantly in a small display window. Most pocket calculators are of this type. Other models, called *printing calculators*, provide tapes that show the numbers involved in problems and the results. The tapes allow an operator to check if the problems were correctly fed into the calculator. They also provide a permanent record of the results. Most of these calculators are desk-top models, but some handheld calculators provide tapes. *Print/display* calculators provide both a display and a tape output.

Texas Instruments Incorporated

A Handheld Calculator flashes the answer to many kinds of mathematical problems. Most of these tiny calculators can perform a wide range of both simple and complicated functions.

One type of electronic calculator can handle complicated, multistep tasks similar to those done by small computers. Such a calculator is called a *programmable calculator*. It carries out difficult tasks by using numbers and *programs*, sets of instructions that tell the calculator what jobs to perform with the numbers. After the instructions are programmed into the calculator, it can automatically perform the steps necessary to solve certain kinds of problems. Most models have several memories in which different programs can be stored for repeated use. Programmable calculators are available in both desk-top and pocket-sized models and have either a display or both a display and tape output.

Adding machines are sometimes called *mechanical calculators*. These machines were widely used before the development of electronic calculators (see ADDING MACHINE).

EILEEN FERETIC

CALCULUS, *KAL kyuh luhs*, is one of the most important branches of mathematics. Students usually learn it in college after they have mastered algebra, plane geometry, trigonometry, and analytic geometry. The word *calculus* comes from Latin and means *pebble*. People once used pebbles to solve problems in mathematics. Mathematicians usually call calculus *the calculus* to distinguish it from other methods of computation.

Calculus deals with changing quantities. For example, imagine an airplane traveling at a constant speed of 1,000 kilometers an hour. It covers 1,000 kilometers in one hour, 2,000 kilometers in two hours, and 3,500 kilometers in $3\frac{1}{2}$ hours. From algebra you can derive the following formula to give the distance (d) in kilometers that the airplane travels in t hours: $d = 1{,}000t$. But suppose that the airplane does not travel at a constant speed because of wind conditions and other factors. Then it is no longer a problem in algebra to predict how far the airplane will go in a given period of time. It becomes a problem to be computed by calculus.

Calculus has two main branches—differential calculus and integral calculus. The central problem of *differential calculus* is to find the rate at which a known, but varying, quantity changes. *Integral calculus* has just the reverse problem. It tries to find a quantity knowing the rate at which it is changing.

For example, imagine a man cruising in a spaceship near the surface of a planet with no atmosphere. Because of gravitational pull, a ball dropped from the spaceship will fall toward the planet. With his instruments, the spaceman determines the formula $d = 7t^2$ for the distance (d) in feet the ball falls from rest in t seconds. He notes that the ball falls 7 feet in one second, 28 feet in two seconds, and 700 feet in 10 seconds. Clearly, the ball is not falling at a constant speed.

But the spaceman wants to know the speed of the ball at any instant. Using differential calculus he derives in his head the formula $s = 14t$ for the ball's speed (s) in feet per second t seconds after it is dropped. Thus, the ball has a speed of 14 feet per second after one second, 28 feet per second after two seconds, and 140 feet per second after 10 seconds. From the formula $s = 14t$, the spaceman again uses differential calculus to show that the ball has a constant acceleration of 14 feet per second per second, written 14 (ft./sec.)/sec. That is, in each second the speed of the ball increases 14 feet per second (14ft./sec.).

If the spaceman had first known that the acceleration of the ball due to the gravitational pull of the planet was 14 (ft./sec.)/sec., then he could have used integral calculus to show that $s=14t$ is the formula for the speed of the ball and $d=7t^2$ is the formula for the distance the ball falls.

The Importance of Calculus

Since the development of calculus in the 1600's, mathematics has grown by leaps and bounds. Calculus introduced new methods into mathematics that stimulated much of this growth.

Physics, many other branches of science, and all branches of engineering use calculus to develop theories and to solve practical problems. For example, an airplane designer uses principles from aerodynamics, a branch of physics, to help him design an airplane wing. He uses mathematical equations to help him find how the wing will react under various conditions. Calculus gives the designer the means to derive the equations from the principles of aerodynamics.

Differential Calculus

Functions. Calculus deals with functions. A function resembles a formula and every formula defines a function. To a mathematician, a function (f) is a correspondence that associates with each number t some number $f(t)$, read "f of t." For example, the formula $d=7t^2$ associates with each number t some number d. If we use f to label this function, then $f(t)=7t^2$. Thus, $f(1)=7\times1^2=7$, $f(2)=7\times2^2=28$, $f(10)=7\times10^2=700$.

Rate of Change of a Function is the concern of differential calculus. If $f(a)$ and $f(b)$ are two values of the function f, then $f(b)-f(a)$ equals the *change* in f brought about by the change from a to b in the number at which f is evaluated. The *average rate of change* of f between a and b is $\frac{f(b)-f(a)}{b-a}$.

For example, in the function $f(t)=7t^2$, the change in f from $t=2$ to $t=10$ equals $f(10)-f(2)=700-28=672$. The average rate of change of f between 2 and 10 is $\frac{f(10)-f(2)}{10-2}=\frac{672}{8}=84$.

In the problem about the ball dropped from the spaceship, $f(10)-f(2)$ is the distance a ball falls in a period of 8 seconds starting 2 seconds after the ball is released. Thus, the ball falls 672 feet in this period. In an example such as this where t is time and $f(t)$ is distance, scientists call the rate of change of f speed. According to the calculations above, the average speed of the ball in the given period of 8 seconds is 84 ft./sec.

Limits. Suppose a jet airplane makes a flight in which its average speed is 1,100 kilometers an hour. Also suppose that you wanted to know the speed of the airplane at any instant during its flight. You could not find this out by merely knowing the average speed of the jet. You would need other calculations.

Similarly, knowing the average rate of change of a function during some interval tells little about the rate of change of the function at any instant or the *instantaneous rate of change*. However, the idea of limit allows us to find the instantaneous rate of change of a function.

Consider the formula $d=7t^2$ for the distance the ball falls near the planet in the situation already described. The average speed, $s(t)$, of the ball between 2 seconds and t seconds after it is dropped is given by the following:

$$s(t)=\frac{f(t)-f(2)}{t-2}=\frac{7t^2-7\times2^2}{t-2}=7(t+2)\text{ ft./sec.}$$

The following table of values gives the average speed of the ball over a time interval from 2 to t as the values of t get closer and closer to 2.

t	10	8	4	3	2.5	2.1	2.01	2.001
$s(t)$	84	70	42	35	31.5	28.7	28.07	28.007

What is the average speed of the ball, $s(t)$, close to when t is close to 2? From the table, we can clearly see that the answer is 28. In calculus, we would say that the limit of $s(t)$ as t approaches 2 is 28 ft./sec. That is, the closer that t comes to 2, the closer the average speed comes to 28 ft./sec. The instantaneous speed of the ball 2 seconds after it is released is 28 ft./sec. In calculus, the fact that the instantaneous speed of the ball at $t=2$ is 28 ft./sec. is written $\underset{t\to2}{\text{limit}}\ s(t)=28$ ft./sec.

In general, the instantaneous rate of change of a function f at the number a is defined as follows:

$$\underset{x\to a}{\text{limit}}\ \frac{f(x)-f(a)}{x-a}$$

Derivatives. The instantaneous rate of change of a function is so important that mathematicians have given it the special name *derivative*. One of the most common symbols for the derivative of the function f at a is $f'(a)$, which is read "f prime of a." Other notations for the derivative are D_xf and df/dx. If we let $y=f(x)$, then the notation dy/dx is used. The derivative is defined as follows:

$$f'(a)=\underset{x\to a}{\text{limit}}\ \frac{f(x)-f(a)}{x-a}$$

All calculus books contain rules for finding derivatives of common functions. One of the most useful rules tells how to find the derivative of a power function, such as $f(x)=cx^n$, where c is a constant. In this kind of function, $f'(x)=cnx^{n-1}$.

This is the rule the spaceman followed to find the speed of the falling ball. From $f(t)=7t^2$ he found that $f'(t)=7\times2t^1=14t$. Therefore, $s=14t$ is the formula for the speed of the ball at any time, t seconds, after it starts to fall.

Integral Calculus

In physics, work is measured by the formula $W=Fd$, where W is the work done in foot-pounds, F is a constant force, and d is the distance through which the force acts. For example, if a constant force of 50 pounds is needed to push a box 20 feet across a room, then the work done is 20×50, or 1,000 foot-pounds. But if the force varies as the box is pushed, then the formula $W=Fd$ does not apply. For example, you could not use the formula if the box was pushed with an ever-increasing force. But you could find the work done by using integral calculus.

Integral calculus also solves many geometrical problems. For example, it is used to find the area of a region with a curved boundary. In fact, finding such areas is basic to integral calculus because it helps solve many problems, including the one of finding the work done by a variable force.

Finding Areas. The curve shown below is part of a parabola, a shape commonly found in the reflectors of automobile headlights and the mirrors used in telescopes.

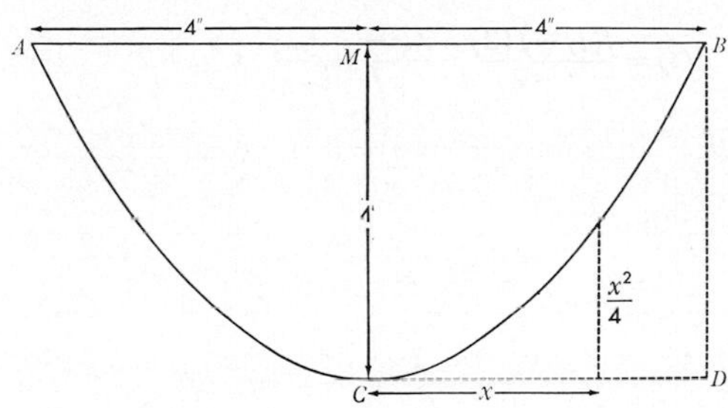

Suppose we want to find the area of the region *ABC* which is bounded by the parabola and the chord *AB*. First, we shall find the area of the region *BCD* which has one curved side *BC*.

Onc way of finding the approximate area of *BCD* is to plot it on graph paper of different dimensions.

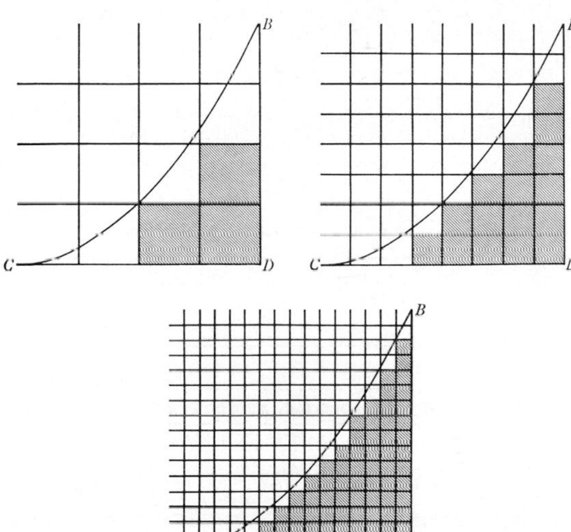

In the graph on the left, suppose that the lines are 1 inch apart and each square has an area of 1 square inch. In the graph on the right, the lines are $\frac{1}{2}$ inch apart and each square has an area of $\frac{1}{4}$ square inch. In the bottom graph, the lines are $\frac{1}{4}$ inch apart and each square has an area of $\frac{1}{16}$ square inch.

In the left-hand graph, *BCD* contains three squares with some area left over. Thus, *BCD* has an area of at least 3 square inches. In the right-hand graph, *BCD* contains 16 squares with some space left over. Since each square in this graph has an area of $\frac{1}{4}$ square inch, *BCD* has an area of at least 4 square inches. In the bottom graph, you can count 74 small squares, each with an area of $\frac{1}{16}$ square inch. Thus, *BCD* has an area of at least $4\frac{5}{8}$ square inches. If you kept plotting *BCD* on graph paper with smaller and smaller squares, you could get a closer approximation to its actual area.

A slightly different way of approximating the area of *BCD* is shown below:

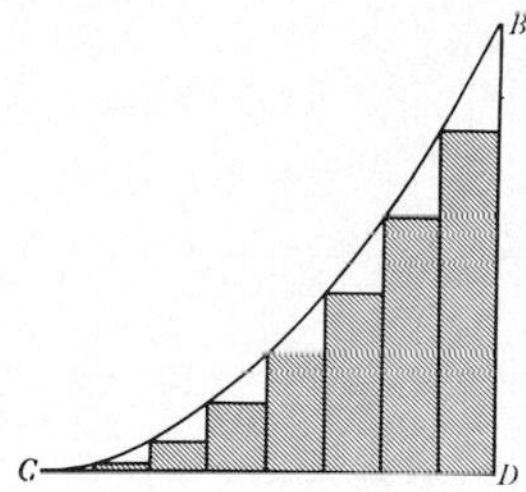

Divide the line segment *CD* into eight equal parts, each $\frac{1}{2}$ inch long. In the original parabola, it can be shown geometrically that any point on the parabola *BC* is $\frac{x^2}{4}$ inches above the line *CD* at any point x inches from *C*. Using this fact, we find that the eight rectangles drawn in *BCD* have heights of 0, $\frac{1}{16}$, $\frac{1}{4}$, $\frac{9}{16}$, 1, $\frac{25}{16}$, $\frac{9}{4}$, and $\frac{49}{16}$ inches. The sum of the areas of these eight is given by the following:

$$S_8 = 0\times\tfrac{1}{2} + \tfrac{1}{16}\times\tfrac{1}{2} + \tfrac{1}{4}\times\tfrac{1}{2} + \tfrac{9}{16}\times\tfrac{1}{2} + 1\times\tfrac{1}{2} + \tfrac{25}{16}\times\tfrac{1}{2} + \tfrac{9}{4}\times\tfrac{1}{2} + \tfrac{49}{16}\times\tfrac{1}{2} = \tfrac{35}{8} = 4\tfrac{3}{8} \text{ square inches}$$

Thus, the area of *BCD* must be more than $4\frac{3}{8}$ square inches using this method.

If we divide the segment *CD* into n equal parts, where n is a positivc wholc numbcr, each part has a lcngth of $\frac{4}{n}$ inches. If we draw n rectangles in *BCD* just as we did above for $n=8$, the sum, S_n, of the areas of the n rectangles is given by the following:

$$S_n = 0\times\frac{4}{n} + \frac{1}{4}\left(\frac{4}{n}\right)^2\times\frac{4}{n} + \frac{1}{4}\left(\frac{8}{n}\right)^2\times\frac{4}{n} + \frac{1}{4}\left(\frac{12}{n}\right)^2\times\frac{4}{n} + \dots + \frac{1}{4}\left(\frac{4(n-1)}{n}\right)^2\times\frac{4}{n}$$

In this equation, the three dots indicate that some of the terms might have been left out. For example, if $n=100$, 95 morc tcrms should bc included.

You can show by algebra that $S_n = \frac{16}{3} - \frac{8}{n} + \frac{8}{3n^2}$. As n gets larger and larger, the last two terms of this equation get smaller and smaller. Therefore, mathematicians say that the limit of S_n as n approaches infinity (∞) is $\frac{16}{3}$. They write this:

$$\lim_{n\to\infty} S_n = \frac{16}{3}$$

Since S_n is getting closer and closer to the area of *BCD* as n gets larger and larger, then the limit of S_n as n approaches infinity is the exact area of *BCD*. That is, the area of *BCD* is $\frac{16}{3}$, or $5\frac{1}{3}$ square inches.

We can use this information to find the area of *BCM*. We know the square *BDCM* has an area of 16 square inches. Therefore, region *BCM* has an area of $16-\frac{16}{3}$ square inches, or $\frac{32}{3}$ square inches. The area of the parabolic region *ABC* is twice that size, or $\frac{64}{3}$ square inches.

The Definite Integral. A method similar to that used in the last example can be used to find the area of a more general region such as *ABDC* shown below.

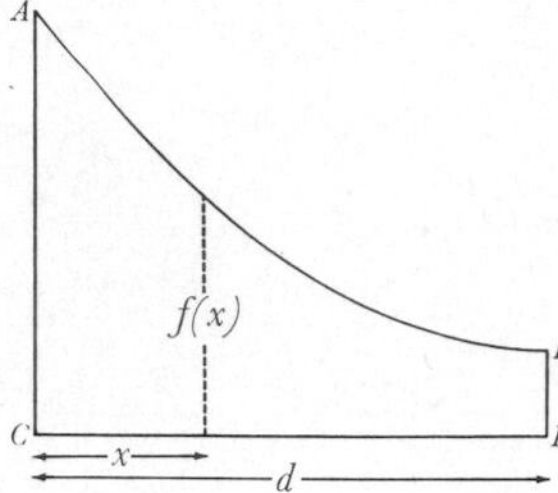

The area of *ABDC* may be approximated by drawing rectangles in it as we did for the parabola. The height of each rectangle is defined by the function $f(x)$, which is the height of the curve x units from C. Therefore, if we draw four rectangles with equal bases, the sum of their areas is given by the following equation:

$$S_4 = f(x_1)\Delta x + f(x_2)\Delta x + f(x_3)\Delta x + f(x_4)\Delta x$$

In this equation, Δx (spoken "delta x") equals $\frac{d}{4}$, the length of each base.

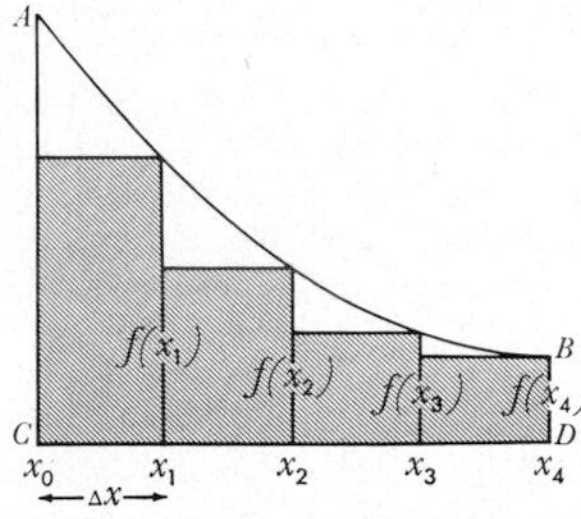

If we divide segment *CD* into n equal parts by the points $x_0, x_1, \ldots, x_n$, and if we draw n rectangles in region *ABDC*, the sum, S_n, of the areas of the n rectangles is given by the following equation:

$$S_n = f(x_1)\Delta x + f(x_2)\Delta x + \ldots + f(x_n)\Delta x$$

Again, $\Delta x = \frac{d}{n}$, or the length of each base.

You can see that S_n is an approximation of the area of *ABDC*. As n gets larger and larger, S_n becomes closer and closer to the actual area of *ABDC*. The actual area a is the limit of S_n as n approaches infinity:

$$a = \lim_{n \to \infty} S_n$$

In words, a is the number that S_n is approaching as we divide segment *CD* into more and more parts, thereby making n larger and larger and Δx smaller and smaller.

The limit of S_n as n approaches infinity is called the definite integral of the function f from 0 to d. It is written with a stretched-out S as follows:

$$\int_0^d f(x)dx$$

The Fundamental Theorem of Calculus. Given any function f, defined between the numbers a and b where a is less than b, we can divide the segment between a and b into n equal parts and form the sum S_n as just shown. The limit of S_n as n approaches infinity is called the definite integral of f from a to b and is written:

$$\int_a^b f(x)dx$$

The integral and the derivative of a function are related by the fundamental theorem of calculus which states that

$$\int_a^b f(x)dx = g(b) - g(a)$$

where g is any function whose derivative is the function f.

For example, if $f(x) = \frac{1}{4}x^2$ is the height function of the parabola we have been studying, then the function g defined by $g(x) = \frac{1}{12}x^3$ has f as its derivative. This is because $g'(x) = \frac{1}{12}3x^2 = \frac{1}{4}x^2 = f(x)$. By the fundamental theorem of calculus:

$$\int_0^4 \frac{1}{4}x^2 dx = g(4) - g(0) = \frac{1}{12}4^3 - \frac{1}{12}0^3 = \frac{64}{12} = \frac{16}{3}$$

This is the area of region *BCD* under the parabola.

History

The first ideas of calculus began with the great Greek mathematician Archimedes. Archimedes found many of our geometrical formulas, such as the formulas for the volume and surface area of a sphere. In his work, Archimedes used methods that foreshadowed those used today in integral calculus.

In the 1500's and 1600's, many mathematicians worked on problems that called for calculus. Then Sir Isaac Newton and Baron von Leibniz discovered the fundamental theorem of calculus. They worked independently of one another. For this discovery, they are called the founders of calculus. RICHARD E. JOHNSON

See also LEIBNIZ, GOTTFRIED W.; MATHEMATICS (History); NEWTON, SIR ISAAC.

CALCUTTA (pop. 3,305,006; met. area 9,194,018) is the third largest city of India. Only Bombay and Delhi have more people. Calcutta serves as India's chief port for trade with Southeast Asia. It also is the gateway to the most heavily populated part of northeastern India. Calcutta lies about 60 miles (97 kilometers) from the mouth of the Hooghly River, on a plain that extends into the Bay of Bengal. For location, see INDIA (political map). Calcutta is the capital of the state of West Bengal. The city has some of the worst living conditions in the world because of overcrowding, poverty, and starvation.

The City covers about 40 square miles (104 square kilometers) on the east bank of the Hooghly, a branch of the Ganges River. Howrah, the second largest city of the Calcutta metropolitan area, is on the west bank. The two cities are connected by a bridge 1,500 feet (457 meters) long. Railroads that serve Calcutta from the west have terminals in Howrah.

The Maidan, a large park, occupies 2 square miles (5 square kilometers) in the center of Calcutta. The

Jehangir Gazdar, Woodfin Camp, Inc.

E. Stering from Carl Östman

Calcutta, the third largest city of India, has some of the most crowded living conditions in the world. Traffic jams occur frequently in downtown Calcutta, *left.* A severe housing shortage forces most of the city's people to live in slum areas, *right,* called *bustees.*

city's finest residential area lies east of the Maidan. Government buildings line the Esplanade, a wide street north of the Maidan.

The Victoria Memorial, an impressive building of white marble, houses a picture gallery and a historical museum. Other important structures include Raj Bhavan, the residence of the governor of West Bengal; and the Ochterlony Monument, a granite column 152 feet (46 meters) high.

Calcutta has a university, founded in 1857, and several colleges. The Indian Museum, built in 1875, features collections of cultural materials.

People. Most of Calcutta's people speak one of three languages—Bengali, Hindi, or Urdu. About two-thirds of the city's adults cannot read or write. Hinduism is the principal religion, but Muslims make up about 15 per cent of the population. Other religious groups include Buddhists, Christians, and Jews.

Wealthy Calcuttans live near the center of the city in pleasant neighborhoods with wide streets and modern houses. But the majority of the people live in slum areas called *bustees.* Most of the slum dwellings are made of scraps of metal or wood. They have no electricity, running water, or sewage disposal. Thousands of people sleep in the streets because they have no shelter. These conditions, plus constant and widespread undernourishment, lead to frequent outbreaks of cholera, malaria, smallpox, and other diseases. During the 1960's, the government began to improve living conditions in the bustees by installing electricity, running water, and sewerage systems.

Economy. Calcutta is the world center of jute production. More than 200,000 people work in mills that process this fiber. Other Calcutta products include electric equipment, metal goods, paint, and shoes.

Calcutta has one of the busiest harbors in the world. Wharves line both banks of the Hooghly River for about 20 miles (32 kilometers). The city is the shipping outlet for the coal and iron mines located in northeastern India.

History. The East India Company, an English trading firm, founded Calcutta in 1690. The settlement grew rapidly in size and importance, and many neighboring villages became part of it.

Calcutta became the capital of India in 1773. By 1900, Calcutta ranked second only to London as the largest city in the British Empire. In 1912, India's capital was moved to Delhi, which had a more central location.

Since the end of World War II in 1945, outbreaks of political and religious violence have occurred frequently in Calcutta. In 1946, a riot between Hindus and Muslims over the proposed division of India into two nations left 4,000 people dead on the city's streets (see INDIA [Independence]). Riots against the government occurred frequently in Calcutta during the 1960's and 1970's.

COLIN MACANDREWS

See also BENGAL; BLACK HOLE OF CALCUTTA.

CALDECOTT, RANDOLPH (1846-1886), an English illustrator, became known for the action, vitality, and humor of his picture books. With Walter Crane and Kate Greenaway, Caldecott began a new era in children's picture books. The Caldecott medal, which is given to the illustrator of the year's outstanding children's picture book, is named for him. Caldecott illustrated such books as *The Diverting History of John Gilpin* (1878), *The House That Jack Built* (1878), and *The Farmer's Boy* (1881).

Detail of a self-portrait sketch in sepia; courtesy of the Harvard College Library

Randolph Caldecott

CALDECOTT MEDAL

Caldecott was born in Chester. From the age of 6, he drew animals and modeled them in clay and wood. For 11 years he worked in a bank, but spent his free time sketching. RUTH HILL VIGUERS

See also LITERATURE FOR CHILDREN (picture: Great Illustrators of the 1800's).

CALDECOTT MEDAL is an annual award for the most distinguished picture book for children published during the previous year. It was the first award recognizing the work of the illustrator of a book. The selection is made by a committee consisting of 15 members of the Association for Library Service to Children (ALSC) of the American Library Association. The winner is announced in January. The ALSC presents the award to the illustrator at a banquet during the association's annual convention.

The Caldecott Medal, *above,* honors the most distinguished children's picture book of the year. It pictures characters from children's storybooks on its face, *left,* and back, *right.*

Winners of Caldecott Medal

Year	Illustrator	Winning Book
1938	Dorothy P. Lathrop	*Animals of the Bible*
1939	Thomas Handforth	*Mei Li*
1940	Ingri and Edgar Parin d'Aulaire	*Abraham Lincoln*
1941	Robert Lawson	*They Were Strong and Good*
1942	Robert McCloskey	*Make Way for Ducklings*
1943	Virginia Lee Burton	*The Little House*
1944	Louis Slobodkin	*Many Moons*
1945	Elizabeth Orton Jones	*Prayer for a Child*
1946	Maud and Miska Petersham	*The Rooster Crows*
1947	Leonard Weisgard	*The Little Island*
1948	Roger Duvoisin	*White Snow, Bright Snow*
1949	Berta and Elmer Hader	*The Big Snow*
1950	Leo Politi	*Song of the Swallows*
1951	Katherine Milhous	*The Egg Tree*
1952	Nicolas Mordvinoff	*Finders Keepers*
1953	Lynd K. Ward	*The Biggest Bear*
1954	Ludwig Bemelmans	*Madeline's Rescue*
1955	Marcia Brown	*Cinderella; or The Little Glass Slipper*
1956	Feodor Rojankovsky	*Frog Went A-Courtin'*
1957	Marc Simont	*A Tree Is Nice*
1958	Robert McCloskey	*Time of Wonder*
1959	Barbara Cooney	*Chanticleer and the Fox*
1960	Marie Hall Ets	*Nine Days to Christmas*
1961	Nicolas Sidjakov	*Baboushka and the Three Kings*
1962	Marcia Brown	*Once a Mouse*
1963	Ezra Jack Keats	*The Snowy Day*
1964	Maurice Sendak	*Where the Wild Things Are*
1965	Beni Montresor	*May I Bring a Friend?*
1966	Nonny Hogrogian	*Always Room for One More*
1967	Evaline Ness	*Sam, Bangs, & Moonshine*
1968	Ed Emberley	*Drummer Hoff*
1969	Uri Shulevitz	*The Fool of the World and the Flying Ship*
1970	William Steig	*Sylvester and the Magic Pebble*
1971	Gail E. Haley	*A Story—A Story*
1972	Nonny Hogrogian	*One Fine Day*
1973	Blair Lent	*The Funny Little Woman*
1974	Margot Zemach	*Duffy and the Devil*
1975	Gerald McDermott	*Arrow to the Sun: A Pueblo Indian Tale*
1976	Leo and Diane Dillon	*Why Mosquitoes Buzz in People's Ears: A West African Tale*
1977	Leo and Diane Dillon	*Ashanti to Zulu: African Traditions*
1978	Peter Spier	*Noah's Ark*
1979	Paul Goble	*The Girl Who Loved Wild Horses*
1980	Barbara Cooney	*Ox-Cart Man*
1981	Arnold Lobel	*Fables*
1982	Chris Van Allsburg	*Jumanji*
1983	Marcia Brown	*Shadow*
1984	Alice and Martin Provensen	*The Glorious Flight: Across the Channel with Louis Bleriot*

The award is limited to artists who are U.S. citizens or residents, and whose work was published within the past year. The book must be the artist's original creation. If two artists worked together, the award is given to both. The illustrator does not have to write the story. The pictures, rather than the text, should be the heart of the book.

The face of the Caldecott medal has a reproduction of Randolph Caldecott's original illustration of John Gilpin's ride from the famous narrative poem "The Diverting History of John Gilpin" by William Cowper. The reverse side has an illustration of "four and twenty blackbirds baked in a pie." The engraving reads "For the most distinguished American picture book for children." René Chambellan designed the medal.

Frederic G. Melcher, co-editor of *Publishers' Weekly* magazine and founder of Children's Book Week, established the medal. Caldecott, for whom the award was named, was an English illustrator of children's books. Melcher also established the Newbery medal, which is awarded for the most distinguished book written for children.

Critically reviewed by the ASSOCIATION FOR LIBRARY SERVICE TO CHILDREN

See also CALDECOTT, RANDOLPH; MELCHER, FREDERIC G.; NEWBERY MEDAL.

CALDER, ALEXANDER (1898-1976), was one of the first American sculptors of international significance, and one of the best-known American artists of the 1900's. Calder became famous for his witty and elegant sculptures called *mobiles.* The works received this name because they actually move when pushed by air currents. Earlier sculptors had given movement to sculpture by using motors or clockworks. Calder's mobiles are delicately suspended abstract constructions of sheet metal parts and wires.

Calder was born in Philadelphia. His father and grandfather were sculptors, and his mother was a painter. Calder received an engineering degree from the Stevens Institute of Technology in 1919. He then studied painting at the Art Students League in New York City, and moved to Paris in 1926. Until 1933, Calder divided his time between Paris and Roxbury, Conn., where he established his first American studio.

Calder in his studio in Roxbury, Conn., John Lewis Stage from *Holiday Magazine* © 1959

Alexander Calder became famous for his delicate and playful metal sculpture. He created both *mobiles* (moving sculpture) and *stabiles* (stationary sculpture).

The early work of Calder in Paris included wooden toys, miniature circuses, and wire sculptures. In 1932, he began constructing mobiles, a term invented by artist Marcel Duchamp. Calder also started to build *stabiles,* a name first used by his friend and fellow artist Jean Arp. Stabiles resemble mobiles except that they do not move. Calder later created works that are combinations of the elements of both mobiles and stabiles. See MOBILE.

Calder's works have been exhibited in many countries, including a major display of his career at the Museum of Modern Art in New York City in 1964 and 1965. Some of his many important public sculptures can be seen in such places as UNESCO headquarters in Paris, Kennedy International Airport and Lincoln Center for the Performing Arts in New York City, and the Festival of Two Worlds in Spoleto, Italy. Calder's sculpture *Red Petals* appears in color in the SCULPTURE article. He also created many lithographs. DOUGLAS GEORGE

CALDERA. See CRATER; VOLCANO (Composite Volcanoes; picture: Shield Volcanoes).

CALDERÓN DE LA BARCA, *KAHL day RAWN day lah BAHR kah,* **PEDRO** (1600-1681), was a Spanish playwright, and the last great writer of Spain's Golden Age. Calderón wrote about 200 plays, including more than 70 *autos sacramentales* (religious plays on the theme of the Eucharist). Calderón dealt with traditional Spanish moral and religious attitudes, rather than with original ideas. He filled his plays with symbolism and elaborate figures of speech. *Life Is a Dream* (1635), his best-known play, explores the mysteries of human destiny and the conflict between free will and predestination. Calderón also wrote tragedies based on the Spanish honor code, including *The Surgeon of His Honor,* and "cloak-and-sword" plays of intrigue.

Calderón was born in Madrid. As a young soldier in France and Italy, he was something of a rowdy. Later, he received a thorough university education in law, logic, and theology. He became a priest at the age of 50. PETER G. EARLE

See also DRAMA (The Golden Age of Spanish Drama); SPANISH LITERATURE (The 1600's).

CALDERONE, MARY STEICHEN (1904-), an American physician, won fame for her efforts to promote sex education in schools. She helped establish the Sex Information and Education Council of the United States (SIECUS) in 1964 and became its executive director. SIECUS provides advice and information about sex education to counselors, physicians, religious groups, and schools. It also publishes books and study guides.

© Karsh, Ottawa

Mary Calderone

Calderone was born in New York City and earned an M.D. at the University of Rochester in 1939. She and her husband, also a physician, both worked in the field of public health. Calderone formerly served as physician to the public schools in Great Neck, N.Y. From 1953 to 1964, she was medical director of the Planned Parenthood Federation of America. She became convinced that a thorough understanding of sex would help people handle their sexual problems responsibly and achieve greater health and happiness. ISAAC ASIMOV

CALDWELL, ERSKINE (1903-), is an American author best known for the sensationalism of his novels about rural Southern life. His most famous works portray the impact of changing cultural and economic conditions on poverty-stricken white tenant farmers. He tells about men and women who are reduced to the basic hungers of life and are starved of the satisfaction of these hungers. His emphasis on sex and violence, even when combined with humor, has been condemned by some as sentimental and by others as immoral.

Over 64 million copies of Caldwell's more than 40 books have been published worldwide. He first became famous with *Tobacco Road* (1932), which features his best-known character, Jeeter Lester. *Tobacco Road* was adapted into a play that ran more than seven years on Broadway during the 1930's. Caldwell's next novel, *God's Little Acre* (1933), increased his fame. His other novels include *Georgia Boy* (1943) and *The Sure Hand of God* (1947). Caldwell's *Complete Stories* appeared in 1953. He was born in White Oak, Ga. JOSEPH N. RIDDEL

See also AMERICAN LITERATURE (Regionalists).

CALDWELL, SARAH (1928-), is an American opera director and conductor. She founded the Opera Company of Boston in 1957 and serves as its artistic director and frequently as its conductor. In 1976, Caldwell

Wide World

Sarah Caldwell

became the first woman to conduct at the Metropolitan Opera House in New York City.

Caldwell emphasizes the dramatic elements of opera in her productions, and many of her stagings include spectacular visual effects. She also is known for producing complete versions of rarely performed operas. For example, she staged the American premieres of such works as Arnold Schönberg's *Moses and Aron*, Sergei Prokofiev's *War and Peace*, Hector Berlioz' *The Trojans*, and Roger Sessions' *Montezuma*.

Caldwell was born in Maryville, Mo. She attended the New England Conservatory of Music, where she studied opera production, stage design, and conducting, and also violin and viola. Caldwell taught at the Berkshire Music Center from 1948 to 1952. From 1952 to 1960, she headed the Opera Workshop Department at Boston University. In 1983, she became artistic director of the New Opera Company of Israel while retaining her Boston position. ELLEN PFEIFER

CALEDONIA, *KAL ih DOH nee uh*, is the ancient Roman name for northern Scotland. It later became a poetic name for all Scotland. The Roman general Agricola invaded Caledonia in A.D. 83. The first Caledonians were the Picts. But the Caledonians of early English history were Picts and Scots. Their raids forced the Britons to seek the help of the Angles and the Saxons.

See also SCOTLAND (The Roman Invasion).

CALENDAR is a system of measuring and recording the passage of time. A major scientific advance was made when people realized that nature furnishes a regular sequence of seasons. The seasons governed their lives, determined their needs, and controlled the supply of their natural foods. They needed a calendar so they could prepare for winter before it came.

Before the invention of the clock, people had to rely on nature's timekeepers—the sun, the moon, and the stars. The daily apparent rotation of the sun provided the simplest and most obvious unit, the solar day. The seasons roughly indicated the length of another simple unit, the solar year. Early people were not aware of the fundamental cause of the seasons, the earth's revolution around the sun. But it was easy to see the changing position and shape of the moon. As a result, most ancient calendars used the interval between successive full moons, the lunar month, as an intermediate measure of time. The month bridged the gap between the solar day and the solar year.

The lunar month, we now know, is about 29½ days long. Twelve such months amount to about 354 days. This interval is almost 11 days shorter than the true solar year which has 365 days, 5 hours, 48 minutes, and 46 seconds. But a year of 13 lunar months would amount to about 383½ days, and would be more than 18½ days

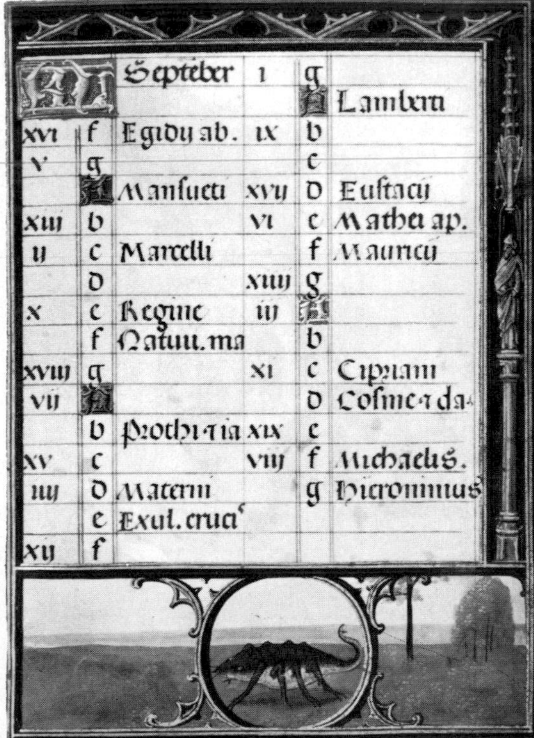

Detail from an illuminated manuscript, *The Hours of the Virgin* (1515); the Pierpont Morgan Library, New York City

A Flemish Calendar from the 1500's Shows the Month of September Illustrated with a Farming Scene.

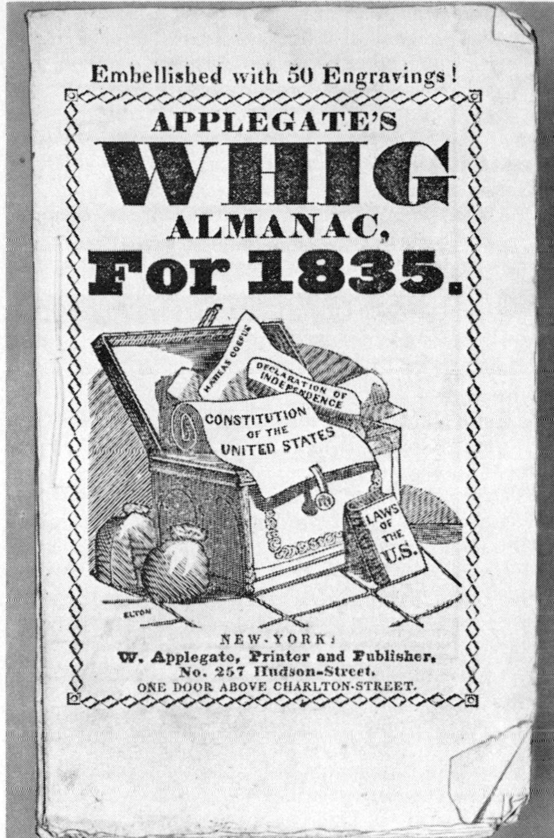

Embellished with 50 Engravings!
APPLEGATE'S
WHIG
ALMANAC,
For 1835.
CONSTITUTION OF THE UNITED STATES
DECLARATION OF INDEPENDENCE
LAWS OF THE U.S.
NEW-YORK:
W. Applegate, Printer and Publisher,
No. 257 Hudson-Street.
ONE DOOR ABOVE CHARLTON-STREET.

Mrs. O. Andreas Garson

Early Printed Calendars often had elaborate pictures. The American almanac shown above boasted 50 of them.

longer than the solar year. The 13-month calendar is even less suited than the 12-month calendar to measure the year. This discrepancy explains the confusion that has existed in the calendar for thousands of years, and still exists in some areas. People have no accurate way to keep both the lunar and solar calendars exactly in step.

The Calendar Today

Most persons in the Western World use the *Gregorian calendar*, worked out in the 1580's by Pope Gregory XIII. It has 12 months, 11 of them with 30 or 31 days. The other month, February, normally has 28 days. Every fourth year, called a *leap year*, it has 29 days. But even this calendar is not quite exact enough. In century years that cannot be divided by 400, such as 1700, 1800, and 1900, the extra day in February must be dropped. The century year 1600 was a leap year, and the year 2000 will be one.

Our calendar is supposed to be based on the year Jesus Christ was born. Dates before that year are listed as B.C., or *before Christ*. Dates after that year are listed as A.D., or *anno Domini* (in the year of our Lord). Non-Christians often write B.C.E., for *before Christian era*, and C.E., for *Christian era*. See B.C.; A.D.; CHRISTIAN ERA.

The Church Calendar is regulated partly by the sun and partly by the moon. *Immovable feasts* include Christmas and such feasts as the Nativity of the Blessed Virgin. They are based on the solar calendar. Such days as Easter are called *movable feasts*, because their dates vary from year to year, according to the phases of the moon. The other principal movable feasts of the church year are Ash Wednesday, Palm Sunday, Good Friday, Ascension, and Pentecost.

The Hebrew Calendar, according to tradition, was supposed to have started with the Creation, at a moment 3,760 years and 3 months before the beginning of the Christian era. To find the year in the Hebrew calendar, we must add 3,760 to the date in the Gregorian calendar. The year 1985 in the Gregorian calendar is the year 5745 according to the Hebrew calendar. But this system will not work to the exact month, because the Hebrew year begins in the autumn, rather than in midwinter. During the winter of 1985-1986, the Hebrew year is 5746.

The Hebrew year is based on the moon, and normally consists of 12 months. These months are *Tishri*, *Heshvan*, *Kislev*, *Tebet*, *Shebat*, *Adar*, *Nisan*, *Iyar*, *Sivan*, *Tammuz*, *Ab*, and *Elul*. The months are alternately 30 and 29 days long. Seven times during every 19-year period, an *embolismic* or extra 29-day month is inserted between Adar and Nisan. The extra month is called *Veadar*. At the same time, Adar is given 30 days instead of 29.

The Islamic Calendar begins with Muhammad's flight from Mecca to Medina. This flight, called *the Hegira*, took place in A.D. 622 by the Gregorian calendar. The year is much shorter than the solar year, with only 354 days. As a result, the Islamic New Year moves backward through the seasons. It moves completely backward in a course of $32\frac{1}{2}$ years. The Islamic calendar divides time into cycles 30 years long. During each cycle, 19 years have the regular 354 days, and 11 years have an extra day each. This method of counting time makes the Islamic year nearly as accurate as the year computed by the Gregorian calendar. The Islamic calendar would be only about one day off every 2,570 years with respect to the moon. The Gregorian calendar would be only a little more accurate with respect to the sun.

The Islamic year is based on the moon, and has 12 months, alternately 30 and 29 days long. These months are *Muharram*, *Safar*, *Rabi I*, *Rabi II*, *Jumada I*, *Jumada II*, *Rajab*, *Shaban*, *Ramadan*, *Shawwal*, *Zulkadah*, and *Zulhijjah*. The extra day in leap years goes to Zulhijjah.

The Chinese Calendar begins with 2637 B.C., the year in which the legendary Emperor Huang-Ti supposedly invented it. This calendar designates years in cycles of 60. For example, 1985 is the second year in the 78th cycle. The years in each cycle are designated by a word combination formed from two series of terms, one of which involves the name of any of 12 animals. The appropriate animal name is assigned to each year. The year 1985 is the *year of the ox*.

The Chinese year is based on the moon and generally consists of 12 months. Each month begins at new moon and has 29 or 30 days. A month is repeated seven times during each 19-year period, so that the calendar stays approximately in line with the seasons. The year starts at the second new moon after the beginning of winter.

Thus, the Chinese New Year occurs no earlier than January 20 and no later than February 20.

History

Ancient Calendars usually represented some sort of compromise between the lunar and solar years, with some years of 12 months and some of 13.

The Babylonians, who lived in the southern part of the valley of the Tigris and Euphrates rivers, developed a calendar that represented many primitive procedures. They *intercalated*, or added, an extra month to their years at irregular intervals. When the royal astrologers discovered that the calendar had run badly out of step, they decreed an intercalary month. A calendar composed of alternate 29-day and 30-day months keeps roughly in step with the 354-day lunar year. To coordinate this calendar with the solar year, the Babylonians intercalated an extra month three times in a cycle of eight years. But even this did not compensate with sufficient accuracy for the accumulated differences, and the Babylonian calendar was quite confused.

The Egyptians were probably the first people to adopt a predominantly solar calendar. They noted that the Dog Star, Sirius, reappeared in the eastern sky just before sunrise after several months of invisibility. They also discovered that the annual flood of the Nile River came soon after Sirius reappeared. They used this event to fix their calendar, and came to recognize a year of 365 days, made up of 12 months each 30 days long, and an extra dividend of five days added at the end. But they did not allow for the extra fourth of a day, and their calendar slowly drifted into error. According to the famed Egyptologist J. H. Breasted, the earliest date known in the Egyptian calendar corresponds to 4236 B.C. in terms of our present-day system.

The Romans apparently borrowed their first calendar from the Greeks. The earliest known Roman calendar consisted of 10 months and a year of 304 days. The Romans seem to have ignored the remaining 60 days, which fell in the middle of winter. The 10 months were named *Martius*, *Aprilis*, *Maius*, *Junius*, *Quintilis*, *Sextilis*, *September*, *October*, *November*, and *December*. The last six names were taken from the words for five, six, seven, eight, nine, and ten. Romulus, the legendary first ruler of Rome, is supposed to have introduced this calendar about 738 B.C.

The Roman ruler Numa added two months to the calendar: January, at the beginning of the year; and February, at the end of the year. To make the calendar correspond approximately to the solar year, he also ordered the addition of a month called *Mercedinus*, which had 22 or 23 days. This month was inserted between February 23 and 24 every other year. The order of months established by Numa was changed in 452 B.C.

The Julian Calendar. By the time of Julius Caesar, the accumulated error caused by the incorrect length

A Perpetual Calendar will show the day of the week for any year desired. This calendar begins with 1753, the year after Great Britain adopted our present calendar. The calendar is easy to use. The letters after each year in the *Table of Years* (*on the opposite page*) refer to the first column of the *Table of Months* (*next to it*). The figures given for each month in the Table of Months refer to one of the seven columns in the *Table of Days* (*below*). For example, to find on what day of the week Christmas fell in 1900, look for **1900** in the Table of Years. The letter **a** follows. Look for **a** in the Table of Months, and, under December, you will find the number **6.** In the Table of Days, column **6** shows that the 25th day of the month, Christmas, fell on Tuesday in 1900.

1	2	3	4	5	6	7
Monday 1	Tuesday 1	Wednesday 1	Thursday 1	Friday 1	Saturday 1	SUNDAY 1
Tuesday 2	Wednesday 2	Thursday 2	Friday 2	Saturday 2	SUNDAY 2	Monday 2
Wednesday 3	Thursday 3	Friday 3	Saturday 3	SUNDAY 3	Monday 3	Tuesday 3
Thursday 4	Friday 4	Saturday 4	SUNDAY 4	Monday 4	Tuesday 4	Wednesday 4
Friday 5	Saturday 5	SUNDAY 5	Monday 5	Tuesday 5	Wednesday 5	Thursday 5
Saturday 6	SUNDAY 6	Monday 6	Tuesday 6	Wednesday 6	Thursday 6	Friday 6
SUNDAY 7	Monday 7	Tuesday 7	Wednesday 7	Thursday 7	Friday 7	Saturday 7
Monday 8	Tuesday 8	Wednesday 8	Thursday 8	Friday 8	Saturday 8	SUNDAY 8
Tuesday 9	Wednesday 9	Thursday 9	Friday 9	Saturday 9	SUNDAY 9	Monday 9
Wednesday 10	Thursday 10	Friday 10	Saturday 10	SUNDAY 10	Monday 10	Tuesday 10
Thursday 11	Friday 11	Saturday 11	SUNDAY 11	Monday 11	Tuesday 11	Wednesday 11
Friday 12	Saturday 12	SUNDAY 12	Monday 12	Tuesday 12	Wednesday 12	Thursday 12
Saturday 13	SUNDAY 13	Monday 13	Tuesday 13	Wednesday 13	Thursday 13	Friday 13
SUNDAY 14	Monday 14	Tuesday 14	Wednesday 14	Thursday 14	Friday 14	Saturday 14
Monday 15	Tuesday 15	Wednesday 15	Thursday 15	Friday 15	Saturday 15	SUNDAY 15
Tuesday 16	Wednesday 16	Thursday 16	Friday 16	Saturday 16	SUNDAY 16	Monday 16
Wednesday 17	Thursday 17	Friday 17	Saturday 17	SUNDAY 17	Monday 17	Tuesday 17
Thursday 18	Friday 18	Saturday 18	SUNDAY 18	Monday 18	Tuesday 18	Wednesday 18
Friday 19	Saturday 19	SUNDAY 19	Monday 19	Tuesday 19	Wednesday 19	Thursday 19
Saturday 20	SUNDAY 20	Monday 20	Tuesday 20	Wednesday 20	Thursday 20	Friday 20
SUNDAY 21	Monday 21	Tuesday 21	Wednesday 21	Thursday 21	Friday 21	Saturday 21
Monday 22	Tuesday 22	Wednesday 22	Thursday 22	Friday 22	Saturday 22	SUNDAY 22
Tuesday 23	Wednesday 23	Thursday 23	Friday 23	Saturday 23	SUNDAY 23	Monday 23
Wednesday 24	Thursday 24	Friday 24	Saturday 24	SUNDAY 24	Monday 24	Tuesday 24
Thursday 25	Friday 25	Saturday 25	SUNDAY 25	Monday 25	Tuesday 25	Wednesday 25
Friday 26	Saturday 26	SUNDAY 26	Monday 26	Tuesday 26	Wednesday 26	Thursday 26
Saturday 27	SUNDAY 27	Monday 27	Tuesday 27	Wednesday 27	Thursday 27	Friday 27
SUNDAY 28	Monday 28	Tuesday 28	Wednesday 28	Thursday 28	Friday 28	Saturday 28
Monday 29	Tuesday 29	Wednesday 29	Thursday 29	Friday 29	Saturday 29	SUNDAY 29
Tuesday 30	Wednesday 30	Thursday 30	Friday 30	Saturday 30	SUNDAY 30	Monday 30
Wednesday 31	Thursday 31	Friday 31	Saturday 31	SUNDAY 31	Monday 31	Tuesday 31

of the Roman year had made the calendar about three months ahead of the seasons. Winter occurred in September, and autumn came in the month now called July. In 46 B.C., Caesar asked the astronomer Sosigenes to review the calendar and suggest ways for improving it. Acting on Sosigenes' suggestions, Caesar ordered the Romans to disregard the moon in calculating their calendars. He divided the year into 12 months of 31 and 30 days, except for February, which had only 29 days. Every fourth year, it would have 30 days. He also moved the beginning of the year from March 1 to January 1. To realign the calendar with the seasons, Caesar ruled that the year we know as 46 B.C. should have 445 days. The Romans called it *the year of confusion.*

The Romans renamed Quintilis to honor Julius Caesar, giving us *July*. The next month, Sextilis, was renamed *August* by the Roman Senate to honor the emperor Augustus. According to tradition, Augustus moved a day from February to August to make August as long as the month of July.

The Julian calendar was widely used for more than 1,500 years. It provided for a year that lasted 365¼ days. But it was actually about 11 minutes and 14 seconds longer than the solar year. This difference led to a gradual change in the dates on which the seasons began. By 1580, the spring equinox fell on March 11, or 10 days earlier than it should.

The Gregorian Calendar was designed to correct the errors of the Julian calendar. In 1582, on the advice of astronomers, Pope Gregory XIII corrected the difference between sun and calendar by ordering 10 days dropped from October. The day that would have been October 5, 1582, became October 15. This procedure restored the next equinox to its proper date. To correct the Julian calendar's error regularly, the pope decreed that February would have an extra day in century years that could be divided by 400, such as 1600 and 2000, but not in others, such as 1700, 1800, and 1900.

The Gregorian calendar is so accurate that the difference between the calendar and solar years is now only about 26 seconds. This difference will increase by .53 second every hundred years, because the solar year is gradually growing shorter.

The Roman Catholic nations of Europe adopted the Gregorian calendar almost immediately. Various German states kept the Julian calendar until 1700. Great Britain did not change to the Gregorian until 1752, Russia until 1918, and Turkey until 1927.

Calendar Reform would simplify the present calendar. Three proposed calendars have received considerable support. In each, months and years would begin on the same day of the week and different months would

YEARS 1753 TO 2030							
	1786g	1821a	1856k	1891d	1926e	1961g	1996h
	1787a	1822b	1857d	1892n	1927f	1962a	1997c
1753a	1788k	1823c	1858e	1893g	1928q	1963b	1998d
1754b	1789d	1824m	1859f	1894a	1929b	1964l	1999e
1755c	1790e	1825f	1860q	1895b	1930c	1965c	2000p
1756m	1791f	1826g	1861b	1896l	1931d	1966f	2001a
1757f	1792q	1827a	1862c	1897e	1932n	1967g	2002b
1758g	1793b	1828k	1863d	1898f	1933g	1968h	2003c
1759a	1794c	1829d	1864n	1899g	1934a	1969c	2004m
1760k	1795d	1830e	1865g	1900a	1935b	1970d	2005f
1761d	1796n	1831f	1866a	1901b	1936l	1971e	2006g
1762e	1797g	1832q	1867b	1902c	1937e	1972p	2007a
1763f	1798a	1833b	1868l	1903d	1938f	1973a	2008k
1764q	1799b	1834c	1869c	1904n	1939g	1974b	2009d
1765b	1800c	1835d	1870f	1905g	1940h	1975c	2010e
1766c	1801d	1836n	1871g	1906a	1941c	1976m	2011f
1767d	1802e	1837g	1872h	1907b	1942d	1977f	2012q
1768n	1803f	1838a	1873c	1908l	1943e	1978g	2013b
1769g	1804q	1839b	1874d	1909e	1944p	1979a	2014c
1770a	1805b	1840l	1875e	1910f	1945a	1980k	2015d
1771b	1806c	1841e	1876p	1911g	1946b	1981d	2016n
1772l	1807d	1842f	1877a	1912h	1947c	1982e	2017g
1773e	1808n	1843g	1878b	1913c	1948m	1983f	2018a
1774f	1809g	1844h	1879c	1914d	1949f	1984q	2019b
1775g	1810a	1845c	1880m	1915e	1950g	1985b	2020l
1776h	1811b	1846d	1881f	1916p	1951a	1986c	2021e
1777c	1812l	1847e	1882g	1917a	1952k	1987d	2022f
1778d	1813e	1848p	1883a	1918b	1953d	1988n	2023g
1779e	1814f	1849a	1884k	1919c	1954e	1989g	2024h
1780p	1815g	1850b	1885d	1920m	1955f	1990a	2025c
1781a	1816h	1851c	1886e	1921f	1956q	1991b	2026d
1782b	1817c	1852m	1887f	1922g	1957b	1992l	2027e
1783c	1818d	1853f	1888q	1923a	1958c	1993e	2028p
1784m	1819e	1854g	1889b	1924k	1959d	1994f	2029a
1785f	1820p	1855a	1890c	1925d	1960n	1995g	2030b

	Jan.	Feb.	Mar.	Apr.	May	Jun.	Jul.	Aug.	Sep.	Oct.	Nov.	Dec.
a	1	4	4	7	2	5	7	3	6	1	4	6
b	2	5	5	1	3	6	1	4	7	2	5	7
c	3	6	6	2	4	7	2	5	1	3	6	1
d	4	7	7	3	5	1	3	6	2	4	7	2
e	5	1	1	4	6	2	4	7	3	5	1	3
f	6	2	2	5	7	3	5	1	4	6	2	4
g	7	3	3	6	1	4	6	2	5	7	3	5
h	1	4	5	1	3	6	1	4	7	2	5	7
k	2	5	6	2	4	7	2	5	1	3	6	1
l	3	6	7	3	5	1	3	6	2	4	7	2
m	4	7	1	4	6	2	4	7	3	5	1	3
n	5	1	2	5	7	3	5	1	4	6	2	4
p	6	2	3	6	1	4	6	2	5	7	3	5
q	7	3	4	7	2	5	7	3	6	1	4	6

have the same or nearly the same number of days. *The Thirteen-Month Calendar* would provide 13 months exactly four weeks long. The extra month, *Sol*, would come before July. A *year day* placed at the end of the year would belong to no week or month. Every four years, a *leap-year day* would be added just before July 1. *The World Calendar* and *The Perpetual Calendar* differ from each other slightly. But both calendars would have 12 months of 30 or 31 days, a year day at the end of each year, and a leap-year day before July 1 every four years. HAROLD F. WEAVER

Related Articles in WORLD BOOK include:

Century	Leap Year	Month	Time
Day	Maya	Moon	Week
Equinox	(Communication	Olympiad	Year
Hegira	and Learning)	Season	

CALENDAR STONE. See AZTEC (Arts and Crafts).

CALENDERING. See PAPER (Processes; picture: How Paper Is Made); PLASTICS (Making Plastics Products; picture: How Plastics Products Are Made); RUBBER (Shaping); TEXTILE (Finishing the Fabric).

CALENDULA, *kuh LEHN juh luh*, is a group of herbs of the composite family. Most kinds grow in the temperate zone from the Canary Islands to Asia Minor.

J. Horace McFarland

Calendulas are common garden flowers in temperate regions around the world.

Calendulas grow from 1 to 2 feet (30 to 61 centimeters) high. The leaves lie one above the other on the stem. The flower heads have yellow or orange rays.

Some calendulas, such as the pot marigold, are favorite annual garden flowers in many parts of the world. Gardeners usually grow them from seeds. The calendula is the flower-of-the-month for October. In Shakespeare's time, the calendula blossom was used in cooking to flavor soups and stews.

Scientific Classification. Calendulas belong to the composite family, *Compositae*. A common calendula is genus *Calendula*, species *C. officinalis*. PAUL C. STANDLEY

CALF, in anatomy. See LEG (The Leg).

CALF. See CATTLE; ELEPHANT (Reproduction); WHALE (Reproduction).

CALF ROPING. See RODEO (Calf Roping; picture).

CALGARY, *KAL guh ree*, is the oil center of Canada and the largest city in the province of Alberta. The oil industry has made Calgary one of the fastest-growing cities in Canada. Calgary lies in the eastern foothills of the Canadian Rocky Mountains and is sometimes called the *Foothills City*. Its location has made the city a leading transportation center and major distribution point of western Canada.

Calgary grew up as a cattle town and is still a major cattle center in Alberta. The city has won fame for the yearly Calgary Exhibition and Stampede, which features horse racing, livestock shows, and rodeo events.

The North-West Mounted Police—now the Royal Canadian Mounted Police—established a fort on the site of Calgary in 1875. Their commander, Colonel James F. Macleod, named the fort after his ancestors' home, Calgary, in Scotland. The Gaelic word *calgary* means *clear, running water*.

The City. Calgary lies at the junction of the Bow and Elbow rivers, which run through the heart of the city. In Calgary, *streets* run north and south, and *avenues* run

City of Calgary

Calgary, the center of Canada's oil industry, lies at the junction of the Bow and Elbow rivers in southwestern Alberta.

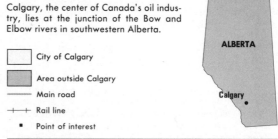

City of Calgary
Area outside Calgary
Main road
Rail line
Point of interest

ALBERTA
Calgary

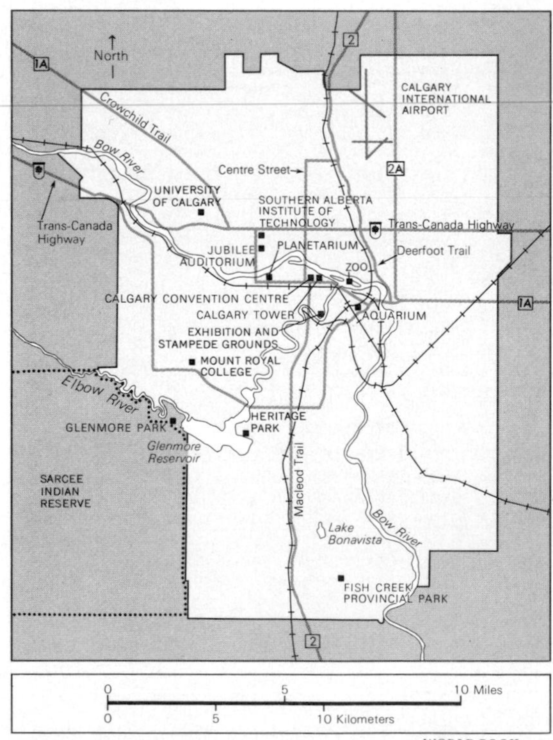

WORLD BOOK map

The City Seal of Calgary shows the city's symbols—the Rockies, a buffalo, a horse, and a steer.

Facts in Brief

Population: 592,743.

Area: 193 sq. mi. (500 km²).

Altitude: 3,441 ft. (1,049 m) above sea level.

Climate: *Average Temperature*—January, 16° F. (−9° C); July, 63° F. (17° C). *Average Annual Precipitation* (rainfall, melted snow, and other forms of moisture)—17½ in. (44.5 cm). For monthly weather in Calgary, see ALBERTA (Climate).

Government: Mayor-council. *Terms*—3 years for the mayor and 12 aldermen.

Founded: 1875. Incorporated as a town in 1884. Incorporated as a city in 1893.

east and west. Many of the streets and avenues have numbers instead of names. The intersection of Centre Street and the Bow River is the starting point of the numbering system. Centre Street divides the east and west numbers, and the Bow divides the north and south numbers. The intersection also divides Calgary into four quarters—northeast (N.E.), northwest (N.W.), southeast (S.E.), and southwest (S.W.)—that help locate most addresses.

The Bow River curves around the city and forms the northern border of downtown Calgary. City Hall stands at the corner of 7 Avenue S.E. and Macleod Trail. The Calgary Tower, a city landmark, rises 626 feet (191 meters) at the intersection of 9 Avenue S.E. and Centre Street. Atop this building are an observation deck and a revolving restaurant.

The People. Most Calgarians are of English descent. After World War II ended in 1945, large numbers of Europeans settled in Canada. These immigrants included Dutch, French, Germans, and Scandinavians, many of whom made their homes in Calgary. Indians make up less than 2 per cent of the city's population. About 800 Indians live on the Sarcee Indian Reserve southwest of Calgary.

Calgary may have more U.S. citizens than any other city outside the United States. The Alberta government estimates that at least 20,000 Calgarians were born in the United States. The growth of the oil industry has brought most of these people to the city.

About 60 per cent of Calgary's people are Protestants. About half of this group belong to the United Church of Canada. Roman Catholics make up about 20 per cent of the city's population.

One of Calgary's major problems is a slum area on the city's east side. In the early 1970's, old, run-down buildings in part of this area were torn down, and the city built a complex called Churchill Park on the site. It includes a high-rise apartment building with inexpensive housing for the poor and elderly.

Economy. More than 450 oil companies have their headquarters in Calgary. The city's many refineries process petroleum from the Turner Valley oil fields and other wells in southern Alberta. During the early 1970's, these refineries helped meet the great demand for petroleum that resulted from oil shortages in Europe and the United States.

About 70 per cent of Canada's engineering, geological, and surveying consultant firms have home offices in Calgary. Most Canadian banks have western headquarters in the city, making it a major financial center.

Calgary is a leading cattle center. Large ranches in southern Alberta send their cattle to Calgary's slaughterhouses and processing plants.

The city's location also makes it a center for trans-

Travel Alberta

Calgary is Alberta's largest city and the center of Canada's oil industry. The city lies in the eastern foothills of the Canadian Rocky Mountains. Calgary Tower, one of Calgary's landmarks, rises 626 feet (191 meters) over the downtown area.

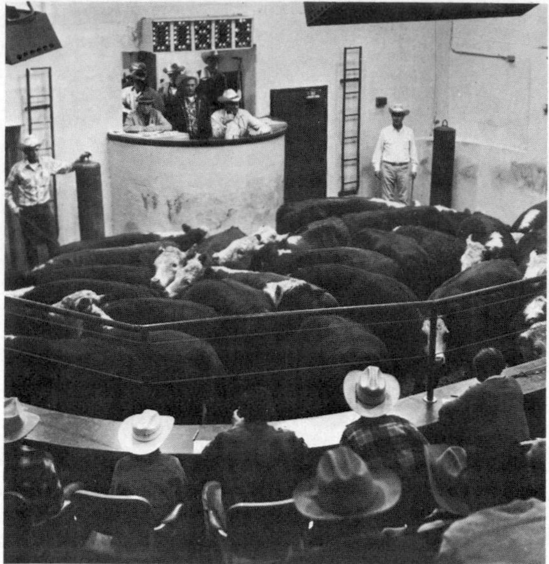

Canadian Government Travel Bureau

Livestock Buyers gather to bid for cattle at an auction in Calgary. The city is one of Alberta's chief cattle centers.

portation and shipping. Seven airlines serve Calgary International Airport. Calgary has two transcontinental railways, four branch railways, and several transcontinental truck lines. The Trans-Canada Highway runs through the city.

Calgary's more than 940 industrial plants manufacture products with a total annual value of about $1 billion. Most of these plants use natural gas for fuel and do not pollute the air with smoke. The Bow and Elbow rivers provide the city with hydroelectric power. The Calgary area also has abundant coal reserves.

Leading Calgary products include building materials, chemicals, electrical equipment, fertilizer, plastics, and sulfur. Calgary lies in a wheat-growing region, and grain elevators and flour mills lie near the city.

Education. Calgary has over 180 public schools and about 50 Roman Catholic schools. Public funds support both systems. The University of Calgary works closely with Calgary's Mount Royal College. The Southern Alberta Institute of Technology is also in Calgary.

The Calgary Public Library, which opened in 1912, was Alberta's first public library. It has 13 branches.

Cultural Life of the city is highlighted by the Calgary Exhibition and Stampede in July. Contestants from throughout North America take part in this 10-day festival, which attracts more than 900,000 persons annually. See ALBERTA (picture: Chuck Wagon Race).

Two daily newspapers, *The Albertan* and *The Calgary Herald*, serve Calgary. The city has seven radio stations and three television stations.

The Calgary Philharmonic Society presents concerts in the Southern Alberta Jubilee Auditorium. A drama group called Theatre Calgary performs in the QR Centre. The Glenbow-Alberta Institute, a cultural organization, has given Calgary an art gallery, a historical library, and a museum.

The Calgary Zoo, Canada's largest zoo, opened in 1918. Its Dinosaur Park features life-size models of the prehistoric animals that once roamed the area. Calgary also has a planetarium and over 100 public parks.

The Calgary Stampeders of the Canadian Football League play in McMahon Stadium. The Calgary Flames of the National Hockey League play in the Olympic Saddledome.

Government. Calgary has a mayor-council form of government. The mayor, whom the voters elect to a three-year term, appoints a four-member board of commissioners, including a chief commissioner. The commissioners administer various departments of the city government. Calgary is divided into six *wards* (voting areas), each of which elects two aldermen to the city council. The aldermen also serve three-year terms. Calgary gets much of its income from business licenses, property taxes, and provincial grants.

History. The Blackfoot Indians and their friends, the Sarcee, lived in the Calgary region before the white people came. Until illness and starvation almost wiped out their people, these tribes hunted the buffalo that roamed the prairie. White traders and trappers first came to the Calgary region during the 1700's, and many Indian wars broke out in the 1800's. Because of the unrest, the North-West Mounted Police established Fort Calgary in 1875.

The Canadian Pacific Railway (now CP Rail) reached Calgary in 1883 while building a railroad across Canada. The Canadian government offered free land to attract settlers to Calgary, and many people moved there from the United States. Calgary was incorporated as a town in 1884, and by 1889 it had a population of nearly 2,000. Its population jumped to almost 3,900 by 1891, and Calgary received a city charter in 1893.

Many large ranches developed in southern Alberta after cattle herds moved north in search of ungrazed land. Calgary became the center of Canada's meat-packing industry. The city's first annual agricultural exhibition was held in 1885. In 1912, four ranchers organized a rodeo. They called this event the Calgary Stampede, and it also became an annual affair. In 1923, the exhibition and the rodeo merged, forming the Calgary Exhibition and Stampede.

Oil was discovered at nearby Turner Valley in 1914. This discovery led to even more important oil strikes, including one at Leduc, near Edmonton, in 1947. These oil strikes attracted thousands of people from the United States and from other parts of Canada.

During the 1960's and early 1970's, construction worth more than $100 million took place in Calgary. In 1967, the city announced plans for major urban renewal in the downtown area. Most of the construction was completed in 1973. The downtown Calgary Convention Centre opened in 1974. A medical school at the University of Calgary opened in 1970. Bow Valley Square, a four-tower downtown office complex, was completed in 1982. The Olympic Saddledome, an indoor arena, opened in 1983. It is the home of the Calgary Flames hockey team. The Olympic Saddledome is also to serve as one of the facilities for the 1988 Winter Olympic Games, to be held in Calgary. The Calgary Center for the Performing Arts is scheduled to open in 1985. The Calgary Philharmonic Society and Theatre Calgary will perform there.

ANDREW SNADDON

CALGARY, UNIVERSITY OF, is a coeducational university in Calgary, Alta. It is supported by the province. The university's *faculties* (divisions) include business, education, engineering, humanities, law, medicine, nursing, science, and social welfare. The university grants bachelor's master's, and doctor's degrees.

The university operates an Environmental Sciences Centre in Kananaskis, a cosmic-ray laboratory on Sulphur Mountain in Banff, and an astrophysical observatory near Priddis. Several research institutes on or near the campus are affiliated with the university.

The University of Alberta established a branch in Calgary in 1945. It became the separate University of Calgary in 1966. For enrollment, see CANADA (table: Universities and Colleges).

Critically reviewed by the UNIVERSITY OF CALGARY

CALHOUN, JOHN CALDWELL (1782-1850), an American statesman, was a major political figure before the Civil War. He played an important part in national affairs for 40 years. He served as a member of the United States House of Representatives and the Senate, and he also served as secretary of war, secretary of state, and as Vice-President.

Detail of an oil portrait (about 1845) by G. P. A. Healy; Virginia Museum of Fine Arts, Richmond

John C. Calhoun

But Calhoun never became President, and this was a bitter disappointment to him during his later years. He is best remembered as the theorist of the doctrines of states' rights and nullification. His leadership in these doctrines helped inspire the South's effort to achieve national independence in the Civil War.

Early Career. Calhoun entered national politics as a member of the House of Representatives from 1811 to 1817. He was an ardent nationalist and, together with other young congressmen, was called a *War Hawk* for advocating the War of 1812 (see WAR OF 1812 [The War Hawks]). He actively supported the government's postwar program, which included such measures as a protective tariff, a national bank, and an enlarged army and navy. He improved the organization of the army while secretary of war from 1817 to 1825.

Calhoun was the vice-presidential running mate of both Andrew Jackson and John Quincy Adams in 1824. He won by a landslide, but the vote for President was indecisive. The House of Representatives picked Adams. In 1828, Jackson again opposed Adams for President. But now Calhoun received support for a second vice-presidential term from Jackson only. Jackson and Calhoun won the election. After Jackson became President, he quarreled with Calhoun because of Calhoun's new attitude. Calhoun had discarded his nationalism, and had become a sectionalist.

Southern Leader. Calhoun felt that his beloved South Carolina, and the South generally, were being exploited by the protective tariff. This favored the manufacturing interests in New England and protected them from foreign competition. Calhoun wrote the South Carolina Exposition for his state's legislature in 1828. It declared that no state was bound by a federal law which it believed was unconstitutional. When another tariff was adopted in 1832, South Carolina acted on Calhoun's *states' rights* theory, and *nullified* the tariff (see NULLIFICATION).

This action caused a constitutional crisis. Calhoun resigned as Vice-President in December 1832. He entered the Senate as the elected spokesman of South Carolina. He had no wish to destroy the Union, and accepted Henry Clay's compromise arrangement of 1833. This quieted the tariff issue, but it did not resolve the states' rights problem Calhoun had raised.

Calhoun served in the Senate until 1843. In 1844, he became secretary of state under John Tyler. He served until March 1845 and then returned to the Senate, serving there until his death. His closing years were marked by strong support of slavery and its extension, and by encouragement of the annexation of Texas. He opposed the Mexican War, the Wilmot Proviso, and the Compromise of 1850 (see COMPROMISE OF 1850; MEXICAN WAR; WILMOT PROVISO).

Calhoun was born near Abbeville District, South Carolina, and was an honor graduate at Yale College in 1804. He practiced law in Abbeville District until his election to the South Carolina legislature in 1808. A statue of Calhoun represents South Carolina in the U.S. Capitol. IRVING G. WILLIAMS

See also JACKSON, ANDREW (Split with Calhoun).

Additional Resources

COIT, MARGARET L. *John C. Calhoun: American Portrait.* Larlin, 1977. First pub. in 1950.

WILTSE, CHARLES M. *John C. Calhoun.* 3 vols. Russell, 1968. Including *Nationalist, 1782-1828.* Reprint of 1944 ed. *Nullifier, 1829-1839.* Reprint of 1949 ed. *Sectionalist, 1840-1850.* Reprint of 1951 ed. The standard biography.

CALICO is a cotton fabric of plain weave. It is related to chintz and percale and, like them, is usually printed on rotary presses. The name *calico* comes from Calicut, India, where calico originated. Early calico was a fine cloth, but today it is a coarse fabric, usually 27 inches (69 centimeters) wide.

CALIFANO, JOSEPH ANTHONY, JR. (1931-), served as United States secretary of health, education, and welfare (HEW) from 1977 to 1979 under President Jimmy Carter. One of Califano's chief concerns as secretary of HEW was to streamline the huge department, which spends more than a third of the annual federal budget.

Califano was born in New York City. He graduated from Holy Cross College and from Harvard Law School. He served in the U.S. Navy from 1955 to 1958 and then practiced law. From 1961 to 1965, Califano held a series of posts in the Department of Defense. He became a special assistant to President Lyndon B. Johnson in 1965. In that position, Califano helped develop the Model Cities project and other programs of what Johnson called the Great Society. He practiced law again from 1969 to 1977.

Califano's writings include two books. They are *The Student Revolution: A Global Confrontation* (1969), a study of student unrest; and *A Presidential Nation* (1975), a discussion of the presidency. LEE THORNTON

Sandy Beach in Sonoma County

California Coastline by Karl Hermann Baumann from the WORLD BOOK Collection

CALIFORNIA

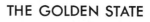

THE GOLDEN STATE

CALIFORNIA has more persons than any other state. Many visitors and new residents are attracted by California's outdoor way of life. The warm, dry climate of southern California permits lightweight clothing and outdoor recreation almost all the year around.

More goods are produced in California than in any other state. Large factories in southern California manufacture airplanes and missiles. Fields of petroleum and natural gas yield thousands of barrels of fuel a day, and help make California a leading mining state. California ranks second only to Alaska in commercial fishing because of a huge tuna and anchovy catch.

California also ranks first among the states in agriculture. A vast farming region, the Central Valley, extends about 500 miles (800 kilometers) from the Cascade Mountains to mountains near Los Angeles. There, peaches, pears, and plums ripen in orchards. Grapevines twist on trellises. Almonds and walnuts hang from nut trees. Fields of barley, cotton, hay, potatoes, rice, sugar beets, tomatoes, and wheat stretch to the horizon. Cattle

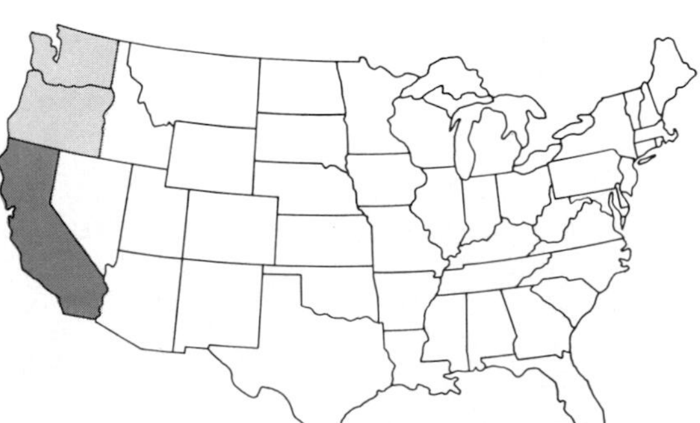

California (blue) ranks third in size among all the states, and is the largest of the Pacific Coast States (gray).

and sheep graze on the fertile pastures of the Central Valley.

Two of the nation's greatest cities—Los Angeles and San Francisco—are located in California. Los Angeles and its suburbs spread across the southern part of the state. San Francisco perches on steep hillsides above San Francisco Bay. Research laboratories, electronic equipment companies, and engineering firms cluster around leading universities in the Los Angeles and San Francisco Bay areas. These companies take advantage of the "brain power" of scientists and engineers from the universities.

California covers a larger area than any other state except Alaska and Texas. High mountains rise near the eastern border. Rocky cliffs and sandy beaches line the shore of the Pacific Ocean in the west. Thick redwood forests cover the Coast Ranges in the northwest. Barren deserts stretch across the southeast.

The state was named by Spanish explorers who first sailed along the coast in the 1500's. They called the land *California*, probably after the name of a treasure island in a popular Spanish tale. California is known as the *Golden State*. Its gold fields attracted thousands of miners, known as the "forty-niners," during the gold rush of 1849. The nickname also suggests the brilliant sunshine, and the golden grass on California pastures in the autumn.

Sacramento is the capital of California. Los Angeles is the largest city.

Facts in Brief

Capital: Sacramento.

Government: *Congress*—U.S. senators, 2; U.S. representatives, 45. *Electoral Votes*—47. *State Legislature*—senators, 40; assemblymen, 80. *Counties*—58.

Area: 158,706 sq. mi. (411,049 km²), including 2,407 sq. mi. (6,234 km²) of inland water but excluding 69 sq. mi. (179 km²) of Pacific coastal water; 3rd in size among the states. *Greatest Distances*—north-south, 770 mi. (1,239 km); east-west, 360 mi. (579 km). *Coastline*—840 mi. (1,352 km).

Elevation: *Highest*—Mount Whitney, 14,494 ft. (4,418 m) above sea level. *Lowest*—282 ft. (86 m) below sea level in Death Valley.

Population: *1980 Census*—23,667,826; 1st among the states; density, 149 persons per sq. mi. (58 persons per km²); distribution, 91 per cent urban, 9 per cent rural. *1970 Census*—19,971,069.

Chief Products: *Agriculture*—beef cattle, milk, grapes, cotton, greenhouse and nursery products, almonds, tomatoes, hay, lettuce, eggs. *Fishing Industry*—tuna, salmon, crabs. *Manufacturing*—transportation equipment; electric machinery and equipment; food products; nonelectric machinery; fabricated metal products; printed materials; chemicals; instruments; lumber and wood products; petroleum and coal products; stone, clay, and glass products; clothing. *Mining*—petroleum, natural gas, sand and gravel, boron.

Statehood: Sept. 9, 1850, the 31st state.

State Abbreviations: Calif. (traditional); CA (postal).

State Motto: *Eureka* (I have found it).

State Song: "I Love You, California." Words by F. B. Silverwood; music by A. F. Frankenstein.

The contributors of this article are Robert W. Durrenberger, Professor of Geography at Arizona State University, and former Professor of Geography at San Fernando Valley State College; and Andrew F. Rolle, Professor of History at Occidental College.

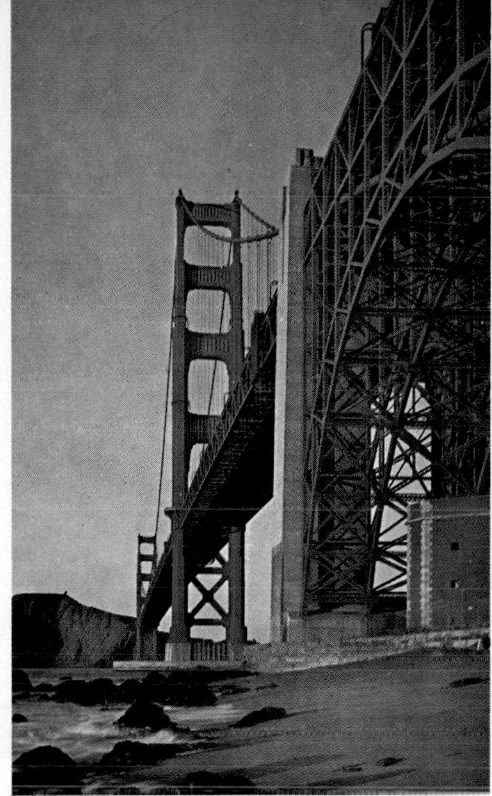

FPG

Golden Gate Bridge in San Francisco

David Muench

Los Angeles at Night

A California Freeway

George Hall, Woodfin Camp, Inc.

Constitution. California's first constitution was adopted by the territorial government in 1849. The present constitution was adopted in 1879. It has been *amended* (changed) over 350 times. A proposed amendment must be placed on the ballot in a regular statewide election. It may be proposed and placed on the ballot in any of three ways: (1) The Legislature may propose it by a two-thirds majority vote in each house. (2) A group of citizens may propose an amendment by submitting a petition. The petition must be signed by at least 8 per cent as many people as voted in the last election for governor. (3) A constitutional convention, approved by two-thirds of the Legislature, may propose an amendment. To become law, an amendment must be approved by a majority of the voters.

Executive. The governor of California is elected to a four-year term. A governor can be reelected any number of times. The governor receives a salary of $49,100 a year. For a list of all the governors of California, see the *History* section of this article.

Other top state officials include the lieutenant governor, secretary of state, attorney general, treasurer, controller, and superintendent of public instruction. All these officials are elected to four-year terms, and can be reelected any number of times. The voters also elect the five-member State Board of Equalization, which administers several important tax laws.

Legislature consists of a Senate of 40 members and an Assembly of 80 members. Each senator and each member of the Assembly represents one senatorial or assembly district. Senators are elected to four-year terms, and members of the Assembly are elected to two-year terms.

Sacramento Chamber of Commerce

The Old Governor's Mansion in Sacramento was the home of California governors from 1903 to 1967. A ranch-style governor's residence was completed in 1975. However, California's governors since then have preferred to live in private residences.

Regular sessions of the Legislature run about two years. They begin on the first Monday in December of each even-numbered year and end on November 30 of the next even-numbered year. The governor may call special sessions at which the Legislature can deal only with subjects specified by the governor. There is no time limit on special sessions of the Legislature.

California citizens can pass laws directly, through their power of *initiative*. To do so, a proposed law must be favored by at least 5 per cent of the persons who voted for governor in the last election. This number of persons must sign a petition in favor of a measure. Then they can put the measure on the ballot in the next state election. If the voters approve the measure, it becomes law. Californians also have the right to challenge most kinds of laws passed by the Legislature. If 5 per cent of the voters challenge a new law, the law does not go into effect until the people have approved it in an election. This process is called the *referendum*. See INITIATIVE AND REFERENDUM.

Courts. The highest court in California is the state Supreme Court. It has a chief justice and six associate justices. The state has six district courts of appeal with a total of 77 justices. Justices of the Supreme Court and of the district courts of appeal are appointed by the governor to 12-year terms, subject to voter approval.

Each county has one superior court. The number of judges for each superior court is fixed by the legislature. The voters elect superior court judges to six-year terms. Lower courts in California include municipal and justice courts. Judicial districts with populations of 40,000 or more have municipal courts. Districts with less than 40,000 persons have justice courts.

Local Government. California has about 430 incorporated cities. The state constitution gives cities of 3,500 or more persons the right to draw up and adopt their own charters. This right is often called *home rule*. About 80 California cities operate under local charters. Most California cities have council-manager governments. The others have mayor-council governments.

California has 58 counties. Most of the counties have a form of government specified by the laws of the state. This form of government includes a five-member board of supervisors and a number of elected executive officials. The elected officials include an assessor, auditor, clerk, coroner, district attorney, sheriff, superintendent of schools, and treasurer. The California constitution provides for county home rule. But only 11 counties have adopted charters under the home-rule law. Most of these counties chose a form of government similar to that of the general-law counties.

Taxation. California taxes personal income, and the income of banks and corporations. It has a state sales tax, and taxes on gasoline, insurance, liquor, and motor vehicles. These taxes account for about three-fourths of the state government's income. Most of the rest of its income comes from federal grants and other assistance programs.

Politics. Until 1959, California did not require political candidates to declare their party affiliation. For example, they could run as candidates of both the Democratic and Republican parties. This practice was

The State Seal

Symbols of California. On the seal, a grizzly bear, symbol of determination, stands near the seated figure of Minerva, Roman goddess of wisdom. The miner represents the state's mining industry. The ships symbolize commercial greatness. The peaks in the background represent the Sierra Nevada. The seal was adopted in 1849. The state flag was adopted in 1911. It was first raised in 1846 by Americans revolting against Mexican rule.

The State Flag

Flag, bird, and flower illustrations, courtesy of Eli Lilly and Company

known as *cross-filing*. Cross-filing kept many California voters from being loyal to one particular party. As a result, political disagreements between various parts of the state tended to be stronger than disagreements among the parties themselves. Today, major political conflicts still occur between northern and southern California. In 1965, southern California gained political power when reapportionment of the Legislature gave the area more seats in the state Senate. For California's electoral votes and voting record in presidential elections, see ELECTORAL COLLEGE (table).

The State Bird
California Valley Quail

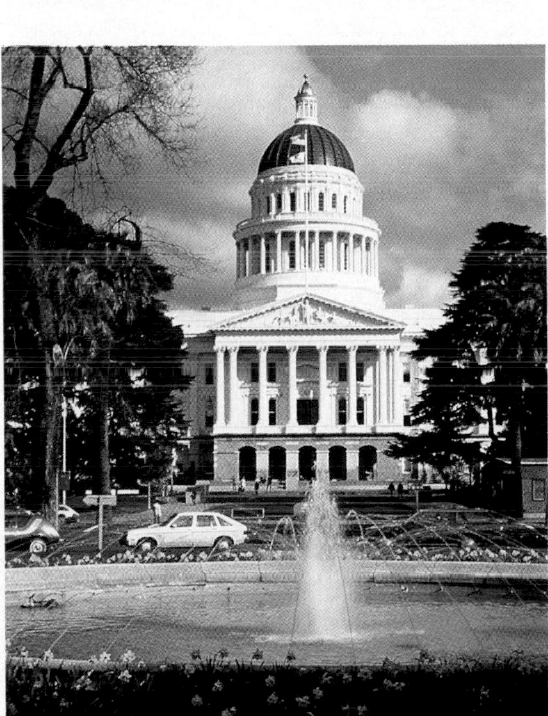

John Palmer

State Capitol in Sacramento stands in a 40-acre (16-hectare) park. The building, first occupied in 1869, has a dome that rises 247 feet (75 meters). Sacramento has been the capital since 1854. Monterey, San Jose, Vallejo, Benicia, and San Francisco served as temporary capitals between 1850 and 1854.

The State Flower
Golden Poppy

The State Tree
California Redwood

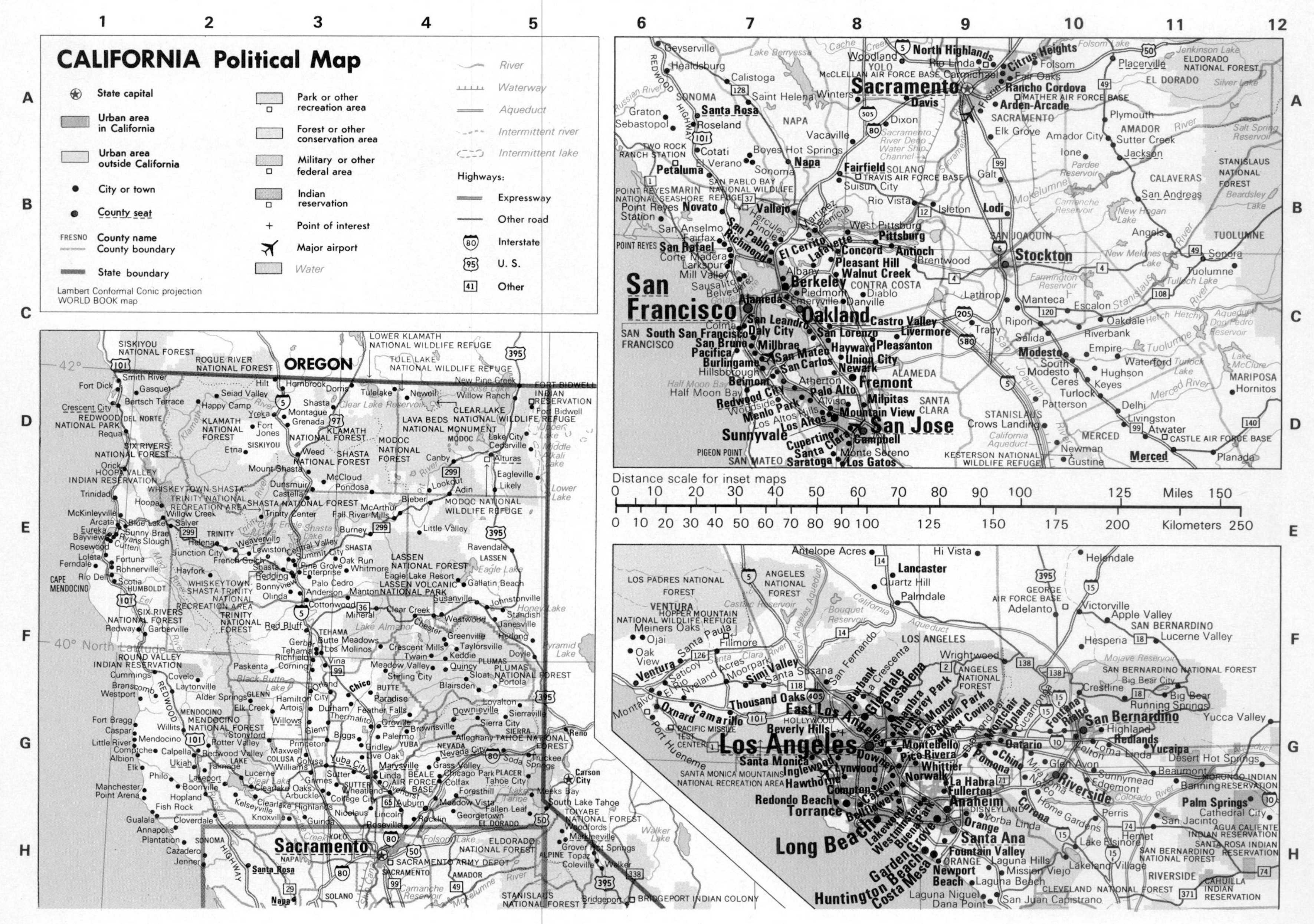

CALIFORNIA Political Map
State capital
Urban area in California
Urban area outside California
City or town
County seat
FRESNO County name
County boundary
State boundary
Park or other recreation area
Forest or other conservation area
Military or other federal area
Indian reservation
Point of interest
Major airport
Water
River
Waterway
Aqueduct
Intermittent river
Intermittent lake
Highways:
Expressway
Other road
Interstate
U. S.
Other
Lambert Conformal Conic projection
WORLD BOOK map
Distance scale for inset maps
Miles 0 10 20 30 40 50 60 70 80 90 100 125 150
Kilometers 0 10 20 30 40 50 60 70 80 90 100 125 150 175 200 250
OREGON
San Francisco
Oakland
San Jose
Sacramento
Stockton
Los Angeles
Long Beach
San Bernardino
Riverside

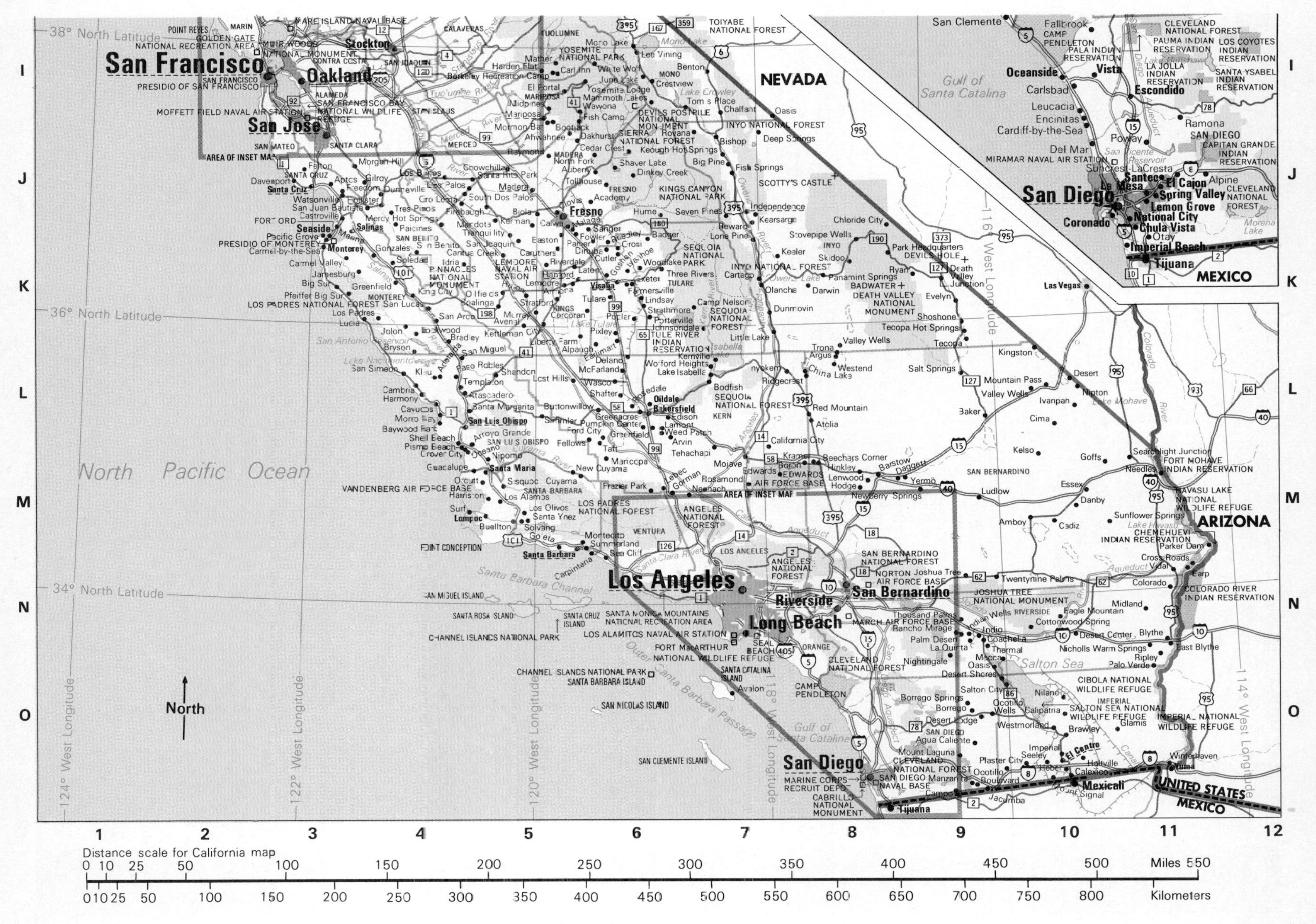

San Francisco
Oakland
San Jose
Stockton
Fresno
Visalia
Bakersfield
Santa Barbara
Santa Maria
San Luis Obispo
Salinas
Monterey
Seaside
Santa Cruz
Los Angeles
Long Beach
Riverside
San Bernardino
San Diego
Tijuana
Mexicali
El Centro
Las Vegas
NEVADA
ARIZONA
MEXICO
UNITED STATES
North Pacific Ocean
Gulf of Santa Catalina
Santa Barbara Channel
Salton Sea
Colorado River
Lake Mohave
Lake Havasu
Oceanside
Carlsbad
Escondido
Vista
Coronado
National City
Chula Vista
El Cajon
Imperial Beach
38° North Latitude
36° North Latitude
34° North Latitude
124° West Longitude
122° West Longitude
120° West Longitude
118° West Longitude
116° West Longitude
114° West Longitude
AREA OF INSET MAP
YOSEMITE NATIONAL PARK
SEQUOIA NATIONAL PARK
KINGS CANYON NATIONAL PARK
DEATH VALLEY NATIONAL MONUMENT
JOSHUA TREE NATIONAL MONUMENT
CHANNEL ISLANDS NATIONAL PARK
VANDENBERG AIR FORCE BASE
EDWARDS AIR FORCE BASE
POINT CONCEPTION
SANTA CATALINA ISLAND
SAN CLEMENTE ISLAND
SAN NICOLAS ISLAND
SANTA ROSA ISLAND
SAN MIGUEL ISLAND
SANTA CRUZ ISLAND
North
I
J
K
L
M
N
O
1
2
3
4
5
6
7
8
9
10
11
12
Distance scale for California map
Miles
Kilometers

California Map Index

Population

23,667,826 ..Census.. 1980
19,971,069 ...." 1970
15,717,204 ...." 1960
10,586,223 ...." 1950
6,907,387 ...." 1940
5,677,251 ...." 1930
3,426,861 ...." 1920
2,377,549 ...." 1910
1,485,053 ...." 1900
1,213,398 ...." 1890
864,694 ...." 1880
560,247 ...." 1870
379,994 ...." 1860
92,597 ...." 1850

Metropolitan Areas

Anaheim-Santa Ana 1,932,709
Bakersfield 403,089
Chico 143,851
Fresno 514,621
Los Angeles-Long Beach 7,447,503
Modesto 265,900
Oakland 1,761,759
Oxnard-Ventura 529,174
Redding 115,715
Riverside-San Bernardino 1,558,182
Sacramento 1,099,814
Salinas-Seaside-Monterey 290,444
San Diego 1,861,846
San Francisco 1,488,871
San Jose 1,295,071
Santa Barbara-Santa Maria-Lompoc 298,694
Santa Cruz 188,141
Santa Rosa-Petaluma 299,681
Stockton 347,342
Vallejo-Fairfield-Napa 334,402
Visalia-Tulare-Porterville 245,738
Yuba City 101,979

Counties

Alameda ..1,105,379..I 3
Alpine ....1,097..H 5
Amador ......19,314..H 4
Butte ....143,851..G 4
Calaveras ....20,710..I 4
Colusa ......12,791..G 3
Contra Costa .....656,331..I 3
Del Norte ......18,217..D 1
El Dorado ....85,812..H 5
Fresno ......514,621..J 6
Glenn ....21,350..G 3
Humboldt ....108,514..H 1
Imperial ......92,110..O 10
Inyo ....17,895..K 8
Kern ....403,089..L 7
Kings ....73,738..K 5
Lake ....36,366..G 2
Lassen ....21,661..E 5
Los Angeles .7,447,503..N 7
Madera ......63,116..J 5
Marin ....222,592..I 2
Mariposa .....11,108..I 5
Mendocino ...66,738..G 2
Merced .....134,558..J 4
Modoc ....8,610..D 4
Mono ....8,577..I 6
Monterey ...290,444..K 4
Napa ....99,199..H 3
Nevada ......51,645..G 4
Orange ...1,932,709..N 8
Placer ......117,247..G 5
Plumas ......17,340..F 5
Riverside ....663,119..N 10
Sacramento .783,381..H 4
San Benito ...25,005..K 4
San Bernardino ......895,016..M 9
San Diego ...1,861,846..O 9
San Francisco .678,974..I 2
San Joaquin ...347,342..I 4
San Luis Obispo ....155,435..M 5
San Mateo ..587,329..J 3
Santa Barbara ...298,694..M 5
Santa Clara ...1,295,071..J 3
Santa Cruz ......188,141..J 3
Shasta ......115,715..E 3
Sierra ....3,073..G 5
Siskiyou ......39,732..D 3
Solano ......235,203..H 3
Sonoma .....299,681..J 2
Stanislaus ...265,900..I 4
Sutter ....52,246..G 3
Tehama ......38,888..F 3
Trinity ....11,858..E 2
Tulare ......245,738..K 6
Tuolumne ....33,928..I 5
Ventura .....529,174..M 6
Yolo ....113,374..H 3
Yuba ....49,733..G 4

Cities and Towns

Adelanto ......2,164..F 10
Agua Caliente, see Fetters Hot Springs [-Agua Caliente]
Alameda .....63,852..C 7
Alamo* ......8,505..I 3
Albany ....15,130..C 7
Alhambra ....64,615..G 8
Alondra Park* 12,096..N 7
Alpine ....5,368..J 11
Alta Hill* ......1,229..G 4
Alta Sierra* ...2,168..G 4
Altadena* ....40,983..G 8
Alturas ....3,025.°D 5
Alum Rock* ..16,890..J 3
American Canyon* ....5,712..I 3
Anaheim ....219,494..H 9
Anderson .....7,381..F 3
Angels ....2,302..B 11
Angwin* ......3,526..H 2
Antioch ....42,683..B 8
Apple Valley ..14,305..E 10
Arbuckle ......1,306..H 3
Arcade, see Arden [-Arcade]
Arcadia* ......45,993..G 9
Arcata ....12,850..E 1
Arden [-Arcade] ..87,570..A 9
Armona ....2,644..K 5
Arnold* ....2,385..I 5
Arroyo Grande ....11,290..M 5
Artesia* ......14,301..H 9
Arvin ....6,863..M 6
Ashland* .....13,893..I 3
Atascadero ...16,232..L 4
Atherton ......7,797..D 8
Atwater ......17,530..D 11
Auburn ....7,540.°H 4
Avalon ....2,022..O 7
Avenal ....4,137..K 5
Avocado Heights* ...11,721..N 7
Azusa* ......29,380..G 9
Bakersfield ..105,611.°L 6
Baldwin Park ......50,554..G 9
Banning ......14,020..G 11
Barstow ......17,690..M 8
Baywood [-Los Osos]* .....10,933..L 4
Beale AFB East* ....6,329..G 4
Beaumont .....6,818..G 11
Bell* ....25,450..G 8
Bell Gardens* ..34,117..G 8
Bellflower ....53,441..H 8
Belmont .....24,505..D 7
Belvedere .....2,401..C 7
Ben Lomond* ....7,238..J 3
Benicia ......15,376..B 8
Berkeley ....103,328..C 7
Bethel Island* ..1,774..I 3
Beverly Hills ..32,367..G 8
Big Bear ......11,151..F 11
Big Pine ....1,510..J 7
Biggs ....1,413..G 3
Bishop ....3,333..J 7
Bloomington* ..12,781..N 8
Blue Lake .....1,201..E 1
Blythe ....6,805..N 11
Bodfish ....1,379..L 7
Bolinas* ......1,225..I 3
Bonadelle Ranchos [-Madera Ranchos]* ...3,272..J 5
Bonita* ....6,257..O 8
Boron ....2,040..M 8
Borrego Springs .....1,405..O 9
Boulder Creek* ......5,662..J 3
Bouquet Canyon, see Saugus [-Bouquet Canyon]
Boyes Hot Springs .....4,177..B 7
Brawley ......14,946..O 10
Brea* ....27,913..G 9
Brentwood .....4,434..C 9
Bridgeport ....°I 6
Brisbane* .....2,969..I 3
Broderick [-Bryte]* ...10,194..H 3
Bryte, see Broderick [-Bryte]
Buellton ....2,364..M 5
Buena Park ...64,165..H 9
Burbank .....84,625..G 8
Burlingame ...26,173..C 7
Burney ....3,187..E 4
Buttonwillow ..1,350..L 6
Calexico .....14,412..O 10
California City . 2,743..M 7
Calipatria .....2,636..O 10
Calistoga ......3,879..A 7
Calwa ....6,640..K 5
Camarillo .....37,797..G 7
Camarillo Heights* ....6,341..G 7
Cambria ......3,061..L 4
Cameron Park* ....5,607..H 4
Camp Pendleton North* ......2,065..O 8
Camp Pendleton South* ......7,952..O 8
Campbell .....26,910..D 8
Canyon Country* ...15,728..N 7
Canyon Lake* .2,039..N 8
Capistrano Beach* .....6,168..I 9
Capitola* ......9,095..J 3
Cardiff-by-the-Sea ....10,054..J 10
Carlsbad .....35,490..I 10
Carmel-by-the-Sea ....4,707..K 3
Carmel Valley ....4,013..K 3
Carmichael ...43,108..A 9
Carpinteria ...10,835..N 6
Carson ....81,221..H 8
Caruthers .....1,514..K 5
Casa Oro [-Mount Helix]* .....19,651..D 8
Casitas Springs* ....1,038..N 6
Castle Park [-Otay]* ....21,049..O 8
Castro Valley .44,011..C 8
Castroville ....4,396..J 3
Cathedral City ....4,130..H 12
Cayucos ....2,301..L 4
Central Valley ......3,424..E 3
Ceres ....13,281..D 10
Cerritos* .....53,020..N 7
Charter Oak* ..6,840..N 7
Chemeketa Park [-Redwood Estates]* ....1,847..J 3
Cherry Valley* .5,012..N 8
Cherryland* ...9,425..I 3
Chester ....1,756..F 4
Chico ....26,716..G 3
Chico North* .....11,733..G 3
Chico West* ...6,319..G 3
China Lake ....4,275..L 8
Chino ....40,165..G 9
Chowchilla ....5,122..J 5
Chula Vista ...83,927..K 11
Citrus* ....12,450..N 7
Citrus Heights ....85,911..A 9
Claremont* ....31,028..G 9
Clayton* ....4,325..I 3
Clearlake Highlands ...4,983..H 3
Clearlake Oaks .1,610..G 3
Cloverdale ....3,989..H 2
Clovis ....33,021..J 5
Coachella .....9,129..N 9
Coalinga ......6,593..K 5
Colton ....21,310..G 10
Colusa ....4,075.°G 3
Commerce* ..10,509..G 8
Compton .....81,347..G 8
Concord ....103,763..B 8
Corcoran .....6,454..K 6
Corning ....4,745..F 3
Corona ......37,791..H 10
Coronado ....18,790..J 10
Corte Madera .....8,074..C 7
Costa Mesa ..82,562..H 9
Cotati ....3,346..B 7
Cotton Center, see Poplar [-Cotton Center]
Cottonwood ....1,553..F 3
Country Club* ....9,585..I 4
Covelo ....1,448..F 2
Covina* ......32,746..G 9
Crescent City ..3,075.°D 1
Crescent North* 2,846..D 1
Crestline ......6,715..G 10
Cucamonga ..55,250..G 9
Cudahy* .....18,275..N 7
Culver City* ....38,139..G 8
Cupertino ....34,297..D 8
Cutler ....3,149..K 6
Cutten ....2,375..E 1
Cypress* ......40,391..H 9
Daly City .....78,427..C 7
Dana Point ...10,602..H 9
Danville ......26,446..C 8
Davis ....36,640..A 9
Deer Park* ....1,454..H 3
Del Aire* ......8,487..N 7
Delano ....16,491..L 6
Delhi ....2,832..D 11
Del Mar ....5,017..J 10
Del Rey Oaks* ......1,557..K 3
Denair* ....2,892..I 4
Desert Hot Springs .....5,941..G 12
Desert View Highlands* ..2,175..N 7
Diamond Bar* ....28,045..N 7
Diamond Springs* ....2,287..H 5
Dinuba ....9,907..K 6
Discovery Bay* ....1,326..I 3
Dixon ....7,541..A 8
Dos Palos .....3,121..J 5
Downey ......82,602..G 8
Downieville ....°G 4
Duarte* ......16,766..G 9
Dublin* ......13,496..I 3
Dunsmuir .....2,253..E 3
Eagle Mountain ....1,890..N 10
Earlimart ......4,578..L 6
East Blythe ......1,660..N 11
East Compton* ...6,435..N 7
East Hemet* ..14,712..N 8
East La Mirada* ..9,688..N 7
East Los Angeles ...110,017..G 8
East Palo Alto* ......18,191..J 3
East Porterville* ..5,218..K 6
Easton ....1,710..K 5
Edgemont .....5,215..G 10
Edwards AFB ..8,554..M 7
El Cajon ......73,892..J 11
El Centro .....23,996.°O 10
El Cerrito .....22,731..C 7
El Dorado Hills* ....3,453..H 4
El Granada* ...3,582..J 3
Elk Grove ....10,959..A 9
El Monte .....79,494..G 9
El Rio ....5,674..G 6
El Segundo* ..13,752..G 8
El Sobrante* ....10,535..I 3
El Toro* ......38,153..O 8
El Toro Station* .....7,632..O 8
El Verano .....2,384..B 7
Emeryville .....3,714..C 7
Encinitas .....10,796..J 10
Escalon ....3,127..C 10
Escondido ....64,355..I 11
Esparto* ......1,303..H 3
Eureka ....24,153.°E 1
Exeter ....5,606..K 6
Fair Oaks .....22,602..A 10
Fairfax ....7,391..B 7
Fairfield ......58,099.°B 8
Fallbrook ....14,041..I 10
Farmersville ...5,544..K 6
Felton ....4,564..J 3
Ferndale ......1,367..E 1
Fetters Hot Springs [-Agua Caliente]* ...1,675..H 2
Fillmore ....9,602..F 7
Firebaugh .....3,740..J 5
Flintridge, see La Canada [-Flintridge]
Florence [-Graham]* .48,662..G 8
Florin* ....16,523..H 4
Folsom ....11,003..A 10
Fontana ......36,991..G 10
Foothill Farms* ....13,700..H 4
Ford City .....3,392..L 6
Fort Bragg ....5,019..G 1
Forest Knolls, see Lagunitas [-Forest Knolls]
Fortuna ....7,591..E 1
Foster City* ....23,287..I 3
Fountain Valley ......55,080..H 9
Fowler ....2,496..K 6
Frazier Park ....1,444..M 6
Freedom ......6,416..J 3
Fremont .....131,945..D 8
Fresno ......217,129.°J 5
Fullerton ....102,034..G 9
Galt ....5,514..B 9
Garden Acres* ......7,361..I 4
Garden Grove ....123,307..H 9
Gardena* ....45,165..N 7
George AFB ...7,061..F 10
Gilroy ....21,641..J 4
Glen Avon .....8,444..G 10
Glen Ellen* ....1,014..H 2
Glendale ....139,060..G 8
Glendora* ....38,500..G 9
Gonzales ......2,891..K 4
Goshen ....1,809..K 6
Graham, see Florence [-Graham]
Grand Terrace* ....8,498..N 8
Grass Valley ...6,697..G 4
Graton ....1,286..A 6
Greenacres ....5,381..L 6
Greenfield .....4,181..K 4
Greenville .....1,537..F 4
Gridley ....3,982..G 4
Grover City ....8,827..M 4
Guadalupe ....3,629..M 5
Gualala ....H 2
Guerneville* ..1,525..H 2
Gustine ....3,142..D 10
Hacienda Heights* ...49,422..N 7
Half Moon Bay ....7,282..D 7
Hamilton City ....1,337..G 2
Hanford ......20,958.°K 6
Hawaiian Gardens* ..10,548..N 7
Hawthorne ....56,447..G 8
Hayfork ....1,788..E 2
Hayward ......94,342..C 8
Healdsburg ....7,217..A 6
Heber ....2,221..O 10
Hemet ....22,454..H 11
Hercules ......5,963..B 7
Herlong ....1,188..F 5
Hermosa Beach* ....18,070..H 8
Hesperia .....13,540..F 10
Hidden Hills* ....1,760..N 6
Highland .....10,908..G 10
Hillmar [-Irwin]* ....1,706..J 4
Hillsborough ..10,372..D 7
Hollister ......11,488.°J 4
Holtville ....4,399..O 10
Home Garden* .1,495..K 5
Home Gardens ....5,783..H 10
Homeland* ....2,616..N 8
Homestead Valley, see Tamalpias [-Homestead Valley]
Hughson ......2,943..D 10
Huntington Beach ....170,505..H 9
Huntington Park* ......45,932..G 8
Huron ....2,768..K 5
Idyllwild [-Pine Cove]* 2,959..N 9
Imperial ......3,451..O 10
Imperial Beach .....22,689..K 11
Independence ....°J 7
Indian Wells ....1,394..N 9
Indio ....21,611..N 9
Inglewood ....94,245..G 8
Ione ....2,207..B 10
Irvine* ....62,134..N 7
Irwin, see Hillmar [-Irwin]
Irwindale* .....1,030..G 9
Ivanhoe ....2,684..K 6
Jackson ....2,331.°B 11
Jamestown* ...2,206..I 5
Jamul* ....1,826..O 9
Johnson Park* ....1,008..E 3
Joshua Tree ...2,083..N 9
Julian* ....1,320..O 9
Kelseyville ....1,567..H 2
Kensington* ...5,200..I 3
Kerman ......4,002..J 5
Kernville ......1,660..L 7
Kettleman* ....1,051..K 5
King City ......5,495..K 4
Kings Beach* .....1,942..G 5
Kingsburg* ....5,115..K 6
La Canada [-Flintridge]* ...20,153..G 8
La Crescenta [-Montrose]* .....16,531..N 7
Ladera Heights* ....6,647..N 7
Lafayette ....20,837..C 8
Laguna Beach .....17,901..H 9
Laguna Hills* ......33,600..O 8
Laguna Niguel .....12,237..H 9
Lagunitas [-Forest Knolls]* .....1,465..I 2
La Habra .....45,232..G 9
La Habra Heights* ....4,786..N 7
Lake Arrowhead* .6,272..N 8
Lake Elsinore .....5,982..H 10
Lake Isabella ..3,428..L 7
Lakeland Village 2,796..H 10
Lakeport ......3,675.°G 2
Lakeside* ....23,921..O 8
Lakewood ....74,654..H 8
La Mesa .....50,308..J 11
La Mirada* ...40,986..G 9
Lamont ....9,616..L 6
Lancaster ....48,027..E 8
La Palma* ....15,399..H 9

La Puente*....30,882..G 9
La Quinta......3,328..N 9
La Riviera*...10,906..H 4
Larkspur.....11,064..C 7
La Selva Beach*.....1,603..J 3
Las Lomas*...1,740..J 3
Lathrop......3,717..C 9
Laton.........1,100..K 6
La Verne*...23,508..G 9
Lawndale*...23,460..G 8
Laytonville....1,096..G 2
Lemon Grove.20,780..J 11
Lemoore......8,832..K 5
Lemoore Station......5,888..K 5
Lennox*.....18,445..G 8
Lenwood.......2,974..M 8
Leucadia......9,478..I 10
Lincoln........4,132..H 4
Lincoln Village*.....6,476..I 4
Linda........10,225..G 4
Lindsay.......6,936..K 6
Live Oak......3,103..G 4
Live Oak*....11,482..J 3
Livermore....48,349..C 8
Livingston....5,326..D 11
Lockeford*....1,852..I 4
Lodi.........35,221..B 9
Loma Linda......10,694..G 10
Lomita*......18,807..H 8
Lompoc......26,267..M 5
London*......1,257..K 6
Lone Pine.....1,684..K 7
Long Beach....361,355..N 7
Loomis*.......1,284..H 4
Los Alamitos*..11,529..H 9
Los Altos.....25,769..D 8
Los Altos Hills........7,421..D 8
Los Angeles.2,968,579.°N 7
Los Banos....10,341..J 4
Los Gatos....26,906..D 8
Los Molinos...1,241..F 3
Los Nietos, see West Whittier [-Los Nietos]
Los Osos, see Baywood [-Los Osos]
Lower Lake*...1,043..H 2
Loyalton......1,030..G 5
Lucas Valley [-Marinwood]*6,409..I 2
Lucerne.......1,767..G 2
Lynwood......48,409..G 8
Madera.......21,732.°J 5
Madera Acres*......2,173..J 5
Madera Ranchos, see Bonadelle Ranchos [-Madera Ranchos]
Mammoth Lakes.......3,929..I 6
Manhattan Beach*....31,542..G 8
Manteca.....24,925..C 10
March AFB....3,607..N 8
Marina.......20,647..K 3
Marina Del Rey*....6,336..N 7
Marinwood, see Lucas Valley [-Marinwood]
Mariposa......1,150.°J 5
Markleeville..........°H 5
Martinez.....22,582.°B 8
Marysville.....9,898.°G 4
Mather AFB...5,245..I 5
Mayflower Village*.....5,018..N 7
Maywood*...21,810..G 8
McCloud......1,656..E 3
McFarland.....5,151..L 6
McKinleyville..7,772..E 1
Meadow Vista..2,683..H 4
Mecca........1,698..N 9
Meiners Oaks [-Mira Monte].....9,512..F 6
Mendocino....1,008..G 1
Mendota......5,038..J 5
Menlo Park.......26,369..D 8
Merced......36,499.°D 11
Mill Valley....12,967..C 7
Millbrae.....20,058..C 7
Milpitas......37,820..D 8
Mira Loma....8,707..G 10
Mira Monte, see Meiners Oaks [-Mira Monte]
Mission Hills*.......2,797..F 5
Mission Viejo*.....50,666..O 8
Modesto.....106,602.°C 10
Mojave.......2,886..M 7
Mono Vista*...1,154..I 5
Monrovia*....30,531..G 9
Montague.....1,285..D 3
Montalvin Manor, see Tara Hills [-Montalvin Manor]
Montara*.....1,972..J 3
Montclair.....22,628..G 9
Monte Rio*....1,137..H 2
Monte Sereno......3,434..D 8
Montebello...52,929..G 9
Monterey....27,558..K 3
Monterey Park.......54,338..G 8
Montrose, see La Crescenta [-Montrose]
Moorpark.....4,030..F 7
Moraga*.....15,014..I 3
Moreno*......1,175..N 8
Morgan Hill...17,060..J 3
Morongo Valley*......1,137..N 9
Morro Bay.........9,064..L 4
Moss Beach*..1,868..I 3
Mount Helix, see Casa Oro [-Mount Helix]
Mount Shasta......2,837..E 3
Mountain View.......58,655..D 8
Mountain View Acres*......1,686..M 8
Mulberry*.....1,946..G 3
Murietta Hot Springs*....1,091..N 8
Murphys*.....1,183..I 5
Muscoy*......6,188..N 8
Myrtletown*...3,959..E 1
Napa........50,879.°H 3
National City.......48,772..J 11
Nebo Center*..1,749..M 8
Needles.......4,120..M 11
Nevada City...2,431.°G 4
Newark......32,126..D 8
Newhall*.....12,029..F 8
Newman.......2,785..D 10
Newport Beach.....62,556..H 9
Niland........1,042..O 10
Nipomo.......5,247..M 5
Norco.......21,126..G 10
North Auburn*....7,619..G 5
North Edwards*...1,107..M 7
North Fair Oaks*.....10,308..J 3
North Highlands..37,825..A 9
Norwalk......85,286..G 9
Novato......43,916..B 7
Nuero*.......1,628..N 8
Oak View......4,671..F 6
Oakdale.......8,474..C 10
Oakhurst......1,959..J 6
Oakland.....339,337.°I 3
Oakley*.......2,816..I 3
Oceano........4,478..M 5
Oceanside....76,698..I 10
Oildale......23,382..L 6
Ojai..........6,816..F 6
Olivehurst.....8,929..G 4
Ontario......88,820..G 9
Opal Cliffs*....5,041..J 3
Orange......91,450..H 9
Orange Cove*..4,026..K 6
Orangevale*..20,585..H 4
Orinda*......16,843..C 8
Orland........4,031..G 3
Orosi.........4,076..K 6
Oroville......8,683.°G 4
Otay, see Castle Park [-Otay]
Oxnard.....108,195..G 6
Pacheco, see Vine Hill [-Pacheco]
Pacific Grove.....15,755..K 3
Pacifica......36,866..C 7
Pajaro*.......1,426..J 3
Palermo......2,572..G 4
Palm Desert..11,801..N 9
Palm Springs....32,359..H 12
Palmdale.....12,277..F 8
Palmdale East*..2,920..M 7
Palo Alto.....55,225..D 8
Palos Verdes Estates*...14,376..H 8
Paradise.....22,571..G 4
Paramount*..36,407..G 8
Parksdale*....1,267..J 5
Parkway [-Sacramento South].....26,815..H 4
Parkwood*....1,146..J 5
Parlier.......2,902..J 5
Pasadena...118,072..G 8
Paso Robles......9,163..L 4
Patterson.....3,908..D 10
Penn Valley*..1,032..G 4
Perris.........6,827..H 10
Petaluma.....33,834..B 7
Pico Rivera...53,387..G 9
Piedmont.....10,498..C 8
Pine Hills......2,686..E 1
Pine Cove, see Idyllwild [-Pine Cove]
Pine Grove....1,049..E 3
Pinole.......14,253..B 7
Piru*.........1,284..M 6
Pismo Beach......5,364..M 4
Pittsburg.....33,034..B 8
Pixley........2,488..L 6
Placentia*....35,041..G 9
Placerville.....6,739.°A 10
Planada.......2,406..D 11
Pleasant Hill........25,124..C 8
Pleasanton...35,160..C 8
Point Dune*....2,438..N 7
Point Mugu*...2,701..G 6
Pollock Pines*......1,941..H 5
Pomona......92,742..G 9
Poplar [-Cotton Center].....1,295..K 6
Port Hueneme..17,803..G 6
Porterville....19,707..K 6
Portola.......1,885..G 5
Portola Valley*......3,939..J 3
Poway.......32,263..J 11
Project City*...1,657..E 3
Quartz Hill.....7,421..F 8
Quincy........4,451.°F 4
Rainbow*.....1,092..O 9
Ramona.......8,173..J 11
Rancho Cordova...42,881..A 9
Rancho Mirage......6,281..N 9
Rancho Palos Verdes*....36,577..N 7
Rancho Santa Fe*..4,014..O 9
Red Bluff.....9,490.°F 3
Redding......41,995.°E 3
Redlands.....43,619..G 10
Redondo Beach.....57,102..H 8
Redway.......1,094..F 1
Redwood City.......54,951.°D 7
Redwood Estates, see Chemeketa Park[-Redwood Estates]
Reedley......11,071..K 6
Rialto.......37,474..G 10
Richgrove*....1,398..L 6
Richmond....74,676..C 7
Ridgecrest....15,929..L 8
Rio Del Mar*..7,067..J 3
Rio Dell.......2,687..F 1
Rio Linda......7,359..A 9
Rio Vista......3,142..B 9
Ripon.........3,509..C 10
Riverbank.....5,695..C 10
Riverdale......1,866..K 5
Riverside....170,591.°N 8
Rocklin.......7,344..H 4
Rodeo*........8,286..I 3
Rohnert Park*.....22,965..H 2
Rolling Hills*...2,049..H 8
Rolling Hills Estates*....7,701..H 8
Romoland*....1,349..N 8
Rosamond.....2,869..M 7
Roseland*.....7,915..H 2
Rosemead*...42,604..G 9
Rosemont*...18,888..H 4
Roseville.....24,347..H 4
Ross*.........2,801..B 7
Rossmoor*...10,457..N 7
Rowland Heights*..28,252..N 7
Rubidoux*....17,048..N 8
Sacramento.275,741.°H 4
Sacramento South, see Parkway [-Sacramento South]
St. Helena.....4,898..A 7
Salinas.......80,479.°K 3
San Andreas...1,912.°B 11
San Anselmo...12,067..B 7
San Bernardino......118,794.°N 8
San Bruno....35,417..C 7
San Carlos...24,710..D 7
San Clemente..27,325..I 9
San Diego...875,538.°O 8
San Dimas*..24,014..N 7
San Fernando..17,731..F 8
San Francisco.678,974.°I 3
San Gabriel*..30,072..N 7
San Jacinto....7,098..H 11
San Joaquin....1,930..K 5
San Jose....629,531.°J 3
San Juan Bautista.....1,276..J 4
San Juan Capistrano.18,959..H 9
San Leandro....63,952..C 8
San Lorenzo..20,545..C 8
San Luis Obispo.....34,252.°L 5
San Marcos*.17,479..O 8
San Marino*..13,307..G 8
San Martin*...1,731..J 4
San Mateo...77,640..D 7
San Pablo....19,750..B 7
San Rafael...44,700.°B 7
San Ramon Village*.....22,356..I 3
Sand Hill*.....2,606..I 3
Sanger.......12,542..K 6
Santa Ana......204,023.°H 9
Santa Barbara....74,414.°M 5
Santa Clara...87,700..D 8
Santa Cruz...41,483.°J 3
Santa Fe Springs*...14,520..G 9
Santa Maria..39,685..M 5
Santa Monica....88,314..G 8
Santa Paula..20,552..F 6
Santa Rosa.......83,320.°H 2
Santa Ynez....3,335..M 5
Santee*......47,080..O 8
Saratoga....29,261..D 8
Saugus [-Bouquet Canyon]*..16,283..M 7
Sausalito.......7,338..C 7
Scotts Valley*.6,891..J 3
Seal Beach*..25,975..H 9
Searles Valley*3,439..L 8
Seaside......36,567..K 3
Sebastopol....5,595..A 6
Sedco Hills*...2,678..N 9
Seely.........1,058..O 10
Selma*......10,942..K 6
Shafter.......7,010..L 6
Shingle Springs*....1,268..H 4
Short Acres*...1,266..K 5
Sierra Madre*.....10,837..G 9
Signal Hill*....5,734..H 8
Simi Valley...77,500..G 7
Solana Beach*....13,047..O 8
Soledad.......5,928..K 4
Solvang.......3,091..M 5
Sonoma.......6,054..B 7
Sonora........3,247.°C 11
Soquel*.......6,212..I 3
South El Monte*....16,623..G 9
South Gate*..66,784..G 8
South Laguna*....6,013..H 9
South Lake Tahoe.....20,681..H 5
South Modesto*..12,492..I 4
South Oroville*....7,246..G 4
South Pasadena*.22,681..G 8
South San Francisco..49,393..C 7
South San Gabriel*.....5,421..N 7
South San Jose Hills*......16,049..N 7
South Taft*.....2,073..L 6
South Turlock*.1,700..J 4
South Whittier*...43,815..N 7
South Yuba City*........7,530..G 3
Spring Valley*40,191..O 8
Stanford*.....11,045..J 3
Stanton*.....23,723..H 9
Stockton....149,779.°I 4
Strathmore.....1,955..K 6
Suisun City...11,087..B 8
Summit City...1,136..E 3
Sun City*......8,460..N 8
Sunnymead...11,554..G 10
Sunnyside [-Tahoe City]..1,836..G 5
Sunnyvale....106,618..D 8
Susanville.....6,520.°F 5
Sutter.........2,226..G 3
Sutter Creek..1,705..A 10
Taft...........5,316..M 6
Taft Heights*..2,111..L 6
Tahoe City, see Sunnyside [-Tahoe City]
Talmage......1,514..G 2
Tamalpias [-Homestead Valley]*.....8,511..I 3
Tara Hills [-Montalvin Manor]*....9,471..I 3
Tehachapi.....4,126..M 7
Temecula*.....1,783..N 9
Temple City*.28,972..G 9
Terra Bella*...1,807..L 6
Thermalito....4,961..G 4
Thousand Oaks......77,072..G 7
Thousand Palms.......1,718..N 9
Tiburon*......6,685..I 3
Tierra Buena*.....2,374..G 3
Tipton*........1,185..K 6
Torrance....129,881..H 8
Tracy........18,428..C 9
Truckee.......2,389..G 5
Tulare.......22,530..K 6
Tulare East*...2,168..K 6
Tulare Northwest*..1,932..K 6
Tuolumne.....1,708..C 12
Turlock......26,287..D 10
Tustin*......32,317..H 9
Tustin Foothills*...26,174..N 7
Twain Harte*......1,369..I 5
Twentynine Palms.......7,465..N 9
Twentynine Palms Base..7,079..N 9
Twin Lakes*...4,502..J 3
Ukiah.......12,035.°G 2
Union City....39,406..C 8
Upland......47,647..G 9
Vacaville...43,367..A 8
Valencia*....12,163..M 7
Valinda*.....18,700..N 7
Valle Vista*....5,474..N 9
Vallejo.......80,303..B 7
Valley Center*.....1,242..O 8
Vandenburg AFB........8,136..M 5
Vandenberg Village*.....5,839..M 5
Ventura......74,393.°F 6
Victorville....14,220..F 10
View Park [-Windsor Hills]*.....12,101..N 7
Villa Park*....7,137..N 7
Vine Hill [-Pacheco]*..6,129..I 3
Visalia.......49,729.°K 6
Vista.........35,834..I 10
Walnut*......12,478..G 9
Walnut Creek......53,490..C 8
Walnut Creek West*......5,893..I 3
Walnut Park*.......11,811..N 7
Wasco........9,613..L 6
Waterford.....2,683..C 11
Watsonville...23,662..J 3
Weaverville....2,787.°E 2
Weed.........2,879..D 3
Weed Patch....1,553..L 6
West Athens*..8,531..N 7
West Carson*....17,997..N 7
West Compton*...5,907..N 7
West Covina..81,292..G 9
West Hollywood*.35,703..G 8
West Parlier...2,811..K 6
West Pittsburg...10,244..D 8
West Puente Valley*....20,445..N 7
West Sacramento*....10,875..H 3
West Whittier [-Los Nietos]*...21,001..N 7
Westminster..71,133..H 9
Westmont*...27,916..N 7
Westmorland..1,590..O 10
Westwood......2,081..F 4
Wheatland.....1,474..H 4
Whittier......68,558..G 9
Williams.......1,655..G 3
Willits........4,008..G 2
Willowbrook*.....30,845..N 7
Willows.........4,777.°G 3
Windsor Hills, see View Park [-Windsor Hills]
Winters.......2,652..A 8
Winton*.......4,995..J 4
Woffard Heights*.....2,112..L 7
Woodacre*....1,300..I 3
Woodbridge*..1,672..I 4
Woodlake.....4,343..K 6
Woodland....30,235.°A 8
Woodside.....5,291..D 7
Woodville*....1,507..K 6
Wrightwood*..2,511..N 8
Yermo........1,092..M 9
Yorba Linda......28,254..H 9
Yosemite Valley*......1,073..I 6
Yountville*....2,893..H 3
Yreka.........5,916.°D 3
Yuba City.....18,736.°G 4
Yucaipa......23,345..G 11
Yucca Valley...8,294..G 12

*Does not appear on map; key shows general location.
°County seat.
Source: 1980 census. Places without population figures are unincorporated areas.

Century City, Inc.

California Art Festivals are often sponsored by merchants. The exhibition shown above was held at the Century City shopping center in Los Angeles.

Amateur Acrobats attract a crowd during a practice session at a Santa Monica beach.

Pacific Pictures

CALIFORNIA/*People*

The 1980 United States census reported that California had 23,667,826 people—more than any other state. The population had increased 19 per cent over the 1970 census figure, 19,971,069. In 1960, California had ranked second to New York in population. Unofficial figures indicated that California passed New York early in 1963. By 1980, California had more than 6 million more people than New York.

About 95 per cent of the people of California live in the state's 22 metropolitan statistical areas (see METROPOLITAN AREA). About a third of California's population lives in the largest metropolitan area—Los Angeles-Long Beach. For the populations of the state's metropolitan areas, see the *Index* to the political map of California.

Los Angeles is the largest city, both in area and in population. It covers 465 square miles (1,204 square kilometers). The U.S. Bureau of the Census reported that Los Angeles had a population of about 3 million in 1980. California has 25 other cities of over 100,000. Only seven of these cities—Bakersfield, Fresno, Modesto, Riverside, Sacramento, San Bernardino, and Stockton—are inland. The others lie on or near the Pacific Coast. Berkeley, Concord, Fremont, Oakland, San Francisco, San Jose, and Sunnyvale are in the San Francisco Bay area. Anaheim, Fullerton, Garden Grove, Glendale, Huntington Beach, Long Beach, Pasadena, Santa Ana, and Torrance cluster around Los Angeles. Oxnard lies on the coast above Los Angeles and San Diego is on the coast near the Mexican border. See the separate articles on California cities listed in the *Related Articles* at the end of this article.

About 85 of every 100 Californians were born in the United States. Mexicans are the largest group from another country. The Los Angeles area has more people of Mexican ancestry than any other urban area in the world, outside Mexico. Many Californians of Chinese and Japanese ancestry live in communities of their own in Los Angeles and San Francisco. Chinatown in San Francisco has a Chinese population of about 32,000. It is one of the largest Chinese communities outside Asia. California also has about 198,000 American Indians—more than any other state.

Most early white settlers in California were Spaniards who belonged to the Roman Catholic Church. Today, Roman Catholics still make up the largest religious group in the state. Major Protestant groups in California include the Baptists, Episcopalians, Methodists, Presbyterians, and Unitarians. Jews form another large religious group in the state.

Katherine Young

Shoppers Browse in the colorful stalls of Olvera Street in Los Angeles. This street has been restored as a typical old Mexican market. Los Angeles has a larger number of persons of Mexican ancestry than any other city outside Mexico.

POPULATION

This map shows the *population density* of California, and how it varies in different parts of the state. Population density means the average number of persons who live in a given area.

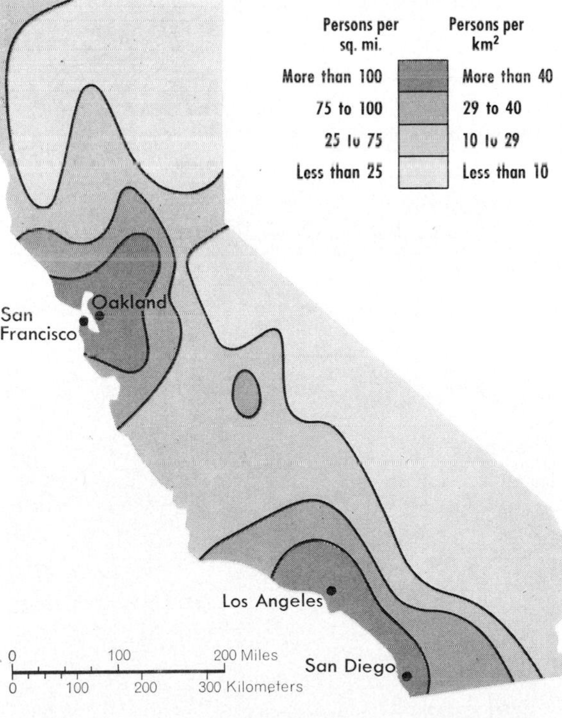

WORLD BOOK map

Colorful Dragon helps celebrate the Chinese New Year in San Francisco's Chinatown, a community of about 32,000 Chinese.

Redwood Empire Association

Migrant Workers harvest lettuce in Salinas. These workers move about the state, harvesting whatever crops are in season.

Alpha Photo Assoc.

U.C.L.A.

Royce Hall is the liberal arts building of the University of California in Los Angeles. This campus is one of nine that make up the university. The campuses are located in various parts of the state.

CALIFORNIA/*Education*

Schools. During the late 1700's and early 1800's, Franciscan friars taught farming, weaving, and other crafts to the Indians of California. A few small schools were established in the region. But most children of the early settlers received instruction from private teachers.

The first tax-supported school in California opened in San Francisco in 1850. It was financed by the city. In 1849, the state constitution provided for a public school system. The state legislature passed a tax law in 1852 to support public schools. But the schools did not become completely free to all children until 1867. The school system then did not include high schools. The first public high school opened in 1856 in San Francisco. In 1910, California established the nation's first tax-supported junior college, in Fresno.

Today, California spends nearly two-fifths of its government income for education, which is more than it spends for any other purpose. A 10-member state board of education develops policies for the elementary and secondary school system. The members of the board are appointed by the governor, subject to the approval of the state Senate. The board members serve four-year terms. A nonvoting student representative also serves on the board. The state department of education provides assistance to the more than 1,000 local school districts and divides state and federal funds among them. An elected superintendent of public instruction heads the department. California law requires children between the ages of 6 and 16 to attend school. Students who pass a special examination are allowed to leave school or to seek admission to a California community college at age 16. Children who have not completed a four-year high school course or who have not passed the special examination must go to school at least part time until the age of 18. For the number of students and teachers in California, see EDUCATION (table).

California has the largest system of state colleges and universities in the nation. Nine campuses of the University of California provide higher education for more than 125,000 students. The California State University system has 19 campuses. A master plan, approved by the legislature in 1960, provides for the orderly expansion of the system. The state also has an outstanding system of community colleges.

Libraries. California has about 170 public libraries. Its outstanding county library system, founded in 1909, has many branch libraries. Bookmobiles serve areas that do not have branch libraries. The University of California in Berkeley has the largest university library in the state. It has over 5½ million volumes, including the Bancroft Library collections of rare materials on the American West. The Hoover Institution on War, Revolution, and Peace at Stanford University has books and documents on world affairs of the 1900's.

Museums. The M. H. de Young Memorial Museum in San Francisco has art objects from many lands. The exhibits include famous paintings by European artists and items made by early American Indians. The California Palace of the Legion of Honor in San Francisco displays antique furniture, paintings, porcelain, sculpture, and tapestries. The Stanford University Museum of Art and Art Gallery has archaeological objects from ancient Egypt, Greece, and Rome.

The Huntington Library and Art Gallery in San Marino exhibits British paintings and French furniture and tapestries of the 1700's. The Southwest Museum in Los Angeles displays items of American Indians who lived in the Southwest. The Los Angeles County Museum of Art has outstanding collections of paintings and other works. The Natural History Museum of Los Angeles County owns perhaps the best collection of Ice Age fossils in the world. These fossils came from the La Brea tar pits in Los Angeles (see LA BREA PITS).

Memorial Church is a center of worship at Stanford University. The San Francisco earthquake destroyed the church in 1906, three years after it was built, but it was restored by 1913.

Stanford University

Art Center College of Design

CALIFORNIA

The Art Center College of Design is in Pasadena, Calif. The school offers courses in advertising and industrial design, illustration, and photography. It was founded in 1930.

Universities and Colleges

California has 96 universities and colleges accredited by the Western Association of Schools and Colleges. For enrollments and further information, see UNIVERSITIES AND COLLEGES (table).

Name	Location	Founded
Armstrong College	Berkeley	1918
Art Center College of Design	Pasadena	1930
Azusa Pacific University	Azusa	1899
Bethany Bible College	Santa Cruz	1954
Biola University	La Mirada	1906
Brooks Institute	Santa Barbara	1945
California, University of	*	*
California Baptist College	Riverside	1950
California College of Arts and Crafts	Oakland	1907
California College of Podiatric Medicine	San Francisco	1914
California Institute of Integral Studies	San Francisco	1968
California Institute of Technology	Pasadena	1891
California Institute of the Arts	Valencia	1957
California Lutheran College	Thousand Oaks	1959
California Maritime Academy	Vallejo	1929
California School of Professional Psychology	*	*
California State University	*	*
Chapman College	Orange	1861
Christ College Irvine	Irvine	1972
Church Divinity School of the Pacific	Berkeley	1893
Claremont Graduate School	Claremont	1925
Claremont McKenna College	Claremont	1947
Cogswell College	San Francisco	1887
College of the Center for Early Education	Los Angeles	1939
Dominican College of San Rafael	San Rafael	1850
Dominican School of Philosophy and Theology	Berkeley	1932
Fielding Institute	Santa Barbara	1974
Franciscan School of Theology	Berkeley	1968
Fresno Pacific College	Fresno	1965
Fuller Theological Seminary	Pasadena	1947
Golden Gate Baptist Theological Seminary	Mill Valley	1944
Golden Gate University	San Francisco	1901
Graduate Theological Union	Berkeley	1962
Harvey Mudd College	Claremont	1955
Hebrew Union College—Jewish Institute of Religion	Los Angeles	1954
Holy Family College	Fremont	1946
Holy Names College	Oakland	1925
Jesuit School of Theology at Berkeley	Berkeley	1934
John F. Kennedy University	Orinda	1964
Judaism, University of	Los Angeles	1947
La Verne, University of	La Verne	1891
Loma Linda University	Loma Linda	1905
Los Angeles Baptist College	Newhall	1927
Loyola Marymount University	Los Angeles	1918
Menlo College	Menlo Park	1927
Mennonite Brethren Biblical Seminary	Fresno	1955
Mills College	Oakland	1852
Monterey Institute of International Studies	Monterey	1955
Mount St. Mary's College	Los Angeles	1925
National University	San Diego	1971
Naval Postgraduate School	Monterey	1909
New College of California	San Francisco	1971
Northrop University	Inglewood	1942
Notre Dame, College of	Belmont	1851
Occidental College	Los Angeles	1887
Otis Art Institute of Parsons School of Design†	Los Angeles	1918
Pacific, University of the	Stockton	1851
Pacific Christian College	Fullerton	1928
Pacific Graduate School of Psychology	Palo Alto	1975
Pacific Oaks College	Pasadena	1945
Pacific School of Religion	Berkeley	1866
Pacific Union College	Angwin	1882
Patten College	Oakland	1944
Pepperdine University	Malibu	1937
Pitzer College	Claremont	1964
Point Loma Nazarene College	San Diego	1908
Pomona College	Claremont	1887
Rand Graduate Institute of Policy Studies	Santa Monica	1970
Redlands, University of	Redlands	1907
St. John's College	Camarillo	1926
St. Joseph's College	Mountain View	1898
St. Mary's College of California	Moraga	1863
St. Patrick's Seminary	Menlo Park	1898
San Diego, University of	San Diego	1952
San Francisco, University of	San Francisco	1855
San Francisco Art Institute	San Francisco	1871
San Francisco Conservatory of Music	San Francisco	1917
San Francisco Theological Seminary	San Anselmo	1915
Santa Clara, University of	Santa Clara	1851
Saybrook Institute	San Francisco	1970
School of Theology at Claremont	Claremont	1885
Scripps College	Claremont	1926
Simpson College	San Francisco	1921
Southern California, University of	Los Angeles	1880
Southern California College	Costa Mesa	1920
Southern California College of Optometry	Fullerton	1904
Stanford University	Stanford	1885
Thomas Aquinas College	Santa Paula	1971
U.S. International University	San Diego	1924
West Coast University	Los Angeles	1909
Western State Univ. College of Law	Fullerton	1966
Westmont College	Santa Barbara	1940
Whittier College	Whittier	1901
Woodbury University	Los Angeles	1884
World College West	San Rafael	1971
Wright Institute	Berkeley	1969

*For the campuses and founding dates, see UNIVERSITIES AND COLLEGES (table).
†See New School for Social Research in UNIVERSITIES AND COLLEGES (table).

Josef Muench

A Street in Disneyland

Ray Atkeson

Ski Lodge in Squaw Valley

San Diego Zoo

Bird Colony in the San Diego Zoo

Golf Course on Monterey Peninsula

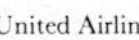

United Airlines

CALIFORNIA / *A Visitor's Guide*

Many people visit California to see such natural wonders as redwood groves and volcanic cones. California also has famous golf courses, resorts, beaches, ski areas, and many other recreational facilities.

California's largest cities, Los Angeles, San Diego, and San Francisco, play host to millions of visitors a year. For information on things to see and do in these cities, see Los Angeles; San Diego; San Francisco.

Places to Visit

Following are brief descriptions of some of California's many interesting places to visit.

Death Valley Scotty's Castle, at Death Valley National Monument, has Spanish-style buildings. It was built by Walter E. Scott, who lived in Death Valley for more than 30 years.

Disneyland, in Anaheim, is an amusement park designed by Walt Disney. Its attractions include a fairyland castle and a boat trip through "jungle" waters.

Knott's Berry Farm, in Buena Park, is California's oldest amusement park. It features rides, a ghost town, and an Indian village.

Marineland, at Palos Verdes Estates, is the world's largest oceanarium. Its aquariums contain sharks, porpoises, and other interesting sea life.

Missions were built in California by Franciscan friars beginning in 1769. These missions are listed in a table in the *History* section of this article.

Monterey Peninsula includes the communities of Carmel, Monterey, Pacific Grove, and Pebble Beach. Carmel is a famous art colony. Monterey has buildings dating from Spanish colonial days. Sights along Seventeen-Mile Drive between Pacific Grove and Carmel include rocks with seals and Pebble Beach Golf Course.

Redwood Highway (U.S. 101), from San Francisco to Oregon, passes through magnificent groves of redwood trees. These trees are the tallest in the world.

San Diego Zoo has a large collection of birds, mammals, and reptiles. Its monkey and ape exhibits rank among the finest in North America.

San Simeon, near San Luis Obispo, is the former estate of newspaper owner William Randolph Hearst. It includes a castle with ancient works of art, a Roman temple, a private theater, and huge swimming pools.

Parklands in California include six national parks. They are Channel Islands, Kings Canyon, Lassen Volcanic, Redwood, Sequoia, and Yosemite. Thousands of miles of trails wind through the parks. California also has several national monuments, including Death Valley, Lava Beds, Muir Woods, and Pinnacles. For more information on these and other California parklands, see the map and tables in the World Book article on National Park System.

National Forests. California has 22 national forests. Congress has set aside several areas in these national forests as national wildernesses, to be preserved in their natural condition.

State Parks, Forests, and Monuments offer a variety of historic and scenic attractions. For information on these areas, write to Department of Parks and Recreation, P.O. Box 2390, Sacramento, Calif. 95811.

FPG

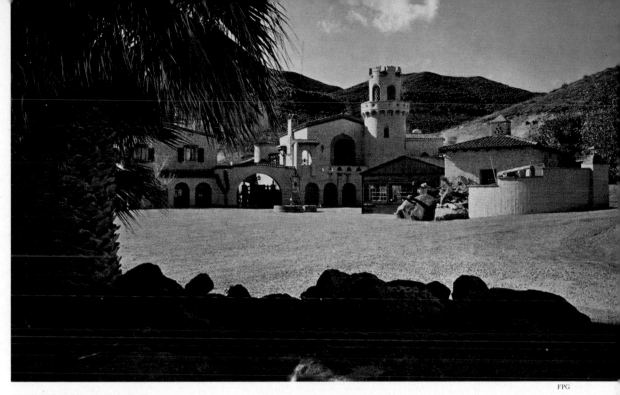

Scotty's Castle in Death Valley

Annual Events

California's most famous annual event is the Tournament of Roses, held in Pasadena on New Year's Day. Colorful floats, decorated with thousands of flowers, compete for prizes. A beauty contest and the Rose Bowl football game are part of the festivities at the Tournament of Roses. Other annual events include:

January-June: New Year Regatta in San Diego (January 1st); Chinese New Year Celebration in San Francisco and Los Angeles (January or February); Swallows return to San Juan Capistrano (March); Great Western Livestock and Dairy Show in Pomona (late March or early April); Kinetic Sculpture Race from Arcata to Ferndale (April); Cherry Blossom Festival in San Francisco (April); Garden Grove Strawberry Festival (May); Calaveras County Fair and Jumping Frog Jubilee in Angels Camp (May); Ojai Music Festival in Ojai (May); Old Sacramento Dixieland Jubilee (May); Festival Season, a series of plays by William Shakespeare and other dramatists, performed in San Diego (June-September).

July-December: California Rodeo in Salinas (July); Santa Barbara National Horse Show and Flower Show (July); Old Spanish Days Fiesta in Santa Barbara (early August); State Fair in Sacramento (late August and early September); Auburn District Fair in Auburn (September); Lodi Grape Festival and National Wine Show in Lodi (September); Los Angeles County Fair (September and October); Monterey Jazz Festival (September); Grand National Livestock Exposition at the Cow Palace in San Francisco (late October and early November); San Francisco Film Festival (October); Mother Goose Parade in El Cajon (November); Christmas Tree Lighting Ceremony in Carmel-by-the-Sea (December).

Visitors at Mission San Juan Capistrano

Alpha Photo Assoc.

New Year's Day Rose Parade in Pasadena

FPG

Amargosa Range ....D 5
American R. ....C 3
Bass Lake ....D 4
Black Butte Lake ...C 2
Bodega Head ....C 2
Breckinridge Mountain ....E 4
Briones Res. ....A 5
Bristol Lake ....E 6
Buchon Pt. ....E 3
Buena Vista Lake ...E 4
Camanche Res. ......C 3
Cascade Range ......B 2
Chanchelulla Peak ..B 2
Channel Islands Nat'l. Park ....E 4
Cherry Valley Res. ...D 4
Chocolate Mts. ......F 6
Clair Engle Lake ....B 2
Clear Lake ....C 2
Clear Lake Res. .....B 3
Claremont ....C 3
Coachella Canal .....F 6
Coast Ranges ....C 2
Colorado R. ....F 6
Colorado R. Aqueduct F 5
Coyote Dam ....C 2
Cuyama R. ....E 4
Cuyamaca Peak .....F 5
Death Valley (Lowest Point in U. S.) ...D 5
Death Valley Nat'l. Mon. ....D 5
Devils Postpile Nat'l. Mon. ....D 4
Diablo Range ....D 3
Donnell Lake ....C 4
Eagle Lake ....B 3
Eagle Peak ....B 3
Eel R. ....B 2
Estero Bay ....E 3
Excelsior Mountain ..C 4
Feather R. ....C 3
Folsom Lake ....C 3
Frazier Mountain ...E 4
Fredonyer Peak .....B 3
Goose Lake ....B 3
Gulf of Santa Catalina ....F 5
Hetch Hetchy Aqueduct ....D 3
Honey Lake ....B 3
Hot Springs Peak....B 3
Ice House Res. ......C 3
Imperial Valley .....F 6
Iron Gate Res. ......B 2
Jenkinson Lake .....C 3
Joshua Tree Nat'l. Mon. ....F 6
Kern R. ....E 4
Kings Canyon Nat'l. Park ....D 4
Kings R. ....D 4
Klamath R. ....B 2
Laguna Mts. ....F 5
Lake Almanor ....B 3
Lake Berryessa ......C 2
Lake Mendocino ....C 2
Lake Oroville ....C 3
Lake Success ....D 4
Lake Tahoe ....C 4
Lassen Peak ....B 3
Lassen Volcanic Nat'l. Park ....B 3
Lava Beds Nat'l. Mon. B 3
Los Angeles Aqueduct E 4
Mammoth Pool Res. .D 4
McKittrick Summit ..E 4
Merced R. ....D 3
Mojave Desert ....E 5
Mojave R. ....E 5
Mokelumne R. ....C 3
Mono Lake ....D 4
Monterey Bay ....D 3
Mt. Humphreys .....D 4
Mt. Linn ....B 2
Mt. Patterson ....C 4
Mt. Ritter ....D 4
Mt. Sanhedrin ......C 2
Mt. Shasta ....B 2
Mt. Vida ....B 3
Mt. Whitney (Highest Point in Calif.) ...D 4
Mt. Williamson .....D 4
Mt. Wilson ....E 4
Nacimiento Res. ....E 3
New Exchequer Res. .D 3
New Melones Lake ...D 3
Olancha Peak ....D 4
Outer Santa Barbara Passage ....F 4
Owens Lake ....D 5
Panamint Range ....D 5
Pescadero Pt. ......D 2
Picacho Peak ....F 6
Pinnacles Nat'l. Mon. D 3
Pit R. ....B 3
Pt. Arena ....C 2
Pt. Conception .....E 3
Pt. Loma ....F 5
Pt. Piedras Blancas .E 3
Pt. Pinos ....D 3
Pt. Reyes ....D 2
Pt. Sal ....E 3
Pt. San Luis ....E 3
Pt. Sur ....D 3
Prosser Creek Res. ...C 3
Pyramid Peak ....C 3
Red Mountain ......B 2
Redwood Nat'l Park B 1
Rogers Lake ....E 5
Russian R. ....C 2
Sacramento R. ......C 3
Sacramento River Deep Water Ship Channel .....C 3
Sacramento Valley ...B 2
Salinas R. ....D 3
Salmon Mts. ....B 2
Salton Sea ....F 6
San Antonio Res. ....E 3
San Benito Mountain D 3
San Bernardino Mts. .E 5
San Clemente Mountain ....F 4
San Diego Aqueduct .F 5
San Gorgonio Mountain ....E 5
San Joaquin R. .....D 3
San Joaquin Valley ..D 3
San Luis Res. ......D 3
San Miguel Island ...E 3
San Nicolas Island ..F 4
San Rafael Mts. .....E 3
Santa Barbara Channel ....E 3
Santa Barbara Island ....F 4
Santa Catalina Island ....F 4
Santa Clara R. ......E 4
Santa Cruz Island ..F 4
Santa Cruz Mts. ....D 2
Santa Lucia Range ..D 3
Santa Rosa Island ...F 3
Searles Lake ....E 5
Sequoia Nat'l. Park D 4
Shasta Lake ....B 2
Sierra Nevada (Mts.) C 3
Siskiyou Mts. ....B 2
Soda Lake ....E 5
Split Mountain .....D 4
Stanislaus R. ....D 3
Telescope Peak ......D 5
Temblor Range ......E 4
Trinidad Head ......B 1
Trinity Mts. ....B 2
Trinity R. ....B 2
Tulloch Lake ....D 3
Warner Mts. ....B 3
Whiskeytown Res. ...B 2
Wishon Res. ....D 4
Yosemite Nat'l. Park ....D 4
Yuba R. ....C 3

CALIFORNIA / *The Land*

California has an area of 158,693 square miles (411,013 square kilometers). It is larger than any other state except Alaska and Texas. California's San Bernardino County covers more than 20,000 square miles (51,800 square kilometers)—almost as large an area as Connecticut, Massachusetts, and New Jersey together. San Bernardino ranks as the largest county in the United States.

Land Regions. California has eight main land regions: (1) the Klamath Mountains, (2) the Coast Ranges, (3) the Central Valley, (4) the Cascade Mountains, (5) the Sierra Nevada, (6) the Basin and Range Region, (7) the Los Angeles Ranges, and (8) the San Diego Ranges.

The Klamath Mountains include several small, forest-covered ranges in the northwestern corner of California.

Land Regions of California

These ranges are higher and steeper than the coastal mountains to the south. Many peaks are from 6,000 to 8,000 feet (1,800 to 2,400 meters) high. Deep canyons break up the ranges. The area also has several valleys that are large and flat enough for farming.

The Coast Ranges extend southward along the Pacific Coast from the Klamath Mountains to Santa Barbara County. Individual sections of this mountain chain have names of their own. These include the Diablo, Santa Cruz, and Santa Lucia ranges. Livestock ranches, orchards, vineyards and truck gardens dot the beautiful valleys that separate the ranges. These valleys include the Napa Valley north of San Francisco, and the Santa Clara and Salinas valleys to the south. California's famous redwood trees grow on the Coast Ranges.

An important feature of the region is the San Andreas Fault. A *fault* is a break in the earth along which movements of the earth's crust have taken place. The San Andreas Fault enters northern California from the Pacific Ocean near Point Arena and extends southeastward into southern California. Movements of the earth's crust along this fault cause earthquakes.

The Central Valley, sometimes called the *Great Valley*, lies between the Coast Ranges and the Sierra Nevada. It has two major river systems—the Sacramento in the north and the San Joaquin in the south. The valley extends about 500 miles (800 kilometers) from northwest to southeast. Much of it is level, and looks like a broad, open plain. This fertile valley forms the largest and most important farming area west of the Rocky Mountains. It has three-fifths of California's farmland, and produces almost every kind of crop.

The Cascade Mountains extend northward from the Central Valley. Unlike other California ranges, the Cascades were formed by volcanoes. Lassen Peak (10,457 feet, or 3,187 meters) is an active volcano in the southern Cascades. Another famous peak, Mount Shasta (14,162 feet, or 4,317 meters), was once an active volcano.

The Sierra Nevada, east of the Central Valley, forms a massive rock wall more than 400 miles (640 kilometers)

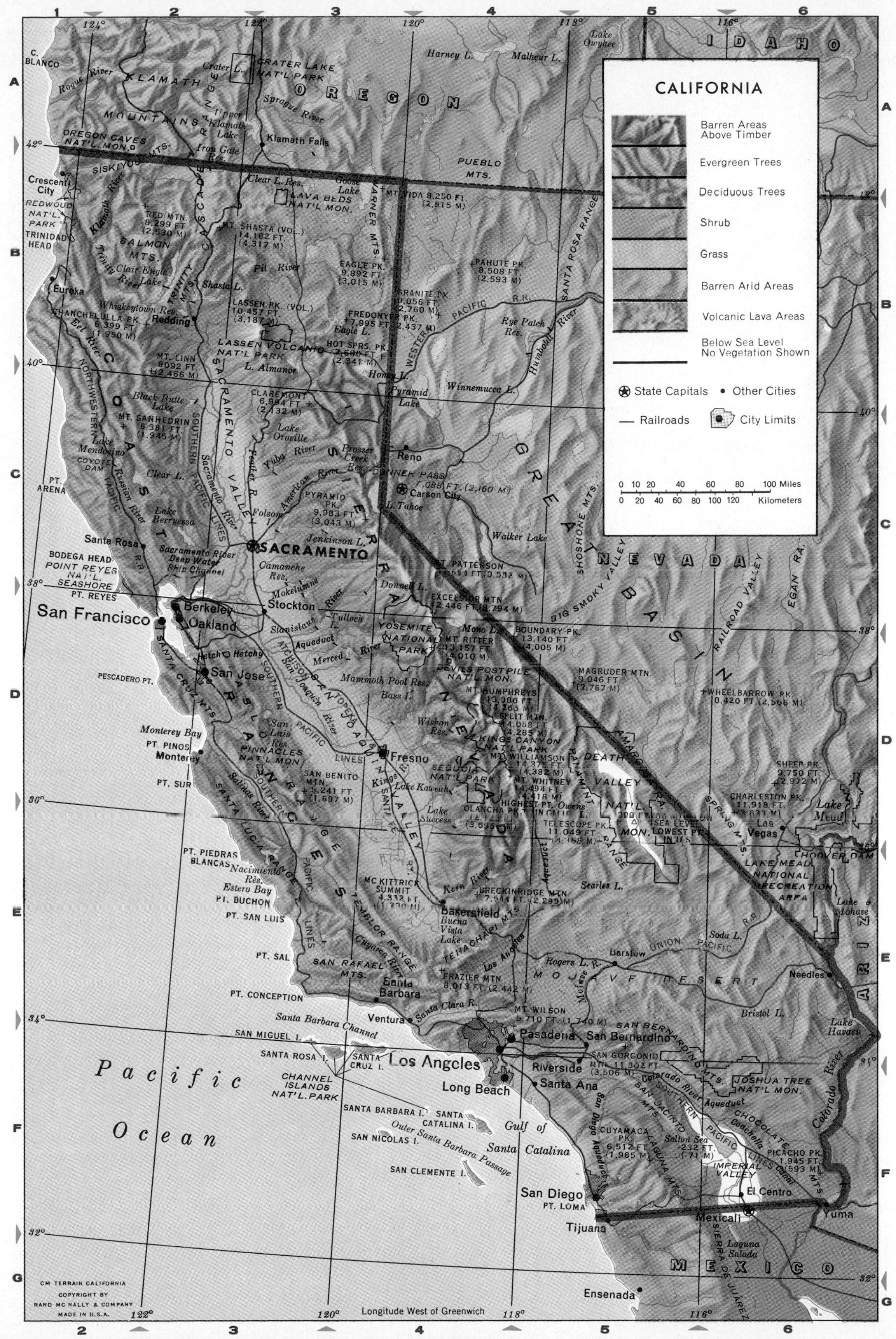

Specially created for **World Book Encyclopedia** by Rand McNally and World Book editors

Winston Pote, Shostal

Bridalveil Fall plunges 620 feet (189 meters) in Yosemite National Park in the Sierra Nevada region. Rivers and glaciers have made deep valleys and steep granite cliffs there. Several peaks in the Sierra Nevada rise over 14,000 feet (4,270 meters).

long and about 40 to 70 miles (64 to 110 kilometers) wide. Several peaks of the Sierra Nevada rise more than 14,000 feet (4,270 meters). These include Mount Whitney (14,494 feet, or 4,418 meters), the highest point in the United States south of Alaska. Rushing mountain rivers have cut deep canyons in the western part of the Sierra. Yosemite Valley is the most outstanding of these canyons. Yosemite originally was cut by streams. Later, glaciers moved down the valley and eroded it further. The glaciers created the sheer granite cliffs that can be seen there today.

The Basin and Range Region is part of a larger region that extends into Nevada, Oregon, and several other states. Much of the northern section is a lava plateau. Thousands of years ago, lava flowed out of great cracks in the earth's surface and flooded the area.

In southern California, much of the Basin and Range Region is a wasteland. The Mojave Desert covers a large area between the southern Sierra and the Colorado River. The Colorado Desert lies to the south. Irrigation has made several valleys in the region suitable for raising crops. These valleys include the fertile Imperial and Coachella valleys near the Mexican border. See Colorado Desert; Imperial Valley; Mojave.

Death Valley is in the Basin and Range Region near the California-Nevada border. Part of Death Valley lies 282 feet (86 meters) below sea level, and is the lowest point in North America. See Death Valley.

The Los Angeles Ranges are a group of small mountain ranges between Santa Barbara and San Diego counties. They are also called the *Transverse Ranges,* because they extend generally in an east-west direction. Other ranges in California run generally north and south. The Los Angeles Ranges include the Santa Ynez, Santa Monica, San Gabriel, and San Bernardino mountains. Some geographers consider the San Jacinto and Santa Ana Mountains to be a part of this group.

The San Diego Ranges, also called the *Peninsular Ranges,* cover most of San Diego County at the southwestern tip of the state. They include the Agua, Tibia, Laguna, and Vallecito mountains. This mountain system extends southward into the Mexican peninsula known as Baja (Lower) California.

Coastline. California's general coastline measures 840 miles (1,352 kilometers). California's *tidal shoreline* (including small bays and inlets) is 3,427 miles (5,515 kilometers) long. Along much of the coast, the Coast Ranges rise from the shore in steep cliffs and terraces. Southern California has many wide, sandy beaches. The California coast has two great natural harbors—San Francisco and San Diego bays. There are smaller natural harbors at Humboldt and Monterey bays.

Two groups of islands are located near the California coast. The small, rocky Farallon Islands rise from the ocean about 30 miles (48 kilometers) west of San Francisco. The eight Channel Islands lie scattered off the coast of southern California. Catalina Island, which is the best known of the Channel Islands, attracts many vacationers.

Rivers, Waterfalls, and Lakes. California's two longest rivers are the Sacramento and the San Joaquin. The Sacramento rises near Mount Shasta and flows south through the Central Valley. The San Joaquin rises in the Sierra Nevada and flows northwest through the Central Valley. The two rivers meet northeast of San Francisco and flow west into San Francisco Bay. Smaller rivers, such as the Feather and the Mokelumne, begin in the eastern mountains and flow west into the Sacramento or the San Joaquin.

The Colorado River forms the border between southern California and Arizona. It is an important source of water for Los Angeles and other cities of southern California. Water from the Colorado is also used to irrigate desert farmlands. Many rivers in southern

California dry up or run underground during the dry season. Water may suddenly pour into the dry riverbeds during the rainy season, and cause serious floods. In desert areas, most rivers have no outlets to other streams or to the sea. They flow above ground for a certain distance. Then they dry up, or sink into the sand.

Yosemite National Park in California has several of the highest waterfalls in North America. Ribbon Falls (1,612 feet, or 491 meters) is the highest on the continent. Other high waterfalls in Yosemite include Bridalveil, Illilouette, Nevada, Silver Strand, Vernal, and Upper and Lower Yosemite.

California has about 8,000 lakes. Lake Tahoe, the deepest, averages 1,500 feet (427 meters) in depth. It lies in the Sierra on the California-Nevada border, and reflects the surrounding mountain peaks. Most of the desert lakes east of the Sierra contain dissolved minerals that give the water a disagreeable taste. Potash, salt, and other minerals are taken from Owens Lake, Searles Lake, and other dry or partly dry lakes in this region. The Salton Sea is a large, shallow lake in southern California. It was formed between 1905 and 1907 by floodwaters from the Colorado River.

California's Coast, *below,* is rugged where the Coast Ranges rise steeply from the ocean. But San Francisco and San Diego bays form natural harbors.

Glen Fishback, Alpha Photo Assoc.

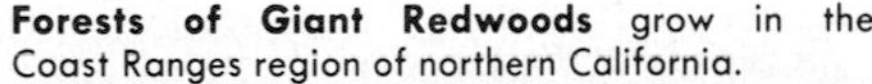

Forests of Giant Redwoods grow in the Coast Ranges region of northern California.

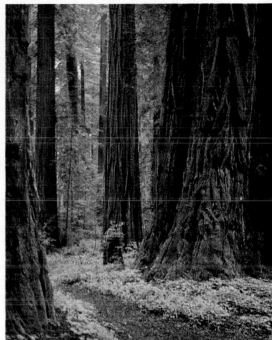

Ray Atkeson

Wasteland makes up much of the Basin and Range Region in southern California. The barren area below is part of the Mojave Desert.

David Muench, Alpha Photo Assoc.

Quiet Farms, like this one near Exeter, lie in the Central Valley, the major agricultural region.

Josef Muench

CALIFORNIA/*Climate*

California has a great variety of climates. Its southern coast has a mild climate. Temperatures in Los Angeles average 55° F. (13° C) in January and 73° F. (23° C) in July. Southeastern California has a hot, dry climate. The highest temperature ever recorded in the United States, 134° F. (57° C), occurred at Greenland Ranch in Death Valley on July 10, 1913.

California's northern and central coast also has a mild climate. But this area is generally cooler than the southern coast. January temperatures in San Francisco average 50° F. (10° C). July temperatures there average 59° F. (15° C). Boca recorded California's lowest temperature, −45° F. (−43° C), on Jan. 20, 1937.

Most parts of California have only two well-marked seasons—a rainy season and a dry season. The rainy season lasts from October to April in the north, and from November to March or April in the south. Yearly *precipitation* (rain, snow, and other forms of moisture) is greatest along the northern coast, where it averages over 80 inches (200 centimeters). At San Francisco, the yearly average is about 22 inches (56 centimeters); at Los Angeles, 15 inches (38 centimeters); and at San Diego, 10 inches (25 centimeters). Some desert basins in the southeast receive almost no rain. From Oct. 3, 1912, to Nov. 8, 1914, Bagdad, in Death Valley, had no measurable precipitation. This 760-day rainless period set the United States record.

Snowfall is rare along the central and southern coast. But at Tamarack, in the Sierra Nevada, the yearly snowfall averages about 450 inches (1,140 centimeters).

Mike Roberts, Shostal

Orange Groves thrive in California's mild weather. The state also has snow-covered mountain regions and hot, dry deserts.

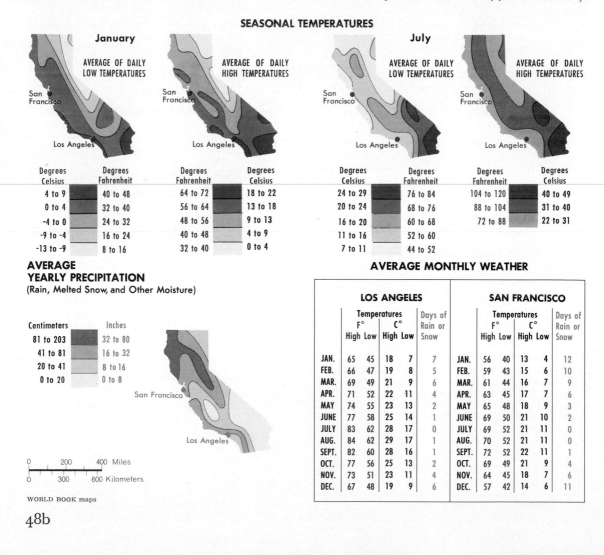

SEASONAL TEMPERATURES

January

AVERAGE OF DAILY LOW TEMPERATURES

San Francisco
Los Angeles

Degrees Celsius	Degrees Fahrenheit
4 to 9	40 to 48
0 to 4	32 to 40
-4 to 0	24 to 32
-9 to -4	16 to 24
-13 to -9	8 to 16

AVERAGE OF DAILY HIGH TEMPERATURES

San Francisco
Los Angeles

Degrees Fahrenheit	Degrees Celsius
64 to 72	18 to 22
56 to 64	13 to 18
48 to 56	9 to 13
40 to 48	4 to 9
32 to 40	0 to 4

July

AVERAGE OF DAILY LOW TEMPERATURES

San Francisco
Los Angeles

Degrees Celsius	Degrees Fahrenheit
24 to 29	76 to 84
20 to 24	68 to 76
16 to 20	60 to 68
11 to 16	52 to 60
7 to 11	44 to 52

AVERAGE OF DAILY HIGH TEMPERATURES

San Francisco
Los Angeles

Degrees Fahrenheit	Degrees Celsius
104 to 120	40 to 49
88 to 104	31 to 40
72 to 88	22 to 31

AVERAGE YEARLY PRECIPITATION
(Rain, Melted Snow, and Other Moisture)

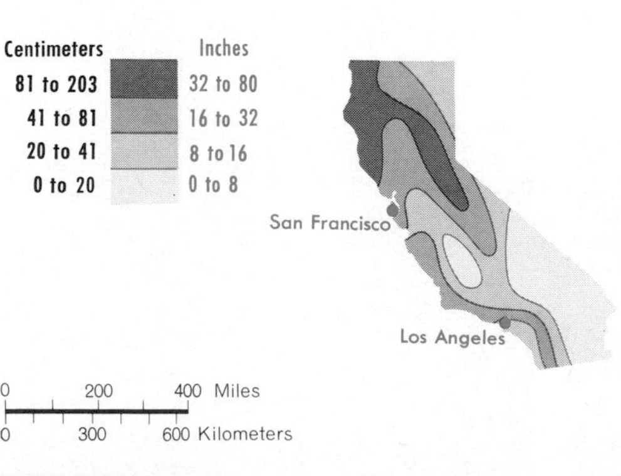

WORLD BOOK maps

AVERAGE MONTHLY WEATHER

	LOS ANGELES						SAN FRANCISCO				
	Temperatures F°		Temperatures C°		Days of Rain or Snow		Temperatures F°		Temperatures C°		Days of Rain or Snow
	High	Low	High	Low			High	Low	High	Low	
JAN.	65	45	18	7	7	JAN.	56	40	13	4	12
FEB.	66	47	19	8	5	FEB.	59	43	15	6	10
MAR.	69	49	21	9	6	MAR.	61	44	16	7	9
APR.	71	52	22	11	4	APR.	63	45	17	7	6
MAY	74	55	23	13	2	MAY	65	48	18	9	3
JUNE	77	58	25	14	1	JUNE	69	50	21	10	2
JULY	83	62	28	17	0	JULY	69	52	21	11	0
AUG.	84	62	29	17	1	AUG.	70	52	21	11	0
SEPT.	82	60	28	16	1	SEPT.	72	52	22	11	1
OCT.	77	56	25	13	2	OCT.	69	49	21	9	4
NOV.	73	51	23	11	4	NOV.	64	45	18	7	6
DEC.	67	48	19	9	6	DEC.	57	42	14	6	11

California produces an enormous quantity and variety of agricultural products, fishery products, manufactured goods, and minerals. All these products have a total yearly value of about $82 billion. This figure is greater than the value of products produced in any other state. The California economy benefits from the state's many natural resources, and from its large population.

Most of the goods manufactured in California are products of modern science and engineering. These products include airplanes, computers, television equipment, and missiles. Private companies maintain several hundred laboratories in California for conducting research and testing new products. Most of these laboratories are located near large universities and draw upon the ideas and skills of university biologists, chemists, engineers, and physicists.

The tourist industry is also a leading business in California. About 30 million persons visit the state annually. These tourists spend more than $21 billion there each year.

Natural Resources. California is unusually rich in minerals, timber, and wildlife. The soil and climate make it possible for California farmers to grow a wide variety of crops.

Soils. Many parts of California, especially in the Central Valley, have *alluvial* (valley) soils. These soils make the best farmland. The Imperial Valley in southern California has rich alluvial soils that produce outstanding crops when irrigated. *Residual* (upland) soils cover the mountain slopes. These soils support forests in areas that have enough rain. In many other places, they provide grazing land.

Minerals. California has important fields of petroleum and natural gas in the southern part of the Central Valley, near the southern coast, and in coastal waters off Long Beach and Santa Barbara. Natural gas also comes from fields around Sacramento. Valuable deposits of boron are found in the desert areas of southeastern California. Commercially important quantities of sand and gravel occur in most California counties. Gemstones, including agate, epidote, garnet, jade, jasper, obsidian, rose quartz, and tourmaline, are found in various counties. Other nonmetallic minerals found in the state include asbestos, barite, clays, diatomite, feldspar, gypsum, peat, potash, pumice, rock salt, salt cake, soda ash, stone, and talc.

California's tungsten deposits are among the largest in the United States. They occur mainly in Inyo County. The state's chief gold deposits are found on the western slopes of the northern Sierra Nevada. Mercury occurs in many parts of the state. Other important metals found in California include copper, iron ore, lead, magnesium, silver, and zinc.

Forests cover about 40 per cent of California. The state has three main forest regions, each named for the tree that is most important in the region. The *redwood region* is a narrow belt that extends south along the coast from Oregon to San Luis Obispo County. The *pine region* covers the Sierra Nevada. It also extends along the inland parts of the Coast Ranges as far south as Lake County. The *coast range pine and fir region* lies between the redwood belt and the inner-coast part of the pine region. California's chief timber trees include the Douglas fir, ponderosa and Jeffrey pine, white fir, redwood, red fir, and sugar pine.

California's most famous trees are its two sequoias, the *coast redwood*, or redwood, and the *sierra redwood*, or giant sequoia. The redwood is the state tree. Coast redwoods are the world's tallest living things. They grow near the coast in northern and central California. Sierra redwoods, often called *big trees*, have larger trunks than coast redwoods, but are not as tall. They grow on the western slopes of the Sierra Nevada. Bristlecone pines in the White Mountains of southeastern California are the world's oldest living things. Some are over 4,600 years old. See BRISTLECONE PINE (with picture).

California's forests are important for timber production and for recreation. But they are especially important for preserving the state's precious water supply. Water does not run off or evaporate so quickly in forest areas as it does in treeless regions. The logging industry and the government work to protect California's forests from fire, harmful insects, and tree diseases. Landowners in California also grow trees on tree farms so there will be a constant supply of timber to replace the trees that are cut.

Water is one of California's most important natural resources. The mountain areas, especially in the north, have plenty of water from rain and melted snow. But most of California's farms, industries, and homes are in the dry southern valleys. One of the state's greatest problems is to transport water from rainy areas to dry places where it is needed. Many *aqueducts* (channels and large pipelines) and canals have been built for that purpose. In 1960, California approved funds for a state water project. The project includes dams to store water, and canals to carry it from rivers in northern California to coastal cities and to southern California. Oroville Dam on the Feather River is the most important part of the project. This dam is 771 feet (235 meters) high—the highest in the United States.

Plant Life. Indigo bushes, Joshua trees, and several kinds of cacti grow in the deserts of southeastern California. California palm trees are also found in this area. Patches of *chaparral* (thick and often thorny shrubs and small trees) cover California's foothills. Many kinds of oaks grow in the state. The oaks make up most of California's hardwood trees.

Animal Life. Desert wildlife in California includes coyotes, lizards, and rattlesnakes. Beavers, bears, deer, foxes, minks, wildcats, wolverines, and a few mountain sheep roam the mountain and forest areas. Small herds of pronghorns and elk live in California, chiefly in the northern part of the state.

The California condor, a huge vulture, is the largest bird in North America. It has a wingspread of about 9 feet (2.7 meters). California condors are very rare. Los Padres National Forest in southern California has the only ones known to exist today. California game birds include ducks, geese, grouse, mourning doves, quail, and turkey. Game fishes in California's streams include black bass, salmon, striped bass, and trout. Abalones, clams, crabs, shrimps, lobsters, oysters, scallops, and other shellfishes are found along the California coast.

Manufacturing accounts for about 77 per cent of the value of goods produced in California. Goods manufactured there have a *value added by manufacture* of about $62½ billion yearly. This figure represents the value created in products by California industries, not counting such costs as materials, supplies, and fuels. California leads the nation in manufacturing. Its chief manufactured products, in order of importance, are (1) transportation equipment, (2) electric machinery and equipment, and (3) food products.

Transportation Equipment made in California has a value added of about $10⅔ billion annually. Southern California is the greatest aircraft-assembly center in the United States. The warm, dry climate of this region permits aircraft companies to fly and test their planes during all seasons. Burbank, Long Beach, San Diego, and other cities have large aircraft factories. California is also a leading center of automobile production. Most of the automobile parts are made outside the state, and shipped to Alameda, Los Angeles, and Santa Clara counties, where the cars are assembled. Long Beach, Los Angeles, San Diego, and San Francisco have shipyards.

Electric Machinery and Equipment produced in California has a value added of about $7¾ billion yearly. Electronic components and communication equipment account for a large part of this output. The state also produces household appliances, electric motors and generators, and wiring devices.

Food Products have an annual value added of about $7½ billion. California is the greatest wine-producing area in the United States. It also has breweries. Meat-packing plants in California process more than 2 million cattle a year. Plants in Los Angeles account for about half this total. California factories also can seafoods, package dairy products and poultry, dry and freeze fruits and vegetables, and refine sugar.

Other Manufactured Products produced in California include nonelectric machinery, such as construction equipment, engines, and office machines; and fabricated metals, such as cans, sheet metal, and tools. Refineries in California process petroleum and extract minerals from seawater. Steel is made in Fontana, Los Angeles, Pittsburg, South San Francisco, and Torrance. California is a fashion center, especially for sportswear. Many companies make clothing and textiles. California firms also make chemicals, lumber and wood products, paper products, rubber and plastics products, and items made from stone, clay, and glass. Printed materials are also important to the state's economy.

Agriculture. California leads the states in farm income. Its farm products have an annual value of about $12⅔ billion. They account for about 15 per cent of the value of all goods produced in the state. California has about 60,000 farms. They average 538 acres (217 hectares) in size. Most Californians call farms *ranches*, even if the farms raise produce rather than livestock.

The wide range of climate and of soil and water conditions allows California farmers to grow over 200 different crops. A few of these crops are grown commercially nowhere else in the United States. Most California farms are highly specialized. Many specialize in fruits or nuts.

California farmers grow some bean and grain crops by dry farming methods (see DRY FARMING). But almost all crop production takes place on farmlands that receive irrigation water. In 1901, an irrigation canal began to bring water from the Colorado River to the Imperial Valley. But the Imperial Valley's future as a farm region was not assured until Hoover Dam, between Arizona and Nevada, began operating in 1936. The All-American Canal opened in 1940. It carries water 80 miles (129 kilometers) from the Colorado River to farms in the Imperial Valley. The Central Valley Water Project includes the Shasta and Friant dams. It supplies water to about 1 million acres (400,000 hectares) in California's Central Valley. See CENTRAL VALLEY PROJECT.

About a third of California's farm income comes from raising beef and dairy cattle, other livestock, and poultry. California ranchers own about 3⅓ million beef cattle. Many of these cattle feed on grass in the foothills and in mountain meadows. Many others are fattened in feedlots in the state. California is one of the leading sheep-raising and wool-producing states. California ranchers raise about 1 million sheep, mainly in the Central Valley. These sheep yield about 10½ million pounds (4.8 million kilograms) of wool yearly. California ranchers also raise hogs and horses.

California has more than 1 million dairy cattle. San

Production of Goods in California

Total annual value of goods produced—$81,514,650,000

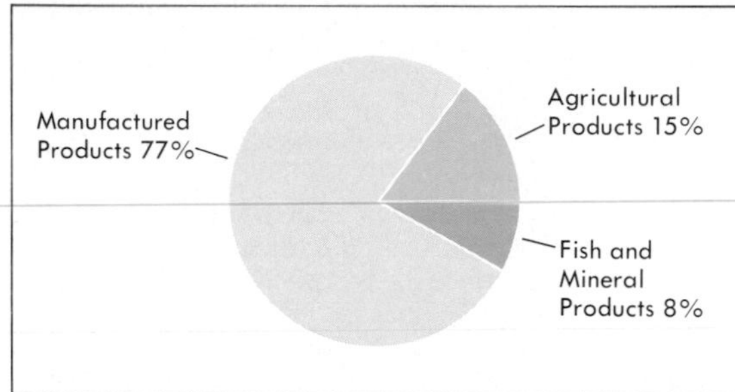

Percentages are based on farm income and value of fish and mineral production in 1979 and on value added by manufacture in 1978. Fish products are less than 1 per cent.

Sources: U.S. government publications, 1980-1981.

Employment in California

Total number of persons employed—10,099,700

	Number of Employees
Wholesale & Retail Trade	2,267,500
Community, Social, & Personal Services	2,164,600
Manufacturing	2,001,100
Government	1,766,900
Finance, Insurance, & Real Estate	620,900
Transportation & Public Utilities	542,500
Construction	431,300
Agriculture	262,000
Mining	42,900

Sources: *Employment and Earnings*, May 1981, U.S. Bureau of Labor Statistics; *Farm Labor*, February 1981, U.S. Department of Agriculture. Figures are for 1980.

U.S. Air Force

A Guided Missile Soars into Space from a launch pad on the testing grounds at Vandenberg Air Force Base. The defense and aerospace industries have played a vital part in California's growth since the 1940's. Today, California receives a larger share of government defense contracts than any other state.

Bernardino County leads all counties in the United States in dairy production. Annual milk production for the whole state is about 1½ billion gallons (4.6 billion liters). California produces about $361 million worth of eggs annually and is the leading state in egg production. California is a leading state in raising turkeys and *broilers* (chickens 9 to 12 weeks old). It also produces much honey. Some farmers specialize in raising unusual or valuable animals, such as chinchillas, earthworms, foxes, frogs, goldfish, and minks.

California farmers raise nearly 70 kinds of fruits and several varieties of nuts. Grapes are California's most valuable fruit. Farmers produce about $1 billion worth of grapes in the state each year. California leads the states in the production of peaches and pears and ranks second only to Florida in orange production. California produces almost all the almonds, apricots, dates, figs, grapes, nectarines, olives, and walnuts grown in the United States. It produces most of the nation's avocados, cantaloupes, honeydew melons, lemons, plums, and prunes.

Almost every major valley in California produces a fruit for which its soil and climate are especially suited. For example, the San Joaquin Valley is known for its almonds, apricots, cherries, figs, grapes, nectarines, olives, oranges, peaches, plums, and walnuts. The Sacramento Valley yields olives, peaches, pears, prunes, and walnuts. The central coast from Lake to San Luis Obispo counties is the leading apple-growing area and also produces apricots, wine grapes, pears, prunes, and walnuts. California's southern counties lead in the production of avocados, grapefruit, and lemons and have a heavy production of oranges. The frost-free parts of southern California have small crops of such tropical fruits as citrons, mangoes, and papayas. Most nut production takes place in the Central Valley and in the counties around San Francisco Bay.

Most vegetable production takes place in the Central and Salinas valleys, along the southern coast, and in such desert areas as the Imperial and Coachella valleys. California produces almost all the artichokes, Brussels sprouts, and garlic grown in the United States. It also leads the states in growing asparagus, broccoli, carrots, cauliflower, celery, lettuce, onions, and tomatoes. Tomatoes are California's most important vegetable crop. In addition, California farms yield valuable quantities of corn, cucumbers, lima beans, peppers, potatoes, and spinach.

Greenhouse nursery products, including flowers and vegetable seeds and plants, rank among California's leading sources of farm income. Cotton is another important crop. Farmers in the state raise about 3 million bales of cotton a year, or about a fourth of all the cotton produced in the United States. Each bale weighs 480 pounds (218 kilograms). Hay, especially alfalfa, is grown in almost every farming area in the state. Farmers grow rice in the Sacramento Valley. They also raise valuable crops of barley, sugar beets, and wheat. California leads the states in sugar beet production.

Mining accounts for about $6 billion a year, or 8 per cent of the value of goods produced in California. California ranks among the leading mining states, and pro-

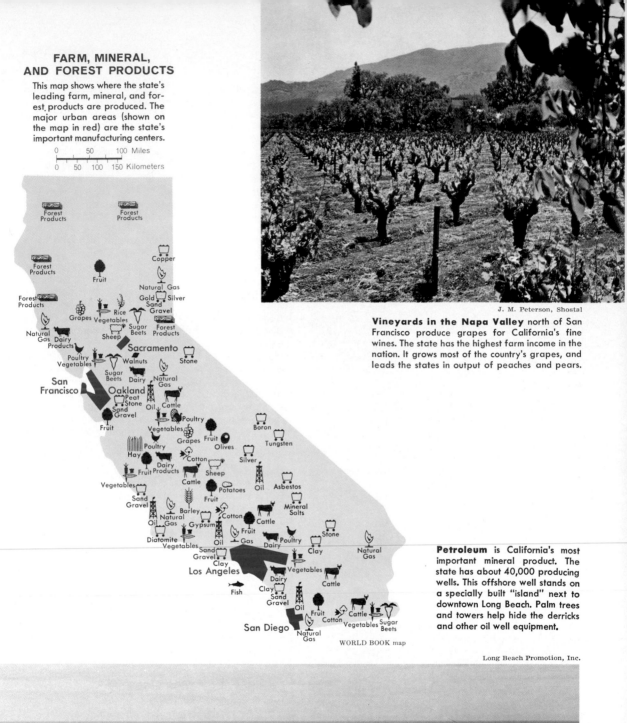

FARM, MINERAL, AND FOREST PRODUCTS

This map shows where the state's leading farm, mineral, and forest products are produced. The major urban areas (shown on the map in red) are the state's important manufacturing centers.

WORLD BOOK map

J. M. Peterson, Shostal

Vineyards in the Napa Valley north of San Francisco produce grapes for California's fine wines. The state has the highest farm income in the nation. It grows most of the country's grapes, and leads the states in output of peaches and pears.

Petroleum is California's most important mineral product. The state has about 40,000 producing wells. This offshore well stands on a specially built "island" next to downtown Long Beach. Palm trees and towers help hide the derricks and other oil well equipment.

Long Beach Promotion, Inc.

duces a greater variety of minerals than any other state. Petroleum is California's most valuable mining product. The state has about 47,000 producing wells that pump about 405 million barrels of crude oil a year. Most of them are in the southern part of the San Joaquin Valley and along the coast near Long Beach, Los Angeles, and Santa Barbara. Much natural gas comes from the petroleum-producing regions. Large amounts of natural gas are also pumped from fields in the Sacramento Valley. California wells yield about 365 billion cubic feet (10.3 billion cubic meters) of natural gas annually.

California mines yield all of the boron that is produced in the United States—about $1\frac{2}{3}$ million short tons (1.5 million metric tons) a year. Boron comes from Inyo, Kern, and San Bernardino counties. It is present in boric acid, an antiseptic; and in borax, a cleaning agent. California is also the leading U.S. producer of asbestos, diatomite, sand and gravel, and tungsten. California is among the leading states in the production of gypsum, iron ore, magnesium compounds, molybdenum, perlite, potash, pumice, and sodium compounds.

Between 1849 and 1859, California mined almost $600 million worth of gold. Today, California produces about $1 million worth of gold annually. Other California mineral products include calcium chloride, carbon dioxide, clays, copper, feldspar, gemstones, lead, lime, lithium compounds, mercury, peat, salt, silver, stone, talc, and zinc.

Fishing Industry. California ranks second only to Alaska in U.S. commercial fishing. The annual seafood catch by the California fishing industry totals about 917 million pounds (416 million kilograms), and has a value of about $227 million.

The tuna industry, one of the largest fishing industries in the United States, centers almost entirely in California. The tuna catch is the most valuable part of California's yearly fish catch. Salmon ranks second in cash value. Other commercially important fishes caught by workers in the California fishing industry include anchovies, bonito, flounder, mackerel, rockfish, sablefish, sea bass, and swordfish. Shellfish caught in California waters include abalones, crabs, oysters, shrimps, and squid.

Electric Power. About two-thirds of California's electric power is generated by steam-turbine plants. Most steam power in the state is produced by burning gas or oil. A few electric companies produce small amounts of steam power with nuclear energy.

Hydroelectric power plants generate about a third of the state's electric power. Hoover, Davis, Glen Canyon, and Parker dams on the Colorado River were built by the federal government to generate electric power. These dams supply power to California, as well as to Arizona, Colorado, Nevada, and Utah. The federal government, and municipal and private power companies, also operate many dams on other California rivers. The Geysers Power Plant near Healdsburg is the only commercial electric plant in the United States powered by *geothermal steam*. This steam is created by heat deep in the earth.

Transportation. California is a state "on the move." It has more motor vehicles than any other state. About $12\frac{1}{2}$ million automobiles are registered in California. The state has only about twice as many people as automobiles.

California's first highway, El Camino Real, began as a path connecting the Spanish missions along the coast during the 1700's. The state's first major freeway, the Arroyo Sero Freeway (now Pasadena Freeway) between Pasadena and Los Angeles, was completed in 1940. Today, the state has about 175,000 miles (282,000 kilometers) of roads and highways, of which about two-thirds are surfaced. Complicated freeway systems, with underpasses, overpasses, and cloverleafs, are a familiar symbol of California's urban areas.

San Francisco Bay has three of the most famous bridges in the world. These are the Golden Gate Bridge between San Francisco and Marin County, the San Francisco-Oakland Bay Bridge, and the Richmond-San Rafael Bridge.

California has about 820 airports. The international airports at Los Angeles and San Francisco are among the busiest in the United States.

California's first railway, completed in 1856, ran 22 miles (35 kilometers) between Sacramento and Folsom. Today, 36 railroads operating on about 7,300 miles (11,748 kilometers) of track in the state provide freight service. Passenger trains serve about 40 of California's cities.

Southern California has major seaports at Los Angeles (San Pedro), Long Beach, and San Diego. The San Francisco Bay area has several deepwater ports that ship millions of tons of goods each year. Besides San Francisco itself, these ports include Oakland, Redwood City, and Richmond. They also include private terminals in Carquinez Strait, Mare Island Strait, and San Pablo Bay.

Sacramento and Stockton are important inland ports. They handle shipments of valuable agricultural and mineral products that come from the Sacramento and San Joaquin valleys. Deepwater channels connect the Sacramento and Stockton ports with San Francisco Bay.

Communication. California's first newspaper, the *Californian*, began publication in Monterey in 1846. Today, the state has about 890 newspapers, including about 625 weeklies and about 135 dailies. Leading California newspapers include the *Los Angeles Times*, Los Angeles *Herald-Examiner*, *San Francisco Chronicle*, *San Francisco Examiner*, *Oakland Tribune*, and *San Diego Union*.

In 1909, David Herrold began operating a radio station in connection with a radio school in San Jose. This was three years before Congress established radio licensing requirements. In 1913, Herrold adopted the call letters SJN. The station's letters were changed to KQW in 1921, and to KCBS in 1949. California's first commercial radio station, KQL in Los Angeles, was licensed in 1921. KWG in Stockton was also licensed in 1921, and is still broadcasting. California's first commercial television station, KTLA in Los Angeles, began operations in 1947. Today, California has about 500 radio stations and 70 television stations.

The motion-picture industry, centered in Hollywood, provides jobs for about 77,000 Californians. Film studios in the southern part of the state also produce many radio and television programs.

CALIFORNIA/*History*

Indian Days. Many Indian tribes lived in the fertile parts of the California region before white people came. Deserts and high mountains separated the California Indian groups from each other and from the tribes farther east. The Hupa Indians lived in the far northwestern part of what is now California. The Maidu lived in the central section, and the Yuma lived in the south. The Pomo Indians occupied the territory that now makes up Lake, Mendocino, and Sonoma counties north of San Francisco. Other Indian groups in the California region included the Míwok, Modoc, and Mohave tribes.

Spanish and English Exploration. Juan Rodríguez Cabrillo, a Portuguese explorer employed by Spain, was probably the first European to see the coast of what is now California. In 1542, Cabrillo sailed north from New Spain (present-day Mexico) along the Pacific Coast. He hoped to find rich cities and a water passage between the Pacific and Atlantic oceans. Cabrillo discovered San Diego Bay and stopped there before sailing farther north. Cabrillo died in 1543, but his men continued the voyage. Some historians believe that Cabrillo's expedition sailed along the entire California coast, as far north as present-day Oregon.

In 1579, Francis Drake, an English sea captain, followed a route along the California coast during his famous voyage around the world. Drake claimed the land for England and named it *New Albion*. The Spaniards then sent several exploring parties along the coast, partly because they feared they might lose California to the English. In 1602, Sebastián Vizcaíno led one of these expeditions. He named many landmarks along the coast, and sent an enthusiastic report about California to the king of Spain. In the report, Vizcaíno urged that Spain colonize California.

Spanish and Russian Settlement. Beginning in 1697, the Spaniards established missions and other settlements in Baja (Lower) California, the Mexican peninsula south of present-day California. Captain Gaspar de Portolá, governor of Baja California, led an expedition that established the first *presidio* (military fort) at San Diego in 1769. He also established one at Monterey in 1770. In 1776, a group of Spanish settlers arrived at the site of what is now San Francisco, then known as Yerba Buena. The settlers founded a presidio and a mission there. Later, other groups of settlers sent by Spain established some *pueblos* (villages) near the coast.

However, Spain did not have a strong hold on the California region. Russia had fur-trading interests in Alaska, and wanted to search for furs farther south along the Pacific Coast. In 1812, the Russians established Fort Ross on the northern California coast. Russian activity in California was one reason for the Monroe Doctrine, proclaimed in 1823. In the Monroe Doctrine, the United States declared that North and South America should be considered closed to European colonization. In 1824, Russia agreed to limit its settlements to Alaska. However, the Russians did not actually leave the California region until the early 1840's.

The California Missions. Franciscan friars of the Roman Catholic Church played an important part in

IMPORTANT DATES IN CALIFORNIA

1542 Juan Rodríguez Cabrillo explored San Diego Bay.

1579 Francis Drake sailed along the coast and claimed California for England.

1602 Sebastián Vizcaíno urged that Spain colonize California.

1769 Gaspar de Portolá led a land expedition up the California coast. Junípero Serra established the first Franciscan mission, near the site of present-day San Diego.

1776 Spanish settlers from New Spain (Mexico) reached the site of what is now San Francisco.

1812 Russian fur traders built Fort Ross.

1822 California became part of New Spain, which won independence from Spain in 1821.

1841 The Bidwell-Bartleson party became the first organized group of American settlers to travel to California by land.

1846 American rebels raised the "Bear" flag of the California Republic over Sonoma. U.S. forces conquered California during the Mexican War (1846-1848).

1848 James W. Marshall discovered gold at Sutter's mill. Mexico gave California to the United States by the Treaty of Guadalupe Hidalgo.

1849 The gold rush began.

1850 California became the 31st state on September 9.

1887 Rapid population growth caused a land boom in southern California.

1906 An earthquake and fire destroyed much of San Francisco.

1915 International expositions at San Diego and San Francisco marked the opening of the Panama Canal.

1945 The United Nations Charter was adopted at the San Francisco Conference.

1960 The legislature provided funds for a project to distribute excess water from the northern mountains to coastal cities and southern California.

1963 California became the state with the largest population in the United States.

1978 California voters approved a $7-billion cutback in state property taxes.

CALIFORNIA'S FRANCISCAN MISSIONS

Missions	At or Near	Founded
San Diego de Alcalá	San Diego	1769
San Carlos Borromeo	Carmel	1770
San Antonio de Padua	Jolon	1771
San Gabriel Arcángel	San Gabriel	1771
San Luís Obispo de Tolosa	San Luis Obispo	1772
San Francisco de Asís	San Francisco	1776
San Juan Capistrano	San Juan Capistrano	1776
Santa Clara de Asís	Santa Clara	1777
San Buenaventura	Ventura	1782
Santa Barbara	Santa Barbara	1786
La Purísima Concepcíon	Lompoc	1787
Santa Cruz	Santa Cruz (replica)	1791
Nuestra Señora de la Soledad	Soledad (partially restored)	1791
San José de Guadalupe	Fremont	1797
San Juan Bautista	San Juan	1797
San Miguel Arcángel	San Miguel	1797
San Fernando Rey de España	San Fernando	1797
San Luís Rey de Francia	Oceanside	1798
Santa Inés	Solvang	1804
San Rafael Arcángel	San Rafael (replica)	1817
San Francisco Solano	Sonoma	1823

HISTORIC CALIFORNIA

The Bear Flag was raised at Sonoma in 1846 by American settlers seeking California's independence from Mexico. The explorer John C. Frémont helped conquer California for the United States that same year.

San Francisco's Earthquake and fire in 1906 left about 300,000 persons homeless and destroyed more than 28,000 buildings.

The Central Valley Water Project, begun in 1937, includes Shasta Dam. It provides water, electric power and flood control.

The 1849 Gold Rush began after James W. Marshall found gold at Sutter's Mill in 1848. He saw the first gold in the American River.

SACRAMENTO

Sonoma

San Francisco

The United Nations adopted its charter at the famous San Francisco Conference in 1945.

First Commercial Film made in California, *The Count of Monte Cristo,* was completed near Los Angeles in 1907.

Richard M. Nixon was born in Yorba Linda.

Los Angeles

San Diego

Early Explorers in California included Spain's Juan Rodríguez Cabrillo (1542) and Sebastián Vizcaíno (1602), and England's Francis Drake (1579).

The Central Pacific, first railroad across the Sierra Nevada, was begun in 1863 with the help of Chinese laborers. It was completed in 1869.

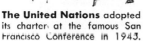

The First Mission, San Diego de Alcalá, was founded by Father Junípero Serra in 1769. By 1823, Franciscan priests had established a chain of 21 missions a day's walk apart.

the Spanish settlement of California. In 1769, during the Portolá expedition, Father Junípero Serra established the first California mission. This mission was San Diego de Alcalá, near the site of present-day San Diego. By 1823, the Franciscans had built a chain of 21 missions. Each mission was about a day's walk from the next. The friars converted many Indians to Christianity. They taught the Indians farming, weaving, and other skills. However, many of the Indians who lived at the missions were forced to work long hours. Some became ill and died.

Many persons in California and Mexico wanted the missions broken up. In the early 1830's, the government began selling mission land to private citizens. By 1846, almost all the mission property had been sold. During this period, the government gave or sold many large estates, called *ranchos*, to private landowners, called *rancheros*. Some rancheros became wealthy by raising cattle for hides and *tallow* (fat used in making candles, soap, and other products).

Mexican Rule. California became a province of Mexico in 1822, after Mexico won its independence from Spain. The province set up its own legislature and established a military force. But, beginning in 1825, Mexico sent a series of governors to California. Many Californians rebelled against having their affairs dictated by these outsiders. Manuel Victoria, who became governor in 1831, ruled with a strong hand and was especially resented by the Californians. A group led by Pío Pico and others clashed with Mexican government troops in 1831. This fighting was not severe. But the continuing opposition forced Victoria to give up the governorship and return to Mexico City. After that, Mexico's control over the region remained weak.

American Settlement. The *Otter*, the first American sailing vessel to reach the coast from the East, appeared in California waters in 1796. After that, American skippers made many trading trips to harbors along the coast of California.

The first American explorer to reach California by land was Jedediah Strong Smith, a trapper who crossed the southeastern deserts in 1826. Other trappers and explorers followed Smith. They included "Kit" Carson, Joseph Reddeford Walker, and Ewing Young.

In 1841, the first organized group of American settlers came to California by land. These settlers were led by John Bidwell, a schoolteacher, and John Bartleson, a wagon master and land speculator. Soon other overland pioneers arrived to make their homes in the Mexican territory. They drove long wagon trains through the mountain passes. The new settlers wanted California to become a part of the United States. The United States offered to buy the land from Mexico, but Mexico refused to sell.

Mexico Surrenders. Between 1844 and 1846, the military explorer John C. Frémont led two surveying parties into California. The Mexicans did not trust Frémont because his parties were made up of U.S. soldiers. In March, 1846, the Mexicans ordered Frémont to withdraw his troops, who were camped near Monterey. Instead, Frémont raised the U.S. flag over Hawk's Peak, about 25 miles (40 kilometers) from Monterey. He began to build a fort there. Fighting was avoided when Frémont withdrew to the north under cover of darkness. On May 13, 1846, the United States and Mexico went to war (see MEXICAN WAR).

In June, 1846, without knowing that war had been declared, a band of American settlers took over Mexico's headquarters in northern California, at Sonoma. The group was led by frontiersman Ezekiel Merritt. After capturing the fort, the settlers unfurled a homemade flag bearing a single star, a grizzly bear, and the words *California Republic*. This action became known as the Bear Flag Revolt.

The real conquest of California was carried out by United States soldiers, sailors, and marines. They were led by Frémont, Commodore Robert F. Stockton, and

California State Library

Discovery of Gold in 1848 lured thousands of prospectors to California. Adventurers, such as these panning for gold near Auburn in 1852, rushed in from many parts of the world.

General Stephen Watts Kearny. After the United States won the Mexican War in 1848, Mexico surrendered its claim to California in the Treaty of Guadalupe Hidalgo. California then became part of the United States.

The Gold Rush. In 1848, just before the United States and Mexico signed the peace treaty, gold was discovered in California. John A. Sutter, a pioneer trader, had received a large land grant in the Sacramento Valley in 1839. He hired James W. Marshall, a carpenter, to help build a sawmill on the American River. There, at Sutter's mill, Marshall found the first gold nuggets. News of his discovery spread, and thousands of persons rushed to establish claims. These "forty-niners," as they were called, poured in from all parts of the world. Between 1848 and 1860, California's population increased from about 26,000 to 379,994. The free spending by the miners who found gold made such communities as San Francisco and Sacramento into flourishing towns. Some miners who were not so lucky in the gold fields became farmers and ranchers in the Central Valley. See FORTY-NINER; GOLD RUSH.

Early Statehood. California became the 31st state on Sept. 9, 1850. Peter H. Burnett, a Democrat, was the first state governor.

Thousands of settlers went west after the Civil War ended in 1865. They sought the high wages paid in California, and a chance to buy land at low prices. In 1869, the first transcontinental railroad system linked Sacramento with the eastern United States. Part of this system, the Central Pacific Railroad, later became part of the Southern Pacific, owned by Charles Crocker, Mark Hopkins, Collis P. Huntington, and Leland Stanford. These men were known as California's "Big Four." They brought many Chinese laborers to California in the 1860's to work on the railroads.

By 1870, California's population had risen to about 560,000. During the next 10 years, a depression caused widespread unemployment and bank failures. Many unemployed workers blamed their troubles on Chinese laborers, who were willing to work for low wages. Anti-Chinese riots took place in Los Angeles in 1871 and in San Francisco in 1877. During the 1880's, a great publicity campaign brought thousands of persons to California. So many came to southern California in 1887 that a land boom occurred. Agriculture and industry flourished as the population increased.

In 1906, the terrible San Francisco earthquake destroyed about 28,000 buildings and killed about 700 persons. However, the city was soon rebuilt.

Progress as a State. During the early 1900's, California grew rapidly in population and in the development of natural resources. Farming increased greatly after irrigation turned many desert areas into fertile land. Development of oil and natural gas was accompanied by the growth of new industries. Other minerals besides gold were found, and mining became more important. By 1910, Hollywood had become the motion-picture capital of the world. In 1910, Californians elected Hiram W. Johnson as governor. Two years later, Johnson joined Theodore Roosevelt in a revolt against the Republican party. Johnson ran for Vice-President under Roosevelt in 1912 on the unsuccessful Progressive party ticket.

In 1914, the completion of the Panama Canal shortened the important sea route between California and the East. To show the importance of the canal to California's progress, the state sponsored the Panama-Pacific International Exposition in San Francisco and the Panama-California Exposition in San Diego in 1915.

After the United States entered World War I in 1917, shipyards, rubber plants, and other factories were established in California. After the war ended in 1918, interest turned to control of the Colorado River. This mighty river had caused serious flood damage for many years. Between 1905 and 1907, floodwaters from the Colorado had even formed the 450-square-mile (1,165-square-kilometer) Salton Sea in southeastern California. In 1928, Congress authorized a huge dam at Boulder Canyon on the Arizona-Nevada border. The dam was completed in 1936. It controls floods and provides water for irrigation and power in southern California and neighboring states (see HOOVER DAM).

During the Great Depression of the 1930's, hundreds of persons without homes or jobs drifted into California. The state passed laws to close its borders to poor persons. But this legislation was later declared unconstitutional by the Supreme Court of the United States.

In 1935 and 1936, the California-Pacific International Exposition was held in San Diego. This fair honored the Pacific Ocean and the countries that border it. The Golden Gate International Exposition was held in 1939 and 1940 on Treasure Island in San Francisco Bay. The Golden Gate Bridge across the bay had been completed in 1937.

The Governors of California

	Party	Term
Peter H. Burnett	Democratic	1849-1851
John McDougal	Democratic	1851-1852
John Bigler	Democratic	1852-1856
John Neely Johnson	Know-Nothing	1856-1858
John B. Weller	Democratic	1858-1860
Milton S. Latham	Democratic	1860
John G. Downey	Democratic	1860-1862
Leland Stanford	Republican	1862-1863
Frederick F. Low	Union	1863-1867
Henry H. Haight	Democratic	1867-1871
Newton Booth	Republican	1871-1875
Romualdo Pacheco	Republican	1875
William Irwin	Democratic	1875-1880
George C. Perkins	Republican	1880-1883
George Stoneman	Democratic	1883-1887
Washington Bartlett	Democratic	1887
Robert W. Waterman	Republican	1887-1891
Henry H. Markham	Republican	1891-1895
James H. Budd	Democratic	1895-1899
Henry T. Gage	Republican	1899-1903
George C. Pardee	Republican	1903-1907
James N. Gillett	Republican	1907-1911
Hiram W. Johnson	Republican	1911-1917
William D. Stephens	Republican	1917-1923
Friend William Richardson	Republican	1923-1927
Clement C. Young	Republican	1927-1931
James Rolph, Jr.	Republican	1931-1934
Frank F. Merriam	Republican	1934-1939
Culbert L. Olson	Democratic	1939-1943
Earl Warren	Republican	1943-1953
Goodwin J. Knight	Republican	1953-1959
Edmund G. Brown	Democratic	1959-1967
Ronald Reagan	Republican	1967-1975
Edmund G. Brown, Jr.	Democratic	1975-1983
George Deukmejian	Republican	1983-

Stanford University

Electronics Laboratory in Stanford produces precision instruments. California has a huge electronics industry.

The Mid-1900's. During World War II (1939-1945), California produced airplanes, ships, and weapons. The state became the nation's aircraft center. Following the Japanese attack on Pearl Harbor in 1941, the government moved thousands of Japanese-Americans from California to detention camps (see WORLD WAR II [Internment of Aliens]). In 1945, representatives of 50 nations approved the United Nations Charter at the San Francisco Conference.

Many people who had come to California as members of the armed forces or to work in defense plants settled there after the war. The population grew tremendously. Farm centers became metropolitan areas with a variety of industries. Rows of ranch-style houses appeared on former orchards and pastures. New freeways linked smaller cities with Los Angeles and San Francisco.

The population growth boosted California's economy, but it also created problems. The state had to provide more schools and highways. Smog became a serious problem in Los Angeles and other cities, as more automobiles and industries discharged fumes and smoke.

Controlling and distributing water resources remained California's biggest problem during the 1960's. Most of the state's rain and snow falls in the northern mountains. But many of California's people live in southern California, where rainfall does not supply enough water. In 1960, the state began work on a system of canals, dams, reservoirs, and power and pumping plants. The system was planned to store and distribute northern California's excess water to the drier areas.

Like many other states, California had racial problems during the 1960's. In 1965, rioting broke out in Watts, a black section of Los Angeles. It resulted in millions of dollars of damage and the deaths of 34 persons. The California Legislature tried to reduce the complaints of minority groups by providing increased education, employment, and housing.

During the 1960's, California greatly expanded its educational system. In 1940, the University of California consisted of three campuses. By 1969, the university had nine major campuses. Between 1940 and 1969, the number of other state universities and colleges also increased rapidly. California's schools became the center of various student movements. The nation's first major college demonstration, organized by the Free Speech Movement, occurred in 1964 at the University of California in Berkeley.

Richard M. Nixon, born in Yorba Linda, served as Vice-President of the United States under President Dwight D. Eisenhower from 1953 to 1961. Nixon won election as President in 1968 and was reelected in 1972. He resigned from the office in 1974 because of his involvement in the Watergate political scandal.

Motion-picture stars gained popularity with California voters during the 1960's. George L. Murphy won election to the United States Senate in 1964 and Ronald Reagan became governor of California in 1967. In 1980, Reagan was elected President of the United States.

California Today still has a strong economy. But large reductions in federal defense spending hurt the state's aerospace industry during the early 1970's. Unemployment became a problem, and the number of people moving to California from other states fell.

In February 1971, an earthquake shook the Los Angeles area. It killed 64 people and caused more than $500 million worth of damage. A drought struck the Western United States in the late 1970's and focused attention on California's water problem. The drought led to water rationing in the San Francisco area.

High taxes and increased government spending became a major issue in California during the late 1970's. In 1978, California voters approved a measure—known as Proposition 13—that called for a $7-billion reduction in state property taxes. At that time, the state treasury had over $5 billion of surplus funds, most of which came from state income and sales taxes. Governor Edmund G. Brown, Jr., proposed that the surplus be distributed to cities, school districts, and other public agencies affected by the cutback. But officials of most school districts and municipalities said the surplus would not make up for expected tax losses, and they announced plans to cut services and reduce the number of employees.

ROBERT W. DURRENBERGER and ANDREW F. ROLLE

CALIFORNIA / *Study Aids*

Related Articles in WORLD BOOK include:

BIOGRAPHIES

Brown (family)
Burbank, Luther
Carson, Kit
Chavez, Cesar E.
Cranston, Alan M.
Disney, Walt
Drake, Sir Francis
Frémont, John C.
Gardner, John William
Hammond (family)
Hayakawa, S. I.
Hearst, William Randolph
Huntington (family)
Johnson, Hiram W.
Kearny, Stephen W.
London, Jack
Nixon, Richard M.
Pauling, Linus C.
Reagan, Ronald W.
Saroyan, William
Seaborg, Glenn T.
Serra, Junípero
Smith, Jedediah S.
Stanford, Leland
Steinbeck, John
Teller, Edward
Urey, Harold C.
Vollmer, August
Warren, Earl

CITIES

Anaheim
Berkeley
Burbank
Carmel
Fresno
Hollywood
Long Beach
Los Angeles
Monterey

Oakland
Palm Springs
Palo Alto
Pasadena
Sacramento
San Bernardino
San Diego
San Francisco
San Jose
San Juan Capistrano
Santa Barbara

HISTORY

Compromise of 1850
El Camino Real
Forty-Niner
Gold Rush
Guadalupe Hidalgo, Treaty of
Indian, American
Mexican Americans
Mexican War
Mission Life in America
Pony Express
Townsend Plan
Western Frontier Life

MILITARY INSTALLATIONS

Camp Pendleton
Edwards Air Force Base
El Toro Marine Corps Air Station
Mare Island Naval Shipyard
San Diego Marine Corps Recruit Depot
San Diego Naval Base
Vandenberg Air Force Base

NATIONAL PARKS AND MONUMENTS

Each national park and monument discussed in the *Visitor's Guide* section has an article in WORLD BOOK.

PHYSICAL FEATURES

Cascade Range
Coast Range
Colorado Desert
Colorado River
Death Valley
Donner Pass
Elk Hills
Golden Gate
Great Basin
Imperial Valley
Lake Tahoe
Lassen Peak
Mojave
Mount Shasta
Mount Whitney
Oroville Dam
Petrified Forest
Pine Flat Dam
Reagan Dam
Ribbon Falls
Sacramento River
Salton Sea
San Andreas Fault
San Joaquin River
Sierra Nevada
Yosemite Falls

PRODUCTS AND INDUSTRY

For California's rank among the states in production, see the following articles:

Agriculture
Alfalfa
Automobile
Barley
Bean
Butter
Cherry
Chicken
Clothing
Cotton
Electric Power
Forest Products
Grape
Grapefruit
Honey
Horse
Lettuce
Lumber
Manufacturing
Milk
Mining
Nut
Onion
Orange
Peach
Pear
Petroleum
Plum
Potato
Publishing
Sheep
Sugar
Sweet Potato
Tomato
Turkey
Vegetable
Wine
Wool

OTHER RELATED ARTICLES

Golden Gate Bridge
La Brea Pits
Motion Picture
Redwood
San Quentin
Sequoia

Outline

I. Government
- A. Constitution
- B. Executive
- C. Legislature
- D. Courts
- E. Local Government
- F. Taxation
- G. Politics

II. People

III. Education
- A. Schools
- B. Libraries
- C. Museums

IV. A Visitor's Guide
- A. Places to Visit
- B. Annual Events

V. The Land
- A. Land Regions
- B. Coastline
- C. Rivers, Waterfalls, and Lakes

VI. Climate

VII. Economy
- A. Natural Resources
- B. Manufacturing
- C. Agriculture
- D. Mining
- E. Fishing Industry
- F. Electric Power
- G. Transportation
- H. Communication

VIII. History

Questions

Where is the lowest point in the United States?
What is the world's largest oceanarium?
Who was the first European to see California?
What is California's most valuable crop?
During what period were California's Franciscan missions built?
What are the two major river systems in the Central Valley of California?
How did the United States obtain California?
Why is southern California a good location for aircraft companies?
What California county is the largest U.S. county?
What are some of California's greatest present-day problems?

Additional Resources

Level I

CARPENTER, ALLAN. *California*. Rev. ed. Childrens Press, 1978.

FRADIN, DENNIS B. *California in Words and Pictures*. Childrens Press, 1977.

LAYCOCK, GEORGE. *Death Valley*. Four Winds, 1976. A natural history and guide.

O'DELL, SCOTT. *The Cruise of the Arctic Star*. Houghton, 1973. A voyage along the California coast.

SANDERLIN, GEORGE W. *The Settlement of California*. Coward, 1972.

SEIDMAN, LAURENCE I. *The Fools of '49: The California Gold Rush, 1848-1856*. Knopf, 1976.

STEIN, R. CONRAD. *The Story of the Gold at Sutter's Mill*. Childrens Press, 1981.

Level II

BEAN, WALTON, and RAWLS, J. J. *California: An Interpretive History*. 4th ed. McGraw, 1982.

HART, JAMES D. *A Companion to California*. Oxford, 1978.

HEIZER, ROBERT F., and ALMQUIST, A. J. *The Other Californians: Prejudice and Discrimination Under Spain, Mexico, and the United States to 1920*. Univ. of California Press, 1971.

HEIZER, ROBERT F., and ELSASSER, A. B. *The Natural World of the California Indians*. Univ. of California Press, 1980.

JACKSON, DONALD D. *Gold Dust*. Knopf, 1980. The California gold rush.

LAVENDER, DAVID S. *California: Land of New Beginnings*. Harper, 1972. *California: A Bicentennial History*. Norton, 1976.

MOORE, CHARLES and KRISTIN. *The Mother Lode: A Pictorial Guide to California's Gold Rush Country*. Chronicle, 1983.

RAWLS, JAMES J. *Indians of California: The Changing Image*. Univ. of Oklahoma Press, 1984.

ROBINSON, WILLIAM W. *Land in California: The Story of Mission Lands, Ranchos, Squatters, Mining Claims, Railroad Grants, Land Scrip, Homesteads*. Univ. of California Press, 1979. Reprint of 1948 edition.

STEWART, GEORGE R. *The California Trail: An Epic with Many Heroes*. Univ. of Nebraska Press, 1983. Reprint of 1963 edition.

WATKINS, T. H. *California: An Illustrated History*. Rev. ed. Crown, 1983.

CALIFORNIA, LOWER. See BAJA CALIFORNIA NORTE; BAJA CALIFORNIA SUR.

CALIFORNIA, UNIVERSITY OF, is a state-supported coeducational institution with nine campuses. Each campus has its own courses of study and grants bachelor's, master's, and doctor's degrees. The university's administrative offices are in Berkeley.

The university has about 150 research centers. It also operates three laboratories for the U.S. Department of Energy. They are the Los Alamos (N. Mex.) National Laboratory, the Lawrence Berkeley Laboratory in Berkeley, and the Lawrence Livermore Laboratory in Livermore, Calif. The university has general extension divisions and agricultural extension services.

The Berkeley Campus offers programs in business administration, chemistry, education, engineering, environmental design, journalism, law, letters and science, librarianship, natural resources, optometry, public health, public policy, and social welfare.

The Davis Campus provides programs in agricultural and environmental sciences, engineering, law, letters and sciences, medicine, and veterinary medicine. Its research facilities include a primate biology center and a nuclear laboratory.

The Irvine Campus has programs in administration, biological sciences, engineering, fine arts, humanities, medicine, physical sciences, and social sciences. It operates research centers in pathobiology, transportation, and other fields.

The Los Angeles Campus is often called UCLA. It offers courses in architecture and urban planning, dentistry, education, engineering and applied sciences, fine arts, law, letters and sciences, library and information sciences, management, medicine, nursing, public health, and social welfare.

The Riverside Campus has courses in administration, education, humanities and social sciences, and natural and agricultural sciences. The campus has centers for research on agriculture and air pollution.

The San Diego and Santa Cruz Campuses consist of several small liberal arts colleges. They have programs in the humanities, natural and physical sciences, and other fields. The San Diego campus has a medical school and several research centers, among them the Scripps Institution of Oceanography. The Santa Cruz campus includes the headquarters and laboratories of the Lick Observatory.

The San Francisco Campus is devoted to the health sciences. It has schools of dentistry, medicine, nursing, and pharmacy. Scientists in the research centers of the San Francisco campus study arthritis, cancer, tropical diseases, and other illnesses.

The Santa Barbara Campus provides programs in creative studies, education, engineering, and letters and science. It is the only college in California that has an undergraduate program in nuclear engineering.

History. The University of California was chartered in 1868. It held its first classes in 1869 in Oakland and moved to Berkeley in 1873. For the enrollment on each campus, see UNIVERSITIES AND COLLEGES (table).

Critically reviewed by the UNIVERSITY OF CALIFORNIA

CALIFORNIA INSTITUTE OF TECHNOLOGY is a private coeducational university in Pasadena, Calif. It has divisions of biology; chemistry and chemical engineering; engineering and applied science; geological and planetary sciences; humanities and social sciences; and physics, mathematics, and astronomy.

The institute, called *Caltech,* was founded in 1891. It operates the Jet Propulsion Laboratory, the Kresge and Donnelley seismological laboratories, a marine biological laboratory in Corona del Mar, a hydraulic and coastal engineering laboratory in Azusa, and a radio astronomy observatory near Bishop. Caltech also operates the Big Bear Solar Observatory at Big Bear Lake and the Palomar Observatory near San Diego. For the university's enrollment, see UNIVERSITIES AND COLLEGES (table).

HAROLD BROWN

See also JET PROPULSION LABORATORY.

CALIFORNIA STATE UNIVERSITY is the largest state-supported system of four-year and graduate-level higher education in the United States. This coeducational system consists of 3 colleges and 16 universities and has a combined enrollment of more than 300,000 students. The system was established in 1960 as the California State Colleges and received its present name in 1982.

The name of each of 12 of the system's 19 campuses is California State College (CSC) or California State University (CSU), followed by the location of the campus. For example, the campus in Long Beach is known as California State University, Long Beach; or CSU, Long Beach.

The 19 campuses are CSC, Bakersfield; CSU, Chico; CSU, Dominguez Hills (located in Carson); CSU, Fresno; CSU, Fullerton; CSU, Hayward; Humboldt State University (located in Arcata); CSU, Long Beach; CSU, Los Angeles; CSU, Northridge; CSU, Sacramento; CSU, San Bernardino; San Diego State University; San Francisco State University; San Jose State University; Sonoma State University (located in Rohnert Park); CSC, Stanislaus (located in Turlock); California State Polytechnic University, Pomona; and California Polytechnic State University, San Luis Obispo.

Each campus grants bachelor's and master's degrees. The campuses in Los Angeles, San Diego, and San Francisco also have programs leading to doctor's degrees, which are granted in association with the University of California. Instruction is offered in the liberal arts and sciences; the humanities; and the professions, including teaching, business administration, computer science, and engineering.

The system also has a division called the Consortium, which provides programs for individuals who cannot attend classes on a campus. The Consortium grants bachelor's and master's degrees. The International Programs section of the system offers instruction in 16 foreign countries for students enrolled at any of the system's campuses. Several of the system's campuses conduct classes in marine studies at the Moss Landing Marine Laboratory in Monterey Bay and at the Southern California Ocean Studies Consortium in Long Beach. Several also operate the Desert Studies Center near Baker. The system has its administrative offices in Long Beach. For enrollments, see UNIVERSITIES AND COLLEGES (table).

Critically reviewed by the CALIFORNIA STATE UNIVERSITY

CALIFORNIA TRAIL. See WYOMING (The Great Trails); PIONEER LIFE IN AMERICA (map).

CALIFORNIUM (chemical symbol, Cf) is a man-made radioactive element. Its atomic number is 98. Its most stable isotope has a mass number of 251. Californium was discovered in 1950 by four American scientists, Stanley G. Thompson, Kenneth Street, Jr., Albert Ghiorso, and Glenn T. Seaborg. It was first produced by bombarding curium, element 96, with helium *ions* (electrically charged atoms). Only 5,000 atoms, or less than one million-billionth of a gram, were produced. Numerous isotopes of californium are produced by charged-particle bombardment of lighter transuranium elements (see TRANSURANIUM ELEMENT). A process of neutron capture in these lighter elements produces weighable amounts of isotopes with mass numbers from 249 through 252. See also ELEMENT, CHEMICAL; RADIOACTIVITY. GLENN T. SEABORG

CALIGULA, *kuh LIHG yuh luh* (A.D. 12-41), was a Roman emperor. He was the great-grandson of the emperor Augustus, and the son of Germanicus and Agrippina the Elder. He was born Gaius Caesar Augustus Germanicus. As a child, he wore military boots, and his father's soldiers nicknamed him *Caligula* (Little Boot). When Caligula was 20, he was adopted by the Roman emperor Tiberius. Caligula became emperor when Tiberius died in A.D. 37.

Detail of a marble sculpture by an unknown Roman sculptor; Uffizi Gallery, Florence (Alinari from Art Reference Bureau)

Caligula

At first, Caligula was popular, but it soon became apparent that he was insane. He spent money on foolish projects, banished many people, and murdered many others, including one of his sisters. Caligula claimed to be all the gods at once, and ordered a statue of himself set up in the Jewish Temple in Jerusalem. This caused riots among the Jews. Caligula claimed he had defeated the British and Germans, but he had not fought them. He also said he had defeated the god Neptune. Caligula was murdered after he insulted the army and threatened to kill the members of the Roman Senate. MARY FRANCIS GYLES

CALIPER, *KAL uh puhr,* is an instrument much like a geometry compass. It is used to take small measurements. The legs, usually curved, are joined at one end by a rivet or screw that can open and close them. *Outside calipers* measure the outside of pipes, boards, and other objects. The open ends are fitted against the object. The legs curve inward so they can circle round objects. *Inside calipers* measure the inside of pipes and other open objects. The legs curve outward. A *double caliper* combines the inside and outside calipers as shown in the accompanying illustration. *Spring calipers* have a spring to automatically open their legs. A *micrometer caliper* is a type of *slide caliper* that has a fine, threaded micrometer screw and can measure to $\frac{1}{10,000}$ inch (0.00254 millimeter). See also MICROMETER; VERNIER. E. A. FESSENDEN

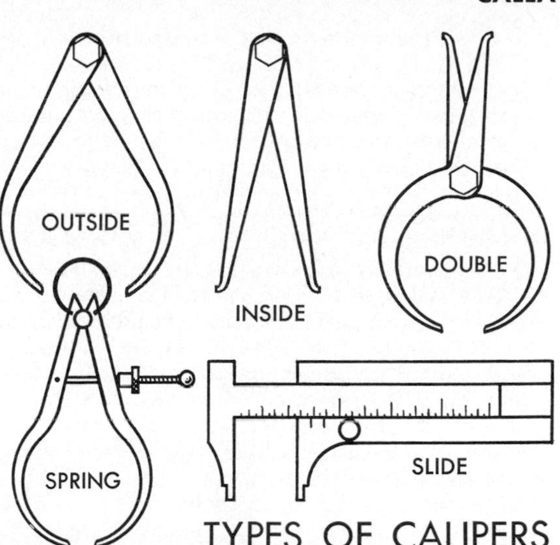

TYPES OF CALIPERS

CALIPH, *KAY lihf,* is the title of Muslim rulers who succeeded Muhammad. The office was abolished in 1924, during the Turkish Revolution. Caliphs were military commanders, and civil and religious leaders of their people. Caliphs performed all the functions of Muhammad, but they were not prophets. The word *caliph* comes from Arabic and means *successor.* A caliph was also called *Commander of the Faithful.*

Only a free, adult, male Muslim of sound mind and body could hold the office of caliph. He had to be skilled in Arabic, and able to understand Muslim law. He also had to belong to Muhammad's tribe, the *Quraysh.* However, such conditions were ignored during the Ottoman caliphate. The Ottoman Turks were not of Arab descent and had almost no association with the family of Muhammad. A caliph usually was elected, but in the Omayyad and Abbasid caliphates, the office was inherited. Abu Bakr, the first caliph, was a trusted companion of Muhammad. ALI H. ABDEL-KADER

See also MUSLIMS (The Spread of Islam); EGYPT (The Middle Ages); ISLAM.

CALISTHENICS, *KAL uhs THEHN ihks,* are exercises that help strengthen and stretch body muscles. Most calisthenics involve slow, rhythmic movements and can be performed without special equipment. Calisthenics are commonly used before and after strenuous physical activity to reduce the risk of injury and muscle soreness.

CALKING. See CAULKING.

CALLA, *KAL uh,* is a flowerlike herb with a large, white leaf shaped like a funnel or bell. The beautiful leaf is often mistaken for the flower. But the real flowers are tiny blossoms inside the flowerlike leaf. The North American calla is called *marsh calla,* or *water arum.* This little plant has heart-shaped leaves about 2 inches (5 centimeters) long. It is closely related to the jack-in-the-pulpit. The marsh calla grows wild in marshy places. The plant is also cultivated as a crop along the edges of ponds. In Lapland, the people grind up the root of the marsh calla to make flour. They use this flour to make bread.

W. Atlee Burpee Co.

Calla Lily

The most common tropical calla comes from the banks of the Nile River in Egypt. It is called *calla lily, Ethiopian lily*, or *common calla*. The plant has a 10-inch (25-centimeter) white leaf. The calla lily causes a burning irritation to the mouth and stomach if eaten.

Scientific Classification. The calla is in the arum family, *Araceae*. The common calla is genus *Zantedeschia*, species *Z. aethiopica*. The golden calla is *Z. elliottiana*. The water arum is *Calla palustris*. ALFRED C. HOTTES

See also ARUM; JACK-IN-THE-PULPIT.

CALLAGHAN, *KAL uh huhn*, **JAMES** (1912-), served as prime minister of Great Britain from 1976 to 1979. He was chosen by the Labour Party to succeed Harold Wilson as prime minister and Labour Party leader after Wilson resigned. During Callaghan's term as prime minister, Britain faced such problems as inflation and major labor strikes. In 1979, the Conservative Party defeated the Labour Party in a general parliamentary election, and Conservative Party leader Margaret Thatcher replaced Callaghan as prime minister. Callaghan remained leader of the Labour Party until 1980, when he resigned from the office.

Wide World

James Callaghan

Leonard James Callaghan was born in Portsmouth, England. He served in the Royal Navy during World War II (1939-1945). In 1945, he was elected to Parliament from Cardiff, Wales. In 1964, he became chancellor of the exchequer, the head of the British Treasury. Economic problems led to the devaluation of the British pound in 1967, and Callaghan resigned from his post. From 1967 to 1970, he was in charge of the Home Office and responsible for British policy toward Northern Ireland. He served as foreign secretary from 1974 until he became prime minister. RICHARD ROSE

CALLAGHAN, *KAL uh huhn*, **MORLEY** (1903-), is a Canadian novelist. His works deal mainly with moral issues and have an urban setting, usually in Montreal or Toronto. Many of his characters are social outcasts who have great moral insight. He has an informal style of writing and is skilled at creating atmosphere.

Callaghan's first novel, *Strange Fugitive*, was published in 1928. During the next 20 years, his works included six novels, two collections of short stories, and two plays. In 1951, Callaghan won the Governor General's award for *The Loved and the Lost*, a novel that explores the relationship between innocence and guilt. Callaghan's later novels include *The Many Colored Coat* (1960) and *A Fine and Private Place* (1975). *That Summer in Paris* (1963) describes Callaghan's life in Paris during the late 1920's, and his association with the American writers Ernest Hemingway and F. Scott Fitzgerald. Callaghan was born in Toronto. CLAUDE T. BISSELL

CALLAO, *kah YAH oh* (pop. 313,316), is the chief port and second largest city of Peru. Only Lima, Peru's capital, is larger. About three-fourths of the country's imports and one-fourth of its exports pass through Callao's harbor. Callao lies on the Pacific Ocean, about 8 miles (13 kilometers) west of Lima. The two cities are part of a large metropolitan area that includes more than half of Peru's industries. For the location of Callao, see PERU (political map). Callao's chief industries are shipbuilding and fish processing.

The Spaniards founded Callao in 1537. Through the years, earthquakes have severely damaged the city, but the people have always rebuilt it. Since the 1950's, many migrants have built crude houses outside the city in settlements called *young towns* or *new towns*. The Peruvian government has encouraged construction of improved housing in this area. WILLIAM MANGIN

CALLAS, *KAL uhs*, **MARIA** (1923-1977), was an American-born soprano. She became one of the world's best-known opera singers because of her fiery temperament and her stirring singing and acting ability.

Wide World

Maria Callas

Callas was born in New York City of Greek parents, making her both a U.S. and Greek citizen. At the age of 13, she returned with her parents to Greece, and won a scholarship at the Royal Conservatory in Athens. At 14, she made her debut in Athens, appearing in the opera *Cavalleria Rusticana*.

Callas made her U.S. debut in Chicago in 1954. She sang the leading soprano role in Bellini's *Norma* and was a great success. The operas she recorded include *Cavalleria Rusticana, Norma, I Puritani*, and *I Pagliacci*. She gave up her United States citizenship in 1966.

CALLES, *KAH yays*, **PLUTARCO ELÍAS,** *ploo TAHR koh ay LEE ahs* (1877-1945), served as president of Mexico from 1924 to 1928. As president, he reformed the nation's army, encouraged labor unions, and organized the official Revolutionary party. Leaders of the Roman Catholic Church bitterly opposed Calles' antichurch measures. His government also took over large estates and regulated the foreign-owned oil industry. Calles was born in Guaymas. HAROLD EUGENE DAVIS

CALLEY, WILLIAM L., JR. See WAR CRIME (The Vietnam War).

CALLIGRAPHY, *kuh LIHG ruh fee*, is the art of beautiful handwriting. In calligraphy, the decorative form of the letters is more important than the clarity of the writing. Calligraphy decorates not only books and manuscripts, but also buildings and works of art. Most calligraphers write with a brush or pen and ink.

Calligraphy developed into an art form more than 2,000 years ago in China. Chinese artists have produced such outstanding calligraphy that the art of handwriting ranks above painting in that country. The Japanese learned calligraphy from the Chinese during the A.D. 600's and became masters of the art.

For hundreds of years, Islamic artists have often used beautiful ornamental handwriting as decoration because their religion prohibits making pictures. The elegant Islamic *Kufic* style of calligraphy was sometimes

Calligraphy is the art of beautiful handwriting. Chinese calligraphy is closely related to Chinese painting. The same type of brush is used in both art forms. The calligraphy pictured here shows Chinese characters that correspond to the words THE WORLD BOOK DICTIONARY.

copied in Europe because of its graceful beauty, even though few Europeans could read it. ELIZABETH BROUN

See also CHINA (Painting; picture: Fine Handwriting); HANDWRITING (picture: The Art of Penmanship); ISLAMIC ART (Calligraphy; picture: Islamic Painting); PAINTING (Chinese Painting; Islamic Painting).

CALLING HARE. See PIKA.

CALLIOPE, in mythology. See MUSES.

CALLIOPE, *kuh LY uh pee* or *KAL ee ohp,* is an organ-like musical instrument that creates sounds by forcing compressed steam through pipes. Calliopes produce loud tones and are often played at such outdoor public events as carnivals and fairs. A calliope has a boiler that creates steam. The steam passes quickly and forcefully through pipes of different lengths, producing musical tones. The flow of steam is regulated by valves that are operated either by a manual keyboard or by a mechanical rotating cylinder. The entire instrument is mounted on wheels.

Bettmann Archive

The Steam Whistles of the Calliope produce loud, harsh tones. It is rarely seen or heard today, except in some circuses.

The calliope was patented in 1855 by Joshua C. Stoddard, an American inventor. The instrument is named after Calliope, the goddess of epic poetry in ancient Greek mythology. F. E. KIRBY

CALLOT, *ka LOH,* **JACQUES,** *zhahk* (1592-1635), was a major French printmaker. He made over 1,400 etchings of beggars, court festivals, landscapes, theater performances, battle scenes, religious subjects, and fashionable aristocrats. Many of his etchings are crowded with tiny figures and amusing details. Callot also made important improvements in the technique of etching.

Callot was born in Nancy, in the historical province of Lorraine, and studied etching in Italy. In 1614, he became an artist for the famous Medici family of Florence (see MEDICI). Callot returned to Lorraine in 1621, during the Thirty Years' War between Protestants and Roman Catholics. He made a series of 18 etchings that showed the effects of the war on the province. These etchings make up one of his most famous works, *The Miseries and Misfortunes of War* (1633). ELIZABETH BROUN

National Gallery of Art, Washington, D.C., Rosenwald Collection

A Callot Etching shows the artist's skill in portraying subjects in great detail. This 1621 etching shows two characters in a type of comic Italian drama called *commedia dell' arte.*

CALLUS, *KAL uhs,* is a hardening and thickening of the skin. It often forms on the feet and hands. Poorly fitted shoes can cause calluses on the heels and soles of the feet. A *corn* is a special kind of callus, usually found on the feet (see CORN). Hand calluses result from prolonged rubbing on some hard object. Many calluses can be treated by soaking them in water and then applying a salicylic-acid solution or other softening preparation. Rubbing calluses with scratchy pads or sponges also helps soften them.

A substance called a *callus* forms around broken bones when they begin to mend. It is a different substance than the skin callus. ORVILLE J. STONE

CALMS, REGIONS OF, are places in the atmosphere which usually have little or no wind. Several areas of the earth's surface are known as regions of frequent calms. These regions of calms include the northern and southern *horse latitudes,* the northern and southern *subpolar regions,* and the equatorial *doldrums.* All of these calms regions may be disrupted by sudden storms.

The Horse Latitudes are regions of calms that lie between the oceanic belts of winds called the *prevailing*

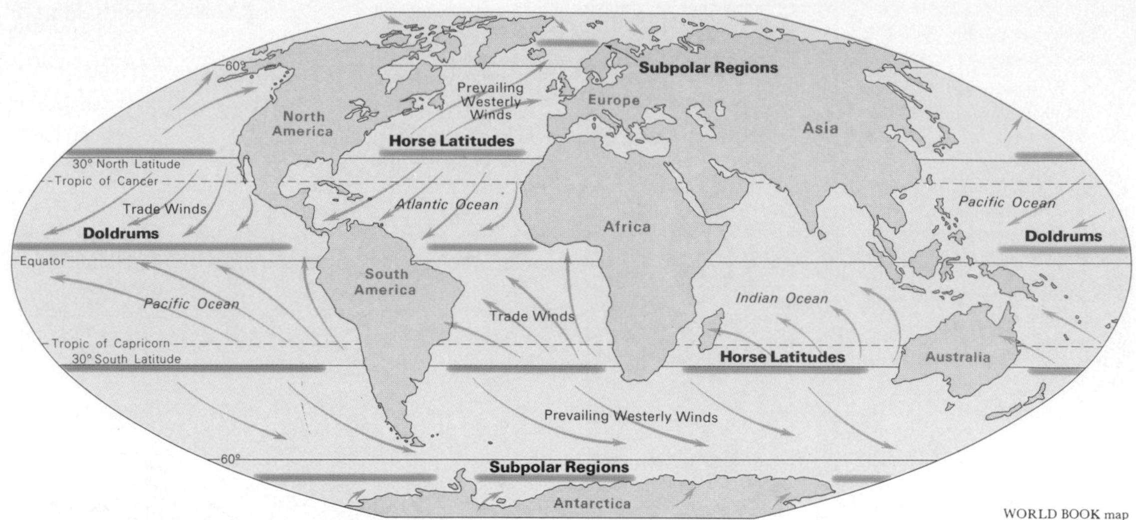

The Regions of Calms occur in certain areas over the world's oceans. These areas are the northern and southern *subpolar regions,* the northern and southern *horse latitudes,* and the equatorial *doldrums.* The positions of the regions of calms change slightly during the summer and winter.

westerlies and the *trade winds* (see PREVAILING WESTERLY; TRADE WIND). These areas are calms because the air above them is gently sinking from high altitudes toward the earth's surface. This results in areas of high barometric pressure. The horse latitudes coincide with the *subtropical maritime anticyclones,* or *subtropical highs.* These high-pressure areas in the atmosphere center over the oceans at about 30° latitude north and south of the equator. They move farther north when it is summer in the Northern Hemisphere, and farther south when it is summer in the Southern Hemisphere. The horse latitudes are sometimes called the *calms of Cancer* and the *calms of Capricorn* because the calms region in the Northern Hemisphere lies near the Tropic of Cancer and the calms region in the Southern Hemisphere lies near the Tropic of Capricorn.

Subpolar Regions. The general circulation of air causes cold air over the North and South poles to sink, forming the *polar anticyclones.* But since this cold air hugs the earth's surface, periods of calms are not so persistent as in warmer regions of calms.

The Doldrums are ocean regions centered slightly north of the equator. One area of doldrums lies in the Pacific Ocean extending westward from Central America and South America to the Philippines. The other area of equatorial doldrums lies in the Atlantic Ocean between South America and Africa. The trade winds that blow from both the northeast and the southeast toward these areas of doldrums bring masses of air into the regions. The air masses are forced upward after being heated in the tropics. This causes a belt of low pressure to form. Tropical storms may occur at the edges of this belt. This belt moves north and south with the sun as the horse latitudes do.

During the days of sailing ships, sea captains avoided the doldrums areas because of the fitful and uncertain winds and heavy downpours. Ships might lie becalmed in these regions for weeks. VANCE E. MOYER

See also DOLDRUMS; HORSE LATITUDES; WEATHER (How Weather Develops and Changes).

CALORIE is a unit used to measure heat energy in the metric system of measurement. A calorie is the amount of energy needed to raise the temperature of one gram of water by one degree Celsius. The word *calorie* comes from the Latin word *calor,* which means *heat.* A *kilocalorie,* or *kilogram calorie,* equals 1,000 calories.

Many chemical *reactions* (changes) produce heat. Scientists measure the amount of heat produced with an instrument called a *calorimeter.* One of the most important uses of the calorimeter is to measure the amount of heat given off by different foods when they burn. This measurement tells how much energy a certain food has when it is completely used by the body. Food scientists measure the heat produced in the calorimeter in kilogram calories, but they report the measurements as *food calories* or simply calories.

Another metric unit that is used to measure heat energy is the *joule.* One joule equals 0.24 calorie. The *British thermal unit* (B.T.U.) is used to measure heat in the customary system of measurement. One B.T.U. equals 252 calories.

Heating engineers make their estimates in calories or B.T.U.'s when designing furnaces, boilers, steam turbines, and other machinery. Air conditioning and refrigeration engineers also use calories or B.T.U.'s when designing cooling systems. KENNETH SCHUG

See also BRITISH THERMAL UNIT; HEAT; JOULE; NUTRITION (tables: Recommended Daily Allowances, Nutritional Values of Common Foods).

CALUMET. See PEACE PIPE.

CALUMET AND HECLA MINE. See AGASSIZ.

CALVARY, called Golgotha in Hebrew, is the spot outside ancient Jerusalem where Christ was crucified. No one knows the actual site, but tradition places it where the Church of the Holy Sepulchre now stands.

See also JERUSALEM (Holy Places).

CALVERT, CECILIUS, CHARLES, and **GEORGE.** See BALTIMORE, LORD.

CALVERT, LEONARD. See MARYLAND (Colonial Days).

CALVIN, JOHN (1509-1564), was one of the chief leaders of the Protestant Reformation. Calvin's brilliant mind, powerful preaching, many books and large correspondence, and capacity for organization and administration made him a dominant figure of the Reformation. He was especially influential in Switzerland, England, Scotland, and colonial North America.

His Life. Calvin was born in Noyon, France, near Compiègne. His father was a lawyer for the Roman Catholic Church. Calvin was educated in Paris, Orléans, and Bourges. After his father's death in 1531, he studied Greek and Latin at the University of Paris. Thus, Calvin's education reflected the influence of the liberal and humanistic Renaissance. Unlike several other Reformation leaders, Calvin was probably never ordained a priest.

By 1533, Calvin had declared himself a Protestant. In 1534, he settled in Basel, Switzerland. There, he published the first edition of his *Institutes of the Christian Religion* (1536). This book achieved immediate recognition for Calvin, and he expanded it throughout his life. The book sets forth Calvin's basic ideas on religion and is a masterpiece of Reformation literature.

In 1536, Calvin was persuaded to become a leader of Geneva's first group of Protestant pastors. In 1538, Geneva leaders reacted against the strict doctrines of the Protestant pastors, and Calvin and several other clergymen were banished. Later that year, Calvin became pastor of a French refugee Protestant church in Strasbourg, Germany. He was deeply influenced by the older German Protestant leaders of Strasbourg, especially Martin Bucer. Calvin adapted Bucer's ideas on church government and worship.

Geneva lacked able religious and political leadership. The Geneva city council begged Calvin to return, and he did so in 1541. From then until his death, Calvin was the dominant personality in Geneva.

Calvinism. From its beginning in 1517, the Reformation brought religious and political opposition from the church and from civil rulers. By 1546, many Protestants in Germany, Switzerland, and France were insisting that the people—not just kings and bishops—should share in political and religious policy-making. This idea influenced Calvin and his followers in France, England, Scotland, and the Netherlands. Calvin's French followers were called *Huguenots*. The English Protestants whom he influenced were called *Puritans*.

The Calvinists developed political theories that supported constitutional government, representative government, the right of people to change their government, and the separation of civil government from church government. Calvinists of the 1500's intended these ideas to apply only to the aristocracy. But during the 1600's, more democratic concepts arose, especially in England and later in colonial America.

Detail of a portrait by an unknown painter of the 1500's; Bibliothèques Municipales, Geneva, Switzerland

John Calvin

Calvin agreed with other early Reformation leaders on such basic religious theories as the superiority of faith over good works, the Bible as the basis of all Christian teachings, and the universal priesthood of all believers. According to the concept of universal priesthood, all believers were considered priests. The Roman Catholic Church, on the other hand, had various ranks of priests that were separate from laypersons. Calvin also declared that people were saved solely by the grace of God, and that only people called the *Elect* would be saved. However, nobody could know who the Elect were. Calvin expanded the idea that Christianity was intended to reform all of society. To promote this reform, Calvin lectured and wrote on politics, social problems, and international issues as part of Christian responsibility.

Many of Calvin's ideas were controversial, but no other reformer did so much to force people to think about Christian social ethics. From this ethical concern and Bucer's ideas, Calvin developed the pattern of church government that today is called *presbyterian*. Calvin organized the church government distinct from civil government, so that an organized body of church leaders could work for social reform. He was the first Protestant leader in Europe to gain partial church independence from the state. L. J. TRINTERUD

Related Articles in WORLD BOOK include:

Foreordination
Predestination
Presbyterians
Protestantism (History)
Puritans
Reformation
Servetus, Michael

Additional Resources

CALVIN, JOHN. *Institutes of the Christian Religion.* 2 vols. Trans. by F. L. Battles. Mellon, 1981. Reprint of 1975 ed.

McNEILL, JOHN T. *History and Character of Calvinism.* Oxford, 1954.

PARKER, T. H. *John Calvin: A Biography.* Westminster, 1976.

WALKER, WILLISTON. *John Calvin: The Organiser of Reformed Protestantism, 1509-1564.* Schocken, 1969. Reprint of 1906 ed. A standard biography.

CALVIN, MELVIN (1911-), an American chemist, received the 1961 Nobel prize in chemistry for his studies of photosynthesis. Using radioactive carbon-14, he traced the chemical reactions that occur when a plant changes carbon dioxide and water into sugar. Calvin studied at the Michigan College of Mining and Technology and the University of Minnesota. He became professor of chemistry and director of the bio-organic division of the Radiation Laboratory at the University of California. He was born in St. Paul, Minn. HERBERT S. RHINESMITH

See also CHEMISTRY (picture: Famous Chemists).

CALVIN COLLEGE. See UNIVERSITIES AND COLLEGES (table).

CALVINISM. See CALVIN, JOHN.

CALYPSO, *kuh LIHP soh,* is a type of folk music that comes from the island of Trinidad in the Caribbean Sea. Calypso songs are in $\frac{2}{4}$ or $\frac{4}{4}$ time, with a strong beat similar to the rhythms of African songs. Experts disagree about the meaning of the word *calypso.* Some think it comes from the African word *Kai-so,* meaning *bravo,* used to praise a good singer.

Characteristics. The words of a calypso song are more important than the music. Cleverness in choosing words and in making up rhymes on the spot marks the champion calypso singer. The lyrics may express a

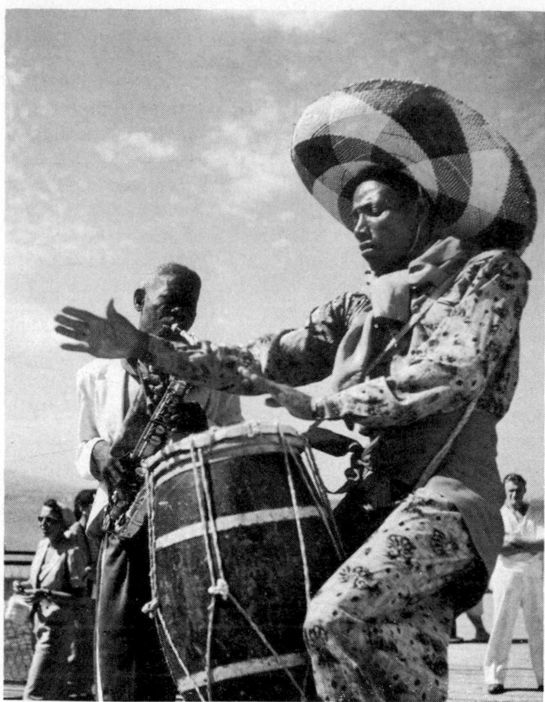

Roger Coster, Monkmeyer

Calypso Musicians in Haiti

personal philosophy or comment on local events and gossip. Calypso songs with nonsense verses are called *bracket*. Songs about serious subjects are known as *ballode*.

Almost any instrument may be used for calypso music. Early instruments included bamboo pieces and rattles. Many calypso singers today use drums, flutes, guitars, saxophones, and rattles for accompaniment.

Development. Calypso originated in the songs of African slaves who worked in the plantation fields of Trinidad. They were forbidden to talk to each other, and used calypso to communicate feelings and information. To fool their masters, they sang in a French-Creole dialect called *patois*. Annual calypso singing competitions were held at carnival time. After slavery was abolished in the 1830's, these competitions became more popular and attracted many visitors to Trinidad. Champion singers today take such names as "Attila the Hun" and "Richard the Lion-Hearted."

Calypso has spread throughout the Caribbean area and to other parts of the world. English versions, such as "Day-O" or "Banana Boat Song" and "Mary Ann," became popular in the United States. MICHAEL HERMAN

CALYPSO, *kuh LIHP soh*, was a sea nymph in Greek mythology. Odysseus was shipwrecked on the lonely island where she lived. She promised him that he would never die if he stayed with her. Seven years later, Zeus sent Hermes to her with an order to let Odysseus go. She helped him build a raft. After Odysseus left, Calypso died of grief. PADRAIC COLUM

See also ODYSSEY.

CALYX. See FLOWER (The Parts of a Flower).

CAMACHO, MANUEL ÁVILA. See ÁVILA CAMACHO, MANUEL.

CAMBODIA. See KAMPUCHEA.

CAMBRIAN PERIOD, *KAM bree uhn*, is one of the geologic periods in the earth's history. Scientists believe that it began about 600 million years ago.

See also EARTH (table).

CAMBRIC, *KAYM brihk*, is a fine white cotton cloth of plain weave. It has a slight luster. Cambric is similar to nainsook, another cotton fabric, except that nainsook has a shinier finish. *Lining cambric*, or *costume cambric*, is used for stage costumes. *Linen cambric*, white and closely woven, is used for embroidery and table linen. Modern cambric may contain synthetic fibers. Cambric gets its name from Cambrai, France, where it was first made of linen. CHRISTINE W. JARVIS

CAMBRIDGE *KAYM brihj*, is a city in England and the home of Cambridge University. It is the chief city in the district of Cambridge, which has a population of 87,194. Cambridge lies on the River Cam, about 50 miles (80 kilometers) north of London. It has radio and electrical industries.

Cambridge was a fort in Roman times, and Roman ruins still stand there. In the 1200's, monks from Ely established the nucleus of the present university. Cambridge University is noted for scholarship in modern literature and science, especially nuclear physics and astronomy (see CAMBRIDGE UNIVERSITY). JOHN W. WEBB

CAMBRIDGE, *KAYM brihj*, Mass. (pop. 95,322), stands on the Charles River opposite Boston. For location, see MASSACHUSETTS (political map). The city is famous for its educational, historical, literary, and scientific contributions. The fame of Harvard University, Massachusetts Institute of Technology, Radcliffe College, and Lesley College has given Cambridge the name *University City*.

Cambridge has many industries. Its products include addressing and billing machines, books, cameras, candy, crackers, electronic measuring instruments, friction tape, and grinding wheels. It also turns out indus-

Stock, Boston

Cambridge, Mass., the home of several famous colleges, is sometimes called *University City*. Skyscrapers in downtown Boston rise behind the Harvard University dormitories shown above.

trial and fire hose, ink, insulated wire and cable, weather balloons, plastic containers, and skates.

The museums of Harvard are world famous. Harvard's Widener Library, with about 6 million books and pamphlets, is the world's largest university library. The Massachusetts Institute of Technology has exhibits on papermaking and on maritime history.

Puritans moving up the river from Boston settled Newtowne in 1630. The present name was adopted in 1638, in honor of Cambridge, England. Stephen Daye printed the first book in the Colonies, *The Bay Psalm Book*, there in 1640.

Cambridge became an armed camp at the outbreak of the Revolution. On July 3, 1775, George Washington took command of the Continental Army under an elm tree on the Common. Prisoners from General John Burgoyne's surrender in 1777 were quartered in Harvard dormitories. In 1779, in Cambridge, a convention drew up Massachusetts' state constitution.

Cambridge contributed to the great literary movement of the mid-1800's. Authors who lived and wrote in the city included Oliver Wendell Holmes, Henry Wadsworth Longfellow, and James Russell Lowell.

Cambridge became a city in 1846. It has a council-manager form of government. Cambridge and Lowell are the seats of Middlesex County. William J. Reid

CAMBRIDGE FLAG. See Flag (First United States Flags; color picture: Flags in American History).

Gullers, Pix

The Bridge of Sighs at Cambridge University, named after the famous bridge in Venice, spans the River Cam.

CAMBRIDGE UNIVERSITY is a world-famous university in Great Britain. Cambridge probably originated in 1209, when some scholars left Oxford University, after several disturbances there between students and townspeople. A number of these scholars moved to the city of Cambridge, about 50 miles (80 kilometers) north of London, where a new university grew up.

Cambridge University has about 11,000 students. Every student must be a member of one of the university's 29 colleges, of which 15 are for men, 3 for women, and 11 for both men and women. Five of the colleges admit only graduate students and, in some cases, older undergraduates. The first college, Peterhouse, was founded in 1284 by Hugo de Balsham, Bishop of Ely. Other well-known colleges of the university include Churchill, Christ's, Corpus Christi, Girton, Jesus, King's, Pembroke, Queens', and Trinity Hall.

Each college is an independent, self-governing corporation, though it must obey the laws of the university. Every college owns its own property, has its own income, and admits its own students. The colleges provide lodging, instruction, and social and sporting facilities for their students. The university provides some library and laboratory facilities. The Cambridge University Library has more than 3 million books and manuscripts.

Each undergraduate at Cambridge is assigned to an instructor called a *tutor*, to a *director of studies*, and to various *supervisors*. The tutor looks after the student's general well-being. The director of studies advises the student on what lectures to attend, and the supervisors give personal instruction. The university grants bachelor's, master's, and doctor's degrees. It first granted degrees to women in 1948. P. A. McGinley

CAMDEN, N.J. (pop. 84,910), is a manufacturing center that covers about 10 square miles (26 square kilometers) on the Delaware River opposite Philadelphia. For location, see New Jersey (political map). About 150 manufacturing plants employ about a third of the city's work force.

Rutgers University has a branch campus and a law school in Camden. The city's museums include the home in which Walt Whitman, the great American poet, lived from 1884 until his death in 1892. Camden's transportation facilities include the Lindenwold High-Speed Line, which is a railway that carries riders between Camden and Philadelphia in about five minutes.

Blacks make up about 53 per cent of Camden's population. The city also has many people of Italian, Polish, or Puerto Rican descent.

Delaware Indians lived in what is now the Camden area before whites first arrived there. In 1681, an English Quaker named William Cooper settled in the area. He soon began operating ferryboats across the Delaware River, and a settlement called Cooper's Ferry grew up around the ferry landing. In 1828, Cooper's Ferry was incorporated and changed its name to Camden. This name honored the Earl of Camden, an English political leader who had been sympathetic to the American Colonies.

Industrial expansion began in Camden after the Civil War ended in 1865. Factories soon lined the waterfront. During the early 1900's, Camden became one of the nation's top shipbuilding centers. During World War I (1914-1918) and World War II (1939-1945), jobs in the city's shipyards brought thousands of workers to Camden. By 1950, the city had 124,555 people.

Camden's shipyards began massive layoffs after World War II and finally closed down in 1967. During the 1960's, many other industries left the city and the number of jobs in Camden dropped by almost a third. In addition, many of Camden's middle-income families moved to the suburbs. By 1980, the city's population had fallen to 84,910. Camden has a mayor-council form of government. Elizabeth Suplee

CAMDEN, BATTLE OF. See Revolutionary War in America (The War in the South; table: Major Battles of the Revolutionary War).

George Holton, Photo Researchers

Herds of Bactrian Camels Graze in the Gobi Desert. These sturdy animals, whose ancestors roamed wild, can carry heavy packs for long distances over rocky mountain trails.

CAMEL is a large, strong desert animal. Camels can travel great distances across hot, dry deserts with little food or water. They walk easily on soft sand where trucks would get stuck, and carry people and heavy loads to places that have no roads. Camels also serve the people of the desert in many other ways.

The camel carries its own built-in food supply on its back in the form of a hump. The camel's hump is a large lump of fat that provides energy for the animal if food is hard to find.

There are two chief kinds of camels: (1) the Arabian camel, which has one hump, and (2) the Bactrian camel, which has two humps. A special kind of Arabian camel called the *dromedary* is raised for riding and racing.

Camels have been tamed by people for thousands of years. Arabian camels may once have lived wild in Arabia, but none are wild today. There are about 3 million Arabian camels, and most of them live with the desert people of Africa and Asia. The first Bactrian camels probably lived in Mongolia and in Turkestan, which was called Bactria in ancient times. A few hundred wild Bactrian camels still roam in some parts of Mongolia, and about a million tame ones live in Asia.

Scientists believe camels lived only in North America until about 175,000 years ago. No one knows why they disappeared. During the 1850's, the U.S. Army brought about 80 camels from Africa and Asia to carry cargo from Texas to California. But the railroads, which were growing rapidly, could carry more goods faster and cheaper than the camels could. The army sold the animals, most of them to circuses and zoos.

Camels belong to the camel family, *Camelidae.* They are the only animals of this family that live in the deserts of Africa and Asia. The four other members of the camel family are (1) alpacas, (2) guanacos, (3) llamas, and (4) vicuñas.

People and Camels

Millions of people who live in Africa and Asia depend on camels to supply most of their needs. In lands at the edge of the deserts, camels pull plows, turn water wheels to irrigate fields, and carry grain to market. Deep in the deserts, camels are almost the only source of transportation, food, clothing, and shelter.

Camels have an unpredictable nature. At times they seem to dislike everything—even other camels. A camel will bite people and animals alike. It often kicks out suddenly and viciously with its hind legs, much as a star-

Donald F. Hoffmeister, the contributor of this article, is Director of the Museum of Natural History of the University of Illinois.

tled mule does. The camel is easily annoyed, and will spit at anything nearby, including visitors at a zoo. Yet at other times a camel will behave quite gently.

Camels do not work willingly, and they never learn to obey people freely as do horses, dogs, and some other animals. A camel whines when anyone mounts it or puts a pack on its back. Then the animal grunts and groans loudly as it rises to its feet. But after the camel starts walking, it carries its load patiently.

Camels are an important source of food in the desert. People eat the meat of young camels, which tastes somewhat like veal. They melt fat from the animal's hump and use it for butter. They drink camel's milk and also make cheese from it. The milk is so rich and thick that it forms hard lumps in tea or coffee.

The camel also supplies wool and leather for clothing and shelter. Camel owners weave the animal's soft, woolly fur into fine cloth and warm blankets. The long fur of the Bactrian camel is especially good for weaving. Arabs use the cloth for much of their clothing, and make tents from it. Camel's hair cloth is sold in many parts of the world for making blankets, coats, and suits.

The strong, tough skin of the camel provides leather for shoes, water bags, and packsaddles. Dried camel bones can be carved like ivory for jewelry or utensils. Camel droppings are dried and used for fuel.

Facts in Brief

Names: *Male,* none; *female,* none; *young,* calf; *group,* herd.

Gestation Period: About 11 months.

Number of Young: Usually 1; rarely 2.

Length of Life: 17 to 50 years.

Where Found: Africa and Asia.

Scientific Classification: Camels belong to the camel family, Camelidae. They are in the genus *Camelus.* The Arabian camel is species *C. dromedarius.* The Bactrian camel is *C. bactrianus.*

The Body of a Camel

A camel stands from 6 to 7 feet (1.8 to 2.1 meters) tall at the shoulders, and weighs from 1,000 to 1,600 pounds (450 to 726 kilograms). Its ropelike tail may be almost 21 inches (53 centimeters) long. Camels seem larger than they are because of their thick, woolly fur, which may be brown or gray. An Arabian camel's fur is short and lies close to its body. A Bactrian camel's fur is longer. It may grow about 10 inches (25 centimeters) long on the animal's head, neck, and humps.

All camels lose their fur in spring and grow a new coat. The fur comes off so fast that it hangs in large pieces, making the animal appear ragged. A camel looks sleek and slender for several weeks after losing its coat, but a thick coat of new fur grows by autumn.

Camels have bare spots on their chests and on their leg joints. These spots look as though the hair had been rubbed off, but they are natural and not signs of wear.

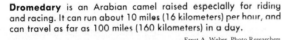

Dromedary is an Arabian camel raised especially for riding and racing. It can run about 10 miles (16 kilometers) per hour, and can travel as far as 100 miles (160 kilometers) in a day.

Ernst A. Weber, Photo Researchers

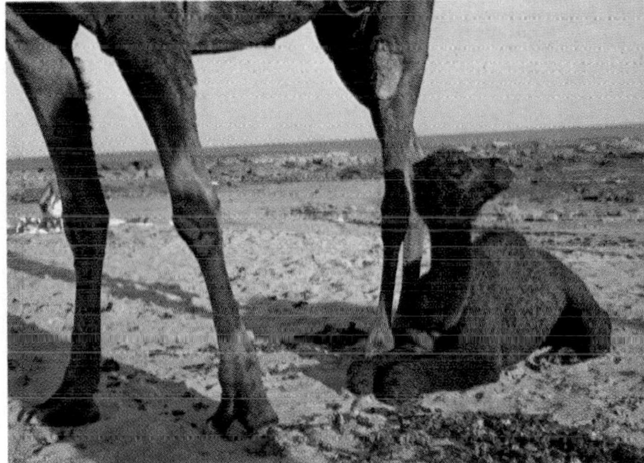

P. J. Holloway, Photo Researchers

A Week-Old Camel Calf, *above,* rests beside its mother. Calves can run soon after birth, but stay with their mothers for about four years.

A Camel's Thick Eyebrows, *right,* help shade its eyes from the sun. The animal can shut its nostrils and lips tightly to keep out blowing sand.

Russ Kinne, Photo Researchers

Even young camels have them. Thick, leathery skin grows there and becomes tough when the animal is about five months old.

Head. A camel has large eyes on the sides of its head. Each eye is protected by three eyelids. The two outer lids have long, curly eyelashes that keep sand from blowing into the eyes. A thin inner eyelid winks over the eyeball and wipes off any dust that may get in. Thick eyebrows shield the eyes from the desert sun. A camel holds its head high and peers out from under its eyebrows, giving the animal a proud appearance.

The camel's small, rounded ears are far back on its head. The ears are covered with hair, even on the inside. The hair helps keep out sand or dust that might blow into the ears. A camel can hear well, but, like the donkey, often pays no attention to commands.

The camel has a large mouth and strong, sharp teeth. It uses the teeth as weapons. A camel owner may cover the animal's mouth with a muzzle to keep it from biting. The camel's upper lip is split somewhat like that of a rabbit. The animal grasps its food with its lips. A camel's nostrils are thin slits above the lips. Special muscles allow the animal to close its nostrils during sandstorms.

Hump of a camel is mostly a lump of fat. Bands of strong tissue hold pads of fat together, forming the hump above the backbone. The hump of a healthy camel may weigh 80 pounds (36 kilograms) or more, and usually makes up about $\frac{1}{20}$ of the animal's weight.

Most kinds of animals store fat in their bodies, but only camels keep most of their fat in a lump. If food is hard to find, the fat in the hump provides energy for the animal. If a camel is starving, its hump shrinks. The hump may even slip off the animal's back and hang down on its side. After the camel has had a few days' rest and some food, its hump becomes firm and plump again. The hump is not a storage place for water, as many persons believe.

Legs and Feet. Camels have long, strong legs. Powerful muscles in the upper part of the legs allow the animals to carry heavy loads for long distances. A camel can carry as much as 1,000 pounds (450 kilograms), but the usual load weighs about 400 pounds (180 kilograms). The animal can travel about 25 miles (40 kilometers) a day, although it may move as slowly as $2\frac{1}{2}$ miles (4 kilometers) per hour. Dromedaries, which usually do not carry heavy packs, can travel as far as 100 miles (160 kilometers) a day. They can run at a speed of about 10 miles (16 kilometers) per hour.

The Body of a Camel

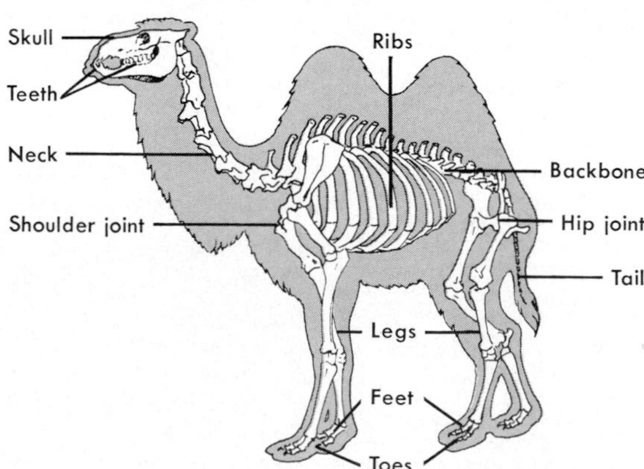

WORLD BOOK illustration by Tom Dolan

When a camel walks or runs, both legs on one side of its body move forward at the same time. Then the legs on the other side swing forward. This leg action produces a swaying, rocking motion that makes some riders "seasick." Camels are sometimes called "ships of the desert."

The tough, leathery skin pads that cover a camel's knees act as cushions when the animal kneels to rest. The camel bends its front legs and drops to its knees. Then it folds its hind legs and falls to the ground. To get up, the camel straightens its hind legs and then jerks up its front legs. A camel can drop to the ground and get up again even with a heavy load on its back.

Camels have two usable toes on each foot. A hoof that looks like a toenail grows at the tip of each toe. Cows, horses, and many other animals walk on their hoofs. But a camel walks on a broad pad that connects its two long toes. This cushionlike pad spreads when the camel steps on it. The pad supports the animal on loose sand in much the same way that a snowshoe helps a person walk on snow. The camel's cushioned feet make almost no sound when the animal walks or runs.

The Life of a Camel

Young. A female camel carries her young inside her body for about 11 months before birth. She almost always has only one calf at a time, but sometimes two are born. The calf's eyes are open at birth, and a thick, woolly coat covers its body. The calf can run when it is only a few hours old, and calls to its mother with a soft "baa" somewhat like that of a lamb. The young camel stays with its mother until it is about 4 years old. The mother guards her calf and keeps it close to her.

When a calf is about a year old, its owner begins to teach it to stand and kneel on command. The young camel also learns to wear a bridle and to carry a saddle or small, light packs. The size and weight of the packs are gradually increased as the camel grows older. A 5-year-old camel can carry a full load of about 400 pounds (180 kilograms).

Food. Camels can go for days or even weeks with little or no food or water. Desert people feed their camels dates, grass, and such grains as wheat and oats. In zoos, the animals eat hay and dry grains—about 8 pounds (3.6 kilograms) of each every day. When a camel travels across the desert, food may be hard to find. The animal may have to live on dried leaves, seeds, and whatever desert plants it can find. A camel can eat a thorny cactus without hurting its mouth. The lining of the mouth is so tough that the sharp cactus thorns cannot push through the skin. If food is very scarce, a camel will eat anything—bones, fish, meat, skin, its bridle, and even its owner's tent.

The camel does not chew its food well before swallowing it. The animal's stomach has three sections, one of which stores the poorly chewed food. This food, called *cud*, is later returned to the mouth in a ball-like glob, and the camel chews it. The chewed food is then swallowed and goes to the other parts of the stomach to be completely digested. Camels, deer, cattle, and other kinds of animals that digest their food in this way are called *ruminants* (see RUMINANT).

Water. A camel can go without water for days or even months. The amount of water a camel drinks varies with the time of year and with the weather. Camels usually need less water in winter when the weather is cool and the plants they eat contain more moisture than in summer. Camels that graze in the Sahara can go all winter without water, and may refuse to drink if water is offered to them. In summer, camels may drink about 5 gallons (19 liters) a day. But they can go without water for two to five days. Then they drink only as much as they need to replace their body moisture.

A camel needs little water because it gets some moisture from its food. Also, it keeps most of the water that is in its body. Most animals sweat when hot, and the evaporation of the water from their skin keeps them cool. But camels do not sweat much. Their body temperature may change as much as 11 Fahrenheit degrees (6 Celsius degrees) without harm. In people, an increase of only two or three degrees is usually a sign of illness.

Working camels in Africa and Asia live for 17 to 50 years. In circuses and zoos, the animals live less than 30 years. DONALD F. HOFFMEISTER

Related Articles in WORLD BOOK include:

Alpaca	Dromedary	Llama
Arabs	Ethiopia (picture)	Sahara (picture)
Asia (pictures)	Guanaco	Vicuña
Camel's-Hair Cloth		

CAMELLIA, *kuh MEEL yuh* or *kuh MEE lee uh,* is a semitropical evergreen tree or shrub related to the tea plant. It is native to China and Japan. Perhaps the best-known kind is the common camellia. Many varieties of this plant are grown as ornamentals in the South and the Pacific Coast regions of the United States. Alabama has adopted the camellia as its state flower. The plants bloom outdoors in winter and spring.

J. Horace McFarland

Camellia

Camellias have shiny, dark green leaves and beautiful roselike flowers with heavy, waxy petals. The blossoms may be red, white, pink, or spotted with color. They sometimes are 5 inches (13 centimeters) across. The blossoms are popular for corsages.

Gardeners usually raise camellias from cuttings or by grafting. The plants thrive in loose, moist, fertile soil and filtered shade. Camellias are usually planted in well-drained acid soils, with *mulch* (straw, leaves, or loose materials) spread around them to keep the soil moist.

Scientific Classification. Camellias belong to the tea family, Theaceae. The common camellia is genus *Camellia*, species *japonica*. The small-flowered camellia is *C. sasanqua*. ROBERT W. SCHERY

CAMELOT. See ARTHUR, KING.

CAMEL'S-HAIR CLOTH is a soft, medium-weight woolen cloth made from the fur of the Bactrian camel. In spring, the camel loses its winter coat and grows a new one. The fur comes off in large pieces, which are gathered and processed. Camel fur consists of long, coarse hairs that yield poor fibers, and short, fine hairs that produce a soft, warm cloth. The cloth is used to make blankets, coats, shawls, and suits. KEITH SLATER

See also CAMEL (People and Camels).

Onyx brooch (mid-1800's), probably by L. Saulini; sardonyx ring (early 1800's) by Niccolò Amastini. The Metropolitan Museum of Art, New York City, the Milton Weil Collection, gift of Mrs. Ethel Weil Worgelt, 1940

Cameos often feature subjects from classical mythology. The brooch on the left shows the head of Medusa, a monster in Greek mythology who had snakes for hair. The ring on the right shows a scene from the education of Bacchus, the Roman god of wine.

CAMEO, *KAM ee oh,* is a gem carved with figures that are *in relief* (raised). The term often refers to a gem that has layers of different colors. The figures are cut from one layer against a background layer of another color. Stones commonly used for cameos include onyx, sardonyx, and agate. Attractive artificial cameos are made from various kinds of shells and fine glass. Shell yields delicate cameos. A famous example of an imitation cameo in glass is the Barberini Vase in the British Museum. It was made in Rome about 100 B.C. Both the Greeks and the Romans produced excellent cameos. See also RELIEF. WILLIAM M. MILLIKEN

CAMERA is an instrument used to take photographs. It ranks as one of the most important means of communication and expression. Basically, a camera is a dark box that holds light-sensitive film at one end and has a small hole at the other end. Light enters the hole through a glass or plastic lens and exposes the film to make a picture. The word *camera* comes from the Latin words *camera obscura*, meaning *dark chamber*.

This article explains how a camera works and discusses various types of cameras. For a discussion of the history and parts of a camera and how to take pictures, see the WORLD BOOK article on PHOTOGRAPHY.

How a Camera Works

A camera can be compared to a dark room into which light enters only through a small hole in the window shade. On the opposite wall of the room, this light produces a dim, inverted image of the scene outside the window. The lens of a camera admits light in much the same way. The light that passes through the lens produces an inverted image on the film at the other end of the camera. The relationship of the distances between the lens, the subject, and the film determines the sharpness of the image. Many cameras have a focusing mechanism by which the photographer can adjust the distance between the film and the lens. A few cameras automatically adjust this distance by means of an electronic or ultrasonic focusing mechanism.

A device called a *shutter* opens to let light enter the camera. The shutter may be behind, in front of, or within the lens. It opens when a shutter release is pressed to take a picture. The speed of the shutter's opening and closing determines how long the film is exposed to light. Many cameras have adjustable shutter speeds, ranging from 10 seconds or more to $\frac{1}{2000}$ of a second. Some cameras have electronic shutters that adjust shutter speeds automatically.

Many cameras also have a *time-exposure* control, which allows photographers to keep the shutter open for long exposures. The extra exposure time makes it possible to take pictures in dim light. A time exposure may require as little as two seconds or as long as several hours.

A device called a *diaphragm* also fits behind or within the lens. In some cameras, it can be expanded or contracted to provide a large or small hole through which light reaches the film. The photographer adjusts the diaphragm to control the overall sharpness of the picture and the amount of light reaching the film. Many cameras have an electric-eye mechanism that automati-

How a Camera Uses Light

A camera is basically a dark box that holds light-sensitive film at one end and has a small *aperture* (hole) at the other. Light enters the camera through the aperture and forms an image on the film. You can see how this process works by shining flashlights through a pinhole in the side of a box.

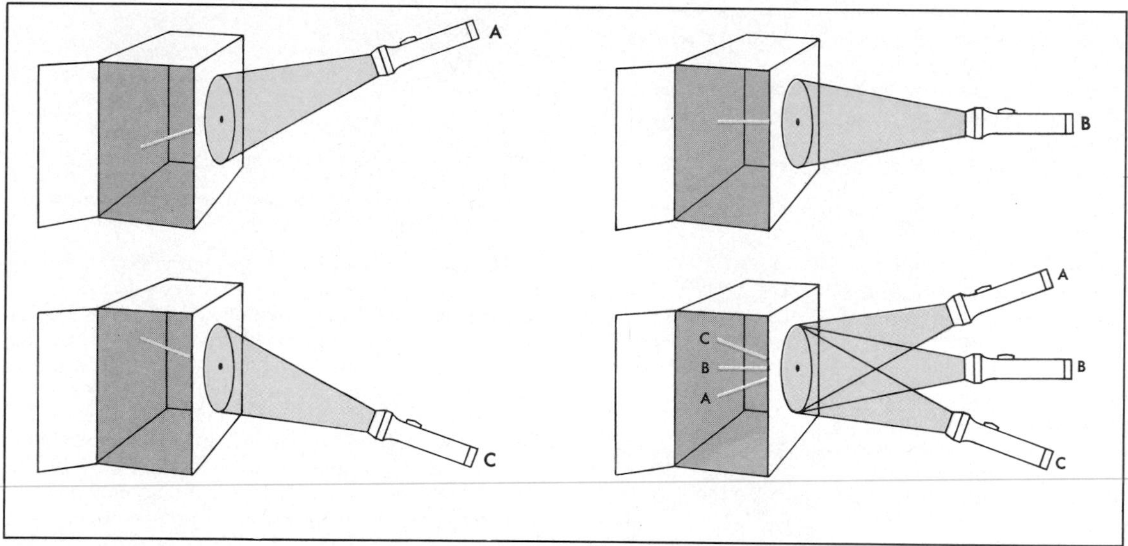

Light Passes Through the Aperture and strikes the opposite side of the box. Light rays travel in a straight line, and so the light reaches the inside wall from the same direction as it entered the box. Light from flashlight A passes downward through the aperture, light from B goes straight across, and light from C travels upward. Light rays coming from all three directions at once cross as they pass through the aperture. As a result, they reverse positions and strike the inside wall at points C, B, and A. Thus, the images formed by light inside a camera are always inverted.

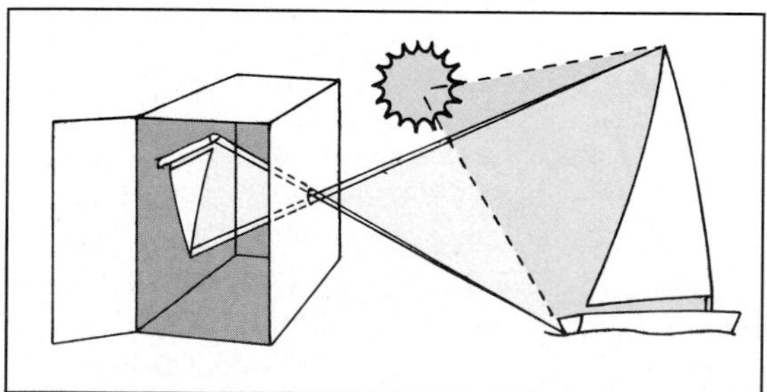

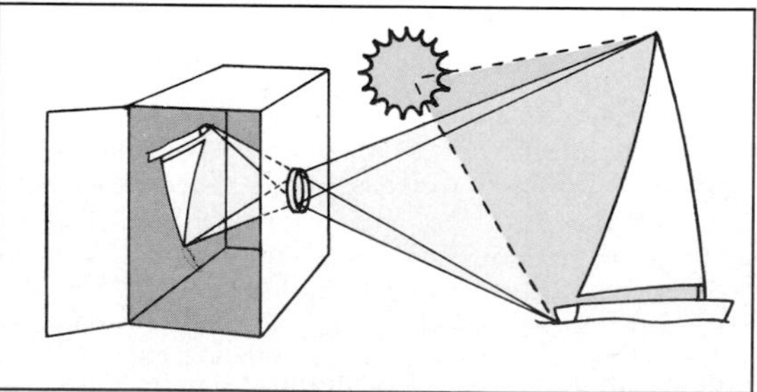

WORLD BOOK diagrams by Richard Fickle

A Pinhole allows sunlight reflected from a sailboat to expose the film in the back of the box, thereby creating a picture of the boat, *above*. A pinhole aperture admits only a small amount of light. For this reason, it may take several seconds for enough light to enter the box to expose the film.

A Lens increases the amount of light that enters the box. A picture of a sailboat can be recorded on film in a fraction of a second by covering the aperture with a lens. A lens also improves the quality of the picture because it focuses the incoming light rays into a sharp image on the film.

Parts of a Single-Lens Reflex Camera

A single-lens reflex camera enables photographers to see their subject through the lens. Light from the subject passes through the lens and is transmitted by a mirror and a prism to the viewfinder. When the shutter release button is pressed, the mirror lifts so that the light will expose the film.

WORLD BOOK diagram by Linden Artists Ltd.

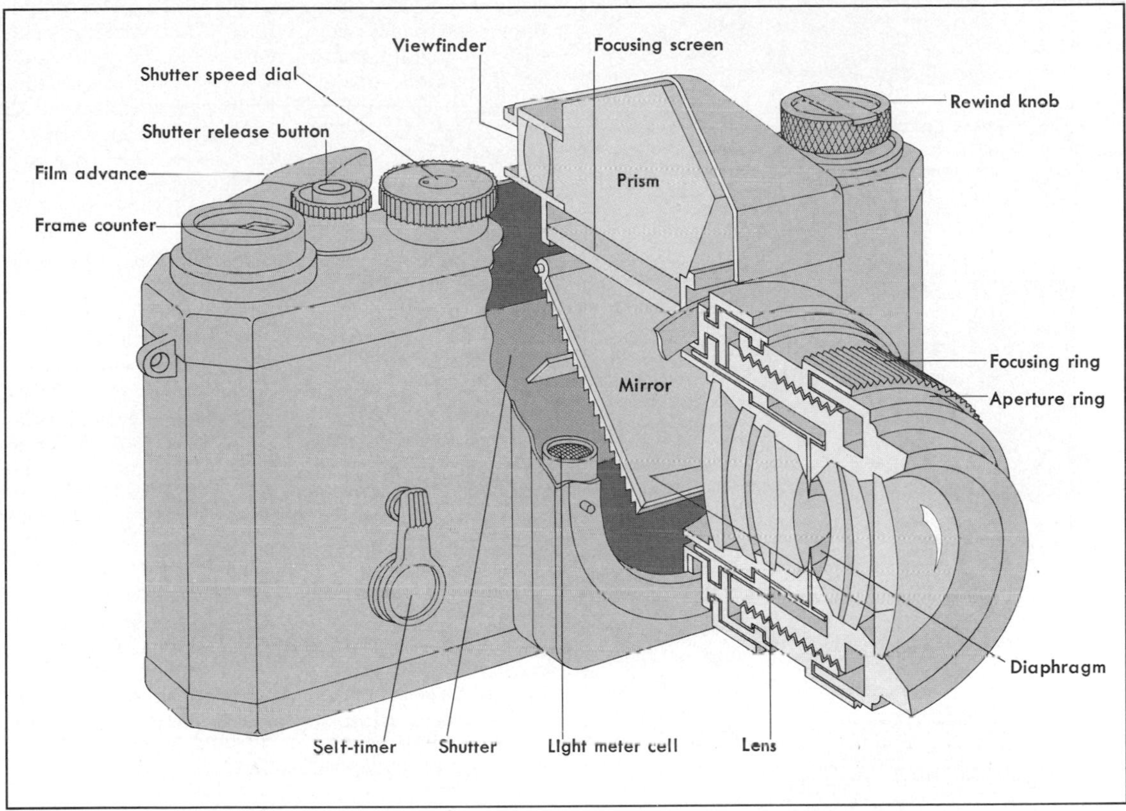

cally adjusts the diaphragm. A flash attachment allows pictures to be taken at short exposures in dim light by firing a bright burst of light as the shutter opens.

In addition, most cameras have a *viewfinder*, a sighting instrument that the photographer looks through to aim at the subject. Most cameras also have a *film advance*. With this device, the photographer winds the film through the camera to put unexposed film in position to take a picture. After each picture has been taken, the film advance moves the exposed film out of the way.

Types of Cameras

Fixed-Focus Cameras, the simplest of all cameras, have a nonadjustable lens. Most models have a single diaphragm setting and only one or two shutter speeds. Fixed-focus cameras include many inexpensive, pocket-sized models that use 110-size film. The negatives of such film are enlarged to provide photographs that measure $3\frac{1}{2}$ by $4\frac{1}{2}$ inches (89 by 114 millimeters).

In general, a fixed-focus camera can take satisfactory photographs in ordinary daylight but not in dim light, because its lens does not admit much light. The camera may produce a blurred picture if the subject is moving or is less than 6 feet (1.8 meters) away. Many fixed-focus cameras can take flash pictures, and some models can take time exposures.

A special type of fixed-focus camera, called a *disc camera*, uses film arranged on a circular disk. Disc cameras are about the size of a pocket calculator, and they include such features as an automatic flash and an automatic film advance. Some provide a second focus for subjects between 2 and 4 feet (0.6 to 1.2 meters) away.

Miniature Cameras are generally defined as those that take pictures ranging in size from 1 by $1\frac{1}{2}$ inches (25 by 38 millimeters) to $2\frac{1}{4}$ by $2\frac{1}{4}$ inches (57 by 57 millimeters). The 35-millimeter camera, which uses film that measures 35 millimeters ($1\frac{1}{2}$ inches) wide, is the most popular model. Most miniatures have an adjustable diaphragm, lens, and shutter speed, as well as a high-quality lens that produces extremely sharp pictures.

The regular lens of many miniature cameras can be replaced by a special-purpose lens, such as a *telephoto* lens or a *wide-angle* lens. A telephoto lens makes the subject appear larger and closer than it really is. A wide-angle lens makes objects appear smaller and farther away. With other special accessories, many miniature cameras can take pictures through a microscope or a telescope, or underwater. A *motor-drive* attachment enables miniatures to rapidly take a sequence of pictures.

Many miniatures have a *single-lens reflex* viewfinder. Such a viewfinder has a mirror mechanism between the lens and the film, allowing photographers to see their subject through the lens. When the shutter release is pressed to take a picture, the mirror lifts out of the way

Some Kinds of Cameras

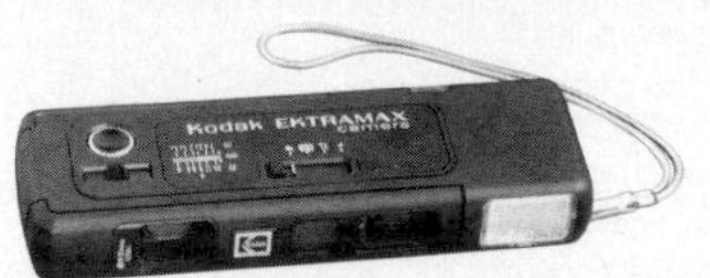

Eastman Kodak Co.

A Fixed-Focus Camera is the easiest camera to use. It takes drop-in film cartridges and focuses automatically on subjects at a certain distance away. It can take satisfactory photographs in ordinary daylight.

Rolleiflex

A Twin-Lens Reflex Camera has a viewing lens directly above the picture-taking lens. A mirror reflects the image from the viewing lens onto a ground-glass screen at the top of the camera. This viewing screen provides an extremely clear and bright view of the subject.

WORLD BOOK photo

A View Camera is the largest and most adjustable type of camera. The lens end and the back end of this camera can be moved forward or backward and tilted at different angles to produce a variety of artistic effects. View cameras are used chiefly by professional photographers.

WORLD BOOK photo

An Instant Camera produces a print almost immediately after a picture is taken. The film used in these cameras contains chemicals that develop and print pictures automatically. Different types of film produce black-and-white prints and color prints. Some provide reusable negatives.

to allow the image to reach the film. Thus, the picture area transmitted to the film corresponds almost exactly with the one seen through the viewfinder.

A miniature camera's compactness and wide range of picture-taking abilities make it the most popular camera among newspaper photographers. Most miniatures can easily photograph a fast-moving or extremely close subject. They also can take fine pictures in lighting too dim for simpler cameras. A 35-millimeter model can take 36 pictures on one roll of film. Many photographers use such a camera to make color slides. A slide requires a projector and a screen for proper viewing.

Subminiature Cameras take pictures smaller than those produced by miniature models. The pictures require considerable enlargement, which can be done with only sharp photographs. Subminiatures use film ranging from about $\frac{3}{8}$ inch to 1 inch (9.5 to 25 millimeters) wide. Many models use 110-size film.

Twin-Lens Reflex Cameras have a viewing lens directly above the picture-taking lens. The image in its viewfinder appears on a flat screen on top of the camera. Photographers find such a viewing screen helpful in composing a picture. Photographers do not hold the viewfinder to the eye, as they do with a fixed-focus, miniature, or subminiature camera. They usually hold the camera at the chest or waist and look down into the viewfinder. The image appears reversed from left to right. In most models, nearby subjects appear lower in the picture area of the viewfinder than in the photograph. Most twin-lens reflex cameras take pictures that measure $2\frac{1}{4}$ by $2\frac{1}{4}$ inches (57 by 57 millimeters).

View Cameras are the largest and most adjustable type of camera. Most have an accordionlike body, with a replaceable lens in front. They have a large *viewing screen* instead of a viewfinder. Most models have an adjustable diaphragm and shutter speed. View cameras must be mounted on a stand for efficient operation.

A photographer focuses a view camera by moving the lens end or the back end of the camera forward or backward to produce a sharp image on the viewing screen. Adjustments in the tilt of the camera give the photographer great control over the image. A view camera can provide artistic distortions of a subject more effectively than any other kind of camera.

Many professional photographers use a view camera for portraits or architectural pictures. Some studio photographers use a large model called a *studio camera.* It may measure up to 6 feet (1.8 meters) long. Its stand may weigh up to 500 pounds (230 kilograms). Studio cameras produce most of the high-quality pictures seen in magazine advertisements. A view camera uses sheets of film that range in size from $2\frac{1}{4}$ by $3\frac{1}{4}$ inches (57 by 83 millimeters) to 11 by 14 inches (279 by 357 millimeters).

Instant Cameras use film that provides a print without first being developed into a negative. The cameras produce a print 15 seconds to 8 minutes after the photographer takes a picture. The time varies according to film type. Instant cameras use film that provides pictures ranging in size from $3\frac{1}{4}$ by $4\frac{1}{4}$ inches (83 by 108 millimeters) to 20 by 24 inches (508 by 610 millimeters). Special types of film for instant cameras also provide negatives.

The convenience of instant cameras makes them widely popular among amateur photographers. Before taking a picture with a studio camera, professionals

Eastman Kodak Co.

A Motion-Picture Camera takes pictures that re-create the movement of subjects when the film is projected on a viewing screen. Most amateur moviemakers use an 8-millimeter motion-picture camera that takes drop-in cartridges of film.

often use instant cameras to quickly see how a subject will look in a photograph. Some instant cameras can take flash pictures and focus automatically as the photographer lines up a subject in the viewfinder.

Motion-Picture Cameras take pictures that re-create the motion of a subject when projected on a viewing screen. Professional moviemakers generally use large cameras that take 35- or 16-millimeter film. Almost all amateurs use smaller, 8-millimeter cameras that take drop-in cartridges of film. Most movie cameras have a motor powered by batteries to wind the film and open and close the shutter. Most of them also have a *zoom lens*, which lets the photographer vary the size of the images.

Stereo Cameras have two identical picture-taking lenses with matched shutters. When a stereo camera takes a picture, each lens photographs the same subject—but from a slightly different angle. When shown on a device called a *stereoscope*, the two images blend in a single picture that seems to have depth. Engineers, scientists, and other specialists use stereo photography to study the depth of a subject.

Special Cameras have been designed for industrial, medical, military, and scientific uses. They include outer-space and underwater cameras. KENNETH POLI

Related Articles in WORLD BOOK include:

Astronomy (Optical Telescopes)	Fairchild, Sherman M.	Motion Picture (The Camera)
Camera Lucida	Flashbulb	Photography
Camera Obscura	Lens	Range Finder
Eastman, George	Light Meter	Television

CAMERA LUCIDA, *LOO suh duh*, is a sketching device that consists of a four-sided prism and a magnifying glass, both attached to a frame. The term means *light chamber*. The device produces a virtual image of the object on the paper where the sketch is made, as in the illustration. Another form uses a right-angled prism with a sheet of glass for a reflector. Artists use it to reduce large drawings to smaller size and to transpose sketches. The reflected image's size is controlled by the distance from the object. See also PRISM. HARRY MUIR KURTZWORTH

CAMERA OBSCURA is a box used for sketching large objects. The term means *dark chamber*. The box contains a mirror set at a 45° angle. A double-convex lens like that in a photographic camera is placed in the front end. The image of the object is transmitted through the lens and appears on the mirror. The mirror then reflects the image upward to a ground-glass screen on the top of the box. There it can be sketched easily. A form of camera obscura that is used today is the *finder*, a camera viewing mirror in which pictures can be composed and focused. HARRY MUIR KURTZWORTH

See also LENS; PHOTOGRAPHY (History).

CAMERON, JULIA MARGARET (1815-1879), a British photographer, pioneered in the field of artistic photography. She was especially noted for dramatic close-up portraits, but her works also include photographs that portray religious scenes or illustrate poems. She photographed many leading British figures of the 1860's and 1870's.

Cameron did not share the widely held belief that a photograph should be a detailed, visually precise representation of a person or scene. Instead, she tried to capture the character and spirit of her subjects. To achieve this effect, she continually experimented with lighting and composition. Cameron valued expressiveness over technical quality in her work, and so many of her photographs were blurred or out of focus. Other photographers criticized these technical flaws, but many artists and critics praised Cameron's works highly. Cameron was born in Calcutta, India, and moved to England in 1848. CHARLES HAGEN

CAMEROON is a country on the western coast of central Africa. It is slightly larger than California, but about as many people live there as in the Los Angeles metropolitan area. More than 100 different ethnic groups live in Cameroon. Most of the people are farm-

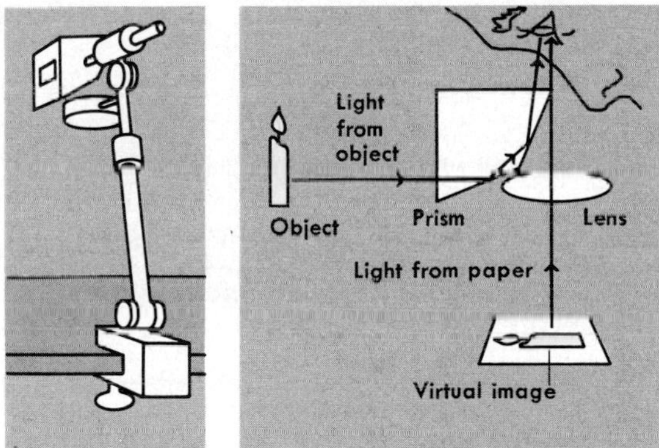

WORLD BOOK diagram

The Camera Lucida Is a Device Used in Sketching.

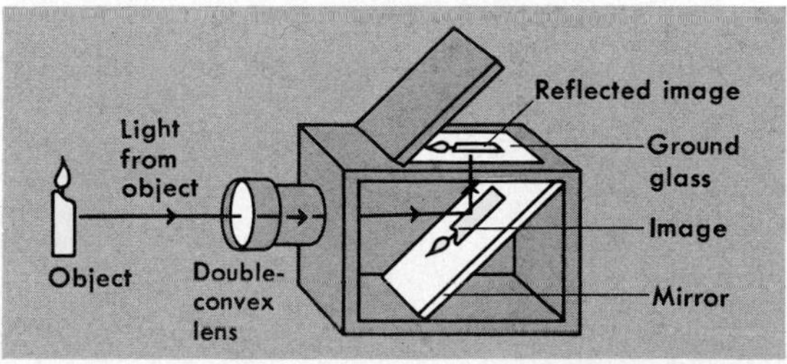

WORLD BOOK diagram

The Camera Obscura was frequently used by artists to reproduce large objects before photographic cameras became common.

Cameroon

National Capital
Other City or Town
Road
Rail Line
River
MOUNTAIN

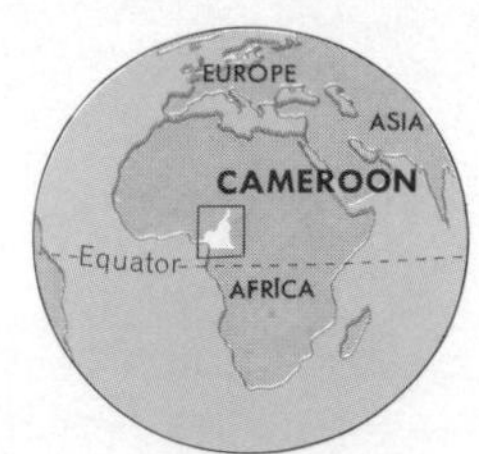

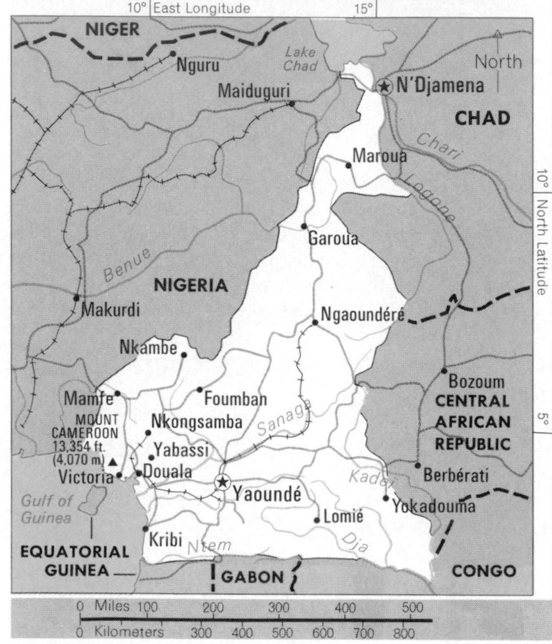

WORLD BOOK map

ers, but their ways of life differ with the regions in which they live. They farm in the south and west, and raise cattle in the north. A marsh-covered plain stretches along the 240-mile (386-kilometer) coast on the Gulf of Guinea. Rain forests cover the plateaus in the south. Fertile grasslands lie in the central region, and hot, dry plains lie in the north. Great Britain and France governed Cameroon from 1919 until 1960, when it became independent. Its official name is United Republic of Cameroon (République Unie du Cameroun in French). Yaoundé (pop. 313,706) is the capital. Douala (pop. 458,426) is the leading port and largest city.

Government. The people of Cameroon elect a president to a five-year term. The president serves as head of the government. A cabinet assists the president. The nation's legislature, the National Assembly, has 120 members elected by the people to five-year terms.

Cameroon is divided into seven provinces. The president appoints provincial governors.

People. Bamiléké, Fulani, and Kirdi ethnic groups live in the northern two-thirds of Cameroon. About half a million Bamiléké live in the western mountains. Bamiléké families live on land assigned by the group's chief. The Bamiléké grow coffee. Their crafts include woodworking, weaving, and embroidery. About half a million Fulani live in northern Cameroon. They live in groups of family huts clustered inside earthen walls for protection from wild animals and thieves. They grow millet and peanuts, and keep horses and cattle. They weave and embroider cloth, and ornament leather and silver. The Fulani are Muslims. See FULANI.

About a million Kirdi people live in Cameroon. Some are nomads in the north. Others live in settlements in the western mountains. They grow cotton, millet, peanuts, and rice, and keep chickens, goats, and sheep. They practice traditional African religions.

More than a million persons live in the southern third of the country. They include the Bassa, the Pahouin, and the Douala peoples. Most of these people grow cassava, cacao, and yams. They live in rectangular dried-mud huts with palm-leaf roofs, or in cement houses with tile roofs. Many are Christians. About 6,500 Pygmies live in small, isolated groups in the forests of southeastern Cameroon.

About 600,000 children attend the more than 3,000 primary schools in Cameroon. Christian missions operate more than half of the schools. About 25,000 students study at secondary schools. The University of Yaoundé, Cameroon's university, was founded in 1962.

Land. Cameroon covers 183,569 square miles (475,442 square kilometers). It has five land regions:

(1) The *coastal plain* borders on the Gulf of Guinea. It is covered with marshes and mangrove forests. Mt. Cameroon, the highest point in western Africa, is on the coastal plain. It is 13,354 feet (4,070 meters) high.

(2) The *southern region* extends from the southern border north to the Sanaga River. It is a region of plateaus covered with dense forests. The plateaus average 2,000 feet (610 meters) above sea level.

(3) The *central Adamaoua plateau* lies between the Sanaga River and the Benue River, and ranges from 2,600 to 5,000 feet (792 to 1,500 meters) above sea level. The region gradually changes from tropical forests near the Sanaga River to *savanna* (grassland) near the Benue.

(4) The *northern savanna*, north of the Benue, has grassy plains. It slopes down to the Lake Chad basin.

(5) Most of the *western mountains* rise in west-central

Facts in Brief

Capital: Yaoundé.

Official Languages: French and English.

Form of Government: Republic. *Head of State*—President (5-year-term).

Area: 183,569 sq. mi. (475,442 km²). *Greatest Distances*—north-south, 770 mi. (1,239 km); east-west, 450 mi. (724 km). *Coastline*—240 mi. (386 km).

Population: *Estimated 1985 Population*—9,548,000; distribution, 58 per cent rural, 42 per cent urban; density, 52 persons per sq. mi. (20 persons per km²). *1976 Census*—7,663,246; *Estimated 1990 Population*—10,803,000.

Chief Products: *Agriculture*—bananas, cassava, cacao, coffee, corn, cotton, livestock, palm oil and kernels, peanuts, sorghum, tea, tobacco. *Forest Products*—lumber, rubber. *Manufacturing*—aluminum. *Mining*—petroleum.

Flag: The flag has green, red, and yellow vertical stripes, with a yellow star in the center of the red stripe. Green stands for the forests of the south, yellow for the savannas of the north, and red for the unity between the two regions. See FLAG (picture: Flags of Africa).

Money: *Basic Unit*—franc. See MONEY (table).

Cameroon. Some are over 8,000 feet (2,400 meters) high.

Some parts of the coastal plain receive as much as 400 inches (1,000 centimeters) of rainfall a year. The southern region gets about half as much rain. Temperatures in Cameroon are hot throughout the year. Temperatures in Yaoundé, in the southern region, range from 63° to 88° F. (17° to 31° C).

Economy. Cameroon's people are poor in terms of money. The average annual income is only about $125.00 per person. However, most farmers raise enough food to feed their families, and the people eat adequately even though they have little cash. The chief export crop is cacao, most of which is raised on about 200,000 small farms. Coffee, the second most important export crop, is grown on small farms and European-owned plantations. Other farm products include bananas, cotton, palm oil and kernels, pepper, and tea.

The government is trying to increase the quantity and the quality of the crops. It has set up agricultural development centers to distribute seeds and plants and to teach farmers better farming methods.

A smelter in Edéa produces aluminum, Cameroon's most important industrial product. Several small industries in the country process agricultural products. Petroleum is Cameroon's most valuable mineral.

Cameroon has over 8,000 miles (13,000 kilometers) of roads, but most of them are dirt. It has about 620 miles (1,000 kilometers) of railroads. Airlines serve Cameroon's main cities. Garoua, a city on the Benue River, is an important inland port during the rainy season.

History. In about the A.D. 900's, the Sao people settled near Lake Chad, in what is now Cameroon. Historians know little else about the Sao except that they produced a distinctive kind of art and cast objects in bronze. The Portuguese arrived in what is now Cameroon in the 1400's.

From the A.D. 1400's to the 1800's many people migrated to what is now Cameroon. The Bamiléké and the Bassa reached Cameroon in the 1400's. The Douala arrived in the 1600's, and the Pahouin reached southern Cameroon in the 1800's. The Fulani settled in northern Cameroon in the early 1800's. Between the 1500's and the 1800's, European slave traders shipped many people from this area to America as slaves. Other Europeans established missions along the coast.

Marc and Evelyne Bernheim, Rapho Guillumette
Yaoundé Shopping District includes a large, three-story open-air clothing store, *background.* Yaoundé is the capital, and a commercial and transportation center of Cameroon.

In 1884, Germany established a *protectorate* (protected country) called *Kamerun* in the area near Douala. German rule was extended to present-day Cameroon by 1914. French and British troops occupied Cameroon during World War I (1914-1918). In 1919, western Cameroon became a British mandate and eastern Cameroon became a French mandate (see MANDATED TERRITORY). In 1946, eastern and western Cameroon became United Nations trust territories (see TRUST TERRITORY). From 1919 to 1960, they were called the Cameroons.

Eastern Cameroon became the Republic of Cameroon in 1960. In 1961, the northern part of western Cameroon joined Nigeria. The southern part united with the east in 1961 to form a federal republic. The republic consisted of two states—East Cameroon and West Cameroon. Ahmadou Ahidjo became the first president of the republic in 1961 and was reelected in 1965, 1970, and 1975. In 1972, Cameroon adopted a new constitution, which abolished the separate states and made the country a unitary republic. During the 1970's, Cameroon began producing petroleum from offshore wells in the Gulf of Guinea. This production has greatly aided the country's economy. KEITH G. MATHER

See also YAOUNDÉ.

CAMÕES, LUIZ DE. See PORTUGAL (The Arts).

CAMOMILE, *KAM uh myl,* is a group of small plants that are sometimes used in folk medicine. The name is often spelled *chamomile.* The most commonly cultivated camomile grows in the eastern and central regions of the United States, where it was brought from Europe. It is called the *common,* or *corn, camomile,* and sometimes the *English,* or *Roman, camomile.* A perennial, it grows about 12 inches (30 centimeters) high and has a slender, trailing stem and many branches. The flowers look much like daisies. The flowers and leaves smell sweet, but taste bitter. They are sometimes applied as a *poultice* (warm, moist mass) to treat toothaches, or made into a tonic. *German camomile* may grow as high as 2 feet (61 centimeters). Its flower heads also are used in folk medicine. The camomile is related to the *mayweed,* a common plant in the Western states.

USDA
The Camomile Plant

Scientific Classification. Camomiles belong to the family Compositae. The common camomile is *Anthemis nobilis.* German camomile is *Matricaria chamomilla.* MARGARET R. BOLICK

CAMORRA, *kuh MAWR uh,* was a secret society of criminals, formed in Naples, Italy, in the early 1800's. Members of the society, called *Camorristas,* divided their time between political activities and deeds of violence for about 100 years. The Camorristas worked openly before 1860, and committed crimes of any sort for payment. The Camorra controlled elections in Naples until 1901. In 1912, the government finally destroyed the power of the Camorra and sentenced many of its members to prison. BENJAMIN WEBB WHEELER

CAMOUFLAGE, *KAM uh flahzh,* is the art of disguising or hiding military equipment and troops from an enemy. People borrowed the idea of camouflage from nature. Many animals have the means of blending into their natural background for protection. The fur of some small animals of northern countries turns white in winter, to blend with the snow. Their fur is brown in summer, to enable them to hide in woods or brush.

Camouflage has always been used in war, but it first became a recognized technique in World War I, when the use of the airplane greatly expanded the possibility of observation by the enemy. During World War II camouflage was applied to nearly every military activity. Camouflage ranged from using white uniforms in Arctic regions and mottled green uniforms in the jungle to concealing cities by smoke screens.

In modern war the purpose of most camouflage is to conceal military forces and equipment from air observation. Roofs of earth and branches are placed over gun emplacements so that enemy pilots cannot locate the guns. Troop movements are concealed by parking trucks and pitching tents in the shadows of trees instead of in the open. The runway of an airfield may be painted so that from the air it looks as if it were an area of fields and roads. The sides and roof of a building may be painted so that a road appears to run across it. War plants have been camouflaged to look like golf courses from the air. People employed to play golf on the roofs make the deception even more realistic. Fleets of ships have been hidden from the enemy by stretching camouflaged nets over a harbor.

Warships of World War I were painted with zigzag lines of many colors to hide them from submarines and enemy ships. This arrangement of colors was called "dazzle paint." World War II ships were painted in softer tones in irregular patterns that blended with sky and sea and made the ships even more difficult to detect.

Most camouflage can be detected by aerial photography. Until recently, an object painted green to blend with a forest showed up when it was photographed with infrared film. Military intelligence officers have learned to detect many kinds of camouflage from such photographs. In 1957, the U.S. Navy developed a paint effective against infrared film. JOHN D. BILLINGSLEY

See also ANIMAL (Ways of Life; picture: Animal Camouflage); BIRD (Protection Against Enemies; Feathers); PROTECTIVE COLORATION; OCTOPUS.

U.S. Army

Camouflage Protects a Soldier practicing war maneuvers in Alaska. His white coveralls blend with the snow-covered terrain.

CAMP. See CAMPING (The Campsite).

CAMP, WALTER CHAUNCEY (1859-1925), was often called the *father of American football.* In 1889, he and sportswriter Caspar Whitney originated all-America football team selections. Camp also suggested many major changes in rules and patterns of play. His books on football and other sports made a valuable contribution to good sportsmanship. They include *American Football* (1891) and *Walter Camp's Book of College Sports* (1893). In 1921 he published the *Daily Dozen,* a series of simple physical exercises.

Camp was born in New Britain, Conn., and graduated from Yale University. He coached football, and later became athletic director at Yale. During World War I, he was chairman of the athletic department of the U.S. Commission on Training Camp Activities, for the physical care of naval personnel. LYALL SMITH

CAMP DAVID is the official retreat of the President of the United States. It lies in a heavily wooded area of Catoctin Mountain in Maryland, about 70 miles (113 kilometers) from Washington, D.C.

Camp David has an office for the President, and living quarters for the first family, staff, and guests. The camp includes a pitch-and-putt golf green, a swimming pool, and facilities for other sports.

Camp David is administered by the Military Office of the White House and is operated by the U.S. Navy. Armed guards from the U.S. Marine Corps patrol the area and permit no unauthorized person to enter.

President Franklin D. Roosevelt established the camp in 1942, as a retreat where he could escape the summer heat of Washington. He chose the site because its elevation made it cool in summer and the isolated high location provided adequate security.

Roosevelt called the camp *Shangri-La,* the name of a perfect mountain kingdom in *Lost Horizon,* a famous novel by the English author James Hilton. In 1945, President Harry S. Truman made Shangri-La the official presidential retreat. President Dwight D. Eisenhower renamed the camp in 1953 for his grandson, David Eisenhower. He also added the golf green.

Presidents have conducted their regular business at the retreat, and several have held important conferences there. In 1943, during World War II, Roosevelt met at the camp with Prime Minister Winston Churchill of Great Britain. Eisenhower conferred at Camp David with Premier Nikita S. Khrushchev of the Soviet Union in 1959. In 1978, President Jimmy Carter used the camp to host peace talks between President Anwar el-Sadat of Egypt and Prime Minister Menachem Begin of Israel. The talks resulted in a major agreement, called the Camp David Accords. For details, see MIDDLE EAST (The Middle East Today). Critically reviewed by the MILITARY OFFICE OF THE WHITE HOUSE

CAMP FIRE is an organization in the United States for young people. It is based on the belief that every individual in the organization has a special personality and special skills to share with others. The national organization is officially called Camp Fire, Incorporated. The organization has groups in cities, suburbs, and rural areas throughout the United States.

The Camp Fire Purpose is to provide opportunities for young people to realize their potential and to develop as responsible individuals. The organization also works to improve the conditions in society that affect young people.

Camp Fire's traditional programs are designed primarily for girls and boys from first grade through high school. However, local councils have a great deal of flexibility in developing programs to meet the needs of their communities. The flexibility of the local Camp Fire councils creates a wide variety of programs that are available to girls and boys of all ages—from birth to 21 years old.

The Camp Fire Law provides a guide to help the organization's members get the most enjoyment out of life. It states: "Worship God. Seek Beauty. Give Service. Pursue Knowledge. Be Trustworthy. Hold on to Health. Glorify Work. Be Happy."

Camp Fire members are taught that enjoyment of life grows out of work, health, and love. The first two letters of these words make up the Camp Fire watchword, *Wohelo*. Camp Fire members follow their slogan, "Give Service," by helping in their homes, schools, and communities. They believe that service develops naturally from love for other people. The Camp Fire symbol is a flame. It stands for the warmth of home and the wonder of the outdoors.

Camp Fire, Inc.

Camp Fire Emblem

More than a half million young people are involved in Camp Fire. The organization has more than 320 local councils in about 30,000 communities throughout the United States. Adult members include paid and volunteer staff, and club and program leaders.

What Camp Fire Members Do

Camp Fire focuses on individual development. It teaches skills in such areas as citizenship, creative arts, interpersonal relations, and leadership. These activities take place in a small group guided by a trained adult leader. Such groups provide an environment in which young people can grow into responsible adulthood.

Camp Fire, Inc.

Camp Fire Costumes differ by club level. This picture shows, *left to right,* two Blue Bird costumes for girls and three Adventurer costumes. The outfits in the center and at the far right are worn by both boys and girls. Each Discovery and Horizon club chooses its own costume.

Camp Fire, Inc.

Blue Birds enjoy camping and other outdoor activities. Boys and girls learn cooperation and build friendships by working together on such tasks as washing the group's camp dishes, *above.*

Camp Fire, Inc.

Adventurers take part in many creative activities. The Adventurers shown above are pressing designs into damp sheets of paper they made from a pulpy mixture.

The organization also provides a variety of other programs. These include day-care centers, career development seminars, and special programs for the handicapped, the mentally retarded, youthful offenders and parolees, and others.

Camp Fire's major youth programs are carried out at four levels: (1) Blue Birds, (2) Adventurers, (3) Discovery Clubs, and (4) Horizon Clubs.

Blue Birds help young people 6 through 8 years old have fun as they learn about the world. Blue Bird leaders encourage members to find their own answers to their questions. For example, a child in the Blue Birds might learn how a plant grows by planting a seed and watching it sprout.

Blue Bird groups play games, tell stories, and make such things as puppets and pictures. They go on picnics and visit factories, museums, parks, zoos, and other places near their homes.

Blue Birds try to follow the Blue Bird Wish: "To have fun; to learn to make beautiful things; to remember to finish what I begin; to want to keep my temper most of the time; to go to interesting places; to know about trees, flowers, and birds; to make friends." The Blue Bird costume for girls consists of a red and blue jumper, white blouse, and blue cap. An alternate Blue Bird costume for girls consists of red pants, white body shirt, and blue cap. Girls and boys also wear denim outfits.

Adventurers are 9 through 11 years old. They learn and have fun through activities in the general areas of business, citizenship, creative arts, games and sports, home, outdoors, and science. Activities include making candles, baking cookies, ice skating, and swimming. Members work alone or in groups and may plan their own new activities.

Adventurers earn an honor bead each time they learn a special skill. They may decorate a ceremonial vest with beads of different sizes and shapes to show what they have achieved. This vest may be worn on ceremonial occasions. The Adventurer costume consists of blue pants, white shirt or blouse, and a blue beret. Boys and girls also wear denim outfits. An alternate costume for girls is a blue skirt, white blouse with a red tie, and a blue beret.

Discovery Clubs encourage 12- and 13-year-olds to learn about their own feelings and ideas. Members try to fulfill the Discovery Club Desire: "I shall strive to discover myself at the fire of adventure and friendship, remembering that what I possess grows in value as I share it with others." Discovery Club members take part in a wide variety of activities, including camping, sports, cooking, and music and the arts. They also do various kinds of volunteer work in the community. Discovery Club members in each council decide on their own costumes.

Horizon Clubs help high school students recognize their desires, abilities, and limitations. Club programs stress that members must begin to make such adult decisions as whether they want a career and how they can change things that they do not like about the world. Members pledge: "As horizons are ever changing and always distant, I shall not stand still and look into their purple shadows. Instead, I shall seek the higher purposes and the new adventures that lie beyond. I shall reach ever outward to the horizon that is always just beyond my grasp."

Members of Horizon Clubs do volunteer work at hospitals, help with community conservation projects, tutor children, and give service in many other ways. They also conduct conferences for youths and adults on social and personal problems. Members continue to learn skills in camping, handicrafts, music, sports, and

Camp Fire, Inc.

Members of Discovery Clubs organize many backpacking and camping trips. They also do volunteer community work.

other areas. The Horizon Club costume is chosen by the members themselves in each council.

Organization

A board of directors manages Camp Fire, Inc. The board establishes national policies, charters local councils, and sets up the requirements and standards that govern the councils.

Camp Fire is divided into zones. The local councils elect delegates in proportion to their membership to represent them at zone meetings. These meetings take place in even-numbered years. A national congress is held in odd-numbered years to discuss and act on matters of national policy.

The local councils supervise the Camp Fire programs in their area. Adult volunteers form the local councils and elect council officers. Professional staff members work with the volunteers and provide services. The charter issued by the national organization allows the local council to organize Camp Fire groups and train leaders. The council also establishes membership dues. In addition, it may develop programs to meet special community needs. However, the local councils must adhere to the Camp Fire Purpose and follow the policies of Camp Fire, Inc.

Adult volunteers from the community serve as club leaders. Most leaders are parents, but some are college students. Qualified high school students—who are members of a special training program—may lead Blue Bird, Adventurer, and Discovery Club groups. Parents, teachers, neighbors, or civic organizations may sponsor a group. The sponsors help the group leaders with special projects and activities and make sure the groups have a place to meet. Meeting places include churches, synagogues, schools, and civic buildings.

Money-raising projects of the councils, contributions from individuals, and funds from the United Way and various foundations help Camp Fire in its work. The organization also receives money from the sale of supplies and publications. Publications include a catalog and *Camp Fire Leadership*, a magazine for adult leaders.

The corporate headquarters and field service division of Camp Fire, Inc., are at 4601 Madison Avenue, Kansas City, Mo. 64112. The field service division provides consultation services to the councils.

History

Originally, membership in Camp Fire groups was open only to girls. Luther Halsey Gulick, a physician and national leader in recreational programs for young people, and his wife, Charlotte Vetter Gulick, founded the organization as the Camp Fire Girls in 1910. For more than 20 years, the Gulicks had operated a family camp in Connecticut. Then, in 1909, they opened one of the first girls' camps in the United States, Camp Sebago-Wohelo, on the shores of Lake Sebago in Maine. There, girls took part in swimming, canoeing, and many other activities that later became part of the Camp Fire program.

In 1910, Gulick had also helped found the Boy Scouts of America. He received many letters asking for a similar organization for girls. As a result, the Gulicks and a group of people known for their work in education and recreation organized Camp Fire groups throughout the country. Camp Fire Girls pioneered in many fields, including child development, group camping for girls, outdoor programs, and social action. In 1975, Camp Fire began admitting boys at all club levels. In 1979, the organization changed its official name from Camp Fire Girls, Inc., to Camp Fire, Inc.

Critically reviewed by CAMP FIRE, INCORPORATED

See also GULICK, LUTHER HALSEY.

CAMP H. M. SMITH, Hawaii, serves as headquarters of the United States Pacific Command. This unified command controls American military forces from the Arctic Ocean to the South Pole, and from the west coast of the United States to the Indian Ocean. The camp covers about 500 acres (200 hectares), and lies on Aiea Heights, 12 miles (19 kilometers) northwest of Honolulu's chief urban area. It was established in 1942 as a naval hospital and depot, and named in 1955 for General Holland M. Smith. RICHARD M. SKINNER

CAMP LEJEUNE, N.C., serves as home base and training center for a combat division and force troops of the United States Fleet Marine Forces, Atlantic. It covers 83,000 acres (33,600 hectares), extending 1 mile (1.6 kilometers) from the center of Jacksonville to the Atlantic Ocean. The marines conduct amphibious training along an 11-mile (18-kilometer) ocean front. In the summer, 10,000 reservists take part in the training program. Major commands at the camp include a Marine Corps base and the largest naval hospital in the South. The 2,670-acre (1,081-hectare) Marine Corps Air Facility there is controlled by the Marine Corps Air Station at nearby Cherry Point (see CHERRY POINT MARINE CORPS AIR STATION). The marines established the camp in 1941, and named it for Lieutenant General John A. Lejeune, who served as Marine Corps commandant from 1920 to 1929. JOHN A. OUDINE

CAMP MEETING was an outdoor religious gathering held in the United States, chiefly in the 1800's. Meetings lasted several days and featured daily open-air services. Camp meetings were intended to revive the spirit of religion, but not take the place of regular church functions. Methodists held most of the meetings. The participants lived in tents or temporary houses in groves. The first camp meeting is said to have taken place in Logan County, Kentucky, in 1800.

See also PIONEER LIFE IN AMERICA (Religion); REVIVALISM.

CAMP PENDLETON, Calif., houses a combat division and other units of the United States Marine Corps. It covers 125,000 acres (50,590 hectares), and lies 30 miles (48 kilometers) north of San Diego. It was once the site of a Spanish ranch and mission. The marines established the camp in 1942, and named it for Major General Joseph H. Pendleton of California. It was the world's largest marine installation until 1957, when the Marine Corps commissioned the 596,638-acre (241,451-hectare) Twentynine Palms Marine Corps Base in the California desert. JOHN A. OUDINE

CAMP ROBBER. See JAY.

CAMPAGNA DI ROMA, *kahm PAH nyah dee ROH mah,* is a large plain in central Italy that surrounds Rome. It covers about 800 square miles (2,100 square kilometers), and extends from the Tyrrhenian Sea to the Sabine and Alban mountains. The Campagna di Roma was highly cultivated in ancient Roman times, but for centuries after was a desolate, malaria-infested region. Reclamation work since the 1800's has restored much farmland.

CAMPAIGN. See ELECTION CAMPAIGN.

CAMPANILE, *KAM puh NEE lee,* is a bell tower. The earliest bell towers belonged to the churches of Italy. Campaniles were built to hold the bells that summoned worshipers to church services. Unlike steeples, they often stand free from the church itself. A passageway of arcades sometimes connects church and campanile. The word *campanile* comes from an Italian word meaning *bell.*

The oldest campaniles were built at Ravenna and Classe in the A.D. 500's. They are round, but later ones are usually square. A famous exception is the Leaning Tower of Pisa, begun in the 1100's (see LEANING TOWER OF PISA). The best known of later campaniles are those of the Cathedral of Florence and of Saint Mark's Cathedral in Venice. Giotto designed the campanile at Florence in the early 1300's. Saint Mark's campanile, begun about 900, was 322 feet (98 meters) high. It collapsed in 1902, but was rebuilt a few years later.

Only a few campaniles were constructed between the 1400's and the 1800's. The campanile of Westminster Cathedral in London was built in 1897. After 1920, many campaniles of various designs were constructed for churches. ALAN GOWANS

See also VENICE (picture: Venice).

CAMPANULA, *kam PAN yuh luh,* or *little bell,* is a group of slender plants that grow wild in Europe, Asia, and North America. There are about 300 species, and many are cultivated as garden plants. The flowers are white, blue, or purple.

Scientific Classification. Campanulas are members of the bellflower family, Campanulaceae. They make up the genus *Campanula.* ROBERT W. HOSHAW

See also BELLFLOWER; BLUEBELL; CANTERBURY BELL.

J. Horace McFarland

The Bluebell of Scotland is a species of campanula.

CAMPBELL, ALEXANDER AND THOMAS. See DISCIPLES OF CHRIST; CHURCHES OF CHRIST.

CAMPBELL, DONALD (1921-1967), became the first speedboat racer to drive faster than 200 mph (320 kph) and live to tell about it. Campbell was born in Povey Cross, Surrey, England. His father, Sir Malcolm Campbell, held the water speed record of 141 mph (227 kph) when he died in 1948. When Stanley Sayres of Seattle set a new mark at 178.497 mph (287.263 kph) in 1952, Donald decided to return the record to the Campbell family. He broke the 200-mph (320-kph) speed barrier in 1955, with a mark of 202.32 mph (325.602 kph). Campbell drove a speedboat at a record of 276.34 mph (444.726 kph) in 1964. Campbell died in a speedboat accident. RICHARD G. HACKENBERG

CAMPBELL, SIR JOHN (1779-1861), an English lawyer, politician, and writer, played an important part in reforming English law. He served as lord chancellor,

Alinari from SCALA

A Famous Campanile (Bell Tower), *far right,* stands next to the Cathedral of Florence, Italy. The Italian artist Giotto designed the tower in 1334, and it was completed in 1359.

Great Britain's highest judicial officer, from 1859 to 1861. His writings include *Lives of the Lord Chancellors* (1845-1847) and *Lives of the Chief Justices* (1849-1857). These biographies provide valuable information about the English judiciary. He was born near Cupar, Scotland. DANIEL J. DYKSTRA

CAMPBELL, MRS. PATRICK (1865-1940), was a strikingly beautiful and sensitive British actress. She became best known for her performances in *Magda, The Second Mrs. Tanqueray,* and *Pygmalion.* George Bernard Shaw wrote the part of Eliza Doolittle in *Pygmalion* especially for her. Mrs. Campbell was born Beatrice Tanner in London. She made her first stage appearance with an amateur dramatic society. During her stage career, Mrs. Campbell made seven successful tours of the United States. RICHARD MOODY

CAMPBELL, ROBERT. See YUKON TERRITORY (History).

CAMPBELL, ROBERT. See ROB ROY.

CAMPBELL, WILLIAM WALLACE (1862-1938), an American astronomer, served as director of the Lick Observatory in California from 1900 to 1923. During the Australian eclipse of 1922, he observed the deflection of starlight by the sun's gravitational field. This observation, first made by Arthur Eddington, gave support to Albert Einstein's theory of relativity. Campbell was born in Hancock County, Ohio. He joined the staff of the Lick Observatory in 1891, and pioneered in the measurement of the motions of stars. HELEN WRIGHT

CAMPBELL-BANNERMAN, SIR HENRY (1836-1908), served as prime minister of Great Britain from 1905 to 1908. His conciliatory attitude toward the Boers during and after the Boer War of 1899 to 1902 helped prepare for the formation of the Union of South Africa in 1910. Born in Glasgow, Scotland, he graduated from Trinity College, Cambridge. A Liberal, he served in Parliament for nearly 40 years. ALFRED F. HAVIGHURST

CAMPECHE, *kahm PAY chay,* is a Mexican state in the Yucatán Peninsula with an area of 19,619 square miles (50,812 square kilometers). The chief industry is lumbering. Most of the 372,277 people live in towns. About a third are Indians, descendants of the Maya (see MAYA). The capital of the state is Campeche (pop. 99,000). For location, see MEXICO (political map).

CAMPHOR, *KAM fuhr* (chemical formula, $C_{10}H_{16}O$), is a substance that comes from the camphor tree. Camphor is almost transparent. The trees grow tall and have white flowers and green leaves. Most grow in Japan and China, and on the island of Taiwan. There are a few camphor trees in southern California and the Southern States.

Camphor is taken from branches of the camphor tree by steaming them until they give off drops of camphor as if they were perspiring. The camphor is drained and pressed to remove the oil and water it contains. Camphor then is left in the form of whitish crystals. These crystals are purified into liquid form.

Albert N. Steward, Oregon State College

Camphor Branch

Camphor is used in cosmetics, lacquers, and pharmaceuticals. *Spirits of camphor*—a mixture of 10 parts camphor, 70 parts alcohol, and 20 parts water—is a mild antiseptic. Camphor is also combined with another compound to make *camphorated parachlorophenol.* This germ-killing drug is sometimes used in dental work. Chemists use camphor to *denature* ethyl alcohol, the type of alcohol used in alcoholic beverages. Denatured alcohol is ethyl alcohol that has been made unfit for drinking but is still useful for other purposes. Large doses of camphor are poisonous, and will cause delirium and convulsions.

Scientific Classification. The camphor tree is a member of the laurel family, *Lauraceae.* It is genus *Cinnamomum,* species *C. camphora.* AUSTIN SMITH

Center panel of an altarpiece (about 1425); the Metropolitan Museum of Art, New York City, the Cloisters Collection

Campin's *Annunciation* shows the angel Gabriel telling the Virgin Mary that she will be the mother of Jesus. Campin's realism and attention to detail greatly influenced painters of the 1400's.

CAMPIN, *KAHM pihn,* **ROBERT** (1375?-1444), was one of the most important painters of the early Renaissance in northern Europe. He introduced a new sense of realism into painting and influenced such Flemish masters as Jan van Eyck and Rogier Van der Weyden.

Except for a few portraits, all Campin's surviving paintings have religious subjects. In all his works, Campin broke away from the abstract, decorative style of earlier Flemish painters and tried to portray everyday reality. Campin's figures have a sculptural solidity. He defined details and textures sharply, and his treatment of space reflected a new emphasis on depth.

Scholars know little about Campin's life except that he worked in Tournai, Belgium. He taught several students there and served as a city councilman and dean of the painters' guild. Until the 1900's, some scholars credited Campin with four paintings that they mistakenly believed had hung in an abbey in Flémalle, Belgium, near Liège. As a result, Campin became known as the Master of Flémalle. ROBERT F. REIFF

See also JOSEPH (picture).

Porterfield-Chickering, Photo Researchers

A Family Camping Vacation can provide an opportunity for water sports and other outdoor recreational activities. But many people go camping simply to relax and enjoy the beauties of nature. National parks, such as Acadia National Park in Maine, *above*, are popular camping sites.

CAMPING

CAMPING is a popular form of outdoor recreation. Various types of camping provide opportunities throughout the year for people to share low-cost outdoor experiences in a natural environment. Camping trips can take many forms. They can range from spending the night in a tent in one's backyard to passing several weeks in the wilderness. Campers may visit forests, deserts, lakes, or mountains.

Some campers remain at one campsite for their entire trip. From this site they visit tourist attractions, participate in water sports, or just relax. They may also spend time in such popular outdoor activities as bird watching, fishing, rock collecting, photography, and hiking.

Many campers prefer to move from place to place each day in motor vehicles. They usually start early in the morning and select a new campsite by early afternoon. Such campers often tour state or provincial parks, national parks, national monuments, and historic sites.

A number of campers prefer to "travel light," carrying all their equipment in backpacks, in canoes, or on bicycles. Usually these campers travel fewer miles than other campers, but enjoy a closer relationship with areas they visit. Most of their activities consist of getting from place to place, enjoying the area, and preparing meals.

Types of Camping

Tent Camping is the most popular type of camping and also one of the least expensive. Tents come in many sizes, shapes, and colors. Some tents can hold only one person while several people can live comfortably in a large tent. Modern tents are made of lightweight materials and are easy to erect, even by beginning campers. The light weight of many modern tents allows campers to carry them almost anywhere.

Recreational Vehicle Camping. A recreational vehicle (RV) is a motor vehicle that provides living quarters for campers. RV's range from small, collapsible trailers to large motor homes with most of the conveniences of permanent homes. For example, many recreational vehicles provide refrigerators and stoves for easy food preparation, showers, and restroom facilities. Most RV's also contain storage tanks for wastewater and sewage.

Numerous North American campgrounds provide electricity and water hookups to serve RV's. Many campers use their RV as a base camp while they explore the countryside by foot, bicycle, motorcycle, or automobile. They return to the RV for meals and to sleep.

Planning a Camping Trip

Campers should plan trips far enough in advance to research campgrounds and make reservations if necessary. Bookstores and sporting goods stores sell guides that list campgrounds, and reference sources in libraries contain information about places to camp. State and provincial tourism bureaus and local chambers of commerce provide maps and other camping information. Local park and recreation agencies usually have information about nearby campgrounds.

At campgrounds that operate on a first-come, first-served basis, it's best to arrive early in the day. But many campgrounds require reservations, especially during the vacation season. Most campgrounds charge a small fee

William Ruskin, the contributor of this article, is the Superintendent of Planning, Design, and Development at the Colorado Springs Park and Recreation Department.

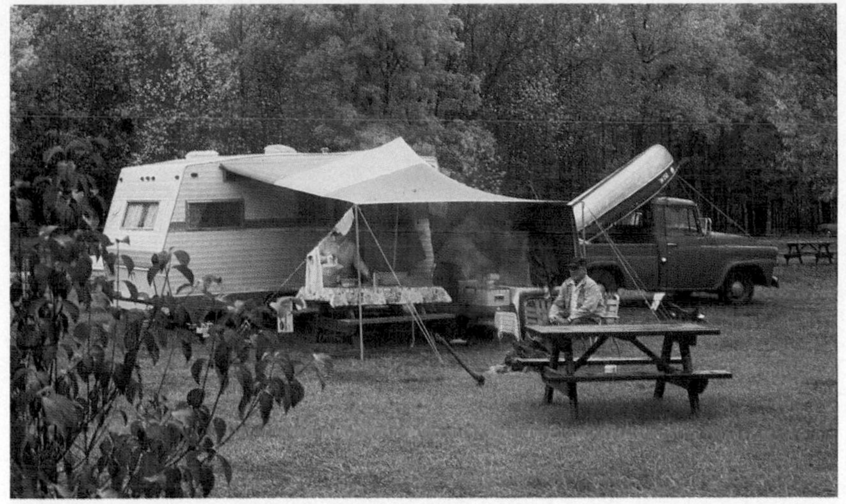

Artstreet

Recreational Vehicles provide many of the conveniences of home during a camping trip. A large number of campgrounds supply hookups for electricity and water for such vehicles. Campers can take all-day outings and return to the recreational vehicle at night to sleep.

for the use of the site. There are additional charges for sites with extra facilities such as electrical hookups and showers. Permits are required to camp in remote parts of national parks or wilderness areas. Campers can obtain permits from the area's ranger.

The information in the following sections refers to tent camping, but it generally applies to most other types of camping.

Camping Equipment and Food

There is a broad range of equipment available, but people need not take a large amount of gear to have an enjoyable camping trip. Beginners often make the mistake of taking more equipment than they need. New campers should start out with a few essential items of high quality. They will learn from experience which additional items would be useful.

Tents today are usually made of canvas, nylon, or cotton. These fabrics supply strength, fireproofing, waterproofing, and adequate ventilation. Modern tents come in different styles designed to serve specific purposes. For example, backpackers need a small and lightweight single-person tent. Such tents may weigh as little as 2.5 pounds (1.1 kilograms). For family camping, tents must be roomy enough to provide comfortable shelter for a group. Some large tents include dining areas and have storage pockets in the walls. This kind of tent is heavier and more difficult to set up.

Before buying a tent, ask for a demonstration to make sure it is easy to erect. Also make sure the tent is well-constructed, and that all the parts are included.

Sleeping Bags are warmer and easier to carry than blankets. A sleeping bag provides efficient insulation to keep campers warm. Goose or duck *down* (soft feathers) is an effective, lightweight insulating material that compresses easily. Several synthetic fabrics insulate nearly as well as down. They also cost less and last longer. In addition, synthetic insulation is easier to clean, and it dries faster than down. The insulation is enclosed in outside coverings made of strong, lightweight fabrics.

Sleeping bags come in three shapes: (1) mummy, which hugs the body and becomes narrow at the bottom, (2) tapered, which is similar to the mummy shape but wider, and (3) rectangular. *Mummy bags* furnish the most warmth, but they limit movement. This lightweight type, often insulated with down, is probably best

Richard Rowan, Photo Researchers

Backpackers carry all of their equipment as they hike from site to site. Backpacking allows people to enjoy wilderness areas that cannot be reached by vehicle.

for backpacking. Mummy bags are also popular for winter camping, and camping at high elevations. *Tapered bags* are designed mainly for the same uses as mummy bags. Tapered bags usually do not provide enough heat for extremely cold temperatures, but they allow more movement. *Rectangular bags* do not insulate as effectively as the other two, but they are the most comfortable. A rectangular bag with synthetic insulation is probably the best choice for the average camper.

Regardless of the style or quality of a sleeping bag, a camper needs additional insulation between the bag and the ground. A *tarpaulin* (piece of canvas or plastic) serves this purpose. Campers also use it as wrap for gear, a windbreak, or a shelter. A foam pad or inflatable air mattress can provide insulation and comfort.

Clothing for camping trips should protect against wind, rain, sun, cold, and insects. The clothing must be sturdy enough to withstand hard wear and weather extremes. The amount needed depends on the length of the trip and whether the clothing will be laundered.

For warm weather, pack at least two pairs of lightweight trousers, as well as comfortable shorts, shirts, and a hat with a wide brim. A warm shirt or jacket should be included for cool evenings, and on visits to high elevations. For colder weather, bring wool shirts and trousers. Wet blue jeans take a long time to dry and do not provide insulation when wet, so avoid wearing them in snowy or rainy weather. A down vest and windproof outer parka provide protection against cold wind without restricting movement. Always carry a hooded, cloak-type raincoat called a *poncho*.

Hiking boots are recommended for hikes in rough terrain. Lightweight nylon boots have generally replaced heavy leather boots in popularity. Any hiking boot should be worn with two pairs of socks—a thin cotton pair under a heavier pair of wool or a wool and cotton blend. Comfortable sports shoes can be worn for relaxing around the campsite. Bring lightweight work gloves for such activities as cooking and chopping wood.

Food and Water. Campers can prepare a great variety of food with the help of portable stoves and ovens and insulated coolers. Each person should bring a complete mess kit, which includes eating utensils. Many campers bring freeze-dried foods, which are prepared with boiling water, for fast cooking. Some plan meals in advance and organize the food in labeled plastic bags.

It is important to select nutritional foods from the basic food groups—dairy products, bread and cereals, meat, and fruit and vegetables. Some good foods for camping include peanut butter, cheese, pancakes, bacon, nuts, and popcorn. Buy canned and freeze-dried foods before the trip. When possible, buy fresh and frozen foods during the trip.

If you are not sure the water will be safe to drink, bring water from home. Additional water should come from an approved source, such as a campground well. Lakes and streams may look, smell, and taste clean, but still be contaminated with disease-causing microscopic organisms. If water must be taken from a questionable source, boil the water for at least five minutes before using it. Carry fresh water in canteens or water bottles.

Other Camp Supplies are necessary for most camping trips. They include a small ax for splitting firewood and such basic tools as a hammer, screwdriver, pliers, flashlight, spade, hunting knife, rope, paper towels, matches in a waterproof container, and extra batteries. In addition, at least one camper in the group should carry a complete first-aid kit. Maps are also important, especially for the first visit to an area. Carry a compass at all times, no matter how familiar the area. A large backpack is necessary for overnight hikes away from the base camp. For shorter hikes, use a smaller pack to carry such items as food, maps, and a camera. Duffel bags can also hold clothing and other equipment.

Keith Gunnar, West Stock

Putting Out a Campfire is an important part of camping safety. The camper should extinguish the coals with water and spread them out with a shovel to make sure there are no burning embers.

The Campsite

Selecting a Location. Many campgrounds rent reserved campsites. Such campsites normally include a picnic table, charcoal grill or fireplace, and a suitable place for a tent. Some campgrounds have special tenting areas with rest rooms and a convenient water supply.

Other locations, such as wilderness areas and forest preserves, do not have reserved campsites. Campers should follow a number of rules in selecting their own sites. Look for a site on high, level ground that is uncluttered and sheltered from the wind. The campsite should be at least 200 feet (50 meters) from hiking trails, scenic attractions, and water. This helps preserve the beauty of the area and the purity of the water. In addition, land next to water is usually low, damp, and a breeding place for insects. The tent should be pitched in sandy soil that is firm enough to hold the stakes securely but still provide good drainage. Always try to avoid disturbing or damaging plant life. Local rangers can usually suggest locations to set up camp.

Building a Campfire. Natural wood supplies are being rapidly used up in many areas, so some campgrounds sell firewood, and some campers bring wood with them. Regulations in some areas prohibit open fires, and other areas require permits to build them.

Camping Equipment

Campers should select suitable food, clothing, shelter, and other equipment for a safe and comfortable camping trip. The equipment should be both durable and easy to carry. Factors that guide campers in the selection of equipment include the duration of the trip, the season, and the surface features of the land in the camping area.

WORLD BOOK illustrations by David Cunningham

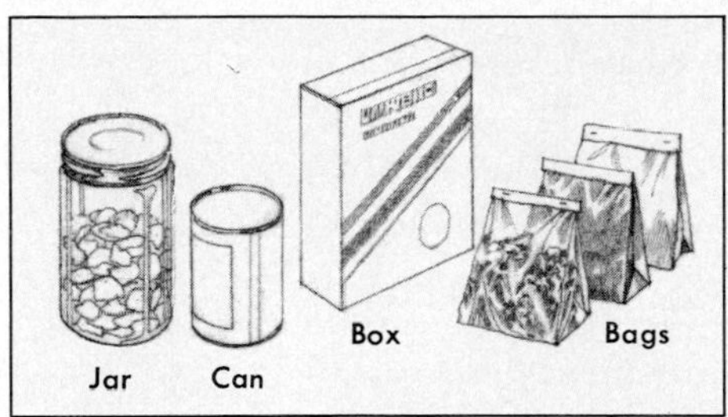

Food should be kept in sanitary containers. Campers can carry lightweight bags and boxes on hikes. Heavier jars and cans should be stored at the campsite.

Clothing should provide protection against insects, bad weather, and the sun. Clothes must also be able to withstand rough use. Campers should carry an extra change of clothing in case the clothes they are wearing become wet.

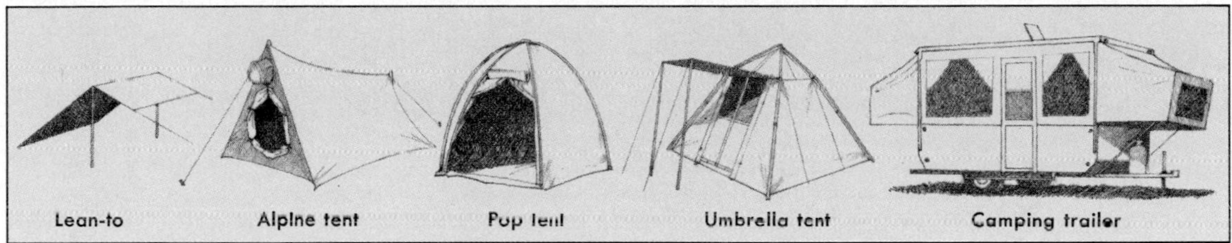

Shelters come in many sizes and styles. The lean-to and the alpine and pop tents can be folded and carried in a pack. The umbrella tent can be collapsed and stored in a car trunk. The camping trailer, which offers many of the conveniences found in a home, must be pulled to a campsite by car or truck.

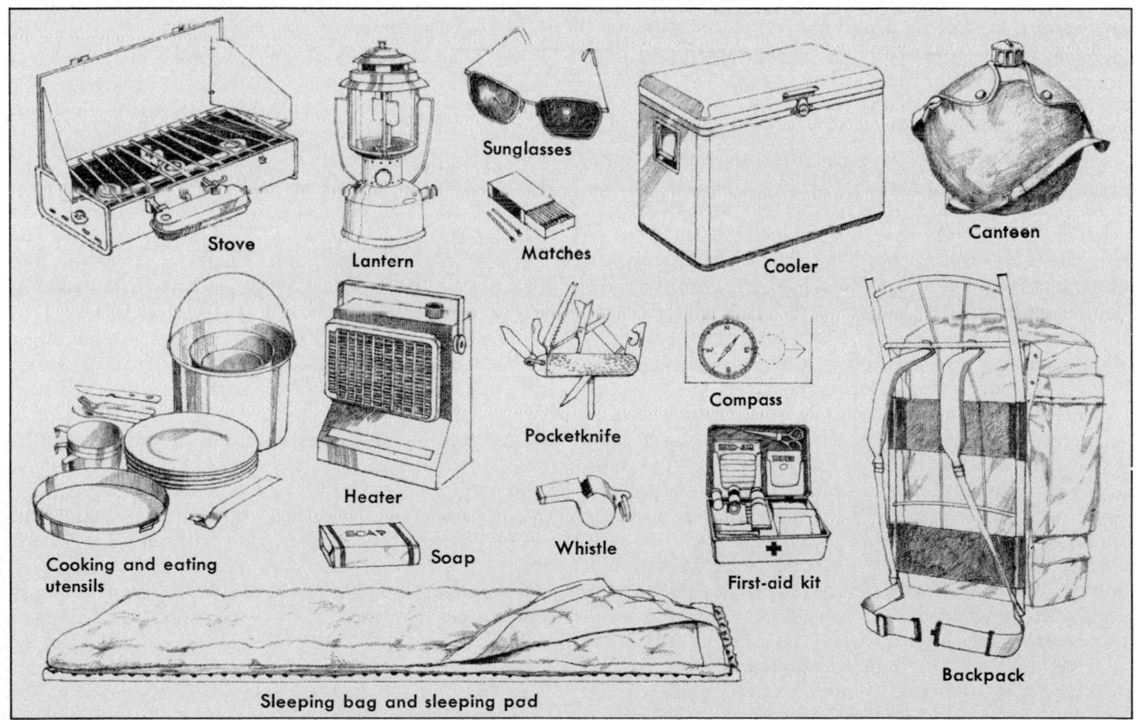

Other Equipment. Heaters, stoves, and lanterns are available in small sizes for hikers and in larger sizes for campers who travel in cars and trailers. Hikers carry most of their supplies in a backpack. Perhaps the single most important item of camping equipment is a first-aid kit.

Girl Scouts of the U.S.A.

Camp Fire, Inc.

Summer Camps offer a wide variety of organized activities for groups who sleep at the campsite for several nights or as long as the entire summer. At the left, a counselor leads a group of campers in a discussion around a campfire. The campers at the right are spending their day horseback riding.

Before building a fire, make certain it will not harm the surroundings. Make pits large enough to keep a fire from spreading. Avoid building fires on windy days. Keep fires small, regularly removing ashes. Someone should be responsible for watching the fire at all times. A bucket of water and a small shovel should be available to control a fire that threatens to spread.

Three types of materials are needed to build a campfire: (1) tinder, (2) kindling, and (3) firewood. Tinder includes dry twigs, pine needles, leaves, and similar materials that ignite quickly. Kindling consists of larger pieces of wood that burn easily and rapidly. Softwoods such as cedar or pine make effective kindling. Firewood consists of woods that burn slowly and evenly and produce a bed of long-lasting coals. Hickory, oak, and sugar maple are examples of woods suitable for campfires.

There are many effective ways to build fires. The following method can be used to build a fire for cooking, for warmth, or simply for enjoyment.

First, place a small pile of tinder on the ground and arrange kindling around it in the shape of a tepee. Then enclose the tepee with four pieces of firewood that form a square. Soon after lighting the tinder, the kindling will begin to burn. Gradually, add firewood to keep the fire burning.

To start a fire in wet weather, find dry materials. Paper milk cartons and wadded paper can serve as tinder, and dry wood can sometimes be found under logs and trees. Damp logs should be split, because the inside of a log stays dry longer in wet weather.

Make sure a fire is out before leaving the campsite. To extinguish a fire, first spread the coals out until they lose their red glow. Then sprinkle water on the dead coals and dump soil over them. Next, stir the mixture, scatter it on the ground, and cover it with fresh topsoil. In areas without designated fire pits, no trace of the campfire should remain.

Camping Safety and Courtesy

Safety. Common sense can prevent most camping injuries. For example, children should never be allowed to use axes or knives, and anyone who is cooking should use gloves and potholders. However, campers must take special precautions to protect against such hazards as poisonous plants, improper food storage, lightning storms, and hiking emergencies.

Poisonous Plants. Because many camping trips take place in the forest, campers should learn to identify poison sumac, poison oak, and poison ivy. If contact occurs, wash the affected skin immediately with soap and water. Then apply a lotion that soothes itching.

Improper Food Storage. Food poisoning can result from lack of refrigeration. Some campers avoid this danger by carrying only freeze-dried foods. Others store all their food in large coolers. Campers with small coolers often pack nonperishable foods separately in airtight containers. The smell of food can attract animals, so never leave food carelessly out in the open or store it in a tent.

Lightning Storms occur more frequently than other types of dangerous weather, and they can take place in any sort of climate or terrain. Immediately seek shelter during a lightning storm. If shelter is not available, sit under trees of similar height. Avoid tall trees in open areas and exposed slopes and hilltops. In addition, get out of water and onto land at the first sign of lightning.

Hiking Safety. Before leaving, tell your destination and expected length of a hike to someone who will not be hiking. If the terrain is unfamiliar, do not hike alone. Carry emergency supplies such as waterproof matches. If you get lost, keep calm, remain in one place, and wait for a search party to arrive. At night, build a fire for warmth, protection, and to signal others. Leave the area only as a last resort.

Courtesy. Regardless of the type of camping trip, always try to preserve the natural environment. Never leave any trace of camping activities. Besides eliminating campfire remains and leaving wildlife undisturbed, save trash until it can be discarded in trash containers. Bury human waste if no rest rooms are available. Out of respect for animals and neighboring campers, keep as quiet as possible.

Organized Camping

Organized camping provides supervised activities for groups. There are three main types of organized camping: (1) summer camps, (2) specialty camps, and (3) school camping.

Summer Camps are sponsored by such organizations as the Boy Scouts, Girl Scouts, Camp Fire, Young Men's Christian Association (YMCA), and Young Women's Christian Association (YWCA). There are also hundreds of private summer camps throughout the United States and Canada. Almost every summer camp has a lake for swimming, boating, and fishing. They also offer such activities as nature hikes, overnight backpacking trips, crafts, horseback riding, and archery. Campers usually sleep in cabins and eat in dining halls.

Specialty Camps combine camping activities with a special activity such as tennis, music, or computer instruction. There are also specialty camps designed for certain groups, such as the handicapped, the elderly, and underprivileged children.

School Camping combines educational programs with camping during the school year. A group of students spends several days, normally at a private camp, learning about the outdoors. Attendance at school camps is usually voluntary, and the school district pays part of the cost of the trip. William Ruskin

Related Articles in World Book include:

Boy Scouts	Hiking	Outward Bound
Camp Fire	Mountain Climbing	Poison Ivy
Canoeing (Canoe Camping)	National Park System (Visiting the Parklands)	Recreational Vehicle
Girl Scouts		Tent

Outline

I. Types of Camping
A. Tent Camping
B. Recreational Vehicle Camping
II. Planning a Camping Trip
III. Camping Equipment and Food
A. Tents
B. Sleeping Bags
C. Clothing
D. Food and Water
E. Other Camp Supplies
IV. The Campsite
A. Selecting a Location
B. Building a Campfire
V. Camping Safety and Courtesy
A. Safety
B. Courtesy
VI. Organized Camping
A. Summer Camps
B. Specialty Camps
C. School Camping

Questions

Why should campers bring water from home on camping trips?
Where can campers find information about campgrounds?
How should campers put out a campfire?
What are the advantages of a recreational vehicle?
What should hikers do if they lose their way?
What shapes do sleeping bags come in?
Why should campers avoid pitching tents near water?
What are some common activities at summer camps?
Where should a camper go in case of lightning?
How can campers avoid food poisoning?

Additional Resources

Level I
Greenbank, Anthony. *A Handbook for Emergencies: Coming Out Alive*. Doubleday, 1976.
Kleeberg, Irene C. *Going to Camp*. Watts, 1978.
Neimark, Paul. *Camping and Ecology*. Childrens Press, 1981.

Level II
Campground and Trailer Park Guide: U.S., Canada, Mexico. Rand McNally. Published annually.
Nourse, Alan E. *The Outdoorsman's Medical Guide: Commonsense Advice and Essential Health Care for Campers, Hikers, and Backpackers*. Harper, 1974.
Riviere, Bill. *The Camper's Bible*. 3rd ed. Doubleday, 1984. All the basics on camping.

CAMPUS SCHOOL. See Laboratory School.

CAMUS, *ka MOO,* **ALBERT,** *al BEHR* (1913-1960), was a French journalist, essayist, novelist, and playwright who was associated with the existentialist movement (see Existentialism). He won the 1957 Nobel prize for literature. Camus wrote moving essays about his native North Africa and set much of his fiction there. But his writing transcends its setting because it deals with moral problems of universal importance.

Camus was concerned with the freedom and responsibility of the individual, the alienation of the individual from society, and the difficulty of facing life without the comfort of believing in God or in absolute moral standards. These themes appear in his novels *The Stranger* (1942), *The Plague* (1947), and *The Fall* (1957); and in his play *Caligula* (1945).

Camus wrote two widely-discussed philosophical essays. In *The Myth of Sisyphus* (1942), he said "There is but one truly serious philosophical problem and that is suicide." He argued that people hang on to life even though life has no meaning or purpose to justify it and is thus "absurd." *The Rebel* (1951) is a critical examination of the forms of human rebellion.

Camus was born in Algeria and went to France for the first time in 1939. In 1942, he joined the French resistance against the Nazis and edited its underground newspaper *Combat*. Ivan Soll

CAN. See Canning; Food Preservation; Tin Can.

CANAANITES, *KAY nuh nyts,* were a people mentioned in the Old Testament. The Canaanites settled in Canaan, the Biblical name for Palestine, about 3000 B.C. They were the chief inhabitants of this land until the Israelites conquered them about 1200 B.C. (see Palestine [Early History and Hebrew Settlement]).

The Canaanites were a Semitic people, related to the Arabs, Assyrians, and Israelites (see Semites). Ancient remains show that the Canaanites had an advanced civilization. They built walls around their cities for protection against invading tribes. But the Israelites finally conquered them. The Israelites adopted many Canaanite laws and customs, and Hebrew language and literature shows much Canaanite influence.

Some Canaanites settled northwest of Palestine before the Israelite invasion. They became known as Phoenicians (see Phoenicia). William F. Rosenblum

Ken Straiton, Image Finders

Scenic Vancouver, the largest city in British Columbia, is Canada's—and North America's—busiest Pacific port.

George Hunter

Fertile Farmlands cover the vast plains of Canada's Prairie Provinces—Alberta, Saskatchewan, and Manitoba.

CANADA

CANADA is the second largest country in the world. Only Russia has a greater land area. Canada extends across the continent of North America, from Newfoundland on the Atlantic coast to British Columbia on the Pacific coast. Canada is slightly larger than the United States, its southern neighbor, but has only about a tenth as many people. Approximately $25\frac{1}{2}$ million people live in Canada, about 80 per cent of them within 200 miles (320 kilometers) of the southern border. Much of the rest of Canada is uninhabited because it has rugged terrain and a severe climate.

Canada is a land of great variety. Towering mountains, crystal-clear lakes, and lush, green forests make Canada's far west a region of great natural beauty. Farther inland, fields of wheat and other grains cover Canada's vast prairies. These fertile farmlands contrast vividly with the Arctic wastelands to the north. The nation's largest population centers and industrial areas lie near the Great Lakes and the St. Lawrence River in central Canada. In the east, fishing villages and sandy beaches dot the Atlantic coast.

Like the country's landscape, Canada's people are also extremely varied. About 45 per cent of all Canadians are of British descent, and about 29 per cent are of French ancestry. French Canadians, most of whom live in Quebec, have kept the language and many customs of their ancestors. About 13 per cent of Canada's people speak both English and French, the nation's two official languages. Other major ethnic groups in Canada include people of German, Italian, Ukrainian, or Dutch descent. Large numbers of Asian immigrants have settled in western Canada. Indians and Eskimos—the original Canadians—today make up about 2 per cent of the nation's population.

More than three-fourths of Canada's people live in cities or towns. Montreal, Que., and Toronto, Ont., are the two largest cities in Canada. They are the centers of two metropolitan areas, each of which has a population of approximately 3 million. Ottawa, Ont., is the nation's capital.

A wealth of natural resources has always been Canada's greatest possession. European settlers first came to Canada to fish in its coastal waters and to trap the fur-bearing animals in its forests. Later, the forests themselves became sources of timber for shipbuilding and other construction. Today, pulpwood from these forests enables Canada to lead the world in the production of *newsprint* (paper on which newspapers are printed). Rich soil helps Canada rank among the world's leading wheat producers. Thanks to power plants on its mighty rivers, Canada ranks third after the United States and Russia in the generation of hydroelectric power. Plentiful resources of petroleum, iron ore, and other minerals provide raw materials that help make Canada a leading manufacturing nation.

Canada is a *federation* (union) of 10 provinces and 2 territories. The nation's name probably comes from *kanata,* an Iroquois Indian word that means *village* or *community.* Today, maintaining a sense of community is one of Canada's major problems because of differences among the provinces and territories. Many Canadians in eastern and western areas feel that the federal government does not pay enough attention to their particular problems and interests. But the greatest challenge to national unity is that many residents of Quebec want their province to become an independent nation. They feel that independence is the only way of guaranteeing full rights to Quebec's many French speakers and ending the domination of their economy and culture by English-speaking Canadians.

The contributors of this article are Adam Karpinski, Regional Planner for Hydro-Quebec; and Patrick Watson, a Canadian writer, filmmaker, and television journalist.

Michael Bertan, Van Cleve Photography

The Changing of the Guard on Parliament Hill is a popular attraction for visitors to Ottawa, Ont., Canada's capital.

Eberhard E. Otto, Miller Services

Tiny Fishing Villages like this one in Newfoundland are found all along the Atlantic Coast of Canada.

Canada is an independent, self-governing nation, but Canadians recognize Queen Elizabeth II of Great Britain as queen of Canada. This position symbolizes the nation's strong ties to Great Britain, which ruled Canada until 1867. Canada and the United States have had a relationship of cooperation and friendship since the 1800's. However, the United States—because of its larger population and greater economic power—has tended to dominate Canada both culturally and economically. Canadians today are striving to maintain control of their economy and to safeguard their Canadian identity.

This article chiefly discusses Canada's people and their way of life as well as the country's geography and economy. For information on the government and the history of Canada, see the articles CANADA, GOVERNMENT OF; and CANADA, HISTORY OF.

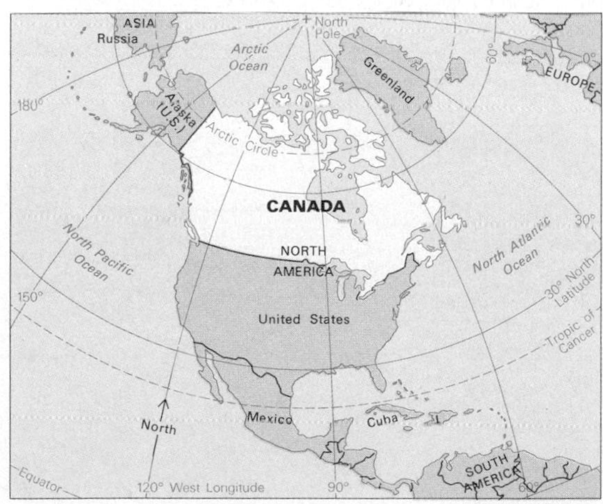

WORLD BOOK map

Canada lies in North America. It borders the United States and the Pacific, Arctic, and Atlantic oceans.

Facts in Brief

Capital: Ottawa.

Official Languages: English and French.

Form of Government: Constitutional monarchy.

Area: 3,831,033 sq. mi. (9,922,330 km²), including 291,571 sq. mi. (755,165 km²) of inland water. *Greatest Distances*—east-west, 3,223 mi. (5,187 km), from Cape Spear, Nfld., to Mount St. Elias, Y.T.; north-south, 2,875 mi. (4,627 km), from Cape Columbia on Ellesmere Island to Middle Island in Lake Erie. *Coastline*—151,488 mi. (243,797 km), including mainland and islands; Atlantic Ocean, 28,019 mi. (45,092 km); Arctic Ocean, 82,698 mi. (133,089 km); Hudson Bay, Hudson Strait, and James Bay, 24,786 mi. (39,890 km); Pacific Ocean, 15,985 mi. (25,726 km). *Shoreline*—Great Lakes, 4,726 mi. (7,606 km).

Elevation: *Highest*—Mount Logan, 19,520 ft. (5,950 m) above sea level. *Lowest*—sea level.

Population: *Estimated 1985 Population*—25,533,000; distribution, 76 per cent urban, 24 per cent rural; density, 8 persons per sq. mi. (3 persons per km²). *1981 Census*—24,343,181. *Estimated 1990 Population*—27,102,000.

Chief Products: *Agriculture*—beef cattle, wheat, milk, hogs, rapeseed, poultry, barley, eggs, corn, vegetables, flowers, fruits. *Fishing Industry*—cod, salmon, lobster, scallops. *Forest Industry*—logs and bolts, pulpwood. *Fur Industry*—mink, fox, lynx, beaver. *Manufacturing*—food products, transportation equipment, petroleum and coal products, paper products, primary metals, fabricated metal products, chemicals, lumber and wood products, electric machinery and equipment, nonelectric machinery, printed materials, textiles. *Mining*—petroleum, natural gas, natural gas liquids, coal, iron ore, copper, zinc, gold, uranium, potash, sulfur, nickel, sand and gravel.

National Anthem: "O Canada."

National Symbols: Beaver and maple leaf.

National Holiday: Canada Day, July 1.

Money: *Basic Unit*—dollar. For its price in U.S. dollars, see MONEY (table: Exchange Rates). See also DOLLAR.

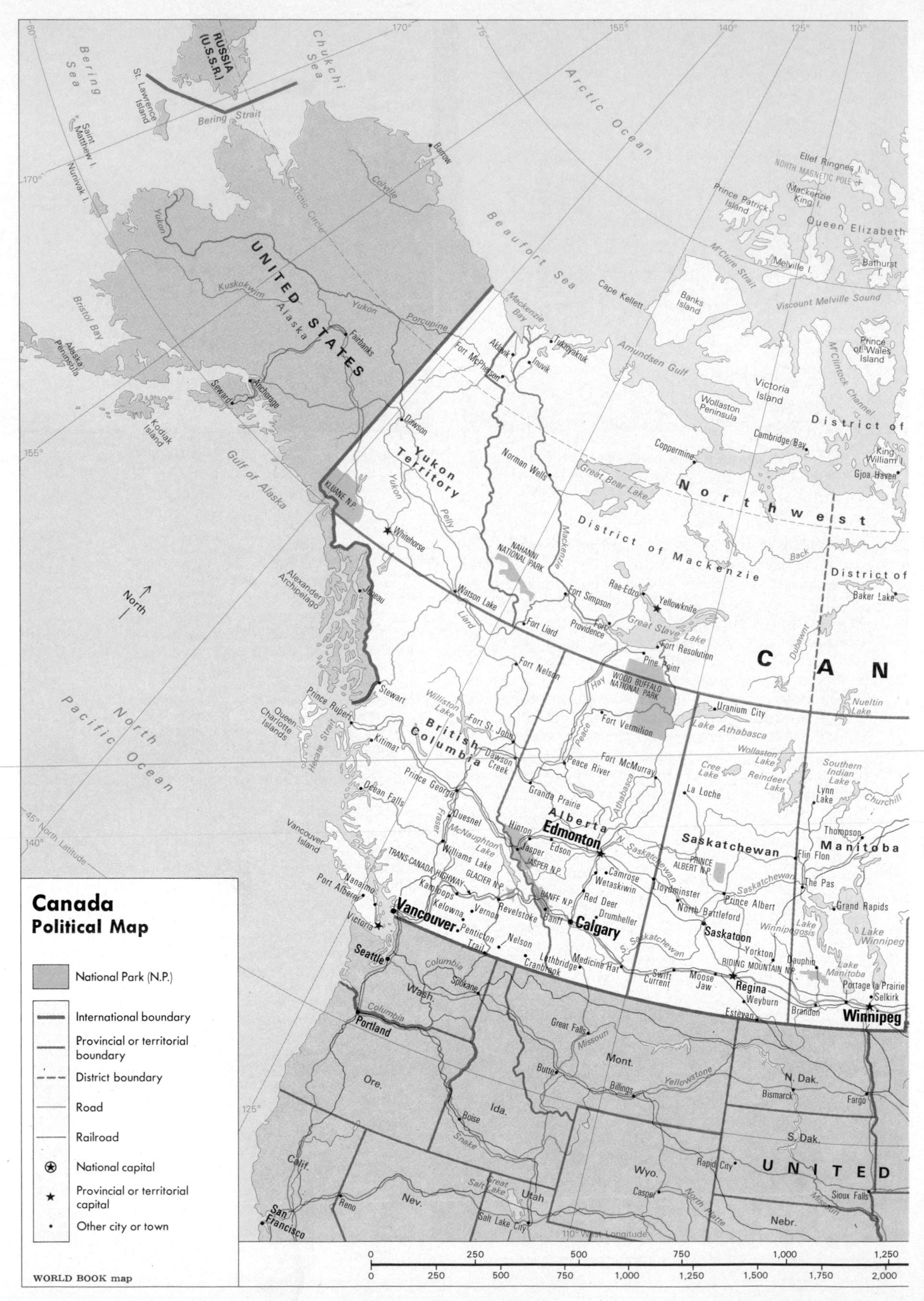
Canada
Political Map
National Park (N.P.)
International boundary
Provincial or territorial boundary
District boundary
Road
Railroad
National capital
Provincial or territorial capital
Other city or town
WORLD BOOK map
Yukon Territory
District of Mackenzie
British Columbia
Alberta
Saskatchewan
Manitoba
Edmonton
Calgary
Vancouver
Victoria
Regina
Winnipeg
Whitehorse
Yellowknife
UNITED STATES
Alaska
Arctic Ocean
Beaufort Sea
Pacific Ocean
Gulf of Alaska
Bering Sea
Chukchi Sea
RUSSIA (U.S.S.R.)

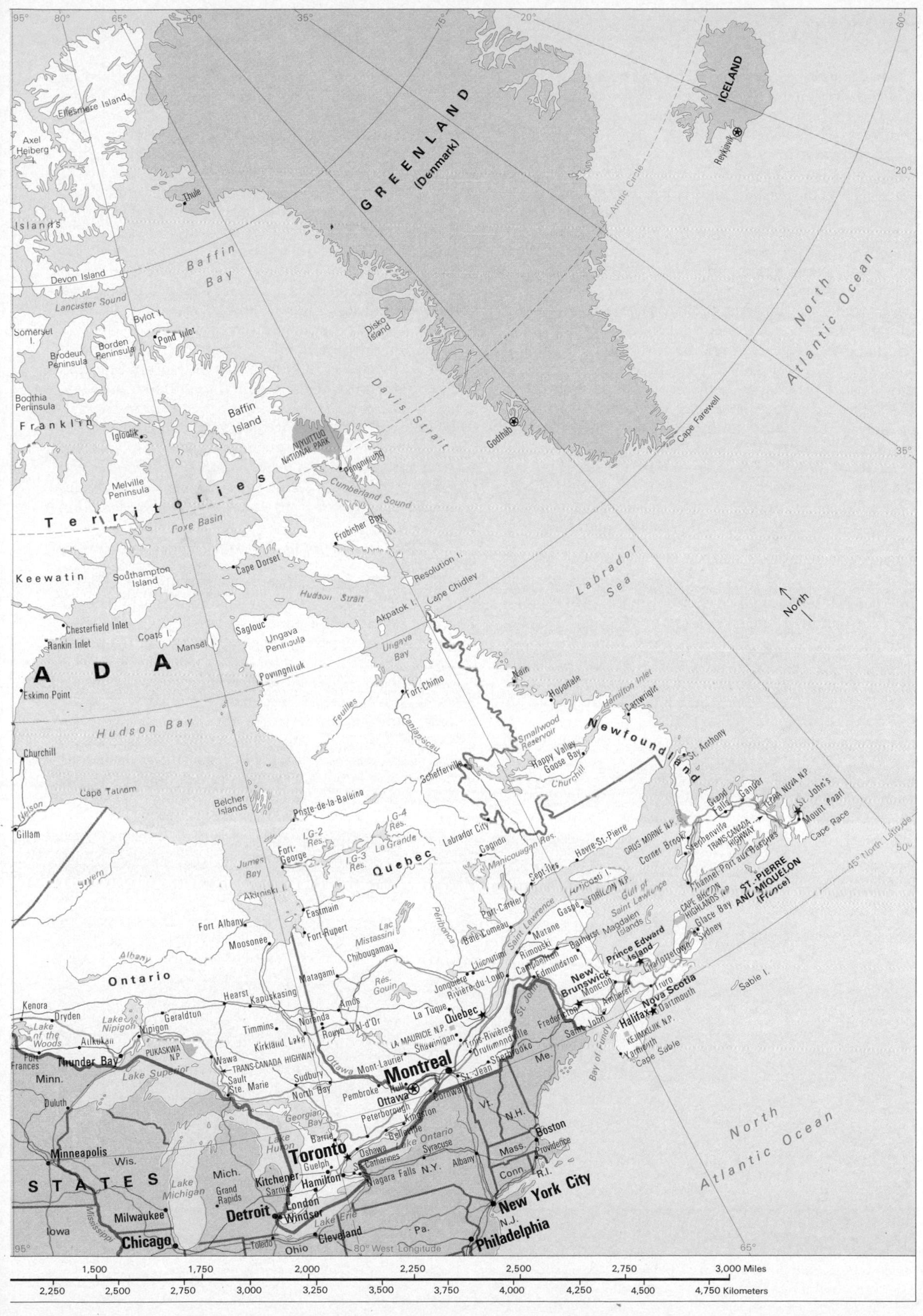

GREENLAND
(Denmark)
ICELAND
Reykjavik
Ellesmere Island
Axel Heiberg I.
Thule
Islands
Devon Island
Baffin Bay
Lancaster Sound
Bylot I.
Pond Inlet
Somerset I.
Brodeur Peninsula
Borden Peninsula
Boothia Peninsula
Franklin
Baffin Island
Igloolik
NAUYUTTUQ NATIONAL PARK
Pangnirtung
Melville Peninsula
Territories
Foxe Basin
Cumberland Sound
Frobisher Bay
Cape Dorset
Disko Island
Davis Strait
Godthåb
Cape Farewell
Arctic Circle
North Atlantic Ocean
Keewatin
Southampton Island
Resolution I.
Hudson Strait
Akpatok I.
Cape Chidley
Labrador Sea
North
Chesterfield Inlet
Rankin Inlet
Coats I.
Mansel I.
Saglouc
Ungava Peninsula
Ungava Bay
ADA
Povungnituk
Eskimo Point
Fort-Chimo
Nain
Hopedale
Hamilton Inlet
Cartwright
Hudson Bay
Feuilles
Caniapiscau
Smallwood Reservoir
Happy Valley Goose Bay
Newfoundland
Churchill
Schefferville
St. Anthony
Cape Tatnam
Belcher Islands
Poste-de-la-Baleine
G-4 Res.
LG-2 Res.
La Grande
Labrador City
Nelson
Gillam
Fort-George
LG-3 Res.
Quebec
Gagnon
Manicougan Res.
Havre-St.-Pierre
GROS MORNE N.P.
Gander
Grand Falls
TERRA NOVA N.P.
St. John's
Mount Pearl
Cape Race
Corner Brook
Stephenville
TRANS-CANADA HIGHWAY
Channel Port aux Basques
ST.-PIERRE AND MIQUELON (France)
James Bay
Akimiski I.
Severn
Sept-Iles
Anticosti I.
FORILLON N.P.
Gaspé
Gulf of Saint Lawrence
Magdalen Islands
CAPE BRETON HIGHLANDS N.P.
Glace Bay
Sydney
Eastmain
Fort Albany
Fort-Rupert
Lac Mistassini
Péribonca
Port-Cartier
Baie-Comeau
Saint Lawrence
Matane
Rimouski
Bathurst
Moosonee
Chibougamau
Chicoutimi
Campbellton
Edmundston
Prince Edward Island
Charlottetown
Albany
Ontario
Matagami
Rés. Gouin
Jonquière
Rivière-du-Loup
New Brunswick
Moncton
Truro
Sable I.
Kenora
Dryden
Hearst
Kapuskasing
Amos
La Tuque
Quebec
Amherst
Nova Scotia
Dartmouth
Halifax
Lake Nipigon
Geraldton
Nipigon
Lake of the Woods
Atikokan
Timmins
Noranda
Rouyn
Val-d'Or
LA MAURICIE N.P.
Shawinigan
Trois-Rivières
Drummondville
St. John
Fredericton
Saint John
KEJIMKUJIK N.P.
Yarmouth
Cape Sable
Bay of Fundy
Fort Frances
Thunder Bay
PUKASKWA N.P.
Wawa
Kirkland Lake
TRANS-CANADA HIGHWAY
Sherbrooke
Me.
Minn.
Lake Superior
Sault Ste. Marie
Sudbury
Ottawa
Mont-Laurier
Montreal
St.-Jean
Hull
North Bay
Pembroke
Ottawa
Cornwall
Duluth
Georgian Bay
Peterborough
Kingston
Vt.
N.H.
Lake Huron
Barrie
Belleville
Lake Ontario
Boston
Minneapolis
Wis.
Toronto
Oshawa
Syracuse
Mass.
Providence
Guelph
St. Catharines
Niagara Falls
N.Y.
Albany
STATES
Lake Michigan
Mich.
Grand Rapids
Kitchener
Hamilton
Sarnia
Conn.
R.I.
New York City
London
Milwaukee
Detroit
Windsor
Mississippi
Iowa
Lake Erie
N.J.
Pa.
Chicago
Toledo
Ohio
Cleveland
Philadelphia
80° West Longitude
45° North Latitude
95°
80°
65°
50°
35°
75°
20°
60°
1,500
1,750
2,000
2,250
2,500
2,750
3,000 Miles
2,250
2,500
2,750
3,000
3,250
3,500
3,750
4,000
4,250
4,500
4,750 Kilometers

Canada has six cultural and economic regions: (1) the Atlantic Provinces, (2) Quebec, (3) Ontario, (4) the Prairie Provinces, (5) British Columbia, and (6) the Territories.

The Atlantic Provinces lie on the Atlantic Ocean. These four provinces—Newfoundland, New Brunswick, Prince Edward Island, and Nova Scotia—make up about 5 per cent of Canada's land area and have about 10 per cent of its people. Most of the region's people are of English, Irish, Scottish, or French descent. New Brunswick, Nova Scotia, and Prince Edward Island are sometimes called the *Maritime Provinces.*

The Atlantic Provinces have been an important fishing center since European explorers arrived there in the late 1400's. The four provinces still provide most of Canada's fish catch, but the fishing industry employs only about 3 per cent of their workers. Manufacturing is the region's leading economic activity. Agriculture, mining, shipping, and tourism also have an important role in its economy. Economic problems have troubled the Atlantic Provinces throughout most of the 1900's. A period of economic growth began there during the 1950's. However, the region still has a lower standard of living, lower wages, and a higher rate of unemployment than any other part of Canada.

Quebec differs greatly from the rest of Canada because of the strong influence of French culture. The French explorer Samuel de Champlain founded Quebec City, the first permanent settlement in Canada, in 1608. Quebec remained a French colony until the British gained control of it in 1763. Today, about 80 per cent of Quebec's people are of French descent. French is the official language of Quebec, and most of the people belong to the Roman Catholic Church.

Quebec is the largest province in area and the second largest in population. Only Ontario has more people. Montreal, Quebec's largest city, is the hub of the province's economic and cultural life. It also is the leading Canadian transportation center. The largest industries in the Quebec region are manufacturing and *service industries,* such as banks, hospitals, and advertising agencies. Other important economic activities there include agriculture, mining, forestry, and fishing.

Ontario has a larger population than any other Canadian province. About a third of the nation's people live there. Fur traders explored Ontario during the 1600's, but major settlement did not begin until the late 1700's. About 60 per cent of Ontario's people have British or Irish ancestry, and 10 per cent are of French descent. In addition, Ontario has about 96,000 American Indians, a greater number than any other province.

The southern boundary of Ontario passes through four of the five Great Lakes—Superior, Huron, Erie, and Ontario. The province's principal manufacturing area, called the *Golden Horseshoe,* lies on the western shore of Lake Ontario. Ontario produces approximately half of Canada's manufactured goods and also ranks as the leading agricultural province. Toronto, the capital and largest city of Ontario, is the chief manufacturing, financial, and communications center of English-speaking Canada.

The Prairie Provinces are Alberta, Saskatchewan, and Manitoba. About 17 per cent of Canada's people live in these three provinces, which make up about a fifth of the country's land area. The southern part of the Prairie Provinces has many wheat farms and cattle ranches, and lakes and evergreen forests cover the northern area.

Until the late 1800's, the Prairie Provinces remained isolated from eastern Canada, and the fur trade was the region's only important economic activity. The completion of Canada's first transcontinental railroad in 1885 made it easy to reach the region. Millions of people settled on the fertile Canadian prairies during the late

NFB Photothèque

Canada's Oldest City, Quebec, lies on the north bank of the St. Lawrence River. One of the city's most famous landmarks is the Château Frontenac, *center,* a hotel built in the style of an old French *château* (castle).

Boris Spremo, Lensman

Shoppers in Toronto can visit more than 100 stores in Eaton Centre, a shopping and office complex. Toronto is Canada's commercial center.

The Provinces and Territories of Canada

Provinces

Province	Capital	Area In sq. mi.	Area In km²	Rank in Area	Population (1981 Census)	Rank in Pop.	Floral Emblem	Date Became Province	Province Abbr.
Alberta	Edmonton	255,285	661,185	4	2,237,724	4	Wild Rose	1905	Alta.
British Columbia	Victoria	366,255	948,596	3	2,744,467	3	Flowering Dogwood	1871	B.C.
Manitoba	Winnipeg	251,000	650,087	6	1,026,241	5	Pasqueflower	1870	Man.
New Brunswick	Fredericton	28,354	73,436	8	696,403	8	Violet	1867	N.B.
Newfoundland	St. John's	156,185	404,517	7	567,681	9	Pitcher Plant	1949	Nfld.
Nova Scotia	Halifax	21,425	55,491	9	847,442	7	Trailing Arbutus	1867	N.S.
Ontario	Toronto	412,582	1,068,582	2	8,625,107	1	White Trillium	1867	Ont.
Prince Edward Island	Charlottetown	2,184	5,657	10	122,506	10	Lady's-Slipper	1873	P.E.I.
Quebec	Quebec	594,860	1,540,680	1	6,438,403	2	White Garden Lily	1867	Que.
Saskatchewan	Regina	251,700	651,900	5	968,313	6	Prairie Lily	1905	Sask.

Territories

Territory	Capital	Area In sq. mi.	Area In km²	Population (1981 Census)	Floral Emblem	Territory Abbreviation
Northwest Territories	Yellowknife	1,304,903	3,379,684	45,741	Mountain Avens	N.W. Ter. or N.W.T.
Yukon Territory	Whitehorse	186,300	482,515	23,153	Fireweed	Y.T.

1800's and the early 1900's. The majority of these settlers came from eastern Canada, the United States, Germany, Italy, the Netherlands, Poland, the Ukraine, and the Scandinavian countries—Denmark, Norway, and Sweden.

For years, the economy of the Prairie Provinces was based on agriculture. The region still produces most of Canada's grain and cattle. During the late 1940's, the discovery of petroleum and natural gas in the region added a new source of wealth. Alberta's oil reserves have made it the most prosperous province. Calgary and Edmonton, the main cities of Alberta, are two of the fastest-growing cities in Canada. Calgary, Alta., is the largest city in the Prairie Provinces and a major Canadian transportation center.

Andy Turnbull, Miller Services

Rugged, Snow-Covered Terrain makes up much of Canada's territories. These dog sleds are traveling through the mountains near the border of the Yukon and the Northwest Territories.

British Columbia is Canada's westernmost province and its third largest in both area and population. British Columbia lies on the Pacific Ocean. Its largest city, Vancouver, is the busiest port on the Pacific coast of North America. The natural beauty of British Columbia's rugged coastline and lofty mountains attracts many tourists. Southern British Columbia has Canada's mildest climate, and large numbers of older Canadians move there after they retire.

People of British ancestry make up most of the province's population. Major groups in the region also include those of Chinese, German, Italian, or Scandinavian descent. Evergreen forests cover much of British Columbia, and many of the province's people work in the logging and wood-processing industries. Other major economic activities in British Columbia include agriculture, fishing, and mining.

The Territories. The Yukon Territory and the Northwest Territories make up more than a third of Canada's land area. However, because of the remote location and severe climate of the territories, less than 1 per cent of the nation's people live there. The terrain in the Yukon and in the southwestern part of the Northwest Territories consists mainly of forest-covered mountains. Most of the rest of the region is a frozen wasteland throughout much of the year. The territories have rich mineral deposits, and mining is the chief economic activity.

Indians and Eskimos made up almost the entire population of the territories until the region's great mineral wealth was discovered during the late 1800's and the early 1900's. Whitehorse, the capital of the Yukon Territory, was founded during the Klondike gold rush of the late 1890's. Yellowknife, the capital of the Northwest Territories, was established during another gold rush in the 1930's.

Population. In 1985, Canada had an estimated population of 25,533,000. The 1981 Canadian census reported a population of 24,343,181. Canada's population has almost doubled since World War II ended in 1945. This rapid growth has resulted from heavy immigration and a high birth rate.

From 1951 to 1977, about 4 million persons immigrated to Canada. Large numbers of new Canadians came from Great Britain, as they have throughout Canada's history. Others arrived from Germany, Greece, Italy, the Netherlands, and Portugal. Canada has become a new home for political refugees from many nations. For example, thousands of Hungarians settled in Canada after the 1956 revolution in Hungary. Between 1975 and 1980, Canada admitted about 60,000 refugees from Kampuchea, Laos, and Vietnam.

Canada's baby boom peaked in 1947, when the nation had almost 29 births per 1,000 persons. The birth rate remained steady during the 1950's, but by 1974 it reached a record low of 15.4 per 1,000 persons.

Ancestry. Almost all Canadians are of European descent. Indians and Eskimos, the original people of Canada, make up about 2 per cent of the nation's population. About 45 per cent of Canada's people have British ancestry, and about 29 per cent are descendants of French colonists. The ancestors of another 23 per cent came from other European countries.

Europeans. People whose ancestors came from the British Isles make up the majority of the population of every province except Quebec. Many are descendants of Scottish settlers who began arriving in Canada during the late 1700's. The ancestors of many others were Eng-

© Michael Philip Manheim

Canadians of Scottish Ancestry celebrate their heritage at the Highland Games, which are held annually in various parts of Canada. One of the most popular events at these games is tossing a heavy wooden pole called a *caber.*

Where Canadians Live

Most Canadians live near the nation's southern border in an area that covers only about a tenth of the country. Canada's vast northern regions are very thinly populated because they have such a severe climate and rugged terrain.

Major Urban Centers

- ● More than 2 million inhabitants
- • 500,000 to 2 million inhabitants
- ○ Less than 500,000 inhabitants

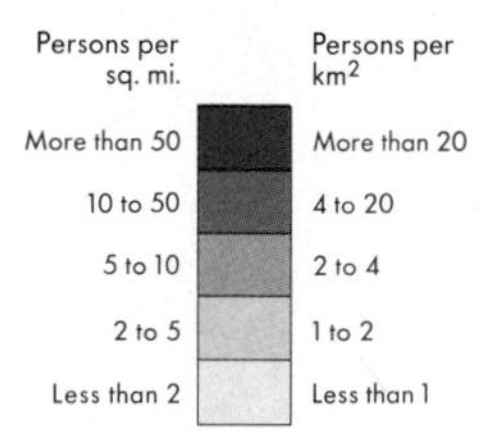

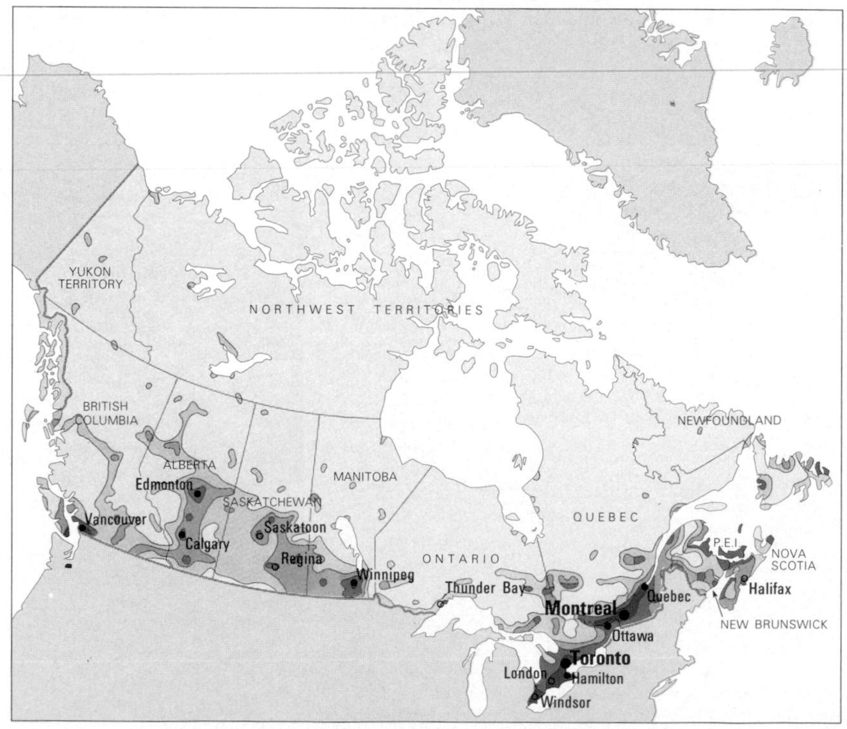

WORLD BOOK map; adapted from *The National Atlas of Canada*, 4th edition lish and Irish settlers who flocked to Canada during the 1800's. Still others are descendants of United Empire Loyalists—people who moved from the United States to Canada during and after the Revolutionary War in America (1775-1783). See UNITED EMPIRE LOYALISTS.

About 65,000 French colonists lived in Quebec when France lost that region to the British in 1763. Since that time, the nation's French population has grown to about 6 million. About 5 million of these people live in Quebec. Another 500,000 live in Ontario, and more than 200,000 live in New Brunswick. Alberta, Manitoba, Nova Scotia, and Saskatchewan have a few largely French areas.

Large numbers of immigrants from other European nations began to arrive in Canada during the late 1800's. The greatest wave of immigration occurred after World War II. Today, about 1,300,000 persons of German descent live in Canada, mostly in Ontario, the Prairie Provinces, and Nova Scotia. Italian immigrants have settled chiefly in the cities, particularly Toronto and Montreal. They and their descendants number more than 700,000. Most of the over 500,000 Canadians of Ukrainian origin live in the Prairie Provinces.

Indians and Eskimos had been living in what became Canada for thousands of years when Europeans first arrived. Today, Canada has nearly 370,000 Indians and about 25,000 Eskimos. The word *Eskimo* comes from an Indian word meaning *eaters of raw meat.* However, the Eskimos call themselves *Inuit,* which means *people.*

About two-thirds of the Eskimos live in the territories, and the rest live in the northern areas of Newfoundland, Ontario, and Quebec. Most of Canada's Indians belong to one of ten major groups—the Algonquian, the Athapaskan, the Haida, the Iroquoian, the Kootenayan, the Salishan, the Siouan, the Tlingit, the Tsimshian, and the Wakashan. Most of the Indians live on the nation's more than 2,200 *reserves* (reservations).

Other Canadians include Chinese, Japanese, and other Asians, who make up about 3 per cent of the population of British Columbia. Many immigrants from China, the East Indies, and the West Indies have settled in Toronto. Canada had about 35,000 black citizens in the mid-1970's. Since that time, thousands of blacks have immigrated to Canada from Haiti.

The Population of Canada

Canada's population has grown steadily since the first census was taken in 1851. Rapid growth occurred between 1851 and 1861, between 1901 and 1911, and between 1951 and 1961.

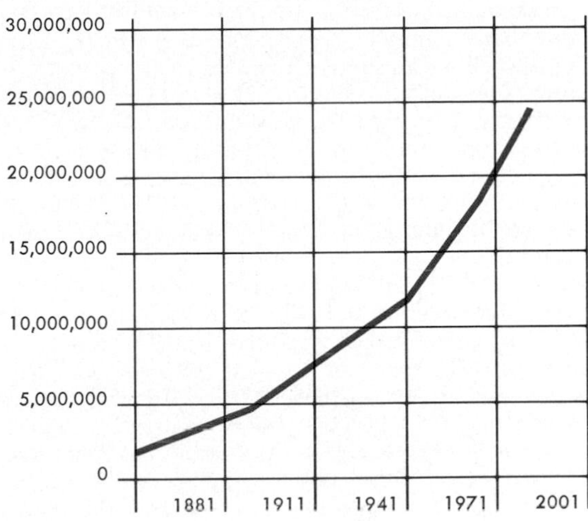

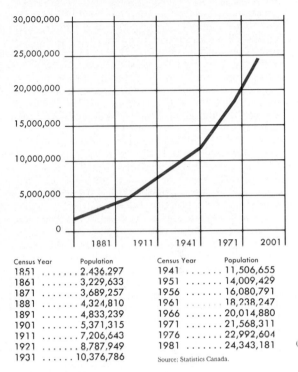

Census Year	Population	Census Year	Population
1851	2,436,297	1941	11,506,655
1861	3,229,633	1951	14,009,429
1871	3,689,257	1956	16,080,791
1881	4,324,810	1961	18,238,247
1891	4,833,239	1966	20,014,880
1901	5,371,315	1971	21,568,311
1911	7,206,643	1976	22,992,604
1921	8,787,949	1981	24,343,181
1931	10,376,786		

Source: Statistics Canada.

Languages. Canada has two official languages, English and French. The Official Languages Act of 1969 guarantees all Canadians the right to communicate with the national government in either French or English. About 67 per cent of the Canadian people speak only English, about 18 per cent speak only French, and more

Camilla Smith, Rainbow

The Indians of Canada's Pacific Coast are famous for their fine wood carvings. The skilled Indian craftsman shown above is using traditional techniques to carve ceremonial wooden masks.

David Burnett, DeWys, Inc.

Eskimo Children attend elementary school in their own communities. Those who wish to continue their education go to high schools or vocational schools in larger towns.

than 13 per cent speak both languages. The rest of the people speak other languages.

Most of the approximately 6 million French-speaking Canadians live in Quebec. As a result, Quebec's French-speaking citizens, called *Québécois* (*KAY beh KWAH*), consider themselves the guardians of the French language and culture in Canada. During the 1960's, many Québécois began to campaign to make French the sole official language of Quebec and to end the domination of Quebec's economy by English-speakers. Some Québécois even demanded independence for Quebec from Canada. In 1968, several groups favoring independence united to form a political party called the Parti Québécois. In addition, an organization called the *Front de Libération du Québec* (*FLQ*) used violence to draw attention to their demands for Quebec's independence.

In the elections of 1976, the Parti Québécois won control of the Quebec legislature. In 1977, the legislature passed a law that restricted the use of languages other than French in Quebec. This law gave Québécois a new sense of pride, but it also made many English-speaking Quebeckers feel unwanted. Some moved out of the province. Many business operations also left Quebec, including the headquarters of the Bank of Montreal and the Sun Life Company, an insurance firm. The independence movement suffered a setback in 1980. That year, Quebec voters refused to give the provincial government the authority to negotiate with the national government for *sovereignty association* with the rest of Canada. Such an arrangement would have given political independence to Quebec but maintained the province's economic ties with Canada.

City Life. Canada began as a nation with a largely rural population. But today, more than 75 per cent of the nation's people live in urban areas. This population shift occurred mainly as a result of the rapid development since the 1940's of manufacturing industries in urban areas. Skyscrapers have risen in Canada's cities during this period, and expressway systems have been contructed to link the cities with the many suburbs that have sprung up.

Canada has 23 metropolitan areas with a population of more than 100,000. The three largest metropolitan areas are Montreal, Que.; Toronto, Ont.; and Vancouver, B.C. The fourth largest metropolitan area consists of Ottawa, Ont., and Hull, Que., which lie across the Ottawa River from each other. Other major Canadian metropolitan areas include Calgary, Alta.; Edmonton, Alta.; Hamilton, Ont.; Quebec City, Que.; and Winnipeg, Man.

City people in Canada have a wide range of cultural and recreational activities. These include plays and concerts, visits to parks and museums, and many types of athletic events. Canadian cities, in spite of their rapid growth, have not suffered from social problems as badly as have many American cities. However, there have been signs of future problems. Some of Canada's cities have had reductions in funds available for education, health care, transportation, and welfare. Tension among various ethnic groups has appeared with the immigration to the cities by people from many nations. In addition, the decreasing supply of energy resources has caused many Canadians to oppose the unlimited growth of urban areas.

Barbara K. Deans

Apartment Buildings provide housing for large numbers of people in Canada's cities. This picture shows a residential street in Montreal.

Harold V. Green

Farming in Canada is largely a family activity. Modern machinery enables members of the nation's farm families to do nearly all the work themselves. About 6 per cent of the Canadian people live on farms.

Photo Librarium, Canada

A Procession to the Notre Dame Parish Church in Montreal reflects the importance of Roman Catholicism in Quebec. More than half of Canada's approximately 10 million Catholics live in Quebec. Canada also has over 10 million Protestants.

Rural Life. About 24 per cent of Canada's people live in rural areas, but only about 6 per cent live on farms. Others work in such industries as fishing, mining, and lumbering. A growing number of Canadians live in rural communities and commute to work in the cities.

In Canada, most farmers own their own farms, and farming is largely a family activity. Modern machinery enables a family to do nearly all the work on their farm themselves. The largest Canadian farms are in the Prairie Provinces and cover an average of 850 acres (344 hectares). Farms in central and eastern Canada are much smaller, averaging from about 180 to 300 acres (73 to 120 hectares).

About 75 per cent of Canada's farmland lies in the Prairie Provinces. Wooden farmhouses dot the golden wheatlands of this region. The homes are surrounded by buildings where farmers store grain and machinery. Grain is also stored in elevators that stand alongside the railroads, which link the farms to ports on the Great Lakes and the Pacific Ocean. Farm people shop, go to school and church, and participate in many community activities in small market towns that have grown up along the railroads.

Arctic Life. Canada's vast Arctic region is extremely thinly populated. Indians and Eskimos have lived there for thousands of years, and today they make up nearly half of the region's population. Most of the other people of the Canadian Arctic are traders, miners, and members of the armed forces and the Royal Canadian Mounted Police.

Many Eskimos and Indians still follow their traditional occupations—fishing, hunting, and trapping. But in general, the old ways of life in the Arctic have ended. The people live in modern houses rather than in tents or igloos. They wear modern clothing and eat food bought in stores. Snowmobiles and motorboats have largely replaced dog sleds and kayaks as their principal means of transportation.

The end of the traditional ways of life has brought many social problems to the Eskimos. They have a high unemployment rate, and their rates of alcoholism and crime are rising. The future may bring improved economic conditions as the result of the discovery of petroleum in the Arctic region. Many Eskimos may find jobs in the construction of pipelines to transport oil and natural gas to markets in southern Canada. But this construction also threatens to displace communities and perhaps further disrupt the traditional Eskimo way of life.

Education. Religious groups operated the earliest schools in Canada. In 1867, the British North America Act made education a responsibility of the provincial governments. Today, each province and territory in Canada has its own school system. Every system is supervised by the provincial or territorial department of education. A Cabinet minister heads each department and reports to the legislature of the province or territory. The Canadian government directs the education of children on Indian reserves, the children of members of the Canadian armed forces, and the inmates of federal penitentiaries. See EDUCATION (Development of Canadian Education).

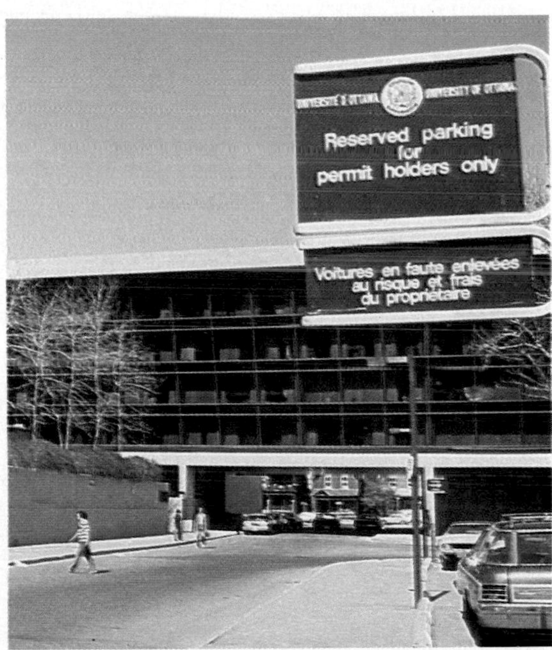

Photo Librarium, Canada

The University of Ottawa is the largest university in Canada that offers courses in both English and French. Courses at the majority of Canadian universities are taught in only one of the two languages.

CANADA

The school systems of most of the provinces have 12 grades. The systems of Quebec and Newfoundland have 11 grades, and those of Ontario have 13. In some provinces, the law provides for the public school system to include separate schools for certain religious groups. Communities in Alberta, Ontario, Saskatchewan, and the territories have separate schools for Roman Catholics in addition to public schools that are open to all students. The school system of Quebec consists of separate schools for Roman Catholics and Protestants. Most of the province's Catholic schools teach in French, and most of the Protestant schools use English. Newfoundland has four different types of schools. Pentecostals, Roman Catholics, and Seventh-day Adventists each operate their own schools, and the fourth system is run cooperatively by the major Protestant denominations.

Classes are taught in English in some Canadian universities and in French in others. Still other universities provide instruction in both languages. The major English-language universities include the University of Alberta, the University of British Columbia, the University of Manitoba, the University of Toronto, and McGill University. The principal French-language institutions are Laval University and the University of Montreal. Laval, founded in 1663, is Canada's oldest university. The University of Ottawa is the nation's largest bilingual institution.

The province of Quebec has *collèges d'enseignement général et professionel* (colleges of general and professional instruction). They offer a two-year course that high-

Universities and Colleges

The following degree-granting universities and colleges are members of the Association of Universities and Colleges of Canada.

Name	Location	Enrollment
Acadia University	Wolfville, N.S.	3,253
Alberta, University of	Edmonton, Alta.	22,857
Athabasca University	Edmonton, Alta.	176
Bishop's University	Lennoxville, Que.	1,010
Brandon University	Brandon, Man.	1,480
Brescia College	London, Ont.	477
British Columbia, University of	Vancouver, B.C.	21,803
Brock University	St. Catharines, Ont.	3,944
Calgary, University of	Calgary, Alta.	14,566
Campion College	Regina, Sask.	498
Cape Breton, University College of	Sydney, N.S.	1,845
Carleton University	Ottawa, Ont.	10,348
Concordia University	Montreal, Que.	12,285
Dalhousie University	Halifax, N.S.	8,822
Dominican College of Philosophy and Theology	Ottawa, Ont.	124
Guelph, University of	Guelph, Ont.	9,789
Huron College	London, Ont.	672
King's College	London, Ont.	1,320
King's College, University of	Halifax, N.S.	501
Lakehead University	Thunder Bay, Ont.	3,544
Laurentian University	Sudbury, Ont.	3,864
Laval University	Ste. Foy, Que.	19,590
Lethbridge, University of	Lethbridge, Alta.	1,850
Luther College	Regina, Sask.	357
Manitoba, University of	Winnipeg, Man.	15,987
McGill University	Montreal, Que.	16,353
McMaster University	Hamilton, Ont.	11,515
Memorial University of Newfoundland	St. John's, Nfld.	9,005
Moncton, University of	Moncton, N.B.	3,095
Montreal, University of	Montreal, Que.	20,348
Mt. Allison University	Sackville, N.B.	1,646
Mt. Saint Vincent University	Halifax, N.S.	1,592
New Brunswick, University of		6,550
at:	Fredericton, N.B.	
	Saint John, N.B.	
Nova Scotia, Technical University of	Halifax, N.S.	1,093
Nova Scotia Agricultural College	Truro, N.S.	475
Nova Scotia College of Art and Design	Halifax, N.S.	474
Ontario Institute for Studies in Education	Toronto, Ont.	*
Ottawa, University of	Ottawa, Ont.	12,817
Prince Edward Island, University of	Charlottetown, P.E.I.	1,676
Quebec, University of		22,993
at:	Abitibi-Témiscamingue, Que.	
	Chicoutimi, Que.	
	Hull, Que.	
	Montreal, Que.	
	Quebec, Que.	
	Rimouski, Que.	
	Trois-Rivières, Que.	
Queen's University at Kingston	Kingston, Ont.	11,314
Regina, University of	Regina, Sask.	4,811
Royal Military College of Canada	Kingston, Ont.	826
Royal Roads Military College	Victoria, B.C.	270
Ryerson Polytechnical Institute	Toronto, Ont.	8,789
St. Francis Xavier University	Antigonish, N.S.	2,539
St. Jerome's College, University of	Waterloo, Ont.	495
St. John's College	Winnipeg, Man.	†
St. Mary's University	Halifax, N.S.	3,131
St. Michael's College, University of	Toronto, Ont.	2,778
St. Paul University	Ottawa, Ont.	416
St. Paul's College	Winnipeg, Man.	588
St. Thomas More College	Saskatoon, Sask.	1,005
St. Thomas University	Fredericton, N.B.	1,200
Ste.-Anne, University of	Church Point, N.S.	218
Saskatchewan, University of	Saskatoon, Sask.	11,917
Sherbrooke, University of	Sherbrooke, Que.	6,808
Simon Fraser University	Burnaby, B.C.	7,517
Sudbury, University of	Sudbury, Ont.	**
Toronto, University of	Toronto, Ont.	35,672
Trent University	Peterborough, Ont.	2,437
Trinity College, University of	Toronto, Ont.	1,078
Victoria, University of	Victoria, B.C.	7,200
Victoria University	Toronto, Ont.	2,515
Waterloo, University of	Waterloo, Ont.	15,896
Western Ontario, University of	London, Ont.	19,482
Wilfrid Laurier University	Waterloo, Ont.	4,468
Windsor, University of	Windsor, Ont.	8,300
Winnipeg, University of	Winnipeg, Man.	3,090
York University	Toronto, Ont.	20,294

Source: Association of Universities and Colleges of Canada
*Enrollment included in Toronto, University of.
†Enrollment included in Manitoba, University of.
**Enrollment included in Laurentian University.

school graduates must complete before enrolling in a Quebec university. In addition, these colleges provide three-year technical and commercial courses. The other provinces also have two-year or three-year institutions of higher learning. Most of these schools are called *community colleges*.

Canada has an extensive system of public libraries. The National Library of Canada in Ottawa was established in 1953. It publishes *Canadiana*, a monthly and annual listing of new books, pamphlets, and music published in Canada. The Canada Institute for Scientific and Technical Information operates an outstanding science library in Ottawa. See LIBRARY (Canadian Government Libraries).

There are about 1,300 museums and art galleries in Canada. National museums in Ottawa include the National Gallery of Canada, the National Museum of Man, the National Museum of Natural Science, and the National Museum of Science and Technology. Among the nation's other distinguished museums, the Royal Ontario Museum in Toronto is known for its exhibits in such fields as archaeology, geology, and zoology.

Religion. The early French settlers brought the Roman Catholic faith to Canada, and Catholics are the nation's largest religious group today. About 10 million Canadians belong to the Roman Catholic Church. Most other Canadians are Protestants. The largest Protestant denominations are the United Church of Canada, which has about $3\frac{3}{4}$ million members, and the Anglican Church of Canada, with about $2\frac{1}{2}$ million members. Other major Protestant groups in Canada include Presbyterians, Lutherans, and Baptists. In addition, Canada has approximately 300,000 Jews, more than 100,000 Muslims, and growing numbers of Buddhists, Hindus, and Sikhs.

Recreation and Sports. Canadians take part in a wide variety of recreational activities. During the long winters, many people enjoy skiing, snowshoeing, skating, and tobogganing. Favorite summertime activities include swimming, canoeing, fishing, hiking, tennis, and golf. Canada's extensive national park system includes areas ideal for many of these activities. The system began in 1885 with the establishment of Banff National Park in Alberta. Today, all the provinces and territories have at least one national park. Each province also has its own park system.

Canada's first national game was lacrosse, which the Indians played before the arrival of the Europeans. Today, hockey is by far the most popular sport. Starting at the age of 7, players can compete in hockey leagues. On the professional level, 21 teams from Canada and the United States belong to the National Hockey League (NHL). Most players in the league are Canadians. Such stars as Ken Dryden, Gordie Howe, Guy Lafleur, and Bobby Orr have become national heroes in Canada.

Other popular professional sports in Canada include football, baseball, and soccer. Teams from nine Canadian cities compete in the Canadian Football League. The Montreal Expos and Toronto Blue Jays attract baseball fans from throughout Canada. Teams representing Calgary, Edmonton, Montreal, Toronto, and Vancouver play in the North American Soccer League.

Photo Librarium, Canada

Hockey is Canada's most popular sport. Professional hockey games draw huge crowds, and thousands of Canadians start to play in amateur leagues at the age of 7.

© Michael Philip Manheim

Breathtaking Ski Slopes, such as this one near Lake Louise, Alta., attract thousands of skiers to the Canadian Rockies yearly. Skiing is a favorite sport in many areas of Canada.

George Hunter, FPG

Fishing on Canadian Lakes and Streams ranks high among summer sports in North America. These fishermen are trying their luck on Lake St. Louis on Quebec's Gaspé Peninsula.

CANADA / *National Park System*

Canada's park system includes 28 national parks and about 700 national historic parks and sites. These attractions preserve historic, natural, and scientific landmarks of Canada. All the national parks and 53 major national historic parks and sites are described below.

National Parks

Name	Area In acres	Area In hectares	Location	Established	Outstanding Features
Auyuittuq*	5,305,600	2,147,100	Baffin Island in the Northwest Territories	1972	Massive icecap and glaciers; fiords; only park above Arctic Circle
Banff*†§	1,640,960	664,073	Western Alberta near Calgary	1885	Rocky Mountain scenery with glaciers and hot springs; Banff and Lake Louise resort areas
Cape Breton Highlands*†	234,880	95,053	Cape Breton Island in Nova Scotia	1936	Rugged coastline and forested hills; seascapes from Cabot Trail
Elk Island*	48,000	19,400	Central Alberta near Edmonton	1913	Rolling hills with aspen and spruce forests and many lakes; buffalo, deer, elk, and moose
Forillon*	59,392	24,035	Southeastern Quebec	1970	Scenic tip of Gaspé Peninsula that juts into Gulf of St. Lawrence
Fundy*†	50,880	20,590	Southeastern New Brunswick	1948	Rugged Bay of Fundy shoreline with coves and cliffs; some of world's highest tides
Georgian Bay Islands*	3,520	1,424	Georgian Bay in Ontario	1929	Rock pillars, glacier-scraped rock, ancient Chippewa Indian ruins
Glacier*†	333,440	134,938	Southeastern British Columbia	1886	Alpine region in Selkirk Mountains with snow-capped peaks and more than 100 glaciers
Gros Morne*	480,000	194,000	West coast of Newfoundland	1970	Scenic Long Range Mountains, fiordlike lakes, waterfalls, beaches, and rugged seacoast
Jasper*†§	2,688,000	1,087,800	Western Alberta	1907	Rocky Mountain landscape with hot springs and lakes; Jasper resort area
Kejimkujik*	94,272	38,151	Southwestern Nova Scotia	1968	Rolling landscape with many islands and lakes; Indian rock etchings
Kluane*	5,440,000	2,201,000	Southwestern Yukon Territory	1972	Mount Logan in St. Elias Mountains; large glacier system; Dall sheep
Kootenay*†	340,480	137,787	Southeastern British Columbia	1920	Rocky Mountain scenery with broad valleys, glaciers, deep canyons, and hot springs
Kouchibouguac*	55,680	22,533	East coast of New Brunswick	1969	Lagoons and bays; 15½-mile (24.9-kilometer) sweep of offshore sandbars
La Mauricie*	166,309	67,303	Near Trois-Rivières, Que.	1970	Heavily wooded section of Laurentian Mountains with numerous lakes
Mount Revelstoke	64,896	26,262	Southeastern British Columbia	1914	Mountaintop plateau in Selkirk Mountains with alpine meadows and lakes
Nahanni*	1,177,600	476,558	Southwestern Northwest Territories	1972	Deep canyons; hot springs; Virginia Falls and Hell's Gate on South Nahanni River
Pacific Rim*	96,000	38,800	Southwestern British Columbia	1970	Long Beach and historic Life Saving Trail on west coast of Vancouver Island; sea lions
Point Pelee	3,840	1,554	Near Leamington, Ont.	1918	Bird migration flyways; Lake Erie beaches
Prince Albert*†	957,440	387,462	Central Saskatchewan	1927	Interesting transition between northern forests and prairie grasslands; lakes and streams
Prince Edward Island*†	4,480	1,813	North shore of Prince Edward Is.	1937	Beaches, cliffs, dunes, and marshes; 25-mile (40-kilometer) strip on Gulf of St. Lawrence
Pukaskwa*	464,000	187,800	Near Marathon, Ont.	1978	Many lakes and rivers and wide variety of wildlife in wilderness area on Lake Superior
Riding Mountain*†	735,360	297,590	Southwestern Manitoba	1929	Forests, grasslands, and lakes on summit of Manitoba Escarpment
St. Lawrence Islands*	1,250	506	Eastern Ontario	1914	Scenic islands and islets on St. Lawrence River
Terra Nova*†	97,984	39,653	East shore of Newfoundland	1957	Spruce forest and bogs along rugged coastline; icebergs off shore in spring
Waterton Lakes*†	129,920	52,577	Southern Alberta	1895	Waterton-Glacier International Peace Park
Wood Buffalo*	11,072,000	4,480,680	Alberta-Northwest Territories border	1922	Largest buffalo herd in North America and nesting grounds of rare whooping crane
Yoho*†	324,480	131,312	Southeastern British Columbia	1886	Rocky Mountain scenery with lakes, waterfalls, natural stone bridge, and Yoho Valley

National Historic Parks and Sites

Name	Area In acres	Area In hectares	Location	Established	Outstanding Features
Alexander Graham Bell	24.7	10.0	Baddeck, N.S.	1956	Museum with models of Bell's experiments
Artillery Park‡	8.1	3.3	Quebec City, Que.	1972	French and British army buildings
Batoche‡	2,700.0	1,090.0	Batoche, near Duck Lake, Sask.	1951	Headquarters of métis during Saskatchewan Rebellion in 1885
Battle of the Chateauguay	3.3	1.3	Near Valleyfield, Que.	1977	Site of War of 1812 battle
Battleford‡	50.0	20.0	Battleford, Sask.	1951	Fort of North-West Mounted Police during Saskatchewan Rebellion in 1885

*Camping permitted. †Has overnight lodging. §Has an article in WORLD BOOK. ‡Closed part of the year.

National Historic Parks and Sites

Name	Area In acres	Area In hectares	Location	Established	Outstanding Features
Bellevue House	2.0	0.8	Kingston, Ont.	1967	Home of first prime minister of Canada, Sir John A. Macdonald, 1848-1849
Cape Spear‡	121.0	50.0	Near St. John's, Nfld.	1975	Lighthouse on Canada's most easterly point
Carleton Martello Tower‡	5.6	2.3	Saint John, N.B.	1924	Defense post built during War of 1812
Cartier-Brébeuf Park	17.8	7.2	Quebec City, Que.	1958	Winter camp of Jacques Cartier in 1535-1536
Castle Hill‡	68.0	27.5	Placentia, Nfld.	1968	French and British fortifications of 1700's
Coteau-du-Lac‡	11.6	4.7	Coteau-du-Lac, Que.	1965	Site of British military post; historic canal
Fort Amherst‡	223.0	90.2	Near Rocky Point, P.E.I.	1967	Ruins of British fort built in 1758
Fort Anne‡	32.2	13.0	Annapolis Royal, N.S.	1917	Site of early Acadian settlement
Fort Beauséjour‡	611.0	247.3	Near Sackville, N.B.	1926	Site of French fort built in 1750's; museum
Fort Chambly	9.7	3.9	Chambly, Que.	1940	Site of French fort of early 1700's; museum
Fort Edward	26.0	10.5	Windsor, N.S.	1925	Oldest blockhouse in Canada, built in 1750
Fort Espérance	——	——	Near Regina, Sask.	1972	Important North West Company post
Fort George‡	50.0	20.2	Niagara, Ont.	1969	Reconstructed British fort from War of 1812
Fort Langley	12.0	4.9	Fort Langley, B.C.	1925	Reconstruction of Hudson's Bay Company post
Fort Lennox‡	163.1	66.0	Near Saint-Jean, Que.	1921	Site of British fort built during the early 1800's
Fort Lévis No. 1	——	——	Lauzon, Que.	1977	Fortifications built by British, begun in 1865
Fort Malden	10.4	4.2	Amherstburg, Ont.	1940	Defense post built between 1797 and 1799
Fort Prince of Wales‡	66.1	26.7	Near Churchill, Man.	1940	Fort built by Hudson's Bay Company, 1732-1772
Fort Rodd Hill	44.4	18.0	Esquimalt, near Victoria, B.C.	1962	First lighthouse on Canada's west coast; fortifications built in late 1800's
Fort St. James‡	14.0	5.7	Fort St. James, B.C.	1969	Hudson's Bay Company post built in 1806
Fort St. Joseph‡	863.0	349.2	Near Sault Sainte Marie, Ont.	1928	Trading post built in 1796; most westerly British fort
Fort Témiscamingue‡	66.1	26.7	Ville-Marie, Que.	1970	Last of a series of posts built by fur traders
Fort Walsh‡	1,600.0	647.0	Maple Creek, Sask.	1924	Early post of North-West Mounted Police
Fort Wellington‡	12.7	5.1	Prescott, Ont.	1940	British fort of the late 1830's
Fortress of Louisbourg‡	15,000.0	6,070.0	Louisbourg, N.S.	1940	Reconstruction of last French fort in Canada
Grand Pré‡	28.0	11.3	Grand Pré, near Wolfville, N.S.	1961	Acadian village; home of Evangeline, heroine of Henry Wadsworth Longfellow's poem
Halifax Citadel	40.0	16.0	Halifax, N.S.	1956	Restored British stone fort built in 1800's
Jacques Cartier Cross	——	——	Near Gaspé, Que.	1978	Commemorates Cartier's landing
Klondike Gold Rush International Historic Park‡	——	——	Yukon Territory	1970	Commemorates Klondike Gold Rush of 1897 and 1898; sites at Bonanza Creek, Dawson, Lake Bennett, and Whitehorse; Chilkoot and White Pass Trails; S.S. *Keno*, S.S. *Klondike*
L'Anse aux Meadows	20,000.0	8,100.0	Near St. Lunaire, Nfld.	1978	Authenticated Viking remains
Les Forges du Saint-Maurice‡	78.2	31.6	St. Maurice, Que.	1973	Site of Canada's first iron industry, 1729-1883
Lower Fort Garry‡	86.0	34.8	Near Selkirk, Man.	1951	Hudson's Bay Company fort built in 1830's
Maison Sir Wilfrid Laurier‡	0.5	0.2	Laurentides, Que.	1938	Early home of Sir Wilfrid Laurier, Canada's seventh prime minister
National Battlefields Park	235.0	95.1	Quebec City, Que.	1908	Site of 1759 Battle of Plains of Abraham
Port au Choix	5,397.0	2,184.1	On Great Northern Peninsula, Nfld.	1974	Maritime Archaic Indians Burial site (2000? B.C.)
Port Royal Habitation‡	25.4	10.3	Near Annapolis Royal, N.S.	1940	Reconstruction of Habitation, French fur-trading settlement of the early 1600's
Prince of Wales Martello Tower‡	6.0	2.4	Halifax, N.S.	1956	Restored defense fortification of early 1800's
Province House	1.1	0.4	Charlottetown, P.E.I.	1974	Birthplace of Confederation in 1864
Quebec City Walls and Gate	14.5	5.9	Quebec City, Que.	**	Defense fortifications built by British in 1820's
Queenston Heights and Brock's Monument‡	12.8	5.2	Queenston, Ont.	1969	Site of major British victory in War of 1812; monument honors General Isaac Brock
Rideau Canal	——	——	Links Ottawa and Kingston, Ont.	1972	Alternate shipping route to Upper Canada, built after War of 1812
Rocky Mountain House‡	542.0	219.3	Rocky Mountain House, Alta.	1970	Site of rival North West Company and Hudson's Bay Company trading posts
St. Andrews Blockhouse‡	2.5	1.0	Saint Andrews, N.B.	1962	Fortifications built at start of War of 1812
St. Roch	——	——	Vancouver, B.C.	1965	First ship to sail through Northwest Passage from both west and east
Signal Hill	243.2	98.4	Near St. John's, Nfld.	1956	Site of last battle of French and Indian War (1754-1763); reception of first transatlantic wireless telegraph message in 1901
Woodside	10.2	4.1	Kitchener, Ont.	1954	Boyhood home of William Lyon Mackenzie King, prime minister of Canada for 21 years
York Factory‡	108.0	43.7	York Factory, Man.	1968	Hudson's Bay Company fur-trading post, 1682-1957
York Redoubt‡	195.0	78.9	Halifax, N.S.	1956	Defense post dating from 1793

Source: Parks Canada. **Not available. ‡Closed part of the year.

Oil painting on canvas (1915); Hart House Permanent Collection, University of Toronto

Canadian Painting largely followed European trends until the mid-1800's, but later painters emphasized Canadian subject matter and developed their own styles. *The Pointers, left,* by Tom Thomson, is a fine example of his brilliantly colored landscapes of the Canadian wilderness. *The Habitant Farm, below,* by Cornelius Krieghoff, shows a scene of French-Canadian farm life during the 1800's.

Robert Buchbinder, Tom Stack & Assoc.

Soapstone Carvings by Eskimo artists portray objects and activities from the traditional life of these people.

Oil painting on canvas (1854); The National Gallery of Canada

The arts have flourished in Canada during the 1900's, especially since the end of World War II in 1945. Government support has played a vital role in this development. In 1957, the Canadian government set up the Canada Council to promote the advancement of the arts, humanities, and social sciences. The council provides financial assistance to individual artists and to orchestras, theaters, and other organizations. Every province except Prince Edward Island supports the arts through grants to individuals and groups.

In 1969, the federal government opened the National Arts Centre in Ottawa. Drama, music, opera, ballet, and motion pictures are presented there. The National Gallery, also in Ottawa, has an excellent collection of European art and a large number of Canadian works.

Literature. Canada has two great literatures, one written in French and the other written in English. For a discussion of Canadian writers and their works, see CANADIAN LITERATURE.

Painting and Sculpture. The works of most early Canadian painters followed European trends. During the mid-1800's, Cornelius Krieghoff, a Dutch-born artist in Quebec, painted scenes of the life of the *habitants* (French-Canadian farmers). At about the same time,

Stratford Festival, Canada from Miller Services

Théâtre du Nouveau Monde, Montreal

Theater flourishes in both the English- and French-speaking areas of Canada. The photo on the left shows a scene from a production of William Shakespeare's *A Midsummer Night's Dream* at the Stratford Festival in Stratford, Ont. The scene pictured on the right is from a performance of *Les Rustres* by Carlo Goldoni staged by Le Théâtre du Nouveau Monde in Montreal.

National Ballet of Canada from Miller Services

Canadian Ballet Stars include Karen Kain and Frank Augustyn, shown above in a performance of *Sleeping Beauty*.

Inventaire des Oeuvres d'Art

Eberhard E. Otto, Miller Services

Architecture in Canada includes both traditional and modern styles. The Maison L'Heureux in Charlesbourg, Que., *left*, is typical of the French-style homes built in Quebec during the 1600's and 1700's. The Place Ville Marie, *above*, is a modern office, shopping, and entertainment complex in Montreal.

Roger Ressmeyer, Sygma

Folk Music and Rock Music are popular in Canada, and Canadian performers have achieved success in the United States as well as their own country. Joni Mitchell, one of the best-known Canadian musicians, is shown above.

National Film Board of Canada

Award-Winning Motion Pictures produced by the National Film Board of Canada include dramas, documentaries, and animated films. The scene above is from *Strangers at the Door,* a 30-minute drama that examines the experiences of immigrants in Canada.

the Canadian artist Paul Kane painted pictures of Indian life in western Canada.

A group of landscape painters called the Group of Seven developed the first distinctively Canadian style of painting. Tom Thomson, one of Canada's best-known painters, was associated with the group. However, he died three years before their first exhibition in 1920. All these artists painted large, brilliantly colored scenes of the Canadian wilderness. See Group of Seven.

Since the 1930's, Canadian painters have developed a wide range of highly individual styles. Emily Carr became famous for her paintings of the totem poles of British Columbia. Other noted painters have included the landscape artist David Milne and the abstract painters Jean-Paul Riopelle and Harold Town.

The finest works of Canadian sculpture are perhaps the ivory and soapstone carvings by Eskimo artists. These carvings show objects and activities from the daily life of Eskimos.

Theater. Canada's best-known theatrical event is the Stratford Festival, held annually in Stratford, Ont., from June to November. Famous performers appear in the plays of William Shakespeare and other noted dramatists. Summer drama festivals also include the Shaw Festival in Ontario and the festival Lennoxville in Quebec. The leading theater organization in French-speaking Canada is Le Théâtre du Nouveau Monde in Montreal. Many regional theater companies have developed throughout Canada since the 1950's.

Music. Canada's outstanding orchestras are the Montreal Symphony Orchestra, the National Arts Centre Orchestra, the Toronto Symphony Orchestra, and the Vancouver Symphony Orchestra. Solo performers who have gained fame include the pianist Glenn Gould and the singers Maureen Forrester, Lois Marshall, Louis Quilico, and Jon Vickers. Canadians who have achieved stardom in popular music include the folk singers Gordon Lightfoot, Joni Mitchell, Anne Murray, and Buffy Saint-Marie. Robert Charlebois and Pauline Julien became famous singers in French-speaking Canada.

Ballet and Opera. Canada has three professional ballet companies. The oldest, the Royal Winnipeg Ballet, was founded in 1938 and is known for its performances of original Canadian works. The National Ballet of Canada in Toronto and Les Grands Ballets Canadiens in Montreal have both toured extensively. The National Ballet features many international stars as well as such outstanding Canadian dancers as Frank Augustyn, Karen Kain, and Veronica Tennant.

The Canadian Opera Company in Toronto performs six operas during their season, which lasts from September to May. Several other Canadian cities have local opera companies.

Motion Pictures. The Canadian motion-picture industry began in 1939 with the founding of the National Film Board. The board, a government-sponsored organization, has won hundreds of awards for documentaries and animated films. In 1967, the government set up the Canadian Film Development Corporation, which helped establish Canada's feature-length film industry.

Architecture. Familiar examples of traditional architecture in Canada include the French-style homes of Quebec and the neo-Gothic Parliament buildings in Ottawa. Modern Canadian architecture is international in style. The Toronto Dominion Centre in Toronto and the Place Ville Marie in Montreal reflect the sleek, uncluttered style originated by Ludwig Mies van der Rohe of Germany. The Toronto City Hall, one of Canada's most impressive structures, was designed by Viljo Revell of Finland (see Toronto [picture]).

Photri

The Rocky Mountains of western Canada offer some of the world's most beautiful scenery. The magnificent setting shown above is in Jasper National Park in southwestern Alberta.

Canada covers most of the northern half of North America. It borders Alaska on the northwest and the rest of the continental United States on the south. From east to west, Canada extends 3,223 miles (5,187 kilometers) from the rocky coast of Newfoundland to the St. Elias Mountains in the Yukon Territory. The nation includes six time zones. At noon in Vancouver, the time in St. John's, Nfld., is 4:30 P.M. From its southernmost point, Middle Island in Lake Erie, Canada extends 2,875 miles (4,627 kilometers) north to Cape Columbia on Ellesmere Island. Of all the world's land areas, only the northern tip of Greenland is nearer the North Pole than is Cape Columbia.

Canada has one of the longest coastlines of any country—151,488 miles (243,797 kilometers), including island coasts. Canada faces the Pacific Ocean on the west, the Arctic Ocean on the north, and the Atlantic Ocean on the east. In addition, Hudson Bay, Hudson Strait, and James Bay form a great inland sea in Canada. Hudson Bay remains frozen for about eight months of the year. But in the summer it is a waterway that provides an entrance to Canada's vast interior regions.

Mountains and wastelands make up more than half the land area of Canada, and forests cover about a third. About 11 per cent of the land has been permanently settled. Most Canadians live in southern agricultural areas and along the Atlantic and Pacific coasts. About 7 per cent of the land is used for agriculture.

Land Regions

Canada has eight major land regions. They are (1) the Pacific Ranges and Lowlands, (2) the Rocky Mountains, (3) the Arctic Islands, (4) the Interior Plains, (5) the Canadian Shield, (6) the Hudson Bay Lowlands, (7) the St. Lawrence Lowlands, and (8) the Appalachian Region.

The Pacific Ranges and Lowlands form Canada's westernmost land region. They make up most of British Columbia and the southwestern part of the Yukon Territory. The region includes the Queen Charlotte Islands and Vancouver Island. All these islands are the upper portions of a mountain range that is partly covered by the Pacific Ocean. The Coast Mountains rise along the coast of British Columbia. The St. Elias Mountains in the Yukon include Canada's highest peak, Mount Logan. It towers 19,520 feet (5,950 meters) above sea level near the Alaskan border. Glaciers cover many of the higher slopes in the St. Elias Mountains.

Because the Coast Mountains are on the seashore, the coastline of British Columbia has many long, narrow inlets called *fiords*. The fiords provide a water route to Canada's most valuable forests. These forests consist of tall red cedars, hemlocks, and other evergreen trees that grow on the lower slopes of the mountains. Black bears, foxes, and a variety of other fur-bearing animals live in the forests.

The Interior Plateau, an area of plains, river valleys, and smaller mountains, lies east of the Coast Mountains. This area has valuable mineral resources, including Canada's largest deposits of bismuth and molybdenum. The southern part of the Interior Plateau has many farms and orchards as well as large grasslands where cattle graze. Forests grow in the northern part of the plateau area.

The Rocky Mountains rise east of the Pacific Ranges and Lowlands. These two regions together are sometimes called the *Cordillera*. In Canada, the snow-capped Rockies vary in height from 7,000 to more than 12,000 feet (2,100 to 3,660 meters) above sea level. The tallest peak, Mount Robson in eastern British Columbia, is 12,972 feet (3,954 meters) high. Thousands of people visit the Rockies every year to view the magnificent scenery and to enjoy such activities as camping, hiking, and skiing.

The Rocky Mountain Chain extends for more than 3,000 miles (4,800 kilometers) from New Mexico to northern Alaska. The Canadian portion of the chain includes several separate ranges. The major range, the Canadian Rockies, stretches from Canada's southern border to the Liard River in northern British Columbia. Railroads and highways cross the Canadian Rockies at Crowsnest, Kicking Horse, Vermillion, and Yellowhead passes. Between the Liard River and the Alaskan border are several other ranges, including the Selwyn Moun-

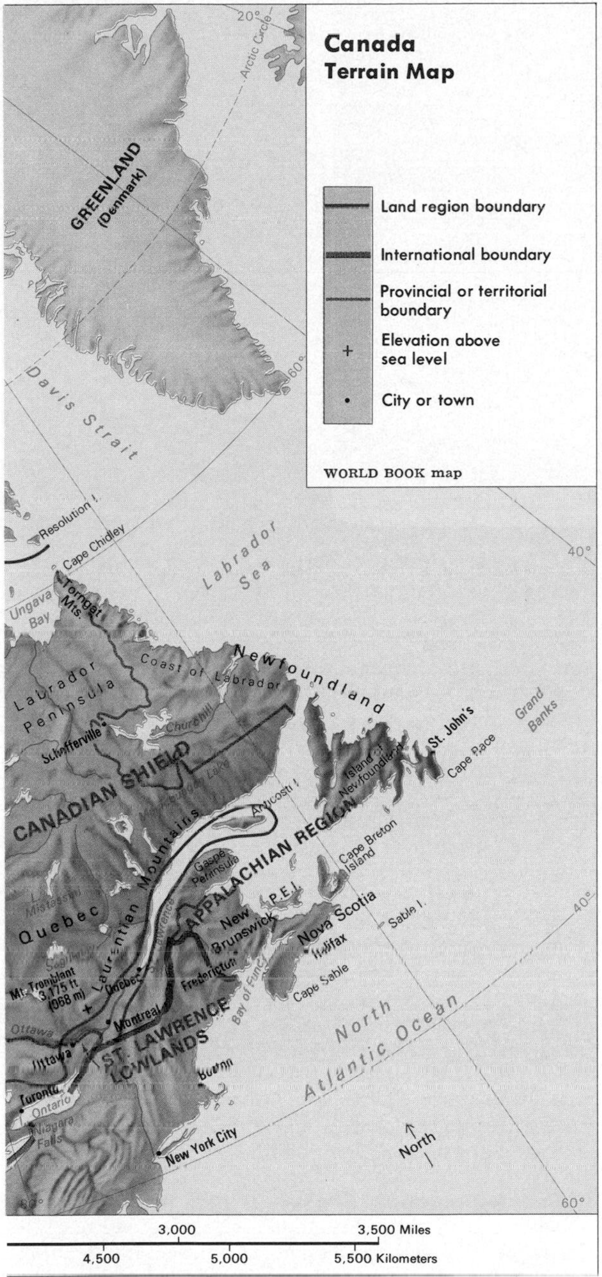

tains and the Mackenzie Mountains. The Columbia Mountains in southern British Columbia are separated from the Canadian Rockies to the east by a long, narrow valley called the Rocky Mountain Trench.

The Rockies contain important deposits of coal, lead, silver, zinc, and other minerals. Forests of juniper and pine trees grow on the lower slopes, and firs and spruces thrive at higher elevations. Bears, deer, minks, mountain lions, squirrels, and other animals inhabit the forests on the upper slopes. Rocky Mountain goats and bighorn sheep live above the *timber line*, the elevation above which trees cannot grow. Rainbow trout, cutthroat trout, grayling, and other fishes swim in the swift-flowing mountain streams.

The Arctic Islands lie almost entirely within the Arctic Circle. They include about a dozen large islands and hundreds of smaller ones. All the islands are barren, and most remain unexplored. Two of the largest islands, Baffin Island and Ellesmere Island, have many glaciers, tall mountains, and deep fiords. In contrast, Victoria Island and the other western islands are extremely flat. The seas surrounding the islands remain frozen most of the year.

The Arctic Islands are *tundras*, which are places too cold and dry for trees to grow. The subsoil of the islands is permanently frozen, and only a thin surface layer of soil thaws during the brief, cool summers. Only simple plants called *lichens* grow on the northernmost islands. The other islands have lichens, mosses, grasses, and grasslike plants known as *sedges*. Herds of caribou and musk oxen graze on the tundras. Other wildlife includes Arctic foxes and hares, lemmings, polar bears, ptarmigans, seals, walruses, and whales. Insects thrive on the Arctic Islands during the summer.

Deposits of petroleum and natural gas, as well as such minerals as lead and zinc, have been discovered in the Arctic Islands. However, little of this mineral wealth has yet been tapped because of the high production costs and the difficulty of transporting the products to distant markets.

The Interior Plains include the northeastern corner of British Columbia, much of Alberta and Saskatchewan, and the southwestern part of Manitoba. The region extends north through the Northwest Territories to the Arctic Ocean.

Grasslands form the natural cover of the vast prairies in the southern Interior Plains. Farmers have plowed most of the grasslands to grow wheat and other grains in the fertile black soil. Ranchers graze cattle on the remaining grasslands in the drier areas of southern Alberta. Farther north, evergreen forests form part of the great northern forest that sweeps across Canada from Alaska to the coast of Labrador. White spruces and jack pines are the most common trees in these forests. Deer, elk, moose, and many kinds of fur-bearing animals live there. Near the Arctic Ocean, the forests gradually give way to tundras that are covered by snow for more than half the year.

The Interior Plains have many mineral resources. Deposits of petroleum, natural gas, and coal have made Alberta Canada's richest province. In addition, the world's largest known deposits of *bituminous sands* or *tar sands* (sands that contain oil) lie along the Athabasca River in Alberta. These deposits may contain as much as 200 billion barrels of petroleum. Southern Saskatchewan has the largest potash deposits in the world. The Northwest Territories has petroleum and major deposits of lead and zinc.

The Canadian Shield is a vast horseshoe-shaped region. It curves around Hudson Bay from the Arctic coast of the Northwest Territories to the coast of Labrador, the mainland part of Newfoundland. The Canadian Shield

The Interior Plains are the major grain-producing region of Canada. Small towns like this one in southern Saskatchewan dot the region's broad, fertile prairies. The tall buildings in the picture are grain elevators, where farmers store grain until it can be shipped to market.

NFB Photothèque

covers about half of Canada and is made up of extremely ancient rock. Much of the region lies between 600 and 1200 feet (180 and 366 meters) above sea level. The eastern part of the region forms the Great Laurentian Uplands north of the St. Lawrence River.

The Canadian Shield consists largely of low hills and thousands of lakes. These lakes are the sources of rivers that break into great rapids and waterfalls at the edge of the region. The rapids and waterfalls provide power for pulp and paper mills as well as a variety of other industrial operations.

Few people live in the Canadian Shield because of its poor soil and cold climate. Only a few areas near the southern edge of the region have soil that is good enough for farming. The northern areas of the Canadian Shield are tundras, and the plant and animal life there resembles that of the Arctic Islands. Valuable evergreen forests cover most of the rest of the Canadian Shield. Deer, elk, moose, wolves, and many smaller animals live in the forests.

The Canadian Shield has much of Canada's mineral wealth. For example, approximately 85 per cent of the nation's iron ore comes from mines near the border between Quebec and Newfoundland. Deposits of cobalt, copper, nickel, and platinum are mined near Sudbury, Ont., a major smelting center. The Canadian Shield also contains valuable deposits of copper, gold, silver, uranium, zinc, and other metals.

The Hudson Bay Lowlands form a flat, swampy region between the Canadian Shield and the southwestern coast of Hudson Bay. It extends about 800 miles (1,300 kilometers) from the Churchill River in Manitoba to the Nottaway River in Quebec. Much of the region is covered by poor-quality forests and huge deposits of decayed vegetable matter called *peat*. The only permanent settlements are several small villages, a few old trading posts and forts, and the ports of Churchill, Man., and Moosonee, Ont.

The St. Lawrence Lowlands make up the smallest Canadian land region, but about 60 per cent of the nation's people live there. This region includes the flat-to-rolling countryside along the St. Lawrence River and the peninsula of southern Ontario. Another part of the region, Anticosti Island at the mouth of the St. Lawrence, remains a wilderness because of its isolation and colder climate. Southern Ontario has Canada's only major *deciduous forests*, which consist of trees that shed their leaves every autumn. The most plentiful trees in these forests include beeches, hickories, maples, oaks, and walnuts. Rabbits, raccoons, squirrels, and other small animals inhabit the forests.

The St. Lawrence Lowlands have excellent transportation facilities and lie near markets in the eastern United States. These features help make the region the manufacturing center of Canada. Its factories produce about three-fourths of the nation's manufactured goods. Because of the region's rapid industrial growth, however, Ontario and Quebec have had to limit the spread of urban development into farm areas. Fertile soil and a relatively mild climate enable farmers in the St. Lawrence Lowlands to produce about a third of Canada's agricultural output. The most important crops include barley, corn, oats, tobacco, and a wide variety of fruits and vegetables. The region also has a large number of dairy farms.

The Appalachian Region includes southeastern Quebec and all of the Atlantic Provinces region except Labrador. The region forms part of an ancient mountain chain that extends from the island of Newfoundland south to Alabama. The terrain of the Appalachian Region varies but is generally hilly. The effects of glaciers and erosion have rounded the mountains. The Shickshock Mountains on the Gaspé Peninsula of Quebec have the region's highest peaks, which reach just over 4,000 feet (1,220 meters).

Most residents of the Appalachian Region live along the coast, where hundreds of bays and inlets provide excellent harbors for fishing fleets. In most areas, the land rises gradually from the Atlantic Ocean, but parts of Newfoundland and Nova Scotia have steep, rocky coasts. The Bay of Fundy, between New Brunswick and Nova Scotia, is famous for its high tides, which reach 70 feet (21 meters) in some areas.

Mixed evergreen and deciduous forests cover much of the Appalachian Region. Valuable farmland lies on the plains of Prince Edward Island and along the St. John River in New Brunswick and the Annapolis River in Nova Scotia. The area around the town of Thetford Mines in Quebec has some of the world's richest deposits of asbestos. Nova Scotia has important coal and gypsum resources. Copper, lead, zinc, and other minerals are mined in Newfoundland and New Brunswick.

Rivers, Waterfalls, and Lakes

Large numbers of rivers, waterfalls, and lakes add to the scenic beauty of the Canadian countryside. Until the first railroads were built during the 1800's, the rivers and lakes also provided the only means of reaching Canada's vast interior. Many of these waterways still serve as major transportation routes. In addition, they have great economic importance as sources of water for the generation of electric power and, in the western provinces, for irrigation.

The water from each of Canada's lakes and rivers eventually drains into one of four major bodies of water. Therefore, the country has four major drainage areas or basins: (1) the Atlantic Basin, (2) the Hudson Bay and Hudson Strait Basin, (3) the Arctic Basin, and (4) the Pacific Basin.

The Atlantic Basin covers about 678,000 square miles (1,756,000 square kilometers) in eastern Canada. The most important waterway in this drainage area is the Great Lakes-St. Lawrence River system. The Great Lakes, the largest group of freshwater lakes in the world, cover 94,510 square miles (244,780 square kilometers). Lake Michigan lies entirely within the United States, but the border between Canada and the United States passes through the other four Great Lakes and the rivers that connect them. These rivers are the Saint Marys, the Detroit, the St. Clair, and the Niagara. Between Lake Erie and Lake Ontario, the Niagara River plunges over a rocky ledge and forms Niagara Falls, a world-famous tourist attraction.

The St. Lawrence River flows about 725 miles (1,167 kilometers) from Lake Ontario to the Gulf of St. Lawrence, an arm of the Atlantic Ocean. The St. Lawrence is sometimes called the *Mother of Canada* because it was the chief route of the European explorers, fur traders, and colonists who came to Canada several hundred years ago. Today, the St. Lawrence forms part of the St. Lawrence Seaway and carries more freight than any other Canadian river. The St. Lawrence Seaway enables huge ocean-going ships to travel between the Atlantic and such Great Lakes ports as Toronto and Chicago. The Thousand Islands, which lie in the St. Lawrence River near Lake Ontario, are a popular resort area.

Dams on the major tributaries of the St. Lawrence provide much hydroelectric power for eastern Canada. Loggers also use such tributaries as the Ottawa, the St. Maurice, and the Saguenay to float wood to pulp and paper plants downstream. Hydroelectric plants operate on several other tributaries and on the St. Lawrence itself. Power projects are planned for a number of rivers on the north shore of the Gulf of St. Lawrence, including the Natashquan and the Romaine.

The Montmorency River plunges 274 feet (84 meters) near Quebec City to form Montmorency Falls. Churchill Falls, on the Churchill River in Labrador, is the site of one of the largest power projects in the Western Hemisphere. New Brunswick is famous for its Reversing Falls at the mouth of the St. John River. Twice each day, high tides from the Bay of Fundy force the river backward through the falls. See REVERSING FALLS OF SAINT JOHN.

The Hudson Bay and Hudson Strait Basin covers about a third of mainland Canada. The chief river in

Eberhard E. Otto, Miller Services

The St. Lawrence Lowlands include large areas of rolling farmland. Fertile soil and a relatively mild climate help this region rank high in Canadian agricultural production.

Photo Librarium, Canada

The Appalachian Region consists primarily of forests and farmland. The forests of this region are a mixture of evergreens and trees that shed their leaves each autumn.

this basin is the Nelson, which flows from Lake Winnipeg to Hudson Bay. During the 1700's and 1800's, the Nelson served as an important transportation route for the Hudson's Bay Company. Today, the river is used mainly as a source of hydroelectric power. The Nelson's principal tributaries—the Assiniboine, the North and South Saskatchewan, the Red, and the Winnipeg rivers—flow into Lake Winnipeg rather than directly into the Nelson. The headwaters of the South Saskatchewan provide water for the irrigation of the dry farmlands in the southern part of Alberta. Dams on the Winnipeg River supply most of the electric power for the city of Winnipeg.

Other major rivers that flow into Hudson Bay include the Churchill and the Hayes in Manitoba, the Severn and the Winisk in Ontario, and the Thelon in the Northwest Territories. Several rivers empty into James Bay. Among them are the Albany and Moose in Ontario, and the Eastmain, La Grande, Nottaway, and Rupert in Quebec.

The Arctic Basin includes parts of British Columbia, the Prairie Provinces, and the territories. The Mackenzie River system drains about half the basin. The sources of this river system, Canada's longest, are high in the Rocky Mountains, where the Peace and Athabasca rivers begin. These two rivers flow into the Slave River, which in turn empties into Great Slave Lake. The Mackenzie River itself flows northwest from Great Slave Lake for approximately 1,000 miles (1,600 kilometers) to the Arctic Ocean. Along the way, it receives water from many tributaries, the largest of which is the Liard River. The Great Bear River flows into the Mackenzie from Great Bear Lake, the largest lake that lies entirely in Canada.

Barges operated by the Canadian government carry cargo for 1,700 miles (2,740 kilometers) of the Mackenzie River system. The route extends between the Arctic Ocean and Waterways, Alta., near Fort McMurray. Along the way, cargo must be transported by land for only 16 miles (26 kilometers)—around a rapids on the Slave River.

The Pacific Basin covers much of British Columbia and the Yukon Territory. The northern third of the region is drained by the Yukon River. This river rises from a series of lakes in northwest British Columbia and flows west through the Yukon Territory and Alaska to the Pacific Ocean. During the gold rush of the late 1890's, riverboats brought thousands of prospectors up the Yukon to Dawson, a boom town near the Klondike gold fields.

The longest river in the southern part of the Pacific Basin is the Fraser. It flows through a deep valley from the Canadian Rockies to Vancouver, B.C., where it empties into the Pacific. The Columbia River rises in the mountains of southeastern British Columbia and flows south into the United States. Hydroelectric plants operate at several points on the Columbia. The Columbia goes through Upper Arrow Lake and Lower Arrow Lake, two of the long, narrow lakes in the interior valleys. Other important rivers of the Pacific Basin include the Kootenay, the Skeena, the Stikine, and the Thompson.

Canada's northern location gives the country a generally cold climate, but conditions vary considerably from region to region. During the winter, westerly winds bring frigid Arctic air to most of Canada. Average January temperatures are below 0° F. (−18° C) in more than two-thirds of the country. January temperatures average above freezing only along the coast of British Columbia. This area has a moderate climate because of mild winds from the Pacific Ocean.

Northern Canada has short, cool summers. In the northern Arctic Islands, July temperatures average below 40° F. (4° C). Permanent icecaps cover parts of Baffin, Devon, and Ellesmere islands. Southern Canada has summers that are long enough and warm enough for raising crops. Summer winds from the Gulf of Mexico often bring hot weather to southern Ontario and the St. Lawrence River Valley. Southern Ontario has average July temperatures above 70° F. (21° C) and a frost-free growing season nearly six months long.

Some coastal areas of British Columbia receive more than 100 inches (250 centimeters) of precipitation annually. Most of it falls during the autumn and winter. The Canadian prairies have from 10 to 20 inches (25 to 50 centimeters) of precipitation a year. Little snow falls there, and most of the rain comes during the summer. These conditions help make the prairies ideal for growing grain.

Southeastern Canada has a humid climate. The average annual precipitation ranges from about 30 inches (76 centimeters) in southern Ontario to about 60 inches (150 centimeters) on the coasts of Newfoundland and Nova Scotia. Heavy snow covers eastern Canada in winter. More than 100 inches (250 centimeters) of snow falls annually on large areas of New Brunswick, Newfoundland, Quebec, and Ontario.

Gerry Souter, Van Cleve Photography

The Arctic Climate of Northern Canada keeps much of the region a frozen wasteland most of the year. January temperatures average below 0° F. (−18° C) in more than two-thirds of Canada.

Average January Temperatures

Most of Canada has long, cold winters. January temperatures average below 0° F. (−18° C) in more than two-thirds of the country. Only the coastal areas of British Columbia have average January temperatures above 32° F. (0° C).

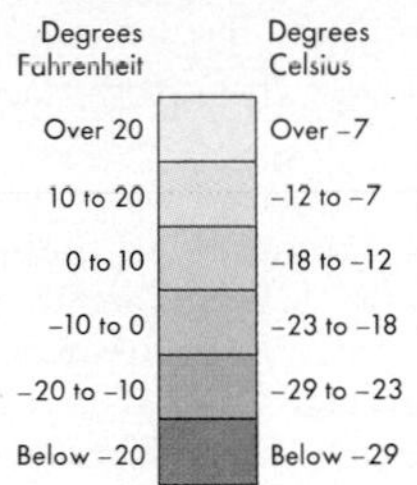

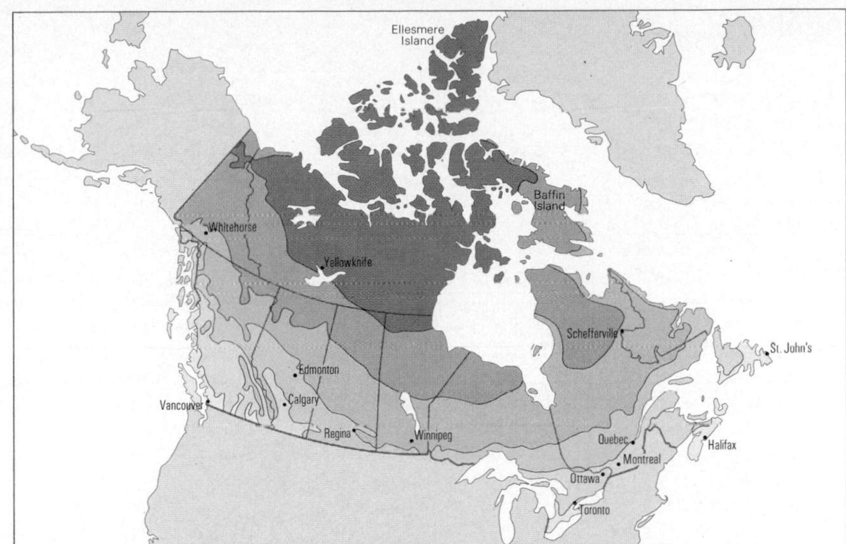

Average July Temperatures

Summers are cool in northern Canada but warm enough for farming in the southern areas of the country. Average July temperatures range from about 40° F. (4° C) in the northern Arctic Islands to more than 70° F. (21° C) in southern Ontario.

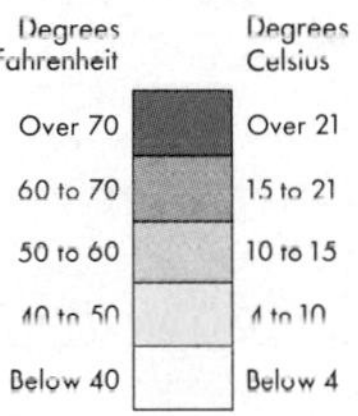

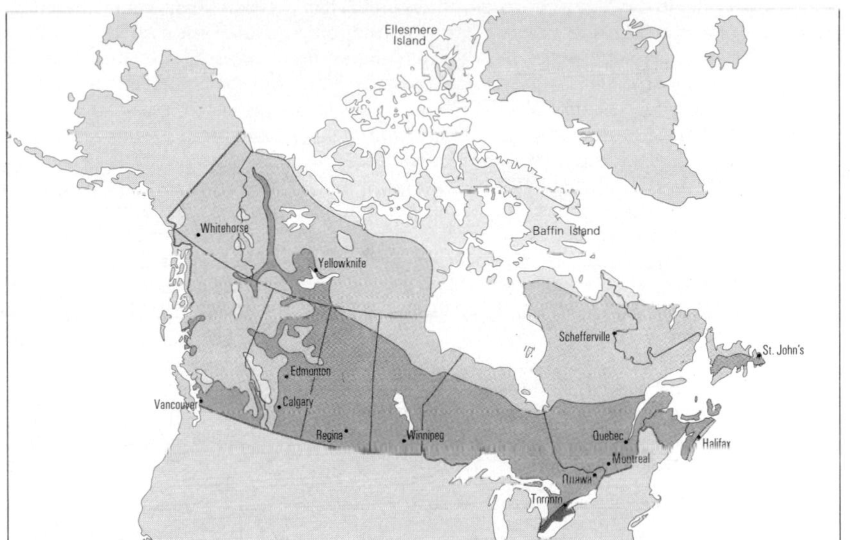

Average Yearly Precipitation

Precipitation in Canada is heaviest along the Pacific coast, where it averages more than 80 inches (200 centimeters) per year. The Prairie Provinces receive only 8 to 20 inches (20 to 50 centimeters), most of which falls in summer.

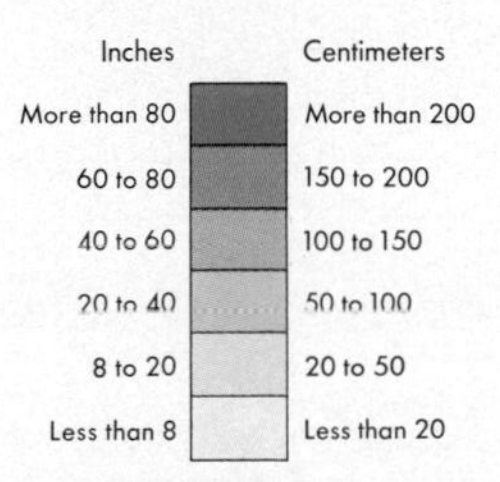

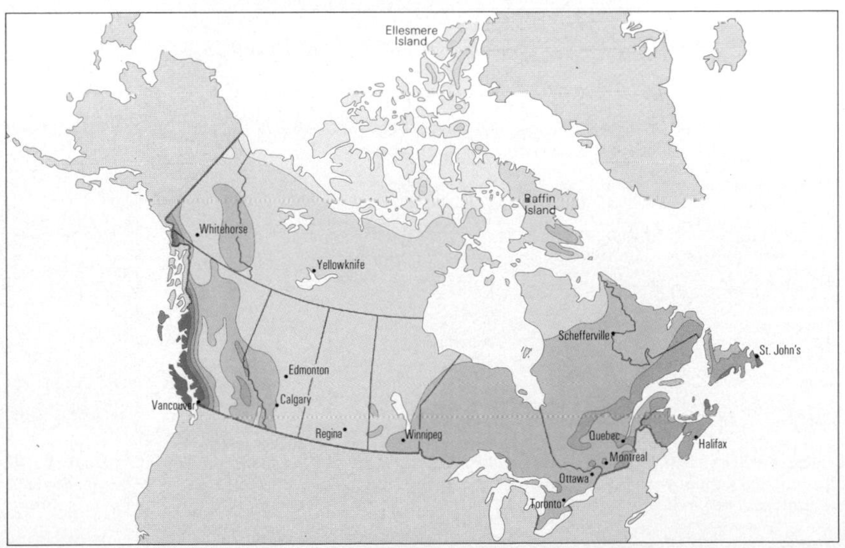

WORLD BOOK maps

During colonial times, most Canadians earned their living by farming, fishing, logging, or fur trapping. Today, these industries still serve the needs of Canada's people and produce valuable exports. But the main economic fields in Canada are service industries and manufacturing. Canada's *gross national product (GNP)* —that is, the total value of all goods and services produced—ranks among the top 10 in the world. The production percentages given in this section are based on Canada's *gross domestic product (GDP)*—the gross national product adjusted for net income sent or received from other countries.

The Canadian economy is based on private enterprise. But the national and provincial governments play an increasingly active role in many economic activities. For example, they provide health insurance that guarantees medical care to all Canadians. The federal and provincial governments also own broadcasting companies, transportation firms, and utilities. They have entered such fields as resource development and the financing of housing construction and steel production. The national government established Petro-Canada, a petroleum company, to gain some control over the production and sale of oil within Canada.

Foreign investment and ownership have a major influence on Canada's economy. U.S. firms affect the economy, both through ownership and through financing of Canadian-owned corporations. Great Britain, Japan, and West Germany also have large investments in Canada. Most Canadians feel that foreign-controlled businesses do not know or care enough about the nation's needs. Canada also suffers from the outflow of interest payments and profits, mostly to the United States. In 1974, the Canadian government created the Federal Foreign Investment Review Agency. This agency can prohibit foreign purchases of Canadian firms or the establishment of foreign-owned companies in Canada if such transactions do not benefit Canada.

The money values in this section are expressed in Canadian dollars. For the value of the Canadian dollar in U.S. currency, see MONEY (table: Exchange Rates).

Service Industries employ about 66 per cent of Canada's workers and account for about 63 per cent of its gross domestic product. The nation's largest and fastest-growing group of service industries provide community, business, and personal services. This group consists of a wide variety of business establishments. They include schools, hospitals, advertising agencies, data-processing services, and restaurants.

Financial institutions, such as banks and insurance companies, form another major group of service industries. Canada's commercial banking system consists of 12 banks, which have a total of nearly 7,500 branches throughout the country. The main Canadian stock exchange is in Toronto, and smaller exchanges operate in Montreal, Vancouver, and Calgary.

Other service industries include trade, transportation, and communications. Each is discussed later in this section. Most government activities are also considered service industries.

Manufacturing employs about 19 per cent of Canada's workers and accounts for about 21 per cent of the country's gross domestic product. Manufacturing in Canada is divided about equally into two broad fields. The first involves processing minerals and other natural resources for export, and the second provides products for use by Canadians. Factories in Ontario and Quebec produce more than three-fourths of Canada's manufactured goods. Food processing ranks as the nation's top manufacturing industry, followed by paper and related products and transportation equipment.

The Canadian food-processing industry handles chiefly meat and poultry products. Its other leading products include baked goods, dairy products, canned fruits and vegetables, soft drinks, beer, and whiskey.

Canada produces more *newsprint,* the paper used for newspapers, than any other country. About a third of the world's newsprint comes from Canada. The nation

Canadian Steel Mills produce about 13 million short tons (12 million metric tons) of steel annually. The plant shown above is in Hamilton, Ont., the center of the nation's steel industry.

George Hunter

Oil Derricks like these are a common sight in Alberta. More than 85 per cent of Canada's petroleum and natural gas comes from this province.

ranks third behind the United States and Japan in total paper production. Quebec is the center of the paper industry, but paper plants operate all along the southern edge of Canada's vast forests.

In the transportation equipment industry, U.S. automobile manufacturers operate plants in Ontario and Quebec. More than a million automobiles roll off the assembly lines of these plants yearly. The industry also produces trucks, aircraft, and farm machinery.

Other industries in Canada produce chemicals, electric and electronic equipment, iron and steel, metal products, and petroleum. Most steel comes from mills in Hamilton and Sault Ste. Marie, Ont., and Sydney, N.S. Major petroleum refineries are located in Montreal and two Ontario cities, St. Catharines and Sarnia.

Mining. Canada is the world's leading exporter of minerals. Since 1945, foreign markets eager for Canadian minerals have brought economic growth to Canada and settlement of its more remote regions.

Canada leads the world in the production of nickel and zinc. The nation ranks second in the world in production of asbestos and uranium. However, more than half of Canada's income from minerals comes from oil, natural gas, and by-products of natural gas. Canadian mines also produce coal, copper, gold, iron ore, lead, magnesium, molybdenum, potash, silver, titanium, and tungsten.

Agriculture employs about 5 per cent of Canada's workers and accounts for about 3 per cent of the nation's gross domestic product. Canada has about 300,000 farms, which cover approximately 169 million acres (68.3 million hectares). Its farmers are leading producers of barley, oats, rapeseed, and wheat. Canadian farmers and ranchers also rank high in production of livestock and dairy products.

More than three-fourths of Canada's farmland lies in the Prairie Provinces. Saskatchewan produces more than half of Canada's wheat, and farmers in Alberta and Manitoba raise most of the rest. Barley, flaxseed, oats, rapeseed, and rye grow in a belt north of the wheat-growing areas. Alberta is Canada's leading producer of beef cattle. Alfalfa, sugar beets, and vegetables come from irrigated areas of southern Alberta. Farmers in the Prairie Provinces also raise hogs and poultry.

The St. Lawrence Lowlands form Canada's other major agricultural region. Farmers in Ontario raise chiefly beef cattle. Southern Ontario's warm summers and long growing season also enable farmers to grow a variety of specialty crops, including fruits, vegetables, and tobacco. Quebec leads the provinces in the production of dairy products, and Ontario ranks second. Quebec farmers also raise hogs, poultry, beef cattle, apples, and vegetables.

Potato farming and dairying are the chief agricultural activities in the Atlantic Provinces. Farmers raise potatoes on Prince Edward Island and in the St. John River Valley of New Brunswick. The Annapolis River Valley in Nova Scotia is known for its apples.

Farmers in the interior of British Columbia and on Vancouver Island produce dairy products, eggs, livestock, and poultry. Cattle ranches prosper on the plateaus of British Columbia. The Okanagan Valley of British Columbia is Canada's leading apple-growing region.

Government marketing agencies establish production quotas and price supports to protect Canadian farmers from the effects of changing prices. The federal and provincial governments also provide credit, as well as technical and management assistance, to farmers. In many areas, farmers have formed cooperatives. These organizations market the farmers' products and supply goods and services needed in farming.

Forestry. Canada is a leading wood-producing nation. The federal and provincial governments own about 90 per cent of the forests and lease them to private companies. British Columbia, Ontario, and Quebec lead the provinces in timber production. Loggers cut down firs, hemlocks, pines, spruce, and many other kinds of trees. Mills process the logs into lumber, paper, plywood, and wood pulp.

Canada's Gross National Product

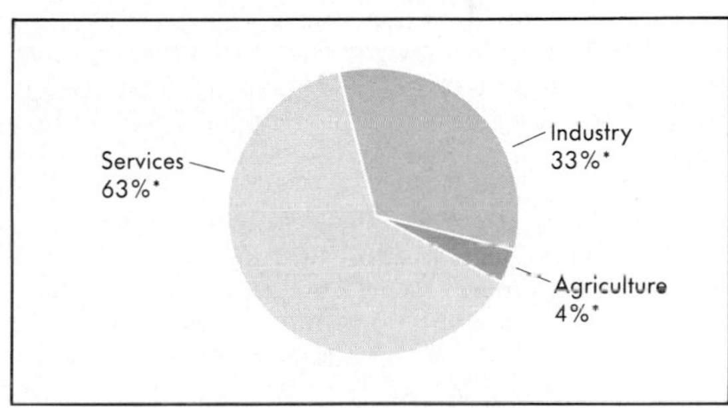

The gross national product (GNP) is the total value of goods and services produced by a country in a year. The GNP measures a nation's total economic performance and can also be used to compare the economic output and growth of countries. Canada's GNP was $281,168,000,000 in 1982.

Production and Workers by Economic Activities

Economic Activities	Per Cent of GDP* Produced	Employed Workers: Number of Persons	Employed Workers: Per Cent of Total
Community, Business, & Personal Services	21	3,238,000	30
Manufacturing	21	2,120,000	20
Finance, Insurance, & Real Estate	11	592,000	5
Trade	11	1,875,000	17
Government	8	761,000	7
Transportation & Communication	8	777,000	7
Construction	7	645,000	6
Mining	5	202,000	2
Agriculture, Fishing, Forestry, & Trapping	4	596,000	5
Utilities	4	127,000	1
Total	100	10,933,000	100

*Based on gross domestic product (GDP) in 1981. GDP is gross national product adjusted for net income sent or received from abroad.
Source: Statistics Canada.

Fishing Industry is one of Canada's oldest industries. The Grand Banks, off the coast of Newfoundland, ranks among the world's best fishing grounds. It has attracted fishing crews since the 1500's. Cod is the most valuable product of Canada's Atlantic waters. Other major catches include herring, lobsters, and scallops.

The main product in the Pacific waters of Canada is salmon. Crews catch most of the salmon near the mouths of the Fraser and Skeena rivers in British Columbia. Coastal canneries and freezing plants prepare the salmon for market. Other fish taken in the Pacific include halibut and herring.

Canada's lakes provide fish chiefly for the central part of the country and the United States. The principal products of these inland fisheries include perch, pickerel, pike, smelts, and whitefish.

Fur Industry. Fur-bearing animals trapped or hunted in Canada include beavers, coyotes, foxes, lynxes, martens, muskrats, and raccoons. The furs of wild animals account for about half of the value of Canada's total fur production. Minks and foxes raised on fur ranches provide the rest.

Energy. Canada uses energy at a high rate per person. The high rate of energy consumption results largely from the huge quantities needed for certain activities. These include providing heat during the severe winters, traveling between distant regions of the country, and processing natural resources. Canada has vast energy resources, but the rising costs of energy and the need to protect the environment make conservation of these resources essential.

Petroleum furnishes about 44 per cent of Canada's energy. Canada produces about 450 million barrels of oil yearly, of which more than 85 per cent comes from Alberta. Eastern Canada imports much oil from Venezuela and other nations. Alberta and British Columbia supply natural gas, which fills about 19 per cent of the nation's energy needs. Natural gas is plentiful and relatively nonpolluting.

Coal provides only about 9 per cent of Canada's energy. Alberta, British Columbia, and Saskatchewan produce most of Canada's coal.

Power generated by hydroelectric and nuclear plants supplies about 80 per cent of the nation's electricity. The nation has about 49 million kilowatts of hydroelectric capacity. Three new dams on La Grande River in northern Quebec will provide an additional 10 million kilowatts of electric power beginning in 1985. Canada's nuclear generators produce about 16 million kilowatts of electric power.

Canada has many possible new sources of energy. For example, the tides of the Bay of Fundy apparently could be used to generate electricity. Other future energy sources may include solar energy, the burning of wood waste and peat, as well as the use of windmills to generate electricity.

Trade. Canada ranks among the leading countries in the world in international trade. The nation's imports and exports total more than $100 billion annually. Fabricated materials—such as chemicals, petroleum, and textiles—and manufactured products account for nearly three-fourths of the nation's exports. Canadian manufactured goods make up about two-thirds of the nation's imports.

U.S. imports and exports provide about 70 per cent of Canada's foreign trade. Automobiles and automobile parts are the major products in trade between Canada and the United States. Canada's other leading exports to the United States include aluminum, iron, lumber, machinery, natural gas, newsprint, and wood pulp. The United States supplies Canada with chemicals, coal, computers and other electronic products, and many manufactured goods for industry and the home. Canada's other major trading partners include Belgium, Great Britain, France, Italy, Japan, the Netherlands, and West Germany.

Transportation. Canada's landscape includes many features that are barriers to travel. These barriers include mountains, forests, and bodies of water. In spite of these problems, however, Canadians have built an outstanding system of railroad, highway, water, and air transportation.

Railroads. Canada's railroad system has about 43,000 miles (69,000 kilometers) of track, more than any other

Herds of Beef Cattle graze on the grasslands of southern Alberta, where cattle ranching is the chief agricultural activity. Ontario and Saskatchewan are also leading producers of beef cattle.

Koos Dykstra, Image Finders

Logging is an important industry in many regions of Canada. This photograph shows a logging operation on the coast of British Columbia, the site of Canada's most valuable forests.

country except the United States and Russia. Canadian railroads carry about 30 per cent of the nation's freight. The government-owned Canadian National Railways (CN) provides freight service in all 10 provinces and the Northwest Territories. Its main competitor, the privately owned CP Rail (formerly Canadian Pacific Railway), operates in all the provinces except for Newfoundland and Prince Edward Island. A government-owned corporation called VIA Rail Canada provides all of Canada's passenger rail service except for commuter services in urban areas.

Roads and Highways. Canada has about 550,000 miles (885,000 kilometers) of highways, roads, and streets. The Trans-Canada Highway extends about 5,000 miles (8,000 kilometers) between Victoria, B.C., to St. John's, Nfld. The nation has about 10 million cars, $2\frac{1}{2}$ million trucks and buses, and 438,000 motorcycles and mopeds. The Canadian trucking industry transports about 119 million short tons (108 million metric tons) of freight annually.

Waterways and Ports. The Great Lakes and the St. Lawrence Seaway form one of the world's greatest in-

The Economy of Canada

The Canadian economy is based on a wealth of natural resources. This map shows some of the major products of each region of Canada. It also indicates how the land is used and points out the nation's chief manufacturing centers.

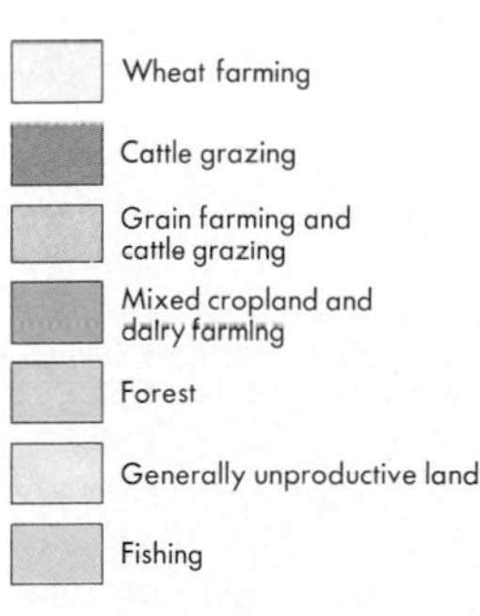

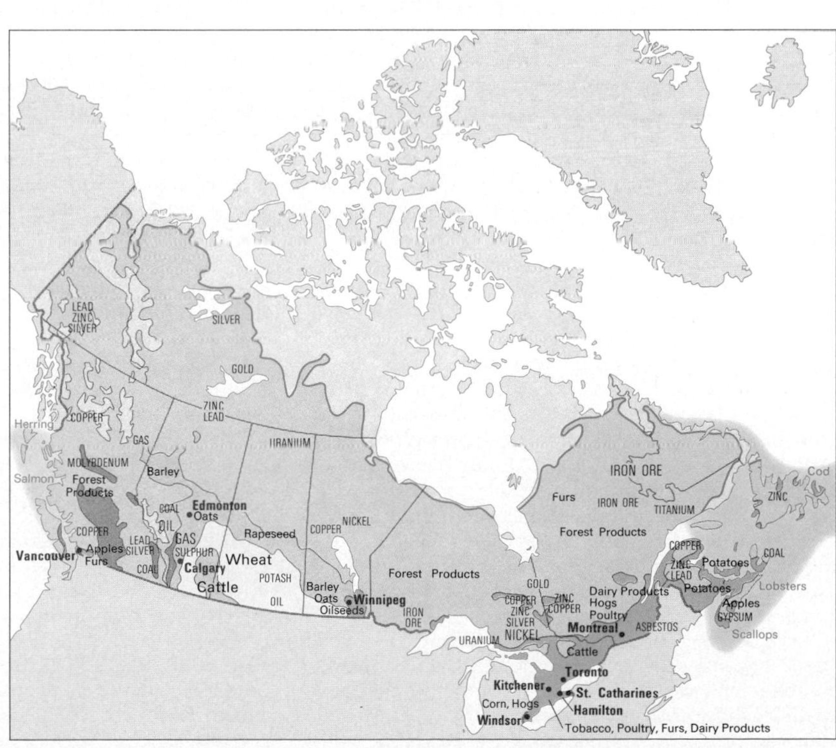

WORLD BOOK map; adapted from *The National Atlas of Canada*, 4th edition.

George Hunter

Canada's Fishing Industry produces about $1\frac{1}{2}$ million short tons (1.4 million metric tons) of fish and other seafood annually. The workers shown above are preparing salmon for canning.

land waterways. The seaway enables huge ocean-going ships to sail between the Atlantic Ocean and Great Lakes ports. These ships transport mainly wheat, iron ore, and other bulk cargoes. Other vessels, called *lakers*, transport cargo between ports on the Great Lakes and the St. Lawrence River. For example, lakers carry iron ore from ports on Lake Superior and the St. Lawrence to steel mills on the Great Lakes.

Canadian ports handle about 252 million short tons (229 million metric tons) of cargo annually. The port of Vancouver, including the facilities at nearby Roberts Bank, is Canada's busiest port. Other important Pacific ports include New Westminster and Victoria, B.C. Major ports on the St. Lawrence River include Sept-Îles, Montreal, Port Cartier, and Quebec City, Que. The leading Great Lakes ports are Thunder Bay, Hamilton, Sarnia, Sault Ste. Marie, and Toronto, Ont. Canada's busiest Atlantic ports are Halifax, N.S., and Saint John, N.B.

Air Travel. Two Canadian airlines—Air Canada and CP Air (formerly Canadian Pacific Air Lines Limited)—provide both domestic and international service. The government owns Air Canada and CP Air is privately owned. Five regional airlines and more than 35 foreign airlines also serve Canada. Toronto International Airport is the nation's busiest terminal, followed by Vancouver International and Montreal International (Dorval). Montreal International (Mirabel) is one of the largest airports in the world in area.

Communication plays a vital role in linking the various parts of a nation as vast as Canada. Canadians have one of the world's most advanced communication systems, including telephone and telegraph service, television and radio, mail service, and publishing.

Telephone and Telegraph Service. More than 150 telephone systems provide service for Canada's nearly 17 million telephones. The 10 major companies that make up the TransCanada Telephone System furnish more than 90 per cent of the service. Telegraph service is provided by CNCP Telecommunications, a company owned cooperatively by the Canadian National Railway and CP Rail.

The TransCanada Telephone System operates the world's longest microwave relay system. The network extends about 3,980 miles (6,400 kilometers) across southern Canada. It not only handles phone conversations but also transmits television and radio programs and computer data from coast to coast. Telesat Canada runs a satellite communications system that broadcasts television programs throughout Canada and provides telephone service in northern areas. Canada's telecommunications systems are linked by cable and satellite to those of almost every other country.

Television and Radio. The Canadian Broadcasting Corporation (CBC) operates national television and radio networks in both English and French. The CBC, though financed largely by the government, functions independently in its programming. Canada's satellite communications system enables CBC broadcasts to reach about 98 per cent of the population. The governments of Ontario and Quebec operate educational television networks, and Alberta has a government-operated educational radio network. Commercial networks serve various heavily populated areas of Canada. About half the nation's households subscribe to cable TV networks, which offer American programs.

The Canadian Radio-television and Telecommunications Commission (CRTC), a government agency, regulates all electronic communication systems in Canada. The CRTC issues licenses to radio and television stations and makes sure that certain percentages of their programs have Canadian content. These *Canadian content quotas* are intended to help maintain a Canadian cultural identity in the face of overwhelming U.S. influence. The quotas also are designed to create jobs in Canada by encouraging production there of TV and radio shows.

Mail Service in Canada is provided by the Post Office, a department of the federal government. Canada has about 8,300 post offices. See POST OFFICE (Canadian Postal System).

Publishing. Canada has more than 100 daily newspapers that are printed in English and over 10 in French. The leading English-language dailies include *The Toronto Star*, *The Globe and Mail*, and *The Sun* of Toronto; *The Sun* of Vancouver; and *The Journal* of Edmonton. The leading French-language dailies are *Le Journal de Montreal* and *La Presse* of Montreal and *Le Soleil* of Quebec. About 700 weekly newspapers serve small communities or certain areas of major Canadian cities. About 275 foreign-language papers are read by a wide range of ethnic groups.

More than 1,000 magazines are published in Canada, the best known of which include *Chatelaine*, *Maclean's*, *L'Actualité*, and *Nous*. American magazines are also widely read in Canada, and magazines from France have many readers in Quebec. Nearly 190 major Canadian publishing houses produce about 4,900 new titles annually. Many American, British, and French publications are printed in Canada at the same time as in their own country.

ADAM KARPINSKI and PATRICK WATSON

CANADA/*Study Aids*

Related Articles. See Canada, Government of; Canada, History of; and the separate province articles with their lists of *Related Articles*. See also the following articles:

PHYSICAL FEATURES

See Lake; Mountain; and River with their lists of *Related Articles*. See also:

Anticosti
Baffin Bay
Bay of Fundy
Boothia Peninsula
Canadian Shield
Cape Breton Island
Ellesmere Island
Gaspé Peninsula
Georgian Bay
Grand Banks
Hudson Bay
James Bay
Labrador
Magdalen Islands
Manitoulin Islands
Melville Island
Niagara Falls
Queen Charlotte Islands
Reversing Falls of St. John
Sable Island
Southampton Island
Thousand Islands
Vancouver Island

OTHER RELATED ARTICLES

Alaska Highway
Atlantic Provinces
Bank (Banks in Canada)
Bank of Canada
Canada, Armed Forces of
Canada Day
Canadian Broadcasting Corporation
Canadian Education Association
Canadian Library Association
Canadian Literature
Conservation (Canada)
Eskimo
Flag (picture: Flags of Canada)
Labor Movement (In Canada)
Library
O Canada
Petroleum (In Canada)
Prairie Provinces
Railroad (In Canada; History)
Remembrance Day
Rideau Canal
Royal Canadian Legion
Royal Society of Canada
Saint Lawrence Seaway
Soo Canals
Trans-Canada Highway
United Church of Canada
Welland Ship Canal

Outline

I. The Nation
- A. The Atlantic Provinces
- B. Quebec
- C. Ontario
- D. The Prairie Provinces
- E. British Columbia
- F. The Territories

II. People
- A. Population
- B. Ancestry
- C. Languages

III. Way of Life
- A. City Life
- B. Rural Life
- C. Arctic Life
- D. Education
- E. Religion
- F. Recreation and Sports

IV. National Park System
- A. National Parks
- B. National Historic Parks and Sites

V. The Arts
- A. Literature
- B. Painting and Sculpture
- C. Theater
- D. Music
- E. Ballet and Opera
- F. Motion Pictures
- G. Architecture

VI. The Land
- A. Land Regions
- B. Rivers, Waterfalls, and Lakes

VII. Climate

VIII. Economy
- A. Service Industries
- B. Manufacturing
- C. Mining
- D. Agriculture
- E. Forestry
- F. Fishing Industry
- G. Fur Industry
- H. Energy
- I. Trade
- J. Transportation
- K. Communication

Questions

How many Canadians speak French as their native language? In which province do most of them live?

How does Canada compare with the United States in size? In population?

What is the *Golden Horseshoe?* Where is it?

Who developed the first distinctively Canadian style of painting?

What kinds of plants and animals live on Canada's Arctic Islands?

Which province produces most of Canada's petroleum?

What is the most popular sport in Canada?

Why is the St. Lawrence River sometimes called the *Mother of Canada?*

What percentage of Canadians live on farms?

Which nations are Canada's main trading partners?

Reading and Study Guide

See *Canada* in the Research Guide/Index, Volume 22, for a *Reading and Study Guide*.

Additional Resources

Level I

Ferguson, Linda W. *Canada*. Scribner (New York City), 1979. Geography, climate, and history are discussed.

Houston, James, ed. *Songs of the Dream People: Chants and Images from the Indians and Eskimos of North America*. Academic Press (Don Mills, Ont.), 1972; Atheneum (New York City), 1972.

Lower, Joseph A. *Canada: An Outline History*. Rev. ed. McGraw (Scarborough, Ont.), 1973.

Owen, I. M., and Toye, William. *A Picture History of Canada*. 2nd ed. Oxford (Don Mills, Ont.), 1968.

Tanner, Ogden. *The Canadians*. Little, Brown (Boston), 1977.

Turner, Wesley B. *Life in Upper Canada*. Watts (New York City), 1980. Culture of the European pioneers and the native peoples from 1791-1841.

Level II

Bothwell, Robert, and others. *Canada Since 1945: Power, Politics, and Provincialism*. Univ. of Toronto Press, 1981. Political and economic history since World War II.

Fodor's Canada. McKay (New York City). Pub. annually.

Hiller, Harry H. *Canadian Society: A Sociological Analysis*. Prentice-Hall (Scarborough, Ont.), 1976.

Krueger, Ralph R., and Corder, R. G. *Canada: A New Geography*. 2nd ed. Holt (Toronto), 1976.

Livingston, John. *Canada: The Sub-Continent*. Natural Science of Canada (Toronto), 1971.

Patterson, E. Palmer. *The Changing People: A History of the Canadian Indians*. Collier (Cambridge, Ont.), 1971.

Ruggeri, Giusseppe C. *The Canadian Economy: Problems and Policies*. Gage (Agincourt, Ont.), 1976.

Watson, Jessie and Wreford. *The Canadians: How They Live and Work*. Griffin (Toronto), 1977.

Winks, Robin W. *The Blacks in Canada: A History*. Yale (New Haven), 1971.

CANADA, ARMED FORCES OF

CANADA, ARMED FORCES OF, are responsible for defending Canada and its interests throughout the world. Canada's air, ground, and naval services have been merged in one military force called the *Canadian Armed Forces* since 1968.

Until 1968, Canada had a separate army, navy, and air force. The Canadian Army was permanently organized in 1871, the Royal Canadian Navy in 1910, and the Royal Canadian Air Force in 1924. Canada's military forces fought gallantly in World Wars I and II and the Korean War. They have also served with peacekeeping forces of the United Nations in such trouble spots as Cyprus and the Middle East.

The Canadian Forces (CF) service dress uniform and rank insignia are the same for all branches of the service. The CF uniform is worn on all occasions except when working clothing, such as combat uniforms or flying suits, is needed.

Organization. The chief of the defence staff commands the Canadian Armed Forces. The chief is responsible to the minister of national defence, a member of the prime minister's Cabinet.

The Canadian Armed Forces has five commands. The commands are:

The Air Command supervises the military forces that defend Canada from air attack. It also cooperates with United States military forces in defending North America. In addition, the Air Command provides air transportation and aircraft training for other commands in the Canadian Armed Forces.

The Canadian Forces Communication Command maintains, manages, and operates strategic communications for the Canadian Armed Forces. It also serves the federal and provincial governments of Canada in emergency situtations.

The Canadian Forces Europe, stationed in Germany, serves as part of the forces of the North Atlantic Treaty Organization (NATO). This command consists of land and air forces.

The Maritime Command operates naval forces on the Atlantic and Pacific coasts to defend Canada against sea attack. It also helps support NATO forces against submarine warfare. In addition, the Maritime Command controls aircraft used in naval operations.

The Mobile Command stands ready to move combat land and air forces to any part of Canada or overseas on short notice. It also trains other Canadian troops for mobile operations.

Training and Enlistment. Officers receive their commissions after (1) graduating from a university and agreeing to active service for at least four years, (2) completing Officers Candidate Training, or (3) graduating from the Royal Military College in Kingston, Ont., Royal Roads Military College in Victoria, B.C., or Collège militaire royal de Saint-Jean in Saint-Jean, Que.

A Canadian citizen from 17 to 24 years old who has completed eighth grade may enlist in the Canadian Armed Forces for 5 years. Recruits receive 11 weeks of basic training.

Critically reviewed by the DEPARTMENT OF NATIONAL DEFENCE, CANADA

See also BISHOP, BILLY; MCNAUGHTON, ANDREW GEORGE LATTA; FLAG (picture: Flags of Canada).

National Defence Headquarters

Women in the Canadian Forces take part in almost all the same programs as men. The women shown above are in a training program for air traffic controllers.

Canadian Forces Command Badges

Mobile Command

Maritime Command

Canadian Forces

Communication Command

Air Command

Canadian Forces Rank and Grade Insignia

Worn on cap peak, sleeves, or shoulder straps

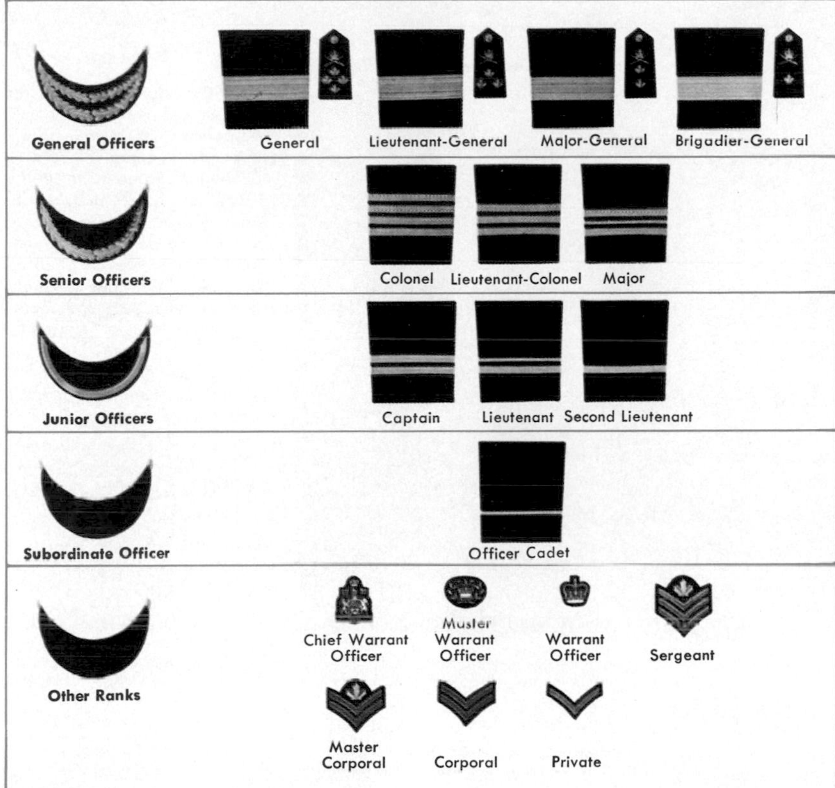

Canadian Forces Uniforms are the same for officers, *above*, and other ranks, *below*.

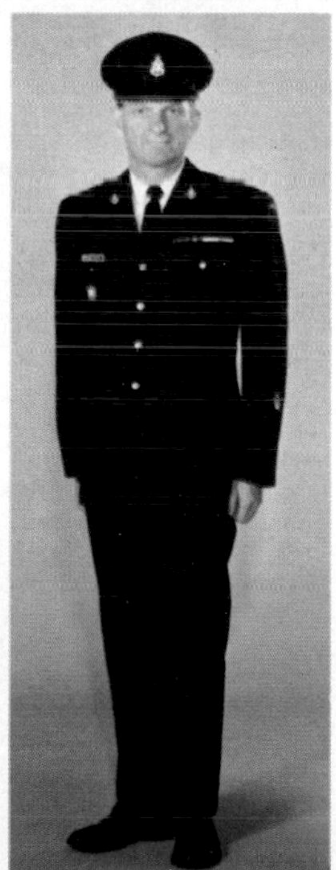

National Defence Headquarters

Branch Cap and Collar Badges

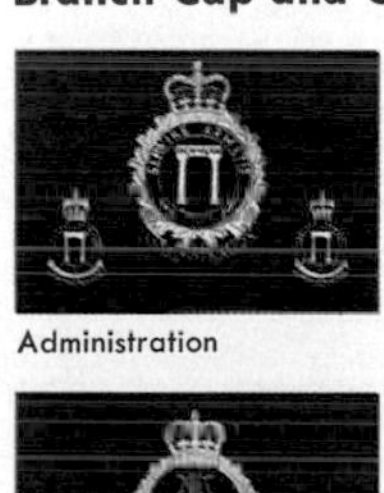

Administration

Air Operations

Armoured

Artillery

Band

Chaplain

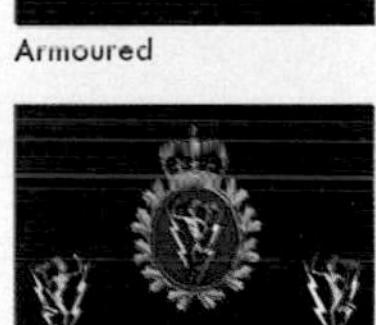

Communications and Electronics Engineering

Dental

Infantry

Land Ordnance Engineering

Legal

Logistics

Medical

Military Engineering

Naval Operations

Security

The Citizen, Ottawa

The Governor General of Canada opens each session of Parliament. This picture shows Governor General Edward R. Schreyer, seated next to the Canadian flag, speaking to government leaders at the opening of the 1980 session. Schreyer's wife is seated alongside him. The governor general serves as the representative of Queen Elizabeth II of Great Britain. In 1984, Jeanne Sauvé became the first woman to serve as Canada's governor general.

CANADA, GOVERNMENT OF

CANADA, GOVERNMENT OF. Canada combines a federal form of government with a cabinet system. The federal form is patterned on that of the United States, and the cabinet system on that of Great Britain.

As a federation, Canada is made up of 10 provinces and two territories. The country works out its national problems through its central government in Ottawa, which represents all the people of Canada. Each province has its own government. The territories have some self-government, but they are controlled largely by the central government.

The cabinet system of Canada unites the legislative and executive branches of the government. The prime minister and all members of the Cabinet are usually members of the House of Commons. Occasionally a senator may be in the Cabinet or serve as prime minister. Ministers are responsible for all their actions to the House, which is elected by the people. The House of Commons has the highest authority in the government. If the House defeats a piece of important government-supported legislation, or if it passes a vote of no confidence in the prime minister, the prime minister must either resign or request that the governor general call a new general election.

Queen Elizabeth II of Great Britain is also queen of Canada. She is the official head of state, but a governor general acts as her representative. However, the governor general performs only certain formal and symbolic tasks. The prime minister actually directs the government.

The people of Canada elect members of the House of Commons. They use the Australian ballot, the type of ballot used in the United States, Great Britain, and other countries. To vote in national elections, a person must be at least 18 years old and a Canadian citizen. Each province in Canada sets its own voting requirements for provincial elections. A voter must be at least 19 in British Columbia and at least 18 in the other provinces.

Canada is a member of the Commonwealth of Na-

The contributor of this article, John T. Saywell, is Professor of History and Environmental Studies, York University, Toronto, and the author of several books on Canadian government.

The Flag of Canada features a red, 11-pointed maple leaf, a national symbol of the country. It became Canada's official flag in 1965.

The Canadian Coat of Arms includes three red maple leaves below the royal arms of England, Scotland, Ireland, and France.

Canapress Photo

The Supreme Court of Canada hears final appeals in civil and criminal cases. The Supreme Court is composed of the Chief Justice of Canada and eight associate judges, called *puisne* judges. All the judges are appointed for life.

Facts in Brief

Form of Government: Constitutional monarchy.

Capital: Ottawa.

Divisions: 10 provinces, 2 territories.

Head of State: Elizabeth II of Great Britain, who is also queen of Canada, appoints a governor general as her representative.

Head of Government: Prime minister, leader of the majority party in the House of Commons.

Parliament: *Senate*—104 members appointed by the governor general. *House of Commons*—282 members elected by the people.

Coat of Arms: The shield bears the royal arms of England (upper left); Scotland (upper right); Ireland (lower left); and France (lower right). A British lion holds the Union Jack. A unicorn holds the fleur-de-lis of France. Canada received the coat of arms in 1921.

Anthems: "O Canada" (national); "God Save the Queen" (royal).

National Motto: *A Mari Usque ad Mare* (From Sea to Sea).

Flag: A red, 11-pointed maple leaf appears on a white field. At each end is a broad, vertical red stripe. The maple leaf is a national emblem. This flag became Canada's official flag February 15, 1965.

tions, but it is not a dependency of Great Britain. Canada is an independent, self-governing democracy, equal in rank to Great Britain and all other nations.

The Constitution

Canada's constitution is partly unwritten (like that of Great Britain) and partly written (like that of the United States). The unwritten part consists mainly of usage and customs, including the Cabinet system of government. The basic written section is the *Constitution Act of 1982*. It includes the *British North America Act*, which was the basic document governing Canada's federal system from 1867 to 1982. Other written parts include ordinary laws and judicial decisions.

The founding fathers of the Canadian confederation wanted to create a strong central government. They were wary of seeming weaknesses exposed in the United States federation by the Civil War. As a result, in the British North America Act, they made the federal government almost all-powerful. The provincial governments received only 16 powers that were then considered to be of relatively minor importance. The federal government received all other powers—called *residual powers*. It also received power to *disallow* (reject) any provincial legislation it believed to be undesirable.

Hans Blohm, Miller Services

The Canadian Parliament Buildings lie along the Ottawa River in Ottawa, Ont. The central tower houses a set of 53 bells.

Through the years, however, the powers given to the provinces—over such matters as education, health, and natural resources—became more and more important. The provinces became stronger and richer, and debates on the divisions of power between the federal and provincial governments increased. The Constitution Act of 1982 did not end the debates. But it achieved another long-sought goal—ending British control over amendments to Canada's constitution. Previously, the British Parliament had to approve all such amendments. Now approval requires the agreement of only the Canadian Parliament and any seven Canadian provinces with at least 50 per cent of the nation's population.

Executive Offices

The Governor General. The prime minister recommends a candidate for this office. The queen appoints the governor general as her representative, usually for five years. Until 1952, the governor general came from Great Britain. In that year, Vincent Massey became the first Canadian-born governor general. In 1959, Georges Philias Vanier became the first French-Canadian governor general. In 1984, Jeanne Mathilde Sauvé became the first woman to hold the post.

The governor general originally had far-reaching powers. But these powers gradually dwindled as the House of

Commons gained authority. Today, most of the governor general's powers have disappeared. The governor general acts in the name of the monarch, but follows the directions and advice of the Cabinet.

The Prime Minister of Canada is the actual executive head of the government. As the leader of the majority party in the House of Commons, the prime minister is indirectly elected by the people. No law establishes this office. It is simply a necessity, worked out long ago in England. No government could carry on without Parliament's support. The leader of the majority in the House gradually became the *prime* (first) minister of the Cabinet.

The prime minister is appointed by the governor general, who follows the wishes of the majority in the House. The prime minister holds office only with the backing of this majority. A prime minister who loses this backing must either resign or request that the governor general call a new general election.

Parliament can control the actions of the prime minister by giving or withholding support. But the prime minister also has a control over the actions of the House of Commons. The prime minister may request that the governor general dissolve the House of Commons and call a new general election. See PRIME MINISTER OF CANADA.

The Cabinet helps the prime minister direct the government. The Cabinet consists of about 30 ministers chosen by the prime minister from members of the majority party in the House—or occasionally the Senate—and appointed by the governor general. These ministers usually head government departments. They lose their offices if the prime minister dies or resigns.

Ministers hold political offices, and may lose their positions if the Cabinet changes. Therefore, a deputy minister is the permanent head of each department. These officers are civil servants. Cabinet ministers perform the following duties:

The Leader of the Government in the Senate is a Senator who sponsors legislation in the Senate that has been passed by the House of Commons.

The Minister of Agriculture supervises federal programs of land reclamation and price stabilization.

The Minister of Communications coordinates research on communications technology, operates the national galleries and museums, and regulates the broadcasting industry.

The Minister of Consumer and Corporate Affairs administers regulations concerning pure food standards and deceptive advertising.

The Minister of Employment and Immigration handles all matters concerning immigration and the development of Canada's labor resources.

The Minister of Energy, Mines, and Resources supervises the development of Canada's energy supply and the surveying of natural resources. The minister is assisted by the Minister of State for Mines. The Minister of State for Mines heads two special agencies—the Advisory Council on the Status of Women and the Office of the Coordinator, Status of Women.

The Minister of the Environment oversees programs to protect the environment.

The Minister of Finance presents the annual budget to Parliament. The minister is assisted by the Minister of State for Finance.

The Minister of Fisheries and Oceans administers programs to control water pollution and to manage the nation's fisheries.

The Minister of Indian Affairs and Northern Development administers the Northwest Territories, Yukon Territory, and Eskimo and Indian affairs.

The Minister of Justice interprets laws passed by Parliament and acts as legal adviser to the national government.

The Minister of Labour helps prevent or settle labor disputes, and watches over the interests of labor.

The Minister of National Defence controls and manages the Canadian Armed Forces.

The Minister of National Health and Welfare manages national public-health and social-welfare activities.

The Minister of National Revenue assesses and collects federal taxes and customs and excise duties.

The Minister of Public Works controls the construction and repair of public roads, buildings, and bridges.

The Minister of Regional Industrial Expansion supervises manufacturing, tourism, and trade in Canada. The minister is assisted by the Minister of State for Trade.

The Minister of State for Economic and Regional Development develops policies for promoting the Canadian economy.

The Minister of State for Science and Technology coordinates research on science and technology within the federal government.

The Minister of State for Social Development directs programs in aid of individual, family, and community development.

The Ministers of State. The Cabinet includes two Ministers of State, who handle special government assignments.

The Minister of Supply and Services handles government purchases and provides management services to other departments.

The Minister of Transport regulates nearly all commercial transportation and communications. The minister is assisted by the Minister of State for the Canadian Wheat Board.

The Minister of Veterans Affairs has charge of all matters concerning war veterans.

The President of the Queen's Privy Council for Canada supervises preparation of the government's legislative program and manages it in the House of Commons.

The President of the Treasury Board reviews proposed spending programs of all government agencies.

The Secretary of State of Canada controls state records and documents. The secretary is assisted by the Minister of State for Multiculturalism, who directs programs to promote the preservation and sharing of cultural heritages.

The Secretary of State for External Affairs handles relations with the Commonwealth nations, with other countries, and with the United Nations.

The Solicitor General of Canada supervises federal prisons and the Royal Canadian Mounted Police.

The Parliament

The Parliament is the national legislature of Canada. The Parliament has two houses, an upper house called the Senate, and a lower house called the House of Commons.

The Senate has 104 members. Senators are appointed by the governor general on the recommendation of the prime minister. The *speaker*, who is the presiding officer in the Senate, is also appointed by the governor general on the prime minister's recommendation. A new prime

CANADIAN PROVINCE SYMBOLS

Designs Cut into Stone on the curving walls of the Canadian House of Commons at Ottawa show the main industries of each of the 10 provinces. William Oosterhoff created the designs.

Alberta

A cowboy and his horse symbolize the ranches along the eastern slopes of the Rockies.

British Columbia

An airplane shows the growth of transportation and industry on the west coast.

Manitoba

A farmer with hayfork and spade stands for farming on Manitoba's prairies.

New Brunswick

A sailing ship shows the importance of water transportation and fishing to the province.

Newfoundland

A lumberman and his ax represent Newfoundland's forest resources.

Nova Scotia

A sailor and a pair of anchors show the importance of shipping in "The Old Colony."

All photos by Dominion-Wide

Ontario

A miner represents the province that leads in mining and manufacturing.

Prince Edward Island

A fisherman hauling in his nets suggests the wealth taken from seas near the island province.

Quebec

A turbine pictures the province that produces the most electric power.

Saskatchewan

A farmer and his tractor tell of agricultural plenty from "Canada's Breadbasket."

How a Bill Becomes Law in Canada

The Canadian Parliament considers two general types of bills—*public bills,* which concern the entire nation, and *private bills,* most of which concern only a person or a small group. The Cabinet sponsors most important public bills. All bills go through the same basic steps—three readings in the House of Commons, three in the Senate, and acceptance by the governor general. Most bills can begin in either the House of Commons or the Senate. But all bills dealing with expenses or taxes must start in the House of Commons. The Senate cannot reject these bills.

WORLD BOOK illustrations by David Cunningham

Action Begins on most public bills when a Cabinet minister gives formal notice of the bill to the House of Commons. This notice appears in the *Notice Paper.* But a bill to adopt a tax or spend money starts as a recommendation from the governor general to a Cabinet minister. Actually, the Cabinet decides what expenses and taxes to call for.

Introduction of the Bill. The Cabinet minister seeks permission to introduce the bill for the first reading. The minister's motion includes the bill's title and a brief explanation of the bill's purpose. The House then grants permission.

The Senate Reviews the Bill during the third reading. Amendments may be offered and put to a vote. If the Senate passes the bill without any amendments, the bill goes to the governor general. If the bill is defeated, it goes back for another first reading in the Senate. If the bill is amended, it is sent to the House of Commons.

One of 10 Standing Committees in the Senate reviews the House-passed bill and submits a report on it. The committee may suggest reductions—but not increases—for a money bill. It also may recommend amendments.

House-Senate Action. If the House of Commons does not accept the Senate's amendments, representatives from the House and the Senate meet and try to reach a compromise. If their compromise includes more changes, the revised bill must be given three readings in each house. If the representatives cannot reach a compromise, the bill is killed.

The Governor General receives the bill after it has been passed by both houses and, by tradition, accepts it. The bill, now a law, takes effect immediately or when the Cabinet proclaims it.

First and Second Readings. The bill is read for the first time. No debate is allowed, and no amendments may be considered. During the second reading, the most important stage, the House debates the bill's chief purpose but not its details. The bill may be passed or defeated. If passed, it goes to a standing or special committee.

One of 19 Standing Committees discusses the bill in detail and submits a report on it to the House. Each of these committees deals with a separate activity, such as agriculture. A special committee may be formed to obtain more information for the standing committee. The standing committee may suggest amendments in its report to the House.

The House of Commons discusses the bill after the committee review. It decides whether to accept the committee's report or to return the bill to the committee for another report. Amendments may be debated and put to a vote. After these proceedings have been completed, the bill goes through a third reading. Some debate is allowed at this time, and other amendments may be put to a vote. If the House passes the bill, it goes to the Senate.

Senate Action follows the same pattern, beginning with a first reading. If the bill originates in the Senate, the first reading occurs at once. Senate permission is not required to introduce bills. During the second reading, the Senate debates the bill's purpose. If passed, the bill goes to a committee.

National Film Board Photothèque

The House of Commons meets in its chamber in the Parliament buildings. Most of the important bills that are introduced in the Canadian Parliament start in the House. The public may observe sessions of the House from galleries.

THE GOVERNMENT OF CANADA

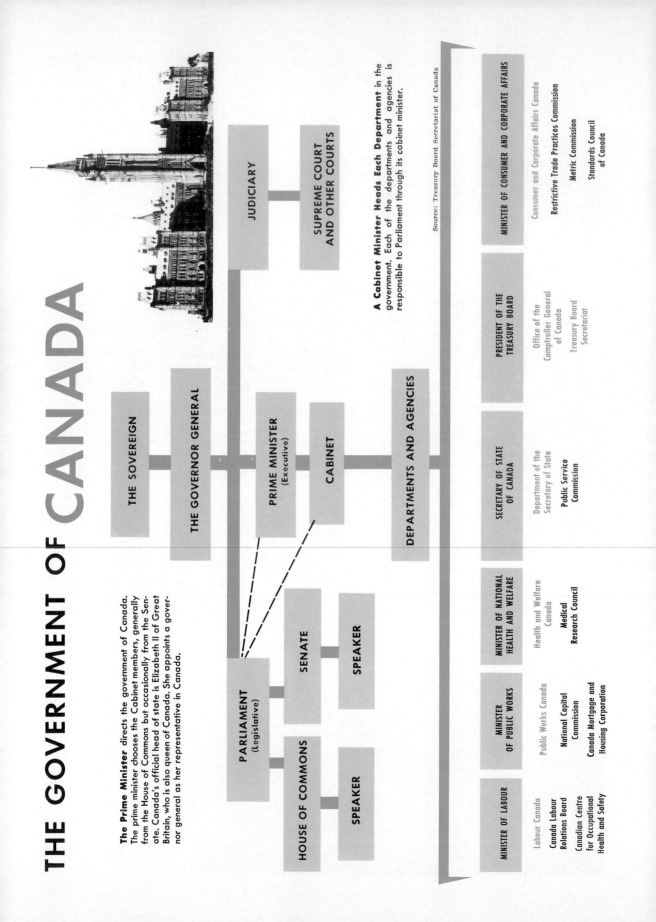

The Prime Minister directs the government of Canada. The prime minister chooses the Cabinet members, generally from the House of Commons but occasionally from the Senate. Canada's official head of state is Elizabeth II of Great Britain, who is also queen of Canada. She appoints a governor general as her representative in Canada.

THE SOVEREIGN

THE GOVERNOR GENERAL

PARLIAMENT (Legislative)

HOUSE OF COMMONS

SPEAKER

SENATE

SPEAKER

PRIME MINISTER (Executive)

CABINET

DEPARTMENTS AND AGENCIES

JUDICIARY

SUPREME COURT AND OTHER COURTS

A Cabinet Minister Heads Each Department in the government. Each of the departments and agencies is responsible to Parliament through its cabinet minister.

Source: Treasury Board Secretariat of Canada

MINISTER OF LABOUR
- Labour Canada
- Canada Labour Relations Board
- Canadian Centre for Occupational Health and Safety

MINISTER OF PUBLIC WORKS
- Public Works Canada
- National Capital Commission
- Canada Mortgage and Housing Corporation

MINISTER OF NATIONAL HEALTH AND WELFARE
- Health and Welfare Canada
- Medical Research Council

SECRETARY OF STATE OF CANADA
- Department of the Secretary of State
- Public Service Commission

PRESIDENT OF THE TREASURY BOARD
- Office of the Comptroller General of Canada
- Treasury Board Secretariat

MINISTER OF CONSUMER AND CORPORATE AFFAIRS
- Consumer and Corporate Affairs Canada
- Restrictive Trade Practices Commission
- Metric Commission
- Standards Council of Canada

MINISTER OF COMMUNICATIONS

Department of Communications

National Film Board
National Library
Public Archives of Canada
Canada Council
National Arts Centre Corp.
Canadian Film Development Corp.
National Museums of Canada
Canadian Broadcasting Corp.
Canadian Radio-Television and Telecommunications Commission
Teleglobe Canada

MINISTER OF STATE FOR SCIENCE AND TECHNOLOGY

Science and Technology Canada

Science Council of Canada
National Research Council of Canada
Natural Sciences and Engineering Research Council

MINISTER OF THE ENVIRONMENT

Environment Canada

National Battlefields Commission

MINISTER OF FINANCE

Department of Finance Canada

Bank of Canada
Dept. of Insurance
Tariff Board
Canada Deposit Insurance Corp.
Anti-Dumping Tribunal
Office of the Auditor General of Canada

MINISTER OF SUPPLY AND SERVICES

Supply and Services Canada

Crown Assets Disposal Corporation
Canadian Arsenals, Ltd.
Royal Canadian Mint
Statistics Canada

MINISTER OF NATIONAL REVENUE

Revenue-Canada (Customs & Excise)

Revenue-Canada (Taxation)

MINISTER OF STATE FOR ECONOMIC AND REGIONAL DEVELOPMENT

Ministry of State for Economic and Regional Development

Northern Pipeline Agency

MINISTER OF TRANSPORT

Transport Canada

Canadian National Railways
National Harbours Board
The St. Lawrence Seaway Authority
Air Canada
Canadian Transport Commission
Northern Transportation Company, Ltd.
The Canadian Wheat Board
Seaway International Bridge Corp., Ltd.
Pilotage Authorities
—Atlantic
—Great Lakes
—Laurentian
—Pacific
Via Rail Canada, Inc.

MINISTER OF JUSTICE

Department of Justice Canada

Law Reform Commission of Canada
Tax Review Board
Office of the Commissioner for Federal Judicial Affairs
Canadian Human Rights Commission

MINISTER OF ENERGY, MINES, AND RESOURCES

Energy, Mines, and Resources Canada

Atomic Energy Control Board
Atomic Energy of Canada, Ltd.
National Energy Board
Eldorado Nuclear, Ltd.
Eldorado Aviation, Ltd.
Uranium Canada, Ltd.
Petro-Canada
Petroleum Compensation Board
Petroleum Monitoring Agency

MINISTER OF REGIONAL INDUSTRIAL EXPANSION

Department of Regional Industrial Expansion

Foreign Investment Review Agency
Export Development Corporation
Federal Business Development Bank
Canadian Commercial Corporation
Canadian Patents and Development, Ltd.
Cape Breton Development Corp.
Atlantic Development Council

MINISTER OF NATIONAL DEFENCE

Department of National Defence

Defence Construction (1951), Ltd.
National Emergency Planning Establishment

MINISTER OF VETERANS AFFAIRS

Veterans Affairs Canada

Canadian Pension Commission
War Veterans Allowance Board
Bureau of Pensions Advocates
Pension Review Board

SOLICITOR GENERAL OF CANADA

Solicitor General of Canada

Correctional Service of Canada
National Parole Board
Royal Canadian Mounted Police

MINISTER OF STATE

MINISTER OF INDIAN AFFAIRS AND NORTHERN DEVELOPMENT

Indian and Northern Affairs Canada

Government of the Northwest Territories
Government of the Yukon Territory
Northern Canada Power Commission

MINISTER OF AGRICULTURE

Agriculture Canada

Farm Credit Corp.
Canadian Dairy Commission
Canadian Livestock Feed Board
National Farm Products Marketing Council

PRESIDENT OF THE QUEEN'S PRIVY COUNCIL FOR CANADA

Office of the President

Office of the Chief Electoral Officer
Public Service Staff Relations Board

MINISTER OF STATE

MINISTER OF FISHERIES AND OCEANS

Department of Fisheries and Oceans

Canadian Saltfish Corp.
Fisheries Prices Support Board
Fisheries and Oceans Research Advisory Council
Freshwater Fish Marketing Corp.

LEADER OF THE GOVERNMENT IN THE SENATE

SECRETARY OF STATE FOR EXTERNAL AFFAIRS

External Affairs Canada

International Joint Commission
Canadian International Development Agency
International Development Research Centre

MINISTER OF EMPLOYMENT AND IMMIGRATION

Employment and Immigration Canada

Immigration Appeal Board
Canada Employment and Immigration Commission

MINISTER OF STATE FOR SOCIAL DEVELOPMENT

Ministry of State for Social Development

minister generally seeks the appointment of a new speaker. Senators must retire at the age of 75.

The Atlantic Provinces—Prince Edward Island, New Brunswick, Newfoundland, and Nova Scotia—send a total of 30 members to the Senate. The Western Provinces—Alberta, British Columbia, Manitoba, and Saskatchewan—send 24. Quebec and Ontario each send 24 members. The Northwest Territories and the Yukon Territory each have one senator.

The Senate has less power than the House. It cannot introduce or reject bills that involve the spending of money, and experts in Canadian constitutional law question the Senate's power to amend such bills.

The House of Commons is made up of members who are elected by the people for terms of five years, unless an election is called earlier. A House of Commons rarely lasts for five years without a new election. The number of members for each province is determined after each Canadian census. For the number of members of Parliament for each province, see the *Facts in Brief* section of each province article.

Each House member represents a *constituency* (district) of a province. Members do not have to live in the constituency, or in the province, they represent. The House elects a speaker to preside over its meetings. The speaker holds office until general elections are called.

The Courts

The courts of Canada include the Supreme Court of Canada, the Federal Court of Canada, and the provincial courts. Judges of these courts are appointed for life by the governor general in council (on the recommendation of the prime minister and the Cabinet).

The Supreme Court of Canada is the highest court of appeal in Canada. It has nine judges. They include the Chief Justice of Canada and eight associate judges, called *puisne* (pronounced *PYOO nee*) judges. The term *puisne* means *junior*, or *associate*. The Supreme Court hears appeals in civil and criminal cases.

The Federal Court of Canada has two divisions—a trial division and an appeals division. The trial division hears all claims against or affecting the Canadian government. It consists of an associate chief justice and seven puisne judges. The appeals division mainly hears appeals from the trial division. It has a chief justice and three puisne judges.

Provincial Courts administer federal and provincial law. The Canadian government appoints the judges. Appeals from these courts go to the Supreme Court.

Money and Taxation

Only the federal government can coin money in Canada. Coins are made at the Royal Canadian Mint in Ottawa and in Winnipeg. The Bank of Canada, a central bank which controls credit and currency, issues all paper money. See BANK OF CANADA.

The taxation powers of the Canadian government are unlimited, but provincial governments may impose only direct taxes. The federal government and each of the 10 provincial governments levy individual and corporate income taxes. Under the tax collection agreement of 1962, the federal government agreed to collect all the income taxes for itself and also for those provinces requesting such service. These provinces are then given their share of the tax money collected.

Provincial and Territorial Governments

The Ten Provinces. Each province has a lieutenant governor who is appointed by the governor general in council. The lieutenant governor once served the federal government as the governor general once served the British, but now holds an honorary position much like the governor general. A premier actually heads the government in nine provinces. Quebec has a prime minister. Each premier or prime minister leads the majority party in the legislature. Each province has an elected one-chamber legislature. This body is called the *Legislative Assembly*, except in Quebec where it is called the *National Assembly*.

Each province controls such matters as education, administration of justice, municipal institutions, property, and civil rights. The federal government has authority to *disallow* (reject) any law passed by a provincial legislature. However, it has disallowed only about 100 of the thousands of bills adopted by the provinces.

The Two Territories have separate governments, but with much less power than those of the provinces. Generally, they provide for law enforcement, medical services, and schools in the towns. The Yukon Territory government is headed by an official called the government leader, who is the leader of the majority political party. A commissioner appointed by the federal government heads the government of the Northwest Territories. Yukon Territory has an elected Legislative Assembly of 16 members. The assembly for the Northwest Territories is made up of 22 elected members. The Yukon Territory sends one representative to the House of Commons in Ottawa, and the Northwest Territories sends two.

Local Government

The provinces and territories regulate local government. Each has a different system. Generally, each province is divided into counties or districts. These counties or districts are further divided into cities, towns, villages, and townships. Elected councils govern the municipalities. The head of the local government is usually a mayor, reeve, warden, or overseer. Other council members are called controllers, aldermen, or councillors. Municipal governments direct such activities as road repair, water supply, and police and fire protection. They gain much of their revenue from property taxes.

Political Parties

Canada has four important political parties. The two largest are the Liberals and the Progressive Conservatives. The differences between them are not always clear. However, the Liberals have favored more free trade, lower tariffs, and provincial rights. They have been sympathetic to the hopes of French Canadians and to social welfare problems. The Progressive Conservatives have strongly supported the British tradition and the industrial and financial interests of Canada.

The New Democratic Party was formed in 1961 by trade unions, a socialist party called the Co-operative Commonwealth Federation (CCF), and independent left wing Canadians. The party favors social welfare measures. It opposes Canadian participation in such military alliances as the North Atlantic Treaty Organization (NATO) and the North American Air Defense Command (NORAD). It held office in Saskatchewan during the early 1960's and from 1971 to 1982. The party controlled the provincial government in Manitoba from 1969 to 1977, and regained power there in 1981. It headed British Columbia's government from 1972 to 1975.

The Social Credit Party, a right wing party, controlled the government of Alberta from 1935 to 1971. It held office in British Columbia from 1952 to 1972, and regained power there in 1975.

International Relations

Canada has been a completely free nation since the Statute of Westminster in 1931 ended the last British controls over Canada. Canada now conducts its foreign relations with Great Britain and other Commonwealth nations in the same manner as it conducts relations with other nations in the world.

Relations with the United States. Canada's closest economic and social ties link it with the United States. The two countries share more than 4,000 miles (6,400 kilometers) of common border, and their relations are exceptionally friendly. Boundary problems are settled by the International Joint Commission, created as a result of a treaty signed in 1909 (see INTERNATIONAL JOINT COMMISSION).

In recent years, Canadians have become increasingly concerned about American ownership of Canadian businesses and American control of parts of the Canadian economy. Many Canadians criticize U.S. foreign policy and oppose Canada's part in NORAD. In general, Canadian-U.S. relations have been close and friendly.

Relations with Other Countries. Canada conducted relations with other foreign countries through the British diplomatic service until the close of World War I. After that, Canada sent its own diplomatic representatives to foreign countries, and received their representatives in return. The first exchange was with the United States, in 1927. Diplomats now represent Canada in nearly all the leading countries of the world. Canada became a charter member of the United Nations in 1945, and of the North Atlantic Treaty Organization in 1949.

Armed Forces

Until 1968, Canada had a separate army, navy, and air force. But in that year all Canadian military forces were merged into one unit called the Canadian Armed Forces. The chief of the defence staff directs the armed forces. He reports to the minister of national defence. Canada and the United States formed the Permanent Joint Board on Defence in 1940 to cooperate in North American defense.

Canada has three professional military colleges. They are the Royal Military College of Canada in Kingston, Ont.; Royal Roads Military College near Victoria, B.C.; and Collège militaire royal de Saint-Jean in Saint-Jean, Que. The Canadian Armed Forces also maintains staff colleges, cadet corps, and officer-training programs in colleges and universities. JOHN T. SAYWELL

Related Articles in WORLD BOOK include:

Attorney General
Bill of Rights (The Canadian Bill of Rights)
British North America Act
Canada, Armed Forces of
Census (Censuses in Other Countries)
Civil Service (Civil Service in Other Lands)
Commonwealth of Nations
Income Tax (Income Taxes in Canada)
National Museums of Canada
New Democratic Party
Political Party (Political Parties in Canada)
Post Office (Canada)
Prime Minister of Canada
Privy Council
Royal Canadian Mounted Police
Social Security (Social Security in Canada)
Welfare (Welfare in Canada)
Woman Suffrage

Outline

I. The Constitution
II. Executive Offices
A. The Governor General
B. The Prime Minister
C. The Cabinet
III. The Parliament
A. The Senate
B. The House of Commons
IV. The Courts
A. The Supreme Court of Canada
B. The Federal Court of Canada
C. Provincial Courts
V. Money and Taxation
VI. Provincial and Territorial Governments
A. The Ten Provinces
B. The Two Territories
VII. Local Government
VIII. Political Parties
IX. International Relations
A. Relations with the United States
B. Relations with Other Countries
X. Armed Forces

Questions

Who is the Canadian head of state?
Who is the administrative head of the government?
How does the Senate of Canada differ from the Senate of the United States?
How does the House of Commons maintain supreme authority in the Canadian government?
What is the International Joint Commission?
What did the British North America Act do?
How long does the prime minister remain in office?
How do voting requirements differ in Canada and the United States?
Who directs the armed forces of Canada?
Who was the first Canadian-born governor general?

Additional Resources

HOCKLIN, THOMAS A. *Apex of Power: The Prime Minister and Political Leadership in Canada.* Prentice-Hall (Scarborough, Ont. and Englewood Cliffs, New Jersey), 1977.

LANGFORD, J. STUART. *The Law of Your Land: A Practical Guide to the New Canadian Constitution.* Gage (Agincourt, Ont.), 1982.

MARCHAND, EDWARD S. *Working for Canadians: A Study of Local, Provincial, and Federal Governments.* Prentice-Hall (Scarborough, Ont. and Englewood Cliffs, New Jersey), 1979. Also suitable for younger readers.

RICKER, JOHN C., and SAYWELL, J. T. *How Are We Governed?* Clarke, Irwin (Toronto), 1966. For younger readers.

STATISTICS CANADA. *Canada Handbook.* Univ. of Washington Press (Seattle). Pub. annually.

TOOKE, MOYRA, ed. *Politics Are People: An Illustrated Guide to Canadian Elections.* Griffin House (Toronto), 1974.

WHITE, WALTER L., and others. *Introduction to Canadian Politics and Government.* 3rd ed. Holt (Toronto and New York City), 1976.

WINN, CONRAD, and others. *Political Parties in Canada.* McGraw (Scarborough, Ont. and New York City), 1976.

Champlain in Huronia (1967), detail of an oil painting on canvas by Rex Woods; Confederation Life Collection

Trading Ceremony at York Factory 1780's (about 1955), an oil painting on canvas by Adam Sherriff Scott; Hudson's Bay Company

The European Settlement of Canada was led by the French and English. In 1608, French explorer Samuel de Champlain, *left center,* founded Quebec and made friends with nearby Indians. Hudson's Bay Company, an English firm formed in 1670, built fur-trading posts like the one at the right.

HISTORY OF CANADA

CANADA, HISTORY OF. Canada's history is an exciting story that traces the development of a vast wilderness into a great nation. The first people to live in what is now Canada came from Asia more than 20,000 years ago. These people spread across the entire country. Their descendants became known as Indians. The Eskimos came to Canada after the Indians. They originally lived on a land bridge that once connected Asia and North America at what is now Alaska. The Eskimos first settled in the Arctic region of Canada about 5,000 years ago. For details on the first Americans, see INDIAN, AMERICAN; ESKIMO.

In 1497, John Cabot, an Italian navigator in the service of England, found rich fishing grounds off Canada's southeast coast. In time, his discovery led to the European exploration of Canada. France took the lead in exploring the country and set up a colony in eastern Canada in the early 1600's. Daring French fur traders traveled westward and came upon many of Canada's sparkling lakes, rushing rivers, and majestic, snow-capped mountains. Great Britain gained control of the country in 1763, and thousands of British immigrants began to join the French who remained in Canada. In 1867, the French- and English-speaking Canadians helped create a united colony called the Dominion of Canada. The two groups worked together to settle the country from coast to coast and to develop its great mineral deposits and other natural resources.

Canada gained its independence from Britain in 1931. During the mid-1900's, hard-working Canadians turned their country into an economic giant. Today, huge harvests from western Canada make the nation a leading producer of wheat, oats, and barley. Canada also ranks among the world's top manufacturing nations, and it is a major producer of electric power.

Throughout its history, Canada has often been troubled by a lack of unity among its people. French Canadians, most of whom live in the province of Quebec, have struggled to preserve their French culture. They have long been angered by Canadian policies based on British traditions, and many of them support a movement to make Quebec a separate nation. People in Canada's nine other provinces also frequently favor local needs over national interests.

Canada and the United States have generally enjoyed a long history of cooperation. They have worked together in the defense of North America and have strong economic ties. Canada has tried to develop independently of its southern neighbor. But its economy is so closely linked to the U.S. economy that severe U.S. business slumps usually cause hard times in Canada. In addition, the popularity of U.S. culture in Canada has challenged the efforts of Canadian leaders to establish a separate identity for their country.

This article traces the history of Canada from European exploration to the present. For detailed information on the people, economy, and government of Canada today, see CANADA; and CANADA, GOVERNMENT OF.

Early European Exploration

About A.D. 1000, Vikings from Iceland and Greenland became the first known Europeans to reach North America. The Vikings, led by Leif Ericson, landed

David Jay Bercuson, the contributor of this article, is Professor of History at the University of Calgary and coeditor of the Canadian Historical Review.

Fathers of Confederation (1969), an oil painting on canvas by Rex Woods; Confederation Life Collection

The Fathers of Confederation were Canadian leaders who planned the union of Great Britain's Canadian colonies under one government. Their plan led to the creation of the Dominion of Canada in 1867. John A. Macdonald, *standing center,* became the Dominion's first prime minister.

somewhere on the northeast coast, a region Ericson called Vinland. The Vikings established a colony in Vinland, but they lived there only a short time. Some historians believe that Vinland was located in what is now Maine or Massachusetts. Others think it was in Newfoundland. Ruins of a Viking settlement have been found at L'Anse aux Meadows, on the northern tip of the island of Newfoundland. See ERICSON, LEIF; VIKINGS; VINLAND.

Lasting contact between Europe and America began with the voyage of Christopher Columbus in 1492. Columbus sailed west from Spain to find a short sea route to the Indies, as Europeans called eastern Asia. This region was known for its jewels, silks, spices, and other luxury goods. When Columbus landed in America, he thought he had reached the Indies. News of his voyage excited most Europeans.

In 1497, King Henry VII of England hired an Italian navigator, John Cabot, to cross the Atlantic Ocean in search of a shorter route to Asia than the one Columbus had taken. Cabot landed somewhere between what are now Newfoundland and Nova Scotia and claimed the area for England. Cabot found no such luxuries as jewels or spices. But he saw an enormous amount of cod and other fishes in the waters southeast of Newfoundland. Reports of the rich fishing grounds soon brought large European fishing fleets to Canada.

By the early 1500's, some Europeans realized that Columbus had reached an unknown land, which they called the New World. In 1534, King Francis I of France sent Jacques Cartier, a French navigator, to the New World to look for gold and other valuable metals. Cartier sailed into the Gulf of St. Lawrence. He landed on the Gaspé Peninsula and claimed it for France. In 1535, on a second trip, Cartier became the first European to reach the interior of Canada. He sailed up the St. Lawrence River to the site of present-day Montreal. In 1541, on a third visit, Cartier joined a French expedition that hoped to establish a permanent settlement in Canada. But the colony lasted only until 1543.

The Development of New France (1604-1688)

Many French fishermen sailed to Canada during the early 1500's. They helped develop a thriving fishing industry off the east coast. But the fishermen played an even more important role in Canada's growth by establishing the fur trade. The fur trade led to the development of a vast French colonial empire in North America. This empire became known as New France. It lasted about 150 years and established the French culture and heritage in Canada.

Start of the Fur Trade. The French fishermen who came to Canada landed on the coast to preserve their

Period Facts in Brief (1604-1688)

Important Dates

- **1604** Sieur de Monts of France founded Acadia.
- **1608** Samuel de Champlain of France founded the city of Quebec.
- **1610** Henry Hudson of England sailed into Hudson Bay.
- **1642** French missionaries founded Montreal.
- **1673** Louis Jolliet and Jacques Marquette sailed down the Mississippi River to its junction with the Arkansas River.
- **1682** Sieur de La Salle sailed to the mouth of the Mississippi River and claimed all the land drained by the river and its branches for France.

Population

1688 About 10,000

Encampment on River Winnipeg (mid-1800's), an oil painting on canvas by Paul Kane; Royal Ontario Museum, Toronto

The Fur Trade in Canada began during the 1500's as an exchange of furs for manufactured goods between Indians and Europeans. The Europeans gave the Indians such items as tools, weapons, and kettles in exchange for beaver, fox, mink, and other pelts. Much of the trading took place at camps like the one at the left.

catches by drying them in the sun. They met Indians who wanted to trade furs for fishhooks, kettles, knives, and other European goods. A brisk trade soon developed. During the second half of the 1500's, felt hats made from beaver fur became tremendously popular in Europe. As a result, the value of Canadian beaver pelts soared. During the late 1500's, more and more French ships sailed to Canada to pick up beaver fur. Traders also supplied such furs as fox, marten, mink, and otter. See FUR TRADE.

Meanwhile, English explorers searched for a water passage to Asia through northern Canada. During the late 1500's, these explorers included Humphrey Gilbert, Martin Frobisher, and John Davis. In 1610, an English sea captain named Henry Hudson sailed into Hudson Bay in his search for the passage. England later based its claim to the vast Hudson Bay region on this voyage.

Early Settlements. In 1603, King Henry IV of France completed plans to organize the fur trade and to set up a colony in Canada. The next year, a French explorer named Pierre du Gua, Sieur de Monts, led a small group of settlers to a site near the mouth of the St. Croix River in what is now the province of New Brunswick. In 1605, the settlers left that spot and founded Port Royal (now Annapolis Royal in Nova Scotia). The French called their colony Acadia. See ACADIA.

In 1608, another French explorer, Samuel de Champlain, founded a settlement along the St. Lawrence River. He named the village Quebec. Champlain made friends with the Algonquin and Huron Indians living nearby and began to trade with them for furs. The two tribes also wanted French help in wars against their main enemy, the powerful Iroquois Indians. In 1609, Champlain and two other French fur traders helped their Indian friends defeat the Iroquois in battle. After this battle, the Iroquois were also enemies of the French.

The Huron lived in an area the French called Huronia. Champlain persuaded the Huron to allow Roman Catholic missionaries to work among them and introduce them to Christianity. The missionaries, especially an order known as the Jesuits, explored much of what is now southern Ontario.

Threats to Expansion. Champlain hoped Quebec would become a large settlement, but it remained only a small trading post for many years. By 1625, about 60 people lived there.

New France failed to attract settlers partly because of threats from English colonists as well as from the Iroquois. Like France, England claimed much of what is now eastern Canada. England based its claims on explorations dating from Cabot's landing in 1497. During the early 1600's, many English colonists settled along the east coast of North America south of New France. Numerous disputes over fur-trading rights broke out between the French and the English. In 1629, English forces captured the town of Quebec. The French regained the town in 1632.

During the late 1640's, the Iroquois conquered Huronia and killed most of the French missionaries. The Algonquin and Huron fled, leaving the French to fight the Iroquois alone. During the next 10 years, the Iroquois increased their attacks on the French. Many settlers were killed, and the French fur trade was destroyed.

The Royal Province. In 1663, King Louis XIV made New France a *royal province* (colony) of France. He sent troops to Canada to fight the Iroquois and appointed administrators to govern and develop the colony. The chief official was the governor. A bishop directed the church and missionary work, and a person called an *intendant* managed most other local affairs. The French troops mounted attacks on Iroquois country, forcing some tribes to make peace with the French in the late 1660's. Afterward, frontiersmen known as *coureurs de bois* again developed the fur trade into the chief economic activity of New France (see COUREURS DE BOIS).

Louis XIV also promoted the *seigneurial system* to encourage farming in New France. Under this system, the king gave land in the colony chiefly to French military officers or merchants. The landholders, called *seigneurs*, brought farmers from France and rented them large sections of the land. Most of the farmers, called *habitants*, became prosperous. The population of New France grew from about 3,000 in 1666 to about 6,700 in 1673. See SEIGNEURIAL SYSTEM.

The boundaries of New France expanded rapidly to the west and south after Louis de Buade, Comte de Frontenac, became governor in 1672. The loss of the Huron fur trade forced the French to go farther inland to get new sources. As a result, Frontenac sent explorers to scout the Great Lakes and the Ohio and Mississippi river valleys.

In 1673, Louis Jolliet, a French-Canadian fur trader, and Jacques Marquette, a French missionary, sailed down the Mississippi River to its junction with the Arkansas River. The French soon built forts and fur-trading posts along the Great Lakes and along the Illinois and Mississippi rivers. In 1682, René-Robert Cavelier, Sieur de La Salle, reached the mouth of the Mississippi at the Gulf of Mexico. He claimed all the land drained by the river and its branches for France.

The Growing French-English Rivalry. The boundaries of English colonies south of New France also expanded during the late 1600's. Settlers poured into the English colonies and pushed the frontier westward, nearer New France. In 1670, an English firm called the Hudson's Bay Company opened fur-trading posts north of New France on the shores of Hudson Bay.

Clashes between England and France in Europe contributed to their rivalry in North America. Other factors also created tension between the English and French colonists. For example, most of the French were Roman Catholics, and the majority of the English were Protestants. Most of the French wanted land for fur trading. The English wanted it for farming. In addition, French and English fur traders competed against each other.

During the 1730's, French-Canadian fur traders traveled farther inland and claimed more land for France. By 1738, Pierre Gaultier de Varennes, Sieur de La Vérendrye, had established a chain of fur-trading posts between Montreal and what is now Saskatchewan.

For details on life in New France, see NEW FRANCE.

British Conquest and Rule (1689-1815)

The French and English colonists fought each other in four wars between 1689 and 1763. These conflicts led to Great Britain's conquest of New France. The British government then worked hard to win the support of its new French-Canadian subjects. During the late 1700's and early 1800's, Canadian explorers pushed westward across the continent.

The Colonial Wars. The first three of the four wars between the French and English colonists broke out in Europe before spreading to America. These wars were the War of the League of Augsburg (1689-1697), the War of the Spanish Succession (1702-1713), and the War of the Austrian Succession (1744-1748). Only after the second war did either side gain territory. In 1713, under the Treaty of Utrecht, France gave Britain Newfoundland, the Nova Scotia region of Acadia, and the Hudson Bay territory.

The fourth war began in the Ohio River Valley in 1754 and lasted until 1763. It spread to Europe in 1756 and became known as the Seven Years' War there and in Canada. The conflict, called the French and Indian War in the United States, marked the final chapter in the struggle between the French and British colonists in America. The British had a number of advantages during the war. For example, there were more than a million British colonists compared with about 65,000 French settlers. The British colonies also received greater military support from Britain than New France did from France. In addition, the British had the help of the Iroquois, the strongest Indian group in the east.

The French did well at first, but the tide of battle slowly turned against them. British armies, backed by the British Royal Navy, captured Quebec City in 1759. Both opposing generals, the Marquis de Montcalm of France and James Wolfe of Britain, were fatally wounded in the battle (see QUEBEC, BATTLE OF). The British seized Montreal in 1760, and the fighting in America ended. In the Peace of Paris, signed in 1763, France surrendered most of New France to Britain. See FRENCH AND INDIAN WARS.

The Quebec Act. Great Britain gave the name Quebec to the area that made up most of its new territory in Canada. It added some of the new territory to Nova Scotia and Newfoundland. At first, Britain governed Quebec under British laws, which denied Catholics the rights to vote, to be elected, or to hold public office. This

Period Facts in Brief (1689-1815)

Important Dates

- **1689-1763** A series of wars between British and French colonists ended with Britain's conquest of New France, the French colonial empire in America.
- **1774** The Quebec Act gave French Canadians political and religious rights.
- **1775-1783** During the Revolutionary War in America, an American invasion of Canada in 1775 failed.
- **1784** The colony of New Brunswick was established.
- **1791** The Constitutional Act split Quebec into the colonies of Upper Canada and Lower Canada.
- **1812-1815** During the War of 1812, British and Canadian troops turned back two major invasion attempts of Canada by the United States.

Population

1698 15,355
1812 75,000

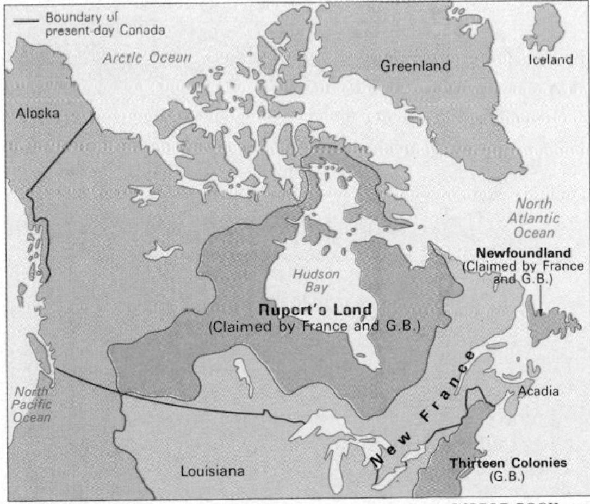

WORLD BOOK map

During the Early 1700's, France and Great Britain dominated eastern North America. The French colonial empire on the continent was known as New France. France also claimed the mostly British-held areas of Rupert's Land and Newfoundland.

Detail of an engraving by Hervey Smyth from a painting (late 1700's) by Francis Swaine; Picture Division, Public Archives of Canada, Ottawa

In the Battle of Quebec in 1759, British troops defeated the French forces at Quebec City. The British approached Quebec from the St. Lawrence River, *above*. Their victory enabled Great Britain to take over France's empire in Canada at the end of the Seven Years' War (1756-1763).

policy affected nearly all the colony's French Canadians. Quebec's first two British governors, Generals James Murray and Guy Carleton, opposed the policy because they wanted Britain to gain the loyalty of the French. Carleton also was aware of discontent in the 13 colonies to the south, then known as the American Colonies. He knew that Britain would need the support of the French Canadians if an American rebellion broke out.

In 1774, Carleton persuaded the British Parliament to pass the Quebec Act. This act recognized French civil and religious rights. It also preserved the seigneurial landholding system and extended Quebec to include much of what is now Quebec, Ontario, and the Midwestern United States. See Quebec Act.

The Revolutionary War in America began in 1775. The Americans asked the French Canadians to join their rebellion against Britain. But the French regarded the war mainly as a conflict between Britain and British colonies and chose to remain neutral. An American invasion of Canada in 1775 failed. See Revolutionary War in America (Canada Invaded).

The United Empire Loyalists. After the Revolutionary War began, many people in the American Colonies remained loyal to Britain. These colonists became known as United Empire Loyalists. About 40,000 of them moved to Canada during and after the war. They settled mainly in western parts of the colonies of Nova Scotia and Quebec. Those who moved to Nova Scotia soon demanded a colony of their own. In 1784, the British government created the colony of New Brunswick out of western Nova Scotia for the Loyalists.

The Loyalists in Quebec also became unhappy. The Quebec Act gave the Catholic Church a special position in the colony. However, most of the Loyalists were Protestants. In addition, the Quebec Act did not permit the colony to have its own elected legislature. The Loyalists demanded a government like they had before the revolution—one that allowed them to choose their own public officials.

The British solution was the Constitutional Act of 1791. This act divided Quebec into two colonies, Lower Canada and Upper Canada. Lower Canada occupied the area along the lower St. Lawrence River. Upper Canada covered the area near the Great Lakes and the upper St. Lawrence. Each colony had its own elected assembly, though the legislatures had little real power. Each colony also had a lieutenant governor and Legislative Council. The lieutenant governor and council members, who were appointed by the British, controlled the government. French Canadians formed the vast majority of the population in Lower Canada. The government there was based on principles of French civil law, Catholicism, and the seigneurial system. English-speaking Canadians made up the majority in Upper Canada.

Color print (late 1800's) by Henry Sandham; Public Archives of Canada, Ottawa (C168)

The United Empire Loyalists were American colonists who remained loyal to Britain during the Revolutionary War (1775-1783). Thousands of them, like this group, moved to Canada.

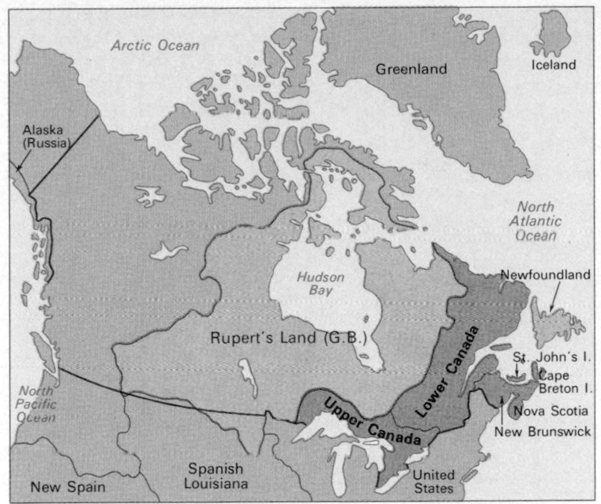

WORLD BOOK map

In 1791, the British government created the colonies of Upper and Lower Canada. Great Britain had gained eastern Canada from France in the Seven Years' War (1756-1763). The British also won undisputed control of Newfoundland and Rupert's Land.

Local officials followed the traditions of English law and property systems. See UNITED EMPIRE LOYALISTS.

Exploration of the West. The Revolutionary War in America led to major developments in the Canadian fur trade. After Britain conquered New France in 1763, hundreds of British merchants settled in Montreal and soon took over the French fur trade. Like the French, they obtained most of their furs from Indians in the Ohio and Mississippi river valleys. But most of this area became part of the United States after the Revolutionary War. British merchants in Montreal thus had to look elsewhere for furs. By 1784, they had formed a firm called the North West Company to trade north and west of the Great Lakes. The Hudson's Bay Company already had trading posts in that territory, and a great rivalry developed between the two companies.

In its search for new and better fur-trading areas, the North West Company sent explorers across the unknown western lands. Alexander Mackenzie reached the Mackenzie River in 1789 and the Pacific Ocean in 1793. Simon Fraser followed the Fraser River to the Pacific in 1808. David Thompson mapped the west and navigated the full length of the Columbia River in 1811.

In 1812, Lord Selkirk, a British colonizer, sent a group of Scottish and Irish immigrants to establish a settlement on the Red River in what is now Manitoba. The settlement became known as the Red River Colony. In 1821, the Hudson's Bay Company took over the North West Company and gained control of nearly all Canadian territory west of the Great Lakes.

The War of 1812 developed out of fighting between Great Britain and France in Europe. During this conflict, the British set up a naval blockade of France and so interfered with U.S. ships bound for French ports. They also stopped American ships and seized sailors of British birth on them. As a result of these actions, the United States declared war on Britain on June 18, 1812. American troops tried to capture Upper and Lower Canada during the war, but British and Canadian troops defeated two major invasion attempts. The war ended in 1815. The Canadian and British forces claimed victory because they had held off much larger American forces. Neither side actually won, but the war promoted a sense of unity and patriotism in Canada. See WAR OF 1812.

The Struggle for Responsible Government (1816-1867)

Canada's population began to soar during the early 1800's as thousands of immigrants came from Great Britain. During the 1840's, leaders in some Canadian colonies pushed for *responsible government* (self-government) in local affairs. In a system of responsible government, the executive is *responsible* (answerable) to an elected assembly. Britain gradually granted all the colonies such government. During the mid-1860's, some colonial leaders argued that Canada needed a strong central government to deal with domestic matters. They started a movement for a *confederation* (union) of the Canadian colonies. This movement led to the formation of the Dominion of Canada in 1867.

Growing Discontent. After the War of 1812, Canada began to attract large numbers of immigrants from England, Ireland, and Scotland. French Canadians resented the flood of English-speaking newcomers. Many of the French believed that the British government wanted to destroy the French heritage in Canada.

By the 1820's, most French Canadians had become very bitter toward the English-speaking Canadians in Lower Canada. The French controlled the legislature, but the English controlled the Legislative Council. The council, in turn, ran the government. It spent much of the colony's tax money on projects to benefit commerce. French Canadians owned few businesses, however, and so opposed these expenses. The French also feared that the council intended to help English-speaking Canadians take over French-Canadian farms.

Upper Canada also faced serious political problems during the early 1800's. Church leaders, merchants, and landowners there formed a group known as the Family Compact. This group controlled the colonial government. It often cooperated with the lieutenant governor to block the demands of the farmers in the assembly. The Family Compact also used tax money to support Church of England schools, though many Upper Canadians belonged to other religious groups.

The Uprisings of 1837. By the late 1830's, many people in Upper and Lower Canada had lost faith in their colonial governments. In November 1837, a revolt

Period Facts in Brief (1816-1867)

Important Dates

1837 Revolts broke out in Upper and Lower Canada.
1841 The Act of Union joined Upper and Lower Canada into the Province of Canada.
1848 The Province of Canada and Nova Scotia gained self-government.
1858 The colony of British Columbia was established.
1864 Conferences in Charlottetown and Quebec City planned for the *confederation* (union) of the Canadian colonies.
1867 The British North America Act established the Dominion of Canada.

Population

1824 151,000
1867 3,463,000

Attack on St. Charles, a lithograph (mid-1800's) by Nathaniel Hartnell from a sketch by Lord Charles Beauclerk; Public Archives of Canada, Ottawa (C393)

Short-Lived Revolts against the government broke out in Lower and Upper Canada in 1837. Rebels in both colonies fought to end harsh British rule. British troops easily defeated the rebels at St. Charles in Lower Canada, *left*, and at other sites.

broke out in Lower Canada. It was headed by Louis Joseph Papineau, a fiery French-Canadian leader in the assembly. Papineau's followers briefly controlled parts of the countryside of Lower Canada. But the seigneurs and the high church officials remained loyal to Britain. British troops and colonial militia quickly crushed the revolt, and the rebel leaders fled to the United States.

News of the fighting in Lower Canada triggered a rebellion in Upper Canada in December 1837. William Lyon Mackenzie, a member of the Reform Party in the assembly, led the revolt. The colonial militia defeated the rebels in a brief battle, and Mackenzie escaped to the United States. See Rebellion of 1837-1838.

Lord Durham's Report. The rebellions in Upper and Lower Canada convinced the British government that it had serious problems in Canada. In 1838, Queen Victoria sent Lord Durham, a British diplomat, to investigate the causes of the uprisings. Durham finished his report in 1839. He recommended that Upper and Lower Canada be united. He also recommended that the Canadian colonies be allowed to handle their local affairs. Both of these ideas had been suggested earlier, and Durham's report did little to influence their eventual adoption by the British government. In 1840, the British Parliament passed the Act of Union. This law, which took effect in 1841, united the two Canadas into one colony, the Province of Canada. See Union, Act of.

The Beginning of Self-Government. During the 1840's, several colonial leaders fought for responsible government for their colonies. These leaders included Robert Baldwin and Louis H. Lafontaine in the Province of Canada and Joseph Howe in Nova Scotia. Many officials in Britain had come to regard the colonies more as a burden than as a benefit, and they supported the self-government movement. The Province of Canada and Nova Scotia gained responsible government in 1848. Nearly all the other Canadian colonies received it soon afterward.

During the mid-1800's, the Canadian colonies expanded trade with the United States. Railways linked more and more towns in the colonies, and new canals became busy transportation routes. These developments and the rapid growth of the fishing, flour-milling, lumber, and textile industries brought prosperity to the Canadian colonies. The American Civil War (1861-1865) also greatly increased demands for Canadian goods.

In spite of responsible government, political problems still troubled the Province of Canada. The main opposing political parties had nearly equal representation in the legislature. As a result, no party could gain a majority of seats or direct the government more than a few months. By the early 1860's, some political leaders had suggested that the colony's problems could be solved only by splitting it again and creating a confederation of the two colonies. Such a union would give French- and English-speaking Canadians the same central government but would allow them to control their own local affairs.

Confederation. The fear of United States expansion into Canada helped attract support for a Canadian confederation. Many Canadians felt certain that the United States wanted to control all North America and would invade Canada after the Civil War ended.

John A. Macdonald, George Étienne Cartier, and other leaders from the Province of Canada headed the campaign for a federal union. In September 1864, they attended a conference of leaders from the Atlantic colonies who were meeting in Charlottetown, Prince Edward Island, to plan a union of their own. The Canadians persuaded them to abandon their plan in favor of a larger union. Another conference was held in Quebec City. The final details for confederation were worked out there in October (see Quebec Conference).

In 1865, the Province of Canada approved the confederation plan. However, Newfoundland and Prince Edward Island rejected it, fearing that they would lose control over local affairs. New Brunswick and Nova Scotia adopted the plan in 1866. Later that same year, officials from Canada, New Brunswick, and Nova Scotia went to London, where they presented the plan to the British government.

In March 1867, the British Parliament passed the British North America Act. This act established the Dominion of Canada. The Dominion used the British parliamentary form of government. It had an elected House of Commons and an appointed Senate, each with almost equal power. A prime minister, usually the leader of the political party with the most seats in the House of Commons, headed the new federal government. Britain continued to handle the colony's foreign affairs, and the British monarch served as head of state.

The British North America Act took effect on July 1, 1867. The new Dominion had four provinces—New Brunswick, Nova Scotia, Ontario, and Quebec. Quebec had formerly been Lower Canada, and Ontario had been Upper Canada. The British North America Act

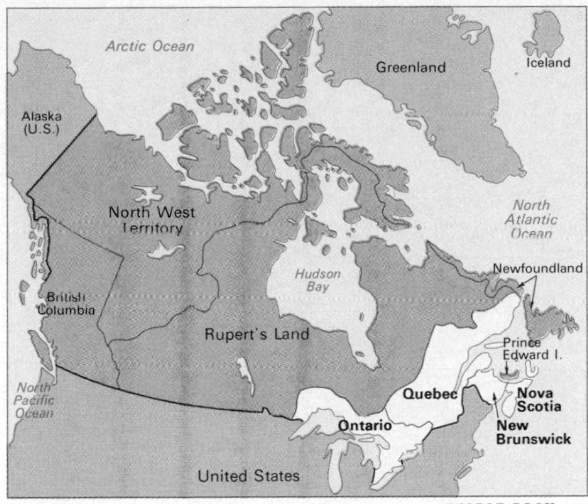

WORLD BOOK map

In 1867, a union of British North American colonies led to the formation of the Dominion of Canada. The Dominion had four provinces—New Brunswick, Nova Scotia, Ontario, and Quebec. Britain ruled its other Canadian territories separately.

provided that other provinces could join the Dominion. Macdonald, leader of the Liberal-Conservative Party, became the country's first prime minister. See BRITISH NORTH AMERICA ACT; CONFEDERATION OF CANADA.

Growth of the Dominion (1868-1913)

The young Dominion of Canada developed rapidly during the late 1800's. A railway connected western and eastern Canada, and courageous pioneers spread across the west. By the early 1900's, the Dominion had nine provinces spanning the continent. Huge wheat crops, rich mines, and new industries brought further economic expansion during this period. In addition, Canada became increasingly involved in international affairs.

Period Facts in Brief (1868-1913)

Prime Ministers (with parties, dates of service)

- Sir John A. Macdonald, Conservative, 1867-1873
- Alexander Mackenzie, Liberal, 1873-1878
- Sir John A. Macdonald, Conservative, 1878-1891
- Sir John J. C. Abbott, Conservative, 1891-1892
- Sir John S. D. Thompson, Conservative, 1892-1894
- Sir Mackenzie Bowell, Conservative, 1894-1896
- Sir Charles Tupper, Conservative, 1896
- Sir Wilfrid Laurier, Liberal, 1896-1911
- Sir Robert L. Borden, Conservative, 1911-1917

Provinces in the Dominion

New Brunswick (1867), Nova Scotia (1867), Ontario (1867), Quebec (1867), Manitoba (1870), British Columbia (1871), Prince Edward Island (1873), Alberta (1905), Saskatchewan (1905)

Important Dates

- **1869** Louis Riel led the métis in the Red River Rebellion in Manitoba.
- **1870** The North West Territories (now Northwest Territories) was established.
- **1885** Riel led a métis revolt in Saskatchewan. The Canadian Pacific Railway (now CP Rail) spanned Canada.
- **1898** The Yukon area became a territory of Canada.

Population

1871 3,700,000
1911 7,200,000

New Provinces. Macdonald's chief goal as prime minister was to extend the Dominion to the west coast. He immediately turned his attention to the vast, largely unsettled northwest. This territory, called Rupert's Land, was owned by the Hudson's Bay Company. In 1868, Macdonald worked out an agreement to buy the region.

About 10,000 people lived in or near the settlement of Red River in Rupert's Land. Most of them were *métis* (people of European and Indian ancestry). The métis feared that the transfer of the area to Canada would bring a flood of white settlers who would take their lands. In 1869, Louis Riel, a settler of French and Indian descent, led the métis in a revolt against the Canadian government. British and Canadian troops easily put down the rebellion (see RED RIVER REBELLION.)

In 1870, the Dominion took possession of Rupert's Land. At the same time, it acquired the North West Territory from Great Britain. This vast territory lay north, west, and south of Rupert's Land. The government combined these two new possessions into the North West Territories, which later became the Northwest Territories. Later in 1870, the government created Manitoba, Canada's fifth province, from part of Rupert's Land. The government also set aside 1,400,000 acres (567,000 hectares) in Manitoba for the métis.

In 1871, the Pacific coast colony of British Columbia became Canada's sixth province. It agreed to join the Dominion in return for construction of a railway to the Pacific coast. In 1873, the eastern colony of Prince Edward Island became Canada's seventh province.

The Pacific Scandal. Macdonald led the Conservative Party to victory in the election of 1872. Afterward, the government chose a company headed by Sir Hugh Allan to build the railway wanted by British Columbia to the Pacific coast. But the so-called Pacific Scandal stalled the project. The scandal broke out in 1873, when it was revealed that the Conservative Party had accepted a campaign contribution of about $300,000 from Allan in 1872. Leaders of the opposing Liberal Party charged that Allan's group got the railroad contract because of its campaign gift. Macdonald did not use any of the money for his own election, but he resigned as prime minister. In November 1873, Alexander Mackenzie, leader of the Liberal Party, became prime minister.

The Return of Macdonald. Mackenzie's government promoted honest and efficient elections by introducing the secret ballot and the one-day national election. It also won Great Britain's approval of a policy limiting the authority of the governor general—the British monarch's representative in Canada. The new policy required the governor general to respect decisions made by Canadian officials in the country's internal affairs. In 1875, Mackenzie established the Supreme Court of Canada. The court lessened British control over Canada's legal matters.

The Mackenzie government became increasingly unpopular after 1875, when a worldwide depression caused a severe business slump in Canada. Mackenzie had little success in reversing the decline, and Macdonald led the Conservatives to victory in the election of 1878.

In 1879, Macdonald began the National Policy, a program calling for high *tariffs* (taxes) on imported goods. The program was designed to encourage Canadians to buy less costly domestic products and so help Canada's industries grow. Macdonald was also determined to complete the stalled coast-to-coast railroad. In 1880, the government gave the Canadian Pacific Railway Company (now CP Rail) a contract to finish the job.

The Saskatchewan Rebellion. During the 1870's, many of the métis in Manitoba moved westward into what is now Saskatchewan. But they again began to fear the loss of their land during the mid-1880's because of the near completion of the transcontinental railroad and government plans to attract settlers to the prairies.

In March 1885, Riel led another métis uprising, the Saskatchewan Rebellion. More than 7,000 government troops ended the rebellion within two months. Riel was found guilty of treason and was hanged on Nov. 16, 1885. See SASKATCHEWAN REBELLION.

Progress Under Laurier. Workers laid the final stretch of Canadian Pacific Railway tracks in 1885. Regularly scheduled passenger service began the next year. The transcontinental railroad in time led to a great rush to settle Canada's fertile western prairies. This activity contributed to a major period of progress that began after the Liberal Party won the election of 1896. Wilfrid Laurier, the Liberal Party leader and a Quebec Catholic, became the country's first French-Canadian prime minister.

Canada's population soared during Laurier's administration. More than 2 million immigrants, most of them from Europe, flocked to Canada between 1896 and 1911. Many settled in such cities as Montreal, Toronto, and Winnipeg. But hundreds of thousands of others took up farming on the prairies. In 1905, the government created two new provinces out of the prairies, Alberta and Saskatchewan.

Canada's economy flourished under Laurier. Farmers in the Prairie Provinces produced huge wheat harvests, and Europe became a great market for Canadian wheat. Aided by the continuing high tariffs, Canada's flour-milling, steel, and textile industries grew quickly. Nova Scotia coal mines thrived, and mining areas opened or expanded in Ontario, British Columbia, and the Klondike region of northern Canada. New hydroelectric power plants and two new transcontinental railroads, the Grand Trunk Pacific and the Canadian Northern, helped make the early 1900's Canada's most prosperous period since 1867.

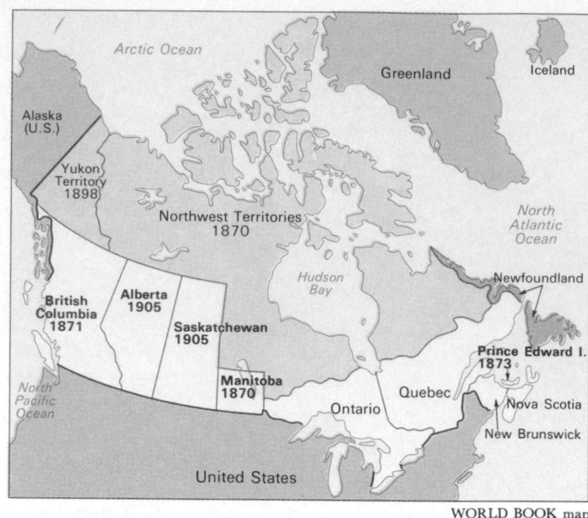

WORLD BOOK map

By 1905, Canada consisted of nine provinces and two territories. The dates indicate when each new province and territory joined Canada. The rapidly growing country spanned the continent, but Newfoundland remained a separate British colony.

Foreign Relations. Canada's role in the British Empire became an issue in 1899, when the Boer War broke out between the British and the Boers in southern Africa. Many Canadians had great pride in the empire and wanted Canada to send troops to help the British forces. But a large number of French Canadians opposed Canada's participation in foreign wars. Laurier compromised by deciding to equip and transport volunteers but not to send the Canadian Army.

In 1910, a controversy developed over a trade treaty between Canada and the United States. The treaty allowed each country to export numerous products to the other without paying high tariffs. But many Canadian business executives feared the trade agreement would destroy industries in Canada aided by the tariffs.

Another dispute involving Canada's obligations to the empire arose in 1910. Britain faced the threat of war with Germany and asked Canada to supply ships and sailors for the British Royal Navy. Laurier responded by announcing a plan to build a separate Canadian navy that could be lent to Britain in time of war. But English-speaking Canadians insisted that Canada contribute directly to the Royal Navy. Many French Canadians also opposed Laurier's plan, charging that it would involve Canada in foreign wars.

Opposition to the trade agreement and the naval plan

Public Archives of Canada, Ottawa (C14464)

Coast-to-Coast Rail Service for passengers began in Canada in 1886. The first passenger train to cross the country from the Atlantic coast to the Pacific coast is shown at the left at a stop in Port Arthur, Ont. The service was provided by the Canadian Pacific Railway (now CP Rail).

Provincial Archives of Alberta, E. Brown Collection

European Immigrants rushed to Canada during the late 1800's and early 1900's. Many of them settled in such big eastern cities as Toronto and Montreal. But hundreds of thousands of others headed west and took up farming on the prairies. The immigrants at the left settled in Alberta in 1906.

led to the defeat of Laurier's party in the election of 1911. Robert L. Borden, head of the victorious Conservative Party, became prime minister.

World War I and Independence (1914-1931)

Canada entered World War I (1914-1918) to aid Great Britain and its allies. Canada's participation in the war enabled it to act more freely in establishing its own foreign policies. In 1931, the Dominion won complete independence from Britain.

World War I. Great Britain's declaration of war on Germany on Aug. 4, 1914, created a tremendous burst of patriotism in Canada. Thousands of Canadians rushed to volunteer for military duty. Canadian troops first saw combat in April 1915. They helped halt the first German gas attack of the war during the Second Battle of Ypres in Belgium. The greatest Canadian triumph came in the Battle of Vimy Ridge in France on April 9, 1917. In the battle, about 130,000 Canadian troops captured the strong German positions on a hill called Vimy Ridge (see VIMY RIDGE, BATTLE OF). Billy Bishop, a Canadian flier, shot down 72 German planes during the war and became one of its most famous combat pilots (see BISHOP, BILLY). Over 600,000 Canadians served in the armed forces during World War I, and about 63,000 died.

World War I contributed enormously to Canada's industrial strength. The country's steel industry thrived through the sale of ships, artillery shells, and other equipment to Britain. Wartime demand also greatly expanded agricultural output, especially the production of beef cattle and wheat.

The Conscription Issue. When World War I began, Borden promised that Canada would not *conscript* (draft) men for overseas military service. He knew that French Canadians bitterly opposed conscription. Early in the war, large numbers of volunteers made a draft needless. By early 1917, however, Canadian forces had suffered high casualties, and the number of volunteers had dropped sharply. As a result, Borden established conscription in July 1917. He received strong support from English-speaking Canadians, but French Canadians strongly objected.

To make conscription work, Borden decided to form a *coalition* (joint) Conservative-Liberal government, which he called the Union government. Borden tried to bring Wilfrid Laurier and other Liberal Party leaders into the coalition. But Laurier opposed conscription and refused to join. The Liberals then split into two groups. One group, the Unionist Liberals, backed conscription. The other group remained loyal to Laurier. Borden appointed a number of Unionist Liberals to his government and called for an election in December 1917. The Unionists won every province except Quebec.

A Larger Role in the Empire's Affairs. Borden became increasingly dissatisfied with Canada's colonial status in view of its major contribution to the British war effort. In 1917, Borden and the leaders of other dominions in the British Empire began to demand greater participation in developing the empire's foreign and defense policies. The British needed the soldiers and weapons that the dominions provided and so agreed to their demands.

After World War I, Borden and the other dominion prime ministers were members of the British Empire's

Period Facts in Brief (1914-1931)

Prime Ministers (with parties, dates of service)

Sir Robert L. Borden, Conservative, 1911-1917
Sir Robert L. Borden, Unionist, 1917-1920
Arthur Meighen, Unionist, 1920-1921
W. L. Mackenzie King, Liberal, 1921-1926
Arthur Meighen, Conservative, 1926
W. L. Mackenzie King, Liberal, 1926-1930
Richard B. Bennett, Conservative, 1930-1935

Provinces of Canada

Number at start of period: 9
Provinces added during the period: none

Important Dates

1914-1918 More than 600,000 Canadians served in World War I.
1920 Canada became a member of the League of Nations.
1931 The Statute of Westminster made Canada an independent nation.

Population

1914 7,879,000
1929 10,029,000

peace delegation in Paris in 1919. They signed the Treaty of Versailles, which officially ended the war with Germany. In addition, all the dominions became original members of the League of Nations, an international peacekeeping agency formed in 1920.

Labor and Farm Unrest. While Borden attended the peace conference in Paris, trouble mounted at home. Workers throughout Canada demanded higher wages, better working conditions, and recognition of their unions. Farmers wanted relief from low crop prices and urged reductions in freight rates. Dissatisfied farmers formed political parties in almost every province. Farmer parties won control of the provincial government in Ontario in 1919 and in Alberta in 1921. In the national election of 1921, the Liberal Party gained a majority of the seats in the House of Commons, and William Lyon Mackenzie King became prime minister.

Independence. King was determined to establish Canada's independence in foreign affairs. In 1922, he refused to support Britain in a possible war with Turkey and rejected a request for Canadian troops. On King's insistence, Canada for the first time signed a treaty alone with another country in 1923. The treaty was with the United States and regulated halibut fishing in the northeast Pacific Ocean.

In 1926, King and representatives from the other dominions met with British representatives at an Imperial Conference in London. At the conference, King joined a successful fight for dominion independence. The dominion and British representatives declared the dominions to be independent members of the British Commonwealth of Nations, as the British Empire then became known. In 1931, the British Parliament passed the Statute of Westminster, which legalized the declaration. This act thus officially recognized Canada and the other self-governing dominions as independent nations.

The Young Nation (1932-1957)

During the 1930's, the young Canadian nation suffered through the Great Depression. The hard economic times ended when production rose during World War II (1939-1945). After the war, an industrial boom at home helped make Canada a major economic power. The nation also became greatly involved in world affairs.

The Great Depression began in 1929 with the stock market crash in the United States and spread throughout the world. The depression caused a sharp drop in foreign trade and especially hurt the demand for Canadian food products, lumber, and minerals. The decline in export income forced thousands of Canadian factories and stores, plus many coal mines, to close. Hundreds of thousands of Canadians lost their jobs and homes. A rapid fall in grain prices and a severe drought worsened the depression in the Prairie Provinces.

Unemployment was the chief issue in the election of 1930. King's government was defeated, and the Conservatives came to power under Richard B. Bennett. Bennett's government established more than 200 relief camps for single, unemployed men and spent hundreds of millions of dollars to aid the needy.

Bennett dealt harshly with strikers and demonstrators and earned the nickname "Iron Heel Bennett." But he also saw the need for reform. His government created a number of important federal agencies, including the Canadian Radio Broadcasting Commission in 1932, the Bank of Canada in 1934, and the Canadian Wheat Board in 1935. Canada's economic problems continued, however, and many Canadians blamed Bennett for failing to ease the hard times. Bennett's unpopularity led to the formation of new political parties, including the Co-operative Commonwealth Federation in 1933 and the Social Credit Party in 1935. In the election of 1935, the Liberal Party regained control of the House of Commons. King then began his third term as prime minister. See Great Depression (In Canada).

World War II. Canada declared war on Germany on Sept. 10, 1939. It declared war on Japan on Dec. 8, 1941, the day after Japan attacked U.S. bases at Pearl Harbor in Hawaii. The Canadian Army first saw action in December 1941, when it participated in the unsuccessful attempt to defend Hong Kong against a Japanese invasion. In August 1942, the Canadian Army suf-

Period Facts in Brief (1932-1957)

Prime Ministers (with parties, dates of service)
- Richard B. Bennett, Conservative, 1930-1935
- W. L. Mackenzie King, Liberal, 1935-1948
- Louis S. St. Laurent, Liberal, 1948-1957
- John G. Diefenbaker, Progressive Conservative, 1957-1963

Provinces of Canada
- Number at start of period: 9
- Number at end of period: 10
- Province added during the period: Newfoundland (1949)

Important Dates
- **1930's** Canada suffered through the Great Depression.
- **1934** The Bank of Canada was established.
- **1939-1945** More than a million Canadians served in World War II.
- **1940** A social security system was started.
- **1945** Canada joined the United Nations (UN).
- **1949** Canada signed a treaty that set up the North Atlantic Treaty Organization (NATO).

Population
- 1932 10,510,000
- 1957 16,610,000

Toronto Star

The Great Depression of the 1930's left hundreds of thousands of Canadians jobless and homeless. Soup kitchens, like this one in Port Arthur, Ont., provided free food for many of the needy.

Public Archives of Canada, Ottawa (PA 122765)

During World War II, the Third Canadian Division took part in the Allied landing at Normandy in France on June 6, 1944, *left.* By the end of the war in 1945, over a million Canadian men and women had served in the armed forces.

fered heavy losses in the bloody Allied assault on the French port of Dieppe.

Canadian troops also took part in the Allied invasion of Sicily in 1943 and in the battle for Italy. The Third Canadian Division participated in the Allied landing at Normandy in France on June 6, 1944. The First Canadian Army, commanded by General H. D. G. Crerar, advanced into northern Germany and accepted the surrender of the German northern front commander on May 7, 1945. The Royal Canadian Air Force aided the Allies, and the Canadian Navy helped protect Allied ships in the Atlantic Ocean. By the end of the war, more than a million Canadian men and women had served in the armed forces. Nearly 100,000 had been killed or wounded.

The Canadian government lent billions of dollars to the war cause. It sent the British people large quantities of food during the Battle of Britain. Canadian factories built thousands of planes, ships, and weapons.

When World War II began, King pledged to keep recruiting voluntary for overseas service. In 1942, however, the government proposed conscription for duty abroad. The vast majority of the Canadian people approved the proposal, though many French Canadians opposed it. However, no Canadian draftees went overseas until November 1944.

The war was especially tragic for Canadians of Japanese descent and for newly arrived immigrants from Japan. Japanese Canadians came under widespread distrust after Japan attacked Pearl Harbor. In February 1942, the Canadian government began to place about 21,000 of them in camps and isolated towns in Alberta, Manitoba, and Ontario. Their rights were not restored until 1949. Most of the Japanese Canadians lost their homes and businesses.

The government adopted several important social programs during the war. It established the beginning of a social security system by introducing unemployment insurance in 1940. In 1944, it adopted a program that assisted families by providing financial aid for children. As the war ended, the government began a vast benefits program to help veterans return to civilian life.

The Postwar Boom. Canada's economy thrived after World War II. Canadians spent their wartime savings on appliances and other household goods. A great demand for housing created a construction boom. The development of Canada's incredibly rich mineral deposits also flourished. The country became an important producer of asbestos, copper, iron ore, nickel, oil, uranium, and other minerals. Foreign investors, mainly from the United States, helped finance the development of many new industries. By the late 1950's, Canada had changed from a chiefly agricultural country to one of the world's great industrial nations.

Meanwhile, Canada experienced another great wave of immigration. From 1945 to 1956, more than a million people from Germany, Italy, and other war-torn European countries moved to Canada. Many of the immigrants settled in Toronto, Montreal, and other large cities. Suburbs grew rapidly outside the central cities.

Increasing Foreign Involvement. King retired as prime minister in November 1948. Louis St. Laurent, the new Liberal Party leader, became Canada's second French-Canadian prime minister. One of the first highlights of his administration occurred in March 1949, when Newfoundland became Canada's 10th province. Under St. Laurent, Canada played an ever-larger role in international affairs.

Canada's prestige and economic strength after World War II convinced many Canadians that their nation's interests required active involvement in foreign affairs. In 1945, Canada became an original member of the United Nations (UN). In 1949, it signed a treaty with the United States and 10 Western European nations that set up the North Atlantic Treaty Organization (NATO). NATO was the first military alliance Canada had joined in peacetime.

During the Korean War (1950-1953), Canada contributed about 22,000 soldiers to the UN forces fighting North Korea's invasion of South Korea. Canada helped bring about peace in the Middle East after Britain, France, and Israel invaded Egypt in 1956. Lester B. Pearson, Canada's secretary of state for external affairs, won the 1957 Nobel Peace Prize for proposing and organizing a UN peacekeeping force for the troubled area.

The End of Liberal Rule. Canadians took pride in the government's accomplishments in foreign affairs. But they were stunned in 1956, when the government broke the rules of Parliament to push through a bill to finance construction of a natural gas pipeline. John G. Diefen-

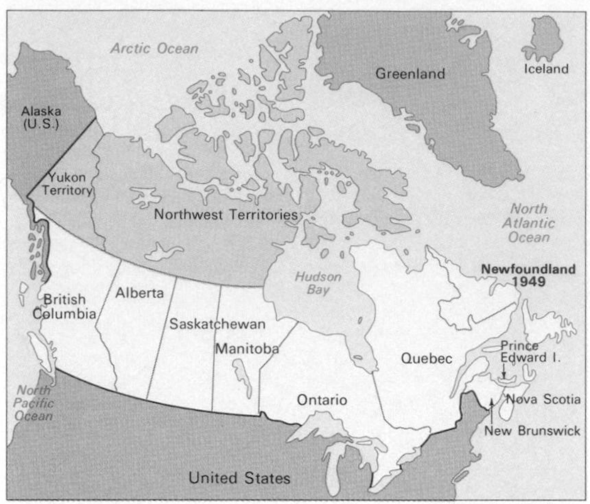

WORLD BOOK map

In 1949, Newfoundland became the 10th province of Canada. Newfoundland had gained control of Labrador in the settlement of a boundary dispute with Quebec in 1927. The Northwest Territories was reduced in size by the expansion of the provinces.

baker, leader of the Progressive Conservative Party, charged that St. Laurent's government had abused its authority and insulted Parliament. Many of the nation's voters agreed. In the election of 1957, Diefenbaker thus led his party to a narrow victory and ended 22 years of Liberal rule.

Challenges of the 1960's

Major economic and social problems troubled Canada during the 1960's. A business slump struck the country, and unemployment rose sharply. Meanwhile, French Canadians began a movement to increase their political power. In Quebec, many French Canadians began to support a campaign to make their province a separate nation.

Period Facts in Brief (1958-1969)

Prime Ministers (with parties, dates of service)

John G. Diefenbaker, Progressive Conservative, 1957-1963
Lester B. Pearson, Liberal, 1963-1968
Pierre E. Trudeau, Liberal, 1968-1979

Important Dates

1958 The Progressive Conservatives won the largest majority in the House of Commons in Canadian history.
1959 The St. Lawrence Seaway, a joint U.S.-Canadian project, opened.
1962 The Trans-Canada Highway, the country's first ocean-to-ocean road, was completed.
1964 A national pension plan was introduced.
1965 A new official Canadian flag flew for the first time on February 15.
1967 Canadians celebrated the 100th anniversary of Confederation with Expo 67, a world's fair in Montreal.
1969 The Official Languages Act required federal facilities in Canada to provide service in both French and English if 10 per cent of the people in a particular area speak either language.

Population

1958 17,080,000
1969 21,001,000

The New Conservative Government. Diefenbaker hoped to broaden his support in Parliament and called an election in 1958. The Progressive Conservatives won 208 of the 265 seats in the House of Commons, the largest majority in Canadian history. In 1959, Diefenbaker joined Queen Elizabeth II of Britain and U.S. President Dwight D. Eisenhower at the opening of the St. Lawrence Seaway. The seaway enables large commercial ships to sail between the Atlantic Ocean and the Great Lakes by way of the St. Lawrence River.

Diefenbaker faced a major political problem in 1959 when his government chose to buy American-made Bomarc missiles for defense at home instead of the more expensive Canadian-built Avro Arrow fighter planes. The government also bought U.S. fighters for Canada's contribution to NATO forces. The rejection of the Avro Arrow planes led to heavy criticism.

In 1960, a sagging economy challenged the Diefenbaker government. By 1961, 11 per cent of Canadian workers had no jobs. The government responded by trying to increase foreign trade. It developed new markets for Canadian wheat in China and the Communist countries of Eastern Europe. In 1962, during an election campaign, the government attempted to boost the economy by lowering the value of the Canadian dollar. In the election, held in June, the Conservatives won the most seats in the House of Commons but not a majority. The Diefenbaker government stayed in power only with the aid of the Social Credit Party, which had won 30 seats.

The Quebec Separatist Movement. Diefenbaker also faced rising discontent in Quebec. In 1960, the Quebec Liberal Party gained control of the provincial government. Led by Jean Lesage, the new government started the Quiet Revolution, a movement to defend French-Canadian rights throughout the country. Many French Canadians believed they were barred from jobs in government and some large corporations because they spoke French. They also wanted English Canadians to recognize and respect Quebec's French heritage. Lesage also worked to increase Quebec's control over its own economy and to reduce such control by the federal government.

The Quiet Revolution awakened deep feelings of French-Canadian nationalism. In Quebec, it influenced the rise of *separatism*, the demand that the province separate from Canada and become an independent nation. During the early 1960's, several separatist groups entered candidates in provincial elections. Other groups, especially the Front de Libération du Québec (FLQ), used terrorist tactics to promote separatism. In 1963, the FLQ began to bomb federal buildings and symbols of Canada that reflected the country's British traditions.

The Return of the Liberals. Early in 1963, a controversy developed over whether Canada had agreed in 1959 to accept nuclear warheads for its Bomarc missiles. The missiles were effective only with such warheads. Diefenbaker had refused to accept the weapons because some members of his Cabinet opposed the use of nuclear arms. The Liberals in Parliament argued that Canada had agreed to take the warheads for use in the defense of North America. Lester B. Pearson, the Liberal leader, accused the government of failing to show leadership. In February, the House of Commons gave Diefenbaker's government a vote of no confidence. Diefenbaker was then forced to call a general election.

In the election of 1963, the Liberals won the most seats in the House but not a majority. Pearson became prime minister with support from several small opposition parties. His government accepted the nuclear warheads. It also expanded social welfare programs, introducing a national pension plan in 1964 and a national health insurance program in 1965.

Pearson achieved a personal goal when Canada adopted a new national flag. The country had long used the British Red Ensign with a coat of arms representing Canada's provinces. The Conservatives wanted to keep the Red Ensign as a symbol of Canada's British heritage. But in 1964, Parliament approved a design that featured a red maple leaf, a symbol of Canada. On Feb. 15, 1965, Canada's new flag flew for the first time.

Canada marked the 100th anniversary of Confederation in 1967 with national celebrations. A highlight was Expo 67, a world's fair held in Montreal.

In April 1968, Pearson resigned as prime minister. His successor, Pierre Elliott Trudeau, became Canada's third French-Canadian prime minister. Trudeau called a national election for June 25. The campaign was marked by widespread enthusiasm that became known as "Trudeaumania." Canadians seemed to be madly in love with Trudeau, a dashing 48-year-old bachelor, and gave his party a majority of the seats in the House.

Trudeau was determined to curb the Quebec separatist movement. He pledged to create equal opportunities for both French- and English-speaking Canadians throughout the nation. His first important move toward this goal was winning Parliament's approval of the Official Languages Act in 1969. This act requires federal facilities to provide service in French in areas where at least 10 per cent of the people speak French. It also requires service in English in areas where at least 10 per cent of the people speak that language. The law brought major changes to the government, but it had little effect on the growing separatist movement.

Wide World

The Maple Leaf Flag became Canada's official flag in 1965. It omitted any symbol of Canadian ties with Great Britain.

Canada Since 1970

Canada headed into the 1970's with high hopes of economic expansion. But sharply rising prices and high unemployment caused problems. Canadian national unity was still threatened by the Quebec separatist movement. The increasingly independent policies of the western provinces also weakened unity.

Foreign Affairs. Canada broadened its relations with the two leading Communist nations, China and the Soviet Union, during the early 1970's. In 1970, Canada and China agreed to resume diplomatic relations, which had ended when the Communists gained control of China in 1949. In 1971, Trudeau and Soviet Premier Aleksei N. Kosygin exchanged visits. Canada increased trade with both China and the Soviet Union.

American magazines, motion pictures, music, and television programs remained tremendously popular in Canada during the 1970's. But relations between the Canadian and U.S. governments became increasingly strained. The U.S. government disapproved of Canada's willingness to accept American men who crossed the border to avoid being drafted in the Vietnam War (1957-1975). The United States also objected to new policies that limited foreign ownership and financing of Canadian industries. In 1973, the Canadian Parliament established the Foreign Investment Review Agency to end conditions that had enabled U.S. companies to gain control of over half of Canada's manufacturing plants.

Canadians, in turn, became disturbed by threats to their environment from the United States. Trudeau objected to the Garrison Diversion Project in North Dakota, which threatened to pollute Canadian rivers. He also protested the polluting of Canadian lakes and rivers by acid rain resulting from chemicals released into the air by U.S. factories and power plants. Control of fishing grounds and other offshore resources in the northeast Pacific and northwest Atlantic also became an issue between Canada and the United States.

Period Facts in Brief (Since 1970)

Prime Ministers (with parties, dates of service)

Pierre E. Trudeau, Liberal, 1968-1979
Charles Joseph Clark, Progressive Conservative, 1979-1980
Pierre E. Trudeau, Liberal, 1980-1984
John N. Turner, Liberal, 1984
Martin Brian Mulroney, Progressive Conservative, 1984-

Important Dates

1970 Militant separatists in Quebec kidnapped two government officials and murdered one of them.
1970 Canada and China resumed diplomatic ties.
1980 Voters in Quebec rejected a proposal to give provincial leaders authority to negotiate with the federal government for political independence.
1982 The Constitution Act ended British control over amendments to Canada's Constitution. The act included a new bill of rights.
1982 Unemployment in Canada reached its highest rate since the Great Depression.

Population

1970 21,297,000
1984 (estimated) 24,754,000

The Separatist Threat. Canada experienced one of its most serious political crises in October 1970, when the FLQ kidnapped two officials in Montreal. The officials were James R. Cross, the British trade commissioner in Montreal; and Pierre Laporte, Quebec's labor minister. The terrorists offered to exchange the two men for $500,000 and the release of 23 jailed FLQ members.

Trudeau rejected the offer. Instead, he put Canada's War Measures Act into effect. This act allows the government to suspend the civil liberties of people judged dangerous during wartime. The law had never been applied in peacetime. Police used it to arrest hundreds of FLQ sympathizers during their search for the kidnapped officials. FLQ members murdered Laporte. They released Cross unharmed in December, when the government permitted the kidnappers to go to Cuba.

FLQ terrorism ended, but the separatist movement continued. The Parti Québécois, a separatist political party organized in 1968, won control of Quebec's government in 1976. René Lévesque, a member of the Quebec legislature and the party's leader, became prime minister of the province. In 1980, Lévesque's government held a provincewide vote on a proposal to give provincial leaders authority to negotiate with the federal government for political independence for Quebec. But about 60 per cent of the voters rejected the proposal. See Lévesque, René.

Economic Problems. During the early 1970's, Canada's economy did not expand fast enough to keep pace with increases in the labor force. The country's difficulties grew after a recession and rapid inflation developed during the mid-1970's.

The soaring price of imported oil led the government to protect Canadians from high fuel costs by holding down the price of Canadian-produced oil and gas. The energy-rich provinces of Alberta, Saskatchewan, and British Columbia sharply criticized the program. But in spite of the low oil and gas prices, the three provinces benefited from an energy boom. Their populations grew rapidly, and numerous corporations shifted their head offices from eastern to western Canada. Nevertheless, many westerners charged that various federal economic policies discriminated against their region. A rising spirit of independence in the west weakened national unity.

In eastern Canada, the economy was no better in the 1970's than in earlier decades. The region suffered from low production and high unemployment. Newfoundland and Nova Scotia hoped that discoveries of oil and natural gas off their coasts would bring prosperity. But disputes between the provinces and the federal government over control of the deposits delayed production.

In 1975, Trudeau began a three-year program of wage and price controls to curb inflation. But prices again rose rapidly after the program ended.

Recent Developments. Trudeau's popularity began to decline during the mid-1970's. The Liberals lost the election of 1979 to the Progressive Conservatives, and Charles Joseph Clark became prime minister. Later that year, Clark announced a plan to conserve energy by raising fuel taxes. But strong opposition to the plan led the House of Commons to give the government a vote of no confidence. Clark then called a general election for February 1980. The Liberals won a majority in the House of

Canapress

The Constitution Act, signed by Queen Elizabeth II on April 17, 1982, *above,* gave Canada the sole power to amend its Constitution. Canadian Prime Minister Pierre E. Trudeau looked on.

Commons, and Trudeau returned as prime minister.

The Liberals continued to work for national unity and cut more traditional ties with Britain. In 1980, the government changed Canada's national anthem from "God Save the Queen" to "O Canada." In 1981, Trudeau won acceptance of proposed changes in Canada's Constitution from all provincial heads of government except Lévesque of Quebec. The proposals became part of the Constitution Act of 1982, which the British Parliament passed in March. The act eliminated the need for British approval of constitutional amendments. The act also included a new bill of rights called the Canadian Charter of Rights and Freedoms (see Bill of Rights [Canada's Constitution]). The revised Constitution took effect on April 17, 1982, and replaced the British North America Act as the basic governing document of Canada. In October 1982, the Canadian government changed the name of the country's main national holiday from Dominion Day to Canada Day.

Canada's economic problems worsened during the early 1980's, when another recession struck the nation. The recession eased inflation, but unemployment soared. In December 1982, 12.8 per cent of Canada's workers had no jobs—the highest unemployment rate since the Great Depression. The recession eased in 1983, and the jobless rate dropped slightly.

Politically, Canada suffered from deep divisions in the early 1980's. The Progressive Conservatives had almost no support in Quebec, and Liberals could count on little support in western Canada. But this situation changed after Trudeau resigned in June 1984 and was succeeded by John N. Turner. In the general election of September 1984, the Progressive Conservatives won 211 of the 282 seats in the House of Commons. The Conservatives, led by Martin Brian Mulroney, captured a majority of the seats in every Canadian province. Mulroney succeeded Turner as prime minister. David Jay Bercuson

Related Articles in World Book. See the *History* section of the province articles. See also:

Early Canada

Acadia
Bienville, Sieur de
Brulé, Étienne
Cadillac, Antoine de la Mothe
Cartier, Jacques

Champlain, Samuel de
Cornwallis, Edward
Coureurs de Bois
Duluth, Sieur
French and Indian Wars
Frontenac, Comte de
Groseilliers, Sieur des
Iberville, Sieur d'
Jolliet, Louis
La Salle, Sieur de
Laval de Montmorency, François
La Vérendrye, Sieur de
Le Moyne, Charles
Louisbourg
Marquette, Jacques
Money (The Development of Paper Money; picture)
Montcalm, Marquis de
Monts, Sieur de
New France
Poutrincourt, Jean de Biencourt de
Quebec, Battle of
Radisson, Pierre E.
Seigneurial System
Talon, Jean Baptiste
Verchères, Marie Madeleine Jarret de
Wolfe, James

British Rule

Amherst, Lord Jeffery
Baldwin, Robert
Brock, Sir Isaac
Carleton (family)
Cartier, Sir George É.
Douglas, Sir James
Dumont, Gabriel
Durham, Earl of
Elgin, Earl of
Fraser, Simon
Hearne, Samuel
Henry, Alexander
Hincks, Sir Francis
Lafontaine, Sir Louis H.
Mackenzie, Sir Alexander
Mackenzie, Roderick
Mackenzie, William L.
McGillivray, William
McKay, Alexander
Murray, James
North West Company
Papineau, Louis J.
Quebec Act
Quebec Conference
Rebellion of 1837-1838
Secord, Laura I.
Selkirk, Earl of
Simpson, Sir George
Sydenham, Baron
Taché, Sir Étienne-P.
Thompson, David
Union, Act of
United Empire Loyalists
War of 1812
Webster-Ashburton Treaty

Confederation and After

There is a separate biography of each governor general listed in the *table* with the article Governor General. There is also a separate biography of each prime minister listed in the *table* with the article Prime Minister of Canada. See also the following:

Assiniboia
Bourassa, Henri
British North America Act
Brown, George
Confederation of Canada
Crowfoot
Duff, Sir Lyman P.
Foster, Sir George E.
Galt, Sir Alexander T.
Howe, Joseph
Lévesque, René
Liberal Party
Macdonald, John S.
MacPhail, Agnes C.
Mowat, Sir Oliver
Murphy, Emily G.
Poundmaker
Progressive Conservative Party
Prohibition (Prohibition in Canada)
Red River Rebellion
Richards, Sir William B.
Riel, Louis
Rose, Sir John
Saskatchewan Rebellion
Stanfield, Robert L.
Strathcona and Mount Royal, Baron of
Tilley, Sir Samuel L.
Vimy Ridge, Battle of
Woodsworth, James Shaver

Other Related Articles

Canada Day
Hudson's Bay Company
Indian, American
Northwest Passage
Remembrance Day
Rupert's Land
Victoria Day

Outline

I. Early European Exploration

II. The Development of New France (1604-1688)
- A. Start of the Fur Trade
- B. Early Settlements
- C. Threats to Expansion
- D. The Royal Province
- E. The Growing French-English Rivalry

III. British Conquest and Rule (1689-1815)
- A. The Colonial Wars
- B. The Quebec Act
- C. The United Empire Loyalists
- D. Exploration of the West
- E. The War of 1812

IV. The Struggle for Responsible Government (1816-1867)
- A. Growing Discontent
- B. The Uprisings of 1837
- C. Lord Durham's Report
- D. The Beginning of Self-Government
- E. Confederation

V. Growth of the Dominion (1868-1913)
- A. New Provinces
- B. The Pacific Scandal
- C. The Return of Macdonald
- D. The Saskatchewan Rebellion
- E. Progress Under Laurier
- F. Foreign Relations

VI. World War I and Independence (1914-1931)
- A. World War I
- B. The Conscription Issue
- C. A Larger Role in the Empire's Affairs
- D. Labor and Farm Unrest
- E. Independence

VII. The Young Nation (1932-1957)
- A. The Great Depression
- B. World War II
- C. The Postwar Boom
- D. Increasing Foreign Involvement
- E. The End of Liberal Rule

VIII. Challenges of the 1960's
- A. The New Conservative Government
- B. The Quebec Separatist Movement
- C. The Return of the Liberals

IX. Canada Since 1970
- A. Foreign Affairs
- B. The Separatist Threat
- C. Economic Problems
- D. Recent Developments

Questions

Who were the United Empire Loyalists?
What were some effects of the Quiet Revolution?
What was the Pacific Scandal?
What was the aim of the Official Languages Act?
What led to the start of the fur trade in Canada?
Why was the Peace of Paris important in Canadian history?
How many provinces formed the Dominion of Canada in 1867?
When did Canada become an independent nation?
What serious political crisis did Canada face in 1970?
In what ways did Trudeau try to strengthen national unity in Canada?

Additional Resources

Level I

Bliss, Michael. *Confederation, 1867: The Creation of the Dominion of Canada.* Watts (New York City), 1975.

Dodds, Gordon, and Hall, Roger. *Canada: A History in Photographs.* Hurtig (Edmonton), 1981.

Doughty, Howard A. *The First Canadians.* Wiley (Rexdale, Ont.), 1979.

Ferguson, Linda W. *Canada.* Scribner (New York City), 1979. History for American readers.

Stewart, Roderick, and McLean, Neil. *Forming a Nation: The Story of Canada and Canadians.* 2 vols. Gage (Agincourt, Ont.), 1977-1978.

Level II

Bercuson, David Jay, ed. *Canada and the Burden of Unity.* Macmillan (Toronto), 1977.

Bothwell, Robert, and others. *Canada Since 1945: Power, Politics, and Provincialism.* Univ. of Toronto Press, 1981.

Marr, William L., and Paterson, D. G. *Canada: An Economic History.* Macmillan (Toronto), 1980.

McInnis, Edgar W. *Canada: A Political and Social History.* Rev. ed. Holt (Toronto), 1982.

McNaught, Kenneth. *The Pelican History of Canada.* Penguin (Markham, Ont.), 1978.

CANADA DAY, one of Canada's most important national holidays, is celebrated on July 1 of each year. It honors the day that the British colonies of New Brunswick, Nova Scotia, and the Province of Canada were united in one government called the Dominion of Canada. On July 1, 1867, the Dominion of Canada was created by terms of the British North America Act. The national holiday, called *Dominion Day* until 1982, is a time for patriotic programs and events. DAVID JAY BERCUSON

CANADA GOOSE is the common wild goose of North America. It grows 35 to 43 inches (89 to 109 centimeters) long, and has a grayish-brown coat and white patches on its cheeks. Its head, neck, and tail are black, its under parts gray. This goose usually makes its nest on a mound in a marsh. It uses twigs, weeds, grass, and reeds, and lines the nest with down. The nest holds from five to nine pale green, yellowish, or buff-white eggs. The best breeding grounds are in northern Canada.

In the autumn, the families fly south. Canada geese fly as far south as northern Florida and northern Mexico. Their varied diets include grasshoppers and other insects, grasses and water plants, corn, and wheat.

Canada geese have been introduced into Europe from America. There are five kinds. (1) The *common* Canada goose usually weighs about 9 pounds (4 kilograms). Its wingspread is from 5 to 6½ feet (1.5 to 2 meters). (2) The *white-cheeked*, or *Western*, Canada goose is about the same size, but a little darker. It seldom flies south in the winter, but stays along the Pacific Coast from Alaska to British Columbia. (3) The *lesser* Canada goose weighs about 5 pounds (2.3 kilograms). It nests on the Arctic Coast from Alaska to Hudson Bay, and winters in Washington, California, and northern Mexico. (4) *Hutchins'*, or *Richardson's*, goose weighs about 4 pounds (1.8 kilograms). It breeds in the central Canadian Arctic, and flies south to the Gulf Coast of Mexico. (5) The *cackling* goose, a darker bird about the size of a 3-pound (1.4-kilogram) duck, nests on the coast and islands of western Alaska, and winters mainly in California.

Scientific Classification. The Canada goose belongs to the duck family, *Anatidae*. It is genus *Branta*, species *B. canadensis*. JOSEPH J. HICKEY

See also BIRD (picture: Birds of the Arctic); GOOSE; LAKE ATHABASCA.

CANADA PENSION PLAN. See SOCIAL SECURITY (The Canada Pension Plan).

CANADA POST CORPORATION. See POST OFFICE (Canada).

CANADA THISTLE is one of the most troublesome of weeds. It is native to Europe and Asia but now grows throughout most of the northern United States and southern Canada. The thistle has prickly leaves and small pink, purple, or white flowers.

Saint Clair
Canada Thistle

The Canada thistle annoys farmers because it grows in cultivated areas as well as in wasteland, and it is difficult to control. The thistle spreads easily because new plants can grow from bits of the many long roots of old plants. If a plant is only partly uprooted, several plants can still spring up from its remaining roots.

The plant can be destroyed in several ways. One way is to kill its roots through starvation. The leaves supply the food that keeps the roots alive. This food supply can be cut off by cutting down the green stems of the plant as soon as they appear. This method can be combined with the growing of crops, such as corn, that require cultivation between rows. Cultivation brings the thistle seeds nearer the surface so they may start growing. Later, the stems are cut down. Chemical weed killers are also used to destroy the plant.

Scientific Classification. The Canada thistle belongs to the composite family, Compositae. It is classified as *Cirsium arvense*. MARGARET R. BOLICK

See also THISTLE; WEED.

CANADIAN BROADCASTING CORPORATION (CBC) operates radio and television networks and provides several other broadcasting services. The CBC receives most of its funds from the Canadian government. It also gets money from the sale of advertising.

The CBC operates two AM radio networks, one of which broadcasts in English and the other in French. These networks furnish programs for about 150 Canadian stations. The CBC owns about 50 of the stations, and about 100 are privately owned.

The corporation also operates two television networks. One of them presents programs in English, and the other uses French. The TV networks provide programs broadcast by about 20 CBC-owned stations and about 40 independent stations.

The CBC operates FM radio stations in several major cities. It provides medium- and short-wave radio service to northern areas of Canada in English and French and in Eskimo and Indian languages. The CBC Armed Forces Service broadcasts to Canadian troops at home and in other countries. The CBC also operates Radio Canada International, a short-wave service that broadcasts in 11 languages to many parts of the world.

The Canadian Broadcasting Corporation was founded in 1936. It has headquarters in Ottawa, Ont.

Critically reviewed by the CANADIAN BROADCASTING CORPORATION

CANADIAN EDUCATION ASSOCIATION is a national association of education authorities that promotes cooperation among the provinces. It is supported by grants from the 10 provincial departments of education and by about 80 school systems. The association collects and distributes information on various aspects of public education. It publishes the magazine *Education Canada*, a newsletter, and many bulletins and reports. The association was founded in 1891 as the Dominion Educational Association. Its headquarters are at 252 Bloor Street West, Toronto, Ont. M5S 1V5.

Critically reviewed by the CANADIAN EDUCATION ASSOCIATION

CANADIAN FOOTBALL. See FOOTBALL.

CANADIAN LIBRARY ASSOCIATION (CLA) is a national organization that promotes high standards of librarianship and of library and information service. The CLA has more than 4,500 members, including librarians, library trustees, and publishers.

The association develops standards for libraries and librarian training programs, offers library school scholarships, and presents book awards. It publishes the

Canadian Periodical Index, the *Canadian Library Journal*, and other professional and reference materials. The CLA also produces microfilms of early Canadian newspapers and documents of historical importance. The association was founded in 1946. It has headquarters at 151 Sparks Street, Ottawa, Ont. K1P 5E3.

Critically reviewed by the CANADIAN LIBRARY ASSOCIATION

CANADIAN LITERATURE may be divided in two parts, somewhat like a tree with two great roots. One root is deeply buried in the culture of France. The other is just as deeply buried in the traditions of England. One part of Canadian literature is written in French, the other in English. But the branches of this tree are purely Canadian. Authors and readers of each literature are gaining more and more knowledge of the other, in the original or in translation.

Characteristics of Canadian Literature

Canada's literature, whether written in French or in English, reflects three main parts of Canadian experience: (1) nature, (2) frontier life, and (3) Canada's position in the world.

First, Canadian authors often emphasize the effects of climate and geography on the life and work of their people. Canada's rugged mountains, roaring rivers, and harsh winters contrast sharply with its rich valleys, peaceful lakes, and mild summers.

Second, frontier life is part of Canada's experience that appears frequently in its literature. Many authors have taken themes from the steady march westward across Canada. Others have found drama in continuing battles to win a living on the sea. Still others have emphasized the ever-present frontier to the north, the constant challenge to expand a foothold in the Arctic. Canadian authors do not regard new lands as the only frontier. They feel that people face exciting challenges in the outposts of experience.

Third, Canada's position in the world profoundly affects many Canadian writers. French Canadians often feel surrounded by their English-speaking neighbors. They have made a determined effort to preserve their own institutions and culture. But English Canadians frequently have a similar feeling of being surrounded by the people and culture of the United States. Many novels and poems show how Canadian writers feel about such problems.

French-Canadian Literature

The history of literature in French Canada may be divided into four general periods: (1) from 1608 to 1760; (2) from 1760 to 1860; (3) from 1860 to 1900; and (4) the 1900's. These periods correspond roughly with those of Canadian history: (1) from the earliest settlement to the end of French rule, (2) from then to confederation, (3) a period of adjustment, and (4) the period of Canada's emergence as a world power.

Before 1760, Canadians had little chance to think of culture. They were too busy establishing homes and villages in their vast new wilderness. As a result, almost the only literature consisted of reports from explorers and missionaries. In 1535, Jacques Cartier became the first European to reach the St. Lawrence River, and he reported on it in *Bref Récit de la Navigation de Canada* (1545). Samuel de Champlain founded Quebec in 1608, and supplied early information about the Indians in *Des Sauvages, ou Voyage de Samuel de Champlain* (1603). Marie de l'Incarnation, who established the Ursuline order in Canada, left a deeply religious autobiography, *Rélations* (1633, 1654). Her work was the first picture of Canada as seen through the eyes of a woman. The Jesuit martyrs of the 1600's, such as Jean de Brébeuf, penned stirring tales of missionary work among the Indians. The only major historian of the period, Pierre F. X. de Charlevoix, published his *Histoire et Description Générale de la Nouvelle-France* in 1744.

The Rise of French-Canadian Literature began after Great Britain won Canada from France in the 1760's. French Canadians found themselves surrounded by a people with language, religion, and traditions that differed from their own. As a result, their authors began a struggle to preserve the French cultural heritage in Canada. In 1822, Étienne Parent became editor of the *Canadien*, a journal in Quebec. Its motto, "Our institutions, our language, and our law," sounded the keynote in this struggle.

French-Canadian historical writing flourished during the 1830's and 1840's. Authors re-created the past from old parish records, diaries, and memoirs, singing the praises of French achievements in Canada. They allowed their prejudices to cloud their judgment, and lost much historical truth. F. X. Garneau published his *Histoire du Canada* from 1845 to 1848. It suffers from his prejudices, but many French Canadians still regard it as their standard history.

Good poetry did not appear until 1854. That year, Octave Crémazie began to contribute religious and patriotic poems to *Le Journal de Québec*. His "Le Drapeau de Carillon" (1858) remains one of the best-loved songs of French Canada.

Crémazie's influence lasted throughout the remarkable literary movement that began about 1860. Religion and patriotism always appeared in this poetry, even though the main theme might be nature. Writers of the Romantic movement in France also exerted strong influence over French-Canadian poetry.

Literary Expansion. A group of poets called *the School of Quebec* arose in the 1860's. These poets were inspired by Crémazie and Alfred Garneau, son of the historian. French-Canadian patriotism was their dominant theme. The best poets of this movement were Léon-Pamphile Lemay and Louis-Honoré Fréchette. Lemay started a new poetry of the soil. Fréchette's lyrics dealt with friendship, nature, and patriotism.

Many historians also wrote during this period. Abbé Henri-Raymond Casgrain wrote *Montcalm et Lévis* (1891), Antoine Gérin-Lajoie wrote *Dix Ans d'Histoire du Canada* (1888), and Benjamin Sulte wrote *Histoire des Canadiens-Français* (1882-1884).

Most novelists of the period wrote historical romances similar to the works of Scotland's Sir Walter Scott. Some novelists wrote works of melodrama or social propaganda. Only two of the novels have permanent value: *Les Anciens Canadiens* (1863), a historical romance by Philippe Aubert de Gaspé, and *Jean Rivard* (1862), a back-to-the-soil novel by Gérin-Lajoie.

Since 1900, novelists and short-story writers of French Canada have attracted more attention than poets have. First came Louis Hémon with his *Maria*

CANADIAN LITERATURE

Annette & Basil Zarov, Montreal

Gabrielle Roy

Chapdelaine (1914), a sensitive story of simple pioneer men and women. Then came the more realistic *Trente Arpents* (1938) by Ringuet (pseudonym of Philippe Panneton). Similarly realistic novels of country life have come from such writers as Germaine Guèvremont, Yves Thériault, and Félix-Antoine Savard. Realistic novels of contemporary city life have also appeared. The best known of these include *Les Plouffe* (1948) by Roger Lemelin, *Bonheur d'occasion* (1945) by Gabrielle Roy, *Le Libraire* (1960) by Gérard Bessette, and *Le Couteau sur la table* (1965) by Jacques Godbout. Excellent psychological novels include those by Robert Charbonneau, Robert Élie, and Marie-Claire Blais. Most of these works have been translated into English and are widely read in both languages.

In poetry, a group of writers called *the School of Montreal* came together about 1895. These poets rejected the broad patriotic and religious themes of the earlier School of Quebec, and turned instead to the psychology of the individual. Representative poets of the School of Montreal include Emile Nelligan and Albert Lozeau. They were inspired by the French poets Charles Baudelaire, Arthur Rimbaud, and Paul Verlaine.

French-Canadian poetry flourished during the period after the end of World War II in 1945. Some poets, such as Guy Delahaye and René Chopin, carried on the tradition of Nelligan and Lozeau. Some sang of the joys and sorrows of rural life, and others of the problems of city life. Perhaps the most successful poets wrote brilliant but difficult poems about the human soul and its quest for understanding. These poets include François Hertel (pseudonym of Rodolphe Dubé), Roger Brien, St. Denys Garneau, Alain Grandbois, and Anne Hébert.

Historians include Sir Thomas Chapais, with *Cours d'Histoire du Canada* (1919-1933); Abbé Lionel Groulx, with *La Naissance d'une Race* (1919); and Marcel Trudel, with *Histoire de la Nouvelle-France* (1963).

English-Canadian Literature

Literature in English Canada began with the accounts explorers wrote about their travels and discoveries. Alexander Henry, Samuel Hearne, and Sir Alexander Mackenzie wrote vivid descriptions of their journeys north and west. After these early writings, English-Canadian literature falls into the same periods

Canadian Literature

Two Literatures have flourished side by side in Canada from about 1800 to the present. One developed from the culture of England, and the other from France. But both literatures reflect the history and experience of Canada. The names in each category of the table are listed in chronological order.

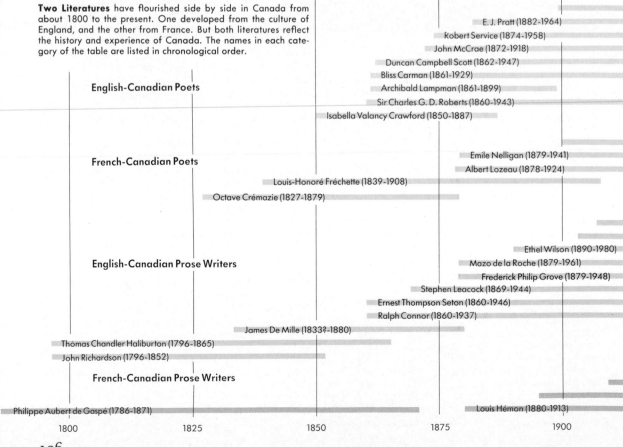

English-Canadian Poets

- E. J. Pratt (1882-1964)
- Robert Service (1874-1958)
- John McCrae (1872-1918)
- Duncan Campbell Scott (1862-1947)
- Bliss Carman (1861-1929)
- Archibald Lampman (1861-1899)
- Sir Charles G. D. Roberts (1860-1943)
- Isabella Valancy Crawford (1850-1887)

French-Canadian Poets

- Emile Nelligan (1879-1941)
- Albert Lozeau (1878-1924)
- Louis-Honoré Fréchette (1839-1908)
- Octave Crémazie (1827-1879)

English-Canadian Prose Writers

- Ethel Wilson (1890-1980)
- Mazo de la Roche (1879-1961)
- Frederick Philip Grove (1879-1948)
- Stephen Leacock (1869-1944)
- Ernest Thompson Seton (1860-1946)
- Ralph Connor (1860-1937)
- James De Mille (1833?-1880)
- Thomas Chandler Haliburton (1796-1865)
- John Richardson (1796-1852)

French-Canadian Prose Writers

- Louis Hémon (1880-1913)
- Philippe Aubert de Gaspé (1786-1871)

1800 1825 1850 1875 1900

as the last three periods in French-Canadian literature: (1) the early 1800's; (2) from 1860 to 1900; and (3) the 1900's.

The Early 1800's saw the first important English-Canadian novel. It was *Wacousta* (1832) by John Richardson, a tale of Pontiac's Indian conspiracy. But Thomas Chandler Haliburton ranks as the most distinguished literary figure of the period. He was a Nova Scotian judge who later served in the British Parliament. Haliburton's fame rests largely upon the humorous stories in *The Clockmaker, or The Sayings and Doings of Sam Slick of Slickville* (1836).

In poetry, Oliver Goldsmith wrote *The Rising Village* (1825), a short epic of the United Empire Loyalists. Goldsmith was a grandnephew of the great English writer of the same name. Charles Heavysege won considerable acclaim for his Biblical drama, *Saul* (1857). Charles Sangster wrote lilting descriptions of Ontario scenery and customs.

After Confederation, Canadian poets produced many fine works. Isabella Valancy Crawford wrote a pastoral epic of pioneer life, *Malcolm's Katie* (1884), which contains some of the finest lyrical passages in Canadian literature. Other poets include Charles Mair and George F. Cameron.

The first novel by James De Mille appeared in 1865. Of the 20 or more that followed, *A Strange Manuscript Found in a Copper Cylinder* (1888) usually ranks as the best. The only other important fiction early in the period was *The Golden Dog* (1877), a long romance written by William Kirby.

A new group of poets appeared in 1880, when Sir Charles G. D. Roberts published *Orion and Other Poems*. These poets usually wrote lyrics about nature, often in sonnet form. Roberts, who wrote over a 60-year period, was the most productive of the group. Some of his best writing appeared in *Songs of the Common Day* (1893), a sonnet sequence. Archibald Lampman, the second poet of the group, was the master of sonnets among Canadian poets. "The Frogs," "Winter Uplands," and "January Morning" rank among his best works. His original and sensitive verses mark Lampman as Canada's supreme nature poet. The third poet of the group, Duncan Campbell Scott, dealt with a wider range of subject matter. His work may seem intellectual, but it carries strong feelings. Some of his finest poems deal with Indian themes and the somber impressiveness and silence of forest and lake, as in "The Forsaken," "An Onondaga Madonna," and "Night Burial in the Forest." An Indian poet, Emily Pauline Johnson, also tried to interpret the spirit of her people in poetry.

During his lifetime, Bliss Carman was often regarded as Canada's finest lyric poet. All his work, and especially his first volume, *Low Tide on Grand Pre* (1893),

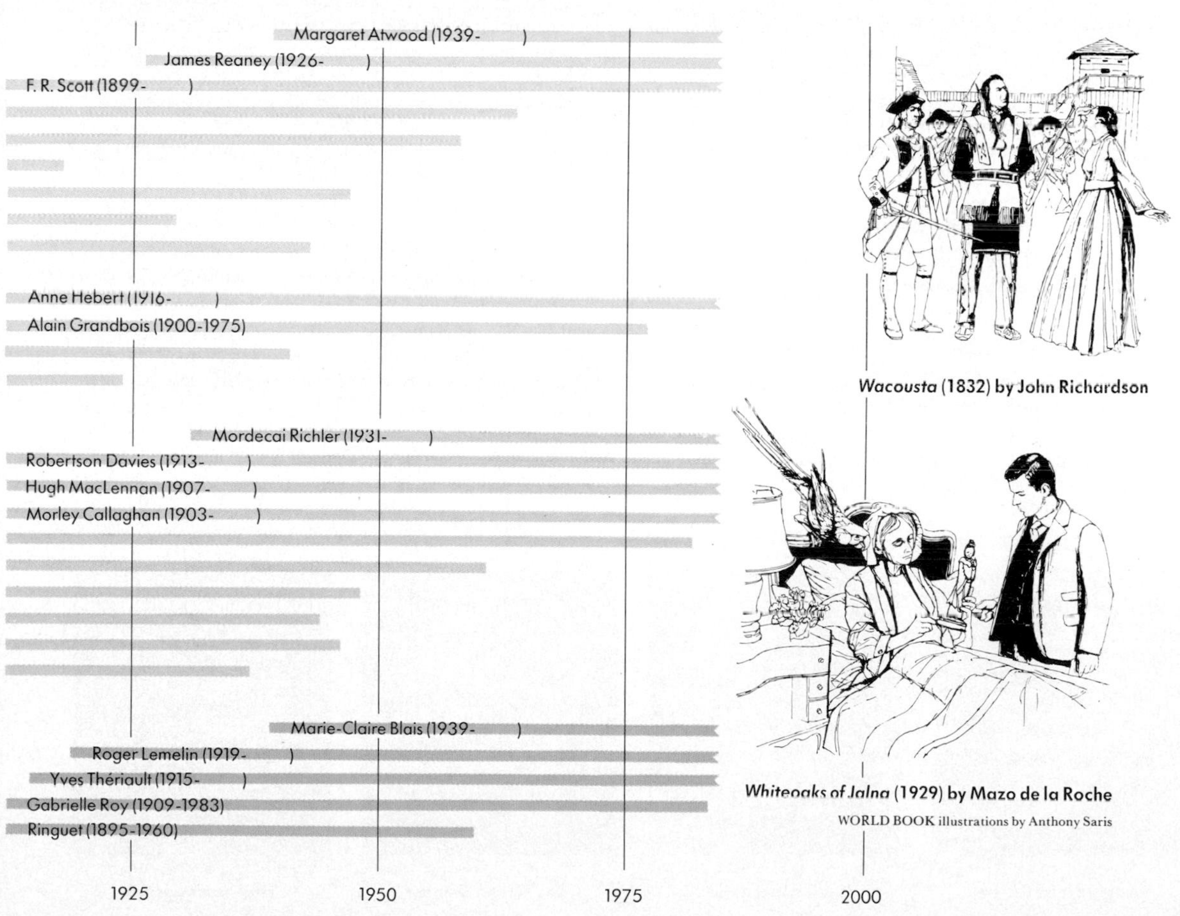

Wacousta (1832) by John Richardson

Whiteoaks of Jalna (1929) by Mazo de la Roche

WORLD BOOK illustrations by Anthony Saris

has pictorial and melodic beauty. Frederick George Scott was a poet with a message—the consolation of the human spirit. Even his nature poetry has a strong religious and moral flavor. William Wilfrid Campbell wrote some fine descriptive poems and a few powerful narratives.

The reading public met three popular new Canadian novelists during the late 1800's. Sir Gilbert Parker published *When Valmond Came to Pontiac* (1895) and *The Seats of the Mighty* (1896). Parker dealt mainly with historical themes. Ralph Connor (pseudonym of Charles W. Gordon) was the first Canadian novelist to write of the expanding West, notably in *Black Rock* (1898) and *The Sky Pilot* (1899). The story of *The Man from Glengarry* (1901) takes place in his native Ontario. Connor became one of Canada's most popular writers of fiction. The third novelist, Lucy Maud Montgomery, won world fame with *Anne of Green Gables* (1908).

Fiction of the 1900's. During the 1800's, fiction had been a comparatively minor form in Canadian literature. However, fiction, especially the novel, assumed a central position in Canadian writing of the 1900's.

During the early and mid-1900's, several novelists wrote historical fiction. They based their work on careful research and avoided sentimental celebrations of the past. Important historical novelists included Philip Child, who wrote *The Village of Souls* (1933), and Thomas Raddall, the author of *His Majesty's Yankees* (1942). Mazo de la Roche wrote a family chronicle of 16 novels, beginning with *Jalna* (1927). She continued an earlier tradition of domestic romance, but brought to her series a sharp psychological insight and a sensitive awareness of nature.

Beginning in the 1930's, many novelists turned to modern themes. They preferred familiar regional settings and became increasingly experimental in their narrative methods. However, no literary schools emerged as writers developed strongly individual qualities in their fiction.

F. P. Grove and Morley Callaghan dominated the Canadian novel in the 1930's. Grove, a German immigrant, wrote about settlers in the western prairies. His novels are serious in tone and reflect a tragic view of life. Grove's grim stories include *The Yoke of Life* (1930) and *Fruits of the Earth* (1933). Callaghan wrote realistic novels with moral and religious implications. His works of the 1930's include *Such Is My Beloved* (1934) and *More Joy in Heaven* (1937).

Sinclair Ross and Hugh MacLennan emerged as major novelists in the 1940's. Ross gained acclaim for his first novel, *As for Me and My House* (1941), a penetrating study of human alienation in a small western town. MacLennan wrote about important social issues in terms of Canadian society in the province of Quebec, where tensions between the French and the English were strongest. *Two Solitudes* (1945) explores conflicts between the two cultures.

Mavis Gallant and Alice Munro both gained recognition as short-story writers. Typical collections include Munro's *Dance of the Happy Shades* (1968) and Gallant's *Home Truths: Selected Canadian Stories* (1981).

Several major novelists established their reputations in the 1950's and 1960's. Ethel Wilson set her novels in British Columbia. Such works as *Swamp Angel* (1954) show a poetic sensitivity to landscape and to the inner lives of her heroines. Adele Wiseman wrote a vivid study of Jewish life in *The Sacrifice* (1956). Mordecai Richler satirized Jewish middle-class life in Montreal in *The Apprenticeship of Duddy Kravitz* (1959) and other novels. Ernest Buckler's *The Mountain and the Valley* (1952) is a classic regional novel about rural life in Nova Scotia. Robertson Davies, who began his literary career writing light comic novels in the 1950's, later became noted for his philosophical satires. His major work is the *Deptford Trilogy*, which consists of the novels *Fifth Business* (1970), *The Manticore* (1972), and *World of Wonders* (1975).

A number of writers who appeared in the 1960's and 1970's wrote experimental fiction. Rudy Wiebe combined history and unconventional narrative techniques in *The Temptations of Big Bear* (1973). Robert Kroetsch blended irony, fantasy, and realism in such novels as *The Studhorse Man* (1969). Michael Ondaatje combined prose and poetry in *The Collected Works of Billy the Kid* (1970). Hugh Hood announced a 12-volume fictional study of Canadian life from the early 1900's to the end of the century. The series, called *The New Age*, began with *The Swing in the Garden* (1975).

Margaret Laurence and Margaret Atwood gained international recognition for their novels about women in modern society. Laurence wrote a powerful study of a middle-aged woman who struggles with her creative instincts in *The Diviners* (1974). In *Life Before Man* (1980), Atwood explored with satiric humor a number of human relationships against a sharply observed Toronto setting.

Poetry of the 1900's. Many critics rate E. J. Pratt as the leading Canadian poet of the first half of the

Little, Brown & Co.

Mazo de la Roche

Nakash, Montreal

Hugh MacLennan

© Karsh from Rapho Guillumette

Robertson Davies

© Karsh, Miller Services

Stephen Leacock

1900's. Pratt wrote long narrative poems in traditional verse forms. In his poems, he showed individuals at their best when confronting overwhelming odds. Pratt's characters battle many antagonists, including nature and their own brutal instincts. Two of his finest epic poems on Canadian themes are *Brébeuf and His Brethren* (1940) and *Towards the Last Spike* (1952).

Poets A. J. M. Smith and F. R. Scott edited an anthology called *New Provinces* (1936) that introduced the work of many poets who became influential in the 1940's and 1950's. These poets favored the short lyric form and experimented with technique and with the use of image and metaphor. Poets represented in the anthology included Robert Finch and A. M. Klein, as well as Smith and Scott.

A. M. Klein was probably the most distinctive poet of his time. He was a learned writer with a knowledge of the cultural traditions of English Canada, French Canada, and Judaism. Klein's *The Rocking Chair* (1948), a portrait of French Canada, has been called the best single volume of poetry in Canadian literature.

The two leading Canadian poets today are probably Earle Birney and Irving Layton. Birney is noted for his mastery of form and language. His poems fiercely protest against human brutality, but occasionally they portray noble qualities in humanity. Layton became known for his brilliant use of language in poems that range from satire to emotionally moving lyrics.

Other Writings of the 1900's. Humorists, journalists, and scholars wrote some of the best Canadian prose of the 1900's. Stephen Leacock ranks as the finest humorist in Canadian literature. His *Sunshine Sketches of a Little Town* (1912) is a portrait of a southern Ontario town that mixes nostalgia with ironic humor.

Several journalists became noted for their vivid prose. Pierre Berton wrote about Canadian history in *The National Dream* (1970) and *The Last Spike* (1971). Peter Newman explored Canadian big business in *The Canadian Establishment* (1975, 1981). Farley Mowat wrote many highly praised books on nature and the Canadian Arctic territory. A selection from his writings was published as *The World of Farley Mowat* (1980).

Canadian scholars produced outstanding works in history, literature, and literary criticism. Donald Creighton wrote *John A. Macdonald* (1952, 1955), a biography of the first prime minister of Canada. Northrop Frye and Marshall McLuhan became internationally respected literary and social critics. Frye wrote a classic of modern literary theory in *Anatomy of Criticism* (1957). McLuhan wrote several famous works on communications and society, including *The Gutenberg Galaxy* (1962) and *Understanding Media* (1964).

Drama did not become an important Canadian literary activity until the mid-1900's. James Reaney, who was primarily a poet, wrote several plays in verse, notably *The Killdeer* (1962). Robertson Davies wrote a number of witty and sophisticated dramas, such as *Fortune My Foe* (1949). Beginning in the 1970's, many small theaters developed in major Canadian cities, and a group of young dramatists emerged to write for them. The best known were David Fennario, David French, John Murrell, and Erika Ritter.

CLAUDE T. BISSELL

Related Articles in WORLD BOOK include:

See also *Canadian Literature* in the RESEARCH GUIDE/INDEX, Volume 22, for a *Reading and Study Guide*.

Additional Resources

KLINCK, CARL F., ed. *Literary History of Canada: Canadian Literature in English.* 3 vols. Univ. of Toronto Press, 1976.

SMITH, A. J. M. *Towards a View of Canadian Letters: Selected Critical Essays, 1928-1971.* Univ. of British Columbia Press (Vancouver), 1973. Critical examination of various genres of Canadian literature, mainly poetry.

STORY, NORAH. *The Oxford Companion to Canadian History and Literature.* Oxford (Don Mills, Ont.), 1967.

TOYE, WILLIAM, ed. *The Supplement to The Oxford Companion to Canadian History and Literature.* Oxford (Don Mills, Ont.), 1974.

WATERSTON, ELIZABETH. *Survey: A Short History of Canadian Literature.* Methuen (Agincourt, Ont.), 1973.

CANADIAN MOUNTED POLICE. See ROYAL CANADIAN MOUNTED POLICE.

CANADIAN SHIELD is a huge, rocky region that curves around Hudson Bay like a giant horseshoe. The Shield covers half the land area of Canada. It includes most of Baffin Island, all of Labrador, nine-tenths of Quebec, over half of Ontario and Manitoba, and large areas in Saskatchewan and the Northwest Territories. About 1,771,000 square miles (4,586,900 square kilometers) of the Shield's 1,864,000-square-mile (4,827,738-square-kilometer) area lie in Canada. It also dips into the United States to form the Adirondack Mountains of New York and the Superior Uplands of Michigan, Wisconsin, and Minnesota. The Shield is also called the *Laurentian Plateau*, after the Laurentian Mountains of southern Quebec. See CANADA (Canadian Shield).

Geologists estimate that the rock formations that make up most of the Shield are 500 million to 5 billion years old. Most of the rocks have undergone one or more periods of mountain-building. During these periods, extreme heat and pressure produced high mountains of granite, diorite, quartzite, and other crystalline rocks. Weathering and erosion wore down the mountains. Today, much of the Shield's central and northwestern part is low and flat. Mountains in the northeastern part rise as high as 8,500 feet (2,590 meters).

Relatively few people live in the region. Only small areas are suitable for agriculture. The Shield is dotted with lakes, some of which have become famous resorts. Large forests in the southern section rank among Canada's most important natural resources. The Canadian Shield is also rich in copper, gold, iron, nickel, uranium, and other minerals.

D. F. PUTNAM

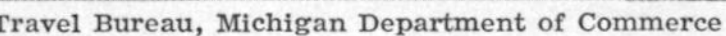

Travel Bureau, Michigan Department of Commerce

Emil Schulthess, Black Star

Canals have served as a means of transporting goods, people, and water for thousands of years. The modern Soo Canals on the United States-Canadian border, *left*, link Lakes Superior and Huron. The centuries-old Grand Canal, *right*, extends for over 1,000 miles (1,600 kilometers) through China.

CANAL is a waterway dug across land. Canals have served as important means of transporting goods and water for thousands of years.

There are two major types of canals: *navigation canals* and *water conveyance canals*. Navigation canals link bodies of water, enabling vessels to travel between them. Water conveyance canals, which include irrigation canals and drainage canals, carry water from one place to another. This article deals mainly with navigation canals.

Navigation canals may connect two similar bodies of water, such as two lakes, or two different waterways, such as a lake and a river. Navigation canals also link oceans with seaports that lie near, but not directly on, the oceans. In addition, many navigation canals are parts of *canalized rivers*—that is, rivers whose navigable stretches are connected by a series of dams and locks. These structures enable vessels to travel an entire river by avoiding waterfalls, shallow areas, and other navigation hazards. Such major inland waterways as the Mississippi and Ohio rivers in the United States and the Rhine River in Europe are canalized rivers.

Early canals were ditches 3 to 5 feet (0.9 to 1.5 meters) deep and 15 to 40 feet (4.6 to 12 meters) wide. Through the years, boats and canals have become larger. For example, the Panama Canal, opened in 1914, is about 40 feet (12.2 meters) deep and about 500 feet (152.4 meters) wide. Its locks are about 110 feet (33.5 meters) wide.

Most navigation canals are built and operated by government agencies. The Corps of Engineers designs, builds, and maintains the navigation canals of the United States. These waterways are used by industry and by private citizens. Many water conveyance canals, however, are privately owned and used by such agencies and businesses as irrigation districts and public utilities.

Planning and Building a Canal

When planning a canal, builders first decide whether a canal is needed in an area. They consider such factors as the kinds of goods to be shipped in and out of an area and what other forms of transport are available. Canals are usually used for shipping large quantities of goods when the speed of movement is not important. In such cases, canals are cheaper than such alternatives as railroads or trucks.

Engineers study the terrain to determine the course of a canal and to decide whether it will need locks. The width and depth of a canal are based on the size of the vessels it will handle. Engineers also consider how a canal will affect surrounding plant and animal life. For example, a canal might disrupt the migration of certain animals and alter their food supply.

The construction of a canal primarily involves the digging and moving of earth and rock. Such materials as clay or crushed rock may be added to a canal to reduce leakage and prevent erosion. Some canals are lined with asphalt or concrete.

Canal Locks

Canal locks are rectangular chambers that enable ships to move from one water level to another by varying the amount of water in the lock. Most locks are made of concrete and have watertight gates at each end. Water flows in and out of locks by gravity, and so no pumps are needed. Locks do, however, require a supply of water at the upper level of the canal. As a result, some locks have special reservoirs and auxiliary canals to ensure an adequate water supply when the normal supply runs low.

Locks are used to overcome changes of elevation along the course of a canal and variations in tide level near a seacoast. To move a vessel upstream, where the water level is higher, the water level in the lock is lowered to that of the water just downstream. The downstream gates are opened and the ship moves slowly into the lock. After the ship is secured to posts, the gates close and valves open to fill the lock with water from upstream. The flow of water is carefully controlled to prevent the ship from colliding with another vessel or from ramming the gates. As the lock fills, the ship rises to the level of the water upstream. The upstream gates are then opened and the ship passes through. To move a ship downstream, the process is reversed. After a ship enters the lock, the water is drained out and the ship is lowered to the downstream level.

Major Canals of the World

The Panama and Suez Canals are the most important canals in the world. Both of them provide valuable navigation short cuts and have figured prominently in military affairs and international politics.

The Panama Canal links the Atlantic and Pacific oceans. It extends from Limón Bay on the Atlantic to the Bay of Panama on the Pacific, a distance of about 51 miles (82 kilometers). It is the busiest canal in the world. About 14,000 ships pass through the canal annually.

The Panama Canal reduces the sea route between New York City and San Francisco by more than 7,800 miles (12,600 kilometers). Without the canal, ships traveling between the two cities would have to pass around the southern tip of South America. The Panama Canal played a strategic role during World War II (1939-1945) by enabling United States naval forces to move quickly and easily between the Atlantic and Pacific oceans.

The Suez Canal extends for about 100 miles (160 kilometers) between Port Said, Egypt, and the Gulf of Suez, an arm of the Red Sea. It allows ships to move directly between the Mediterranean and Red seas and serves as an important water link between Europe and Asia. For example, the canal shortens sea voyages between Great Britain and India by about 6,000 miles (9,700 kilometers). Without the canal, ships traveling between the two countries would have to pass around the southern coast of Africa. The Suez Canal was blocked by sunken ships in 1967, during the Arab-Israeli War, and sea traffic between Asia and Europe was disrupted. Egypt reopened the canal in 1975.

Major Canals in the United States and Canada include the Soo Canals, the Chicago Sanitary and Ship Canal, and the All-American Canal. Canals also form an important part of the St. Lawrence Seaway and other major waterways.

The Soo Canals, on the United States-Canadian bor-

How a Ship Moves Through a Canal Lock

To move upstream, a vessel enters a lock in which the water level has been lowered to that of the water just downstream. The downstream gates are then closed and the lock is filled with water. After the water level in the lock reaches that of the water upstream, the upstream gates are opened and the ship passes through. To move a ship downstream, the process is reversed.

WORLD BOOK diagram by George Suyeoka

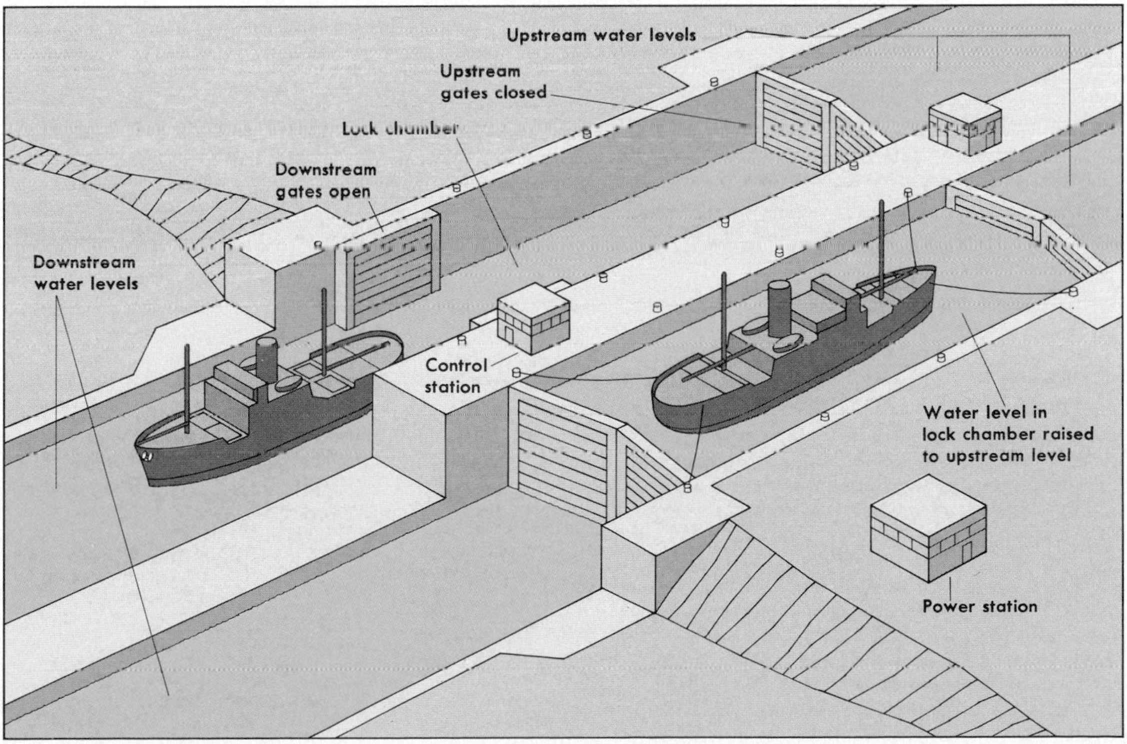

Important Ship Canals of the World

Canal	Location	Length In mi.	Length In km	Minimum Width In ft.	Minimum Width In m	Minimum Depth In ft.	Minimum Depth In m	Number of Locks	Year Opened	Tonnage Carried* Short tons	Tonnage Carried* Metric tons
Albert	Belgium	80.8	130	335	102	15	4.5	6	1939	31,458,000	28,538,000
Amsterdam-Rhine	Netherlands	45	72.4	246	75	7.2	2.2	4	1952	31,526,000	28,600,000
Cape Cod	Massachusetts	17.5	28.2	450	137	32	10	0	1914	15,245,000	13,830,000
Chesapeake and Delaware	Delaware, Maryland	14	23	450	137	35	10.7	0	1829	16,963,000	15,389,000
Chicago Sanitary and Ship	Illinois	30	48	202	61.5	24	7.3	1	1900	19,064,000	17,295,000
Corinth	Greece	3.9	6.3	81	24.6	26	8	0	1893	4,291,000	3,893,000
Houston Ship Channel	Texas	50.6	81.4	300	91.4	36	11	0	1914	94,650,000	85,865,000
Inner Harbor Navigation	New Orleans, La.	5.2	8.4	200	61	32	10	1	1923	2,259,000	2,049,000
Kiel (Nord-Ostsee)	West Germany	61.3	98.6	336.3	102.5	36	11	8	1895	64,595,000	58,600,000
Lake Washington Ship	Seattle, Wash.	8	13	300	91.4	30	9.1	2	1917	1,317,000	1,195,000
Manchester Ship	England	36	58	120	36.6	22	6.7	5	1894	12,821,000	11,631,000
Moscow	Russia	80	128	98	30	18	5.5	7	1937	19,000,000	17,000,000
New York State Barge System	New York	524	843	45	13.7	12	3.7	57	1918	777,000	705,000
North Sea	Netherlands	15.3	24.7	525	160	49.5	15.1	4	1876	58,090,000	52,700,000
Panama	Panama	50.7	81.6	550	168	45	13.7	12	1914	163,470,000	148,300,000
Sabine-Neches Waterway	Texas	93	150	400	122	40	12.2	0	1916	79,527,000	72,146,000
Sacramento River Deepwater Ship	California	42.8	68.9	200	61	30	9.1	0	1963	1,928,000	1,749,000
Saint Lawrence Seaway	Canada, New York	182	293	200	61	27	8.2	7	1959	49,671,000	45,061,000
Soo (Sault Sainte Marie)	Canada	1.4	2.2	61	18.6	19	5.8	1	1895	682,000	619,000
Soo (St. Marys Falls Canal and Locks)	Michigan	1.8	2.9	80	24.4	23.1	7	4	1855	43,825,000	39,757,000
Suez	Egypt	117.9	189.8	741	226	64	19.5	0	1869	179,926,880	163,226,913
Volga-Baltic	Russia	528	850	70	21.4	11	3.5	7	1964	15,500,000	14,000,000
Volga-Don	Russia	62.8	101	59	18	11	3.5	13	1952	9,900,000	9,000,000
Welland Ship	Canada	26	42	200	61	27	8.2	8	1932	55,275,000	50,145,000
White Sea-Baltic	Russia	138	222	46	14	10	3.2	19	1933	5,500,000	5,000,000

*Figures are for 1983 and earlier years.
Sources: Canal officials; U.S. Corps of Engineers; Transport Canada; *Soviet Geography*.

der, connect Lakes Superior and Huron. The Chicago Sanitary and Ship Canal enables ships to travel between Lake Michigan and the Mississippi River via the Chicago, Illinois, and Des Plaines rivers. The All-American Waterway, in southern California, carries water from the Colorado River to the Imperial and Coachella valleys, important agricultural areas.

The St. Lawrence Seaway consists of a system of canals and locks, the St. Lawrence River, and several lakes. It extends for about 450 miles (724 kilometers) from the eastern end of Lake Erie to Montreal, Que. It links the Great Lakes and the Atlantic Ocean.

Major Canals in Other Countries include the Grand Canal in China and several canals in Russia, and in Western Europe. The Grand Canal is a system of canals and navigable sections of the Yangtze, Yellow, and Huai rivers. It extends more than 1,000 miles (1,600 kilometers) through China. It is the world's longest artificially created waterway.

In Russia, a system of canals links the Volga River with the Arctic Ocean, the Baltic Sea, the Don River, and Moscow. Major rivers in Western Europe are also connected by many canals, including the Amsterdam-Rhine Canal in the Netherlands and the Albert Canal and Charleroi-Brussels Canal in Belgium. The Kiel Canal in Germany connects the Baltic and the North seas.

History

People have built and used canals for thousands of years. The ancient Egyptians constructed a navigation canal around a waterfall on the Nile River more than 4,000 years ago. About the same time, the ancient Babylonians built navigation and water conveyance canals in the fertile area between the Tigris and Euphrates rivers. The Chinese began construction of the Grand Canal during the 500's B.C., but the canal was not completed until the A.D. 1200's. During the 900's, the Chinese built the first known canal locks.

Important European canal systems were built in the 1100's and 1200's in the region that includes present-day Belgium and the Netherlands. The Canal du Midi, completed in 1681, became an important waterway in France. It enabled ships to travel from the Mediterranean Sea at Sète to the Bay of Biscay by way of Toulouse and the Garonne River. Today, however, its size permits only small barge and tourist traffic.

The first canal in the United States was built in 1793 on the Connecticut River in Massachusetts. The Erie Canal in New York, completed in 1825, opened up the Great Lakes region to ships from the Atlantic Ocean. It also helped make New York City the nation's financial center. In addition, the success of the Erie Canal led to a great burst of canal building in the country. During the 1830's, however, railroads began to replace canals as a major means of transporting goods in the United States. Goods could be moved faster by railroad than by canal. Today, nevertheless, canals still play an important role in shipping goods, especially in Belgium, the Netherlands, and other European countries.

JOHN S. MCNOWN

Related Articles in WORLD BOOK include:

Atlantic Intracoastal Waterway
Chesapeake and Ohio Canal
Chicago Sanitary and Ship Canal
Corinth Canal
Erie Canal
Inland Waterway
Irrigation
Kiel Canal
Netherlands (Transportation)
New York State Barge Canal System
Ohio River
Panama Canal
Saint Lawrence Seaway
Soo Canals
Suez Canal
Welland Ship Canal

CANAL ZONE. See PANAMA CANAL ZONE.

CANARY is one of the most popular bird pets. People keep canaries for their songs, and because they make cheerful companions. Canaries belong to the finch family. They are named for the Canary Islands, where they once lived untamed. Tame canaries live in all parts of the world. Wild canaries can sing, but their songs are not nearly so melodious as those of the tamed birds which are bred for the quality of their song. Wild canaries are dark green and olive-colored, and are seldom over 8 inches (20 centimeters) long. Wild canaries live in pairs, but often flock together like their distant relatives, the American goldfinches. Canaries build nests of dry moss and grass in branches about 10 feet (3 meters) from the ground. A canary lays four or five eggs.

R. T. French Co.

Canaries are popular bird pets in all parts of the world. They are bred carefully to produce a lively, cheerful song.

Tame canaries are usually a bright yellow, but sometimes they may be orange, reddish, or pale yellow. They were introduced into Europe in about the 1500's. Careful breeding has produced many types of canaries. English, French, Scottish, and Belgian canary breeders have developed many birds with strange appearances. Some tame canaries bred in Lancashire, England, grow 8 inches (20 centimeters) long. Scottish canaries are long, thin birds with tails that curl between their legs.

Belgian canaries have such long necks that their heads droop. French canaries have curly patterns of feathers all over their bodies.

The best singing canaries, such as the St. Andreasburg variety, are bred in the Harz Mountains of Germany. Different kinds of singing canaries are named for the qualities of their songs. *Rollers*, for example, have a rolling, gurgling song.

Canaries should be kept in clean cages that are large enough to let the birds fly for exercise. Although canaries eat canary seed, they also need green food. They should also be given water for drinking and bathing.

Canaries have been used to detect poison gases in time of war, and to detect dangerous gases in coal mines. They are also used for laboratory experiments.

In the United States, the name *wild canary* is often given to the American goldfinch, which looks much like a tame canary.

Scientific Classification. Canaries belong to the family *Fringillidae*. The common canary is genus *Serinus*, species *S. canarius*.

GEORGE J. WALLACE

See also BIRD (picture: Birds as Pets); GOLDFINCH; PET (Pets for the Home; Cleanliness).

CANARY, MARTHA JANE. See CALAMITY JANE.

CANARY ISLANDS make up two provinces of Spain. This group of 13 islands lies in the Atlantic Ocean about 60 miles (97 kilometers) off the coast of northwest Africa. The islands cover 2,808 square miles (7,273 square kilometers) and have 626 miles (1,007 kilometers) of coastline. Seven are inhabited. They have a population of 1,343,000. Ships going down the West African coast can stop there to refuel.

The islands were divided into two provinces in 1927. The province of Santa Cruz de Tenerife includes the islands of Tenerife, La Palma, Gomera, and Hierro. The capital also is called Santa Cruz de Tenerife. Las Palmas province includes Gran Canaria, Lanzarote, and Fuerteventura. Its capital is Las Palmas de Gran Canaria. The largest island in the Canaries is Tenerife, which has the port of Santa Cruz de Tenerife.

The Canaries are mountainous, and many of the mountains are volcanic. The highest peak is 12,162-foot (3,707-meter) Pico de Teide.

The Canary Islands have fertile soil and a mild and healthful climate. Crops include grain, fruit, vegetables, and flowers. The people are of Spanish descent, mixed with the Gaunches, a tall, blond people who originally lived there. The inhabitants of Gomera communicate over distances with a whistled language that imitates spoken Spanish.

The ancients named the Canary Islands *Canaria* from the Latin word *canis* (dog) because they found large, fierce dogs there. Canary birds are so called because

H. W. Neal, Bruce Coleman, Inc.

Las Palmas Is the Chief Port of the Canary Islands. The city's mild climate and seaside location make it a popular resort.

they were first found on the Canary Islands. The islands once belonged to Queen Catherine of Castile, and later to the Portuguese prince, Henry the Navigator. In 1479 they were returned to Spain. RUPERT CLAUDE MARTIN

See also COLUMBUS, CHRISTOPHER (Sailing Westward; Second Voyage to America; AFRICA (terrain map).

CAÑAS, *KAHN yahs,* **JOSÉ SIMEON** (1767-1838), was a scholar and statesman who took part in the Central American independence movement. In 1821, he signed the area's declaration of independence. He also led in freeing the slaves of the United Provinces of Central America. Cañas was born in Zacatecoluca, now in El Salvador. He was president of the University of San Carlos in Guatemala City. DONALD E. WORCESTER

CANASTA, *kuh NAS tuh,* is the name of a high-scoring card game that originated in Latin America. It is a variation of rummy and may be played by two, three, four, or six persons. The object of canasta is to score a seven-card set of one number. A player cannot build sequences of numbers as may be done in other rummy games. For example, seven fours make a canasta score, but a run of four through ten does not count. A seven-card set is called a *canasta,* which is Spanish for *basket.*

The players use two decks of cards and four jokers. The jokers and twos are "wild" cards, and can be used as substitutes for other cards in forming canastas. The object of the game is to make 5,000 points.

CANBERRA, *KAN behr uh* or *KAN buhr uh* (pop. 219,331), is the capital of Australia and the nation's leading example of large-scale city planning. The city lies within the Australian Capital Territory in southeastern Australia (see AUSTRALIA [political map]).

The City is built around several hills and ridges on rolling plains. The Molonglo River flows through Canberra. A dam on the river forms Lake Burley Griffin in the central part of the city.

Lake Burley Griffin divides the central part of Canberra into northern and southern sections. Two bridges span the lake and connect these sections. The northern section includes the commercial center of Canberra, the city hall, and the Australian National University. The southern section, built around Capital Hill, includes the meeting place of Australia's Parliament and most of the other principal national government buildings, as well as the Australian National Gallery.

Australian Tourist Commission

Lake Burley Griffin, *above,* is part of Canberra, the capital of Australia. Several government buildings stand near the lake.

Residential areas of bungalows and apartment buildings extend north and south of the center of Canberra. Some small industrial plants operate near the center of the city, but most industrial activity is in the suburbs. Several new towns are being developed northwest and southwest of Canberra. These projects began during the 1960's and were scheduled for completion in the 1980's. Each town will have its own commercial center and be linked to Canberra by highways.

Economy of Canberra is based primarily on the activities of the national government, which employs about two-thirds of the city's workers. Leading nongovernment economic activities include construction, retail and wholesale trade, and tourism.

Buses provide public transportation in Canberra. The streets have special lanes reserved for buses. An airport and railroad station serve the city.

History. Aborigines, the earliest inhabitants of Australia, lived in the Canberra area at least 4,000 years ago. In 1820, British explorers became the first white people to reach the area. White settlers soon established ranches and farms there. In 1901, when the Commonwealth of Australia was established, Canberra was still a small rural community. But in 1908, the government selected the area as the site for a national capital. In 1912, a city plan by the Chicago architect Walter Burley Griffin was chosen for the capital.

Construction of the new capital began in 1913. In 1927, the Australian Parliament met in Canberra for the first time, and many government agencies were transferred there from Melbourne. The growth of Canberra proceeded slowly during the Great Depression of the 1930's and World War II (1939-1945). The pace of development increased in the late 1950's. Since then, Canberra's population has grown from about 40,000 to more than 200,000. ALAN FITZGERALD

See also AUSTRALIA (picture).

CANCELLATION is a method of shortening mathematical problems by striking out terms or factors. To multiply the fractions $\frac{3}{10}$ and $\frac{4}{3}$, a person would get 12, or 4 times 3, for the numerator, and 30, or 10 times 3, for the denominator. The fraction $\frac{12}{30}$ may be reduced by dividing the 12 and 30 by the common factors of 3 and 2. But it is easier to do the divisions before multiplying, rather than after. This is done by cancellation, or by striking out the old terms and replacing them by new ones. The 3's can be divided by 3, and 10 and 4 can be divided by 2:

$$\frac{\overset{1}{\cancel{3}}}{\underset{5}{\cancel{10}}} \times \frac{\overset{2}{\cancel{4}}}{\underset{1}{\cancel{3}}} = \frac{2}{5}$$

If you want to calculate the value of the expression $26 + 7 + 4 - 7$, you can cancel the 7's to save the trouble of adding and then subtracting them. In an equation, you can cancel factors or divisors common to both sides, or equal terms that are added to or subtracted from both sides. For example, in the equation $x^2 + y^2 + x - 2 = x^2 + y^2 + 4$, you could cancel the x^2 and y^2 terms. ROBERT L. SWAIN

See also FRACTION (Cancellation).

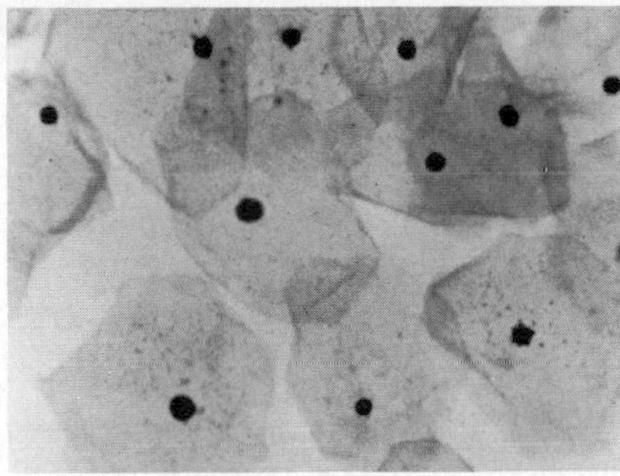

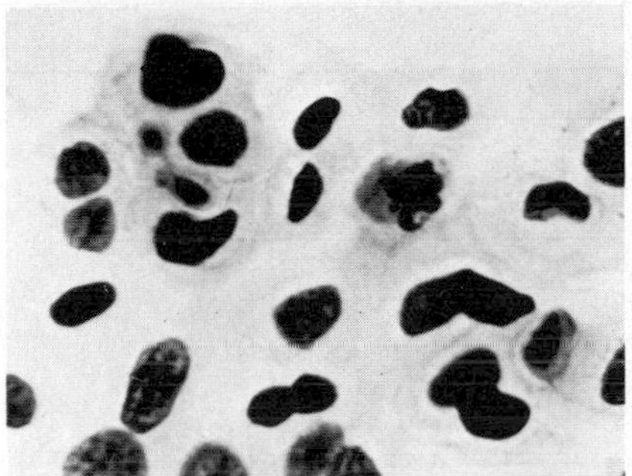

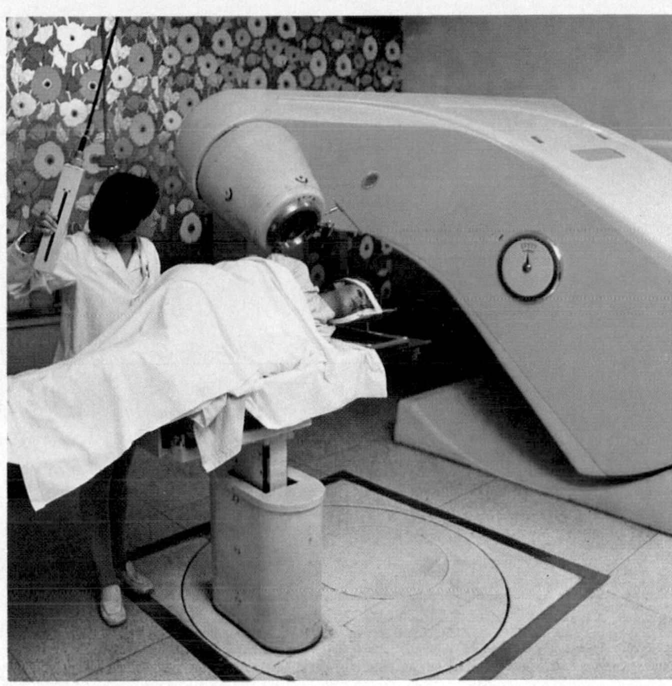

American Cancer Society

Methods of Diagnosing and Treating Cancer have improved steadily during the 1900's. With the help of improved microscopes, doctors can quickly and accurately diagnose whether the cells in a tissue sample are normal, *top left,* or cancerous, *bottom left.* At the right, a modern engineering device called a *linear accelerator* destroys cancer cells with high energy radiation.

CANCER

CANCER is a disease in which cells multiply without control, destroy healthy tissue, and endanger life. About 100 kinds of cancer attack human beings. The disease is a leading cause of death in many countries. In the United States and Canada, only diseases of the heart and blood vessels kill more people. Cancer occurs in most species of animals and in many kinds of plants as well as in human beings.

Cancer strikes people of all ages but especially middle-aged persons and the elderly. It occurs about equally among people of both sexes. The disease can attack any part of the body. However, the parts most often affected are the skin, the digestive organs, the lungs, and the female breasts. Scientists do not know exactly why cancer develops. But they have found that certain *agents* play an active role in causing the disease. These agents include the tars in tobacco smoke, a variety of other chemicals, and certain kinds of radiation. In many cases, cancer can be prevented if a known agent is avoided or eliminated. The elimination of cigarette smoking, for example, would prevent most cases of lung cancer.

Without proper treatment, most kinds of cancer are fatal. In the past, the methods of treatment gave patients little hope for recovery. But the methods of diagnosing and treating the disease have improved greatly since the 1950's. Today, about a third of all persons treated for cancer recover completely or live much longer than they would have lived without treatment. But much research remains to be done to find methods of preventing and curing the disease. To help further this research, many countries have anticancer programs.

This article discusses how cancer develops, the major kinds of cancer, the causes of the disease, and the main methods of diagnosis and treatment. The article also discusses cancer research and the chief U.S. cancer organizations and programs.

Frank J. Rauscher, Jr., the contributor of this article, is Senior Vice-President for Research of the American Cancer Society.

How Cancer Develops

Cancer develops as a result of abnormal cell reproduction. The body of an adult human being is made up of hundreds of billions of cells. Each minute, several billion of these cells die and are replaced by several billion new cells. The new cells are produced by division. In this process, a cell divides and forms two identical cells. Each of these new cells then doubles in size and becomes capable of dividing. In this way, the new cells that are constantly being produced replace those that die. Normal cells reproduce at exactly the rate required to replace dying cells, never at a faster rate. Like normal cells, cancer cells reproduce by dividing. But they have lost the ability to reproduce at a controlled rate.

Whenever anything interferes with the reproductive control of cells, the cells multiply and gradually build up a mass of tissue called a *tumor*. Some tumors are noncancerous, or *benign*. A benign tumor does not

How Lung Cancer Develops

Lung cancer, like all other forms of cancer, results from uncontrolled cell growth. Most cases of lung cancer start in the tissue that lines the *bronchi*—that is, the tubes that supply the lungs with air, *below left*. The four pairs of drawings at the right illustrate various stages in the development of such a cancer. The drawings across the top show changes in a portion of the affected tissue. The bottom drawings show, greatly enlarged, changes in the cells that make up the tissue.

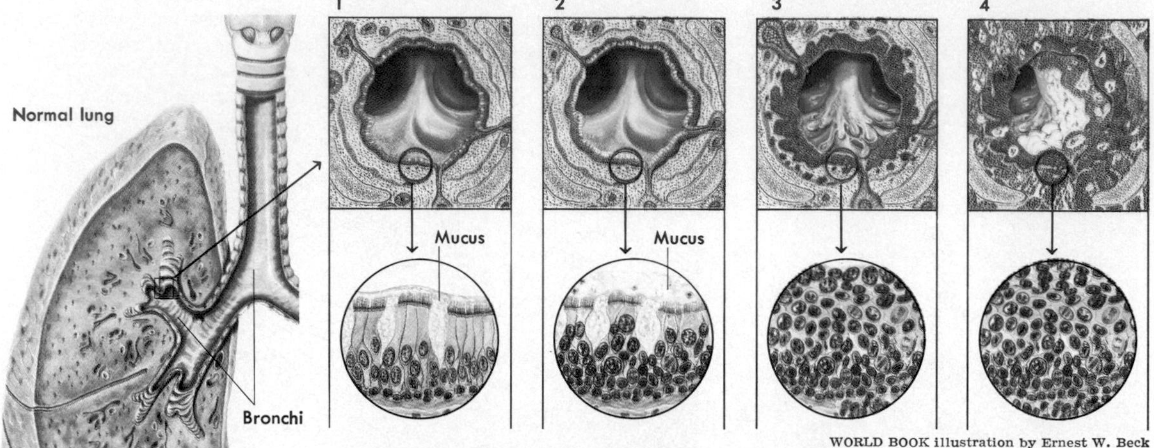

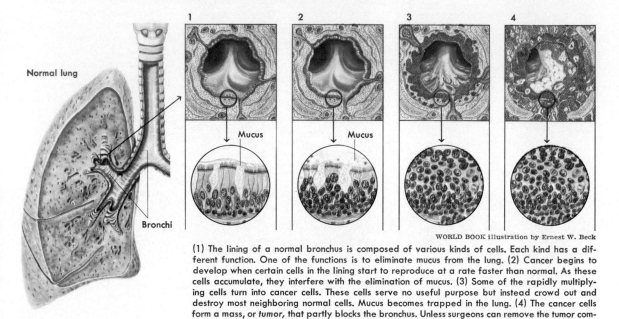

WORLD BOOK illustration by Ernest W. Beck

(1) The lining of a normal bronchus is composed of various kinds of cells. Each kind has a different function. One of the functions is to eliminate mucus from the lung. (2) Cancer begins to develop when certain cells in the lining start to reproduce at a rate faster than normal. As these cells accumulate, they interfere with the elimination of mucus. (3) Some of the rapidly multiplying cells turn into cancer cells. These cells serve no useful purpose but instead crowd out and destroy most neighboring normal cells. Mucus becomes trapped in the lung. (4) The cancer cells form a mass, or *tumor*, that partly blocks the bronchus. Unless surgeons can remove the tumor completely, cancer cells will spread to other sites in the body and eventually cause death.

spread to surrounding healthy tissue or to other parts of the body.

Cancer produces *malignant* tumors. A malignant tumor invades, compresses, and eventually destroys surrounding healthy tissue. In addition, cells can break away from a malignant tumor. These cells are carried by the blood or *lymph* (fluid from body tissues) to other parts of the body, where they continue to multiply and so form new tumors. The spread of cancer from the original tumor to one or more other body sites is called *metastasis*. Cancer's ability to spread to other parts of the body makes the disease extremely difficult to treat unless it is detected early.

Kinds of Cancer

As has been noted, about 100 kinds of cancer attack human beings. The various cancers are classified in two ways: (1) by a cancer's *primary body site*—that is, the part of the body where the cancer first develops; and (2) by the type of body tissue in which the cancer originates.

Classification by Body Site. The primary body sites that cancer strikes most often are the skin; the female breasts; and the organs of the digestive, respiratory, reproductive, blood-forming, lymphatic, and urinary systems. The occurrence of cancer in these sites varies from country to country. Cancer of the stomach, for example, is much commoner in Japan than in the United States. But a far higher percentage of Americans than Japanese develop lung cancer. The following discussion deals with the kinds of cancer that occur most often in the United States. However, each kind also occurs frequently in many other countries.

Skin Cancer occurs more often among Americans than does any other kind of cancer. But most skin cancers grow slowly and do not spread to other parts of the body. As a result, these cancers are easier to treat than are most other kinds. About 95 per cent of all persons treated for skin cancer recover completely.

Cancers of the Digestive System are the most common kinds of cancer in the United States after skin cancer. The *colon* (large intestine) and rectum are the organs generally affected. About 45 per cent of all people treated for cancer of the colon and rectum survive five years or longer after treatment without a return of the disease. Patients who remain free of cancer this long after treatment have a good chance of remaining permanently free of the disease. Other cancers of the digestive system are those of the esophagus, liver, pancreas, and stomach.

Cancers of the Respiratory System involve the larynx and lungs. Lung cancer is by far the more common of the two kinds. It occurs mainly in men, but a growing number of women also develop the disease. The death rate among lung cancer patients is exceptionally high. In most cases, the disease has already spread to other parts of the body before it is detected. As a result, only about 10 per cent of all lung cancer patients are saved. The disease kills more American men than does any other kind of cancer.

Breast Cancer occurs in both sexes but attacks far more women than men. It is the chief cause of cancer deaths among American women. But nearly 70 per cent of all female breast cancer patients recover and remain free of the disease five years or longer after treatment.

Cancers of the Reproductive System occur at a relatively high rate among both men and women in the United States. The male organ most often affected is a sex gland called the *prostate*. More than 60 per cent of the men treated for prostate cancer recover and show no signs of the disease at the end of five years.

The most common cancers of the female reproductive system are those that affect the childbearing organ, the *uterus*. Most cancers of the uterus affect the organ's *cervix* (neck). Cervical cancer patients have a five-year survival rate of about 65 per cent. Some cancers of the uterus affect the main part of the organ. These cancers generally occur much later in life than do cervical cancers. About 85 per cent of the women treated for this form of the disease survive five years or longer after treatment.

Cancers of the Blood-Forming and Lymphatic Systems. Cancer of the bone marrow and other blood-forming organs is called *leukemia*. It involves the multiplication of immature white blood cells at the expense of vital blood elements. Cancer of the lymphatic organs, and of other organs composed of *lymphoid* tissue, is called *lymphoma*. It involves the overproduction of certain cells in this tissue (see LYMPHATIC SYSTEM).

Both leukemia and lymphoma have several forms. One of the most common forms of leukemia is *acute* leukemia. This disease attacks more children in the United States than does any other kind of cancer. The most common form of lymphoma is *Hodgkin's disease*, named after the English physician Thomas Hodgkin, who first described it. More young adult Americans are struck by Hodgkin's disease than by any other kind of cancer.

How Cancer Spreads

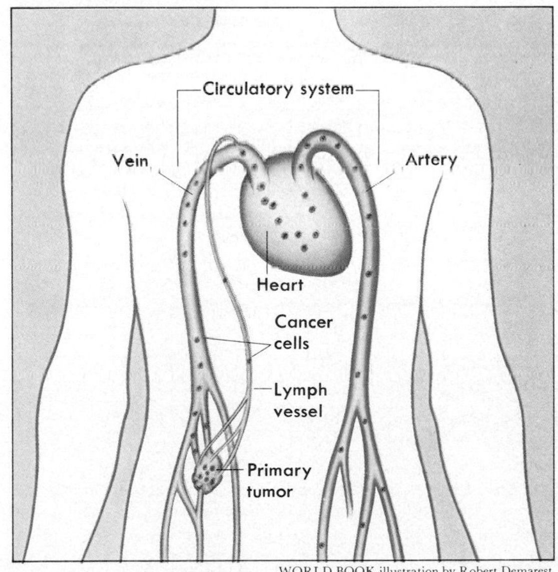

WORLD BOOK illustration by Robert Demarest

Cancer starts to spread when one or more cancer cells break away from the original, or *primary,* tumor and enter the circulatory system through a blood or lymph vessel. The blood or lymph carries the cells to other body sites, where they may form new tumors.

In the past, leukemia and lymphoma were among the most difficult of all cancers to cure. But methods of treatment developed since the early 1960's have greatly increased the survival rate. Many children with acute leukemia now survive five years or longer after treatment. Americans treated for early Hodgkin's disease now have a five-year survival rate of better than 90 per cent. For advanced cases, the survival rate is about 70 per cent. See HODGKIN'S DISEASE; LEUKEMIA.

Cancers of the Urinary System occur less often than do cancers of the other major body systems. The bladder is the organ usually affected. Approximately three-fourths of all bladder cancer patients are men. The five-year survival rate is about 70 per cent.

Classification by Body Tissue. Cancers are identified scientifically according to the type of body tissue in which they originate. They can thus be divided into two main groups: *carcinomas* and *sarcomas*. Carcinomas are cancers that start in *epithelial* tissue—the tissue that forms the skin and the linings of inner organs. Sarcomas are cancers that begin in *connective* tissue—the tissue that forms the body's supporting structures, such as bones and cartilage. Leukemia and lymphoma are sometimes classed separately from carcinomas and sarcomas. But they are also classed as forms of sarcoma because the tissues they affect—blood and lymph—are forms of connective tissue.

The great majority of cancer cases are carcinomas. They include most cancers of the skin and breast and of the digestive, reproductive, respiratory, and urinary systems. Sarcomas also occur in all these organs and systems but far less often than carcinomas do.

Causes of Cancer

Most experts agree that people develop cancer mainly through repeated or prolonged contact with one or more cancer-causing agents, called *carcinogens*. In addition, scientists suspect that a person may inherit a tendency to develop the disease.

Carcinogens attack normal cells and may eventually cause one of them to become cancerous. Scientists believe that most cancers start in this way—that is, with changes in a single cell. The changes are then passed on to all the cell's descendants. Some carcinogens are introduced into the body through the nose, mouth, or some other opening. Others attack through the skin. Many cancers are probably caused by a combination of two or more agents rather than by a single one.

If a particular population group shows an unusually high cancer rate, experts look for substances in the group's environment that may be a cause of the cancer. To determine whether a suspected substance is a carcinogen, scientists test it in laboratory animals. If a high percentage of the animals develop cancer, scientists strongly suspect that the agent might also cause cancer in human beings.

Laboratory tests and population studies indicate that two main groups of carcinogens can cause cancer in human beings. These groups consist of (1) various chemicals and (2) certain forms of radiation. Viruses make up a third group of potential carcinogens.

Chemicals. Scientists have identified hundreds of chemicals that can cause cancer in animals. These chemicals are also a cancer hazard to human beings if they become widespread in the food supply, the general environment, or the living or working environments of individual groups of people.

In most cases, a chemical carcinogen enters the food supply as a *food additive* (chemical used in food processing) or through use in agriculture. Some widely used food additives have been discovered to be carcinogens, as have certain insecticides and other chemicals widely used in agriculture. Because these carcinogens could endanger great numbers of Americans, the U.S. government prohibits or limits their use. Molds that sometimes develop on such food crops as corn and peanuts are also suspected of containing carcinogens. Scientists are seeking ways to control these molds.

In discharging waste products, some factories release chemical carcinogens into the environment. These carcinogens may pollute the air or drinking water and so endanger entire communities. Federal, state, and local government agencies act to stop this practice if it becomes a serious threat.

Other chemical carcinogens that may occur in a person's living or working environment include (1) the tars in tobacco smoke, (2) certain industrial chemicals, (3) certain natural food chemicals, and (4) certain chemicals used in drugs.

In the United States, cigarette smoking is responsible for nearly half the cancers associated with environmental agents. Cigarette smoking causes most cases of lung cancer and is associated with cancers of the esophagus, larynx, mouth, pancreas, and urinary bladder.

Some industrial chemicals create a cancer hazard for people who work with them. Such chemicals include aniline dyes, arsenic, asbestos, chromium and iron compounds, lead, nickel, vinyl chloride, and certain products of coal, lignite, oil shale, and petroleum. Unless industrial plants carefully control the use of such chemicals, excessive amounts may escape or be released into the general environment. The chemicals then create a cancer hazard for people in surrounding areas.

Some chemicals naturally present in food may become a cancer threat if consumed in large quantities. Diets high in fats, for example, have been associated with cancers of the breast, colon, and prostate gland.

Drug chemicals that may cause cancer include artificial forms of the female hormones called *estrogens*. Hormones, including estrogens, are chemicals that the body produces to regulate various body functions. Artificial estrogens are used in birth control pills and in drugs to relieve symptoms of the female *menopause* (end of the menstrual cycle). If taken in large doses, the chemical may cause cancer. For example, cancer of the main part of the uterus occurs at a high rate among women who have taken estrogens regularly to relieve menopause symptoms. A few cases of liver cancer have been associated with the taking of birth control pills.

Radiation. Certain kinds of radiation produce cancer in people exposed to these radiations for long periods. For example, most cases of skin cancer are caused by ultraviolet rays from the sun. The disease therefore occurs most often among sunbathers and people who work outdoors. X rays are a cancer hazard if they are allowed to strike healthy tissue in large doses. The usefulness of X rays in medical and dental diagnosis is believed to outweigh any hazards connected with their use.

Viruses. Experiments have shown that certain kinds of viruses cause cancer in animals, and a virus has been linked to a rare form of leukemia in human beings.

Major Kinds of Cancer in the United States

Primary Body Site	Annual Rates Per 100,000 Population		Signs and Symptoms	Precautionary Measures
	New Cases*	Deaths*		
Lung	57	50	Persistent cough or long-lasting respiratory ailment.	Avoidance of cigarette smoking; regular medical checkup.
Colon and Rectum	54	25	Change in bowel habits; bleeding from the rectum; blood in the stool.	Regular medical checkup, including examination of the colon and rectum.
Breast	49	16	Lump or thickening in the breast.	Monthly self-examination of the breasts; regular medical checkup.
Prostate	32	10	Difficulty in urinating.	Regular medical checkup, including a rectal examination.
Bladder and Kidney	24	8	Difficulty in urinating; blood in the urine.	Regular medical checkup, including analysis of the urine.
Uterus	23†	4	Unusual bleeding or discharge from the vagina.	Regular medical checkup, including a Pap test.
Lymphatic Organs**	17	9	Enlarged lymph nodes.	Regular medical checkup.
Mouth (including pharynx)	12	4	Sore that does not heal; difficulty in swallowing.	Regular medical and dental checkup.
Pancreas	11	10	Yellowing of skin and eyes; abdominal pain.	Regular medical checkup.
Stomach	10	6	Persistent indigestion.	Regular medical checkup.
Blood-Forming Organs	10	7	Fatigue; tendency to bruise and bleed easily; frequent infections.	Regular medical checkup, including examination of the blood.
Skin	7††	3	Sore that does not heal; change in a wart or mole.	Avoidance of excessive sunbathing; regular medical checkup.
Larynx	5	2	Hoarseness; difficulty in swallowing.	Regular medical checkup, including examination of the larynx.

*1982 estimates.
†Excludes cases where cells of uterus show changes but are not yet cancer cells.
**Includes multiple myeloma, a disease of bone marrow.
††Includes only melanoma, which occurs in birthmarks, black or dark-brown moles, and warts.
Source: American Cancer Society.

Certain other cancerous human tissues contain viruses similar to those that cause cancer in animals. However, most cancer experts feel that viruses are not a major cause of human cancers.

Inherited Tendencies. Some cancers, including those of the breast and colon, occur among blood relatives at a higher than average rate. Scientists therefore conclude that some people inherit a tendency to develop a certain type of cancer. But only a few kinds of cancer have been proved to be hereditary. One such kind is *retinoblastoma,* a rare cancer of the eye that occurs mainly in children under 3 years of age.

In addition, researchers have found evidence that people inherit genes that are vital to early tissue development but that may become modified and cause cancer later in life. Such genes, called *oncogenes,* normally remain inactive in cells of adults. But chemicals, viruses, hormones, or other agents may activate them. The oncogenes then produce proteins that can transform a healthy cell into a cancerous one. Some scientists believe that oncogenes are involved in all cancers.

Cancer Detection and Diagnosis

Only a doctor can diagnose cancer. But in many cases, a doctor is consulted only after the disease is far advanced. A person should therefore be alert to any physical change that may be a symptom of cancer. Early detection greatly increases the chances of a cure.

Cancer's Seven Warning Signals. Cancer shows no symptoms in its beginning stages. But symptoms may appear before the disease starts to spread. The American Cancer Society lists seven such warning signals. They are:

(1) Change in bowel or bladder habits
(2) A sore that does not heal
(3) Unusual bleeding or discharge
(4) Thickening or lump in breast or elsewhere
(5) Indigestion or difficulty in swallowing
(6) Obvious change in wart or mole
(7) Nagging cough or hoarseness

A person who has any of these symptoms longer than two weeks should consult a physician promptly.

Preliminary Diagnosis. About 50 per cent of all cancers start in parts of the body that a physician can routinely examine during an office visit. Doctors rely on various laboratory techniques for further examination of suspected cancers. X rays are used to detect many kinds of cancer and are especially valuable for the detection of lung cancer. A special X-ray technique called *mammography* enables doctors to detect breast cancer in an early stage. Routine use of mammography is generally limited to women whose age or family history indicates a high risk of breast cancer.

The *Pap* test has greatly helped reduce the death rate from cancer of the uterus. The test is named after its inventor, George Papanicolaou, a Greek-born American doctor. For the Pap test, fluid taken from the *vagina* (opening to the uterus) or cells scraped from the cervix are examined under a microscope. The technique can detect cancer of the uterus 5 to 10 years before symptoms appear. Physicians use a similar technique to help detect cancers of the bladder and lungs in their early stages.

Scientists are working to develop other methods of early cancer detection. Much of this research involves detecting changes in proteins, hormones, and other body chemicals that may indicate the development of the disease.

Final Diagnosis. The various methods of detection may reveal the presence of a tumor. But doctors need the results of a special test called a *biopsy* to determine whether the tumor tissue is malignant. For this test, a small piece of tissue is surgically removed from the tumor. The tissue is then examined under a microscope to check for the presence of cancer cells, which have an appearance unlike that of normal cells. Similar tests are performed to diagnose leukemias and lymphomas. In suspected cases of leukemia, tissue is removed from a blood-forming organ or a blood sample is taken. The tissue or blood is then checked under a microscope for the presence of cancer cells. Tissue from a lymphatic organ is examined in tests for lymphoma.

Cancer Treatment

Doctors use three main methods to treat cancer: (1) surgery, (2) radiation therapy, and (3) drug therapy. In many cases, treatment consists of two or all three of these methods, a procedure called *combination therapy.*

Surgery is the main method of treating cancers of the breast, colon and rectum, lung, stomach, and uterus. Cancer surgery chiefly involves removal of the tumor and repair of the affected organs. But in addition to the tumor itself, certain types of apparently healthy tissue may also have to be removed to help prevent the disease from spreading. For example, breast cancer operations may involve removing not only the cancerous breast but also certain neighboring lymph organs. Cancer cells may have spread to these organs and could spread from there to other parts of the body.

Radiation Therapy, or *radiotherapy,* involves attacking cancers with X rays or with rays or particles from such radioactive substances as cobalt 60 and radium. Radiotherapy is one of the main methods of treatment in cases involving the bladder, the cervix, the skin, or parts of the head and neck. Radiation kills cancer cells. But it also kills normal cells. To be effective, therefore, radiotherapy must destroy as many cancer cells as possible without endangering the patient's life.

Improvements are constantly being made in radiation equipment to increase its effectiveness. For example, the *supervoltage* X-ray machine and the *cobalt bomb* produce radiation that has greater penetrating power and is less damaging to normal tissue than ordinary radiation. Two other modern engineering devices, the *linear accelerator* and the *cyclotron,* are even more efficient in this respect. Beams of high-energy electrons produced by linear accelerators are increasingly used in treating deep-seated tumors. High-energy neutron beams produced by cyclotrons are being used experimentally to treat advanced cancers of the head and neck, breast, esophagus, lung, and rectum.

Drug Therapy, or *chemotherapy,* has become an increasingly important method of cancer treatment. More than 50 drugs are used against a variety of cancers. Drugs have proved especially effective in treating leukemia and lymphoma.

Anticancer drugs are designed to destroy cancer cells with as little injury to normal cells as possible. Nevertheless, the drugs injure normal cells to some degree and so produce various undesirable side effects, ranging from nausea to high blood pressure. Chemists are working to develop anticancer drugs that are less harmful to normal cells.

Combination Therapy involves using two or three methods to treat individual cancer patients. Doctors have long used surgery and radiotherapy in this way. But in more and more cases involving either or both of these methods, doctors also prescribe follow-up drug therapy. Because the drugs circulate to all parts of the body, they attack cancer cells that may have spread to distant organs. This type of combination therapy is used in the treatment of certain breast cancer patients and also in treating certain kinds of bone cancer. It is being used experimentally to treat cancers of the colon and rectum, lung, and stomach.

Basic Cancer Research

Cancer research includes a wide range of projects, from identifying carcinogens to developing improved anticancer drugs. Some of the most important work is in the field of *basic* cancer research—that is, research to discover how cancers develop. Many scientists believe that the answers to this question will pave the way for the development of cancer cures.

One of the chief areas of basic cancer research is *cell biology*—the study of the composition and behavior of cells. By studying normal cells and cancer cells under microscopes, scientists have discovered important differences in their behavior. They have found, for example, that in the process of cell division, normal cells continue dividing until they come into contact with neighboring cells. Cell division then stops. This characteristic of normal cells is called *contact inhibition*. It apparently is a part of the control system that regulates cell reproduction. Cancer cells have lost contact inhibition. Instead, they continue dividing after they come into contact with neighboring cells. During the early and mid-1980's, much research focused on the role of oncogenes in causing normal cells to become cancerous. Scientists believed that such research might lead to an understanding of why cancer cells reproduce in an uncontrolled way. It might also lead to treatments that would restore normal controls to cancer cells and thus prevent them from spreading to other parts of the body.

Another important area of basic cancer research is in *immunology*. Immunology is the study of how the body resists disease. Researchers have found that many cancer cells contain substances that activate the body's *immune system*—that is, its system of defenses against disease. The substances that activate the immune system are called *antigens*. The immune system produces substances, called *antibodies*, that react with the antigens and make them harmless. Scientists have long known that such *immune responses* are the body's chief defense against disease-causing bacteria and viruses. But research has shown that immune responses are also an important defense against cancer.

Most people who never develop cancer probably have an immune system that reacts strongly to cancer antigens. Immune responses are also believed to be responsible for the rare cases in which cancers unexpectedly stop growing and disappear without treatment. People who develop cancer may do so because their immune system responds weakly to cancer antigens. Scientists are seeking ways to strengthen the immune system's defenses against cancer.

Cancer Organizations and Programs

Numerous organizations throughout the United States are involved in fighting cancer. They include hospitals, medical schools, research institutes, government agencies, and voluntary groups. Some of these organizations deal chiefly with cancer research. Others are concerned mainly with the control of cancer—that is, with organized campaigns to prevent, detect, and help treat the disease. The National Cancer Institute, a part of the National Institutes of Health, is the chief federal agency dedicated to cancer research and control. The largest voluntary organization engaged in this work is the American Cancer Society.

Many of the anticancer efforts in the United States are carried out as part of a National Cancer Program established by Congress in 1971. This program awards federal funds to private and public organizations engaged in cancer research and control. The program also provides for the coordination of research and control activities at the national level. The National Cancer Institute manages the program. FRANK J. RAUSCHER, JR.

Related Articles in WORLD BOOK include:

Biopsy
Cancer Society, American
Cell
Disease (graph)
Epithelioma
Hodgkin's Disease
Laetrile
Leukemia
Malignancy
Mastectomy
Prostate Gland
Radiation
Radioactivity (In Medicine)
Radium
Rous, F. Peyton
Smoking
Tumor

Outline

I. **How Cancer Develops**
II. **Kinds of Cancer**
  A. Classification by Body Site
  B. Classification by Body Tissue
III. **Causes of Cancer**
  A. Carcinogens
  B. Inherited Tendencies
IV. **Cancer Detection and Diagnosis**
  A. Cancer's Seven Warning Signals
  B. Preliminary Diagnosis
  C. Final Diagnosis
V. **Cancer Treatment**
  A. Surgery
  B. Radiation Therapy
  C. Drug Therapy
  D. Combination Therapy
VI. **Basic Cancer Research**
VII. **Cancer Organizations and Programs**

Questions

What are the three main methods of treating cancer?

What kind of cancer causes the most deaths among American men? Among American women?

How is cell reproduction involved in the development of cancer?

What are cancer's seven warning signals?

How do scientists determine whether a particular substance can cause cancer?

Why is cancer extremely difficult to treat unless it is detected early?

What are *carcinomas*? Sarcomas?

Why may many people be immune to cancer?

What are *oncogenes*?

What causes most cases of lung cancer in the United States?

Reading and Study Guide

See *Cancer* in the RESEARCH GUIDE/INDEX, Volume 22, for a *Reading and Study Guide.*

Additional Resources

BEATTIE, EDWARD J., JR., and COWAN, S. D. *Toward the Conquest of Cancer.* Crown, 1980.

CREASEY, WILLIAM A. *Cancer: An Introduction.* Oxford, 1981.

MCKHANN, CHARLES F. *The Facts About Cancer: A Guide for Patients, Family and Friends.* Prentice-Hall, 1981.

PRESCOTT, DAVID M. *Cancer: The Misguided Cell.* Scribner, 1982.

ROSENBAUM, ERNEST H. and ISADORA R. *A Comprehensive Guide for Cancer Patients and Their Families.* Bull, 1980.

CANCER is the fourth sign of the zodiac. Cancer, a water sign, is symbolized by a crab. Astrologers believe that the moon, which they consider a planet, rules Cancer.

Astrologers regard people born under the sign of Cancer, from June 21 to July 22, as intuitive and artistic. Cancerians also love home and family life. They are emotional, and their moods change quickly. They rely more on their feelings than on reason.

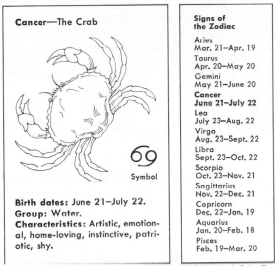

Cancer—The Crab
♋
Symbol
Birth dates: June 21–July 22.
Group: Water.
Characteristics: Artistic, emotional, home-loving, instinctive, patriotic, shy.

Signs of the Zodiac

Aries
Mar. 21–Apr. 19

Taurus
Apr. 20–May 20

Gemini
May 21–June 20

Cancer
June 21–July 22

Leo
July 23–Aug. 22

Virgo
Aug. 23–Sept. 22

Libra
Sept. 23–Oct. 22

Scorpio
Oct. 23–Nov. 21

Sagittarius
Nov. 22–Dec. 21

Capricorn
Dec. 22–Jan. 19

Aquarius
Jan. 20–Feb. 18

Pisces
Feb. 19–Mar. 20

WORLD BOOK illustration by Robert Keys

Cancerians can be hard to get along with. They often try to seem shy, but they are hiding feelings that are easily hurt. Their sensitivity makes them successful in business because they are aware of public needs. Cancerians can be selfish. They often prefer to dwell on their own dreams and memories instead of facing reality. CHRISTOPHER MCINTOSH

See also ASTROLOGY; HOROSCOPE; ZODIAC.

CANCER, TROPIC OF. See TROPIC OF CANCER.

CANCER SOCIETY, AMERICAN, is a voluntary health organization. It supports research through grants to individuals and institutions. It also supports a program of service for cancer patients and their families. It directs educational programs for the public, doctors, and others who have an interest in treating the disease.

The society is governed by a national board of 114 volunteer directors. Half the volunteers are laypeople and half are physicians and scientists. Most society funds are raised in an annual drive during April, which was designated as Cancer Control Month by Congress in 1938. The society was founded in 1913. Headquarters are at 777 Third Avenue, New York, N.Y. 10017.

Critically reviewed by the AMERICAN CANCER SOCIETY, INC.

CANDELA, *kan DEHL uh,* is the unit of measurement of *luminous intensity,* the amount of light produced in a certain direction by a glowing object. The more luminous intensity a light has, the brighter the light appears. Luminous intensity is sometimes called *candlepower.*

The candela is one of the seven base units in the metric system. Its symbol is cd. One candela is the amount of light that shines out through a hole in one side of a ceramic container after it has been heated to 1772° C under a pressure of 101,325 newtons per square meter. The container is called a *blackbody radiator,* and the hole measures $\frac{1}{600,000}$ of a square meter. The radiating surface consists of platinum and is heated until the metal begins to melt. The container then is cooled slowly until the platinum begins to solidify. The platinum begins to solidify at a temperature of 1772° C. At such a temperature, the platinum inside the container glows with intense light. This light shines out through the hold in the container.

The candela is used to calculate other units of light measurement. These units include *lumens* and *foot-candles.* The unit of measurement for luminous intensity was once the *candle,* the amount of light produced by a certain kind of candle. But scientists found this unit too difficult to standardize. In 1948, the International Commission on Illumination adopted the candela. One candela is slightly less than 1 candle. RONALD N. HELMS

See also FOOT-CANDLE; LIGHT (The Brightness of Light; diagram: Basic Units of Light Measurement).

CANDLE is an object made of wax or a similar material that is burned to give light. When a candle is lighted, wax melted by the flame is drawn up an embedded cotton wick. This liquid wax burns, producing light. Candles are made in various colors, scents, shapes, and sizes.

WORLD BOOK photo

Candles are made in a variety of colors, shapes, and sizes. This photograph shows some of the many types of candles available.

Candles have been used since prehistoric times. Through the centuries, they have been made of many substances, including bayberry wax, beeswax, paraffin, spermaceti, stearin, and tallow. Candles are made by hand by (1) dipping the wick repeatedly into liquid wax, (2) pouring liquid wax into a mold that contains a suspended wick, or (3) rolling sheets of softened wax around the wick. Candle manufacturers use machines that produce several dozen candles at a time.

Before electric lighting became common in the early 1900's, people used candles as one source of artificial light. Today, candles are used for such purposes as birthday celebrations, holiday and home decorations, and for religious services. Many people enjoy candlemaking as a hobby. The safest way to extinguish a candle flame is to smother it with a metal device called a *snuffer*. William E. Webster

Related Articles in World Book include:

Beeswax	Paraffin
Candlefish	Pioneer Life in America (picture)
Christmas (Religious Practices)	Spermaceti
Colonial Life in America (picture: Candle Mold)	Stearin
Hanukkah	Tallow Tree

U.S. Fish and Wildlife Service

Candlefish Are Members of the Smelt Family.

CANDLEFISH is a salt-water fish about 8 inches (20 centimeters) long. It lives in the North Pacific from the Bering Sea to the northern tip of California. From February to April, it swims up rivers to spawn. Fishermen catch candlefish then with dip nets and seines in shallow parts of certain tributaries of the lower Columbia and Fraser rivers. This fish has tasty meat.

The West Coast Indians used dried candlefish as candles. Their name came from this use.

Scientific Classification. Candlefish belong to the smelt family, *Osmeridae*. They are genus *Thaleichthys*, species *T. pacificus*. Leonard P. Schultz

CANDLEMAS DAY is a Christian festival that honors the purification of the Virgin Mary after the birth of Jesus. It falls on February 2, forty days after Christmas. In the Roman Catholic Church, candles blessed by the pope or a priest are given to the poor. The candles symbolize the words of Simeon to Mary that Jesus would be "a light to lighten the Gentiles, and the glory of thy people Israel" (Luke 2: 32). In early days, people carried the blessed candles in procession before Mass. See also Ground-Hog Day. Raymond Hoyt Jahn

CANDLEPOWER. See Candela.

CANDY is a popular sweet-tasting food. Candy is also called *confection*. The main ingredient in most candies is sugar, but a number of confections are made with saccharin and other artificial sweeteners. People in the United States buy about $3\frac{1}{4}$ billion pounds (1.5 billion kilograms) of candy annually. In Canada, about 490 million pounds (222 million kilograms) of confections are eaten each year.

Candy is sold in a variety of forms and packages, including bars, bags of wrapped candies, boxes of assortments, and rolls. Candymakers also produce single *penny-per-piece candies*, which once sold for a penny, but now cost up to 4 cents. Manufacturers often sell candy in special packages for certain holidays or special occasions, such as Easter and Valentine's Day.

Although candy is often called "junk food," it actually contains many wholesome ingredients. For example, various confections include eggs, fruits, milk, and nuts. In addition, vitamins and minerals are added to many candies to make them more nutritious. Candy serves as a source of quick energy because the body digests sugar faster than any other food. But people who eat too much candy may become overweight or develop tooth decay or other health problems (see Teeth [A Good Diet]).

Types of Candies

Candies vary in their ingredients and the way they are manufactured. There are four major types of candies: (1) chocolate candies, (2) hard candies, (3) chewy candies, and (4) whipped candies. Candies also may be *grained* or *nongrained*. Grained candies, such as creams and fudges, contain fine sugar crystals. Nongrained candies have no sugar crystals. They include marshmallows and caramels.

Sugar is the main ingredient in most candies. The most commonly used sugar is *sucrose*, which comes from sugar cane and sugar beets. Manufacturers also sweeten candy with such ingredients as corn syrup, honey, and *invert sugar*. Invert sugar consists of the sugars fructose and glucose. Some candies also contain cereals, fats, flour, fruits, milk products, nuts, and peanut butter. Such natural ingredients as cocoa, peppermint, and

WORLD BOOK photo

The Many Varieties of Candy differ in shape, texture, and taste. Some popular types, such as chocolates, caramels, and mints, are shown above. One of the most attractive candies is *marzipan, lower left,* an almond paste that is molded into various shapes.

Knechtel Laboratories (WORLD BOOK photos)

Candy Manufacturers Use Machines to Produce Most Candies. Some chocolate-covered candies are made by using a *chocolate enrober, above left,* which pours melted chocolate over cookie pieces. Many taffy producers use a machine with rotating bars to pull the taffy, *above right.*

vanilla provide the flavor and color of many confections. However, some candies contain artificial dyes and flavorings.

Chocolate Candies are the best-selling confections. Solid chocolate and chocolate-covered bars are the most popular. Chocolate consists mainly of roasted cacao beans, cacao butter, and sugar. In making chocolate candies, these ingredients are mixed and ground into fine particles. Additional grinding produces heat, which melts the cacao butter, forming melted chocolate, also known as *chocolate liquor.*

To form chocolate bars, melted chocolate is poured into molds and allowed to harden. A process called *enrobing* is used to make many chocolate-covered candies. In this process, pieces of candy or cookie are placed on a screenlike conveyor belt, and melted chocolate is poured over them. Chocolate candies with liquid centers are produced by *shell molding.* In this process, molds are partly filled with melted chocolate, which is allowed to cool. The chocolate shells are filled with syrup and then sealed with a layer of chocolate.

Hard Candies include fruit drops, mints, and sticks. They are made from a solution of sugar, corn syrup, and a small amount of water. This mixture is boiled and forms a hot syrup, to which flavoring and color are added. After the syrup cools somewhat, it becomes easy to shape. The candy is then pulled into long, thin cords and cut into various shapes by machines.

Butterscotch and brittles are hard candies made with butter or a vegetable fat. Most brittles contain nuts, and some also include milk.

Chewy Candies include caramels, toffees, jellies, and gums. Caramels and toffees contain milk cooked with sugars and vegetable fats. The cooked mixture is flavored, cooled, and cut into pieces. Jellies and gums are made with a solution of sugars and a jelling agent, such as gelatin or starch. The solution is boiled, and the jelling agent, color, and flavoring are added. The mixture is then poured into molds and allowed to set.

Whipped Candies, such as creams, fudges, and marshmallows, are *aerated* (mixed with air) to produce a smooth texture and to increase their volume. Most whipped candies are concentrated syrups that contain a whipping agent, which makes them easier to aerate. Common whipping agents include gelatin and egg whites.

In one method of producing whipped candy, air is beaten into the hot syrup with a *vertical whisk.* This device resembles an electric food mixer. In another method, the syrup is aerated inside a closed mixing chamber and then poured into molds or onto sheets and allowed to set.

Other Candies. *Cotton candy* is made from sugar crystals that are spun in a heated whirling device called a *centrifuge* and then wound on a stick. *Marzipan* is produced by grinding almonds and sugars into a paste. *Licorice* contains wheat flour dough that has been sweetened, dyed, and flavored. Its flavoring comes from the roots of the licorice herb (see LICORICE).

Jellybeans, malted milk balls, and sugared or chocolate-covered nuts are known as *panned candies.* The center of the candy is placed in a rotating pan and sprayed with chocolate or syrup. Repeated coatings form the outer shell.

History

The earliest records of candymaking date back 3,000 years to ancient Egypt, where confections were made by mixing fruits and nuts with honey. People in ancient India made the first candy with sugar cane. Candymaking remained a fairly small industry until the 1800's, when advances in technology enabled large quantities of candy to be produced cheaply.

During the 1900's, candymaking has developed from a craft involving much handwork to a chiefly automated, computer-controlled industry. Modern candy factories have long production lines, on which machines perform such tasks as measuring and mixing ingredients and packing shipping cases.

During the 1970's, the rising costs of raw materials, particularly cacao beans and sugar, led to the development of new candies. For example, many candymakers began to substitute carob beans and imitation cacao butter for cacao beans in chocolate candies (see CAROB). Sugar-free candies also were developed for people who must limit the amount of sugar they eat. R. J. GROVES

See also CHOCOLATE; SUGAR.

CANDYTUFT is any one of several flowering plants that belong to the mustard family. Gardeners often use the perennial, *evergreen candytuft,* as a border plant. It grows about 12 inches (30 centimeters) high, has small

J. Horace McFarland

Candytuft Blossoms. The name comes from *Candia,* the old English name for Crete in the Mediterranean.

narrow leaves, and pure white flowers borne on upright heads. Another popular candytuft for gardens is the annual *globe candytuft.* It may grow 16 inches (41 centimeters) high and bears lavender, pink, or red blossoms.

Scientific Classification. Candytufts belong to the mustard family, Cruciferae. They make up the genus *Iberis.* The edging candytuft is genus *Iberis,* species *I. sempervirens.* The globe candytuft is *I. umbellata.* DONALD WYMAN

CANE SUGAR. See SUGAR (Making Cane Sugar).

CANEBRAKE is a dense growth of cane in swamps and along river beds in the southern United States. The canes may grow 25 feet (7.6 meters) high.

CANIFF, MILTON ARTHUR. See CARTOON (Comic Strips and Panels).

CANINE. See TEETH (Permanent Teeth); DOG (table: Dog Terms).

CANINE PARVOVIRUS. See PARVOVIRUS.

CANIS MAJOR, *KAY nihs,* is a constellation in the Southern Hemisphere. It contains Sirius, the Dog Star, the brightest star in the heavens, excluding the sun. Canis Major is the Great Dog, companion of the Great Hunter, Orion, who stands nearby. The three familiar stars that form the belt of Orion point to Sirius, an ornament in the collar of the dog. Sirius is one of the stars nearest to Earth, yet it is so distant that its light takes almost nine years to reach us. I. M. LEVITT

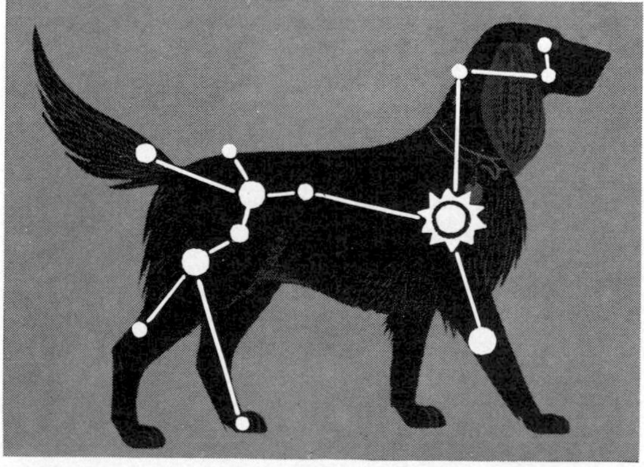

The Constellation Canis Major Contains the Dog Star.

See also ASTRONOMY (map: The Stars and Constellations of the Southern Hemisphere); ORION; SIRIUS.

CANISIUS, *kuh NIHSH uhs,* **SAINT PETER** (1521-1597), was the founder of the first German house of Jesuits, and the foremost promoter of the reform of the Roman Catholic Church in Germany, Austria, and Bohemia. Saint Ignatius Loyola, founder of the Jesuits, sent him as a missionary to help check the spread of Lutheranism in Germany. There Saint Canisius founded Jesuit colleges to meet the need for educated Roman Catholics.

His most effective tool in strengthening the Roman Catholic faith was his *Summa Doctrinae Christianae* (1555), a catechism with more than 200 editions in 12 languages. His teaching and preaching contributed greatly to halting the spread of Protestantism in Germany, Austria, and Bohemia. Canisius was born in Nijmegen, now in the Netherlands. He was canonized in 1925. JAMES A. CORBETT and FULTON J. SHEEN

CANKER is a small, painful sore in the mouth. One or several cankers may form at the same time on the tongue or on the inside of the lips. Cankers also may appear on the inside of one or both sides of the cheeks. The first sign of a canker is a burning or tingling sensation in the affected area. A red spot then appears, and its center becomes inflamed and turns gray or whitish. Physicians are not certain what causes cankers, but they suspect that the sores result from viral infections. Most cankers heal by themselves in about a week, but some people suffer repeated attacks.

People who have cankers should avoid eating grapefruit, oranges, and other foods that contain large amounts of acid. Acid causes pain when it comes into contact with the sores. Physicians treat severe cankers with painkillers and an antibiotic called *tetracycline,* which aids healing. YELVA LIPTZIN LYNFIELD

CANKERWORM is the *larva* (caterpillar) of a moth. It crawls by humping its back and bringing its hind feet up to its forefeet to make a loop of its body. Then it pushes the front feet forward again. Two kinds of cankerworms damage orchards and shade trees. They are the *spring cankerworm* and the *fall cankerworm.* The adult females of both these insects have no wings. They climb trees to lay their eggs. The spring cankerworm hatches about the time the elm leaves grow, and eats the leaves. The fall cankerworm usually comes from eggs laid by adults that have appeared from their cocoons the autumn before. It hatches in early spring as the leaves unfold. These caterpillars can strip an orchard or a grove of shade trees in a few days. When they are molested, they drop from the leaves and hang in the air by silken threads. Bands of cloth or paper smeared with a sticky substance and wrapped around the tree

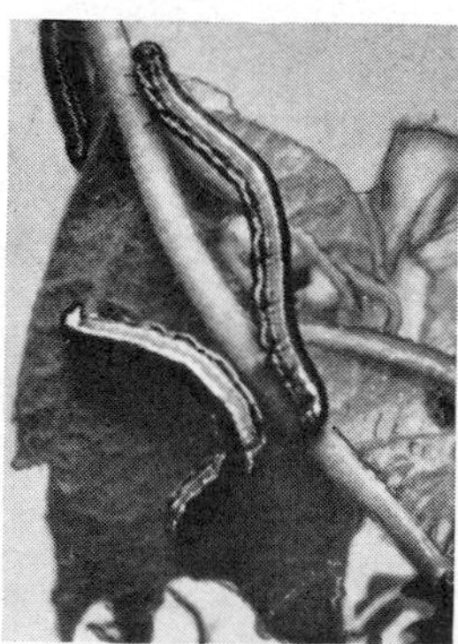

Davey Tree Expert Co.

The Cankerworm is a greedy eater. It attacks fruit trees and shade trees.

trunks will keep the females from laying eggs in the trees. Spraying the trees with arsenate of lead kills the caterpillars. See also MOTH (color pictures).

Scientific Classification. Cankerworms belong to the family Geometridae. The spring cankerworm is genus *Paleacrita*, species *P. vernata*. The fall cankerworm is *Alsophila pometaria*. E. GORTON LINSLEY

CANNA, *KAN uh*, is a tall ornamental plant with brilliantly colored flowers. The *Indian canna* grows wild in the United States. It may be 4 feet (1.2 meters) high and bears bright red flowers tipped with orange. It has large leaves that sometimes grow 2 feet (61 centimeters) long and 8 inches (20 centimeters) wide.

Florists sell many hybrid varieties of cannas. These plants often grow from $2\frac{1}{2}$ to 10 feet (76 to 300 centimeters) high, and have green, yellow-green, or bronze foliage. The leaves grow densely on stout stems. The blossoms of the hybrid plants vary in color and marking. Two to five petal-like stamens make up the flower.

Cannas can be grown easily, and are widely cultivated as garden plants in all parts of the United States. They grow best in rich, warm soil, and need plenty of moisture. In cold regions, the big root must be dug and kept in a warm, dry place during the winter to prevent freezing.

Ferry-Morse Seed Co.

The Canna. The largest variety of this tall ornamental plant grows as high as 10 feet (3 meters).

Scientific Classification. Cannas make up the canna family, Cannaceae. The Indian canna is a member of genus *Canna*, species *C. indica*. GEORGE A. BEACH

See also FLOWER (picture: Garden Perennials).

CANNABIS. See MARIJUANA.

CANNAE. See HANNIBAL.

CANNERY. See FOOD PRESERVATION (Canning); FISHING INDUSTRY.

CANNES, *kan* (pop. 70,527; met. area pop. 258,479), is a luxurious resort city on the French Riviera in southeastern France. For location, see FRANCE (political map). Cannes is famous for its annual film festival, which features movies from all parts of the world.

Cannes lies on the Gulf of Napoule, an arm of the Mediterranean Sea. The city is noted for its mild, dry climate and its broad, tree-lined boulevards. The best-known boulevard is the Promenade de la Croisette, which runs along the shore and has elegant hotels and casinos. Other interesting features of Cannes include the Hôtel de Ville (City Hall); the nearby Lérins Islands; and a castle called the Chateau des Abbés de Lérins on Mont Chevalier, a hill overlooking the gulf.

Tourism is Cannes's leading economic activity. Other activities include perfume and soap manufacturing, metalworking, and fishing. The first settlement at what is now Cannes was a fortress built on Mont Chevalier by an ancient Italian people called *Ligurians*. It was probably established about the 700's B.C. MARK KESSELMAN

CANNIBAL is a person who eats human flesh. Throughout history, many individuals and societies in all parts of the world have committed acts of cannibalism. Archaeologists have found evidence of cannibalism that occurred more than 500,000 years ago. Today, cannibalism no longer exists except perhaps among some societies in isolated areas of Africa, Asia, and the Pacific Islands.

Cannibalism may also be practiced today by people who can obtain no food except human flesh. Survivors of a plane crash in the Andes Mountains in 1972 ate their dead companions to survive.

Through the centuries, most cases of cannibalism have been connected with religious or other traditional beliefs. Most cannibals ate only the parts of the body that they considered important. For example, some cannibals believed that the heart contained such qualities as courage and wisdom. They ate the hearts of the dead in order to acquire those qualities themselves. The inhabitants of ancient Gaul (now France) thought that eating parts of another human being cured various diseases.

Some cannibals showed respect to dead relatives and friends by eating parts of them. The Aborigines of central Australia thought this practice strengthened the ties between the dead members of the family and the living ones. Some mothers ate their dead babies to get back the strength they thought they had given the infants during pregnancy.

Some societies thought that eating the corpses of enemies prevented the souls of the slain foes from seeking revenge. The Maoris of New Zealand felt they insulted their enemies by cooking and eating them. Some cultures in southern Africa believed that their members gained such qualities as courage and wisdom by eating the enemies they had killed.

The word *cannibal* comes from *Carib*, the name of a warlike society whose members ate human flesh. The Caribs, whose name means *strong men*, lived on islands in the Caribbean Sea when Christopher Columbus sailed there in the late 1400's. Columbus called them *Canibales* by mistake. The Spaniards continued to call them Canibales probably because the old Spanish word for dog was *can*. They thought the practice of cannibalism among the Caribs seemed more doglike than human. The term *cannibal* also refers to any animal that eats others of its own kind. WADE C. PENDLETON

CANNING is a method of preserving food by heating it in airtight containers. Airtight sealing prevents organisms that spoil food from entering the containers. The heating process destroys organisms that are already present in food and would eventually spoil it. In the United States, almost all canned food is prepared by food-manufacturing companies, but some canning is done at home. This article discusses home canning. For information about commercial canning, see the WORLD BOOK article on FOOD PRESERVATION.

Home canning is a convenient, economical way to preserve fresh foods. Many people enjoy canning home-grown fruits and vegetables. A wide variety of fruits, vegetables, and meat may be canned at home. However, heat causes chemical and texture changes that ruin such foods as avocados, lettuce, and milk. These foods should not be canned at home. Certain foods, including artichokes, cucumbers, and peppers, are also ruined by high temperatures. But they may be safely canned at lower temperatures if they are *pickled*—that is, preserved in vinegar or lactic acid.

Food that has been properly canned may be stored for as long as three years. Correct methods of canning prevent the growth of organisms and enzymes that spoil food. Such organisms include bacteria, molds, and yeasts. A dangerous kind of bacteria can grow in certain foods, but such bacteria grow only where there is no air. While growing, these bacteria produce a poison that causes a type of food poisoning called *botulism,* which can be fatal (see BOTULISM). Molds and certain yeasts may also grow in food. Enzymes may change the color, flavor, and texture of food. Proper heating destroys bacteria, molds, yeasts, and enzymes. The heating of food in sealed containers is called *processing.*

Airtight seals prevent such organisms as molds and certain kinds of bacteria and yeasts from entering containers and spoiling food. The seals also prevent the growth of microbes that require oxygen. A chemical reaction called *oxidation* may occur in food packed in containers that have not been sealed properly. Oxidation causes changes in the color and flavor of food and may also reduce the vitamin content.

The U.S. government issues publications that provide information about home canning. They can be obtained from the Office of Communication, U.S. Department of Agriculture, Washington, D.C. 20250.

Containers

Two types of containers—glass jars and tin cans—are used in home canning. Most foods may be canned in either jars or cans.

Glass Jars, the most common containers used for home canning, can be used time after time. These jars are manufactured in half-pint, pint, 1½-pint, quart, and half-gallon sizes. In Canada, they also are available in ¼-liter, ½-liter, ¾-liter, liter, 2-liter, 3-liter, 4-liter, and 5-liter sizes. The rims should be smooth and even, and jars with cracks, bubbles, or other defects must not be used.

Three types of seals are used with glass jars: (1) flat metal lids with a sealing compound and metal screw bands, (2) porcelain-lined zinc screw caps with rubber rings, and (3) glass lids with rubber rings and wire devices called *bails.*

Flat metal lids, the most widely used kind of seal, have a rubber or plastic sealing compound that fastens them to the rim of the jar. The metal bands are screwed on over these lids. Do not use a metal lid if it is bent, or if the sealing compound is dried or cracked or has bare spots. The screw bands should not be rusty or bent. Metal lids should not be reused, but the screw bands may be used repeatedly.

Porcelain-lined zinc caps are screwed on over a rubber ring that fits below the jar rim. These caps should not be used if they are dented or if the porcelain is chipped or cracked. Check the rubber rings for brittleness or splitting, but do not stretch them while doing so. Zinc screw caps may be reused, but the rubber rings should be used only once.

Glass lids are placed on rubber rings that fit below the jar rim. A bail around the neck of the jar is adjusted to secure the lid. Do not use lids with cracks or other defects. Check the rings for brittleness or splitting, but do not stretch them. Glass lids are reusable, but the rings should be used only once.

Tin Cans for home canning are made in three sizes. The Number 2 size holds 20½ fluid ounces (606 milliliters). A Number 2½ can holds 29¾ fluid ounces (880 milliliters), and a Number 303 can holds 16 fluid ounces (473 milliliters). Some cans have an enamel lining.

Tin cans, unlike glass jars, require a machine called a *sealer* to attach their lids. Cans are lightweight and unbreakable. They cool more quickly than jars. However, they cannot be reused.

Preparing Food for Canning

Food used for canning should be fresh and undamaged, and vegetables should be crisp. If you are canning home-grown vegetables, do so on the day they are picked. If this is not possible, they can be stored for several days at a temperature of about 35° F. (2° C).

Most fruit should be firm and ripe for canning. Fruit

National Presto Industries, Inc.

A Steam-Pressure Canner is used to can meats and most vegetables. This device heats food with steam under pressure. The canner shown above has a dial gauge that measures the pressure.

used in making jelly or jam should be soft and ripe. Trim damaged areas from fruit and vegetables. Discard heavily damaged or overripe foods. Wash and rinse all fruit and vegetables thoroughly to remove dirt and soil.

Such vegetables as beets, eggplant, hardshell squash, potatoes, and turnips must be peeled before canning. Apples, carrots, peaches, pears, and tomatoes to be canned may or may not be peeled. Apricots, beets, peaches, and tomatoes can be peeled easily by dipping them in boiling water for a few seconds. Then dip them in cold water for easy handling and pull off the skins with a knife. To prevent peeled apples, peaches, or pears from becoming discolored, put them in cold water that contains a little salt or lemon juice.

If you plan to can meat, fish, or poultry but cannot do so within a few days, store such foods at a temperature of about 32° to 40° F. (0° to 4° C). If they will not be canned for a longer period of time, freeze them at −5° to 0° F. (−21° to −18° C).

Packing and Sealing

There are two methods of packing food into jars and cans, *cold packing* and *hot packing*. In cold packing, foods are put into containers while raw. In hot packing, foods are cooked just before being put into jars or cans. Containers of both hot- and cold-packed foods are then filled with a *covering liquid* before being sealed. You should fill and seal only as many containers as can be processed at one time.

Cold packing is easier than hot packing because it involves no cooking. But cooking the food for hot packing shrinks it and, therefore, enables more to be packed into a container. Cooking the food also keeps it from floating above the liquid in the container during processing and storage. Floating darkens food and causes it to lose some flavor.

Most foods may be canned safely by either hot packing or cold packing. However, such vegetables as corn, pumpkin, and spinach should always be hot-packed. If these foods are cold-packed, heat may not thoroughly penetrate the containers during processing.

Cold Packing. Most fruits and vegetables should be packed firmly into jars or cans. When cold-packing tomatoes, press them into containers until they are covered with their own juice. Fish should also be firmly packed. Meat and poultry should be packed loosely. If meats and vegetables are packed too tightly, they may not receive enough heat during processing to kill dangerous organisms.

Hot Packing. Fruits and vegetables to be hot-packed may be cooked in gently boiling water. They also can be held in a strainer over boiling water and heated by steam. Meat, fish, and poultry should be cooked in water or broth.

Fruit may also be cooked in syrup or in its own juice before being canned. Tomatoes should be cooked in their own juice. Syrup for fruit is made by boiling a mixture of sugar and water. Honey or corn syrup may also be dissolved in water to make syrup. Do not use brown sugar or molasses, which would darken the fruit and kill its flavor. All hot-packed foods except fruits should be packed loosely into jars or cans. Fruits should be packed firmly.

The Covering Liquid should be boiling when it is added to cold-packed containers of food and hot when added to hot-packed foods. Water is the covering liquid for vegetables. Fruits should be canned in water, syrup, or their own juice. Use water or broth for meat, fish, and poultry. When hot-packing foods, you can use the liquid in which the food was cooked.

Jars of fruit should be filled with the covering liquid so it is $\frac{1}{4}$ to $\frac{1}{2}$ inch (6 to 13 millimeters) from the rim. Add liquid to vegetables until it is $\frac{1}{2}$ to 1 inch (13 to 25 millimeters) from the rim. Meat in jars should be covered with liquid up to about 1 inch (25 millimeters) from the rim. All food packed in cans should be covered with liquid up to $\frac{1}{4}$ to $\frac{1}{2}$ inch (6 to 13 millimeters) from the rim. After adding the liquid to hot- or cold-packed foods, run a dull knife around the inside of the container to release air bubbles from the liquid. Vitamin C in crystal form, or lemon juice, may be added to jars of apricots, apples, peaches, and pears to prevent discoloration of the fruit.

Sealing the Jars. After filling the jars with food, wipe the rims with a damp cloth. Food left on the rim may prevent airtight sealing. Metal lids with a sealing compound should be placed briefly in hot or boiling water. Place the lid on the jar so that the sealing compound touches the rim. Then screw on the metal band firmly. However, if the band is screwed on too tightly, gases in the jar may not be able to escape during the processing of the food.

If you use a porcelain-lined zinc cap, place the rubber ring briefly in boiling water and then put the ring on a filled jar. Screw on the zinc cap firmly and then turn it back $\frac{1}{4}$ inch (6 millimeters) to allow gases to escape. After the jar has been processed, screw the cap down tightly.

If you are using a glass lid, heat the ring in boiling water before putting it on a filled jar. Place the lid on the ring and adjust the bail so that the lid fits firmly on the jar. After processing, pull down the bail to completely secure the lid.

Sealing the Cans. A sealing machine should be tested several times before sealing cans of food. Test the sealer by sealing an empty can or one that contains water. The seam between the lid and the can should be smooth and even. Submerge the can for several seconds in boiling water. If you see air bubbles, the machine should be adjusted to tighten the seal.

When a can is sealed, the temperature of the food must be at least 190° F. (88° C). Cans of cold-packed food may have to be heated to this temperature before being sealed.

Processing Methods

There are three ways of processing canned foods: (1) the hot water-bath method, (2) the steam-pressure method, and (3) the open-kettle method.

The Hot Water-Bath Method is used to process preserves, rhubarb, tomatoes, and most fruits. Such foods may be heated in gently boiling water.

A *water-bath canner* is a metal container deep enough so that jars or cans are completely covered with water during processing. Any deep metal container may be used. Some water-bath canners have close-fitting lids to enable the water to heat rapidly. A water-bath canner has a metal or wooden rack to keep the jars or cans from touching the hot bottom of the canner. Several layers of clean cloth also may serve as a rack.

To process food by the hot water-bath method, put water in the canner and heat it on a stove. Containers of cold-packed food may be placed in the canner when the water is warm or cold. Put hot-packed food in when the water is hot. The water must completely cover the tops of the jars or cans. Start to time the processing when the water begins to boil gently. The time required for processing varies among foods and also often depends on the size of the container.

The Steam-Pressure Method is used to process *low-acid foods*. The bacteria that cause botulism can grow in these foods, which include meat, fish, poultry, and most kinds of vegetables. To kill these bacteria in a reasonable amount of time, process such foods at a temperature above the boiling point of water. The foods are usually processed at 240° F. (116° C). A *steam-pressure canner*, which processes food with steam under great pressure, is used for this method.

A steam-pressure canner has a lid that can be sealed airtight. It also has either a *dial gauge*, which measures pressure inside the canner, or a *weighted gauge*, which controls the pressure. A dial-gauge canner has a vent that can be closed to raise the pressure. In a weighted-gauge canner, the pressure is raised by placing the gauge into a vent in the lid. Steam-pressure canners have a wooden or metal rack to hold the jars or cans.

How to Can Peaches by the Cold-Packing Method

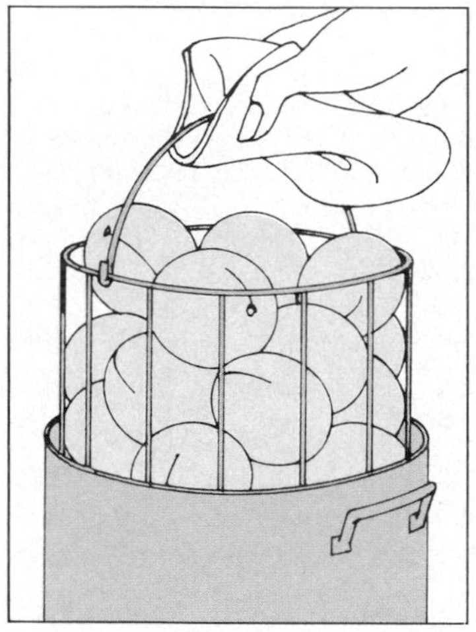

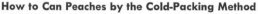

Wash and Rinse the Peaches thoroughly in cool water. To make them easy to peel, dip the peaches in boiling water and then in cold water.

Peel the Peaches, and then cut them in half and remove the pits. Keep the peaches in cold water containing salt or lemon juice to keep them from turning dark.

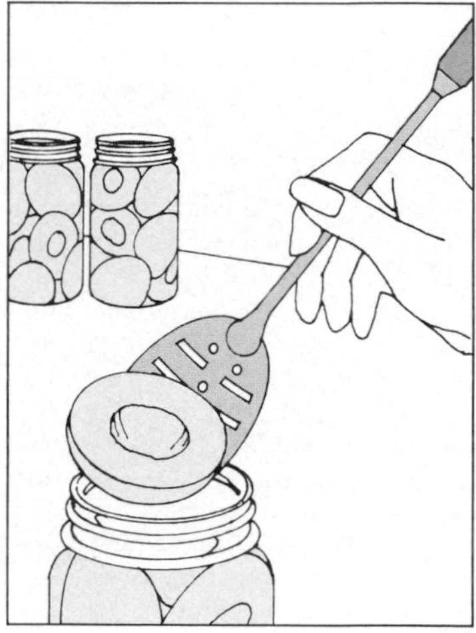

Drain the Peaches and pack them firmly into jars. Then boil the *covering liquid* for the fruit. This liquid may be syrup or water.

Add the Covering Liquid so it is ¼ to ½ inch (6 to 13 millimeters) from the rim. Run a knife around the jar to release air bubbles. Then seal the jar.

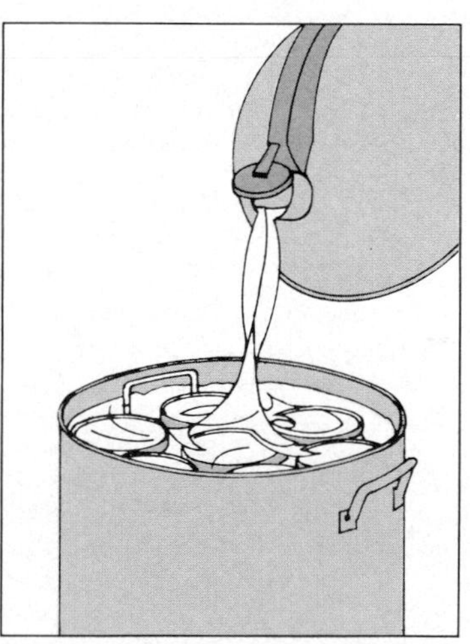

Put the Jars in Water in the canner. The water must completely cover the tops of the jars. Begin timing when the water is boiling gently.

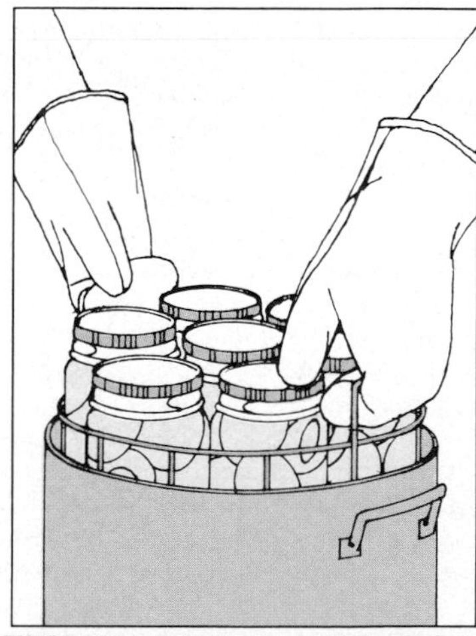

WORLD BOOK illustrations by David Cunningham

Remove the Jars from the Canner, set them slightly apart, and let them cool at room temperature. Finally, check the seals and label the jars.

To process low-acid foods, put 2 to 3 inches (5 to 8 centimeters) of water in the canner and fill it with containers. Fasten the lid securely and heat the canner on a stove. Allow a steady flow of steam to escape from the vent for 5 to 15 minutes, depending on the size of the canner. This action allows air in the canner to escape so that the food is heated only by the remaining steam. For safe processing, the canner should contain no air.

After enough steam has escaped from a dial-gauge canner, close the vent and allow the pressure to rise in the canner. If you are using a weighted-gauge canner, put on the gauge. When the desired pressure has been reached, start to time the processing.

After the food has been processed for the recommended period of time, turn off the heat source on the stove. When the pressure returns to normal, open the vent or remove the weighted gauge. Then remove the lid of the canner.

A type of canner called a *pressure saucepan* may also be used to process low-acid foods. However, this device can hold only small jars and cans.

The Open-Kettle Method may be used for jelly or jam. The jelly or jam is heated in a kettle and then poured into hot glass jars, which are sealed with hot lids. Each jar should be filled and sealed individually, rather than filling several jars at the same time and then sealing them. The jars may also be sealed with melted wax or paraffin. Jelly or jam preserved by the open-

How to Can Beans by the Hot-Packing Method

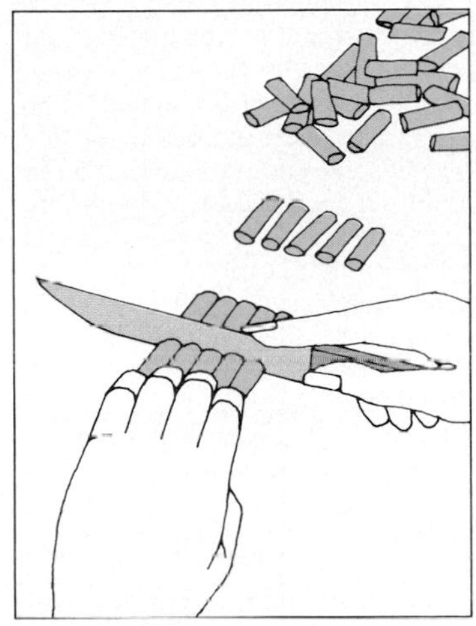

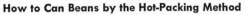

Wash and Rinse the Beans thoroughly in cool water to remove any dirt or insects. Cut off the ends and slice the beans into 1-inch (25-millimeter) pieces.

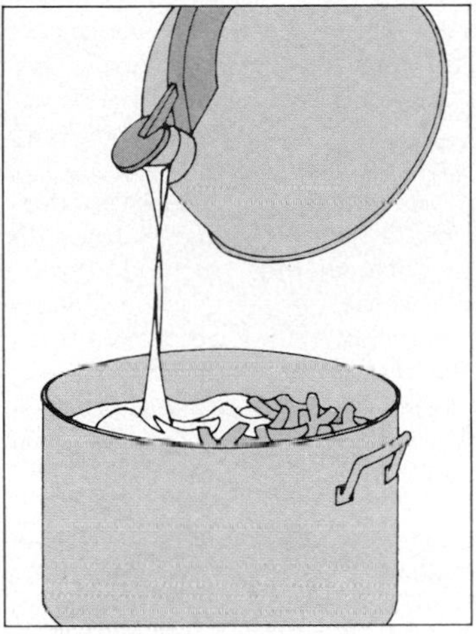

Put the Beans in a Pot and add boiling water until all are covered. Boil the beans for about 5 minutes. Then drain them and save the cooking liquid.

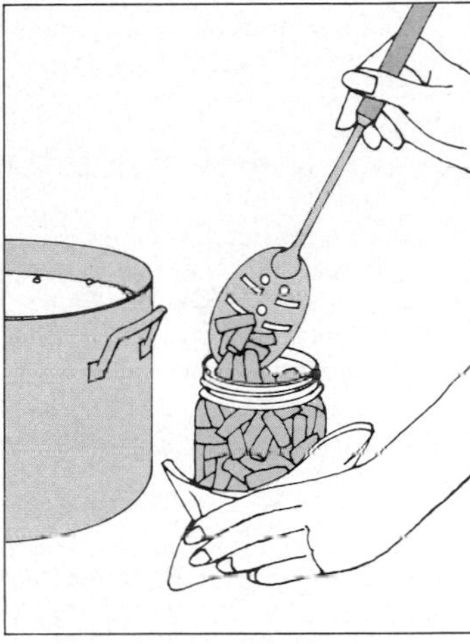

Pack the Beans Loosely into Jars. Add the boiling cooking liquid so it is ½ to 1 inch (13 to 25 millimeters) from the rim. Then seal the jars.

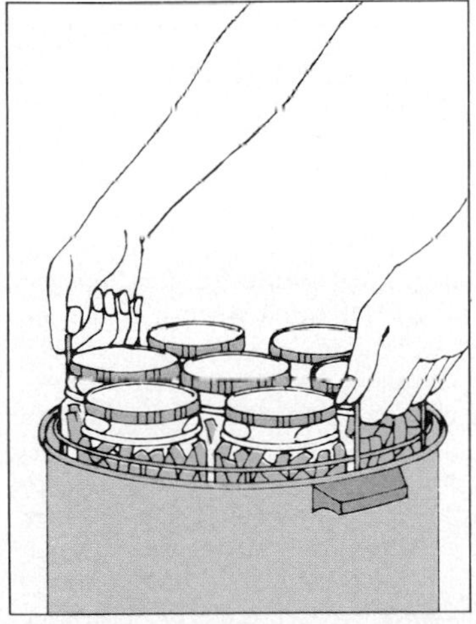

Loading the Canner. Put 2 to 3 inches (5 to 8 centimeters) of water in the steam-pressure canner and fill it with jars. Fasten the canner lid and heat the canner.

Let Steam Escape from the Vent for 5 to 15 minutes. Then close the vent. Begin timing when the pressure inside the canner reaches the correct level.

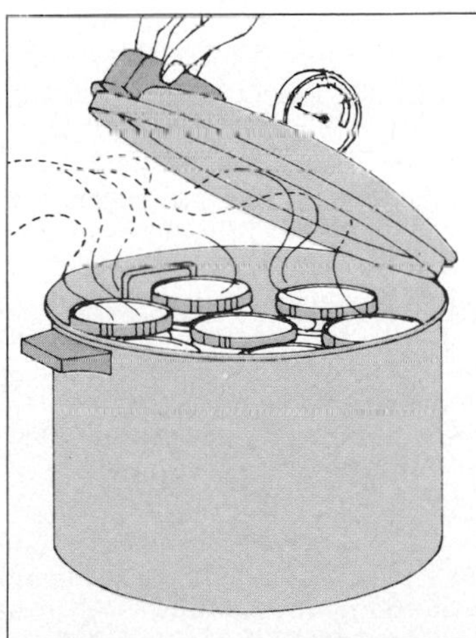

WORLD BOOK illustrations by David Cunningham

Remove the Canner from the Heat. Open the vent after the pressure returns to normal and remove the lid of the canner. Then take out the jars.

kettle method requires no further processing. However, jars of jelly or jam may also be processed by the water-bath method.

Handling Foods After Canning

After being processed, containers of food are removed from the canner and are cooled. The seals should be checked immediately after cooling and periodically during storage. Be sure to label the containers and store them properly. Before using any canned food, check it for spoilage.

Cooling. Jars of food are cooled by letting them stand at room temperature. Place them a few inches apart in a wood or plastic surface, or on a surface covered with cloth towels or paper towels. Do not cool the jars on a glass, metal, or tile surface.

Tin cans should be cooled under cold running water until they are warm. Then place the tin cans a few inches apart at room temperature and let them cool completely.

Checking the Seals. Wait until glass jars of food have cooled at least 12 hours and then check the seals. To test metal lids that have a sealing compound, first remove the screw bands. If a metal lid bends slightly inward, the jar is probably sealed correctly. To be sure, carefully lift the jar by holding the edges of the lid with the fingers of one hand. Keep your other hand under the jar in case it falls. If your fingers can support the weight of the jar, it is properly sealed. Glass jars sealed with such lids may be stored with or without the screw bands.

To test a jar sealed with a porcelain-lined zinc cap and a rubber ring, turn the jar over in your hands. If liquid leaks from the lid, the jar has not been properly sealed.

Even if cans are checked for proper sealing on the day after processing, a faulty seal might not be seen. About a week after processing, check for liquid leaking from the seam or lid. The seals of all jars and cans should be checked occasionally during storage.

If you spot an inadequate seal on a jar or can the day after processing, refrigerate the food and use it as soon as possible. If a container loses its seal any time after that, discard the food. However, a jar that contained such food may be washed and reused.

Labeling. After checking the seals, label all the jars or cans. The label should include the type of food, the date it was canned, and the name or initials of the person who canned it. If more than one batch was processed that day, include the number of the batch. The method used to process the food should also be recorded on the label.

Storing. Canned foods should be stored in a dark place that has a temperature of 55° to 70° F. (13° to 21° C) and humidity below 70 per cent. Poor storage conditions may not spoil food, but they can affect its quality, flavor, and vitamin content.

Checking for Spoilage. All food canned at home should be checked for spoilage before being eaten, and any spoiled food must be thrown out. Be sure to check low-acid foods for signs of the poison that causes botulism. These signs include bulging lids on jars or cans. Also, the liquid in the container may be cloudy, and the food may have a foul smell. However, the poison may be present without any signs. Therefore, all low-acid foods should be thoroughly heated before eating so that any poison in the food can be destroyed. Such foods should be brought to a boil and then simmered for 20 minutes.

Molds and certain yeasts may grow in inadequately sealed containers. These organisms produce a white, gray, black, or green growth on food. Other yeasts produce gases and turn sugar in food into alcohol and carbon dioxide.

Food can also be spoiled by *flat-sour bacteria*. Signs of these bacteria include a sour taste in food in cans or a cloudy liquid in food in jars.

History

The first processed food in sealed containers was prepared about 1795 by Nicolas Appert, a French chef. In 1809, Appert won the prize offered by the government for a simple way of preserving food for the French Army. Appert won with his method of using boiling water to heat food in glass bottles and then sealing them. He believed air caused food to spoil and, therefore, food in airtight containers would not spoil. In 1810, Peter Durand, an English merchant, obtained a patent for a method of preserving food in metal cans.

About 1860, the great French scientist Louis Pasteur discovered that organisms caused food spoilage. Pasteur found that heating food in closed containers killed such organisms and kept others from entering.

In 1858, John L. Mason, an American glass blower, introduced the first glass jar with a screw-on cap. This container, called the Mason jar, had a threaded top onto which the cap screwed. Today, Mason jars are widely used for home canning. In 1874, A. K. Shriver, an American canner, developed the first pressure canner. Metal lids with a sealing compound were introduced in the mid-1930's. GEORGE K. YORK

See also JELLY AND JAM.

Additional Resources

HERTZBERG, RUTH, and others. *Putting Food By*. 3rd ed. Stephen Greene, 1982.

KLUGER, MARILYN. *Preserving Summer's Bounty*. M. Evans, 1979.

U.S. DEPARTMENT OF AGRICULTURE. *Complete Guide to Home Canning, Preserving, and Freezing*. Dover, 1973.

CANNING INDUSTRY. See FOOD PRESERVATION (Canning).

CANNIZZARO, *KAN uh ZAH roh*, or *KAHN need DZAH roh*, **STANISLAO** (1826-1910), was an Italian chemist whose ideas laid the basis for modern chemistry. Amedeo Avogadro had shown the difference between atoms and molecules in 1811, but his work had been neglected. Cannizzaro developed Avogadro's ideas. The acceptance of Cannizzaro's work led to proper use of atomic weights and chemical formulas. He was born in Palermo, Sicily. HENRY M. LEICESTER

CANNON is a weapon of more than 1 inch (2.5 centimeters) in caliber that has a barrel, breech, and firing mechanism. The big guns that are now classed as artillery and the larger guns fired from World War II airplanes were once called *cannon*.

Cannon comes from the Latin word *canna*, which means *a tube* or *reed*. Large cannons were first used in warfare about 1350. Cannons of this time were cast of bronze and of wrought iron. Cannons firing heavy

Culver

An Early Giant Cannon, the *Dulle Griete* fired 700-pound (320-kilogram) balls at the Battle of Ghent in 1411.

balls were used extensively by Union and Confederate forces during the Civil War. JOHN D. BILLINGSLEY

See also AMMUNITION; ARTILLERY; CIVIL WAR (picture); GUN; HOWITZER.

CANNON, ANNIE JUMP (1863-1941), was a leading American woman astronomer. Known as "the census taker of the sky," she discovered 300 variable stars, five new stars, and a double star. She analyzed 286,000 stars to show the relation between their spectral type, brightness, and distribution. She compiled a bibliography of 200,000 references on variable stars. In 1896, she joined the staff of the Harvard Observatory. She was born in Dover, Del. HELEN WRIGHT

CANNON-BALL TREE is a South American tree that sheds its leaves more than once a year. Its pink or reddish flowers are about 3½ inches (9 centimeters) wide. Its round fruits grow up to 7 inches (18 centimeters) in diameter with thin, woody shells. The juicy pulp has a disagreeable odor. The cannon-ball tree is related to the Brazil-nut tree. See also BRAZIL NUT.

Field Museum of Natural History

The Cannon-Ball Tree bears a large, round fruit. South Americans make a drink from the fresh pulp.

Scientific Classification. The cannon-ball tree belongs to the lecythis family, *Lecythidaceae*. It is genus *Couroupita*, species *C. guianensis*. K. A. ARMSON

CANO, JUAN SEBASTIÁN DEL. See EXPLORATION (Magellan's Globe-Circling Expedition); MAGELLAN, FERDINAND (The End of the Voyage).

CANOEING is a popular sport in the United States, Canada, and many other countries. Large numbers of campers, fishermen, and hunters take canoe trips deep into wilderness areas. Others enjoy a peaceful canoe trip across a lake or an exciting canoe race down a river.

Canoes are easy to operate, maintain, store, and transport. They also cost little, compared to other kinds of boats. Most canoes hold from one to four persons.

Canoeing Equipment

A canoeist needs only two basic pieces of equipment —a canoe and a paddle. Manufacturers produce several kinds of each. Many canoeists also use a variety of other equipment.

WORLD BOOK photo

A Family Canoe Ride across a lake is a relaxing form of recreation. Canoes are also used for camping trips and racing.

Canoes. Most canoes measure from 11 to 20 feet (3.4 to 6.1 meters) long. They range from 35 to 40 inches (89 to 102 centimeters) in *beam*, the width at the widest point. Their depth varies from 12 to 14 inches (30 to 36 centimeters). Canoes may be made of aluminum, fiberglass, plastic, inflatable rubber, or wood and canvas. An aluminum canoe about 17 feet (5.2 meters) long would be ideal for a family of four.

Most canoes are open boats—that is, they have no deck. Some have an enclosed deck and a snug cockpit where the canoeist sits. Decked canoes closely resemble kayaks and are used in rough water where an open canoe would quickly fill with water (see KAYAK). Other canoes have one square end to which a small motor can be attached. Still other craft, called *sailing canoes*, have a mast and a sail but can also be paddled.

The design of a canoe varies according to the maneuverability and stability of the craft. Maneuverability is the ease with which a canoe can be operated. Stability is the quality that prevents it from turning over. A canoe's design may stress one of these principles over the other. For example, some canoes have a flat piece of metal or wood called a *keel* that extends into the water from the bottom of the hull. Such canoes are stable in the water and hold a straight course. They are good for traveling on a lake but difficult to maneuver on a river.

Paddles. Most canoe paddles are made of wood, but some are aluminum or plastic. Paddles made of a hard-

American National Red Cross (WORLD BOOK illustration)

To Enter a Canoe, a canoeist grips the near rim and places one foot in the middle of the craft, *left*. He then shifts his weight onto the foot in the canoe and grips the far rim, *right*.

wood, such as ash or maple, are limber and sturdy but may be too heavy for children and inexperienced paddlers. Those made of a softwood, such as pine or spruce, are lighter but may break more easily. Canoe paddles vary greatly in length. In general, a canoeist should choose one that extends from the ground to eye level.

The type of paddle blade depends on a person's needs and experience. A wide blade provides a powerful stroke but requires strength and skill to operate. A narrow blade requires less strength, but it does not provide so much power. A popular type called the *beaver tail blade* measures from 6 to 8 inches (15 to 20 centimeters) wide.

Other Equipment. Federal law requires that a flotation device, such as a life jacket, be carried for each person in a canoe. Other important equipment includes a *bailer*, which may be a coffee can or a small pump, to empty water from the canoe. On a camping trip, a canoeist may take waterproof storage bags to hold food, clothing, and camping equipment. Straps are used to fasten equipment so it does not float away if the canoe overturns. Many canoes are fitted with a device called a *yoke* for carrying the craft. When canoeing in cold water, a person may wear a tight-fitting garment called a *wet suit* for protection. A backrest and kneeling pad may be used for comfort.

Handling a Canoe

A skilled canoeist follows certain procedures in handling a canoe safely and efficiently. The most important one involves maintaining balance in the canoe so it remains *trim* (level). This is done by evenly distributing the weight of the people and equipment in the craft. Other procedures include (1) entering and leaving a canoe, (2) paddling and steering, and (3) *portaging* (carrying) a canoe.

Entering and Leaving a Canoe. When entering a canoe, the canoeist faces the bow of the canoe, grips the near *gunwale* (rim of the craft), and puts one foot in the middle of the canoe. Then, with one hand on the near gunwale, the canoeist reaches for the far gunwale with the other hand. At the same time, the canoeist shifts weight onto the foot in the canoe and lifts the other foot aboard. When two canoeists are entering, the first on board sits in the stern and steadies the canoe for the second, who sits in the bow.

When leaving a canoe, a canoeist follows the same procedure in reverse. If two persons are leaving, the one in the bow goes first.

Paddling and Steering. A canoeist should take a comfortable paddling position, either kneeling or sitting. Whatever position is used, the canoe must be kept trim at all times. When two canoeists are paddling, the one in the stern may use a slightly longer paddle, which enables the craft to be steered more easily.

Canoeists use several kinds of paddle strokes. The most basic one is the *bow stroke*, which moves the canoe forward. The canoeist holds the paddle with one hand near the *grip* (top) and the other hand near the blade. The hands should be about as far apart as the width of the shoulders. The paddle is drawn through the water by pulling back with the lower arm and pushing forward with the other.

Each bow stroke turns the canoe away from the side on which the stroke is made. Therefore, various strokes must be used to hold a straight course. One such stroke is the *J-stroke*, in which the canoeist pushes the paddle sideways at the end of each stroke. Other strokes are used to maneuver the canoe backward or sideways. A canoe can be stopped by pushing the paddle forward in the water.

Portaging a Canoe. On some canoe trips, the canoe may have to be carried overland. On a river trip, for example, canoeists may want to avoid such obstacles as rapids or falls. Or they may want to reach a lake that lies several miles from the river. When portaging a canoe, the canoeists may use a padded yoke, which enables the canoe to be carried upside down on their shoulders.

Canoe Camping

Canoe camping became increasingly popular during the early 1970's. Many people found they could use canoes to reach quiet, scenic sites far from crowded campgrounds. Canoe camping includes long trips through wilderness areas, as well as quiet weekends on a local lake or river. Information on the many campsites in North America may be obtained from various state agencies or from the American Canoe Association, 4260 E. Evans Avenue, Denver, Colo. 80222.

The equipment taken on a canoe trip depends on such factors as the season, the amount of cargo space,

Wil Blanche, DPI

White Water Racing down rough rapids provides excitement for both canoeists and spectators. This challenging form of canoeing requires great endurance, strength, and skill.

and the amount of portaging involved. For a discussion of camping equipment, see the WORLD BOOK article on CAMPING (Camp Supplies).

Canoe Racing

Canoe racing provides challenge and excitement. The several kinds of competition include (1) marathon racing, (2) white water racing, (3) flat water racing, and (4) poling and sailing.

Marathon Racing takes place on a river. The contestants speed over a course of about 20 miles (32 kilometers), with the winner determined by the fastest time. Men, women, and children compete in separate events.

White Water Racing was named for the rough, rapid water on which it takes place. Decked canoes or kayaks compete in these races. The winner is determined by the fastest time. There are two types of white water racing, *wildwater* and *slalom.* A wildwater race is based on the endurance, skill, and strength of the racers. A slalom race features precise maneuvering of canoes through a series of poles called *gates*, which hang over the water.

Flat Water Racing, which is an event of the summer Olympic Games, takes place on the smooth water of a lake or lagoon. One, two, or four racers paddle their canoes over a course of 500 to 10,000 meters.

Poling and Sailing are special types of canoe racing. In poling, a canoeist propels the craft with a pole that measures from 12 to 14 feet (3.4 to 4.3 meters) long. Contestants maneuver up and down stream and around floating markers called *buoys.* Races for sailing canoes are held in several classes of competition.

History

The canoe developed from the seagoing dugouts of the Carib Indians of the Caribbean islands. These dugouts were made from large tree trunks, which had been shaped and then hollowed out. The word *canoe* comes from *kanu*, the Carib term for such a dugout. The early Indians of North America made canoes by fastening bark, mostly birchbark, to a wooden frame or by hollowing out tree trunks. These light, swift canoes were ideal for the continent's vast system of lakes, rivers, and streams.

During the 1600's, canoes played an important part in the exploration of North America. In 1673, Louis Joliet, a French-Canadian explorer, and Father Jacques Marquette, a French missionary, traveled the Mississippi River in birchbark canoes. MIKE MICHAELSON

See also INDIAN, AMERICAN (Transportation); OLYMPIC GAMES (table); PIROGUE.

CANON. See BIBLE.

CAÑON. See CANYON.

CANON is a form of vocal or instrumental music. Two or more parts, or voices, are used. The first voice begins a melody. When the first voice has sung a few notes, the second voice begins the same melody. If there is a third voice, it begins the melody a few notes after the second voice starts. All the voices then sing the melody through to the end. Sometimes the canon finishes with a *coda*, or concluding passage. But in a *perpetual* or *circular canon*, each voice begins the entire melody again as soon as it has been sung through. A *round* is a kind of canon (see ROUND). RAYMOND KENDALL

CANON LAW is the collection of laws and regulations for the religious government of members of the Roman Catholic Church. These laws are set forth in the *Codex Juris Canonici*, which became effective on May 19, 1918, by order of Pope Benedict XV. Before that time, the canon law of the Church was based on the *Corpus Juris Canonici*, a collection of the scattered laws of many centuries. FULTON J. SHEEN

CANONIZATION is a ceremony in the Roman Catholic Church by which persons are declared saints after their death. Canonization follows the ceremony of *beatification*, by which persons are declared *blessed.* Certain proof of two miracles is necessary before canonization can take place (see MIRACLE). Proof of three miracles is required if the person has not been beatified formally. The Congregation of Rites must accept the proof of the occurrence of the miracles. After that, the pope can canonize. A thorough examination of the person's mode of life and of the genuineness of the miracles is made even before beatification. Delays of many years generally occur in the process of canonization, so that additional proof of the candidate's fitness can be obtained. After the person is canonized, a day is set aside on which the saint's memory is honored. Usually this day is the anniversary of the person's death. The new saint's name is placed in the list of saints. Churches may be dedicated to the saint as their patron, and public prayers may be said to the saint's honor or to seek the saint's intercession with God. FULTON J. SHEEN

See also SAINT.

CANOSSA. See GREGORY (Saint Gregory VII).

CANOVA, *kuh NOH vuh,* **ANTONIO** (1757-1822), was one of the most famous and influential European sculptors of the Napoleonic period. Canova's sculpture is usually called "neoclassical" because it shows the strong influence of classical Greek and Roman work. Many of his statues represent the gods and heroes of ancient times. Even when portraying Napoleon and other people of his own time, Canova usually presented them as though they were ancient Romans. Canova's greatness lies in his ability to fill these forms from another time with a distinct grace and vitality.

Canova was born in Possagno in northern Italy and spent much of his life in Rome. But he was known and admired all over Europe. Most of his statues are in European collections, but the Metropolitan Museum of Art in New York City owns important works, including *Perseus* and *Cupid and Psyche.* ROBERT R. WARK

CANSO, STRAIT OF. See CAPE BRETON ISLAND.

CANTABRIAN MOUNTAINS. See SPAIN (The Northern Mountains; Natural Resources).

CANTALOUPE. See MUSKMELON.

CANTATA, *kuhn TAH tuh,* is a short musical composition for one or more soloists and an orchestra, usually with a chorus. A cantata resembles an opera, but it does not have the stage action that an opera has. A cantata is similar to an oratorio. However, a cantata is usually much shorter than an oratorio. See OPERA; ORATORIO.

Cantatas developed in the early 1700's. They became especially popular for use in Protestant church services.

Dietrich Buxtehude wrote fine examples of the *cantata da chiesa* (church cantata) based on sacred subjects. A cantata on a secular subject is called a *cantata da camera* (chamber cantata).

Many persons regard Johann Sebastian Bach as the greatest composer of cantatas. He wrote almost 300 of them, including five complete series for the Sundays and holy days of the church year. Only about 200 have survived. They include *Christ lag in Todesbanden* (Christ lay in the bonds of death) and *Wachet auf* (Sleepers, awake!). Such composers as Claude Debussy, George Frideric Handel, Alessandro and Domenico Scarlatti, and Igor Stravinsky also wrote cantatas.

CANTERBURY is the ancient religious center of Great Britain. It is the chief town in the district of Canterbury, which has a population of 114,304. The town of Canterbury lies in the county of Kent, southeast of London (see GREAT BRITAIN [political map]). The archbishop of Canterbury is the spiritual head of the Church of England. Canterbury's main attraction is its huge Gothic cathedral, which was built between the 1000's and the 1400's. Canterbury attracted many pilgrims during the Middle Ages. It was the destination of Geoffrey Chaucer's travelers in his famous *Canterbury Tales*. See also ENGLAND (picture: Canterbury Cathedral). JOHN W. WEBB

CANTERBURY BELL is a plant about 4 feet (1.2 meters) high, with leaves that sometimes grow 10 inches (25 centimeters) long. The Canterbury bell is native to southern Europe. It grows wild and in gardens in the United States. See also BLUEBELL.

Scientific Classification. Canterbury bells belong to the bellflower family, *Campanulaceae*. They are genus *Campanula*, species *C. medium*. ALFRED C. HOTTES

CANTERBURY TALES is a group of stories by the English poet Geoffrey Chaucer. Scholars consider it the outstanding work in Middle English, the form of English used from about 1100 to about 1485. Chaucer worked on *The Canterbury Tales* from about 1385 until his death in 1400. He did not complete the work, but his plan is suggested in the general prologue. He gathered 29 pilgrims at the Tabard Inn in south London for a pilgrimage to Canterbury. Each pilgrim agreed to tell two tales going and two tales returning.

Chaucer wrote only 24 tales, and four of these are incomplete. The pilgrims approach Canterbury on the fourth day. There is no return journey. Many critics believe this one-way pilgrimage actually represents Chaucer's intended plan—a pilgrimage of human life that suggests the journey from earth to heaven.

The Canterbury Tales are a collection of stories by the English author Geoffrey Chaucer. The tales are told by a group of pilgrims during a journey from London to Canterbury. A squire tells one of the stories. This picture of the squire appears in an early edition of the tales that was published about 1400.

Henry E. Huntington Library and Art Gallery, San Marino, Calif.

Chaucer introduced the pilgrims in the prologue. The knight, the parson, and the plowman are idealized portraits representing the medieval *three estates*—aristocracy, clergy, and workers. Other pilgrims are traditional characters of medieval society. Chaucer provided much detail about the characters' appearance and private lives. Most of the tales reflect the personalities of the pilgrims who tell them. For example, the nun tells a story about a saint. Some of the tales are arranged in groups and give different viewpoints on a subject. Love, marriage, and domestic harmony are the most common themes in the tales. DONALD R. HOWARD

See also CHAUCER, GEOFFREY.

CANTICLES. See SONG OF SOLOMON.

CANTILEVER, *KAN tuh LEE vuhr*, is a structural beam which is supported at one end and free at the other end. It is fastened at one end so that the beam will be supported even when it projects straight out into the air. A *cantilever bridge* has two towers on opposite sides of the river. Each tower supports beams that meet in the middle of the bridge. The two cantilevers do not get any of their ability to support loads from being joined together. If half the bridge were raised, the other half could carry as much weight as before. See also BRIDGE (Cantilever Bridges). E. A. FESSENDEN

CANTON, in flags. See FLAG (table: Flag Terms; diagram: Parts of a Flag).

CANTON, *KAN tuhn*, is a political division in some countries of Europe. The name comes from the Italian word *contone*, meaning a *corner* or *angle*. Each of the 23 states that make up the Swiss republic is known as a *canton*. The French canton is a division of the political unit known as an *arrondissement*, and is the seat of a justice of the peace. There are about 3,000 cantons in France. Each canton has an average of 12 smaller divisions, or *communes*. ROBERT G. NEUMANN

CANTON, *kan TAHN* (pop. 1,840,000), is the largest city in southern China and a major center of international trade. It is also an industrial center and one of China's principal ports. Canton, which the Chinese call *Kuangchou*, lies at the head of the Chu Chiang (Pearl River) Delta. It is about 75 miles (121 kilometers) northwest of Hong Kong and the South China Sea. For location, see CHINA (political map).

The City is the capital of Kwangtung Province. Canton is one of China's most modern cities. Many of its people live in three- or four-story concrete apartment buildings. Until 1960, thousands of Cantonese lived on boats anchored in the Chu Chiang. Since then, the government has moved these people into apartments.

The city has a sports stadium and several public parks and museums. It also has many national monuments, including the Peasant Movement Training Institute. In 1925 and 1926, Chairman Mao Zedong of the Chinese Communist Party taught Communist beliefs to party workers at the institute. Another monument marks the burial site of the people who died in the Communist-led Canton Uprising of 1927. That year, the Communists failed in an attempt to take over the city's government. Colleges in Canton include Chi Nan University and Chung Shan University.

Economy of Canton is based largely on trade, and the city has an ideal location as a trade center. Tributaries of four rivers—the Chu Chiang, the North, the East, and

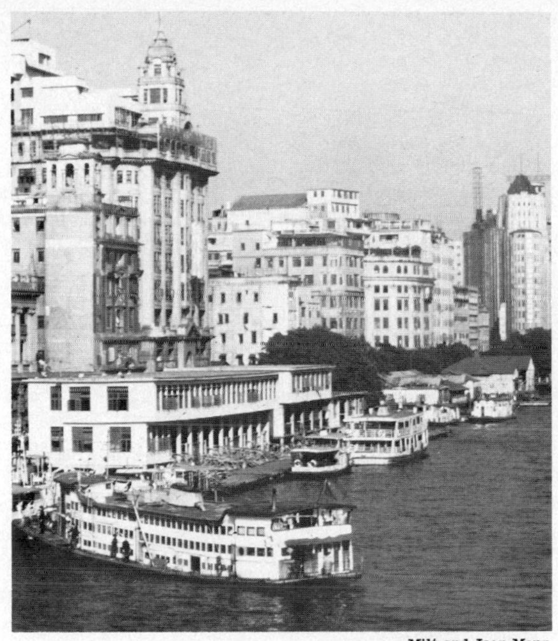

Milt and Joan Mann

Canton is a major port of China and one of the country's most modern cities. The city's downtown area, shown above, lies along the Pearl River. Canton is also an important Chinese center of industry and of trade with other nations.

the West—connect Canton and nearby Kwangsi province. Just east of Canton is the deepwater port of Whampoa, which serves ocean-going ships. A railroad links Canton to Hong Kong and to the industrial center of Wu-han, which lies about 600 miles (966 kilometers) north of Canton.

China's largest foreign trade fair takes place twice annually in Canton. This event, called the Export Commodities Fair, is held for a month each spring and fall. It attracts thousands of foreign merchants.

Canton has long been a center of handicraft industries. The city's craftworkers are famous for their ivory and jade carvings, lacquerware, and porcelain.

The establishment of new industries has modernized the city's economy since 1950. Recently built factories include a paper mill, a sewing machine plant, and a textile mill. Shipbuilding and sugar refining are also important industries in Canton.

History. Canton was founded about 214 B.C. by Shih Huang Ti, the emperor of China's Ch'in dynasty. During the time of the Roman Empire, from about 27 B.C. to A.D. 476, Roman merchants went to Canton for silks, spices, and tea. Arab and Persian traders visited the city during the A.D. 600's. Portuguese merchants first went to Canton in 1516. By the early 1800's, British, Dutch, French, and Portuguese traders controlled most of the trade between Canton and the West. From 1759 to 1842, Canton was the only Chinese port open to foreign trade. See CHINA (Clash with Western Powers).

Many leaders of the 1911 revolution came from Canton. This revolt led to the establishment of the Chinese republic in 1912. One of the leaders was Sun Yat-sen, who helped form the Nationalist Party that year and became its first leader. The party had its headquarters in Canton from 1917 to 1926. The Japanese occupied Canton from 1938 until World War II ended in 1945. In 1949, Chiang Kai-shek, head of the Nationalist Party since the mid-1920's, moved his government from Nan-ching to Canton. The Chinese Communists took over China later in 1949, and the Chinese Nationalists fled from Canton to Taiwan. RICHARD H. SOLOMON

CANTON, Ohio (pop. 94,730; met. area pop. 404,-421), is a city in northeastern Ohio. It lies 60 miles (97 kilometers) southeast of Cleveland and 75 miles (121 kilometers) northwest of Pittsburgh. See OHIO (political map).

The chief products manufactured in Canton include electric-furnace alloy steel; titanium steel; roller bearings; iron castings and forgings; machine tools; metal lockers, shelving, and furniture; vacuum cleaners; electrical appliances; gasoline and diesel motors; steel presses; safes and vaults; paving and building brick and glazed tile; water softeners and cleansers; rubber gloves; paints; household and cooking wares; and meats.

Canton lies in a rich agricultural area where pascal celery and other vegetables flourish. The region also has important deposits of bituminous coal, clay, and limestone. Canton serves as the trading center for a region of about 460,000 people.

McKinley Memorial, a monument to former President William McKinley, stands in Canton. McKinley and his wife are buried in the granite tomb. The city is the site of the National Professional Football Hall of Fame. Walsh College is also in Canton. Canton has about 700 acres (280 hectares) of parks.

Four airlines serve the Akron-Canton Airport, which lies about 10 miles (16 kilometers) northwest of the business district. Railroad passenger trains and three rail freight lines also serve the city.

Canton was founded in 1805. It became the seat of Stark County in 1809, and was incorporated as a village in 1822. A thriving metal-plow factory drew many settlers to the town in the 1830's. Canton received a city charter in 1854. The city operates under a mayor-council form of government. JAMES H. RODABAUGH

CANTOR, EDDIE (1892-1964), was an American stage, radio, television, and motion-picture star. He became known for tears-and-laughter comedy and popping eyeballs. His parents came from Russia. He was born Edward Iskowitz in New York City, and grew up on New York's lower East Side. After appearing in vaudeville and burlesque, Cantor starred in musical comedies, such as *Kid Boots* and *Banjo Eyes*, in the 1920's. He was active in charity work and named the campaign against polio the "March of Dimes." NARDI REEDER CAMPION

CANUTE, *kuh NYOOT*, or CNUT (994?-1035), became the King of England in 1016. He completed the Danish conquest of the English kingdom that same year. Canute divided England into military districts ruled by earls. In 1019, he succeeded his brother as king of Denmark. He acquired Norway in 1028, thus uniting a great Scandinavian empire. In England, Canute ruled wisely and enjoyed the strong support of the church. His code of laws restored and enforced Anglo-Saxon customs. He was the first Norse ruler to be accepted as a civilized Christian king. ROBERT S. HOYT

See also ENGLAND (The Anglo-Saxon Period).

Arizona Photographic Associates

Steep Canyon Walls drop into a valley at the Canyon de Chelly National Monument in northeastern Arizona.

CANVAS is a strong, coarse cloth. The name comes from the Latin word *cannabis*, meaning *hemp*, which was originally used to make canvas. Most canvas is made of cotton and is called *duck*. More expensive canvas fabrics are made from synthetic fibers. Artists paint oil pictures on cotton or linen canvas. Canvas is also used for clothing and tennis shoes. Heavy grades of canvas are used for conveyer belts, sails, tents, and awnings. KENNETH R. FOX

CANVASBACK is a large duck of North America that dives under water to get the plants it eats from the bottom of lakes and ponds. It makes its home from Nevada east to Nebraska, and north as far as Alaska. In winter it flies to the Atlantic and Pacific coasts of the United States. It is a large duck, from 20 to 24 inches (51 to 61 centimeters) long and weighing 2 to 3 pounds (0.9 to 1.4 kilograms). The canvasback gets its name from the canvas-colored body of the male bird. The male has a reddish-brown head and a black collar around his breast. The female is gray and brown.

Canvasbacks usually build their nests in clumps of weeds and grass in marshes. They line the nests with gray down. The birds lay seven or more greenish or olive-gray eggs. Canvasbacks cannot fly while they are growing new feathers after the nesting season. At other times they can fly high and fast, often traveling in V-shaped lines. These birds like to eat wild celery. Canvasbacks have a fine flavor and hunters prize them.

Scientific Classification. The canvasback belongs to the surface duck family, *Anatidae*. It is classified as genus *Nyroca*, species *N. valisineria*. JOSEPH J. HICKEY

See also BIRD (picture: Birds of Inland Waters and Marshes).

CANYON, or CAÑON, *KAN yun*, is a deep valley with steep sides. The word *canyon* is from the Spanish *cañón*, which means *hollow tube*. A narrow canyon with almost perpendicular walls is called a *gorge*. Canyons are worn to great depths by the erosion of thousands of years. They form some of the grandest scenery in the world. The Grand Canyon of the Colorado River in Arizona is in some places over 1 mile (1.6 kilometers) deep, and it is 2 to 18 miles (3 to 29 kilometers) wide at the top. The canyon of Snake River in Oregon and Idaho averages 5,500 feet (1,680 meters) deep for 40 miles (64 kilometers). Beautiful small canyons are found in the Canadian Rockies. Great canyons occur in the ocean. ELDRED D. WILSON

See also BRYCE CANYON NATIONAL PARK; EROSION; GRAND CANYON NATIONAL PARK; ROYAL GORGE; YELLOWSTONE NATIONAL PARK.

CANYON DE CHELLY NATIONAL MONUMENT, *duh SHAY*, is in northeastern Arizona. Its caves and crevasses contain records of an ancient civilization covering a longer period than any other ruins discovered in the Southwest. There are walls of red sandstone 800 feet (240 meters) high. The monument was authorized in 1931. For area, see NATIONAL PARK SYSTEM (table: National Monuments).

See also CLIFF DWELLERS (picture).

CANYONLANDS NATIONAL PARK lies in southeast Utah. It is near Moab, Utah, around the junction of the Green and Colorado rivers. This scenic area has red rock canyons, sandstone spires, and series of canyons called the Maze. Much of the area is unexplored. The region became a national park in 1964. For the area of the park, see NATIONAL PARK SYSTEM (table: National Parks).

CANZONIERE. See PETRARCH.

CAOUTCHOUC. See RUBBER (First Uses).

CAP-HAÏTIEN, *kayp HAY shuhn* (pop. 44,123), is the second largest city of Haiti. It lies on the north coast, about 170 miles (274 kilometers) north of Port-au-Prince (see HAITI [map]). Many of the crops of northern Haiti are shipped from this port. Columbus established a settlement near Cap-Haïtien in 1492. The ruins of Henri Christophe's Citadel and his palace are nearby. Cap-Haïtien was the capital of Haiti until 1770.

CAPACITANCE, *kuh PASS uh tuhns*, is the property of an electrical capacitor that determines the amount of electric charge it can store. A simple capacitor can be made by placing two flat metal plates parallel to each other. When a wire is connected from each plate to the terminals of a battery, an electric charge will be put in the capacitor. If the plates are made larger or moved closer together, the capacitance is increased and the capacitor can hold a larger charge.

Capacitance is determined by dividing the charge in the capacitor, measured in coulombs, by the voltage of the battery. The basic unit used to measure capacitance is the *farad.* A capacitor has a capacitance of 1 farad if 1 volt gives it a charge of 1 coulomb. However, the farad is such a large unit that it is seldom used to measure the capacitors used in ordinary electronic devices. These capacitors are measured in *microfarads* or in *picofarads.* A microfarad (mF) equals one-millionth of a farad, and a picofarad (pF) is one-millionth of a microfarad. ROBERT M. BURGER

See also CAPACITOR.

CAPACITOR, once called a *condenser,* is a device that stores an electric charge. Capacitors perform many functions in electrical and electronic circuits. They can smooth the flow of fluctuating current. They are used in circuits that tune a television or radio to the desired station. They can block a continuous flow of direct current, but allow an alternating current to flow through them. Almost all electronic devices from small transistor radios to giant television transmitters and electronic computers use capacitors.

How a Capacitor Works. One kind of capacitor, often called a *plastic-film capacitor,* consists of a piece of plastic film sandwiched between two sheets of aluminum foil. The sheets are rolled into a tight roll, with the plastic film insulating the two aluminum sheets. A wire is attached to each piece of foil, and the device is sealed with plastic. The aluminum foil sheets are the *plates* of the capacitor, and the plastic film is the *dielectric.*

If the wires from the plates are attached to the terminals of a battery, current will flow into the capacitor for a short time. The current builds up an *electrostatic* charge in the dielectric. The charge is called electrostatic because it does not flow past the capacitor. After the charge has built up, current no longer flows from the battery. If the wires are disconnected from the battery and touched together, a spark will jump between them. The spark discharges the capacitor.

Kinds of Capacitors. Capacitors are made from many materials and in a variety of shapes and sizes. They are classified according to the insulating material used as the dielectric. These materials include ceramics, glass, mica, plastics, and paper saturated with oil.

Some capacitors are designed for special purposes. *Oil capacitors* have mineral oil as the dielectric. Most

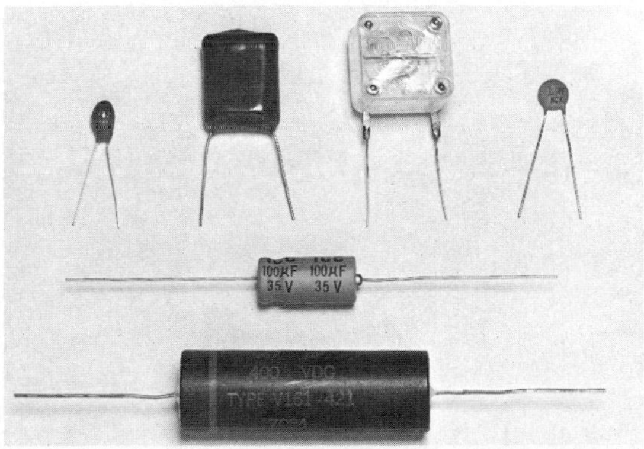

WORLD BOOK photo

Capacitors used in electronic equipment vary in size and shape, but they all work in basically the same way.

of them are used in devices that require high-potential alternating current.

Air capacitors have an air space between the plates. Most of these capacitors have two groups of plates. One group is attached to a shaft that moves the plates between the second group. Turning the shaft changes the area where the plates overlap. This change, in turn, varies the *capacitance* of the capacitor (see CAPACITANCE). Variable air capacitors are often used to tune in different stations on a radio.

Electrolytic capacitors have their plates in a liquid or moisture-retaining material. When voltage is applied to the capacitor, a thin coating of oxide forms on the metal plates and acts as the dielectric. These capacitors are used in circuits that require a large capacitance in a small space. ROBERT M. BURGER

See also FARAD; INSULATOR, ELECTRIC; LEYDEN JAR.

CAPACITY MEASURE. See WEIGHTS AND MEASURES (Volume and Capacity); LITER.

CAPE is a headland, cliff, or point of land that projects prominently into a lake, sea, or ocean. Tips of islands (Cape Race, Newfoundland) and continents (Cape Agulhas, Africa) are good places to find capes.

People sometimes use other terms for a cape: *point* (Montauk Point, N.Y.); *head* (Duncansby Head, Scotland); and *promontory* (Wilson's Promontory, Australia).

Capes may be formed in several ways. (1) Offshore bars or barrier beaches occasionally form points projecting far into the sea. They apparently result from converging shore currents depositing sandy materials in shallow water. Cape Hatteras, N.C., is an example. (2) River deposits may accumulate in shallow offshore waters until a point of land has been created, as at Cape Gracias a Dios, Honduras. (3) Cape Cod in Massachusetts is an example of a cape formed by rocks, gravels, and sands deposited along the margins of a continental glacier. (4) Huge rock cliffs, which withstand wave erosion better than softer coastal material, may slowly project away from the shoreline to form headlands. Australia's Cape York is an example. J. ROWLAND ILLICK

CAPE AGULHAS, *uh GULL us,* is the southernmost point of Africa. It is in Cape of Good Hope Province, South Africa. Cape Agulhas lies about 100 miles (160 kilometers) east of the Cape of Good Hope, and about 30 miles (48 kilometers) farther south. See SOUTH AFRICA (color map).

CAPE ALAVA is the farthest point west on the United States mainland, except Alaska. It is in the Ozette Lake region of northwestern Washington.

CAPE BRETON HIGHLANDS NATIONAL PARK. See CANADA (National Parks).

CAPE BRETON ISLAND, *BRIHT'n,* or *BREHT'n,* is a large, forest-covered island off the east coast of Canada. It forms a part of the province of Nova Scotia. A stone causeway, built in 1955 over the Strait of Canso, provides a road and railroad link between Cape Breton and the mainland. An arm of the Atlantic Ocean, called Bras d'Or Lake, covers about a sixth of the island, and almost cuts it in half (see BRAS D'OR LAKE). The rugged coastline has many inlets. A highway called the Cabot Trail leads to Cape Breton Highlands National Park in the northwestern part of the island. Cape Breton Island

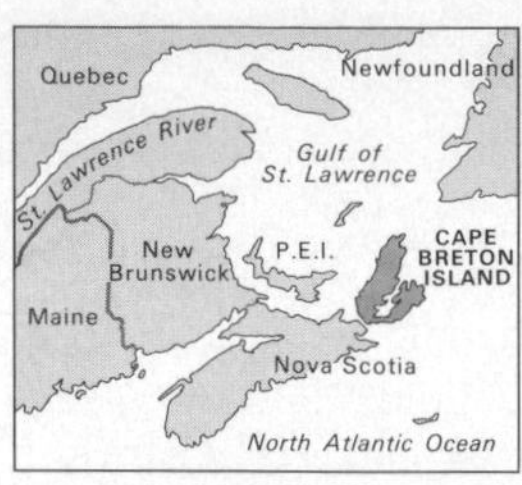

Cape Breton Island lies off the eastern coast of Canada. The island forms the northeastern part of the province of Nova Scotia.

WORLD BOOK map

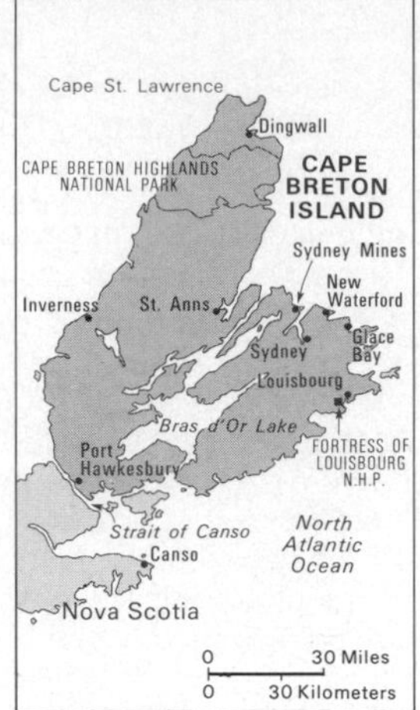

covers 3,981 square miles (10,311 square kilometers), about half the size of Massachusetts.

The People. The population of 170,088 includes many persons of Scottish descent, a lesser number of French Acadians, and a few hundred Indians. Sydney is the third largest city of Nova Scotia. Major towns include Glace Bay, New Waterford, North Sydney, and Sydney Mines. St. Anns holds an annual *Mod*, or gathering, in July, at which the people of Scottish descent enjoy bagpipe contests, Highland dancing, and folk songs.

Industry. The fishing industry, which employs about a third of the people, concentrates on herring, cod, mackerel, and swordfish. Most of the province's rich coal fields lie beneath the island and the surrounding water. Nova Scotia ranks first among the provinces in coal production. Gypsum also is mined on the island. A large steel industry operates at Sydney.

History. John Cabot was probably the first European to see Cape Breton Island, in 1497. European fishermen soon visited the island. A party of Scots made the first settlement in 1629. But the French made the first permanent settlements, and built the fortress of Louisbourg in the early 1700's to guard the sea approach to the St. Lawrence River. An army of New Englanders, with the aid of a British fleet, took Louisbourg in 1745, but France regained it by treaty in 1748. British troops led by Major General Jeffery Amherst regained Louisbourg in 1758. The island was part of Nova Scotia from 1763 to 1784, when it became a separate British colony. It was reunited with Nova Scotia in 1820. THOMAS H. RADDALL

See also LOUISBOURG; NOVA SCOTIA (color picture: The Atlantic Upland Area).

CAPE BUFFALO. See BUFFALO (animal).

CAPE CANAVERAL, formerly called Cape Kennedy, is the site of the John F. Kennedy Space Center. It lies on the east-central coast of Florida, 10 miles (16 kilometers) north of Cocoa Beach, Fla. The space center includes the first tracking station in the Atlantic Missile Range, and the National Aeronautics and Space Administration (NASA) Launch Operations Center. For a map of Cape Canaveral, see SPACE TRAVEL (Launch Operations).

The missile range extends 9,000 miles (14,000 kilometers) across the South Atlantic, and includes tracking stations on Jupiter, Grand Bahama, Eleuthera, San Salvador, Mayaguana, Grand Turk, St. Lucia, Fernando de Noronha, and Ascension islands, and in Mayagüez, Puerto Rico, and the Dominican Republic. A temporary station is in Pretoria, South Africa.

The United States began its large-scale space explorations at the cape in 1958, when the first U.S. satellite was launched. Alan B. Shepard, Jr., made the first U.S. suborbital space flight from the cape in 1961. In 1962, John H. Glenn, Jr., the first American to orbit the earth, was launched from the cape. In 1969, Edwin E. Aldrin, Jr., Neil A. Armstrong, and Michael Collins rocketed from the cape to begin the journey that placed Armstrong and Aldrin on the surface of the moon.

The Air Force Missile Test Center operates the missile range, which was established in 1949. Army and Navy ordnance units are also stationed at the cape. The entire area was called Cape Canaveral until President Lyndon B. Johnson renamed it Cape Kennedy in November 1963, after the assassination of President John F. Kennedy. In 1973, the name was changed back to Cape Canaveral. The change represented the preference of Floridians. However, the cape's rocket complex continued to be known as the John F. Kennedy Space Center. JOHN H. THOMPSON

See also PATRICK AIR FORCE BASE.

CAPE COD is a hook-shaped peninsula on the coast of Massachusetts. Cape Cod Bay lies in the hooked arm of Cape Cod (see MASSACHUSETTS [physical map]). The cape is about 65 miles (105 kilometers) long and from 1 to 20 miles (1.6 to 32 kilometers) wide. The long, sandy beaches attract many visitors each summer, especially artists. The cape received its name because of the codfish caught off the shores. Cranberries are gathered in the Cape Cod marshes. The cape's most important towns are Provincetown and Hyannis.

Bartholomew Gosnold, an Englishman who sailed around Cape Cod in 1602, is usually credited as the first European to sight it. However, some historians believe that Basque and Norse fishermen visited the cape long before Gosnold's voyage. Cape Cod was a center of the whaling industry in the 1800's. WALTER F. DOWNEY

See also GOSNOLD, BARTHOLOMEW.

CAPE COD CANAL is one of the world's widest artificial waterways. It ranges from 450 to 700 feet (137 to 213 meters) in width. It cuts through the strip of

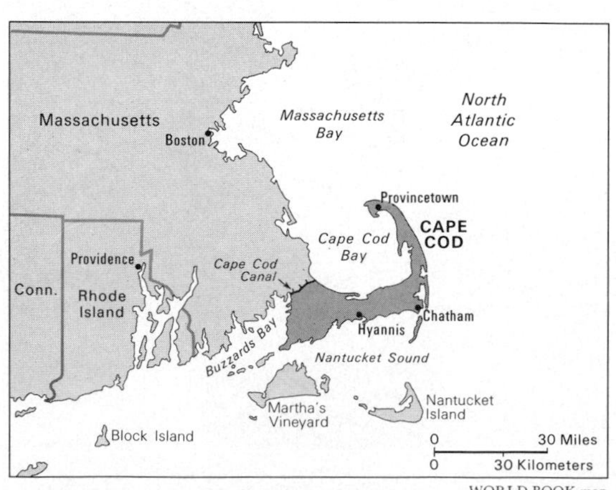

WORLD BOOK map

Location of Cape Cod

land that joins Cape Cod to the rest of Massachusetts. The canal decreases the sea route between Boston and New York City by 70 miles (110 kilometers), and enables ships to avoid the dangerous shoals off Cape Cod. The total length of the canal is $17\frac{1}{2}$ miles (28.2 kilometers). The land cut between Cape Cod Bay on the east and Buzzards Bay on the west measures 8.6 miles (13.8 kilometers). The canal, a sea-level waterway, has no locks. Its *channel* (deepest part) is 32 feet (9.8 meters) deep at low water. The channel permits two-way passage of all but the largest vessels. Annual commercial traffic averages about 7,700 ships carrying about $11\frac{1}{4}$ million short tons ($10\frac{1}{4}$ million metric tons). The federal government owns and operates the canal toll-free.

Work on the canal began in 1909 when August Belmont, a banker, sponsored the project. It opened in 1914 as a toll waterway. The U.S. government purchased the canal in 1928 for $11,400,000, and spent $22 million deepening and widening it. WILLIAM J. REID

CAPE HATTERAS, *HAT uhr uhs*, is a scenic promontory at the southern tip of Hatteras Island. It lies over 30 miles (48 kilometers) east of the North Carolina coast, across Pamlico Sound (see NORTH CAROLINA [physical map]). The nearby Diamond Shoals are dangerous for ships. The many shipwrecks have earned the area the name *Graveyard of the Atlantic*. Lighthouses and an offshore light station warn ships away. Cape Hatteras National Seashore is located there. HUGH T. LEFLER

CAPE HORN is the most southerly part of South America. It lies at the southern tip of Horn Island in Chile. Willem Schouten, a Dutch sailor, named it in 1616 for his native town of Hoorn. The cape runs far into the sea. It has steep sides which rise 500 to 600 feet (150 to 180 meters) in some places. Plant life is sparse on Cape Horn because of the cold climate. The region is so stormy that sailors have dreaded "rounding the Horn." Many ships now use the Panama Canal.

CAPE JASMINE. See GARDENIA.

CAPE KENNEDY. See CAPE CANAVERAL.

CAPE OF GOOD HOPE is a peninsula that lies about 100 miles (160 kilometers) northwest of Cape Agulhas, the southern tip of Africa. It extends southward from Table Mountain, which overlooks the city of Cape Town. South Africans call this peninsula *Cape Peninsula*. They call the peninsula's southern tip *Cape Point*. The peninsula forms the west side of False Bay. Cape of Good Hope is famous for its fine roads and beaches.

According to tradition, when the Portuguese explorer Bartolomeu Dias discovered the cape in 1488, he named it the Cape of Storms. But King John II of Portugal gave the cape its present name in the hope that a sea route to India had been found. In 1497, Vasco da Gama, another Portuguese explorer, proved this hope a fact when he sailed around the cape and continued on to Calicut (Kozhikode). HIBBERD V. B. KLINE, JR.

See also DA GAMA, VASCO; DIAS, BARTOLOMEU.

CAPE PROVINCE is the oldest province of South Africa. Sometimes called Cape of Good Hope Province, it lies on the southern tip of Africa (see SOUTH AFRICA [map]). The shores of the province touch the Indian and Atlantic oceans. The province covers 276,686 square miles (716,613 square kilometers). A low plain lies along the southeastern coast. Behind it are several mountain ranges, including the Langeberg, Groote Zwarte Bergen, and the Nieuwveld.

The People. Cape Province has a population of 7,443,500. About $1\frac{1}{4}$ million of the residents are *whites* (persons of European descent), and about 2 million are persons of mixed ancestry, called *Coloreds*. Nearly 4 million blacks live in Cape Province. Most of the people farm the land, raise stock, or work as miners. The whites own most of the land. Blacks own land in the eastern part of the province. Many of the blacks work for whites on farms or in the cities. The largest cities are Cape Town, Port Elizabeth, East London, and Kimberley. Cape Town is the capital of the province and the legislative capital of South Africa.

History. Dutch settlers founded the Cape Colony in 1652. The British took over the colony in 1795, gave it back in 1803, and regained possession of it in 1806. Boers invaded the Cape Colony during the Boer War (1899-1902). Many Boers who lived in the colony rose against the British government in sympathy with the invading Boer forces.

Cape Province once made up a separate colony, with a governor, council, and house of assembly of its own. It became part of the Union of South Africa in 1910. During World War II (1939-1945), when the Suez Canal route became too dangerous, Britain used the Cape

Cape Horn is the southernmost tip of South America. The cape lies at the southern end of Horn Island, which belongs to Chile.

WORLD BOOK map

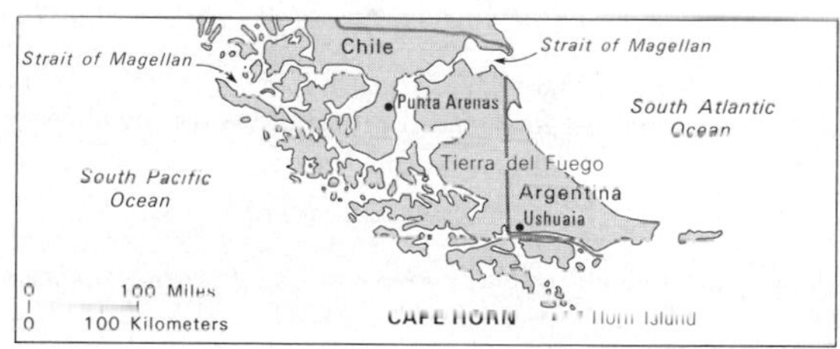

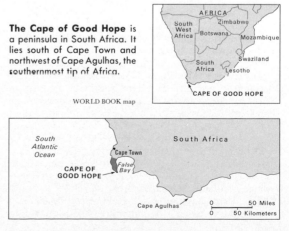

The Cape of Good Hope is a peninsula in South Africa. It lies south of Cape Town and northwest of Cape Agulhas, the southernmost tip of Africa.

WORLD BOOK map

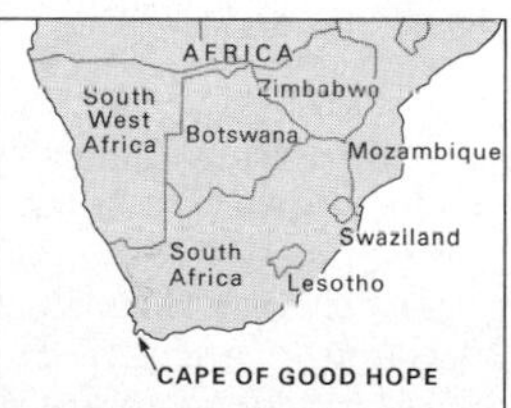

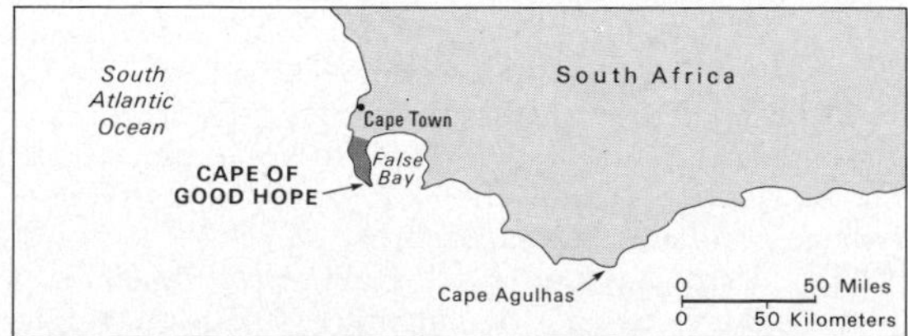

route in order to send soldiers and supplies to India and Australia. LEONARD M. THOMPSON

See also BOER WAR; CAPE OF GOOD HOPE; CAPE TOWN; KIMBERLEY; PORT ELIZABETH.

CAPE TOWN (pop. 789,580; met. area pop. 1,490,-935) is the legislative capital of South Africa. Parliament meets in Cape Town. Pretoria is South Africa's administrative capital, and Bloemfontein is its judicial capital (see SOUTH AFRICA [introduction]). Cape Town is also the capital of Cape Province. One of the main ship routes from Europe to the Far East passes near Cape Town. Cape Town lies at the foot of Table Mountain on Africa's southwest coast. For location, see SOUTH AFRICA (political map).

More people live within the city limits of Cape Town than live within the city limits of any other South African city. But Johannesburg has the country's largest metropolitan area population, and so South Africans consider it to be the country's largest city.

South African Tourist Corporation

Downtown Cape Town has many modern buildings. The city lies at the foot of rugged Table Mountain, *left background.*

Many Cape Town houses have graceful, rounded gables patterned after the Dutch-style homes of the original white settlers. Cape Town's sandy beach and sunny climate make it a favorite vacation spot. Over two-thirds of the people are nonwhites.

Cape Town's excellent docks and harbor make the city an important shipping and trading center. With its crowded business streets, Cape Town resembles cities in North America. It has many fine buildings, including the houses of Parliament, a museum, a cathedral, and several *mosques* (Muslim houses of worship). The Royal Observatory and University of Cape Town are near the city. Jan van Riebeeck, a naval surgeon, founded Cape Town in 1652 as a supply base for Dutch East India Company ships. LEONARD M. THOMPSON

See also SOUTH AFRICA (picture: Scenic Cape Town).

CAPE VERDE is an African country that consists of 10 main islands and 5 tiny islands. It lies in the Atlantic Ocean, about 400 miles (640 kilometers) west of Dakar, Senegal, on the African mainland.

Cape Verde has a population of about 365,000 and a total land area of 1,557 square miles (4,033 square kilometers). São Tiago, the largest island, covers 383 square miles (992 square kilometers). Santo Antão is the second largest island, followed by Boa Vista, Fogo, São Nicolau, Maio, São Vicente, Sal, Brava, and Santa Luzia. Santa Luzia and the five islets are uninhabited.

Praia, the capital and largest city of Cape Verde, is on São Tiago. It has a population of about 55,300 and is an important seaport and trading center. Portugal ruled the islands from the 1460's until they gained independence in 1975.

Government. Cape Verde is a republic. The people elect a 56-member legislature called the People's Assembly, which selects a president and a premier. It also appoints a Cabinet of eight members, headed by the premier. The president is the chief of state.

Cape Verde has only one legal political party, the African Party for the Independence of Cape Verde. It is usually called the PAICV, the initials of the party's name in Portuguese. Until 1981, the party was called the African Party for the Independence of Guinea and Cape Verde, or PAIGC. It had ties with the PAIGC of Guinea-Bissau, an African mainland nation southeast of Cape Verde.

People. About 70 per cent of the people of Cape Verde have mixed black African and Portuguese ancestry. Black Africans make up most of the rest of the population.

Cape Verde has an extremely low standard of living because many of its people cannot find work. The country's chief industries, farming and fishing, provide workers with only a bare income. Famines have occurred frequently through the years, and many of the people are undernourished. Since the mid-1900's, hundreds of thousands of Cape Verdeans have emigrated to Brazil, Portugal, the United States, and other countries.

Most Cape Verdeans speak a local Creole dialect based on ancient Portuguese and various African languages. The majority of the people are Roman Catholics, but many also practice *animism*, the belief that everything in nature has a soul.

Cape Verde has about 500 elementary schools and several high schools and technical schools. About 75 per cent of the people can read and write.

Land and Climate. The islands of Cape Verde were formed by volcanic eruptions that occurred from $2\frac{1}{2}$ to 65 million years ago. The only remaining active vol-

Facts in Brief

Capital: Praia.

Form of Government: Republic.

Total Land Area: 1,557 sq. mi. (4,033 km²). *Coastline*—600 mi. (966 km).

Elevation: *Highest*—Pico, 9,281 ft. (2,829 m). *Lowest*—sea level.

Population: *Estimated 1985 Population*—365,000; distribution, 80 per cent rural, 20 per cent urban; density, 236 persons per sq. mi. (91 per km²). *1980 Census*—296,093. *Estimated 1990 Population*—414,000.

Chief Products: Bananas, salt, sugar cane.

Flag: A black star and a yellow seashell, framed by two curved cornstalks, lie on a red vertical stripe at the left. A yellow horizontal stripe appears over a green one at the right. See FLAG (picture: Flags of Africa).

Money: *Basic Unit*—escudo.

cano is on Fogo Island. Most of the islands have rugged, mountainous land, with tall cliffs along the coastlines.

Cape Verde has a warm, dry climate, with average annual temperatures that range from 68° F. (20° C) to 77° F. (25° C). A continual shortage of rain makes most of the land too dry to support plant life.

Economy of Cape Verde is underdeveloped. Agriculture is the country's major industry, but most of the land is too dry to farm. A drought that began in 1968 and continued into the 1970's caused about a 90 per cent drop in agricultural production. Most of the country's livestock died. Cape Verde's chief crops include coffee beans; sugar cane; bananas and other fruits; and such vegetables as beans, corn, and tomatoes.

During the mid-1900's, Cape Verde worked to develop its fishing industry. Lobsters and tuna are the main catches. The country's mining industry produces salt and *pozzuolana*, a volcanic rock used by the cement industry. Both these products are exported.

Before Cape Verde became independent in 1975, it relied almost entirely on Portugal for economic support. Since then, it has received food aid from the United Nations and financial aid from various countries.

Cape Verde has three radio stations and two newspapers. The islands have about 920 miles (1,480 kilometers) of roads. There are no railroads. Boats operate among the islands infrequently. Sal Island has an airport, and several other islands have landing strips.

History. Portuguese explorers discovered the islands of Cape Verde about 1460. The islands were uninhabited at the time, and the Portuguese began to settle there about two years later. They planted cotton, fruit trees, and sugar cane and brought slaves from the African mainland to work the land.

Slave trading became Cape Verde's most important commercial activity during the 1500's and 1600's, and

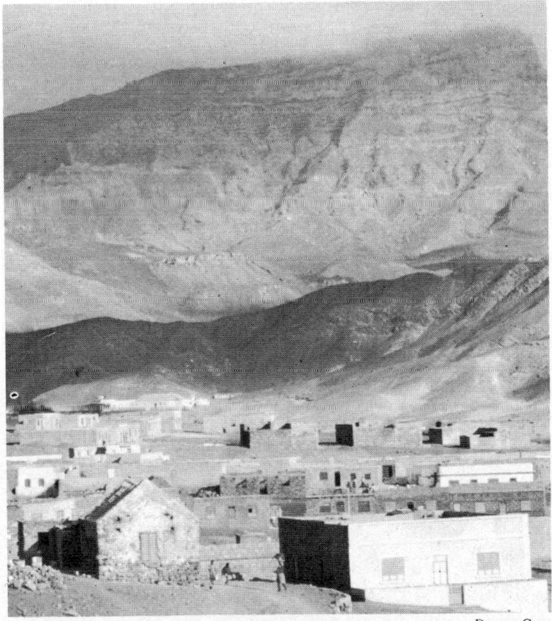

Duncan Carse

Cape Verde's Rugged, Mountainous Land lies barren after years of drought. Few plants can grow in the volcanic ash that covers São Vicente, *above*, and most of the country's other islands.

Cape Verde

⊛	National capital
•	Settlement
+	Elevation above sea level
——	Road

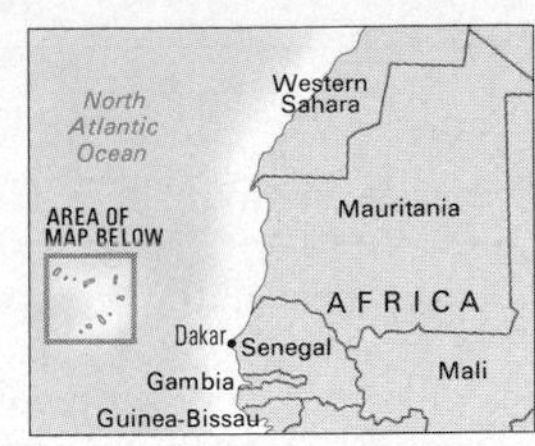

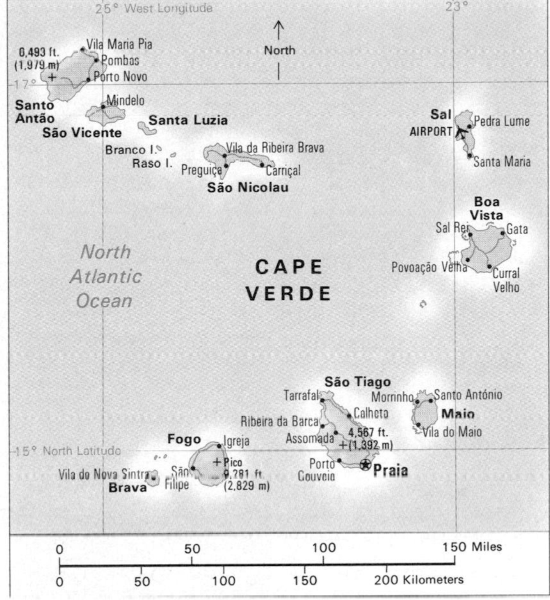

WORLD BOOK map

the islands prospered. Slaves learned how to work on plantations there before being shipped elsewhere. The slave trade declined in the late 1600's, and the prosperity ended. Economic conditions improved slightly in the mid-1800's, when Mindelo became an important refueling port for ships crossing the Atlantic.

Portugal ruled Cape Verde and what is now Guinea-Bissau under one government until 1879, when each became a separate Portuguese colony. Cape Verde became a Portuguese overseas province in 1951, and its people assumed a greater role in the government. The PAIGC (now called the PAICV) fought to overthrow Portuguese rule from the mid-1950's until 1975, when Cape Verde became independent. Guinea-Bissau had won independence in 1974.

During the 1970's, the two nations held discussions about uniting under one government. In the early 1980's, disagreements between the two countries ended the discussions. Kristin W. Henry and Clement Henry Moore

CAPE YORK is a mountainous, ice-covered point of land that extends into Baffin Bay. The cape is on the northwest coast of Greenland at 76° north latitude, well north of the Arctic Circle (see Arctic Ocean [color map]). Admiral Robert E. Peary used this lonely point as a base for many of his explorations around the North Pole. Peary's party discovered huge meteorites there. The largest meteorite he found weighed about 34 short tons (31 metric tons). John Edwards Caswell

ČAPEK, *CHAH pehk,* **KAREL,** *KAIR uhl* (1890-1938), a Czech writer, became famous for his symbolic, fantastic plays and novels. In his best-known play, *R.U.R.*, he introduced the word *robot* to describe his mechanical characters without souls. He foresaw the use of atomic energy in his novel *The Absolute at Large* (1922).

Čapek feared the loss of individuality in the machine age. He wrote *R.U.R.* in 1921 as a protest against tendencies toward regimentation. His other dramatic masterpiece, *The Insect Comedy*, which he wrote with his artist-brother Josef in 1921, portrayed the loves, vices, and wars of humanity. His play, *The Makropoulos Secret* (1922), dealt with extending the life span of human beings. Čapek was born in Bohemia. JOHN W. GASSNER

CAPELLA, *kuh PEHL uh,* is the brightest star in the constellation Auriga and the sixth brightest in the heavens, excluding the sun. Capella's diameter is 12 times the diameter of the sun. The star is approximately 46 light-years away from Earth. *Capella*, which is Latin for *little she-goat*, sometimes represents the goat that suckled the infant Zeus (Jupiter).

CAPER, *KAY puhr,* is a flower bud used in a meat sauce. The unopened buds are pickled in salt and vinegar to make the sauce. The buds come from a low, trailing shrub called the caper bush which grows in the southern United States, the Mediterranean countries, Canada, and Great Britain. The caper plant blooms early in summer. The plant has pinkish-white flowers with long stamen tassels and four petals.

The Caper Bush

Scientific Classification. The caper bush belongs to the caper family, Capparidaceae. It is classified as *Capparis spinosa*. HAROLD NORMAN MOLDENKE

CAPET, HUGH. See HUGH CAPET.

CAPETIAN DYNASTY, *kuh PEE shuhn,* is the name given to a long line of kings that ruled France from 987 to 1328. Between 987 and 1316, son followed father without a break in the royal succession. A surprising number of the Capetian kings had very long reigns. Several of them, notably Philip II (Augustus), Louis IX (St. Louis), and Philip IV (The Fair), were men of considerable administrative ability. Hugh Capet, the first of the line, ruled only a small territory and was surrounded by feudal lords much more powerful than he. Later Capetians enlarged the royal holdings, increased the powers of the rulers, and gave France a strong centralized government. See also HUGH CAPET; LOUIS (IX); PHILIP (II; IV) OF FRANCE. WILLIAM C. BARK

CAPILLARITY, *KAP uh LAR uh tee,* in physics, is the tendency of liquids to rise in small tubes and into the hairlike openings that are present in porous matter.

When a narrow tube is dipped into a liquid, the liquid rises if it wets the tube. The liquid is depressed if it does not wet the tube. The amount of capillarity depends on *surface tension* in the liquid (see SURFACE TENSION). If the liquid wets the tube, the molecules on the outside surface cling together tightly, and tend to pull up all the liquid. The liquid rises until the weight of the liquid in the tube balances the surface tension.

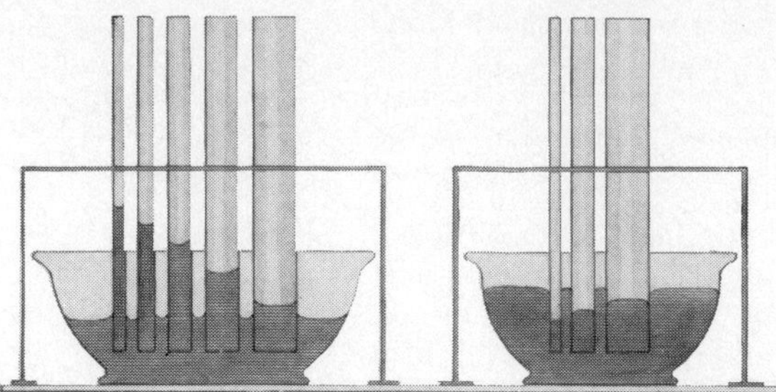

How Capillarity Works. If a number of straws which have different widths are placed in a bowl of water, *left,* the water will rise in the straws above the surface of the water in the bowl. It will rise highest in the narrowest tube. Water wets the straws, so surface tension pulls the water up. But mercury does not wet the straws, *right.* Surface tension pulls the mercury in the straws down below the level in the bowl.

Liquid rises higher in narrow tubes than in wide tubes, because there is more surface tension. When liquid molecules attract each other more than they do the wall of the tube, the liquid does not wet the tube. In this case, the surface tension causes the liquid to be depressed. Mercury is a liquid that sinks in a glass tube.

Capillarity is very useful. It causes blotters to absorb ink, and plants to draw up water. Water is drawn upward in the earth by capillarity. Particles of earth act as capillary tubes. The *capillaries* of the blood vessels carry blood through the body. ROBERT L. WEBER

CAPILLARY, *KAP uh lehr ee,* is the smallest blood vessel in the body. It can be seen only under the microscope. Most capillaries are so small that only one blood cell can pass through them at a time. Capillaries connect the smallest arteries with the smallest veins. They make up a network of blood vessels throughout the body. The largest capillaries are in the bone marrow and skin. The smallest are in the brain and lining of the intestine.

Capillaries have thin walls. Foods which are carried in the blood stream are able to pass through their walls into the tissues. Waste materials from the tissues also pass into the blood stream through capillary walls. In the capillaries of the lungs, oxygen goes through the walls into the blood and carbon dioxide goes out. Other waste products pass through tiny capillary walls into the kidneys, intestine, and skin. JOHN B. MIALE

See also BLOOD (pictures); CIRCULATORY SYSTEM; VEIN.

CAPISTRANO. See SAN JUAN CAPISTRANO.

CAPITAL. See COLUMN; CAPITOL.

CAPITAL is an economic term for wealth, other than land, that is used to produce more wealth. People's invested savings are capital, because they produce more wealth through the interest or dividends that they earn. Land and other natural resources are not considered capital, because people did not produce them. Most assets used by a business represent capital, because they are used to produce earnings. Such items as personal food, furniture, and clothing are considered wealth but not capital. They do not produce added wealth. There are two types of business capital, *fixed* and *working*.

Fixed Capital includes industrial or commercial buildings, machinery, equipment, and other facilities used to produce goods and services. By producing goods and services, these fixed-capital items create new wealth. Items of fixed capital must be replaced from time to time, when they wear out or become outdated. The owner of a fixed-capital item tries to estimate the economic life of such an item when acquiring it. Guided by this estimate, the owner can set aside enough money to replace the item when it becomes useless.

Working Capital consists of cash, inventories, and *accounts receivable* (money owed to the business). These items usually do not produce wealth themselves, but they make it possible for fixed capital to do so. Businesses must have cash to pay for labor and other expenses. They need inventories of raw materials, supplies, work in production, and finished products. Businesses usually keep accounts receivable, so customers can purchase goods and services and pay later.

Total Capital. The extent of a company's ownership of capital is usually expressed in terms of money. For example, a company may have been capitalized at $10 million. This means that investors have invested $10 million in the company. This money has been used to buy fixed and working capital goods and other items. Money invested in businesses or available for investment is often called *capital funds.* LEONARD C. R. LANGER

Related Articles in WORLD BOOK include:

Bank	Economics	Industry (Capital)
Business	Industrial Revolution (The Role of Capital)	Interest
Capitalism		
Corporation		

CAPITAL GAINS TAX is a tax on gains from the sale of certain property. Such property includes houses, stocks, bonds, and certain other possessions usually owned more than a year. The U.S. government and many state and local governments tax gains from the sale of such property at a lower rate than other income.

The entire amount of ordinary income, such as wages, interest, and dividends, is subject to taxation. But only 40 per cent of the profit from the sale of property covered by the capital gains tax is taxable. To qualify for this treatment, an item must be owned longer than six months before it is sold. The profit is called a *long-term capital gain.* The profits from the sale of property owned six months or less are taxed the same as ordinary income. Such amounts are called *short-term capital gains.* A loss on the sale of one item may be deducted from the gain on the sale of another when calculating the tax on the gain. Capital losses up to $3,000 a year may be deducted from ordinary income if no capital gains occur.

Some people criticize the capital gains tax, charging that it benefits chiefly wealthy individuals and others who own a great amount of property. People who favor the tax argue that it encourages investment and thereby strengthens the economy. They also say that many capital gains result largely from inflation rather than from actual profits, and that it would be unfair to tax such gains at the normal rate. ARTHUR D. LYNN, JR.

CAPITAL PUNISHMENT is punishment by death. Since the early 1800's, most executions have resulted from convictions for murder. The death penalty has also been imposed for such serious crimes as armed robbery, kidnapping, rape, and treason.

Many persons oppose the death penalty, chiefly because they consider it cruel. Other persons favor it because they believe it prevents crime. Criminologists have never established a direct relationship between the death penalty and the murder rate. Studies have shown no unusual increase in murders when capital punishment is abolished.

In the mid-1980's, 37 states of the United States had laws that permitted the death penalty. These laws were greatly influenced by a 1972 decision of the Supreme Court of the United States, which had banned the death penalty as it was then imposed. The court ruled that "the imposition and carrying out of the death penalty" was cruel and unusual punishment in violation of the Eighth Amendment to the Constitution. But the court left open the possibility that the death penalty might be constitutional—if imposed for certain crimes and applied uniformly.

After the 1972 decision, many state legislatures passed new capital punishment laws designed to satisfy the Supreme Court's requirements. Most of these laws limit the death penalty to murder and other specified crimes if they result in a person's death. Such crimes include armed robbery, hijacking, and kidnapping. The laws of several states specify the circumstances under which a judge or jury may impose the death penalty.

In 1976, the court upheld death sentences for three men convicted of murder under new laws in Florida, Georgia, and Texas. The court ruled that capital punishment for murder was "not unconstitutionally severe." However, the court struck down laws that made the death penalty *mandatory* (required) for certain crimes.

Many other countries, including most European and Latin-American nations, have repealed the death penalty since 1900. Canada abolished capital punishment in 1976. In Australia, the federal government and all of the six states except Western Australia have repealed the death penalty.

Capital punishment was widely used during the Middle Ages, especially for crimes against the state and church. In the 1700's, England had more than 200 capital offenses. Most of these were abolished in the

Capital Punishment in the United States

This table shows the states that had capital punishment in mid-1984 and the method of execution used. Thirteen states and the District of Columbia did not have a death penalty.

State	Method of Execution	State	Method of Execution
Alabama	Electrocution	Nevada	Drug injection
Arizona	Gas chamber	New Hampshire	Hanging
Arkansas	Drug injection	New Jersey	Drug injection
California	Gas chamber	New Mexico	Drug injection
Colorado	Gas chamber	North Carolina	††
Connecticut	Electrocution	Ohio	Electrocution
Delaware	*	Oklahoma	Drug injection
Florida	Electrocution	Pennsylvania	Electrocution
Georgia	Electrocution	South Carolina	Electrocution
Idaho	†	South Dakota	Electrocution
Illinois	Drug injection	Tennessee	Electrocution
Indiana	Electrocution	Texas	Drug injection
Kentucky	Electrocution	Utah	Firing squad
Louisiana	Electrocution	Vermont	Electrocution
Maryland	Gas chamber	Virginia	Electrocution
Massachusetts	**	Washington	*
Mississippi	Drug injection	Wyoming	Gas chamber
Missouri	Gas chamber		
Montana	*		
Nebraska	Electrocution		

*Drug injection or hanging
†Drug injection or firing squad
**Drug injection or electrocution
††Drug injection or gas chamber

1800's. Great Britain abolished capital punishment on an experimental basis in 1965 and permanently abolished it in 1969.

In the United States, the number of executions had been dropping steadily even before the 1972 Supreme Court ruling outlawing the death penalty as it was then imposed. In 1935, 199 persons were put to death. The number of executions dropped to seven in 1965, one in 1966, and two in 1967. There were no executions from 1968 through 1976. After the Supreme Court reapproved the use of the death penalty in 1976, executions resumed. Today, about 1,200 persons sentenced to death are awaiting execution in the United States. Many of these people have appealed their sentences and are seeking executive reviews. George T. Felkenes

Related Articles in World Book include:

Drowning	Garrote	Guillotine
Electrocution	Gas Chamber	Hanging

Additional Resources

Berns, Walter F. *For Capital Punishment: Crime and the Morality of the Death Penalty*. Basic Books, 1979.

Gettinger, Stephen H. *Sentenced to Die: The People, the Crimes and the Controversy*. Macmillan, 1979. A balanced presentation.

Sellin, Johan Thorsten. *The Penalty of Death*. Sage, 1980. Against capital punishment.

CAPITAL STOCK. See Stock, Capital.

CAPITALISM is an economic system controlled chiefly by individuals and private companies instead of by the government. Under capitalism, individuals and companies own and direct most of the resources used to produce goods and services. These resources include land and other natural resources, labor, and *capital*. Capital includes factories, equipment, and money used in business activities. The term *capitalism* comes from *capital*.

Capitalism stresses private economic choices. People are free to decide how they will earn and spend their income. Companies may choose which goods and services to produce and how much to charge for them. Companies also compete with one another to sell their products. Nations whose economies are based on capitalism include the United States, Canada, West Germany, and Japan.

The government controls some aspects of the economy in every nation. But capitalism's emphasis on private economic decisions makes it different from the two other major economic systems—*Communism* and *mixed economies*. In a Communist economy, the government owns or controls most of the resources used in production and develops national plans for their use. In a mixed economy, the government does some economic planning and controls some industries, but it also allows some individual choice.

Capitalism is sometimes called *free enterprise* because it permits people to engage in economic activities largely free from government control. Other names for capitalism include *free market system*, *competitive system*, *entrepreneurial system*, and *laissez faire*.

How Capitalism Works

A number of factors influence economic decisions under capitalism. The most important factors are (1) individuals, (2) businesses, (3) the market, (4) income, and (5) the government.

Individuals influence the economy as consumers, workers, and investors. For example, if consumers show by their purchases that they prefer small cars to large cars, dealers will order more small cars and fewer large ones. Manufacturers, in turn, will step up production of small cars and cut production of large cars.

As workers, individuals may decide which jobs to prepare for and where to try to find a job. As investors, they decide how much of their income to save and how to invest their savings. Private investors provide much of the money that businesses need to grow.

Businesses decide what to produce and where to conduct their activities. They also buy the necessary equipment and hire workers. Businesses try to influence what consumers buy through advertising and by creating new and improved products.

The driving force of a capitalist economy is the desire for profits. Profits are a firm's earnings after it has paid all its expenses. The desire for profits, called the *profit motive*, ensures that companies produce the goods and services that consumers are willing and able to buy. To succeed, businesses must sell enough of their products at a price high enough to yield a profit. A firm may lose money instead of earn a profit if sales fall too low or costs run too high. The profit motive also encourages firms to operate efficiently. By saving time, energy, and materials, a company can reduce its production costs. Lower production costs can lead to greater sales and profits.

Business plays a large role in determining how fast a capitalist economy grows. An economy grows when it increases its production of goods and services. Growth requires investment in buildings, equipment, and other resources used to increase production. In a capitalist nation, businesses decide for themselves when and how much to invest for this purpose.

The Market is a term used by economists for places and situations in which people buy and sell goods and services. In a capitalist economy, the prices of goods and services are determined mainly by such market conditions as *supply and demand* and *competition*.

Supply is the amount of a good or service offered for sale. Demand is the amount that people are willing and able to buy. Prices tend to change whenever supply and demand are unequal. Generally, the market forces prices to fall when supply exceeds demand and to rise when demand exceeds supply. See Supply and Demand.

Competition exists when many producers try to sell the same kinds of products to the same buyers. Capitalist economies depend on competition to discourage companies from charging unreasonable prices. A company that charges lower prices or improves the quality of its products can take customers away from its competitors.

Without competition, a *monopoly* or *cartel* may develop. A firm has a monopoly when it supplies the total output in a market. A monopoly can limit output and raise prices because it has no fear of competition. A cartel is a group of companies that band together to control output and raise prices. Many countries have laws that prohibit monopolies and cartels.

Despite antimonopoly laws, giant corporations form near monopolies in some industries. Such firms can temporarily afford to reduce prices and accept losses.

Smaller firms that cannot afford losses cannot compete. In many capitalist nations, public utilities, such as electric, gas, and telephone companies, are allowed to operate as monopolies under government regulation. See also MONOPOLY AND COMPETITION.

Income in a capitalist economy depends chiefly on the supply of and demand for skills that society values most. People who have skills that are in scarce supply and worth a lot in the market can attract high incomes. For example, the players on a professional basketball team earn high salaries. However, the team's equipment managers earn comparatively low salaries because they contribute little to the team's earnings.

Competition among employers for workers and among workers for jobs also helps set wage rates. Businesses need to pay wages high enough to attract the workers that they need. When jobs are scarce, however, workers may accept lower wages than they would when jobs are plentiful.

Labor unions and the government also influence wages in many capitalist countries. Unions bargain with employers to establish wage scales and working conditions acceptable to their members. In addition, the United States government has established minimum wages for most workers. Government agencies also enforce safety standards.

The Government in a capitalist nation allows individuals to use their property largely as they wish and to work where they please. The government generally permits companies to set wages for their workers and prices for their products.

The government also performs a number of important economic functions. For example, it issues money, supervises public utilities, and enforces business contracts. Laws protect competition and forbid unfair business practices. Government agencies regulate standards of service in such industries as airlines, drugs, and radio and television broadcasting. The government also finances a wide variety of programs and regulates the flow of credit and money in the nation. In addition, the government can use its powers to fight such problems as inflation and unemployment.

Problems of Capitalism

Capitalism allows much personal freedom and provides a high standard of living for many people. But capitalist economies often face several problems. These problems include (1) economic instability, (2) inequalities in the distribution of wealth, and (3) neglect of the public interest.

Economic Instability. Capitalist economies experience ups and downs. Sometimes they grow rapidly and produce widespread prosperity. But economic expansion often leads to inflation and causes money to lose value. Capitalist nations also have suffered a number of severe business slumps, which have led to high unemployment. Economists and political leaders disagree on what causes swings in business activity and on how to control them. Thus, governments in capitalist countries frequently have to deal with either high inflation or rising joblessness.

Inequalities in the Distribution of Wealth. Some people in capitalist nations can afford a great many luxuries. But other people lack adequate food, housing, and other necessities. This unequal distribution of wealth results largely from capitalism's emphasis on individual economic freedom. To a great extent, people are free to enjoy—or suffer from—the results of their economic decisions. Such decisions are influenced by ability, ambition, and willingness to take risks. However, racial and sexual discrimination and differences in education and inherited wealth also contribute to inequalities in income distribution.

Some government welfare programs aid the poor in capitalist nations. But many needy persons rely on help from relatives and private charities.

Neglect of the Public Interest. Most companies in a capitalist economy try to earn as much profit as they can. But sometimes government actions are necessary to ensure that the profit motive works in the public interest. For example, low-cost housing, community health facilities, and other public services usually become profitable only with government financial support. In addition, without government regulations, many industries might pollute the air, water, or soil, rather than introduce unprofitable pollution controls. Other critics point out that a capitalist economy may waste precious natural resources in its desire to increase production and profits.

How Other Systems Differ from Capitalism

There are three main types of economic systems today—capitalism, Communism, and the mixed economy. Each system has some government control and some private choice. But capitalism relies more on private decisions and less on government planning than the other two systems do.

In a Communist Economy, the government controls nearly all the resources used in production. For example, the government owns most of the industries, land, and natural resources. It also controls trade and operates the major communication and transportation systems. Individuals and businesses make no major economic decisions. Instead, government planners decide which goods and services and how much of them should be produced. They also establish wage and price scales and determine the desired rate of economic growth.

Communism produces most goods and services less efficiently than capitalism does. Shortages and surpluses occur frequently because supply and demand have little influence on decisions. Consumers may spend their money largely as they wish, but they can choose only among the goods and services that the government makes available. Workers cannot change jobs freely. China and the Soviet Union are the largest Communist nations.

In a Mixed Economy, the government might own such important industries as coal mines, railroads, steel mills, and oil wells and refineries. But it allows private firms to own most other industries. Many countries with mixed economies tax citizens heavily but also provide extensive welfare benefits.

Most nations of the world have mixed economies. Some countries with mixed economies are democracies, including Great Britain and Sweden. In these nations, the people can vote to increase or reduce government control over the economy. The economic system of such countries with mixed economies is often called *democratic socialism.* Other countries with mixed economies are dictatorships.

History of Capitalism

From the 1400's to the 1700's, the major European trading nations used an economic system known as *mercantilism.* Under this system, governments regulated their economic affairs to ensure that exports exceeded imports. They placed high tariffs on imported goods to make them cost more at home, and gave financial aid to local farms and industries so they could lower the prices of their exports. Nations enriched their treasuries by selling more goods than they bought.

The Development of Capitalism. During the mid-1700's, a group of French economists known as *physiocrats* urged governments to stop interfering in foreign trade. Their policy, called *laissez faire,* demanded an end to tariffs and other trade restrictions.

The Scottish economist Adam Smith also argued that a nation could increase its wealth most rapidly by allowing free trade. He believed that people who followed their economic best interests would automatically act in the economic best interest of society. In his book *The Wealth of Nations* (1776), Smith described how laissez faire should work. His ideas first became influential during the early 1800's. During that period, the British government began to remove its mercantilist controls and to develop the first capitalist economy. Capitalism soon spread to other major trading nations.

Changing Attitudes Toward Capitalism began to develop during the 1800's, when new technology in industrialized nations helped create many new products. The increased production brought prosperity to many businesses. But unfavorable situations also developed. Several depressions occurred, and many workers earned low wages and labored under unhealthful conditions.

As a result of these developments, the German social philosopher Karl Marx claimed that laissez-faire capitalism would be destroyed. He predicted that owners of businesses would become wealthier while their workers grew poorer. Finally, the workers would overthrow the capitalist system. Marx was wrong in predicting that workers in capitalist economies would not share in rising standards of living. However, his ideas influenced the revolutions that led to the introduction of Communism in Russia in 1917 and in China in 1949.

Capitalism faced its most serious challenge during the Great Depression, a worldwide business slump that began in 1929. During the 1930's, many banks, factories, and stores closed. Millions of people lost their jobs, homes, and savings. Many also lost faith in capitalism, and political leaders sought new economic theories. As a result, the British economist John Maynard Keynes gained notice. In his book *General Theory of Employment, Interest, and Money* (1936), Keynes rejected the capitalists' belief that government should keep out of economic affairs. He said a nation's level of economic activity depends on the total spending of consumers, business, and government. Keynes urged increased government spending to fight the depression.

The Great Depression lasted until the early 1940's, when huge amounts of government military spending for World War II finally stimulated the world economy. Many capitalist governments continued to move away from laissez-faire policies after the war ended. Since then, they have greatly increased their spending and control of their economies. On the other hand, government leaders in some capitalist countries have tried to reduce government involvement in their economies. Even some Communist governments have begun to rely increasingly on forces in the market to distribute goods and services in their countries. WILLIAM G. DEWALD

See also ECONOMICS with its list of *Related Articles.* For a *Reading and Study Guide,* see *Capitalism* in the RESEARCH GUIDE-INDEX, Volume 22.

Additional Resources

FORMAN, JAMES D. *Capitalism: Economic Individualism to Today's Welfare State.* Watts, 1972. Historical treatment with an explanation of the contemporary system.

FRIEDMAN, MILTON and ROSE. *Free to Choose: A Personal Statement.* Harcourt, 1980. Presents the argument for free-market capitalism.

CAPITALIZATION means the use of *capital* (large) letters in writing. Capital letters are usually used at the beginnings of certain words. There are many capitalization rules in the English language.

The First Word of a sentence or direct quotation is capitalized, as in *The boy asked, "Do you think I should go?"* The first word in each line of most poems or in each part of an outline is capitalized.

Proper Nouns and words used as proper nouns are capitalized. This includes names of persons (*Mary Smith*), places (*416 Maple Street, Cincinnati, Ohio*), and particular things (*my dog, Rover*). One of the largest groupings of proper nouns includes the specific names of rivers, mountains, buildings, schools, business organizations, and commercial products.

Names of special political, social, or religious groups are capitalized, such as the *Political Action Committee* or the *Lutheran Church.* The collective name of members of a group is also capitalized, as in *Democrats* or *Lutherans.* Holidays (*Fourth of July*), days of the week (*Monday*), and months (*June*) are capitalized, but not names of seasons (*autumn*). Geographical regions are capitalized (the *West*), but not the names of geographical directions (*going west*). Names of special events in history (*Battle of the Bulge*) are capitalized, as well as names of meetings (the *Yalta Conference*), congresses (the *Seventy-Fourth Congress*), alliances (the *Holy Alliance*), and expositions (the *Golden Gate Exposition*). Periods in history are capitalized, as in the *Restoration.* Nationalities and languages are capitalized, as in *African* and *Japanese.* Names of school studies are capitalized when they refer to a specific subject (*Mathematics 2*).

Titles of persons are capitalized in certain uses. Titles that precede a name are capitalized, as in *President Woodrow Wilson.* Titles that immediately follow a name or take the place of a name are sometimes capitalized when they show high distinction, as in *Woodrow Wilson, President* or the *President.* Words that modify a proper noun and are usually used as part of that name are capitalized, as in *Frederick the Great.* Names of the Deity are always capitalized, as in *God* or *Jehovah.*

All Important Words in a Title are capitalized, including the first word.

Adjectives Taken from Proper Nouns are capitalized, such as *French* or *English.* When a prefix is used, the prefix is not capitalized, as in *un-American* or *pro-German.*

Personification means treating an object that is not human as a human being. A personified noun is capitalized, as in *Death, be not proud.*

Formal Statements begin with capital letters, as in *Resolved: That this club meet on the first of every month.*

O and I are always capitalized when used as words.

Many Abbreviations are capitalized, especially those that refer to proper names, such as *U.S.A.* for *United States of America.* See ABBREVIATION. GARY TATE

CAPITALS OF THE STATES. See UNITED STATES (table: Facts in Brief About the States).

CAPITALS OF THE UNITED STATES. See UNITED STATES CAPITALS.

CAPITOL is the government building where a legislature makes laws. *Capital* refers to the city where the building stands, while the building is the *Capitol.* The name *Capitol* comes from the *Capitolium,* the ancient temple of Jupiter in Rome. HOWARD M. DAVIS

For a description of the United States Capitol, see CAPITOL, UNITED STATES. See also pictures of state Capitols with the articles on U.S. states, such as ALABAMA.

CAPITOL, UNITED STATES, is the building where Congress meets. It stands on Capitol Hill near the center of Washington, D.C. Besides its importance as a government office building, the Capitol serves as a symbol of the United States. Each year, about 10 million people visit this famous building. Many of the rooms in the Capitol are open to the public. These rooms include the chambers where the House of Representatives and the Senate meet. Visitors may attend sessions of Congress if they have passes from their representative or senator.

The Capitol's architecture follows the classical style of ancient Rome. The building consists of two wings that extend north and south of a central section. A huge, cast-iron dome rests on the central section of the building. The dome's white-painted surface resembles the white marble exterior of the rest of the Capitol. On top of the dome stands the Statue of Freedom, 19½ feet (5.9 meters) high. The statue is the figure of a woman wearing a headdress of eagle feathers and holding a sword and shield. The distance from the top of the Statue of Freedom to the ground is almost 300 feet (91 meters).

The Capitol has 540 rooms, including visitors' galleries, offices, and reception rooms. Many rooms hold mementos of the American past as well as paintings and sculptures by some of the world's greatest artists. The Great Rotunda, which forms the center of the Capitol, consists of the circular area under the dome. It measures more than 95 feet (29 meters) in diameter and over 183 feet (56 meters) high. Funeral ceremonies for a number of American citizens have taken place in the Great Rotunda. Citizens honored in this way include Presidents Abraham Lincoln and John F. Kennedy.

The Senate wing of the Capitol extends to the north of the Great Rotunda. This wing houses the Senate Chamber, the room in which the Senate meets. The Senate Chamber has galleries where visitors may watch the Senate in session. Another room in this wing, the President's Room, is one of the most richly furnished rooms. It displays a huge, gold-plated chandelier and portraits of a number of American political leaders. The Senate wing also includes the former Supreme Court chamber, where the court met from 1810 to 1860. The room has been restored to look as it did in the 1850's.

The House of Representatives wing of the Capitol extends to the south of the Great Rotunda. This wing includes the House Chamber, the room in which the House of Representatives meets. The House Chamber, like the Senate Chamber, has galleries for visitors. The House wing also includes Statuary Hall, which exhibits statues of some outstanding Americans (see STATUARY HALL).

In 1792, the federal government held a contest for a Capitol design. William Thornton, an American doctor and amateur architect, submitted the winning entry. President George Washington laid the building's cornerstone in 1793. Congress first met in the Capitol in 1800. In 1814, during the War of 1812, British troops captured Washington, D.C., and set fire to the Capitol. Congress began meeting in the Capitol again in 1819, though workers did not finish rebuilding it until 1829. In 1863, the Capitol received a new dome and the Statue of Freedom. In 1962, builders completed a 32½-foot (9.9-meter) extension to the eastern side of the Capitol's central section.

Critically reviewed by the OFFICE OF THE ARCHITECT OF THE CAPITOL

See also CONGRESS OF THE UNITED STATES (diagram: Capitol Floor Plan); HOUSE OF REPRESENTATIVES; SENATE; WASHINGTON, D.C. (pictures; map).

CAPITOL HILL. See WASHINGTON, D.C. (A Visitor's Guide; map).

CAPITOL REEF NATIONAL PARK lies near Torrey, Utah. It includes a white-sandstone-capped ridge 20 miles (32 kilometers) long that resembles a capitol dome. The area was established as a national monument in 1937 and became a national park in 1971. For area, see NATIONAL PARK SYSTEM (table: National Parks).

CAPON. See CHICKEN (Meat Chickens).

CAPONE, *kuh POHN,* **AL** (1899?-1947), controlled the Chicago underworld in the 1920's. His gang ran most of the illegal operations in the city. They killed many rival gangsters, and were blamed for the *St. Valentine's Day Massacre* of seven men in 1929. In 1931, a federal jury convicted Capone of income tax evasion. After almost eight years in prison, he retired to his home in Miami, Fla., where he died of syphilis.

Wide World
Al Capone

There is no clear record of Capone's real name, birthdate, or birthplace. His given first name was either Alphonse or Alphonso, and his last name was Caponi or Capone. Capone insisted that he was born in Brooklyn, N.Y., but several of his biographers believe he was born in Naples, Italy, and came to the United States with his parents when he was very young. Capone became known as *Scarface Al*—a nickname he resented—after his left cheek was slashed in a fight. J. JOSEPH HUTHMACHER

CAPOTE, *kuh POH tee,* **TRUMAN** (1924-1984), an American author, was best known for *In Cold Blood*

(1966), an account of the brutal murder of a Kansas farm family. Because it combines journalistic accuracy and literary imagination, the book has been called the finest American "nonfiction novel."

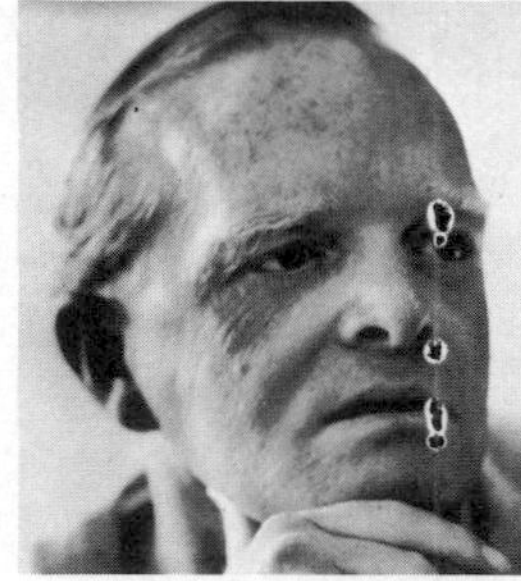
Mike Salisbury, Black Star
Truman Capote

Capote was born in New Orleans and spent most of his childhood in the South. His early novels, *Other Voices, Other Rooms* (1948) and *The Grass Harp* (1951), are set in the South. Many of their characters are eccentric, some sinister and others comic. The atmosphere is filled with grotesque, supernatural elements, and the style is vivid and fanciful. *A Tree of Night and Other Stories* (1949) makes even greater use of weird, supernatural elements. *Breakfast at Tiffany's* (1958) traces the decline of Holly Golightly, a New York City playgirl.

Capote also wrote *The Muses Are Heard* (1956), an account of his experiences with the cast of *Porgy and Bess* touring Russia. He adapted his story *House of Flowers* into a musical produced in 1954. A collection of Capote's stories and nonfiction pieces was published as *Music for Chameleons* (1980). EUGENE K. GARBER

CAPP, AL (1909-1979), an American cartoonist, created the comic strip "Li'l Abner" in 1934. Capp centered the comic strip on the humorous adventures of Li'l Abner Yokum, a hillbilly from "Dogpatch U.S.A." Other major characters included his wife Daisy Mae and his parents Mammy and Pappy Yokum. Capp often used "Li'l Abner" to satirize famous persons and events of the day. He created the character of Fearless Fosdick in "Li'l Abner" as a satire on another comic strip character, detective Dick Tracy.

Capp was born in New Haven, Conn. His real name was Alfred Gerald Caplin. He attended two art schools before joining the Associated Press as a cartoonist in 1932. He helped create the comic strip "Abbie an' Slats" in 1937 and created another strip, "Long Sam," in 1954. ROY PAUL NELSON

See also SATIRE.

CAPRA, *KAP ruh,* **FRANK** (1897-   ), is an American motion-picture director. He became noted for his comedies dealing with the individual's fight against corruption in society. These comedies include *Mr. Deeds Goes to Town* (1936), *You Can't Take It with You* (1938), *Mr. Smith Goes to Washington* (1939), and *State of the Union* (1948). Capra won Academy Awards for his direction of *Mr. Deeds Goes to Town, You Can't Take It with You,* and *It Happened One Night* (1934). He also directed *Lost Horizon* (1937), *Meet John Doe* (1941), *Arsenic and Old Lace* (1942), and *It's A Wonderful Life* (1946). During World War II, he produced the *Why We Fight* series for the United States Army.

Capra was born in Palermo, Sicily, and moved to the United States at the age of six. He studied chemical engineering in California before entering the motion-picture industry in 1923. Capra directed comedian Harry Langdon's best silent films, including *Tramp, Tramp, Tramp* (1926). His autobiography, *The Name Above the Title,* was published in 1971. HARVEY R. DENEROFF

CAPRI, *KAH pree* or *kuh PREE* (pop. 12,144), is an Italian island in the Bay of Naples. Its climate and scenery attract thousands of visitors. The famous Blue Grotto is a wave-cut cave that is filled with a sapphire-blue coloring when the sun shines through its waters. For the location of Capri, see ITALY (physical map).

The island covers about 4 square miles (10 square kilometers). Mount Solaro (1,932 feet, or 589 meters) is the highest point. The capital, which is also named Capri, lies in the eastern part of the island. The town of Anacapri, in the western portion, is 738 feet (225 meters) above sea level. It stands on a plateau. Products of the island include red and white wine, olive oil, and fruits. In Greek mythology, Capri was the home of the lovely maidens called the Sirens, whose music enchanted Ulysses and his sailors. The Roman emperors Augustus and Tiberius built splendid palaces on Capri. BENJAMIN WEBB WHEELER

CAPRICORN, *KAP ruh kawrn,* is the 10th sign of the zodiac. Its symbol is a goat. Astrologers believe the planet Saturn rules Capricorn. They consider Saturn to have a stern influence. Capricorn is an earth sign.

According to astrologers, people born under the sign of Capricorn, from December 22 to January 19, take life seriously and do not have much of a sense of humor. They overcome hardship well and enjoy the challenge

Signs of the Zodiac

Aries
Mar. 21–Apr. 19
Taurus
Apr. 20–May 20
Gemini
May 21–June 20
Cancer
June 21–July 22
Leo
July 23–Aug. 22
Virgo
Aug. 23–Sept. 22
Libra
Sept. 23–Oct. 22
Scorpio
Oct. 23–Nov. 21
Sagittarius
Nov. 22–Dec. 21
Capricorn
Dec. 22–Jan. 19
Aquarius
Jan. 20–Feb. 18
Pisces
Feb. 19–Mar. 20

WORLD BOOK illustration by Robert Keys

of difficult problems. Capricorns do not rush into friendships, but they remain loyal after their confidence has been gained.

Capricorns behave with dignity and do not like to hurry. Their stubbornness often leads them to insist that their opinions are right. They can sometimes be too stern. CHRISTOPHER MCINTOSH

See also ASTROLOGY; HOROSCOPE; ZODIAC (diagram: The Signs of the Zodiac).

CAPRICORN, TROPIC OF. See TROPIC OF CAPRICORN.

CAPS AND GOWNS are the official and traditional costumes for students in many nations. In most cases,

WORLD BOOK photo courtesy Collegiate Cap & Gown Company

High School Graduates of many schools wear caps and gowns to add dignity and color to their commencement ceremonies.

students wear caps and gowns only at graduation exercises and on special occasions. A student wears a long, full-flowing robe and a skullcap attached to a stiff square piece called a *mortarboard.* A tassel dangles from the center of the mortarboard. In addition to the cap and gown, a college graduate wears a cape or hood that is lined with colored silk and trimmed with velvet.

Most collegiate caps, gowns, and hoods are black. The cut of the robe and its sleeves, as well as its trimming, indicate various academic degrees. The color of the hood's silk lining indicates the school that conferred the degree. The velvet binding of the hood indicates the graduate's field of study. The tassel may be black or the color that represents the graduate's field. Some schools have graduates change their tassel from the right side to the left after receiving their diploma. In the United States, the Intercollegiate Commission set the standards for academic costume in 1894.

Doctor's Degree. A doctor wears a gown with full, round sleeves. The gown shows velvet facings on the front. Three velvet bars decorate the sleeves. The color of the gown's velvet trim indicates the doctor's field of study. A doctor wears a 4-foot (122-centimeter) silk hood with a velvet binding that is 5 inches (13 centimeters) wide.

Master's Degree. A master wears a gown with full-length square sleeves. A crescent-shaped piece hangs down from each sleeve. The gown has no velvet trim. The $3\frac{1}{2}$-foot (107-centimeter) hood has velvet bindings that are 3 inches (8 centimeters) wide.

Bachelor's Degree. A bachelor wears a gown with long, pointed sleeves and a single button at the neck. It has no velvet trim. Women wear white collars. Bachelors wear hoods 3 feet (91 centimeters) long, with velvet edging 2 inches (5 centimeters) wide.

History. During the 1100's, men and women wore gowns and hoods as everyday clothing. Styles have changed over the years, but Oxford University still has its students wear gowns and hoods. The costume implies that the students are individuals of learning, dignity, and maturity, who are not affected by passing fads and changing tastes.

Early American colleges and universities followed the

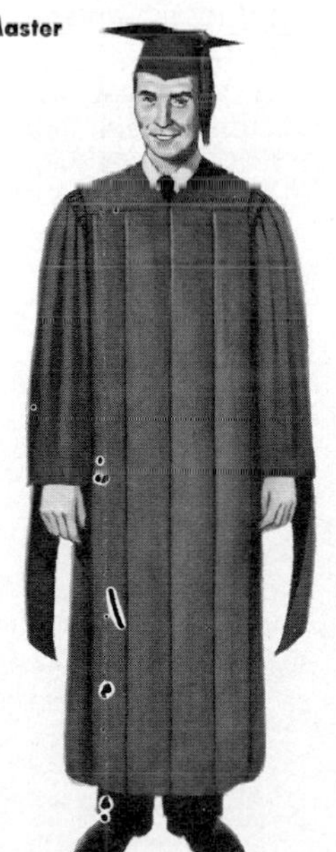

Styles of Gowns worn by college graduates show whether a person holds a bachelor's, master's, or doctor's degree. The colors on the gown's hood indicate the graduate's school and field of study.

same customs in regard to dress. American students liked caps and gowns as a simple, dignified, and economical dress for graduation ceremonies. Since 1900, caps and gowns have increased in popularity for use at high school and grammar school graduations. High school caps and gowns are usually blue-gray or blue. Girls sometimes wear white gowns. E. R. MOORE

CAPSICUM, *KAP sih kum*, is the name of a group of small, shrubby plants that grow in tropical America. They have long, pointed leaves and bear wheel-shaped flowers that have five petals. Most fruits of capsicum plants are called peppers and are used as food.

Douglas Dawn

Capsicum

Cayenne, or red pepper, is made from the dried fruits of two kinds of capsicum plants. These plants can be grown in colder climates. Cayenne has a strong, burning taste. Other capsicum fruits are used in making sauces and mixed pickles. A Hungarian seasoning called *paprika* is made from other kinds of capsicum fruits that taste milder. A few types of capsicum fruits are used in various forms to treat neuralgia, rheumatism, and sore throat.

Scientific Classification. Capsicum plants are in the nightshade family, *Solanaceae*. Cayenne is genus *Capsicum*, species *C. frutescens*. HAROLD NORMAN MOLDENKE

See also CAYENNE PEPPER; NIGHTSHADE; PAPRIKA; PEPPER.

CAPSULE. See SPACE TRAVEL (table: Space Travel Terms; pictures).

CAPTAIN. See RANK IN ARMED SERVICES.

CAPTAIN JACK (1837-1873) was a leader of the Modoc Indians. He led his tribe against the United States Army during the Modoc War (1872-1873).

The tribe lived in the Lost River Valley, on the California-Oregon border. In 1864, the government moved the Modocs to the Klamath reservation in Oregon, but they could not support themselves there. Captain Jack led part of his tribe back to the Lost River Valley in 1872.

Fighting broke out when the Army tried to force the Modocs to return to the reservation. The Indians fled to an area near Tule Lake in California. At a peace council, Captain Jack killed General E. R. S. Canby when the general said he could not withdraw his troops from the area. Captain Jack fled, but the Army captured and hanged him.

Smithsonian Institution National Anthropological Archives, Washington, D.C.

Captain Jack

Captain Jack was born near what is now Tulelake, Calif. His Indian name was *Kintpuash*. W. JEAN HURTADO

CAPTAIN KIDD. See KIDD, WILLIAM.

CAPUCHIN, *KAP yu chihn* or *KAP yu shihn*, or SAPAJOU, is a type of monkey that lives in Central and South America. Some zoologists consider capuchins the most intelligent New World monkeys. Capuchins have a dark patch of hair on top of their head that resembles a *capuche* (monk's hood).

There are four species of capuchins, all of which have white or beige hair on their face. Three species also have white or beige hair on their chest and upper arms, and black or brown body hair elsewhere. The fourth species has brown or black body hair, and tufts of black hair on the top of the head. A capuchin measures about 17 inches (43 centimeters) long, not including the tail, which is about 18 inches (46 centimeters) long. It weighs about 5 pounds (2.2 kilograms).

Capuchins live in tropical forests from Honduras to Paraguay. They spend most of their time in the trees but may come to the ground during the day. Capuchins eat fruit, seeds, insects, and occasionally small backboned animals, such as lizards and young squirrels.

Capuchins live in groups of 5 to 30 or more monkeys. Each group has about the same number of young and adults, with two or three times as many adult females as adult males. A female capuchin gives birth about six months after mating. She has one baby every one or two years. Young capuchins form social ties with one another while playing. The adults, especially the females, spend much time grooming one another's fur. Capuchins enjoy this physical contact, and it helps preserve social ties among the adult members of the group.

New York Zoological Society

The Capuchin is regarded by some zoologists as one of the most intelligent members of the monkey family.

Scientific Classification. Capuchins are genus *Cebus* of the New World monkey family, Cebidae. The tufted species is *C. apella*. The untufted species are *C. capucinus*, *C. albifrons*, and *C. nigrivittatus*. JOHN R. OPPENHEIMER

See also MONKEY.

CAPUCHINS are members of the Roman Catholic order of friars of the same name. The order was founded in 1525. The Capuchins form a branch of the Order of Saint Francis. Their name comes from the pointed hood, or *capuche,* that is part of their brown or gray habit. According to the rules of the order, they must live by charity, and use no gold, silver, or silk about their altars. They are noted for the piety and simplicity of their religious teaching. With the Jesuits, they were among the most effective preachers and missionaries of the Roman Catholic Church in the 1500's. There are Capuchin monasteries in Milwaukee, New York, Pittsburgh, and other cities in the United States. See also FRIAR. FULTON J. SHEEN

CAPULIN MOUNTAIN NATIONAL MONUMENT is in northeastern New Mexico. The mountain is a cinder cone of geologically recent formation. It rises 8,215 feet (2,504 meters) above sea level and 1,500 feet (457 meters) above the surrounding plain. It has a rim diameter of 1,450 feet (442 meters). The monument was established in 1916. For area, see NATIONAL PARK SYSTEM (table: National Monuments).

CAPYBARA, *KAP ih BAH ruh,* is the largest of all rodents. It grows up to 4 feet (1.2 meters) long and may weigh over 100 pounds (45 kilograms). It lives in eastern Panama and in South America east of the Andes.

Robert Wright, NAS

The Capybara is the largest rodent in the world. It may weigh more than 100 pounds (45 kilograms). Capybaras live in groups.

The capybara looks like a small pig or a large guinea pig. Its thick body is covered with coarse hair that is reddish-brown or gray on its upper parts and yellowish-brown on its under parts. The animal has a large head with a blunt, square muzzle, and a short tail. Its hind legs are somewhat longer than its front legs. The capybara has webbed toes and swims well. It grazes near lakes and rivers, and plunges into the water at any sign of danger. Some people call the capybara a *water pig* or *water hog*.

In prehistoric times, capybaras lived in southeastern North America. They are a favorite food of jaguars.

Scientific Classification. Capybaras are in the Capybara family, Hydrochoeridae. They are genus *Hydrochoerus,* species *H. hydrochaeris.* DANIEL BRANT

CAR. See AUTOMOBILE; CABLE CAR; RAILROAD (Passenger and Freight Cars; pictures); STREETCAR.

CARABAO, *KAH rah BAH oh,* is a water buffalo of the Philippine Islands. It is a little smaller than the Indian water buffalo, which is often 6 feet (1.8 meters) high. The carabao is a slaty bluish-black, and becomes almost hairless when old. A slow animal, it will not work in the heat of the day. But it will travel through bogs and marshes where no other large animal can pass. Like the Indian buffalo, the carabao loves the water and is a good swimmer. This animal is fearless in the wild state. When wounded it becomes dangerous, and charges fiercely with great speed. In the Philippines, people tame the carabao and use it to draw carts and carry loads. Some farmers use tame carabaos to cultivate rice fields. See also WATER BUFFALO.

Bern Keating, Black Star

The Faithful Carabao, or Water Buffalo, is the most common beast of burden in the Philippine rice fields.

Scientific Classification. The carabao is a member of the bovid family, Bovidae, and is classified as *Bubalus bubalis.* DONALD F. HOFFMEISTER

CARACAL, *KAR uh kal,* sometimes called *Persian lynx,* is a member of the cat family related to the lynxes. It lives in India, and is also found in many places

W. Suschitzky

The Caracal Lives in India and Many Parts of Africa.

throughout Africa. Like the lynxes, the caracal has tufts of long hair on the tips of its ears. The lynx has brown tufts, but the caracal's are black. The caracal has reddish-brown body fur. It is one of the *Carnivora*, a group that eats meat and hunts other animals. Its fur is never used in women's coats, and should not be confused with *caracul*, a commonly used fur that comes from the karakul, a breed of Asiatic sheep. See also LYNX.

Scientific Classification. Caracals are in the cat family, Felidae. They are species *Lynx caracal*. HAROLD E. ANTHONY

CARACARA, *KAHR uh KAHR uh*, is the name given to several large birds of South and Central America and the southern United States. They often eat the dead of other animals as vultures do, but they also capture and kill small animals. They have long legs and some caracaras can run faster than most birds.

Cruickshank, NAS

Caracara

Scientific Classification. Caracaras are members of the caracara and falcon family, Falconidae. The common caracara is classified as species *Polyborus tharus*. JOSEPH J. HICKEY

See also FALCON AND FALCONRY.

CARACAS, *kuh RAH kuhs*, (pop. 1,279,600; met. area pop. 2,755,000) is the capital, largest city, and economic center of Venezuela. It lies in a narrow valley in far northern Venezuela, about 7 miles (11 kilometers) inland from La Guaira, a port on the Caribbean Sea. For location, see VENEZUELA (political map).

The City. Caracas is one of the most modern cities in Latin America. Since the 1950's, many new high-rise office and apartment buildings have been erected throughout the city. This construction boom and a rapidly growing population have changed Caracas from a quiet colonial city to a crowded, busy urban center. Traffic jams occur frequently, and the city's water and power systems sometimes break down.

Caracas still has a few sections that date from its colonial period, which lasted from the 1500's to the 1800's. Much of what remains of these older sections is in the center of the city, near an attractive park called the Plaza Bolívar. The old buildings in this area include the gold-domed Venezuelan Capitol, a historic cathedral, and City Hall. A few blocks from the plaza is the Miraflores Palace, a beautifully decorated old building that houses the offices of the president and his chief advisers. Caracas has several museums that feature art, natural history, and other subjects. The Central University of Venezuela is nearby.

Many of Caracas' middle-class residents live in high-rise apartment buildings. Most of the wealthier families live in large, traditional Spanish-style houses. Many poor people live in slums called *barrios*, which consist of flimsy shacks built on the slopes of mountains that surround the city.

Economy. The commercial life of Caracas is based on the activities of the Venezuelan government. Most of the city's people work for government agencies, in government construction projects, or in the government-owned oil industry. Caracas produces such products as beer, cement, paper, and textiles.

Modern highways serve the major residential and business areas of Caracas. The *Autopista*, or Caracas-La Guaira Expressway, winds through steep mountains and connects Caracas with La Guaira, its port.

History. Caracas was founded in 1567 by Spaniards who came to the Western Hemisphere in search of gold. Venezuela gained independence from Spain in 1821, and Caracas became the capital in 1829. Since the 1920's, Venezuela has been an important oil producer and has steadily gained wealth. Throughout this period, especially since the 1950's, the government has used income from the oil industry to make Caracas a modern city. Through the years, new jobs became available in Caracas and attracted large numbers of people. The city's population has almost doubled since the early 1960's. NATHAN A. HAVERSTOCK

See also VENEZUELA (pictures).

CARACUL. See KARAKUL.

CARAMANLIS, *kahr uh MAHN lees*, **CONSTANTINE** (1907-), also spelled *Karamanlis*, is a Greek political leader. He served as prime minister of Greece from 1955 to 1963 and from 1974 to 1980. In 1980, he became president. During Caramanlis' terms as prime minister, Greece maintained close ties with the United States. His first term as prime minister was a period of political stability that brought much economic development to Greece.

Caramanlis was born in Prote, near Serrai, and received a law degree from Athens University in 1932. He won election to the Greek parliament in every election from 1935 to 1963.

In 1963, following a minor dispute with King Paul of Greece, Caramanlis resigned as prime minister. He went into voluntary exile after his political party lost the election that year. He returned from exile and became prime minister in 1974 after Greek military leaders asked him to form a civilian government. The military government had resigned following the Turkish invasion of Cyprus. Caramanlis retained his office through elections in 1974 and 1977. In 1980, he resigned as prime minister and was elected president. The president has less involvement in government operations than does the prime minister. KEITH R. LEGG

United Press Int.

Constantine Caramanlis

CARAT, *KAR uht*, is a measure used by jewelers in weighing precious stones and pearls. The term is derived from the Arabic *carat*, meaning a *bean* or *seed*. In ancient times, the seeds of coral trees and carob trees were used as weights for precious stones. The stones were described as being of so many "beans' weight" or "carats." The metric carat weighs 200 milligrams, or 0.2 gram. It equals 3.086 troy grains, or 0.00705 avoirdupois ounce.

The term is also used to express the amount of gold

The Louvre, Paris

Caravaggio's Paintings are noted for realism and emphasis on light and shadow. *The Fortune Teller, left,* was one of his early works, completed in the mid-1590's. In his later paintings, Caravaggio concentrated on religious subjects.

in an alloy. In this sense, the word is spelled *karat* in most Western countries except Great Britain. A karat is $\frac{1}{24}$ of the total weight of the alloy. For example, an 18-karat gold ring has 18 parts gold and 6 parts alloy. Pure gold is 24 karats. E. G. STRAUS

See also ALLOY; DIAMOND; GOLD.

CARAVAGGIO, *KAH rah VAHD joh,* **MICHELANGELO MERISI DA** (1573-1610), was an Italian painter known for the powerful realism of his religious pictures. Caravaggio refused to idealize his religious figures in the tradition of earlier European art. He supposedly used peasants and people from the streets as models for his unorthodox interpretations of Biblical stories.

In most of his paintings, Caravaggio grouped his figures against a plain, dark background and spotlighted them with an intense, revealing light. An example of his style, *The Supper at Emmaus,* is reproduced in color in the PAINTING article. Caravaggio's realistic approach influenced such artists as Peter Paul Rubens and Diego Velázquez and helped establish the baroque movement in European art (see BAROQUE).

Caravaggio's real name was Michelangelo Merisi. He named himself after his birthplace, the northern Italian town of Caravaggio. ROBERT F. REIFF

See also BACCHUS (picture); PAINTING (The 1600's and 1700's).

CARAVAN is the term used in Britain and the Commonwealth for a house trailer. See TRAILER.

CARAVAN, *KAR uh van,* is a long train of people and pack animals that travels through wild or barren country. The name comes from the Persian word for *people* or *army.* Caravans protect the people in them against the hazards of travel. Among the animals used for caravans are camels, mules, and llamas. Caravans of as many as 5,000 camels once brought goods out of Persia, China, and India to ports for shipment to Europe. JOHN H. WHITE

See also GOBI (picture: The Gobi).

CARAVEL was a type of ship used by Columbus on his first voyage across the Atlantic and by Spanish and Portuguese sailors of the 1500's and 1600's. Some caravels, used for fishing and coastal shipping, weighed about 10 long tons (10.2 metric tons). Those used for ocean voyages weighed about 50 long tons (51 metric tons). The ocean caravel had a high structure at the bow called the *forecastle.* A higher structure of two decks at the stern was called the *sterncastle.* The true caravel had four masts. The foremast carried square sails, and the other three carried *lateen,* or triangular sails. Three-masted caravels like Columbus' *Niña* and *Pinta* usually had square sails on the first two masts and lateen sails on the rear mast. The flagship of Columbus, the *Santa María,* was larger than a caravel and had a deck amid-

WORLD BOOK illustration by Richard Fickle

A Caravel Had a Two-Deck Structure at Its Stern.

ships. It was called a *nao* (ship). See also COLUMBUS, CHRISTOPHER. ROBERT H. BURGESS

CARAWAY, *KAR uh way*, an herb of the parsley family, is famous for its spicy seeds. Caraway seeds are used to flavor pastry and some kinds of cheese. The plants grow in Europe, Asia, and in the northern United States. See also HERB (picture).

Scientific Classification. Caraway belongs to the parsley family, *Umbelliferae*. It is classified as genus *Carum*, species *C. carvi*. HAROLD NORMAN MOLDENKE

CARAWAY, HATTIE OPHELIA WYATT (1878-1950), was the first woman elected to the United States Senate. Caraway, a Democrat, was also the first woman to head a Senate committee. In 1943, she became the first woman to preside over a Senate session.

Arkansas History Commission

Hattie Caraway

Hattie Wyatt was born and raised on a farm near Bakersville, Tenn., southwest of Waverly. She received a B.A. degree from Dickson Normal School. In 1920, her husband, Thaddeus, a lawyer, was elected to the U.S. Senate from Arkansas. He died in 1931, and Governor Harvey Parnell of Arkansas appointed Caraway to replace her husband. In a special election in January 1932, she was elected to serve the remaining year of the term. In November 1932, she was reelected to a full six-year term.

Caraway served in the Senate from 1931 to 1945. She was defeated in a Democratic primary election for her Senate seat in 1944. JUNE SOCHEN

CARBAMIDE. See UREA.

CARBERRY, JOHN JOSEPH CARDINAL (1904-), served as the Roman Catholic archbishop of St. Louis from 1968 until he resigned in 1979. He was appointed a cardinal by Pope Paul VI in 1969.

Cardinal Carberry was born in Brooklyn, N.Y. He was ordained a priest in 1929 after studying at Cathedral College in New York City, and in Rome. From 1956 to 1965, he served as bishop coadjutor and then bishop of Lafayette, Ind. In 1965, he became bishop of Columbus, Ohio. THOMAS P. NEILL

CARBIDE, *KAHR byd*, is a chemical compound made up of carbon and a metal. Iron carbide consists of carbon and iron. Different amounts of carbon in iron change the properties of the iron. Pig iron, wrought iron, and steel contain iron carbides made up of different amounts of carbon, and so have different properties. Calcium carbide contains carbon and calcium. Industry uses it to make products such as acetylene gas and calcium cyanamide. See also CARBON.

CARBINE, *KAHR byn* or *KAHR been*, is a short, lightweight rifle. It weighs about five pounds, or about half as much as the U.S. Army's M1 rifle. Carbines shoot much farther and more accurately than a pistol, but only half as far as an M1. Carbines are being replaced by the M14 and M16 rifles. The early carbines were short muskets. By World War I, few carbines were in use, but they were used in World War II as gas-operated semiautomatic weapons that were similar to the Garand rifle. See also GARAND RIFLE. JOHN D. BILLINGSLEY

CARBOHYDRATE is one of three main classes of foods essential to the body. The others are fats and proteins. Carbohydrates include all sugars and starches and also some other substances, such as cellulose and glycogen. They are the main source of energy for animals and plants.

Carbohydrates are made during *photosynthesis*, the process by which green plants make food. Animals obtain carbohydrates by eating these plants or other animals. Animals and plants also store carbohydrates for future use. All carbohydrates contain the chemical elements carbon, hydrogen, and oxygen.

Carbohydrates make up about 45 per cent of the total number of calories in a well-balanced diet. Foods high in carbohydrate content include bananas, bread, corn, macaroni, potatoes, and rice. Some sources of carbohydrates, such as fruits, vegetables, and whole cereal grains, also contain important amounts of vitamins and minerals.

Most candy and soft drinks have a high sugar content. However, they serve only as a source of energy for the body and so do not provide the health benefits of other carbohydrate foods.

Kinds of Carbohydrates. There are two kinds of carbohydrates, *simple* and *complex*. Simple carbohydrates have a simple molecular structure. Complex carbohydrates have a complicated molecular structure that consists of simple carbohydrates joined together in long chains.

Simple Carbohydrates. There are two kinds of simple carbohydrates, *monosaccharides* and *disaccharides*, and all are sugars. Monosaccharides are simple sugars. A disaccharide consists of two monosaccharides.

The principal monosaccharides include *glucose*, *fructose*, and *galactose*. Glucose, a mildly sweet sugar, is the most important carbohydrate in the blood. It is also called *blood sugar*. Fructose, an extremely sweet sugar, comes from fruits and vegetables. Large amounts of both glucose and fructose are in honey. Galactose occurs in food only as part of a disaccharide called lactose.

Among the most important disaccharides are *sucrose*, *lactose*, and *maltose*. Sucrose is table sugar. A molecule of sucrose consists of a molecule of glucose linked to a molecule of fructose. Much sucrose comes from sugar cane and the juices of the sugar beet plant. Pure sucrose has an extremely sweet taste and almost no odor. Lactose, also called *milk sugar*, makes up about 5 per cent of cow's milk. A molecule of lactose consists of a molecule of glucose and a molecule of galactose. Maltose, or *malt sugar*, remains after the brewing process. It is used to flavor some candy. A molecule of maltose consists of two molecules of glucose.

Complex Carbohydrates, also called *polysaccharides*, are made up of many monosaccharides. Polysaccharides include *starch*, *cellulose*, and *glycogen*. A molecule of starch consists of hundreds or even thousands of glucose molecules joined end to end. It is the chief form of carbohydrate stored by plants. Starch occurs in such foods as beans, corn, potatoes, and wheat. Molecules of cellulose and glycogen, like those of starch, consist of many glucose molecules. Cellulose makes up much of the cell walls of plants. Glycogen, sometimes

Carbon
Oxygen
Hydrogen

A monosaccharide molecule of glucose

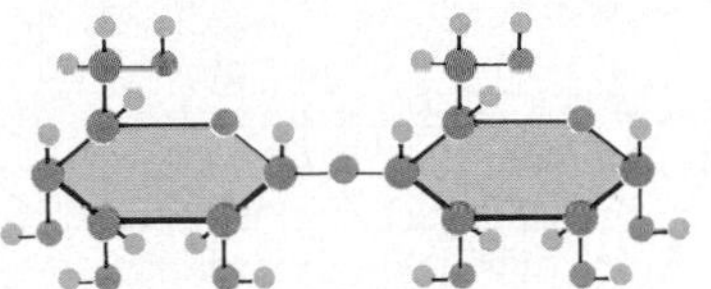

A disaccharide molecule of maltose

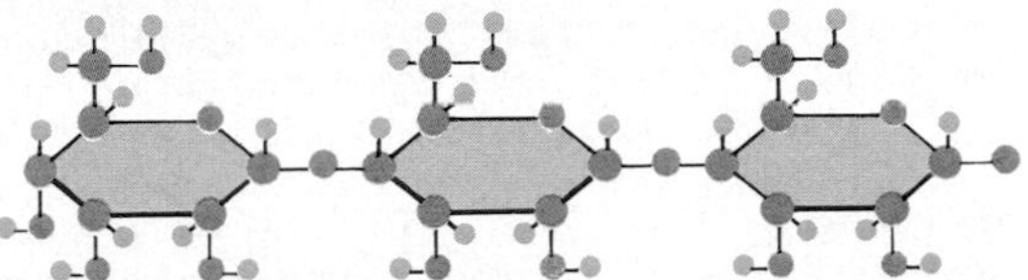

Part of a polysaccharide molecule of starch

WORLD BOOK diagram

Carbohydrates consist of carbon, oxygen, and hydrogen atoms arranged in "building blocks" called *saccharides.* A *monosaccharide* consists of only one saccharide. A *disaccharide* is made up of two saccharides, and a *polysaccharide* has hundreds or more.

called *animal starch,* is the chief form of stored carbohydrate in animals.

How the Body Uses Carbohydrates. Carbohydrates are used by the body as fuel. However, only monosaccharides can enter the bloodstream directly from the digestive system. Disaccharides and starch must be digested in the small intestine before the body can use them. For example, sucrose must first be broken down into glucose and fructose. Lactose must be broken down into glucose and galactose. Starch has to be broken down first into maltose and then into glucose.

After carbohydrates have been broken down into simple sugars in the small intestine, the blood transports them to the liver. The liver changes fructose and galactose into glucose, which is carried by the blood to all the cells of the body. The cells use glucose as fuel for the muscles and nerves and to build and repair body tissues. The liver changes excess glucose into glycogen and stores it. When the level of sugar in the blood is low, the liver changes glycogen back into glucose and releases it into the blood. Glycogen is also stored in the muscles as an emergency reserve of energy. Some of this glycogen is changed back into glucose when the body needs energy quickly.

Cellulose differs from most other carbohydrates because it cannot be digested by the human body and has no food value. However, certain amounts of it are useful. Cellulose helps maintain the health and tone of the intestines and thus aids digestion. Cattle, goats, and many other animals that eat plants have bacteria in their digestive systems that break down cellulose. The bodies of such animals use the digested cellulose as fuel.

RICHARD A. AHRENS

Related Articles in WORLD BOOK include:

Bread	Glucose	Saccharides	Sucrose
Cellulose	Glycogen	Starch	Sugar
Dextrose	Nutrition		

CARBOLIC ACID. See ANTISEPTIC (History).

CARBON is one of the most important chemical elements. Industry uses it in a wide variety of products, and all living things contain carbon. Yet carbon makes up less than 0.03 per cent of the earth's crust.

Forms of Carbon. Pure carbon exists in nature in the form of *diamonds,* and in *graphite,* such as that used in some lead pencils. Both forms are pure carbon with different crystal structures. Another form of pure carbon, called *amorphous carbon,* consists of graphitelike particles too tiny to see without a microscope.

Diamonds and graphite have important industrial uses. But much of the carbon used in industry is amorphous carbon. Amorphous carbon and ash result when materials containing carbon are burned or heated without enough oxygen for them to burn completely. For example, if oil, natural gas, or other petroleum fuels are burned in limited supplies of air, a powdery-black soot of amorphous carbon, called *carbon black,* is formed. Carbon black is also called *lampblack, gas black,* or *channel black.* It is used in rubber products and paint.

Animal charcoal or *bone charcoal,* also called *boneblack,* results from heating bones without exposing them to air. *Wood charcoal* results from heating wood without enough air to burn it completely. The various kinds of charcoal are used to remove the brown color from sugar and to filter impurities and odors from the air. Charcoal is also used as a cooking fuel.

Coke, an important fuel used in making steel, results from heating soft coal without oxygen, as in making charcoal. *Ivory black,* made by heating ivory, is sometimes used as a *pigment* (coloring matter) in paint.

Occurrence. Most carbon occurs in combination with other elements. For example, the carbon dioxide in the air is a compound of carbon and oxygen. Other compounds containing carbon include minerals such as limestone (calcium carbonate), and fuels such as coal and petroleum. Carbon compounds make up the living tissues of all animals and plants. There are about 1 million known carbon compounds. These compounds combine in various ways to produce an almost unlimited number of carbon-containing substances. Organic chemistry is primarily the study of carbon compounds.

Properties. The forms of pure carbon vary widely depending upon which crystal structure the atoms take. In diamond, the carbon atoms are arranged in a close framework that makes diamond one of the hardest substances known. Diamonds are used to cut other hard materials. In contrast, graphite is so soft that it can be used to lubricate moving machine parts. Its carbon atoms are arranged in flat sheets or layers that can easily slide back and forth over each other.

At room temperature, pure carbon does not react chemically, but its compounds unite easily with other elements and compounds. Pure carbon will not dissolve in any common solvent. At higher temperatures, carbon combines with oxygen, sulfur, certain metals, and elements of the halogen group. Carbon also forms many organic compounds which usually contain hydrogen and may contain other elements.

Carbon has the chemical symbol C. It does not melt, but it *sublimes* at about 3500° C. That is, it changes from a solid directly to a gas. Carbon's atomic number is 6 and its atomic weight is 12.01115. Its density is 2.25 grams per cubic centimeter at 20° C. Its most common *isotope* (type of atom), carbon 12, was adopted in 1961 as the standard for atomic weights with an assigned weight of 12.0000.

A radioactive isotope called carbon 14 provides archaeologists with a method of finding the age of many ancient objects. See RADIOCARBON. STANLEY KIRSCHNER

Related Articles in WORLD BOOK include:

Bitumen	Carbon Tetrachloride	Diamond
Carbide	Carbonate	Graphite
Carbohydrate	Charcoal	Hydrocarbon
Carbon Dioxide	Chemistry	Iron and Steel
Carbon Disulfide	Coal	
Carbon Monoxide	Coke	

CARBON 14. See RADIOCARBON.

CARBON BISULFIDE. See CARBON DISULFIDE.

CARBON BLACK. See CARBON.

CARBON DATING. See RADIOCARBON.

CARBON DIOXIDE is an odorless, colorless, and tasteless gas. Human beings and animals inhale oxygen and exhale the carbon dioxide that is produced by *oxidizing* (burning) food in their bodies. Green plants take carbon dioxide from the air and give off oxygen when light shines on them. In the light, plants combine carbon dioxide with water to make food.

Carbon dioxide has many everyday uses. For example, cakes rise in an oven because baking powder or yeast in the cake batter releases carbon dioxide. Carbon dioxide produces the fizz or sparkle in soft drinks, beer, and sparkling wines. Some fire extinguishers use carbon dioxide because it will not burn and it can put out fires. Carbon dioxide settles over a fire and shuts off the supply of oxygen in the air that a fire must have to burn. It does this because it is over one and a half times as *dense* (heavy) as air.

Because of its higher density, carbon dioxide sometimes collects in the bottom of wells, silos, caves, and mines. These places can be dangerous to humans and animals because a concentration of carbon dioxide will suffocate them. The carbon dioxide itself is not poisonous, but it cuts off necessary supplies of oxygen.

Carbon dioxide is useful in other forms. It becomes a solid when cooled to −109.3° F. (−78.5° C) at atmospheric pressure. This solid is called *dry ice* because it does not melt to form a liquid as frozen water does. Instead, it changes directly back to a gas. This process, in which a solid changes to a gas without first becoming a liquid, is called *sublimation*. Carbon dioxide is also known as *carbonic-acid gas* because it produces a weak acid when dissolved in water.

Carbon dioxide is produced when wood, oil, gasoline, or any fuel containing carbon burns with a large supply of oxygen. If fuels containing carbon burn without enough oxygen, they produce carbon monoxide. Decaying plants and animals give off carbon dioxide. The air is about 0.035 per cent carbon dioxide.

Carbon dioxide molecules contain one atom of carbon and two of oxygen. The chemical formula of carbon dioxide is CO_2. The gas was discovered in the early 1600's by Jan Baptista van Helmont, a Belgian chemist and physician. A. L. Lavoisier discovered its composition in 1781. STANLEY KIRSCHNER

See also DRY ICE; FIRE EXTINGUISHER; PHOTOSYNTHESIS.

CARBON DISULFIDE, or CARBON BISULFIDE is a colorless, inflammable liquid. It has a pleasant odor when pure, but usually contains impurities which have the unpleasant odor of rotten eggs. Industries use carbon disulfide in making rayon, insecticides, and carbon tetrachloride, an important solvent. Carbon disulfide can dissolve sulfur, iodine, waxes, and India rubber.

Carbon disulfide is made by heating coke and sulfur in an electric furnace. It can also be produced by heating iron disulfide (FeS_2) and carbon. Its chemical formula is CS_2. It boils at 46.3° C and melts at −111.6° C. It is 1.27 times as dense as water. STANLEY KIRSCHNER

See also SULFIDE.

CARBON MONOXIDE is a colorless, odorless, tasteless, and extremely poisonous gas. Because it has no odor or color, persons breathing it usually fall asleep without realizing they are being poisoned. Carbon monoxide prevents *hemoglobin* (the oxygen-carrying substance in the blood) from supplying oxygen to the body. Without oxygen, people and animals soon die.

Carbon monoxide results when fuels containing carbon such as coal or oil burn in stoves or furnaces that do not contain enough oxygen. Automobile engines

Plants Absorb Carbon Dioxide exhaled by people and animals. People and animals take in oxygen given off by plants. Thus, the supply of oxygen and carbon dioxide stays fairly stable.

also produce deadly amounts of carbon monoxide. This gas contributes greatly to air pollution. U.S. automakers are required to equip vehicles with devices that reduce carbon monoxide emissions. Cigarette smoke contains a small amount of carbon monoxide. But even this small quantity can be harmful, especially to persons suffering from *arteriosclerosis* (hardening of the arteries) and a lung disease called *emphysema*.

Industry burns carbon monoxide to provide heat for manufacturing processes. The carbon monoxide is usually in a fuel gas such as water gas or producer gas. These gases are sometimes used to heat homes and to cook food (see GAS [How Gas Is Manufactured]). Carbon monoxide is also used to separate metals such as iron and nickel from their ores and to purify them. Carbon monoxide can be used to make other chemical compounds. Industry heats carbon from coal with carbon dioxide, oxygen, or water to make carbon monoxide.

The chemical formula of carbon monoxide is CO. The gas was first prepared in the laboratory in 1776 by J. M. F. de Lassone, a French chemist. Its composition was identified in 1800 by William Cruikshank, an English chemist. STANLEY KIRSCHNER

CARBON TETRACHLORIDE, *TEHT ruh KLAWR eyed,* is a clear, colorless liquid that does not burn. Industries use it to dissolve oils and rubber. They also use it to manufacture refrigerants, and to produce propellants that make liquids spray from containers.

Carbon tetrachloride was once widely used as a cleaning fluid. But inhaling its fumes can cause severe illness or death. In addition to being nonflammable, carbon tetrachloride will not mix with water, but it changes into poisonous gases when heated. In 1970, the U.S. government banned the use of carbon tetrachloride in household products.

Manufacturers make carbon tetrachloride by passing chlorine through glowing coke, or by combining chlorine with carbon disulfide or methane. Carbon tetrachloride has the chemical formula CCl_4. OTTO THEODOR BENFEY

CARBONATE, *KAHR buh nayt,* is any compound which contains the carbonate *ion*. An ion is one or a group of atoms with an electric charge. The carbonate ion has two negative charges and consists of one carbon atom and three oxygen atoms. Its chemical formula is $CO_3^{=}$. Chalk, marble, and other limestones are examples of a naturally abundant carbonate, calcium carbonate. Animal bones and teeth as well as egg and oyster shells have large amounts of calcium carbonate.

Carbonate ions combined with metal ions form the most common carbonates, including calcium carbonate. These metal carbonates can be produced by allowing a water solution of a chemical base, such as sodium hydroxide, to combine with carbon dioxide. The reaction produces a *bicarbonate* (carbonate which includes a hydrogen ion, HCO_3^-). A carbonate compound results from heating a bicarbonate compound. For example, common washing soda (sodium carbonate, Na_2CO_3) results from heating baking soda (sodium bicarbonate, $NaHCO_3$). STANLEY KIRSCHNER

See also CALCIUM CARBONATE; SODA.

CARBONIC-ACID GAS. See CARBON DIOXIDE.

CARBONIFEROUS PERIOD. See EARTH (table: Outline of Earth History).

CARBORUNDUM, *KAHR buh RUHN duhm* (chemical formula, SiC), is a trade name for silicon carbide, an abrasive. It is prepared from sand and carbon. Carborundum is almost as hard as a diamond, and is one of the most important abrasives used for grinding and cutting hard materials such as metal. Carborundum grains are sometimes pressed together to make grinding wheels. They may also be glued to cloth or paper to make sheets or belts used for polishing, grinding, and sanding. In electronics, resistors known as *thermistors* are often made of silicon carbide. Carborundum is also used as a furnace lining. ARTHUR C. ANSLEY

CARBUNCLE, *KAHR buhng kuhl,* is a painful infection of the skin and tissues just under the skin. A carbuncle is a warm, tender, dark red lump that looks like a group of boils. Carbuncles most often develop on the back of the neck. They usually break through the skin in several places and discharge pus.

Carbuncles are caused by a type of bacteria called *staphylococci*. The bacteria enter through the opening around a hair or through a break in the skin. They multiply and move into deeper tissues. Carbuncles are most common in elderly or malnourished individuals. They also affect people who suffer from diabetes and certain other *chronic* (long-term) diseases.

Carbuncles are dangerous because the infection can spread through the bloodstream to other parts of the body. They should be treated by a physician. Antibiotics can cure most carbuncles. YELVA LIPTZIN LYNFIELD

See also ABSCESS; BOIL.

CARBURETOR, *KAHR buh RAY tuhr,* is part of a gasoline engine. It provides the mixture of gasoline vapor and air that is burned inside the cylinders of the engine. The gasoline must be mixed with about 15 times its weight in air in order for all the fuel to burn. Complete combustion of the gasoline results in better fuel economy and lower exhaust emissions.

This article describes a simple automobile carburetor. The main parts of a carburetor are (1) the float chamber, (2) the venturi tube, (3) the choke valve, and (4) the throttle valve.

The Float Chamber of the carburetor is a small fuel storage tank. A *fuel line* carries gasoline to the float chamber from the main fuel tank of the automobile. When the chamber is full, a float resting on top of the gasoline closes a valve in the fuel line. When gasoline is used by the engine, the fuel level drops and so does the float, causing the valve in the fuel line to open. More gasoline then flows into the chamber. The float thus keeps a steady amount of gasoline in the carburetor.

The Venturi Tube is the section of the carburetor where the gasoline and air are mixed. The venturi tube has an hourglass shape. Air enters the tube through an *air cleaner* that removes dirt that could damage the engine. Gasoline from the float chamber flows into the venturi through several nozzles called *jets*. The *pump jet* is located in the first wide section of the venturi. The *main jet* empties into the narrow central section of the tube. The *idle jet* meets the venturi where the tube widens out again.

The narrow part of the venturi tube increases the speed of the air flowing through the carburetor and lowers its pressure (see BERNOULLI'S PRINCIPLE). This decrease in air pressure creates a vacuum that draws gasoline from the main jet into the venturi. The main jet

The Parts of a Carburetor

A carburetor consists of four main parts: (1) the float chamber, (2) the venturi tube, (3) the choke valve, and (4) the throttle valve. The float chamber serves as a small fuel storage tank. The float regulates the amount of gasoline that goes to the venturi tube. Gasoline and air are mixed in the venturi. Gasoline flows from the float chamber to the venturi through nozzles called *jets,* and air enters the venturi through the air cleaner. The amount of air that enters the tube is determined by the choke valve. The throttle valve controls the amount of fuel-air mixture that flows from the venturi to the intake manifold and on to the engine's cylinders.

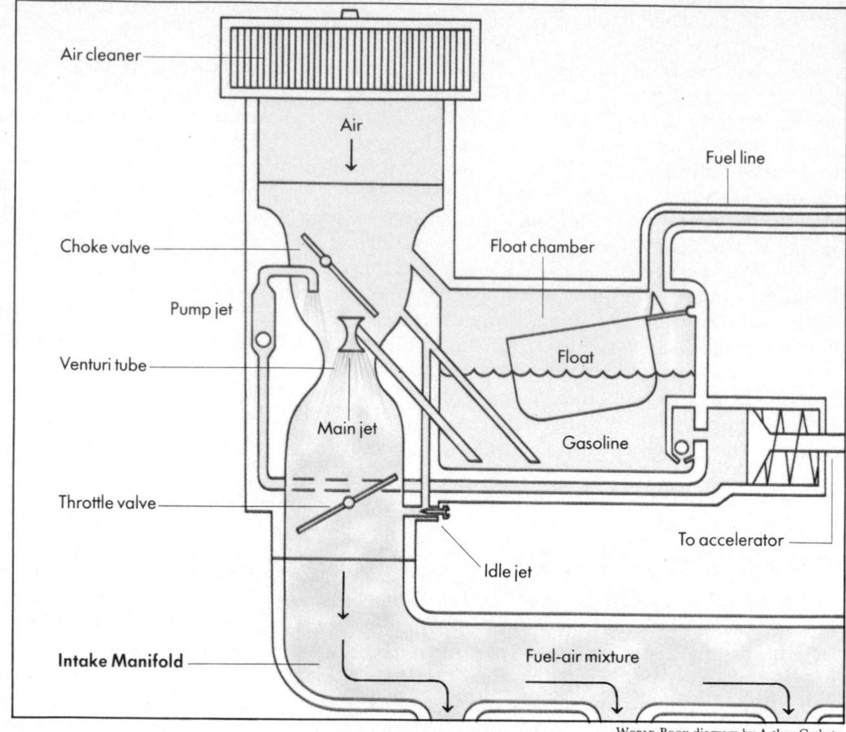

World Book diagram by Arthur Grebetz

supplies fuel to the venturi at most operating speeds of the engine. During rapid acceleration, the pump jet, which is connected to the accelerator, furnishes additional gasoline. When the engine is running at low speeds, the vacuum in the narrow part of the venturi is not strong enough to suck fuel from the main jet. Instead, the moving pistons in the engine create a vacuum that draws gasoline from the idle jet.

Heat from the engine vaporizes the liquid gasoline in the venturi. The fuel vapor mixes with the air in the tube, and the fuel-air mixture then flows out of the carburetor into the *intake manifold.* The manifold distributes the mixture to the engine's cylinders.

The Choke Valve controls the amount of air that enters the carburetor. The choke valve is located between the air cleaner and the venturi. In most cars, the choke is controlled automatically by the temperature of the engine. A cold engine needs more gasoline and less air to start it than a warm engine does. Thus, when the engine is cold, the choke is partially closed, reducing the amount of air flowing through the carburetor.

The Throttle Valve regulates the amount of fuel-air mixture that enters the intake manifold. It lies between the main jet and the idle jet in the venturi. Opening the throttle allows more of the fuel-air mixture to flow to the engine, resulting in greater engine speed and thus a faster-moving car. A driver presses on the accelerator to open the throttle and lets up on the accelerator to close it. MARGARET L. A. MACVICAR and PATRICIA CANTY WYATT

See also AUTOMOBILE (diagram: How an Automobile Runs); FUEL INJECTION; GASOLINE ENGINE.

CARCASSONNE, *kahr kah SAWN* (pop. 42,154), is a city in southern France that includes one of the finest examples in Europe of a medieval walled town. The walled town lies southeast of the rest of the city. For location, see FRANCE (political map). Two walls, both including towers, surround the southeastern section. Landmarks within the walls include the Cathedral of St.-Nazaire, which dates from the 1000's; and the Château Comtal, a castle built in the 1100's. Many tourists visit Carcassonne to see its medieval structures. Carcassonne serves as the capital of the Aude *department* (administrative district). It is a center of the wine trade of its region.

Roman soldiers built a walled town at what is now Carcassonne in the first century before Christ. To keep out invaders, the people of Carcassonne rebuilt the walls and towers in the A.D. 600's and enlarged them in the 1100's and 1200's. The area outside the walls began to develop in the 1200's. It became the city's main commercial and residential district. In the late 1800's, most sections of the walls and towers were repaired or rebuilt for historical preservation purposes. MARK KESSELMAN

CARCINOGEN. See CANCER (Causes of Cancer).

CARCINOMA. See CANCER (Classification by Body Tissue).

CARD CATALOG. See the section *A Student Guide to Better Writing, Speaking, and Research Skills* in the RESEARCH GUIDE/INDEX, Volume 22.

CARD GAME is a game of chance or skill played with oblong pieces of thin cardboard. Each piece, or card, has certain *spots* and figures. Hundreds of games can be played with cards. Various numbers of players take part, depending on the game. *Solitaire*, or *patience*, as it used to be called, provides entertainment for one person. *Casino* is usually played by two persons. Two, three, or four may play *cribbage* or *pinochle*. Four players take part in *bridge* or *whist*. The game of *canasta* calls for from two to six players. *Poker* can be played by as many as ten.

Other popular card games include *gin rummy, hearts,*

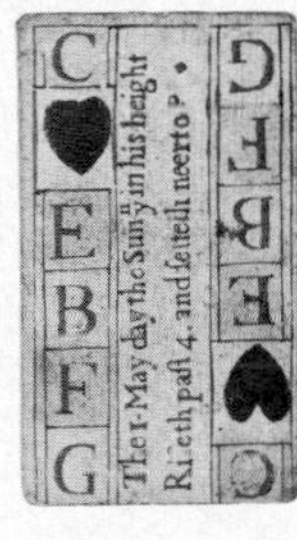

Unusual playing cards include a Chinese domino card, *above left,* a disk card from India, *center,* and an English card of 1656, *above right.* The French card, *below left,* is a woodcut printed about 1480. The American card, *below right,* dates from 1800.

Illustrations courtesy of the Cincinnati Art Museum

euchre, skat, blackjack, five hundred, red dog, and *piquet.* Each game has its own set of rules.

Playing Cards. There are 52 playing cards in a set, also called a *deck* or *pack.* The 52 cards are divided into four *suits* of 13 cards each. There are two black suits (*spades* and *clubs*) and two red suits (*hearts* and *diamonds*). Each suit includes 10 *spot cards* that range from 1 (*ace*) through 10. Each suit also has three *face* (picture) cards: *jack* (knave), *queen,* and *king.* These cards do not picture modern royalty, but are stylized drawings that probably originated during the Middle Ages. In many games, such as poker, the ace is the highest card. But, in some, the ace is used as 1 and the king ranks highest. Some games, such as canasta and pinochle, use parts of two decks, or a combination of decks.

History. Playing cards probably originated in Hindustan about A.D. 800. Their use in Europe was first mentioned in Italy in 1279. Cards next appeared in Germany, then in France and Spain. The four suits originated in France in the 1500's. An object shaped like a clover leaf marked the suit called *trèfle,* now known as the *club* suit. The tip of a pike marked the *pique* suit, now called the *spade.* The third suit was called *coeur,* the French word for *heart.* The name of the fourth suit, *carreau,* means square, but the suit is called *diamond* because of its diamond-shaped spot. LILLIAN FRANKEL

See also BRIDGE; CRIBBAGE; HOYLE, EDMOND; PINOCHLE; POKER.

CARDAMOM, *KAHR duh muhm,* is the fruit of several plants in the ginger family. The fruit and seeds grow in a small shell about $\frac{3}{4}$ inch (19 millimeters) long. The seeds give an oil that is used in medicine as a stimulant. American and English medicine recognize only the cardamom which grows in Malabar, India, as the *true,* or *official, cardamom.* This kind of cardamom also grows in Jamaica. It reaches a height of 10 feet (3 meters) and has white flowers with blue stripes and a yellow margin. Other forms of cardamom grow in the East Indies, the Bengal region, and Sri Lanka.

People in some countries use the fruit of the cardamom as a seasoning for sauces, curries, and cordials. In northern Germany, the people like pastry that is flavored with cardamom.

Scientific Classification. Cardamom is in the ginger family, *Zingiberaceae.* Official cardamom is *Elettaria cardamomum.* Cardamom from Sri Lanka is *E. cardamomum,* variety *major.* East Indian cardamom is *Amomum cardamomum.* Cardamom from Bengal is *A. subulatum.* HAROLD NORMAN MOLDENKE

CARDBOARD is a popular name for any stiff paper or paperboard that is more than 0.006 inch (0.1524 millimeter) thick. It usually does not mean paper used for special purposes, such as *wallboard* or *corrugated boxboard.* Papermakers use various names for different kinds of cardboard. The name may be based on the raw material used, such as *strawboard* or *newsboard.* It may indicate useful characteristics, such as *bending board.* Or it may designate the final use, such as *poster board* or *shoe board.* A familiar type of cardboard is *bristol board,* used for index cards, postal cards, and a great variety of printed matter.

Manufacturers make cardboard by pressing several layers of paper together. They often coat it for decoration or to improve the surface for printing. JOHN B. CALKIN

CÁRDENAS, *KAHR day nahs,* **LÁZARO,** *LAH sah ROH* (1895-1970), served as president of Mexico from 1934 to 1940. More than any other president since the beginning of the Mexican Revolution in 1910, he carried out the revolution's reform aims. His greatest accomplishments were a program that gave land to the poor, and the construction of schools. Controversy arose over his support of a petroleum strike which led to Mexico's seizure of foreign oil properties in 1938, and over enforced state control of large cotton, sugar, henequen, and rice plantations. Cárdenas' support of inter-American cooperation during World War II strengthened Mexico's international position.

Cárdenas was born in Jiquilpan, Michoacán, on May 21, 1895. He joined the revolutionary army in 1913, and took an active part in many of its military and political developments. HAROLD EUGENE DAVIS

See also MEXICO (Economic and Social Changes).

CARDIAC. See HEART.

CARDIAC ARREST. See HEART (Beat of the Heart).

CARDIFF, *KAHR dihf* (pop. 269,459), is the capital and largest city of Wales. It is also the country's chief economic, industrial, and cultural center. Cardiff lies on the southeast coast of Wales. It borders the Bristol Channel, an arm of the Atlantic Ocean. For the location of the city, see WALES (map).

Three rivers—the Taff, the Ely, and the Rhymney—flow through Cardiff into the Bristol Channel. A

City of Cardiff

Cardiff's Civic Center consists of a group of cultural and government buildings that stand near the center of the city. The two domed buildings in the foreground are City Hall, *left*, and the National Museum of Wales, *right*.

number of docks line the coast, and many factories are nearby.

A large area of parkland lies near the center of Cardiff. The Civic Center and many of the city's major commercial buildings are clustered around Cathays Park in this area. The Civic Center includes the Law Courts, City Hall, National Museum of Wales, and the University College. Nearby are the National Sports Center, National School of Medicine, many fashionable shops and modern hotels, and Cardiff Castle. The castle was built in 1090. Castell Coch (Red Castle), built in the 1200's, is just outside the city. Cardiff is also the home of the medieval Llandaff Cathedral, the Welsh Industrial and Maritime Museum, and the Welsh Folk Museum.

Factories in Cardiff produce automobile parts, chemicals, electronics equipment, engineering products, and processed food and tobacco. The city is a busy shipping center. Modern railroad and highway systems connect Cardiff with the rest of Great Britain. An airport lies outside the edge of the city.

About A.D. 75, Roman soldiers built a fort on the site of what is now Cardiff. The name *Cardiff* means *fort on the Taff*. Normans settled the area in the late 1000's. They built Cardiff Castle on the site of the old Roman fort. A walled town grew up around the castle and served as a market and port for Welsh farm products.

By the early 1800's, Cardiff was still a small town. Then, Wales became a major center of coal mining and iron and steel production. Cardiff served as the shipping center for these products and grew rapidly. By 1890, it had become known as the *Coal Metropolis of the World*.

Cardiff coal trade declined after World War I ended in 1918, and the city soon developed new industries. Since the mid-1940's, Cardiff has grown steadily as the administrative and commercial center of Wales. In 1955, it became the capital of Wales. J. GERAINT JENKINS

CARDIGAN WELSH CORGI, *KAWR gee*, is a breed of dog that was first raised in the area of Cardigan, Wales. Since about A.D. 1000, farmers there have used Cardigan Welsh corgis to herd cattle. These dogs bite the heels of the cattle to drive them. Cardigans are also excellent watchdogs and make extremely loyal companions.

The word *corgi* comes from two Welsh words meaning *dwarf dog*. Cardigan Welsh corgis stand about 12 inches (30 centimeters) high and weigh from 20 to 26 pounds (9 to 12 kilograms). They have short, rough hair, and most have red and white coats. Their long, furry tails resemble those of foxes.

The Cardigan Welsh corgi closely resembles the Pembroke Welsh corgi. However, the Cardigan has a slightly longer body, a coarser textured coat, and a much longer tail. JOAN MCDONALD BREARLEY

See also PEMBROKE WELSH CORGI.

CARDINAL is one of a group of Roman Catholic clergymen who serve as counselors to the pope and rank next to him within the church. The cardinals as a group form the Sacred College, or College of Cardinals.

Many cardinals head Roman Catholic dioceses throughout the world. Other cardinals help govern the church from the Vatican in Rome. Individual cardinals have no lawmaking power, but their high rank gives them great influence in church affairs. Since 1059, the Sacred College has elected every pope. In 1970, Pope Paul VI ruled that no cardinal past the age of 80 could vote for a new pope.

The pope appoints all cardinals. For hundreds of years, a pope could make any Roman Catholic a cardinal, and some popes even appointed laypersons to the office. In 1917, the church adopted a rule that went into effect in 1918 providing that cardinals must be at least priests. In 1962, Pope John XXIII declared that all cardinals must be bishops. Cardinals who were not bishops were given that rank.

Walter Chandoha

The Cardigan Welsh Corgi Has a Long Foxlike Tail.

Canadian Cardinals

Cardinal	Life Dates	Elevated	Archdiocese
Bégin, Louis N.	1840-1925	1914	Quebec
*Carter, Gerald E.	1912-	1979	Toronto
*Flahiff, George B.	1905-	1969	Winnipeg
*Léger, Paul - Émile	1904-	1953	Montreal
McGuigan, James C.	1894-1974	1946	Toronto
Rouleau, Félix R.	1866-1931	1927	Quebec
*Roy, Maurice	1905-	1965	Quebec
Taschereau, Elzéar A.	1820-1898	1886	Quebec
Villeneuve, Jean M.	1883-1947	1933	Quebec

American Cardinals

Cardinal	Life Dates	Elevated	Archdiocese
*Aponte Martinez, Luis	1922-	1973	San Juan, P.R.
*Baum, William W.	1926-	1976	†
*Bernardin, Joseph L.	1928-	1983	Chicago
Brennan, Francis J.	1894-1968	1967	†
*Carberry, John J.	1904-	1969	St. Louis
*Cody, John P.	1907-1982	1967	Chicago
*Cooke, Terence J.	1921-1983	1969	New York
Cushing, Richard	1895-1970	1958	Boston
Dearden, John F.	1907-	1969	Detroit
Dougherty, Dennis J.	1865-1951	1921	Philadelphia
Farley, John M.	1842-1918	1911	New York
*Gibbons, James	1834-1921	1886	Baltimore
Glennon, John J.	1862-1946	1946	St. Louis
Hayes, Patrick J.	1867-1938	1924	New York
*Krol, John J.	1910-	1967	Philadelphia
*Manning, Timothy	1909-	1973	Los Angeles
*McCloskey, John	1810-1885	1875	New York
*McIntyre, James F.	1886-1979	1953	Los Angeles
*Medeiros, Humberto S.	1915-1983	1973	Boston
Meyer, Albert G.	1903-1965	1959	Chicago
*Mooney, Edward	1882-1958	1946	Detroit
Muench, Aloisius J.	1889-1962	1959	†
Mundelein, George W.	1872-1939	1924	Chicago
O'Boyle, Patrick A.	1896-	1967	Washington, D.C.
O'Connell, William H.	1859-1944	1911	Boston
*O'Hara, John F.	1888-1960	1958	Philadelphia
Ritter, Joseph E.	1892-1967	1961	St. Louis
*Shehan, Lawrence J.	1898-1984	1965	Baltimore
*Spellman, Francis	1889-1967	1946	New York
Stritch, Samuel A.	1887-1958	1946	Chicago
Wright, John J.	1909-1979	1969	†

*Has a separate biography in THE WORLD BOOK ENCYCLOPEDIA
†Member of the Roman Curia at the Vatican

In 1586, Pope Sixtus V set the number of cardinals at 70. In the mid-1900's, Pope John XXIII and Pope Paul VI increased the number several times to provide more widespread representation of Roman Catholics.

No one really knows the origin of the term *cardinal.* At one time, many church scholars believed the term came from the Latin word *cardo,* meaning *hinge* or *pivot.* This word referred to the office as a crucial part of the operation of the church. Today, most scholars believe the title originated from the fact that many bishops were *incardinated*—that is, named to serve a diocese other than the one in which they had been or-

Pictorial Parade

Cardinals Celebrate Mass in St. Peter's Church in Vatican City. This Mass was part of the ceremonies during which Pope Paul VI elevated 33 bishops to the rank of cardinal in 1969.

dained. Such a situation occurred as early as the 500's for bishops whose original dioceses had been destroyed by barbarian invasions.

The power of cardinals has varied during different periods in church history. Some cardinals have participated in church councils organized to reform the church. At the height of this *conciliar movement* in the 1400's and 1500's, some church members considered cardinals as a group to be higher in authority than the pope. The church never officially accepted this viewpoint.

Today, the privileges, functions, symbols, and dress of cardinals are undergoing many changes. These changes are largely the result of trends toward simplification and modernization within the church introduced during Vatican Council II (1962-1965). Francis L. Filas

Related Articles in World Book include:

Address, Forms of (Cardinal)
Bellarmine, Saint Robert Francis Romulus
Langton, Stephen Cardinal
Mazarin, Jules Cardinal
Mindszenty, Joseph Cardinal
Newman, John H. Cardinal
Pope
Rampolla, Mariano Cardinal
Richelieu, Cardinal
Roman Catholic Church (Church Government)
Stepinac, Aloysius Cardinal
Wyszyński, Stefan Cardinal

CARDINAL is a bird of the finch family. It is sometimes called *redbird*. Cardinals live in the Eastern United States from South Dakota, southern Minnesota, and Massachusetts southward to Florida and the Gulf of Mexico. Since the early 1900's, they have been spreading farther north and west through the United States.

The cardinal grows about 8 inches (20 centimeters) long. It has a crest of feathers on its head that looks like a peaked cap. The males are mostly red, with tints of gray on their backs. A distinctive black marking around the base of the bill resembles a beard. The females are a brownish color, with a little red in their wings, tails, and crests. Both males and females have bright red or orange bills.

Cardinals usually build their nests 4 to 5 feet (1.2 to 1.5 meters) above the ground in bramble thickets or in the lower branches of trees. The nests are made from dead leaves, grass, and weed stems and are lined with grass or roots. The female lays from three to five eggs that are colored white or pale blue with spots of reddish-brown and lilac. The female sits on the eggs, and the male feeds her during this time, usually away from the nest. The eggs hatch in 12 to 13 days, and the male helps feed the young. The young birds leave the nest after about 10 days. The male continues to feed them while the female builds a new nest. Cardinals may have several broods during a nesting season.

Cardinals feed on insects, worms, waste grain, and the seeds of weeds and wild fruits. In winter, they often go to barnyards and corncribs in search of corn. They are also fond of sunflower seeds and visit feeding stations to get them. Young cardinals eat many harmful insects, including boll worms, cotton worms, codling moths, and potato beetles.

The cardinal has a cheerful song. The birds were once trapped and sold as songbirds, and their feathers were used to decorate women's hats. Cardinals are now protected by law.

Scientific Classification. The cardinal belongs to the finch family, *Fringillidae*. It is genus *Richmondena*, species *R. cardinalis*. George J. Wallace

See also Bird (table: State and Provincial Birds; pictures: Birds of Urban Areas; Birds' Eggs).

Dan Sudia, Photo Researchers

The Cardinal is one of the most popular songbirds of North America. The female, *left,* is dull brown, and the male, *right,* is bright red. Each has a crest of feathers on its head.

CARDINAL FLOWER is a tall plant that grows along marshes and riverbanks in eastern and central North America. The plant has become a rare wild flower. It grows 3 to 4 feet (91 to 120 centimeters) high. Erect stems from 2 to 5 feet (61 to 150 centimeters) high bear cardinal-red flowers. See also LOBELIA.

Scientific Classification. The cardinal flower is a member of the lobelia family, *Lobeliaceae*. It is genus *Lobelia*, species *L. cardinalis*. JULIAN A. STEYERMARK

CARDINAL NUMBER. See NUMBER AND NUMERAL.

CARDINAL POINTS. See COMPASS.

CARDING. See COTTON (Cleaning; picture); WOOL (Processing of Wool; picture).

CARDIOPULMONARY RESUSCITATION. See FIRST AID (Heart Attack).

CARDIOVASCULAR DISEASE. See HEART (Heart Diseases).

CARDOZO, *kahr DOH zoh,* **BENJAMIN NATHAN** (1870-1938), served as an associate justice of the Supreme Court of the United States from 1932 until his death. He became a leading member of the court's liberal wing, and wrote the court's opinion upholding the federal Social Security Act in 1937.

Oil painting on canvas by Eben F. Comins; Supreme Court Building, United States Supreme Court

Benjamin Cardozo

Cardozo was born in New York City, and was graduated from Columbia University. In 1914, he became a member of the New York Court of Appeals, and served as chief justice of the court after 1927. President Herbert Hoover appointed him to the Supreme Court in 1932 to succeed Oliver Wendell Holmes. MERLO J. PUSEY

CARDS. See CARD GAME.

CARDSTON, Alberta (pop. 3,267), is a Mormon community about 140 miles (225 kilometers) south of Calgary. See ALBERTA (political map). Most of the people near Cardston work on ranches and farms. A group of Mormon families founded the town in 1887. Charles Ora Card, a son-in-law of Brigham Young, led them to Canada. Cardston is called the *Temple City of Canada,* because a Mormon temple towers above the housetops of the town. W. D. MCDOUGALL

See also MORMONS.

CARDUCCI, *kahr DOOT chee,* **GIOSUÈ,** *jaw SWEH* (1835-1907), an Italian poet and scholar, won the 1906 Nobel prize for literature. His verse is variously lyrical, political, and historical. Carducci's poetry shows his political liberalism, and his belief in the ideals of classicism and opposition to romanticism. The poetry was greatly influenced by his familiarity with European literature, especially Greek, Latin, and Italian works. Carducci's major collections include *New Verses* (1887) and *Barbarian Odes* (1877-1889). His critical works had a strong influence on Italian attitudes toward literature.

Carducci was born in Tuscany. He served as professor of Italian literature at the University of Bologna from 1860 to 1904. In 1890, he was named a senator by the Italian government. SERGIO PACIFICI

CARE is a private, nonprofit agency founded in 1945 by 22 leading cooperative, labor, relief, and religious organizations. Its letters mean the *C*ooperative for *A*merican *R*elief *E*verywhere.

Originally, CARE supplied packages of food and clothing to needy persons in Europe. Later, it extended its service to Africa, Asia, and Latin America. CARE features feeding programs, self-help, and medical aid and development assistance. It also provides immediate aid to refugees and disaster victims. In 1962, MEDICO (Medical International Cooperation Organization) merged with CARE. Founded by two American doctors, Peter Comanduras and Tom Dooley, it provides medical care and training in developing areas.

Donors may select the type of aid and the countries to which they wish their gifts sent, or they may let CARE decide. The agency is registered with the U.S. government's Advisory Committee on Voluntary Foreign Aid. CARE has headquarters at 660 First Avenue, New York, N.Y. 10016. Critically reviewed by CARE

CAREER EDUCATION is instruction to help young people choose and prepare for a career. Such education occurs in the family, in the community, and in schools. Career education in school is not a separate course, though many schools provide a special unit or course dealing with careers. Instead, career education consists of attitudes, knowledge, and skills that are incorporated into many courses. For example, a science class might investigate careers in environmental fields, health, and marine sciences. Career education helps students develop self-understanding and use it to plan their education and working life.

A comprehensive career education program begins in kindergarten and continues at least through high school. In kindergarten and elementary school, youngsters learn about different types of work and how school subjects relate to occupations. In middle school or junior high school, children begin to explore the careers that interest them most. School counselors and teachers work to help each child determine which educational and occupational choices fit his or her abilities and interests. In high school, students receive information and experiences with which they can make specific plans. They also should obtain the skills they need for further study or for a job after graduation. Counselors provide information on such matters as how to locate and apply for jobs and how to be successful in interviews.

Teachers and counselors use a variety of instructional methods to provide career education. They may show films about occupations and industries. Children may invite their parents or other adults to come to school and describe their jobs. A student may accompany a worker on the job for a day or more. Another important method is *cooperative education,* which combines classroom study with practical work experience.

Career education differs from vocational education, though many people confuse them. Vocational education is designed to teach specific occupational skills. Career education works to give students an understanding of many different types of work and how to choose among them. EDWIN L. HERR

See also CAREERS; COOPERATIVE EDUCATION; VOCATIONAL EDUCATION.

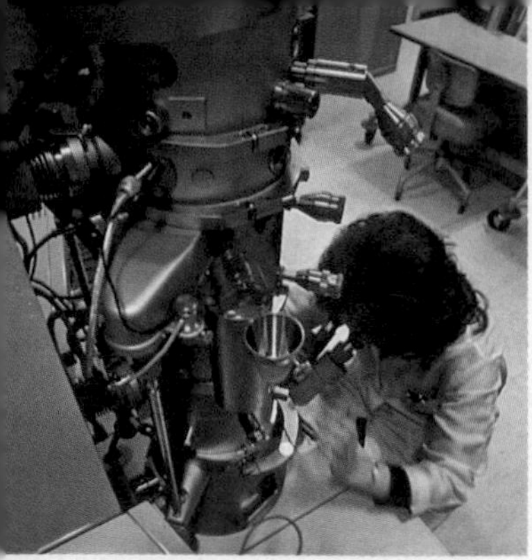

WORLD BOOK photo

Ted McDonough, Webb Photos

First Federal Savings & Loan Assn. of Chicago

Milt and Joan Mann

Zenith Radio Corporation

Milt and Joan Mann

The World of Work offers people the chance to choose a career that suits individual abilities, interests, and goals. A person seeking a career can select from a wide range of opportunities that include all kinds of settings and require various levels of preparation.

CAREERS

CAREERS. Many people use the term *career* to mean the job, occupation, or vocation a person has. However, a career involves much more than does a job, an occupation, or a vocation. A career is the pattern of work and work-related activities that develops throughout a lifetime. It includes the job or series of jobs a person has until retirement. It also involves the way a person's work roles affect other life roles, such as being a student, a parent, or a community leader. There are as many kinds of careers as there are people. They vary greatly in the type of work involved and in the ways they influence a person's life.

Almost every adult has a career of some kind. Most people build a career to help them satisfy certain goals. Such goals might include earning a living or helping others. The best-known career pattern develops around work for pay. Most workers in such a career hold a job to support themselves and their family. However, some people build a career around activities for which they receive no money. For example, many people work to create a comfortable home life for their family. Others spend much of their time on charitable projects.

The kind of career you have can affect your life in a great number of ways. For example, it can determine where you live and the friends you make. It can reflect how much education you have and can determine the amount of money you earn. Your career can also affect the way you feel about yourself and the way other people act toward you. By making wise career decisions, you can thus help yourself build the life you want.

Important career decisions include choosing a career field and deciding how you want your career to develop. Other decisions involve selecting the educational and job opportunities that will advance your career. Knowing your abilities, interests, and goals gives you a foundation on which to base your career decisions. In addition, a broad knowledge of the world of work can help you find job possibilities that suit your abilities, interests, and goals.

This article deals mainly with careers based on work for pay. It concentrates on careers in the United States, but much of the material applies also to careers in Canada and other industrial countries. The article provides information that can help you choose and plan a career. It also describes skills that can be useful in getting a job. In addition, the article discusses major career fields and many of the occupations within each field. For more detailed information on an individual career field, see the articles listed in the *Related Articles* at the end of this article.

Edwin L. Herr, the contributor of this article, is Professor and Head of the Division of Counseling and Educational Psychology at Pennsylvania State University. He is also the author of Schools and Careers *and* Vocational Guidance and Human Development.

Choosing and Planning a Career

To make wise career decisions and plans, you need as much information as possible. The more you know about yourself and career opportunities, the better able you will be to choose a satisfying career.

Learning About Oneself

People differ in what they want from a career. Many people desire a high income. Some hope for fame. Others want much leisure or adventure. Still others want to serve people and make the world a better place.

Before you begin to explore career fields, you should determine (1) your values, or goals in life; (2) your interests; and (3) your abilities. Most people are happiest in jobs that fit their values, interests, and abilities.

Values are a person's basic goals. Values include the accomplishment of something important, a life of excitement, and the achievement of fame or wealth. Other values include being active, helping others, being a leader, and following a life of religious devotion. The actions of most people reflect their values.

To learn about your values, ask yourself what your goals in life are. Do you want to be wealthy? Do you desire fame? Do you want to have responsibility and supervise other people? Or would you rather follow orders? Do you desire travel and variety? Or do you prefer to stay at home with familiar people? Would you rather work alone or with others? The answers to such questions can help you discover your values. Counselors can help you learn about your values.

Interests. People's interests, like their actions, reflect their values or help toward the achievement of those values. For example, someone who prefers working with others rather than alone would probably be interested in team sports or various other group activities. Many people have interests in artistic, mechanical, outdoor, or scientific activities. Other interests include helping people and solving problems.

Many people base their career choices on their interests. For numerous workers, job performance and job satisfaction depend on how much their work relates to their interests. It is therefore helpful to identify your strongest and most lasting interests before you select a career field. To find out what your interests are, examine the kinds of activities you have enjoyed. Such activities might include club work, hobbies, and sports. The activities you enjoy most may represent your strongest interests. Counselors can also help you identify your interests.

Abilities, or aptitudes, influence how easily a person can learn to perform various activities. For example, people who have mechanical ability quickly learn how to assemble or repair machines. The term *ability* also means a skill—such as reading or speaking a foreign language—that a person has learned.

Some people have exceptional artistic or musical talent. People who have the ability to record and organize information quickly and correctly are good at *clerical reasoning*. Those with *manual dexterity* can use their hands skillfully. Those with *mechanical comprehension* can easily understand how machines work.

The abilities that indicate how well a person can think and reason are known as *scholastic aptitudes*. One kind of scholastic aptitude, called *verbal reasoning*, is the ability to think and reason with words. *Numerical reasoning* refers to how well a person uses numbers in solving problems. *Abstract reasoning* is the ability to reason with symbols other than words or numbers.

Abilities can influence a person's choice of career. They can also affect a person's success or failure in a chosen career. Students with high scholastic aptitudes tend to prepare for occupations that require advanced education beyond high school. Many students with strong clerical or mechanical abilities take jobs or job-training programs after high school. Most occupations require a combination of abilities. For example, dental students need scholastic aptitudes to graduate from dental school, and they need manual dexterity to perform dental work. A person who lacks these abilities might not succeed in dentistry.

Your performance in schoolwork, in aptitude tests, and in games, sports, and other activities can help you identify your abilities. An honest examination of your strengths and weaknesses can help you choose a career that suits your abilities.

Other Personal Characteristics, such as friendliness, dependability, and honesty, contribute to success in a career. They may even be essential elements of a career in sales, banking, management, or other fields. These kinds of characteristics are difficult to measure. However, a serious look at your past behavior can help you find out if you have such qualities.

Discovering the World of Work

The world of work is vast and constantly changing. There are about 20,000 kinds of occupations in the United States. Scientific advances and other developments constantly eliminate some jobs and create new ones. For a survey of many of the most common occupations and the training they require, see the section *The World of Work* later in this article.

Most people begin to discover the world of work in early childhood. The following discussion deals with how children learn and can be helped to learn about the wide range of career possibilities.

Children start to discover the world of work before they enter elementary school. At home and in the community, they become aware that people work in various occupations. During these years, most children also start to form ideas about life and about themselves as individuals. These ideas can influence their later school success and occupational choices. A realistic view of themselves and the world of work can help prepare children to make successful career choices.

Adults can help children discover the world of work in many ways. For example, parents and teachers can encourage children to notice and talk about different jobs in the community. Children might play games, such as "what's my line?" or "let's pretend," using occupations they have seen. They might also read and discuss stories that deal with different kinds of workers.

Teachers can ask students to select an occupation and give a report on it. Teachers can also assign other projects. For example, students might produce a skit about various kinds of work. They also might interview

John Running Productions

Art Seitz

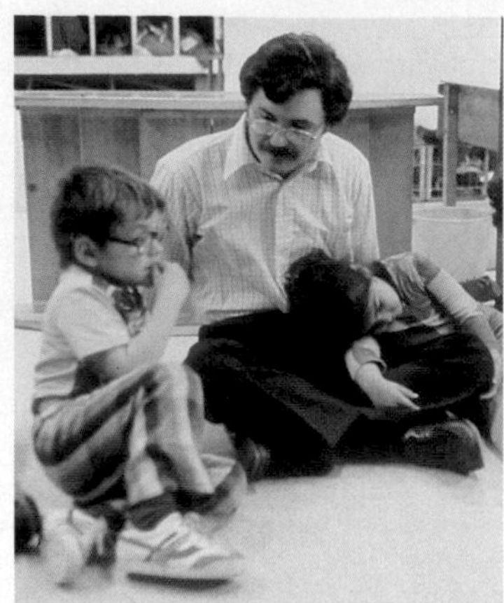

WORLD BOOK photo

Careers for Men and Women now include many jobs formerly limited to one sex. For example, a woman may become a surveyor or a telephone line worker, and a man may teach nursery school.

workers and later discuss these interviews in class. Older students might make a film for which they serve as writers, directors, and other motion-picture workers. This kind of activity can help the students see how various occupations depend on one another.

Children can learn about their own characteristics by listing their abilities and interests. These lists can then be compared with characteristics that are important in certain occupations. In this way, children can begin to discover occupations that might suit them.

Exploring Career Fields

By carefully examining various occupations, you should find the elements of a career that best suits your needs. But it would be hard to study every kind of career opportunity. You can limit the number of occupations you consider by identifying and exploring only those that most interest you. Many students begin to explore career fields when they are in junior high school. Such exploration helps them select high school courses that relate to their career interests.

What to Look For. For most workers, job satisfaction depends on how well the various characteristics of a job meet their own personal characteristics. In exploring an occupation, you should therefore consider the following job characteristics:

The Nature of the Work. Some jobs chiefly involve working with things, and others mainly require dealing with people or ideas. Most jobs combine a variety of work activities. You should look for an occupation that involves activities you enjoy and can do well.

All occupations can be classified into four groups, based on work activities. These groups are (1) white collar, (2) blue collar, (3) farm, and (4) service.

White-collar occupations mainly require dealing with people or ideas. The U.S. Department of Labor classifies administrators, managers, salespeople, and all professional, technical, and clerical workers as white-collar workers. The term *white collar* comes from the fact that such workers have traditionally worn street clothes on the job. Blue-collar occupations chiefly involve working with things. The jobs include such duties as assembling products, operating or repairing machinery, and constructing buildings. Most blue-collar occupations call for work clothes on the job.

Farm occupations involve farm management and farm labor, and most emphasize working with things. Service jobs provide personal, educational, and protective services to people. Workers in service jobs, such as cooks and hairstylists, deal mainly with people and things.

Working Conditions mean the environment in which a particular job is performed. A work environment might be indoors or outdoors, or involve extreme heat or cold. Some jobs involve high levels of dust or noise, physical hazards, or mental stress. Other conditions to consider include the hours involved and whether employees work alone or in groups.

Special Abilities Required. Some occupations call for more intelligence, mechanical aptitude, artistic talent, or other abilities than most people possess. You should therefore be aware of any special requirements in the jobs you consider.

Physical Demands. Some occupations make special physical demands on workers. For example, jobs that involve carrying, lifting, pulling, or pushing objects require strength. Other occupations might require workers who have keen vision or who can stand for long periods. When you consider a job, be sure you can meet any physical demands the work might make.

Preparation Needed. The amount of preparation required to enter an occupation varies from job to job. It can range from a few hours of on-the-job training to more than 10 years of education beyond high school. In addition, workers in some occupations must continue their education to keep their jobs or to advance in them. Some occupations require several years of experience and preparation at lower-level jobs. You should thus consider how much time and money you might have to invest in the careers that interest you.

Chances for Employment. Before you choose a career field, you should consider your chances for getting a job in that field. Most workers are hired to replace employees who have left their jobs. This situation is especially true in occupations and industries with steady or decreasing employment. In growing occupations and industries, however, additional workers are needed to fill newly created jobs. In addition, employment in various occupations is affected by the introduction of new products and advanced technologies. Government spending and economic conditions also affect job opportunities.

Probable Earnings. In exploring an occupation, you will want to know how much money you can expect to earn. Government, professional, and trade publications supply information on probable earnings for various occupations. However, pay scales vary with location and employers. Union agreements and the amount of experience and education required also affect salaries and wages. Many employers provide insurance coverage, paid vacations, and other *fringe benefits,* which you should consider in addition to the probable earnings.

Job Security. For many people, job security is an important consideration in selecting an occupation. You may therefore want to examine whether the occupations you are interested in offer relative security. In some industries, production or spending cuts and various other circumstances can cause employers to lay off or fire workers. In many occupations, workers are protected from losing their jobs by a union contract or other written agreement between workers and employers. Workers under such agreements may not be fired except in certain situations. Many occupations have no written guarantee of job security.

Chances for Advancement. In exploring various occupations, you should examine possible patterns of promotion, known as *career ladders* or *career paths.* In some occupations, workers are promoted to higher positions based on their ability and experience. However, some employers hire people from outside the organization to fill high-level openings. In such cases, a worker can advance only by changing employers. Some occupations allow only limited advancement. Workers in such fields have to obtain additional education or training or completely change occupations in order to advance their careers.

Social Status is a person's position or rank in society. Many people believe that certain jobs have higher social status than do others. Some people who value status seek it through choosing highly regarded occupations. You must decide for yourself how important social status is in making your career choices.

Sources of Information. A number of sources supply information that can help you explore a career field.

Annual Income in the United States by Amount of Education

The advantage of education is shown in the incomes at each educational level. In most groups, college graduates earn about twice as much as people with only an elementary school education.

Education Completed: College High School Elementary

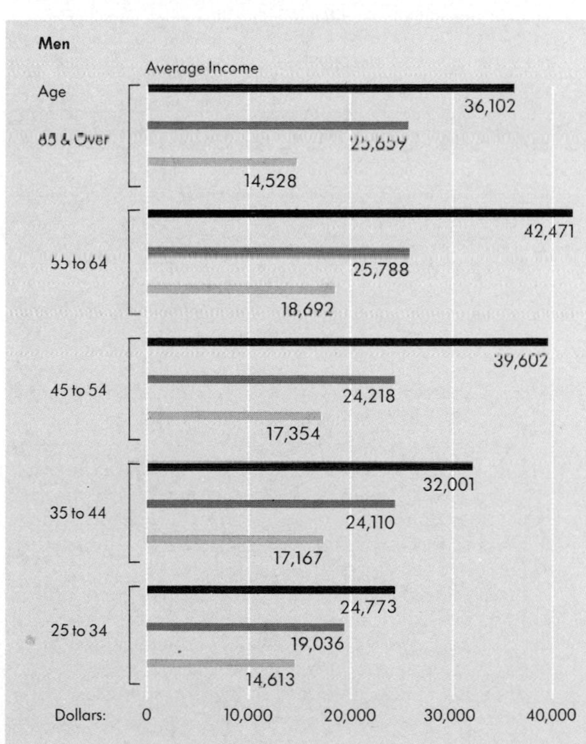

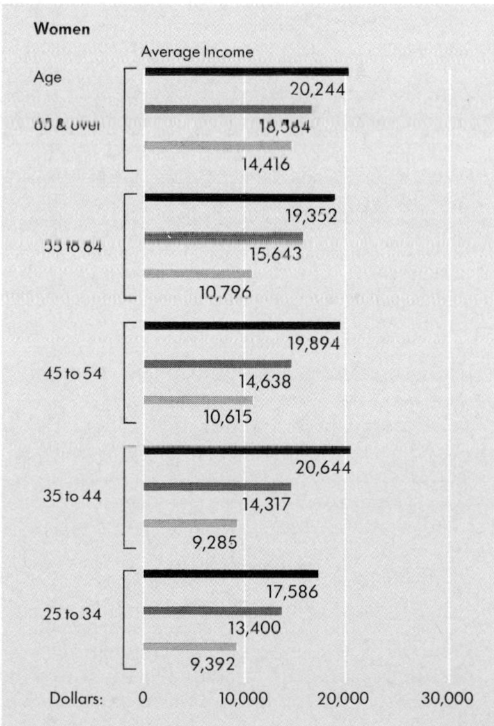

Source: Current Population Survey, U.S. Bureau of the Census. Figures are for full-time workers in 1982.

WORLD BOOK graph

Government agencies, industries, professional organizations, and many employers provide materials that describe various occupations. For example, the U.S. Department of Labor describes about 20,000 jobs in its *Dictionary of Occupational Titles*. It also publishes the *Guide for Occupational Exploration*, which groups occupations by interests and by abilities and traits necessary for success. Every two years, the Bureau of Labor Statistics issues the *Occupational Outlook Handbook*, which discusses job requirements, indicates probable earnings, and predicts employment opportunities for selected occupations. Other helpful publications are listed in the *Additional Resources* section at the end of this article.

Many schools offer career courses, clubs, and field trips to help students learn about job opportunities. Some schools provide computer systems that answer students' questions about careers.

Career information is also available from career and guidance counselors. These experts work in high schools, community agencies, employment offices, and college career development and placement centers. A counselor can help you identify your immediate and future career goals and the qualities you have to offer an employer. A counselor can also advise you on how to prepare for and obtain a job in your chosen field.

You can learn about the characteristics of individual jobs by interviewing workers in those jobs. In addition, you can gain firsthand information about an occupation through part-time jobs and volunteer work. For example, a person considering a career in medicine might volunteer as a hospital aide.

Preparing for a Career

Career preparation involves learning a variety of skills. Some skills, such as being able to accept supervision and knowing how to get along with others, are learned through everyday experiences in school and in the community. Others require specialized training.

For most people, specialized career preparation begins in high school. Business and vocational courses prepare high school students to enter an occupation immediately after graduation. These courses teach skills used in such fields as business, construction, and manufacturing. Most high schools also offer college preparatory courses for students who plan to go to college. In addition, many high schools offer *cooperative education programs*. Under these programs, students continue their classroom education while they hold a part-time job or participate in some community activity.

Certain occupations require only a high school education. But most jobs call for additional training. This section briefly describes the major kinds of career preparation programs. For more detailed information on particular programs, see the articles listed in the *Related Articles* at the end of this article.

On-the-Job Training means that a worker is taught jobs skills after being hired. In most cases, an experienced worker trains and supervises the beginner. The training may last a few hours or many months.

Apprenticeships are formally regulated by the U.S. Department of Labor and combine classroom instruction and on-the-job training. They require two or more years of job experience and instruction. Every apprenticeship is based on a written agreement between the employer and the apprentice. Most apprenticeships train workers for skilled occupations in construction, manufacturing, transportation, and service industries.

Vocational Schools, also called *trade schools*, offer courses in bookkeeping, secretarial work, television repair, and many other skills. Some trade schools specialize in training such workers as beauticians, flight engineers, mechanics, and truck drivers. Courses range from several months to two years. Most vocational schools prepare students to meet any licensing requirements needed to enter a trade or profession. Many schools also award certificates to graduates.

There are two main kinds of vocational schools, *public* and *proprietary*. Public vocational schools are supported by taxes. Proprietary schools are owned by individuals or businesses and operate to make a profit.

Armed Forces Schools provide career education opportunities for people in military service. These opportunities range from on-the-job training and short courses to college and graduate school. In most cases, the training is designed for jobs in military career fields. However, many skills used in military occupations can be applied to civilian jobs.

Home Study and Correspondence Schools enable people to learn certain job skills at home. Correspondence schools mail study guides, assignments, and examinations to students. The students send the completed work back to the school for grading. Some schools offer lectures over the radio or on public television. Home study courses can prepare students for careers in business, skilled trades, and many other areas.

Technical Institutes provide advanced, specialized training in such fields as agriculture, data processing, engineering, and laboratory work. Many graduates of these schools become *technicians*—that is, workers who assist engineers, scientists, and other highly trained specialists. Most technical institutes have two- or three-year programs, and many are associated with a hospital, university, or other institution. Some technical schools offer short courses similar to those in vocational schools.

Community and Junior Colleges provide two years of college-level education. They prepare some students to transfer to a four-year college. They train other students for jobs as technicians and for such specialized occupations as nursing, office management, and police work. Most community colleges are financed by taxes. Most junior colleges are privately owned.

Colleges and Universities offer four-year programs that lead to a bachelor's degree. For the first two years, students study a wide variety of subjects. For the last two, most students take courses in their chosen career fields. College students learn skills for such professions as architecture, journalism, science, and teaching.

Professional and Graduate Schools. Such professions as dentistry, law, and medicine require education beyond college at a professional school. In addition, many students in business, education, science, and other fields attend graduate school for advanced study in their subject areas. Most professional and graduate schools are part of large universities.

CAREERS/*Getting A Job*

Getting a job begins with locating and applying for jobs that will advance your career plans. It also involves convincing employers that you are the best applicant for their job openings. The way you apply for a job and present your qualifications can greatly influence an employer's impression of you. Therefore, you should know how to contact employers, how to complete application forms, and how to make a good impression in job interviews. It is also important to know how to write a good *résumé,* or summary of your background and qualifications. All these skills can improve your chances for employment. However, do not be discouraged if you are not offered the first job you apply for. Most employers consider several applicants for each job opening, and many people make a number of applications before being hired.

Finding Job Opportunities. One of the most common ways to learn about job opportunities is by word-of-mouth. Many jobs are filled by people who have heard of the job openings from friends, relatives, teachers, and acquaintances. You should therefore tell the people you know and meet that you are looking for certain kinds of work.

Another common way to locate job opportunities is through the help-wanted section of newspapers. Many professional and union newsletters, journals, and other trade publications also carry advertisements for job openings. In numerous cases, the information given in help-wanted ads can help you decide whether to contact the employer.

Information about job openings is also available from employment agencies. Public employment agencies are run by the government and do not charge for their services. Private agencies charge the jobseeker or the employer a fee if a person is hired as a result of their efforts. Many high schools, colleges, and other schools have *placement offices,* which are set up to help students and graduates find jobs.

Telephone directories, the *College Placement Annual,* and other directories list the names and addresses of employers in various fields. Jobseekers must contact the employers to learn about possible job openings.

Contacting Employers. Your first contact with an employer will be either to apply for a known job opening or to find out if any jobs are available. Your contacts with employers should be effective and orderly. The most common ways of contacting employers are by mail, by telephone, and by personal visit to an employer's office.

Most applicants for white-collar jobs get in touch with employers by mail. A letter to an employer should be typewritten or neatly handwritten in ink. In the letter, introduce yourself and explain why you are writing. Briefly indicate any experience and skills you have that relate to the kind of job you are seeking. Finally, ask for an interview. Be sure to include your address and telephone number so that the employer can reach you. If you contact an employer by telephone, try to provide the same information that you would cover in a letter.

Many blue-collar, farm, and service jobs require applicants simply to fill out an application form. Most people seeking such jobs apply in person. People who apply in person for other kinds of jobs will probably have to arrange a future interview. They will also likely be asked to fill out an application form or leave a résumé.

PERSONAL RÉSUMÉ

Jerry Williams
1226 34th Street
Indianola, Iowa 50125
515/255-5225

POSITION SOUGHT:	News editor on metropolitan daily newspaper
EXPERIENCE:	
1/83 to Present	Indianola Record Herald & Tribune P.O. Box 259 Indianola, Iowa 50125 News editor for twice-weekly newspaper
6/81 to 12/82	Mediapolis New Era P.O. Box 487 Mediapolis, Iowa 52637 Editor for weekly newspaper
9/79 to 5/81	Daily Iowan Room 111, Communication Center Iowa City, Iowa 52240 Copy editor for daily newspaper published by University of Iowa
EDUCATION:	
9/77 to 5/81	University of Iowa, Iowa City, Iowa Received Bachelor of Arts degree (May 1981) Major in journalism
LANGUAGES:	Spanish (spoken and read)
OUTSIDE ACTIVITIES:	Member of Society for Professional Journalists and Iowa Newspaper Association; amateur radio operator; volunteer for United Way in Indianola
REFERENCES:	Personal references available on request.

A Résumé, *above,* briefly describes a job applicant's work experience, education, and interests. To be effective, a résumé should be neatly typed, well organized, and easy to read.

Writing a Résumé. A résumé describes your background and qualifications in more detail than does a letter of application. It may be enclosed with such a letter or given to an employer before or during an interview. A good résumé is neat, well organized, and easy to read. Most are about one or two pages long. A sample résumé appears on this page.

Begin your résumé with your name, address, and telephone number and indicate the kind of job you are seeking. Then list your work experiences, beginning with the most recent. Give the names and addresses of past employers, dates of employment, and a brief description of your duties and function. Indicate any skills you have that relate to the job you are seeking. Also mention any related volunteer work or other activities.

Next, list the names and locations of all schools and training programs you have attended since high school. Include your attendance dates and major subjects plus any degrees, diplomas, certificates, and honors you received. Finally, list any hobbies, travel experience, or other information that applies to the job you are seeking. Be sure to date your résumé to show how recent the information is.

Many employers ask for the names and addresses of *personal references*—that is, persons the employer may contact to learn more about you. Some job applicants list three or four personal references in their résumés. Other applicants indicate that such references are available on request.

Completing Application Forms. Most employers ask job applicants to fill out an application form. Such forms help employers find out about your qualifications. Application forms should be filled out carefully. Read each question thoroughly before you answer it, and make your answers as brief, neat, and complete as possible.

Most application forms request the same kinds of information, and much of the information duplicates that given in résumés. The forms ask for your address, telephone number, social security number, and the title of the job for which you are applying. Most forms also ask about your previous employment, including your employers' and supervisors' names, the dates of your employment, and your duties. The forms further request that you list the schools you attended, the dates you attended them, and any degrees, diplomas, and certificates you received. Many forms request information about your military experience, health, and hobbies. They may also ask for the names and addresses of personal references.

Being Interviewed. If your résumé or application form indicates you are qualified for a job opening, the employer may ask you to come in for an interview. The interview enables you to learn more about the job opening. It also helps the employer find out if you are the best person to hire for the job.

Most interviewers pay close attention to the way an applicant acts, dresses, and answers questions. You can favorably influence an interviewer by arriving on time and by being polite, sincere, and well organized. Dress as you would for the kind of job you are seeking, unless the workers wear uniforms. The interviewer will probably ask about your interests, your work experience, and your goals. Common questions also include your reasons for applying for the job and what you believe you can contribute to the success of the employer's business. Answer all questions briefly and frankly. You might find it helpful to think out your answers to such questions before an interview.

Many people prepare for a job interview by trying to learn some facts about the employer's business. Such facts might include information on the kinds of products the company manufactures or on the services it provides. This kind of knowledge can help you ask intelligent questions during your interview. It also shows the interviewer that you are interested in the employer's business.

After the interview, send a thank-you letter to the interviewer. If you still want to be considered for the job, say so in your letter. Also ask any further questions you might have.

CAREERS / *The World of Work*

With thousands of career possibilities to choose from, a person exploring career fields could become extremely confused. In an attempt to organize the vast amount of career information, experts have developed various classification systems. Each system groups occupations that are similar in some way. One familiar system classifies jobs into four groups according to work activities. These groups—white collar, blue collar, farm, and service—are discussed earlier in this article in the section *Exploring Career Fields.*

Career education programs in many schools use a classification system that groups jobs with similar goals and similar work activities. This system divides occupations into 15 groups called *clusters.* These clusters commonly are (1) agribusiness and natural resources, (2) business and office, (3) communications and media, (4) construction, (5) environment, (6) fine arts and humanities, (7) health, (8) home economics, (9) hospitality and recreation, (10) manufacturing, (11) marine science, (12) marketing and distribution, (13) personal services, (14) public service, and (15) transportation.

The occupations included in a cluster require similar abilities and interests but different levels of preparation. The main preparation levels are (1) short on-the-job training, (2) long on-the-job training, (3) specialty level, and (4) university level. These levels indicate the amount of training most workers need to perform their jobs with average ability. People who cannot prepare for an occupation in the higher levels of a cluster can find related occupations in the same cluster that require less training.

In jobs with short on-the-job training, a person can learn the work in a few hours or days. Many such occupations do not require a high school diploma. Occupations that call for long on-the-job training can be learned through months or years of work experience or through an apprenticeship, vocational school courses, or a job-training program. Most of the jobs at this level require a high school education. Most specialty-level occupations call for training beyond high school at a technical school or a two-year college. Most jobs at the university level require a college degree. Some of these jobs also require additional training at a professional or graduate school.

This section discusses each career cluster individually, one cluster to a page. Each page covers occupational groups within the cluster and describes common activities and working conditions. Each page also gives examples of jobs at each level of preparation. However, these examples provide only a general guide. Preparation requirements vary among both employers and workers. In addition, some occupations might be included in more than one career cluster, depending on the kind of work that is involved. For example, mechanics who service automobiles are listed within the transportation cluster, and those who repair mining equipment are included in the agribusiness and natural resources cluster.

Agribusiness and Natural Resources

Many workers in agribusiness and natural resources supply raw materials for much of the food, clothing, energy, shelter, and industrial goods that people require. Some of the jobs in this cluster deal with the production or regulation of natural resources. Other jobs help ensure and improve the quality of raw materials.

Agribusiness includes workers who raise livestock, crops, and ornamental flowers, shrubs, and trees. It also includes people who process and market agricultural products. Other workers provide supplies and technical aid to farmers. Still others are involved in the development of new ways to preserve food and in the commercial raising of plants and animals that live in water.

Natural resources occupations include the exploration for and the mining or quarrying of such materials as coal, iron, and gravel. Other jobs include the production of petroleum and natural gas. Forestry occupations involve managing and protecting forests and woodlands and harvesting forest products. Fisheries and wildlife specialists manage and protect fish and wildlife resources. Workers in the area of land and water management are concerned with the administration, conservation, and development of parks, inland and coastal waterways, and hydroelectric power. Research workers look for better ways to produce and use natural resources. Other workers enforce conservation laws and other regulations dealing with natural resources.

Many occupations in this cluster are performed outdoors. In some cases, such as coal mining and fighting forest fires, the work can be unpleasant or dangerous.

The kinds of jobs available in agribusiness and natural resources constantly change. For example, the development of scientific farming methods and modern farm machinery has sharply reduced the need for farm laborers and increased the need for highly trained farmers and other agriculturalists. The development of new equipment and techniques is also expected to decrease opportunities for employment in various mining and quarrying occupations.

Short On-the-Job Training. Agribusiness workers who can learn their jobs through a short training session include fruit pickers, general farm hands, and turkey raisers. Workers in natural resources who need only a brief training period include fish hatchery workers, loggers, park workers, and quarry workers.

Long On-the-Job Training. Many farmers and ranchers learn their jobs through years of experience. Other workers who require a long period of training include game wardens, logging supervisors, and sheep herders. Mining and petroleum workers at this level include drillers, miners, mine supervisors, oil pumpers, and mining equipment mechanics.

Specialty Level. Agricultural aides, dairy technologists, and poultry technicians require specialty-level training. Natural resources workers who need such training include conservation aides, geological technicians, park rangers, and petroleum-engineering aides.

University Level. Many farmers need college courses in agriculture and business to operate modern farms successfully. Other agribusiness workers who require a college education include agronomists and veterinarians. In the natural resources area, such occupations as forester, geologist, mining or petroleum engineer, and zoologist call for a college degree.

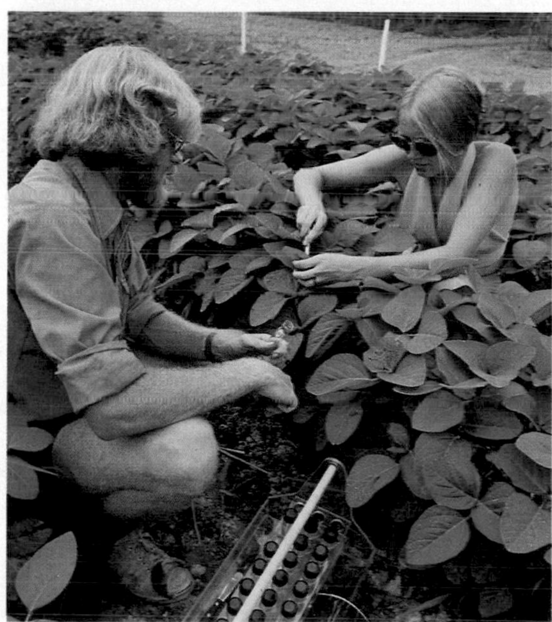

U.S. Dept. of Agriculture

Agricultural Researchers work to improve farm production. These research technicians are collecting soybean samples that will be tested to measure the effect of a special fertilizer.

Leo Touchet, The Photo Circle

Oil-Well Drillers work with heavy machinery. They must be strong and have good physical coordination. These workers, called *roughnecks,* are adding a section of pipe to an oil drill.

Business and Office

Every day, businesses, governments, industries, schools, and other organizations produce vast quantities of documents, letters, reports, and other records. Many business and office occupations involve developing, organizing, and analyzing such records.

Almost every office employs clerical workers to perform such tasks as filing, answering telephones, operating office machines, and receiving or distributing cash. Secretaries keep records, take dictation, and compose and edit documents, letters, and reports. Specialists in the area of records systems use bookkeeping and accounting methods and computers to record or analyze information.

Most businesses need management workers to plan and administer company activities and policies and to train and supervise other employees. Personnel specialists interview, hire, test, and dismiss employees. Some also direct training programs or help employees solve personal or work-related problems.

Banks and other financial institutions employ people who arrange loans, manage funds, and perform other related duties. Insurance workers provide many kinds of insurance, such as accident, automobile, fire, health, life, and theft. Real estate workers help people buy, sell, or rent land and buildings. Some are also involved in building management.

Most workers in this cluster perform their duties in business offices during regular business hours. Many office employees, such as cashiers and typists, work with things and often repeat the same kinds of tasks. Other office workers deal with ideas. For example, they may design computer systems, offer financial or legal advice, or analyze financial reports. Employment in business and office occupations is expected to increase through the 1980's. Workers projected to be in greatest demand include accountants, auditors, bookkeepers, cashiers, general office clerks, secretaries, and typists.

Short On-the-Job Training. Many beginning office workers have had business courses in high school or vocational school but no job experience. In numerous cases, these workers include accounting clerks, bank tellers, cashiers, messengers, receptionists, and typists. Many employees in lower-level occupations advance to more responsible jobs as they gain experience.

Long On-the-Job Training. Most bookkeepers, court clerks, and insurance adjusters learn their job skills in vocational school or through lengthy on-the-job training. Other workers at this level include insurance, personnel, and real estate clerks. Most workers also need special training to learn how to operate complicated business machines.

Specialty Level. Many executive, legal, and medical secretaries are graduates of a two-year college or technical institute. Other workers at this level include some computer programmers and real estate salespeople.

University Level. Most accountants, bankers, business executives, economists, personnel directors, and statisticians have a college education. Many of them also hold a graduate degree. Lawyers must have a degree from a law school.

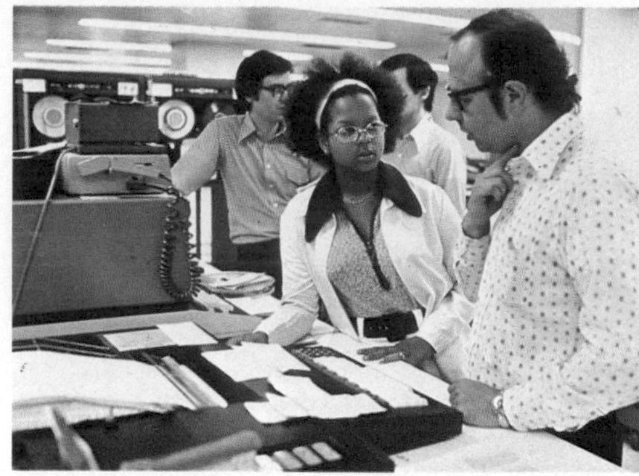

WORLD BOOK photo

Computer Specialists develop systems that help business executives organize information and solve problems. Computer experts need a college education or other advanced training.

First National Bank of Chicago

Bank Employees in the new accounts section of a bank, *above,* open checking and savings accounts for new customers. Most banks hire and train college graduates to fill such positions.

WORLD BOOK photo

Clerical Workers maintain files, sort mail, and perform other tasks that help an office run smoothly. Many high schools offer business courses that prepare students for clerical work.

Communications and Media

The field of communications and *media* (means of communication) involves the processing and transmitting of information. Some workers gather and report the news, provide entertainment, or translate foreign languages. Other workers operate or service equipment used in communications.

Journalism and publishing communicate information through books, magazines, newspapers, and other printed materials. Workers in this area write, edit, illustrate, print, and distribute such materials. Radio and television broadcasting includes developing, producing, and transmitting radio to TV programs. It also involves servicing broadcasting and receiving equipment. Workers in telephone and telegraph communications transmit messages and install, maintain, and repair telephone and telegraph equipment. Workers in the area of satellite and laser transmissions operate and service the equipment used in such communications.

Occupations in the motion-picture industry involve creating and producing films. Workers in the recording industry reproduce sounds on phonograph records or tapes and sell and distribute such recordings. Occupations in the field of language interpretation help people understand foreign languages or signs and symbols, such as those used in braille.

Working conditions differ for various occupations in this cluster. Many workers perform their duties in offices, shops, or studios. Journalists may be sent to combat and disaster areas. Many jobs require well-developed language skills. In general, the employment outlook for jobs in this cluster is favorable. Most occupations in this field will be increasingly affected by the use of computers, lasers, satellites, videotape recorders, and other modern communications technology.

Short On-the-Job Training is required for film projectionists, film splicers, and stagehands. Some of the workers at this preparation level take care of the costumes and sets used in television and motion-picture productions. Other workers include those who assist telephone line installers and repairers.

Long On-the-Job Training. Many workers who operate and repair communications equipment learn their skills through an apprenticeship or other lengthy training program. Other workers at this preparation level include braille translators, camera operators, makeup artists, proofreaders, script clerks, sound effects technicians, and wardrobe personnel.

Specialty Level. Many photographers and radio and television announcers obtain training at a two-year college or a technical institute. Some graduates of technical institutes become technicians who help produce radio or TV broadcasts or movies. Other graduates help develop new communications systems.

University Level. College courses can help students develop their communications skills and gain a better understanding of world affairs. Therefore many journalists and scriptwriters have a college degree. Other workers with college training include producers; program directors; radio, television, and telephone engineers; and radio and TV station managers.

Martin Levick, Black Star

Telephone Line Workers install and repair cables that link together to form a vast communication network. The crew shown above is working on a cable that runs under the street.

Universal Studios (WORLD BOOK photo by John Hamilton, Globe)

The Motion-Picture Industry employs a variety of specialists. This picture shows a director, *right,* supervising camera operators and other crew members during an outdoor filming session.

Milt and Joan Mann

The Editorial Staff of a Newspaper includes writers and editors who produce news stories and feature articles. They must be able to write clearly and work quickly to meet deadlines.

Construction

Construction occupations deal with building, modernizing, and repairing houses, factories, and other kinds of buildings. Construction workers also build and repair such structures as bridges, dams, and highways.

Workers in construction range from unskilled laborers to highly skilled professionals. Employees in the area of design include architects and civil engineers, who draw up plans for a structure and choose the materials to be used. Contractors estimate building costs and schedule and supervise construction work. Workers in the area of materials distribution buy and sell building materials and supplies. Workers in management help construction companies operate smoothly.

Most construction workers specialize in certain building materials. For example, carpenters and other woodworkers use wood in constructing buildings and such building features as floors and frames. Metalworkers perform such jobs as pipe fitting and welding. They also install plumbing, heating, and air-conditioning systems. Masonry workers use bricks, cement, stones, and similar materials to build foundations, sidewalks, walls, and other structures. They also plaster surfaces and lay tiles. Electrical specialists install wiring and electrical fixtures. Finishing workers paint, wallpaper, landscape, install windows, and do other tasks to complete a building. Heavy-equipment operators run and maintain such construction machinery as bulldozers and cranes.

Numerous construction jobs take place outdoors or in partly completed buildings. In many cases, work on such jobs stops during bad weather. Much of the work requires standing, bending, or stooping for long periods. In addition, construction workers are more likely to be injured on the job than are most other kinds of workers. Employment opportunities in construction depend heavily on economic conditions. When money is plentiful, people tend to build new homes and factories. When money is scarce, they try to economize by having their old buildings repaired or remodeled. Some specialists in construction are expected to have more job opportunities through the 1980's than other workers in this field. Such specialists include architects, experts in computerized construction design, installers of solar-energy systems, and refrigeration mechanics.

Short On-the-Job Training. Most construction laborers can learn their jobs in a short training session. Some laborers help prepare a building site by tearing down existing structures. Others load trucks or set up scaffolding. Some laborers assist bricklayers, carpenters, and other skilled workers.

Long On-the-Job Training. Skilled personnel make up the largest group of construction workers. Many learn their trade through an apprenticeship. Others attend vocational school or learn through long on-the-job training. Skilled construction workers include bricklayers, carpenters, electricians, painters, and plumbers. Other skilled workers operate bulldozers or cranes and install windows, elevators, or heating systems.

Specialty Level. Some graduates of technical institutes become drafters or surveyors. Drafters use special instruments to draw diagrams that show how a structure should be built. Surveyors measure a construction site to determine its boundaries and other characteristics. Some plumbers, electricians, and other skilled workers train at vocational schools.

University Level. Architects, civil engineers, and electrical engineers require college training. Many managers and contractors in the construction industry also have a college education.

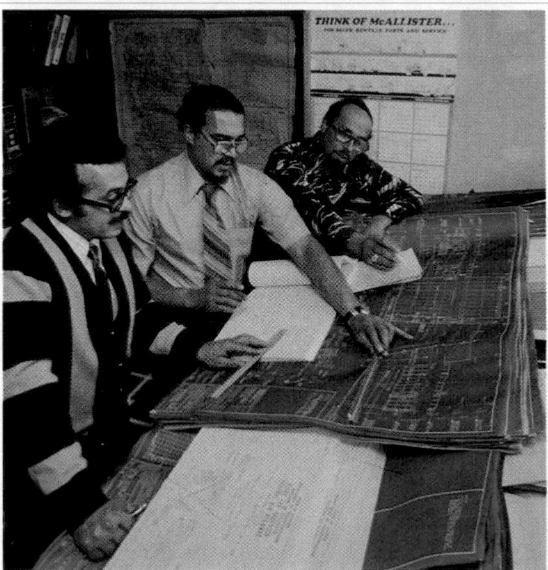

Brent Jones

Architects combine artistic and engineering skills in designing buildings and other structures. These architects are discussing the blueprints for a construction project.

Sam Ashey, Stock, Boston

Construction Workers prepare to work in a trench by propping up boards to keep the sides in place, *above.* Many construction jobs involve outdoor work and require much physical exertion.

Environment

Environmental specialists are concerned with protecting and improving the environment. Some environmentalists do scientific research to increase our knowledge about the environment. Other workers use such knowledge to help solve environmental problems. Still other environmentalists help develop, work for the passage of, and enforce antipollution laws and conservation regulations.

Environmentalists specialize in a variety of fields. Some of them work to prevent and control air, water, soil, and noise pollution. Others conduct experiments to discover how pollutants affect the atmosphere and weather conditions.

In the field of water resources, some workers design and operate water purification systems and water treatment plants. Others develop irrigation and other water supply systems. Environmentalists concerned with soil and mineral conservation work to protect the land from erosion and from pollution by chemical fertilizers and pesticides. They also instruct farmers and mining companies in production techniques that cause the least possible damage to the land.

Such environmental conditions as pests, pollution, and improper waste disposal can present health hazards to members of a community. Experts in the field of disease prevention and health planning work to control and prevent such hazards. Many environmentalists are involved in planning how to make the best present and future use of the environment. Some of them work to preserve forests, rangelands, shorelines, and wildlife and to develop recreational areas. City planners cooperate with sociologists and other experts to develop and provide the best possible environment for urban dwellers. Other specialists plan for the development of rural areas.

Environmentalists are employed by colleges and universities, government agencies, and private industries. Some work in classrooms, laboratories, or offices. Others work mostly outdoors. Employment in many environmental fields is expected to increase through the 1980's as people become more and more concerned about the quality of the environment. In particular, specialists in the disposal of nuclear and other hazardous wastes are expected to be in great demand.

Short On-the-Job Training. Campground caretakers, forest fire fighters, fire patrollers, and tree planters require only a short training session. Other workers at this level include orchard fumigators and sewage disposal workers.

Long On-the-Job Training is required for many workers who operate and service pollution control equipment. Such workers include incinerator and water treatment plant operators and sewage plant attendants. Fire wardens, park maintenance supervisors, and some laboratory assistants also learn their jobs through lengthy work experience.

Specialty Level. Many land use technicians, pest control experts, radiation monitors, safety inspectors, and other environmental specialists are trained at technical institutes or two-year colleges. Most forester aides and park rangers also need such preparation.

University Level. Chemists, ecologists, microbiologists, soil scientists, and other university-trained scientists work as environmental researchers, inspectors, and planners. Most foresters, range managers, and other natural resources managers also need a college education. So do industrial hygienists, mining engineers, park naturalists, and traffic engineers.

Forest Service, USDA

A Forest Ranger cuts down dead trees, *above,* to encourage new growth and to reduce the danger of a forest fire. Careful forest management helps protect the natural environment.

Shell Oil Company

An Industrial Hygienist, *above left,* measures noise levels outside a chemical plant. Such specialists help reduce health hazards by measuring various kinds of pollution in work areas.

Fine Arts and Humanities

Literature, music, painting, sculpture, and other arts enrich the lives of most people. In addition, religious faith, a sense of history, and other cultural values add meaning to many people's lives. The fine arts and humanities are concerned with creating beauty and with expressing, studying, and preserving ideas and cultural values.

Workers in the fine arts convey thoughts and feelings through various creative activities. Many of these workers also entertain people. The fine arts consist of the *visual arts*, the *performing arts*, and *creative writing*. The visual arts include such fields as painting, photography, sculpture, and textile design. Dance, music, and theater are performing arts. Creative writing involves the production of original literary works, such as novels, plays, and poems.

Workers in the humanities are concerned with the moral, social, and artistic values of a culture and its members. Fields in the humanities include history, religion, philosophy, and *linguistics* (the scientific study of language).

Most workers in the fine arts and humanities have to compete intensely for job openings. Competition in the performing arts is especially strong. The number of talented performers seeking employment is much greater than the number of jobs available. As a result, many performers also do other kinds of work to help support themselves. Writers and artists also face serious job competition. Some writers and artists are employed by business firms and receive a salary. Others work on their own and earn money by selling their works. However, many of these people must also hold other jobs to support themselves.

Short On-the-Job Training. Stagehands and certain other workers involved in theatrical and musical productions require only a short training session. Some musicians and singers in the field of popular music also have little or no training beyond high school.

Long On-the-Job Training. Many workers who help produce plays and other artistic performances learn their job skills through an apprenticeship or other long training period. Such workers include stage electricians, stage managers, and operators of sound, lighting, and other production equipment.

Specialty Level. Many commercial photographers, interior designers, and museum technicians have had specialized training at a technical institute or a community college. Other workers at this preparation level include editorial assistants, layout artists, and photograph retouchers.

University Level. In the fine arts, many art directors, authors, composers, conductors, and sculptors have a college education. Numerous illustrators, paintings restorers, and technical writers are also college trained. A college education, as well as a graduate degree, is required for most workers in the humanities. Many of them become college or university teachers. Others work as archivists, curators, historians, or linguists for various organizations. Still others pursue a religious vocation as ministers, nuns, priests, or rabbis.

Ted Thai

Dancing and the other performing arts require years of study, training, and dedicated practice. The scene shown above is from a performance of the dance work *Cloven Kingdom.*

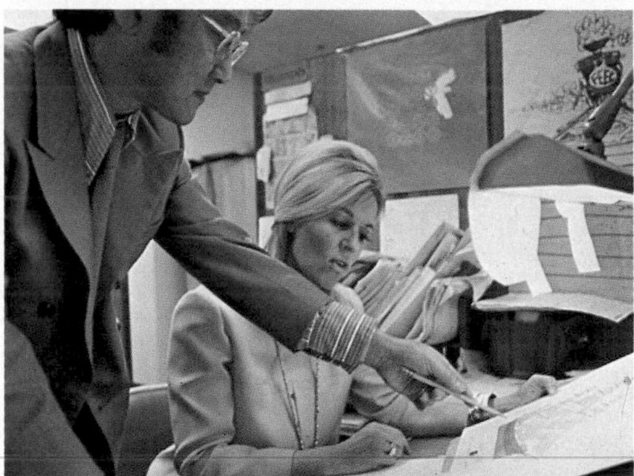

WORLD BOOK photo

Commercial Artists create illustrations that appear in advertisements, books, magazines, and other publications. The artists pictured here are discussing the artwork for a book.

Field Museum of Natural History (WORLD BOOK photo)

Building a Museum Exhibit, such as the one shown above, is a highly specialized job. Museum curators, model makers, and technicians work together in creating such displays.

Health

Workers in health occupations help people live healthier and happier lives. The services involved in health-care occupations range from teaching children how to brush their teeth to transplanting organs.

Physicians and nurses are among the best-known health workers. However, many other kinds of workers are needed to provide complete health care. For example, some workers in the area of medical support help patients learn to use artificial arms or legs. Other workers in this area help patients overcome hearing or sight problems, or they design special diets for individuals. Dentists and other dentistry specialists treat and help prevent diseases and abnormalities of the teeth and gums. Mental health workers help prevent and treat mental illnesses. Medical emergency specialists care for patients in hospital emergency rooms or in ambulances. Personal and community health workers look after patients at home. These workers also help community members develop good health habits.

Research scientists and laboratory assistants study biological processes and the causes of diseases. They also help physicians make diagnoses. Pharmacists fill prescriptions. Pharmacologists study the effects of drugs on living things.

Many occupations keep health services operating efficiently. Hospitals, clinics, and other health-care centers are supervised by administrators. Clerical workers keep patients' records, order supplies, and perform many other tasks. Medical librarians and other workers in the field of health information help doctors keep informed about medical advances.

Many health workers work evening or late-night shifts. Some jobs require workers to stand for long periods or to deal with seriously ill or injured patients. In general, jobs in the health cluster, particularly at the semiprofessional level, are expected to increase considerably through the 1980's. Among the health workers projected to be in greatest demand are dental assistants and hygienists, hospital orderlies, nurses, nurses' aides, physical therapists, and veterinarians.

Short On-the-Job Training is required for some beginning nurses' aides and hospital orderlies. Other workers at this level include diet clerks, home health aides, and medical office clerks and receptionists.

Long On-the-Job Training. Ambulance drivers, medical records clerks, occupational therapy aides, and psychiatric aides require vocational school courses or lengthy job training. *Orthopedic* (bone) cast specialists also need long on-the-job training.

Specialty Level. Many graduates of technical institutes assist doctors or dentists directly or help them by doing laboratory work. Such specialists include dental hygienists, medical assistants, practical nurses, veterinary technicians, and X-ray technicians.

University Level. Dentists, hospital administrators, medical doctors, pharmacists, psychiatrists, and veterinarians require specialized training beyond college. Other health workers at this level include chiropractors, dietitians, medical technologists, optometrists, physical therapists, podiatrists, and registered nurses.

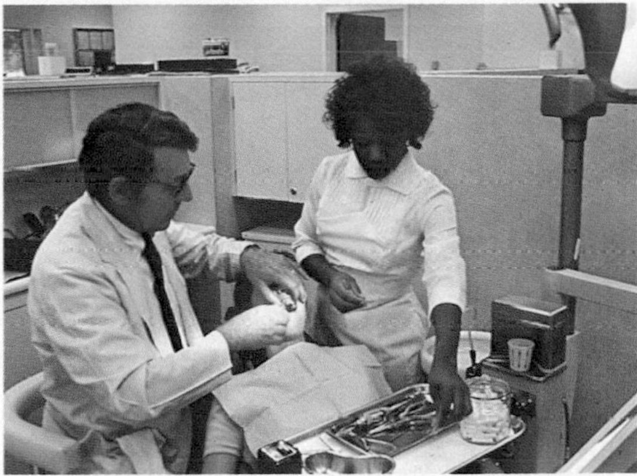

University of Illinois Medical Center (WORLD BOOK photo)

An Orthodontist, *above left,* is a dentist who specializes in correcting irregular positions of the teeth. A dental assistant, *above right,* is specially trained to help the dentist.

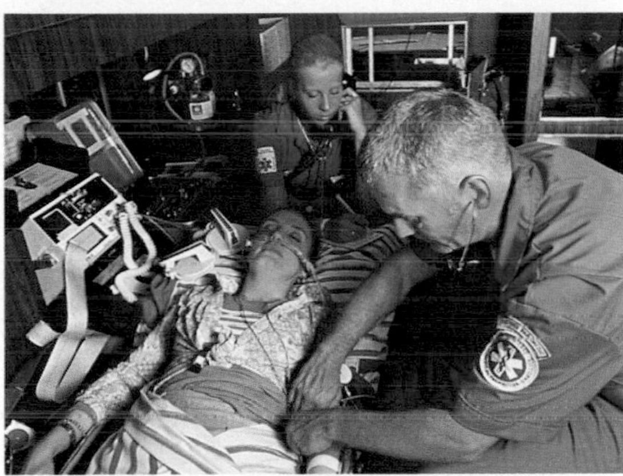

Betz Ambulance Service (WORLD BOOK photo)

Paramedics are trained to take the place of a physician under certain conditions. These paramedics use a mobile telephone to consult a doctor while treating a patient in an ambulance.

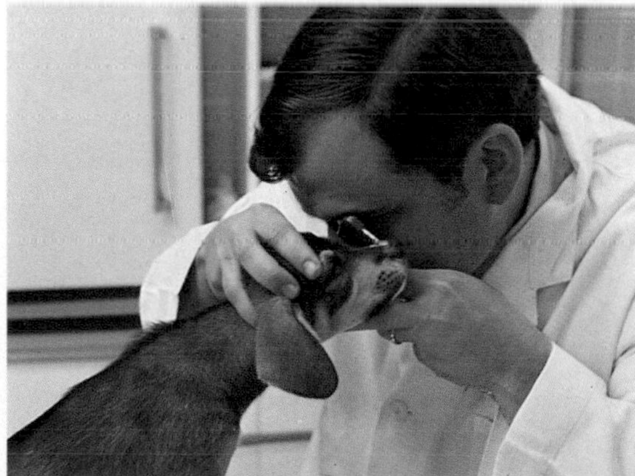

WORLD BOOK photo

Veterinarians treat family pets, livestock, and other animals. Veterinarians must have at least two years of college followed by four years in a college of veterinary medicine.

Home Economics

Home and family life plays an important part in most people's lives. Occupations in home economics deal with managing households effectively and improving the quality of family life. They also are concerned with helping consumers learn how to shop wisely.

Home economics includes many specialized fields. Workers in the field of food service study human nutritional needs and help develop and improve food products. Some of these workers manage food services in schools, hospitals, and other institutions. Other workers maintain, operate, and sanitize food-handling equipment. Still others are involved in the advertising, sale, or delivery of food products.

In the field of clothing and textiles, some workers develop, test, or produce fabrics. Others design or produce clothing. Additional occupations in this field include dry cleaning and the advertising, buying, or selling of clothing or textiles. In the field of housing and household equipment, some workers deal with the design and interior decoration of homes. Others develop, test, and improve household equipment and products.

Many workers in the area of family and community services offer family counseling services, assist elderly citizens, and help parents learn how to care for their children. Many others perform housekeeping and household maintenance tasks. Occupations in the field of child care deal with the emotional and intellectual development of children. Workers care for children in the home, in institutions, or in child-care centers. Another home economics field, extension service, deals with teaching community members such homemaking skills as selecting household appliances, planning and preparing nutritious meals, and managing family finances. Extension service agents also help guide 4-H club programs throughout the United States.

Many people, especially women, choose homemaking as a career. Homemakers work to create a healthful and comfortable home for their family. In doing so, they practice many of the same skills that other home economics workers use.

Some home economics specialists work in offices. Others are employed in test kitchens or laboratories. Still others work in stores or schools or provide their services in people's homes. Openings for many kinds of jobs in this cluster, especially the teaching of home economics at the high school level, are fairly competitive. However, opportunities for workers with the elderly are expected to be favorable through the 1980's. Child-care workers and kitchen helpers and other food service workers are also expected to be in great demand.

Short On-the-Job Training is required for dry-cleaning machine operators and many food service workers. Some nursing home and child-care aides also need only a short training session.

Long On-the-Job Training. Some food service supervisors and management aides learn their jobs through a long training period. Other workers at this level include electric equipment testers, comparison shoppers, and some fashion models.

Specialty Level. Technicians who work in the area of food processing, household products, and textiles commonly require two years of specialized training. Other workers at this level include sewing instructors and some institutional cooks and housekeepers.

University Level. Many home economics workers need four years of college or more. They include directors of consumer education, extension service specialists, fashion designers, nutritionists, and textile chemists.

Baker Knapp & Tubbs (WORLD BOOK photo)

Interior Designers plan attractive settings that best suit the needs of a family or business. The designer shown above helps a couple choose an upholstery fabric.

The Quaker Oats Company (WORLD BOOK photo)

Home Economists try out a cookie recipe in a test kitchen, *above.* Food-processing companies employ such specialists to improve recipes and to develop new uses for their products.

Hospitality and Recreation

Hospitality and recreation workers provide services that help people enjoy their leisure time. Hospitality occupations involve tourism and other travel for pleasure. Jobs in the field of recreation deal with the planning, organizing, and directing of recreational activities. They also involve providing entertainment and amusements.

Workers in travel bureaus and travel agencies help people plan vacations and tours. Travel bureaus provide tourist information about cities, countries, and regions. Travel agencies provide information about restaurants, transportation, hotels and other accommodations, and travel requirements and regulations. They also make airline and hotel reservations and other travel arrangements.

Specialists in tour management, including tour conductors and travel guides, try to make tourists comfortable as they travel. They also help tourists learn about the areas and attractions they visit.

Occupations in the area of public, industrial, and private recreation involve sports and entertainment. This area includes sports instructors, professional athletes, recreation directors, circus and carnival workers, and certain stage performers. Many recreation workers provide services that help people enjoy natural resources. Some of these workers manage and maintain such recreation areas as beaches, forests, and wildlife parks. Other workers include lifeguards, zookeepers, and hunting and fishing guides. People who plan, develop, or sell recreation areas and equipment are also grouped in this cluster.

Most hospitality and recreation occupations involve dealing with people, and some jobs require special physical abilities. Educational requirements vary for occupations in this cluster. However, a college degree in recreation is becoming increasingly important for people entering the recreation field. Employment opportunities for hospitality and recreation workers are dependent on economic conditions but are expected to increase through the 1980's.

Short On-the-Job Training. Attendants at bowling lanes, golf courses, skating rinks, tennis courts, and similar recreation centers require very little training. Deck stewards and stewardesses, ski-tow operators, travel agency clerks, and ushers also need only a short training session.

Long On-the-Job Training. Many hospitality and recreation workers learn their duties through lengthy training on the job or in vocational school. They include railroad ticket clerks, tour conductors, and travel agents. Most animal trainers, hunting and fishing guides, lifeguards, and zookeepers also require special courses or long on-the-job training. In addition, many professional entertainers, such as circus performers, puppeteers, and ventriloquists learn their skills from experienced performers.

Specialty Level. Recreation directors, travel guides, and many professional athletes need about two years of specialized training beyond high school. Numerous camp counselors, golf course managers, and theater managers also have such training.

University Level. Many managers and other workers in hospitality and recreation have a college education. They include numerous advertising and publicity specialists, athletics directors and trainers, recreation center directors, and travel writers. In addition, many professional athletes played on college teams before entering professional sports.

Ask Mr. Foster Travel Service (WORLD BOOK photo)

A Travel Agent, *above left,* helps a customer plan a trip. Agents handle transportation arrangements and hotel reservations. Many travel agencies offer their employees travel benefits.

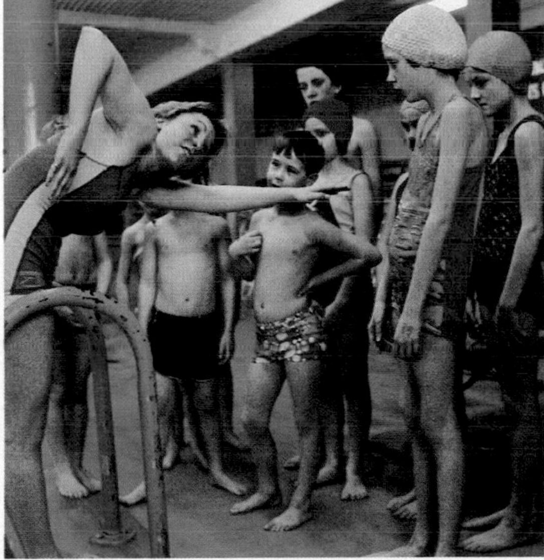

Chicago Park District (WORLD BOOK photo)

A Swimming Instructor at a community recreation center teaches children how to swim, *above.* Many recreation workers must have a college degree in recreation or in physical education.

Manufacturing

Manufacturing includes all occupations that are involved in making products by hand or by machine. Manufactured products range from simple plastic or wooden objects, such as clothespins or toothpicks, to highly complicated electronic computers. Manufactured goods also vary in size, from microscopic electronic parts to giant aircraft carriers and supertankers.

About two-thirds of the workers in manufacturing actually make products. These employees include craftworkers, skilled and semiskilled workers, and unskilled laborers. Craftworkers are highly skilled in such trades as tool designing, tool and die making, and tailoring. Many craftworkers supervise other employees. Skilled workers, who include engravers, machinists, printers, and welders, use special job skills to make items or to operate machinery. Semiskilled workers include machine operators and assistants to skilled workers. Many semiskilled occupations require workers to repeat the same task again and again. Unskilled laborers perform jobs that require no special skills, such as sorting, packing, or moving materials.

Many scientists, engineers, and technicians also work in manufacturing. Scientists perform laboratory tests and other research to develop new products and improve old ones. Engineers design and test airplanes, automobiles, household appliances, machine parts, and countless other products. They also design production equipment and improved manufacturing techniques. Some technicians assist scientists and engineers. Others plan or supervise production activities, such as packing or storing products. The manufacturing cluster also includes management workers. They develop and enforce company policies, plan and direct production activities, purchase equipment and materials, or work in labor relations or public relations.

Most employees in manufacturing work in factories or shops. Common working conditions include high levels of dust, heat, or noise. Some factory jobs require great strength or standing for long periods. Prospects for employment in manufacturing vary according to occupation and industry. But the overall increase in manufacturing jobs is expected to be slow, in part because of the growing use of computers and other forms of mechanization in industry. Workers who develop, improve, and maintain industrial equipment may have more job opportunities than other workers in this cluster.

Short On-the-Job Training. Most unskilled and semiskilled manufacturing workers need only brief training. Such employees include cannery workers, foundry laborers, mill hands, packers, and machinery operators.

Long On-the-Job Training. Most skilled workers and craftworkers in manufacturing learn their trade through an apprenticeship or a long period of on-the-job training. These workers include machinists, patternmakers, tailors, tool designers, and tool and die makers. Other workers at this level include die casters, heavy-duty press operators, instrument makers, and welders.

Specialty Level. Manufacturers employ many graduates of technical institutes. Such workers include engineering and science technicians, electronics technicians, engineering schedulers, and quality technicians. Some skilled workers also learned their trade at technical institutes or in vocational schools.

University Level. Chemists, physicists, and other scientists employed in manufacturing need four or more years of college. Engineers must also have a college degree. In addition, many management workers have had college training.

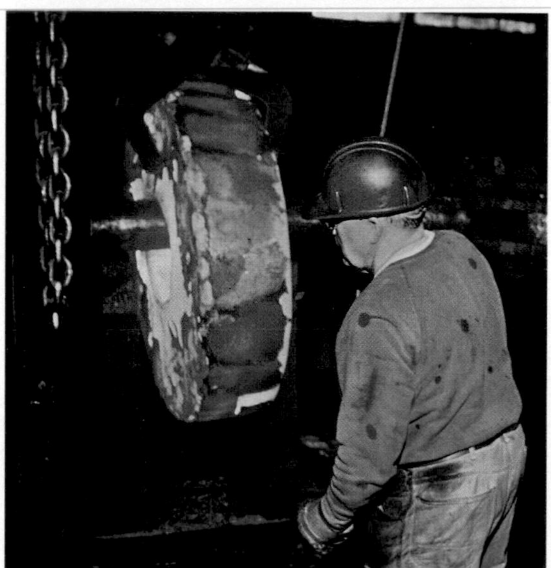

Aramco World Magazine

Heavy Industry includes mills, foundries, and factories that produce steel parts for heavy equipment. This foundry worker operates machinery that handles red-hot metal parts.

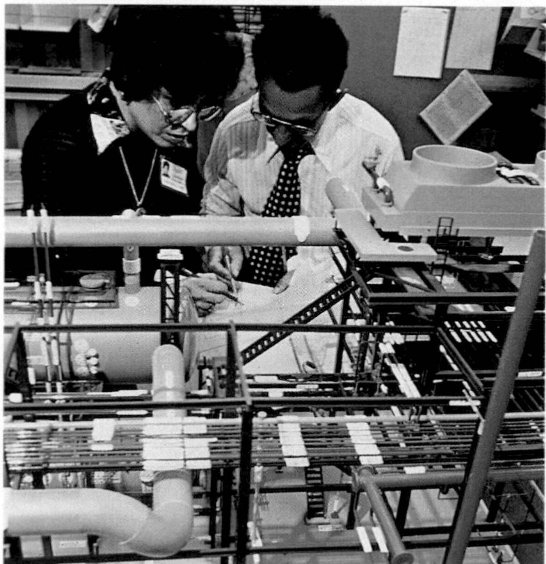

Aramco World Magazine

Engineers work in many industries, designing and testing products and production equipment. These engineers are inspecting a model of equipment they designed for an oil refinery.

Marine Science

Careers in marine science deal with the oceans, lakes, and rivers. These bodies of water cover more than two-thirds of the earth's surface. They affect the weather and provide transportation routes and recreation areas. In addition, many experts believe that the oceans can be developed to help meet growing demands for food, energy, and minerals.

Workers in the field of marine exploration and research explore, survey, and analyze the oceans and other waterways. Some *oceanographers* (ocean scientists) study currents, tides, and waves and how the oceans affect weather patterns. Other oceanographers study the ocean floor or the chemicals in seawater. Marine biologists study fish and other water life. Some seek ways to increase the production of food from the oceans. Other marine biologists study the effects of pollution on water life. Marine architects, engineers, and technologists design and build surface and underwater vessels. They also design instruments and other equipment used in marine exploration, research, and other activities.

Specialists in the field of chemical and mineral extraction explore for and remove chemicals and minerals from seawater and the ocean floor. Specialists in offshore drilling explore and drill for petroleum and natural gas beneath the ocean floor.

Workers in commercial fishing catch fish and other marine animals or process the animals for market. Some also take customers on recreational fishing trips. Other workers are engaged in *aquaculture*—the raising of fish and other marine life on fish farms, in hatcheries, or in similar controlled environments. Many workers in marine science operate, maintain, and repair boats and other vessels. Other workers support marine studies by conducting laboratory experiments or by using computers to analyze information that has been gathered by scientists.

The majority of marine science occupations require workers to live near an ocean or other body of water. Most of the work is done outdoors along the shoreline, aboard a boat, or underwater. In the United States, most scientific marine research is financed by the federal government. As a result, employment in oceanography and related occupations depends on the level of government spending in this field. However, job opportunities in marine science are expected to be favorable through the 1980's.

Short On-the-Job Training. Commercial fishing and aquaculture provide many kinds of occupations that require only a brief training session. Workers in these kinds of jobs include fish cleaners, hatchery helpers, seaweed cutters, shellfish shuckers, sponge gatherers, and wharf laborers.

Long On-the-Job Training is required for divers, dock supervisors, fish farmers, fishing instructors, net or trap makers, and people who catch fish for market. Such training is also common for operators and repairers of clam dredges, derricks, motorboats, and other marine machinery.

Specialty Level. A number of marine occupations call for a two-year training program. Such jobs include research technician, laboratory worker, marine drafter, and surveyor.

University Level. Four or more years of college are required for marine biologists, fishery bacteriologists, marine geologists and geophysicists, and other scientists. Marine architects and engineers also need a college education.

Jeff Foott, Bruce Coleman Inc.

Marine Biology includes the study of the habits of fish. Workers tag a salmon, *above,* so that the fish's spawning journey can be traced.

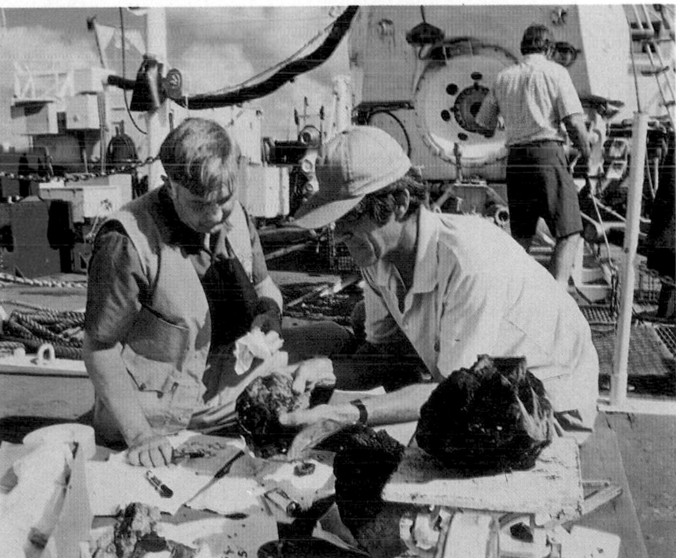

Woods Hole Oceanographic Institution

Marine Geology includes the study of rock samples taken from the ocean floor, *above.* Such research helps scientists learn about the formation of the continents. It also aids in locating offshore deposits of petroleum and natural gas.

Marketing and Distribution

Occupations in marketing and distribution are concerned with moving goods from farmers, manufacturers, and other producers to consumers. Some producers sell their goods directly to consumers. Others market their products through *wholesalers* and *retailers*. Wholesalers buy large quantities of an item. They then sell smaller quantities of that item to stores and other retailers. The retailers sell individual items to customers.

Many kinds of workers are involved in marketing and distribution. Marketing managers plan, organize, and direct marketing activities. Market researchers and analysts collect and analyze market information and predict sales patterns. Manufacturers, wholesalers, and retailers employ buyers, or purchasing agents, who buy materials or equipment from producers or wholesalers. Workers in the area of sales promotion and training try to create a demand for a product or service and to increase sales. Such workers are involved in advertising, the display and demonstration of merchandise, customer service, and the training of salespeople.

Numerous workers in wholesale and retail trade are salespeople. Many call on possible customers and try to persuade them to buy their products. Others work in retail stores. Workers in the area of distribution handle, store, and transport goods between producers and consumers. Other workers in this cluster provide various business services, such as credit, financing, and insurance. They also keep records and perform clerical duties.

Most employees in management, market research, sales promotion, and business services work in offices. Distribution employees mainly work in warehouses or drive delivery trucks. Some salespeople sell in stores or shops. Others sell door-to-door in a community or travel large distances covering a regional sales territory. Employment prospects in this cluster appear to be good through the 1980's. In fact, cashiers and salesclerks are expected to have more employment opportunities than workers in many other fields.

Short On-the-Job Training. Most salespeople who work in retail stores need only a short training session. Cashier-checkers, delivery drivers, shipping clerks, and vending machine attendants also require only limited training.

Long On-the-Job Training. Auctioneers, product demonstrators, inspectors, and mail-order fillers learn their work through long on-the-job training. Other workers at this level include retail supervisors, statistical tabulators, stock control supervisors, and warehouse managers.

Specialty Level. Some graduates of two-year colleges or technical institutes find jobs as advertising assistants, assistant buyers, market research assistants, or window trimmers. Others become commercial artists or market survey workers.

University Level. People who sell airplanes, computers, and other complicated products need college-level training to understand their products thoroughly. College training is also required for foreign trade consultants, market research analysts, statistical report writers, and some merchandising and sales managers.

WORLD BOOK photo

A Supermarket Checkout Clerk totals the cost of a customer's purchases, *above,* and then handles the money transaction. Such cashiers work in a wide variety of retail businesses.

WORLD BOOK photo

Direct Selling involves visiting possible customers in their homes. The saleswoman shown above at the right is demonstrating to a family the special features of a set of reference books.

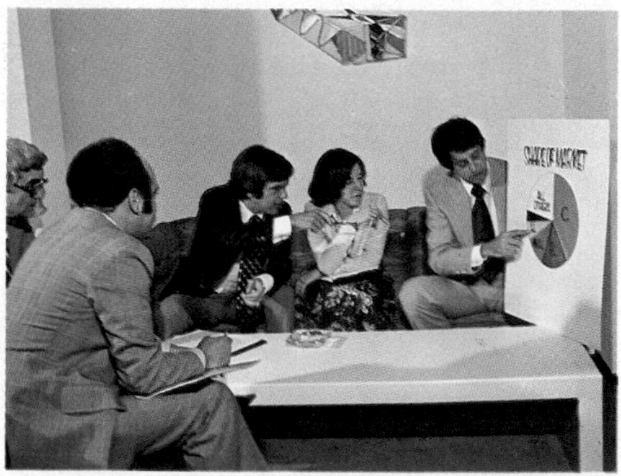

Tatham, Laird, and Kudner (WORLD BOOK photo)

Market Researchers and Analysts study marketing trends and buying habits. They use their findings to help businesses develop new products and plan advertising campaigns, *above.*

Personal Services

Workers in this category perform personal tasks for people. Some workers, such as barbers and manicurists, work to improve a customer's appearance. Others help care for a person's clothing, home, pets, or other possessions. In addition, numerous workers in this cluster attend to the needs of guests in hotels, resturants, and other establishments.

Many personal services include tasks that most people could do themselves. However, some people have personal service workers do these tasks because the jobs may be heavy, difficult, or take a long time to complete. In addition, some personal service jobs require special skills that many people lack.

Barbers and cosmetologists offer beauty, grooming, and related services. Such services include haircutting and hairstyling and facial and scalp treatments.

Workers in the area of domestic services help take care of an employer's home, members of the household, and guests. Domestic workers include cleaning personnel, gardeners, housekeepers, and private cooks. Dry cleaners and launderers clean and repair clothing and such home furnishings as rugs and draperies. Workers in the area of household pet services groom, exercise, train, and sell pets, especially dogs. Some service workers specialize in *mortuary science*. They embalm, cremate, and transport the bodies of dead people. They also plan and arrange funeral and burial services.

When people are away from home, many kinds of personal service workers help make them comfortable. They include employees who provide and care for lodgings in hotels, motels, and similar establishments. Other workers prepare or serve food and drinks in restaurants and cocktail lounges. In addition, flight attendants, bellhops, and restaurant hosts and hostesses greet passengers or guests and offer helpful services.

Some personal service employees work in the employer's home. Many others have jobs in business places or are self-employed. Much of the work includes physical activity. Job opportunities in this cluster are expected to remain steady through the 1980's.

Short On the Job Training. Most babysitters, bellhops, camp attendants, kitchen helpers, and laundry workers need only brief training. Other workers at this level include some housekeepers, janitors, room service clerks, and waiters and waitresses.

Long On-the-Job Training. Many personal service workers learn their skills from experienced workers and lengthy training. Such workers include bartenders, cooks, dog groomers, kitchen supervisors, shoe repairers, stable attendants, and some tailors.

Specialty Level. Some technical institutes offer courses in mortuary science. Graduates of such programs become embalmers and funeral attendants. Many barbers, chefs, cosmetologists, and other personal service workers also train at vocational schools.

University Level. Some college graduates become flight attendants or hotel managers. Others become volunteers in such programs as the Peace Corps and VISTA and work with communities and individuals to improve people's standard of living.

WORLD BOOK photo

Restaurant Employees, such as the waitress and cook above, provide food services in many kinds and sizes of eating places. Most restaurant workers are on their feet for long periods.

R & L Tree Service (WORLD BOOK photo)

Landscape Workers tend lawns and gardens for homeowners and businesses. A special crew may be hired for heavy, difficult jobs, such as uprooting a stump from a yard, *above.*

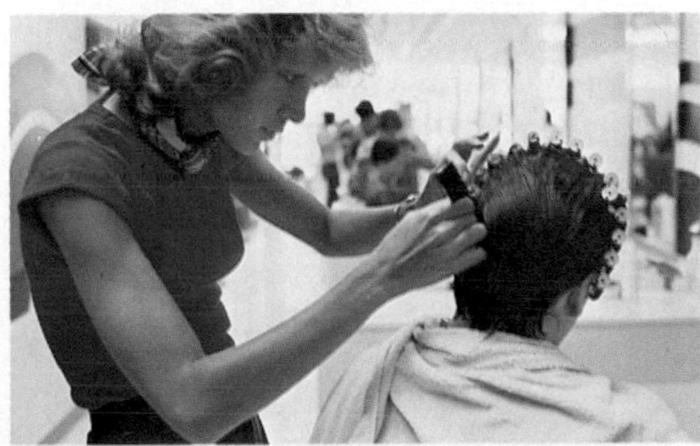

Hair Incorporated (WORLD BOOK photo)

A Hairdresser, *above,* offers such services as styling, cutting, and curling a customer's hair. Beauticians learn their skills at a cosmetology or vocational school or by working as an apprentice.

Public Service

Society has become increasingly complicated. As a result, people depend on public service workers to help meet their needs and improve the quality of life in the community.

Many workers in the area of legislative, administrative, and management services develop laws and direct governmental activities. Other workers in this area set and maintain licensing standards for various occupations. They also keep public records, administer immigration laws, and regulate financial institutions. Specialists in labor affairs regulate labor standards, provide employment information, and operate unemployment insurance programs. Postal service employees collect, process, and distribute the mail.

Some public service workers are concerned with the physical health and safety of citizens. Public health specialists try to reduce health hazards in the community. Workers in the area of protective services enforce laws and safeguard citizens and their possessions. Such workers include police officers, city fire fighters, members of the military, and civil defense workers. Some public utilities employees operate water and sanitation systems. Others provide electricity and gas to consumers. Experts in urban development plan housing, parks, and other city improvements.

The largest number of workers in public service are employed in education. Teachers transmit cultural values and teach many kinds of skills to students of all ages. Workers in the area of social services, rehabilitation, and corrections help individuals and families solve problems. Many of these workers counsel people in prisons and other correctional institutions.

Public service occupations offer a variety of work settings and working conditions. For example, some postal employees have jobs indoors. Others work outside in all kinds of weather to deliver the mail. Fire fighters, police officers, and other people in protective services frequently work in dangerous situations. Employment prospects in public service are expected to be steady through the 1980's, though they may vary according to occupation. Elementary-school teachers, corrections officials, prison guards are among the workers projected to be in greatest demand.

Short On-the-Job Training is required for teacher aides, file clerks, and mail carriers. Other workers at this level include security guards and social service aides.

Long On-the-Job Training. Many public service workers learn their jobs through lengthy training programs. Such workers include city fire fighters, military personnel, and police officers.

Specialty Level. Public services employ graduates of two-year training programs as technicians and assistants in many fields. Workers in such jobs include city-planning aides, institutional child-care technicians, and sanitary inspectors.

University Level. Judges, librarians, social workers, teachers, and urban planners need four or more years of college. City managers, military officers, and many elected officials also have college training.

U.S. Navy

The Armed Forces stand ready to defend the country and also to help provide disaster relief. Military work settings cover a wide range, from office to the deck of an aircraft carrier, *above.*

WORLD BOOK photo

Teachers form the largest group of public service workers. Teachers often work closely with individual students, *above.*

Chicago Fire Department

Fire Fighters put out fires, *above,* an exciting but dangerous job. They also work to eliminate fire hazards.

WORLD BOOK photo

A Post Office Clerk sorts letters for delivery, *above.* Postal clerks must have good reading skills and a good memory.

Transportation

Industrialized societies need fast, safe methods for moving people and goods from place to place. Passengers and goods can travel by air, highway, rail, and water transportation. In addition, some materials, such as natural gas and petroleum, can be transported through a series of tubes called a *pipeline*. Common transportation occupations involve designing, operating, or servicing vehicles; handling freight or baggage; and conducting safety inspections. Other jobs provide passenger services.

Specialists in air transportation deal with the movement of people and cargo by airplanes and other aircraft. Pilots and crew members operate aircraft in flight. Ground support workers direct air traffic and handle other operations at airports. Aerospace specialists develop spacecraft and plan space explorations. Highway transportation involves travel by automobile, bus, taxicab, and truck. Some bus and truck drivers cover a long distance in one trip. Others make several short trips a day. Workers called *dispatchers* tell truck and taxicab drivers where to pick up and where to deliver goods or passengers.

Rail transportation moves freight and passengers by trains, streetcars, elevated railroads, and subways. Employees in rail transportation include conductors, switch tenders, track maintenance and repair workers, and yard managers. Water transportation involves such vessels as barges, general cargo ships, passenger liners, riverboats, and tankers. Merchant ships travel all over the world carrying cargo. Experts called *pilots* guide ships through harbors and difficult waters.

Some transportation workers maintain and repair pipeline systems. Others operate the pumps that push materials through such systems, or they help empty the materials from the pipeline into storage tanks.

Some transportation employers, such as airlines, allow employees to travel as passengers free or at reduced fares. In addition, many transportation workers travel as part of their jobs. However, workers assigned to long-distance trips may have to be away from home for long periods. In general, employment in transportation is expected to increase slowly through the 1980's.

Short On-the-Job Training. Baggage handlers, bus and taxi drivers, cargo agents, and parking attendants need only a short training period to learn their jobs. Other workers at this level include railroad switch tenders, ship loaders, and taxi dispatchers.

Long On-the-Job Training or an apprenticeship is required for many kinds of transportation jobs. Workers in such jobs include air traffic controllers, coal pipeline operators, diesel mechanics, passenger service agents, shipfitters, and truck dispatchers.

Specialty Level. Many airline pilots and flight engineers learn their skills at a technical institute or a trade school. Other workers at this preparation level include automobile mechanics and train conductors.

University Level. College training is necessary for aerospace engineers, airport supervisors, safety engineers, and sales managers. Many ship officers also need a college degree.

EDWIN L. HERR

WORLD BOOK photo

Air Traffic Controllers help provide safe, efficient air transportation. Traffic controllers at airports, *above,* direct the movement of aircraft preparing to take off or land.

Milt and Joan Mann

A Bus Driver on a local run, *above,* carries passengers on short trips along a specific bus route. In most cases, such drivers travel the same route several times a day.

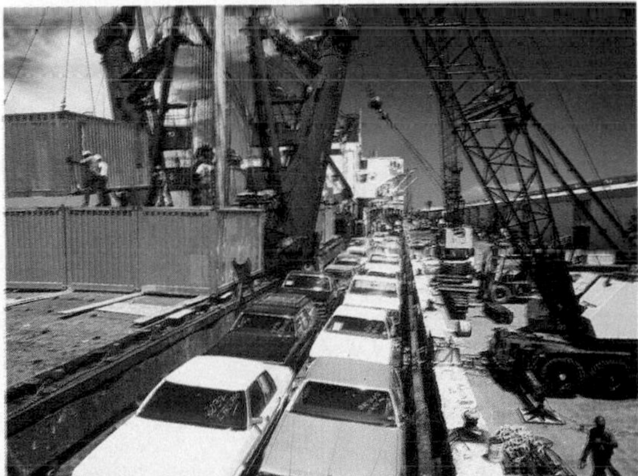

Milt and Joan Mann

Dockworkers called *stevedores* use cranes and other machinery to load containers onto a cargo ship, *above.* Most stevedores learn their jobs during several weeks of on-the-job training.

CAREERS/Study Aids

Related Articles in WORLD BOOK include:

CAREER OPPORTUNITIES

The following articles contain information helpful to a general understanding of a career area. Many of the articles include a *Careers* section and give qualifications and sources of further information.

Accounting
Advertising
Agriculture
Air Conditioning
Air Force, U.S.
Airplane Pilot
Anthropology
Archaeology
Architecture
Army, U.S.
Astronomy
Audiology
Automobile
Aviation
Ballet
Bank
Biology
Bookkeeping
Botany
Building Trade
Business
Chemistry
Chiropractic
City Planning
Clothing
Coal
Coast Guard, United States
Commercial Art
Computer
Conservation
Crime Laboratory
Criminology
Dental Hygiene
Dentistry
Dietitian
Economics
Electronics
Engineering
Entomology
Federal Bureau of Investigation
Fire Department
Flight Attendant
Florist
Forestry
Funeral Director
Geology
Government
Hairdressing
Handicapped
Home Economics
Hospital
Hotel
Industrial Arts
Industrial Design
Industry
Insurance
Interior Decoration
Iron and Steel
Journalism
Law
Library
Marine Corps, U.S.
Mathematics
Mechanical Drawing
Medicine
Merchant Marine
Metallurgy
Meteorology
Mining
Modeling
Motion Picture
Music
Navy, U.S.
Nuclear Energy
Nursing
Occupational Therapy
Ocean
Ophthalmology
Optometry
Osteopathy
Personnel Management
Petroleum
Pharmacy
Photography
Physical Education
Physical Therapy
Physics
Plastics
Police
Psychiatry
Psychology
Public Relations
Publishing
Radio
Railroad
Real Estate
Recreation
Religious Education
Research
Restaurant
Retailing
Salesmanship
Science
Secretarial Work
Social Work
Sociology
Speech Therapy
Surveying
Taxidermy
Teaching
Telephone
Television
Theater
Toolmaking
Veterinary Medicine
Vocational Rehabilitation
Writing
Zoology

OTHER RELATED ARTICLES

Apprentice
Career Education
Civil Service
Community College
Correspondence School
Employment Agency
Fellowship
Foreign Service
Guidance
Job Corps
Letter Writing
Peace Corps
Scholarship
Service Industries
Universities and Colleges
Vocational Education

Outline

I. Choosing and Planning a Career
A. Learning About Oneself
B. Discovering the World of Work
C. Exploring Career Fields
D. Preparing for a Career

II. Getting a Job
A. Finding Job Opportunities
B. Contacting Employers
C. Writing a Résumé
D. Completing Application Forms
E. Being Interviewed

III. The World of Work
A. Agribusiness and Natural Resources
B. Business and Office
C. Communications and Media
D. Construction
E. Environment
F. Fine Arts and Humanities
G. Health
H. Home Economics
I. Hospitality and Recreation
J. Manufacturing
K. Marine Science
L. Marketing and Distribution
M. Personal Services
N. Public Service
O. Transportation

Questions

Why is it important to learn about yourself before exploring career fields?

In what ways can a person learn about job openings?

What are some job characteristics to consider when you explore an occupation?

In what ways can the kind of career you have affect your life?

What is a résumé? Why is it used?

What are some ways high schools can help students prepare for a career?

Why do most people have a career of some kind?

How can abilities influence a person's career choice?

What are the four main levels of career preparation? How do they differ?

What are some sources of information that can help you explore a career field?

Additional Resources

CASS, JAMES, and BIRNBAUM, MAX. *Comparative Guide to American Colleges: For Students, Parents, and Counselors.* 10th ed. Harper, 1981.

HERR, EDWIN L., and CRAMER, STANLEY H. *Career Guidance Through the Life Span: Systematic Approaches.* 2nd ed. Little, Brown, 1984.

The Encyclopedia of Careers and Vocational Guidance, ed. by W. E. Hopke. 5th ed. 2 vols. Doubleday, 1981.

KIMBRELL, GRADY, and VINEYARD, B. S. *Succeeding in the World of Work.* Rev. ed. McKnight, 1981.

LUNNEBORG, PATRICIA W., and WILSON, V. M. *To Work: A Guide for Women College Graduates.* Prentice-Hall, 1982.

MITCHELL, JOYCE SLAYTON. *The Work Book: Trade, Technical and Business Careers.* Bantam, 1978.

SHANAHAN, WILLIAM F. *College — Yes or No.* Arco, 1981.

SPLAVER, SARAH. *Your Personality and Your Career.* Simon & Schuster, 1977.

U.S. DEPARTMENT OF LABOR. *Occupational Outlook Handbook.* U.S. Government Printing Office. Rev. ed.

Several publishers issue a series of books covering a wide range of careers. Some examples are *What Can She Be?* (Lothrop, distributed by Morrow); and *Career Concise Guides* (Watts).

CAREY, JAMES BARRON (1911-1973), an American labor leader, gained wide recognition for his fight against Communist influence in unions. He became president of the United Electrical Workers (UE) in 1936 when it joined the Committee for Industrial Organization. The committee was a forerunner of the Congress of Industrial Organizations (CIO). He lost this post in 1941 because of his anti-Communist stand. When the CIO expelled the UE on charges of Communist domination, Carey organized the International Union of Electrical, Radio and Machine Workers (IUE) in 1949. He served as president of this union from 1949 to 1965. Carey was born in Philadelphia. JACK BARBASH

CARGO. See AIRPLANE; AIRPORT (Cargo Handling; Airport Terms; picture); AVIATION; SHIP (Classification of Cargo Ships; General Cargo Ships; pictures).

CARIB INDIANS, *KAR ihb*, were a warlike group of South American tribes who lived mainly in the Amazon River Valley and the Guiana lowlands. These fierce

Male and Female Caribou both have antlers. The antlers of the female caribou, *left*, are smaller than those of the male, *right*.

M. Stouffer, Animals Animals

Indians ate their victims. Our word *cannibal* comes from the Spanish name for these Indians. About 1300, the Carib moved from northeastern South America to the Caribbean islands, which they captured from the more peaceful Arawak (see ARAWAK INDIANS).

The Carib were farmers, and raised manioc, a root crop. They lived in small, independent villages which were located so they could not be surprised by enemy attack. The people had no tribal chiefs or permanent village chiefs, but followed special leaders in time of war. The Carib, especially those who lived on the islands, were expert canoeists. They used large, planked dugouts. They hunted with traps, javelins, and clubs, and shot fish with poison arrows. The Carib are said to have valued personal independence so highly that they looked down on Spaniards who took orders from others.

Like other aggressive tribes, the Carib trained their sons for war from childhood. A boy had to prove his skill and endurance with weapons when he came of age. If he passed the tests, the tribe accepted him as a warrior and gave him a new name. Most of the Carib died from warfare and disease soon after the Spanish invasion. Today, only a handful survive on the islands, in the Guianas, and in the Amazon Valley. CHARLES WAGLEY

CARIBBEAN SEA, *KAR uh BEE uhn*, or *kuh RIHB ee uhn*, is a part of the Atlantic Ocean between the West Indies and Central and South America. It is about 1,700 miles (2,740 kilometers) long from west to east and between 500 and 800 miles (800 and 1,300 kilometers) wide from north to south. Its greatest depth is 24,720 feet (7,535 meters). The widest entrance is the Yucatán Channel, between Mexico and Cuba. Ships sail the Caribbean carrying sugar from the West Indies; petroleum from Venezuela and Colombia; coffee from Colombia, Costa Rica and Guatemala; and bananas from Panama, Costa Rica, Honduras, and El Salvador. The United States has military bases in Panama and Puerto Rico. In the 1500's and 1600's, many pirates sailed the Caribbean, plundering cargo ships on the Spanish Main. See also SOUTH AMERICA (map); SPANISH MAIN. OTIS P. STARKEY

Location of Caribbean Sea

CARIBE. See PIRANHA.

CARIBOU, *KAR uh boo*, is the French-Canadian name for the wild reindeer of North America. Caribou have broad hoofs to support them in deep snow and spongy tundra. They have broad antlers, and the male's antlers grow much larger than the female's. The female caribou is the only American female deer that has antlers.

A *bull* (male) caribou weighs from 250 to 700 pounds (113 to 320 kilograms), stands 4 to 5 feet (1.2 to 1.5 meters) tall, and measures 6 to 8 feet (1.8 to 2.4 meters) long. A *cow* (female) is smaller than a bull. Cows give birth to one calf in late spring. There are two main types of caribou—*barren ground* and *woodland*.

Barren-ground caribou spend the summer in the Arctic tundra and the winter in the evergreen forests south of the tundra. They may be found from western Alaska to western Greenland. In the western part of their range, they live in large herds. Roaming caribou cover the land for days at a time. They do not overgraze their range because they keep moving from place to place. In summer, they eat mostly grass and leaves of various shrubs. In winter, they live mostly on lichens.

Woodland caribou are slightly larger and darker than barren-ground caribou. They are found in forested regions from Newfoundland to the Northwest Territories and down through British Columbia, northern Idaho, and northeastern Washington.

Some Northern Indians and Eskimos eat caribou meat and make soup from the animal's marrow. They make clothing and tents from its hide. They use its bones for needles and knives, its tendons for thread, and its horns for fishhooks, spears, and spoons.

The number of caribou has declined from about 2 million in the early 1900's to about a million today.

Scientific Classification. Caribou are in the deer family, *Cervidae*. They are genus *Rangifer*, species *R. tarandus*. VICTOR H. CAHALANE

See also ANIMAL (picture: Animals of the Polar Regions); DEER; MAMMAL (picture); REINDEER; TUNDRA.

Lithograph (1834) by Honoré Daumier; The Art Institute of Chicago, the Charles Deering Collection

Ink drawing by David Levine; reprinted with permission from *The New York Review of Books,* © 1969 *The New York Review*

Drawing by Oscar Berger

Caricatures may exaggerate physical characteristics or something associated with a person. The French artist Honoré Daumier caricatured the arrogance he saw in many French legislators of the 1800's, *above.* A caricature of the German philosopher Karl Marx, *upper right,* emphasizes his hair and beard. A caricature of the English statesman Sir Winston Churchill, *right,* highlights his cigar.

CARICATURE, *KAR uh kuh chur,* is any sort of writing or picture which so exaggerates the peculiarities of persons or objects that they appear ridiculous. Written caricatures include such satires as *Don Quixote* and *Gulliver's Travels.* Most commonly, a caricature is an exaggerated satirical portrait.

Not every kind of exaggerated drawing is a caricature. The caricaturist must select and emphasize the peculiar features of a person. A few simple lines are often enough to emphasize certain features, producing a picture that can be easily recognized. A drooping lock of hair and a little mustache clearly suggested Adolf Hitler. Many of the best caricatures portray actual persons, but excellent caricatures have been made of types.

It is possible for a caricaturist to so emphasize peculiar features as to cause scorn and mockery to be heaped upon a person. Politicians have been made to appear so ridiculous that they were forced to give up office. Thomas Nast's clever series of caricatures brought about the downfall of the "Tammany Tiger" (see NAST, THOMAS; TAMMANY, SOCIETY OF).

The Assyrians, Egyptians, Greeks, and Romans used caricature. The satirical art has flourished in the past few hundred years through the work of such fine caricaturists as William Hogarth, Honoré Daumier, George Cruikshank, John Tenniel, George du Maurier, Sir Max Beerbohm, and David Low. MARJORIE HENDERSON BUELL

Related Articles in WORLD BOOK include:

Beerbohm, Sir Max
Cartoon
Comics
Cruikshank, George
Daumier, Honoré
Hogarth, William

CARIES. See TEETH (Diseases and Defects).

CARILLON, *KAR uh lahn,* is a set of fixed bells. It is usually tuned to the chromatic scale and has a range of three octaves or more. A person called a *carillonneur,* who sits at a keyboard, plays tunes on the carillon. Sometimes a mechanical playing device is used.

The carillon developed from the bell and chime. In the Middle Ages, bell ringing was popular in The Netherlands and Belgium. Sets of bells replaced single bells in many churches. Hammers struck single notes. Later developments permitted the playing of simple tunes. The chime is a set of movable bells. It has fewer

Star Weekly, Toronto

bells than the carillon, and it is not tuned so exactly.

Carillonic bells is the name of an electronic device which duplicates the sound of bells. It consists of small pieces of tuned bell metal struck by a tiny rod. The sound is electronically amplified. This device is played from a keyboard like that of a piano, and has a range of two full octaves. CHARLES B. RIGHTER

See also CAMPANILE; SINGING TOWER.

CARL XVI GUSTAF, *GUHS tahv* (1946-), became king of Sweden in 1973. Carl Gustaf succeeded his grandfather, Gustaf VI Adolf. His father died in 1947, when Carl Gustaf was less than a year old.

Carl Gustaf was born near Stockholm. His full name is Carl Gustaf Folke Hubertus. After his great-grandfather, Gustaf V, died in 1950, his grandfather became king and Carl Gustaf became crown prince. He received his early education from tutors and then entered a private boarding school in Sigtuna. He graduated in 1966. For the next two years, he served in the various branches of the Swedish armed forces. He then attended Uppsala University for a year. Carl Gustaf worked in several Swedish government agencies from 1969 to 1971. In 1976, Carl Gustaf married Silvia Renate Sommerlath, the daughter of a West German businessman. RAYMOND E. LINDGREN

CARLETON is the family name of two brothers, soldiers, and British governors of Canadian provinces.

Sir Guy Carleton (1724-1808), BARON DORCHESTER, became lieutenant-governor of Quebec province in 1766. He was governor from 1768 to 1778. In 1786, he was made governor-in-chief of British North America, which included Quebec. He served until 1796. In 1774, Carleton persuaded the British government to grant greater freedom to the French Canadians. In 1791, he helped obtain the laws that gave Canadians representative government.

When the Revolutionary War broke out in 1775, he took command of the British army in Canada. He defeated an American army attacking the city of Quebec and drove it back. He became the British commander-in-chief in North America in 1782. Carleton supervised the evacuation of British troops and loyalists from New York in 1783.

Carleton was born in Strabane, Ireland. He was knighted in 1776. He became a major general in 1772, a lieutenant general in 1777, and a general in 1793.

Thomas Carleton (1735-1817) became the first governor of New Brunswick. He took office in 1784 and served until his death. His title was changed to lieutenant governor in 1786, when his brother became British governor-in-chief in North America. Thomas Carleton was born in Ireland. MICHEL BRUNET

CARLETON UNIVERSITY is a coeducational university in Ottawa, Ont. It is privately controlled, but receives grants from the provincial government. Carleton has programs in arts, architecture, commerce, engineering, industrial design, journalism, music, and science. It also offers evening degree courses and extension courses. The university grants bachelor's, master's, and doctor's degrees. It was founded in 1942. For enrollment, see CANADA (table: Universities and Colleges).

Critically reviewed by CARLETON UNIVERSITY

CARLISLE, *kahr LYL,* Pa. (pop. 18,314), is a manufacturing and farm trading center of the Cumberland Valley. It is in south-central Pennsylvania, about 18 miles (29 kilometers) west of Harrisburg. For the location of Carlisle, see PENNSYLVANIA (political map). Carlisle factories make shoes, electronic components, and carpets.

Carlisle was founded in 1751. It served as headquarters for the force George Washington sent to Pennsylvania to suppress the Whiskey Rebellion (see WHISKEY REBELLION). Dickinson College was founded in Carlisle in 1773. The federal government maintained the Carlisle Indian School from 1879 to 1918. The Army War College is located at Carlisle Barracks. Carlisle is the seat of Cumberland County, and has a council-manager government. S. K. STEVENS

CARLOMAN. See CHARLEMAGNE (Military Conquests).

CARLOS, JUAN. See JUAN CARLOS I.

CARLOTA, EMPRESS. See MAXIMILIAN.

CARLSBAD. See KARLOVY VARY.

CARLSBAD CAVERNS NATIONAL PARK is a chain of huge underground caves in southeastern New Mexico. Stalactites and stalagmites, in white and pastel shades, form shapes like Chinese temples, heavy pillars, and lacy icicles (see STALACTITE; STALAGMITE). One large chamber, called the Big Room, is 4,000 feet (1,200 meters) long and 625 feet (191 meters) wide. At one point, the ceiling is 285 feet (87 meters) high. The caverns became a national park in 1930. For area, see NATIONAL PARK SYSTEM (table: National Parks).

Although many passages in the caverns have been explored, there are still unexplored areas. Two levels, at 750 feet (229 meters) and 829 feet (253 meters) underground, may be reached by trail from the natural entrance, or by elevator. On the lower level, visitors may look down to an unopened passage which has been explored as deep as 1,100 feet (335 meters). One part of the

A 53-Bell Carillon in the House of Commons Peace Tower, *left,* has rung over Ottawa, Canada, since 1927. The bells, *above,* hang in tiers. Guards protect the player's hands, *below.*

Star Weekly, Toronto

caverns contains millions of bats which fly out at dusk in warm weather in search of insects. Paintings on the entrance wall of the cave show that Indians used the cave at one time.

The limestone in the caverns is believed to have formed in a shallow inland extension of the ocean about 200 million years ago. When the Rocky Mountains were formed about 60 million years ago, the cavern area rose above sea level and water began hollowing out the limestone to form the caves. HERBERT E. KAHLER

See also CAVE (table); NEW MEXICO (picture: Rock Formations).

CARLYLE, THOMAS (1795-1881), was a Scottish essayist and historian. He once was considered the greatest social philosopher of Victorian England. Carlyle's reputation has declined in the 1900's, but his works are still read for his distinctive ideas on democracy, heroism, and revolution.

Early Career. Carlyle was born in Ecclefechan, near Dumfries, Scotland. In 1819, he moved to Edinburgh and began writing articles on science and literature for the city's leading magazines and encyclopedias. In 1826, he married Jane Welsh, the daughter of a Scottish physician. Two years later, the couple moved to Craigenputtock, Jane Carlyle's farm near Dumfries.

At Craigenputtock, Carlyle wrote *Sartor Resartus*, which was published in 1833 and 1834. This work brought him fame and is still considered his most original and enduring achievement. The book is an elaborate work of fiction about a German professor. Through this character, Carlyle poured out his own ideas and experiences. He thus made *Sartor Resartus* one of the greatest—and one of the most incomprehensible—autobiographies in literary history. The work introduced readers to *Carlylese*, a writing style characterized by its rich vocabulary and complex sentence structures.

Carlyle moved to London in 1834 and began writing a history of the French Revolution. He lent the completed manuscript to the philosopher John Stuart Mill, and Mill's maid accidentally burned it. Carlyle then rewrote *The French Revolution* largely from memory and published it in 1837. In *The French Revolution*, Carlyle discussed both the dangers and the promise of revolution. During this same period, Carlyle also delivered many public lectures, including a series he published as *On Heroes, Hero-Worship, and the Heroic in History* (1841). In *On Heroes and Hero-Worship*, as the book is often called, he stated that the main cause of social progress is a strong, heroic leader.

Thomas Carlyle

Detail of an oil portrait by Sir John Everett Millais; National Portrait Gallery, London

Later Career. During the 1840's, Carlyle turned to what he called "the condition-of-England question"—the problem of mass poverty existing alongside increasing middle-class wealth. In *Past and Present* (1843), Carlyle attacked the political and social conditions in England. He called for a revival of certain medieval ways of life before the development of machines. The book inspired many people in Victorian England to try to correct the social ills of the time.

Carlyle then wrote a massive study of Oliver Cromwell, who had been England's ruler during the English Civil War of the 1600's. The study is called *Oliver Cromwell's Letters and Speeches, with Elucidations* (1845). In this work, Carlyle discussed his ideas on the need for a hero to lead social change. He suggested that a hero was needed to solve Great Britain's problems.

In 1848, Britain stood on the brink of revolution because of *Chartism*, a movement to extend the vote to workers (see CHARTISM). The prospect of violence over electoral reform turned Carlyle and other formerly progressive intellectuals into conservatives on social issues. Carlyle wrote against electoral reform and the possibility of a society dominated by the working class in *Latter-Day Pamphlets* (1850) and the biography *Frederick the Great*, published from 1858 to 1865. Many readers agreed with Carlyle's conservative views. But others disliked the extremism of his later writings. These works contributed to the decline of his reputation.

In his later years, Carlyle received many public honors, and his writings were widely read. But he remained uneasy over the continuing growth of democracy in Britain. AVROM FLEISHMAN

CARMAN, BLISS (1861-1929), was a Canadian poet whose verse praises the beauty and power he saw in nature. Carman's descriptions of the landscape suggest images of death and lost love. Much of his verse expresses a sense of yearning for the beauty of scenes from his past. His poetry also praises the carefree life of a wanderer. Carman was influenced by the religious and philosophical movement called *transcendentalism*, and by the American poets Ralph Waldo Emerson and Walt Whitman (see TRANSCENDENTALISM).

Carman's first book of verse, *Low Tide on Grand Pré*, was published in 1893. It contained some of his best-known lyrics on nature. Perhaps Carman's most popular books were the Vagabondia series, written with the American poet Richard Hovey. These books include *Songs from Vagabondia* (1894), *More Songs from Vagabondia* (1896), and *Last Songs from Vagabondia* (1901). Carman later won praise for his love poems in *From the Book of Myths* (1902), *Songs of the Sea Children* (1904), and *Sappho* (1904). He also wrote a number of essays, some of which were collected in *The Kinship of Nature* (1904).

William Bliss Carman was born in Fredericton, N.B. He began his career in 1890 as a journalist in New York City. He spent the rest of his life in the United States but often returned to Canada. ROSEMARY SULLIVAN

CARMEL, Calif. (pop. 4,707), is a seaside community on the Monterey Peninsula, about 100 miles (160 kilometers) south of San Francisco (see CALIFORNIA [political map]). Its official name is CARMEL-BY-THE-SEA, but it is usually called Carmel. The mild climate, the rugged coastline, and the white sand beach attract many visitors. The town was founded in 1904 by a group of artists and writers. They wished to keep the community simple and rural, and for many years it had no paved streets, no gas and electric service, and no jail. Carmel still has no jail or neon signs, nor does it have mail delivery, street lights, sidewalks, or street numbers in its residential area. Incorporated in 1916, Carmel has a mayor-council form of government. George Shaftel

CARMEL, MOUNT. See Mount Carmel.

CARMELITES, *KAHR muh lyts,* are members of a Roman Catholic order of friars. Its official name is the Order of Our Lady of Mount Carmel. The order was established at Mount Carmel, Syria, probably in the 1100's, and soon spread through most of Europe. At first the Carmelites followed severe rules for living. In 1431, by order of Pope Eugenius IV, these rules were relaxed. Because of the white cloak worn over their brown robes, Carmelites are sometimes called *White Friars.* In the United States several branches have been established, the first in 1864. Saint Theresa founded a Carmelite order of nuns in 1562. Fulton J. Sheen

See also Friar; Theresa, Saint.

CARMICHAEL, FRANKLIN. See Group of Seven.

CARMICHAEL, HOAGY, *HOH gee* (1899-1981), one of America's leading songwriters, wrote popular music that has a dreamy, relaxed mood. He composed such songs as "Star Dust," "Lazy Bones," "Rockin' Chair," and "Georgia on My Mind." He also appeared in several motion pictures, and starred in his own radio and television programs. Carmichael studied law at Indiana University, and organized several dance bands at the school. Later, he abandoned law to become a songwriter. Hoagland Carmichael was born in Bloomington, Ind. Nardi Reeder Campion

CARMICHAEL, STOKELY (1941-), became a spokesman for the doctrine of Black Power. This doctrine urges black Americans to gain political and economic control of their own communities. It also urges them to form their own standards and reject the values of white America. It rejects complete nonviolence, and calls for blacks to meet violence with violence.

Carmichael was born on the island of Trinidad, in the West Indies. He grew up in Harlem, a New York City ghetto, and graduated from Howard University in 1964. While in college, Carmichael led student protest activities and helped teach black Americans in the South how to register and vote. In 1966, he became chairman of the Student Nonviolent Coordinating Committee (SNCC), a civil rights group he had helped form six years earlier. Under his leadership, SNCC moved toward Black Power ideals.

Carmichael left SNCC in 1968, and became prime minister of the Black Panther Party, a militant Black Power organization. He resigned his post with the Black Panthers in 1969. He and Charles Hamilton wrote the book *Black Power* (1967). C. Eric Lincoln

See also Student Nonviolent Coordinating Committee.

CARMINE. See Dye (Natural Dyes).

CARNATION is a tall, colorful flower with many blossoms. It is related to a group of flowers called *pinks.* Carnations are from 1 to 3 feet (30 to 91 centimeters) high, and may be pink, purple, red, white, or yellow.

Carnations originally came from southern Europe, but several varieties are grown in the United States, both outdoors and in greenhouses. The carnation may bloom throughout the year, depending on its cultivation and the climate. Carnations are usually raised by planting young shoots from the stems of mature plants, or by bending one of the stems into the ground again so that it forms a new root. Carnation plants need a rich, loamy soil mixed with a small amount of manure, leaf mold, and some sand.

The carnation has been cultivated by gardeners since ancient times. It is one of the special flowers of January. The scarlet carnation is the state flower of Ohio.

Scientific Classification. The carnation belongs to the pink family, Caryophyllaceae. It is classified as genus *Dianthus,* species *D. caryophyllus.* Marcus Maxon

See also Pink; Sweet William.

Inter-State Nurseries

The Carnation grows well both outdoors and in greenhouses. Carnations usually need a loamy or sandy soil.

CARNAUBA WAX, *kahr NOW buh,* is a vegetable wax. It is obtained from the leaves of the carnauba palm, which is native to Brazil. To obtain carnauba wax, leaves from the palm are dried in the sun until their waxy coating turns to a flourlike dust. This dust is then melted, cooled, and formed into cakes for shipment.

Carnauba wax is the hardest natural wax known. It is used in polishes, lubricants, plastics, floor and automobile waxes, and other products. Richard F. Blewitt

CARNEADES, *kahr NEE uh DEEZ* (213?-129 B.C.?), was a Greek philosopher who believed that no absolute standard of truth exists. He accepted the doctrine that any action is right if it can be reasonably defended. By describing hideous crimes committed with rational motives, Carneades undermined the Stoic doctrine that reason is the highest gift that God gave to the human race. Carneades' views about testing sense impressions for their reliability as guides to action resemble the beliefs of modern pragmatism (see Pragmatism).

Carneades was born in Athens. He founded and led a school called the third or New Academy from about 155 B.C. until his death. Josiah B. Gould

CARNEGIE, *kahr NAY gee,* **ANDREW** (1835-1919), a steel manufacturer and philanthropist, was one of the most remarkable foreign-born Americans. He entered the United States as a poor boy but became one of the world's richest people by the time he reached middle age. He gave away most of his wealth for the betterment of humanity. He gave millions of dollars to schools and universities. Largely because of Carnegie's financial help, thousands of communities have public libraries.

Carnegie was born on Nov. 25, 1835, in Dunfermline, Scotland, where he received his only regular schooling. His father was a hand weaver. After steam machinery for weaving came into use, the elder Carnegie sold his looms and household goods, and sailed to America with his wife and two sons. Andrew was then 12 years old, and his brother, Thomas, was 5.

Early Achievements. The Carnegies settled in Allegheny City, Pa., a suburb of Pittsburgh, where relatives had already found homes. Before long, young Andrew was working as bobbin boy in a cotton factory for $1.20 a week. His father also worked there, and his mother made a little money by binding shoes at home. She kept the highest ideals of conduct before her children. When Carnegie was 15, he became a telegraph messenger boy in Pittsburgh. He learned to send and decipher telegraphic messages, and became a telegraph operator at the age of 17.

Carnegie next got a job as railroad clerk in the office of the division superintendent of the Pennsylvania Railroad in Pittsburgh. He worked his way up and became train dispatcher. When his chief, Thomas Scott, was appointed vice-president of the company in 1859, Carnegie became division manager. He was then only 24 years old, but he had already made some small investments that laid the foundations of his great fortune. One of these investments was the purchase of stock in the Woodruff Sleeping Car Company, the successful forerunner of the Pullman Company. During the Civil War, Carnegie helped organize the telegraph department of the Union Army.

A Millionaire. In 1864, Carnegie entered the iron business. But he did not begin to make steel for some years. In 1873, after seeing the Bessemer process in action, he built the Edgar Thomson works in Braddock, Pa., to make Bessemer steel. He established other steel plants, including one in Homestead, Pa. In 1892, he merged his interests into the Carnegie Steel Company. This firm became one of the greatest industrial enterprises in America. Carnegie sold it to the United States Steel Corporation in 1901.

When he retired, Carnegie's fortune was estimated to be as large as half a billion dollars. From that time, he devoted himself largely to philanthropy. Most of his fortune went to support education, public libraries, and the world peace movement. He outlined his ideas on how large fortunes should be used for the betterment of society in an article called "Wealth," published in 1889. He also wrote *Triumphant Democracy* (1886), *The Gospel of Wealth* (1900), *The Empire of Business* (1902), *Problems of Today* (1908), and an *Autobiography* (1920). Carnegie was made a Commander of the French Legion of Honor in 1907, and in 1911 received the peace medal of the Fourth International Congress of American States.

Andrew Carnegie

U&U

Carnegie's Gifts, estimated at $350 million, include $135 million to the Carnegie Corporation of New York; $10 million to Hero funds; $11 million to Carnegie Institute of Technology (now Carnegie-Mellon University) in Pittsburgh; $10 million to universities in Scotland, including Saint Andrews and Aberdeen, both of which he served as lord rector; $5 million as a benefit fund for employees of the Carnegie Steel Company; a $2½ million trust for Dunfermline, Scotland; $3¾ million to churches on behalf of permanent peace; and $1½ million for the Peace Palace at The Hague. ROBERT H. BREMNER

See the articles on Carnegie institutions on this and the following page. See also FOUNDATIONS.

Additional Resources

HACKER, LOUIS M. *The World of Andrew Carnegie: 1865-1901.* Lippincott, 1968.

LIVESAY, HAROLD C. *Andrew Carnegie and the Rise of Big Business.* Little, Brown, 1975.

SHIPPEN, KATHERINE B. *Andrew Carnegie and the Age of Steel.* Random House, 1958. For younger readers.

WALL, JOSEPH F. *Andrew Carnegie.* Oxford, 1970.

CARNEGIE, DALE (1888-1955), was a pioneer in public speaking and personality development. He became famous by showing others how to become successful. His book *How to Win Friends and Influence People* (1936) has sold more than 10 million copies and has been translated into many languages. His books became popular because of his illustrative stories and simple, well-phrased rules. Two of his most famous maxims are, "Believe that you will succeed, and you will," and "Learn to love, respect and enjoy other people." His other books include *How to Stop Worrying and Start Living* (1948). Toward the beginning of his career, Carnegie wrote *Public Speaking and Influencing Men in Business* (1931), which became a standard text.

Carnegie attended Warrensburg (Mo.) State Teachers College, and became a salesman for Armour and Company. Later, he taught public speaking to businessmen. He was born in Maryville, Mo. CARL NIEMEYER

CARNEGIE CORPORATION OF NEW YORK is a philanthropic foundation established by Andrew Carnegie for "the advancement and diffusion of knowledge and understanding." It was founded in New York City in 1911, with an endowment of $135 million. Grants are made primarily to colleges, universities, and other educational institutions, and to organizations that conduct basic research and experimental programs dealing with education and public affairs. A small portion of the corporation's funds may be used in certain countries of the Commonwealth of Nations. The corporation has made about $475 million worth of grants. Its offices are at 437 Madison Avenue, New York, N.Y. 10022. For assets, see FOUNDATIONS (table: Leading United States Foundations).

Critically reviewed by the CARNEGIE CORPORATION OF NEW YORK

CARNEGIE ENDOWMENT FOR INTERNATIONAL PEACE is an organization founded to promote international peace and understanding. It conducts programs of research, discussion, publication, and education in international affairs and United States foreign policy. The programs concentrate on such issues as arms control, international law, the Middle East, South Africa, and relations between the United States and Russia. The endowment works with other organizations to further discussion of international affairs in the United States and in other countries. It publishes the quarterly journal *Foreign Policy*.

The Carnegie Endowment for International Peace was founded by the American industrialist Andrew Carnegie. He established the endowment in 1910 with a gift of $10 million. The endowment has its headquarters at 345 E. 46th Street, New York, N.Y. 10017. It also has offices in Washington, D.C. Critically reviewed by the CARNEGIE ENDOWMENT FOR INTERNATIONAL PEACE

CARNEGIE FOUNDATION FOR THE ADVANCEMENT OF TEACHING is an organization that promotes the dignity of the teaching profession and the cause of higher education. It provides retirement pensions for teachers in colleges, technical schools, and universities in the United States and Canada. The foundation has sponsored and published many studies on various educational problems. These studies have had much influence on American higher education.

Andrew Carnegie established the foundation in 1905 with an endowment of $15 million. With the Carnegie Corporation of New York, the foundation established the Teachers Insurance and Annuity Association in 1918. The foundation has headquarters at 437 Madison Avenue, New York, N.Y. 10022. Critically reviewed by THE CARNEGIE FOUNDATION FOR THE ADVANCEMENT OF TEACHING

CARNEGIE LIBRARIES. See LIBRARY (Libraries in the United States).

CARNELIAN, *kahr NEEL yuhn,* is a red or reddish-brown quartz which can be cut and polished as a jewel. This gem is sometimes called a *cornelian*. Most carnelian comes from India, South America, and Japan. It is used in rings, bracelets, and other jewelry. Imitations are made by staining gray or white chalcedony.

The carnelian was one of the first stones to be used as a decoration. People of ancient times believed the carnelian had special powers that would protect its wearer from weapons and evil spirits. Muhammad wore a ring that had a carnelian stone to seal his important papers. FREDERICK H. POUGH

See also CHALCEDONY; GEM.

CARNIVAL is a traditional form of outdoor amusement that consists of exhibits, games, rides, and shows. Most carnivals today are small and are held in towns and small cities, setting up their attractions in streets and parking lots. The term *carnival* also can refer to a time of feasting and merrymaking just before Lent. The Mardi Gras in New Orleans is a famous American carnival of this type.

A carnival is arranged around a main street called a *midway*. The area near the entrance is called the *front end* and includes the games and refreshment and souvenir stands. The rear area, called the *back end*, usually consists of the rides and shows. The most popular rides include the Ferris wheel and merry-go-round (see FERRIS WHEEL; MERRY-GO-ROUND). Side shows that displayed unusual exhibits and acts were once a main attraction of carnivals, but they have become rare.

Carnivals developed from traditional festivals in Europe dating back hundreds of years. The traveling carnival in America began in the late 1800's as a result of improved transportation and technology. The success of the 1893 World's Columbian Exposition in Chicago stimulated people to take special attractions to different cities. Today, there are about 500 carnivals that travel across the United States. However, they are not as elaborate as earlier carnivals. Modern amusement parks include rides and other popular features of the traditional carnival. DON B. WILMETH

Artstreet

A Carnival is a form of outdoor amusement that travels from town to town. Carnivals feature rides, shows, exhibits, and games. Visitors can also purchase refreshments and souvenirs.

CARNIVORE, *KAHR nuh vawr,* is any animal that eats chiefly meat. Most such animals prey on *herbivores* (plant-eating animals). Carnivores thus help regulate the number of herbivores and preserve the balance of nature (see BALANCE OF NATURE). The term *carnivore* also refers to an *order* (group) of mammals. This article discusses such mammals, which include cats and dogs.

All mammals classified as carnivores have well-developed canine teeth. Most of them have several blade-like shearing teeth and a heavy skull, with strong facial and jaw muscles. Most carnivores, including cats, civets, dogs, and weasels, hunt and kill their own prey. Some, such as bears and raccoons, also eat plants. Others, such as hyenas and jackals, usually eat animals that they find dead.

Carnivores live in all parts of the world except Antarctica and some islands. Most dwell on land, but some, such as otters and polar bears, spend much time in water. Most carnivores live alone or in family groups. They range in size from the least weasel, which weighs only 1 or 2 ounces (28 to 57 grams), to the brown bear, which may weigh over 1,500 pounds (680 kilograms).

Most carnivores mate once a year. The number of young born at one time varies among the species. A weasel, for example, may have as many as eight young at a time, but some kinds of bears have only one.

Some carnivores, such as foxes and minks, are sources of valuable fur. People sometimes kill other carnivores, such as coyotes and lions, for sport or because the animals kill livestock.

Scientific Classification. Carnivores make up the order *Carnivora* in the class *Mammalia* and the phylum *Chordata.* To learn where this order fits into the animal kingdom, see ANIMAL (table: A Classification of the Animal Kingdom). WILLIAM O. PRUITT, JR.

See also MAMMAL (illustration: The Teeth of Mammals) and the separate articles in WORLD BOOK on the carnivores mentioned in this article.

CARNIVOROUS PLANT, *kahr NIHV uhr uhs,* is any plant that traps insects for food. Such plants are also called *insectivorous plants.* Carnivorous plants usually live in moist places where they get little or no nitrogen from the soil. The plants must obtain nitrogen from the insects that they trap. Carnivorous plants have special organs with which to capture insects, and glands that give off a digestive fluid to help them make use of their food. Some carnivorous plants have flowers colored or scented in such a way as to appear or smell at a distance like decaying meat. This attracts insects.

Various devices have been developed by carnivorous plants as traps. For example, pitcher plants have tube-shaped leaves that hold rain water in which the insects drown. Rosettes of leaves provided with sticky hairs are borne by the sundews. When an insect is caught by the hairs, the leaf margins curl around it, trapping it inside. Venus's-flytrap has leaves that work like a steel trap. They close tightly about an insect, holding it inside. GEORGE H. M. LAWRENCE

Related Articles in WORLD BOOK include:

Bladderwort	Plant (Insect-Eating Plants; pictures)
Butterwort	Sundew
Pitcher Plant	Venus's-Flytrap

CARNOTITE, *KAHR nuh tyt,* is one of the main mineral sources of uranium and vanadium. This yellow ore has the chemical formula $K_2(UO_2)_2(VO_4)_2 3H_2O$. It usually occurs as a powder, but sometimes in tiny flat crystals. Geologists believe carnotite is formed by the action of surface water working downward on uraninite. For this reason they call carnotite a *secondary* mineral. The chief carnotite deposits in the United States occur in the *four corners* region of the Colorado Plateau, where Colorado, Utah, New Mexico, and Arizona meet. It often appears with similarly formed minerals, chiefly tyuyamunite. Colorado is the chief source of carnotite and for this reason is also the main producing state for vanadium. CORNELIUS S. HURLBUT, JR.

CAROB, *KAR uhb,* is a dark evergreen tree that grows in countries along the Mediterranean Sea. Some carobs are found in the southern United States. The carob has brown, leathery pods that contain a sticky pulp. The pulp, which is also called *carob,* has a taste similar to that of chocolate. After being roasted and ground, it can be substituted for chocolate.

Carob provides a chocolate flavor in many dishes and in such products as beverages and candy bars. During the 1970's, large numbers of consumers and manufacturers began to use carob because of the increasingly high cost of chocolate. Some people prefer carob because they are allergic to chocolate.

The carob tree grows as tall as 50 feet (15 meters) and has small red flowers. Its pods range from 4 to 10 inches (10 to 25 centimeters) long. The pulp, sometimes called *Saint John's-bread,* is fed to cattle and horses and is also eaten raw by people. According to the Bible, John the Baptist ate carob while living in the wilderness.

Scientific Classification. Carob is in the pea family, Leguminosae. It is *Ceratonia siliqua.* MARGARET MCWILLIAMS

CAROL is a traditional song of joyful character, usually associated with a religious or seasonal festival such as Christmas, Easter, or the month of May. The word was also used for an English pagan song-dance performed to celebrate the shortest days of winter. Well-known Christmas carols include "Silent Night," "The First Noel," and "O Little Town of Bethlehem." For more details on Christmas carols, see CHRISTMAS (Christmas Decorations). RAYMOND KENDALL

CAROL I (1839-1914) ruled Romania from 1866 until his death. Under his rule, Romania won its independence from the Ottoman Empire in 1878.

Carol was born in Sigmaringen, east of Freiburg (now in West Germany). He was a prince of the Hohenzollern family, a famous royal family that then ruled Prussia. In 1866, the Romanian parliament chose Carol to rule Romania as Prince Carol I. At that time, Romania belonged to the Ottoman Empire. Carol sent 38,000 Romanian soldiers to fight against the Ottoman Empire in the Russo-Turkish War of 1877-1878. Romania gained its independence as a result of this war. In 1881, Romania became a kingdom, and Carol was crowned king. He built a railroad network and did much to develop industry. GERALD J. BOBANGO

CAROL II (1893-1953) was king of Romania from 1930 to 1940. He tried to prevent Germany from dominating Romania during World War II (1939-1945), but failed.

Carol was born in Sinaia, Romania. In 1925, he gave up his right to the throne because of his love for a commoner, Magda Lupescu. In 1930, the government repealed the law that kept Carol from the throne. The Iron Guard, a patriotic and anti-Communist movement, charged that Carol's rule was corrupt. Carol had its leader assassinated and, in 1938, made himself dictator. He outlawed the Iron Guard and all political parties. In 1940, Germany forced Carol to give parts of Romania to Bulgaria, Hungary, and the Soviet Union. The Iron Guard helped force Carol from the throne. His son, Michael, succeeded him. GERALD J. BOBANGO

CAROLINA. See NORTH CAROLINA; SOUTH CAROLINA.

CAROLINE ISLANDS (pop. 85,932) are an archipelago of more than 930 islands in the Pacific Ocean. They lie just north of the equator, between the Marshall Islands and the Philippines (see PACIFIC ISLANDS [map]). The island group extends over 2,000 miles (3,200 kilometers), but the combined land area is only 463 square miles (1,199 square kilometers). The islands have a total coastline of 375 miles (604 kilometers). There are five large islands or island groups: Kusaie (Kosiae) Island, Ponape Island, the Truk Islands, the Yap Islands, and the Palau Islands. There are also 32 atolls and some isolated islets. The Carolines are part of a larger island group called *Micronesia,* which means *small islands.* Copra, the dried meat of coconuts, is the chief export. Palau produces bauxite and phosphate.

Spanish explorers discovered the Carolines in the

1500's. Spain formally claimed the islands in 1885, and sold them to Germany in 1899. The Japanese captured the islands during World War I. After the war, the League of Nations gave them to Japan as mandates. Japan fortified some of the islands. During World War II, U.S. forces captured some of the islands, including Peleliu. In 1947, the United Nations made the United States trustee of the Carolines as part of the Trust Territory of the Pacific Islands. In 1980, the United States agreed to grant the Caroline Islands a form of self-government called *free association.* The agreement divided the islands into two groups—the Palau Islands and the Federated States of Micronesia. The federated states consists of the Truk Islands, the Yap Islands, and the islands of Kusaie and Ponape. By 1984, the steps involved in establishing the self-governing units were still in process. EDWIN H. BRYAN, JR.

Related Articles in WORLD BOOK include:

Pacific Islands	Peleliu	Truk Islands	Yap Islands
Palau Islands	Ponape	Ulithi	

CAROLINGIAN ART was a style of art created during the late 700's and the 800's in France and Germany. Carolingian art is named for Charlemagne, who was king of the Franks from 768 to 814. Carolingian architects made major contributions to church design and monastic planning. Carolingian scribes created a new type of handwriting. In previous centuries, artists had emphasized abstract geometric patterns and fantastic animals. Carolingian painters, sculptors, and artisans reintroduced the human figure in a natural setting into the visual arts.

Carolingian architects claimed they were copying early Christian buildings, but they changed their models to suit their needs. These architects followed the plan of the early Christian church called the *basilica,* but they added chapels, elaborate crypts, and high towers. They invented an entrance called a *westwork* that included a porch, chapels, two towers enclosing stairways, and, in an imperial church, a throne room. Carolingian abbots developed a monastic plan in which covered walks joined the church, the library, and living quarters.

Carolingian scribes developed a beautiful, legible script, which they used in copying the Bible and other books. Painters added illustrations, such as narrative scenes and a portrait of the ruler. MARILYN STOKSTAD

See also CHARLEMAGNE; ARCHITECTURE (Carolingian Architecture).

Tempera painting (about 870) by an unknown French artist; Abbey of S. Paolo fouri le Mura, Rome (Istituto Poligrafico e Zecca Dello Stato)

Carolingian Art included beautifully painted book illustrations. The painting above portrays episodes from the life of Saint Paul and is from the Bible of Charles I of France.

CAROLINGIAN EMPIRE. See MIDDLE AGES (The Carolingian Empire).

CAROM BILLIARDS. See BILLIARDS.

CAROTENE. See VITAMIN (Vitamin A); LEAF (The Leaf Changes Color).

U.S. Fish and Wildlife Service

The Carp lives in inland waters. It has golden-colored scales. The largest carp weigh from 30 to 80 pounds (14 to 36 kilograms).

CARP is a large fish that lives in inland lakes and streams. The most common kinds of carp are the *scale carp, mirror carp,* and *leather carp.* Scale carp are covered evenly with scales. Mirror carp have larger scales of different sizes. Leather carp have few scales and look almost bare. The goldfish and the roach also are kinds of carp (see GOLDFISH; ROACH).

Carp came from Asia, but are now found in most parts of the Northern Hemisphere. They were brought to California in 1872. The United States Fish Commission brought more carp to America in 1877, and the fish has spread rapidly, especially in the waters of the Mississippi River Valley.

Carp are both useful and harmful. They are used as food, but they destroy the eggs and breeding places of more valuable fish. People who use young carp as live bait for fishing help spread carp. The unused fish are thrown in the water and multiply. Most Americans do not like carp, but Europeans are fond of them. Carp can be eaten either fresh or smoked. Some are canned.

Scientific Classification. The carp is a member of the carp and minnow family, *Cyprinidae.* The leather carp, mirror carp, and scale carp are *Cyprinus carpio.* CARL L. HUBBS

See also FISH (picture: Fish of Temperate Fresh Waters).

CARPAL BONE. See HAND.

CARPATHIAN MOUNTAINS, *kahr PAY thee uhn,* are part of the great mountain system of central Europe. The Carpathians extend for about 900 miles (1,400 kilometers) in a half circle between Czechoslovakia and Poland. Most of these mountains lie in Czechoslovakia and Romania. For location, see EUROPE (physical map). The highest elevations are Gerlachovka (formerly called Stalin) Mountain (8,737 feet, or 2,663 meters) in the Tatra Mountains of Czechoslovakia and Rysy (8,199 feet, or 2,499 meters) in Poland.

The Carpathians are an extension of the mountain range which includes the Alps. But the Carpathian peaks are generally lower than the Alps and have fewer lakes, glaciers, and waterfalls. The Carpathians contain several minerals, including large deposits of coal and salt. Large quantities of timber come from the fir, oak, and beech forests which cover the lower slopes of the mountains. Wolves, lynx, and bears roam through these forests. Many fertile farms lie in the valleys of the Carpathian Mountains. People cross the mountains by using any of the narrow passes. M. KAMIL DZIEWANOWSKI

See also GALICIA.

CARPENTER, M. SCOTT (1925-), one of the first United States astronauts, was the second American to circle the earth in a spacecraft. He made a three-orbit flight in the *Aurora 7* spacecraft on May 24, 1962. Carpenter's trip ended dramatically after his spacecraft landed more than 200 miles (320 kilometers) beyond the intended landing area and beyond radio range of the recovery forces. He was out of contact for almost an hour before a search plane finally spotted him in a life raft beside his spacecraft.

Malcolm Scott Carpenter was born in Boulder, Colo. He served in the Navy during World War II (1939-1945) and then studied aeronautical engineering at the University of Colorado. He served as a Navy pilot during the Korean War (1950-1953) and became a test pilot in 1954. In 1959, the National Aeronautics and Space Administration (NASA) selected Carpenter to be an astronaut in the Mercury program.

In 1965, Carpenter took a leave of absence from NASA to be an aquanaut in the Navy's Man-in-the-Sea program. In 1966, he became branch chief for advanced programs for NASA. He resigned from NASA in 1967 to do deep-sea research for the Navy. Leg injuries received in the Man-in-the-Sea program ended his deep-diving career in 1969. He retired from the Navy that year. WILLIAM J. CROMIE

See also ASTRONAUT; SPACE TRAVEL.

CARPENTER ANT. See ANT (Nests; The Importance of Ants).

CARPENTER BEE. See BEE (Kinds).

CARPENTERS AND JOINERS OF AMERICA, UNITED BROTHERHOOD OF, is one of the unions of the joint American Federation of Labor and Congress of Industrial Organizations. Members work in wood or in other industries which require the skill of a carpenter. The brotherhood has locals, or chapters, in the United States, Canada, Panama, and Puerto Rico.

The union was organized in Chicago in 1881, and it combined with the Amalgamated Wood Workers of America in 1912. Workers in logging and lumber camps became part of the brotherhood in 1935. Some logging and lumber workers' locals broke away from the brotherhood in 1937 and formed the International Woodworkers of America.

The brotherhood holds a convention every four years. It has headquarters at 101 Constitution Ave. NW, Washington, D.C. 20001. For total membership, see LABOR MOVEMENT (table). Critically reviewed by the UNITED BROTHERHOOD OF CARPENTERS AND JOINERS OF AMERICA

CARPENTERS' HALL. See PHILADELPHIA (Downtown Philadelphia); UNITED STATES, GOVERNMENT OF THE (picture).

CARPENTRY is the building and repairing of structures. It involves all types of work done by carpenters, including the construction of buildings and parts of buildings. Carpentry also includes the design and assembly of cabinets, furniture, and other items. Most carpenters work chiefly with wood, but some also work with such materials as metals and plastics.

Carpenters must have a thorough knowledge of construction materials and methods. This knowledge includes the ability to understand technical literature and follow the instructions of a blueprint or scale drawing. Carpenters also must know how to use various hand tools, including chisels, hammers, and planes, and such power tools as drills and power saws. Some carpenters use *pneumatic tools,* which operate by compressed air. These tools include air drills, pneumatic nailers, and pneumatic staplers.

There are two types of carpentry, *rough carpentry* and *finish carpentry.* Rough carpenters assemble the frameworks of buildings and then place coverings called *sheathing* and *siding* on the structures. These carpenters also apply shingles and do other exterior construction work. After the rough carpentry has been completed on a building, finish carpenters do various types of interior work. Their jobs include hanging doors and windows, applying wood trim, installing paneling, and laying floors.

Some finish carpenters specialize in certain types of work. For example, *cabinetmakers* design, shape, and assemble cabinets, furniture, and other items. Large numbers of cabinetmakers are employed by furniture manufacturers, and many work for companies that produce *millwork,* such as doors, windows, and moldings. Other specialists, called *joiners,* cut, fit, and join together pieces of wood to make various items, including stairs and tabletops. Joiners do especially precise and complicated work.

Some carpenters learn their trade through on-the-job training, and others attend a technical or vocational school. Still others receive instruction in a four-year apprenticeship program. ALVA H. JARED

See also HOUSE (Building a House); WOODWORKING.

CARPET. See RUGS AND CARPETS.

CARPET BEETLE is a common insect pest. Its *larvae* (young) live on carpets. They also enter closets and eat woolens, feathers, and furs. In spring, the adult beetles may be found around infested houses. They are brownish-black or marked with red or yellowish-white spots. The adults live on pollen. Protective measures against carpet beetles include good housekeeping and spraying with various insecticides.

Scientific Classification. The carpet beetle belongs to the order *Coleoptera.* It is a member of the skin beetle family, *Dermestidae*. It belongs to the genus *Anthrenus*, species *A. scrophulariae*. H. H. Ross

See also Beetle; Larva.

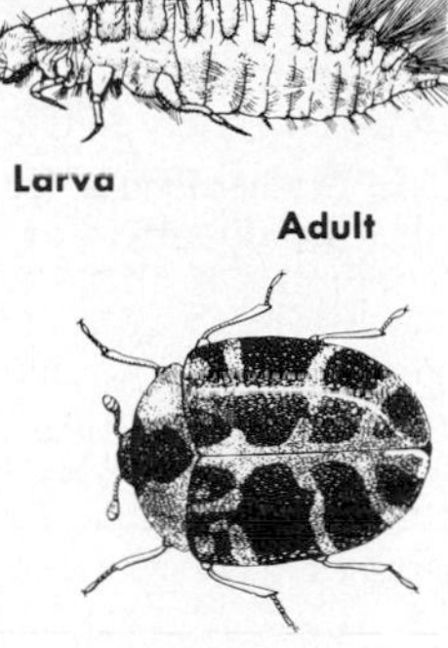

Carpet Beetles are also sometimes called *buffalo bugs*.

CARPETBAGGERS was a term that Southerners scornfully applied to Northerners who moved to the South during the Reconstruction period after the Civil War. Some were business people who wished to invest their money and make their fortunes in the South. Others were schoolteachers who often combined high ideals with a smug hostility toward all things Southern. Still others went South openly seeking plunder or political office. Hostile Southern whites coined the name *carpetbaggers* to suggest that these people could stuff everything they owned when they came south into a *carpetbag*, or suitcase. The term is still used to describe an outsider or a politician who tries to exert unauthorized influence or power.

The carpetbaggers created antagonism in the South, still sensitive from its recent defeat. They aroused the bitterest feeling when they entered Southern politics. In 1867, the United States Congress, controlled by Northern Republicans, put the Southern States under military rule and temporarily took voting rights away from many prominent Southern whites. The newly emancipated blacks, who could now vote, looked to their Northern friends for leadership in setting up new Southern state governments. Several carpetbaggers became governors, and others served in the national and state legislatures. These "carpetbag" governments accomplished a great deal of good in the South. They drew up enlightened constitutions, equalized the tax load, embarked upon the rebuilding of roads and levees destroyed during the war, inaugurated public school systems, and guaranteed blacks their civil rights.

Culver

The Carpetbaggers' trek to the South after the Civil War was satirized in this caricature by the famed cartoonist Thomas Nast.

But the carpetbaggers did not succeed in the long run. They often proved inexperienced, wasteful, or corrupt. By the 1870's, they had alienated the Southern planters, who objected to their heavy tax programs; the Southern white farmers, who disliked concessions to the blacks; and even many blacks, who wanted black leaders in office. One carpetbag regime after another collapsed as federal troops withdrew from the South and Southern whites regained political power. The last three Southern states, Florida, Louisiana, and South Carolina, returned to white Democratic rule in 1877. David Herbert Donald

See also Reconstruction (Republicans in the South).

Additional Resources

Current, Richard N. *Three Carpetbag Governors*. Louisiana State Univ. Press, 1968. Investigates carpetbag rule in Florida, Louisiana, and Mississippi.

Daniels, Jonathan. *Prince of Carpetbaggers*. Greenwood, 1974. Reprint of 1958 ed. The career of one of the best-known carpetbaggers, Milton S. Littlefield.

CARR, EMILY (1871-1945), was a noted Canadian painter and writer. She worked as a painter throughout most of her life and began her writing career only a few years before her death.

Carr was born in Victoria, B.C. In 1904, she made her first of many visits to Indian villages in British Columbia. Most of her early paintings portray the Indian life and culture that she saw there. These works received little favorable attention, and so Carr gave up painting almost completely in 1913.

In 1927, an exhibit of Carr's paintings in Ottawa, Ont., brought her to the attention of the Group of Seven. The members of this group were nationally known Canadian landscape painters. They and their works inspired Carr to resume painting and encouraged her interest in landscapes. Most of her later paintings reflect her desire to capture the spirit of the vast forests of Canada's west coast.

Carr's first book, *Klee Wyck* (1941), is a collection of stories about her experiences among the Indians. She also wrote six other books. Rosemary Sullivan

CARRAGEEN. See Irish Moss.

CARRANZA, *kuh RAN zuh,* **VENUSTIANO** (1859-1920), a Mexican general, became president of Mexico in 1915. He led a revolt against the government of General Victoriano Huerta in 1913, and was named "First Chief" in 1914. Carranza called a congress which adopted the present Mexican constitution in 1917 (see Mexico [The Constitution of 1917]). This constitution provided for many beneficial reforms. Carranza was born in Coahuila, Mexico. Harold Eugene Davis

CARREL, *kuh REHL,* **ALEXIS** (1873-1944), a French surgeon and biologist, proved that tissues could survive apart from their organs if properly nourished. He won the 1912 Nobel prize in medicine for his work in blood-vessel surgery and in transplanting organs and tissues. During World War I, he and the English chemist, Henry Dakin, developed the Carrel-Dakin antiseptic solution for treating injuries and wounds.

Carrel was born in Lyon, France. He came to the United States in 1905, and was appointed to the Rockefeller Institute for Medical Research (now Rockefeller University) in 1906. At the outbreak of World War II, he returned to France, where he died. His works include *Man, the Unknown* (1935). With the aviator Charles A. Lindbergh, Carrel wrote *The Culture of Organs* (1938). HENRY J. L. MARRIOTT

CARRIAGE is a horse-drawn vehicle used for the transportation of people. It developed in the early 1700's from the slow, heavy wagons and coaches used for passenger travel. Better roads permitted the use of the more graceful and speedy carriage.

The carriage was characterized by its light weight, flexibility, and elegant design. The running gear on the vehicle was usually made of strong, springy wood such as oak, ash, or hickory. Wrought iron brackets and fittings braced the slender wooden parts. Early wheels were usually made of hickory and fitted with iron tires, but solid rubber tires came into use after 1875.

The first carriages were imported into America from England and France. Carriages were not manufactured in America until about 1740, but by 1880 the United States produced more horse-drawn vehicles than any other country in the world. Popular American carriages included the *buckboard*, the *buggy*, the *chaise*, and the *rockaway*. Persons of wealth and social standing used fashionable carriages called *landaus* and *victorias*.

Use of the carriage reached a peak in 1905 when about 8,000 builders produced more than 930,000 vehicles. The introduction of the automobile at this time brought the end of the carriage. By World War I, it was no longer an important private carrier. JOHN H. WHITE

See also TRANSPORTATION (pictures).

CARRIER. See DISEASE (Spread of Infectious Diseases).

CARRIER PIGEON is a large, stately pigeon bred as a show bird. The carrier pigeon is descended from the *rock dove* of Europe. Carriers may be black, white, dun-colored, or yellow. The carrier pigeon is larger than other types of pigeons, and it carries itself proudly erect. The bird has a long beak, head, and body, and strong wings and feet. The carrier keeps its feathers in fine trim and always appears sleek and well groomed. It has large, fleshy growths around its big yellow eyes and on its bill. The growths may cover the nose of an old bird.

Scientific Classification. The carrier pigeon is in the pigeon and dove family, Columbidae. It is *Columba livia*. LEONARD W. WING

See also HOMING PIGEON; PIGEON.

L. D. Eldridge

Carrier Pigeon

CARROLL was the family name of three early American leaders, two brothers and their cousin.

Daniel Carroll (1730-1796) signed both the Articles of Confederation and the United States Constitution. He favored a strong central government and opposed election of the President by Congress. He first favored direct election by the people, but later urged the electoral college system. He served in the first Maryland state Senate in 1777, and was president of the Senate in 1783. In 1789, he was elected to the U.S. House of Representatives in the first U.S. Congress. From 1791 to 1795, he was a commissioner of the District of Columbia. He was born in Prince George's County, Md. He is usually called "Daniel Carroll of Rock Creek," to distinguish him from relatives of the same name.

John Carroll (1735-1815), brother of Daniel, became the first Roman Catholic bishop in the United States. American priests elected him bishop in 1789, and he took office the next year. Bishop Carroll founded Georgetown University in 1789 and helped establish other Catholic colleges. He planned and built the Basilica of the Assumption in Baltimore, the first major Catholic cathedral in the United States. In 1808, he was elevated to archbishop. He was born in Upper Marlboro, Md., and was ordained in 1769.

Charles Carroll (1737-1832), was the last surviving signer of the Declaration of Independence. He always signed his name "Charles Carroll of Carrollton" to distinguish himself from several others who had the same name. Carroll went to Canada in 1776 with his cousin John Carroll, Samuel Chase, and Benjamin Franklin to ask Canadians to help America in the Revolutionary War. Their mission failed.

Carroll was elected to Maryland's first state senate in 1777. He served there until 1801. From 1776 to 1778, he was a member of the Continental Congress, where he signed the Declaration of Independence. He was a U.S. senator from Maryland between 1789 and 1792. Carroll retired from politics in 1801, and he devoted the rest of his life to private affairs. A statue of Carroll represents Maryland in the United States Capitol in Washington, D.C. Carroll was born in Annapolis, Md. AUBREY C. LAND

CARROLL, JAMES. See LAZEAR, JESSE W.

CARROLL, LEWIS, was the pen name of CHARLES LUTWIDGE DODGSON (1832-1898), an English author. Carroll wrote two of the most famous books in English literature—*Alice's Adventures in Wonderland* and its continuation *Through the Looking-Glass and What Alice Found There*. People in all parts of the world read these books. *Alice in Wonderland*, as the first book is usually called, has been translated into more than 30 languages, including Arabic and Chinese. The book has even been produced in Braille so that blind persons can read and enjoy it.

Carroll wrote both books to give pleasure to children. But adults also enjoy the humor, fantastic characters, and adventures in the stories. Scholars study the books to find meanings in what seems to be nonsense.

Life. Carroll was born on Jan. 27, 1832, in Daresbury, in northwest England. He graduated from the Christ Church College of Oxford University in 1854. He began teaching mathematics at Christ Church in 1855 and spent most of his life at the school. He became a *deacon*

(officer) in the Church of England in 1861. Carroll died on Jan. 14, 1898.

The *Alice* Books. Carroll enjoyed being with children. He created the character of Alice to amuse a little girl named Alice Liddell, the daughter of the dean of Christ Church. On July 4, 1862, Carroll went rowing on the River Isis with Alice Liddell and two of her sisters. He began to tell the story of Alice that day. Later, he wrote the story down, and called it "Alice's Adventures Underground." Carroll enlarged the story into its present book-length version, which was published in 1865.

Brown Brothers

Lewis Carroll

Alice in Wonderland tells about the adventures of a little girl in a make-believe world under the ground. Alice lands in this "wonderland" after she falls down a hole while following a rabbit. She meets many strange characters, including the Cheshire Cat, the Mad Hatter,

"Now for the evidence," said the King, "and then the sentence."
"No!" said the Queen, "first the sentence, and then the evidence!"
"Nonsense!" cried Alice, so loudly that everybody jumped, "the idea of having the sentence first!"
"Hold your tongue!" said the Queen.
"I won't!" said Alice, "you're nothing but a pack of cards! Who cares for you?"

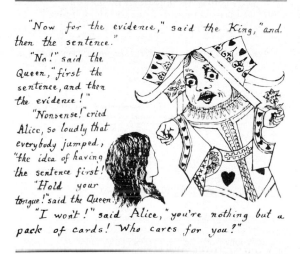

The British Library (Copyright by University Microfilms, Inc., 1964)

Alice's Adventures in Wonderland **was written by Lewis Carroll in the early 1860's. The author decorated his original text with pictures illustrating the story. In one picture, *above,* Carroll showed Alice arguing with the bad-tempered Queen of Hearts.**

the Queen of Hearts, and the Mock Turtle. *Alice in Wonderland* became so well known that the names of some of its characters are part of everyday speech. For example, we hear about persons who "grin like a Cheshire Cat" or who are as "mad as a March Hare."

Through the Looking-Glass (1871), introduced new characters, including the frightened Jabberwock dragon, the silly twins Tweedledee and Tweedledum, and the Walrus and the Carpenter. Sir John Tenniel drew the pictures for both books. His illustrations became nearly as famous as the story. See TENNIEL, SIR JOHN.

Other Works. Carroll also wrote *Sylvie and Bruno*, a fairy tale in verse and prose (two parts, 1889 and 1893). The poem "The Hunting of the Snark" (1876) tells the story of the Banker, Baker, Beaver, Bellman, and other amusing characters in search of a Snark, an animal that does not exist. Carroll wrote many works on mathematics under his real name. They include "Notes on the First Two Books of Euclid" (1860) and *Curiosa Mathematica* (two parts, 1888 and 1894). Carroll also was a fine photographer.

JAMES DOUGLAS MERRITT

Additional Resources

CLARK, ANNE. *Lewis Carroll: A Biography*. Schocken, 1979.

DODGSON, CHARLES L. *The Annotated Alice: Alice's Adventures in Wonderland and Through the Looking Glass.* Intro. and notes by Martin Gardner. Illus. by John Tenniel. Potter, 1960. *The Letters of Lewis Carroll.* Ed. by Morton Cohen. 2 vols. Oxford, 1979.

HUDSON, DEREK. *Lewis Carroll: An Illustrated Biography.* Rev. ed. Potter, 1977.

CARROT is a long, reddish-yellow root vegetable that belongs to the parsley family. People in all parts of the world grow carrots. Carrots have thin, lacy leaves on long stems. The leaves and stems sometimes are sprinkled on meats to improve the flavor. But the root of the carrot plant is the part eaten as a vegetable.

Carrots can live through winters that are not too cold, and can endure much summer heat. Gardeners in the northern United States can raise a crop of carrots in about a hundred days. They also grow fall crops. Most of the fresh carrots that are sold in groceries during the winter come from California and Texas.

Frank Cassidy

Carrot Roots

Carrots grow from tiny seeds planted in rows about $1\frac{1}{2}$ to 2 feet (46 to 61 centimeters) apart. They grow best in deep rich soils that contain sand or muck.

Several pests attack carrots. They include plant lice, carrot caterpillars, carrot rustfly, leafhoppers, and nematodes. They may be killed with parathion.

People eat carrots raw, in salads, or boiled. In some places, carrots have been ground and roasted, and used as a substitute for coffee. A substance called *carotene* comes from carrots. Carotene is used by the human body to produce vitamin A. Carrots also contain vitamin B_1 and small amounts of vitamins B_2 and C. Carrots are rich in sugar and contain much iron.

The ancient Greeks and Romans used carrots for medicine but not for food. Many of the early colonists in Virginia and Massachusetts raised carrots to eat.

Scientific Classification. Carrots are in the parsley family, *Umbelliferae*. They are classified as genus *Daucus*, species *D. carota*.

S. H. WITTWER

See also VITAMIN (Vitamin A); WILD CARROT.

CARSON, JOHNNY (1925-), a popular American entertainer, became famous as host of "The Tonight Show" on television. He is noted for his quick sense of humor and natural performing style.

Carson was born in Corning, Iowa. He began his career in Lincoln, Neb., where he worked as a radio announcer in the late 1940's. During the early 1950's,

Carson worked as a writer and performer in radio and television in Los Angeles. In 1955, he starred in "The Johnny Carson Show," a weekly TV program. Then, for five years, Carson hosted a daytime game show called "Who Do You Trust?" He appeared as a guest host on "The Tonight Show" in 1958 and became the regular host in 1962. TERRENCE O'FLAHERTY

See also TELEVISION (pictures).

CARSON, KIT (1809-1868), was a famous American frontiersman. He became known as a skillful and daring hunter, guide, and soldier. People described Carson as brave, gentle, honest, and wise.

Early Life. Carson, whose real first name was Christopher, was born in Madison County, Kentucky. His family moved to Boon's Lick, Mo., near Arrow Rock, when he was 1 year old. At the age of 14 or 15, Kit was sent to work for a saddlemaker. He hated the job and ran away in 1826 to join a group of traders headed for Santa Fe, in what is now New Mexico. From 1829 to 1841, Carson worked in the fur trade. He trapped beavers in Arizona, California, Idaho, Wyoming, and the Rocky Mountains and took part in many fights with Indians.

Rise to Prominence. John C. Frémont, who became a famous government explorer, hired Carson in 1842 to guide his party along the Oregon Trail to South Pass in the Rockies in Wyoming. The expedition passed safely through land of hostile Sioux Indians. Frémont praised Carson in his official reports, which helped make Carson well known. In 1843 and 1844, Carson helped guide Frémont's second expedition, which included a survey of Great Salt Lake in Utah and part of the Oregon Trail. In 1845, Carson guided the explorer's third expedition. The group traveled from Colorado to California and north into Oregon.

The Mexican War broke out in 1846, and Frémont and his group returned to California. They joined the American settlers there in a revolt against the Mexicans who controlled the region. The Americans defeated the Mexicans, and Frémont sent Carson to Washington, D.C., with messages, including news of the victory. But at Socorro, N. Mex., General Stephen W. Kearny ordered Carson to guide him to California. Kearny's troops were attacked by Mexicans at San Pasqual, Calif., near Escondido. Carson and two others slipped through the enemy lines to seek help from American forces in San Diego. They had to walk or crawl for about 30 miles (48 kilometers), but Kearny's troops were rescued.

Military Career. After the Civil War began in 1861, Carson was made colonel of the New Mexico Volunteer Regiment. In 1862, he fought the Confederate forces in a battle at Valverde, N. Mex., near Socorro. Carson was later ordered to lead a campaign against the Apache Indians to force them to live on a reservation. During the fall of 1862, Carson gathered together about 400 Apache Indians and placed them on a reservation near Fort Sumner, N. Mex. He then led a campaign against the Navajo Indians. By destroying their crops and animals, Carson forced about 8,000 Navajos to accept reservation life (see NAVAJO INDIANS). In November 1864, Carson fought the Kiowas, Comanches, and other Plains Indians at Adobe Walls, an abandoned trading post in Texas. His force of about 400 men retreated after being attacked by 1,500 to 3,000 Indians. Carson

Denver Public Library, Western History Department

Kit Carson won fame as a frontiersman in the West. He was especially known for his skill as a guide, hunter, and soldier.

was made a brigadier general in 1865 and took command of Fort Garland in Colorado the following year. Carson resigned from the Army in 1867 because of illness. HOWARD R. LAMAR

See also FRÉMONT, JOHN C.; KEARNY, STEPHEN W.

Additional Resources

BLACKWELDER, BERNICE. *Great Westerner: The Story of Kit Carson.* Caxton, 1962.

BREWERTON, GEORGE D. *Overland with Kit Carson: A Narrative of the Old Spanish Trail in '48.* Coward, 1930.

CARTER, HARVEY L. *Dear Old Kit: The Historical Christopher Carson, with a New Edition of the Carson Memoirs.* Univ. of Oklahoma Press, 1968.

CARSON, RACHEL (1907-1964), was an American marine biologist and science writer. She wrote several books that reflect her lifelong interest in the life of the seas and the seashores.

In her writings, Rachel Carson stressed the interrelation of all living things and the dependence of human welfare on natural processes. *The Sea Around Us* (1951) describes the biology, chemistry, geography, and history of the sea. *Silent Spring* (1962) called public attention to the wasteful and destructive use of pesticides. The author warned that pesticides poison the food supply of animals and kill many birds and fish. She pointed out that pesticides could also contaminate human food supplies. Her arguments helped lead to restrictions on the use of pesticides in many parts of the world.

Erich Hartmann, Magnum

Rachel Carson

Rachel Louise Carson was born in Springdale, Pa. She graduated from the Pennsylvania College for Women in 1929 and received a master's degree from Johns Hopkins University in 1932. She worked for the U.S. Fish and Wildlife Service during most of her adult life. SHELDON NOVICK

CARSON CITY is the capital of Nevada and a tourist center. It lies at the eastern base of the Sierra Nevada, near the Nevada-California border. For location, see NEVADA (political map). Carson City ranks as one of the fastest-growing cities in Nevada. Many people who vacationed in the Carson City area during the 1970's returned to settle in the city. The population increased from 15,468 in 1970 to about 32,000 in 1980.

The Carson City area has many places of historical interest. Several abandoned mining towns lie near the city. About 30 houses in the city itself date from the mining days of the 1800's. The Nevada State Museum building in Carson City housed a United States mint from 1870 to 1894.

A land speculator named Abraham Curry founded Carson City in 1858. He named it after the famous frontier scout Kit Carson. In 1859, prospectors discovered a rich deposit of silver ore, the Comstock Lode, near Carson City (see COMSTOCK LODE). The town grew quickly as a mining supply center. Carson City became the capital of the Nevada Territory in 1861 and the state capital in 1864.

Carson City served as the seat of Ormsby County until 1969. That year, the city and county merged and became the independent city of Carson City. The city has a council-manager government. STEVEN R. FRADY

See also NEVADA (picture: The State Capitol).

CARTAGENA, *KAHR tuh JEE nuh* or *KAHR tah HAY nah* (pop. 435,361), is the chief seaport on the northwestern coast of Colombia (see COLOMBIA [map]). Its industries produce cotton goods, furniture, leather goods, perfumes, drugs, soap, and tobacco products. Cartagena was founded in 1533. In 1586, the city was plundered by England's Sir Francis Drake.

CARTAGENA, *KAHR tuh JEE nuh* or *KAHR tah HAY nah* (pop. 172,751), stands on a beautiful bay of the Mediterranean Sea in southeastern Spain (see SPAIN [map]). It has a large harbor, and is the site of one of Spain's most important naval bases. The city exports agricultural products, and lead and iron ore. Factories there produce cordage, canvas, and chemicals.

The mines near Cartagena attracted the Carthaginians, who founded the city about 225 B.C. Its people were among the first to rise against Napoleon in 1808. The city served as headquarters of the Republican fleet during the Spanish Civil War. STANLEY G. PAYNE

CARTEL, *kahr TEHL* or *KAHR tuhl*, is an association formed among producers in a particular industry to control the market for their product. Cartels raise the selling price of their product by restricting the available supply. A cartel may consist of privately owned companies in one country or several countries. A cartel also may be formed among governments.

To succeed, a cartel should have relatively few members. However, the cartel must include all or most producers in the industry and so have a monopoly or near monopoly on the product. The product must have no close substitutes, and new supplies must be scarce.

A cartel sets a relatively high selling price for its product. To obtain this price, the cartel limits the output of each member. It also assigns each member a share of the market. The cartel will likely fail if too many members cheat on these arrangements.

Until the late 1930's, international cartels existed among firms in such industries as drugs and steel. However, industrial cartels have become unimportant because they are hard to maintain. Since 1960, some cartels have been formed among governments of countries that produce oil or other natural resource products. These cartels are dominated by nations of the *Third World* (developing countries in Africa, Asia, and Latin America). The most successful of these cartels is the Organization of Petroleum Exporting Countries (OPEC), which largely controls the world market for oil. Cartels within the United States are illegal. In certain special circumstances, however, American firms may join international cartels in order to sell export goods. ROBERT M. STERN

See also MONOPOLY AND COMPETITION; TRUST.

CARTER, ELLIOTT (1908-), is one of the leading American composers of the 1900's. His music is extremely complex, and its performance requires highly skillful musicianship. Carter became especially noted for his chamber music. He won a Pulitzer Prize in 1960 for his *Second String Quartet* and in 1973 for his *String Quartet No. 3*. Several modern composers influenced Carter's style, including Béla Bartok, Arnold Schönberg, and Igor Stravinsky.

Carter's first important compositions were the ballet suite *Pocahontas* (1939) and the choral work *The Defense of Corinth* (1941). Since the late 1940's, he has used complicated rhythmic patterns in his works. Carter calls these patterns *metrical modulations*. In addition to chamber music, Carter has composed several major works for orchestra. They include *Variations for Orchestra* (1955), *Double Concerto for Piano and Harpsichord and Two Chamber Orchestras* (1961), *Piano Concerto* (1967), and *Concerto for Orchestra* (1970). Elliott Cook Carter, Jr., was born in New York City. MILOŠ VELIMIROVIĆ

CARTER, GERALD EMMETT CARDINAL (1912-), was appointed a cardinal of the Roman Catholic Church in 1979 by Pope John Paul II. He had become archbishop of Toronto, Canada, in 1978.

Carter was born in Montreal and was ordained a priest in 1937 after studying at the Grand Seminary there. In 1939, he founded St. Joseph Teachers College in Montreal. He taught at the college until 1961, when he became auxiliary bishop of London, Ont. He was bishop of London from 1964 to 1978. FRANCIS L. FILAS

CARTER, HOWARD (1873-1939), an English archaeologist, specialized in excavating ancient Egyptian tombs. He made his most famous discovery, the tomb of Pharaoh Tutankhamen, in 1922 (see TUTANKHAMEN). His most famous writing was the three-volume work *The Tomb of Tut-ankh-amen* (1923-1933). Carter wrote many other works describing his discoveries.

Carter spent many years in Egypt's Valley of the Kings making a series of excavations. For a time, he directed the Egyptian government's program to preserve the remains of ancient Egyptian civilization. Carter was born in Swaffham, England. He received most of his education privately due to poor health. Much of his early training in archaeology came from the famous archaeologist Sir Flinders Petrie. Carter first went to Egypt in 1890 as a member of an archaeological expedition headed by Petrie. DAVID B. STOUT

JIMMY CARTER

NIXON
37th President
1969—1974

FORD
38th President
1974—1977

CARTER, JAMES EARL, JR. (1924-), was elected President of the United States in 1976, climaxing a remarkable rise to national fame. Carter had been governor of Georgia from 1971 to 1975 and was little known elsewhere at the beginning of 1976. But then he won 18 primary elections and became the Democratic candidate for President. Carter, known by the nickname Jimmy, defeated President Gerald R. Ford in the 1976 election. In 1980, Carter was defeated in his bid for a second term by former Governor Ronald Reagan of California, his Republican opponent.

Before Carter won election as governor, he served in the Georgia Senate. He had managed his family peanut warehouse business and farm before entering politics. Carter also had been an officer in the United States Navy. He was the first graduate of the U.S. Naval Academy to become chief executive.

During Carter's presidency, the United States faced problems both at home and abroad. At home, the economy suffered from unemployment and severe inflation. Abroad, relations between the United States and the Soviet Union plunged to their lowest point in several years following a Soviet invasion of Afghanistan. In Iran, revolutionaries held hostage a group of Americans who worked at the U.S. embassy in Teheran. They had seized the hostages to protest U.S. support for the deposed shah of Iran. Despite these problems, Carter won praise for some achievements in foreign affairs. He helped establish diplomatic relations between the United States and China. He also helped bring about a peace treaty between Egypt and Israel.

In appearance and manner, Carter was calm, reserved, and soft-spoken. His friends knew him as a man of great personal warmth and charm. In politics, Carter was an able, energetic campaigner with an iron will and a determination to win every fight. According to his political aides, he demanded hard work and set high standards but pushed himself the hardest.

Early Life

Boyhood. James Earl Carter, Jr., was born on Oct. 1, 1924, in Plains, Ga. He had two sisters, Gloria (1926-) and Ruth (1929-1983), and a brother, William Alton III (1937-), usually called Billy.

Carter's father, a farmer and small businessman, ran a farm products store on the family farm in the rural community of Archery, a few miles west of Plains. Carter's mother, Lillian Gordy Carter, was a registered nurse.

The Carters lived in Plains when Jimmy was born. Four years later, they moved to the farm in Archery. Jimmy grew up there and helped with the farm chores during his boyhood. He also developed an early interest in business. When the sandy-haired boy was about 5 years old, he began to sell boiled peanuts on the streets of Plains. He earned about $1 a day on weekdays and about $5 on Saturdays. At the age of 9, Jimmy bought five huge bales of cotton for 5 cents a pound. He stored the cotton and sold it a few years later, when the price had more than tripled.

Education. Jimmy went to public school in Plains. He shared his mother's love of reading and received good grades. A schoolmate later remembered that Jimmy "was always the smartest in the class." The boy's favorite subjects included history, literature, and music. As a teen-ager, he played on the high school basketball team.

In 1941, following graduation from high school, Carter entered Georgia Southwestern College in nearby Americus. In 1942, a boyhood dream came true when he received an appointment to the United States Naval Academy in Annapolis, Md. "Even as a grammar school child, I read books about the Navy and Annapolis," Carter recalled. However, he lacked the mathematics courses required for admission to the academy and enrolled at Georgia Institute of Technology to fulfill this requirement. Carter entered the academy in 1943. He did especially well in electronics, gunnery, and naval tactics and graduated in 1946, ranking 59th in a class of 820.

Carter's Family. In 1945, Carter had started to date Rosalynn Smith (Aug. 18, 1927-) of Plains. She was the best friend of his sister Ruth. Rosalynn's father, a garage mechanic, died when she was 13 years old. She took a part-time job as cleaning girl in a beauty shop to help pay the family's expenses.

Jimmy and Rosalynn were married on July 7, 1946, about a month after he graduated from Annapolis. They had four children—John William (1947-); James Earl III (1950-), usually called Chip; Donnel Jeffrey (1952-); and Amy Lynn (1967-).

Naval Career. Carter spent his first two years in the Navy chiefly as an electronics instructor. He served first on the U.S.S. *Wyoming* and later on the U.S.S. *Mississippi.* These battleships were being used to test new equipment. Near the end of his period on the *Mississippi,*

Hugh S. Sidey, the contributor of this article, is Washington Contributing Editor of Time *magazine.*

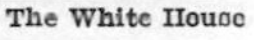

REAGAN
40th President
1981—

39TH PRESIDENT OF THE UNITED STATES 1977-1981

The United States flag had 50 stars when James E. Carter, Jr., became President.

The White House

Carter volunteered for submarine duty. He graduated from submarine-training school in 1948, ranking third in a class of 52. Carter was then assigned to the submarine U.S.S. *Pomfret* and, in 1950, to the U.S.S. *K-1*, a submarine designed for antisubmarine warfare.

In 1952, Carter joined a select group of officers who were developing the world's first nuclear-powered submarines. He became engineering officer of the nuclear submarine *Sea Wolf*. Carter served under Captain Hyman G. Rickover, who pioneered the nuclear project. Carter later wrote that Rickover "had a profound effect on my life—perhaps more than anyone except my own parents. . . . He expected the maximum from us, but he always contributed more."

A turning point in Carter's life occurred in 1953, when his father died of cancer. Carter felt he was needed in Plains to manage the family businesses. But Rosalynn had no desire to return to Plains, and she argued against his leaving the Navy. Carter later called their disagreement "the first really serious argument in our marriage." He resigned from the Navy that year with the rank of lieutenant senior grade.

IMPORTANT DATES IN CARTER'S LIFE

1924 (Oct. 1) Born in Plains, Ga.

1946 Graduated from the United States Naval Academy.

1946 (July 7) Married Rosalynn Smith.

1946-1953 Served in the United States Navy.

1962 Elected to the Georgia Senate.

1964 Reelected to the Georgia Senate.

1970 Elected governor of Georgia.

1976 Elected President of the United States.

1980 Lost presidential election to Ronald Reagan.

Return to Plains

Businessman and Civic Leader. Soon after Carter returned to Plains, he took over the family farm and a peanut warehouse that his father had established in the town. He studied modern farming techniques at the Agricultural Experiment Station in Tifton, Ga. During the late 1950's and the 1960's, Carter expanded the warehouse and bought new machinery for the farm. The family businesses thrived under his management.

Carter devoted much time to civic affairs. He served on the Sumter County Board of Education from 1955 to 1962, the last two years as chairman. Carter also became a deacon and Sunday-school teacher of the Plains Baptist Church and a member of the local hospital and library boards.

Carter was widely respected in Plains. But his views on racial issues often differed from those of most of his neighbors. He disapproved of the segregation laws that separated blacks and whites in schools and other public facilities throughout the South. During the 1950's, these laws came under increasing attack by federal courts and civil rights workers. Many Southerners formed local chapters of the White Citizens' Council, an organization designed to help preserve segregation.

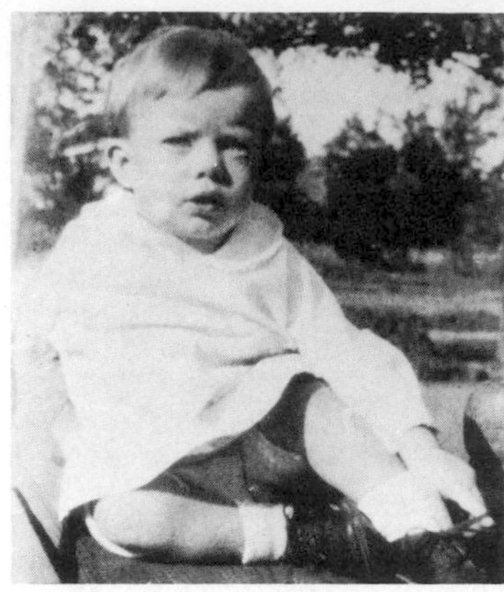

Young Jimmy, shown at the age of 2, lived in the small town of Plains, Ga., for the first four years of his life.

Carter Family Album photos from Charles M. Rafshoon

Carter's Boyhood Home was this wooden clapboard house on a farm in Archery, Ga., just west of Plains. His family lived in the house from 1928 to 1949. Jimmy worked on the farm and sold peanuts in Plains. He also attended school in Plains.

A chapter was established in Plains in 1955, and Carter was asked to join. He refused to do so and declared that he would rather move from Plains.

In 1965, Carter's church considered a proposal to ban blacks from Sunday services. At that time, black civil rights workers were trying to integrate various Southern churches. Carter urged his congregation to defeat the measure, but only his family and one other church member voted against it.

State Senator. In 1962, Carter ran for the Georgia Senate. He received a stormy introduction to state politics. On the day of the Georgia primary election, Carter saw voters marking their ballots openly in front of the election supervisor in the town of Georgetown. He charged that this action violated voting laws. But the supervisor, who was the political boss of the area and a supporter of Carter's opponent, ignored the protest.

The results of the primary election showed that Carter had lost by only a few votes. He angrily challenged the results in court. Just three days before the general election, he was declared to be the Democratic nominee. Carter beat his Republican opponent by about 1,000 votes. He was reelected to the Senate in 1964. As a state senator, Carter worked hard for reforms in education.

Steps to the Governorship. In 1966, Carter became a candidate for the Democratic nomination for governor of Georgia. He was defeated in the primary election. But Carter, determined to win the governorship, decided later that year to run for the office again in 1970.

Carter Family Album from *Chicago Sun-Times*

At the Age of 13, the sandy-haired Carter attended a summer camp near Covington, Ga.

Carter Family Album from Charles M. Rafshoon

Carter's Parents, Lillian and James E. Carter, Sr., were born in Georgia. She was a nurse, and he was a farmer and businessman.

From 1966 to 1970, he worked to increase his understanding of Georgia's problems and made about 1,800 speeches throughout the state.

In 1970, political experts gave Carter little chance of winning the Democratic nomination for governor. The heavily favored candidate was Carl E. Sanders, a liberal who had served as governor from 1963 to 1967. During the campaign, Carter opposed the busing of students to achieve racial balance in schools. He also took other stands that were important to Georgia's rural, conservative voters. Carter's critics charged he was appealing for the support of segregationists. Carter won the nomination. In the general election, he defeated his Republican opponent, Hal Suit, an Atlanta television newscaster, by about 200,000 votes.

Governor of Georgia

Carter began his term as governor in January 1971 and quickly made clear that he would work to aid all needy Georgians. In his inaugural address, he declared: "I say to you quite frankly that the time for racial discrimination is over. No poor, rural, weak, or black person should ever have to bear the additional burden of being deprived of the opportunity of an education, a job, or simple justice." This speech brought Carter his first nationwide attention.

Political Reformer. During Carter's campaign for the governorship, he had promised to make the state government more efficient. Soon after he took office, he set up task forces of leaders from education, industry, and state government to study every state agency. One task force member later recalled that the new governor "was right there with us, working just as hard, digging just as deep into every little problem. It was his program and he worked on it as hard as anybody, and the final product was distinctly his." As a result of this detailed study, Carter merged about 300 state agencies and boards into about 30 agencies.

Carter also pushed a series of reforms through the legislature. One of the most important ones was a law to provide equal state aid to schools in the wealthy and poor areas of Georgia. Other reforms set up community centers for retarded children and increased educational programs for convicts. At Carter's urging, the legislature passed laws to protect the environment, preserve historic sites, and decrease secrecy in government. Carter took pride in a program he introduced for the appointment of judges and state government officials. Under this program, all such appointments were based on merit, rather than political influence.

Concern for Blacks. Carter opened many job opportunities for blacks in the Georgia state government. During his administration, the number of black appointees on major state boards and agencies increased from 3 to 53. The number of black state employees rose by about 40 per cent.

Carter also established a project to honor notable black Georgians. In 1973, he appointed a committee to nominate blacks for the portrait galleries in the State Capitol. Pictures of many prominent Georgia men and women hung there, but none were of blacks. The committee's first choice was Martin Luther King, Jr. A portrait of the famous civil rights leader was hung in the Capitol in 1974.

Plans for the Presidency. While serving as governor, Carter became increasingly active in national activities of the Democratic Party. He headed the 1972 Democratic Governors' Campaign Committee, which worked to help elect the party's candidates for governor. He also served as chairman of the Democratic National Campaign Committee in 1974.

At about the middle of his term as governor, Carter began to consider running for President in 1976. Georgia law prohibited a governor from serving two consecutive terms. But Carter also saw no heavy favorite for the Democratic presidential nomination. In addition, he believed that voters would support a leader from outside Washington, D.C., who offered bold, new solutions to the nation's problems.

Carter's mother later recalled that she learned in September 1973 of his plan to seek the presidency. She asked him what he intended to do after leaving the governorship, and Carter replied, "I'm going to run for President." She asked, "President of what?", and

Carter Family Album from Charles M. Rafshoon

As a Submarine Officer in the United States Navy, Carter, *second from left,* served aboard the U.S.S. *K-1,* a submarine designed for antisubmarine warfare. He later joined a group of officers who were developing the world's first nuclear-powered submarines.

As Governor of Georgia, Carter began a project to honor noted black Georgians by hanging their portraits in the State Capitol. In 1974, a portrait of Martin Luther King, Jr., became the first to be hung. Carter and Mrs. King attended the ceremony, *left.*

Johnson Publishing Co.

he answered: "Momma, I'm going to run for President of the United States, and I'm going to win."

In December 1974, a month before his term as governor expired, Carter announced his candidacy for the 1976 Democratic presidential nomination. He was still little known outside Georgia.

Presidential Candidate

Rise to Prominence. Carter began to work full time for the nomination soon after leaving office as governor in January 1975. He campaigned outside Georgia for about 250 days that year, but his campaign attracted little public attention. In October 1975, a public opinion poll that ranked possible contenders for the Democratic presidential nomination did not even mention Carter.

In January 1976, Carter began a whirlwind rise to national prominence. That month, he received the most votes in an Iowa caucus, the first contest to elect delegates to the 1976 Democratic National Convention. In February, Carter won the year's first presidential primary election, in New Hampshire. By then, 10 other Democrats were seeking the nomination. Carter's chief opponents were Senator Henry M. Jackson of Washington, Representative Morris K. Udall of Arizona, and Governor George C. Wallace of Alabama. In March, Carter beat Wallace in the Florida primary election. Soon afterward, a public opinion poll showed that Carter was the top choice of Democrats for the presidential nomination.

Many voters liked Carter largely because he had not served in Washington, D.C. He became a symbol of their desire for a leader without ties to various interest groups in the nation's capital. Carter also attracted much support with his vow to restore moral leadership to the presidency. Public confidence in government had been shaken by the Watergate scandal, which led to the resignation of President Richard M. Nixon (see WATERGATE). Vice-President Gerald R. Ford succeeded Nixon as President. But Ford's popularity fell sharply after he pardoned Nixon for any federal crimes Nixon may have committed as President.

Carter easily won the nomination for President on the first ballot at the Democratic National Convention in New York City. At his request, Senator Walter F. Mondale of Minnesota was nominated for Vice-President. The Republicans nominated Ford and his vice-presidential choice, Senator Robert J. Dole of Kansas.

The 1976 Election. Many political observers believed that Carter's nomination would unite the Democratic Party. Since 1964, millions of conservative Democrats in the South had supported Republican presidential candidates. But in 1976, most of these men and women were expected to vote for Carter.

In the presidential campaign, Carter charged that Ford had failed to deal effectively with high unemployment. During the autumn of 1976, about 8 per cent of the nation's workers had no jobs. Carter promised to help create more jobs by increasing federal spending and encouraging business expansion. Ford argued that Carter's plans would lead to rapid inflation. Carter also pledged to consider pardons for Vietnam War draft evaders, to reorganize the federal government, and to develop a national energy policy.

In the 1976 presidential election, Carter defeated Ford by 1,678,069 popular votes, 40,825,839 to 39,147,770. Other candidates received about 750,000 votes. Carter won 297 electoral votes and Ford 240. Former Governor Ronald Reagan of California received 1 elec-

Keystone

Nomination in 1976 brought this happy response from Carter and his running mate, Senator Walter F. Mondale of Minnesota.

toral vote. For the electoral vote by states, see ELECTORAL COLLEGE (table).

Carter's Administration (1977-1981)

Early Programs. Carter's first major decision as President was to pardon draft evaders of the Vietnam War period. Later in 1977, he approved a plan to review and possibly upgrade the less-than-honorable discharges of deserters and other military law violators of the Vietnam era. These actions fulfilled one of Carter's most controversial campaign pledges.

The President succeeded in winning quick congressional passage of several major measures. In March 1977, Congress approved his request for the authority to eliminate or consolidate federal agencies that he felt duplicated services. Soon afterward, Carter won congressional passage of legislation to lower federal income taxes. In August 1977, Congress adopted the President's proposal to establish a new executive department—the Department of Energy.

During the 1976 presidential campaign, Carter had often charged that the program to produce B-1 bombers was "wasteful." The cost of the program was estimated at over $25 billion. Many military officials and members of Congress had argued that the U.S. Air Force needed about 245 of these bombers. But in June 1977, Carter halted manufacture of the B-1 and instead supported development of the *cruise missile*. Cruise missiles can be launched from airplanes or submarines and can be directed to avoid enemy defenses.

The National Scene. During Carter's first year as President, the nation's economy improved and unemployment fell. But in 1978, inflation became a major problem. In an attempt to fight inflation, Carter urged businesses to avoid big price increases and asked labor leaders to hold down wage demands. But these steps had little effect on inflation.

In 1978, Carter won congressional approval of a national energy program. The energy legislation was designed largely to reduce U.S. oil imports. The legislation included tax penalties for owners of automobiles that used excessive amounts of gasoline. But, despite this legislation, oil imports remained at a high level, and inflation grew steadily worse. In 1979, continuing high inflation and gasoline shortages contributed to a sharp drop in Carter's performance rating in public opinion polls.

In July 1979, the President asked his entire Cabinet to submit their resignations for his consideration. Carter then made six Cabinet changes in hopes of strengthening his Administration. Carter also named Hamilton Jordan, one of his presidential assistants, to the newly created position of White House chief of staff.

In September 1979, Congress adopted Carter's proposal to establish a Cabinet-level Department of Education. The Department of Health, Education, and Welfare was renamed the Department of Health and Human Services.

In March 1980, Carter announced a new program to fight inflation. The program included cuts in federal spending, a tax on imported oil, and voluntary restraints on wages and prices. Carter also ordered restrictions on credit cards and certain other types of consumer credit. Despite these measures, prices continued to rise. The rate of inflation soared to about 15 per cent for the first half of 1980. In 1976, the year before Carter took office, the inflation rate had been less than 6 per cent. In July 1980, a public opinion poll showed that only 21 per cent of Americans approved of Carter's performance, the lowest score on record for any President.

Foreign Affairs. Carter attracted worldwide attention in 1977 when he strongly supported the struggle for human rights in the Soviet Union and other nations. Carter limited or completely banned U.S. aid and exports to some nations whose governments he believed to be violating human rights. Most of these nations were in Africa, Asia, and Latin America.

The President achieved one of his major foreign policy goals in 1978. In that year, the U.S. Senate ratified two treaties concerning the Panama Canal, which the United States has controlled since its construction in the early 1900's. According to one treaty, Panama will gain control of the canal on Dec. 31, 1999. The other treaty gives the United States the right to defend the canal's neutrality.

Also in 1978, Carter strengthened official ties between the United States and the Communist government of China. The two nations established full diplomatic relations with one another in 1979.

Carter's Election

Place of Nominating Convention	New York City
Ballot on Which Nominated	1st
Republican Opponent	Gerald R. Ford
Electoral Vote*	297 (Carter) to 240 (Ford) and 1 (Reagan)
Popular Vote	40,825,839 (Carter) to 39,147,770 (Ford)
Age at Inauguration	52

*For votes by states, see ELECTORAL COLLEGE (table).

Vice-President and Cabinet

Vice-President	*Walter F. Mondale
Secretary of State	*Cyrus R. Vance *Edmund S. Muskie (1980)
Secretary of the Treasury	W. Michael Blumenthal G. William Miller (1979)
Secretary of Defense	*Harold Brown
Attorney General	Griffin B. Bell Benjamin R. Civiletti (1979)
Secretary of the Interior	Cecil D. Andrus
Secretary of Agriculture	Robert S. Bergland
Secretary of Commerce	*Juanita M. Kreps Philip M. Klutznick (1980)
Secretary of Labor	Ray Marshall
Secretary of Health, Education, and Welfare	*Joseph A. Califano, Jr. *Patricia R. Harris (1979)
Secretary of Health and Human Services†	*Patricia R. Harris
Secretary of Housing and Urban Development	*Patricia R. Harris Moon Landrieu (1979)
Secretary of Transportation	Brock Adams Neil E. Goldschmidt (1979)
Secretary of Energy	*James R. Schlesinger Charles W. Duncan, Jr. (1979)
Secretary of Education	*Shirley M. Hufstedler

*Has a biography in WORLD BOOK.
†The Department of Health, Education, and Welfare was renamed the Department of Health and Human Services in 1979, when Congress created a separate Department of Education.

Bill Fitz-Patrick, The White House

A Peace Treaty Ceremony in 1979 marked the end of a 30-year state of war between Egypt and Israel. Carter helped work out the treaty, which was signed by President Anwar el-Sadat of Egypt, *left,* and Prime Minister Menachem Begin of Israel, *right.*

The President received much praise for his efforts in bringing about a peace treaty between Egypt and Israel. In 1978, he arranged meetings in the United States between himself and President Anwar el-Sadat of Egypt and Prime Minister Menachem Begin of Israel. Carter helped work out a major agreement that included a call for the creation of a peace treaty between Egypt and Israel. The two nations adopted the treaty in 1979. See MIDDLE EAST (The Middle East Today).

Also in 1979, the Carter Administration and Soviet officials negotiated a treaty to limit the use of nuclear weapons by the United States and the Soviet Union. The treaty, called SALT II, resulted from the second round of Strategic Arms Limitations Talks. It would not take effect unless it was approved by the U.S. Senate. Opponents of SALT II argued that it would weaken the U.S. defense system. Supporters believed the treaty was necessary to slow the arms race.

In late 1979 and early 1980, the Soviet Union invaded Afghanistan, and Soviet-American relations plunged to their lowest point in several years. At Carter's urging, the United States and many other nations refused to participate in the 1980 summer Olympic Games in Moscow as a protest against the invasion. Carter also asked the Senate to postpone consideration of the SALT II treaty.

The Iranian Crisis. In February 1979, a movement led by Ayatollah Ruhollah Khomeini, a Muslim religious leader, overthrew the government of the shah of Iran. The shah, Mohammad Reza Pahlavi, had left Iran in January. In October, Carter allowed the deposed shah to enter the United States for medical treatment. The next month, Iranian revolutionaries took over the United States Embassy in Teheran, the capital of Iran. They seized a group of U.S. citizens, most of whom were embassy employees, and held them as hostages. They demanded that the United States return the shah to Iran for trial in exchange for the prisoners.

The White House

The President is shown with Mrs. Carter and their daughter, Amy. The Carters also have three sons, John, James, and Jeffrey.

THE WORLD OF

WORLD EVENTS

1978 Treaties provided for Panama to gain control of the Panama Canal in 1999 and for the U.S. to defend the canal's neutrality.

1979 Egypt and Israel signed a peace treaty.

1979 The Soviet Union invaded Afghanistan.

1979 Iranians took over the U.S. Embassy in Teheran and held a group of Americans as hostages for 444 days.

1979 The U.S. and China began diplomatic relations.

1979 Margaret Thatcher became the first woman prime minister of Great Britain.

UNITED STATES EVENTS

The United States flag had 50 stars throughout Carter's presidency.

1977 Congress created the Department of Energy.

1979 Congress created the Department of Education.

1979 An accident at the Three Mile Island nuclear power plant in Pennsylvania caused concern about the safety of such plants.

1980 The U.S. boycotted the 1980 summer Olympic Games in Moscow to protest the Soviet Union's invasion of Afghanistan.

1980 Women graduated from U.S. military academies for the first time.

PRESIDENT CARTER

The U.S. Population was about 228 million in 1981, the year Carter left the presidency.

Two Panama Canal Treaties won Senate approval in 1978. One gives Panama control of the canal at the end of 1999.

The U.S. and China strengthened ties by establishing full diplomatic relations with one another in 1979.

A Peace Treaty between Egypt and Israel was worked out in 1979 by Carter and heads of the two Middle Eastern nations.

The U.S. Boycotted the 1980 summer Olympic Games in Moscow to protest the Soviet invasion of Afghanistan.

American Hostages taken by Iranian revolutionaries in 1979 were released in 1981 on Carter's last day as President.

Carter denounced the Iranians' action as a violation of international law, and he refused to meet their demands. Trying to force the release of the hostages, he banned imports from Iran. He also cut diplomatic relations between the two countries.

In April 1980, Carter authorized an armed rescue mission to attempt to free the hostages. The mission ended in failure after three of its eight helicopters broke down while flying through a sandstorm. After the project had been canceled, a fourth helicopter crashed into a transport plane. Both aircraft exploded, killing eight men. Secretary of State Cyrus R. Vance, who had opposed the rescue attempt, resigned. Carter named Senator Edmund S. Muskie of Maine as Vance's successor. In July, the former shah died in Egypt, but the Iranian revolutionaries continued to hold the hostages to protest American policies toward their country. They finally released the Americans on Jan. 20, 1981, the day Carter left office.

Life in the White House. Carter ended much of the ceremony and pageantry that had marked official receptions in the White House. For example, he eliminated the practice of having trumpeters announce the presidential family and of having a color guard precede it. Most state dinners ended about 11 P.M., far earlier than those of most previous Presidents. Carter conducted official business during some state functions in the White House and worked after others.

The Carters' daughter, Amy, was 9 years old when her father became President. She attended public schools near the White House. Amy often enlivened the White House by bringing classmates there to play.

Rosalynn Carter became an active representative of Carter's Administration. In 1977, she led a U.S. delegation on a tour of Latin America. She also worked to help women gain equal rights and to improve care for the elderly and the mentally ill.

The 1980 Election. Senator Edward M. Kennedy of Massachusetts challenged Carter for the 1980 Democratic presidential nomination. In August 1979, polls showed that Democrats preferred Kennedy over Carter by a huge margin. But Carter regained popularity during late 1979 and early 1980, partly for his handling of the Iranian crisis. He won enough delegates in primary elections to gain renomination on the first ballot at the Democratic National Convention in New York City. Mondale again became his running mate. The Republicans chose former Governor Ronald Reagan of California for President and George Bush, former U.S. ambassador to the United Nations (UN), for Vice President. Representative John B. Anderson of Illinois and his running mate, former Governor Patrick J. Lucey of Wisconsin, ran as independent candidates.

In the presidential campaign, Carter stressed such achievements as his energy program and the Egyptian-Israeli peace treaty. Reagan charged that Carter had failed to deal effectively with severe inflation and high unemployment. Carter lost the 1980 presidential election by a wide margin. He received about 35 million popular votes to about 44 million for Reagan, but he got only 49 electoral votes to Reagan's 489. Carter carried six states and the District of Columbia, while Reagan carried 44 states. For the electoral vote by states, see ELECTORAL COLLEGE (table).

Later Years

Carter returned to Plains after leaving the White House. In 1982, he published *Keeping Faith: Memoirs of a President*. That same year, he founded the Carter Center of Emory University as a forum for the discussion of national and international issues. HUGH S. SIDEY

Related Articles in WORLD BOOK include:

Democratic Party
Ford, Gerald R.
Mondale, Walter F.
President of the United States

Outline

I. Early Life
A. Boyhood
B. Education
C. Carter's Family
D. Naval Career

II. Return to Plains
A. Businessman and Civic Leader
B. State Senator
C. Steps to the Governorship

III. Governor of Georgia
A. Political Reformer
B. Concern for Blacks
C. Plans for the Presidency

IV. Presidential Candidate
A. Rise to Prominence
B. The 1976 Election

V. Carter's Administration (1977-1981)
A. Early Programs
B. The National Scene
C. Foreign Affairs
D. The Iranian Crisis
E. Life in the White House
F. The 1980 Election

VI. Later Years

Questions

What boyhood dream came true for Carter in 1942?
How did Carter receive a stormy introduction to statewide politics in Georgia?
What special project did Carter join in the navy?
What conditions influenced Carter's decision to seek the presidency?
How did Carter help honor notable black Georgians while he was governor of Georgia?
How did Carter first gain nationwide attention?
Which of Carter's views often differed with those of most of his neighbors in Plains?
Why was Carter's nomination for President expected to unite the Democratic Party in the 1976 election?
What were some ways Carter earned money as a boy?
Why did Carter resign from the Navy in 1953?

Additional Resources

CARTER, JIMMY. *Keeping Faith: Memoirs of a President.* Bantam, 1982.
GERMOND, JACK W., and WITCOVER, JULES. *Blue Smoke and Mirrors: How Reagan Won and Why Carter Lost the Election of 1980*. Viking, 1981.
GLAD, BETTY. *Jimmy Carter: In Search of the Great White House*. Norton, 1980. A biography.
JORDAN, HAMILTON. *Crisis: The Last Year of the Carter Presidency*. Putnam, 1982. Covers the Iranian hostage crisis.
KRAUS, SIDNEY, ed. *The Great Debates: Carter vs. Ford, 1976.* Indiana Univ. Press, 1979.

CARTER, JIMMY. See CARTER, JAMES EARL, JR.

CARTESIAN PHILOSOPHY. See DESCARTES, RENÉ.

CARTHAGE, *KAHR thihj*, was one of the greatest cities of ancient times. A wealthy trading center, it stood on a peninsula in North Africa, near the present city of Tunis, Tunisia. Carthage was one of the colonies founded by Phoenician seamen as a trade and shipping outpost. The Phoenician name for Carthage is *Kartha-dasht*. It means *New Capital* or *New City*.

Legend says that Dido, daughter of a king of Tyre, another Phoenician city, founded Carthage. The story of her tragic love for Aeneas, a Trojan prince whose family founded Rome hundreds of years later, is sung in Virgil's poem, the *Aeneid*.

Importance. Carthage grew quickly because of its location on a peninsula and its two excellent harbors. One harbor, inside the city walls, was large enough to shelter hundreds of military vessels. The city was well protected. A wall about 40 feet (12 meters) high and 30 feet (9 meters) wide stretched across the peninsula. Another wall enclosed the *Byrsa*, an inner fortress.

Carthage was probably the first city-state to control an empire. Much of western North Africa, southern Spain, Sardinia, Corsica, and the western half of Sicily came under Carthage's rule. The Carthaginians were more interested in trade than in conquest, but they used military power when they felt it was necessary.

History. According to tradition, colonists from Tyre founded Carthage in 814 B.C. But archaeologists who have searched the ruins of Carthage have found no remains earlier than from about 750 B.C.

Tyre and the other cities of Phoenicia were weakened by the repeated attacks of the Assyrians and Babylonians (or Chaldeans). Carthage, therefore, became independent without a struggle after about 600 B.C. It became the leader of the western Phoenician territories.

Leadership brought new responsibilities, and Carthage often fought with Greek forces on Sicily. Carthage made

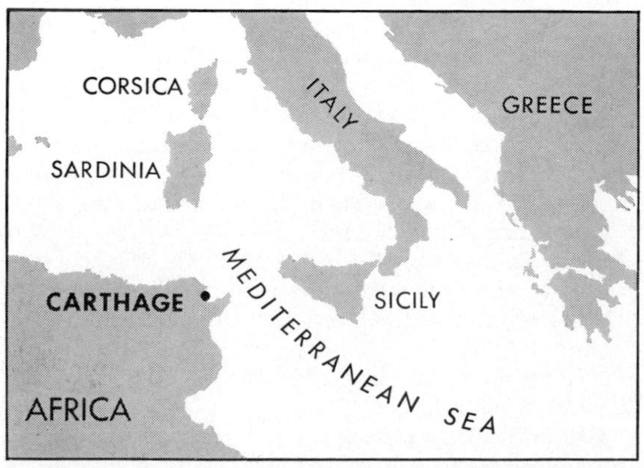

The Ancient City of Carthage Lay on the Mediterranean.

an alliance with the Etruscans, a people who lived in central Italy. But Etruscan power declined after 500 B.C. In 480 B.C., the Greeks crushed a Carthaginian army at Himera, in Sicily. Carthage could not get help from eastern Phoenicians, who lost many ships while taking part in the Persian invasion of Greece.

Carthage then went through a period of isolation and decline. The government system changed from a one-man rule to an *oligarchy* (rule by a few). There was an assembly of citizens, but the real power lay with the *sufets* (magistrates), the generals, and a council of nobles.

Carthage expanded in Sicily again about 410 B.C., and ruled much of Sicily at times. After 265 B.C., the Romans also wanted Sicily. Carthage fought and lost three wars called the Punic Wars with Rome, from 264 to 241, from 218 to 201, and from 149 to 146 B.C. The genius of Hannibal, a Carthaginian general, nearly won the second war for Carthage. But Carthage was destroyed in the third war.

Carthage later became an important city in the Roman Empire. St. Augustine was one of its famous inhabitants. Carthage was overrun by the Vandals around A.D. 430. The final destruction of Carthage came in A.D. 698 at the hands of Arabs. HENRY C. BOREN

Related Articles in WORLD BOOK include:

Aeneid	Dido	Hannibal	Punic Wars
Cato	Hamilcar Barca	Phoenicia	

Additional Resources

PICARD, GILBERT C. and COLETTE. *The Life and Death of Carthage: A Survey of Punic History and Culture from Its Birth to the Final Tragedy*. Taplinger, 1969.

WARMINGTON, BRIAN H. *Carthage*. Rev. ed. Praeger, 1970.

CARTHUSIANS, *kahr THOO zhuhnz,* are members of a Roman Catholic order of monks. The name comes from the village of Chartreuse, in the French Alps. There, Saint Bruno of Cologne, with six companions, founded the first Carthusian monastery in A.D. 1084. They wore plain garments, ate vegetables and bread, and slept on straw. They fasted, prayed, and kept watch at night. The modern Carthusians lead a life almost as severe. Their monasteries were once the finest in the world, but in Europe now number less than 20. The most famous were La Grande Chartreuse, in France, and Certosa di Pavia, near Milan. The monks of La Grande Chartreuse first produced the liqueur known as *chartreuse*. FULTON J. SHEEN

CARTIER, *kahr TYAY,* **SIR GEORGE ÉTIENNE,** *zhawrzh ay TYEHN* (1814-1873), was a French-Canadian political leader. He was one of the Fathers of Confederation, the men whose plan for a union of British North American colonies led to the formation of the Dominion of Canada in 1867. He played the key role in winning French-Canadian support for the dominion.

Cartier was born at St.-Antoine-sur-Richelieu in Lower Canada (now Quebec). As a young man, he became a critic of British rule in Canada. In 1837, Cartier joined a rebellion against the government and was forced to flee to the United States. Later pardoned, he became a member of the Legislative Assembly and a cabinet minister in the government of the Province of Canada. From 1857 to 1862, he served as joint prime minister of the province with John A. Macdonald.

From 1867 to 1873, Cartier served as minister of militia in the first cabinet of the Dominion of Canada. He strongly supported westward expansion and arranged the government's purchase of Rupert's Land, a vast territory in the northwest owned by the Hudson's Bay Company. Cartier also encouraged the construction of a Canadian transcontinental railroad. He was made a baronet of Great Britain in 1868. ANDRÉE DÉSILETS

CARTIER, *kahr TYAY,* **JACQUES,** *zhahk* (1491?-1557), was a French navigator. His explorations established the basis for France's claims to territory in what is now Canada. In 1535, he led the first European expedition up the St. Lawrence River.

Cartier was born in the seaport of St.-Malo and studied navigation in Dieppe, a French center for navigators. He became a respected navigator and may have sailed to Newfoundland with a fishing fleet in the early 1500's. Some historians believe Cartier accompanied the Italian navigator Giovanni da Verrazano on French expeditions to the New World during the 1520's.

Exploration of Canada. In 1534, King Francis I of France sent Cartier to North America to search for

Robert Davis Productions

A Phoenician Sanctuary containing grave markers and vases filled with human ashes was found among the ruins of Carthage. Archaeologists worked for many years uncovering the city's ruins.

Vance Henry, Taurus

Ruins at Carthage include this public bathing facility built by the ancient Romans. The Romans destroyed Carthage during the A.D. 100's, but they later constructed many buildings there.

Engraving from the *Vallard Atlas* (1546); the Huntington Library, San Marino, Calif.

Cartier Landed in Canada in 1534. This map of the 1540's shows Cartier, *center,* wearing a red hat and short black coat, surrounded by members of his expedition. Cartier explored the Gulf of St. Lawrence and claimed the region for France.

gold and other precious metals. Cartier left St.-Malo in April with two ships. The expedition sailed into what is now the Gulf of St. Lawrence and landed on the Gaspé Peninsula, which Cartier claimed for France.

Cartier met a group of Iroquois Indians, who told him that precious jewels and metals could be found farther northwest. The French gave gifts to the Indians and established friendly relations with them. Their chief let two of his sons sail to France with Cartier in August. Cartier's men brought a supply of corn that was probably the first corn ever seen in northern Europe.

In May 1535, the king sent Cartier on a second expedition to Canada. The two Indian boys returned home on this voyage. On August 10, Cartier reached the northern coast of the Gaspé Peninsula and entered a nearby bay. He named the bay for Saint Lawrence because the expedition had arrived there on the saint's feast day. Cartier then saw the mouth of the great river that also became known for the saint. Cartier sailed up the river to the foot of a mountain, which he named Mont Réal (Mount Royal). It became the site of the city of Montreal. Cartier and his men sailed back to what is now Quebec City and spent the winter there. They returned to France the next summer.

Attempts at Colonization. In 1541, the king organized an expedition to establish a permanent settlement in Canada. He appointed a nobleman named Jean François de la Rocque, Sieur de Roberval, in command over Cartier. However, Cartier sailed in May before Roberval had completed plans for his own voyage.

Cartier sailed up the St. Lawrence River to what is now Cap Rouge, near Quebec City. Some of his men remained there and built a settlement. Cartier and the others continued to search for gold. They sailed to Mont Réal and traveled farther west on foot but found no precious metals. He then returned to the settlement.

During the winter, the Iroquois became hostile and killed several Frenchmen. Roberval had not arrived by spring, and Cartier decided to sail back to France.

On his return voyage, Cartier met Roberval in Newfoundland. Roberval ordered Cartier to remain in Canada, but Cartier refused and warned the nobleman about the Indians. Cartier then returned to France. He was pardoned for disobeying Roberval and lived the rest of his life in and around St.-Malo. FRANKLIN L. FORD

See also NEW BRUNSWICK (Exploration and Settlement); ROBERVAL, SIEUR DE.

Additional Resources

BAXTER, JAMES P. *Memoir of Jacques Cartier, Sieur de Limoilou: His Voyages to the St. Lawrence.* Dodd, 1906.

MORISON, SAMUEL ELIOT. *The European Discovery of America: The Northern Voyages, A.D. 500-1600.* Oxford, 1971. Includes two chapters on Cartier.

CARTIER-BRESSON, HENRI (1908-), is a French photographer. He became known for his ability to cap-

Hyères, France, 1930, **a photograph by Henri Cartier-Bresson, captures the elements of the scene in a lively visual balance.**

ture the significance of an event by the arrangement of people and objects in a scene. Cartier-Bresson takes a picture when these elements are in a lively visual balance.

Cartier-Bresson works with a small, hand-held camera. He chiefly uses black-and-white film because he believes color film takes attention away from the subject of a photograph. He rarely uses lens filters or other equipment that provides special effects.

Cartier-Bresson became a photographer in 1930. Until then, he had studied painting. He has photographed news events throughout the world for newspapers and magazines. Many books of his photographs have been published, including camera studies of the United States and China. In 1947, Cartier-Bresson helped found *Magnum*, an agency that provides publishers with photos. He was born in Chanteloup, near Paris. CHARLES HAGEN

CARTILAGE, *KAHR tuh lihj*, commonly called *gristle*, is a bluish-white rubbery tissue found in human beings and animals that have backbones. It is found at the ends of long bones, between the *vertebrae* (bones) of the spine, and in the ears, nose, and internal respiratory passages. Cartilage cushions long bones against shock, and prevents them from rubbing against one another. It also makes an elastic but firm framework for the ear and respiratory passages, ensuring that these openings do not collapse. *Vertebrates* (animals with backbones) have skeletons of cartilage before they are born. Some vertebrates, such as sharks, lampreys, and hagfishes, retain this skeleton throughout their lives. But in all other vertebrates, bone gradually replaces the cartilage as the animal grows. Cartilage cells are round and are enclosed in capsules. Groups of cartilage cells lie embedded in a noncellular framework called a *matrix*. MARSHALL R. URIST

See also BONE; KNEE; LARYNX.

CARTOGRAPHY is the art of making maps. See MAP.

CARTOON is a drawing or series of drawings that tells a story or expresses a message. Cartoons may entertain, teach, or comment about a person, event, or state of affairs. Most cartoons combine words and drawings, but some express their messages through drawings alone. Each separate scene in a cartoon is called a *panel*.

Most cartoonists do not draw things as they appear in real life. These artists use fewer details and may exaggerate some feature of a character, such as the head, hands, or feet. A person's head actually measures only about an eighth of the length of the body. But the head of a cartoon character may be a third or even half of the body length. Oversized heads help the cartoonist direct the reader's attention to important facial expressions, such as a smile, a sneer, a squint, or raised eyebrows. Oversized hands and feet are often drawn to stress action.

Sometimes cartoonists use symbols as a type of shorthand to help them tell the story. For example, they use a light bulb above a character's head to indicate a bright idea. A dark cloud over a character's head shows despair.

Cartoonists create cartoons for books, magazines, newspapers, and motion pictures. Advertisers, educators, and governments often use cartoon messages because they attract attention and are easy to read. Cartoon messages also communicate quickly and effectively.

In the fine arts, the word *cartoon* refers to a drawing that an artist sketches as a guide for a painting or some other work. Such an artist differs from a cartoonist because the cartoon is drawn as only a first step. A cartoonist, on the other hand, works in the field of commercial art and produces cartoons as finished drawings for publication.

Kinds of Cartoons

Cartoonists draw five major kinds of cartoons: (1) *editorial* or *political*, (2) *comic strips and panels*, (3) *gag*, (4) *illustrative*, and (5) *animated*. For a discussion of animated cartoons and the steps in their production, see the WORLD BOOK article on MOTION PICTURE (Animation).

Roy Paul Nelson, the contributor of this article, is Professor of Journalism at the University of Oregon and the author of Cartooning.

PROFESSOR BUTTS STEPS INTO AN OPEN ELEVATOR SHAFT AND WHEN HE LANDS AT THE BOTTOM HE FINDS A SIMPLE ORANGE SQUEEZING MACHINE. MILK MAN TAKES EMPTY MILK BOTTLE (A) PULLING STRING (B) WHICH CAUSES SWORD (C) TO SEVER CORD (D) AND ALLOW GUILLOTINE BLADE (E) TO DROP AND CUT ROPE (F) WHICH RELEASES BATTERING RAM (G). RAM BUMPS AGAINST OPEN DOOR (H) CAUSING IT TO CLOSE. GRASS SICKLE (I) CUTS A SLICE OFF END OF ORANGE (J) AT THE SAME TIME SPIKE (K) STABS PRUNE HAWK (L) HE OPENS HIS MOUTH TO YELL IN AGONY, THEREBY RELEASING PRUNE AND ALLOWING DIVER'S BOOT (M) TO DROP AND STEP ON SLEEPING OCTOPUS (N). OCTOPUS AWAKENS IN A RAGE AND SEEING DIVER'S FACE WHICH IS PAINTED ON ORANGE, ATTACKS IT AND CRUSHES IT WITH TENTACLES, THEREBY CAUSING ALL THE JUICE IN THE ORANGE TO RUN INTO GLASS (O).
LATER ON YOU CAN USE THE LOG TO BUILD A LOG CABIN WHERE YOU CAN RAISE YOUR SON TO BE PRESIDENT LIKE ABRAHAM LINCOLN.
A
B
C
D
E
F
G
H
I
J
L
M
N

Rube Goldberg's Cartoons were a popular feature in many American newspapers during the early 1900's. Goldberg drew ridiculously complicated contraptions that were designed to accomplish simple tasks. In the cartoon above, he explained how his orange-juice squeezer worked.

Editorial Cartoons do in pictures what editorials do in words. They encourage the reader to develop an opinion about someone or something prominent in the news. Most editorial cartoons appear on the editorial pages of newspapers as single drawings with or without captions or titles. They may support a main editorial of the day, or they may deal with some event in the day's news. Many editorial cartoons, called *caricatures*, poke fun at well-known people by exaggerating their physical characteristics or facial expressions (see CARICATURE).

Editorial cartoonists use a variety of symbols to help get their messages across quickly. For example, a hungry vulture identified as a large corporation might show that the company has gobbled up smaller firms. In many cartoons, a bear symbolizes Russia. A thin, bearded man in a red, white, and blue tuxedo is Uncle Sam, who stands for the United States. Thomas Nast, a famous editorial cartoonist, introduced the elephant as the symbol of the Republican Party in an 1874 cartoon for *Harper's Weekly* magazine. Nast also made the donkey popular as a symbol of the Democratic Party. Examples of Nast's work appear with the WORLD BOOK articles on DEMOCRATIC PARTY and REPUBLICAN PARTY.

National Safety Council

Illustrative Cartoons express a specific idea in a direct, simple way. The cartoon at the left carries an important message about bicycle safety.

"YOO HOO! MISS DAVIS! WHAT'S THIS SAY?"

© 1972 Field Newspaper Syndicate

Panel Comics regularly feature the same chief characters. "Dennis the Menace," *right*, drawn by Hank Ketcham, describes the amusing activities of a mischievous boy.

"HELP!"

From the *Herblock Gallery* © 1968, Simon & Schuster

Editorial Cartoons, such as the one above, call attention to an important current event or problem. Most of these cartoons appear daily on the editorial pages of newspapers.

© 1964 The New Yorker Magazine, Inc.

Gag Cartoons may have new characters in each panel. Charles Addams has drawn many gag cartoons, including the one above, that treat mysterious or frightening subjects in a comic manner.

The Pulitzer prizes awarded each year include a cartoon category. Leading cartoonists who have won the prize include Herbert L. Block (who signs his work Herblock), Ding Darling, and Bill Mauldin. A complete list of winners appears in the PULITZER PRIZES article.

Comic Strips and Panels appear in newspapers and magazines as regular features with established characters. Some comics, such as Milton Caniff's "Steve Canyon," are adventure stories that continue from one day to the next. In other comic strips, including Charles Schulz's "Peanuts" and Johnny Hart's "B. C.," the characters appear in different humorous situations each day.

Most newspapers publish a number of comic strips together on one or two pages. Each strip includes a series of panels with the characters' words printed near their heads in white areas called *balloons*. A *panel comic* consists of only one panel. Some panel comics appear on the comic pages. Others are used to brighten pages that have nothing but type, such as pages of classified advertisements. Panel comics had their greatest popularity in the early 1900's. But some, such as Brad Anderson's "Marmaduke," have large audiences today. See COMICS.

Gag Cartoons are single panels accompanied by a one-line or one-sentence caption. The caption consists of words spoken by a character in the panel. Some gag cartoons have no captions, and others are a series of pantomime panels. Such a series differs from a comic strip because it—and its characters—appear only once, not as a continuing feature.

Gag cartoons make fun of people in general, not of specific persons, as do editorial cartoons. They create humor by overstatement and understatement. The main function of a gag cartoon is to entertain, but the cartoon may also poke fun at human faults. The best-known gag cartoonists of the 1900's include Charles Addams and Virgil Partch. Addams became famous for the ghoulish but amusing characters he drew for *The New Yorker* magazine. Partch created weird situations with ridiculous characters for a number of magazines and newspapers.

Illustrative Cartoons help explain stories, teaching materials, or advertisements. Most illustrative cartoons have little meaning by themselves. They serve to draw attention to—and to develop the meaning of—the text they accompany. Such cartoons illustrate important points in many schoolbooks.

Some illustrative cartoons use comic strip characters. For example, the Soil Conservation Society of America has used Hank Ketcham's "Dennis the Menace" in a series called "Dennis the Menace and Dirt."

Many companies use popular comic strip characters to illustrate their advertisements. Governments sometimes use cartoon figures to help establish certain programs or to spread information about them.

Creating a Cartoon

Developing the Idea. A cartoonist must be able to visualize an idea and then produce a finished drawing of it. Most editorial cartoonists meet with their editors to discuss the day's news. The group decides which events deserve editorial comment. Then the cartoonist

How a Cartoonist Tells A Story

Facial Expressions tell a reader immediately how a cartoon character feels. A cartoonist can illustrate almost any mood by drawing a character's eyes and mouth in a certain way.

Movement is illustrated largely through the use of lines of different sizes. For example, long thin lines trailing a running horse show speed. Short broken lines indicate a jumping frog.

WORLD BOOK illustrations by Fred Womack

The Senses are illustrated by lines, symbols, and words. The lines and stars around the thumb suggest pain. The words "snif snif" and the lines leading from the dog's nose represent smell.

DRAWING A COMIC STRIP

Cartoons consisting of several related drawings are called comic strips. In creating a comic strip, the cartoonist must present the action so that the reader can easily follow the story from drawing to drawing. Most comic strips go through three major stages before they are finished. These stages are illustrated below in the development of an episode for "B. C.," a comic strip by Johnny Hart.

In the first stage, the cartoonist determines the content of each drawing in the strip. Using a pencil, he draws the strip's basic elements—dialogue, figures, and major objects.

During the second stage, the cartoonist adds backgrounds and strengthens his lines. He also may make minor changes to improve the content of the cartoon.

Finally, the cartoonist applies ink over the pencil lines. He adds textures and tones to indicate the surfaces of clothes, objects, and skin. He also erases any unwanted pencil marks.

By permission of John Hart and Field Enterprises, Inc.

sketches several ideas, and the editor of the editorial page selects one to be completed.

Gag cartoonists and comic strip artists may develop their own ideas or work with the ideas of writers. A comic strip artist may team with a writer who provides the story. Most gag cartoonists who use gags written by others give the writer a fourth of their payment for the finished cartoon.

Most gag cartoonists do not work for just one publication. They send several rough sketches at a time to a magazine editor. The editor may buy a sketch, or he may ask the cartoonist to redraw the cartoon in a more complete form.

Cartoonists who draw illustrative cartoons work from manuscripts supplied by writers or editors. An illustrative cartoonist must create cartoons that emphasize or clarify key points of the text.

Producing the Finished Cartoon. Depending on his own style—and his editor's requirements—a cartoonist may take from 30 minutes to a day to create a cartoon. In general, adventure comic strip cartoonists use a fairly detailed, realistic style. Humorous comic strip artists, gag cartoonists, and most editorial cartoonists favor a less detailed style.

Most cartoonists begin with a penciled outline. They go over the outline with a pen or brush dipped in India ink or with a felt- or nylon-tip marker.

The cartoonist may draw some parts of his cartoon over and over again and then piece the parts together. This piecing does not show in the printed version. Shaded areas and areas of solid black create contrast in a cartoon. Common methods of shading include drawing a series of thin lines close together or pasting down pieces of thin plastic on which a pattern of dots or lines has been printed. Many editorial cartoonists draw with a brush on rough-textured paper and then shade with a grease crayon.

Many magazines and newspapers use a process called *photoengraving* to reproduce cartoons for publication. The engraver photographs the cartoon to make a negative. Then a platemaker uses the negative to transfer the drawing to a metal plate used for printing. For color cartoons, such as the Sunday comic section of a newspaper, staff artists make copies of the original cartoon. Then the platemaker uses these copies to make separate plates for yellow, red, and blue ink. He uses the original to print a black plate. When the four plates are printed over one another, they combine to provide all the correct colors. See PHOTOENGRAVING and PHOTOLITHOGRAPHY.

History

Comic art dates back to ancient times. For example, caricatures have been found on ancient Egyptian walls

New York Public Library

Many Early Cartoons dealt with political issues. In 1754, Benjamin Franklin urged the American Colonies to unite against the French and the Indians in his cartoon, "Join, or Die," *above.* In an 1835 cartoon, *right,* the French artist Honoré Daumier attacked what he considered to be the French government's restriction of free speech.

"You are free to speak" (1835), a lithograph by Honoré Daumier; collection of Howard P. Vincent

and Greek vases. But cartoons did not gain wide popularity until the 1800's.

Early Cartoons. During the 1700's and early 1800's, several British artists, including George Cruikshank and William Hogarth, drew and sold prints of caricatures. In 1754, Benjamin Franklin drew one of the first cartoons in the American Colonies. Franklin's cartoon urged the colonies to unite against the French and Indians. It showed each colony as part of a snake, with the caption "Join, or Die." At that time, people thought a snake cut into pieces would live if the pieces were rejoined. Paul Revere engraved a version of the cartoon during the Revolutionary War in America (1775-1783) to urge the colonies to unite against England.

During the first half of the 1800's, many American artists created political cartoons in the form of engravings, prints, and woodcuts. But a French artist, Honoré Daumier, who worked from the 1830's to 1870's, became known as the father of modern cartooning. He drew caricatures of French leaders for French newspapers and humor magazines. Daumier served six months in prison in 1832 because of a caricature he drew of King Louis Philippe.

Modern Cartooning. In 1841, cartoons began appearing regularly in the English comic magazine *Punch.* Weekly magazines in the United States started to feature cartoons during the 1850's. Thomas Nast of *Harper's Weekly* and Joseph Keppler of *Puck* ranked among the most influential weekly cartoonists.

Toward the end of the 1800's, editorial cartoons became regular features of daily newspapers. Newspaper cartoonists used less detail, fewer characters, and a looser style than did magazine cartoonists. Using editorial cartoons in magazines declined because cartoons in daily newspapers could comment on news far more quickly. But such comic weekly magazines as *Judge, Life*, and *Puck* carried thousands of cartoons in the 1890's.

Newspaper comics grew as a result of circulation wars between the *New York World* and the *New York Journal.* The two papers competed for Richard Outcault's strip "Hogan's Alley," which appeared first in the *New York World* in 1895. The earliest comic strips featured wild, slapstick humor. They included the mischievous "Katzenjammer Kids," whose pranks delighted millions of readers. The cartoonist, Rudolph Dirks, based the kids on two illustrative cartoon characters created by a German author in the 1870's.

By 1900, editorial and comic cartoons had firmly established themselves in American newspapers. Homer Davenport and Frederick Opper stood out as editorial cartoonists. Davenport's most famous cartoon showed Uncle Sam standing behind President Theodore Roosevelt and saying, "He's good enough for me." The Republican Party used this cartoon in the 1904 presidential campaign. Opper mastered both editorial and comic cartooning and created the popular strips "Happy Hooligan" and "Alphonse and Gaston."

Newspaper comic strips based on family life appeared in the early 1900's. In 1904, George McManus began one of the first family strips, "The Newlyweds."

In the 1920's *The New Yorker* magazine introduced the gag cartoon, and *Vanity Fair* began publishing caricatures of show business personalities. Today, some magazines use more than 20 gag cartoons in one issue.

Adventure comic books and strips became popular in the 1930's and 1940's. After World War II (1939-1945), humorous comics regained popularity. In the 1960's and 1970's, some comic books and comic strips commented on political and social issues. Roy Paul Nelson

Related Articles in World Book include:

Beerbohm, Sir Max
Block, Herbert L.
Capp, Al
Caricature
Carpetbaggers (picture)
Comics
Computer (picture: A Computer Can Produce Drawings)
Cruikshank, George
Darling, Ding
Daumier, Honoré
Disney, Walt
Held, John, Jr.
Hogarth, William
Mauldin, Bill
Motion Picture (Animation; pictures)
Nast, Thomas
Oliphant, Patrick B.
Outcault, Richard F.
Ripley, Robert L.
Schulz, Charles M.
Seuss, Dr.
Steig, William
Steinberg, Saul
Tenniel, Sir John
Thurber, James

CARTOUCHE, *kahr TOOSH,* in architecture, is an ornament shaped like a scroll with rolled-up ends. Architects also use the term for an inscribed tablet shaped like a partly-unrolled scroll.

In Egyptian archaeology, a cartouche is an oval frame with the name or symbol of a ruler on it. In heraldry, the term refers to an oval shield used by popes and churchmen of noble descent to display their coats of arms (see HERALDRY). The word also means a map title, drawn in the form of a scroll.

The word *cartouche* comes from the Italian word *cartoccio* (roll of paper). It first referred to the wadded roll of parchment or paper containing the explosive charge of a firearm. The word *cartridge* originally came from this Italian term. ARTHUR E. DUBOIS

The Cartouche of Khufu (Cheops), King of Egypt, was used as a name plate on a monument.

CARTRIDGE is a metal or paper case that holds a charge of explosive powder and a bullet or a charge of shot. The cartridge used in rifles and machine guns is a brass cylinder with a percussion cap at the base. The explosive is placed in the cartridge and the bullet is placed on top of it. The brass is *crimped* (pressed) against the bullet to hold it firmly.

Cartridges for shotguns usually consist of several thicknesses of stout paper with a brass base to give additional strength and to hold the percussion cap. A *blank cartridge* contains a charge of explosive, but no ball or shot. Cartridges made of paper were first used in muskets in 1585. JACK O'CONNOR

See also AMMUNITION (Cartridges; illustrations; table: Important Dates); BULLET; CARTOUCHE.

CARTWRIGHT, ALEXANDER. See BASEBALL (Alexander Cartwright; table: National Baseball Hall of Fame).

CARTWRIGHT, EDMUND (1743-1823), was an English inventor and clergyman. He developed a steam-powered loom for weaving cotton that led to the invention of more effective power looms and to the development of the modern weaving industry.

Cartwright was born at Marnham, in Nottinghamshire. He was graduated from Oxford University, and became pastor of a rural parish in Goadby Marwood in Leicestershire. In 1784, Cartwright learned of the need for a weaving machine that could make cloth faster than the hand loom. He became convinced that he could make a power loom even though he had never seen a loom in operation. His first machine, which was patented in 1785, required two strong people to operate it for a short time and was not much more effective than a hand loom. However, in 1786, Cartwright invented a steam-powered loom, and the next year he used it in a spinning and weaving factory that he opened at Doncaster.

In 1791, a mill at Manchester ordered 400 of Cartwright's looms. But the factory was burned down by workers who feared the new power machinery would eliminate their jobs. A few other manufacturers tried to use Cartwright's loom, but their efforts failed and Cartwright closed his mill in 1793. Although Cartwright's looms were never fully practical, Parliament recognized his pioneering work in 1809 by awarding him the equivalent of $50,000.

Cartwright also invented a wool-combing machine and a grain-cutting machine for farmers, but neither brought him much money. MONTE A. CALVERT

CARTWRIGHT, PETER (1785-1872), was a frontier American Methodist circuit rider and presiding elder. After his conversion in 1801, be became a Methodist preacher and rode circuits in Kentucky and Tennessee. In 1824, Cartwright moved to Sangamon County, Illinois. He was twice elected to the Illinois state legislature, but lost to Abraham Lincoln in 1846 in a contest for a congressional seat. His *Autobiography* is an interesting account of pioneer life. Cartwright was born in Amherst County, Virginia. EARLE E. CAIRNS

CARUSO, *kuh ROO soh,* **ENRICO,** *ehn REE koh* (1873-1921), an Italian tenor, was one of the greatest opera stars of the 1900's. He became famous for his powerful voice, his ringing high notes, and his extraordinary breath control. Caruso performed mainly in French and Italian operas. His most famous roles included Canio in *I Pagliacci* and Rhadames in *Aida.* Caruso was one of the first opera singers to record extensively.

Brown Bros.

Enrico Caruso

Caruso was born into a poor family in Naples. He received little formal education, and less musical training than most opera stars of his time. Caruso made his debut in 1894, in Naples in *L'Amico Francesco.* By 1902, he had acquired international fame. In 1903, Caruso performed for the first time at the Metropolitan Opera in New York City, taking the role of the Duke of Mantua in *Rigoletto.* He became closely associated with the Metropolitan Opera, regularly appearing there from 1903 to 1920. ELLEN PFEIFER

Additional Resources

CARUSO, DOROTHY. *Enrico Caruso: His Life and Death.* Simon & Schuster, 1945. Written by his wife, this standard biography includes a discography of his recordings.

GREENFELD, HOWARD. *Caruso.* Putnam, 1983.

JACKSON, STANLEY. *Caruso.* Stein & Day, 1972.

ROBINSON, FRANCIS. *Caruso: His Life in Pictures.* Bramhall, 1957.

CARVER, GEORGE WASHINGTON (1864-1943), was a black American scientist who won international fame for his agricultural research. He was especially noted for his work with peanuts. Carver made more than 300 products from peanuts, including a milk substitute, face powder, printer's ink, and soap. In addition to his scientific contributions, Carver also worked to promote the interests of black people and to improve relations between blacks and whites.

Early Years. Carver was born a slave on a farm near Diamond, Mo. Shortly after Carver's birth, his father was killed in an accident and his mother was kidnapped by night raiders. The child was reared by Moses and Susan Carver, who were his owners until slavery was abolished in 1865.

As a young boy, George showed a keen interest in plants and a great desire to learn. The Carvers taught him to read and write. When he was about 11 years old, he moved to Neosho, Mo., to attend a school for black children.

For the next 20 years, Carver worked at various jobs to support himself and pay for his education. In 1890, he entered Simpson College in Indianola, Iowa. Carver showed promise as a painter but decided to pursue a career in agriculture instead. In 1891, he transferred to Iowa State Agricultural College (now Iowa State University) in Ames. Carver received a bachelor's degree in agriculture in 1894 and a master's degree in 1896.

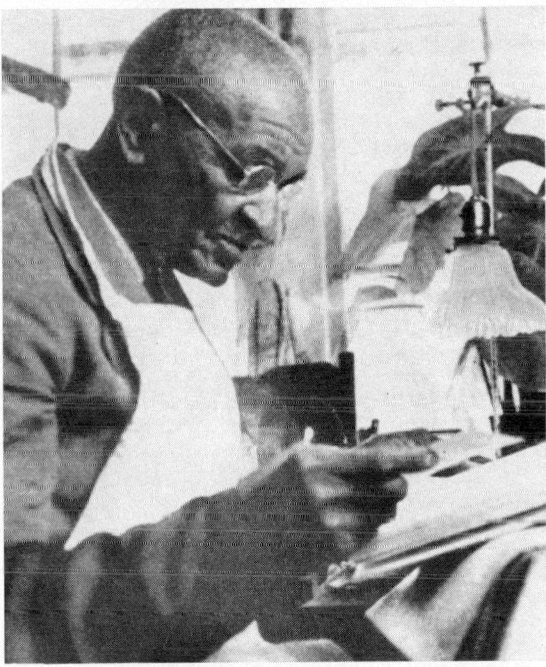

Brown Bros.

George Washington Carver worked many long hours in his laboratory to improve agricultural methods in the South.

Tuskegee Instructor and Researcher. In 1896, Carver moved to Alabama to join the faculty of the Tuskegee Institute, an industrial and agricultural school for blacks. Carver became head of the Tuskegee agricultural department and director of a state agricultural station. At first, Carver continued his research on fungi, the topic in which he had specialized in Iowa. However, he gradually began to direct his attention toward soil conservation and other ways to improve crop production. At the same time, he wrote a number of pamphlets and bulletins on applied agriculture and distributed these publications to farmers in Alabama and other states. Carver also sought to teach more productive agricultural practices to Southern farmers—particularly black farmers—through conferences, traveling exhibits, demonstrations, and public lectures.

In 1910, Carver became head of Tuskegee's newly created Department of Research. After 1914, he began to focus his research on peanuts. He received national attention in 1921, when he lectured about the many uses of peanuts before a committee of Congress. He later gave lectures throughout much of the country in an effort to promote peanuts. He also spent much time during the 1920's working to improve race relations. He was especially active in his work for the Commission on Inter-Racial Cooperation and the Young Men's Christian Association (YMCA).

Carver never married. In 1940, he gave his life savings of $33,000 to the Tuskegee Institute to establish the George Washington Carver Foundation for Agricultural Research there.

Awards and Honors. Carver received many awards for his accomplishments. In 1916, he was named a fellow of the Royal Society of Arts of London. In 1923, the National Association for the Advancement of Colored People (NAACP) awarded him the Spingarn Medal for distinguished service in agricultural chemistry. In 1939, Carver received the Theodore Roosevelt Medal for his valuable contributions to science. In 1951, the George Washington Carver National Monument was established on 210 acres (85 hectares) of the Missouri farm where Carver was born. JOHN W. KITCHENS

See also GEORGE WASHINGTON CARVER NATIONAL MONUMENT; TUSKEGEE INSTITUTE; SWEET POTATO.

Additional Resources

ELLIOTT, LAWRENCE. *George Washington Carver: The Man Who Overcame.* Prentice-Hall, 1966.

GRAHAM, SHIRLEY, and LIPSCOMB, G. D. *Dr. George Washington Carver: Scientist.* Messner, 1971. Reprint of 1944 edition.

HOLT, RACKHAM. *George Washington Carver: An American Biography.* Rev. ed. Doubleday, 1963.

MCMURRY, LINDA O. *George Washington Carver: Scientist and Symbol.* Oxford, 1981.

CARVER, JOHN (1576?-1621), became the first governor of Plymouth Colony immediately after the signing of the Mayflower Compact. As governor, he made a peace treaty with the Indian chief Massasoit which lasted many years. Carver's piety and wisdom greatly aided the colonists during a difficult period of adjustment in America.

Carver was born in Nottinghamshire, England. He became a merchant before joining the Pilgrim church in Leiden, Holland, about 1610. A few years later, he became a deacon in the church and helped negotiate with the merchants who financed the Pilgrim voyage. Carver died four months after he arrived in Massachusetts. BRADFORD SMITH

See also MASSASOIT; PLYMOUTH COLONY (The Founding of Plymouth Colony).

CARVING is the art of cutting figures, ornaments, or decorative objects by hand from such materials as stone, marble, wood, ivory, bone, and shell. The term *sculpture* designates large carvings in stone, marble, or wood. The term *carving* applies to small sculptures and

American Seating Co.

A Skilled Carver uses a special chisel to apply details to a historical scene he has carved from a panel of wood.

to decorations that are carved on furniture or buildings.

Early History. The art of carving is older than recorded history. Archaeologists have found examples of carved bone and horn which early peoples made during the Stone Age. Primitive peoples of today carve many objects from wood. Carved masks are outstanding examples of art from Africa. Islanders in the South Pacific Ocean work with simple tools to make ceremonial objects, as well as everyday tools and utensils. Craftworkers carve intricate decorations on houses, coconut shells, and canoe prows.

The ancient Egyptians cut beautiful objects from wood, ivory, alabaster, stone, turquoise, and other materials. Many such pieces are remarkable because they were carved from extremely hard stone, such as diorite or porphyry. Egyptian craftworkers made gems with *intaglios*, or designs cut in their surfaces (see INTAGLIO). People used the gems to make an impression in sealing wax. Mesopotamian civilizations also used intaglios. The ancient Sumerians and Babylonians carved cylinder seals from colored stone. When these were rolled over soft clay, they left impressions. Early peoples in the Western Hemisphere also made use of carving. The Aztec, Maya, and Zapotec Indians chiseled figures on stone pyramids. These tribes also carved in jade and *obsidian* (volcanic glass).

Many Indians of Alaska and Canada carved wood. The Haida Indians of the Northwest Coast were famous totem-pole makers, and were known for their high-prowed canoes.

The Greeks and Romans carved precious stones. They also worked with ivory, and produced many pieces of beautiful sculpture. Japanese craftworkers are noted for their ivory figures and fans.

The early Christians in Egypt, called *Copts*, used wood carvings for ceilings and for openwork screens. Wood carving spread throughout the Arab world and into Spain. Outstanding examples of Arabic achievements in carving include the Mudéjar wood ceiling in the Archbishop's Palace in Alcalá, and the carved wonders of the Alhambra in Granada (see ALHAMBRA). The latter has especially beautiful arches, ceilings, and doors. The carved ceiling of the Capella Palatina in Palermo, Sicily, is another masterpiece of Arab influence.

Later Carvings. Wood carvers decorated church stalls in Gothic churches. They also produced simple, sturdy, and massive pieces of furniture during the Gothic period. During the Italian Renaissance, craftworkers paneled rooms with carved decorations. Baroque and rococo architecture also featured wood carvings.

Oriental art has produced many examples of carving. The Ajanta Caves in India, which artists cut out of cliffs, contain examples of great artistry. So do many Oriental temples. Craftworkers have decorated outside walls of many of these structures. They have also carved figures on stone *stelae*, or pillars, to tell religious stories. The decorations of the Taj Mahal are another example of this art (see TAJ MAHAL). They include delicate paneling and pierced marble windows and screens. The Chinese used simple tools to produce many beautiful jade pieces (see JADE [pictures]).

Carving as a Hobby. The beginner usually prefers to carve in materials which are easy to cut. Wood carving, or *whittling*, has always been popular in the United States. A form of gypsum called *alabaster* is easy to carve and takes a high polish. Soap is an inexpensive and easily molded material. WILLIAM M. MILLIKEN

Related Articles in WORLD BOOK include:

Alabaster
Eskimo (Art; picture: Soapstone Sculpture)
Ivory (pictures)
Lacquer (pictures)
Sculpture
Wood Carving

CARVING, MEAT. See MEAT (pictures).

CARY, JOYCE (1888-1957), ranks among the leading British novelists of the 1900's. Cary combined great verbal gifts, humor, and striking realism with his lively style. Sometimes the view of life he showed in his novels was blurred by a sentimentality for the past. For example, Cary tended to picture the 1800's as a simpler and happier time than it really was.

Cary's major works are two *trilogies* (groups of three related novels). The first trilogy includes *Herself Surprised* (1941), *To Be a Pilgrim* (1942), and *The Horse's Mouth* (1944). The second trilogy includes *Prisoner of Grace* (1952), *Except the Lord* (1953), and *Not Honour More* (1955). All six novels deal with the traditional literary themes of conflict between generations, the relations between the individual and society, the artist and the middle class, and freedom and authority.

Cary was born in Londonderry, Northern Ireland, and studied art at the University of Edinburgh and in Paris. He worked in Africa as a member of the Nigerian Political Service from 1913 to 1920. Cary's early novels are about Africa and Africans. FREDERICK R. KARL

CARY, MARY ANN SHADD (1823-1893), was an American teacher and journalist known for helping fugitive slaves living in Canada. She was the first black woman in North America to establish and edit a weekly newspaper. In 1853, she helped found the *Provincial Freeman*, a weekly in Windsor, Ont., for blacks in Canada.

Mary Ann Shadd was born to free parents in Wilmington, Del. From 1839 to 1851, she taught in and established schools for blacks in Delaware, New York, and Pennsylvania. She moved to Windsor in 1851. She became an active worker for slaves who escaped to Canada after the United States Congress passed the Fugitive Slave Act of 1850. This legislation provided for the return of slaves who escaped from one state to another. Many slaves fled to Canada to avoid being returned to their owners. She married Thomas F. Cary, a Toronto barber, in 1856.

In 1869, Cary moved to Washington, D.C., where she taught elementary school for the next 15 years. She also worked for women's right to vote. Cary studied law at Howard University and received an LL.B. degree in 1883. JUNE SOCHEN

CARYATID. See SCULPTURE (As Part of Architecture; picture).

CASA GRANDE NATIONAL MONUMENT, in southern Arizona, includes the ruins of an adobe tower that was built by Indians who irrigated and farmed the land in the Gila Valley 600 years ago. The tower was discovered in 1694. The monument was established in 1918. For the area of the Casa Grande National Monument, see NATIONAL PARK SYSTEM (table: National Monuments).

CASABA, *kuh SAH buh,* sometimes called CASABA MELON, is a large, round melon that has a delicious thick yellow flesh. Most casabas eaten in the United States grow in California, where they were brought about 1871 from Kasaba, near Izmir, in Turkey. The casaba has the shape of a muskmelon, but does not have the musk odor. Grooves run down the melon from the stem and mark the smooth yellow skin. The casaba matures for harvest in autumn. It will keep for several weeks during the cool months if cared for properly, and is called a winter melon because it can be bought in the winter. California growers usually ship casabas in November and December.

Scientific Classification. The casaba belongs to the gourd family, *Cucurbitaceae.* It is classified as genus *Cucumis,* species *C. melo,* variety *inodorus.* JULIAN C. CRANE

See also GOURD; MELON; MUSKMELON.

CASABLANCA, *KAS uh BLANK uh* (pop. 1,506,373), is the largest city in Morocco and a major port in North Africa. About 70 per cent of Morocco's trade passes through this Atlantic port. For location, see MOROCCO (map).

Wide avenues branch out from the *Place de France,* the business and amusement center, to all other sections of the city. Arabs and Moors live in two crowded sections of Casablanca, *Old Medinah* and *New Medinah.* Jews live in the *Mellah.* Europeans live near the center of the city.

Morocco's only glass factory and blast furnace are in Casablanca. Other industrial plants in the city include brickworks, canneries, sawmills, and furniture factories.

Casablanca was the site of a meeting between President Franklin D. Roosevelt and Prime Minister Winston Churchill in January 1943. The two leaders met there to decide the course of World War II. The Portuguese founded Casablanca in 1515. KEITH G. MATHER

CASABLANCA CONFERENCE was a meeting at which U.S. President Franklin D. Roosevelt and British Prime Minister Winston Churchill planned World War II strategy. The Casablanca Conference took place during the war, in Casablanca, Morocco. It lasted from Jan. 14 to Jan. 24, 1943.

The Allies had invaded North Africa in November, 1942. At the conference, Roosevelt and Churchill decided to invade Sicily and the Italian mainland after completion of the North African campaign. Roosevelt, with Churchill's support, also declared that the war could end only with the unconditional surrender of the enemy nations. In the end, only Germany surrendered unconditionally. Italy and Japan surrendered after some peace negotiations. ROBERT HUGH FERRELL

CASALS, *kah SAHLS,* **PABLO** (1876-1973), a Spanish cellist, became one of the outstanding string players of the 1900's. Casals set the modern style for cello playing and greatly influenced contemporary cellists and violinists. Casals founded the Barcelona Orchestra in 1919. In 1950, he organized the famous chamber music festivals in Prades, France. He also founded the Festival Casals in Puerto Rico in the 1950's. Casals was awarded the U.S. Presidential Medal of Freedom in 1963.

Karsh, Ottawa

Pablo Casals

Casals was born in Vendrell, Spain, on Dec. 29, 1876. His father, the local organist and choirmaster, taught him to play the flute, violin, piano, and cello. He made his debut at the Concerts Lamoureux in Paris in 1899. In 1901, he made the first of several concert tours of the United States.

Casals left Spain in 1939 after the Spanish Civil War because of his opposition to Spain's ruler, Francisco Franco. Casals lived in Prades, France, and also in Puerto Rico. DOROTHY DELAY

CASANOVA, *KAZ uh NO vuh,* **GIOVANNI JACOPO** (1725-1798), is considered the greatest of romantic lovers. As a youth he held many jobs, ranging from soldiering to playing the violin. But he had to leave them all, usually because of entangling affairs with women. His memoirs, published between 1826 and 1838 in 12 volumes, tell much about his exploits as a lover and about the customs of his day. He was born in Venice. A man who is called a "Casanova" is usually quite popular with women. FRANK GOODWYN

Detail of a portrait (1775) by Alessandro Longhi; The Toledo Museum of Art, Toledo, Ohio. Gift of Edward Drummond Libbey, 1965

Giovanni Casanova

CASBAH. See ALGERIA (Cities).

CASCADE. See WATERFALL.

CASCADE RANGE is a chain of mountains that extends from northern California through western Oregon and Washington into southern British Columbia. The mountains are made up of lavas and volcanic materials. Many of the peaks are extinct volcanoes, but two have erupted during the 1900's. Mount St. Helens in southwestern Washington erupted in 1980 and caused widespread damage. After its eruption, the mountain measured 8,364 feet (2,549 meters) above sea level. Lassen Peak (10,457 feet, or 3,187 meters) in northern California last erupted in 1921. Mount Rainier (14,410 feet, or 4,392 meters), in west-central Washington, and Mount Shasta (14,162 feet, or 4,317 meters), in northern California, are the highest peaks in the range. Other peaks include Mount Adams (12,307 feet, or 3,751 meters), in Washington, and Mount Hood (11,239 feet, or 3,426 meters), in Oregon.

Rainfall is heavy in the mountains. Streams have cut deep valleys, which are covered with heavy fir and pine forests. The Columbia River cuts through the range, and several long railroad tunnels have been built through the mountains. Among the most important tunnels are the Cascade and Snoqualmie. JOHN H. GARLAND

Related Articles in WORLD BOOK include:

Cascade Tunnel	Mount Saint Helens	Washington (pictures)
Lassen Peak	Mount Shasta	
Mount Rainier		

CASCADE TUNNEL in Washington is the longest tunnel in the Western Hemisphere, and one of the longest in the world. The tunnel runs under the Cascade Range. It cuts through 7.79 miles (12.54 kilometers) of granite in Chelan and King counties. The Great Northern Railway completed the tunnel in 1929 at a cost of $25 million.

Old Cascade Tunnel cuts under the crest of the Cascades for 2.6 miles (4.2 kilometers) from a point about 50 miles (80 kilometers) southeast of Everett to about 55 miles (89 kilometers) east of Seattle. Old Cascade Tunnel is 16 feet (4.9 meters) wide and 21½ feet (6.6 meters) high. WALLACE E. AKIN

CASCARA SAGRADA, *kas KAIR uh suh GRAY duh,* is an important drug plant that grows in the northwestern United States. It is also called *cascara buckthorn* and *chittam*. It grows as a shrub or a small tree about 25 feet (7.6 meters) high, and it thrives in rich, moist soil. Its oval leaves may be 3 to 6 inches (8 to 15 centimeters) long and have straight side veins. The small, green flowers form black, berrylike fruits.

Eli Lilly & Co.

Cascara Sagrada

The Spanish term *cascara sagrada* means *sacred bark*. Substances from the bark are used in medicines as a laxative. The bark is peeled from the trunk and branches. Then the tree dies. If it is cut down and the stump left with its bark whole, the roots send up new shoots. Cascara sagrada can be grown from seed.

Scientific Classification. Cascara sagrada belongs to the buckthorn family, *Rhamnaceae*. It is genus *Rhamnus*, species *R. purshiana*. ELBERT L. LITTLE, JR.

CASE is a feature of nouns and pronouns that helps show their relation to other parts of speech in a sentence. The case of a noun is shown by the inflectional ending attached to it (see INFLECTION). For instance, in some languages a noun may have one ending when it is the subject of a verb, another when it is the direct object, a third when it is the indirect object, and so on. Languages differ widely in the number of cases they have. Old English nouns have five cases, but modern English nouns have only two. Latin has six cases. Some languages, such as Hungarian, have as many as 25 or 30 cases.

Cases in Latin

Latin provides a good example of a case system. The Latin word *servus*, which means *slave*, has the following forms in the singular:

nominative	*servus*
vocative	*serve*
genitive	*servi*
dative	*servo*
accusative	*servum*
ablative	*servo*

The *nominative* form occurred when the word was the subject of a verb: "The slave was waiting." The *vocative* was used when a person called or addressed someone else: "Get me my toga, slave." The *genitive* resembled the English possessive, and denoted possession or origin: "The slave's clothes," "A child of the slave." The *dative* corresponded to the English indirect object: "He gave the slave his freedom." The *accusative* was used when the word was the object of a verb: "I saw the slave." The *ablative* followed certain prepositions: "He went with the slave." The ablative and dative are listed as separate cases, although the forms for this particular noun are the same, because some nouns had different forms. For example, the word for *foot* (*pes*) is *pedi* in the dative and *pede* in the ablative.

Cases in English

Nouns. Over a period of about 1,000 years, the case forms of English nouns were reduced from five to two —*common* and *possessive*. The common, or all-purpose, case is the base form of the noun used in either the subject or object position. The possessive case is the base form, plus, in writing, *'s*. For example, the common case nouns *girl*, *boy*, and *monkey* become *girl's*, *boy's*, and *monkey's* in the possessive case. If the form is both plural and possessive, an apostrophe follows the plural ending: *girls'*, *boys'*, *monkeys'*. In speech, the possessive ending is identical with the plural ending. The following pairs are pronounced alike: *boy's* and *boys*, *rat's* and *rats*, *witch's* and *witches*.

As the name suggests, the possessive ending usually indicates that the noun names a possessor or owner of something else: "the boy's car," "the rat's nest." Often, however, the possessive indicates meanings other than physical possession. Thus we have the possessive in "the boy's picture," though the boy may not own the portrait of himself. Other examples showing the varied meaning of the possessive are "a day's work," "land's end," and "a stone's throw." Notice that the expression "Shakespeare's plays" has two meanings: plays owned by Shakespeare and plays written by Shakespeare.

Proper nouns ending in *s* are sometimes written in the possessive with just the apostrophe and no additional *s*.

For example, either "Keats's poems" or "Keats' poems" is correct. Common nouns ending in *s* are generally written *'s* (the waitress's husband), though the ending may sometimes drop out in speech.

An interesting feature in English is illustrated by the expression "the king of Spain's hat." The possessive ending is attached to *Spain*, not to *king*, although the hat belongs to the king, not to Spain. A rule in English states that the possessive always follows the whole possessive phrase occurring just before the noun modified by the possessive: "someone else's hat," "the man in the back row's remark."

Pronouns. Some English personal pronouns and the relative pronoun *who* retain three case forms instead of two. The subject forms are *I*, *he*, *she*, *we*, *they*, and *who*. These pronouns are said to be in the *subjective*, or *nominative*, case. The object forms are *me*, *him*, *her*, *us*, *them*, and *whom*. These pronouns are in the *objective* case. The pronouns *you* and *it* have a common case form for subject and object positions. All pronouns show a possessive form (*my*, *your*, *his*, *her*, *its*, *their*, *whose*). Most have a variant form of the possessive (*mine*, *yours*, *hers*, *ours*, *theirs*). This form is used for special positions ("*my* book," but "The book is *mine*" and "*Mine* is lost").

Generally, the subject form is used when the pronoun is the subject of a verb ("*She* sang") or when it is a complement after the verb *to be* ("This is *she*"). The object form is used when the pronoun is the object of a verb ("The light blinded *her*"), the indirect object of a verb ("John did *her* a favor"), or the object of a preposition ("The class gave special recognition to *her*"). The possessive forms are often used as modifiers ("*their* house," "This is *his*"). They also serve in the subject position ("*Hers* has been destroyed") or the object position ("I bought *mine*").

Informal usage often interferes with the orderly use of case forms. For example, many persons use *who* in a question like "*Who* are you going with?" because *who* occupies what is ordinarily a subject position, even though it is the object of the preposition *with*. Despite such trends in usage, many writers still maintain careful case distinctions. They prefer "*Whom* are you going with?" or "With *whom* are you going?" William F. Irmscher

CASE, CLIFFORD PHILIP (1904-1982), a New Jersey Republican, served in the United States Senate from 1955 to 1979. Case was a member of the United States House of Representatives from 1945 to 1953. He began his political career in 1938, when he won election to the Rahway, N.J., common council. He served in the New Jersey house of assembly in 1943 and 1944. In 1953 and 1954, Case was president of the Ford Foundation's Fund for the Republic, an organization that studies threats to American liberties. Case was born in Franklin Park, N.J. Richard P. McCormick

CASE HISTORY. See Psychology (Systematic Assessment).

CASE METHOD, in law schools, uses actual case decisions for study. Law students read these decisions and discuss the reasoning by which they were reached. For nearly a hundred years before 1870, law schools in the United States had taught by lectures and individual reading of the few law books available. In that year, Christopher C. Langdell, a professor at the Harvard Law School, introduced the case method of study. He collected decisions, or cases decided by appellate courts, in a *case book*. Law students studied these decisions and discussed the cases in class. By the early 1900's, most law schools had adopted the case method. Students now study statutes and administrative regulations in addition to cases. The case method is also used in other social sciences. William Tucker Dean

See also Law (Common-Law Systems).

CASE WESTERN RESERVE UNIVERSITY is a private coeducational university in Cleveland, Ohio. It has two undergraduate colleges. Western Reserve College offers degrees in the arts and sciences. Case Institute of Technology offers degrees in engineering, management, mathematics, and the natural sciences. The graduate school and the schools of applied social science, dentistry, engineering, law, library science, management, medicine, and nursing offer advanced degrees.

In 1967, Western Reserve University and Case Institute of Technology united to form Case Western Reserve University. Western Reserve was founded at Hudson, Ohio, in 1826, and moved to Cleveland in 1882. Case Institute of Technology was founded in Cleveland in 1880. For enrollment, see Universities and Colleges (table). Critically reviewed by Case Western Reserve University

CASEIN, *KAY seen*, is the chief protein in milk. It is also the main ingredient in cheese. Casein separates as curd when milk sours, or when acid is added. It also separates from sweet milk when the enzyme *rennin* is added. Casein contains carbon, hydrogen, nitrogen, oxygen, phosphorus, and sulfur. Pure casein is a tasteless, odorless, white solid. Cow milk contains about 3 per cent casein. See Cheese; Milk.

Casein is produced commercially from skim milk. The curd is washed, dried, and ground. Commercially prepared casein is pale yellow and has a pleasant odor. It is widely used in medicines, cosmetics, and as a *sizing* (coating) for paper. Casein is also used in waterproof glues, casein paints, and certain plastic articles such as buttons. Critically reviewed by the National Dairy Council

CASEWORK. See Social Work.

CASEY JONES. See Jones, Casey.

CASH refers to money, especially ready money. The word *cash* is most commonly used to describe money that is paid promptly after making a purchase.

CASH REGISTER is a machine that makes and keeps sales records automatically. There are two basic kinds of cash registers. One shows the amount of each sale on a sign that pops up. It prints an *audit strip*, which gives a record of every sale. A meter records the total sales made. The totals can be used to arrange records in different ways, such as sales of different departments, or different kinds of sales. The second kind of cash register prints a record on a tape, but no sign pops up. In most cases, two tapes are printed. One tape is given to the customer, and the other is kept by the store. Some cash registers of both types print the amount the customer paid to the cashier, and show the change owed the customer. James Ritty of Dayton, Ohio, invented the first practical cash register in 1879 (see Ritty, James).

During the 1960's and 1970's, several manufacturers developed computerized cash registers called *electronic data processing point-of-sale terminals*. These machines work faster than mechanical cash registers and can per-

Milt and Joan Mann

An Electronic Cash Register records the price and inventory number of each item and then calculates the total sale.

NCR Corporation

The First Model of the Cash Register resembled a clock. One hand indicated dollars and the other indicated cents.

form many additional tasks. Some machines have an electronic device called a *scanner,* which "reads" the price or other information about an item from a specially-printed code on the package. One such code, the *Universal Product Code,* consists of a series of numbers and an arrangement of lines and bars. Electronic cash registers also can check a customer's credit, issue an itemized receipt, and help a store keep track of its inventory and sales trends.
WILLIAM H. FISH

CASHEW, *KASH oo,* is a bean-shaped nut that grows on a tropical evergreen tree. Cashew nuts are delicious when roasted and are a popular food in the United States. India and South America produce most of the world's cashew nuts. The cashew tree is related to poison ivy, and the shell of the cashew nut contains an irritating poison. People who touch the shell sometimes develop skin blisters. But roasting removes all poison from the nuts.

The cashew tree is native to Central America and other tropical regions. The first cashew trees in India were brought from South America. In the United States, cashew trees grow mostly in Florida.

The trees sometimes reach a height of 40 feet (12 meters). They have large, leathery, green leaves up to 6 inches (15 centimeters) long and 4 inches (10 centimeters) wide. Each fruit of the cashew contains one nut. In addition to the nut, people eat the fleshy red or yellow base of the fruit, called the cashew apple. The apple may be eaten raw or made into a preserve. Cashew trees also yield a gum used in varnishes.

Scientific Classification. Cashew trees belong to the cashew family, Anacardiaceae. The most important kind is genus *Anacardium,* species *A. occidentale.*
RICHARD A. JAYNES

U.S. Dept. of Agriculture

Cashews grow in bean-shaped shells attached to fruitlike cashew apples. The apple's stem grows at the end opposite the nut.

CASHIER'S CHECK. See CHECK (Special Checking Services).

CASHMERE, *KASH mihr,* is a soft, fine wool fabric with a diagonal weave. Cashmere woven with a pattern is called *tapestry twill.* Sweaters, dresses, and scarves are often made of cashmere. The name *cashmere* also applies to fabrics made of the wool of Cashmere goats. See also CASHMERE GOAT.

CASHMERE GOAT, *KASH mihr,* is a long-haired goat, famous for its fine, silky wool. Cashmere goats live in Tibet and India. Some have also been raised in France and in Germany.

The Cashmere goat is a medium-sized animal. It has drooping ears and spirally twisted horns. The goats from the high plateaus and mountains are colored deep yellow. Goats that do not live in such high places are lighter colored, and those that live in the valleys and plains below the mountains are pure white. The goats that live in cold places have the heaviest fleece. The meat can be eaten, and the milk is rich. See also CASHMERE; GOAT.
VICTOR H. CAHALANE

CASIMIR THE GREAT. See POLAND (History).

CASING. See MEAT PACKING (Sausage Making).

CASKET. See FUNERAL CUSTOMS.

CASPER (pop. 51,016) is the largest city in Wyoming. It serves as an administrative and production center for companies that develop coal, gas, oil, and uranium deposits in Wyoming. Many tourists visit Casper to enjoy camping, hunting, and winter sports. The city lies along a bend of the North Platte River in east-central Wyoming. For location, see WYOMING (political map).

Casper began as a military post called Platte Bridge Station. In 1865, the name was changed to Caspar to honor Caspar W. Collins, a soldier who died fighting Cheyenne Indians nearby. A clerical error probably caused the spelling change to Casper. The first oil well near Casper was drilled in 1883. The development of more oil wells in the area caused the city to grow rapidly. The oil boom ended during the Great Depression of the 1930's.

In the 1970's several companies moved to the Casper area to explore and develop new sources of energy, and the city started to expand again. Casper has a council-manager government and is the county seat of Natrona County. DIANE P. NESTE

CASPIAN SEA

Area: 143,630 sq. mi. (372,000 km²)

Elevation: 92 ft. (28m) below sea level

Deepest point: • 3,264 ft. (995m)

— Road
Salt marsh
Oil fields

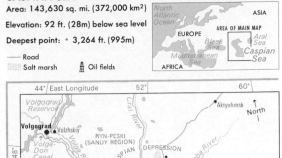

North Atlantic Ocean
ASIA
AREA OF MAIN MAP
EUROPE
Black Sea
Aral Sea
Caspian Sea
Mediterranean Sea
AFRICA

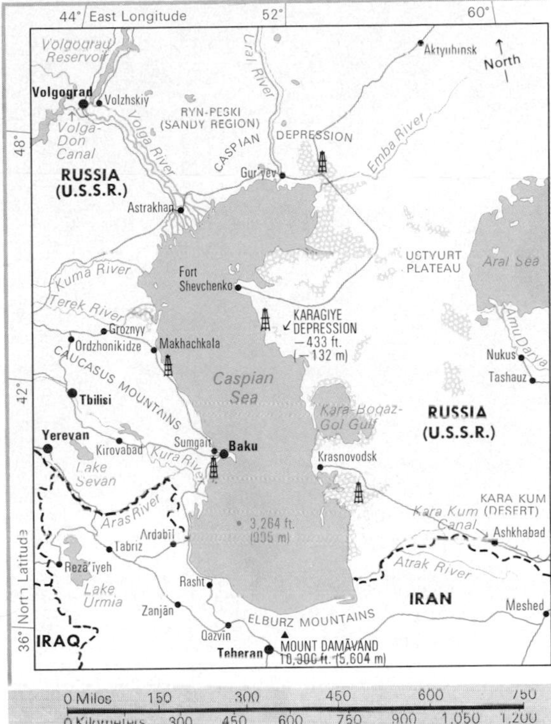

WORLD BOOK map

CASPIAN SEA, *KAS pih un*, a great salt lake below sea level, is the largest inland body of water in the world. It lies between Europe and Asia east of the Caucasus Mountains. Russia surrounds the Caspian Sea on three sides, and Iran lies against its southern shore. See RUSSIA (physical map).

The Caspian Sea covers 143,630 square miles (372,000 square kilometers), an area almost the size of the state of California. It is about 750 miles (1,210 kilometers) long at its greatest extent, and varies from 130 to 300 miles (209 to 483 kilometers) in width. During the past several centuries, the Caspian has been shrinking in size because the rivers that empty into it bring it less water than it loses by evaporation. Large irrigation projects built by Russia in the Caspian Basin drain off much water from these rivers. The most important rivers that empty into the Caspian include the Volga, Ural, Terek, and Kura.

The Caspian Sea lies 92 feet (28 meters) below sea level, and has no outlet to any ocean. Because seals live in its waters, some scientists believe the lake was once linked to the Arctic Ocean. The waters of the Caspian are less salty than ocean waters, and abound with both fresh-water and salt-water fish. The Caspian Sea has no tides. Scattered small islands in the lake have a combined area of about 850 square miles (2,201 square kilometers).

Astrakhan, on the delta of the Volga River which extends into the Caspian, is an important port on the lake. JOHN D. ISAACS

CASS, LEWIS (1782-1866), was an American statesman. He served from 1813 to 1831 as governor of the Territory of Michigan, which included what later became the states of Michigan, Wisconsin, Iowa, and Minnesota. Cass helped bring civilization to that area. He built roads and organized local governments. From 1831 to 1836, Cass served as secretary of war under President Andrew Jackson. He was a United States senator from Michigan from 1845 to 1848 and from 1849 to 1857. He was the Democratic candidate for President in 1848, and served as secretary of state under President James Buchanan. A statue of Cass represents Michigan in Statuary Hall in the United States Capitol in Washington, D.C.

Cass was born in Exeter, N.H., and studied at Phillips Academy. He became a lawyer in Marietta, Ohio, and served in the War of 1812. He first proposed the doctrine of *Popular Sovereignty* by which the people of a territory could decide for themselves if they would permit slaveholding. W. B. HESSELTINE

CASSANDER. See SALONIKA.

The Cashmere Goat supplies cashmere wool, the downy fleece that lies under the goat's long hair. An average-sized goat gives only 3 ounces (85 grams) of the fleece. For this reason, cashmere wool is an expensive product.

Dickason, Ewing Galloway

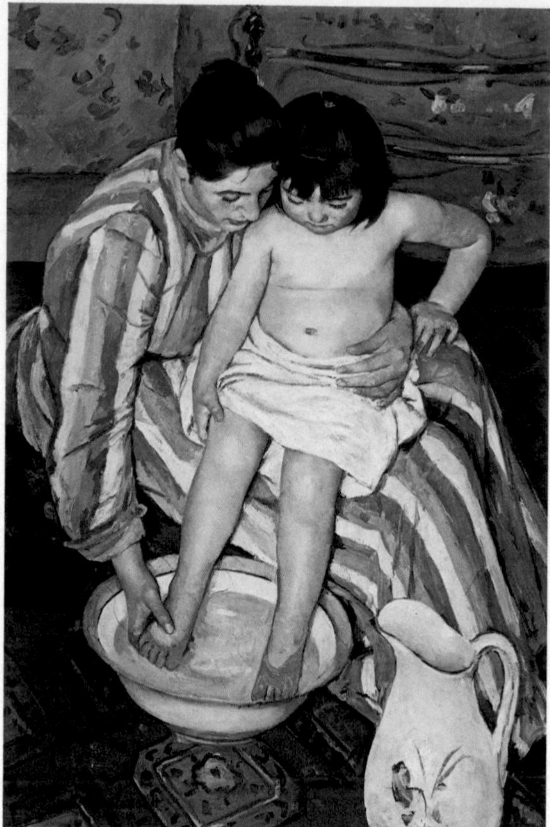

Oil painting (about 1892) by Mary Cassatt; The Art Institute of Chicago, Robert A. Waller Fund

Mary Cassatt became famous for her paintings of mothers and children in everyday situations. *The Bath, above,* shows how she used flat, delicate colors and strong, clear lines. The French painter Edgar Degas, a friend of Miss Cassatt's, painted her portrait, *left.*

A detail of an oil portrait by Edgar Degas; collection of André Meyer, New York City (WORLD BOOK photo by Robert Crandall)

CASSANDRA, *kuh SAN druh,* was the daughter of Priam and Hecuba, king and queen of Troy in Greek epic poetry. According to Homer, her beauty was so great that Apollo fell in love with her and gave her the power to foretell the future. But she would not love him in return. Apollo angrily punished her by ordering that no one should ever believe her prophecies.

Cassandra repeatedly warned her countrymen not to keep Helen of Troy captive or take the Trojan Horse inside the walls of Troy. But they paid no attention.

Cassandra was praying at the altar of Athena when Troy fell. Agamemnon took her to Mycenae as a slave. There Clytemnestra and Aegisthus murdered her.

The story of Cassandra has been told often in literature. Schiller, Rossetti, and Oliver Wendell Holmes made her the subject of poems. Euripides tells of her fate in his play *The Trojan Women.* O. M. PEARL

See also TROY.

CASSATT, *kuh SAT,* **MARY** (1845-1926), probably America's most famous woman painter, is best known for her sensitive pictures of mothers and children. She brought a delicate feeling and color sense to her etchings and color prints. Miss Cassatt was associated with the French impressionist movement in painting. She became a close friend of Edgar Degas, who influenced her style greatly. She exhibited with the impressionist group.

Miss Cassatt was born in what is now Pittsburgh, and studied at the Pennsylvania Academy of Arts. She spent most of her life abroad, and settled in Paris in 1868, against her father's wishes. ROBERT GOLDWATER

CASSAVA, *kuh SAH vuh,* is a small shrub of South America, the roots of which are eaten and are used to make tapioca. Cassava is related to the *castor bean* and the *Pará rubber tree.* It is raised in the southern United States and other warm regions.

There are two main kinds of cassava. *Bitter cassava* is used to make tapioca, and *sweet cassava* has roots that are eaten like potatoes. To make tapioca, the bitter cassava root is ground and thoroughly washed to remove the prussic acid that it contains. Because of this acid, it cannot be eaten raw in the way people eat sweet cassava.

Scientific Classification. Cassava belongs to the spurge family *Euphorbiaceae.* Bitter cassava is genus *Manihot,* species *esculenta.* Sweet cassava is *M. dulcis.* JULIAN C. CRANE

See also TAPIOCA.

The Cassava Plant grows only in a warm, tropical climate. Roots of the *bitter cassava* are ground and washed to make tapioca.

Ewing Galloway

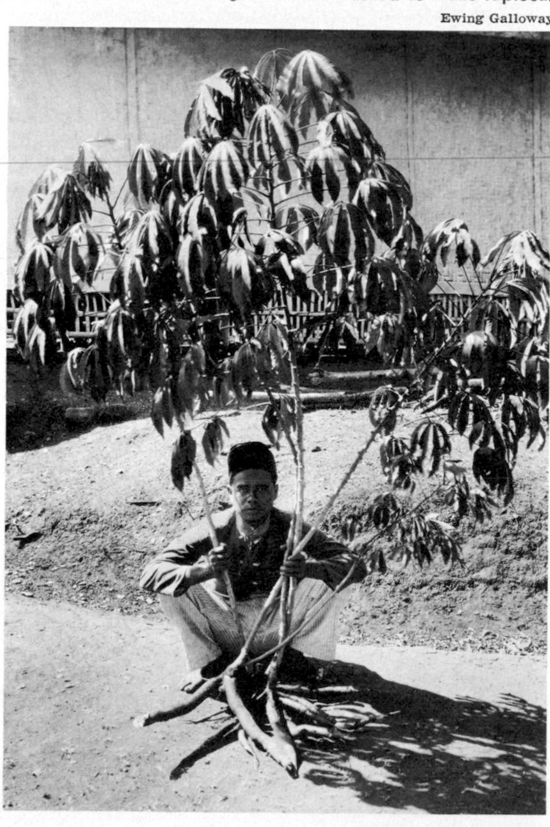

CASSETTE. See Tape Recorder; Television.

CASSIA, *KASH uh,* is any one of a group of plants that includes many trees, shrubs, and herbs. They grow in tropical and warm temperate climates. Some botanists place over 400 different species in this group.

Cassias from Africa and from India supply the *senna* (dried leaves) used as a laxative. Several kinds of cassia grow wild in the United States. These include wild senna and partridge peas. *Cassia bark* is the bark of a plant of the laurel family. It tastes like cinnamon.

Scientific Classification. True cassias belong to the pea family, *Leguminosae*. The African cassia is genus *Cassia*, species *C. acutifolia*. The Indian cassia is *C. angustifolia*. The wild senna is *C. marilandica*. The partridge pea is *C. fasciculata*. Harold Norman Moldenke

See also Cinnamon; Partridge Pea.

CASSIN, RENÉ. See Nobel Prizes (table: Nobel Prizes for Literature—1968).

CASSINI, JEAN DOMENIQUE. See Saturn (Rings).

CASSINO, *kuh SEE noh* (pop. 25,992), is an Italian town about 75 miles (121 kilometers) southeast of Rome. For location, see Italy (political map). The famous Benedictine monastery of Monte Cassino has been the home of Benedictine monks since A.D. 529. Fierce fighting took place in Cassino during World War II, when German troops made a stronghold of the city and resisted Allied attempts to seize it. Shepard B. Clough

See also Monte Cassino.

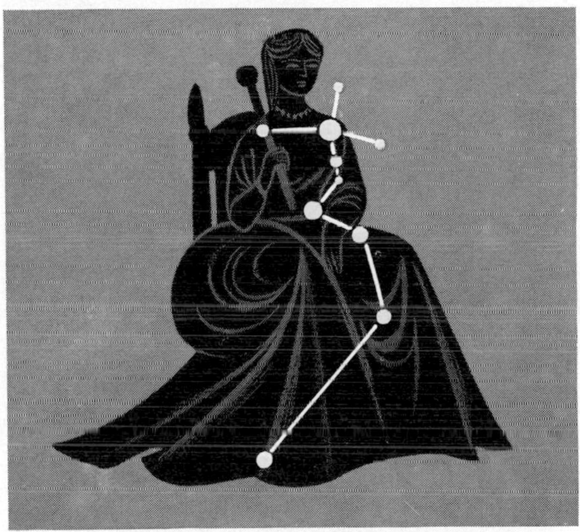

Cassiopeia Is Called "The Lady in Her Chair."

CASSIOPEIA, *KAS ee uh PEE uh,* is an easily seen constellation of the Northern Hemisphere. It is located on the side of the North Star opposite the Big Dipper, and about the same distance away. Five of the brightest stars in Cassiopeia form a sprawling, irregular letter *W*. In Greek mythology, Cassiopeia was the mother of Andromeda and the wife of Cepheus. Because of her mother's vanity, Andromeda was chained to a rock in the sea. I. M. Levitt

CASSITERITE, *kuh SIHT uh ryt* (chemical formula, SnO_2), is the only important mineral ore of tin. It is sometimes called *tinstone*. Cassiterite usually has a slight metallic luster, with a brown or black color. It usually occurs in veins associated with quartz, and is either in or near granite rocks. Malaysia provides about one-fourth of the world's supply of cassiterite. Bolivia, Indonesia, Russia, and Thailand are also major sources. See also Tin. Walter J. Moore

CASSIUS LONGINUS, *KASH ih uhs lahn JY nuhs,* **GAIUS** (? -42 B.C.), was a Roman general who, with Marcus Junius Brutus, led the conspiracy against Julius Caesar. During the civil war between Caesar and Pompey, Cassius commanded a fleet for Pompey. Caesar won the war, pardoned Cassius, and made him *praetor* (administrator of the courts) in 44 B.C. But Cassius helped murder Caesar later in 44 B.C. Cassius and his brother-in-law Brutus fled east and raised a large army. Mark Antony and Octavian defeated them at Philippi. Cassius committed suicide when his camp was taken. See also Caesar, Julius. Chester G. Starr

CASSOWARY, *KAS uh WEHR ee,* is a large, shy bird that lives in the thick forests of Australia, New Guinea, and nearby islands. Cassowaries cannot fly. All three species of cassowaries have a massive body, long legs, and a featherless neck and head. A bony helmet, used for butting through undergrowth, covers the head.

The largest species, the one-wattled cassowary of New Guinea, stands about 5 feet (1.5 meters) tall and weighs about 120 pounds (54 kilograms). Its wings and tail are small and almost hidden. Brownish-black, bristlelike feathers cover the body. Each foot has three toes armed with sharp claws. These claws are deadly weapons in a fight.

Scientific Classification. Cassowaries make up the cassowary family, *Casuariidae*. The one-wattled cassowary is classified as genus *Casuarius*, species *C. unappendiculatus*. R. A. Paynter, Jr.

See also Emu.

The Cassowary can sprint at nearly 40 miles (64 kilometers) per hour and leap 6 feet (1.8 meters) or more in the air.

George Leavens, Photo Researchers

CAST AND CASTING. Casting is a method of shaping an object by pouring a liquid into a mold and letting it harden. The shaped object is called either a *cast* or a *casting*. Casting is used to make thousands of articles, including tools, machine parts, toys, and art objects such as statuary. The Egyptians cast bronze in molds over 3,500 years ago. Today, plastics, iron, steel, aluminum, ceramics, and many other materials are used.

Patterns for Casting. Before materials are cast, workers make a wood or metal pattern of the article to be cast. These patterns are later used to make the molds from which the actual castings are made. Patterns may be made in several ways, depending on the size of the article and on how many times the mold will be used. Solid, or one-piece, patterns are called *loose patterns*. They are generally used when the object is very large and when only a few pieces of the object will be needed. A *match-plate* pattern is made by splitting the pattern in two halves. A *split pattern* consists of two halves that can be fitted and held together with pins.

Types of Molds. Most metals are cast in *green sand*, which is a mixture of sand, clay, water, and a binder to hold the sand grains together. A *dry sand* mold makes a smoother casting surface. It contains a special binder. The surfaces of a dry sand mold are dried with an open flame before the mold is poured. *Permanent molds*, made of metal, are used for special types of castings.

How Castings Are Made. Metal is usually cast in a sand mold. If an object, such as an iron dumbbell, is to be cast from a split pattern, one half of the pattern is placed on a board, with its flat side down. The board is surrounded by two loose-fitting wooden or metal boxes. Together, these boxes make up a *flask*. Damp sand is packed firmly around the pattern to fill the space between the pattern and the sides of the flask. The board is removed, and the other half of the pattern is fitted to the first half. Sand is then packed around it.

The top half of the flask with its sand is called the *cope*. The bottom half is called the *drag*. The cope and the drag of the mold are fitted together after the pattern has been removed from the sand. A small opening called a *gate* is formed in each end of the cope so the metal can be poured into the mold. A cavity can be made in a casting by suspending a hard sand object called a *core* in the mold. When the metal is poured into the mold, it cools quickly and forms a solid. The sand is then broken away.

Other Types of Casting. In *pit molding*, extremely large castings are molded in a deep pit. It takes several days or even a week to make a mold and complete the casting in a pit mold. In *centrifugal casting*, molds are rotated rapidly while the metal is being poured. The centrifugal force of the rotation forces the metal to the inner surface of the mold.

Three processes are used to make *precision castings:* (1) shell molding, (2) die casting, and (3) the lost wax

Sand Casting

Sand casting is one of the methods used to make castings. Some of the steps in sand casting are shown below. The mold for a casting is made by pressing a pattern into two beds of firmly packed sand. Each bed contains half a mold. The beds are matched and locked together tightly, *below left*. A worker then pours molten metal into the mold, *below right*. After the metal cools, the mold and casting are emptied onto a shakeout screen. The screen vibrates and the sand mold is shaken from the casting.

Osborn Manufacturing Co.

Link-Belt Co.

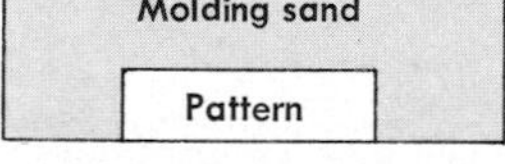

A Sand Mold is made from a pattern of the object to be cast. Damp sand is packed around the pattern in a wooden or metal box.

The Drag is the bottom half of the mold. It has a pouring gate and the mold cavity, which will be filled with metal.

The Cope is the top half of the mold. It has a pouring basin and a *sprue* (channel through which metal is poured).

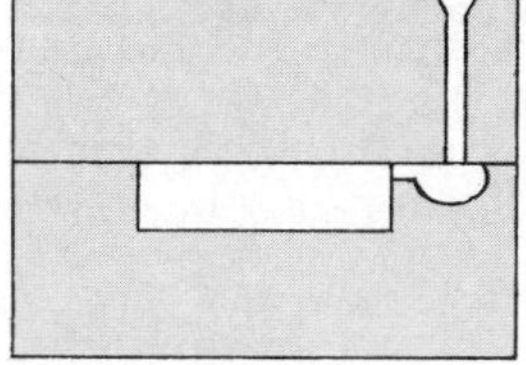

The Flask consists of the cope and the drag, which are fastened together. Molten metal is poured into the mold.

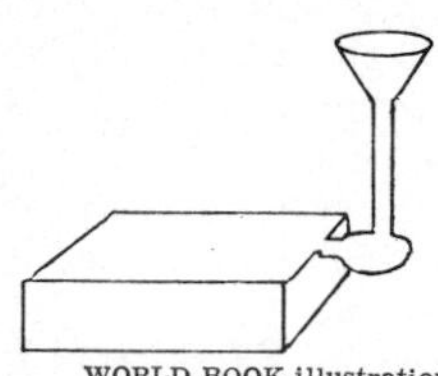

WORLD BOOK illustrations

The Casting has the same shape as the original pattern. The sprue is later removed from the casting.

The Lost Wax Process

The lost wax process is a method used to make *precision castings.* Precision castings are more accurate and have a better surface finish than sand castings. In the lost wax process, it is possible to make parts accurate up to $\frac{2}{1,000}$ inch (0.05 millimeter). Four basic steps in the lost wax process are shown below.

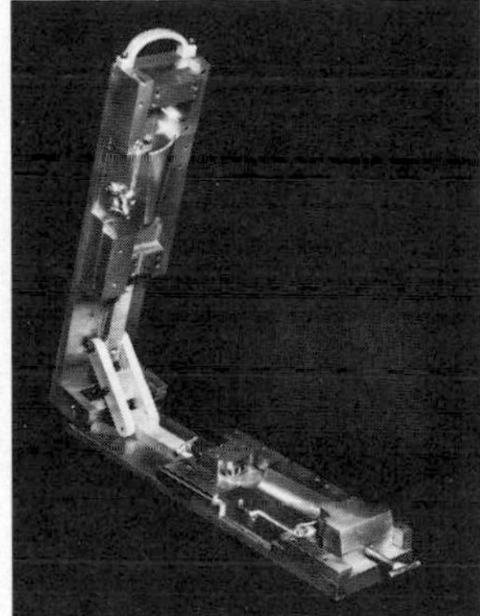

A Steel Die is used to make a wax pattern. Liquid wax is injected into the die and allowed to cool.

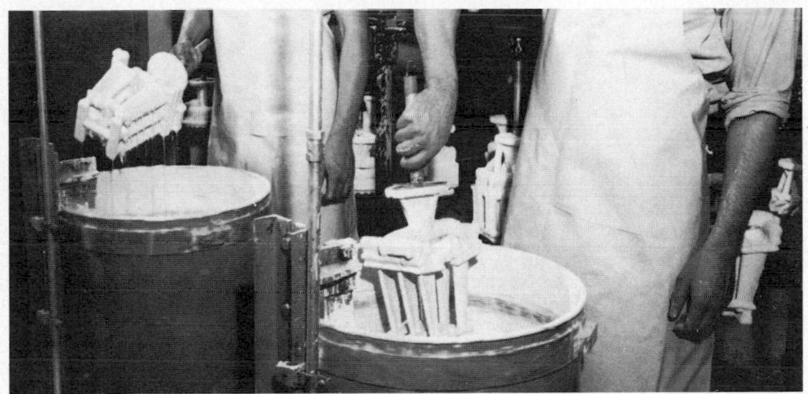

The Wax Pattern is removed from the die and used to make a mold. The patterns are dipped into a plasterlike material until they are covered with a thin coating, *above.* After the coating dries, it forms a hard finish that will not melt under high temperatures.

The Pattern Is Heated in a furnace to melt the wax from inside of the plaster shell. The wax runs out, leaving a precise mold.

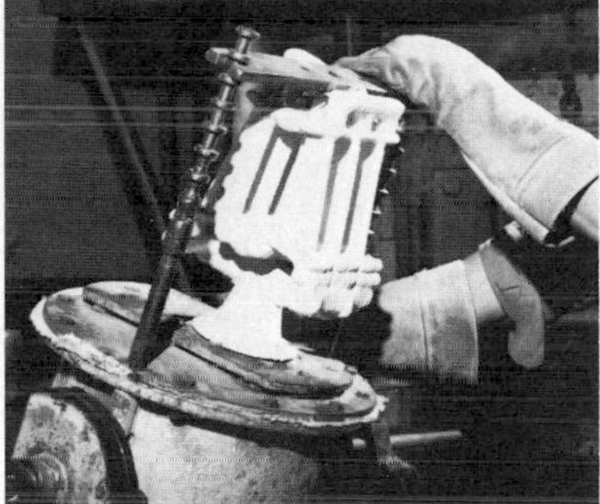

Hot Metal Is Poured into the mold. After the metal has cooled, the mold is broken away from the finished casting.

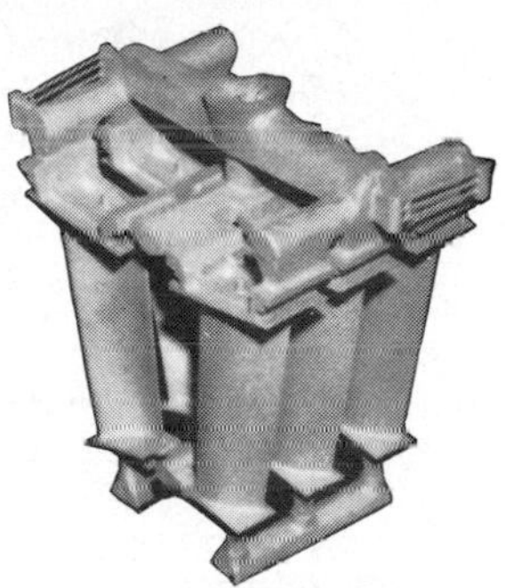

Misco Precision Casting Co.

The Finished Casting is a precise copy of the pattern made in the die.

process. In *shell molding*, the copes and drags are from $\frac{1}{4}$ to $\frac{1}{2}$ inch (6 to 13 millimeters) thick, and are held in place by clamps or weights. The pattern is heated and placed in the molding material. This material consists of fine sand and a plastic substance that holds the sand together when heat is applied. In *die casting*, the melted metal is forced into a mold, and the castings are removed when they cool. In the *lost wax process*, moist plaster of Paris is placed around a wax pattern. The mold is heated or baked, and the wax runs out, leaving a precise mold. This process is used to make dental plates and to shape metals that cannot be shaped by the usual factory methods.

William G. N. Heer

Related Articles in World Book include:

- Aluminum (Casting)
- Die and Diemaking
- Cast Iron
- Foundry
- Glass (How Glass Is Shaped; pictures)
- Iron and Steel (Cast Iron; Shaping and Finishing Steel)
- Plastics
- Pottery
- Sculpture (The Sculptor at Work)
- Silver (pictures)

CAST IRON is an iron that contains so much carbon that it cannot be shaped at any temperature. Commercial cast iron is an alloy of iron, carbon, and silicon, and contains small amounts of manganese, phosphorus, and sulfur. There are several different alloys. Cast iron is known for its hardness, brittleness, and heaviness. It is an important construction material, because it is cheap and can absorb great shocks. It is widely used for engine blocks and machinery frames.

William G. N. Heer

See also Iron and Steel (Cast Iron).

CASTALIA. See Parnassus.

CASTANETS, *KAS tuh NEHTS*, are a small percussion instrument of indefinite pitch. Each castanet is a spoon-shaped clapper made of a hard wood. In the original Spanish form, two castanets are tied together in pairs. A dancer carries a pair of castanets in each hand and clicks

Ludwig & Ludwig

Castanets are so called because they look like chestnuts, the Latin word for which is *castanea.*

them together to add a rhythmic accompaniment. For orchestral use, castanets are tied on both sides of a small wooden paddle, and the performer uses only one pair. The instrument is ancient and characteristically Spanish. THEODORE M. FINNEY

CASTE, *kast,* is a word from the Portuguese that means *family, strain,* or *race.* It usually refers to the groups of society into which the people of India are divided by religious laws. But in a general sense, it means a hereditary division of any society into classes on the basis of occupation, color, wealth, or religion.

India has a more firmly established *caste system* than any other country. It originated about 3,500 years ago when the Aryans came into India. The Aryans developed the caste system to control the Indians and keep them separate. However, the two racial groups mingled, and caste came to be based on means of livelihood.

Four castes were formed. Priests and scholars, who were supposed to establish and preserve the ideals of the nation, were the *Brahmans.* The rulers and warriors were called *Kshatriyas.* Artisans and merchants became the *Vaisyas.* Servants and laborers were called *Sudras.* All others who did not belong to any of these groups were called *pariahs,* or outcastes and "untouchables." Persons who committed serious crimes were made pariahs and called *Chandalas* (criminals).

As time went by, the castes became rigid social divisions. No one could rise to a higher caste than the one into which he or she was born. No marriages took place between castes. The Hindu legal code, called the *Code of Manu,* said that people would be born again into a higher caste, if they lived righteously and followed the code rigorously (see MANU).

Major castes later divided into subcastes. In southern India, more than 2,000 subcastes developed. As a result, the caste system, intended to stabilize and strengthen society, degenerated into class hatred and rigid division that hindered the progress of the entire Indian nation.

Buddhism, India's principal religion at one time, struck a blow at the caste system, because it taught universal brotherhood and love. Some courageous Hindu leaders, such as Mohandas K. Gandhi, disregarded caste rules in their effort to aid the outcastes. As a result of these efforts, the Indian Constitution of 1950 outlawed untouchability, and granted full social status to outcastes. In 1955, the government passed a law making discrimination against untouchables a punishable offense. GEORGE NOEL MAYHEW

See also BUDDHISM; GANDHI, MOHANDAS K.; HINDUISM.

CASTIGLIONE, *KAHS tee LYOH nay,* **BALDASSARE,** *BAHL dahs SAH ray* (1478-1529), was a writer of the Italian Renaissance. He is best known for *The Book of the Courtier* (completed about 1518), in which he set forth standards of conduct for the perfect courtier. This work is in the form of dialogues and has four sections. The first two sections are addressed to the courtier. The third deals with the requirements of the perfect court lady and her role in her husband's achievement of excellence. The fourth relates this excellence to the courtier's responsibility to his prince. Translations of the book became guides to social refinement in Spain, France, and England.

Castiglione was born near Mantua. He spent much of his life in the courts of Milan and Urbino. The Urbino court was the setting for *The Courtier.* ALDO S. BERNARDO

CASTILE AND ARAGON, *kas TEEL, AR uh gahn,* were two separate and powerful kingdoms of Spain. They were united in 1479 under the rule of Ferdinand and Isabella, the monarchs who later earned a place in American history through their association with Christopher Columbus. The combined territories formed the heart of the modern kingdom of Spain. Aragon extended over the northeastern part of the peninsula, and Castile occupied the greater part of present-day Spain, extending from the Bay of Biscay southward. Castile had always been a leader in the struggle against the Moors. The strength gained from its union with Aragon made possible the death blow to Moorish dominion in Europe (see MOORS). The language of Castile is still the literary language of Spain. The modern region of Castile is divided into Castile-Leon and Castile-La Mancha and subdivided into provinces. Aragon is divided into three provinces. WALTER C. LANGSAM

See also FERDINAND V; ISABELLA I; MADRID; SPAIN (History).

CASTILLA, *kahs TEE yah,* **RAMÓN,** *rah MAWN* (1797?-1867), one of Peru's great statesmen, served as president of Peru from 1845 to 1851 and from 1855 to 1862. A moderate liberal, he gave Peru its first period of peace and stability. He encouraged the guano and nitrate industries, railroads, and the telegraph. He abolished black slavery, extended suffrage, and ended payment of tribute by the Indians. Castilla was born in Tarapacá, Peru (now part of Chile). In 1821, he joined the independence forces in Peru led by General José de San Martín (see SAN MARTÍN, JOSÉ DE). See also PERU (The Early Republic). HAROLD EUGENE DAVIS

CASTILLO DE SAN MARCOS NATIONAL MONUMENT, *kas TEE yoh duh san MAHRK uhs,* is in Saint Augustine, Fla. It includes the oldest masonry fort in the continental United States. The Spaniards started its construction in 1672. The monument was established in 1924. It was formerly called Fort Marion National Monument. For area, see NATIONAL PARK SYSTEM (table: National Monuments).

CASTILLON DAM, *KAS tee YOHN,* is situated in the limestone gorge of the Verdon River in the southeastern section of France. It lies about 18 miles (29 kilometers) southwest of Puget Théniers. The dam is 325 feet (99 meters) high. It is 51 feet (16 meters) wide at the base, and 600 feet (183 meters) across at the crest. This arch-type dam forms a reservoir that can store about 109,000 acre-feet (134 million cubic meters) of water. There is a small hydroelectric power plant at the dam, and the dam also furnishes water for irrigation. Work began on the dam in 1926, but was stopped in 1930. Construction of the dam was resumed in 1945, and completed in 1948. See also DAM. ROBERT E. DICKINSON

CASTING. See CAST AND CASTING.

CASTING, in fishing. See FISHING (Reels).

CASTLE was the home and stronghold of a feudal lord during the Middle Ages. The word *castle* comes from the Latin *castellum,* meaning *fort.*

Castles became important in feudal times, when Europe was in a state of almost constant warfare and the people needed protection. A castle served as home and fortress, prison, armory, treasure house, and center

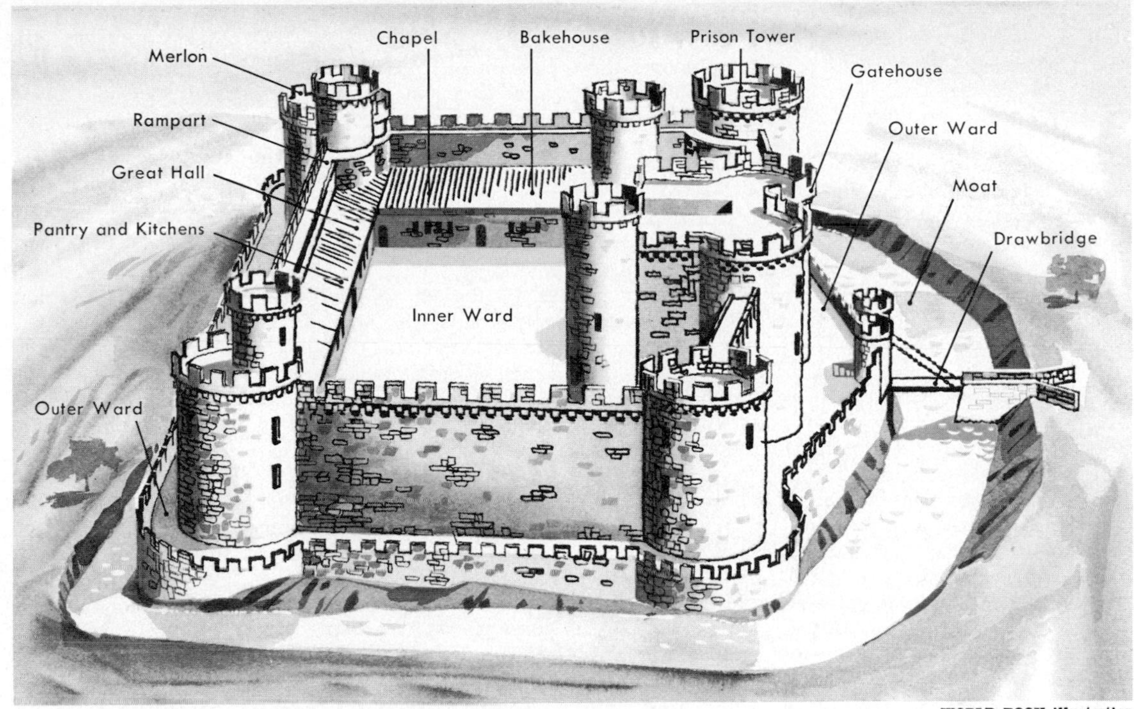

WORLD BOOK Illustration

A Castle Built in Europe had high, stone walls. The lord and his family lived in the gatehouse, the strongest part of the castle. A donjon or keep was the strongest part of many earlier castles.

of local government. Villages often grew up around castles. Later, when towns became important, castles became part of a town's defenses. See FEUDALISM.

Defense of a castle depended on its position. Some castles were built on top of steep hills. Others were built on level ground. In Anglo-Saxon England, earthworks protected the earliest castles, which were built partly of wood. In the 1000's and 1100's, the Normans built heavy walls around their castles. Norman castles were called *motte and bailey* because a *bailey* (walled court) was built at the foot of a *motte* (natural or artificial hill). A *moat* (deep ditch filled with water) surrounded the castle. A *drawbridge*, which could be raised, lay across the moat.

The outer walls of the castle were crowned by *battlements* (defensive walls). The solid parts of the battlements, called *merlons*, protected defenders who stood behind them. Open spaces between the merlons were

Aerofilms Ltd.

Pickering Castle in northern England had living quarters in a tower that was built on a high mound in the center of the court.

Burton Holmes, Ewing Galloway

Turreted Alcazar Castle towers over Segovia, Spain. Kings of Castile and Leon once lived in this fairy-tale castle.

called *embrasures*. Battlements projected out over the walls, and defenders could drop stones or boiling liquids on attackers through holes in the floors. The defenders stood on ledges called *ramparts*, which ran along the inside of the battlements. People hurled arrows, spears, and rocks through narrow slits in the towers that stood at intervals along the walls. A *portcullis* (armored gate) protected the main entrance of the castle.

The strongest part of the castle was the *donjon* or *keep*, a high towerlike structure with thick walls. It could be easily defended even if the rest of the castle was captured or destroyed. The feudal lord and his family lived on the upper floor of the keep. The servants and a garrison of soldiers usually lived on the first floor. The basement contained wells and storage space.

Europeans who went to Asia Minor during the first four crusades later adopted the principles used in Byzantine fortresses in building European castles. A crusader castle had a second and a third wall within the main defensive walls. Round projecting towers were placed at strategic points along the walls. In some of these later castles, a huge gatehouse replaced the keep as the strongest part of the castle.

In the later Middle Ages, a castle became more of a stately home than a fort. Builders then preserved the fortifications merely for tradition. BRYCE LYON

For more pictures of castles, see CRUSADES; SPAIN; WINDSOR CASTLE; DENMARK; GERMANY. See also CHÂTEAU; MIDDLE AGES.

Additional Resources

ANDERSON, WILLIAM. *Castles of Europe: From Charlemagne to the Renaissance*. Random House, 1970. Heavily illustrated vol. covering the development of castles.

BURKE, JOHN F. *Life in the Castle in Medieval England*. Rowman & Littlefield, 1978. Describes castles and castle life in the context of medieval society.

GIES, JOSEPH and FRANCES. *Life in a Medieval Castle*. Harper, 1974. Emphasis on the architecture and the interior.

LONG, ROBERT P. *Castle Hotels of Europe: Ancient Castles, Abbeys, Baronial Mansions, Ancestral Homes, Chateaux, and Palaces in Western Europe Which Offer Hotel Accommodations*. 5th ed. The Author, 1977.

CASTLE CLINTON NATIONAL MONUMENT is in New York City. It was originally a fort that was built to defend New York City during the War of 1812. The fort served as military headquarters for the United States Army in New York during the war.

In 1815, the fort was named Castle Clinton in honor of De Witt Clinton, then mayor of New York City. It was later named Castle Garden and used as an entertainment center. Beginning in 1855, it served as an immigration station, and from 1896 until 1941, it was the site of the New York Aquarium. The monument was established in 1946. For area, see NATIONAL PARK SYSTEM (table: National Monuments).

CASTLEREAGH, *KASuhlray*, **VISCOUNT** (1769-1822), was a noted British statesman. He served as both foreign secretary and leader of the House of Commons from 1812 to 1822. He worked out many of the peace settlements at the Congress of Vienna in 1815, and later allied Britain with the small states of Europe. See VIENNA, CONGRESS OF.

Castlereagh was born Robert Stewart in County Down, Ireland (now Castlereagh District, Northern Ireland). He studied at Cambridge University. He persuaded the Irish Parliament to unite with the English Parliament in 1800, and served in the united Parliament from 1801 until his death. Castlereagh served as war secretary in 1805 and from 1807 to 1809. He resigned in 1809 after he wounded Foreign Secretary George Canning in a duel over a war policy. Castlereagh's mind gave way under strain in 1822, and he committed suicide. VERNON F. SNOW

CASTOR AND POLLUX were twin heroes in Greek mythology. They are often called the *Dioscuri*, which means the *sons of Zeus* (Jupiter). Yet it was said that only Pollux was Zeus' son, and that Castor was the son of Tyndareus, the husband of their mother Leda. Helen of Troy and Clytemnestra were their sisters. The two brothers were good companions and became, as gods, patrons of athletes and protectors of sailors at sea. Castor and Pollux had power over winds and waves.

They quarreled with their cousins, Idas and Lynceus. Idas killed Castor. Then Pollux and Zeus killed Idas and Lynceus. Pollux, an immortal as the son of Zeus, begged to die so that he would not be separated from his brother. They were placed together in the sky in the constellation *Gemini*, or *The Twins*. Another version of the story is that the brothers spend one day in heaven, and then descend the next day into the lower world. JOSEPH FONTENROSE

CASTOR OIL is a colorless oil that is used as a laxative. When fresh, it is clear and sticky. Castor oil gently irritates the walls of the intestines and causes them to function. If used too frequently, it may cause constipation. Castor oil is used as a medicine, but a large number of industrial processes use most of the supply.

The castor-oil plant grows in many tropical countries, especially Brazil and India. The plant grows up to 30 feet (9.1 meters) high in tropical climates. In colder climates, the plant grows no more than 15 feet (4.6 meters) high. The spiny *beans* (fruits) contain the seeds. The seed is extremely poisonous if eaten. Industry uses castor oil in the preparation of certain foods and in the manufacture of paints and dyes. It is also used as a lubricant for boat and airplane engines.

Scientific Classification. The castor-oil plant belongs to the spurge family, *Euphorbiaceae*. It is genus *Ricinus*, species *R. communis*. AUSTIN SMITH

Spencer Kellogg and Sons

Castor-Oil Plants bear spiny fruits that contain the oil-producing beans. Much castor oil comes from Brazil and India.

CASTRATION. See CAT (Birth Control); DOG (Social and Moral Responsibilities); PET (Birth Control).

CASTRIES, *ka STREE* or *KAHS trees* (pop. 47,000), is the capital and largest city of St. Lucia, an island country in the Caribbean Sea. The city borders a fine harbor on the northwest coast of the country.

Castries has a busy port, which plays an important role in the nation's economy. Fires almost destroyed Castries in 1948 and 1951. It has since been rebuilt into a new community. Modern commercial and government buildings line the streets of the business district. Unlike most Caribbean cities, Castries has few slums.

French settlers founded Castries in 1651. From the 1600's to 1814, France and Great Britain fought for possession of St. Lucia. Britain governed the island from 1814 to 1979, when St. Lucia became an independent nation. THOMAS G. MATHEWS

CASTRO, FIDEL (1926-), became the dictator of Cuba in 1959, when he overthrew the military dictatorship of Fulgencio Batista. Castro promised freedom for the Cuban people, but he has changed Cuba into a Communist state. Tall and bearded, Castro became famous for his long, fiery anti-American speeches.

Castro was born Fidel Castro Ruz in Oriente Province, Cuba. He graduated from the University of Havana with a Doctor of Laws degree in 1950. While at the university, Castro became a popular student leader and entered Cuban politics. On July 26, 1953, he tried to start a revolution against the Batista government by attacking the Moncada Army Barracks in Santiago de Cuba. Castro's attack with a band of about 170 young followers failed. He was captured and sentenced to 15 years in prison. But Batista released him in 1955, and Castro went into exile in Mexico.

Castro then organized the *26th of July Movement*, training a small rebel force near Mexico City. On Dec. 1, 1956, he invaded Cuba with about 80 rebels. Many were killed, and the survivors fled to the Sierra Maestra mountains. The group grew as supporters from the surrounding countryside joined the movement. The band hid in the mountains and waged guerrilla warfare until Batista fled from Cuba on Jan. 1, 1959. Castro then became head of the Cuban government.

Castro's government seized property owned by Americans, other foreigners, and wealthy Cubans. The United States stopped buying Cuban sugar and finally ended all relations with Cuba. Castro turned to Russia for economic and military aid, and declared himself a Communist. He built a strong military force that defeated an invading band of Cuban exiles at the Bay of Pigs in 1961, and he boasted of starting revolutions in other Latin-American countries.

Castro provided improved education, housing, and health facilities in Cuba. But the Cuban economy lagged despite the economic aid from Russia. THOMAS G. MATHEWS

See also CUBA (The Castro Revolution); KENNEDY, JOHN FITZGERALD (Foreign Affairs).

Owen Franken, Sygma

Fidel Castro

Additional Resources

GONZALEZ, EDWARD. *Cuba Under Castro: The Limits of Charisma*. Houghton, 1974.

HALPERIN, MAURICE. *The Rise and Decline of Fidel Castro: An Essay in Contemporary History*. Univ. of California Press, 1972. *The Taming of Fidel Castro*. 1981. Traces how Castro changed from an independent rebel to a pro-Soviet head of state.

MARTIN, LIONEL. *The Early Fidel: Roots of Castro's Communism*. Lyle Stuart, 1978.

CASTRO, RAUL HECTOR (1916-), served as governor of Arizona from 1975 to 1977. Castro, a Democrat, was the first Mexican American to hold that office. In 1977, President Jimmy Carter appointed Castro to serve as U.S. ambassador to Argentina.

Castro was born in Cananea, Mexico. His family moved to Pirtleville, Ariz., in 1926, and Castro became a United States citizen in 1939. He graduated from Arizona State Teachers' College (now Northern Arizona University) in 1939 and earned a law degree from the University of Arizona in 1949.

From 1949 to 1955, Castro practiced law in Tucson, Ariz., and served as an assistant attorney for Pima County. He became county attorney in 1955 and was judge of the Pima County Superior Court from 1959 to 1964.

Marltow Photography

Raul H. Castro

Castro served as United States ambassador to El Salvador from 1964 to 1968 and ambassador to Bolivia from 1968 to 1969. He opened a law office in Tucson in 1969 and practiced there until he was elected governor of Arizona. GUY HALVERSON

CASTRO, ROSALÍA DE. See SPANISH LITERATURE (Romanticism).

CASWELL, HOLLIS LELAND (1901-), an American educator, became an authority on curriculum planning in schools. He directed surveys of curriculum practices in a number of school systems and wrote several books on the subject.

Caswell was born in Woodruff, Kans. He graduated from the University of Nebraska and Teachers College, Columbia University. Caswell taught and conducted research at George Peabody College for Teachers from 1929 to 1937. He joined the staff at Teachers College in 1937, and he served as president of Teachers College from 1954 to 1962. Caswell became a member of the editorial advisory board of THE WORLD BOOK ENCYCLOPEDIA in 1936. He served as chairman of the editorial advisory board from 1948 to 1966. DOUGLAS SLOAN

Fabian Bachrach

Hollis L. Caswell

Hediye Kerman

A Kitten Staring Curiously at a Vase

Pete Pearson, Van Cleve Photography

A Cat Hunting in a Field

© Hans Reinhard

A Tabby Clawing at a Tree

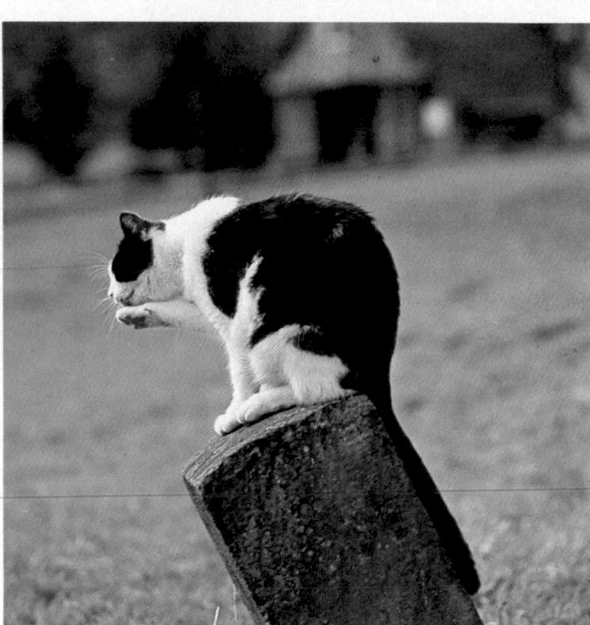

© Hans Reinhard

A Cat Washing Itself

CAT

CAT is a favorite pet of people around the world. Cats are intelligent and have an independent nature. These small animals can also be playful and entertaining. Many cats make affectionate, loyal pets, providing companionship for people of all ages. Cats rank second only to dogs in popularity as pets. About 40 million cats are kept as pets in the United States. About 2 million pet cats live in Canada.

The word *cat* also refers to a family of meat-eating animals that includes tigers, lions, leopards, and panthers. This family also includes *domestic cats*—that is, those that people keep as pets. Domestic cats and their wild relatives share many characteristics. All have long, powerful bodies and somewhat rounded heads. They have short, strong jaws equipped with 30 sharp teeth. Members of the cat family are skillful hunters. They are able to catch other animals by approaching them swiftly and quietly on padded feet. Or they may wait motionless until an animal comes close and then spring upon it suddenly.

This article deals with domestic cats. These animals have many special physical abilities. They see better in dim light than people do. They can climb trees, run at a high speed, and leap long distances. Cats also have a keen sense of balance and can easily walk along the tops of narrow fences or along narrow ledges. When cats fall, they almost always land on their feet.

Terri McGinnis, the contributor of this article, is a veterinarian and the author of The Well Cat Book. *She also writes "Ask the Vet," a column on pets in* Family Health Magazine.

Cats vary in personality and in certain physical features, such as the length and color of their coats. There are many breeds of cats. Special characteristics set each breed apart from all others. Among the favorite breeds are the Siamese and the Persian.

No one knows exactly when the first cats were tamed. But some authorities believe cats were tamed about 5,000 years ago. Throughout history, people have valued cats for their skill at hunting and killing mice, rats, and snakes. Cats help keep farms, homes, and businesses free of these pests. The ancient Egyptians considered cats sacred. Today, people in many societies believe cats bring good fortune. But some people associate cats with bad luck and so fear them. Many people find cats mysterious because they move swiftly and silently and because their eyes seem to glow in the dark.

The grace and beauty of cats have made them favorite subjects of artists throughout history. Cats have also been featured in almost every type of literature. They appear in the mythology of ancient Greece and Rome. Hundreds of years ago, Oriental writers praised cats in their stories and poems. Cats are also commonly mentioned in the fairy tales, folklore, and legends of many countries. In modern times, books, comic strips, motion pictures, and television programs have featured these popular animals.

The Body of a Cat

Body Size and Structure. Adult cats average about 8 to 10 inches (20 to 25 centimeters) tall at the shoulder. Most cats weigh from 6 to 15 pounds (2.7 to 7 kilograms). But some cats weigh more than 20 pounds (9 kilograms).

Cats have the same basic skeleton and internal organs as human beings and other meat-eating mammals. The skeleton of a cat has about 250 bones. The exact number of bones varies, depending on the length of the cat's tail. The skeleton serves as a framework that supports and protects the tissues and organs of a cat's body. Most of the muscles attached to the skeleton are long, thin, and flexible. They enable a cat to move with great ease and speed. Cats can run about 30 miles (48 kilometers) per hour.

The arrangement of the bones and the joints that connect them permits a cat to perform a variety of movements. Unlike many animals, a cat walks by moving the front and rear legs on one side of its body at the same time, and then the legs on the other side. As a result, a cat seems to glide. Its hip joint enables a cat to leap easily. Other special joints allow a cat to turn its head to reach most parts of its body.

A cat has five toes on each forepaw, including a thumblike toe called a *dewclaw*. Each hindpaw has four toes. Some cats have extra toes. Each of a cat's toes ends in a sharp, hooklike claw. The claws usually are *retracted* (held back) under the skin by elastic ligaments, which are a type of connective tissue. However, when the claws are needed, certain muscles quickly pull the *tendons* (cordlike tissues) connected to the claws. This action extends the claws. A cat uses its claws in climbing, in catching prey, and in defending itself. Several spongy pads of thick skin cover the bottoms of a cat's feet. The pads cushion the paws and enable a cat to move quietly.

A cat's tail is an extension of its backbone. The flexible tail helps a cat keep its balance. When a cat falls, it whips the tail and twists its body so that it lands on its feet.

Head. A cat's head is small and has short, powerful jaws. Kittens have about 26 needlelike temporary teeth, which they shed by about 6 months of age. Adult cats have 30 teeth, which are used for grasping, cutting, and shredding food. Unlike human beings, cats have no teeth for grinding food. But a cat's stomach and intestines can digest chunks of unchewed food. Tiny hooklike projections called *papillae* cover a cat's tongue, making it rough. The rough surface helps a cat lick meat from bones and groom its coat.

A cat has a small, wedge-shaped nose. The tip is covered by a tough layer of skin called *nose leather*.

WORLD BOOK illustration by James Teason and John D. Dawson

The Skeleton of a Cat

The body of a cat includes about 250 bones. The exact number of bones varies, depending on how long a cat's tail is. The skeleton supports and protects the tissues and organs of the body.

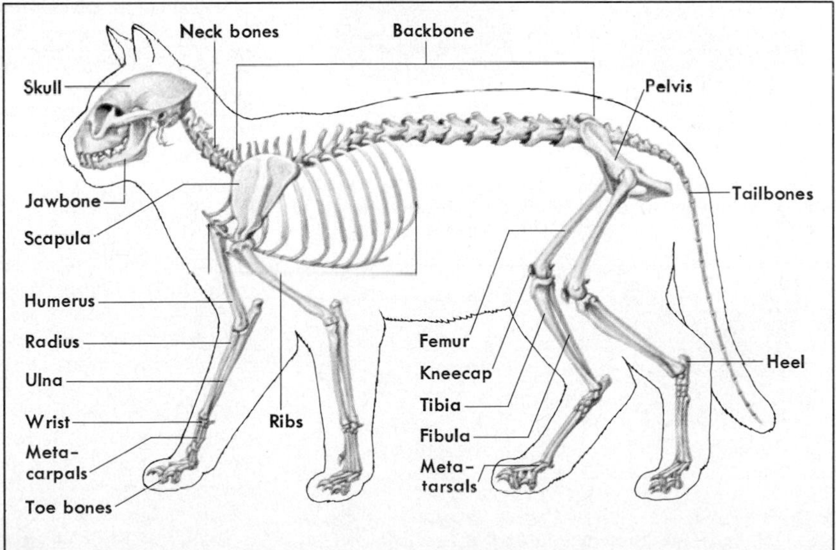

The Paws of a Cat

Spongy footpads, *right,* enable a cat to walk quietly. Each of a cat's toes ends in a sharp, hooked claw. When retracted, *below left,* the claws are held under the skin by ligaments. The claws extend when muscles tighten the tendons, *below right.*

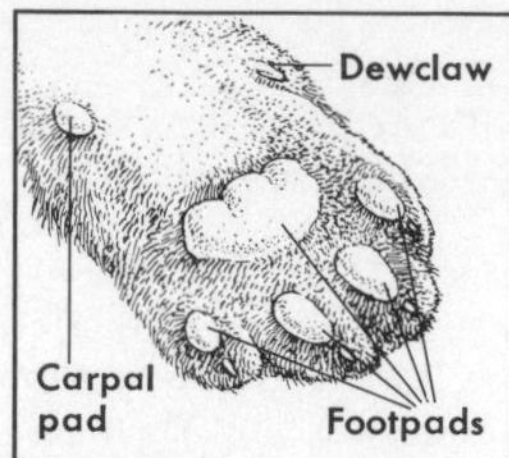

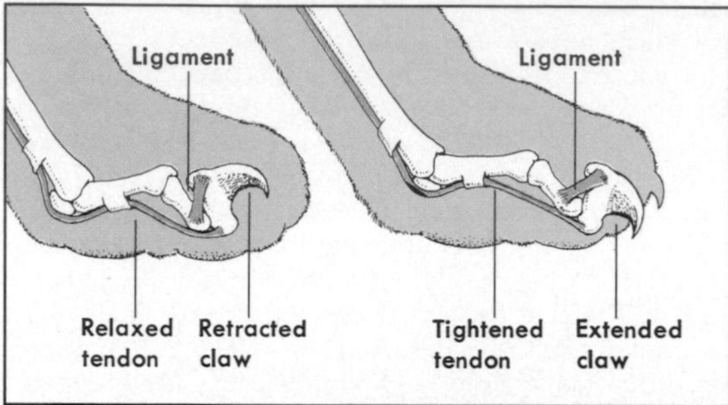

WORLD BOOK illustrations by John D. Dawson

The nose leather may be various colors. It is usually moist and cool. A sick cat may have a warm, dry nose.

The colored part of a cat's eyes, called the *iris,* may be various shades of green, yellow, orange, copper, blue, or lavender. *Odd-eyed* cats have irises of different colors. For example, one eye may be green and the other blue. Muscles in the iris control the amount of light that enters a cat's eye through an opening called the *pupil.* In bright light, the iris protects the eye from glare by making the pupil contract and form a vertical slit. In dim light, the pupils widen and so permit more light to enter.

The Eyes of a Cat

The illustrations below show some of the special features of a cat's eyes. Cats can see well in normal and dim light.

WORLD BOOK illustrations by Keith Freeman

Narrowing of the Pupils in bright light allows less light into the eyes.

Widening of the Pupils in dim light permits more light to enter the eyes.

A Third Eyelid, in the inner corner of each eye, protects and lubricates the eyes.

Irises of Different Colors are a feature of *odd-eyed cats.* The cats have normal vision.

At the back of each eye, a cat has a special mirror-like structure called the *tapetum lucidum.* This structure reflects light and so helps a cat see in dim light. It also produces *eyeshine,* the glow a person sees when light strikes the eyes of a cat at night. Each of a cat's eyes has a third eyelid at the inner corner. This structure, called the *nictitating membrane,* protects and lubricates the eyes.

A cat's ears are near the top of its skull. Each ear can move independently. A cat can aim the cup of its ears in the direction from which a sound is coming and so improve its hearing.

Coat. A cat's coat protects its skin and provides insulation. The coats of most cats have two types of hairs. The outer part of the coat is made up of long, stiff *primary,* or *guard,* hairs. The undercoat consists of softer and shorter *secondary,* or *down,* hairs. The color, length, and texture of the coat vary greatly among cats. The terms commonly used to describe the color of a cat's coat are *solid* or *self, smoke, shaded, tabby, parti-color,* and *colorpoint.*

Solid, or self, coats have only one color. The solid colors are black, *blue* (dark gray), brown, *cream* (tan), *lilac* (light gray), *red* (shades of orange), and white.

Smoke coats consist of a white undercoat covered by guard hairs of a dark color. In most cases, the guard hairs are black, blue, or red.

Shaded coats are similar to smoke coats except that the dark color is limited to the tips of the guard hairs. *Chinchilla* is a type of shaded coat that has a sparkling appearance because only the extreme tips of the guard hairs are dark. Red chinchilla coats are sometimes called *shell cameos.*

Tabby coats are symmetrically patterned with stripes and blotches of a dark color on a lighter background. The patterns are formed by bands of a dark color on individual hairs. Tabby colors include blue, brown, cream, red, and silver. *Mackerel* tabbies have extremely narrow markings.

Parti-color coats have two or more clearly defined colors, such as black and white or blue and cream. *Tortoise-shell* coats are black, red, and cream. *Calico* coats have patches of white, black, red, and cream.

Colorpoint coats consist of a solid color over the trunk of the body and a contrasting color on the *points.* The points include the face, ears, feet, and tail.

Senses. A cat's vision is not as keen as that of a human being. Cats see most colors as various shades of gray. However, they can detect the slightest motion, which is helpful in hunting. They see well in dim light but cannot see in total darkness.

Cats have a highly developed sense of smell. Newborn kittens, for example, are able to recognize their nest by scent alone. In addition to its nose, a cat has another sense organ in its mouth that detects scents.

Cats also have a keen sense of hearing. They hear a much broader range of sounds than people do. Deafness is rare among cats. However, it is an inherited defect among some white cats, particularly those with blue or odd-color eyes.

The whiskers of a cat are special hairs that serve as highly sensitive touch organs. These hairs, called *vibrissae* or *tactile hairs,* grow on the chin, at the sides of the face, and above the eyes. The hairs are attached to nerves in the skin, which transmit signals to the brain when the whiskers brush against objects. The whiskers may help a cat protect its eyes, feel its way in the dark, and detect changes in wind direction.

Breeds of Cats

The many breeds of cats vary greatly in appearance. Cat breeders have developed numerous breeds by selectively mating animals with certain desirable and distinctive characteristics. These characteristics appear consistently in the offspring of *purebred* cats. A purebred cat is one whose mother and father belong to the same breed. The offspring of cats that have mated randomly are known as *crossbreds* or *alley cats*.

Many people prefer the special features of a certain breed of cats. For example, such purebreds as the Abyssinian and the Birman are among the most beautiful and unusual animals in the world. But crossbreds may be just as beautiful and lovable as purebreds.

Certain associations officially recognize cat breeds and establish standards for the ideal characteristics of each breed. However, different cat associations recognize different breeds, and breed standards also vary somewhat. In the United States, cat breeds are commonly divided into two major groups: (1) short-haired breeds and (2) long-haired breeds.

Short-Haired Breeds. Most cat associations in the United States commonly recognize 10 short-haired breeds. They are the (1) Abyssinian, (2) American Shorthair, (3) Burmese, (4) Havana Brown, (5) Japanese Bobtail, (6) Korat, (7) Manx, (8) Rex, (9) Russian Blue, and (10) Siamese.

Abyssinian is a slender, muscular, medium-sized cat with a long, tapering tail. *Aby* cats, as they are sometimes called, have a rounded, wedge-shaped head and large, pointed ears. Their almond-shaped eyes may be green or gold. These cats are known for their melodic voices and their *agouti* coat pattern, which is common in wild animals. Each hair of an Aby's soft coat has two or three bands of alternating light and dark colors. The coat may have red and chocolate bands, or reddish-brown and black or dark brown bands.

Abyssinians have been bred in Ethiopia (formerly called Abyssinia) for thousands of years. Many people believe the quiet, graceful Aby is descended directly from the sacred cats of ancient Egypt.

American Shorthair, also called the *Domestic Shorthair*, is the best known breed of cats. American Shorthairs resemble many alley cats but are purebreds. The American Shorthair is a muscular, medium- to large-sized animal. Its large head features full cheeks; a broad, squarish muzzle; large, round eyes; and rounded, medium-sized ears. The coat and eyes may be any color. The breed probably developed from cats originally brought to the American Colonies by Europeans. The *British Shorthair* is similar to the American Shorthair but is stockier and has a thicker coat.

The Coats of Cats The coats of cats vary in color and pattern, as shown in the illustrations below. Most cats have an undercoat of short, soft *down* hairs and an outer coat of longer, stiffer *guard* hairs.

WORLD BOOK illustrations by Keith Freeman

A Solid Coat has only one color, such as the red coat shown above. Other common solid colors are black, cream, and white.

A Smoke Coat consists of a white undercoat covered by dark guard hairs. This cat has a blue smoke coat.

A Shaded Coat is white with a dark color on the tips of the guard hairs. This cat has a silver chinchilla coat.

A Tabby Coat has patterns of dark stripes and blotches on a lighter ground color. A brown tabby is shown above.

A Parti-Color Coat consists of two or more clearly defined colors. This calico cat has white, black, red, and cream patches.

A Colorpoint Coat has a solid color on the trunk of the body and a contrasting color on the face, ears, feet, and tail.

Short-Haired Breeds

The pictures below show some of the most common short-haired breeds of cats. The short coats of these animals vary greatly, ranging from the tight curls of the Rex to the thick, plush fur of the Russian Blue. The breeds also differ in other physical features. For example, the Siamese has a wedge-shaped head, slender body, and tapering tail; and the Manx has a round head, muscular body, and no tail.

All photos on this page, unless otherwise credited, are WORLD BOOK photos by Alice Su.

Rex

Russian Blue

Burmese

Havana Brown

WORLD BOOK photo

Korat

Siamese

Manx

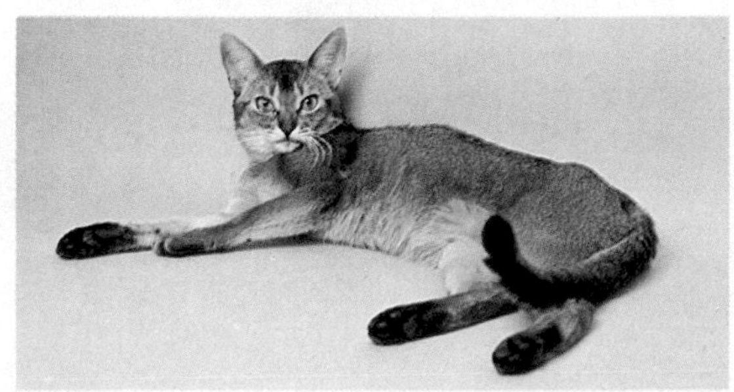

Abyssinian

Long-Haired Breeds

The pictures below show some of the most common long-haired breeds of cats. The coats of these cats differ in color, length, and texture. The breeds also vary in body size and shape. The large, muscular Maine Coon has an almost rectangular shape. The Persian and the Himalayan are both stocky animals. The Balinese and the Turkish Angora have a long, slender body.

All photos on this page, unless otherwise credited, are WORLD BOOK photos by Alice Su.

Maine Coon

Birman

Persian

Balinese

Somali

WORLD BOOK photo

Himalayan

Turkish Angora

Burmese is a medium-sized animal with a muscular body. The cat has a very short, sleek, dark brown coat and round, golden eyes. The breed was developed from a female cat named Wong Mau, which was brought to the United States from Burma in 1930.

Havana Brown is so named because its coat has the reddish-brown color of Havana cigars. The cat has medium-length fur and a medium-sized body. Its long head features oval green eyes. The breed resulted from the crossbreeding of Russian Blues, Siamese, and other short-haired cats. In Great Britain, where Havana Browns were developed in the 1950's, the breed is also called *Chestnut Brown*.

Japanese Bobtail has a short, rigid tail with bushy hair. This slender, medium-sized animal has been raised in Japan for hundreds of years. Some Japanese believe the Bobtail brings good luck. Many works of art portray this cat seated with a paw raised in greeting.

The Bobtail has a triangular head with a long nose, slanted eyes, and large ears. Its medium-length, silky fur may be any color. But the traditional "good luck" color is white with patches of red and black.

Korat is a quiet, gentle animal that originated in Thailand, where it is believed to bring good luck. It is a muscular, medium-sized cat with a rounded back. The Korat has a heart-shaped face and large green eyes. Its short, silvery-gray coat lies flat.

Manx is named for the Isle of Man in the Irish Sea, where the breed originated. There are four varieties of Manx cats—*rumpy*, *rumpy-riser*, *stumpy*, and *longie*. The most common is the rumpy, which is the only kind of cat without a tail. The cat has a notch where the tail would normally be. The rumpy-riser has a short knot at the tail base. The stumpy has an extremely short tail, and the rare longie has a full-length tail.

The playful Manx has a small body with a round head, broad chest, arched back, and high rump. The heavily muscled rear legs are longer than the front legs. The cat runs with a rabbitlike hop. Its coat and eyes may be any color.

Rex has short, tightly curled fur. The cat's soft, silky coat has no visible guard hairs. The Rex is a slender, small- to medium-sized animal. It has an arched back, tapering tail, and thin legs. Its small, narrow head features a curved nose and large ears. Rex cats vary in the color of their coat and eyes. The breed originated in Great Britain about 1950.

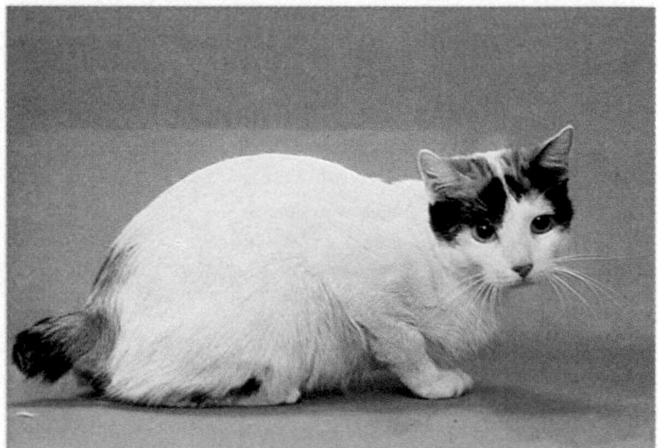

WORLD BOOK photo

The Japanese Bobtail has a short, bushy tail. This cat has been a symbol of good luck in Japan for hundreds of years.

Russian Blue has short, extremely thick, bluish-gray fur that is unlike the fur of any other cat. The plush coat seems to glitter because the guard hairs are silver-tipped. The Russian Blue has a large, muscular body and a long tail. It moves gracefully on long legs. The cat's wedge-shaped head features large ears, a flat forehead, and round green eyes. Despite its name, the origin of this breed is unclear. Some people believe sailors brought the animal from Russia to England and the Scandinavian countries.

Siamese is the most popular short-haired cat. It is best known for its fine, glossy colorpoint coat. The Siamese is a loving pet that seems less independent than other breeds. Siamese cats often utter loud, mournful meows until they get attention.

The Siamese has a long, slender, medium-sized body and a thin tail. Its legs are slim and its paws small. The cat's long, wedge-shaped head has straight sides and large, pointed ears. Its eyes are almond-shaped and deep blue. The fur on the trunk of the cat's body is a solid light color. The points are one of four colors—blue, chocolate, lilac, or *seal* (dark brown). Siamese kittens are born white but develop their adult color within a year. A *Colorpoint Shorthair* resembles a Siamese, but its points may be any color or pattern.

The Siamese originated in Thailand, which was formerly called Siam. There, these cats were royal property and guarded palaces and temples. In 1884, a pair of Siamese, Pho and Mia, were brought to Great Britain. Their offspring won many prizes at cat shows, and the breed soon gained worldwide popularity.

Long-Haired Breeds. Seven long-haired breeds of cats are commonly recognized in the United States. They are the (1) Balinese, (2) Birman, (3) Himalayan, (4) Maine Coon, (5) Persian, (6) Somali, and (7) Turkish Angora.

Balinese was developed from the Siamese and has the same body structure and coloring. But the fine, silky fur of the Balinese is about 2 inches (5 centimeters) long and has no undercoat. The hair on its long tail spreads out like a plume. The Balinese became an established breed in the United States during the 1960's.

Birman is a large, long-bodied cat with a bushy tail and short legs. Its head is round with a curved nose, blue eyes, and rounded ears. The cat's long, silky coat has a colorpoint pattern, except that the large, rounded paws are always white. The Birman is an affectionate animal. The breed originated in Burma, where it is considered sacred. The Birman is not related to the short-haired Burmese.

Himalayan is a cross between the Persian and the Siamese. It has the body and long coat of a Persian and the colorpoint pattern of a Siamese. The Himalayan may have points that are red, *tortie* (tortoise-shell), or one of the four Siamese point colors. Cat associations also recognize solid chocolate or lilac Himalayans. American and British breeders began to develop this cat in the 1930's.

Maine Coon, the largest cat, looks somewhat like a raccoon. Its heavy, silky coat is medium length and may be any color. Its fur falls smoothly over most of the body but is shaggy on the *ruff*, stomach, and tail.

WORLD BOOK photo

The Scottish Fold has ears that are folded forward. This stocky breed was developed in Scotland during the 1960's.

A ruff is a fringe of long hairs that circles the neck.

The broad, muscular body of the Maine Coon has an almost rectangular shape. Its head features a long nose and large eyes and ears. The cat stands on sturdy, medium-length legs. Tufts of fur cover its large, round paws, which are well suited to running across ice and snow. The breed developed in New England during the 1800's, probably as a result of matings between American Shorthairs and Turkish Angoras.

Persian is the most popular breed of long-haired cats. This animal has a stocky, medium- to large-sized body with short, strong legs. Its large, round head includes a snubbed nose; large, wide-set, round eyes; and small, rounded ears. The Persian is admired for its extremely long, fine-textured, glossy coat. Its fur stands out from the body and forms a large ruff and a full, brush-like tail. The coats of Persians vary in color and pattern. The solid white Persian has blue, copper, or odd-color eyes. Most other Persians have copper eyes.

The exact origin of the Persian is unknown. But the breed probably came from the Middle East. Persians have been carefully bred for hundreds of years to develop their present distinctive look.

Somali is like the Abyssinian in all ways except for its long, thick coat. Breeders in the United States developed this cat from the Aby during the mid-1900's.

Turkish Angora is one of the oldest breeds. The cat originated in Turkey and spread throughout Europe during the 1700's and 1800's. Beginning in the early 1900's, Angoras were commonly crossed with Persians. As a result, the pure Angora nearly became extinct. Only a few remained by the early 1960's. Then, cat breeders and officials of the zoo in Ankara, Turkey, established a breeding program that saved these cats.

The Turkish Angora has a long, slender body. Its tiny, wedge-shaped head includes a long nose and long ears. Its silky, medium-length hair forms slight waves on the stomach and big tufts on the ears and between the toes. The color of the coat and eyes varies.

Other Breeds. There are many other breeds of cats around the world. Some breeds are extremely rare and unusual. Other breeds are popular in only one country or area. Still others have been developed recently and have not yet gained wide recognition.

The rare *Sphynx*, or *Canadian Hairless*, has almost no hair. The Chinese *Lopear* cat has long, droopy ears. The *Chartreux* is a stocky, blue-coated shorthair common in France. The *Turkish Van*, an Angora-like cat, enjoys swimming. The *Cymric* is a long-haired version of the Manx. The elegant *Egyptian Mau* has a spotted coat. The *Scottish Fold* has a large, round head with folded ears.

The Life of a Cat

Most healthy cats live from 12 to 15 years. But many reach 18 or 19 years of age, and some have lived as long as 30 years.

Reproduction. A *queen* (female cat) can begin mating when it is between 5 and 9 months old, and a *tomcat* (male cat) can begin when it is between 7 and 10 months old. Tomcats can mate at any time. Queens mate only during a period of sexual excitement called *estrus* or *heat*. Estrus occurs several times a year and usually lasts from 3 to 15 days. If a queen is prevented from mating while she is in heat, she will probably come into heat again very soon. In most cases, this cycle recurs until she becomes pregnant.

The pregnancy period among cats lasts about nine weeks. When a queen is ready to give birth, she selects a quiet, safe spot as a nest. On the average, a queen bears from 3 to 5 kittens at a time. However, litters of more than 10 kittens have been reported. The mother can deliver the kittens herself with no human assistance, unless complications develop.

Most newborn kittens weigh about $3\frac{1}{2}$ ounces (99 grams). The mother licks the kittens and so dries them and stimulates their breathing and other body functions. Like other mammals, cats feed their young on milk produced by the mother's body. Newborn kittens cannot see or hear because their eyes and ears are sealed. They depend completely on their mother to nurse, clean, and protect them. The father cat plays no role in caring for the kittens.

Growth and Development. Healthy kittens show a steady, daily weight gain. Their eyes open from 10 to 14 days after birth. Soon afterward, their ears open and the first teeth begin to appear. Kittens start to walk and explore their environment at about 3 weeks of age. But the mother watches over them and retrieves kittens that stray too far from the nest.

By about 4 weeks of age, kittens have their full set of temporary teeth. They then begin to eat solid foods and to lap water. The mother usually begins to *wean* (stop nursing) them at about this age.

When kittens are about 4 weeks old, owners should begin to handle them frequently and play with them gently. Kittens that receive such attention tend to become good pets. They learn faster and have fewer behavior problems than kittens that are ignored or overprotected. A kitten that has contact with a variety of people will be less fearful of strangers and new situations as an adult. Kittens can even learn not to fear dogs if they are allowed to play with a friendly dog.

By about 6 weeks of age, kittens have a fully devel-

Edward O. King, Alpha

A Mother Cat Nurses Her Kittens, *above,* until they can eat solid foods. Healthy kittens show a steady weight gain.

© Hans Reinhard

A Mother Cat Carries a Kitten back to the nest if it strays too far, *above.* Kittens begin to walk at about 3 weeks of age.

oped brain and nervous system and can be safely separated from their mother. However, if possible, kittens should remain with their mother and littermates until they are 9 or 10 weeks old. Kittens develop important physical skills by playing with one another. They also learn to get along with other cats in this way. In addition, kittens learn many skills, especially hunting, by watching and imitating their mother. Most cats reach their adult body size at about 1 year of age.

Communication. Cats communicate with one another, with other animals, and with human beings in a variety of ways. Cats use sounds, body signals, and scents as means of communication.

Some experts estimate that a cat can make more than 60 different sounds, ranging from a soft purr to a loud wail, or *caterwaul.* Most of these sounds originate in the *larynx* (voice box) in the throat. But some scientists believe purring arises from vibrations in the wall of a blood vessel in the chest. The vibrations result when the speed of the blood flow increases.

The sounds a cat makes may have various meanings. For example, depending on the situation, a meow can be a friendly greeting, or it may express curiosity, hunger, or loneliness. Purring usually means contentment, but some cats also purr when they are sick. Hisses, growls, and screams indicate anger and fear.

Cats also communicate through various body and tail positions and facial expressions. A contented cat often lies on its chest with its eyes half closed. To invite play or petting, some cats roll over on one side and wave a paw in the air. However, a similar posture accompanied by extended claws, a direct stare, and ears folded back indicates a fearful cat ready to defend itself. A friendly cat may greet someone with its tail raised vertically. It may also bump its head against the person and lick an extended hand. An angry or frightened cat flicks its tail from side to side, arches its back, and puffs up its fur. A submissive cat crouches down, flattens its ears, and avoids direct eye contact.

Cats commonly communicate with one another by means of odors. Cats have scent glands on the forehead, around the mouth, and near the base of the tail. A cat rubs these glands against people and objects and so marks them with its scent. Only cats and a few other animals can smell these odors. A tomcat sprays urine on objects and so marks his mating territory. People as well as cats can smell the strong, unpleasant odor of the urine.

Caring for a Cat

Cats depend on their owners for shelter and protection. Owners are also responsible for feeding, grooming, training, and providing veterinary care for their pets. In addition, owners have an obligation to prevent their cats from mating if a good home cannot be provided for the kittens.

Feeding. Cats need a balanced diet. Such a diet supplies the proper amount of various nutrients, which provide energy and are essential for growth and replacement of body tissues. Cats require proteins, fats, vitamins, and minerals in their diet. The easiest way to meet a cat's nutritional needs is to buy high-quality commercial cat food. The label should indicate that the food is "complete and balanced." Cats should not be fed dog food because it does not meet their dietary requirements. A diet of only meat or mostly meat is also nutritionally unbalanced.

Cats are not naturally finicky eaters. But owners should give them a variety of commercial foods to prevent them from developing fussy appetites. Cats may occasionally be fed small amounts of such cooked foods as beef liver, eggs, fish, and vegetables. Many cats also enjoy milk, cheese, and other dairy products. However, such foods cause diarrhea in some cats. Owners should provide fresh drinking water at all times. Food and water bowls should be cleaned daily.

Kittens that have been weaned should be fed small amounts four times a day until they are 3 months old. They should eat three times daily until they are 6 months old, and then twice a day until they are full grown. Adult cats require only one meal a day, but many seem happier with two smaller meals. Food may be kept available at all times for a healthy cat that does not overeat. Sick cats, pregnant and nursing queens, and old cats often need special diets.

Grooming. Cats instinctively clean themselves. They do so by licking their fur with their tongue. They also rub and scratch their fur with their paws. At least once a day, a cat licks a paw and washes its face and head with the wet paw. However, not all cats groom themselves well.

Owners should brush or comb a cat's fur daily to

clean it and to remove loose hairs. In the case of long-haired cats, such care is essential to prevent the coat from tangling and matting. Daily brushing or combing also reduces the amount of loose hairs that cats swallow when they clean themselves. Swallowed hair may wad up and form a *hairball* in the cat's stomach. Hairballs can cause gagging, vomiting, and loss of appetite. If a cat cannot spit up a hairball, surgery may be required to remove it. Owners may feed their cat a small amount of mineral oil, petroleum jelly, or a commercial preparation once a week to prevent hairball formation. A veterinarian can suggest safe methods of administering such products. If necessary, owners may clean their cat's ears and teeth with a soft cloth. Owners may also trim the tips of a cat's claws.

Some cats—especially those allowed outdoors—become so soiled that they need a bath. Most cats dislike bathing and swimming. But if cats are bathed about once a month when they are kittens, they will become accustomed to water. Kittens also should be brushed or combed so that they will be easier to care for after they grow older.

Training should begin when a kitten is about 8 weeks old. A cat can learn to respond to its name. Some cats have been trained to walk on a leash and to do such tricks as shaking hands and retrieving a ball.

The most effective way to train a cat is with praise, petting, and food rewards for good behavior. Correct a cat immediately with a sharp "No" if it misbehaves. Always react to a particular action in the same manner so that the cat can learn what to expect. Owners should be patient with their pet and avoid using physical punishment. Squirting a cat with water is a good way to stop undesirable behavior.

Indoor cats should learn to use a litter box. Cats instinctively bury their body wastes, and so training them to use a litter box is easy. Kittens raised with a mother that uses a litter box will usually begin to use it themselves before they are 5 or 6 weeks old.

Any smooth-surfaced plastic or enamel pan can be used as a litter box. Put the pan in a quiet spot. Place a layer of commercial clay litter, sand, sawdust, shredded newspaper, or sterilized soil in the bottom. Sift the litter clean with a strainer each day. Clean the pan and change the litter whenever a third of the litter is damp or, at least, every fourth day. Most cats will not use a wet or dirty box.

Cats that have not learned to use a litter box at an early age must be trained. Place the cat in the box after it eats, when it wakes up, and after play. Praise the cat when it uses the box. The cat will soon learn to go to the box by itself.

Cats should also be trained to claw a scratching post instead of carpeting, draperies, and furniture. Cats naturally scratch at objects to pull off the worn outer layers of their claws and to mark their territory. A bark-covered log or a piece of wood covered with carpeting, cork, or fabric makes a good scratching post. Rub some *catnip*, a strongly scented herb that many cats love to sniff, into the post to attract the cat's interest. Guide the cat's front paws down the post. Whenever the cat begins to claw another object, correct the animal immediately and take it to the post. Some cats cannot be trained to use a post, however, and so some owners take their pet to a veterinarian for *declawing*. Declawing is a surgical procedure in which the claws are entirely removed from the paws. A declawed cat may have difficulty defending itself, and so the animal should not be allowed outdoors unattended.

Some cats enjoy chewing plants. But owners can train their cat to leave house plants alone, especially if they provide a pot of grass or oats for the pet.

Veterinary Care. A cat that is kept indoors faces fewer health risks than an outdoor cat. Outdoor cats may be struck by automobiles, poisoned by pesticides, or attacked by sick or unfriendly animals. But even indoor cats are not entirely safe. They can fall from open

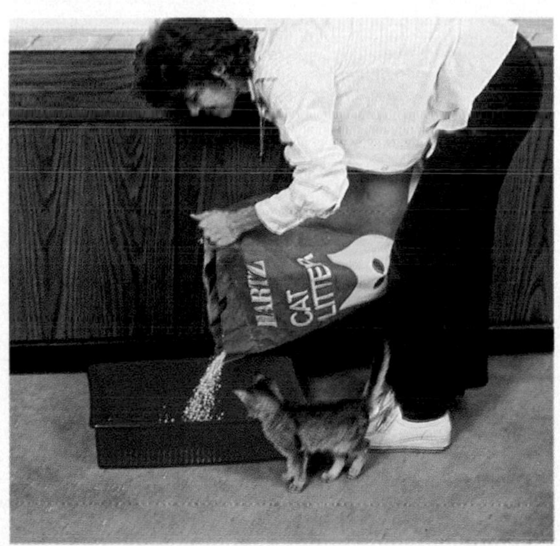

Caring for a Cat includes providing a clean litter box, *above*. Cats also need fresh water and a balanced diet.

WORLD BOOK photos

Training helps a cat become a good pet. Many cats can be trained to claw a scratching post, *above*, instead of furniture.

windows and unenclosed balconies. In addition, many cleaning products and certain houseplants, such as ivy and philodendron, are poisonous to cats. Owners should place such items out of the reach of cats.

Kittens should be taken to a veterinarian when they are about 8 to 10 weeks old for a physical examination. They should also receive vaccinations to protect them from common cat diseases. An adult cat should visit a veterinarian once a year for a checkup and additional shots. Veterinary care protects an owner's health as well as a cat's because some animal diseases can be transmitted to people. Such a disease is called a *zoonosis*.

Cat owners should learn to recognize signs of illness in their pet. A healthy cat has clean ears, clear eyes, a moist nose, pink tongue and gums, and a clean, glossy coat. Whenever a cat shows any change in appearance or behavior for more than 24 hours, the owner should consult a veterinarian.

One of the most serious and widespread cat diseases is *panleukopenia*, also called *feline enteritis* or *cat distemper*. This highly contagious infection is caused by a virus and is often fatal. Symptoms of panleukopenia include listlessness, loss of appetite, high fever, and severe vomiting and diarrhea. If a cat has several of these symptoms, call a veterinarian at once. All cats should be vaccinated yearly against panleukopenia.

Another deadly disease that strikes cats is *rabies*. Rabies is an infection of the nervous system and is the most dangerous cat zoonosis. Rabies is commonly transmitted by a bite from an infected animal. All cats permitted outdoors require periodic rabies vaccinations. See Rabies.

Respiratory infections, ranging from mild colds to pneumonia, are common among cats. Signs of such infections include sneezing, a runny nose, watery eyes, and fever. A veterinarian can give vaccinations to prevent respiratory infections.

Many kinds of parasites may cause health problems in cats. Certain types of worms, including roundworms and tapeworms, can infect a cat's intestines and other organs. Worms may cause listlessness, weight loss, vomiting, and diarrhea. Some other parasites may live on a cat's skin and cause severe itching. Fleas and ear mites are the most common external parasites. Cats may also develop *ringworm*, a skin disease caused by a fungus. A veterinarian should be consulted about the treatment of these health problems. See Flea; Mite; Ringworm; Roundworm; Tapeworm.

WORLD BOOK photo

A Judge at a Cat Show examines an Egyptian Mau, *above.* Shows promote interest in owning and breeding cats.

Birth Control. Each year, millions of unwanted cats are abandoned. Animal shelters must destroy many of these homeless cats. Countless other strays die of starvation, injury, or disease. Because the problem of unwanted cats is so serious, owners should not allow their cats to mate unless a good home can be provided for the kittens.

Owners can try to prevent cats from mating by keeping them indoors. But this method of birth control is difficult. It also does not prevent such undesirable sex-related behavior as the spraying of urine by tomcats and the howling of queens during estrus.

A veterinarian can permanently prevent a cat from reproducing by *neutering* it—that is, by surgically removing some of its sex organs. Neutering also ends sex-related behavior. The operation is called *spaying* when performed on a female cat, and *castration* when done on a male cat. Many veterinarians recommend that females be spayed before their first estrus, but not before 5 months of age. Male cats can be neutered any time after about 6 months of age.

Cat Associations and Shows

Cat lovers throughout the world have formed many associations to promote interest in cats. The largest of these groups is the Cat Fanciers' Association, Incorporated, which has more than 600 member clubs in the United States, Canada, and Japan. Cat associations *register* purebreds—that is, they record the ancestries of the animals—to ensure the preservation of the breeds. The associations also sponsor cat shows and establish standards for judging each breed. These standards cover such features as the shape of the body and the head, eye color, and coat type and color.

Breeders and pet owners display their finest cats at shows. The animals compete in groups based on such factors as age, sex, and breed. Most shows also have a household pet category in which almost any healthy cat, including crossbreds, may compete. Show judges award points for healthiness, for pleasant temperament, and for how closely the animal meets the standards of its breed. Cats that earn enough points in shows may become champions or grand champions.

History

Scientists believe that members of the cat family gradually developed from a small weasellike animal called *Miacis*, which lived more than 50 million years ago. Miacis also was probably the ancestor of such mammals as bears, dogs, and raccoons. Members of the cat family first appeared about 40 million years ago.

No one knows exactly how or where cats were first tamed. But many authorities believe the domestic cat is a direct descendant of an African wildcat that the Egyptians tamed—possibly as early as 3500 B.C. Domesticated wildcats killed mice, rats, and snakes and so prevented these pests from overrunning Egyptian farms and grain storehouses. The cats became pampered pets and were honored in paintings and sculptures.

By about 1500 B.C., the Egyptians had begun to con-

Charles Edwin Wilbour Fund, The Brooklyn Museum, New York City

The Ancient Egyptians Worshiped Cats and honored them in works of art. This bronze statue of a standing cat was created more than 2,000 years ago by an unknown Egyptian sculptor.

sider cats sacred. They worshiped a goddess of love and fertility called *Bastet*, or *Bast*, who was represented as having the head of a cat and the body of a woman. Egyptians were punished for harming cats. If a person killed a cat, the punishment was usually death. When a pet cat died, the Egyptians shaved off their eyebrows as a sign of mourning. They made dead cats into mummies. Scientists have found an ancient cat cemetery in Egypt containing more than 300,000 cat mummies. See EGYPT, ANCIENT (picture: Cats).

Greek and Phoenician traders probably brought domestic cats to Europe and the Middle East about 1000 B.C. The ancient Greeks and Romans valued cats for their ability to control rodents. In Rome, the cat was a symbol of liberty and was regarded as the guardian spirit of a household.

Domestic cats spread from the Middle East throughout Asia. In the Far East, cats were used to protect temple manuscripts from destruction by rats and mice. Cats also were used to prevent rodents from attacking silkworm cocoons, from which silk is made. People of the Orient admired the beauty and mystery of the cat. The animal became a favorite subject of artists and writers in China and Japan.

In Europe during the Middle Ages, the cat was considered a symbol of evil. Superstitious people associated the cat with witchcraft and the Devil. For this reason, people killed hundreds of thousands of cats. Experts believe that the destruction of so many cats led to a huge increase in the rat population of Europe and contributed to the spread of the *black death*, a form of *bubonic plague*. This disease, which is transmitted to people by rat fleas, killed about a fourth of the people who lived in Europe during the 1300's.

By the 1600's, Europeans had begun to realize once again the importance of cats in controlling rodents. Cats gradually regained popularity. European explorers, colonists, and traders brought domestic cats to the New World during the 1600's and 1700's. Throughout the 1800's, settlers took cats with them as they moved westward. Most cats in the United States and Canada today are descendants of these cats.

The first cat show was held in London in 1871. In 1887, the National Cat Club of Great Britain was formed. Interest in breeding and owning cats increased greatly. Today, the cat's ever-growing popularity has produced a billion-dollar industry that provides services and products for cats and their owners.

Scientific Classification. Cats belong to the cat family, Felidae. Domestic cats of all breeds are classified as *Felis domesticus*.

TERRI McGINNIS

Related Articles in WORLD BOOK include:

Animal (pictures: The Cat and Its Relatives)	Cheetah	Ocelot
Bobcat	Jaguar	Panther
Brain (picture: Some Animal Brains)	Jaguarundi	Pet
Caracal	Leopard	Saber-Toothed Cat
Catnip	Lion	Serval
	Lynx	Snow Leopard
	Margay	Tiger
	Mountain Lion	Wildcat

Outline

I. The Body of a Cat
- A. Body Size and Structure
- B. Head
- C. Coat
- D. Senses

II. Breeds of Cats
- A. Short-Haired Breeds
- B. Long-Haired Breeds
- C. Other Breeds

III. The Life of a Cat
- A. Reproduction
- B. Growth and Development
- C. Communication

IV. Caring for a Cat
- A. Feeding
- B. Grooming
- C. Training
- D. Veterinary Care
- E. Birth Control

V. Cat Associations and Shows

VI. History

Questions

How long do most healthy cats live?
What is the only kind of cat without a tail?
What produces *eyeshine* in a cat?
Why did people kill many cats in Europe during the Middle Ages?
How are tabby coats patterned?
How many teeth do adult cats have?
How do cats clean themselves?
What are some serious cat diseases?
What are some of the ways in which cats communicate?
What purpose do the whiskers of a cat serve?

Additional Resources

Level I

JOHNSON, NORMAN H., and GALIN, SAUL. *The Complete Kitten and Cat Book*. Harper, 1979.
ROCKWELL, JANE. *Cats and Kittens*. Watts, 1974.
SILVERSTEIN, ALVIN and VIRGINIA. *Cats: All About Them*. Morrow, 1978.
STEVENS, CARLA. *The Birth of Sunset's Kittens*. Addison-Wesley, 1969.

Level II

FOX, MICHAEL W. *Understanding Your Cat*. Coward, 1974.

LOEB, JO and PAUL. *You Can Train Your Cat.* Simon & Schuster, 1977.
MCGINNIS, TERRI. *The Well Cat Book.* Random House, 1975.
WRIGHT, MICHAEL, and WALTERS, SALLY, eds. *The Book of the Cat.* Simon & Schuster, 1980.

CAT BRIER. See GREENBRIER.

CAT SCANNER. See X RAYS (History).

CATACOMBS, *KAT uh kohmz,* are systems of underground passages or rooms once used as burial places. The most famous catacombs lie on the outskirts of Rome. The early Christians cut them into the soft tufa rock in the 200's and 300's. The catacombs formed a network of connecting corridors and rooms covering about 600 acres (240 hectares). Graves were cut into the walls. Bricks or marble slabs were used to close some of the graves. When more space was needed, additional *galleries* (halls) were dug beneath the first.

The Christians used the catacombs for funeral and memorial services. The fresco paintings on the walls are important examples of early Christian art. Such scenes as *Daniel in the Lions' Den* and *Moses Striking the Rock* symbolize God's salvation of people and nations. The paintings also show *orante* (praying) figures of the dead resurrected in Paradise, standing with their arms upraised in adoration.

During the periods of persecution, Christians took refuge in the catacombs because Roman law held all burial places sacred. But the catacombs lost their usefulness when Christianity became the established religion of the Roman Empire. Their existence was completely forgotten after about 400. When they were accidentally rediscovered in 1578, it was first thought that they were the ruins of ancient cities.

Catacombs have been found in other Italian cities and in Sicily, Malta, Egypt, North Africa, and Palestine. The burial chapels of some monasteries and nunneries in Europe are sometimes called catacombs. The *catacombs of Paris* are abandoned stone quarries that were first used for burials in 1787. ALAN GOWANS

See also BIBLE (picture: Scenes from Biblical Stories); ROME (The Catacombs).

Roman Catacombs contain frescoes of the late 200's and early 300's portraying Jesus, the apostles, and episodes from the Bible.

Leonard Von Matt

CATALEPSY, *KAT uh LEHP see,* is a condition in which a person loses the desire to move, not even to adjust the body into appropriate and comfortable positions. The person's arms and legs can be placed in bizarre postures, as though he or she were a wax figure. A patient with catalepsy is said to be in a *catatonic state.* The cataleptic person can hold the trunk and limbs for long periods of time in almost any position in which they are placed. The person is not paralyzed. He or she can move, but lacks the will to move. Catalepsy usually occurs in association with a form of mental illness called *schizophrenia.* It sometimes occurs in *hysteria.* Catalepsy differs from cataplexy, with which it is often confused. FREDERIC A. GIBBS

See also CATAPLEXY; HYSTERIA; MENTAL ILLNESS (Schizophrenia).

CATALOG. See ADVERTISING (Direct Mail); MAIL-ORDER BUSINESS. For information about using a card catalog, see *A Student Guide to Better Writing, Speaking, and Research Skills* in the RESEARCH GUIDE/INDEX, Volume 22.

CATALPA, *kuh TAL puh,* also called *Indian bean,* is the name of a group of rapidly growing shade trees. There are seven species of catalpa. They grow in the United States, the West Indies, and China. The trumpet-shaped flowers bloom in early summer.

The catalpa grows long, narrow fruit capsules 8 to 20 inches (20 to 51 centimeters) long, which resemble pea and bean pods. The many seeds inside are flat and bearded at each end with hairlike growths. The trees have stout branches and thin, scaly bark. Catalpa wood is chocolate-colored and soft, but it is durable.

Scientific Classification. Catalpas belong to the bignonia family, *Bignoniaceae.* The North American catalpas are classified as genus *Catalpa,* species *C. speciosa* and *C. bignonioides.* WILLIAM M. HARLOW

See also TREE (Familiar Broadleaf Trees [picture]).

CATALYSIS, *kuh TAL uh sihs,* is a process in which a substance increases the speed of a chemical reaction without being consumed by the reaction. Any substance that accelerates a reaction in this way is called a *catalyst.* In industry, catalysts are used to speed up many chemical reactions that otherwise would take place too slowly to be practical. Enzymes serve as catalysts in many complex reactions that occur in all animals and plants (see ENZYME).

In most cases, there are several possible sequences of steps by which a reaction can take place. A catalyst participates in some or all of the steps of a particular sequence. By doing so, the catalyst provides a chemical pathway along which the overall reaction can proceed far more rapidly than it otherwise could.

A typical example of catalysis is the effect of nitric oxide (NO) on the decomposition of ozone (O_3) in the upper atmosphere of the earth. An oxygen atom (O) and an ozone molecule combine slowly by themselves and produce two oxygen molecules (O_2). But in the presence of nitric oxide, a catalyst, a rapid two-step reaction takes place instead. First, a nitric oxide molecule combines with an oxygen atom, producing nitrogen dioxide

(NO_2). Then the nitrogen dioxide reacts with ozone and forms two molecules of oxygen and one molecule of nitric oxide. The second step of the reaction produces exactly as much nitric oxide as is consumed by the first step. Thus, the overall reaction does not change the amount of nitric oxide.

There are two types of catalysis, *homogeneous* and *heterogeneous*. In homogeneous catalysis, the catalyst and the *reactants* (reacting substances) are in the same physical state. For example, the catalytic decomposition of ozone is homogeneous because nitric oxide, oxygen, and ozone are all gases. On the other hand, heterogeneous catalysis involves two physical states, such as a solid catalyst affecting gaseous reactants.

Heterogeneous catalysts are generally used in industry because they can easily be separated from the products of reactions and then reused. Such catalysts are widely used in refining petroleum (see PETROLEUM [Conversion]). In the production of ammonia, iron catalyzes the reaction of nitrogen with hydrogen. In the manufacture of nitric acid, platinum speeds the oxidation of ammonia. GARY L. HALLER

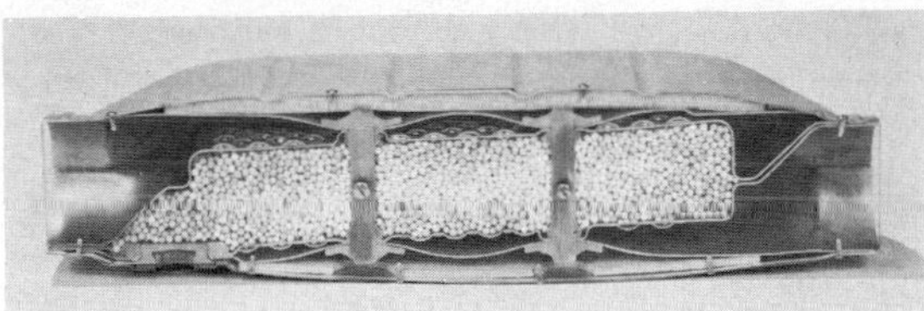

General Motors Corp. (WORLD BOOK photo)

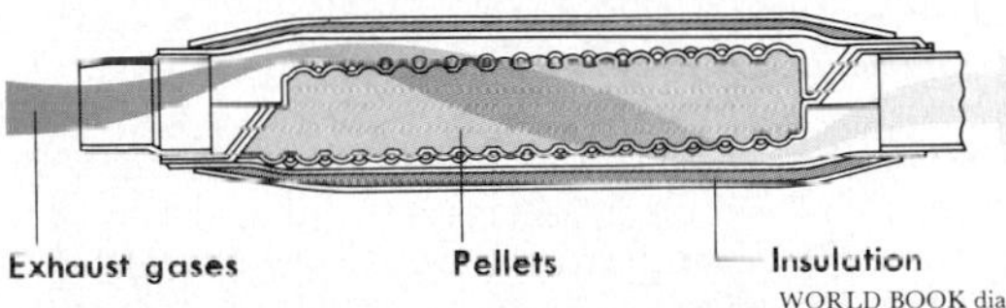

WORLD BOOK diagram

A Catalytic Converter consists of a mufflerlike chamber that contains pellets coated with a platinum-palladium mixture, *top*. Pollutants are chemically converted into nonpollutants when a car's exhaust gases flow among the pellets, *bottom*.

CATALYTIC CONVERTER, *KAT uh LIHT ihk*, is a device that helps reduce the pollutants given off by an automobile engine. It changes harmful carbon monoxide and unburned *hydrocarbons* (compounds of hydrogen and carbon) into nonpollutants.

A catalytic converter is installed in the exhaust system of a car. The device consists of a mufflerlike chamber that contains porous, heat-resistant materials coated with a substance called a *catalyst* (see CATALYSIS). The catalyst used in most converters is a mixture of two metallic elements, platinum and palladium. These elements cause the carbon monoxide and hydrocarbons in an automobile's exhaust to combine with oxygen, which converts them into carbon dioxide and water vapor.

Cars with catalytic converters must use gasoline that is free of lead and phosphorus. These elements can cause the catalyst to become ineffective. Catalytic converters first appeared in many 1975 cars to meet auto emission standards established by the U.S. government (see AUTOMOBILE [Air Pollution]). OTTO A. UYEHARA

CATAMARAN, *KAT uh muh RAN*, is a raftlike boat that has two hulls. In the United States, catamarans are used mainly as pleasure boats and as floating and landing gear on planes that land on water. Their balanced design allows fast, smooth sailing, and the two hulls reduce the chance of tipping over. United States manufacturers make catamarans up to 35 feet (11 meters) long with sails. Catamarans driven by engines are up to 45 feet (14 meters) long. The design was developed from outrigger boats used by the Polynesians and Malays for thousands of years. CARL D. LANE

See also BOATING (picture).

CATAMOUNT is the folk name given to the mountain lion and the lynx. See LYNX; MOUNTAIN LION.

CATAPLEXY, *KAT uh PLEHK see*, is the condition in which a person loses muscular power and control without loss of consciousness. It often occurs in persons who have attacks of *narcolepsy* (an irresistible urge to sleep). Cataplectic attacks usually last only a few seconds. In most cases, they are caused by a sudden emotional disturbance. For example, people subject to cataplectic attacks may slump to the floor if they should get a surprisingly good hand in a card game.

Cataplexy is not a form of epilepsy, and the condition is not usually helped by medication. Cataplexy differs from catalepsy, with which it is sometimes confused (see CATALEPSY). FREDERIC A. GIBBS

See also NARCOLEPSY.

CATAPULT, *KAT uh puhlt*, is a machine that works like a slingshot or a bow and arrow. In ancient times, warriors used catapults to hurl heavy rocks and pieces of metal across moats and over walls into castles or cities. In World War I, soldiers at the front made catapults that flung grenades and poison-gas bombs great distances. These catapults sometimes threw tin cans filled with gunpowder or dynamite. One form of cata-

WORLD BOOK illustration by Tak Murakami

Catapults were used by warriors in ancient times and during the Middle Ages to attack walled cities and castles. The catapult worked like a giant slingshot to hurl heavy stones over the walls and into the city or castle.

pult used was a limber young tree. A leather loop, or pocket, was fastened to the top. The tree was bent back, and the pocket loaded with its tin-can missile. The soldiers then let the tree spring forward. The thrust of the spring cast the tin-can missile into the enemy lines.

In naval warfare, a catapult is used to launch planes from the decks of the aircraft carriers. This type of catapult is a huge steel framework, equipped with tracks. A car carrying the plane runs on the tracks. By means of steam, a strong spring, or explosive charge, car and plane are shot forward and the plane is launched into the air. PAUL D. STROOP

CATARACT. See WATERFALL.

CATARACT is the clouding of the lens of the eye. Many cataracts begin as small spots in the lens that interfere slightly with vision. They may cause blindness by spreading until the entire lens becomes milky white and *opaque* (nontransparent).

The lens helps the eye focus. Light rays from an object first strike the *cornea*, the transparent part of the outside of the eyeball. The cornea bends the light rays toward each other, but not enough to focus them into an image. The light rays then pass through the lens, which bends them further and causes them to focus an image on the *retina* (back layer of the eyeball). Because the lens is flexible, it can change shape to help a person focus on objects at different distances. Thus, clear vision depends on light passing through the cornea and lens easily and on the lens focusing correctly.

Cataracts occur for a variety of reasons. *Senile cataract* results from aging. It occurs more frequently than any other form of the condition and eventually produces complete opaqueness of the lens. Some cataracts result from such eye inflammations as *iritis* or from injuries to the eye. Diabetes can also cause cataracts. Cataracts may develop if the parathyroid gland, which controls the amount of calcium in the body, does not work properly. Some babies are born with cataracts. Such cataracts may be caused by an infection before birth or by abnormal chemical processes in the body.

Doctors do not know how to prevent or cure most kinds of cataracts, but sight can be restored to most cataract patients. The lens must be removed by surgery. Light can then reach the retina, but it cannot be focused properly. Special glasses or contact lenses can provide good focusing. In some cases, eye surgeons *implant* (place) an artificial plastic lens in the eye. Most persons who have had cataract surgery can see well enough to carry on their normal activities. But glasses, contact lenses, and implanted lenses are not flexible—as the natural lens was—and so the patient cannot see objects equally well at all distances. SIDNEY LERMAN

See also BLINDNESS; EYE; CONTACT LENS.

CATARRH, *kuh TAHR*, is thick mucus that collects in the throat, or may run from the nose of a person with a long-continued head cold. In *acute catarrh*, the membranes first swell, but do not give off more mucus than usual. Doctors call this the *dry* stage. In the second, or *moist*, stage there is an unusually free flow of mucus. The word *catarrh* is gradually being replaced by more specific terms. See also COLD, COMMON; SINUS. ALBERT P. SELTZER

CATBIRD is a North American songbird that is related to the mockingbird. The catbird is about 9 inches (23 centimeters) long and is slate-gray in color. The top of its head is black, and it has a brick-red patch beneath the base of its long tail feathers. Catbirds breed in the United States and southern Canada, as far west as the Rocky Mountains. They fly south in the fall, and winter in the Gulf States, West Indies, Mexico, and Central America.

The catbird hides its loosely made nest of twigs and rootlets in tangled thickets and thick brush. Catbirds lay three to five bluish-green eggs. They sometimes eat strawberries, raspberries, blackberries, and cherries. But they help man by eating beetles, ants, crickets, and other harmful insects.

The catbird is an excellent singer, and has a delightful song. It can imitate the songs of other birds. The catbird gets its name from one of its mewing call notes, which sounds like a cat. The catbird sometimes sings for hours on warm, moonlit nights.

Scientific Classification. The catbird belongs to the mockingbird and thrasher family, *Mimidae*. It is genus *Dumetella*, species *D. carolinensis*. ALBERT WOLFSON

See also BIRD (pictures: Birds of Brushy Areas; Birds' Eggs); MOCKINGBIRD.

CATBOAT. See SAILING (Kinds of Sailboats).

CATCHUP is a spiced sauce made from tomatoes. The name originated in the Orient from a word pronounced like "Kaychup." It is often spelled *catsup*, *katchup*, or *ketchup*. Catchup consists of tomato pulp, sugar, salt, mustard, vinegar, and spices. There is no standard formula for its manufacture. The U.S. Food and Drug Administration has established a "Standard of Identity" for catchup. This standard specifies what optional ingredients may be included in catchup. It also specifies, for some ingredients such as dextrose, the maximum amount that may be used. RICHARD A. HAVENS

CATECHISM, *KAT ee kiz'm*, is a system of questions and answers used for religious instruction in Christian churches. The first regular catechisms were compiled in the 700's and 800's.

Among the chief catechisms are the Lutheran, published by Martin Luther (1529); the Genevan, the work of John Calvin (1537); the Heidelberg or Palatinate Catechism (1563), used in the Dutch Reformed Church; the Anglican (1549-1661), found in the Book of Common Prayer; the Tridentine (1566), prepared at the Council of Trent, and of high authority in the Roman Catholic Church; the Shorter (1647) and Larger (1648) Catechisms, used in the Presbyterian Church; and the Methodist Catechism. FULTON J. SHEEN

CATECHU, *KAT ee choo*, is a brown, sticky substance obtained chiefly from the wood of tropical trees called acacias. *Cutch* is another name for catechu. This material is used in dyeing and tanning, and in medicines. The heartwood of the acacia is cut into pieces and boiled in water until a substance like tar or resin is produced. When catechu is partly hardened, it is formed into rough blocks or balls and wrapped in large leaves. It is marketed in this form. Catechu makes rich brown dyes used in coloring leather. It is also used to dye and print cotton cloth such as calico. FRED FORTESS

See also ACACIA.

CATERPILLAR is a wormlike creature that is the second, or *larval*, stage in the life history of butterflies and moths. When a butterfly egg hatches, a tiny caterpillar crawls out and begins to eat. The caterpillar grows, but its skin does not grow with it as does the skin of most animals. Soon the skin becomes too tight, and the caterpillar prepares to throw it off. A split appears on the upper part, near the head end, and the caterpillar wriggles out. It appears in a new soft skin formed under the old one. In a few days this, too, is outgrown, and the process is repeated a number of times. In the temperate regions, most species remain in the caterpillar stage from two to four weeks. In very cold climates, some species take from two to three years to pass from the egg to the butterfly stage.

Lee Smiley

Caterpillar

Appearance. A caterpillar usually has 12 rings or segments, not including the head. To each of the first three segments is attached a pair of five-jointed legs. These develop later into the legs of the adult insect. But the leg-like *prolegs* on the abdomen are not really legs, and are shed with the last skin. Occasionally, as in the so-called measuring worms, there are two pairs of prolegs on the abdomen, and the larva moves by drawing these hind legs up to the front pair.

The head has six simple eyes on each side. The caterpillar guides itself by a pair of short, jointed feelers. Its strong, biting jaws differ from the sucking mouth parts of the butterfly. The body may be naked or covered with hairs, bristles, or spines.

Some caterpillars have glands that secrete an unpleasant fluid. Others have a sickening taste which saves them from being eaten by birds and other animals. False eyespots help frighten away attackers of some caterpillars, while long, whiplike appendages on the backs of other larvae are lashed about as a means of defense. But, in spite of these devices, very few caterpillars that are hatched ever reach the adult stage. Larger animals eat them, and parasites burrow into their bodies and kill them.

Habits. Caterpillars are heavy eaters. A butterfly or moth does all its growing during the caterpillar stage. The larva stores up the tissues that later are transformed into the adult insect. The adult grows no more after it grows wings. A few larvae, such as the silkworms, are valuable, but most are not. Sometimes, in years when caterpillars are numerous, fields are made bare of vegetation, and trees are stripped of their leaves. The cabbage worm, the cotton worm, the army worm, and the cutworms are especially troublesome. E. Gorton Linsley

Related Articles in World Book include:

Army Worm	Jumping Bean	Silk (Raising Silkworms)
Butterfly	Larva	Tent Caterpillar
Cankerworm	Measuring Worm	
Chrysalis	Moth	
Cutworm	Rotenone	

CATFISH is the name of a large group of fish, most of which have two to four pairs of whiskers. These whiskers, called *barbels*, resemble the whiskers of a cat. Many of the more than 2,000 species of catfish also have sharp spines on the back fins and on the fins near the gills. The spines of some kinds of catfish give off a poison when they pierce another animal. Unlike most other fish, catfish have no scales over their skin.

The smallest kinds of catfish, including the *pygmy corydoras*, measure only 1 to 1½ inches (2.5 to 3.8 centimeters) long and weigh about $\frac{1}{10}$ ounce (3 grams). The largest species, the European catfish, may grow more than 10 feet (3 meters) long and weigh 400 pounds (180 kilograms). Many people keep such small catfish as the *glass catfish* in home aquariums.

Catfish are found in most parts of the world. Some kinds live in fresh water, and others in salt water. Most species dwell in quiet waters and feed on tiny animals and bits of animal flesh. They find their food near the bottom of a pond or a slow-moving river. A few species of catfish live in swift streams. They include the *channel catfish*, which lives in North America. Such catfish eat other fish, frogs, crayfish, and insects.

Some kinds of catfish have unusual features or ways of life. For example, the *armored catfish* has overlapping bony plates that cover its body. The *upside-down catfish* swims upside down. The *electric catfish* can send out a strong electric shock. The *eelcat*, a West African catfish, is so long and slim that it resembles an eel. The *candiru*, a small South American catfish, swims into the gills of larger fish. It then rips the gills with its sharp spines and drinks the victim's blood. Among some species of ocean catfish, the male carries the eggs in his mouth and does not eat until they hatch.

The *walking catfish* of tropical Asia can move overland to another body of water if its pond dries up. This fish pushes itself along the ground with its tail, using its strong front fins to lift the front part of its body. The walking catfish has gills, but it also has lunglike breathing organs. These organs enable the fish to stay out of

Field Museum of Natural History

The Channel Catfish lives in swift, clear streams in North America. It has a slender body and a forked tail. Many small speckles dot its bluish or silvery skin.

Charles Trainor, Rapho Guillumette

A Walking Catfish moves on land by wriggling its body and thrashing its tail. It uses its front fins as supports. Lunglike organs enable the fish to stay out of water for long periods of time.

water for days if the surroundings are wet or rainy. Even under dry conditions, the fish can survive out of water as long as 12 hours. Walking catfish have escaped into rivers in southern Florida. They have replaced other kinds of fish in some Florida waters.

Many people consider catfish delicious to eat. Fishermen in the eastern United States, especially in the Mississippi River Valley, fish for channel catfish, *blue catfish*, and *yellow catfish*. The *bullhead*, a type of catfish, is also a popular food fish in the Eastern States. Catfish farms, most of them in the Southern States, raise channel catfish for use as food.

Scientific Classification: There are many families and genera of catfish. The channel catfish is genus *Ictalurus*, species *I. punctatus*. The walking catfish is genus *Clarias*, species *C. batrachus*. WARREN J. WISBY

See also BULLHEAD.

CATGUT is a tough cord made from the intestines of certain animals and used mainly for the strings of musical instruments and for sewing up wounds. Most catgut is made from the intestines of hogs or sheep. The intestine casings are split into ribbons that are cleaned, cured, and spun into string. The string is dried and polished. Catgut is also used for stringing tennis rackets, on looms, in the controls of artificial limbs, and in the mechanisms of clocks and typewriters.

CATHARINE. See CATHERINE.

CATHARSIS, *kuh THAHR sihs*, literally means a *cleaning out*. In psychoanalysis, the term signifies the healing process by which the mind is cleansed of factors that tend to disrupt mental functioning and cause a person anguish, anxiety, or unhappiness. These disruptive factors, which are mostly unconscious, include early harmful experiences, threatening impulses, and disturbing complexes. ALEXANDER A. SCHNEIDERS

CATHAY, *kuh THAY*, is the name Europeans once gave to China, especially the part north of the Yangtze River. From the early A.D. 700's to the early 1100's, a pre-Mongol people called *Khitan* controlled parts of China. The term *Cathay* came into the English language when it was used in a report by William of Rubruck in 1253. Marco Polo also called the country Khitai, or Cathay, in his account of his travels to the land of Kublai Khan. H. F. SCHURMANN

See also KUBLAI KHAN; POLO, MARCO.

CATHEDRAL is the church of a bishop of some Christian religions. It is also the administrative headquarters of a *diocese*, a church district headed by a bishop. The bishop's throne, a symbol of the office, is in the cathedral. The word *cathedral* comes from the Greek word *kathedra*, meaning *seat*. Only the Anglican, Eastern Orthodox, and Roman Catholic religions and some Lutheran groups use the title cathedral.

Historical Importance of Cathedrals. A great era of cathedral building occurred in Europe during the Middle Ages from about 1000 to 1500. Medieval architects believed extreme grandeur would inspire greater faith. They designed many majestic cathedrals and decorated them with sculptures and other art treasures.

The medieval cathedral served as a center of public life. Public meetings, as well as daily church services, were held there. The cathedral was also an educational center. Its walls were lined with paintings or stained-

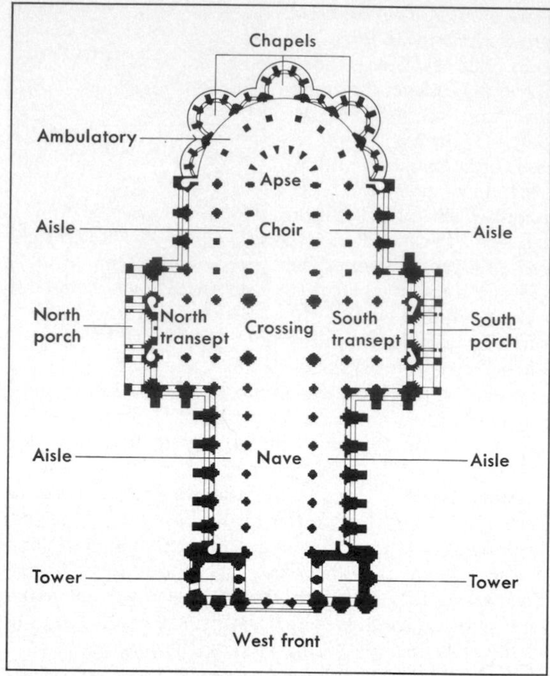

WORLD BOOK diagram

A Cathedral is shaped like a cross. The entrance faces west. At the east end, chapels and an aisle called an *ambulatory* are outside a semicircular area known as the *apse*.

Cathedral of Notre Dame, Reims, France (Tony Stone Associates Ltd.)

The Cathedral in Reims, France, is a masterpiece of Gothic architecture. The cathedral was built during the 1200's. More than 5,000 statues decorate its doorways, towers, and walls.

glass windows that portrayed scenes from the Bible and the lives of the saints. These scenes made up a visual encyclopedia of medieval knowledge for the many worshipers who could not read.

The role of the cathedral has declined through the years. However, it is still considered the most important church in a diocese and must receive a special blessing before being used.

The Plan of a Cathedral. No church laws refer to the design of a cathedral. However, many of these churches in Western religions have traditionally been built according to the general plan of a medieval cathedral. For a description of Eastern Orthodox cathedrals, see BYZANTINE ART.

Most cathedrals are built in the shape of a cross. A long central aisle, called the *nave*, and two side aisles extend from the entrance, which is at the bottom of the cross. The two arms of the cross, called the *transept*, meet the nave at the *crossing*. Worshipers assemble in the nave and transept to hear the service.

The altar and the seats for the choir are at the end of the nave in a semicircular area known as the *apse*. A walkway called the *ambulatory* extends behind the altar and opens into several chapels. The bishop's throne, which stands on top of three steps and has a canopy over it, is on one side of the altar.

Through the years, architects have made changes in the basic plan of a cathedral. For example, architects of the 1600's designed cathedrals with extremely short transepts so the entire congregation could see the altar. However, many of the most modern cathedrals have some features of the medieval design.

Famous Cathedrals. Many cathedrals of western Europe are famous for their great beauty. France is the home of some of the most magnificent ones, including those in Amiens, Chartres, Reims, and Strasbourg. Other famous European cathedrals include the Cologne Cathedral in Germany and the Milan Cathedral in Italy. The Seville Cathedral in Spain is the largest in Europe.

A number of North American cathedrals were built in the grand style of European cathedrals. Outstanding U.S. cathedrals include St. John the Divine and St. Patrick's Cathedral, both in New York City. A well-known Canadian cathedral is the Cathedral-Basilica of Mary, Queen of the World, in Montreal. The National Cathedral in Mexico City dates from the 1500's and is the oldest in North America. SAMUEL Y. EDGERTON, JR.

Related Articles. Many of the cities and countries mentioned above have articles in WORLD BOOK with pictures of famous cathedrals. See also the following articles:

Architecture (pictures)
Coventry
Gothic Art
Hagia Sophia
Lateran
Milan Cathedral
Notre Dame, Cathedral of
Romanesque Architecture
Saint Mark, Cathedral of
Saint Patrick's Cathedral
Spire
Stained Glass
Washington Cathedral

Church of Our Lady, Munich, Germany
(Marburg from Art Reference Bureau)

St. Michael's Cathedral, Coventry, England
(Heinz Zinram)

Cathedral Interiors present a feeling of harmony and soaring height through the arrangement of arches and pillars. The cathedral in Munich, Germany, *left*, was built in the 1400's. The one in Coventry, England, *right*, was finished in 1962, replacing a 600-year-old church destroyed in 1940.

CATHER, WILLA (1873-1947), an American author, became famous for her novels set on the Nebraska prairies or in the Southwest. In *O Pioneers!* (1913), she first used the theme for which she became famous. The novel tells about hardy but sensitive immigrant women who match their strength and determination against the harsh, lonely life of the prairies during pioneer days.

In her fiction, Cather portrayed the beauty of the land and the simplicity of pioneer life, as well as the bitter, hard existence of the pioneers. *My Ántonia* (1918) is probably her best-known work. With lyricism and simple realism, Cather tells the story of a young Bohemian immigrant girl who grows up on a farm, becomes a hired girl in town, and returns to the vast, lonely land as a wife and mother. Many critics consider *Death Comes for the Archbishop* (1927) Cather's finest work. This novel is the story of a missionary priest in early New Mexico. Cather won the 1923 Pulitzer prize for fiction for *One of Ours* (1922), the story of a young Nebraska farmer who dies in battle during World War I.

Steichen, courtesy Alfred Knopf
Willa Cather

Willa Sibert Cather was born in Gore, Va., and moved to Nebraska with her family in 1883. She grew up among the immigrants who appear in her works. After graduating from the University of Nebraska in 1895, she was a high-school teacher in Pittsburgh from 1901 to 1906. She then joined the staff of *McClure's Magazine*, and later became managing editor. She left the magazine in 1912, the year her first novel, *Alexander's Bridge*, was published.

DEAN DONER

CATHERINE was the name of two rulers of Russia.

Catherine I (1683?-1727) became the ruler of Russia in 1725 after the death of her husband, Peter the Great. During her reign from 1725 to 1727, she achieved little, leaving the administration to her favorites. Catherine was born of peasant parents in Livonia. She was made a prisoner by the Russians, and lived for some years among the soldiers. Finally, she came to the attention of Peter, who married her in 1712. She possessed patience, courage, and caution, and was a steadying influence on Peter. See PETER I, THE GREAT.

Catherine II (1729-1796), called "the Great," was a German princess who became empress of Russia. During her rule, Russia expanded greatly. Catherine promoted European culture in Russia.

Catherine was born in Stettin, Prussia (now Szczecin, Poland). At the age of 16, she came to St. Petersburg (now Leningrad) and married Peter, the weak and incompetent successor to the throne. He became emperor in 1762, but was quickly deposed by Catherine and her friends and later was murdered. Catherine succeeded Peter to the Russian throne.

Catherine was a gifted person, devoted to art, literature, science, and politics. Although extravagant, she proved to be a conscientious ruler. Early in her rule, she became interested in the liberal ideas of the Age of Reason. She built schools and hospitals, encouraged smallpox inoculation, promoted the education of women, and extended religious tolerance. Teachers, scientists, writers, artists, and actors from other countries came to Russia.

Detail of an oil portrait by Johann Baptist Lampi I; Russian State Museum, Leningrad (Library of Congress)
Catherine the Great

But Catherine did little to grant wider freedoms to the majority of the Russian people. She preserved and extended serfdom, and brutally suppressed peasant revolts (see SERF). Except for raising the status of merchants, she carried out few social reforms. Instead, she promoted the interests of the upper classes.

Catherine's achievements consisted mainly in modernizing the administration, but she did nothing to curb its corruption. She also extended the frontiers of Russia. She acquired most of Poland through three partitions. Her successful wars on Turkey gained the Crimea and lands along the Black Sea for Russia. She also conquered Siberian tribes.

W. KIRCHNER

See also RUSSIA (Catherine the Great; picture); RUSSO-TURKISH WARS.

CATHERINE DE MÉDICIS, or, in Italian, DE' MEDICI (1519-1589), was the wife of King Henry II of France, and the mother of three French kings. Catherine was a daughter of Lorenzo, Duke of Urbino, of the famous Medici family of Florence, and a niece of Pope Clement VII. She knew well the selfish political principles practiced in Italy during her time. Her whole career was directed by her ambition and by her abnormal affection for her sons. When her son Francis II became king in 1559, Catherine began to meddle in state affairs. Francis II died the next year, leaving a 10-year-old brother, Charles IX, as king. Catherine then took over the rule of France.

She began to stir up trouble between the Roman Catholics and the Protestants, in order to strengthen her position as ruler. Catherine's plan to kill the Protestant leader Gaspard de Coligny failed. Then she decided that all his followers should die, and King Charles IX was forced to order a massacre on St. Bartholomew's Day. Her plotting continued through the reign of a third son, Henry III. Catherine and Henry III died in 1589, ending one of the most tragic eras in French history.

ANDRÉ MAUROIS

See also HENRY (II) of France; HUGUENOTS; SAINT BARTHOLOMEW'S DAY, MASSACRE OF.

CATHERINE OF ARAGON (1485-1536) was the first of the six wives of King Henry VIII of England. She was the daughter of Ferdinand and Isabella of Spain. At the age of 16, she became the wife of

Brown Bros.
Catherine of Aragon

Arthur, Prince of Wales, the oldest son of Henry VII. Arthur died five months later, and the king arranged for Catherine to marry his second son, Henry.

They were married in 1509, when Henry became king, and lived together for 18 years. Of the five children born to Catherine, only Mary lived. She became Queen Mary I (see MARY [I]). King Henry, wanting a male heir and enchanted by Anne Boleyn, decided to annul his marriage to Catherine. After he broke with the Roman Catholic Church to divorce her, Catherine lived in retirement. PAUL M. KENDALL

CATHERINE OF SIENA, *SYEH nah,* **SAINT** (1347-1380), is a saint of the Roman Catholic Church who was born in Siena, Italy. At the age of 16, she joined the Dominican Tertiaries. She spent much of her time caring for the sick. She also held a unique position as adviser to religious and civil rulers. Her efforts helped to bring the pope back from Avignon in 1377, and to reconcile Florence and the Holy See in 1378. She is the patroness for the prevention of fires, and her feast day is April 30. FULTON J. SHEEN

CATHERINE THE GREAT. See CATHERINE (II).

CATHODE. See ELECTROLYSIS; ELECTRONICS (Early Experiments); VACUUM TUBE.

CATHODE RAYS, *KATH ohd,* is the name of an invisible radiation emitted from the negative electrode (cathode) of Crookes tubes (see CROOKES TUBE). The rays can be produced by connecting the electrodes with high-voltage sources of electric energy. Cathode rays cause a yellowish-green fluorescence to form wherever they strike the glass of the tube. When they are focused on a piece of platinum, the metal becomes red-hot. A boldly defined shadow is produced in the fluorescence on the end of the tube when platinum is placed in the path of these rays. Cathode-ray tubes are used in television cameras and sets.

Cathode rays are streams of negative units of electricity (electrons) shot off from the surface of the cathode at high speeds. These cathode rays are identical with the beta rays which are emitted by radium and other radioactive elements. MARCEL SCHEIN

See also FLUORESCENCE; VACUUM TUBE (Kinds of Vacuum Tubes); X RAYS.

CATHOLIC CHURCH, ROMAN. See ROMAN CATHOLIC CHURCH.

CATHOLIC CONFERENCE, UNITED STATES, is an agency that coordinates Roman Catholic programs in education, religious communication, and social welfare in the United States. It is administered by the nation's bishops. The conference was established in 1919 as the National Catholic Welfare Conference. It adopted its present name in 1966. Headquarters are at 1312 Massachusetts Avenue NW, Washington, D.C. 20005.

Critically reviewed by the UNITED STATES CATHOLIC CONFERENCE

CATHOLIC LIBRARY ASSOCIATION (CLA) is an organization interested in encouraging good literature and improving Roman Catholic libraries in the United States. It has over 4,000 members. Publications include *The Catholic Library World, The Catholic Periodical Index, The Guide to Catholic Literature,* and *The CLA Booklist.* The CLA sponsors Catholic Book Week and the Regina medal, a children's literature award (see REGINA MEDAL). The CLA was founded in 1921, and has headquarters at 461 W. Lancaster Avenue, Haverford, Pa. 19041. Critically reviewed by the CATHOLIC LIBRARY ASSOCIATION

CATHOLIC UNIVERSITY OF AMERICA, in Washington, D.C., was founded as the national Roman Catholic university in 1887. It was chartered by Pope Leo XIII in 1889, on the recommendation of American Catholic church leaders. The university is coeducational and admits students of all faiths.

Catholic University has schools of arts and sciences, education, engineering and architecture, law, music, nursing, philosophy, religious studies, and social service. Courses lead to bachelor's, master's, and doctor's degrees.

The university is noted for its research programs. It also has centers for Byzantine and medieval studies, organizational ethics, and various religious interests. The university library has special collections, ranging from canon law to physical chemistry. For enrollment, see UNIVERSITIES AND COLLEGES (table).

Critically reviewed by the CATHOLIC UNIVERSITY OF AMERICA

CATHOLIC WOMEN, NATIONAL COUNCIL OF, is a federation of Roman Catholic women's organizations. It was founded in 1920 to unite the endeavors of these organizations and to stimulate them to greater activity in fields of current interest. The council has about 8,500 local organizations. The organization's headquarters are at 1312 Massachusetts Avenue NW, Washington, D.C. 20005.

Critically reviewed by the NATIONAL COUNCIL OF CATHOLIC WOMEN

CATHOLIC YOUTH ORGANIZATION (CYO) is the parish youth group of many dioceses of the Roman Catholic Church in the United States. CYO offers social, cultural, spiritual, recreational, and community service activities. It includes athletics, camping, drama, retreats, and service projects to help the aged and the poor.

More than 4 million young people belong to CYO groups. The groups are united under the National Catholic Youth Organization Federation. The CYO was founded in Chicago in 1930. Critically reviewed by the NATIONAL CATHOLIC YOUTH ORGANIZATION FEDERATION

CATILINE, *KAT uh LYN* (? -62 B.C.), was a Roman who led an unsuccessful plot against his government in 63 B.C. Catiline was a member of a *patrician* (aristocratic) family. His name in Latin was Lucius Sergius Catilina. Catiline sought Rome's highest political office, the consulship. He was not allowed to run for consul in 66 B.C. because he faced a trial on charges of misgovernment while he was governor in Africa. In 65 B.C., Catiline plotted the murder of government leaders in Rome, but the plot was not carried out.

Catiline lost the election for consul in 64 B.C. to Cicero. When he failed again in 63 B.C., Catiline renewed his plot against the state. He tried to gain the support of discontented Romans by calling for the cancellation of debts.

Cicero publicly denounced Catiline in a famous speech before the Roman Senate, but he lacked proof of Catiline's treason. Catiline fled from Rome. When new evidence about the plot was found, the Senate gave Cicero extraordinary power. Cicero seized and executed the plotters in Rome. Catiline managed to raise a small army in Etruria, in northern Italy. But in 62 B.C., he and his men were killed by Roman troops. HENRY C. BOREN

CATION. See ION (Behavior of Ions).

J. Horace McFarland

Catkins hang from the branches of certain trees, such as the Carolina poplar. They appear early in the spring.

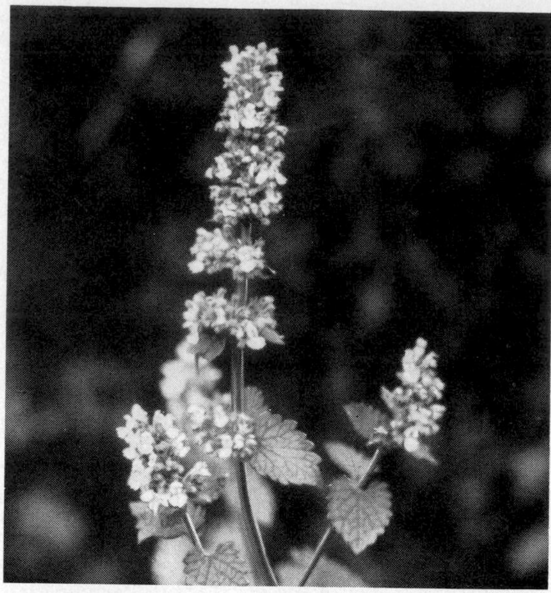

St. Clair

Catnip received this name because cats like to roll and play in the leaves. They also enjoy eating them.

CATKIN is a tassel-like flower cluster that consists of numerous small flowers arranged around a long central axis. Each flower lacks the colored petals so typical of most familiar wild flowers. For this reason, the grayish- or yellowish-green catkins are rarely thought of as flowers. Each catkin is either *staminate* (male, producing pollen) or *pistillate* (female, producing seeds). The wind pollinates the female catkins. The most familiar catkin is the pussy willow. Catkins appear on the branches of willows, alders, and poplars long before other spring flowers appear. Most catkins are long and drooping. They are also called *aments*. See also POLLEN AND POLLINATION; PUSSY WILLOW. ARTHUR W. GALSTON

CATLIN, GEORGE, (1796-1872), was an American artist known for his paintings and drawings of American Indians. His works rank among the most important studies of North American Indian culture.

Catlin was born in Wilkes-Barre, Pa. He practiced law and, until 1823, painted only as a hobby. That year, he gave up law and became a portrait painter. By 1826, he had decided to study Indian culture after seeing a group of Indians traveling to Washington, D.C.

From 1830 to 1836, Catlin spent several summers among various Indian tribes. He painted Indians in St. Louis, along the Missouri River, in Texas, and in the upper Mississippi River region. By 1837, he had made almost 500 portraits and sketches and had gathered information from almost 50 tribes. He used these materials in an exhibition called "Catlin's Indian Gallery," which he took to major cities in the United States and Europe. From 1852 to 1857, Catlin traveled in South America and painted Indians there. Except for those years, he lived in Europe from 1839 to 1870. Many of his paintings hang in the Smithsonian Institution in Washington, D.C., and several appear in the article on INDIAN, AMERICAN. EDWARD H. DWIGHT

CATNIP, or CATMINT, is a plant of the mint family that grows to a height of 2 or 3 feet (61 to 91 centimeters). The catnip bears little clusters of whitish flowers tinged with a delicate rose color. The downy, heart-shaped leaves are green above and whitish below. Catnip was once used to make a valuable home tonic. It also furnished a seasoning for cooking. The plants are harvested when in full bloom. Catnip has become a common roadside weed in North America and Europe.

Scientific Classification. The catnip plant belongs to the mint family *Labiatae*. It is classified as genus *Nepeta*, species *N. cataria*. HAROLD NORMAN MOLDENKE

See also MINT.

CATO, *KAY toh*, was the family name of two statesmen and soldiers of ancient Rome.

Marcus Porcius Cato the Elder (234-149 B.C.) was a prominent Roman statesman. He began his political career under Valerius Flaccus, a Roman with great influence. Flaccus was impressed with Cato's service to Rome in the war against Hannibal of Carthage. Cato was known as a *conservative* because he generally opposed change. For 50 years after the war, Cato fought against the luxury Romans enjoyed as the city's wealth increased. As *censor* (a high administrative official) he tried to restore simplicity to Roman life. He became known as "Cato the Censor."

Toward the end of his life, he was alarmed by the recovery of Carthage. He is said to have ended every speech with the phrase, "Carthage must be destroyed." His warnings encouraged Rome to fight Carthage again, and the city was destroyed by the Romans in 146 B.C.

Cato opposed the influence of the Greeks, but he learned Greek himself at the age of 80. He published his speeches and wrote a book on farming which gives a picture of life in the ancient Italian countryside. Cato also wrote a book on early Roman history which has been lost. HERBERT M. HOWE

Marcus Porcius Cato the Younger (95-46 B.C.) was the great-grandson of Cato the Elder. He became a Stoic philosopher and was a stubborn conservative in politics. He considered principles more important than compromise. He became quaestor in 65 B.C. and helped reform the treasury. As a tribune, he supported Cicero against Catiline and opposed the First Triumvirate (see TRIUMVIRATE). In 54 B.C., Cato was made praetor.

When Pompey and Julius Caesar quarreled, Cato supported Pompey. When the news of Pompey's defeat at Pharsalus in 48 B.C. reached him, Cato fled to North Africa. There he received command of the defense of Utica. After the defeat of Pompey's forces at Thapsus in 46 B.C., Cato committed suicide by stabbing himself. He became a hero to those who idealized the dying Roman Republic. CHESTER G. STARR

See also CAESAR, JULIUS; PRAETOR; STOIC PHILOSOPHY; TRIBUNE.

CAT'S-CLAW. See ACACIA.

CAT'S-EYE is a prized gem stone that is an opalescent variety of chrysoberyl, a beryllium-aluminum compound. When cut in a certain way, this gem resembles a cat's eye. It has a silky luster and shows a greenish, reddish, and yellowish play of colors. The true cat's-eye is found in Sri Lanka. See also GEM (color picture).

CATSKILL MOUNTAINS form a chain of low mountains along the western shore of the Hudson River in New York. The southern end of the Catskills lies about 100 miles (160 kilometers) from New York City. The chain is about 50 miles (80 kilometers) long and 30 miles (48 kilometers) wide. The highest peaks include Slide Mountain (4,204 feet, or 1,281 meters) and Hunter Mountain (4,025 feet, or 1,227 meters).

The Catskill Mountains once formed part of a plateau that was carved out by rivers thousands of years ago. Trees, woodland plants, and flowers cover the slopes of the Catskills. This is one of the most beautiful natural regions in New York. Catskill State Park covers 596,120 acres (241,241 hectares) in the region.

Many summer resorts and sanitariums are in the Catskills. The Schoharie and Ashokan Reservoirs are artificial bodies of water that have been dug in the Catskills region. The Catskill Aqueduct carries water from the Ashokan Reservoir to New York City. Thunder Mountain in the Catskills is the *Dunderberg* of Washington Irving's famous story, "Rip Van Winkle," published in 1819. WILLIAM E. YOUNG

CATSUP. See CATCHUP.

CATT, CARRIE CHAPMAN (1859-1947), was an American leader in the campaign for woman suffrage. She served as president of the National American Woman Suffrage Association from 1900 to 1904, and from 1915 to 1920, when Amendment 19 to the United States Constitution was passed, giving women the right to vote.

Carrie Chapman Catt
Clinedist

Mrs. Catt began her suffrage work as an organizer of clubs in 1887. She became one of the suffrage movement's most effective lecturers and organizers. Her work extended to Canada and Europe. From 1904 to 1923, she served as president of the International Woman Suffrage Alliance. In 1920, she founded the National League of Women Voters (now called the League of Women Voters) to teach women an understanding of public affairs so they could vote intelligently. In 1925, she founded the National Committee on the Cause and Cure of War. This became the Women's Action Committee for Victory and a Lasting Peace.

Mrs. Catt was born in Ripon, Wis., and attended Iowa State College. She taught school and became the first woman superintendent of schools in Mason City, Iowa. She married Leo Chapman, a newspaper editor, who died in 1886. She married George William Catt, an engineer, in 1890 in Seattle, Wash. LOUIS FILLER

See also LEAGUE OF WOMEN VOTERS; WOMAN SUFFRAGE.

CATTAIL is a wild plant that grows in swamps and marshes throughout the United States and southern Canada. In some places, cattails cover large areas with their waving green leaves. The larger cattails are about 6 feet (1.8 meters) high, and have long, broad leaves. The smaller ones have narrow leaves. Cattail flowers enlarge and become the long brown spikes sometimes used for winter decorations. On the Pacific Coast, cattails are known as *tule-reeds*.

The roots of cattails contain starch, and are eaten by the Cossacks of Russia. The English eat them under the name of *Cossack asparagus*. Cattails provide a silky down used to dress wounds and for upholstering. During World War I this down was used in the manufacture of artificial silk and served as a substitute for cotton. In some places in Europe and India, people use the highly inflammable pollen of cattails for tinder.

Cattails are often used for decorations in homes.
J. Horace McFarland

Scientific Classification. Cattails belong to the cattail family, *Typhaceae*. The larger cattail is genus *Typha*, species *T. latifolia*; the smaller, *T. angustifolia*. FRANK THONE

See also BULRUSH.

CATTALO. See BUFFALO.

CATTELL, *kuh TELL,* **JAMES MCKEEN** (1860-1944), an American scientist, professor, editor, and publisher, pioneered in the field of experimental psychology. He taught psychology at the University of Pennsylvania, Cambridge University, and Columbia University. He served as editor of several scientific publications, including *Science*, *The Scientific Monthly*, and *The American Naturalist*. He also was editor and publisher of *American Men of Science*. Cattell was born in Easton, Pa. CLAUDE A. EGGERTSEN

Grant Heilman

Hereford Cattle Graze in a Pasture.

CATTLE

CATTLE are among the most important farm animals. We eat the meat of cattle as roast beef, veal, hamburger, and hot dogs. We drink the milk of cattle, and use it to make butter, cheese, and ice cream. The hides of cattle provide leather for our shoes. Cattle also furnish materials for such useful items as medicines, soap, and glue. In some countries, cattle supply a main source of power by pulling plows, carts, and wagons. In some parts of the world, a man's wealth is judged by the number of cattle he owns.

All cattle have heavy bodies, long tails, and *cloven* (divided) hoofs. Cattle chew their food two separate times to digest it. After they chew and swallow the food, they bring it up from the stomach and chew it again. This once-swallowed food is called a *cud.*

Cattle graze lazily in green pastures and on the plains. Their mooing, or *lowing,* often breaks the silence of the countryside. *Beef cattle* are raised for their meat. *Dairy cattle* are raised for their milk. *Dual-purpose* cattle provide both meat and milk. But almost all cattle eventually are killed for meat.

People on every continent raise cattle. Cattle live in cold lands such as Iceland, and in hot countries such as India. Hindus in India believe cattle are holy animals. They do not kill cattle or eat their meat.

Cattle possess less intelligence than most other domestic animals. People sometimes give them names. But cattle rarely learn to respond to their names as horses and dogs do.

In the United States, the word *cattle* usually means cows, bulls, steers, heifers, and calves. A *cow* is a female and a *bull* is a male. *Steers* are males whose reproductive organs have been removed by an operation. A young cow is called a *heifer* until she gives birth to a calf. A *calf* is a young cow or bull. The mother of a calf is called a *dam,* and the father is called a *sire.* A group of cattle is known as a *herd.*

Beef cattle and dairy cattle that can be traced through all their ancestors to the original animals of a breed are called *purebred.* A *registered* animal is one whose family history has been recorded with the appropriate breed association in its register, or *herdbook.*

In the late 1970's, about $1\frac{1}{2}$ million purebred cattle were registered with national associations. Not all purebred cattle are registered. Some farmers and ranchers have no interest in registering their cattle.

The Bodies of Cattle

Cattle have muscular backs and hindquarters. Most cattle reach a height of about 5 feet (1.5 meters). Cows weigh from about 900 to 2,000 pounds (410 to 910 kilograms). Bulls may weigh 2,000 pounds or more.

Most cattle have a coat of short hair that grows thicker and somewhat longer during the winter. A few breeds have long hair. The long, shaggy hair of Galloway cattle enables them to survive the extremely cold weather in Scotland, where the breed developed and where most of them are raised. Cattle also have a long tail, which they use to shoo away insects.

Teeth. Adult cattle have 32 teeth—8 in the front of the lower jaw and 12 each in the back of the upper and lower jaws. A cow cannot bite off grass because it does not have cutting teeth in the front of its upper jaw. It must tear the grass by moving its head. Cattle chew their cud with their *molars* (back teeth).

Horns. The horns of cattle are hollow and have no branches, as do those of some other horned animals such as deer. Cattle born without horns are called *polled* cattle. Cattle owners have increased the number of polled animals through selective breeding. They *dehorn* (remove the horns of) most horned cattle to keep them from injuring other cattle or people. The horns are removed with chemicals or a hot iron. In most cases, dehorning occurs when a calf is less than 3 weeks old.

Stomach. Cattle have a stomach with four compartments. This kind of stomach enables them to bring swallowed food back into their mouth to be chewed and swallowed again. Animals with such stomachs are called *ruminants*. The four compartments are the *rumen*, the *reticulum*, the *omasum*, and the *abomasum*.

When cattle eat, they first chew their food only enough to swallow it. The food goes down the *esophagus* (food pipe) into the rumen. The rumen and the reticulum form a large storage area. In that area, the food is mixed and softened. At the same time, microorganisms that grow in the rumen break down complex carbohydrates into simple carbohydrates. Such simple carbohydrates as sugars and starches provide the major source of energy for the animal. The microorganisms also build protein and many B-complex vitamins.

After the solid food has been mixed and softened, stomach muscles send it back up into the animal's mouth. The animal rechews this cud and swallows it. The swallowed cud goes back to the rumen and reticulum, where it undergoes further chemical breakdown. The food and fluids then move down into the omasum, where much of the water is absorbed. The food then enters the abomasum. The walls of the abomasum produce digestive juices. These juices further digest the food. The abomasum is called the *true stomach*, because it functions in much the same way as the stomach of creatures that are not ruminants. From the stomach, the food goes to the intestine, where digestion is completed.

Udder. Cows have a baggy organ called an *udder*, which holds their milk. The udder hangs from the cow's

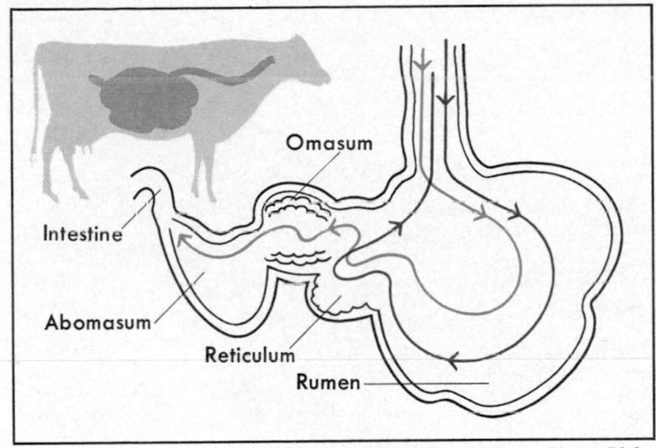

WORLD BOOK diagram by Steven Liska

A Cow's Stomach has four compartments. Food first enters the two sections shown by the red line. The cow then rechews the food as a *cud*, which follows the path shown by the blue line. In the drawing, the animal's stomach has been stretched out of its actual shape to show how food travels through it.

Grant Heilman

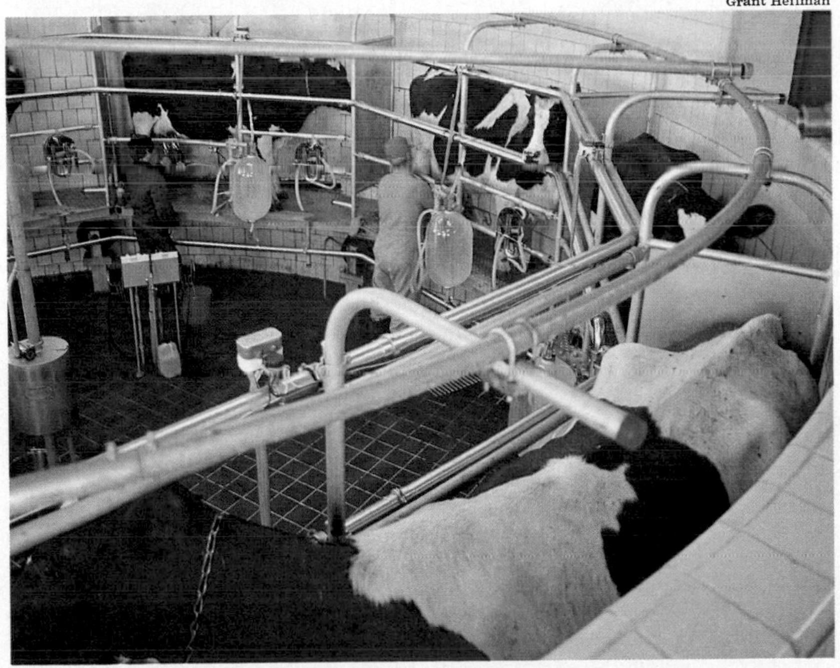

A Milking Parlor on a dairy farm has sanitary equipment that milks cows, such as the Holsteins shown at the left. The milk is stored in a refrigerated tank until it is delivered to a processing plant.

American Angus Association

Aberdeen-Angus

American Brahman Breeders Association

Brahman

Grant Heilman

Charolais

body a little in front of the hind legs. The udder has four sections that hold milk. When a cow is milked by hand, pressure causes the milk to squirt out of the udder through large nipples called *teats*. Some farmers still milk their cows by hand. But large dairy farms use electrically operated milking machines. Milking machines use suction to draw the milk from the cow's udder into a container (see MILKING MACHINE). Beef cows, which produce milk only for their calves, have smaller udders than dairy cows.

Beef Cattle

Most beef calves graze on large areas of open grassland that are unsuitable for growing crops. This method of feeding enables ranchers to raise stock without using large numbers of workers and expensive feeds and equipment. Beef calves have been bred to produce meat under such ranching conditions.

Beef cattle have also been bred to mature and fatten earlier than dairy cattle and to produce less milk than dairy cattle. However, steers and heifers from dairy breeds also provide excellent beef and supply much of the beef eaten in the United States.

Meat from calves that are less than 3 months old is called *veal*. Meat from older animals is called *beef*. Butchers classify beef into various *cuts*, such as steaks and roasts. People also eat the brains, heart, kidneys, liver, *sweetbread* (pancreas and thymus), tongue, and *tripe* (stomach lining) of cattle.

The chief breeds of beef cattle in the United States are the *Aberdeen-Angus*, *Brahman*, *Charolais*, *Hereford*, *Shorthorn*, and *Simmental*.

Aberdeen-Angus cattle, often called simply *Angus*, are polled animals with black coats. These cattle mature and fatten early. Their fat tends to *marble* (mix with lean meat), a desirable quality in beef. Many cattle raisers consider the Angus the typical beef animal. But others believe the breed is not large enough. A number of breeders crossbreed the Angus with certain larger breeds to produce larger offspring.

Breeders developed the Angus in the Highlands of Northern Scotland. The breed was brought to America in 1873. Today, cattle owners throughout the nation raise Angus cattle.

The *Red Angus*, a separate breed, was developed from red calves born to Aberdeen-Angus cattle. Except for their red color, these Angus resemble Aberdeen-Angus.

Brahman cattle thrive in the hot, humid climate of the southern United States, especially in states bordering the Gulf of Mexico. Brahman cattle have short hair and well-developed sweat glands that enable them to withstand heat and humidity. The Brahman has a fleshy hump over its shoulders. Most of these cattle are light gray or nearly black, although a few are red. American breeders developed the Brahman by crossing various kinds of *Zebus*, the humped cattle of India, which were imported into the United States from 1854 to 1926.

Charolais cattle are a very large, white breed that originated in France. Commercial cattle producers seek Charolais for crossbreeding because of their great size, their heavy muscular system, and the rapid growth of Charolais calves. No other breed has gained such widespread popularity in the United States in so short a time. In 1936, the first Charolais were brought to the United States from Mexico. In the mid-1960's, a number of them were imported from Canada.

Hereford cattle have red bodies and white faces. They often are called *whitefaces*. Herefords also have white patches on their chests, flanks, lower legs, and on the *switches*, or tips, of their tails. They have short necks and broad heads.

Herefords can be raised on the grasslands of the western United States until they are ready for market. But their meat is tastier if they are fattened on corn and other grains. Herefords are especially popular as "baby beef." Packing houses buy baby beef when the animals are 8 to 18 months old and weigh from 600 to 1,100 pounds (270 to 499 kilograms).

The Hereford breed was developed in the county of Hereford in England. The breed first was brought to the United States when Henry Clay imported Herefords in 1817 for his Kentucky farm. But they were not brought in on a large scale until 1850.

A *strain* (variety) of Herefords called *Polled Herefords* are born without horns. They are not a separate breed. Warren Gammon of Des Moines, Iowa, developed purebred polled Herefords in 1901 by crossbreeding Herefords that had been born without horns.

Shorthorn cattle include three strains. The term *Shorthorn* alone applies to cattle raised for meat. *Milking Shorthorns* are raised for beef and milk. *Polled Shorthorns* are raised for beef. Shorthorns may be white, red, or *roan* (yellow-red), or combinations of white and red.

Shorthorn cattle were brought to America from England in 1783. The Shorthorn became popular with the early American pioneers. Settlers crossed the breed with the Longhorn, which was the most plentiful breed at that time. Shorthorns can be found in most parts of the United States and in many parts of Canada.

Simmental cattle were introduced into the United States from Canada in 1967. The breed originated in Switzerland and is found in many parts of Europe, where it is raised for beef, milk, and *draft* (pulling loads). In the United States, the large-bodied Simmental is raised mainly for beef. The cattle range in color from red and white to *fawn* (light yellowish brown) and white. The American Simmental herd has grown rapidly because of such breeding techniques as *artificial insemination* and *embryo transfer* (see BREEDING).

Other Beef Cattle. The *Limousin* is a large, well-muscled French breed popular for crossbreeding in the United States. The Limousin was brought to the United States in 1969. Other imported breeds popular among U.S. cattle owners include the *Devon*, from England; the *Galloway* and the *Highland*, from Scotland; the *Maine-Anjou*, the *Normandy*, the *Salers*, and the *Tarentaise*, from France; the *Gelbvieh*, from Germany; the *Beef Friesian*, from Ireland; the *Chianina*, the *Marchigiana*, and the *Romagnola*, from Italy; and the *Murray Grey*, from Australia.

Breeders have crossed cattle from major breeds to create such new American breeds as the *Barzona*, the *Beefmaster*, the *Brangus*, the *Charbray*, and the *Santa Gertrudis*. The *Droughtmaster*, a cross between a Brahman and a Shorthorn, is a popular breed in Australia.

Dairy Cattle

The five most important breeds of milk cows in the United States are the *Holstein-Friesian*, *Jersey*, *Guernsey*,

Danny Weaver, Agri-Graphic Services

Hereford

American Simmental Association

Simmental

American Shorthorn Association

Shorthorn

Danny Weaver, Agri-Graphic Services

Holstein-Friesian

The American Jersey Cattle Club

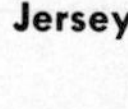

Jersey

Danny Weaver, Agri-Graphic Services

Guernsey

Ayrshire, and *Brown Swiss*. All breeds are considered good milk producers, but some breeds, such as the Holstein-Friesian, produce more milk than others.

The cows brought to America in colonial days produced little milk. Dairy farmers increased the milk output and butterfat content by improving herds. The butterfat content is important because butterfat is used to make butter. The average annual output of milk per cow increased from 8,305 pounds (3,767 kilograms) in the mid 1960's to 12,147 pounds (5,510 kilograms) in the early 1980's. Milk production is measured by weight because farmers are paid for their milk by weight at creameries and receiving stations. One gallon (3.8 liters) of milk weighs 8.6 pounds (3.9 kilograms).

Dairy cows normally give milk for about five or six years, but some still give it at the age of 20 or older. When cows no longer give milk, they usually are sent to a livestock market for slaughter. Dairy cattle provide between 25 and 30 per cent of our beef and veal.

Holstein-Friesian cattle, usually called *Holsteins*, are identified by their black-and-white coats. Some Holsteins are nearly all black or all white. A few are red and white. Holsteins are the largest dairy breed. They have broad hips and long, deep *barrels*, or body trunks. Their horns slant forward, but curve inward.

There are more Holsteins in the United States than any other dairy breed. Many farmers favor them because a Holstein cow produces more milk than other breeds. However, their milk contains less butterfat than that of other breeds.

Holsteins probably were developed from a strain of black-and-white cattle found in the province of Friesland in The Netherlands. Cattle raisers of Schleswig-Holstein in Germany also helped develop the breed.

Holsteins were brought to the United States in 1795. They are now raised in every state. Holsteins are also popular in Canada. The Holstein-Friesian Association of America has headquarters in Brattleboro, Vt.

Jersey cattle range in color from gray to dark fawn, or reddish-brown. Some appear almost black. The Jersey is the smallest major dairy breed. Its broad face is unusually short from its forehead to its nostrils. The small horns curve inward.

Jersey cows produce less milk than the four other major breeds, but their milk contains the most butterfat. A thick mass of cream rises to the top of a container of Jersey milk.

Jersey cattle came from the tiny British island of Jersey in the English Channel. They were brought to the United States in 1850. Jerseys thrive in all sections of the country. Many are raised in Canada. The American Jersey Cattle Club has headquarters in Columbus, Ohio.

Guernsey cattle are slightly larger than Jerseys. The Guernsey's fawn-colored coat is spotted with white markings. The Guernsey has a long head. A white shield often appears on its broad forehead. The horns curve upward and forward.

Guernseys produce a little more milk than Jerseys, but the rich milk of the Guernsey ranks second to that of the top-ranking Jersey in butterfat content.

Guernseys probably originated on Guernsey, an island in the English Channel. Breeders crossed the red brindle cattle of Normandy with the small brown-and-white cattle of Brittany. Guernseys were brought to the

United States in 1831. They are raised in every state, as well as in Canada. The American Guernsey Cattle Club has headquarters in Peterborough, N.H.

Ayrshire cattle are red and white or brown and white. Some are nearly all red or all white. The Ayrshire's long, curving horns give it an impressive appearance. Its body is sturdy, but somewhat lean. Production of milk from Ayrshire cattle ranks between Brown Swiss and Guernsey.

Ayrshires came from the hilly country of Ayr in southwest Scotland. They are more rugged than other breeds, and they thrive in hilly country. Ayrshires were brought to the United States in 1822. They later spread to the Pacific Coast, and are also popular in Canada. The Ayrshire Breeders' Association has headquarters in Brandon, Vt.

Brown Swiss may be light brown, dark brown, or brownish-gray. A light gray stripe may run along the back. The nose, horn tips, and tail switch are black. Brown Swiss are larger than most dairy cattle. The horns slant forward and upward.

Brown Swiss milk production ranks second only to that of Holsteins. The milk is pure white, and is rich in nonfat solids, minerals, and *lactose*, or milk sugar. These qualities make the milk of Brown Swiss cattle excellent for cheese.

Like the Holstein, the Brown Swiss is one of the oldest breeds of dairy cattle. It was first raised in the *canton* (state) of Schwyz in Switzerland.

Brown Swiss cattle were brought to New England in 1869. They now are raised throughout the United States and also in Canada. The Brown Swiss Cattle Breeders' Association of America has headquarters in Beloit, Wis.

Other Dairy Cattle. *Dutch Belted* cows are black, with a wide belt of white around the middle. Their milk contains about as much butterfat as that of the Brown Swiss and Ayrshire. Dutch Belted cows were brought to the United States from The Netherlands in the late 1830's. This breed is raised mostly in the eastern United States.

French Canadian cattle are a small, dark brown breed, much like the Jersey and the Guernsey. They are raised mostly in Quebec. The milk of these cows is rich in butterfat. French Canadian cattle are not common in any sections of the United States.

Kerry cattle, a black breed, originated in Ireland. They are closely related to *Dexter* cattle, which are small and have short legs. Dexters produce about one half Dexter offspring, one fourth Kerry-type offspring, and one fourth abnormal "bulldog" calves that die at birth. Kerry and Dexter cattle are not commonly raised in the United States.

Red Sindhi is a red, Brahman-type of cattle that originated in the province of Sind in Pakistan. It produces more milk than the Brahman, and has been crossed with other breeds in the United States to develop cattle with greater resistance to high temperatures.

Dual-Purpose Cattle

Some cattle can be raised for beef or kept as dairy cattle. They are called *dual-purpose cattle*. These animals have many of the qualities of beef cattle, but they also are good milk producers. The most important dual-purpose breeds are the *Milking Shorthorn* and the *Red Poll*. Many farmers raise dual-purpose breeds only for meat. These breeds produce calves that grow rapidly and can be slaughtered for veal or baby beef sooner than some beef cattle breeds.

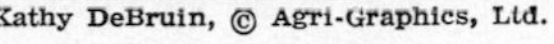
Kathy DeBruin, © Agri-Graphics, Ltd.

Ayrshire

© Agri-Graphic Services (Brown Swiss Cattle Breeders' Association)

Brown Swiss

Dairy cattle provide much of our beef and veal. But they are not classified as dual-purpose cattle, because they are bred and raised chiefly for milk.

Milking Shorthorns produce large amounts of milk and beef. They are popular with farmers who do not specialize either in fattening beef cattle for market or in producing milk for big cities.

Milking Shorthorns are red, white, roan, or red and white spotted. They were brought to Virginia and Maryland from England in 1783. Milking Shorthorns are raised in the Middle West and the eastern and southeastern sections of the United States. The American Milking Shorthorn Society has headquarters in Springfield, Mo.

Red Polls are red, hornless cattle. Horned Norfolk cattle were crossed with polled Suffolk to produce Red

Danny Weaver, Agri-Graphic Services

Milking Shorthorn

Danny Weaver, Agri-Graphic Services

Red Poll

Polls. Red Polls are smaller than Shorthorns, and are less numerous than Milking Shorthorns.

The breed originated in the counties of Norfolk and Suffolk in England. Red Polls were brought to the United States in 1873. Most of the Red Polls in the United States are raised on farms in the Middle West. The Red Poll Cattle Club of America has its headquarters located in Lincoln, Nebr.

Breeding and Care of Cattle

Breeding. Cattle breeders select and mate the best types of cattle for a special purpose, such as producing large quantities of milk or high-grade beef. Then they mate the best of the offspring until, after several generations, the cattle possess the desired qualities. In this way, beef cattle have been bred to mature earlier. They thus can be sold at a greater profit than they could if they had to be fattened over a longer time. Selective breeding has increased milk output and the percentage of butterfat.

Heifers usually are mated when they are between 15 and 27 months old. A cow carries her calf in her body for nine months before it is born. Cows usually have one calf every year. Sometimes twins are born. Bulls may start breeding at the age of 1 year, but they are most active between 2 and 6 years of age.

A cow cannot produce milk unless it has given birth to a calf. Such a cow is known as a "fresh" cow. After the birth of the calf, the cow usually gives milk for about 10 months. A cow that does not give milk is called a "dry cow."

Feeding. Feeding methods have greatly improved the production of both meat and milk. Cattle are hearty eaters. Here is a recommended daily diet for fattening a 2-year-old beef steer: 25 pounds (11 kilograms) of corn or sorghum silage, 4 pounds (1.8 kilograms) of red clover hay, 14 pounds (6 kilograms) of corn or ground grain sorghum, and 1¼ pounds (0.57 kilogram) of linseed meal or cottonseed meal.

The fattening diet of younger cattle contains more grain and less *roughage*, or coarse feed such as hay.

Six Main Breeds of Beef Cattle

Breed	Aberdeen-Angus	Brahman	Charolais	Hereford	Shorthorn	Simmental
Color	Black	Light gray to nearly black	White to straw-colored	Red and white	Roan, red, or white; or red and white	Red and white to fawn and white
Place of origin	Scotland	United States	France	England	England	Switzerland
Rank in size	5	3	1	4	6	2
Year brought into United States	1873	—	1936	1817	1783	1967
Rank in number registered in United States	2	5	4	1	6	3
National registry association formed	1883	1924	1957	1881	1882	1968

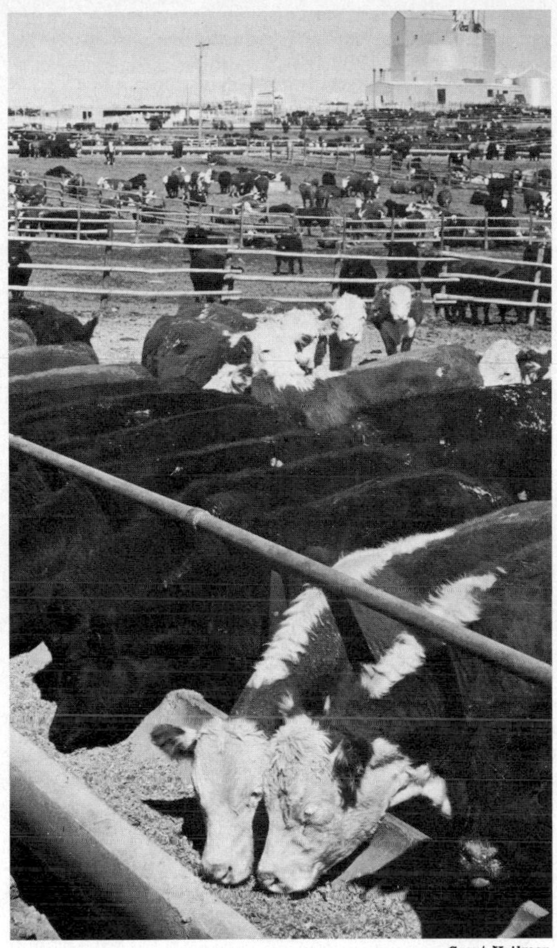

Grant Heilman

In a Feed Lot, cattle eat carefully selected feed that makes them gain weight much faster than they would by grazing. Feed lots are an efficient means of fattening cattle before they are sent to a packing house.

Cattle feeders watch the appetites of their cattle closely. They often add "blackstrap" molasses, a low-grade sugar solution, to encourage cattle to eat more. The best feeders use the latest scientific methods to make their cattle gain weight rapidly at the lowest cost.

Certain chemicals may be added to cattle feed to make cattle eat more and fatten more quickly. Antibiotics are also added to feed to increase gains in weight.

The amount of milk and butterfat produced each year by a cow can be increased by a proper diet. The average dairy cow eats 3 pounds of silage and 1 pound of hay a day for every 100 pounds of its body weight. Dairy cows usually receive 1 pound of grain or other concentrated feed for every 4 to 6 pounds of milk. Both dairy and beef cattle eat large amounts of *forage*, or rough feed such as clover and alfalfa. They eat huge amounts of grass every year and turn it into meat and milk for us to eat and drink.

Many cattle have been poisoned by eating certain kinds of plants found in dry regions of the western United States. Weeds that may poison cattle include locoweed, death camas, prince's-plume, and some lupines and larkspurs. Cattle owners sometimes destroy these plants with chemicals. See LOCOWEED.

Diseases sometimes attack cattle. The most serious cattle diseases include *anthrax*, *blackleg*, *bloat*, *brucellosis*, *foot-and-mouth disease*, and *mastitis*. All except bloat and mastitis are contagious.

Anthrax is caused by a germ that is usually picked up from the soil. It generally enters an animal's body through the mouth. Anthrax causes a high fever and often stops the flow of milk. It may be fatal to cattle. See ANTHRAX.

Blackleg is one of the deadliest diseases. It usually strikes animals between 6 and 18 months of age. It causes lameness, convulsions, rapid swelling, and high fever. Blackleg, carried by a germ in the soil, usually causes death within 36 hours.

Bloat is a condition in which gas swells the paunch,

Five Main Breeds of Dairy Cattle

Breed	Ayrshire	Brown Swiss	Guernsey	Holstein-Friesian	Jersey
Color	Red and white spotted	Brownish-gray	Orange, fawn, and white spotted	Black and white spotted	Light to dark grayish-fawn
Place of origin	Scotland	Switzerland	Isle of Guernsey	The Netherlands	Isle of Jersey
Rank in size	3	2	4	1	5
Average per cent butterfat of milk	4.0	4.0	4.7	3.7	5
Average annual yield of milk	6,500 lbs. (2,950 kg)	7,000 lbs. (3,200 kg)	5,750 lbs. (2,608 kg)	8,500 lbs. (3,860 kg)	5,250 lbs. (2,381 kg)
Rank in number registered in United States	4	5	2	1	3
National registry association formed	1875	1880	1877	1885	1868

causing the animal to stagger and gasp for breath. Cattle may be stricken with bloat after grazing in moist pastures. A change in feed when cattle are very hungry also may cause them to bloat.

Brucellosis, or *Bang's Disease*, attacks the lymph glands, udders, and reproductive organs of cows. Cattle pick up the brucellosis germ from dirty feed or other objects. Cows with brucellosis often cannot bear calves. See BANG'S DISEASE.

Foot-and-Mouth Disease is caused by a virus. The disease causes lameness and reduces milk output. The United States Department of Agriculture does not allow the import of cattle from countries where the disease is known to exist. See FOOT-AND-MOUTH DISEASE.

Mastitis is the most costly disease of dairy cattle in the United States. The disease is caused by germs that enter the udder. The germs do the greatest damage when the udder is injured or exposed to cold, wet surfaces. The udder then becomes hard, swollen, and painful. Mastitis causes a drop in milk production and quality. Antibiotics can be used effectively in treatment.

Insects spread such diseases as *anaplasmosis*, which is similar to malaria. *Texas fever* is an infectious disease caused by the cattle tick (see CATTLE TICK). Many kinds of flies annoy cattle. Some flies merely cause cattle to produce less meat or milk. But heel flies lay eggs on the heels of cattle. The larvae work up through the body and bore holes in the hide.

Cattle owners spray cattle with insecticides to kill flies and other insects. Veterinarians use modern vaccines, drugs, and antibiotics to help keep cattle healthy and to cure sickness.

Dwarf Cattle are undersized animals that never develop fully. They are stunted at birth, and many die soon after they are born. Cattle owners have become alarmed because more and more dwarf cattle have appeared in purebred herds. Dwarfs appear in every major breed. Some breeders believe that efforts to develop better beef cattle may lead to dwarfism. Some bulls with otherwise desirable qualities seem to produce many dwarfs.

Raising and Marketing Cattle

Most beef calves are born on Western ranches in the spring. The young spend the summer with cows in fenced pastures, or on an open range. Most calves are *branded* (marked) with a hot iron to show ownership (see RANCHING [picture: Famous Ranch Brands]). In the fall, the calves are *weaned* (taken from their mothers).

Feeder Cattle. The rancher sells the weaned calves to farmers, or *feeders*, in the Middle West, on the West Coast, or elsewhere. Such calves, called *feeder cattle*, are raised in *feed lots*. A feed lot is an enclosed area where cattle are fed special feed to fatten them for market. The farmer then sends them to a *stockyard* (market). Meat packers at the market buy cattle for slaughter. The largest stockyards are in Omaha, Nebr.; South St. Paul, Minn.; Oklahoma City, Okla.; and Sioux City, Iowa. See MEAT PACKING.

Ranchers sometimes send their calves directly to a market instead of selling them to farmers. Farmers, in turn, may buy feeder cattle from a carefully chosen market instead of from a rancher. The farmers fatten such calves, then sell them back to a market at a profit.

A farmer usually fattens feeder cattle for 90 to 180 days. The farmer tries to sell them when market con-

Leading Beef Cattle States and Provinces

Number of beef cattle in the state or province on Jan. 1, 1980*

Texas	12,795,000
Iowa	6,635,000
Nebraska	6,244,000
Kansas	6,043,000
Oklahoma	5,355,000
Missouri	5,036,000
South Dakota	3,807,000
Alberta	3,545,000
California	3,335,000
Montana	2,606,000

*State figures include all beef cattle, plus all dairy calves under 500 pounds (230 kilograms). Province figures include all beef cattle, plus all dairy calves under 1 year old.
Sources: U.S. Department of Agriculture; Statistics Canada.

Leading Dairy Cattle States and Provinces

Number of dairy cattle in the state or province on Jan. 1, 1980*

Wisconsin	2,548,000
New York	1,268,000
Minnesota	1,250,000
California	1,215,000
Pennsylvania	978,000
Quebec	960,000
Ontario	785,000
Michigan	593,000
Ohio	519,000
Iowa	515,000

*State figures include all dairy cows and heifers except calves under 500 pounds (230 kilograms). Province figures include all dairy cows and heifers except calves under 1 year old.
Sources: U.S. Department of Agriculture; Statistics Canada.

ditions give the biggest profit. A steer is normally ready for slaughter by the time it is 18 months old, but it may be 2 years old or older. Cattle reach full growth in two to three years. But many cattle are fat enough before they reach *maturity* (full growth). Such cattle, called *finished* cattle, may be as young as 8 months, and may weigh only 600 pounds (270 kilograms).

Some farmers in the East and Middle West breed and raise their own cattle. But most farmers find it more profitable to buy feeder cattle and use their land for growing feeds to fatten the stock.

Grass-Fed Cattle. Cattle owners sometimes feed their stock on grass for one or two years, and sell the animals as "grass fattened." Some grass-fattened cattle also receive grain feed for several weeks before they are fat enough to send to market. Farmers in southern coastal areas raise many calves that are sold for early slaughter or for grazing on richer pastures. Their land is not suitable for raising feeds on which to fatten cattle.

Dairy Cows. Most dairy cows spend their lives on one farm. Heifers from cows that have produced little milk are sent to market to be slaughtered for veal when only a few weeks old. It is probable that such calves, like their mothers, would be poor milk producers. Most male calves also are sent to market. Dairy farmers are careful to save the female calves of the best cows for herd replacements. When a cow fails to produce milk economically, it is sent to a livestock market and sold for slaughter. Such dairy cows produce much of our low-grade beef.

Show Cattle. Cattle owners exhibit prize animals at county fairs, state fairs, and livestock expositions. A champion dairy cow has a wide chest, strong head, and well-developed udder. A blue-ribbon beef animal has a solid, compact body, with short legs and broad head. Exhibitors such as Four-H Club members start developing show cattle as soon as the calves are born. The animals are carefully fed, exercised, and groomed. Their coats are trimmed and their horns are polished.

Leading Cattle Countries

Number of beef and dairy cattle in 1979

India	181,849,000*
Russia	114,086,000
United States	110,864,000
Brazil	90,000,000*
China	63,718,000*
Argentina	60,174,000*
Bangladesh	31,741,000
Mexico	29,920,000
Australia	27,107,000
Colombia	26,137,000

*Estimate.
Sources: U.S. Department of Agriculture; FAO.

Grant Heilman

Longhorn Cattle, such as the steer shown above, were an important breed in the American West until the early 1900's.

History

Early Cattle. Cattle belong to the genus *Bos*. Modern breeds descended from two species: *Bos indicus*, the humped cattle of Asia; and *Bos taurus*, the wild cattle of Europe. Most U.S. breeds descended from European cattle, especially the subspecies *B. taurus primigenius* and *B. taurus longifrons*. *B. taurus primigenius* were large, long-horned cattle. They were also called *auroch* (giant ox). *B. taurus longifrons*, also called the *celtic ox*, were smaller and had short horns.

People have raised cattle for thousands of years. Prehistoric drawings of cattle have been found on the walls of the Lascaux Cave in France and the Altamira Cave in Spain. Pictures carved in ancient Egyptian tombs show oxen pulling plows and treading grain.

Cattle raisers once followed their herds from land to land as the cattle searched for grass to eat. Later, some of these herders and their families settled in one place. They fed their cattle grain in addition to grass.

Beginning of Breeding. The first cattle were used as work animals as well as for producing milk and beef. The same kind of animal performed all three tasks. Gradually, people began to breed cattle either as beef animals or for producing milk. Robert Bakewell, a farmer who lived in Leicestershire, England, first used modern livestock breeding methods. He began improving his cattle during the late 1700's. He used a breed of cattle called *Longhorns* (different from Texas Longhorns), and tried to develop cattle that would give larger amounts of meat.

American Cattle. Some historians believe that cattle were first brought to the Americas by Norwegian Vikings in the early 1000's. In 1493, Christopher Columbus brought long-horned cattle from Spain to Santo Domingo (now part of the West Indies) on his second voyage to America. Descendants of these cattle later were taken into Mexico and eventually into Texas. They were ancestors of the famous Texas Longhorns.

Governor Edward Winslow of Plymouth Colony brought cattle to New England in 1624. Cattle raising spread westward as the pioneers moved across the continent. They used oxen to pull their wagons and plows.

Railroads helped cattle ranchers on the plains by providing transportation to the eastern markets. Refrigerated railroad cars made it possible to ship meat products safely over long distances. Breeders' organizations encouraged the improvement of beef and dairy cattle. Livestock shows spurred interest in breeding prizewinning cattle.

In the West, ranchers came to realize that the Texas Longhorn grew slower and was less profitable than such breeds as the Hereford and Aberdeen-Angus. The Longhorn produced little beef in proportion to its bulk. By the 1920's, the Texas Longhorn had nearly disappeared from the western ranges. However, the number of Texas Longhorns began to increase during the 1970's. Today, ranchers use Longhorns chiefly for crossbreeding with other cattle.

Growth of Herds. In 1900, there were about 59,739,000 cattle in the United States. The United States Department of Agriculture in the early 1980's estimated the number of cattle in the country at about 116 million. It valued them at about $48 billion.

United States cattle owners have worked to improve breeds and to increase beef and milk production. By the early 1950's, Americans were eating more beef than pork. People in the United States eat about 104 pounds (47.1 kilograms) of beef and drink about 108 quarts (102 liters) of milk every year.

The World Supply. There are about 1.2 billion beef and dairy cattle in the world. Asia raises three-tenths of the world's cattle. Africa and North and South America also have large numbers of cattle.

India has the most cattle of any country. But India's cattle are undernourished and have little work value. There is also little demand for meat in India because the cow is considered sacred. Other countries with large numbers of cattle include the United States, Russia, Brazil, and China. The United States, Russia, and Brazil have the most beef cattle. Russia, the United States, and France have the most dairy cattle.

Scientific Classification. Domestic cattle belong to the genus *Bos* of the bovid family, Bovidae. H. M. Briggs

Related Articles in World Book include:

Kinds of Cattle

Buffalo
Carabao
Kouprey
Musk Ox
Ox
Water Buffalo
Yak

Diseases and Pests

Actinomycosis
Anthrax
Bang's Disease
Botfly
Face Fly
Foot-and-Mouth Disease
Mange
Rinderpest
Tsetse Fly
Warble Fly

Industry

Agriculture
Breeding
Dairying
Livestock
Meat Packing
Ranching

Products

Beef
Butter
Casein
Cheese
Gelatin
Leather
Milk
Tallow
Veal

Other Related Articles

DES
Farm and Farming (pictures)
Horn
Pasture
Ruminant
Ungulate
Western Frontier Life (The Cattle Boom; Life in the Country; picture: Texas Longhorn Cattle)

Outline

I. The Bodies of Cattle
A. Teeth B. Horns C. Stomach D. Udder

II. Beef Cattle
A. Aberdeen-Angus
B. Brahman
C. Charolais
D. Hereford
E. Shorthorn
F. Simmental
G. Other Beef Cattle

III. Dairy Cattle
A. Holstein-Friesian
B. Jersey
C. Guernsey
D. Ayrshire
E. Brown Swiss
F. Other Dairy Cattle

IV. Dual-Purpose Cattle
A. Milking Shorthorns
B. Red Polls

V. Breeding and Care of Cattle
A. Breeding
B. Feeding
C. Diseases
D. Dwarf Cattle

VI. Raising and Marketing Cattle
A. Feeder Cattle
B. Grass-Fed Cattle
C. Dairy Cows
D. Show Cattle

VII. History

Questions

What are polled cattle?

What do cattle owners strive for in breeding beef cattle? In breeding dairy cattle?

Why are Charolais cattle popular for crossbreeding?

What was the original meaning of the word *cattle*?

About how many beef and dairy cattle are there in the world?

How can Holsteins be identified? How do they rank in size among the dairy breeds? In milk production?

Why had Texas Longhorns nearly disappeared in the United States by the 1920's?

What are purebred cattle? Are they always registered?

How long do cows usually produce milk? What usually happens to a cow that no longer gives milk?

What country has the most cattle?

Additional Resources

Dale, Edward Everett. *The Range Cattle Industry: Ranching on the Great Plains from 1865 to 1925.* Rev. ed. Univ. of Oklahoma Press, 1969. Reprint of 1960 ed.

Rouse, John E. *World Cattle.* 2 vols. Univ. of Oklahoma Press, 1970. *World Cattle III: Cattle of North America,* 1973.

Scuro, Vincent. *Wonders of Cattle.* Dodd, 1980. For younger readers.

Simpson, James R. *The World's Beef Business.* Iowa State Univ. Press, 1982.

CATTLE DRIVE. See Cowboy (The Cattle Drive; picture); Western Frontier Life (The Cattle Boom; Life in the Country).

CATTLE GRUB. See Warble Fly.

CATTLE PLAGUE. See Rinderpest.

CATTLE RANCH. See Ranching.

CATTLE TICK, also called *Texas fever tick,* carries Texas fever, a disease of cattle. The tick is round and chestnut brown in color. It carries a one-celled animal that causes the disease. The female tick leaves the one-celled animals in the cow's body when it sucks the cow's blood.

Texas fever is an infectious disease. The one-celled animals multiply in the cattle's blood and destroy the red blood corpuscles. The disease became serious in the southwestern part of the United States about the middle of the 1800's. It once threatened all the cattle in the country, but has been brought under control. To prevent the disease, ranchers bathe their cattle in a liquid that contains arsenic, which kills the ticks. Cattle can remain on a pasture containing ticks if they are dipped in the solution every two weeks.

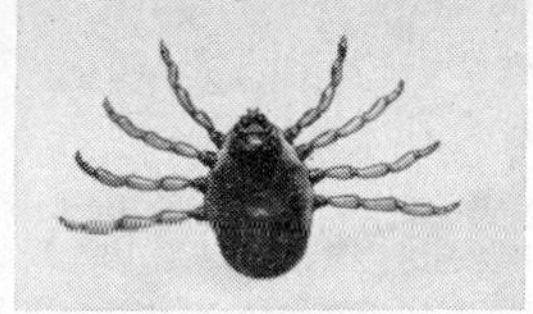

USDA

The Cattle Tick causes Texas fever when it bites cows and sucks their blood.

Scientific Classification. Cattle ticks belong to the tick family, *Ixodidae.* They are genus *Boophilus,* species *B. annulatus.* EDWARD A. CHAPIN

See also SMITH, THEOBALD; TICK.

CATTON, BRUCE (1899-1978), an American historian and journalist, won the Pulitzer prize in 1954 and the 1954 National Book Award for *A Stillness at Appomattox.* He wrote many other books about people and events of the Civil War. These include *Mr. Lincoln's Army* (1951), *Glory Road* (1952), *U. S. Grant and the Military Tradition* (1954), *Grant Moves South* (1960), *The Coming Fury* (1961), *Terrible Swift Sword* (1963), and *Never Call Retreat* (1965). Catton's vivid narratives were the result of a close study of original documents, letters, and diaries.

Catton was born in Petoskey, Mich. From 1926 to 1941, he served as Washington correspondent and special writer for the Newspaper Enterprise Association. He was editor of the *American Heritage* magazine from 1954 to 1959, when he became senior editor. MERLE CURTI

CATULLUS, *kuh TUHL uhs,* **GAIUS VALERIUS,** *GAY uhs vuh LEER ee uhs* (84? B.C.-54 B.C.), a Roman lyric poet, wrote personal and passionate poetry. His best-known poems tell of his love for Clodia, an aristocratic Roman matron called Lesbia in his poems. He wrote about the affair from its beginning to his final disillusionment in her.

Catullus also wrote long poems on mythological themes, a wedding chant, and many epigrams. One of the epigrams attacked Julius Caesar, who later forgave him. Catullus also wrote a famous farewell to his dead brother. A famous quotation from his works is: "What woman says to fond lover should be written in wind and running water."

He was born in Verona, Italy. The only surviving manuscript of his work was found there. MOSES HADAS

See also CLASSICISM (Rome); LATIN LITERATURE (The Age of Cicero).

CAUCASIA, *kaw KAY zhuh,* is a region in southwestern Russia, with a population of about 25 million. Caucasia is divided by the Caucasus Mountains, which extend 750 miles (1,210 kilometers) from the Black Sea to the Caspian Sea. The portion to the north of the mountains is called *Northern Caucasus;* that to the south, *Transcaucasia,* or *across the mountains.* After the Bolshevik Revolution, the southern section was organized as the "republics" of Georgia, Armenia, and Azerbaijan. In 1922, they were reorganized as the Transcaucasian Soviet Federated Socialist Republic of Russia. In December 1936, they were reorganized again as three separate states within the Soviet dictatorship. Caucasia is rich in natural resources, including oil and nonferrous metals. Most of the oil is produced near the city of Baku. See also ARMENIA; AZERBAIJAN; GEORGIA. THEODORE SHABAD

CAUCASOID RACE. See RACES, HUMAN (How Races Are Classified).

CAUCASUS MOUNTAINS, *KAW kuh suhs,* are a great mountain range in Russia. They rise between the Black and Caspian seas, and extend from northwest to southeast for about 750 miles (1,210 kilometers). The chief peak is Mount Elbrus (18,481 feet, or 5,633 meters, above sea level), which also ranks as the highest spot in Europe. Many geographers consider the Caucasus as the boundary line between Europe and Asia.

The mountains have a number of passes over 10,000 feet (3,000 meters) high. Roads cross a few passes, but railroads skirt around the mountains. The glaciers of the Caucasus rival those of the Alps in size, but there are almost no lakes. Among the Caucasus' rich mineral resources are the oil fields of Baku, Groznyy, and Maykop; the rich manganese deposits of Georgia; and valuable tungsten and molybdenum reserves. The mountains have been important historically as a barrier to migration, but numerous invasions swept over them in ancient times and in the Middle Ages. THEODORE SHABAD

See also MOUNT ELBRUS.

CAUCUS, *KAW kuhs,* is a meeting of members of a political party to name candidates for office or to decide on policy. The term *to caucus* means to hold a caucus.

In the early days of the United States, voters of each party in a city or village met in a local caucus to choose delegates for a county or state caucus which picked the party candidates. As the population grew, it became hard to get all the voters together. One person or a small group of people sometimes got control of the caucus and used it for private advantage. Partly for this reason, the direct primary was set up instead of the caucus as the method of nominating candidates. In some states, however, caucuses still choose delegates to the national conventions of the two major parties.

Until 1824, candidates for President and Vice-President were chosen by a caucus of the political parties in Congress. Caucuses are still active in Congress and in the parliaments of many nations. In the United States, the members of each party in Congress traditionally hold a caucus to decide on candidates for speaker of the House and other offices. Party caucuses in Congress also decide policy questions. CHARLES O. JONES

See also PRIMARY ELECTION (History).

CAUDAL ANESTHESIA. See ANESTHESIA (Local Anesthesia).

CAULIFLOWER is a garden vegetable. It is grown for its head of tightly clustered, juicy flowers and its fleshy stem. Large green leaves surround the head of the cauliflower.

Cauliflower may be cooked, pickled, or eaten raw. It provides large amounts of vitamin C and sulfur, and smaller amounts of vitamin A and phosphorus.

Cauliflower plants are usually grown from seed. Growers start the plants in a hotbed or greenhouse. Then, they transplant them to the field. Most growers

The Cauliflower Is a Garden Vegetable. Cauliflowers have been cultivated and eaten for several hundred years.

tie the large leaves around the head while the plant is growing to keep the flowers white.

Cauliflower grows best in cool, moist weather such as that found in some of the Pacific Coast states. Cauliflower is also grown in Southern states during the late fall and the winter. Leading cauliflower producing states include Arizona, California, Michigan, New York, Oregon, and Texas.

Scientific Classification. Cauliflower belongs to the mustard family, Cruciferae. It is *Brassica, oleracea,* variety *botrytis.* William Raymond Kays

CAULKING, *KAW kihng,* also spelled *calking,* is a technique of sealing seams and joints to make them watertight. Asphalt, mastic glazing, and special plastic-base compounds are the most commonly used caulking materials. Asphalt and such mastics as putty are usually applied with a putty knife or a device called a caulking gun. Workers often use putty to seal joints around windows and doors (see Putty). The plastic-base compounds, called *elastomeric* caulking, are used to seal joints that are likely to shrink or swell. Alva H. Jared

CAUSTIC, *KAWS tihk,* is any chemical that can burn or destroy flesh. The term comes from the Greek word *kaustos,* meaning *burning.* In chemistry, the word caustic usually refers to sodium hydroxide (caustic soda or lye) or to potassium hydroxide (caustic potash).

Caustic soda is used in refining petroleum and in making textiles, soap, and paper. In homes, hard white grains of caustic soda are poured into drains to clean out grease. Caustic soda is made from common salt (sodium chloride).

Caustic potash is used in making *soft* soaps that dissolve easily in water. It is made from potassium chloride. When concentrated, both caustic potash and caustic soda can slowly destroy glass and porcelain.

Doctors sometimes destroy warts and other unwanted body tissues with a chemical called *lunar caustic.* This caustic is crystallized silver nitrate. Esmarch S. Gilreath

See also Alkali; Base; Lye; Potassium; Silver Nitrate.

CAVALIER, *KAV uh LIHR,* meaning *horseman,* was a name used in England in the 1640's for the colorfully dressed troops devoted to King Charles I, as opposed to *Roundhead,* the name given to a follower of the Parliamentary cause during the English Civil War. Today, the term *cavalier* often applies to a courteous escort for a woman. See also Charles (I) of England; England (The Civil War). J. Salwyn Schapiro

CAVALIER POETS. See English Literature (Metaphysical and Cavalier Poets).

CAVALLERIA RUSTICANA. See Opera (The Opera Repertoire).

CAVALRY is a unit of soldiers mounted on horseback. The word *cavalry* comes from the French word *cavalerie* and the Latin word *caballus,* meaning *horse.* The expense of maintaining horses and the greater speed and mobility of motorized units made horse cavalry obsolete by the mid-1900's.

Tribes of nomads in Asia were the first to use cavalry. King Philip II of Macedonia used cavalry as major

Detail of an oil painting on canvas (1881) by Lady Butler; Leeds City Art Gallery, Yorkshire, England

The Cavalry Charge became an important military tactic during the 1600's. This painting shows the Scots Greys, a Scottish regiment, attacking the French in the Battle of Waterloo in 1815.

military units for the first time in Europe in the 300's B.C. Cavalry units became a leading part of the Roman army in the late A.D. 300's. During the Middle Ages, only knights and their squires fought on horseback. Later, common soldiers rode horses to the battlefield, then dismounted to fight. Oliver Cromwell developed the cavalry charge, which the Duke of Marlborough, Frederick the Great, and Napoleon improved further. The cavalry charge was abandoned when machine guns and barbed wire were developed in the late 1800's.

Cavalry units called *dragoons* fought in the Revolutionary War in America. During the Civil War, both Union and Confederate armies used cavalry units extensively. The U.S. Cavalry patrolled the Mexican border and chased the bandit Pancho Villa in Mexico during the early 1900's. Automobiles and trucks began to replace horses in the U.S. Army in 1920. The Army has not had horse cavalry units since 1943. Armored units have inherited the honors and traditions of the U.S. Cavalry. Armored units are considered cavalry because they use the same tactics as the horse cavalry used.

Historians consider the Russian Cossack and the German Uhlan cavalries among the world's greatest. During World War II, the Russians are believed to have used 300,000 horse cavalrymen. MARK M. BOATNER III

CAVE, or CAVERN, is a naturally hollow area in the earth that is large enough for a person to enter. Some caves consist of a single chamber only a few yards or meters deep. Other caves are vast networks of passages and chambers. The longest cave ever explored, the Mammoth-Flint Ridge cave system in Kentucky, extends more than 190 miles (306 kilometers).

The interior of a cave is a dark, damp place where sunlight never enters. However, artificial light supplied by explorers may reveal a strange underground landscape filled with beautiful, oddly shaped rock formations called *speleothems*. Many caves also have underground lakes, rivers, and waterfalls.

Some of the most spectacular caves are popular tourist attractions. These caves have been equipped with pathways and electric lights to enable people to walk through them easily and safely. However, thousands of caves remain in their natural state, and many caves have passages that have never been seen by a human being.

The scientific study of caves is called *speleology*. Scientists who study caves and the organisms that live in them are known as *speleologists*. Many people enjoy *spelunking*, the hobby of exploring and mapping caves.

How Caves Are Formed. The vast majority of caves are formed in limestone or in a related rock, such as marble or dolomite. Such caves, called *solution caves*, form as underground water slowly dissolves the rock. This process takes thousands of years. It begins when surface water trickles down through tiny cracks in the rock to the *water table*, the level at which the underground area is saturated. There the water slowly dissolves some of the rock, forming passages and chambers. The water may form deep pits in places where the rock tilts sharply.

Limestone and similar rock are only slightly soluble in water. But the water that trickles down from the surface contains carbon dioxide, which has been absorbed from the air and soil above the rock. The carbon dioxide forms a mild acid in the water, and this acid helps dissolve the rock.

Luray Caverns, Virginia

A Cave may consist of an enormous chamber filled with colorful, strangely shaped rock formations. The Giant's Hall, *above*, is one of many such chambers of the Luray Caverns in Virginia.

Eventually, the water table may drop below the level of the cave. Or, the cave may be raised above the water table by an earthquake or, more often, by a gradual uplifting of the ground. Most of the water then drains out, and air fills the cave. A surface stream may enter the cave and flow through it. The stream continues the process of dissolving the rock and thus enlarges the cave. Connections from the cave to the surface may develop in several ways. For example, the rock above part of the cave may collapse, forming a vertical entrance called a *sinkhole*. A horizontal entrance may develop on a hillside or a valley slope, especially at a point where a spring or stream flows from the cave.

Other caves, called *lava caves*, form from molten lava. As lava flows down a slope, its outer surface cools and hardens, but the lava beneath remains molten. The molten lava continues to flow and eventually drains out, creating a cave. Lava caves are near the surface of the earth and have many openings in their thin

A Sectional View of a Solution Cave A solution cave, such as the one shown below, is formed in limestone when water dissolves sections of the rock. Many of the cave's features develop from minerals deposited by the water.

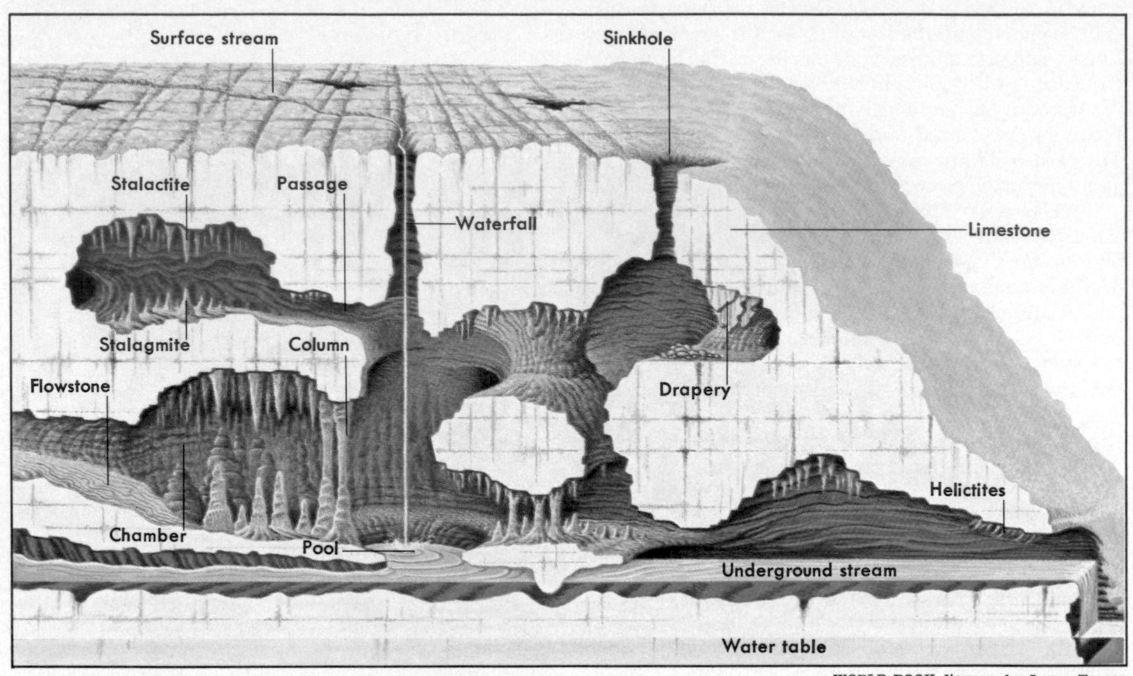

WORLD BOOK diagram by James Teason

roof. *Sea caves* form along rocky shores as the surf and wind wear away weak areas of the rock.

Speleothems. If the water table drops below the level of a cave, water may continue to seep in through cracks in the rock. The water contains dissolved minerals. As it enters the cave, some of the minerals crystallize and are deposited as speleothems. A speleothem may be white, brown, red, or multicolored, depending on the minerals that form it.

The best-known kinds of speleothems are *stalactites* and *stalagmites*. Stalactites are iciclelike formations that hang from the ceiling of a cave. Stalagmites are pillars that rise from the floor. A stalactite and a stalagmite may join and form a column. See STALACTITE; STALAGMITE.

Many other kinds of speleothems also may form in a cave. *Drapery* consists of thin sheets of rock that hang from the ceiling. *Flowstone* develops where a thin film of water flows over the walls and floor of a cave, depositing sheets of minerals. *Gypsum flowers* are delicate spiral crystals that sprout from porous rock. *Helictites* are strangely twisted cylinders that grow from the walls,

Interesting Caves of the World

Cave or Cave Area	Location	Outstanding Features
Blue Grotto	Isle of Capri, Italy	Sea cave that fills with sapphire-blue light when the sun shines through its waters
Carlsbad Caverns	Southeastern New Mexico	Contains some of the world's largest and most spectacular stalactites and stalagmites
Lascaux Cave	Southwestern France	Has prehistoric wall paintings believed to be tens of thousands of years old; closed to the public
Lava Beds National Monument	Northern California	Includes more than 300 lava caves, as well as other volcanic formations
Luray Caverns	Northern Virginia	Contains a large number of exceptionally beautiful and colorful speleothems
Mammoth-Flint Ridge Cave System	Central Kentucky	Longest cave system ever explored, with more than 190 miles (306 kilometers) of interconnected passages and chambers; includes underground lakes and rivers
Waitomo Cave	North Island, New Zealand	Thousands of tiny glowworms cling to the cave ceiling, resembling stars in the night sky
Gouffre de la Pierre St. Martin	Border of France and Spain	One of the world's deepest caves, measuring about 1 mile (1.6 kilometers) in depth

ceiling, or floor of a cave, or from other formations.

Life in Caves. Wallpaintings, stone tools, and skeletal remains found in caves show that people lived there thousands of years ago. Today, many kinds of animals, including a small number of human beings, use caves as permanent shelters. See CAVE DWELLERS.

Animals that live in caves include birds, crickets, lizards, raccoons, rats, salamanders, and spiders. Many bears hibernate in caves. Large numbers of bats roost in caves during the day and fly out at night to hunt for insects. The *guano* (manure) of bats provides food for the countless beetles, millipedes, flatworms, and other creatures that make their home in caves.

Various species of animals known as *troglobites* live in the dark innermost part of most caves, where there is no light, wind, or change in temperature and humidity. Such animals include certain beetles, fish, salamanders, and spiders. Most troglobites are blind and have a thin, colorless skin or shell. They rely on highly developed senses of smell and touch to make up for their lack of sight.

Green plants, such as algae, ferns, and mosses, may grow in the outer parts of caves, which receive some sunlight. Only fungi and other plants that do not require light can live in the dark inner areas.

Spelunking is an exciting but relatively dangerous hobby. Persons who wish to explore caves should always do so in groups headed by experienced leaders.

Spelunkers use some of the techniques and equipment of mountain climbing. For example, they use sturdy ropes or cable ladders to scale steep underground cliffs. They wear hardhats and rugged, heavy clothing for protection against dripping water and jagged rocks in caves. A spelunker should always carry at least two sources of light—a headlamp attached to the hardhat plus a flashlight held in the hand.

Experienced spelunkers want a cave to be in the same condition before and after they explore it. Therefore, they neither damage nor remove anything they may find. Speleothems are fragile and, if broken, cannot be restored. Also, many cave animals are extremely rare, and can be easily harmed. NICHOLAS SULLIVAN

R. Norman Matheny, *The Christian Science Monitor*

A Group of Spelunkers explore the dark interior of a cave. Their hardhats have headlamps, and they wear heavy, rugged clothing for protection against jagged rocks and dripping water.

Related Articles in WORLD BOOK include:

Alabama (picture)	Luray Caverns
Carlsbad Caverns National Park	Mammoth Cave National Park
Jewel Cave National Monument	Oregon Caves National Monument
Lehman Caves National Monument	Prehistoric People
	Russell Cave National Monument
	Wind Cave National Park

Additional Resources

LAYCOCK, GEORGE. *Caves.* Four Winds, 1976. For younger readers.

MOHR, CHARLES E., and POULSON, T. L. *The Life of the Cave.* McGraw, 1967.

MOORE, GEORGE W., and SULLIVAN, G. N. *Speleology: The Study of Caves.* Zephyrus, 1978. Includes a list of U.S. caves open to the public.

WALTHAM, ANTHONY C. *The World of Caves.* Putnam, 1976.

CAVE DWELLERS are people who live in caves or in the shelter provided by overhanging rocks at the bottom of cliffs. Prehistoric people are often incorrectly called "cave men," though some did live in caves.

The earliest known cave used by people is on the French Riviera in southern France. Stone tools found in this cave are about 500,000 years old. Scientists know much more about a cave site near Peking, China, which Peking people occupied about 375,000 years ago. About 100,000 years ago, some Neanderthal people lived in caves in Europe and western Asia. Some Cro-Magnon people occupied caves in those regions from about 35,000 years ago until about 8,000 B.C. The Neanderthal and Cro-Magnon people built tents and other shelters in the cave entrances. They used the dark interiors for ceremonial purposes. The Cro-Magnons painted pictures of animals on the cave walls and probably thought the paintings had magic qualities.

However, relatively few people have ever been cave dwellers. Caves are uncommon in most parts of the world. In addition, people have found most caves too cold, damp, and dark to live in. Such animals as cave bears, cave hyenas, and cave lions also discouraged cave dwelling.

In the New World, some Pueblo Indians lived in cave villages in what is now the Southwestern United States from about A.D. 1000 to 1300 (see CLIFF DWELLERS). Today, a few cave dwellers live in parts of Africa, Asia, Europe, and the Near East. In Spain, about 3,000 Gypsies make their homes in caves near Granada. Their dwellings range from single rooms to caves of about 200 rooms. These Gypsies also have churches, schools, and stores in caves. In the Philippines, some members of a people called the Tasaday live in caves located near Cotabato. KARL W. BUTZER

See also TROGLODYTE.

Additional Resources

FORD, T. D., and CULLINGFORD, C. H. D. *The Science of Speleology.* Academic Press, 1976. Physical aspects of caves and their use as habitats.

STENUIT, ROBERT, and JASINSKI, MARC. *Caves and the Marvelous World Beneath Us.* Barnes, 1966. How "living fossils" found in caves throw light on early human development.

CAVE MAN. See CAVE DWELLERS.

CAVE PAINTING. See PREHISTORIC PEOPLE (Religion and Art); PAINTING (Prehistoric Painting).

CAVEAT EMPTOR, *KAY vee at EHMP tawr,* is a Latin term meaning *let the buyer beware.* Unless an expressed or written guarantee accompanies goods or services for sale, the purchaser buys at his or her own risk. Present-day marketing conditions, processes, and principles protect the buyer to a large extent. The doctrine of *implied warranties* is incorporated in the commercial laws affecting business activities in the United States. Implied warranties are guaranteed by law. JOHN H. FREDERICK

CAVELIER, RENÉ-ROBERT. See LA SALLE, SIEUR DE.

CAVELL, *KAV ul,* **EDITH LOUISA** (1865-1915), was an English nurse. Her tragic death made her one of the martyrs of World War I. Miss Cavell was in charge of a hospital in Brussels, Belgium, when German troops occupied the city in 1915. For several months she assisted Allied soldiers, about 200 in all, to escape to the Dutch border. Arrested by the Germans, she admitted her activities, and was sentenced to die. "Patriotism is not enough" were the last words she spoke before a German firing squad shot her. Her body later was taken to Norwich, England, her birthplace, and a statue was erected to her memory in London. Mount Edith Cavell in Jasper National Park, Alberta, Canada, is named for her. ANDRÉ MAUROIS

CAVENDISH, HENRY (1731-1810), an English physicist and chemist, discovered many fundamental laws of electricity. He also conducted important experiments in chemistry and heat. In 1766, Cavendish discovered the properties of hydrogen and identified it as an element, calling it *inflammable air.* Later he showed that water is a compound of hydrogen and oxygen. In 1798, using a torsion-balance type of apparatus, Cavendish measured the density of the earth (see TORSION BALANCE). Much of his work in electricity remained unpublished until the late 1800's, when another physicist, James Clerk Maxwell, edited his papers (see MAXWELL, JAMES CLERK). Cavendish was born on Oct. 10, 1731, in Nice, France. He attended college at Cambridge University. R. T. ELLICKSON

CAVERN. See CAVE.

CAVIAR, *KAV ee ahr,* is the salted eggs, called *roe,* of the sturgeon and other large fish. This salty food has been popular in Russia for hundreds of years. Caviar was once a rare delicacy. Since the 1800's, caviar has been made in quantity from the roe of lake sturgeon in the United States. The eggs are rubbed through a screen to free them from an enclosing tissue. Then they are washed, rubbed with salt, and drained, dried, and packed. LEONE RUTLEDGE CARROLL

CAVITY. See TEETH (Diseases and Defects of the Teeth).

CAVOUR, *kah VOOR,* **COUNT DI** (1810-1861), CAMILLO BENSO CAVOUR, an Italian statesman, helped unite the peoples of Italy under a single kingdom. He served as prime minister of Sardinia from 1852 to 1859 and from 1860 to 1861. Under his leadership, Sardinia and France fought a war against Austria in 1859. As a result, Austria was expelled from its province of Lombardy. Sardinia then annexed Lombardy and all the states of central Italy except the area around Rome. Cavour, Giuseppe Garibaldi, and others helped bring about the unification in 1861 of all Italy except Venetia and Rome. Cavour was born in Turin. R. JOHN RATH

See also ITALY (History); SARDINIA, KINGDOM OF.

CAVY, *KAY vee,* is the general name for several related South American *rodents* (gnawing animals). The best-known cavies are *guinea pigs.* Other cavies include *maras (Patagonian hares)* and *mocos.* Most cavies have thick bodies, short legs, and short, bristly hair. But maras have long, thin legs. A few kinds of *domesticated* (tamed) guinea pigs have long hair. All cavies are plant eaters. See also GUINEA PIG; RODENT.

Scientific Classification. Cavies make up the cavy family, *Caviidae,* of the order *Rodentia.* DANIEL BRANT

Bruce Coleman Inc.

Cavies live in South America. The kind called maras, or Patagonian hares, *above,* have long, thin legs and large ears.

CAWDREY, ROBERT. See DICTIONARY (History).

CAWNPORE. See KANPUR.

CAXTON, WILLIAM (1422?-1491), introduced printing into England. He published many old, popular tales, including those of Geoffrey Chaucer and the King Arthur legends. Caxton also translated other stories into English and helped fix the literary form of the language.

The first book printed in the English language was a translation of the story of Troy, *The Recuyell of the Historyes of Troye.* Caxton helped produce the book in Flanders about 1475. He then returned to England and set up a press near Westminster Abbey. In 1477, he published *The Dictes or Sayings of the Philosophers,* the first book printed in England.

Caxton began printing after retiring from a career as a merchant. He was born in the Weald of Kent, England. As a youth, he was apprenticed to a London merchant. He then went to Bruges, Belgium, and lived abroad for 30 years. In 1471, he went to Cologne, Germany, to learn printing. RAY NASH

See also ADVERTISING (The Impact of Printing); BOOK (Printed Books); ENGLISH LITERATURE (The Beginning of Modern English).

CAYAMBE. See MOUNTAIN (table).

CAYENNE, *ky EHN* or *kay EHN* (pop. 30,000), is the capital, largest city, and chief port of French Guiana. It lies on an island near the mouth of the Cayenne River. See FRENCH GUIANA (map). Cayenne pepper, an important product, is named for the city.

CAYENNE PEPPER is a hot-tasting red powder made from the fruits or pods of a kind of capsicum plant.

It is used to flavor foods such as tamales and chili con carne. It may be made by powdering the dried fruits or by grinding and baking them into cakes. The cakes are then ground and sifted. See also CAPSICUM; PEPPER.

Scientific Classification. Cayenne pepper plants belong to the nightshade family, Solanaceae. They are genus *Capsicum*, species *C. frutescens*. HAROLD NORMAN MOLDENKE

CAYLEY, *KAY lee*, **SIR GEORGE** (1773-1857), is often called the *father of modern aeronautics*. He contributed many ideas to the early history of aviation. Cayley wrote about helicopters, parachutes, and streamlining. He conceived the biplane and built a glider that carried his unwilling coachman 900 feet (270 meters). But he abandoned the idea of airplanes until a lightweight engine could be developed. In the lighter-than-air field, he suggested the subdivision of the gas bag for safety. Cayley was born in Brompton, England. ROBERT B. HOTZ

See also AIRPLANE (First Manned Flights); GLIDER (Early Days).

CAYMAN. See ALLIGATOR; CROCODILE.

CAYMAN ISLANDS, *ky MAHN* or *KAY muhn*, a British dependency, lies about 200 miles (320 kilometers) northwest of Jamaica in the Caribbean Sea. The three islands that form the group—Grand Cayman, Little Cayman, and Cayman Brac—cover about 100 square miles (259 square kilometers), and have 19,000 persons. The capital and largest city, Georgetown, lies on Grand Cayman, the largest island.

CAYUGA INDIANS. See IROQUOIS INDIANS.

CAYUSE INDIANS. See OREGON (Indian Days; Indian Wars).

CB RADIO. See CITIZENS BAND RADIO.

CBR WARFARE. See CHEMICAL-BIOLOGICAL-RADIOLOGICAL WARFARE.

CBS INC. is a corporation that operates the CBS radio and television networks. It also publishes books and magazines, and manufactures musical instruments, phonograph records, and tape recordings.

The CBS radio and television networks provide program service for approximately 275 radio stations and about 200 television stations. Most of these stations are independently owned, but CBS owns AM and FM radio stations in seven U.S. cities and television stations in five U.S. cities. Since 1952, the CBS television network has been the world's largest advertising medium in terms of dollar value of advertising.

CBS produces Columbia and Epic records and tapes. CBS Laboratories, the company's research division, has developed the long-playing record and a color TV system used by the astronauts to transmit pictures from space. CBS owns Holt, Rinehart and Winston, Inc., which publishes textbooks, paperback books, and general books; and W. B. Saunders Co., the world's largest medical publisher. CBS also publishes several magazines. It distributes educational films and, through CBS Educational Services, operates business and technical training institutions. CBS Theatrical Films produces motion pictures. The CBS Musical Instruments Division manufactures drums, guitars, and Steinway pianos. CBS also owns Creative Playthings, a toy company.

CBS began in 1927 as United Independent Broadcasters, Inc., a network of 16 radio stations. The name was later changed to the Columbia Broadcasting System. In 1974, it became CBS Inc. CBS has headquarters in New York City. Critically reviewed by CBS INC.

CCC. See CIVILIAN CONSERVATION CORPS.

CEAUSESCU, *chow SHEHS koo*, **NICOLAE,** *NEE kaw LY* (1918-), became head of state in Romania in 1967. He has served as general secretary and leader of the Romanian Communist Party since 1965. Ceausescu maintains close political relations with Russia. But he believes Romania should be free to conduct its own national affairs, without Russian interference.

Ceausescu was born in Scorniceşti, near Piteşti. He served in the Union of Communist Youth from 1933 to 1936, and then joined the Communist Party. In 1948, he was elected to the party's Central Committee. He served as a committee secretary from 1954 to 1965. He became a member of the Politburo in 1955. Ceausescu was a close associate of former premier Gheorghiu-Dej before Gheorghiu-Dej died in 1965. WALTER C. CLEMENS, JR.

CEBU, *say BOO* (pop. 413,025), is the fourth largest city in the Philippines. It stands on the east coast of Cebu Island. For the location of Cebu, see PHILIPPINES (map). Cebu serves as the commercial center and port of Cebu Island. The Spaniards established their first permanent settlement in the Philippines at Cebu in 1565. RUSSELL H. FIFIELD

CEBU ISLAND. See PHILIPPINES (The Main Islands).

CECCHETTI, *chayk KEHT tee*, **ENRICO,** *ayn REE koh* (1850-1928), was one of the greatest ballet teachers. He helped train many of the great dancers of the 1900's. Cecchetti was noted as a dancer for his technique and speed. He was the leading male dancer with La Scala in Milan from 1885 to 1887 and created the role of the Bluebird in *The Sleeping Beauty* in 1890 in Russia.

Cecchetti began teaching in Russia in 1890. His students at the Imperial School of Ballet in St. Petersburg included Anna Pavlova and Vaslav Nijinsky. Cecchetti became instructor for the Ballets Russes de Diaghilev in 1909. In 1918, he opened a private school in London, where all leading Russian dancers of the day studied during their London seasons. Cecchetti was born in Rome. He was the last great teacher in the strict Italian tradition, the oldest in ballet. P. W. MANCHESTER

CECIL, *SEHS uhl*, is the name of one of England's most famous families. One member of the family was a prime minister.

William Cecil (1520-1598), Lord Burghley, guided England's foreign and domestic policies for 40 years under Elizabeth I (see BURGHLEY, LORD).

Thomas Cecil (1542-1623), Earl of Exeter, was Burghley's eldest son. He helped crush a rebellion led by the Earl of Essex in 1601.

Robert Cecil (1563-1612), Earl of Salisbury, was Burghley's younger son. He served as secretary of state from 1596 to 1608 and as lord treasurer from 1608 until his death.

Robert Arthur Talbot Gascoyne-Cecil (1830-1903), 3rd Marquess of Salisbury, a leader of the Conservative Party, served as prime minister three times (see SALISBURY, MARQUESS OF).

Robert Arthur James Gascoyne-Cecil (1893-1972), 5th Marquess of Salisbury, served as Conservative leader in the House of Lords from 1942 to 1945 and from 1951 to 1957. VERNON F. SNOW

CECIL, LORD DAVID (1902-), a British author and critic, became known for his lively and scholarly biographies. His best-known works include *The Stricken Deer: The Life of Cowper* (1929), *Sir Walter Scott* (1933), *Melbourne* (1954), and *Max* (1964). He also edited *The Oxford Book of Christian Verse* (1940). Edward Christian David Cecil was born in London.

CECILIA, *see SIHL ih uh,* **SAINT,** is a saint and martyr of the Roman Catholic Church. She was cruelly put to death about A.D. 230. Her singing of the praises of God has led her to be considered a patron of music. Many musical societies have been named in her honor.

The artists Raphael, Domenichino, Dolce, and Mignard have represented Saint Cecilia in noted paintings. Her praises were sung by Chaucer in one of his *Canterbury Tales*, by Dryden in "Alexander's Feast" and "Song for St. Cecilia's Day," and by Alexander Pope in "Ode for Music on St. Cecilia's Day." Her tomb is in the Church of Saint Cecilia in Rome. Saint Cecilia's feast day is November 22. FULTON J. SHEEN

CECROPIA MOTH. See MOTH (Giant Silkworm Moths; color picture).

CECROPS, *SEE krahps,* in Greek mythology, founded the city of Athens. He was the first king of Attica and the builder of the great fortress of Athens. He called the fortress *Cecropia* in his honor. He was half man and half snake. Legend says he introduced the customs of marriage and burial of the dead, and did away with sacrifices of blood. PADRAIC COLUM

CECUM. See COLON.

CEDAR is any of a variety of large evergreen trees that grow in many parts of the world. There are two major groups of cedars, the *cupressineous cedars* of the cypress family and the *true cedars* of the pine family.

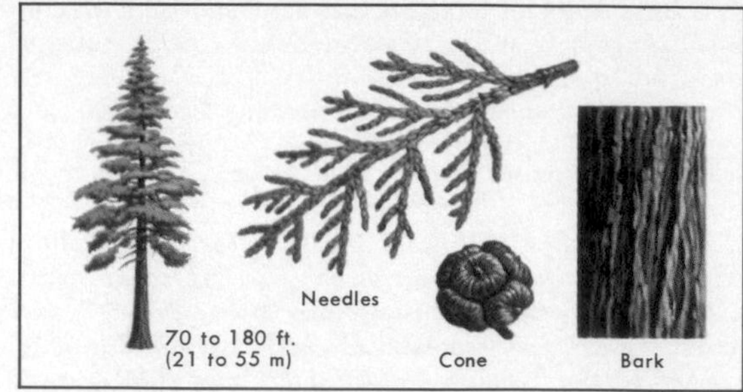

The Main Kinds of Cedars, cupressineous and true cedars, differ in structure. Cupressineous species include the Port-Orford cedar, *above.* The cedar of Lebanon, *below,* is a true cedar.

WORLD BOOK illustrations by John D. Dawson

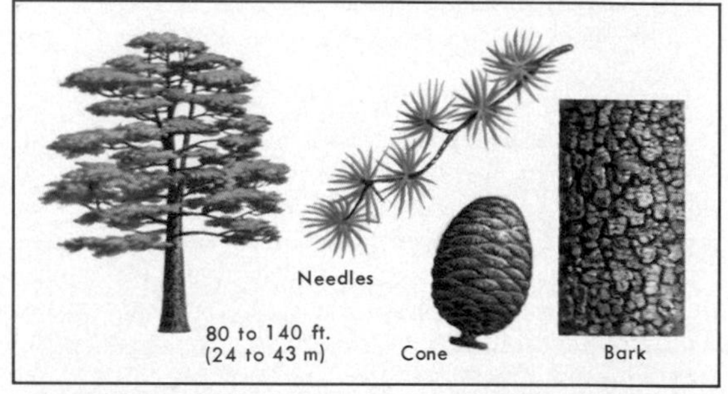

Red Cedar Shingle & Handsplit Shake Bureau

Cedar Shingles make excellent roofing and siding material because the wood can withstand extreme weather conditions. In the picture above, a worker stacks the shingles for packaging.

Cupressineous Cedars have small, scalelike leaves that grow flattened against the branches. They also have small cones, most of which are less than $\frac{1}{2}$ inch (1.3 centimeters) long.

Several species of cupressineous cedars grow in North America. Most of these trees have shallow roots and thrive in moist soil. Four kinds grow in the mountains of western North America from Alaska to northern California. They are the *Alaska cedar*, the *incense cedar*, the *Port-Orford cedar*, and the *western red cedar*. Three other cedars are found in eastern North America. The *northern white cedar* grows in eastern Canada and the northeastern United States. The *Atlantic white cedar* is found in the Atlantic and Gulf coastal plains. The *eastern red cedar* grows in the central and eastern United States. The western red cedar and northern white cedar are sometimes called *arborvitae*. The eastern red cedar belongs to the same group of trees as the juniper.

The wood of North American cedars resists rotting better than many other woods, and it can be easily sawed, planed, and carved. Many clothing chests and closets are lined with cedar because the wood's pleasant odor seems to keep moths away. The wood is also used in making boats, pencils, shingles, and telephone poles.

True Cedars have tufts of needlelike leaves that measure from $\frac{1}{2}$ to $1\frac{1}{2}$ inches (1.3 to 4 centimeters) long. Their cones are 3 to 5 inches (8 to 13 centimeters) long and grow straight up on the branches. There are four species —the *Atlas cedar* of the Atlas Mountains in northern Africa; the *Cyprus cedar* of the island of Cyprus; the *cedar of Lebanon*, which grows in the Middle East and Asia Minor; and the *deodar cedar* of the Himalaya. Some true cedars are planted as ornamentals in warm regions of the United States. The cedar of Lebanon, the best-known true cedar, has attractive, fragrant, durable wood. The people of early Middle East civilizations used it for building palaces, ships, temples, and tombs.

Scientific Classification. North American cedars belong to the cypress family, Cupressaceae. The western red cedar is *Thuja plicata*, and the northern white cedar is *T. occidentalis*. The Port-Orford cedar is *Chamaecyparis lawsoniana;* the Alaska cedar, *C. nootkatensis;* the Atlantic white cedar, *C. thyoides*. The incense cedar is *Libocedrus decurrens*. True cedars make up the genus *Cedrus* in the pine family, Pinaceae. The cedar of Lebanon is *C. libani*. DONALD B. ZOBEL

See also ARBORVITAE; JUNIPER; PINE.

CEDAR BREAKS NATIONAL MONUMENT is on the Markagunt Plateau in southwestern Utah. It includes a great amphitheater of sandstone and limestone, eroded to a depth of nearly 2,000 feet (610 meters) in Utah's Pink Cliff formation. It also has spectacular canyons. The monument was established in 1933. For the area of the monument, see NATIONAL PARK SYSTEM (table: National Monuments). C. LANGDON WHITE

CEDAR OF LEBANON. See CEDAR.

CEDAR RAPIDS, Iowa (pop. 110,243; met. area pop. 169,775), is a manufacturing and distributing city, and the center of a large farming and dairying area. It lies on the Cedar River in Linn County, in east-central Iowa. For location, see IOWA (political map). Oatmeal mills, established in the 1870's, were the start of the city's thriving cereal-processing industry. Other foods processed include corn, meat, and sorghum. Factories in the city make machinery, farm implements, radios, and earth-moving equipment. Cedar Rapids is the home of Coe College and Mount Mercy College. The Iowa Masonic Library has a large collection of books on Freemasonry.

Cedar Rapids was first settled as Rapids City in 1841, and was incorporated under the present name in 1849. The rapids in the Cedar River inspired both names. The city has a commission form of government, and is the seat of Linn County. WILLIAM J. PETERSEN

CEDAR WAXWING. See WAXWING; BIRD (picture: Birds of Forests and Woodlands).

CEDRELA. See MAHOGANY.

CELA, CAMILO JOSÉ. See SPANISH LITERATURE (Spanish Literature Today).

CELANDINE, *SEL un dine*, is an herb in the poppy family. Its juice was once used to treat warts, jaundice, and other ailments. The plant grows from 1 to 2 feet (30 to 61 centimeters) high. It has thin, grayish-green leaves, and bright yellow flowers. Celandine thrives in rich, damp soil. It grows wild in Europe and in eastern North America.

Scientific Classification. Celandine is in the poppy family, Papaveraceae. It is *Chelidonium majus*.

WORLD BOOK illustration by James Teason

Celandine Leaves and Buds

CELEBES. See INDONESIA (The Islands).

CELEBRATION. See FEASTS AND FESTIVALS; HOLIDAY; and articles for each month of the year.

CELERY is a popular vegetable related to parsley and parsnips. People eat the stiff, crisp leafstalks either raw or cooked. Full-grown celery plants may be from 20 to 30 inches (51 to 76 centimeters) high. They bear coarsely toothed leaves at the tip of each stalk.

Celery thrives in moist, fertile soil. But the plants grow quite slowly. Growers often soak celery seed in lukewarm water to hasten sprouting. Then they sow the seed in greenhouses or outdoor seed beds. In 8 to 12 weeks, the plants are large enough to be transplanted to the field. Farmers place the plants 6 inches (15 centimeters) apart in rows 18 to 36 inches (46 to 91 centimeters) apart in the field.

Pascal, or *green, celery* is most often seen in stores. *Blanched*, or *white, celery* contains less *chlorophyll* (green color). Sometimes growers bleach white celery by placing boards, black plastic, or soil against the plants to prevent chlorophyll from forming. Neither type of celery has much food value.

W. Atlee Burpee Co.

Crisp Celery Stalks are a favorite food in salads.

Scientific Classification. Celery belongs to the parsley family, Umbelliferae. It is genus *Apium*, species *A. graveolens*. ARTHUR J. PRATT

CELESTA, *see LESS tuh*, is a pianolike musical instrument played by means of a keyboard. Small hammers striking against steel plates instead of strings produce the tone. The plates rest above hollow boxes that *resonate* (increase) the sound. The celesta produces a clear, sweet sound, and its name comes from a French word meaning *heavenly*. Its range covers four octaves, but it sounds the notes one octave higher than the music indicates. Composers use the celesta in compositions for symphony orchestras, but it is rarely heard as a solo instrument. Auguste Mustel, a Frenchman, invented the celesta in 1886. F. E. KIRBY

G. C. Jenkins Co.

The Celesta, a keyboard instrument, has a sweet, clear tone.

CELESTIAL EQUATOR. See ASTRONOMY (table: Astronomy Terms; Locating Objects in the Sky).

CELESTIAL NAVIGATION. See NAVIGATION (Celestial Navigation).

CELESTIAL POLES. See ASTRONOMY (table: Astronomy Terms; Locating Objects in the Sky).

CELIBACY, *SELL uh buh see*, is the state of being unmarried. All faiths that have monks and nuns require them to be celibate. The Roman Catholic Church requires its clergy to take the vow of celibacy. In Eastern Orthodox Churches, bishops must be celibate, but priests may marry before ordination. Protestant churches rejected celibacy. Judaism, Hinduism, and other religions permit their clergy to marry. R. PIERCE BEAVER

CELL. See BEE (The Nest); BATTERY; PRISON.

General Biological Supply

CELL

Cells, the Building Blocks of All Living Things, stand out clearly in this photograph of an onion root tip. The cells have been stained, and magnified about 1,200 times. The reddish stains show structures called *chromosomes* in cells that are dividing and becoming two cells.

CELL is the basic unit of all life. All living things—tigers, trees, mosquitoes, and people—are made up of cells. Some animals and some plants consist of only one cell. Other plants and animals are made up of many cells. The body of a human being has more than 10 million million (10,000,000,000,000) cells.

Most cells are so small that they can be seen only under a microscope. It would take about 40,000 of your red blood cells to fill this letter *O*. It takes several million cells to make up the skin on the palm of your hand.

Irwin Rubenstein, the contributor of this article, is Professor of Genetics and Cell Biology at the University of Minnesota, Twin Cities Campus. The diagrammatic illustrations were prepared for WORLD BOOK *by Cynthia Fujii.*

Some one-celled plants and animals lead independent lives. Others live in loosely organized groups. In plants and animals made up of many cells, the cells are specialists with particular jobs to do. As you read these words, for example, nerve cells in your eyes are carrying messages of what you are reading to your brain. Muscle cells attached to your eyeballs are moving your eyes across the page. Nerve cells, muscle cells, and other specialized cells group together to form *tissues*, such as nerve tissue or muscle tissue. Different kinds of tissues form *organs*, such as the eyes, heart, and lungs. All the specialized cells together form you—or a giraffe, a daisy, or a bluebird.

All cells have some things in common, whether they are specialized cells or one-celled plants and animals. A cell is alive—as alive as you are. It "breathes," takes in food, and gets rid of wastes. It also grows and *repro-*

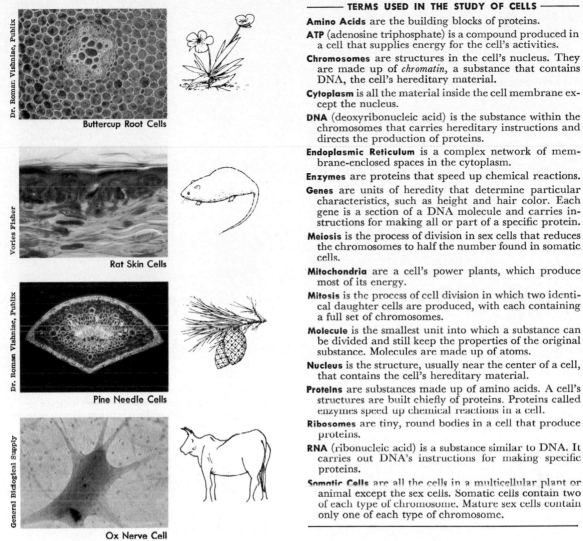

Dr. Roman Vishniac, Publix

Buttercup Root Cells

Vories Fisher

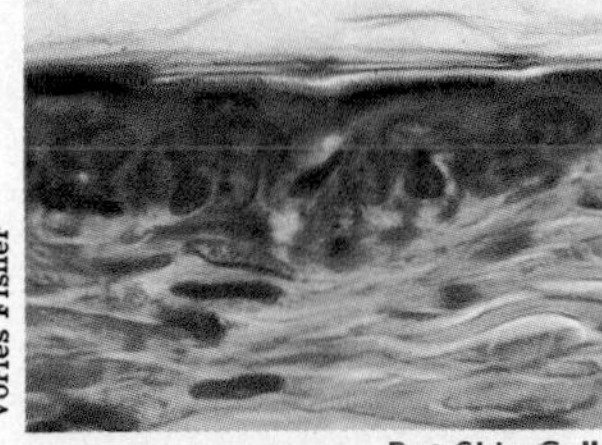

Rat Skin Cells

Dr. Roman Vishniac, Publix

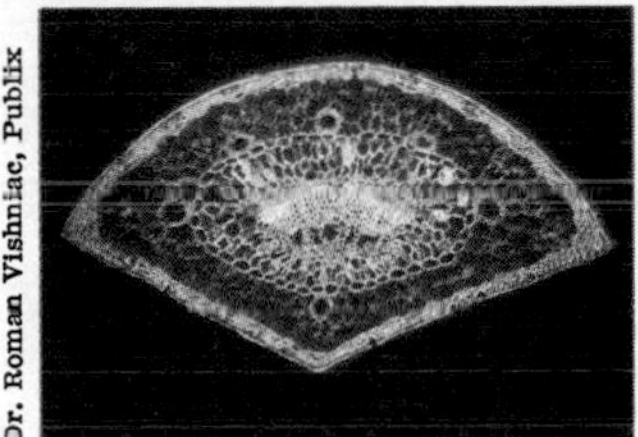

Pine Needle Cells

General Biological Supply

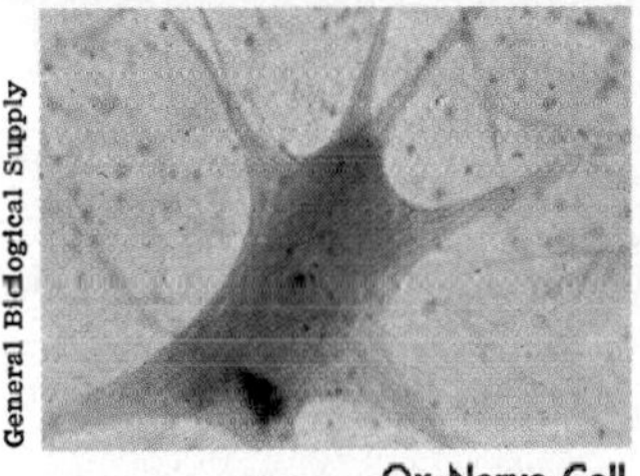

Ox Nerve Cell

TERMS USED IN THE STUDY OF CELLS

Amino Acids are the building blocks of proteins.

ATP (adenosine triphosphate) is a compound produced in a cell that supplies energy for the cell's activities.

Chromosomes are structures in the cell's nucleus. They are made up of *chromatin*, a substance that contains DNA, the cell's hereditary material.

Cytoplasm is all the material inside the cell membrane except the nucleus.

DNA (deoxyribonucleic acid) is the substance within the chromosomes that carries hereditary instructions and directs the production of proteins.

Endoplasmic Reticulum is a complex network of membrane-enclosed spaces in the cytoplasm.

Enzymes are proteins that speed up chemical reactions.

Genes are units of heredity that determine particular characteristics, such as height and hair color. Each gene is a section of a DNA molecule and carries instructions for making all or part of a specific protein.

Meiosis is the process of division in sex cells that reduces the chromosomes to half the number found in somatic cells.

Mitochondria are a cell's power plants, which produce most of its energy.

Mitosis is the process of cell division in which two identical daughter cells are produced, with each containing a full set of chromosomes.

Molecule is the smallest unit into which a substance can be divided and still keep the properties of the original substance. Molecules are made up of atoms.

Nucleus is the structure, usually near the center of a cell, that contains the cell's hereditary material.

Proteins are substances made up of amino acids. A cell's structures are built chiefly of proteins. Proteins called enzymes speed up chemical reactions in a cell.

Ribosomes are tiny, round bodies in a cell that produce proteins.

RNA (ribonucleic acid) is a substance similar to DNA. It carries out DNA's instructions for making specific proteins.

Somatic Cells are all the cells in a multicellular plant or animal except the sex cells. Somatic cells contain two of each type of chromosome. Mature sex cells contain only one of each type of chromosome.

duces (creates its own kind). And, in time, it dies.

A thin covering encloses each cell. Within the covering is a jellylike fluid called *cytoplasm*. This fluid contains many tiny structures. Each structure has a job to do, such as producing energy. Most cells have a structure called the *nucleus*, which is the cell's control point. The nucleus contains the cell's *genetic program*, a master plan that controls almost everything the cell does. The entire living substance that makes up the cell is often called *protoplasm*.

Just as all living things are made up of cells, every new cell is produced from another cell. Most cells reproduce by dividing, so that there are two cells where there once was one. When a cell divides, each of the two new cells gets a copy of the genetic program.

The genetic program is "written" in a chemical substance called *DNA* (deoxyribonucleic acid). All DNA, whether it comes from an animal cell or a plant cell, looks much alike, and is made up of the same building blocks. But the genetic program carried in DNA makes every living thing different from all other living things. This program makes a dog different from a fish, a zebra different from a rose, and a willow different from a wasp. It makes you different from every other person on the earth.

Scientists are beginning to understand the genetic program and the chemical code in which it is written in DNA. After they have solved it, they may be able to control cancer and many other diseases that arise in the cell. Scientists also may be able to change the characteristics of plants and animals. They may even be able to create life in a test tube.

This article describes the cell and how it works. For further information, see also the WORLD BOOK articles on HEREDITY and LIFE.

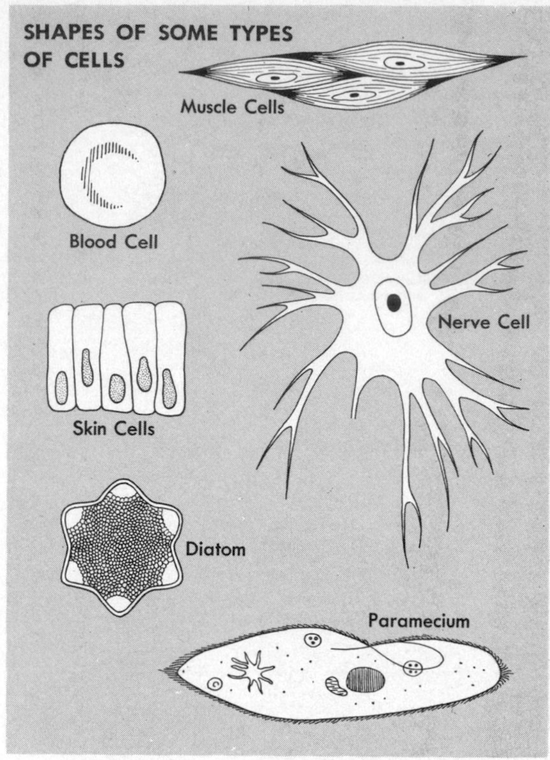

Looking at a Cell

More than 1½ million species of plants and animals live on the earth. They differ greatly in shape, in size, and in the way they live. But they all have one thing in common—they are all made up of cells.

One of the most important tools scientists use to study cells is the microscope. An *optical microscope* can magnify a cell up to 2,000 times. An *electron microscope* can magnify a cell more than 200,000 times on photographic film. An ant magnified 200,000 times would be more than ½ mile (0.8 kilometer) long. But even with such tremendous magnification, the detailed structure of some cell parts still cannot be seen. See MICROSCOPE.

Another tool used to study cells is the *centrifuge*. This instrument separates the various substances in a mixture by whirling the mixture at high speeds. It is used to study the chemical content and chemical reactions of cell parts. Scientists first grind up the cells. Then they put the bits and pieces into a centrifuge and whirl them rapidly. The particles separate into layers. The heaviest particles settle at the bottom, and the lightest ones gather at the top. After they have been separated, the particles can be checked for their chemical content. See CENTRIFUGE.

Scientists also use dyes to study cells. When various parts of a cell are stained with certain dyes, these parts stand out clearly under a microscope.

Shapes of Cells. Cells may be shaped like cubes, coils, boxes, snowflakes, corkscrews, rods, saucers, rectangles, or blobs of jelly. Many *unicellular* (one-celled) plants and animals look like tiny balls. They include some yeasts and certain water plants. The ameba, a unicellular animal, has no particular shape at all. It is a flattened jellylike mass that changes its shape to move about. Bacteria are shaped like balls, rods, or coils. Diatoms are one-celled water plants shaped like boxes of almost any shape—square, round, oblong, triangular.

Most cells of *multicellular* (many-celled) plants are shaped like cubes or rectangles. The greatest variety in cell shapes occurs in human beings and other multicellular animals. Animal cells may be round, egg-shaped, square, or rectangular. Some muscle cells are long and thin, and pointed at each end. Some nerve cells, with their long branches, resemble trees.

A cell's shape is related to its needs or to the job it does. For example, the long, thin muscle cells can contract to do work. The long, many-branched nerve cells relay messages throughout the body.

Sizes of Cells. Cells vary widely in size, just as they do in shape. Most cells are about $\frac{1}{1,000}$ of an inch (0.0025 centimeter) long. About 500 of these average-sized cells would fit within the period at the end of this sentence. Bacterial cells are among the smallest of all cells. Certain kinds of bacterial cells are so small that a row of 50,000 of them would measure only 1 inch (2.5 centimeters) long. The largest cells are the yolks of birds' eggs. The largest cell of all is the yolk of an ostrich egg, which is about the size of a baseball.

The size of any multicellular plant or animal depends on the total number of cells it has, not on the size of the cells. An elephant is a giant compared with a mouse because it has trillions more cells, not because its cells are larger.

Inside A Living Cell

We have seen that cells differ greatly in size, in shape, and in the special jobs they do. But we can imagine a typical living cell that has the features found in almost all cells except those of bacteria and blue-green algae. Such a cell can be thought of as a tiny chemical factory. It has a control center that tells it what to do and when. It has power plants for generating energy, and it has machinery for making its products or performing its services.

A thin covering called the *cell membrane* or *plasma membrane* encloses the cell and separates it from its surroundings. The cell has two main parts: (1) the nucleus and (2) the cytoplasm.

The Nucleus is the control center that directs the activities of the cell. A *nuclear membrane* surrounds the nucleus and separates it from the cytoplasm. The nucleus contains two important types of structures, *chromosomes* and *nucleoli*.

Chromosomes are long, threadlike bodies that normally are visible only when the cell is dividing. Chromosomes consist chiefly of two substances—DNA and certain proteins. Lined up along the chromosomes are the *genes*, the basic units of heredity. Genes control the passing on of characteristics from parents to offspring. Each gene consists of part of a DNA molecule. The DNA that makes up the genes determines that a dog will give birth to a dog instead of a fish. It determines

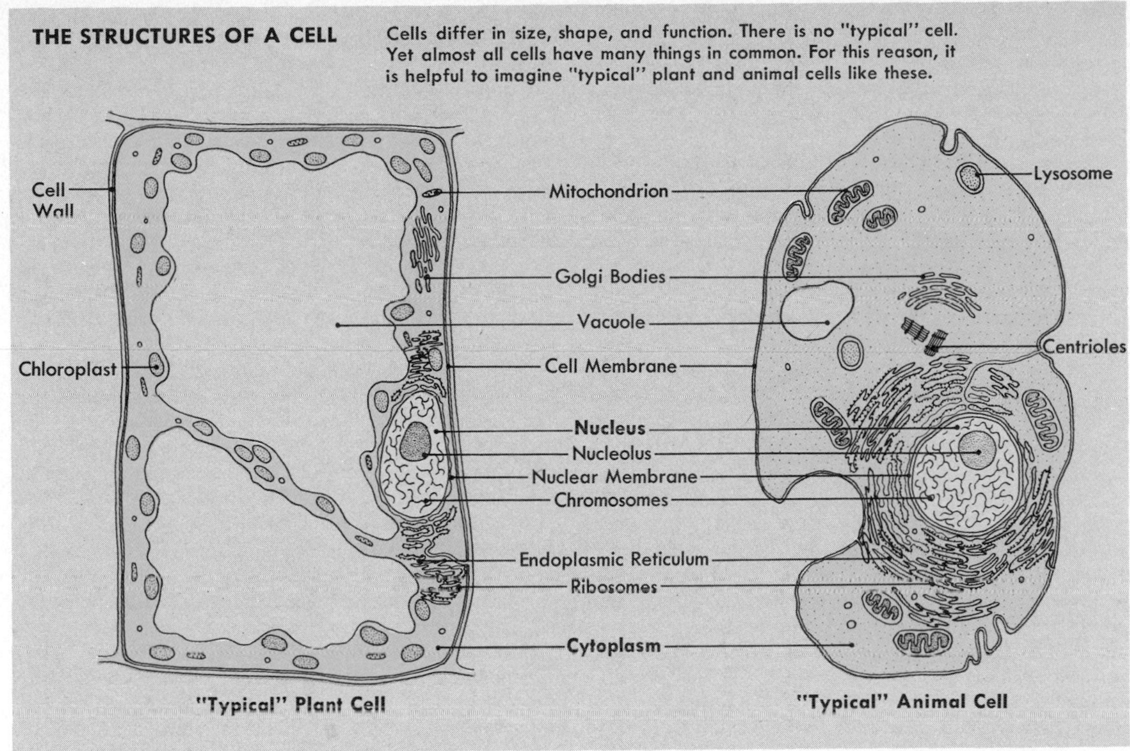

your height, the color of your eyes, the shape of your hands, the texture of your hair, and thousands of other characteristics.

DNA works its wonders chiefly by directing the production of complicated chemical substances called *proteins*. The cell's structures are built mostly of proteins. In addition, certain proteins called *enzymes* speed up chemical reactions in the cell. Without enzymes, these reactions would occur very slowly, and the cell could not function normally (see ENZYME). Thus, the kinds of proteins a cell makes largely determine the nature of the cell.

Nucleoli are round bodies that form in certain regions of specific chromosomes. Each nucleus may contain one or more nucleoli, though some cells have none at all. Nucleoli help in the formation of *ribosomes*, the cell's centers of protein production. Nucleoli are made up of proteins and *RNA* (ribonucleic acid). RNA is chemically similar to DNA and plays an important role in making proteins.

The Cytoplasm is all the cell except the nucleus. Proteins are made in the cytoplasm, and many of the cell's life activities take place there. Many tiny structures called *organelles* are located in the cytoplasm. Each has a particular job to do. These organelles are called *mitochondria*, *lysosomes*, the *endoplasmic reticulum*, *centrioles*, and *Golgi bodies*.

Mitochondria are the power producers of the cell. A cell may contain hundreds of mitochondria. These sausage-shaped structures produce almost all the energy the cell needs to live and to do its work.

Lysosomes are small, round bodies containing many different enzymes, which can break down many substances. For example, lysosomes help white blood cells break down harmful bacteria.

Endoplasmic Reticulum is a complex network of membrane-enclosed spaces in the cytoplasm. The surfaces of some of the membranes are smooth. Others are bordered by ribosomes—tiny round bodies that contain large amounts of RNA. Ribosomes are the cell's manufacturing units. The proteins the cell needs in order to grow, repair itself, and perform hundreds of chemical operations are made on the ribosomes.

Centrioles look like two bundles of rods. They lie near the nucleus, and are important in cell reproduction.

Golgi Bodies, also called *Golgi complex* or *Golgi apparatus*, consist of a stack of flat, baglike structures that store and eventually release various products from the cell.

Membranes enclose the entire cell, the nucleus, and all the organelles. The membranes hold the cell and each of its parts together. Most membranes consist of a double layer of a fatty substance called *phospholipid* (see LIPID). Proteins occur at various points and extend to different depths within the double layer of phospholipids. Only needed materials can enter the cell and its parts because of the structure and chemical composition of the membranes.

Plant Cells have certain special structures. *Chloroplasts*, found in the cytoplasm, are organelles that contain a green substance called *chlorophyll*. In a process called *photosynthesis*, chlorophyll uses the energy of sunlight to produce energy-rich sugars (see PHOTOSYNTHESIS). All life on the earth depends on these sugars. Plant cells also have a *cell wall* surrounding the cell membrane. The cell wall of most plants contains *cellulose*, a substance manufactured in the cytoplasm. Cellulose makes plant stems stiff. *Vacuoles* are common in plant cells. These large, fluid-filled cavities often take up a large part of the plant cell.

Bacteria and Blue-Green Algae Cells lack a well-defined nucleus and cytoplasmic organelles. The small, simple cells of these unicellular organisms are called *procaryotic*, which means *before the nucleus*. All other cells are called *eucaryotic*, which means *having a true nucleus*. All multicellular animals and plants consist of eucaryotic cells, as do such unicellular organisms as amebas and diatoms. Despite their differences, both procaryotic and eucaryotic cells have their genetic program written in the same DNA code. Thus, a similar basic plan directs protein production and heredity in both types of cells.

Cell Division

Every living thing is made up of one or more cells, and each of these cells was produced by an already existing cell. New cells are formed by dividing, so that there are two cells where there once was one. One-celled plants and animals begin and complete their lives as single cells. Human beings and many-celled plants and animals also develop from a single cell. But after this cell grows to a certain size, it divides and forms two cells. These two cells grow and divide, forming four cells. The cells grow and divide over and over again, and during this process they begin to specialize. A dog, a fish, or a human being finally develops from the single cell. There are two main types of cell division: (1) mitosis and (2) meiosis.

Mitosis. Most cells are produced by a process called mitosis. In mitosis, a cell divides and forms two identical daughter cells. Each daughter cell then doubles in size and becomes capable of dividing. Most one-celled plants and animals reproduce by mitosis. This is also the way most cells in your body and in many-celled plants and animals reproduce.

Mitosis in animal cells takes place in four stages: (1) prophase, (2) metaphase, (3) anaphase, and (4) telophase. During the period between divisions, the cell grows and carries on its normal activities. The chromosomes are extremely long and thin. At this time, they can be seen only as grainy particles in the nucleus. Yet sometime during this period, called *interphase*, the chromosomes duplicate. The cell then has two identical sets of genes, which are carried on the chromosomes. It is ready to divide and give each daughter cell a complete copy of the DNA genetic program.

The first stage of mitosis is called *prophase*. The chromosomes begin to condense into visible threads that become progressively shorter and thicker. Every kind of organism has a certain number of chromosomes in each of its *somatic* (body) cells. For example, human beings have 46; frogs, 26; and pea plants, 14.

Because of the duplication that occurs during interphase, each of the condensing chromosomes consists of two identical structures called *sister chromatids*. The sister chromatids are joined together near the middle or end by a structure called a *centromere*.

The centrioles, the two bundles of rods just outside the nucleus, have also duplicated before the division process begins. Each pair of centrioles now begins to move apart. As they do, long fibers appear in the cell. The centrioles move to opposite sides of the cell and form structures called *poles*. The network of fibers then extends across the cell between the two poles, forming a *spindle*. Toward the end of prophase, the nuclear membrane dissolves.

In *metaphase*, the second stage of mitosis, the sister chromatids move to the middle of the spindle, called the *equator*. They are still joined, but they line up on opposite sides of the equator. Each sister chromatid is

MITOSIS Most eucaryotic cells reproduce by *mitosis*. In this process, a cell divides and forms two identical *daughter* cells. Each daughter cell receives a set of *chromosomes* identical with those of the original cell. The bottom pictures show the mitosis of a cell with a large number of chromosomes.

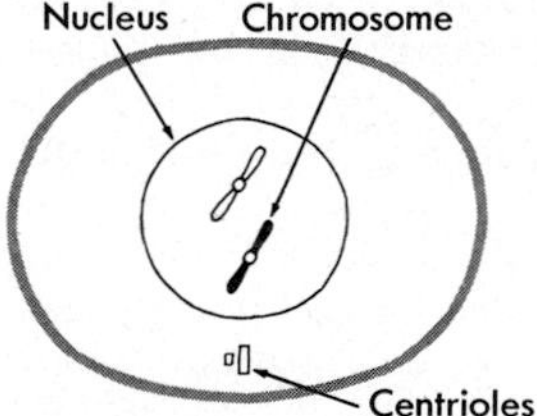

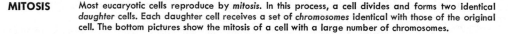

1. An animal cell with two chromosomes, *above*, is about to divide. Before the process begins, the chromosomes and the pair of centrioles duplicate.

Spindle
Chromatids
Centrioles

2. The centrioles move to opposite sides of the cell, forming a *spindle* across it. The duplicated sister chromatids go to the middle of the spindle.

Spindle
Chromosome
Centrioles

3. The sister chromatids now separate. The members of each pair move to opposite sides of the cell, and each becomes a new chromosome.

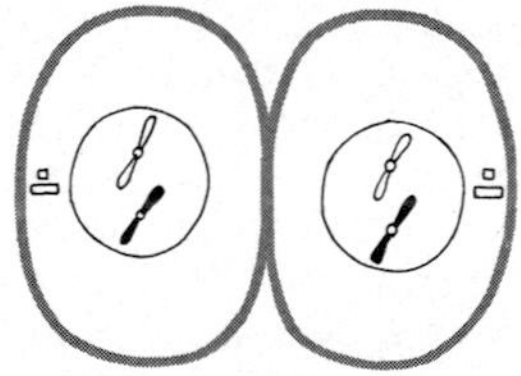

4. The cell splits in two. Each new daughter cell receives identical chromosomes. They are exact duplicates of those of the parent cell, *far left*.

General Biological Supply

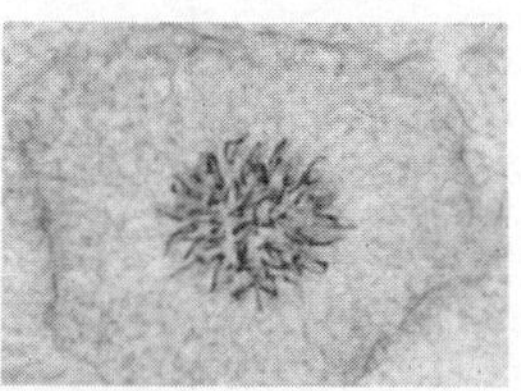

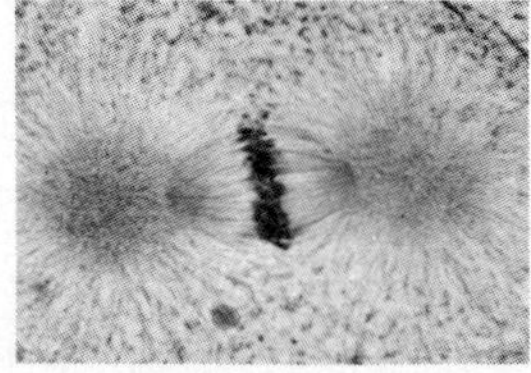

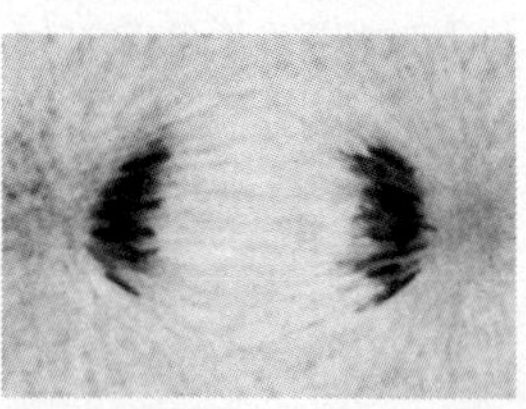

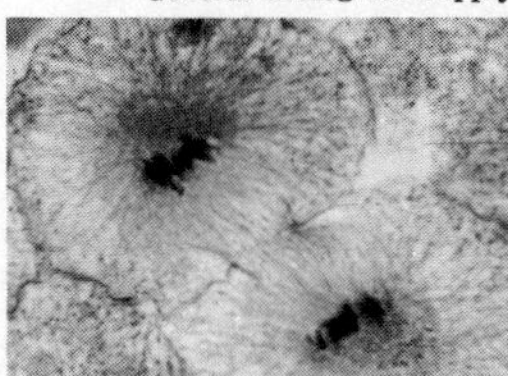

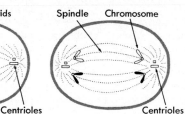

attached at its centromere to a spindle fiber. Now the third stage, called *anaphase*, begins. The centromeres divide, and each sister chromatid becomes a new chromosome. The new chromosomes separate and move to opposite poles. In *telophase*, the final stage of mitosis, the cell splits at the equator. Two new cells are produced. Each new cell has a full set of chromosomes and contains the same hereditary information as the original cell. The chromosomes gradually become elongated and almost invisible.

Mitosis in plant cells differs somewhat from that in animal cells. For example, cells in multicellular plants do not have centrioles, but they do form a spindle similar to that formed in animal cells.

Meiosis. Human beings and many other living things reproduce sexually. A new individual can be created only if a male sex cell, called a *sperm*, unites with a female sex cell, called an *egg*. Sex cells, also called *germ cells*, are produced in special reproductive tissues or organs. At first, new sex cells are produced by mitosis. But before a sex cell matures, it goes through a special kind of cell division called *meiosis*. To understand why, we must understand something about heredity.

We have seen that every species of life has a certain number of chromosomes in its somatic cells. These chromosomes exist in pairs. The members of each pair are similar in size, shape, and hereditary content. Human beings have 23 pairs of chromosomes; frogs, 13 pairs; and pea plants, 7 pairs. Suppose the egg and sperm cells had the same number of chromosomes as all the other cells in an organism. If they united, the somatic cells in the offspring would have twice the number of chromosomes that they should have.

For example, human beings have 46 chromosomes in their somatic cells. If the father's sperm cells and the mother's egg cells also contained 46 chromosomes, their child's somatic cells would have 92 chromosomes. The next generation would have 184, and so on. Thus, the sex cells must have half the chromosomes found in the somatic cells. This is accomplished by meiosis.

Meiosis consists of two separate divisions of sex cells. Each chromosome duplicates before the first division. Then each chromosome, which now consists of two joined sister chromatids, lines up side by side with the other chromosome of its pair. Each pair of doubled chromosomes moves to the equator. The paired chromosomes then separate. One chromosome, still consisting of two chromatids, goes to one pole. The other chromosome moves to the opposite pole. The cell divides. Each daughter cell thus receives one chromosome, made up of two sister chromatids, from each original pair. These new cells then divide. In this second division, one of each of the sister chromatids goes to each new daughter cell. Thus, the two divisions of meiosis produce four sex cells. Each cell contains half the number of chromosomes found in all the other cells of an organism.

Human sperm and egg cells have 23 chromosomes each. When a sperm and an egg combine in a process called *fertilization*, they produce a *fertilized egg* with 46 chromosomes, or 23 similar pairs. The child develops from this egg. See HEREDITY (The Physical Basis).

Growth and Specialization are the processes by which a single fertilized egg develops into a particular plant or animal. The fertilized egg from which you developed contained all the instructions on how you were to grow. The single cell divided by mitosis. Cell after cell divided. Then the dividing cells began to *differentiate* (specialize), and became muscle cells, skin cells, nerve cells, and so on. The different kinds of cells grouped into tissues. These tissues, in turn, formed organs, such as your heart and lungs.

Understanding differentiation is one of the most challenging problems facing scientists. Every time a cell

MEIOSIS Sex cells are formed in a special type of division called *meiosis*. It requires two separate divisions to reduce the chromosomes in sex cells to half the number found in all the other kinds of cells in an organism. When a male and female sex cell unite, the full number of chromosomes is restored.

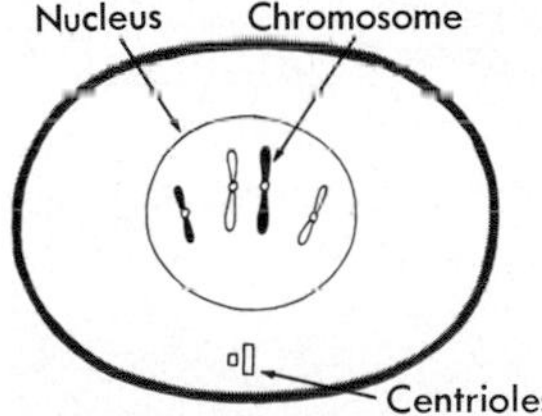

Spindle Chromosomes Centrioles

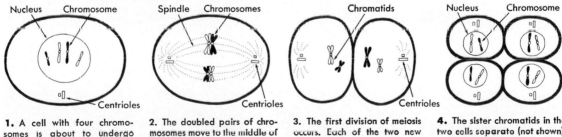

Chromatids Centrioles

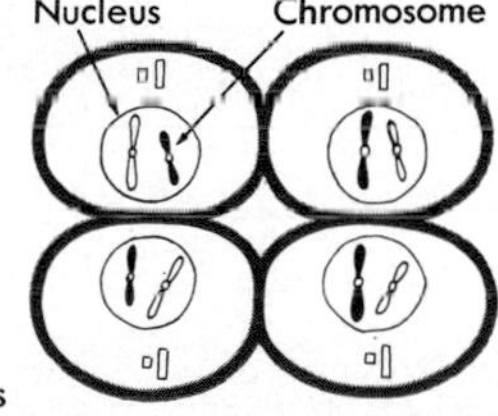

1. A cell with four chromosomes is about to undergo meiosis. In preparation, the chromosomes duplicate. The similar ones then pair up.

2. The doubled pairs of chromosomes move to the middle of the spindle. The doubled members separate and go to opposite sides of the cell (not shown).

3. The first division of meiosis occurs. Each of the two new cells receives one member of each original pair. Each member consists of two chromatids.

4. The sister chromatids in the two cells separate (not shown). The cells divide. The four resulting cells thus get one chromosome of each pair.

General Biological Supply

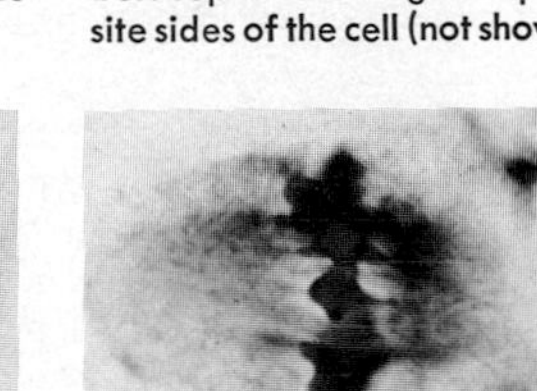

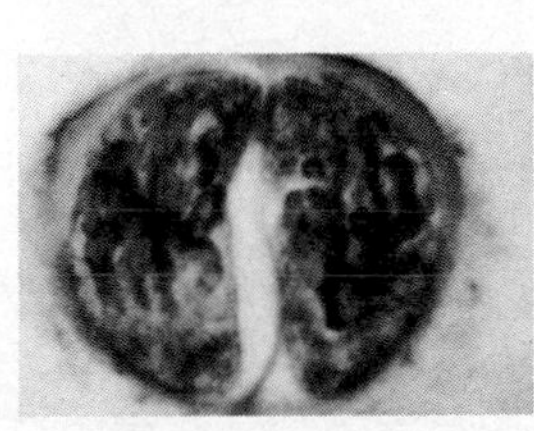

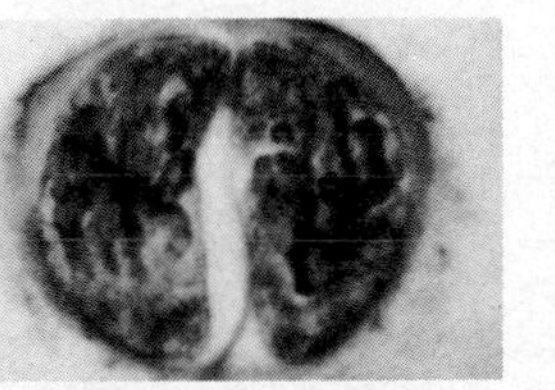

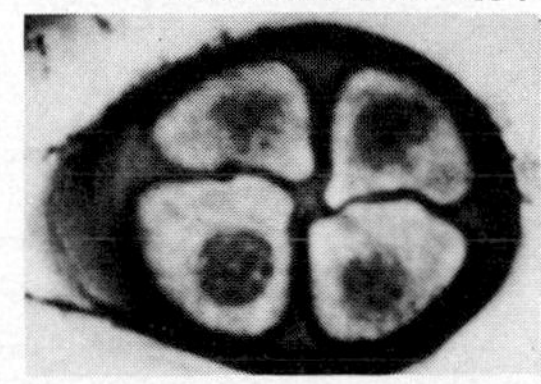

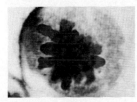

divides, it passes on the same hereditary material. Scientists think that DNA, the hereditary material carried by the chromosomes, controls differentiation partly by directing the production of certain enzymes. As these enzymes appear in a cell, their chemical reactions cause the cell to become a specialist. All the cells in an organism have the same DNA, so what makes the DNA in one cell order different enzymes than it orders in another cell? Scientists do not yet know.

Death of a Cell. Like all other living things, cells die. Every minute, about 3 billion cells in your body die. During the same minute, about 3 billion new cells are born by mitosis and replace them. Dead skin cells flake off. Dead cells from internal organs pass out of the body with waste products. White blood cells live about 13 days; red blood cells live about 120 days; and liver cells live about 18 months. Nerve cells can live about 100 years. But they can never be replaced if they are destroyed, because nerve cells do not reproduce after they have become mature.

Cell Research

The mystery of the cell has long been a challenge. More than 2,000 years ago, people debated how a human being grew from a single egg cell. Some thought this cell contained a tiny, completely formed human being. Others argued that the heart, legs, arms, and all other parts of the body developed successively. But only with the development of the microscope could scientists begin to solve the mysteries of the cell.

Before 1900. In 1665, Robert Hooke, an English scientist, observed a thin slice of cork under his microscope. He saw that it was composed of neat holes enclosed by walls. He called these holes *cells*. Other scientists also studied cells and tiny living things under the microscope. But for many years, few guessed the significance of the cell.

In 1838, the German botanist Matthias Schleiden stated that the cell was the basic unit of all life. The next year, Theodor Schwann, a German physiologist, advanced the same idea. Schleiden and Schwann did not originate this idea. A number of other scientists had already come to believe that all organisms were made up of cells. But from that time on, biologists regarded the cell as the building block of life.

In the mid-1800's, Gregor Mendel, an Austrian monk, discovered the laws of heredity through experiments with garden peas. Mendel's work, translated into modern terms, suggested that there is a basic unit of heredity—the *gene*. Genes occur in pairs, with each parent supplying one member of every pair. In 1866, Mendel published a paper explaining his findings. But his work went unrecognized until 1900.

Meanwhile, using ever more powerful microscopes, scientists had discovered much about cells. They learned that cells reproduced by division. They found that the nucleus of every cell contained a substance they called chromatin. During cell division, the chromatin condensed into a certain number of visible pairs of chromosomes, depending on the species of life. Each daughter cell received the same number of chromosomes that the parent cell had. Scientists also discovered that when egg and sperm cells were produced, they received only half the number of chromosomes that the body cells had.

Near the end of the 1800's, a number of scientists argued that chromosomes must be the basis of heredity.

BREAKTHROUGHS IN CELL RESEARCH

The Structure of a Piece of Cork was drawn 300 years ago by Robert Hooke. Looking through the microscope he had built, Hooke noted that the cork consisted of "little Boxes." He called these "little Boxes" *cells.*

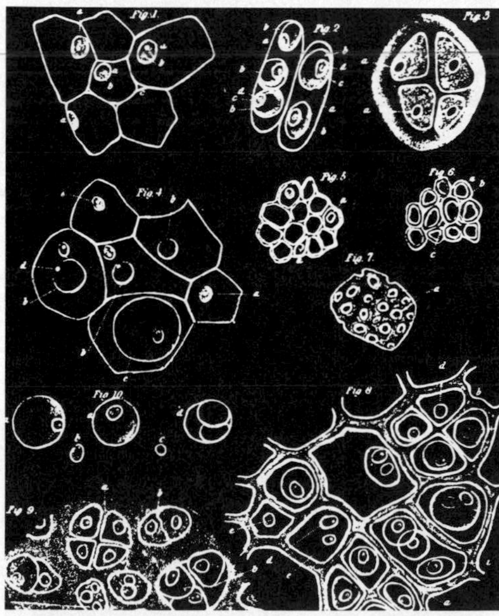

Theodor Schwann's Drawings of plant and animal cells helped convince scientists that all living things are made up of cells. Schwann and Matthias Schleiden advanced this idea, called the *cell theory,* in the 1830's.

However, this opinion was not yet generally accepted.

The 1900's. Mendel's work was rediscovered three times in 1900—by Hugo de Vries of The Netherlands, Carl Correns of Germany, and Erich Tschermak of Austria. Each of these botanists, working independently on the problem of heredity, came across Mendel's findings. In 1902, Walter S. Sutton, an American scientist, pointed out that during cell division chromosomes behaved the way genes were thought to behave, according to Mendel's findings. A few years later at Columbia University, Thomas Hunt Morgan and his associates proved that genes are the units of heredity. They also proved that genes are arranged in an exact order along the length of the chromosomes.

The question then became: How do genes determine the structure and behavior of living things? Two American scientists, George W. Beadle and Edward L. Tatum, found the answer in the early 1940's. They discovered that genes control chemical reactions in cells by directing the formation of enzymes. Beadle and Tatum found that there is a specific gene for each enzyme.

Scientists now became increasingly interested in the chemistry of the gene. They knew that chromosomes consisted of DNA and protein. In fact, DNA had been discovered in 1868 by a Swiss biochemist, Friedrich Miescher. But scientists had dismissed DNA as unimportant, knowing how essential proteins were in the life processes. The turning point came in 1944. At the Rockefeller Institute (now Rockefeller University), a team of scientists headed by Oswald T. Avery found evidence that DNA alone determined heredity.

Scientists knew that the DNA molecule consisted of *phosphate*, *deoxyribose*, and four compounds called *bases*—adenine, cytosine, guanine, and thymine. But they did not know how these six units fitted together. In 1953, James D. Watson, an American, and Francis H. C. Crick, an Englishman, made a model of the DNA molecule. They showed that it resembled a twisted ladder. Experiments have proved their model correct.

In 1957, Arthur Kornberg, an American biochemist, produced DNA in a test tube. He mixed DNA units with an enzyme, and added a bit of natural DNA as a *primer* (starter). The DNA units linked together into a chain resembling the primer DNA. Ten years later, Kornberg manufactured DNA that was *biologically active* (able to reproduce naturally). Until this time, only inactive DNA could be made.

Many scientists have worked on unraveling the genetic code, found in the bases of DNA. In 1962, Marshall W. Nirenberg, an American biochemist, discovered the code for one amino acid. He and others eventually broke the code for the 20 amino acids involved in protein production. They also discovered how RNA copies the DNA code to produce proteins.

The Future holds enormous challenges and exciting promises for cell research. Tomorrow's great medical triumphs will probably be in controlling disorders that arise in the cell. The genetic code has been broken, but other aspects of how genes operate and the detailed function of all the tiny parts of the cell remain a mystery. Many questions must still be answered, including: What causes a cell to die? Can errors in the genetic code that cause mental and physical disorders be corrected? What makes a cell differentiate?

If scientists can discover what causes a cell to die, they may be able to slow the aging process and increase the

The Electron Microscope became a vital tool of cell research in the 1950's. With its tremendous magnifying power, it opened a new world to scientists. It revealed that cells contained many highly elaborate structures.

WORLD BOOK photo by Arthur Siegel

A Model of DNA, showing how its parts fitted together, was built by James D. Watson and Francis H. C. Crick in 1953. The balls represent the individual atoms of the parts.

Arnold Ryan Chalfant & Associates

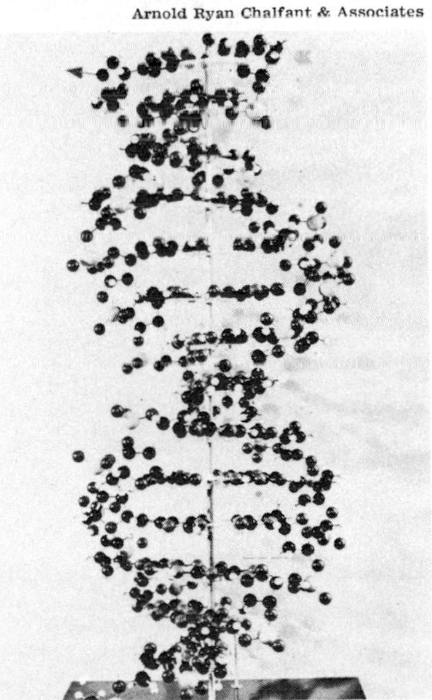

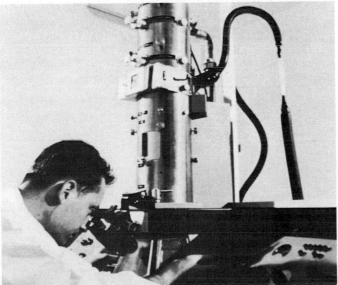

span of human life. As scientists learn more about DNA and the genetic code, they may be able to alter the code and erase hundreds of inherited mental and physical defects. They may find how to control cancer. If scientists learn how a cell differentiates, they may be able to alter mature nerve cells, which do not reproduce. Then these cells could be replaced if damaged or destroyed. Or perhaps scientists may be able to replace worn-out or diseased tissues, or encourage the stump of an amputated leg to regrow. By manipulating hereditary processes, scientists may free farm crops and livestock of hereditary diseases. Thus, agricultural production may be greatly increased.

One of the most promising areas of future cell research is the field of genetic engineering. This field developed during the 1970's after scientists discovered techniques for removing genes from one organism and inserting them into another. This procedure is called *recombinant DNA research.* Experiments with recombinant DNA have helped scientists to learn more about the structure and function of genes. Many researchers believe that recombinant DNA research will lead to advances in agriculture, medicine, and industry. However, many people feel that such research is dangerous, and the government has placed strict guidelines on recombinant DNA research in the United States. See Genetic Engineering.

The following sections on *The Work of a Cell*, *The Code of Life*, and *The Cell in Disease* summarize current theories about the cell and how it works.

The Work of a Cell

A cell is intensely active. It carries out most of life's functions, including growth and reproduction. In addition, cells of multicellular organisms have special jobs. To live and to do its work, a cell must produce energy. It also must manufacture proteins for the construction of its parts and to speed up the hundreds of chemical reactions that occur in the cell.

Producing Energy. Most of your energy comes from the mitochondria, the power producers of a cell. The mitochondria are like a power plant which burns fuel to produce the electricity that runs machines. The food you eat is the fuel that is "burned" inside the mitochondria. A product of this burning is a compound called *adenosine triphosphate* (ATP). ATP is the "electricity" that runs the cell's activities. It supplies the energy when a protein is made, a muscle cell contracts, a nerve cell sends a message, or a gland cell produces a chemical.

An ATP molecule consists of three substances: (1) adenine, (2) ribose, and (3) three phosphate groups. *Chemical bonds* (forces that hold atoms together) link the phosphate groups together like railroad cars. The bonds that attach the second and third phosphate groups are especially rich in energy. When they are broken, energy is released. See Chemistry (Chemical Bonds).

PRODUCING ENERGY

This diagram traces the steps by which the energy a cell needs to live and to work is produced. Most of this energy is produced in the *mitochondria*. The energy is stored in a compound called *ATP*. To make ATP, the mitochondria must have fuel. In an animal cell, the fuel comes from food.

The left side of the diagram shows that an animal's digestive system first breaks down food into amino acids, fatty acids, and simple sugars. The blood carries these substances to the cells. They enter the cytoplasm. The sugars are broken down into pyruvic acid, and a little ATP is produced.

The right side of the diagram shows that amino, fatty, and pyruvic acids enter the mitochondria. There, in the presence of oxygen, they are broken down further in a series of chemical reactions. The reactions produce carbon dioxide and water as waste products, and molecules of ATP.

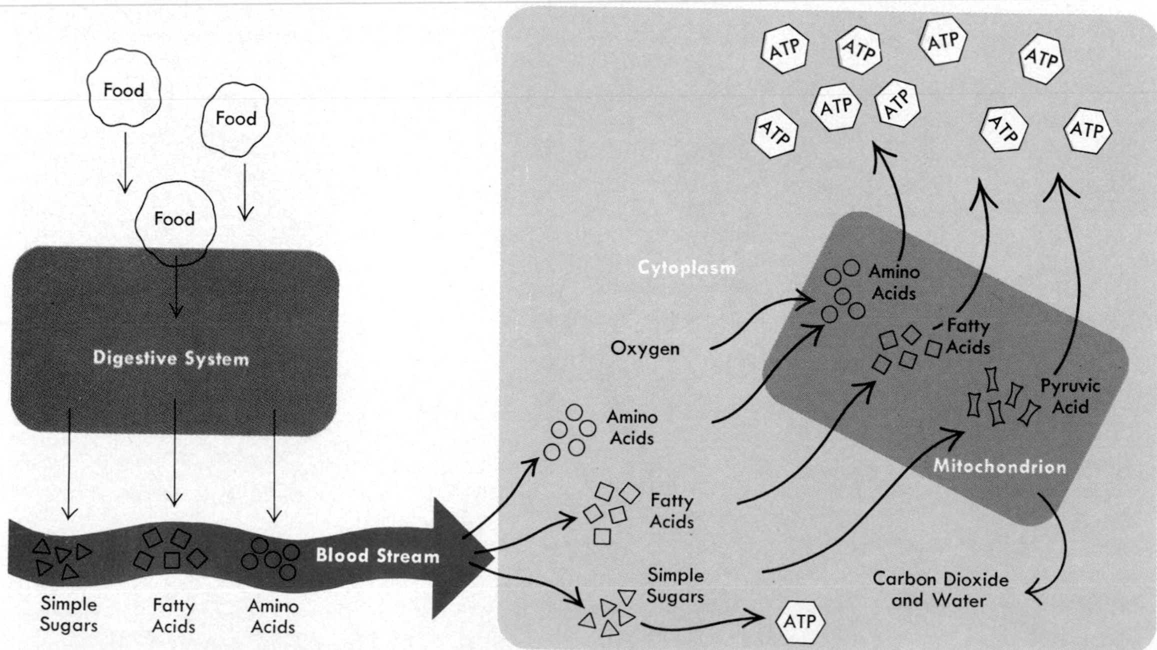

PRODUCING PROTEINS

A cell's form and function are determined by the proteins it produces. Proteins, in turn, are made up of tiny units called *amino acids*. DNA contains the blueprints for all the proteins made in a cell. These blueprints direct the order in which the amino acids will be linked together to form particular proteins.

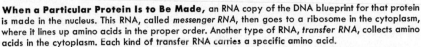

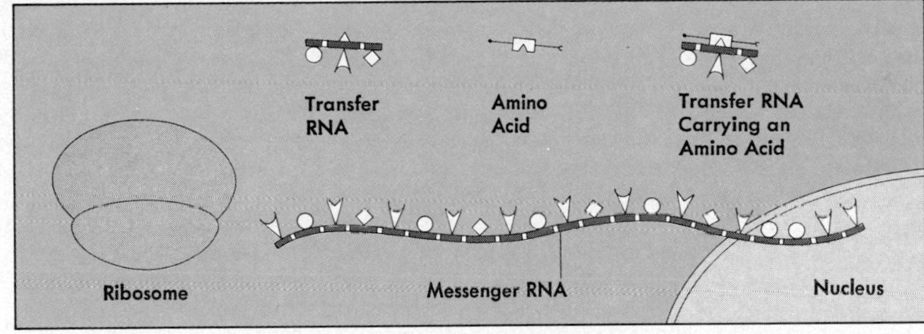

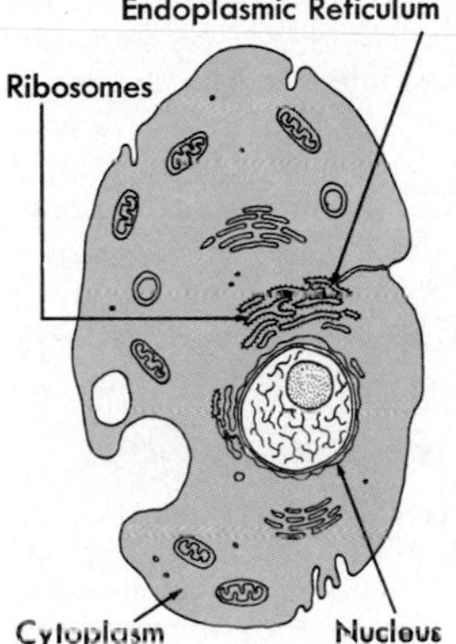

When a Particular Protein Is to Be Made, an RNA copy of the DNA blueprint for that protein is made in the nucleus. This RNA, called *messenger RNA*, then goes to a ribosome in the cytoplasm, where it lines up amino acids in the proper order. Another type of RNA, *transfer RNA*, collects amino acids in the cytoplasm. Each kind of transfer RNA carries a specific amino acid.

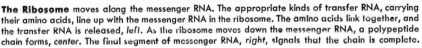

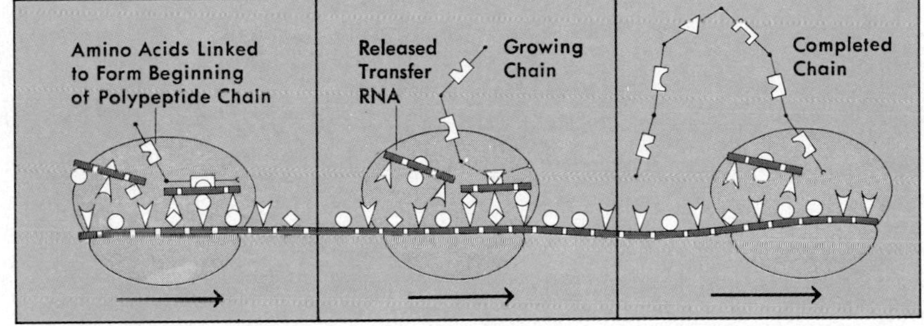

The Ribosome moves along the messenger RNA. The appropriate kinds of transfer RNA, carrying their amino acids, line up with the messenger RNA in the ribosome. The amino acids link together, and the transfer RNA is released, *left*. As the ribosome moves down the messenger RNA, a polypeptide chain forms, *center*. The final segment of messenger RNA, *right*, signals that the chain is complete.

Animal cells produce ATP in a very complicated process. First, an animal's digestive system breaks down the food the animal eats. Proteins are broken down into amino acids, fats into fatty acids, and sugars and starches into simple sugars. The blood carries these substances to all the cells in the body. In the cytoplasm, the sugars are broken down into pyruvic acid, and a small amount of ATP is produced. The amino, fatty, and pyruvic acids then enter the mitochondria. Enzymes in the mitochondria break down these substances further in a series of chemical reactions. Oxygen must also be present in the mitochondria for these reactions to take place. The reactions produce carbon dioxide, water, and many molecules of ATP. The ATP molecules then leave the mitochondria and provide power wherever it is needed in the cell. For every job that is done, enzymes break the ATP phosphate bonds and release the energy.

ATP is also produced during photosynthesis, the process by which green plants make sugars. When sunlight strikes a chlorophyll molecule in a chloroplast, it sets off a series of chemical reactions. A result of these reactions is the formation of ATP. ATP provides the energy by which plants then turn carbon dioxide from the air, and water from the soil, into sugars. Some other organisms, including certain bacteria, also produce ATP during photosynthesis. See PHOTOSYNTHESIS.

Producing Proteins. All living things contain proteins. The structures of a cell are built largely of proteins. The proteins called enzymes speed up the chemical reactions of life. They help digest your food, help produce energy, and assist in building other proteins. A single cell may contain hundreds of enzymes. Many *hormones*, the substances that regulate chemical activities throughout your body, are proteins. So are the antibodies your body makes to fight disease germs.

Proteins are complex, three-dimensional substances composed of one or more long, folded *polypeptide chains*. These chains, in turn, consist of small chemical units called *amino acids*. All amino acids contain carbon, hydrogen, oxygen, and nitrogen, and some also contain sulfur. The amino acids link together in a line to form polypeptide chains. There are 20 kinds of amino acids involved in protein production, and any number of them may be linked in any order to form a polypeptide chain. Some polypeptide chains may contain only 10 amino acid "links." Others contain more than 100. Each different arrangement of amino acids forms a different polypeptide chain. The number of different chains—and thus, different proteins—that can be formed is practically unlimited. The kinds of proteins actually produced are determined by the DNA in the cell's nucleus. See AMINO ACID; PROTEIN.

DNA contains the blueprint for every protein made in the cell. The proteins are manufactured in the cytoplasm of the cell, according to the DNA structure of the cell's genes. But the DNA of the genes does not leave the nucleus to help make the proteins. This job is done by DNA's chemical cousin, RNA. RNA is made in the nucleus and is present in both the nucleus and the cytoplasm.

To understand how proteins are made, let us trace the production of a protein that consists of one polypeptide chain. The first step takes place in the nucleus. There, an RNA copy of the DNA blueprint for the polypeptide chain is made. The RNA then leaves the nucleus and enters the cytoplasm. This RNA, called *messenger RNA*, goes to the ribosomes, the cell's centers of protein production. A ribosome moves along the messenger RNA, "reading" the information coded on it. The messenger RNA acts as a *template* (mold) to line up the amino acids in the exact order called for by the DNA of the genes. The amino acids are linked together one by one to form the polypeptide chain.

Another type of RNA, called *transfer RNA*, collects the amino acids in the cytoplasm and brings them to the messenger RNA in the ribosome. There is at least one transfer RNA molecule for each kind of amino acid. The specific transfer RNA and the correct amino acid are brought together with the help of ATP and an enzyme designed for the job.

At any one time, the ribosome covers two coding segments of messenger RNA. Each of these coding segments, which are called *codons*, specifies one amino acid. The correct transfer RNA, with its amino acid attached, lines up on the first codon of the messenger RNA template. After a second transfer RNA and its amino acid have lined up on the other codon, the two amino acids are linked together. The first transfer RNA is then set free to collect more amino acids.

The second transfer RNA holds the growing polypeptide chain to the ribosome. The ribosome then moves one codon further down the messenger RNA. The appropriate transfer RNA, with its attached amino acid, lines up on this codon. The amino acid is joined to the first two amino acids, and the second transfer RNA is now set free.

The ribosome moves one position further, covering the next codon on the messenger RNA template. This process continues until the ribosome has passed over the entire length of the messenger RNA. The last codon on the messenger RNA does not code for an amino acid. It signals that the chain is complete. The finished polypeptide chain is then released. In this case, the protein is now complete. In most proteins that consist of more than one polypeptide chain, the chains are manufactured separately, and then they combine to make the protein. The finished protein then starts to do its particular job. Some proteins are used inside the cell. Others, such as hormones and digestive enzymes, are released from the cell to do their work.

The Code of Life

As we have seen, DNA controls the life of the cell—and the lives of organisms made up of cells—in two ways. First, it passes on all hereditary information from one generation of cells to the next. Second, DNA determines the form and function of the cell by regulating the kinds of proteins it produces. Thus, DNA is the master plan of all life.

DNA—The Wondrous Ladder. DNA molecules lie tightly coiled in the chromosomes of a cell. Each chromosome probably contains one extremely long DNA molecule. On the average, a single human chromosome consists of a DNA molecule that is about 16 inches (41 centimeters) long. But the DNA molecule is a thread so thin that its details cannot be seen even when magnified by a powerful electron microscope. Scientists have figured out its structure on the basis of its chemical composition. They also have bounced X rays off the atoms in a DNA molecule and studied the patterns the scattered X rays made on photographic plates.

The patterns show that the molecule is a *double helix*—that is, a double thread, held together by crosspieces and coiled like a spring. In other words, DNA looks like a twisted rope ladder. All DNA molecules have this shape, whether they come from the cells of a cactus, a turtle, or a human being.

The DNA ladder consists of six pieces. The long threads that make up the sides of the ladder contain alternating units of *phosphate* and a sugar called *deoxyribose*. The rungs of the ladder are made up of four compounds called *bases*. The bases are *adenine*, *cytosine*,

DNA'S SIX PARTS

A DNA molecule consists of *phosphate*, a sugar called *deoxyribose*, and four bases—*adenine*, *cytosine*, *guanine*, and *thymine*.

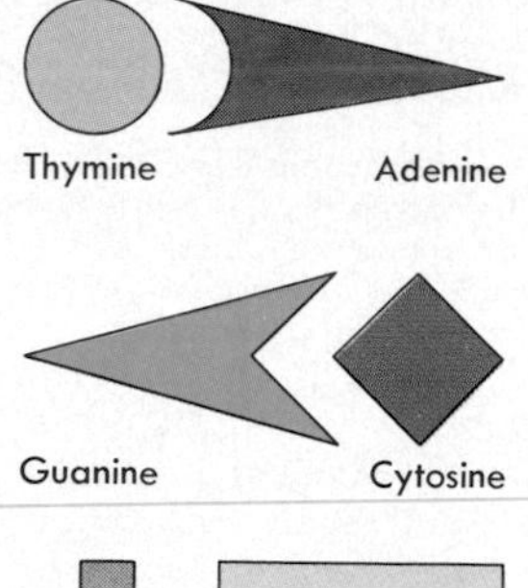

RNA'S SIX PARTS

RNA differs from DNA in two chief ways. The sugar in RNA is *ribose*, and RNA contains the base *uracil*, instead of thymine.

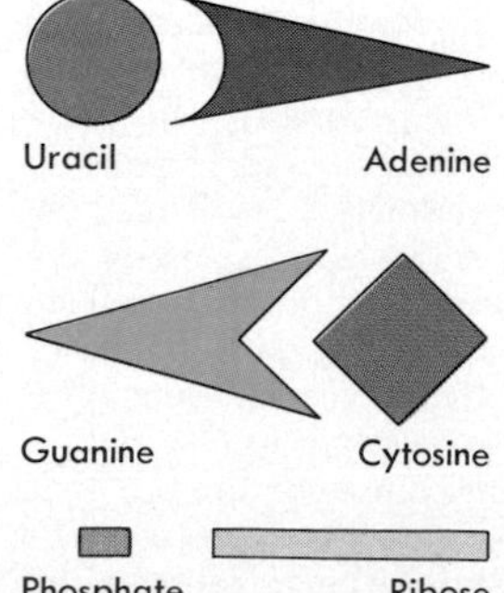

THE DNA LADDER

DNA's parts link together like a twisted ladder. Each rung consists of two matching bases. The sides are sugar and phosphate.

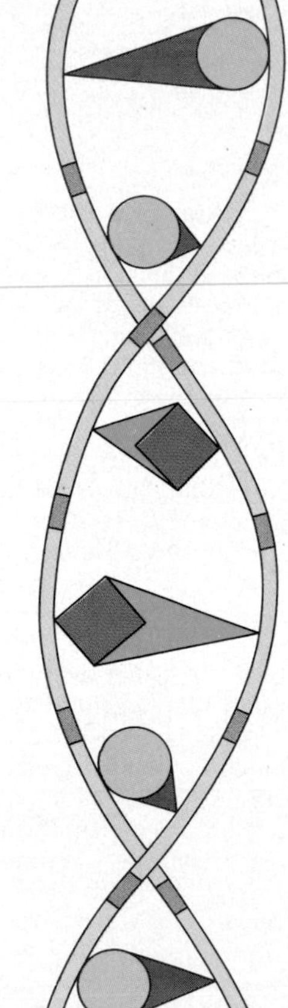

guanine, and *thymine* (abbreviated A, C, G, and T). They are attached to the sugar units of the ladder's side pieces. Each rung consists of two bases: A-T, T-A, C-G, or G-C. No other combination is possible, because only the A-T and C-G pairs are chemically attracted to each other. In addition, only these pairs make rungs of the proper length to fit between the ladder's side pieces. Any other combination is too big or too small. The order of the bases in one *strand* (half) of the ladder determines the order of the bases in the other strand. For example, if the bases in one strand are ATCGAT, the bases in the opposite strand would be TAGCTA.

Before a cell divides, the DNA duplicates. The ladder splits lengthwise, separating the bases of each strand. Then, with the help of special enzymes, each half ladder picks up free bases with their attached sugars and phosphates. But the bases in each half ladder can pick up only their matching mates. The A's attach to T's, the T's to A's, the G's to C's, and the C's to G's. In this way, each new ladder becomes a duplicate of the original ladder. When the cell divides, each of the new daughter cells receives identical DNA molecules.

RNA—The Master Copy. RNA, the substance that carries out DNA's instructions for protein production, resembles DNA in chemical structure. But there are two major differences. The sugar in RNA is *ribose* instead of deoxyribose, and RNA contains the base *uracil* (abbreviated U) instead of thymine. Like thymine, uracil will pair only with the base adenine. RNA's other three bases—A, C, and G—and the phosphate unit are identical to those in DNA.

How does messenger RNA copy the DNA blueprints for making proteins? Scientists think a part of the DNA molecule may unwind and split. One of the halves then serves as a mold for lining up the RNA bases. Free bases, with their sugars and phosphates, attach to the exposed DNA bases. For example, the RNA bases AUCGAU attach to the DNA bases TAGCTA. An RNA strand is formed, and it is a reverse copy of the DNA master plan. The messenger RNA, which may consist of hundreds of

DNA DUPLICATION

1. Just before a cell divides, the DNA duplicates. The ladder splits lengthwise, separating the bases of each rung.

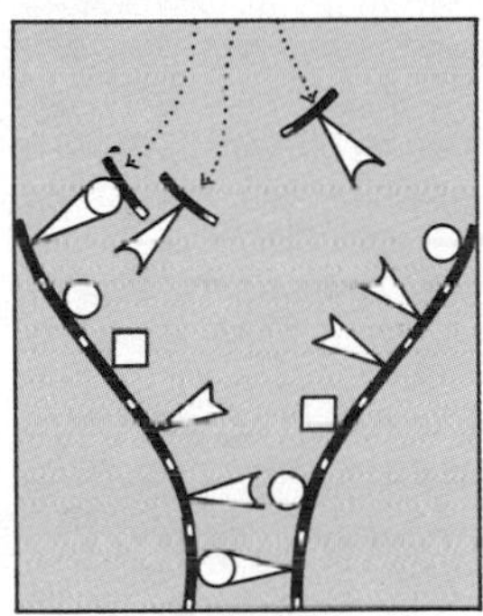

2. Free bases, with their sugars and phosphates, attach to the bases of each half ladder. But only matching bases can pair up.

3. Two ladders are built, each a duplicate of the original. Thus, when the cell divides, each new cell gets identical DNA.

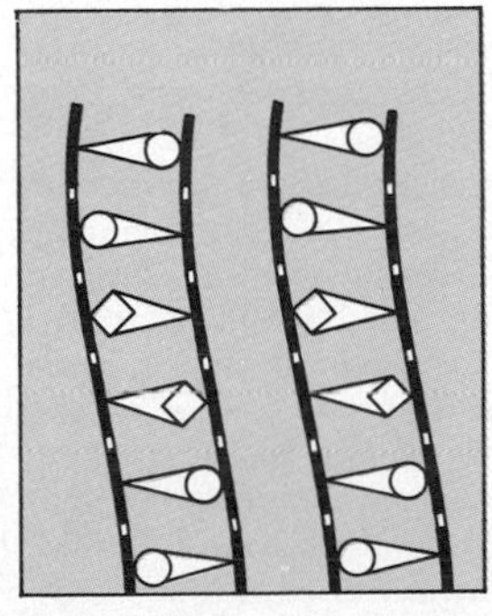

HOW MESSENGER RNA IS FORMED

1. When RNA copies DNA's blueprint for making a protein, the DNA ladder first splits lengthwise through its bases. One half of the ladder then serves as a mold to form messenger RNA. Free RNA bases, with their attached sugars and phosphates, match up with the exposed DNA bases. A strand of messenger RNA thus begins to form.

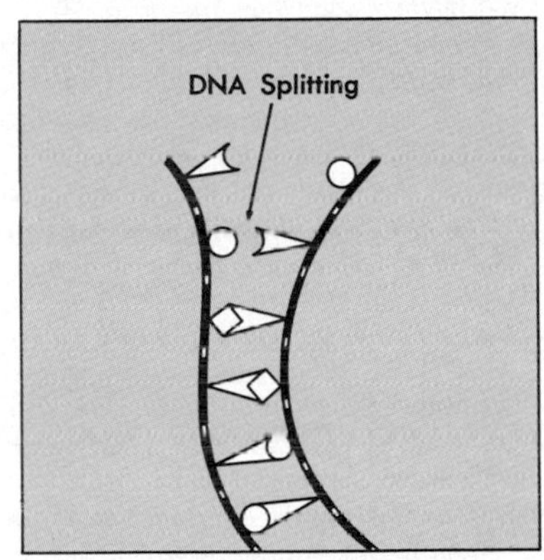

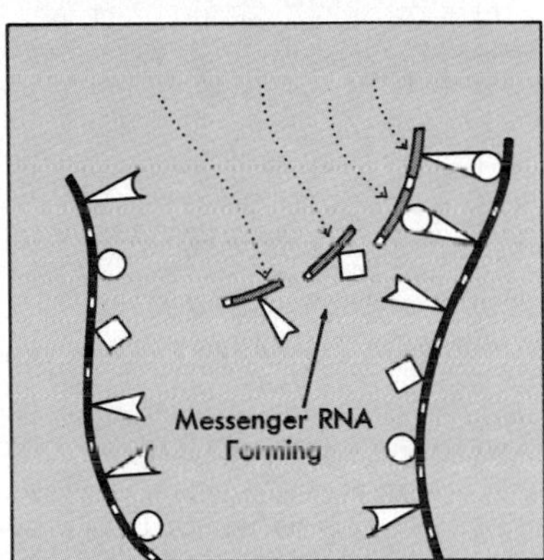

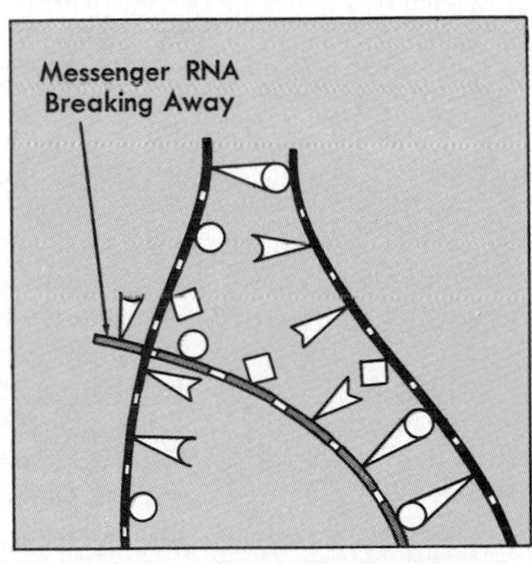

2. As messenger RNA forms, it becomes a reverse copy of the DNA blueprint, and begins to peel off the DNA mold. As it breaks away, the bases of the DNA ladder start to rejoin.

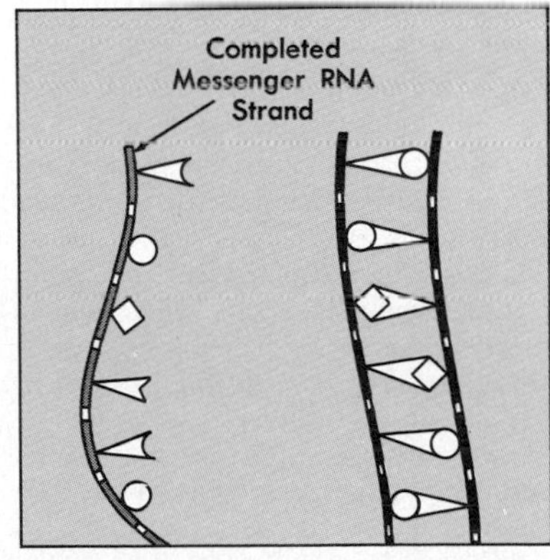

3. The completed strand of messenger RNA leaves the nucleus and goes to the ribosomes. There, it will serve as a mold on which amino acids will be linked into a protein chain.

bases, peels off the DNA mold and carries the instructions for making a protein to the ribosomes on the endoplasmic reticulum. The bases of the DNA molecule rejoin, the ladder rewinds, and the master plan is again locked away. Meanwhile, transfer RNA molecules, carrying amino acids, find their correct position on the messenger RNA mold. Thus, the protein ordered by DNA is built.

The Genetic Code lies in the order of the bases in the DNA molecule. This order of bases is passed on from one generation of cells to the next, and from one generation of organisms to the next. The order of bases makes an elephant give birth to an elephant, not a zebra, a goldfish, or an elm tree. It is this order that determines the color of your eyes, the shape of your ears, and thousands of other traits.

The order of the 4 bases determines the order of the 20 amino acids when the cell produces specific proteins. These instructions for making specific proteins are carried by specific genes. A gene is a particular segment of the DNA ladder, and contains a certain number of bases in a certain order.

But how can the order of 4 bases determine the order of 20 amino acids in a protein chain? Obviously, a single base cannot direct the position of a specific amino acid. The answer lies in a *triplet code*. In other words, a group of three bases in a certain order forms the codon for a specific amino acid. Each codon is given a three-letter name that corresponds to the abbreviation of the names of its bases.

Scientists have broken the genetic code. The first codon to be solved was UUU of RNA. Scientists used an RNA chain consisting of only the base uracil repeated over and over again. They added this RNA to a mixture containing the 20 amino acids and the cell's protein-making machinery. The RNA produced a protein chain consisting of only the amino acid phenylalanine. So, UUU turned out to be the RNA codon for phenylalanine. Messenger RNA is a reverse copy of DNA. Thus, the DNA codon for phenylalanine is AAA. Other RNA codons include UAU, which stands for the amino acid tyrosine; CAC, which stands for histidine; and UGG, which stands for tryptophan.

A total of 64 three-letter codons can be formed from the 4 letters of the DNA bases. Because there are only 20, not 64, amino acids, there is more than one codon for most amino acids. Three of the codons, UAA, UAG, and UGA, do not code for any amino acid. They act as signals for the release of the polypeptide from the ribosome.

One of the most striking findings in modern biology is that the genetic code is universal. The same three-letter codons specify the same amino acids in all organisms that have been studied—from bacteria to human beings. Thus, underlying the vast variety of life is a common unit, the cell, whose activities are directed by a common language—the genetic code written in DNA.

The Cell in Disease

A cell usually functions perfectly. It grows and reproduces in an orderly fashion and performs its tasks with remarkable efficiency. But sometimes things go wrong. Instead of dividing in an orderly fashion, a cell may go wild and multiply without stopping—and form a cancer. A virus may take over the machinery of the cell for its own purposes and kill it. The genetic code may contain an error, and a needed protein may not be produced, or an abnormal one may be formed.

Cancer is a disease marked by a disorderly growth of cells. It occurs in plants as well as in human beings and other animals. Many cancer cells look like immature cells. The cytoplasm is thin, and the nucleus occupies most of the cell. In cancerous tissue, many nuclei are in the process of mitosis. The wildly dividing cells eventually pile up and form a tumor. Cells in the tumor may break away, invade other tissues, and disrupt their function. Many factors, including smoking, exposure to certain chemicals, or excessive use of X rays, may cause cells to go on a rampage of reproduction. Many scientists believe that whatever the cause or causes may be, they produce a change in the genetic code. The altered code is then duplicated and passed on to daughter cells. See CANCER.

Virus Diseases occur when a virus invades a cell. Viruses are tiny parasites. They are not cells. They occupy a twilight zone between the living and the lifeless. By themselves, viruses are lifeless particles. But inside a living cell, viruses become active and capable of reproduction. Most viruses consist only of hereditary material —DNA or RNA—and protein. After a virus enters a cell, it may take over the cell's machinery to produce viruses like itself. Soon, many viruses are produced, and the cell is destroyed in most cases. The new viruses then invade other cells. Viruses that attack human beings cause chicken pox, measles, mumps, poliomyelitis, and many other diseases. Scientists have proved that certain viruses cause cancer in laboratory animals. See VIRUS.

Metabolic Diseases. *Metabolism* is the chemical process by which all living things transform food into living matter and energy. Metabolism depends on specific proteins, which are made according to the genetic code. Sometimes the code contains an error that may cause a metabolic disease. Many of these errors are inherited and are brought about by a *mutation* (change) in the code. Most mutations are caused by radiation or chemicals, which scramble a part of the genetic code and result in an error. If the DNA in a parent's reproductive cells contains an error in the plans for making a protein, the error may be passed on to the offspring.

Several metabolic diseases occur because the code does not call for a needed enzyme. For example, *galactosemia*, a disease of infants, is caused by a lack of the enzyme needed to convert galactose, a milk sugar, to glucose. *Phenylketonuria*, another disease of infants, is caused by the lack of the enzyme needed to convert the amino acid phenylalanine to the amino acid tyrosine. Both these diseases cause mental retardation and poor physical development.

Some metabolic diseases are caused when the instructions for making a protein are misspelled in the genetic code. *Sickle cell anemia*, an almost always fatal human disease, is an outstanding example. Normal red blood cells are disk-shaped. But in a sickle cell victim, some red blood cells become twisted into a hooked, or sickle, shape. These deformed cells die quickly, causing severe anemia. Red blood cells contain a protein called hemoglobin, which carries oxygen to the body's tissues. Hemoglobin is made of several hundred amino acids.

The deadly sickling occurs when, in only one part of this long chain, the genetic code calls for the amino acid valine instead of glutamic acid. IRWIN RUBENSTEIN

Related Articles in WORLD BOOK include:

Amino Acid	Human Body
Beadle, George W.	Life
Biology	Mendel, Gregor J.
Biosynthesis	Microscope
Blood	Microtome
Cancer	Microtomy
Cellulose	Mutation
Chromosome	Nervous System
Crick, Francis H. C.	Nucleic Acid
Cytology	Photosynthesis
Enzyme	Protein
Evolution	Protoplasm
Franklin, Rosalind E.	Reproduction
Gene	Sickle Cell Anemia
Genetic Engineering	Spontaneous Generation
Genetics	Tatum, Edward L.
Golgi, Camillo	Tissue
Growth	Virus
Heredity	Watson, James D.
Histology	Wilkins, Maurice H. F.
Hooke, Robert	

Outline

I. Looking at a Cell
A. Shapes of Cells
B. Sizes of Cells
II. Inside a Living Cell
A. The Nucleus
B. The Cytoplasm
C. Membranes
D. Plant Cells
E. Bacteria and Blue-Green Algae Cells
III. Cell Division
A. Mitosis
B. Meiosis
C. Growth and Specialization
D. Death of a Cell
IV. Cell Research
V. The Work of a Cell
A. Producing Energy
B. Producing Proteins
VI. The Code of Life
A. DNA—The Wondrous Ladder
B. RNA—The Master Copy
C. The Genetic Code
VII. The Cell in Disease
A. Cancer
B. Virus Diseases
C. Metabolic Diseases

Questions

What is a cell?
What structures do most cells have in common?
What are the two main types of cell division?
How does a cell make proteins?
What is the genetic code?
Why is ATP so important in the life and work of a cell?
How do viruses cause disease?
In what two ways does DNA control the life of a cell?
Why are Matthias Schleiden and Theodor Schwann so important in the history of cell research?
What is *differentiation*? Why is it such a challenging problem?

Additional Resources

BOREK, ERNEST. *The Code of Life*. Columbia, 1969. *The Sculpture of Life*. 1973.
COBB, VICKI. *Cells: The Basic Structure of Life*. Watts, 1970. For younger readers.
GUNNING, BRIAN E. S., and STEER, M. W. *Ultrastructure and the Biology of Plant Cells*. Arnold, 1975.
HOAGLAND, MAHLON BUSH. *Discovery: The Search for DNA's Secrets*. Houghton, 1981.
LECHTMAN, MAX D., and others. *The Games Cells Play: Basic Concepts of Cellular Metabolism*. Benjamin/Cummings, 1979.
SHEELER, PHILLIP, and BIANCHI, D. E. *Cell Biology: Structure, Biochemistry, and Function*. Wiley, 1980.
SILVERSTEIN, ALVIN and VIRGINIA B. *Cells: Building Blocks of Life*. Prentice-Hall, 1969. For younger readers.

CELLINI, *chuh LEE nee,* **BENVENUTO,** *BEHN vuh NOO toh* (1500-1571), was an Italian goldsmith and sculptor. He was not regarded as an outstanding sculptor during his lifetime, and it is doubtful if his name would mean much today except for his writings. Cellini began writing his *Autobiography* in 1558. It was published in 1728.

Kunsthistorisches Museum, Vienna

Cellini's Saltcellar is the artist's only major surviving work as a goldsmith. It was created for King Francis I of France.

The *Autobiography* follows the bragging, arrogant Cellini through adventure after adventure in the courts of Rome, Florence, and Paris. He dramatized each incident as if it were an event that moved the world.

Cellini's story is instructive as well as entertaining. It takes the reader through such historical events as the siege of Rome in 1527, and introduces people of his time in such a way that they seem to live again. He vividly describes every step of the casting of his masterpiece, *Perseus*. Cellini says that the completion of *Perseus* was hailed with joy throughout Italy. This is typical of his exaggerations. The reader must be on guard, especially when the artist appraises his own deeds. However, critics have praised *Perseus* for its expressive outlines and striking *patina* (oxidized surface). It is reproduced in color in the SCULPTURE article.

Cellini's only identifiable work as a goldsmith, except for some coins and medals, is an elaborate silver and gold table ornament known as the *Saltcellar of Francis I*. It was done in the 1540's. The forced poses, elongated proportions, and rich ornamentation show the influence of both the movement known as *mannerism* and of Michelangelo. The same ornamentation appears in Cellini's bronze relief of the goddess Diana, called *Nymph of Fontainebleau* (1543-1544), which was made for King Francis I of France. Cellini was born in Florence. G. HAYDN HUNTLEY

CELLO, *CHEHL oh,* is a stringed musical instrument of the violin family that is played with a bow. It is also called *violoncello* (pronounced *VY uh luhn CHEHL oh*).

The cello is shaped like a violin but is much larger. The cello measures about 4 feet (1.2 meters) long and about $1\frac{1}{2}$ feet (0.5 meter) across its widest part. It has four strings and produces full, rich sounds, starting with a note an octave and a fifth below the lowest note of the violin. The cello, supported by an end pin, is held between the knees in an upright position.

WORLD BOOK photo, courtesy Chicago Symphony Orchestra

The Cello, or Violoncello, became popular as a solo instrument in the late 1600's. It has a rich, deep tone.

The cello probably originated in northern Italy in the 1530's. It was first used as a supporting bass instrument. During the late 1600's, composers began writing music for the cello as a solo instrument. It became prominent in chamber music groups and symphony orchestras in the 1700's and 1800's. ABRAM LOFT

See also CASALS, PABLO.

CELLOPHANE is a thin, flexible, synthetic material. It is made from *cellulose*, a substance in the walls of plant cells. Most cellophane is coated with special chemicals to make it airproof and moisture-resistant. These chemicals also make cellophane *heat sealable*—that is, they enable cellophane to be sealed to itself and to certain other materials through the application of heat and pressure.

About 95 per cent of the cellophane made in the United States is used to package products that require protection from air and moisture to remain fresh. Such products include baked goods, candy, and cigarettes. Most cellophane is transparent and colorless and is about $\frac{1}{1,000}$ inch (0.03 millimeter) thick.

Manufacturers of cellophane chemically remove cellulose from wood pulp and mix it with caustic soda. This mixture is aged and treated with carbon disulfide to create a thick, sticky liquid called *viscose*. After the viscose has been aged and filtered, it is formed into a thin liquid sheet by forcing it through a long, narrow slit. The liquid sheet is immediately treated with sulfuric acid, which hardens it into cellophane. The product then undergoes various chemical processes to remove impurities and make it flexible. Finally, cellophane is dried and wound onto rolls.

A Swiss chemist named Jacques E. Brandenberger discovered cellophane in 1908, when he sprayed viscose on a tablecloth he was trying to make stain-resistant. He found he could peel the coating from the cloth in the form of a thin, transparent sheet. In 1911, Brandenberger designed a machine to produce the material.

Cellophane was produced in the United States for the first time in 1924. Originally, it was neither moisture-resistant nor heat-sealable. Products packaged in it had to be wrapped by hand because there were no wrapping machines. As a result, cellophane was used to package only perfume and other luxury items. After the invention of heat-sealable and moisture-resistant coatings in 1927 and of wrapping machines during the 1930's, the cellophane industry grew rapidly.

By the early 1960's, the U.S. cellophane industry had reached its peak production of 440 million pounds (200 million kilograms) a year. Since then, competition from plastics and other less expensive packaging materials has led to a decline in the use of cellophane. Today, about 150 million pounds (68 million kilograms) of cellophane are produced annually in the United States. FRED M. REITER

See also CELLULOSE.

CELLULOSE, *SEHL yuh lohs*, is a substance that forms a major part of the cell walls of trees, grasses, vegetables, and many other plants. Cellulose is a *carbohydrate*—that is, a substance composed of carbon, hydrogen, and oxygen. All fruits and vegetables contain cellulose. Industries use cellulose in the manufacture of hundreds of products, including paper, textiles, and plastics.

Biological Importance. Cellulose fibers strengthen the stems, roots, and leaves of many kinds of plants. Plants make cellulose from glucose, a sugar that they first produce from carbon dioxide and water through the process of photosynthesis (see PHOTOSYNTHESIS). Cellulose consists of glucose molecules linked in long chains called *polymers*. Its chemical structure resembles that of starch, another polymer of glucose. However, the glucose molecules in cellulose are linked differently than those in starch.

The foods most abundant in cellulose are vegetables that consist of stalks or leaves, such as celery and spinach. The human body cannot digest cellulose. However, cellulose serves as bulk that stimulates the intestines and aids in elimination.

Industrial Uses. Cellulose makes up an important part of many familiar products. For example, it makes up about 42 per cent of wood, which is used in buildings and in furniture and hundreds of other objects. Cotton, the fiber most widely used in textile manufacturing, contains more than 95 per cent cellulose. Paper also consists largely of cellulose. The highest quality papers are almost pure cellulose. In addition, manufacturers process cellulose obtained from cotton and wood to make a wide range of products.

Industries use strong acids and alkalis to modify the properties of cellulose for various purposes. For example, textile producers strengthen cotton fibers by treating them with *caustic soda* (sodium hydroxide). This process is called *mercerizing*. A solution called *viscose* is made by treating cellulose with caustic soda and carbon disulfide. Manufacturers process viscose to produce rayon fibers for use in textiles and tire cord. Cellophane is also made from viscose.

Manufacturers produce substances called *cellulose derivatives* by combining cellulose with certain chemicals. The most widely used cellulose derivative is *cellulose acetate*, a plastic made by treating cellulose with acetic anhydride. Products made of cellulose acetate include photographic film, magnetic sound-recording tape, electrical insulation, and textile fibers. *Cellulose acetate butyrate*, a tougher and more water-resistant plastic than cellulose acetate, is used in such items as steering wheels and tool handles. Manufacturers cast a plastic called *ethyl cellulose* to produce tough, rigid items, such as luggage and flashlight cases.

Other common cellulose derivatives include *carboxy-*

methyl cellulose and *cellulose nitrate*. Carboxymethyl cellulose dissolves in water and so can be used as a thickener in foods and paints. Cellulose nitrate is used in lacquers and other coatings. It is made by treating cellulose with a mixture of nitric and sulfuric acids. A form of cellulose nitrate called *guncotton* is an explosive used in smokeless gunpowders.

During the late 1940's, synthetic substances made primarily from petroleum began to replace cellulose in the manufacture of some plastics, fibers, and photographic films. In many cases, the petroleum-based substances were cheaper and easier to process than cellulose. Today, however, some experts believe that a shortage of petroleum and rising oil prices will probably lead to greater use of cellulose. JOHN BLACKWELL

See also CELLOPHANE; FIBER (Cellulosics); GUNCOTTON; RAYON.

CELLULOSE ACETATE. See CELLULOSE; PLASTICS (table: Kinds of Plastics); RAYON.

CELSIUS SCALE, *SEHL see uhs*, is a scale for measuring temperature. The Celsius scale is a part of the metric system of measurement. People in most major countries of the world use the Celsius scale for everyday temperature measurement. Scientists throughout the world also use this temperature scale. In the United States, the Fahrenheit temperature scale is generally used for everyday purposes. However, the Celsius scale is gradually coming into greater use.

On the Celsius scale, 0° is the freezing point of water and 100° is its boiling point. The scale is divided into 100 equal parts between those fixed points. The Celsius scale is often called the *centigrade* scale because this word means *divided into 100 parts*.

Sometimes it is necessary to change a Celsius temperature to a Fahrenheit temperature, or vice versa. To change a temperature on the Celsius scale to one on the Fahrenheit scale, multiply the Celsius temperature by $\frac{9}{5}$ and then add 32. We multiply by $\frac{9}{5}$ because 1 Celsius degree equals 1.8 (or $\frac{9}{5}$) Fahrenheit degrees. We add 32 because 0° C equals 32° F. These steps can be expressed as an equation: °F. = $\frac{9}{5}$ (°C) + 32. Suppose we want to know the temperature in Fahrenheit if a Celsius temperature is 20° C. Using the equation, we see that °F. = $\frac{9}{5}$ (20) + 32, which equals 9 (4) + 32, or 68° F.

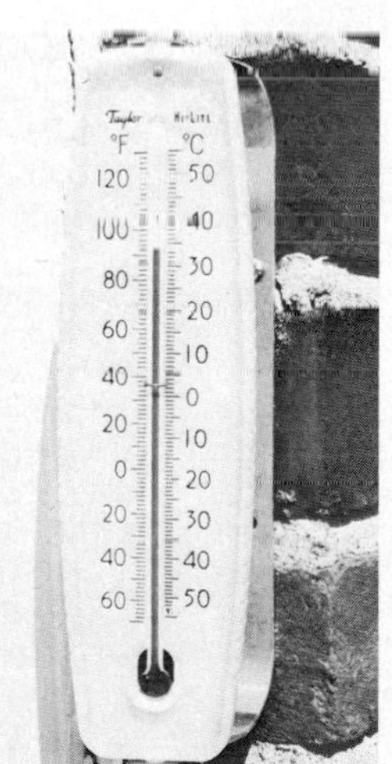

© Robert Lee II

The Celsius Scale is a common scale for measuring temperature. A double-scale thermometer, *above,* gives both Celsius and Fahrenheit readings.

This equation is used to change Fahrenheit readings to Celsius readings: °C = $\frac{5}{9}$ (°F. − 32). Suppose we want to change 77° F. to a Celsius temperature. The equation tells us that °C = $\frac{5}{9}$ (77 − 32), which equals $\frac{5}{9}$ (45), or 25° C.

Temperatures below the freezing point of water have a minus sign on the Celsius scale. For example, the lowest temperature possible in theory is called *absolute* zero. It is −273.15° C.

The Celsius scale was originally developed in 1742 by the Swedish astronomer Anders Celsius. It was later changed and improved. The ninth General Conference on Weights and Measures officially named the scale the Celsius scale in 1948. JOSEPH J. SNOBLE

See also THERMOMETER.

CELTS, *sehlts* or *kehlts*, are a people—or their descendants—who are native speakers of a Celtic language. The Celtic languages, which include Breton, Irish, Welsh, and Scottish Gaelic, form a branch of the Indo-European family of languages.

The oldest known evidence of the Celts comes from Hallstatt, Austria, near Salzburg. Excavations there revealed hundreds of Celtic graves dating from about 700 B.C. The Hallstatt Celts were one of the first peoples in northern Europe to make iron. By about 500 B.C., the Celts had spread to France, Portugal, Spain, and the British Isles. They also settled in northern Italy and raided as far south as Rome, which they looted in 390 B.C. During the 300's and 200's B.C., some Celtic groups moved into the Balkans, including what are now Bulgaria and Greece. Between about 300 B.C. and about A.D. 100, the Romans conquered much of Europe. The only Celts who preserved their own culture were those of Ireland, Scotland, and western England.

Bronze decorated with silver, gold, and jewels by an unknown Irish artist (early 1100's), National Museum of Ireland; © Lee Boltin

Celtic Metalwork, such as this shrine for a bell that belonged to Saint Patrick, features patterns of interwoven spirals.

Early Celtic society had several classes, including aristocrats; common people; and a learned class that included lawyers, poets, and priests. The Celts were divided into small tribes, each of which consisted of families with a common ancestor. The Scottish clans developed from such tribes. Some tribes formed loose federations, but the early Celts never became a united nation. The Celts built a few towns, but most of the people lived in small rural settlements, raising crops and livestock.

The early Celts had no system of writing. Information about them comes from ancient Greek and Roman authors and from remains discovered by archaeologists. In the early centuries of the Christian Era, some Celts used a primitive form of writing called *ogam*, which survives in stone inscriptions. During the Middle Ages, the Celts adopted the Latin alphabet and developed a large body of written literature, including many ancient Celtic myths and legends.

About 500 B.C., the Celts developed the *La Tène style* of art. It was named after the La Tène region of Switzerland, near Lake Neuchâtel, where much metalwork decorated in that style was discovered. The La Tène style emphasized elaborate patterns of interwoven curves and spirals. It also featured highly stylized plants and animals that had little resemblance to those in nature.

The La Tène style lasted into the Middle Ages and became a major element of medieval Celtic art (see PAINTING [Celtic Painting]). Celtic artists produced decorated manuscripts, elaborate metalwork, and sculptured stone crosses. B. WAILES

See also DRUIDS; ENGLAND (The First Invaders); HALLOWEEN (The Celtic Festival); MYTHOLOGY (Celtic Mythology).

Additional Resources

CUNLIFFE, BARRY. *The Celtic World*. McGraw, 1979.
FINLAY, IAN. *Celtic Art: An Introduction*. Noyes, 1973.
LAING, LLOYD. *Celtic Britain*. Scribner, 1979.
ROSS, ANNE. *Everyday Life of the Pagan Celts*. Putnam, 1970.

CELTUCE. See LETTUCE (Kinds of Lettuce; picture).

CEMENT AND CONCRETE are among the most important building materials. Cement is a fine, gray powder. It is mixed with water and materials such as sand, gravel, and crushed stone to make concrete. The cement and water form a paste that binds the other materials together as the concrete hardens. People often misuse the words *cement* and *concrete*. For example, a person may speak of "a cement sidewalk." But the sidewalk actually is made of concrete.

Concrete is fireproof, watertight, and comparatively cheap and easy to make. When first mixed, concrete can be molded into almost any shape. It quickly hardens into an extremely strong material that lasts a long time and requires little care.

Nearly all the cement used today is *portland cement*, which is a *hydraulic* cement, or one that hardens under water. This cement was named *portland* because it has the same color as the natural stone quarried on the Isle of Portland, a peninsula on the south coast of Great Britain.

The word *cement* comes from the Latin word *caementum*, which means *pieces of rough, uncut stone. Concrete* comes from the Latin word *concretus*, which means *to grow together.*

Uses of Cement and Concrete

Nearly all skyscrapers and factories and many homes stand on concrete foundations. These buildings may also have concrete frames, walls, floors, and roofs. Concrete is used to build dams to store water and bridges to span rivers. Cars and trucks travel on concrete highways, and airplanes land on concrete runways.

Concrete tunnels run through mountains and under rivers. Concrete pipe distributes water, carries away sewage, drains farmland, and protects underground telephone wires and electric-power lines.

Portland cement is used chiefly to make concrete, but it can also be used in other ways. For example, asbestos fibers can be combined with cement and water to make shingles for roofing.

Kinds of Concrete

There are special ways of strengthening concrete or of making concrete building materials. These include (1) reinforced concrete, (2) prestressed concrete, (3) precast concrete, and (4) concrete masonry. Engineers have also developed special kinds of concrete for certain uses. These include (1) air-entrained concrete, (2) high-early-strength concrete, and (3) lightweight concrete.

Reinforced Concrete is made by casting concrete around steel rods or bars. The steel strengthens the concrete. Almost all large structures, including skyscrapers and bridges, require this extra-strong type of concrete.

Prestressed Concrete usually is made by casting concrete around steel cables stretched by hydraulic jacks. After the concrete hardens, the jacks are released and the cables compress the concrete. Concrete is strongest when it is compressed. Steel is strong when it is stretched, or in tension. In this way, builders combine the two strongest qualities of the two materials. The steel cables can also be bent into an arc, so that they exert a force in any desired direction, such as upward in a bridge. This force helps counteract the downward pressure of the weight of the bridge. Prestressed concrete beams, roofs, floors, and bridges are often cheaper for some uses than those made of reinforced concrete.

Precast Concrete is cast and hardened before being used for construction. Precasting firms make concrete sewer pipes, floor and roof units, wall panels, beams, and girders, and ship them to the building site. Sometimes builders make such precast pieces at the building site and hoist them into place after they harden. Precasting makes possible the mass production of concrete building materials. Nearly all prestressed concrete is precast.

Concrete Masonry includes many shapes and sizes of precast block. It is used to make about two-thirds of all the masonry walls built each year in the United States. Some concrete masonry is decorative or resembles brick.

Air-Entrained Concrete contains tiny air bubbles. These bubbles are formed by adding soaplike resinous or fatty materials to the cement, or to the concrete when it is mixed (see RESIN). The bubbles give the water in concrete enough room to expand as it freezes. The bub-

Freshly Mixed Concrete is poured into forms that hold it in shape until it hardens. Workers spread the wet concrete, which has a rough texture, working it into the corners of the form, *left*. To produce a flat surface, workers smooth the concrete before it dries completely, *center*.

Robert H. Glaze, Artstreet

bles also protect the surface of the concrete from chemicals used to melt ice. Such qualities make air-entrained concrete a good material for roads and airport runways.

High-Early-Strength Concrete is chiefly used in cold weather. This concrete is made with high-early-strength portland cement, and hardens much more quickly than ordinary concrete. It costs more than ordinary concrete. But it is often cheaper to use, because it cuts the amount of time the concrete must be protected in cold weather.

Lightweight Concrete weighs less than other kinds of concrete. Builders make it in two ways. They may use lightweight shales, clays, pumice, or other materials instead of sand, gravel, and crushed rock. Or they may add chemicals that foam and produce air spaces in the concrete as it hardens. These air spaces are much larger than the air spaces in air-entrained concrete.

How Concrete Is Made

Materials. Concrete is a mixture of portland cement, water, and aggregates. *Aggregates* are materials such as sand, gravel, crushed rock, and blast-furnace *slag* (waste). The cement and water form a paste that binds the aggregates into a rocklike mass as the paste hardens. Builders generally use both a fine aggregate such as sand, and a coarse aggregate such as crushed rock, to make concrete. The aggregates must be free from silt, mud, clay, dust, and other materials that might weaken the concrete. The water used to make concrete should also be free from dirt and other impurities.

Mixing. Before concrete is mixed, workers measure the proper amounts of the materials. The strength and durability of concrete depend chiefly on the amount of water used. If too much water is added, the cement paste will be too weak to hold the aggregates together firmly when it hardens. The less water used, within reasonable limits, the stronger the concrete will be.

Concrete can be mixed either by hand or by machine. Machine mixing makes more uniform batches. Proper mixing coats every particle of aggregate and fills all the spaces between them with cement paste. For most home repairs, concrete can be hand mixed.

The methods for mixing concrete by machines vary. The concrete may be mixed by machines at the place

Recommended Concrete Mix

This mix makes about 4 cubic feet (0.1 cubic meter) of concrete.

Material	By Volume	By Weight
Cement	1 bag, or 1 cu. ft. (0.03 m^3)	94 lbs. (43 kg)
Water	5½ gals. (21 l.)	46 lbs. (21 kg)
Sand	2 cu. ft. (0.06 m^3)	200 lbs. (91 kg)
Coarse Aggregate*	3 cu. ft. (0.08 m^3)	260 lbs. (118 kg)

*Particles graded ¼ to ¾ inch (6 to 19 millimeters) in size.

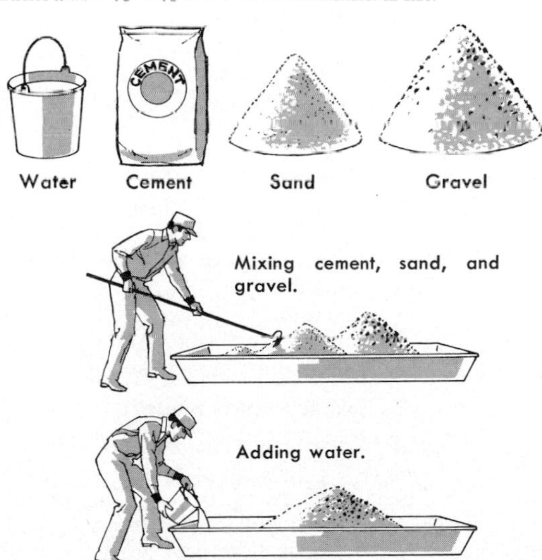

Concrete is a combination of portland cement, water, and such materials as sand and gravel, mixed in measured amounts.

where the concrete will be used. *Ready-mix* companies make huge batches of concrete at mixing plants, and haul it to the work site in trucks. Some firms use mixing machines mounted on trucks. These machines mix the concrete as the truck carries it to the building site.

Homeowners can buy prepared mixtures of cement and aggregates for small repair jobs. Only water has to be added to such mixtures.

Placing. Workers place the wet concrete into forms made of wood, plywood, or steel. The forms hold the concrete in shape until it hardens. The concrete may be dumped directly into the forms, or poured down chutes. Workers use wheelbarrows, two-wheeled carts called *buggies*, small rail cars, trucks, or buckets lifted by cranes. The concrete may also be pumped through steel pipes.

After the concrete is placed, it must be worked into the corners and sides of the forms with wooden spades and *puddling sticks*. The concrete should also be *tamped*, or packed down, to prevent open spaces called *honeycombs*. Sometimes workers stick *vibrators* into the concrete or fasten them to the forms in order to help settle the concrete.

Concrete placed for floors, sidewalks, and driveways should be leveled off with a straight-edged board. Next, it should stand until the film of moisture on its surface has disappeared. Then, the concrete should be smoothed off with a wooden trowel called a *wood float*. The float produces a rough surface that prevents slipping or skidding after the concrete hardens. A smoother surface can be made by using a *steel trowel* after the wood float. Motorized rotary steel floats are often used.

Curing makes concrete harden properly. After the concrete becomes firm enough to resist marring, it should be sprinkled with water, then covered with wet canvas, wet burlap, or wet sand. This cover keeps the concrete from drying too rapidly. A chemical reaction between portland cement and water makes concrete harden. For this reason, the longer concrete remains moist, the stronger it becomes. In hot weather, concrete should be kept moist at least three days. Cold weather slows the rate at which concrete hardens. Hardening concrete must be protected by canvas or straw when the temperature drops near freezing.

Concrete shrinks as it hardens. This results from the loss of moisture as the concrete dries, or from the cooling of the concrete. The chemical reaction of water and portland cement produces heat. When large amounts of concrete are used, as in dams, this heat must be drained away to make the concrete harden properly. This is usually done by running cold water through pipes stuck into the concrete. Cement companies have developed a special portland cement that produces less heat than other cements.

How Cement Is Made

Raw Materials. Portland cement contains about 60 per cent lime, 25 per cent silica, and 5 per cent alumina. Iron oxide and gypsum make up the rest of the materials. The gypsum regulates the *setting*, or hardening, time of cement. The lime used to make cement comes from materials such as limestone, oyster shells, chalk, and a type of clay called *marl*. Shale, clay, silica sand, slate, and blast-furnace slag provide silica and alumina. Iron oxide is supplied by iron ore, pyrite, and other materials.

Most cement plants are located near limestone quarries. They may also be near deposits of clay and other raw materials. Ships, trains, trucks, and conveyer belts haul the limestone and other raw materials to the plants. In the plants, the materials go through a chemical process that consists of three basic steps: (1) crushing and grinding, (2) burning, and (3) finish grinding.

Crushing and Grinding. The quarried limestone is dumped into *primary crushers* that can handle pieces as large as an upright piano. This first crushing smashes the rock into pieces about the size of a softball. *Secondary crushers*, or *hammer mills*, then break the rock into pieces about $\frac{3}{4}$ inch (19 millimeters) wide.

Next, the crushed rock and other raw materials are mixed in the right proportions to make portland cement. This mixture is then ground in rotating *ball mills* and *tube mills*. These mills contain thousands of steel balls that grind the mixture into fine particles. The materials can be ground by either a wet or dry method. In the *wet process*, water is added during the grinding until a soupy mixture called a *slurry* forms.

Burning. After the raw materials have been ground, they are fed into a *kiln*, a huge cylindrical furnace made of steel and lined with firebricks. A cement kiln rotates about one turn a minute, and is the largest piece of moving machinery used in any industry. It may be over 25 feet (8 meters) in diameter and 750 feet (229 meters) in length. The kiln is mounted with one end higher than the other. The ground, raw materials are fed into the higher end and slide slowly toward the lower end as the kiln revolves. It takes about four hours for the materials to travel through the kiln. Oil, gas, or powdered coal is burned at the lower end of the kiln. This produces a blast of flame that heats the materials to 2600 to 3000° F. (1430 to 1600° C). The heat changes the materials into a substance called *clinker*, in pieces about the size of marbles.

Finish Grinding. Large fans cool the clinker after it leaves the kiln. The clinker may be stockpiled for future use, or it may be reground at once in ball or tube mills. A small amount of gypsum is added to the clinker before the regrinding. This final grinding produces powdery portland cement that is finer than flour. The cement is stored in silos until it is shipped.

Shipping. Cement plants ship cement either *in bulk* (unpackaged) or packed in strong paper sacks. Unpackaged cement is shipped by railroad, truck, or barge. Packaged cement is shipped in sacks containing 94 pounds (43 kilograms), or 1 cubic foot (0.03 cubic meter), of cement to the sack.

History

The ancient Romans developed cement and concrete similar to the kinds used today. Their cement had such great durability that some of their buildings, roads, and bridges still exist. To make cement, the Romans mixed *slaked lime* (lime to which water has been added) with a volcanic ash called *pozzuolana*. The ash produced a hydraulic cement that hardened under water. People lost the art of making cement after the fall of the Roman Empire in the A.D. 400's. In 1756, John Smeaton, a British engineer, again found how to make cement.

Construction of the Erie Canal created the first big

demand for cement in the United States. In 1818, Canvass White, an American engineer, discovered rock in Madison County, New York, that made natural hydraulic cement with little processing. Cement made from this rock was used in building the canal.

Portland Cement. Joseph Aspdin, a British bricklayer, invented portland cement in 1824 and gave the cement its name. Aspdin made a cement superior to natural cement by mixing, grinding, burning, and regrinding certain amounts of limestone and clay. David O. Saylor probably established the first portland cement plant in the United States at Coplay, Pa., in 1871.

At first, portland cement manufacturers developed their own formulas. In 1898, manufacturers used 91 different formulas. In 1917, the United States Bureau of Standards and the American Society for Testing Materials established a standard formula for portland cement. The Portland Cement Association was formed in Chicago in 1916. Its research laboratories perfected air-entrained concrete in the early 1940's.

Joseph Monier, a French gardener, developed reinforced concrete about 1850. In 1927, Eugene Freyssinet, a French engineer, developed prestressed concrete.

The Cement and Concrete Industry. The United States produces about 67 million short tons (61 million metric tons) of portland cement a year, about one-tenth of the world's total. Other major cement-producers include China, France, Italy, Japan, Russia, and West Germany. The leading states are California, Michigan, Pennsylvania, and Texas.

The production of ready-mixed concrete ranks as the biggest single concrete industry in North America. About 5,000 firms in the United States and Canada produce ready-mixed concrete. More than 60 per cent of the cement produced in the United States is sold to ready-mix producers. The second largest branch of the concrete industry is the manufacture of precast concrete for construction. MAX D. MOORE

Related Articles in WORLD BOOK include:

MATERIALS USED TO MAKE CEMENT AND CONCRETE

Alumina	Gypsum	Sand
Chalk	Lime	Silica
Clay	Limestone	Slate
Gravel	Marl	

OTHER RELATED ARTICLES

Building Construction	Road
Dam (Masonry Dams)	Street
Plaster	Stucco

CEMENTUM. See TEETH (Cementum; picture: Parts of a Tooth).

CEMETERY RIDGE. See CIVIL WAR (Gettysburg; color picture).

CENOZOIC ERA, *SEE nuh ZOH ihk* or *SEHN uh ZOH ihk,* is the most recent era in the geologic time scale of the earth's history. Geologists believe this era began about 65 million years ago. It is sometimes called the Age of Mammals. See also EARTH (The Cenozoic Era; table); MAMMAL (The Age of Mammals).

CENSER, *SEHN suhr,* is a vessel in which incense is burned during religious ceremonies. The ancient Jews used censers in their tabernacles and temples. They burned perfume in them as a sacrifice. Today, censers of various kinds are used in the services of the Roman Catholic, Anglican, and other churches.

The censer is usually ornamental in form. The attached chains are used to swing it back and forth. Holes pierced in the top allow the perfumed smoke to stream out. In Elizabethan times, a censer was an ornamental bottle used by women for sprinkling perfume. FLOYD H. ROSS

Eastern Rites Information Service
Censer

CENSOR. See ROMAN EMPIRE (The Republic).

CENSORSHIP is the control of what people may say or hear, write or read, or see or do. In most cases, such control comes from a government or from various types of private groups. Censorship can affect books, newspapers, magazines, motion pictures, radio and television programs, and speeches. It also may influence music, painting, sculpture, and the other arts. Censorship can even affect such things as the clothing that people wear.

Whenever a government or a private group feels endangered by free expression, it may turn to censorship to protect its basic beliefs. Every society, including democratic ones, has had some kind of censorship when its rulers have felt it would benefit the nation—or themselves. But the strictest control of expression and information occurs in dictatorships and during wartime. The difference between censorship in democracies and in dictatorships is that democracies have ways to limit such action. In the United States, for example, the Bill of Rights and the Supreme Court serve as checks on unlimited censorship.

There are four major types of censorship: (1) moral, (2) military, (3) political, and (4) religious.

Moral Censorship is the most common kind of censorship today. Many governments or groups try to preserve their standards of morality by preventing people from learning about or following other standards. Moral censorship may result when some people believe they have the right to force their values on others. It also may result if most of the people of a country believe that their government should promote certain moral codes.

Many countries, including the United States, have obscenity laws. A number of U.S. cities have official censorship groups that ban books and movies they consider obscene. See OBSCENITY AND PORNOGRAPHY.

Military Censorship. During a war, battle plans, troop movement schedules, weapons data, and other information could help the enemy. The armed forces of every country have *censors* who read the letters written and received by servicemen and servicewomen. The censors snip out or blot out any information that might be valuable to the enemy. The military also may withhold information from the press for security reasons. In Canada, the United States, and some other countries, the press, radio, and TV voluntarily censor themselves in wartime. Most nations have some military censorship during peacetime as well.

Political Censorship is used by governments that fear free expression of criticism and opposing ideas. Such censorship is common in nondemocratic countries, where unapproved forms of expression are forbidden. Russia, for example, has political censorship (see Russian Literature [Recent Soviet Literature]).

Democracies do not officially permit political censorship. But many democratic governments try to discourage the expression of certain radical ideas. In the United States, various laws prohibit speeches or writings that might lead to violence. During wartime, many democratic governments carry on political censorship. They believe that criticism of the government or opposition to the war could aid the enemy.

Religious Censorship occurs in some nations where the government is close to one religion or where religious feelings run high. Those in power may censor the ideas and practices of other religions. Spain, almost all of whose people are Roman Catholics, did not allow Protestants or Jews to hold public religious services throughout much of its history. The Spanish government dropped this ban in 1967.

Censorship Methods. There are two main kinds of censorship methods, *formal* and *informal*. Formal censorship occurs when government officials follow the law to control free expression. Informal censorship takes place if no specific law covers an offense. Officials may act informally because of pressure from a private group to censor something the group dislikes. Some groups also pressure various companies by threatening not to buy their products. A number of businesses, including the motion-picture and television industries, censor themselves in an effort to avoid public disapproval.

Censorship can occur before or after something is released to the public. In checking material before release, officials may approve it, reject it, or approve it with certain changes. Censors may also act against a book, magazine, or motion picture after its release. The U.S. Postal Service may refuse to deliver objectionable mail, and the United States Customs Service may prevent the importation of certain materials. Loren P. Beth

See also Freedom; Freedom of Religion; Freedom of Speech; Freedom of the Press; Motion Picture (Censorship); World War II (Censorship).

Additional Resources

Berninghausen, David K. *The Flight from Reason: Essays on Intellectual Freedom in the Academy, the Press, and the Library*. American Library Assn., 1975.

Dewhirst, Martin, and Farrell, Robert, eds. *The Soviet Censorship*. Scarecrow, 1973.

Haight, Anne L. *Banned Books, 387 B.C. to 1978 A.D.* Bowker, 1978.

Hoyt, Olga G. and Edwin P. *Censorship in America*. Seabury, 1970.

CENSUS is a survey conducted by a national government to gather information about the society that it governs. Censuses examine such aspects of a nation as population, housing, agriculture, and manufacturing. A population census determines the size of a population and such information as the age, employment, income, race, and sex of people. Other censuses gather such data as the quality of housing or transportation, the level of agricultural or industrial production, or the form of organization of local governments. About 90 per cent of the world's nations conduct at least one kind of census—a population count in most cases.

Only governments conduct censuses. Federal administration of a census helps ensure that (1) the census serves the entire society, and (2) special interest groups do not influence census procedures. In addition, most private organizations could not afford the expense of taking a census. Most people realize that their government has the authority to conduct censuses, and so they cooperate with the operation.

National, state, and local governments analyze census data to determine the extent of economic and social problems. These data also help identify resources available to solve such problems. Most national governments publish census information to make it available to the public. Business executives use census statistics to help them plan company policies. Economists and sociologists apply census data to the analysis of economic and social conditions. Labor unions and welfare agencies also use census information.

Most governments follow certain procedures to obtain accurate and complete census information. First, a government tries to contact every individual—either directly or indirectly. For example, a population census questions some individuals personally and gathers data about others by questioning the heads of households. The census seeks out people rather than depending on them to come forward with information. Second, the government attempts to gather information from everyone at the same time. Most censuses do this by asking about conditions as they existed on a certain date. Third, a census does not question people about taxation, selection for military service, or anything else that could affect their responses. For instance, a government would not conduct an agricultural census just to establish taxes on farmers. Finally, most governments conduct censuses at regular intervals, such as once every 10 years. This policy ensures regular measurement of changes and trends in a society.

United States Censuses

The United States collects more varied and complete census information than any other nation. The Bureau of the Census, an agency of the Department of Commerce, conducts all U.S. federal censuses.

Kinds of Censuses. The Bureau of the Census conducts censuses of population, housing, agriculture, governments, business, construction, manufactures, mineral industries, and transportation.

The Census of Population gathers such population data as the total number of people and their age, education, employment, income, marital status, race, and sex. The United States Constitution provided for a count of the population "within three years after the first meeting of the Congress of the United States, and within every subsequent term of ten years. . . ." The first census took place in 1790. In 1976, the federal government passed legislation requiring a population census every 5 years instead of every 10. It would be conducted in years ending with zero or five, such as 1990 or 1995. However, the 1985 census was canceled because Congress did not appropriate funds for the project.

The Census of Housing gathers various information for each housing unit—the year it was built; how it is financed; the number of rooms; the condition of the unit; the type of plumbing facilities and heating equipment; and the number of air conditioners and television sets

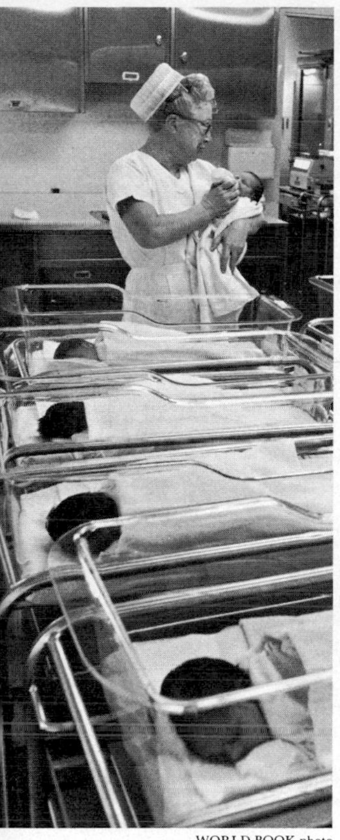

WORLD BOOK photo

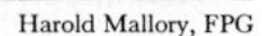

Harold Mallory, FPG

Charles Harbutt, Magnum

I. Howard Spivak, FPG

Population, Agriculture, Business, and Manufacturing are some of the topics covered by censuses. A population census counts the people of a country. Other censuses gather such information as the level of a nation's agricultural and industrial production or the value of total retail sales.

in the unit. The Census Bureau has conducted a housing census every 10 years since the first Census of Housing in 1940. In 1976, the government authorized a housing census every five years, but the 1985 census was canceled because funds were not appropriated.

The Census of Agriculture, begun in 1840, is conducted every five years. It gathers such information as the number of farms, the amount of crops harvested and the amount of fertilizer used during the preceding year, the type of equipment used, the number of farmworkers, and the amount of irrigated farmland.

The Census of Governments collects information on all units of local government every five years. This information includes the form of government organization, the number of people employed, and the financial arrangements of the government. The first Census of Governments was conducted in 1850.

The Census Bureau conducts censuses of business, construction, manufactures, mineral industries, and transportation every five years. These surveys collect data on the output and resources of the various industries. The information includes the form of ownership, the volume of business, the size of the payroll, and the quantity and type of equipment available for use.

Conducting Censuses requires detailed planning. The Census Bureau first decides what topics to cover and what questions to ask. Then it surveys people to collect information. Next, it processes the information and tabulates the statistics. Finally, the bureau publishes census information to make it available to other government agencies and the general public.

Census Content. The Federal Reports Act of 1942 established guidelines for census questions. The Census Bureau, with the approval of the Office of Management and Budget and of Congress, determines the content of each census.

The Bureau of the Census periodically adds census topics and changes the established content. Before choosing the topics, the bureau consults many public and private groups that use census information. Agencies at all levels of government—federal, state, and local—have the greatest influence on the choice of topics. Other users of census data, including business executives, labor unions, and research workers, work with the Census Bureau through advisory committees. These committees meet regularly with bureau specialists to discuss census needs and uses. The bureau also receives thousands of letters yearly requesting the addition or removal of various census questions.

After selecting the topics for a census, the Census Bureau develops questions that will obtain the desired information. The bureau asks questions that people can answer quickly and easily. It tries to avoid asking annoying questions.

Taking a Census. The Census Bureau chooses the

method of questioning—either mailing questionnaires or sending out interviewers. Sometimes both methods are used. The bureau may hire and train temporary workers for a particular census. It also informs the public about the purpose and method of the census, so that people will know what to expect.

For a population census, the bureau tries to contact each household in the United States. For other censuses, the bureau obtains accurate information by questioning a representative sample of the group to which the census applies. For example, the bureau may conduct a housing census by gathering information from every fourth or fifth home. It then adjusts the results statistically to apply to the entire population. This procedure saves the bureau time, effort, and money.

The Census Bureau uses two methods of questioning. In an *enumerator census*, interviewers go from door to door, asking questions and recording the answers. In a *self-enumerated census*, the bureau mails census forms to businesses, households, or other survey groups. Individuals fill out the forms and return them to the bureau. The Census Bureau uses the self-enumerated method for most censuses—agriculture, business, construction, governments, manufactures, mineral industries, and transportation.

The bureau conducts population censuses chiefly by the self-enumerated method. Most households in the United States receive a census form through the mail. The bureau sends enumerators to contact persons whom it cannot reach by mail, who do not return their completed census forms, or who make mistakes in completing their forms. The bureau also tries to contact citizens living outside the United States, especially military personnel and employees of the federal government. These persons mail their census forms to the bureau. But the bureau cannot locate all civilians who live overseas.

Until 1960, the Census Bureau used enumerators to conduct the population census. That year, the bureau used a combination of enumerator and self-enumerated procedures. The 1970 and 1980 censuses were largely self-enumerated, with most enumerators working in small towns and rural areas.

Occasionally, the bureau must hire and train temporary employees to assist with a census, especially the population census. It employed about 470,000 temporary workers for the 1980 population count.

Processing the Results. The Census Bureau processes all census information, tabulating statistics and organizing them into usable form. The bureau once processed all data by hand. Following the invention of card-sorting equipment about 1890, machines processed increasingly large portions of census information. By

How the United States Population Changed from 1970 to 1980

This map shows how the population of the United States changed from 1970 to 1980. Although the population of the nation increased by 11.4 per cent, the populations of two states—New York and Rhode Island—and of the District of Columbia decreased.

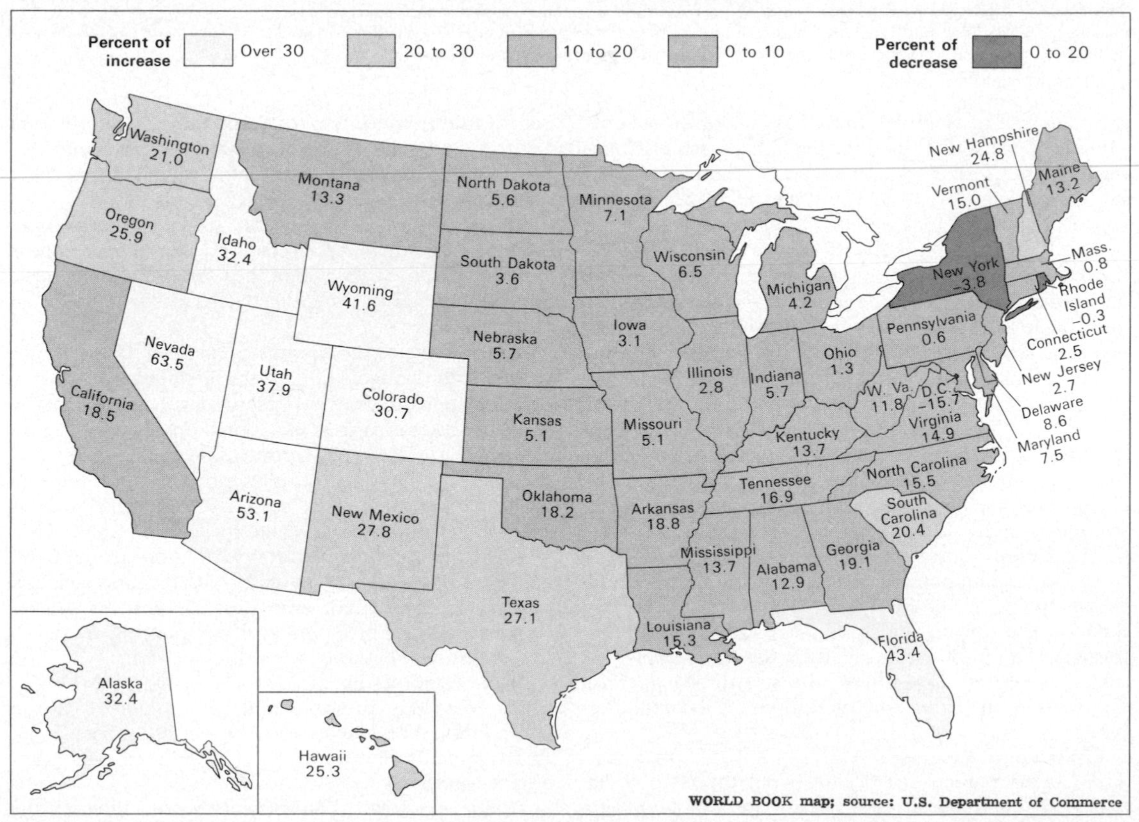

WORLD BOOK map; source: U.S. Department of Commerce

1960, electronic computers processed most census data.

In 1970 and 1980, people answered most census questions by blackening in small circles on the forms. The completed forms were photographed and recorded on microfilm. A special machine called *FOSDIC* (*F*ilm *O*ptical *S*ensing *D*evice for *I*nput to *C*omputers) processed the microfilm. FOSDIC transmitted information from the film onto magnetic tape in a form that could be read by computers. The computers then produced tables of census statistics from information on the tape.

Publishing Census Information. The Bureau of the Census publishes census results so that anyone can obtain the information. The government published the 1790 census results in a single 56-page volume. The amount of published census information increased steadily during the 1800's and 1900's.

The bureau follows special procedures to make sure that personal records remain confidential. Concern that census taking might invade individual privacy led the bureau to establish these procedures. For example, the bureau withholds personal identification data, such as names and addresses, when it feeds information into the computers. It never publishes these data. According to law, no one other than bureau employees may examine census records.

Uses of Census Information. Many organizations—both public and private—and individuals use census information in their daily activities. The need for increasingly extensive and detailed census data has grown steadily since the 1790's. The first census asked only a few questions, and the general public had little need for census data. The nation's rapidly expanding population and growing number of social problems has brought a greater need for reliable census statistics. Through the years, the government has increased the amount of information it collects by conducting such additional censuses as those of business, governments, and transportation.

Federal, state, and local governments make the greatest use of census data. Census information helps government agencies administer various programs, plan future programs, distribute revenues, and study social and economic problems. The statistics provided by a population census may affect the assignment of funds for economic development programs, housing, school aid, or such public services as welfare and social security. Population size determines the number of representatives each state may have in the U.S. House of Representatives. Membership in state legislatures is also apportioned on the basis of population. The censuses of business, manufactures, and mineral industries tell much about the nation's economic condition. The Census of Agriculture provides a picture of agricultural production and resources.

Business leaders study census figures in making such decisions as where to locate new facilities, where to direct their advertising, and how to plan production. The construction industry uses census data to decide where to build new housing. Utility companies determine service requirements on the basis of census data.

Census statistics also help social scientists analyze economic and social problems and plan solutions. These experts study census statistics on such subjects as marriage and divorce, population movement, residential and educational segregation patterns, and the relationship of education to income and employment.

Many groups are concerned about the accuracy of census figures, because the figures are used to draw voting districts and to determine the distribution of federal aid. Officials of large cities and leaders of minority groups challenged the accuracy of the 1980 census in court, charging that the Census Bureau had failed to count many minority residents. Like all censuses, the 1980 census failed to count some people—especially among the poor and members of minority groups—for several reasons. People with little education or whose native language is not English may have difficulty completing self-enumeration forms. In addition, many people refuse to give the government information about themselves. But over the years, census-taking procedures have been improved to reduce such undercounting, and the 1980 census was considered the most nearly complete in U.S. history.

The First United States Census was a population count that began in 1790. The government used population size to determine the amount of taxation and congressional representation of the states.

The counting process began on Aug. 2, 1790, and lasted about 18 months. Fewer than 4 million persons lived in the United States in 1790, but they were scattered throughout a largely undeveloped country. Enumerators on horseback had to ride through the countryside to count most of the population. Many people refused to cooperate because they did not know why the government needed information about them.

The first population count provided little information other than number of people. The enumerators counted the number of (1) free persons, (2) slaves, and (3) free white males under and over 16 years of age. They also recorded the sex and color of free persons and the names and addresses of heads of families.

Censuses in Other Countries

Early Censuses. In ancient Rome, census takers prepared lists of persons and property, chiefly for purposes of taxation and enforcement of military service requirements. The word *census* comes from the Latin word *censere*, meaning *to tax.* After William the Conqueror defeated England in 1066, his officials made a count of the country's land, people, and property. They listed this information in the Domesday Book (see DOMESDAY BOOK).

During the 1400's and 1500's, various European cities began to count their populations. The first such count took place in Nuremberg, Germany, in 1449. In 1666, a French official named Jean Baptiste Talon completed a census of the people of Canada, then called New France. In 1749, the Swedish government conducted the first national census. It based the census on church records of births, deaths, and migration.

Modern Censuses. The first modern census—one that was complete, direct, and periodic—was the United States census of 1790. Great Britain has conducted a modern census every 10 years since 1801, except in 1941 during World War II. France took its first modern census in 1836. Belgium followed with one in 1846, Italy in 1861, Germany in 1871, Russia in 1897, and Japan in 1920.

The colonial powers, particularly England, helped spread census taking to Africa, Asia, and Latin America. These powers established census procedures in areas where they had large investments of resources and personnel and had a role in the government.

The number of countries with censuses has increased since the 1850's. From 1855 to 1864, 51 nations—with about 17 per cent of the world's population—conducted censuses. From 1965 to 1976, 187 nations, colonies, or territories—with about 67 per cent of the total population—took censuses. Almost all these censuses were population counts.

In Canada, the Census Division of Statistics Canada conducts periodic censuses. This federal agency takes censuses of agriculture, housing, and population every five years in years ending with 1 and 6, such as 1971 and 1976. Canadian censuses in years ending with 6 are only partial surveys. The Manufacturing and Primary Industries Division of Statistics Canada conducts an annual Census of Manufactures.

The United Nations (UN) encourages all nations to conduct complete, periodic censuses. The UN publishes manuals of recommended census procedures. It works to establish standard censuses so it can collect accurate world statistics. JAMES A. SWEET

Critically reviewed by KARL E. TAEUBER

See also CENSUS, BUREAU OF THE; POPULATION.

CENSUS, BUREAU OF THE, is an agency of the U.S. Department of Commerce that is best known for its publication of population and housing statistics. It also conducts censuses of agriculture, business, governments, manufactures, mineral industries, and transportation. The Bureau of the Census publishes statistical data in the annual *Statistical Abstract of the United States*, the monthly "Business Conditions Digest," and other reports.

The bureau was established in 1902 as part of the Department of the Interior. It became part of the Department of Commerce and Labor in 1903 and of the Department of Commerce in 1913.

Critically reviewed by the BUREAU OF THE CENSUS

See also CENSUS.

CENT is a small coin that represents one-hundredth of a dollar. It is the coin of smallest value in the United States and Canada. The name *cent* was first suggested by the Revolutionary War patriot Gouverneur Morris in 1782, when he was assistant to Superintendent of Finance Robert Morris. He may have taken the word from the Latin word *centum* (hundred). The people of the United States and Canada say *penny* and *cent* to mean the same thing.

The first cent to be minted in the United States was the so-called Washington cent of 1783. In 1785, Vermont and Connecticut authorized the coinage of cents. The Fugio cent of 1787 was the first coin issued by authority of the United States. In 1792, Congress authorized the establishment of a United States mint to issue coins regularly. The first regularly issued cents from the mint, each worth a hundredth part of a dollar, were issued in 1793. Half cents also were issued until 1857, two-cent pieces from 1864 to 1873, and three-cent pieces from 1851 to 1889.

The weight and metal content of the cent have

Sterling Publishing Co., Inc.

The U.S. Chain, or Link, Cent, *above,* was the first cent issued by the United States mint. It appeared in 1793.

Western Publishing Company, Inc.

The Indian Head Cent was minted from 1859 to 1909. It had an Indian head on the front and a wreath on the back.

changed many times. But in 1864 the law provided that the cent contain 95 per cent copper and 5 per cent tin and zinc, and weigh 48 grains (3 grams). Any number of cents has been legal tender since 1933.

The content of the cent was changed to zinc-coated steel in 1943, when copper was scarce. In 1944 and 1945, the government minted cents that were 70 per cent copper and 30 per cent zinc. Because of their high proportion of zinc, these coins were lighter in color than the usual bronze cents. The United States returned to making cents with prewar amounts of copper in 1946. In 1981, the United States Mint began making pennies of copper-coated zinc containing 2.4 per cent copper. FRED REINFELD

See also MONEY (picture); PENNY.

CENTAUR, *SEHN tawr*, was a creature in Greek mythology that was half man and half horse. Centaurs lived in northern Greece. Most of them were wild and lawless. At the wedding feast of the king of the Lapiths, a drunken centaur attacked the bride. In the battle that followed, the Lapiths defeated the centaurs. Scenes of this battle appear in the magnificent sculptures of the Parthenon and those of the temple of Zeus at Olympia.

The most famous centaur was Chiron. Unlike the others, he was wise and just. He taught many famous Greek heroes, including Achilles. NATHAN DANE II

See also MYTHOLOGY (picture).

CENTAVO, *sehn TAH voh*, is a minor coin of Guinea-Bissau, the Philippines, Portugal, and of a number of countries of Latin America, including Mexico. Its value is one-hundredth of the unit of money used in those countries.

CENTENNIAL EXPOSITION was a world's fair held in Philadelphia in 1876 to celebrate the hundredth anniversary of the signing of the Declaration of Independence. Nearly 50 other nations joined the United States in exhibiting products of the arts and sciences, of nature, and of industry. The exposition covered 236 acres (96 hectares) and had 167 buildings. About 10 million persons attended it.

Working models of new machines included the continuous-web printing press, the self-binding reaper, the typewriter, the telephone, the Westinghouse air brake, the refrigerator car, and Thomas A. Edison's duplex telegraph. The exposition was the first successful world's fair held in America. HELEN AUGUR

CENTER OF GRAVITY. See GRAVITY, CENTER OF.

CENTER OF MASS. See GRAVITY, CENTER OF.

CENTER OF POPULATION. See UNITED STATES (color map: Population).

CENTER OF THE UNITED STATES. See GEOGRAPHIC CENTER OF THE UNITED STATES.

CENTERS FOR DISEASE CONTROL, frequently referred to as the CDC, is an agency of the Public Health Service and part of the U.S. Department of Health and Human Services. It works to protect the public health by administering national programs for the prevention and control of disease.

The agency provides health information and conducts research to track down the sources of epidemics. It helps train doctors in *epidemiology*, the study of the causes, distribution, and control of the spread of disease. The CDC also works with state and local agencies to develop immunization services and programs to eliminate rats and other causes of disease.

The National Institute for Occupational Safety and Health, a unit of the agency, develops standards for safe and healthful working conditions. The CDC also cooperates with foreign governments and international agencies in a worldwide effort to control disease and improve health. The agency was established in 1946. Its headquarters and laboratories are in Atlanta, Ga.

Critically reviewed by the CENTERS FOR DISEASE CONTROL

CENTIGRADE SCALE. See CELSIUS SCALE.

CENTILITER. See WEIGHTS AND MEASURES.

Bronze statue in The Louvre, Paris (Alinari)

A Statue of the Centaur by Antoine Louis Barye stands in the Louvre in Paris. It shows the death of a centaur that attacked the intended bride of the king of the Lapiths during a wedding feast.

CENTIME, *SAHN teem*, is a minor coin used in some countries that use the franc. It represents a hundredth of a franc. In Haiti, the centime represents a hundredth of a gourde, and in Algeria, a hundredth of a dinar. See MONEY (table: Exchange Rates).

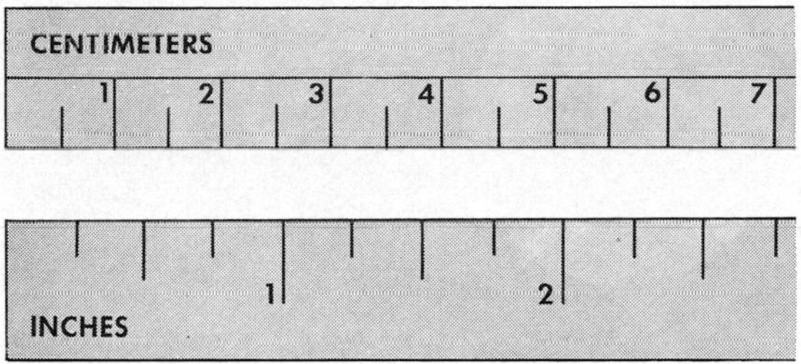

There Are About Two and a Half Centimeters in an Inch.

CENTIMETER, also spelled *centimetre*, is a measure of length in the metric system of measurement. Its symbol is *cm.* A centimeter is one one-hundredth of a meter. One centimeter equals 0.3937 inch. To convert centimeters to inches, multiply by 0.3937. E. G. STRAUS

See also METRIC SYSTEM.

CENTIMETER-GRAM-SECOND. See DYNE.

CENTIPEDE, *SEHN tuh peed*, is one of a group of small animals that look like worms or caterpillars. Their narrow bodies are divided into many sections or segments that lie behind each other down the back. Each section has a pair of thin legs.

Cornelia Clarke

A Full-Grown Centipede may have from 15 to 170 pair of legs. A young centipede may have only 7 pair of legs.

The centipede has a pair of *antennae* (jointed feelers) on its head, and two pair of jaws. The first pair of legs behind the head have claws and are used for fighting, not for walking. They are called *poison claws*, because a gland in the centipede's head fills these claws with poison. Centipedes eat mollusks, worms, and insects, which they kill with their poison claws. The centipede hunts its food at night. In the tropics, there are some centipedes whose bite can be very dangerous to human beings.

Scientific Classification. Centipedes are members of the phylum *Arthropoda*. These animals make up the class *Chilopoda*. EDWARD A. CHAPIN

CENTO. See CENTRAL TREATY ORGANIZATION.

Central African Republic

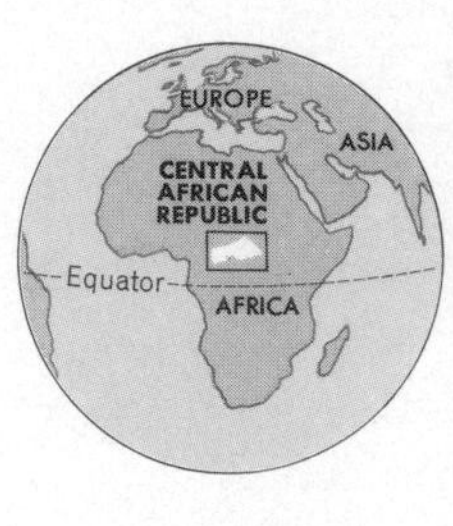

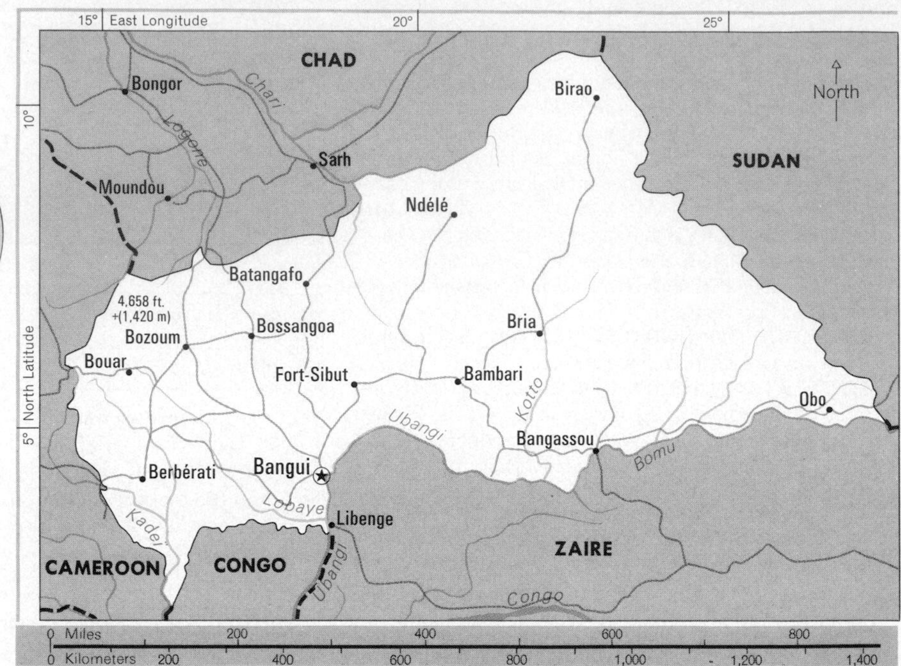

WORLD BOOK map

CENTRAL AFRICAN REPUBLIC is a thinly populated country in the center of Africa. It is about as large as the state of Texas, but only has about one-fifth as many people as that state.

Most of the Central African Republic is a vast, rolling plateau broken by deep river valleys. Grass and scattered trees cover most of the country. Thick rain forests grow in the southwest, and the extreme northeast section is semidesert, much like the Sahara. Tourists visit the country to hunt or photograph antelope, buffalo, elephants, gorillas, lions, rhinoceroses, and other animals that run wild over the countryside.

The Central African Republic is one of the poorest countries in Africa. Most of the people are farmers who can raise only enough food to feed their own families. The country was formerly a territory in French Equatorial Africa called Ubangi-Shari. It became an independent country in 1960. Bangui, a river port, is the capital and largest city.

Government. A committee made up of army officers heads the government of the Central African Republic. It was established in 1981, after army officers overthrew the country's civilian government.

People. About half of the 2,672,000 Central African Republic citizens live in country areas. They hunt, fish, raise food crops, and gather insects and caterpillars to feed their families. They also raise some goats, pigs, sheep, and poultry.

Most of the people are black Africans. They belong to many ethnic groups and speak many languages or dialects, of which the most common is *Sango*. About a fourth of the people are Christians and a twentieth are Muslims. But most of the people practice traditional African religions. Most of the older people of the Central African Republic cannot read or write. About 40 per cent of the children receive an elementary school education. The country has a few secondary schools.

Land. The Central African Republic covers 240,535 square miles (622,984 square kilometers). The plateau has an average altitude of about 2,000 feet (610 meters) above sea level. Areas in the northeast and on the country's western border with Cameroon rise more than 4,500 feet (1,370 meters) above sea level.

Jacqueline M. C. Thomas, the contributor of this article, is Director of Research at the National Center of Scientific Research in Paris, and author of Les Ngbaka de la Lobaye, *a book about the forest people of the Central African Republic.*

Facts in Brief

Capital: Bangui.

Official Language: French.

Official Name: La République Centrafricaine (The Central African Republic).

Form of Government: Republic.

Area: 240,535 sq. mi. (622,984 km²).

Population: *Estimated 1985 Population*—2,672,000; distribution, 54 per cent rural, 46 per cent urban; density, 10 persons per sq. mi. (4 persons per km²). *1975 Census*—2,054,000. *Estimated 1990 Population*—3,024,000.

Chief Products: *Agriculture*—bananas, coffee, cotton, livestock, palm kernels, peanuts, rubber, sesame, yams. *Forestry*—timber. *Mining*—diamonds, gold.

Flag: Horizontal blue, white, green, and yellow stripes are divided at the center by a red vertical stripe. A yellow star represents the guiding light of the future. Red, white, and blue recall the French flag. Green, yellow, and red are for the people and their unity. See FLAG (color picture: Flags of Africa).

Money: *Basic Unit*—franc. See MONEY (table).

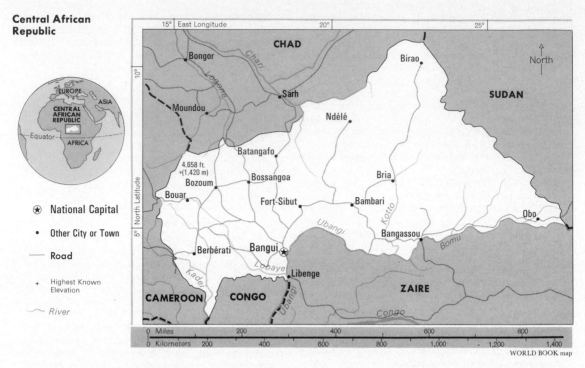

Many rivers flow through the Central African Republic. Most rivers in the north are tributaries of the Chari River, which flows inland to the Lake Chad basin (see LAKE CHAD). A divide separates the northward flowing rivers from those that flow south from the central and southern parts of the country into the Congo River basin. Many of these rivers are tributaries of the Ubangi River (spelled Oubangui there), which joins the Congo River. The Ubangi and its tributary, the Bomu (Mbomou) River, form most of the country's southern boundary with Zaire.

The country has a fairly comfortable climate even though it lies near the equator. This is due chiefly to its altitude. The average temperature is 80° F. (27° C). Each year, the country receives about 31½ inches (80 centimeters) of rainfall in the north and about 63 inches (160 centimeters) in the south. The rainy season extends from June through October in most parts of the country. In the southwest, where the rainfall is heaviest, rain sometimes falls throughout the year.

Economy. The Central African Republic is an isolated country with no railroads and many roads that are impassable during the rainy season. A few plantations raise coffee, cotton, and rubber products for export. The country has few known mineral resources. Diamond mining is the only important mining industry.

A few farmers raise livestock in regions where there are no tsetse flies. These insects spread the dread African sleeping sickness (see SLEEPING SICKNESS; TSETSE FLY). There are a few manufacturing plants in the Central African Republic. One of these is a textile mill.

Rivers form the most important transportation routes. Boats can navigate the Ubangi River throughout the year from Bangui to Brazzaville, in Congo. From Brazzaville, exports are carried by railroad to the port of Pointe Noire. Bangui has an international airport. Bambari, Bouar, and several other smaller towns also have airports.

History. Little is known of the history of what is now the Central African Republic before the arrival of European explorers in the 1800's. For several centuries, slave raids caused the people living there to flee to safer areas. France established an outpost at Bangui in 1889. In 1894, the French created the territory of Ubangi-Shari. In 1910, France linked Ubangi-Shari with the present-day territories of Chad, Congo, and Gabon to form French Equatorial Africa.

The French established a local parliament in Ubangi-Shari in 1946. Elected members represented the country in the French parliament. In 1958, the country gained internal self-government as the Central African Republic. It became a member of the French Community, an organization that linked France and its overseas territories. The Central African Republic became fully independent on Aug. 13, 1960.

The first prime minister and leading political figure, Barthelemy Boganda, was killed in an air accident in 1959. His nephew David Dacko succeeded him. Dacko became the country's first president in 1960.

The country became a one-party state in 1962 and, in 1964, Dacko was elected to serve a seven-year term as president. But in 1966, army officers overthrew his government. Jean-Bedel Bokassa, head of the army, became president. He was named president for life in 1972. In 1976, he changed the country's name to the Central African Empire. He declared himself emperor. In 1979, supporters of Dacko overthrew Bokassa and took control of the government. Dacko again became president. The country's name was changed back to Central African Republic. In March 1981, the country became a multiparty state again, and Dacko was elected president. In September 1981, army officers overthrew Dacko once more and took control of the government. The new government banned all of the country's political parties. JACQUELINE M. C. THOMAS

See also BANGUI; UBANGI RIVER.

Peter Larsen, Nancy Palmer

Bangui, Capital City of the Central African Republic, nestles at the foot of a hill on the banks of the Ubangi River. Bangui is the country's largest city, and its leading shipping and commercial center.

CENTRAL AMERICA

CENTRAL AMERICA is the narrow bridge of land at the southern end of North America. It borders Mexico on the north and Colombia on the south. The Pacific Ocean lies to the west, and the Caribbean Sea—an arm of the Atlantic Ocean—lies to the east. Central America consists of seven countries: Belize, Costa Rica, El Salvador, Guatemala, Honduras, Nicaragua, and Panama. The region covers 201,976 square miles (523,115 square kilometers) and has a total population of about 25 million.

On both coasts of Central America, there are lowlands. Inland, rugged mountains crisscross the region. They make transportation and economic development difficult. Many of the mountains are active volcanoes. Severe earthquakes and volcanic eruptions sometimes strike Central America, causing much damage.

Central America has a diverse population. The people of Guatemala are primarily of Indian origin. Most of the people of Honduras and El Salvador are *mestizo* (mixed Indian and European ancestry). Large numbers of blacks live in Belize, Nicaragua, and Panama. Costa Ricans are mainly of European descent.

Spanish is the official language of all the Central American countries except Belize, where the official language is English. Many Indians in Guatemala speak their own tribal languages.

Most of the people of Central America live in the highlands of moutainous regions, where they earn their living on tiny farms. However, Central America's main sources of income are large plantations, and forests and mines. Plantations in the highlands produce about 10 per cent of the world's coffee, and those in the lowlands produce about 10 per cent of the world's bananas.

A small percentage of Central America's people have great wealth, and the region has a growing middle class. However, large numbers of the people live in poverty. A high population growth rate contributes to unemployment, especially among young people.

The constitution of every Central American country except Nicaragua, which has no constitution, provides

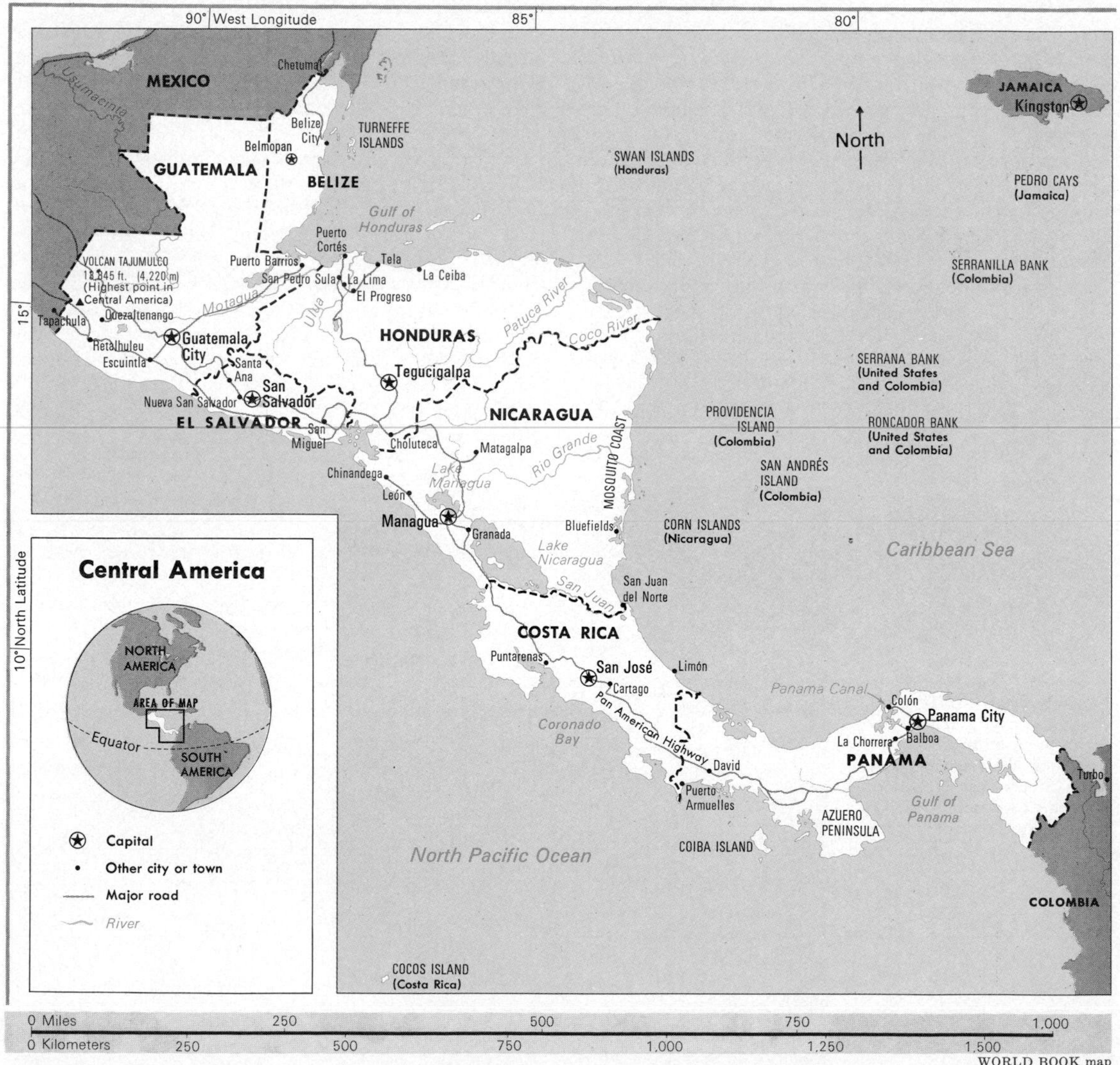

WORLD BOOK map

for the democratic election of representatives. However, in many cases governments have disregarded their constitutions. Some countries have been ruled by military dictators. In the middle and late 1900's, economic problems and civil wars have caused widespread suffering in many parts of Central America.

This article traces the history of Central America. For additional information on the region, see the articles on LATIN AMERICA and NORTH AMERICA, and the articles on each Central American country.

Early History

Thousands of years ago, the ancestors of today's Central American Indians migrated to Central America from Asia. About 400 B.C., the Maya Indians emerged as the dominant culture of Central America. Their culture especially flourished from about A.D. 250 to 900. The Maya were accomplished engineers and architects, building many magnificent cities. The ruins of hundreds of Maya palaces, pyramids, and temples still stand. The Maya also constructed a vast system of canals to irrigate their fields of corn, beans, and squash. The Maya were skilled astronomers and mathematicians. They developed a solar calendar and a system of hieroglyphic writing. About A.D. 900, the Maya mysteriously abandoned their cities. Today, their descendants live in the mountains of Mexico as well as in Central America. Many of these people still wear traditional costumes and speak Maya languages.

The Colonial Period

In 1501, Rodrigo de Bastidas and Juan de la Cosa of Spain became the first Europeans to explore the Central American coast. In 1502, the Italian explorer Christopher Columbus sailed the Caribbean coast from Honduras to Panama, and claimed the land for Spain, the country sponsoring his voyage. For the next 13 years, Spanish *conquistadors* (conquerors) invaded Central America, fighting the Indians throughout the region. The Spanish completed their conquest in 1525. By then, many Indians had been killed or sent as slaves to plantations in the West Indies.

In 1570, the Spanish established an administrative center, called an *audiencia*, in Guatemala. The Audiencia of Guatemala ruled over all of Central America except Panama. It was a subdivision of the Viceroyalty of New Spain, which governed most of the Spanish colonies in North America from its headquarters in Mexico City.

Spain paid more attention to Mexico and Peru, which had treasures of gold and silver, than it paid to Central America, which had far less mineral wealth. Administrative matters were often handled locally in Central America. Gradually, missionaries established an educational system in Central America and converted the Indians to the Roman Catholic religion. Colonists developed a plantation system of agriculture.

Panama owed its early development to its strategic position and its land as a narrow isthmus. The Spaniards built a stone road across the isthmus, near the site of the present Panama Canal. Under Spain, Panama became an important shipping route for provisions for colonies on the west coast of South America and for gold and other treasures bound for Spain. Panama also became a center for the distribution of black African slaves in the New World. However, Spain let Panama govern itself in most matters.

Independence

In 1808, Napoleon I of France occupied Spain and forced the Spanish king into exile. As a result, Spain's control over its colonies weakened. In Central America, conservatives remained loyal to Spain. However, liberals resented the taxes and trade restrictions that Spain had imposed. They saw in Spain's conflict with France an opportunity to break away from the mother country. On Sept. 15, 1821, the Audiencia of Guatemala declared its independence, removing from Spanish control all of Central America except what is now Panama. That same year, Panama broke away from Spanish rule and became a province of the newly independent nation of Colombia. The independence movement succeeded throughout Central America with little bloodshed.

What is now Belize had belonged to the Audiencia of Guatemala. But the Spaniards did not establish settlements there and did little to exercise their rule over the area. In 1638, British sailors, who had been shipwrecked off the coast of Belize, established the first known European settlement in the area. The British built other settlements in the area during the next 150 years. In the mid-1800's, they took formal possession of the Belize area. They made it a colony called British Honduras. Belize did not become independent until 1981.

During the first years after independence, Central Americans generally favored union with newly independent Mexico because they felt loyalty toward the former seat of the viceroyalty in Mexico City. From January 1822 to March 1823, Costa Rica, El Salvador, Guatemala, Honduras, and Nicaragua were legally part of Mexico. In 1823, these states separated from Mexico and formed a united federation among themselves. They called the federation the United Provinces of Central America. There were disagreements between those who favored states' rights and those who wanted a strong central government. The constitution, which provided for strong states' rights, was completed in November 1824. The federation freed the slaves and ended the special privileges of the powerful landowners and the Roman Catholic Church. The federation began to collapse under various pressures, including efforts by rich landowners and the priests to regain their former privileges. Rivalries also developed between local governments and the federal government. In the late 1830's, the federation broke up and the individual states became independent republics.

In the early 1900's, the United States wanted to build a canal across Panama. With U.S. support, Panama separated itself from Colombia in 1903 and formed an independent nation. Panama granted the United States a strip of land 10 miles (16 kilometers) wide upon which to build the canal. The Panama Canal was completed in 1914.

Attempts at Unification

Since the early 1800's, various combinations of Central American countries have tried at least 25 times to achieve political unification. All these unions were short-lived, most lasting only a few months and none more than a few years. In 1842, for example, El Salvador, Honduras, and Nicaragua created the Central American Confederation. This government proved too weak to enforce its rule and it collapsed in 1845.

In 1907, Costa Rica, El Salvador, Guatemala, Honduras, and Nicaragua set up the Central American Court of Justice. This court had jurisdiction in cases between the nations. It was dissolved in 1918, after Nicaragua had ignored its findings in a dispute over canal-building rights. In 1921, El Salvador, Guatemala, and Honduras united under a central government called the Central American Federation. But rivalries and disagreements among members caused its collapse in less than a year.

Regional Organizations

In 1948, all the Central American states except Belize joined with other Latin American countries and the United States to form the Organization of American States (OAS). The OAS works for cooperation among member nations (see ORGANIZATION OF AMERICAN STATES). In 1951, Costa Rica, El Salvador, Guatemala, Honduras, and Nicaragua established the Organization of Central American States. This organization promotes cultural, economic, and political understanding among member nations.

In 1960, El Salvador, Guatemala, Honduras, and Nicaragua formed the Central American Common Market. Costa Rica joined in 1963. This organization provides for free trade among member nations. It created the Central American Bank for Economic Integration. This bank promotes economic cooperation and invests in industries needed to supply the area as a whole.

Recent Developments

The countries of Central America experienced economic growth during the 1960's and early 1970's. Later in the 1970's, however, several factors combined to end this growth. The nations of Central America had to pay much higher prices for imported oil and agricultural chemicals. At the same time, the prices they received for their exports dropped. These nations had borrowed billions of dollars at high interest rates to finance their development. In the early 1980's, they began to have trouble paying back these loans.

The population of Central America is increasing dramatically. The number of people has more than tripled since the early 1900's. This population explosion has led to widespread unemployment and contributed to the area's other problems.

In an effort to reduce tensions and help the economy of Panama, the United States signed treaties in 1977 to restore the Canal Zone to Panama. In 1973, British Honduras changed its name to Belize. Britain granted Belize complete independence in 1981. Guatemala, however, strongly protested this action. It had always claimed Belize as its own territory. In 1983, it reduced its claim to the southern fifth of Belize.

In 1979, rebels overthrew the government of Nicaragua. Much fighting has since taken place between the new government and Nicaraguans who oppose the government. The United States has given aid to the opposition, and Cuba and the Soviet Union have aided the government. Widespread fighting between rebels and the government has also taken place in El Salvador. The United States has provided aid to El Salvador's government, and Cuba and the Soviet Union have supported the rebels.

NATHAN A. HAVERSTOCK

Related Articles in WORLD BOOK include:

COUNTRIES

Belize	El Salvador	Honduras	Panama
Costa Rica	Guatemala	Nicaragua	

OTHER RELATED ARTICLES

Central America, United Provinces of	Organization of American States
Latin America	Pan American Union
Maya	Panama Canal
North America	Panama Canal Zone

CENTRAL AMERICA, UNITED PROVINCES OF, was formed in 1823. The federation included Costa Rica, El Salvador, Guatemala, Honduras, and Nicaragua. Its government was modeled after that of the United States. But the people failed to develop a feeling of unity, and their leaders engaged in bitter rivalry. Francisco Morazán of Honduras became president of the federation in 1830. He worked to hold the union together for almost 10 years. When he was driven into exile, all hopes for the federation collapsed. Morazán tried to form another union in 1842, but failed. The Central American Federation, a union formed in 1921, lasted only a few months.

CHARLES P. SCHLEICHER

See also HONDURAS (Independence).

CENTRAL BANK. See BANK (Kinds of Banks).

CENTRAL HEATING. See HEATING.

CENTRAL INTELLIGENCE AGENCY (CIA) gathers political and military information about certain countries and evaluates it for other U.S. government agencies. Such information, called *intelligence*, involves national security, and much of it is secret. The CIA also conducts various secret operations in support of U.S. foreign policy.

The CIA was established in 1947. The United States was determined to avoid another surprise attack like the Japanese bombing of Pearl Harbor in 1941. Much important information about some countries—Communist nations, for example—can be obtained only by secret methods.

Few of the activities or finances of the CIA are made public. The director reports to the National Security Council, which includes the President (see NATIONAL SECURITY COUNCIL). The CIA reportedly spends about $2 billion a year.

Publicity received by some CIA operations has embarrassed the government. In 1960, a Russian missile shot down a U.S. spy plane piloted by a CIA agent photographing Russian territory. In 1961, Cuban refugees, sponsored by the CIA, tried to invade Cuba and overthrow dictator Fidel Castro. Castro's forces trapped them near the Bay of Pigs.

Other CIA actions, some of which were not discovered until years after they occurred, included aid in the overthrow of an Iranian prime minister in 1953, of the Guatemalan government in 1954, and of the Chilean government in 1973. In 1975, it was revealed that the CIA had been involved in several attempts to assassinate Cuban Prime Minister Fidel Castro in the early 1960's.

Also in 1975, a commission headed by Vice President Nelson A. Rockefeller investigated charges that the CIA had spied illegally on American citizens. The agency's charter forbids such domestic intelligence work. The commission confirmed that the CIA had investigated thousands of Americans who were involved in antiwar or other political groups. The panel also reported that the CIA had used such illegal means as break-ins, wiretaps, and the opening of mail to gather the information. The commission recommended a number of steps, including stricter congressional supervision of CIA operations. HARVEY GLICKMAN

See also INTELLIGENCE SERVICE.

Additional Resources

CONFERENCE ON THE CIA AND WORLD PEACE. *Uncloaking the CIA.* Macmillan, 1978.

EVELAND, WILBUR C. *Ropes of Sand: America's Failure in the Middle East.* Norton, 1980. A critical view of the CIA.

LEFEVER, ERNEST W., and GODSON, ROY. *The CIA and the American Ethic: An Unfinished Debate.* Georgetown Univ. Press, 1979.

MEYER, CORD. *Facing Reality: From World Federalism to the CIA.* Harper, 1980. A defense of the CIA's actions from 1951 to 1977.

CENTRAL PARK. See NEW YORK CITY (Parks; picture: Manhattan's Central Park).

CENTRAL POWERS. See WORLD WAR I.

CENTRAL TIME. See TIME (map: Standard Time Zones).

CENTRAL TREATY ORGANIZATION (CENTO) was a mutual defense treaty among several nations, most of which lie south of Russia. It was designed to provide protection against possible attack by Russia. The alliance began in 1955 and ended in 1979.

In 1955, Iraq and Turkey signed the Baghdad Pact, a defense treaty that marked the start of what became the CENTO alliance. Later in 1955, Great Britain, Iran, and Pakistan joined the pact between Iraq and Turkey. The United States took part in the organization without being a full member.

The CENTO alliance was known as the Baghdad Pact until 1958, when its headquarters were moved from Baghdad, Iraq, to Ankara, Turkey. Iraq withdrew from the alliance in 1959. In 1979, Iran, Pakistan, and Turkey withdrew from CENTO, and the alliance was dissolved. NORMAN D. PALMER

CENTRAL VALLEY PROJECT is a federal irrigation and electric-power system in California. Central Valley is 500 miles (800 kilometers) long and 100 miles (160 kilometers) wide. In the north is Sacramento Valley, which usually has surplus water. San Joaquin Valley in the south has about two-thirds of Central Valley's land, but gets only about a third of its water supply. To permit better distribution, water stored behind Shasta Dam in the north is directed down the Sacramento River, and channeled into the San Joaquin River. This river flows back north through the San Joaquin Valley. But from Friant Dam on the upper San Joaquin, part of the water is channeled into the Friant-Kern Canal and taken south to the Bakersfield area. This project, under construction for 14 years, began operating in 1951. In 1955, the project was expanded to include the Trinity River. See also SHASTA DAM.

CENTRAL WASHINGTON UNIVERSITY. See UNIVERSITIES AND COLLEGES (table).

CENTRALIZATION is a feature of organization that places control under one head or system. Decisions are made at the top of an organization. A certain amount of centralization is essential for the effective function of a large-scale organization. *Overcentralization,* the extreme of centralization, produces poor morale, general inefficiency, and red tape. To counteract this, experts advise *decentralization,* in which minor decisions are made on lower levels.

See also RED TAPE.

CENTRIFUGAL FORCE, *sehn TRIHF uh guhl,* is often incorrectly defined as the force that pulls an object outward when it moves in a circle. Actually, an object moving in a circle is being pulled inward. If no force pulled it inward, it would continue to move in a straight line with constant speed. Physicists call the force that pulls the object inward *centripetal force.*

If you tie a string to a stone and whirl the stone around, you must exert a centripetal force to keep the stone from moving in a straight line. In the same way, the earth's gravity exerts a centripetal force on a speeding satellite and keeps it from flying into space.

Physicists find the idea of centrifugal force useful in certain situations. For example, when you ride on a merry-go-round, you can feel yourself being thrown away from the center of rotation. If you observe your motion with respect to the merry-go-round, you could say that centrifugal force pulls you away from the center. Physicists would call the merry-go-round *a rotating reference frame.* You do not need the idea of centrifugal force if you observe your motion with respect to the ground instead of to the merry-go-round. You would then say the merry-go-round exerts centripetal force, the result, let us say, of friction between your shoes and the platform. This keeps you from moving in a straight line with a constant speed. LEON N. COOPER

See also CENTRIPETAL FORCE; INERTIA; MOTION (Newton's Laws of Motion).

CENTRIFUGE, *SEHN truh fyooj,* is an instrument used to separate two liquids mixed together, or solid particles that are mixed in a liquid. The centrifuge causes the heavier liquid or the solid particles to move to the bottom of the container, leaving the lighter substances on top. It usually consists of a large wheel connected to an electric motor. The mixtures to be separated are balanced in containers on each side of the wheel. When the motor is turned on, the wheel rotates rapidly and the containers swing out from the center. A smaller centrifuge consists of a small rotating top in which test tubes of material can be placed at an angle. Centrifuges turn from 800 to 6,000 times per minute.

Centrifuges are commonly used in chemical and biological laboratories. They are used in medicine to prepare serums and plasma. Centrifuges separate the heavier blood cells or blood clot from the blood plasma or serum. They separate heavy bacteria from lighter kinds without destroying them. The cream separator is a centrifuge that is used to take cream out of whole milk, the cream being lighter than the skim milk that remains.

The *ultracentrifuge* is a newer kind of centrifuge with tremendous speed. It can spin at around 80,000 turns per minute. The rotating part of an ultracentrifuge

A Centrifuge for Physiologic Research provides information about the effects acceleration has on the human body.

Mayo Clinic

touches nothing solid. It is balanced on a cushion of air. The ultracentrifuge whirls by means of jets of compressed air that touch the outer surface. Ultracentrifuges are used in the study of viruses. LEON N. COOPER

See also PLASMA; SVEDBERG, THEODOR.

CENTRIPETAL FORCE, *sehn TRIHP uh tuhl,* is the force that compels a body to move in a circular path. According to the law of inertia, in the absence of forces, an object moves in a straight line at a constant speed. An outside force must act on an object to make it move in a curved path. When you whirl a stone around on a string, you must pull on the string to keep the stone from flying off in a straight line. The force the string applies to the object is the *centripetal force.* The word *centripetal* is from two Latin words meaning *to seek the center.*

Centripetal force acts in other ways. For example, a speeding automobile tends to move in a straight line. Centripetal force must act on the car to make it travel around a curve. This force comes from the friction between the tires and the pavement. If the pavement is wet or icy, this frictional force is reduced. The car may then skid off the road because there is not enough centripetal force to keep it moving in a curved path.

You can use the following formula to calculate the centripetal force, F, necessary to make an object travel in a circular path:

$$F = \frac{mv^2}{r}$$

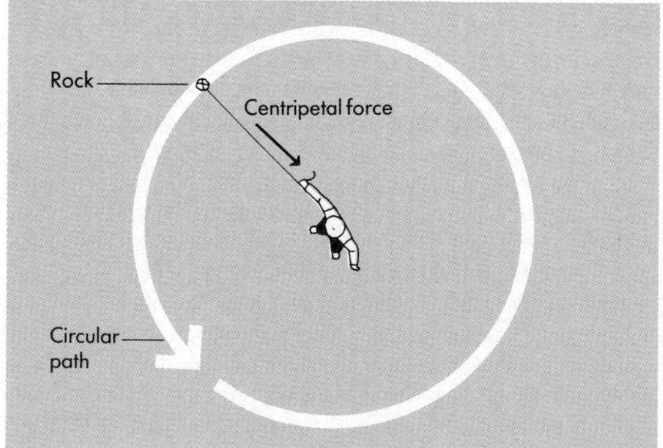

WORLD BOOK diagram by David Cunningham

Centripetal Force compels an object to move in a circular path. The person in the illustration above exerts a centripetal force on the rock by pulling on the string.

Multiply the object's mass, m, by the square of its velocity (the velocity multiplied by itself), v^2, and divide this product by the radius of the circle in which the object moves, r. In the metric system, the centripetal force is given in newtons when the object's mass is expressed in kilograms, the velocity in meters per second, and the radius in meters. LEON N. COOPER

See also INERTIA; MOTION (Newton's Laws of Motion).

CENTROSPHERE, *SEHN truh sfihr,* is the inner core of the earth. It is also called the *barysphere* (pronounced *BAR uh sfihr*). Its diameter is about 1,630 miles (2,623 kilometers). Scientists believe that it is composed mainly of iron and nickel. See also SEISMOLOGY.

CENTURION, *sehn TYUR ee uhn,* was a captain in the Roman army who commanded a *century* (a force numbering approximately 100 soldiers).

See also LEGION.

CENTURY ordinarily means 100 years. The word is from the Latin *centuria,* meaning a hundred. The years 1 through 100 after the birth of Christ are called the first century; from 101 through 200 was the second century. The present century is the 20th century. C. R. O'DELL

CENTURY CITY. See LOS ANGELES (West Los Angeles; picture: Century City).

CENTURY OF PROGRESS EXPOSITION marked the *centennial* (100th anniversary) of Chicago. The fair opened in 1933 on a strip of reclaimed land about 6 miles (10 kilometers) long and 600 feet (180 meters) wide along Lake Michigan. More than a fifth of the area was devoted to lagoons. The exhibits of science and industry were regarded as the best ever assembled in the United States up to that time. Appealing to nonscientific minds, they emphasized the union of science and industry and its remarkable developments.

In 1933, the United States was in the midst of a severe depression. Unlike most previous major expositions, the Century of Progress was an outstanding financial success. It was held over for the next summer, and not only paid off its underwriters, but yielded a surplus. Its construction and operation, together with the many people it brought to the city, proved strong business stimulants. The fair enabled many Chicago business people to avoid bankruptcy. HERBERT J. DOTTEN

See also FORT DEARBORN (picture: A Replica of Fort Dearborn).

CENTURY PLANT is the name of a group of desert plants in the agave family. It is also called *agave* (pronounced *ah GAH vee*). The name *century plant* came from the mistaken idea that the American century plant blooms only once in 100 years. Some kinds of century plants flower every year. Other kinds bloom less often. But none blooms so rarely as once in 100 years.

The American century plant has thick, fleshy leaves with sharp-spined edges. The white or greenish flowers grow in an open cluster on the upper portion of the stalk. The leaves die after the plant has bloomed. The roots remain alive and produce a new plant. The American century plant is also known as the *American aloe*.

The people of Mexico use the sap of certain agaves to make beverages, such as *pulque* and *mescal*. The long, tough fibers of agaves may be formed into thread, cord, and ropes. The green leaves of the plants are used as fodder.

Josef Muench

Century Plant stems reach their full height—20 to 30 feet (6 to 9 meters)—in one season.

Scientific Classification. Agaves belong to the agave family, Agavaceae. The American century plant is genus *Agave*, species *A. americana*. EDMUND C. JAEGER

See also HENEQUEN; MAGUEY; SISAL.

CEPHALOPOD. See MOLLUSK (Octopuses and Squids); OCTOPUS.

CEPHALOSPORIN, *SEHF uh luh SPAWR ihn*, is any of a group of widely used antibiotics. Doctors use cephalosporins to treat a variety of bacterial infections, including diseases of the respiratory system, urinary tract, bloodstream, and skin. In addition, doctors often use cephalosporins to prevent infections following surgical operations.

Cephalosporins are chemically similar to penicillins, and the two types of antibiotics have many similar properties. But cephalosporins fight more kinds of bacteria than penicillins. Doctors frequently use cephalosporins in treating patients who are allergic to penicillins. In some patients, however, both antibiotics cause an allergic reaction.

Like penicillins, cephalosporins fight bacteria by preventing the bacteria from making the rigid cell walls they need to live. Human cells do not have rigid walls and are not damaged by the antibiotics. The first cephalosporin was discovered in 1948. EUGENE M. JOHNSON, JR.

See also ANTIBIOTIC.

CERAM. See INDONESIA (The Moluccas; table: The Chief Islands).

CERAMIC ENGINEERING. See ENGINEERING (table: Specialized Engineering Fields).

CERAMICS, *suh RAM ihks*, are one of the three most important types of primarily synthetic materials. The others are metals and plastics. The chief feature of ceramics is their great resistance to chemicals and high temperatures. The word *ceramics* comes from the Greek word *keramos*, meaning *potter's clay*. The term *ceramic* describes a material that is neither a metal nor a plastic.

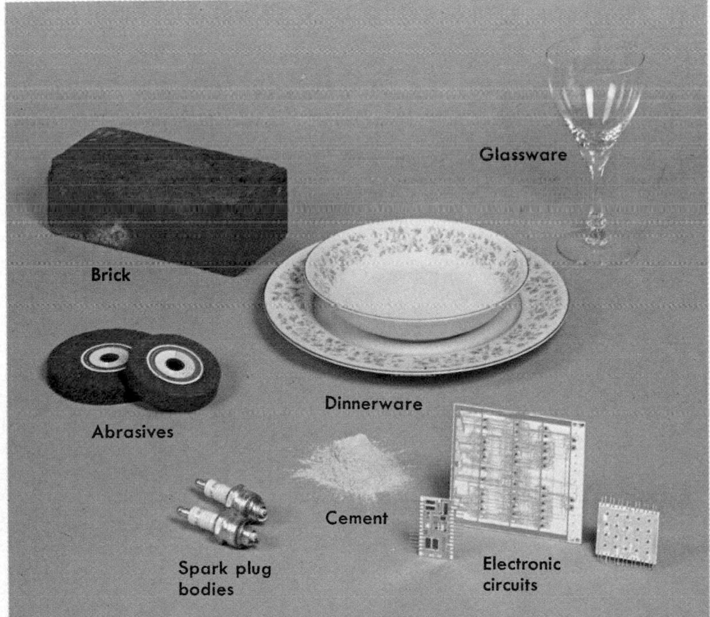

WORLD BOOK photo

Ceramics are useful materials that can be tailored to fit many specific purposes. All the products shown above contain ceramics. But the items differ greatly in chemical resistance, heat resistance, durability, strength, and other properties.

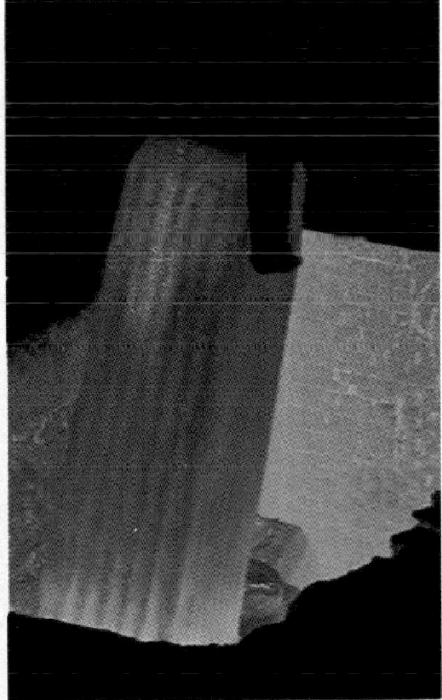

Harbison-Walker Refractories

Ceramic Brick serves as an excellent lining for steelmaking furnaces because it can withstand extremely high temperatures.

Commonwealth Edison

Doulton & Co. Limited

Doulton & Co. Limited

Ceramic Insulators, *left,* enable high-voltage lines to operate safely and efficiently. Workers shape such insulators on a machine, *center,* and then spray them with a glaze, *right.* The glaze makes the insulators airtight and watertight. Finally, the insulators are baked in an oven.

Most ceramics are compounds of carbon, oxygen, and nitrogen in combination with other chemical elements. Ceramics are made into useful materials or products through high-temperature processing.

Ceramics have a wide variety of artistic and industrial uses. This article discusses the industrial uses of ceramics. For information on how artists use ceramics, see the WORLD BOOK article on POTTERY.

The United States ceramics industry produces about $11 billion worth of products annually. These products range from bricks to nose cones for rockets.

Properties of Ceramics. Manufacturers make ceramics from such minerals as bauxite, clay, feldspar, silica, and talc. These minerals, called *silicates,* form most of the earth's crust and occur almost limitlessly. Most ceramics are made from clays that consist of one or more silicates. But not all ceramic materials consist of clay. For example, glass is made from sand.

Most ceramic products, like their mineral ingredients, can withstand acids, gases, salts, water, and high temperatures. Not all ceramic products have the same characteristics. Ceramic engineers control the properties of a product by controlling the proportion and type of materials used.

Kinds of Ceramic Products. The properties of ceramics make them more suitable than other materials for certain products. Products made of ceramic materials include *abrasives* (materials used for grinding), construction materials, dinnerware, electrical equipment, glass products, and *refractories* (heat-resistant materials).

Abrasives. Manufacturers use some extremely hard ceramic materials for cutting metals and for grinding, polishing, and sanding various surfaces. These ceramic materials include alumina and silicon carbide.

Construction Materials. Clay and shale are used in making strong, durable bricks and drainpipes for homes and other buildings. Tiles are made of clay and talc. Cement consists chiefly of calcium silicates and is used primarily in making concrete (see CEMENT AND CONCRETE). Gypsum is used in the production of plaster for the surfaces of walls and ceilings. Bathtubs, sinks, and toilets are made of porcelain, which consists chiefly of clay, feldspar, and quartz.

Dinnerware. Ceramics make excellent containers for food and drinks. They do not absorb liquids, and they resist acids, salts, and extremely high or low temperatures. Most ceramic dinnerware, such as bowls, cups, and plates, is made from a mixture of clays, feldspar, and quartz.

Electrical Equipment. Certain types of ceramics do not conduct electricity. They are used as insulators in automobile spark plugs, on electric power lines, and in television sets. Such ceramics include alumina and porcelain. Another ceramic material, barium titanate, is used in making *capacitors,* which store electric charges in electronic equipment.

Glass Products. Glass is one of the most important materials, chiefly because of its transparency. The countless products made of glass include food containers, light bulbs, windows, and lenses for eyeglasses and telescopes. Fiberglass insulates the walls of many homes. The main ingredient in glass is silica. See GLASS.

A glasslike coating called *porcelain enamel* serves as a protective surface on many metal products. These products include such appliances as refrigerators, stoves, and washing machines. Porcelain enamel, which consists of silica and many other ingredients, also makes outdoor signs weather-resistant.

Refractories. The property of heat-resistance makes refractories suitable for the manufacture of industrial boilers and furnaces, such as the furnaces used to make steel. Certain types of refractories serve as rocket nose cones, which must withstand the high temperatures created by high-speed travel. Ceramics used in making refractories include alumina, magnesium compounds, and silica.

Other Products. Ceramic engineers continually develop new uses for ceramics. For example, different types of porcelain are used to make false teeth and artificial bone joints. Uranium oxide ceramics serve as fuel elements for nuclear reactors. Computer manufacturers use iron oxides as magnetic memory cores. Refractories made from carbides are used to make parts for aircraft engines. Alumina is used in making certain *lasers* (instruments that produce intense light beams).

Making Ceramics. The clays and other materials used in ceramics are dug from the earth. Machines crush and grind the minerals into fine particles. The particles are mixed in the proper proportions, and water is added to them to make them *plastic* (flexible) for shaping.

The most common methods used to shape clay ceramics are *jiggering*, *slip casting*, *pressing*, and *extrusion*. In jiggering, a machine presses the clay into a rotating mold of the desired shape. Jiggering shapes dinnerware products. Slip casting consists of pouring *slip* (liquid clay) into a mold. The clay hardens next to the mold, and the surplus slip is poured off to form hollow items, including coffeepots and vases. Some products, such as abrasives and insulators, are shaped by pressing the clay into a mold of the desired shape. Extrusion shapes such objects as bricks and drainpipes by forcing the clay through an opening in a shaping tool.

After the product has dried, it is strengthened by *firing*, a process that takes place in special furnaces called *kilns*. Ceramics are fired at temperatures ranging from about 1200° to 3000° F. (649° to 1649° C). Firing hardens the product permanently and gives it strength, durability, and other desired qualities.

Manufacturers cover many ceramic products with a glassy coating called *glaze*. Glaze prevents the item from absorbing liquids and makes it smoother and easier to clean. Glazes are also used for decoration.

History. Pottery, the oldest form of ceramic products, dates back to prehistoric times. Examples of pottery more than 6,000 years old have been found in several parts of the world. Other early ceramic materials included sun-dried clay bricks.

Industrial uses of ceramics began during the 1900's. Military requirements of World War II (1939-1945) created a need for high-performance materials and helped speed the development of ceramic science and engineering. During the 1960's and 1970's, advances in atomic energy, communications, and space travel required new kinds of ceramics. For example, the introduction of high-speed spacecraft required heat-resistant ceramic coatings and engine linings. During the early 1980's, researchers worked to develop ceramic engines for cars, trucks, pumps, and electric generators. Willis E. Moody, Jr.

Related Articles in World Book include:

Brick	Clay	Porcelain
Cement and Concrete	Enamel	Pottery
Cermet	Glass	Tile

Additional Resources

Charleston, Robert J., ed. *World Ceramics: An Illustrated History*. McGraw, 1968.

Conrad, John W. *Contemporary Ceramic Techniques*. Prentice-Hall, 1979.

Kenny, John B. *The Complete Book of Pottery Making*. 2nd ed. Chilton, 1976.

Nelson, Glenn C. *Ceramics: A Potter's Handbook*. 5th ed. Holt, 1983.

CERAMOPLASTICS. See Plastics (table: Plastic Terms).

CERATOPSIAN. See Dinosaur (Kinds of Dinosaurs).

CERBERUS, *SUR buhr uhs*, was the three-headed dog who guarded the gate to Hades, the lower world of Greek mythology. Cerberus allowed only *shades*, or spirits, to enter Hades, and savagely barred their escape. But Orpheus, a mortal, charmed all the underworld with his music, and Cerberus let him leave Hades with his wife, Eurydice. Hercules forced his way into Hades to capture Cerberus and bring him for Eurystheus to see. He squeezed Cerberus with such force that Cerberus became manageable. Eurystheus was so terrified at the sight of Cerberus that he immediately sent Hercules back to Hades with the monster. See also Hades; Hercules; Orpheus. O. M. Pearl

CEREAL is a food made from such cereal grains as wheat, oats, corn, rice, barley, and buckwheat. People in the United States eat more than 20 billion bowls of cereal yearly. There are two main types of breakfast cereals, *ready-to-eat* and *hot*. Both are served with milk or cream.

Ready-to-eat breakfast cereals require no cooking and are more popular than hot cereals. Manufacturers use various processes, including grinding and rolling, to form the grains into flakes, puffs, and other shapes. Sugar or another sweetener is added to some cereals.

Some ready-to-eat cereals contain no artificial substances, such as colorings or preservatives. Most of these *natural cereals* consist of oats and wheat and may be mixed with honey, nuts, or other ingredients.

Hot cereals, most of which are made of oats or wheat, are manufactured in three main forms—*regular*, *quick-cooking*, and *instant*.

Manufacturers make regular hot cereals by steaming the oats or wheat and then rolling the grains into flakes. Wheat grains may also be prepared by exploding them in moist heat. Regular hot cereals take about 15 minutes to prepare at home. The grains for quick-cooking cereals are precooked or are exploded in a vacuum. Such cereals take 3 minutes or less to cook. Instant hot cereals require only the addition of hot water. They are made of grain that has been cut into three or more pieces and pressed into thin flakes.

Hot cereals and *whole-grain* ready-to-eat cereals are made from all parts of the grain, and so they keep their natural nourishing qualities. However, many ready-to-eat cereals are made from only portions of the grain. These cereals lose some of their nutrients during the manufacturing process. In 1941, manufacturers began to restore to cereals such important nutrients as iron and the B vitamins *niacin* and *thiamine*. Such *restored cereals* contain about the same amount of nutrients as does the whole grain.

By 1973, more than 85 per cent of the ready-to-eat cereals manufactured in the United States had been fortified with extra nutrients. Fortified cereals are sprayed with synthetic nutrients, including vitamins A, B_6, C, niacin, riboflavin, and thiamine. Some cereals, called *high-protein cereals*, are strengthened with such protein foods as soy flour and sesame.

Breakfast cereals consist largely of energy-producing carbohydrates and may contain from 5 to 25 per cent protein, depending on the ingredients. Adding milk or cream to a cereal provides calcium, protein, vitamins, and other nutrients. Fortified cereals contain significant amounts of vitamins and iron. Cereals that contain bran provide fiber, a natural laxative. L. R. Hackler

See also Bran; Ceres; Grain; Nutrition; Oatmeal.

CEREBELLUM. See Brain (The Cerebellum).

CEREBRAL HEMORRHAGE, *SEHR uh bruhl,* or *suh REE bruhl, HEHM uh rihj,* is bleeding that results from a broken blood vessel in the brain. Blood escapes into the brain and destroys or damages the surrounding tissue. In addition, other brain tissue suffers damage because of the interruption of normal circulation. The victim suffers a stroke (see Stroke).

Most victims of cerebral hemorrhage suffer from *hypertension* (high blood pressure). In many cases, the victim also has *arteriosclerosis,* or "hardening of the arteries." Arteriosclerosis makes the arteries stiff and more likely to rupture under continued high blood pressure. In other cases, the victim may have a weak spot in the wall of a blood vessel in the brain. Hypertension may cause this weak spot to swell like a bubble. This swollen area, called an *aneurysm,* may eventually burst (see Aneurysm). Cerebral hemorrhages can occur at any age but are most common in people over 50 years old.

A cerebral hemorrhage occurs without warning. Within six hours, it can cause unconsciousness and paralysis of the limbs. Many cerebral hemorrhages cause death. Others leave the victim with various disabilities, depending on what areas of the brain are damaged. The speed and extent of recovery depend on the amount of the damage. Vincent V. Glaviano

See also Arteriosclerosis; Hypertension.

CEREBRAL PALSY, *SEHR uh bruhl,* or *suh REE bruhl, PAWL zee,* is a general term for a variety of disorders caused by damage to the brain. The damage occurs before, during, or soon after birth. It may cause severe crippling and mental retardation, or the symptoms may be so mild that they hardly interfere with the patient's activities. Cerebral palsy cannot be cured.

There are several types of cerebral palsy, and all involve lack of muscle control. Common effects of the disorder include a clumsy walk, lack of balance, shaking, jerky movements, and unclear speech. In many victims, cerebral palsy also affects intelligence and the senses, including sight and hearing. About half of 1 per cent of the people in the world have cerebral palsy.

Causes. The type of brain damage that can produce cerebral palsy may result from disease, faulty growth, or injury. One or more of these causes may occur before birth, during the birth process, or shortly after birth. Cerebral palsy cannot be inherited.

Before birth, brain damage may result from a disease of the mother. For example, German measles can severely harm an unborn child, even though the mother may have had only mild symptoms or none at all during pregnancy. Faulty growth of the child's brain may occur if the mother does not follow the proper diet. Brain damage occurs in many cases of *premature* (early) birth.

During the birth process, brain damage may result from the baby's being in an unusual position. The brain may also be damaged if the baby's head is too large to pass through the mother's *pelvis* without being squeezed abnormally. The pelvis is the framework of bones through which a child is born. In some cases, a too rapid or a too slow delivery can harm the infant's brain. All these situations can lead to a lack of oxygen in the brain. Brain cells die if they do not have oxygen—even for a few seconds—and the body can never replace them. Problems during birth can also cause tearing in parts of the baby's brain.

After birth, a baby may develop cerebral palsy if disease or injury damages the brain. During the first year of life, infections and accidental dropping of the child are the most frequent causes of the condition. In some cases, child beating has caused cerebral palsy.

Types. Cerebral palsy varies in seriousness and in the parts of the body affected. A victim's physical and mental condition depend on the part or parts of the brain involved, the amount of damage, and the stage of brain development when the damage occurred.

There are four chief types of cerebral palsy that involve some kind of muscle disorder: (1) *atactic,* (2) *athetoid,* (3) *hypotonic,* and (4) *spastic.* In the atactic form, the victim's voluntary movements are jerky, and a loss of balance is suffered (see Ataxia). In the athetoid type, the person's muscles move continually. These movements prevent or interfere greatly with voluntary actions. A person with hypotonic cerebral palsy appears limp. The person can move little or not at all because the muscles cannot contract. A victim of spastic cerebral palsy has stiff muscles and cannot move some body parts (see Spastic Paralysis). A person with cerebral palsy may have more than one muscle disorder. The person may be only slightly disabled or completely paralyzed.

Cerebral palsy can involve sight and hearing problems in addition to muscle disorders. Many victims also suffer speech disorders because they cannot control their tongue, lip, or breathing muscles.

Brain damage seriously affects the intelligence of some cerebral palsy victims. But many victims have little or no loss of mental ability. More than a third of all cerebral palsy patients also suffer convulsions.

Treatment of cerebral palsy aims at helping the child make the best use of damaged muscles and limited mental abilities. Each type of cerebral palsy requires different therapy. Each patient needs individual care.

Most victims of cerebral palsy can be helped by physical therapy. If possible, the patient learns to maintain balance and to move about unaided. The patient may develop such self-help skills as dressing, eating, and toilet care. See Physical Therapy; Occupational Therapy (Helping the Physically Disabled; picture).

A child with cerebral palsy may face the task of conquering problems of speech, sight, and hearing that could interfere with other learning. Speech therapy, glasses, and hearing aids may correct some of these problems. The child can then learn to communicate in order to continue an education. Later, the child may receive training that can help in finding a suitable job.

Physicians may prescribe drugs for cerebral palsy patients to relax muscles and to control their convulsions. Braces and other mechanical devices provide support and help the victim walk. Surgeons also use *brain pacemakers* to treat cerebral palsy victims. The pacemaker electrically stimulates the *cerebellum,* a part of the brain, and helps relieve spastic paralysis.

The future of cerebral palsy victims depends largely on the extent of their physical and mental disabilities. Many can lead almost normal lives and can become happy, productive members of society.

Prevention of brain damage before, during, and soon after birth is the most important way of fighting cerebral palsy. Before becoming pregnant, a woman should be vaccinated against any disease that could harm her unborn baby. An expectant mother should keep herself in top condition and avoid injury. She should only take drugs prescribed by her physician. A pregnant woman should not smoke heavily because too much nicotine from cigarettes could cause a premature delivery. A woman under the age of 16 or over 40 also has a greater chance than other women of giving birth to a premature baby. After birth, a baby can be protected from brain damage by careful handling, proper care, and vaccination against common childhood diseases. Ernst A. Rodin

Additional Resources

Cruickshank, William M., ed. *Cerebral Palsy: A Developmental Disability*. 3rd ed. Syracuse Univ. Press, 1976.

Finnie, Nancie R. *Handling the Young Cerebral Palsied Child at Home*. Rev. ed. Dutton, 1975.

Haynes, Una H. *Holistic Health Care for Children with Developmental Disabilities: With Special Reference to Young Children with Neuromotor Dysfunctions*. University Park Press, 1982.

Schleichkorn, Jay. *Coping with Cerebral Palsy: Answers to Questions Parents Often Ask*. University Park Press, 1983.

CEREBROSPINAL FLUID, *SEHR uh broh SPY nuhl*, is the liquid in the body that surrounds the entire surface of the brain and the spinal cord. It flows between the *meninges*, or membranes, that cover these nerve centers. The fluid serves as an extra cushion to protect the brain and spine from damage. Doctors sometimes withdraw a little fluid by inserting a hypodermic needle in the spinal canal. This is called a *spinal tap*, or *lumbar puncture*. Doctors analyze the fluid to diagnose many diseases, including meningitis. Pressure on the brain may be detected from the pressure of the fluid.

See also Brain (How the Brain Is Protected); Spine.

CEREBRUM. See Brain (The Cerebrum).

CERES, *SIHR eez*, was the goddess of grain, the harvest, and agriculture in Roman mythology. The worship of Ceres dates back to early Roman history. The Romans dedicated a temple to her in the 400's B.C. She was one of the six children of Saturn and his sister Ops. Ceres resembled the Greek goddess Demeter.

Ceres was worshiped primarily by the common people of Rome and by farmers outside the city. A festival that was called the *Cerealia* honored Ceres each year from April 12 to April 19. The word *cereal* comes from her name.

The most important story about Ceres tells of her search for her daughter Proserpina, who was called Persephone in Greek mythology. The girl had been kidnaped by Pluto, the Roman god of the dead. For details of this myth, see Persephone. Paul Pascal

See also Demeter; Saturn.

CERES, *SIHR eez*, is one of thousands of *asteroids* (small planets) that are located mostly between the orbits of Mars and Jupiter. About 2,700 asteroids have known orbits. Ceres, the largest, was the first asteroid to be found. It has a diameter of about 600 miles (970 kilometers).

Giuseppe Piazzi first saw it by accident, on Jan. 1, 1801, from Palermo, Sicily. The printer of Piazzi's new catalog of stars had accidentally listed an extra star. When Piazzi looked for it, he found Ceres. The asteroid was lost, but mathematician Karl F. Gauss predicted the place in the sky where Ceres was found again by astronomers a year later. Ceres is named in honor of the Roman goddess of agriculture. Charles A. Federer, Jr.

CERIUM, *SIHR ee uhm*, is a soft, gray metal of the rare-earth group of chemical elements. It was discovered in 1803 by the Swedish chemist Jöns Berzelius and the Swedish geologist Wilhelm von Hisinger, and independently by the German chemist Martin Klaproth. Cerium is named for Ceres, an *asteroid* (small planet).

Cerium is the most abundant of the rare-earth elements. It is found in many minerals, and is obtained commercially from the minerals monazite and bastnasite. Radioactive *isotopes* (forms) of cerium occur during the *fission* (nuclear splitting) of uranium, thorium, and plutonium. Cerium is added to alloys to strengthen them. It is also used to remove fission products from melted uranium. Cerium oxide is used in making porcelain and in polishing glass.

The chemical symbol for cerium is Ce. Its atomic number is 58, and its atomic weight is 140.12. Cerium has a melting point of 798° C (±3° C), and a boiling point of 3257° C. It has a density of 6.768 grams per cubic centimeter at 20° C. Frank H. Spedding

See also Element, Chemical; Rare Earth.

CERMET, *SUR meht*, is a hard material that can withstand high temperatures. The name comes from the words *ceramic* and *metal*. Ceramic materials are hard and brittle. A cermet consists of a *refractory ceramic* and a metallic binder. See Ceramics; Refractory.

Typical cermets are made by mixing an oxide or carbide with a powdered metal. Examples include aluminum oxide and chromium, and titanium carbide and nickel. The mixture is then pressed and baked at extremely high temperatures. It does not melt but undergoes certain changes because of the heat and pressure. Cermets behave much like metals but resist heats that would melt metals. They are especially useful in jet engines and for certain electrical devices that must withstand high temperatures.

Cermets also have several drawbacks. They shrink when baked, so it is difficult to mold precision parts. They are also extremely hard and can be smoothed only with grinding wheels. William B. Shook

CERN. See European Organization for Nuclear Research.

CERRO GORDO, BATTLE OF. See Mexican War (Principal Battles).

CERRO TOLOLO INTER-AMERICAN OBSERVATORY, *SAY roh toh LOH loh*, is an astronomical observatory in Chile. It is operated by the Association of Universities for Research in Astronomy, an organization of 12 United States universities.

The observatory stands on Cerro Tololo Mountain, about 50 miles (80 kilometers) east of La Serena. It houses several telescopes, the largest of which has a mirror 157 inches (400 centimeters) in diameter. This instrument is the world's most accurately ground large reflecting telescope. The observatory's other telescopes include an instrument with a 39-inch (100-centimeter) mirror, which is designed to measure the positions and motions of stars.

Astronomers at the observatory study high-energy

stars that give off strong radio waves and X rays. They also study the central portions of the Milky Way galaxy, which are best observed from the Southern Hemisphere. The U.S. National Science Foundation provides funds for the observatory. FRANK D. DRAKE

CERTIFIED MAIL. See POST OFFICE (Extra Protection).

CERTIFIED PUBLIC ACCOUNTANT is an accountant who has passed a state examination and received a certificate confirming his or her abilities. Certified public accountants are allowed to use the letters *CPA* after their names. They examine and report on the financial records of businesses and individuals. The reports are accepted for tax purposes, dividend payments, and other uses. See also ACCOUNTING. J. R. MEANY

CERTIORARI, *SUR shee uh RAIR ee,* **WRIT OF,** in its original form, is a written command by a higher court to a lower court, public board, or public officer. It orders them to send up for review the record of a proceedings. The higher court then examines the record and decides whether the decision was according to law. Courts use the writ to review decisions involving rights, but not legislative or executive decisions. State laws have made many changes in the form of the writ of certiorari. EDWARD W. CLEARY

CERVANTES, *suhr VAN tees,* **MIGUEL DE,** *mih GEHL day* (1547-1616), ranks as the outstanding writer in Spanish literature. His masterpiece, *Don Quixote,* is a novel about a middle-aged country landowner who imagines himself a knight in armor and goes into the world to battle injustice. *Don Quixote* ranks among the great works in literature, and has been a major influence on the development of the novel. See DON QUIXOTE.

The Bettman Archive, Inc.
Miguel de Cervantes

His Early Life. Miguel de Cervantes Saavedra was born in Alcalá de Henares, probably on Sept. 29, 1547. Unlike most writers of his time, he did not attend a university. He must have read widely, because his writings show the influence of many other works, including pastoral romances and epics of chivalry.

Cervantes joined the army in 1570, and fought in the naval battle of Lepanto against the Turks in 1571. He was wounded in the left hand and came to be called the *Maimed of Lepanto.* Fond of military and heroic deeds, Cervantes remained in the army, and fought in Tunis, Sicily, Italy, and Greece.

Homesick, Cervantes resigned from the military in 1575, and sailed for Spain. Pirates captured his ship and sold him into slavery in Algiers. Cervantes spent five years as a slave. He tried to escape several times before his family and an order of friars raised enough money to ransom him. Incidents from Cervantes' captivity became episodes in *Don Quixote.*

Cervantes reached Madrid in 1580, a poor and sick man burdened by the memory of years of misfortune. He asked the government for permission to go to America, but the government refused and made him a tax collector. In this job, Cervantes visited many parts of Spain and met all kinds of people. He gained an understanding of human nature that enabled him to ponder in *Don Quixote* and other works the conflict between hope and disillusionment, dreams and reality.

His Literary Career. Cervantes' first long work was *La Galatea* (1585), a prose pastoral romance. Cervantes wrote many plays during the next 20 years, but could find no one to produce them. The publication of the first part of *Don Quixote* in 1605 made him famous. But he published nothing else for eight years.

Old and lonely, Cervantes became incredibly active during his last three years. *Novelas ejemplares* (*Exemplary Novels*) appeared in 1613. This collection of stories ranks as Cervantes' major work after *Don Quixote.* The stories vary in style and subject matter, ranging from crude naturalism to romanticism. The best stories are noted for their realism and satirical flavor.

Critics do not regard Cervantes' poetry highly. *Journey to Parnassus* (1614), a long poem, is of interest chiefly for its critical appraisals of Spanish poets. In 1615, he published the second part of *Don Quixote* and *Eight Comedies and Eight Entremeses,* a collection of plays. His *Entremeses* (one-act comedies) are among his best works and much superior to his longer, more serious plays.

Cervantes' last work was *Persiles and Sigismunda,* a romantic adventure novel published in 1617 after his death. One of the book's highlights is its eloquent and moving introduction, completed four days before the author's death. In the introduction, Cervantes foresaw his death and offered his farewell to life. GERMÁN BLEIBERG

See also SPANISH LITERATURE (The Golden Age).

CESIUM, *SEE zee uhm,* is a soft, silvery metallic element. Dissolved cesium salts, such as cesium carbonate and cesium chloride, are widely distributed in low concentrations in brines and mineral waters. The German scientists Robert Bunsen and Gustav Kirchhoff first detected cesium in 1860. In 1882, the chemist Carl Setterberg isolated the pure metal.

Cesium has an atomic number of 55 and an atomic weight of 132.905. Its chemical symbol is Cs. Cesium belongs to the group of elements called *alkali metals* (see ELEMENT, CHEMICAL [Periodic Table of the Elements]). It reacts vigorously with air and water. Cesium melts at 28.40° C and boils at 678.4° C. At 20° C, it has a density of 1.873 grams per cubic centimeter (see DENSITY).

Most cesium metal is obtained from cesium chloride through a special chemical process. Cesium ionizes readily when heated or struck by light. Because of this property, it is used in *photomultiplier tubes* that measure very weak light (see PHOTOMULTIPLIER TUBE). Scientists are studying the use of cesium as a fuel in ion-propulsion engines for space vehicles. They also are experimenting with methods of power generation that involve the ionization of cesium. DUWARD F. SHRIVER

CETA. See COMPREHENSIVE EMPLOYMENT AND TRAINING ACT.

CETACEAN, *suh TAY shuhn,* is a member of the order of mammals made up of whales, dolphins, and porpoises. Cetaceans bear their young alive, and the babies nurse on the mother's milk. Cetaceans live entirely in water and breathe air through lungs. Their fishlike bodies have a thick layer of fat called *blubber* that keeps them warm. Cetaceans have flippers for front limbs, and no hind limbs. They have almost no hair.

Scientific Classification. The cetaceans are in the phylum *Chordata*. They belong to the class *Mammalia* and make up the order *Cetacea*. RAYMOND M. GILMORE

See also DOLPHIN; MAMMAL; RIVER DOLPHIN; WHALE.

CEYLON. See SRI LANKA.

CÉZANNE, *say ZAHN,* **PAUL** (1839-1906), was a French painter who created a style of composition that changed the course of art. Cézanne's paintings led to the development of cubism and much abstract art.

During the 500 years before Cézanne, most artists believed that a painting should show the world realistically. They therefore tried to create the illusions of atmosphere, light, mass, space, and texture as these elements appear in nature. But Cézanne felt that a painting should reflect the artist's sensations or impressions, which are translated into pictorial form through brushstrokes, color, and line.

In his paintings, Cézanne made no attempt to tell a story or express a point of view. He even avoided the suggestion of mood or atmosphere. Cézanne deliberately distorted the natural appearance of his subject matter in an effort to create a more forceful, exciting composition. However, Cézanne never totally rejected recognizable subject matter. His paintings, particularly his last works, seem midway between realistic representation of nature and abstraction.

Cézanne was born in Aix-en-Provence and lived there most of his life. His father was a banker and wanted him to become a lawyer. But Cézanne was determined to become a painter. He had some art training, but was basically self-taught. Cézanne's first paintings were dark and crudely drawn. These works dealt largely with sexual themes based on Italian paintings of the 1500's and the works of the French artist Eugène Delacroix.

About 1872, Cézanne fell under the influence of the French impressionist painters, particularly Camille Pissarro. Cézanne's *House of the Hanged Man* (1873) is characteristic of his rather solemn approach to the lighthearted, spontaneous impressionist style.

Cézanne mastered his art from the 1880's to about 1900. He painted most of his best-known pictures during this period. They include views of Mont Sainte-Victoire and of the bay of l'Estaque in Provence, many outstanding portraits and still lifes, pictures of men playing cards, and huge pictures of bathers. *The Clockmaker* (1900) appears in color in the WORLD BOOK article on PAINTING.

Cézanne's work attracted little attention during his life. His work received much criticism from other artists, critics, and the public, and he became a rather solitary person. A year after Cézanne's death, a large exhibition of his paintings was held in Paris. The exhibition had great impact on many leading painters of the 1900's, including Georges Braque, Fernand Léger, Henri Matisse, and Pablo Picasso. ROBERT F. REIFF

See also IMPRESSIONISM (Postimpressionism); BRAQUE, GEORGES.

Additional Resources

REWALD, JOHN. *Paul Cézanne*. Springbook, 1948.

RUBIN, WILLIAM. *Cézanne: The Late Work*. Museum of Modern Art, 1977.

VENTURI, LIONELLO. *Cézanne*. Rizzoli, 1979. An analytical study with reproductions of his works.

CHACO. See GRAN CHACO; PARAGUAY (Land Regions; Military Ruin).

CHACO CULTURE NATIONAL HISTORICAL PARK, in northwestern New Mexico, has ruins of pueblos, including the world's largest aboriginal apartment houses. Pueblo Bonito, the best known, had about 800 rooms.

The Art Institute of Chicago, The Albert Hern Fund

Paul Cézanne was a leader of the postimpressionism school of painting. The pencil sketch above is a self-portrait from one of his notebooks. *Mont Sainte-Victoire, right,* shows the feeling for depth and the attention to form that appear in Cézanne's landscapes.

The Metropolitan Museum of Art, New York City, The H. O. Havemeyer Collection, 1929

The area was established as a national monument in 1907 and became a national historical park in 1980. For area, see National Park System (table: National Historical Parks).

CHAD is an independent country in the heart of northern Africa. It is the fifth largest country in Africa in area. The country gets its name from Lake Chad, a large, shallow lake on the southwestern border. Chad is *landlocked* (has no borders on the sea).

Chad's scenery varies greatly. *Savannas* (grasslands with few trees) cover most of the south, where rainfall is the heaviest. Grassy plains cover central Chad, and the dry sands of the Sahara extend into northern Chad. In the north, people live only around oases. The country has many different kinds of wild animals. Many tourists visit Chad to hunt or photograph African buffaloes, cheetahs, elephants, leopards, and lions.

Chad was once part of French Equatorial Africa. It became independent as the Republic of Chad in 1960. Its name in French, the official language, is République du Tchad. N'Djamena, a city of about 242,000 people, is the capital and largest city.

Government. Chad is a republic. A president heads Chad's government. A 31-member cabinet assists the president. The National Consultative Council, which has 30 members, serves as the country's legislature.

People. Chad has about 5 million people. About three-fourths of the people are farmers or *nomadic* (wandering) herders. Most of the people live in the southern part of the country.

The differences between the people who live in the north and the south made it difficult in the past to unite the country politically. In the north, nomadic Arabs and persons of Hamitic origin live in tents and raise livestock (see Hamites). In the south, most persons are black Africans who raise crops on small farms. Most of the people who live in northern and central Chad are Muslims. Residents of central Chad live in houses made of dried mud. In the south, most of the people live in circular houses with mud walls and thatched roofs. Most of those who live in the south practice traditional African religions. Some are Christians. Chad has about 50 ethnic groups, each with its own language or dialect.

The Muslims include Arabs and Baguirmi, Kanembou, Toubou, and Waday peoples. Most of them wander across the dry northern and central regions in search of water and grazing land for their livestock. The Sara make up the largest ethnic group in southern Chad. Persons in the south raise such food crops as sorghum, millet, rice, beans, and cassava. The raising of livestock has been limited by the tsetse fly, which infests some parts of the south. See Tsetse Fly.

About 18 per cent of the people can read and write. About a third of the children receive some elementary education. Southern Chad has the best schools.

Land. Chad covers 495,800 square miles (1,284,000 square kilometers). Much of Chad is a level plain. The Chari and the Logone rivers flow into Lake Chad, a large, inland basin that has no outlet to the sea. The lake is only about 4 feet (1.2 meters) deep, and is surrounded by broad stretches of marshy land (see Lake Chad). The highest land is in the Tibesti Mountains in northern Chad, where Emi Koussi towers 11,204 feet (3,415 meters) above sea level. In central Chad, a few hills are over 5,000 feet (1,500 meters) high.

Most of northern Chad is desert sand where no farming is possible. It has a hot, dry tropical climate, and gets less than 10 inches (25 centimeters) of rain a year. Temperatures often range from about 130° F. (54° C) during the day to near freezing at night. Central Chad averages about 20 inches (51 centimeters) of rain a year.

Chad

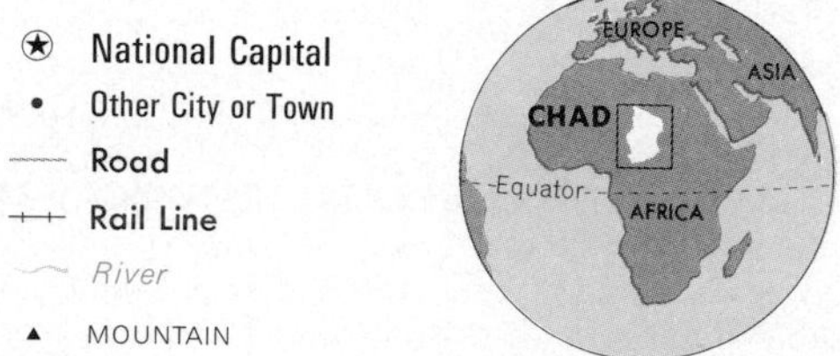

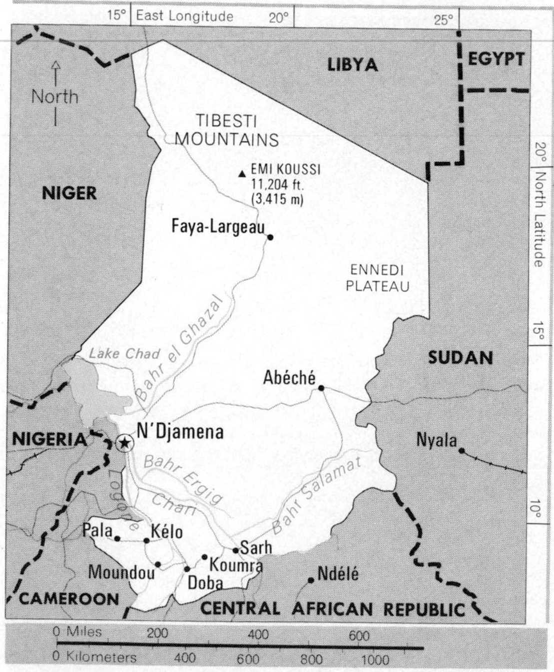

WORLD BOOK map

Facts in Brief

Capital: N'Djamena.

Official Language: French.

Area: 495,800 sq. mi. (1,284,000 km²).

Population: *Estimated 1985 Population*—4,941,000; distribution, 78 per cent rural, 22 per cent urban; density, 10 persons per sq. mi. (4 per km²). *1963-64 Census*—3,254,000. *Estimated 1990 Population*—5,482,000.

Chief Products: *Agriculture*—beans, cassava, cotton, dates, livestock (cattle, goats, sheep), millet, peanuts, rice, sorghum, tropical fruit, wheat. *Mining*—natron (washing soda), tungsten. *Fishing*—fresh and dried fish.

Flag: The flag has vertical blue, yellow, and red stripes. Blue symbolizes the sky and hope. Yellow stands for the sun. Red represents fire and unity. See Flag (picture: Flags of Africa).

Money: *Basic Unit*—franc. See Money (table).

Most of the south gets about 40 inches (100 centimeters). The rainy season in Chad extends from June to September. The average annual temperature in central and southern Chad is 82° F. (28° C).

Economy. Chad is one of the least economically developed countries in Africa. Its isolated location and its lack of transportation slow down economic development. Its few industries process farm products. The lack of water has slowed agricultural development in many areas.

Farmers raise cotton, Chad's most important export, in the southwest. Other exports include cattle, meat, hides and skins, and peanuts. Most trade is with France. Chad also exports fish to Cameroon and Nigeria, and it has a small trade with the United States.

Chad has no railroads and few all-weather roads. Many of the roads are impassable during and after the rainy season. River transportation is important, and sections of the Chari and Logone rivers are navigable for parts of the year. N'Djamena has an international airport, and Abéché, Moundou, and Sarh also have airports. N'Djamena has a radio station.

History. The Chad region was part of several early African empires. The most important was the Kanem empire, which began in the 700's in the Lake Chad area. It had a powerful central government and traded with Asia, Europe, and North Africa (see KANEM). Other peoples who controlled parts of Chad included the Bulala and the Baguirmi.

The first European explorers arrived in the 1800's. Many traders moved through the area taking slaves, ostrich plumes, and ivory. In 1897, Gaorang, the last Baguirmi ruler, signed a treaty with France making Chad a French-protected state. In 1910, France linked Chad with what are now the Central African Republic, Congo, and Gabon to form French Equatorial Africa.

In 1958, Chad became a self-governing republic within the French Community, an organization that linked France with its overseas territories. In 1960, Chad became a fully independent member of the French Community. François Tombalbaye, a southern leader, became the first president of Chad.

In the 1970's, a severe drought caused food shortages and other problems in Chad. In 1973, President Tombalbaye changed his first name from François to Ngarta. His action was part of a government campaign to replace European names with African names. In 1975, military forces killed President Tombalbaye, and military officers took control of the government.

Some Muslim groups of northern Chad organized a rebellion against the southern-dominated government in the mid-1960's. Much fighting took place between the rebels and government troops during the 1960's and 1970's. France gave Chad's government military equipment, and French troops aided the government from 1968 to 1972 and in the late 1970's. Some fighting also took place between rival northern rebel groups. Libya—which claims part of northern Chad—provided some of the rebels with troops and military equipment.

In 1979, the rebels and the government agreed to a cease-fire. A new government that included representatives of both sides was formed. Goukouni Weddeye, the leader of a northern rebel group, became president. During 1980, heavy fighting took place between Goukouni's group and northern rebels led by Defense Minister Hissene Habre. Libya supported Goukouni's group with troops and military equipment. It helped the group defeat Habre's rebels in a major battle for control of N'Djamena. In 1982, after the Libyans withdrew from Chad, Habre's rebels attacked N'Djamena and defeated Goukouni's group there. They took control of Chad's government and Habre became president. But fighting continued between the forces of Habre and Goukouni. Goukouni's forces gained control of part of the north. In 1983, Libya again sent troops and equipment to aid Goukouni. France supported Habre's government with troops and military equipment. IGOR DE GARINE

See also N'DJAMENA.

Marc & Evelyne Bernheim, Rapho Guillumette

A Market in N'Djamena was designed to match the Arabic patterns of other buildings in the city. N'Djamena is the largest city and the center of most of the country's commercial activity.

CHAD, LAKE. See LAKE CHAD.

CHADRON STATE COLLEGE. See UNIVERSITIES AND COLLEGES (table).

CHADWICK, SIR JAMES (1891-1974), a British physicist, won the 1935 Nobel prize in physics for his discovery of the neutron, one of the particles making up an atom. In 1925 he became assistant director of radioactive research at the Cavendish Physics Laboratory at Cambridge, England. There he bombarded various chemical elements with alpha particles (see ALPHA RAY). He studied the *transmutation* (change) of these materials into different chemical elements. This work on nuclear structure led him to discover the neutron and determine its mass (see NEUTRON). Born in Manchester, England, he studied at Manchester, Berlin, and Cambridge universities. G. GAMOW

CHAERONEA. See BOEOTIA.

CHAFER, *CHAY fuhr*, is a general name for several large, slow beetles. Chafers feed mostly on leaves and flowers. The *larvae* (young) live in the soil and feed on roots. They are thick, fleshy grubs with curved bodies and well-developed legs. Common chafers include June bugs, rose chafers, and cockchafers.

Scientific Classification. Chafers belong to the beetle and weevil family, *Scarabaeidae*. R. E. BLACKWELDER

See also BEETLE; JUNE BUG; ROSE CHAFER.

CHAGALL, *shah GAHL*, **MARC** (1887-), a Russian-born artist, won fame for his dreamlike, fanciful paintings. Chagall's rich imaginative art has a joyous quality seldom found among paintings of the 1900's.

Pix

Marc Chagall

Many of Chagall's fantastic, brilliantly colored scenes contain objects recalled from his childhood in the Russian-Jewish village of Vitebsk. Such objects include floating animals, lovers, and musicians. An example of Chagall's graceful and topsy-turvy world is his painting, *Birthday*, which is reproduced in color in the PAINTING article. Chagall also is a religious artist of real distinction.

Chagall paints in a style all his own. But his use of symbols and dream images makes him a forerunner of the *surrealism* movement. The geometric planes used in the composition of many of his earlier works show *cubist* influences. See CUBISM; SURREALISM.

Chagall illustrated books, designed sets and costumes for ballets and operas, and became one of the leading lithographers of the 1900's. In the early 1960's, he designed stained-glass windows for the Hadassah-Hebrew University Medical Center in Jerusalem (see STAINED GLASS; picture). In 1964, he completed a huge painting for the ceiling of the Paris Opera.

Chagall has lived most of his life in France. In the 1940's, he lived for a time in the United States and Mexico. In *My Life*, an autobiography, Chagall describes his life up to 1922. JOSEPH C. SLOANE

Oil painting on canvas (1911); the Museum of Modern Art, New York City, Mrs. Simon Guggenheim Fund

Chagall's *I and the Village* shows scenes of life in Vitebsk, the Russian village where the artist grew up. The bright colors and topsy-turvy figure are typical of his style. The influence of the cubist art movement appears in the painting's geometric shapes.

CHAGOS ARCHIPELAGO. See BRITISH INDIAN OCEAN TERRITORY.

CHAGRES RIVER, *CHAH grehs*, is a chief source of water for the Panama Canal. The Chagres rises in the mountains of eastern Panama, flows southwest, and empties into Gatun Lake—a part of the Panama Canal route.

See also PANAMA CANAL (Gatun Lake).

CHAIKOVSKY, PETER ILICH. See TCHAIKOVSKY, PETER ILICH.

CHAIN is a flexible length of links or rings joined together. The links of a chain are usually made from metal bent into loops, with the ends of each link welded together inside the loop of the next link.

The size of a chain is measured by the thickness of its links. A half-inch chain has links made from a metal bar $\frac{1}{2}$ inch (13 millimeters) in diameter. Chains vary in size from small ones used in jewelry to huge steel chains used in cables, pulleys, and other types of machinery. Iron, brass, steel, and bronze make strong chains. Gold, silver, platinum, and alloys are used in making ornamental chains.

The links of chains sometimes consist of several pieces. Bicycle chains, for example, are made this way. In anchor chains, a metal brace called a *stud* is sometimes put in each link to make it stronger. Such links are called *stud links*. WALTER R. WILLIAMS, JR.

CHAIN is the term for a unit of measurement in surveying, and for the measuring instrument itself. A surveyor's chain has 100 links. Each link is 7.92 inches (20.12 centimeters) long. Ten *square chains*, or 100,000 *square links*, make 1 acre (0.4 hectare). This length comes from the first surveyor's chain, called *Gunter's chain.* It was 66 feet (20 meters) long.

A steel band or a tape has replaced the cumbersome chain in surveying, but the term "chain" is still used. Many country roads and some village streets are 66 feet (20 meters) wide, because surveyors found it easiest to measure them with one length of chain. E. G. STRAUS

See also SURVEYING.

CHAIN, ERNST BORIS (1906-1979), a British biochemist, shared the 1945 Nobel prize for physiology or medicine with Sir Alexander Fleming and Sir Howard Florey. Beginning in 1938, Chain worked with Florey on antibiotic substances produced by various microorganisms. The Nobel prize was awarded for their discovery of the healing properties of penicillin. These properties had previously been described by Fleming. Chain was born in Berlin, Germany, and was graduated from the Friedrich-Wilhelm University. HENRY H. FERTIG

CHAIN GANG was a group of prisoners who were chained together for labor. The convicts wore leg shackles connected by a short chain. Another longer chain connected each convict to the next convict. Chain gangs were frequently used to build roads in the southern United States.

CHAIN HOIST. See BLOCK AND TACKLE.

CHAIN MAIL. See ARMOR.

CHAIN REACTION. See NUCLEAR ENERGY (Nuclear Fission).

CHAIN STITCH. See CROCHETING; EMBROIDERY.

CHAIN STORE is one of a group of retail stores managed and usually owned by a single company. Some chain-store companies have no more than three stores, but others own thousands. Most chain stores specialize in groceries, clothing, and shoes. The familiar "five-and-ten" or "dime" store and many department stores are chain stores. So are many drugstores and stores that sell automobile parts and accessories. There are two main types of chain-store systems. These are *corporate chains* and *voluntary chains.*

Corporate Chain Stores are directed and supervised from a central office. Specialists in certain types of goods buy these goods for the chain. In a grocery chain, for example, one or more persons may buy meats, while others specialize in buying fruits, vegetables, dairy products, and canned goods. For a "five-and-ten" or variety-store chain, one or more persons may buy clothing. Other persons skilled in buying different kinds of products may purchase hardware, candy, jewelry, toys,

Three Types of Chains: *top,* twisted links which permit chain to lie flat; *center,* straight links, the commonest type; *bottom,* stud links, which form the strongest chain.

housewares, cosmetics, stationery, and school supplies.

Some chain-store companies own factories that manufacture goods sold by the stores. It is common for a grocery chain to own a bakery. Some drugstore chains own ice cream factories to help supply their soda fountains. Sometimes factories own chain stores. Shoe manufacturers own most large shoe chains, and tire manufacturers own chains of automobile tire and automotive supply stores.

Each store in a corporate chain is under the control of a manager who must follow the instructions of the central office. The central office sets the prices at which the stores must sell their goods. The central office also decides how the stores display the merchandise and how they sell it. Supervisors visit the stores to see that the goods are priced and displayed according to the instructions sent out by the central office.

Voluntary Chain Stores. In voluntary chains, the managers of the stores are also the store owners. The owners have agreed or volunteered to adopt methods of operation similar to those used by the corporate chains. Owners of stores that are in voluntary chains agree to buy the same kind of goods, buy from the same wholesale merchants and manufacturers, advertise alike, and display their goods in the same way. Voluntary chains are important in the retailing of groceries and hardware.

Growth of Chain Stores. No one knows for certain what firm was the first chain-store company. Instances are known of three or more stores being owned by one person or firm as far back as the early 1800's. It was not until after 1900, however, that chain stores became important. People after that time bought more of the things they needed. They did not make as many items in their homes as did their pioneer ancestors. Factories began to make more and more of the food, clothing, and other items used in the home. The factories that sold the goods to the chain stores could manufacture on a large scale, so they could make savings that enabled them to sell at low prices to the stores. The chain stores also operated on a large scale, and could make savings in operating expenses. Both these factors resulted in goods being sold to customers at low prices. The sales volume of the chain stores and the number of chain stores increased because the low prices at which they could sell goods attracted customers.

It is difficult to determine how many chain stores are in operation today. New chain stores are constantly being established. At the same time, old chain stores are being discontinued.

Chain stores do not have a monopoly on retail trade. Many independent stores are in operation. Anybody can open a store at any time. This single store may very well become the first of a new chain. Almost all chain-store companies have been established by people who, when they started in the business, had only a single store. FRED M. JONES

See also DEPARTMENT STORE; FOOD (table: 10 Leading Food-Store Chains in the United States); MAIL-ORDER BUSINESS; RESTAURANT (Chains and Franchises); RETAILING; FRANCHISE.

CHAIR. See FURNITURE.

CHALAZA. See EGG (The White).

CHALCEDONY, *kal SEHD uh nee,* is a variety of quartz used to make gem stones. The mineral was named for the ancient town of Chalcedon in what is now Turkey, which has large deposits of chalcedony nearby. Other deposits of chalcedony have been found in California, Colorado, Iceland, and Scotland.

Common chalcedony, sometimes called *white agate,* is semitransparent and clouded with circles and spots. Other kinds of chalcedony are nearly transparent, and may be stained many colors. Varieties of chalcedony include agate, bloodstone, carnelian, chrysoprase, onyx, and sardonyx.

The petrified forests of Arizona were formed in part by water depositing chalcedony in place of the woody fibers of the trees. The Bible (Rev. 21:19) mentions that the third foundation of the wall of the Holy City was made of chalcedony.

Related Articles in WORLD BOOK include:

Agate	Onyx
Carnelian	Quartz
Gem	Sardonyx

CHALCOCITE, *KAL koh site,* is an important mineral ore of copper. Its chemical formula is Cu_2S. Chalcocite has a shiny lead-gray color that turns black when the ore is exposed to the air. Some chalcocite is soft and sooty. Chalcocite is found in copper deposits throughout the world. The ore is sometimes called *copper glance.* MARIA LUISA CRAWFORD

See also COPPER (Copper Ores).

CHALCOPYRITE. See COPPER (Copper Ores); MINERAL (picture).

CHALDEA, *kal DEE uh,* was the ancient name given to the sea lands at the head of the Persian Gulf, south of Babylonia. The Chaldeans were famous for studying the stars to foretell the future.

Little is known of the earliest Chaldeans, but they probably spoke Aramaic. In the 700's B.C., the Chaldeans overpowered Babylonia. The first Chaldean king to rule the Babylonians was Merodachbaladan, about 721 B.C. Nabopolassar founded the Chaldean (or New Babylonian) Empire in 625 B.C. His famous son Nebuchadnezzar, mentioned in the Old Testament, succeeded him. Under Nebuchadnezzar's rule, Babylonia reached its greatest glory and power. Because of the Chaldean rule over Babylonia in the 700's and the 600's B.C., the names Chaldean and Babylonian are closely associated and sometimes mixed in usage. After the Persians conquered Babylonia in the 500's B.C., the terms Chaldean and Babylonian came to mean the same thing. JACOB J. FINKELSTEIN

See also NEBUCHADNEZZAR (II).

CHALET, *sha LAY,* is a country house built mostly of wood. Chalets are found in many parts of Switzerland. The style differs with the region, but chalets usually have several floors, low ceilings, small windows, and roofs with broad gables and deep overhangs that must be partly supported by brackets. Craftworkers may decorate a chalet with carving or cut-out open work. The beams or other parts of construction, often roughly hacked out, show plainly.

Some chalets are solidly built of heavy squared timbers resting lengthwise on each other and locked at the corners. Others have heavy wood framing covered with thick boarding. Some structures in Europe and America imitate the chalet style. BERNARD LEMANN

CHALIAPIN, *shuh LYAH pyin,* **FEODOR IVANOVICH** (1873-1938), a Russian opera singer, became a leading interpreter of bass roles in Russian and Italian opera. Many persons believe that Chaliapin's characterizations of Boris Godunov, Ivan the Terrible, and Mephistopheles have never been equaled.

He had little musical training before joining a small-town opera company in 1890. He won attention singing at St. Petersburg (now Leningrad), Russia, and as a member of Mamontov's opera troupe in Moscow. He sang for the first time outside Russia at La Scala in Milan, Italy, in 1901. He appeared in the United States for the first time in 1907, with the Metropolitan Opera of New York. Chaliapin was born of peasant parents in Kazan on Feb. 11, 1873. SCOTT GOLDTHWAITE

CHALICE OF ANTIOCH. See ANTIOCH, CHALICE OF.

CHALK is a soft, fine-grained white limestone. It was formed as a mud on the bottom of an ancient sea. It differs from many pure, fine-grained limestones only in still being soft and easily rubbed off. That is, it did not change into hard rock.

Chalk consists largely of tiny shells and crystals of calcite. Both of these materials are made up of the compound calcium carbonate. The white cliffs of Dover are thick layers of chalk. This gave the name *Albion* to England. Albion probably means *white land.* The chalk deposits of western Kansas contain preserved skeletons of extinct sea serpents, flying reptiles, birds, and fishes.

Most deposits of chalk formed during the Cretaceous Period of time. The Cretaceous Period got its name from the Latin word for chalk, *creta.*

Chalk is made into *whiting,* a substance used to manufacture rubber goods, paint, putty, soft polishing powders, and tooth powder. Industry also uses chalk, like

Solidly Built Swiss Chalets are protected from the deep snows of the fierce Alpine winters by wide, overhanging eaves.

Swiss National Tourist Office

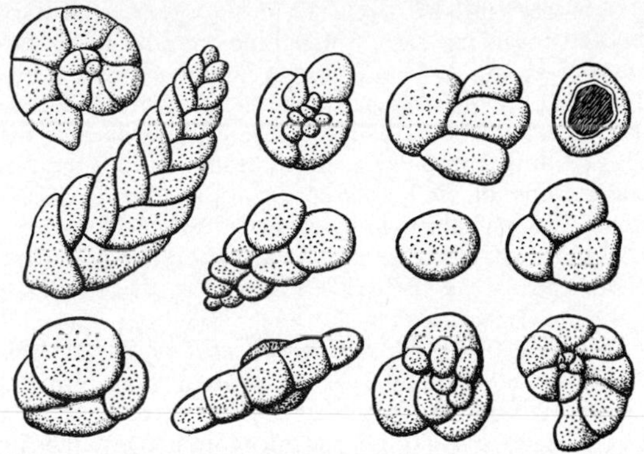

Chalk contains a variety of shells of tiny sea animals. These tiny Foraminifera shells are formed in many unusual shapes.

any other limestone, in the manufacture of Portland cement and as a top dressing for soils. Chalk is also used to make crayons for writing on chalkboard.

Some substances called "chalk" actually contain a different material. For example, "French chalk," used by tailors, is a type of talc. A. J. EARDLEY

See also CALCITE; CALCIUM CARBONATE.

CHALKBOARD is a smooth, dark board usually made of slate, glass, or wood. Crayon or chalk is used to write or draw on the board. The chalkboard is probably the world's most widely used visual aid to education. Instructors use chalkboards to help emphasize classroom talks.

Chalkboards were once black, but many are now green. The chalkboard grew out of the hornbook of the Middle Ages. It was in fairly common use in Europe by the 1600's, but was not widely used in the United States until the early 1800's.

CHALMERS, THOMAS (1780-1847), a Scottish preacher and philanthropist, founded the Free Church of Scotland in 1843. He left the Established Church of Scotland during a dispute over the method of choosing ministers. Chalmers favored their election by the people. He also won fame as a supporter of Sunday schools and as an organizer of relief for the poor. He taught theology at the University of Edinburgh from 1828 to 1843. He was born at East Anstruther, Scotland. F. A. NORWOOD

CHÂLONS, BATTLE OF. See ARMY (table: Famous Land Battles).

CHAMBER MUSIC is a type of classical music written for small groups of musicians. These groups, called *ensembles*, may vary in size from two to nine performers. Most ensembles consist of three to five musicians who play string or wind instruments. One musician plays each part.

Chamber music is generally classified according to the number of performers in the ensemble. Music performed by two musicians is called a *duet* or *duo*. Other forms of chamber music include *trios*, *quartets*, and *quintets*. Chamber music may be further classified by the type of instruments played. For example, a *string quartet* is performed by two violins, a viola, and a cello. A *brass quintet* calls for two trumpets, a French horn, a trombone, and a tuba.

Since about 1750, most great composers have written chamber music. Some of the best works are string quartets by Joseph Haydn, Wolfgang Amadeus Mozart, Ludwig van Beethoven, Johannes Brahms, and Béla Bartók.

The term *chamber music* was first used during the 1500's, when small groups performed in private homes. Until about 1900, musicians played chamber music chiefly for their own enjoyment and for small gatherings of music lovers. Today, many ensembles perform in concert halls before large audiences. R. M. LONGYEAR

See also CLASSICAL MUSIC (pictures: A String Quartet; Chamber Music).

CHAMBER OF COMMERCE is an association of business people which promotes the interests of its members and of business in general. Chambers of commerce have been organized in towns, cities, regions, and countries. In many European countries, chambers of commerce are official agencies, supported by taxes. Chambers of commerce are sometimes called boards of trade, merchants' associations, or associations of commerce. The International Chamber of Commerce is an organization of business people from many countries who want to bring about closer international economic ties.

Chambers of commerce work to bring new industries to their communities. These organizations also furnish information about their communities that may help those planning to move into their area. The first associations of this kind were formed in the days of the Roman Empire. The first group to have the name "Chamber of Commerce" was organized in Marseille, France, in 1599. ALAN GRIFFIN

CHAMBER OF COMMERCE OF THE UNITED STATES is a national organization that speaks for American business and industry. Its chief purpose is to improve and protect a free enterprise system. It finds out what business people in the country think about legislation, and makes these views known to members of Congress. The chamber also works to develop private-business programs to solve social and economic problems.

Individuals, business firms, other organizations of business people, and local, state, and regional chambers of commerce may hold membership in the national chamber. The chamber is controlled by a 63-member board of directors. A chairman and a president are elected by the board of directors each year. The chamber's headquarters are at 1615 H Street NW, Washington, D.C. 20062.

The chamber was organized in 1912 at a conference called by President William Howard Taft in Washington, D.C. At that time, there were already many local chambers. Critically reviewed by the CHAMBER OF COMMERCE OF THE UNITED STATES

CHAMBERED NAUTILUS. See NAUTILUS.

CHAMBERLAIN was the family name of a father and two sons in British politics.

Joseph Chamberlain (1836-1914) was prominent in British politics for more than 30 years. Chamberlain entered Parliament and served from 1880 to 1885 in the Liberal Party government under William Gladstone. He split with Gladstone over Irish Home Rule. Chamberlain then organized the Unionist Party, which became allied with the Conservatives. After 1903, his proposals for tariff reform split the Conservative Party. Chamberlain served as Great Britain's colonial secretary from 1895 to 1903. He was born in London.

United Press Int.

Neville Chamberlain, *with umbrella,* went to Munich in 1938 to negotiate with Adolf Hitler. This effort to win peace failed.

Sir Austen Chamberlain (1863-1937), the oldest son of Joseph Chamberlain, served as British foreign secretary from 1924 to 1929. He was largely responsible for the Locarno Treaties of 1925, and shared the Nobel peace prize that year (see LOCARNO CONFERENCE). He was born in London, and entered Parliament in 1892.

Neville Chamberlain (1869-1940), the second son of Joseph Chamberlain, served as prime minister from 1937 to 1940. He was closely associated with the policy of appeasement toward Nazi Germany. This policy led to the Munich Agreement of 1938, by which Chamberlain hoped to achieve "peace for our time." His government took Britain into World War II. He was forced to resign in 1940. Chamberlain was born in London. A Conservative, he served as minister of health and twice as chancellor of the exchequer. ALFRED F. HAVIGHURST

See also MUNICH AGREEMENT; WORLD WAR II (Aggression on the March).

CHAMBERLAIN, *CHAYM buhr lihn,* **OWEN** (1920-), an American physicist, shared the 1959 Nobel Prize in physics with Emilio Segrè. They discovered the antiproton in 1955 at the University of California (see ANTIPROTON). Chamberlain was born in San Francisco.

CHAMBERLAIN, *CHAYM buhr lihn,* **WILT** (1936-), was one of the greatest scorers in National Basketball Association (NBA) history. During his 14-year NBA career, he scored 31,419 points. Only Kareem Abdul-Jabbar scored more. Chamberlain, a center, set an NBA record for career rebounds with 23,924. He stands 7 feet 1 inch (216 centimeters) tall.

Don Sparks, Tom Stack & Associates

Wilt Chamberlain

Wilton Norman Chamberlain was born in Philadelphia. He played for the University of Kansas before joining the NBA's Philadelphia (now Golden State) Warriors in 1959. He led the NBA in scoring during his first seven seasons. In the 1961-1962 season, he set league records for average points per game (50.4), most points in regular-season play (4,029), and most points in a single game (100). In 1965, the Warriors traded him to the Philadelphia 76ers. In 1966-1967, he helped lead the 76ers to the NBA title. In 1968, Philadelphia traded him to the Los Angeles Lakers. He helped lead the Lakers to the NBA title in 1972. Chamberlain coached the San Diego Conquistadors of the American Basketball Association (ABA) during the 1973-1974 season. HERMAN WEISKOPF

See also BASKETBALL (picture).

CHAMBERS, WHITTAKER, *HWIHT tuh kuhr* (1901-1961), a confessed spy, was the United States government's chief witness in the 1949 perjury trials of Alger Hiss. Chambers said Hiss, a former Department of State official, gave him United States military secrets. Chambers produced microfilms of secret U.S. government papers he had hidden in a pumpkin on his Maryland farm (see HISS, ALGER).

Whittaker Jay David Chambers was born in Philadelphia. He joined the Communist Party in 1924. He was an editor for the Communist *Daily Worker* newspaper until 1929, and a *courier* (messenger) for the Russian spy system in Washington, D.C., in the 1930's. Disillusioned, he left the Communist Party in 1938. Chambers worked on the editorial staffs of *Time* and *Life* magazines from 1939 to 1948. After the Hiss trials, he lived on his farm. From 1957 to 1959, he helped edit the *National Review* magazine. CAROL L. THOMPSON

CHAMELEON, *kuh MEE lee uhn,* is any of about 100 kinds of lizards. Most species of chameleons live in the forests of Africa and Madagascar. A few species live in the Middle East, in southern Asia, and in southern Spain.

Chameleons are known for their ability to change color, but many other kinds of lizards also have this ability. A chameleon may be green, yellow, or white one minute, and the next minute it may be brown or black. Chameleons also may become spotted or blotched. Many people believe chameleons change color to blend with their surroundings. However, the changes occur in response to variations in light or temperature, or as the result of fright or some other reaction

Angabe A. Schmidecker, Alpha

The Three-Horned Chameleon, *above,* lives in eastern Africa. Unlike most kinds of lizards, a chameleon has feet that grip like hands rather than cling by means of sharp claws.

Stephen Dalton, Oxford Scientific Films

A Chameleon Shoots Out Its Tongue to capture an insect. The chameleon's tongue, which is controlled by powerful neck muscles, moves so rapidly that the human eye can hardly see it.

© Robert L. Dunne, Bruce Coleman Inc.

A Male Anole Displays Its Throat Flap to attract a mate or to scare away other males. Anoles are closely related to chameleons and are often called *American chameleons.*

to the environment. The color of a chameleon is controlled by body chemicals called *hormones*, which affect pigments in the skin.

A lizard called the *anole* (pronounced *uh NOH lee*) is closely related to the chameleon. There are more than 225 species of anoles, and they live in South America, Central America, and the southeastern United States. Anoles are often called *American chameleons.*

The Body of a Chameleon is short and flat. Chameleons range from $1\frac{1}{4}$ to 25 inches (3.2 to 63 centimeters) long. As many as three horns may grow from a chameleon's head. The eyes stick out and function independently, so that the animal can look forward and backward at the same time. A chameleon's feet grasp like hands rather than cling with sharp claws, as do those of most other lizards. The chameleon is one of the few lizards that have a grasping tail.

The Life of a Chameleon. Chameleons move extremely slowly. Most species live in trees and bushes, where they lie in wait to prey on insects. Some kinds make their home on the ground and eat wild grasses. Chameleons that live in trees have a long, sticky tongue with which they capture prey. The tongue, which may be as long as the entire body, is controlled by powerful muscles in the throat. It shoots out so rapidly that the human eye can hardly see it.

Chameleons rarely fight one another. The males establish feeding territories, which they defend by trying to outbluff their rivals. They puff out their throat and the rest of their body to look larger in an attempt to scare away other males.

Males of the tree-dwelling species of chameleons rarely come to the ground. But the females of many species dig nests in the ground for the 30 to 40 eggs that they lay yearly. Among other species of chameleons, the female keeps the eggs in her body until they are ready to hatch.

Anoles, like chameleons, can change color quickly. Anoles are similar in size to chameleons but have a long, slender body. They also have sticky footpads that enable them to cling to leaves and branches. Anoles move quickly and generally prey on insects. Larger species sometimes catch frogs and young birds. Many male anoles have a colorful throat flap called a *dewlap.* They display the dewlap when defending their feeding territory or to attract females during the mating season.

Scientific Classification. Chameleons make up the family Chamaeleonidae. Anoles make up the genus *Anolis* in the iguana family, Iguanidae. CARL H. ERNST

CHAMOIS, *SHAM ee,* is a shy animal noted for its swiftness and keen sense of smell. It is often called a *goat-antelope,* but it looks a little more like an antelope than a goat. The chamois lives in the high mountains of Europe and Western Asia, and was once common in the Swiss Alps. In summer, the chamois lives in the snowy parts of the mountains. In winter, it goes down to the forests.

The chamois stands about 30 inches (76 centimeters) high at the shoulder, and weighs about 65 pounds (29 kilograms). The chamois is reddish brown, with black tail and horns. The fur changes to a dark brown in the winter. Its head is a pale yellow with a black band around the eyes from the nose to the ears. The chamois has round, smooth horns about 7 inches (18 centimeters) long. The horns grow straight up and curve backward into a sharp hook at the tip. The longest chamois horns ever found were $12\frac{3}{4}$ inches (32.4 centimeters) long.

Leonard Lee Rue III, Tom Stack & Associates

A Chamois resembles an antelope in appearance and speed. The chamois lives in the mountains of Europe and western Asia.

Hunting chamois is difficult because the animals are so light and quick that they can easily jump across a wide ravine. Chamois live in bands of about 10 to 15 animals. The flesh of the chamois is good food, but the skin is the most valuable part of the animal. It is used to make the soft, warm leather called *chamois skin*. Much sheepskin is sold as chamois skin.

Scientific Classification. The chamois belongs to the bovid family, *Bovidae*. It is classified as genus *Rupicapra*, species *R. rupicapra*. DONALD F. HOFFMEISTER

CHAMOMILE. See CAMOMILE.

CHAMORROS, *chah MAWR rohz*, are the peoples of the Mariana Islands in the western Pacific Ocean. The Chamorros include most of the people of Guam and Saipan, and small groups on other islands. They number more than 38,000. The Chamorros are descendants of the original Micronesian population, mainly of the Asian geographical race. The Chamorros of today also include a mixture of other peoples, mainly Spanish and Filipino. The term *Chamorro* also refers to the language spoken by these peoples. FELIX M. KEESING

CHAMP DE MARS. See PARIS (Gardens, Squares, and Parks).

CHAMPAGNE, *sham PAYN*, is a sparkling white wine which was first made in the province of Champagne, France. The sparkling effervescence of the best champagne comes from a natural secondary fermentation which takes place in the bottle. Cheaper grades are made to sparkle by adding carbon dioxide. Champagne may be either sweet or dry. *Sparkling burgundy* is a type of champagne made from red wine. J. BERNARD ROBB

CHAMPLAIN, LAKE. See LAKE CHAMPLAIN.

CHAMPLAIN, SAMUEL DE (1570?-1635), was a French explorer who founded the Canadian city of Quebec. He helped colonize French North America, once known as *New France*, and is often called the *Father of New France*.

Early Life. Champlain was born in Brouage, France, near Rochefort. His father, a sea captain, taught him navigation. Champlain joined the French Army at the age of about 20 and served until 1598. The next year, he sailed to the Spanish colonies in America on a French trading ship. From 1599 to 1601, he made several voyages to the West Indies, Mexico, and Panama.

Champlain returned to France in 1601 and wrote a book about his voyages. He described the splendor of Mexico City and was one of the first persons to propose the construction of a canal across Panama. Champlain's book interested King Henry IV, who was eager for France to acquire wealth in America. Henry also hoped the French could find a "Northwest Passage"—that is, a waterway through North America to Asia.

In 1603, Champlain sailed to Canada and explored the St. Lawrence River for the king. Champlain also became one of the first Europeans to write about Niagara Falls. He sailed back to Canada in 1604 and then explored the New England coast. In 1605, Champlain helped found a settlement at Port Royal (now Annapolis Royal, N.S.). In 1605 and 1606, he made two more voyages along the New England coast in search of a better site for the settlement.

The Founding of Quebec. Champlain returned to Canada in 1608 to establish a fur-trading post. He chose a site along the St. Lawrence River and named it Quebec. It became the first permanent settlement in New France. Champlain and his men built a fort and storehouse. The first winter was extremely cold, and only 8 of the 24 settlers survived.

Champlain became friendly with the Algonquin and Huron Indians living near Quebec. He believed his friendship could prevent Indian attacks on the settlement. He also thought that peaceful relations would make it easier for the French to trade furs with the Indians and to explore the country. In 1609, Champlain and two French companions joined the Algonquin and Huron in a raid on the Iroquois, who lived in what is now New York. Champlain and his friends had muskets and easily defeated the Iroquois, who knew nothing about firearms. On this raid, he became the first European to reach Lake Champlain, which he named for himself. Champlain won the lasting friendship of the Algonquin and Huron Indians by helping them.

Later Life. From 1610 to 1624, Champlain made several trips to France to obtain aid for Quebec. He also explored Lake Ontario and the Georgian Bay of Lake Huron.

War broke out between France and England in 1626, and the English began to seize French settlements in Canada. In 1628, an English fleet cut off supplies to Quebec and ordered Champlain to surrender the fort. The settlers held out for a year but finally surrendered after they ran out of food. The English took Champlain to England but allowed him to return to France in 1629. In 1632, the Treaty of Saint-Germain-en-Laye returned Quebec to France. Champlain sailed back to

Samuel de Champlain, *right*, founded Quebec, the first permanent settlement in New France. The map shows his explorations of the St. Lawrence River, parts of the North American coast, and the Great Lakes region.

Detail of an oil painting by Theophile Hamel; Public Archives of Canada, Ottawa

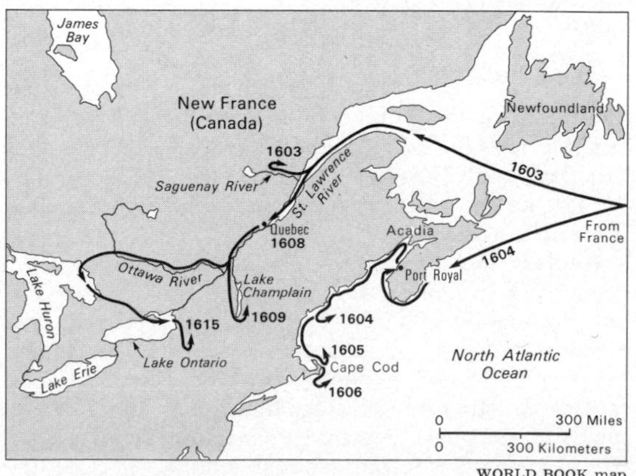

WORLD BOOK map

Quebec in 1633 and rebuilt the fort, where he lived until his death. FRANKLIN L. FORD

See also CANADA, HISTORY OF (Early Settlements; picture); MONTS, SIEUR DE; NOVA SCOTIA (Exploration and Settlement); BRULÉ, ÉTIENNE.

Additional Resources

BISHOP, MORRIS. *Champlain: The Life of Fortitude.* Octagon, 1979. Reprint of 1948 edition.

GARROD, STAN. *Samuel de Champlain.* Fitzhenry & Whiteside (Markham, Ont.), 1981. For younger readers.

MORISON, SAMUEL ELIOT. *Samuel de Champlain: Father of New France.* Little, Brown, 1972. Includes Champlain's drawings.

PARKMAN, FRANCIS. *Pioneers of France in the New World.* Corner House Publications, 1970. Originally published in 1865, has extensive coverage of Champlain's activities in North America.

CHAMPOLLION, JEAN FRANÇOIS. See ROSETTA STONE.

CHAMPS ÉLYSÉES. See PARIS (Gardens, Squares, and Parks).

CHANCE, FRANK (1877-1924), a baseball player and manager, became known as the *Peerless Leader.* He is best remembered as the first baseman in the famous Tinker-to-Evers-to-Chance double-play combination of the Chicago Cubs. He was elected to the baseball Hall of Fame in 1946. Chance managed the Chicago Cubs from 1905 through 1912, and led them to National League championships in 1906, 1907, 1908, and 1910. His lifetime batting average was .297. Frank Leroy Chance was born in Fresno, Calif. ED FITZGERALD

CHANCE MUSIC. See ALEATORY MUSIC.

CHANCELLOR, *CHAN suh luhr,* is a title given certain administrators in governments, universities, and churches. For example, West Germany calls its government leader chancellor. In Great Britain, the lord chancellor presides over the House of Lords, and is also a Cabinet member. Great Britain's chancellor of the exchequer is the minister of finance. Most European countries have had officials called chancellors.

In the United States, the presiding judge in some courts of chancery and courts of equity is called chancellor. The head of a university is sometimes called chancellor, and in some states the title is used for the official in charge of the state's colleges and universities. The Anglican, Episcopal, and Roman Catholic churches have chancellors who keep legal records. The word *chancellor* comes from the Latin word *cancellarius,* the title of a court usher. I. J. SANDERS

CHANCELLOR OF THE EXCHEQUER. See EXCHEQUER.

CHANCELLORSVILLE, BATTLE OF. See CIVIL WAR (The South Strikes Back [Chancellorsville]; table: Major Battles).

CHANCHAN. See PERU (History).

CHANDIGARH, *CHUHN dee guhr,* India (pop. 371,-992; met. area pop. 450,061), became a Union Territory of India and the joint capital of two states, Punjab and Haryana, in 1966. Chandigarh lies near the Ghaggar River on the Delhi-Kalka railroad, about 25 miles (40 kilometers) northwest of Ambāla. For location, see INDIA (political map).

The government announced plans to build Chandigarh in 1948, and engaged Le Corbusier (Charles-Édouard Jeanneret-Gris), a Swiss-born architect, to design the city. Construction began on a 15-square-mile (39-square-kilometer) site in 1950, and the city was inaugurated as the capital of East Punjab in 1953. It incorporates modern ideas of town planning, such as separate roads for cars and pedestrians. Its styling is adapted to the environment. ROBERT I. CRANE

CHANDLER, RAYMOND (1888-1959), was one of the leading writers of the "hard-boiled" school of detective fiction. His stories are noted for their realism and violence. Chandler created the *private eye* (private investigator) Philip Marlowe. Marlowe is a modern knight who roams the Los Angeles area, protecting the helpless and bringing the guilty to justice.

Chandler was born in Chicago and spent several years as an oil company executive in southern California. He published his first story in 1933 in *Black Mask,* a magazine that specialized in detective stories. Chandler wrote slowly and carefully. He produced only seven novels. They are *The Big Sleep* (1939), *Farewell, My Lovely* (1940), *The High Window* (1942), *The Lady in the Lake* (1943), *The Little Sister* (1949), *The Long Goodbye* (1953), and *Playback* (1958). A collection called *The Simple Art of Murder* (1950) includes several short stories and a famous essay on Chandler's philosophy of detective-story writing. PHILIP DURHAM

CHANDLER, ZACHARIAH, *ZAK uh RY uh* (1813-1879), an American businessman and politician, was an early leader of the Republican Party. He served as a United States senator from Michigan from 1857 to 1875, and interior secretary from 1875 to 1877. In 1861, he opposed any compromise that would prevent the Civil War. As a member of the Committee on the Conduct of the War, he favored punishing the Southern leaders. He was born in Bedford, N.H. A statue of Chandler represents Michigan in the U.S. Capitol. W. B. HESSELTINE

CHANDRAGUPTA MAURYA, *CHUHN druh GUP tuh MAH oor yuh* (? -298? B.C.), was the first great emperor

Peter Schmidt, Pix

An Indian Woman In Chandigarh drives her donkeys past a modern building designed by the famous architect Le Corbusier.

of India. He founded the Maurya Empire and ruled from about 321 to 298 B.C. Chandragupta imposed heavy taxes on the people and provided severe punishment for crimes, including the crime of nonpayment of taxes. He used spies and informers to ensure obedience to his will. However, Chandragupta also provided great economic benefits for his people by improving irrigation canals and roads.

Chandragupta established the Maurya Empire by seizing control of the Punjab region after the death of Alexander the Great, and then conquering Magadha, a kingdom in the Ganges Valley. He eventually controlled much of North India, what is now Pakistan, and part of Afghanistan. J. F. RICHARDS

See also MAURYA EMPIRE.

CHANGAMIRE EMPIRE. See ZIMBABWE (History).

CH'ANG-CH'UN, *chahng chun* (pop. 1,000,000), is an important trade and railway center in northeastern China (see CHINA [political map]). Ch'ang-ch'un became the capital of the Japanese puppet state of Manchukuo in 1932, and its name was changed to Hsinking, which means *new capital.* After World War II, Ch'ang-ch'un resumed its old name. THEODORE H. E. CHEN

CHANGE OF LIFE. See MENOPAUSE.

CH'ANG-SHA, *chahng shah* (pop. 300,000-1,000,000), is the capital of Hunan province in southeastern China. Ch'ang-sha is a major trading and industrial city. It is located on the Hsiang River (see CHINA [political map]).

Factories in Ch'ang-sha produce brassware, glass, machine tools, and textiles. Riverboats handle trade between Ch'ang-sha and Wuhan to the north. The Peking-Canton railroad runs through Ch'ang-sha. The Chinese leader Mao Zedong attended schools in Ch'ang-sha and was involved in his first political activities there between 1911 and 1921. RICHARD H. SOLOMON

CHANNEL. See RADIO (Broadcasting Power and Frequency); TELEVISION (Broadcasting).

CHANNEL BASS. See REDFISH.

CHANNEL ISLANDS are a group of islands in the English Channel. The islands are British Crown dependencies, but they lie only about 10 to 30 miles (16 to 48 kilometers) off the French coast. The four main islands are Jersey, Guernsey, Alderney, and Sark. The group also includes several smaller islands and a number of tiny, rocky isles.

The Channel Islands have a total land area of 75 square miles (195 square kilometers) and a population of about 130,000. English is the official language of all the islands except Jersey. French serves as Jersey's official language. Tourism is the islands' leading industry. The mild climate and fertile soil help make farming important as well. Farmers on the islands grow fruit, vegetables, and flowers for export. Jersey, Guernsey, and Alderney have long been famous for their fine breeds of dairy cattle. Banking and other financial services are also major economic activities in the Channel Islands.

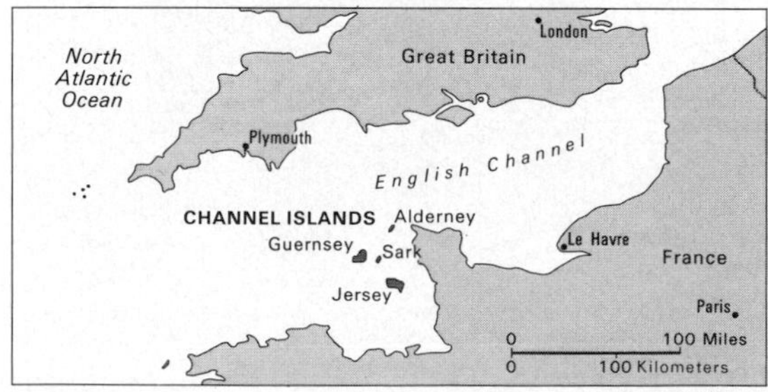

WORLD BOOK map

The Channel Islands Lie in the English Channel.

England gained control of the Channel Islands during the 1000's, and the islands have remained British territory ever since. However, they have been largely self-governing since the 1200's. The islanders pay allegiance to the British monarch. But British laws do not apply to the Channel Islands unless the islands are specifically named in them. H. R. JONES

See also GUERNSEY; JERSEY; SARK.

CHANNEL ISLANDS NATIONAL PARK is located off the coast of Southern California, west and southwest of Los Angeles. It consists of Anacapa, San Miguel, Santa Barbara, Santa Cruz, and Santa Rosa islands. The islands feature sea lions, nesting sea birds, and animal fossils. Anacapa and Santa Barbara islands were established as a national monument in 1938. The five islands became a national park in 1980. For the area of the park, see NATIONAL PARK SYSTEM (table: National Parks).

CHANNING, WILLIAM ELLERY (1780-1842), an American clergyman, was a leader of the Unitarian Church, which emphasizes the Oneness of God rather than the Trinity. In a sermon in Baltimore in 1819, he set forth the theology of Unitarianism. In 1825, he founded the American Unitarian Association and became its first president. He worked for world peace, and opposed human slavery. He also influenced such American writers as Ralph Waldo Emerson, Henry Wadsworth Longfellow, and James Russell Lowell. Channing served as pastor of the Federal Street Church in Boston from 1803 until his death. He was born in Newport, R.I. EARLE E. CAIRNS

See also UNITARIANS (History).

CHANTEY, *SHAN tee* or *CHAN tee*, is the name for the songs sailors sang at work in the days of sailing ships. It is also spelled *chanty* or *shanty.* A favorite chantey was *Blow the Man Down.* The songs disappeared from common usage when steamships replaced sailing vessels.

CHANUKAH. See HANUKKAH.

CHANUTE, *shuh NOOT,* **OCTAVE,** *ahk TAYV* (1832-1910), an American civil engineer, became famous as a scientific student of gliding. He began studying aerodynamics during his late 30's, but he did not build and fly a glider until after he was 60. He built multiwing gliders and then a biplane glider which shifted the wings for control. His structural-design experience helped him to create the lightest, strongest airframes of his day. Chanute was born in Paris, France. ROBERT B. HOTZ

CHAO TZU-YANG. See ZHAO ZIYANG.

CHAOS. See MYTHOLOGY (The Creation Myth).

CHAPARRAL, *CHAP uh RAL,* is a thick growth of brush and small trees that occurs mostly in southern California. It also grows in other Western states and in Mexico.

In California, chaparral includes such plants as chamise, manzanita, scrub oak, and wild lilac. Most chaparral plants have small, hard leaves that do not fall off in winter. Few of the plants are more than 10 feet (3 meters) tall. But in some places, their strong, crooked branches grow so densely that people cannot walk through them. Many cowhands wear leather *chaps* to protect their trousers and legs from chaparral and similar plants. Many kinds of animals, including deer, foxes, quail, and rabbits, live in chaparral.

Vegetation similar to chaparral thrives in areas that have hot, dry summers and mild, moist winters. Such areas occur around the Mediterranean Sea and in Australia, Chile, and South Africa, as well as in North America. In the Mediterranean area, the plants are called *maquis*. RAYMOND F. DASMANN

CHAPARRAL COCK. See ROADRUNNER.

CHAPATTY. See BREAD (Kinds of Bread; picture); PAKISTAN (Food).

CHAPBOOK is a pamphlet, originally sold by *chapmen* (peddlers) from the 1500's through the 1700's. The contents ranged from almanacs to sensational stories. Many also contained songs, ballads, and children's stories. Chapbooks today are mainly religious tracts. See also STORYTELLING (The Middle Ages).

CHAPLAIN is a minister, a rabbi, or a priest attached to a unit in the armed forces. The title of chaplain also is given to the religious officer of a club, an institution, or a prison. The word *chaplain* has an interesting history. Saint Martin of Tours was the patron saint of the French kings in the Middle Ages. The French carried his cloak into battle as a banner. The cloak, called a *cappella*, was kept by men called *cappellani*, or chaplains, who also tended the kings' religious needs. They worshiped in a *chapel*.

Chaplains in the United States armed forces are commissioned officers. But they are called *chaplain*, or the title they hold in civilian life, such as *father*, regardless of their rank. The armed forces choose enough chaplains to represent the various religious denominations fairly. In the Army and Air Force, chaplains may hold any rank from first lieutenant to colonel. The chief of chaplains is a major general. In the Navy, chaplains hold rank from lieutenant junior grade to captain. The chief is a rear admiral. CHARLES B. MACDONALD

CHAPLIN, CHARLIE (1889-1977), became one of the most famous stars in motion-picture history. During the era of silent comedies, he was often called "the funniest man in the world." Chaplin was also one of the most versatile men in movie history. He wrote and directed nearly all his films, and he composed the music scores for all his sound pictures.

Chaplin's stardom began in 1914, when he first appeared as "the Tramp" or "the Little Fellow." Looking undersized and undernourished, Chaplin wore a battered derby hat, a coat too small for him, and pants much too large. He walked in a shuffling manner that suggested he had never worn a pair of shoes his own size. But this figure of poverty always wore gloves and carried a bamboo cane that seemed to reflect a spirit that bounces back from the most crushing defeats. The last shot in many of Chaplin's early silent films shows him walking down a road into the distance. The Tramp was homeless and penniless once more, but with hat tilted and cane flourishing, he again was ready for whatever mischief lay around the corner.

In 1919, Chaplin formed the United Artists Film Corporation with actor Douglas Fairbanks, Sr., actress Mary Pickford, and director D. W. Griffith. He made fewer pictures, and those he made were longer and more serious. He continued to create laughter, but he also seemed to be commenting on why the world of respectability and authority offered so little to the human soul. His films during this time included *The Kid* (1920) and *The Gold Rush* (1925). Chaplin played the Tramp in these films and in his first two sound films, *City Lights* (1931) and *Modern Times* (1936). In *The Great Dictator* (1940), he played two roles, a humble Jewish barber and a tyrant based on the German dictator Adolf Hitler. Chaplin played a murderer in *Monsieur Verdoux* (1947) and an elderly music hall comedian in *Limelight* (1952).

Charles Spencer Chaplin was born into a poor London family. He toured English music halls before moving to the United States in 1910. He lived in the United States for more than 40 years but never became a citizen. In 1943, Chaplin married Oona O'Neill, the daughter of American playwright Eugene O'Neill. It was Chaplin's fourth marriage.

In the 1940's and early 1950's, Chaplin aroused great controversy. Some people criticized Chaplin's personal life as immoral and accused him of supporting Communism. In 1952, Chaplin traveled to Europe. While he was in Europe, the U.S. government announced that Chaplin could not reenter the United States unless he agreed to have his personal life and political views investigated. Chaplin refused, and he and his family settled in Switzerland.

In 1972, Chaplin returned to the United States to participate in ceremonies in his honor in New York City and Los Angeles. Chaplin received an honorary Oscar at the annual Academy Award ceremonies in April. The

Pictorial Parade; Wide World

Charlie Chaplin was famous for his comic character "the Tramp," *left.* The character appeared with child star Jackie Coogan in *The Kid* (1920), *right,* one of Chaplin's most popular films.

award praised Chaplin "for the incalculable effect he has had in making motion pictures the art form of this century." In 1975, Chaplin was knighted by Queen Elizabeth II. RICHARD GRIFFITH

See also MOTION PICTURE (The Rise of Stars; Mack Sennett and Silent Comedy).

Additional Resources

CHAPLIN, CHARLES. *My Autobiography.* Simon & Schuster, 1978. First pub. in 1964.
MANVELL, ROGER. *Chaplin.* Little, Brown, 1974.
MCDONALD, GERALD, and others. *The Films of Charlie Chaplin.* Citadel, 1971.
SOBEL, RAOUL, and FRANCIS, DAVID. *Chaplin: Genesis of a Clown.* Horizon, 1977.

CHAPMAN, GEORGE (1559?-1634?), was an English poet, playwright, and scholar. He was concerned with both the philosophical and the moral significance of poetry, as well as the importance of classical learning to humanity.

Chapman was born in Hertfordshire. His first publication was a philosophical poem, *The Shadow of Night* (1594). In 1598, he published his continuation of Christopher Marlowe's poem *Hero and Leander* and a translation of part of the *Iliad.* As a playwright, Chapman wrote both comedies and tragedies, including the famous tragedy *Bussy D'Ambois* (1604). His tragedies usually center on a great man's relation to his society. They concern ideals of order in each person and in society, and the corruption of these ideals.

In 1616, Chapman published his impressive translation of the *Iliad* and the *Odyssey.* John Keats expressed his awe at the imaginative world opened to him by these translations in his sonnet "On First Looking into Chapman's Homer." LAWRENCE J. ROSS

CHAPMAN, JOHN. See APPLESEED, JOHNNY.

CHAPS. See CHAPARRAL; COWBOY.

CHAPULTEPEC, BATTLE OF. See MEXICAN WAR (Principal Battles).

CHAR, or CHARR. See TROUT.

CHARCOAL is a black, brittle substance that has many uses. For example, charcoal is used in *pigments* (coloring matter); in filters to remove unwanted colors, flavors, and odors; as a fuel; and as a drawing instrument.

Charcoal consists mainly of *amorphous carbon* and ash. Amorphous carbon is carbon made of tiny, irregularly arranged particles of *graphite* (a form of pure carbon). Charcoal also contains small amounts of impurities, such as sulfur and hydrogen compounds. Manufacturers produce charcoal by heating carbon-rich plant or animal materials, such as wood or bones, in ovens that contain little or no air. During the heating process, most of the hydrogen, nitrogen, and oxygen in the raw materials escape. The end product is a black, *porous* (full of tiny holes) material, which is charcoal.

Types of Charcoal. The two most common types of charcoal are *wood charcoal,* which is made from wood, and *bone charcoal* (also called *animal charcoal* or *boneblack*), which is made from animal remains, chiefly bones. Wood charcoal consists mainly of carbon. It has some ash and impurities. Bone charcoal consists mainly of ash. It has some carbon and impurities.

Activated charcoal is charcoal from which most of the impurities have been removed. Manufacturers make it by treating ordinary charcoal with steam and air heated to above 600° F. (316° C).

Uses of Charcoal. Wood charcoal is the most widely used kind of charcoal. Small chunks of wood charcoal burn well and are an excellent fuel. Many people burn wood charcoal *briquettes* (small, molded pieces) in outdoor barbecues. Artists draw with small sticks of wood charcoal (see DRAWING [picture: A Charcoal Drawing]). In powdered form, wood charcoal is used in filters and as an ingredient in gunpowder.

Manufacturers use bone charcoal in powdered form to make pigments for dyeing leathers and coloring inks and paints. Powdered forms of wood, bone, and activated charcoal are used to *adsorb* (hold on their internal surfaces) unwanted colors, flavors, and odors from gases and liquids. Activated charcoal is the best adsorbent, because its spaces give it a large internal surface area. FRANK C. ANDREWS

CHARD. See SWISS CHARD.

CHARDIN, *shahr DAN,* **JEAN BAPTISTE SIMÉON** (1699-1779), is now regarded as one of the great French painters of the 1700's. Born in Paris, he lived there all his life, content to paint the common scenes and objects of daily life. *The Cardplayer* (1737) and *Grace Before Meat* (1740) are excellent examples of his early style.

Like the Dutch masters of the 1600's, Chardin deals with themes that must attract interest chiefly through the quality of the paintings. He lifts simple people and objects into a painted world of quiet perfection with a sure sense of design, color, and texture. Even the great critic Denis Diderot, who thought that art should deal only with "noble" themes, admired Chardin for his ability to make common things universal through the magic of style. Chardin's intimate subjects show the growing influence of middle-class taste on painting during his time.

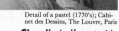

Detail of a pastel (1770's); Cabinet des Dessins, The Louvre, Paris

Jean Chardin (self-portrait)

Chardin's colors are generally low in key so that the effect is subdued rather than brilliant. He applied the paint in a mixture of glazes and thick pigment that suggests the textures of his subjects with amazing accuracy. His paintings are carefully composed, and each form or part has a balanced and proportioned place in the final effect. JOSEPH C. SLOANE

CHARDONNET, *SHAR duh NAY,* **HILAIRE** (1839-1924), was a French chemist and physiologist. In 1884, he patented a synthetic nitrocellulose fiber made from cotton. This fiber became known as rayon, and Chardonnet later manufactured it (see RAYON). His studies of silkworms and of the structure of natural silk fibers helped him develop synthetic fibers. Chardonnet was born in Besançon, France. He studied under Louis Pasteur when Pasteur was carrying on research work on silk and silkworms. PAUL R. FREY

CHARGE ACCOUNT. See CREDIT (Types of Credit).

CHARIOT, a two-wheeled, horse-drawn cart used in ancient times by warriors and kings, is the ancestor of all modern wheeled vehicles. The bed of a chariot was a platform only large enough for one or two passengers to stand on. The back of the chariot was usually open.

Some war chariots had scythelike blades on the axles. Chariots were drawn by two to four horses. In battle, drivers stood up, with the reins tied around their waists, leaving their hands free to use spears or bow and arrows against their enemies.

The Egyptians, Assyrians, Greeks, and Romans all built chariots, more for show than for speed. A description of a Roman chariot race may be found in *Ben-Hur*, by Lew Wallace. The ancient Britons used chariots for war and for transportation. FRANKLIN M. RECK

Stone bas-relief by an unknown artist from the palace of Sennacherib; The British Museum, London (Michael Holford Library)

An Assyrian Ceremonial Chariot of the 600's B.C. was used by King Ashurbanipal. Servants on foot accompanied the king.

CHARISMATIC CHRISTIANITY. See RELIGION (Religion Today; picture: Charismatic Christianity).

CHARITY, SISTERS OF. See SISTERS OF CHARITY.

CHARLEMAGNE, *SHAHR luh MAYN* (742-814), or CHARLES THE GREAT, was the most famous ruler of the Middle Ages and a key figure in European history. He conquered much of western Europe and united it under a great empire. Charlemagne revived the political and cultural life of Europe, which had collapsed after the fall of the West Roman Empire in the A.D. 400's. His activities laid the foundation of the European civilization that arose during the later Middle Ages.

More is known about Charlemagne than most medieval rulers because of a biography written by Einhard, a friend of his son Louis the Pious. This biography describes Charlemagne as more than 6 feet (2 meters) tall, with piercing eyes, fair hair, a thick neck, and a potbelly. He was strong, fond of exercise, and had an alert mind and a forceful personality. Charlemagne could read and speak Latin, the language of educated people of his time. But he never learned to write it, even though he tried.

Military Conquests. Charlemagne was a son of Pepin the Short, who became king of the Franks in 751 (see FRANK). After Pepin died in 768, his two sons, Charlemagne and Carloman, shared the Frankish kingdom. The kingdom covered what is now Belgium, France, Luxembourg, The Netherlands, and part of western Germany. Charlemagne became the sole ruler following Carloman's death in 771.

Bronze statue by an unknown artist, The Louvre, Paris

Charlemagne was one of the greatest military leaders of the Middle Ages. In 800, he became emperor of the Romans.

Charlemagne began to expand his kingdom almost immediately. He conquered Lombardy and Bavaria and added them to his realm. He took land and treasure from the Avars in eastern Europe. Charlemagne waged his longest and bitterest campaign against the Saxons, a pagan people who lived in northwestern Germany. He subdued the Saxons after about 30 years of war and forced them to accept Christianity.

Charlemagne also waged war in Spain. He was returning from an expedition there in 778 when a mountain people called the Basques ambushed and wiped out his rear guard. This incident became the subject of the famous epic poem *The Song of Roland*. In the poem, how-

Empire of Charlemagne

This map shows the growth of Charlemagne's empire. In 768, Charlemagne and his brother Carloman became joint rulers of the Frankish kingdom, shown in yellow. Charlemagne's share of the kingdom consisted of Austrasia, Neustria, and half of Aquitaine. Carloman died in 771, and Charlemagne became king of all the Franks. He enlarged his empire by conquering Saxony, Lombardy, Bavaria, and other areas, shown in light tan.

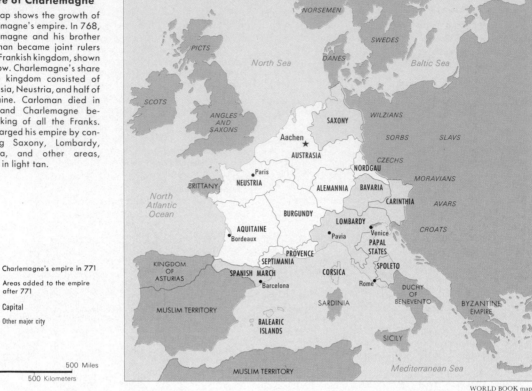

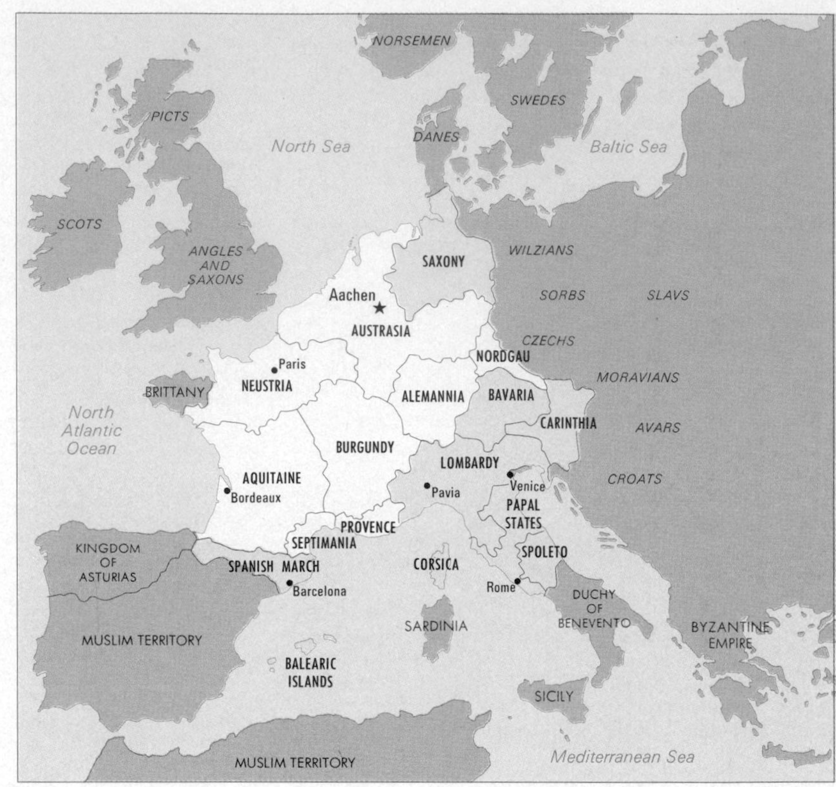

WORLD BOOK map

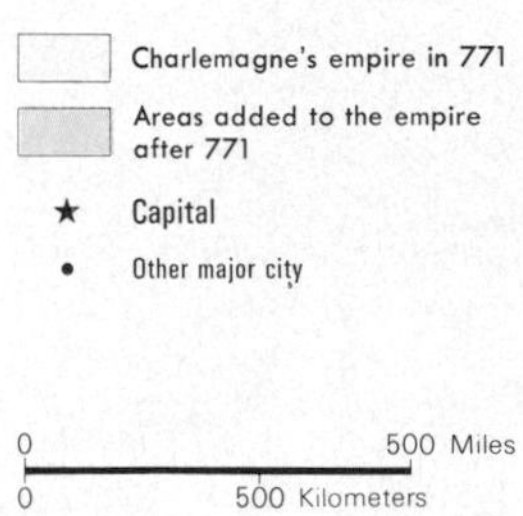

ever, the ambushers were the Moors, a Muslim people who ruled Spain (see ROLAND).

By 800, Charlemagne's realm extended from central Italy north to Denmark and from eastern Germany west to the Atlantic Ocean. Throughout his reign, Charlemagne followed a policy of friendship and cooperation with the Christian church. He protected the church and continually extended its power. In recognition of Charlemagne's vast power, and to strengthen the king's alliance with the church, Pope Leo III crowned him emperor of the Romans on Christmas Day, 800. This act led to the birth of the Holy Roman Empire, which lasted in some form until 1806 (see ROMAN CATHOLIC CHURCH [Charlemagne]; HOLY ROMAN EMPIRE).

Administration and Influence. In Charlemagne's time, Europe had hardly any towns, trade, or industry. Almost all the people made their living by farming, and they raised barely enough to feed themselves. Few people had much money, and the government and laws of the old Roman Empire had disappeared.

To improve conditions, Charlemagne introduced a number of reforms. He granted large estates to loyal nobles, who, in return, provided military and political services to the king. The nobles also maintained the roads, bridges, and fortifications on their land. This arrangement, called *feudalism*, became the basic political and military system of Europe for the next 400 years (see FEUDALISM).

Charlemagne helped increase the supply of food by introducing more efficient methods of farming. To stimulate trade, he coined silver money and encouraged the establishment of markets.

Charlemagne was devoted to justice and good government. He decreed that all courts be held regularly and that judges base their decisions only on accepted law. He divided his realm into districts and appointed efficient officers to administer them. Periodically, Charlemagne sent royal inspectors to carry his orders to the districts and to report on local conditions. In this way, Charlemagne kept control of the distant parts of his empire.

Charlemagne also improved education and culture by establishing a school at his palace in Aachen. This *palace school*, as it was called, attracted the best teachers and students in Europe. It educated clergymen, thus strengthening the church, and trained teachers for other schools throughout the empire. Scholars at the schools collected and copied ancient Roman manuscripts, which otherwise would have been lost forever. They also developed a new style of handwriting, called *Carolingian minuscule*. This style of handwriting later became the model for printing. The revival of learning under Charlemagne is sometimes called the *Carolingian Renaissance*.

By the time Charlemagne died in 814, his empire had started to fall apart. Attacks by Vikings and other invaders further weakened the empire, and in 843, Charlemagne's grandsons divided it into three parts. By the late 800's, it had ceased to exist. However, the cultural revival begun by Charlemagne had a lasting effect on European civilization. Charlemagne's empire also inspired later attempts to unite many European nations.

BRYCE LYON

See also MIDDLE AGES (The Carolingian Empire);

AACHEN; ARCHITECTURE (Carolingian Architecture); CAROLINGIAN ART; PEPIN THE SHORT; VERDUN, TREATY OF. For a *Reading and Study Guide*, see *Charlemagne* in the RESEARCH GUIDE/INDEX, Volume 22.

Additional Resources

BULLOUGH, DONALD. *The Age of Charlemagne*. Putnam, 1966.

EINHARD. *The Life of Charlemagne*. Trans. by Samuel Epes Turner. Univ. of Michigan Press, 1960. A first-hand account, written by a close associate.

HEER, FREDERICK. *Charlemagne and His World*. Macmillan, 1975. Heavily illustrated.

LAMB, HAROLD. *Charlemagne: The Legend and the Man*. Doubleday, 1954. A standard biography.

CHARLES was the name of two English rulers of the House of Stuart (see STUART, HOUSE OF). Both of these rulers believed strongly in the "divine right of kings."

Charles I (1600-1649) became king in 1625. During the next four years, he called three Parliaments and dissolved each one because the members would not submit to his demands. In 1628, he accepted the Petition of Right drawn up by the third Parliament. But he violated it by raising money unlawfully.

From 1629 to 1640, Charles ruled without Parliament. He tried to force Scotland to use English forms of worship, but in 1639 the Scots rebelled. Charles had to call Parliament to obtain the money he needed to fight the rebels. He dismissed one Parliament after three weeks, but had to summon another, the Long Parliament. It met from 1640 to 1653, and held its last session in 1660. When the king tried to seize five parliamentary leaders in 1642, civil war broke out. Charles had the support of most of the nobility, gentry, and clergy. The Puritans and the merchant class supported Parliament. Oliver Cromwell became a leading general of the parliamentary army. He won important battles at Marston Moor in 1644 and Naseby in 1645. Charles fled to Scotland, and the war ended in 1646.

Soon afterward, however, Scottish leaders turned Charles over to Parliament. Later, the army seized the king. But he escaped and made a secret agreement with the Scots. A second civil war began in January 1648 and lasted about seven months. Charles was again seized by the army. He was convicted of treason by Parliament in 1649 and beheaded.

See CROMWELL, OLIVER; DIVINE RIGHT OF KINGS; LONG PARLIAMENT; PETITION OF RIGHT; PAINTING (The 1600's and 1700's [picture]).

Charles I of England was painted in this unusual triple portrait about 1637 by the famous Flemish artist Anton van Dyck.

Charles II (1630-1685), son of Charles I, was the first of the restored Stuart line. In 1651, the Scots proclaimed him king, but Cromwell defeated his army and he fled to France. After Cromwell died in 1658, the English people became dissatisfied with the protectorate. They invited Charles to return, and he became king in 1660. His first Parliament granted him wide powers. The important events of his reign included two wars with the Dutch, the great plague, the Great Fire of London, the Rye House Plot, and the passage of the Habeas Corpus Act. See HABEAS CORPUS; RESTORATION; RYE HOUSE PLOT. W. M. SOUTHGATE

CHARLES was the name of 10 kings of France.

Charles I (823-877), called THE BALD, arranged with his two half brothers to divide the great empire of their grandfather, Charlemagne. He accomplished this by the Treaty of Verdun in 843. Charles received the western portion of Charlemagne's empire, thus becoming the first to rule France as a separate kingdom (see VERDUN, TREATY OF).

Charles II (839-888), called THE FAT, was a failure as a ruler. He could not stop the attacks of the vikings or control his own vassals. The leading nobles deposed him in 887 after two years of rule.

Charles III (879-929), called THE SIMPLE, became king in 893. He recognized the Norsemen's conquest of Normandy, but added to his territory by seizing Lorraine. The mistakes of the previous kings were too costly, however. The nobles had been allowed to gain power, and they deposed Charles in 923.

Charles IV (1294-1328), called THE FAIR, was the last of the Capetians (see CAPETIAN DYNASTY). He ruled from 1322 to 1328. Except for a territorial dispute with King Edward II of England, the reign of Charles IV was uneventful.

Charles V (1337-1380), called THE WISE, governed France as regent for several years before the death of his father, King John II, in 1364. France was torn by internal rivalry. By careful administrative reforms, Charles made the government more just and efficient. He built an army and navy, repressed the unruly nobles, and resumed the Hundred Years' War with England—all with great success. He supported art and literature, and was himself a man of culture. Charles was probably the best of the Valois kings of France.

Charles VI (1368-1422) was only a boy of 12 when his father, Charles V, died. In 1392, he had a mental breakdown, and thereafter he was not a strong ruler. Throughout his long reign, France endured the wrangling of greedy nobles. King Henry V of England quickly renewed the Hundred Years' War.

Charles VII (1403-1461) succeeded his father, Charles VI, as king in 1422. He has been described as "one of the most contemptible creatures" ever to disgrace the title of king. But Joan of Arc made his reign notable. After her death, the French continued the progress she had begun. They rejected English claims to the French throne and French territory, made useful administrative and military reforms, and ended the long war. See HUNDRED YEARS' WAR; JOAN OF ARC, SAINT.

Charles VIII (1470-1498) was only 13 when he succeeded his father, Louis XI, as king in 1483. Louis had made the French monarchy one of the dominant forces of Europe. Charles added Brittany to France. Then he expanded into Italy, where he had a claim to the kingdom of Naples. Though soon forced to flee, he exposed the weakness and division of Italy.

Charles IX (1550-1574) came to the throne in 1560 upon the death of his brother, Francis II. His clever and scheming mother, Catherine de Médicis, directed the kingdom throughout most of his reign. She conspired with Roman Catholic leaders to assassinate the leading Protestants, who favored war with Spain. The result was the Massacre of Saint Bartholomew's Day in 1572. Charles died soon after and religious strife continued. See CATHERINE DE MÉDICIS; SAINT BARTHOLOMEW'S DAY, MASSACRE OF.

Charles X (1757-1836), a younger brother of Louis XVI and Louis XVIII, became king in 1824 at the age of 66. He was head of the conservative nobility who had fled France during the French Revolution. He at once compensated members of the old aristocracy for property they had lost during the Revolution. His unrealistic attempt to turn the clock back failed. In 1830, the republican elements in Paris staged a popular revolt and Charles fled. The older Bourbon royal line ended with him. The moderates selected Louis Philippe of the younger Bourbon line to succeed him. WILLIAM C. BARK

CHARLES was the name of seven rulers of the Holy Roman Empire (see HOLY ROMAN EMPIRE).

Three kings of France—Charlemagne, Charles I, and Charles II—are traditionally listed as rulers of the Holy Roman Empire, even though that name was not used until after their time. As emperors, they are titled Charles I, Charles II, and Charles III. See CHARLEMAGNE; CHARLES (I and II) of France.

Charles IV (1316-1378), or Charles of Luxembourg, became king of Germany and Bohemia in 1346. After 1347, he also ruled as Holy Roman emperor. He issued the Golden Bull of 1356 which regulated imperial elections. He was born in Prague.

Charles V (1500-1558) ruled over more countries than any other European monarch. He was the grandson of Ferdinand and Isabella of Spain and also of Emperor Maximilian I and Mary of Burgundy. Born in Ghent, Belgium, he inherited The Netherlands and Burgundian lands in 1506. He became King Charles I of Spain in 1516, and Holy Roman emperor in 1519.

Charles fought Francis I of France over their rival claims in Italy. He also fought the Turks who threatened central Europe. He tried unsuccessfully to put down the Protestants. See PHILIP (II) of Spain.

Charles VI (1685-1740), emperor after 1711, was born in Vienna, Austria. European rulers agreed to let his oldest daughter inherit the Habsburg possessions if he had no male heirs. But they broke their pledge, and did not allow the daughter, Maria Theresa, to inherit the possessions when Charles died.

Charles VII (1697-1745) was elected Holy Roman emperor in 1742 by European rulers. His previous title had been Charles Albert, elector of Bavaria. He was the first Holy Roman emperor in 300 years who was not a member of the Habsburg family. ROBERT G. L. WAITE

See also AUGSBURG CONFESSION; HABSBURG, HOUSE OF; MARIA THERESA; PRAGMATIC SANCTION; SUCCESSION WARS.

CHARLES was the name of several Swedish kings.

Charles IX (1550-1611), the third son of King Gustavus I, became king in 1604. He restored Lutheranism as Sweden's state religion. His wars with Poland, Russia, and Denmark gained nothing for Sweden.

Charles X (1622-1660), GUSTAVUS, became king in 1654 after his cousin, Queen Christina, abdicated. He fought wars with Poland and Denmark. He forced the Danes to give up their southern provinces in Sweden, and opened a ship route to the Baltic Sea. His reign marked the height of Swedish power in Europe.

Charles XI (1655-1697) succeeded his father, Charles X, in 1660, when he was only 4. At 16, he led Swedish armies against Denmark and Brandenburg and saved Sweden from defeat. During the long peace until his death in 1697, he reduced the power of the nobles, achieved order in state finances and taxation, and aided the improvement of Swedish trade.

Charles XII (1682-1718) became king in 1697, at the age of 15. He was formally crowned when he came of age in 1700. That year, he led Swedish armies against Denmark, Poland, and Russia and defeated them all. After a long war in Poland and Saxony, Charles invaded Russia. Peter the Great defeated him in 1709 at Poltava. Charles fled to Turkey, and tried to gain Turkish aid for an attack on Russia. His plan failed. He returned to Sweden in 1714, and renewed the war with Denmark and Russia. He was killed in a battle in Norway.

Charles XIV (1763-1844) founded the present royal line of Sweden. He reigned from 1818 to 1844 (see BERNADOTTE, JEAN BAPTISTE JULES). RAYMOND E. LINDGREN

See also CARL XVI GUSTAV.

CHARLES, PRINCE (1948-), CHARLES PHILIP ARTHUR GEORGE, is the heir apparent to the British throne. When Charles was 3 years old, his mother,

Snowden, Camera Press Ltd.

Prince Charles and his wife, Diana, Princess of Wales, had their first child in 1982. The boy, named William Arthur Philip Louis, is second to Charles in line to the British throne.

Elizabeth, became queen after his grandfather, King George VI, died. His full name and titles are His Royal Highness Prince Charles Philip Arthur George, Prince of Wales and Earl of Chester, Duke of Cornwall, Duke of Rothesay, Earl of Carrick, Baron of Renfrew, Lord of the Isles, and Great Steward of Scotland.

Prince Charles was born on Nov. 14, 1948. He became the first heir to the British throne to receive most of his education away from the royal palace. His father, Prince Philip, wanted to break tradition and expose the boy to life outside the palace. From the age of 8, Charles went to private schools, rather than having tutors at home. In 1956, he attended day classes at Hill House in London. From 1957 to 1962, he went to Cheam, a preparatory school near London. In 1962, Charles enrolled at Gordonstoun, a strict school in the Scottish highlands. He spent six months in 1966 at Timbertop, an Australian school that stresses rugged outdoor activities. He then returned to Gordonstoun, where he became head boy in January 1967. As head boy, Charles supervised student activities and chores and helped settle student disputes.

In 1967, Charles entered Trinity College at Cambridge University and specialized in history. He acted in the drama society, took part in polo and cricket, played the cello, and flew his own airplane.

Queen Elizabeth named Charles Prince of Wales in 1958, when he was 9 years old. In 1969, she presented him to the people of Wales in a colorful and ancient ceremony at Caernarfon Castle in Wales. In 1970, Charles became a member of the House of Lords. He entered the Royal Air Force College in March 1971, and graduated from its advanced flying course in August. Later in 1971, he joined the Royal Navy. He served in the navy until the end of 1976. On July 29, 1981, Charles married Lady Diana Spencer, a British aristocrat. The couple had two sons—William Arthur Philip Louis, born in 1982; and Henry Charles Albert David, born in 1984. NORMAN RUNNION

CHARLES I (1887-1922), ARCHDUKE KARL FRANZ JOSEPH, was the last emperor of Austria and king of Hungary. He succeeded his uncle, Francis Joseph, in 1916. He became heir to the throne through the assassination of the Archduke Francis Ferdinand in 1914. Charles tried to make peace with the Allies in World War I. After his country was defeated, he went into exile in Switzerland. He later made two unsuccessful attempts to regain the throne of Hungary. He was finally interned with his family in the Madeira Islands, where he died. GABRIEL A. ALMOND

CHARLES MARTEL, *mahr TEHL* (688-741), ruled the Merovingian Franks from A.D. 719 to 741. He used only the title of Mayor of the Palace, but he actually had the power of a king. In 732, Charles defeated the invading Muslims in the Battle of Poitiers, also called the Battle of Tours. The fighting began near Tours and ended near Poitiers. For repeatedly attacking the Muslims, Charles later received the title of Martel, meaning *the Hammer*. He raised an army by giving his troops land he had seized from the church. Charles supported Saint Boniface in his conversion of *pagans* (non-Christians) and his reform of the Frankish church. See also BONIFACE, SAINT; FRANK; MEROVINGIAN. WILLIAM C. BARK

CHARLES THE BALD. See CHARLES (I) of France.

CHARLES THE GREAT. See CHARLEMAGNE.

CHARLES'S LAW. See GAS (matter).

CHARLESTON, S.C. (pop. 69,510; met. area pop. 430,462), is an important Atlantic seaport and South Carolina's second largest city. Only Columbia has more people. Charleston lies on a peninsula between the Ashley and Cooper rivers, about midway on the coastline. For location, see SOUTH CAROLINA (political map).

Charleston was founded in 1670 and was named Charles Town for King Charles II of England. The city's people changed the name in 1783. Many houses and other buildings in Charleston date from the 1700's and 1800's. The Civil War began on the Charleston waterfront in 1861 when Confederate soldiers attacked Union troops at Fort Sumter in the city's harbor.

The City. Charleston is South Carolina's chief port. Its harbor handles about $8\frac{1}{2}$ million short tons (7.7 million metric tons) yearly. Charleston's chief products include clothing, diesel engines, gas storage tanks, paper, and polyester fibers. Many of the city's people work at the Charleston Naval and Air Force bases.

Charleston's economy depends heavily on tourism. Old Charles Town, an area on the waterfront, has many of the city's oldest buildings. Many tourists go there in March and April for the annual Festival of Old Houses. The Battery, an area of elegant mansions, is also in Old Charles Town. The Charleston Museum, founded in 1773, is the oldest museum in the United States. Large crowds attend Spoleto U.S.A., an annual festival of art, drama, and music held in May. Charleston is known for its gardens. The Middleton Place Gardens, established in 1741, are the nation's oldest landscaped gardens (see SOUTH CAROLINA [picture]).

The College of Charleston, founded in 1770, is one

Authenticated News Int.

Historic Charleston Homes date back to colonial and pre-Civil War days. Visitors to the city can tour buildings and sites that date from the 1700's and 1800's.

of the nation's oldest colleges. Charleston is also the home of the Baptist College at Charleston, the Medical University of South Carolina, and the Citadel Military College of South Carolina.

Government and History. Charleston has a mayor-council form of government. The city is the county seat of Charleston County.

Kiawah, Sewee, and Wando Indians lived in what is now the Charleston area until the mid-1700's. Most of the first white settlers came from England. Charleston was the capital of South Carolina from 1670 to 1790, when Columbia became the capital.

Charleston was the wealthiest city in the South during the early colonial period. Its wealth came chiefly from exports of rice and indigo. Thousands of slaves worked on vast plantations that grew these products. A deerskin trade with Indians extended to the Ohio and Mississippi rivers and contributed to Charleston's wealth. In 1831, the nation's first regularly scheduled train service began in Charleston. The train's locomotive was named *Best Friend of Charleston.*

During the Civil War, the city suffered great economic loss. After the war ended in 1865, the construction of fertilizer plants and a naval yard helped Charleston recover. Port expansion financed by the federal government encouraged much shipping and many other industries to come to the Charleston area. By the late 1930's, the city's factories were manufacturing asbestos, oil, paint, rubber, and other products. Charleston also had a flourishing trade in fruit, lumber, seafood, and vegetables.

During the 1970's, Charleston's port was expanded, and parts of the downtown area were modernized. The city opened a new shopping mall in 1981. A convention center was among other projects scheduled for completion in the 1980's. JOHN GIRARDEAU LELAND

For the monthly weather in Charleston, see SOUTH CAROLINA (Climate). See also SOUTH CAROLINA (pictures); COLONIAL LIFE IN AMERICA (picture: Charles Town); FORT MOULTRIE; FORT SUMTER.

CHARLESTON, W. Va. (pop. 63,968; met. area 269,595), is the capital and leading industrial, trade, and transportation center of the state. The city's chemical industry ranks as one of the largest in the South. Charleston lies at the meeting place of the Elk and Kanawha rivers (see WEST VIRGINIA [political map]).

In 1787, George Clendenin, a Virginia legislator, bought the land where Charleston now stands. The next year, he and a group of soldiers built Fort Lee there to protect the Kanawha Valley, which was then a frontier area. This valley runs between the Appalachian Mountains and the Ohio River. Clendenin believed it would become a highway to the West.

Settlers soon built cabins near Fort Lee. In 1794, the settlement officially became a town, which Clendenin named Charles Town for his father, Charles Clendenin. The city changed its name to Charleston in 1818.

Description. Charleston, the county seat of Kanawha County, covers 29 square miles (75 square kilometers). The Charleston metropolitan area occupies 1,259 square miles (3,261 square kilometers) and consists of Kanawha and Putnam counties. The State Capitol and the central business district of Charleston are about 2 miles (3 kilometers) apart on the north bank of the Kanawha River. For pictures of the Capitol and other Charleston scenes, see WEST VIRGINIA.

Charleston is the home of the University of Charleston. West Virginia College of Graduate Studies and West Virginia State College are in nearby Institute. The city has a ballet company, a symphony orchestra, and opera and theater groups. A cultural center at an estate called *Sunrise* includes an art gallery, a museum, and a planetarium. The West Virginia Science and Cultural Center in Charleston features the state museum and state library, as well as a theater and art museum.

Economy. About 20 per cent of Charleston's labor force works in retail and wholesale trade. Government and manufacturing each employ about 15 per cent of the city's workers. Charleston has about 180 manufacturing plants. The chemical industry provides about two-thirds of the city's industrial income. It relies heavily on coal, natural gas, and petroleum from the nearby area. Other products of Charleston include beverages, glass, metal products, and processed food.

Twelve barge lines and three railroad freight lines serve the city. Charleston also has passenger train service. Kanawha Airport lies just outside the city.

Government and History. Charleston has a mayor-council form of government. The voters elect a mayor and 24 council members, all to four-year terms. Charleston's main source of income is a city sales tax.

Shawnee Indians and other tribes hunted in the Kanawha Valley when white settlers first arrived there. Charleston grew up around Fort Lee, which was built in 1788. During the 1790's, the famous frontiersman Daniel Boone lived in what is now Charleston and served the area briefly as a state legislator. Charleston had about 50 people in 1794, when it became a town.

A road that crossed the Appalachian Mountains was extended to Charleston in the early 1800's. The town became a transportation center where travelers transferred between wagons and riverboats. Its main industry was the mining and processing of salt. Charleston had 1,050 people in 1850.

The West Virginia region formed part of Virginia until 1863, when West Virginia became a separate state. Charleston served as the state capital from 1870 to 1875 and became the permanent capital in 1885.

Coal mining in the Charleston area expanded greatly after 1873, when rail lines reached the city. Trains provided a practical way to ship the coal to Eastern cities. Charleston had a population of 6,742 by 1890.

During the early 1900's, Charleston's coal, salt, and other natural resources attracted several chemical companies to the area. These factories created many new jobs, and the city's population grew to 60,408 by 1930. But in the 1960's and 1970's, several local industries declined and many families left. Charleston's population decreased from 85,796 to 63,968 during that period.

In the early 1980's, much urban renewal took place in the central business district of Charleston. The Government Square and Project Triangle projects included apartment buildings and office buildings. The Charleston Town Center resulted in the renovation of the civic center, and the construction of a coliseum, a shopping mall, hotels, and office buildings. HARRY G. HOFFMANN

For the monthly weather in Charleston, see WEST VIRGINIA (Climate).

CHARLOTTE, N.C. (pop. 314,447; met. area 971,391), is the largest city in the Carolinas. It ranks as a major financial, transportation, and wholesaling center. Charlotte lies in the Piedmont region, 15 miles (24 kilometers) north of the South Carolina border. For location, see North Carolina (political map).

About 1748, several Scotch-Irish families from Pennsylvania settled in what is now the Charlotte area. They established a farming community on the site because of its fertile soil. Their community became the area's first permanent white settlement. The settlers named Charlotte for Queen Charlotte of Mecklenburg-Strelitz, the wife of King George III of Great Britain.

Description. Charlotte, the county seat of Mecklenburg County, covers about 143 square miles (370 square kilometers). The city is the home of Central Piedmont Community College, Johnson C. Smith University, Queens College, and the University of North Carolina at Charlotte.

Charlotte has an entertainment complex that consists of the Charlotte Coliseum and Ovens Auditorium. The Civic Center opened in 1973. The Mint Museum of Art is a reconstruction of a branch of the U.S. Mint that operated in Charlotte from 1837 to 1861.

Economy. The Piedmont region leads the United States in textile production (see Piedmont Region). Charlotte provides banking, insurance, and wholesaling services for the region's industries. The city's chief manufactured products include, in order of importance, machinery, food products, textiles, and printed materials. The textile industry has helped Charlotte become one of the nation's chief trucking centers. Five airlines and three railroads serve the city.

Government and History. Charlotte has a council-manager form of government. The voters elect a mayor and the seven members of the city council to two-year terms. The mayor votes only to break tie votes of the council. The council appoints a city manager.

Catawba Indians lived in what is now the Charlotte area before white settlers first arrived there in the 1740's. The city was incorporated in 1768. Some people believe that on May 20, 1775, a group of Mecklenburg County patriots signed a resolution called the Mecklenburg Declaration of Independence. This resolution declared Mecklenburg citizens free of British rule. See Mecklenburg Declaration of Independence.

Charlotte became a center of gold mining after the discovery of gold in nearby Cabarrus County in 1799. More than 50 gold mines operated in the Piedmont during the early 1800's. The region led the nation in gold production until the California gold rush of 1849.

In 1900, Charlotte had a population of 18,091. Industry developed rapidly during the early 1900's, and by 1930 the city had 82,675 people. Industry expanded again after the end of World War II in 1945, and the population reached 201,564 by 1960. The city's growth had slowed by the early 1970's. But by the early 1980's, the population had increased by about a third.

In 1970, the Charlotte-Mecklenburg school system began one of the nation's first large-scale programs to integrate schools by busing students. A federal court ordered the countywide system to improve the racial balance in the schools by busing students to schools outside their neighborhood. The Supreme Court of the United States upheld the program in 1971.

In 1961, Charlotte began the construction of Governmental Plaza, an urban renewal complex that replaced the city's worst slum. The plaza includes county and city government buildings. Work on the plaza continued into the 1980's. In 1973, construction started on an expansion of Douglass Municipal Airport. The project was completed in 1982.

In 1983, voters elected Harvey Gantt mayor. Gantt became the first black mayor of the city. James K. Batten

For the monthly weather in Charlotte, see North Carolina (Climate).

CHARLOTTE AMALIE, *uh MAHL yuh* (pop. 11,756), capital of the American Virgin Islands, is a harbor city on the Caribbean Sea. It lies on the central coast of the south side of St. Thomas Island. The island is about 40 miles (64 kilometers) east of Puerto Rico. The city's harbor is partly closed by Hassel Island. Charlotte Amalie surrounds the bay and extends back to the main ridge of the island. It is the chief trading center for the islands. The city also is a famous tourist resort. Charlotte Amalie was named for the princess consort of King Christian V of Denmark. The Danes controlled St. Thomas Island until 1917. See also Virgin Islands (map; picture: Government House). J. Antonio Jarvis

CHARLOTTESVILLE, Va. (pop. 39,916; met. area pop. 113,568), is in the Blue Ridge Mountains foothills. On the top of one of these hills, overlooking the city, is Monticello, Thomas Jefferson's home. Charlottesville is the home of the University of Virginia, founded by Jefferson in 1819. Near Monticello is Ash Lawn, the home of James Monroe. The city is a marketing center for the surrounding area. Charlottesville has a council-manager form of government. It is the seat of Albemarle County. See also Monticello. Francis B. Simkins

CHARLOTTETOWN (pop. 15,282), the capital of Prince Edward Island, is one of Canada's most historic cities. In 1864, representatives from several British North American colonies met in Charlottetown and discussed plans to unite. This meeting led to the formation in 1867 of the Dominion of Canada.

Charlottetown covers 2.7 square miles (7 square kilometers) on the southern coast of Prince Edward Island. For location, see Prince Edward Island (political map). Micmac Indians lived in the area before European colonists first arrived in the early 1700's. The British founded Charlottetown in 1763 and made it the capital of the island. They named the city after Queen Charlotte of England.

Charlottetown has several dairies, food-processing plants, and other small manufacturing plants. About 17 per cent of the city's work force is employed by government agencies.

Charlottetown attracts thousands of tourists during the summer. The Confederation Centre of the Arts in the city includes an art gallery, a library, a museum, and a theater. The Confederation Chamber in Province House, where the historic 1864 meeting took place, is known as the *Birthplace of Canada.* Charlottetown is the home of the University of Prince Edward Island and several other educational institutions. The city has a mayor-council form of government. W. J. Hancox

See also Prince Edward Island (pictures).

CHARMS. See Amulet; Evil Eye; Magic.

CHAROLAIS. See CATTLE (Beef Cattle).

CHARON, *KAIR uhn,* was the old boatman of the Lower World in Greek mythology. He was the son of Erebus (Darkness) and Nyx (Night). Charon ferried the souls of the dead across the River Styx or the Acheron River to Hades. He always demanded a bronze coin called an *obolus* in payment for the trip. In a proper Greek burial, one of these coins was placed under the corpse's tongue. Charon took the money, and then ferried the soul across the river. He forced souls without coins to wander for many years on the shore of the river before he would carry them across.

Aeneas was one of the few living mortals to visit Hades, according to Virgil's *Aeneid.* Aeneas wanted to visit his father Anchises, but Charon refused to take him. Then a sibyl helped Aeneas obtain a magic golden branch. When Charon saw the branch, he agreed to take Aeneas across the river. NATHAN DANE II

See also HADES; STYX; ORPHEUS.

CHART is a diagram, drawing, graph, list, map, or table designed to make information easy to understand. Charts are used to provide data about business, geography, and the weather. They also serve as aids in education.

See also GRAPH; MAP; and the many kinds of charts with WORLD BOOK articles, such as with AIRPLANE; POLITICAL PARTY; WEATHER.

CHARTER, sometimes called *articles of incorporation,* is a written document granted by a government. A charter entitles the holder to certain rights or powers, such as the right to engage in business. It may be granted to a person, corporation, or local government. State charters set up the limits within which banks, corporations, and associations must conduct business. A state or province can charter a village or city government. The charter sets forth the powers and duties of these governments. See also ATLANTIC CHARTER; COLONIAL LIFE IN AMERICA (Land Ownership); CORPORATION; MAGNA CARTA; UNITED NATIONS (The Charter). JOHN ALAN APPLEMAN

CHARTER OAK was a huge tree in Hartford, Conn. It became famous because of a tradition that Connecticut's original charter was hidden there to keep the English governor from seizing it.

When James II became King of England in 1685, the New England colonies were in danger of losing their charters and freedom. The king appointed Sir Edmund Andros governor of the Dominion of New England. Andros came to Hartford in 1687 to seize the Connecticut charter and take control of the colony. He appeared at a legislative meeting and demanded the charter, but met with opposition. Debate lasted into the night, and candles were lighted. Suddenly, the candles went out. When they were relighted, the charter was gone. According to tradition, Joseph Wadsworth took the charter and hid it in a nearby oak tree.

Andros' rule ended in 1689 after James II fell from power. The charter remained Connecticut's supreme law until a new constitution was adopted in 1818. A windstorm destroyed the Charter Oak in 1856. A granite shaft marks the spot where it stood. ALBERT E. VAN DUSEN

See also ANDROS, SIR EDMUND.

CHARTERHOUSE is one of the leading public schools of England. The school was founded for poor boys in 1611 by Sir Thomas Sutton, a wealthy merchant. Later, fee-paying pupils were admitted. Until 1868, the foundation included a hospital for old men, which Thackeray describes in his novel *The Newcomes.* In 1872, the Charterhouse school was moved from London to its present location near Godalming, Surrey. R. W. MORRIS

CHARTISM, *CHAR tihz uhm,* was a political movement of the British working class during the early 1800's. It tried to win voting rights for all men and to reform the House of Commons. Among the movement's chief leaders was Feargus O'Connor. The movement's Charter of 1838 set forth six points: (1) universal manhood suffrage, (2) a secret ballot, (3) no property qualifications for members of parliament, (4) salaries for members of parliament, (5) annual elections, and (6) equal electoral districts. The movement did not achieve these points, but all except the fifth were later adopted. See also LABOUR PARTY. JAMES L. GODFREY

CHARTRES, *SHAHR truh* or *shahrt* (pop. 38,928), is a city in north-central France that is famous for its cathedral, which is a masterpiece of Gothic architecture. Chartres is the capital of the Eure-et-Loir *department* (administrative district). For location, see FRANCE (political map).

Chartres Cathedral, officially called the Cathedral of Notre Dame, stands near the center of Chartres. It features beautiful stained-glass windows and hundreds of sculptured religious figures. The cathedral has two bell towers, one 378 feet (115 meters) high and the other 350 feet (107 meters).

Chartres lies on a hill that is surrounded by grainfields. The Eure River runs next to the city. Chartres serves as a market for products of the surrounding area. Its other economic activities include flour milling; leatherworking; and the manufacture of electronic equip-

Robert L. Perry

The Charter Oak Monument stands in Hartford, Conn., where the Connecticut charter was hidden from the British in 1687.

Art Resource

Chartres Cathedral stands near the center of the city of Chartres. An outstanding example of Gothic architecture, it has huge stained-glass windows and two bell towers.

ment, farm machinery, and home appliances. Chartres was founded by the Carnutes, an ancient tribe of Celts whose activities in Chartres were described by Julius Caesar about 50 B.C. The Chartres Cathedral was originally built in the mid-1100's, but most of it was destroyed by fire in 1194. Most of the cathedral was rebuilt between 1194 and 1230. MARK KESSELMAN

See also SCULPTURE (picture: West Portals of Chartres Cathedral); STAINED GLASS (Technical Improvements).

CHARTRES CATHEDRAL. See CHARTRES.

CHARYBDIS. See SCYLLA.

CHASE, SALMON PORTLAND (1808-1873), was a prominent American statesman and chief justice of the United States. He served as secretary of the treasury under President Abraham Lincoln. Chase is considered one of the greatest secretaries, because of his work during the Civil War. He maintained national credit and raised money to carry on the war. Chase laid the basis of the present national banking system. After he resigned in 1864 because of a policy dispute, Lincoln, who disliked him personally, named him chief justice in recognition of his ability. As chief justice, Chase presided capably over the impeachment trial of President Andrew Johnson.

Chase was born at Cornish, N.H. After studying law in Washington, D.C., he became a lawyer in Cincinnati, Ohio. He was a leader of the antislavery movement, and defended many runaway slaves. As a United States Senator from 1849 to 1855, he opposed the extension of slavery into the new territories. He served as governor of Ohio from 1856 to 1860. In later years, Chase wanted to become President of the United States. A founder of the Republican party, he sought its presidential nomination several times. In 1872, he tried to get the Democratic nomination. JERRE S. WILLIAMS

Brown Bros.

Salmon P. Chase

See also EMANCIPATION PROCLAMATION (picture).

CHASE, SAMUEL (1741-1811), an associate justice of the Supreme Court of the United States, was impeached in 1804 for *malfeasance* (illegal conduct) in presiding over two sedition trials. In acquitting him the following year, the U.S. Senate denied that judges might be removed on largely political grounds. Chase was born in Somerset County, Maryland. He served in the Maryland General Assembly and the Continental Congress. Chase signed the Declaration of Independence. Chase joined the Supreme Court in 1796, and served until his death. See also IMPEACHMENT (History); JEFFERSON, THOMAS (The Courts). RICHARD B. MORRIS

CHASE, WILLIAM MERRITT (1849-1916), was an American painter and art teacher. In his paintings, Chase combined flowing, spontaneous brushwork with glowing colors and dazzling contrasts to create striking visual effects. One of his favorite subjects was the elaborate interior of his studio in New York City. Chase made many paintings that included stylish women examining the room's exotic ornaments. He also painted sunny coastal landscapes of Long Island, city park scenes, and sophisticated portraits of wealthy people.

Chase was born in Nineveh, Ind., near Indianapolis. He studied at the National Academy of Design in New York City and at the Royal Academy in Munich. Chase's early paintings reflect the Munich style and feature dashing brushstrokes, dark tones, and brilliant highlights. In the late 1880's, influenced by French impressionism, he began using lighter colors. Chase taught in New York City and his own art school on Long Island. His students included the famous American painters Charles Sheeler, Edward Hopper, and Georgia O'Keeffe. SARAH BURNS

CHASE MANHATTAN BANK is one of the largest commercial banks in the United States. It operates about 290 offices in the New York City metropolitan area, and has representatives throughout the world. Chase Manhattan was formed in 1955 by a merger of The Chase National Bank and The Bank of Manhattan. The bank is a subsidiary of Chase Manhattan Corp. See also BANK (table: 10 Largest Banks).

CHAT is one of the largest birds of the wood-warbler family. Its full name is *yellow-breasted chat.* It feeds mostly on insects, and builds its nest in brier thickets. During the mating season, the male chat shows off by dangling its legs, singing, and flopping its wings in midair. He has been called the *clown among birds,* and the *buffoon of the brier patch.* The chat gets its name from its song, which is a mixture of whistles, wails, clucks, and chuckles. It spends the winter season in the tropics. See also WARBLER.

Scientific Classification. The yellow-breasted chat belongs to the wood-warbler family, Parulidae. It is genus *Icteria,* species *I. virens.* ALBERT WOLFSON

CHÂTEAU, *sha TOH,* is the French word for *castle.* Generally, château means the country seat of a feudal lord or noble landowner. In the Middle Ages, the *château fort* was a fortress, with a *donjon*, or central tower, a courtyard, defensive walls, and a water-filled *moat*, or trench. Improved living conditions led to the *château de plaisance*, or pleasure castle. BERNARD LEMANN

See also CASTLE; FRANCE (picture: Castles).

CHATEAUBRIAND, *shah toh bree AHN,* **FRANÇOIS-RENÉ DE,** *frahn SWAH ruh NAY duh* (1768-1848), was one of the most important figures in French romantic literature. His novel *Atala* (1801) describes a tragic love affair between two North American Indians. The novel is an example of the European romantic's fascination with primitive and faraway subjects. Chateaubriand's *The Spirit of Christianity* (1802) praises Christianity as a great cultural and moral force. One part of it, called *René*, is the story of a young man whose vague feeling of despair makes him a typical romantic hero. Chateaubriand's autobiography, *Memoirs from Beyond the Grave*, was published soon after his death. It is often called his best work. Chateaubriand was born in St. Malo. He held several diplomatic posts, including that of French foreign minister in 1823. IRVING PUTTER

CHÂTELET, *SHAH tuh LEH,* **MARQUISE DU** (1706-1749), was a French mathematician, physicist, and science writer. She contributed to the revival of French science by promoting the theories of the English physicist Sir Isaac Newton. She also influenced the work of Voltaire, one of France's leading authors and philosophers, and became his mistress.

Du Châtelet began her interpretations of Newton's work in 1735 with an essay on his discoveries in optics. Voltaire incorporated some of her later writings on Newton in his book *Elements of Newton's Philosophy* (1738). From 1745 to 1749, du Châtelet worked on a translation and analytical review of Newton's most important work, *Principia Mathematica*. The translation was published in 1759 after her death.

Du Châtelet was born Gabrielle-Émilie Le Tonnelier de Breteuil in Paris. As an aristocrat, she received an excellent education in literature and science. In 1724, she married Florent-Claude, marquis du Châtelet, the governor of Semur-en-Auxois. ROMUALDAS SVIEDRYS

CHATHAM, EARL OF. See PITT.

CHATTANOOGA, *CHAT uh NOO guh,* Tenn. (pop. 169,728; met. area pop. 426,540), is a chief industrial city of the South. It was a key city in the Civil War. It lies on both banks of the sharp Moccasin Bend of the Tennessee River, north of the Georgia border. For location, see TENNESSEE (political map).

Ranges of the Appalachian Plateau and the Appalachian Ridge and Valley Region surround the city. Lookout Mountain stands to the south. The Creek Indians called this mountain *Chat-to-to-noog-gee*, meaning *mountain rising to a point*. In early days these natural mountain barriers protected settlers against their enemies, but some of the steep ridges have been blasted through for the main highways that enter the city. In addition to the truck and bus lines that use these roads, Chattanooga is joined to other cities by railroads, airlines, and river shipping lines. The city serves as a port of entry into the United States (see PORT OF ENTRY).

Over 500 industries have located in Chattanooga. Factories produce chemicals, clay products, clothing, furniture, and iron and steel products. Chattanooga also makes kitchenware, machinery, paints, paper, petroleum products, and textiles. Chickamauga Dam to the east and Nickajack Dam to the west, both parts of the Tennessee Valley Authority, help harness the Tennessee River to control navigation and floods at all seasons.

About 100 schools make up the Chattanooga public school system, which serves both city and county students. The University of Tennessee at Chattanooga is located there. Chattanooga also has a civic chorus and a symphony orchestra.

Chattanooga has a commission form of government. It serves as the seat of Hamilton County.

The first inhabitants of the Chattanooga area were the Chickamauga, a branch of the Cherokee Indians. They were conquered in 1794 and moved west in 1838, but during this period John Ross, a chief, operated a trading post on the site of the city. It was called Ross' Landing. Chattanooga received its present name when it was incorporated as a town in 1839. It received its city charter in 1851.

Chattanooga had only 5,545 inhabitants when the Civil War broke out. But it had a strategic location, and metal industries soon developed to supply the Confederacy. The Battle of Chattanooga took place in November, 1863 (see CIVIL WAR [Chattanooga]). About 1,500 lived in the city at the end of the war, but it had a population of 13,000 by 1880. The most rapid growth in the city began in the 1930's after the establishment of the Tennessee Valley Authority. JEWELL PHELPS

CHATTANOOGA, BATTLE OF. See CIVIL WAR (Chattanooga; table: Major Battles of the Civil War).

CHATURANGA. See CHESS (History).

CHAUCER, *CHAW suhr,* **GEOFFREY,** *JEHF rih* (1340?-1400), was the greatest English poet of the Middle Ages. He wrote *The Canterbury Tales*, a group of stories that ranks among the masterpieces of literature.

Life. Chaucer was born in London sometime between 1340 and 1343. He lived most of his life there. He came from a prosperous middle-class family, and was trained as a civil servant and diplomat. Chaucer was controller of customs from 1374 to 1386 and clerk of the King's Works from 1389 to 1391. In the latter position, he administered the royal properties. Chaucer was appointed a justice of the peace in 1385, and was appointed to Parliament in 1386. His experiences in all these positions probably developed his fascination with people, his wide knowledge of English life, and the tone of charitable irony in his works.

Chaucer wrote for the courts of Edward III and, especially, Richard II. He was a close friend of the powerful nobleman John of Gaunt. Chaucer viewed the aristocratic fashion called "courtly love" with polite and amused skepticism. In his poetry, he often satirized the fashion's lofty ideals, elaborate etiquette, and literary style. Chaucer viewed the corruption he saw in the medieval church with less tolerance than he had for the fashion of courtly love. In *The Canterbury Tales*, he satirized church abuses in his portrayals of the friar, monk, pardoner, and summoner.

Chaucer was one of the most learned men of his age. He traveled in Flanders, France, Italy, and Spain on diplomatic missions. He was influenced first by French writers and then by Italian writers, especially Boccaccio, Dante, and Petrarch. Chaucer may have studied law. He was familiar with the Latin classics, medieval science, and theology. His prose works include a translation of Boethius' *Consolation of Philosophy* and an essay on the astrolabe, an astronomical instrument that was the forerunner of the sextant.

Poetry. Chaucer wrote in Middle English, the form of English used from about 1100 to about 1485. He was the first English poet to use *heroic verse* (rhymed couplets in iambic pentameter).

The Book of the Duchess (1369), one of Chaucer's earliest works, is a graceful elegy on the death of John of Gaunt's first wife. Chaucer modeled it on the French dream-vision form of poetry. He gradually developed his individual style in the poems *The House of Fame* (1379?), *The Parliament of Fowls* (1382?), *The Legend of Good Women* (1386?), and other shorter lyrics.

Apart from *The Canterbury Tales*, Chaucer's greatest poem is *Troilus and Criseyde* (1386-1387). Adapted from a love story by Boccaccio, this poem is both a medieval romance and a philosophical tragedy. Set in ancient Troy just before its fall, it tells of the love of Prince Troilus for Criseyde. In the poem, Chaucer explored the beauty of love, the mysterious workings of fortune, and the sad brevity of earthly joy.

The Canterbury Tales (about 1385-1400) is a collection of stories told by a group of pilgrims on a journey to the shrine of Thomas à Becket in Canterbury. One of the pilgrims represents Chaucer himself. Chaucer pictured this pilgrim as a simple fellow who takes everything at face value. This device allowed Chaucer to describe the other pilgrims objectively, while allowing the reader to see the pilgrims' real personalities. For more information, see CANTERBURY TALES. DONALD R. HOWARD

Additional Resources

BOWDEN, MURIEL. *A Reader's Guide to Geoffrey Chaucer.* Farrar, 1964.
BREWER, DEREK. *Chaucer and His World.* Dodd, 1978.
GARDNER, JOHN. *The Life and Times of Chaucer.* Knopf, 1977.
ROWLAND, BERYL, ed. *Companion to Chaucer Studies.* Oxford, 1968.

Henry E. Huntington Library and Art Gallery, San Marino, Calif.

Portrait of Chaucer appears on a page of the Ellesmere manuscript of *The Canterbury Tales,* dating from 1400 to 1410.

CHAUTAUQUA, *shuh TAW kwuh,* is a system of summer school and correspondence school education founded at Chautauqua Lake, N.Y., in 1874. The term also refers to traveling groups, called Tent Chautauquas, which had no connection with the original educational movement.

The Chautauqua Institution. Rev. John H. Vincent, a Methodist clergyman, and Lewis Miller of Akron, Ohio, first conceived the idea of setting up a summer school to give instruction to Sunday school teachers. The first assembly was held at Chautauqua in August 1874. The movement rapidly expanded to include a school of languages (1878), a summer school for public school teachers (1879), a school of theology (1881), and a series of clubs for young people interested in reading, music, fine arts, physical education, and religion. In 1883, the Chautauqua University was established.

Many of these activities have since been curtailed. The university closed in 1898. But the Chautauqua Institution continues to maintain a summer adult education program. It also makes its facilities available to other groups interested in such activities.

The Chautauqua Literary and Scientific Circle is a correspondence school that offers courses in such fields as history, literature, science, and art. Founded in 1878, it is one of the oldest U.S. correspondence schools. It influenced adult education leaders in many countries.

Tent Chautauquas were traveling groups that operated in the United States from 1903 to 1930. They moved from town to town giving lectures, concerts, and recitals in a tent. These traveling groups brought shows of mixed quality to rural areas. Their popularity decreased with the development of radio and other forms of entertainment. MERLE L. BORROWMAN

CHAUVINISM. See PATRIOTISM.

CHÁVEZ, *CHAH vehz,* **CARLOS** (1899-1978), a Mexican composer, was one of the most important influences on the musical life of Mexico in the 1900's. Many of Chávez' works reflect his interest in Mexican folk music. Some of Chávez' other compositions were written in a strong romantic style. The use of complex rhythms became a dominant element in his mature compositions.

Chávez wrote seven symphonies, several ballets, and cantatas, songs, and chamber works. Several of his pieces use native Mexican folk instruments. For example, *Xochipilli Macuilxochitl* (1940) is an orchestral composition that requires traditional Indian drums.

Chávez was born in Mexico City. In 1928, he organized the first permanent symphony orchestra in Mexico, and he served as its conductor until 1949. He also directed the National Conservatory of Music almost continuously from 1928 to 1934 and the National Institute of Fine Arts from 1947 to 1952. In addition, Chávez was a music and art critic for a Mexico City newspaper. Chávez served as guest conductor for several major symphony orchestras in the United States, often conducting his own compositions. VINCENT MCDERMOTT

CHAVEZ, *SHAH vehz,* **CESAR ESTRADA** (1927-), is a labor union organizer and spokesman for the poor—especially his fellow Mexican-American farmworkers. He has supported nonviolent action to achieve his aims.

Chavez was born on a farm near Yuma, Ariz.

When he was 10 years old, his parents lost their farm and the family became migrant workers in California.

Chavez began to organize grape pickers in California in 1962, when he established the National Farm Workers Association. In 1966, his union merged with another one into the United Farm Workers Organizing Committee (UFWOC). The two earlier unions had been on strike since 1965 against California grape growers. After the merger, California's wine grape growers agreed to accept the UFWOC as the collective bargaining agent for the grape pickers. But the table grape growers refused to do so. Chavez then organized a nationwide boycott of California table grapes. In 1970, most table grape growers agreed to accept the union, and the boycott ended. Later that year, Chavez called for a nationwide boycott of lettuce produced by growers without union contracts. In 1973, the union changed its name to the United Farm Workers of America (UFW). Many grape growers failed to renew their contracts in 1973, and Chavez led a new grape boycott. He ended the boycotts of lettuce and grapes in 1978.

Wide World

Cesar Chavez

Chavez remained committed to nonviolence in spite of pressures to abandon it. He declared that the "truest act of courage, the strongest act of manliness, is to sacrifice ourselves for others in a totally nonviolent struggle for justice." FELICIANO RIVERA

See also MEXICAN AMERICANS (The Chicano Movement); LABOR MOVEMENT (picture).

Additional Resources

LEVY, JACQUES E. *Cesar Chavez: Autobiography of La Causa.* Norton, 1975.

MATTHIESSEN, PETER. *Sal Si Puedes: Cesar Chavez and the New American Revolution.* Random House, 1969.

TAYLOR, RONALD B. *Chavez and the Farm Workers.* Beacon Press, 1975.

CHAVEZ, *SHAH vehz,* **DENNIS** (1888-1962), served in the United States Senate from 1935 to 1962. Chavez was a Democrat from New Mexico, a state with many Spanish-speaking persons and American Indians. He worked for laws that aided such minority groups. For example, he was an early supporter of federal fair employment laws. Chavez was born in Los Chavez, N. Mex., south of Albuquerque. He served in the U.S. House of Representatives from 1931 to 1935, when he was appointed to fill out a term in the Senate. He won election to the Senate five times between 1936 and 1958. A statue of Chavez represents New Mexico in the U.S. Capitol in Washington, D.C. RICHARD A. BARTLETT

CHAYOTE, *chah YOH tay,* is a climbing vine grown chiefly for its fruit. Chayote has thick roots, cream-colored flowers, and heart-shaped leaves. A single plant may cover a tree 50 feet (15 meters) tall.

Chayote plants produce gourds that are round to pear-shaped. These fruits grow as long as 6 inches (15 centimeters) and weigh as much as 3 pounds (1.4 kilograms). They range in color from ivory-white to dark-green. Chayote gourds are usually cooked, and they are often used in pies, puddings, and salads. The roots, leaves, and young shoots of chayote are also edible, and the plant is sometimes used as livestock feed.

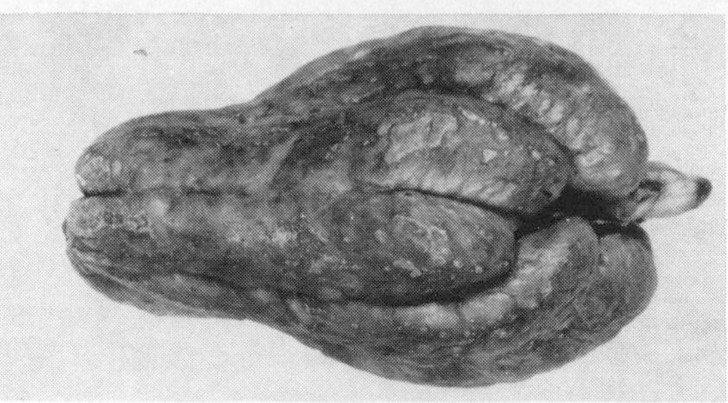

USDA

The Fruit of the Chayote ranges from ivory-white to dark-green, and grows about 6 inches (15 centimeters) long.

Chayote is native to Guatemala, but it now grows throughout Latin America. In the United States, it is raised only in parts of Florida. New chayote vines are produced by planting either entire gourds or cuttings taken from the plant's stem.

Scientific Classification. Chayote belongs to the family Cucurbitaceae. It is *Sechium edule.* GARY W. ELMSTROM

CHECK, is a written order directing a bank to pay money to a person or organization, or to the bearer. A check may be written by any person or organization with money in a checking account. The bank transfers the amount specified on the check from the depositor's account to the *payee,* the designated person or organization. The word *check* is spelled *cheque* in Canada, Great Britain, and some other countries.

Checks are widely used because they are safer and more convenient than cash. For example, a person who has a checking account does not have to carry large sums of money, which could be lost or stolen. Checks can be sent safely through the mail because only the payees can legally cash them. Used checks, called *canceled* checks, serve as convenient records of payment.

How the Checking System Works. When a person or organization opens a checking account, the depositor receives a checkbook containing blank checks. The depositor issues a check by writing in the date, the name of the payee, and the amount of money involved. The depositor also signs the check. Every month, the bank sends the depositor a *statement.* This document lists the deposits made into the account, and the amounts of the checks written against it. The statement also shows the *balance,* the amount remaining in the account. The bank encloses the canceled checks for the month.

The payee may *cash* the check—that is, exchange it for cash—or deposit it in a bank account or transfer it to another person or organization. To cash, deposit, or transfer a check, the payee *endorses* it by signing it on the back. The endorser becomes responsible for the payment of the check if the issuer's checking account lacks enough money to cover it.

After a check has been deposited in a bank, the bank collects its money by sending the check back to the bank of the check writer. The check writer's bank then

BARBARA W. THOMPKINS
1443 N. ONTARIO ST.
CHICAGO, ILLINOIS 60634
1653
DATE January 12 19 82
PAY TO THE ORDER OF Illinois Bell $24.37
Twenty-four 37/100 DOLLARS
CONTINENTAL BANK
CONTINENTAL ILLINOIS NATIONAL BANK AND TRUST COMPANY OF CHICAGO
MEMO Dec.-Jan. Telephone Barbara W. Thompkins
⑆071000039⑆ 12⑈34567⑈ 1653

Continental Illinois National Bank and Trust Co. of Chicago

A Check is a document directing a bank to pay money to a certain person or organization. Every check has a code printed in magnetic ink, *bottom left.* The code identifies the check writer and his or her bank. Machines sort checks by reading the codes.

charges the depositor's account for the amount involved. If the two banks are in the same community, the check is routed through a clearing house. The clearing house collects checks and determines how much money the banks owe each other. Out-of-town checks are collected by a Federal Reserve Bank or some other large bank.

Numbers printed on checks with magnetic ink identify the bank and the owner of the checking account. These numbers enable checks to be sorted electronically.

Special Checking Services. Some payments are required to be made by *certified check* or by *cashier's check.* Such checks are accepted almost as readily as cash because banks guarantee their payment. A certified check is an ordinary check made out by a person or organization and then stamped *Certified* by a bank. The bank sets aside sufficient funds from the depositor's account to pay for a check that it certifies. A cashier's check is the bank's own check. The bank charges the depositor's account for the amount. Cashier's checks may also be purchased with cash.

Banks and travel agencies sell blank *traveler's checks* in denominations of $10, $20, $50, and $100. The person who buys the checks signs them immediately at the bank or agency. He or she signs them again to obtain cash or to make purchases. The second signature verifies the person's identity. Traveler's checks can be used throughout the world because the issuing bank or company guarantees payment. The bank or travel agency replaces lost or stolen traveler's checks.

Checks and the Economy. Checks serve as the chief method of payment in many parts of the world. For this reason, economists consider *checkbook money* (funds in checking accounts) as part of a nation's money supply. Such funds make up about 75 per cent of the total amount of money in circulation in the United States.

Federal law once prohibited U.S. banks from paying interest on money in checking accounts, unlike funds in savings accounts. In 1980, however, Congress lifted the ban on interest-paying checking accounts. It authorized banks to offer *negotiable order of withdrawal accounts,* usually called *NOW accounts.* Like a savings account, a NOW account pays interest. But the depositor can transfer funds to someone else by writing a *negotiable order of withdrawal,* which is like a check.

For many years, checking accounts were offered only by *commercial banks* (banks that offer a full range of banking services). Since the 1970's, however, other institutions have provided accounts that compete with the checking accounts of commercial banks. For example, savings banks and savings and loan associations offer NOW accounts. Banks and other financial institutions also offer special interest-bearing accounts known as *money market accounts,* from which withdrawals may be made by check. Credit unions use *share drafts,* which also are similar to checks. William G. Dewald

See also Clearing House; Negotiable Instrument; Traveler's Check; Alaska (picture: The United States Used This Check to Purchase Alaska from Russia).

CHECK, TRAVELER'S. See Traveler's Check.

CHECKERS is a game played on a checkerboard by two persons. It is also called *draughts* (pronounced *drafts*). The checkerboard has 64 alternating black and red squares. Each player has 12 round, flat pieces, called *men* or *checkers.* One set is black, the other red. The players sit opposite each other, and each arranges his or her men on the first three rows of black squares. Two rows in the center remain open.

The player with the black men starts by moving one of the black checkers one space diagonally forward toward the red checkers. Then the other player moves a red man toward the black. The men can be moved only forward, and only on the black squares.

The object of the game is to capture all the men of the opponent, or to block their progress. If a red man moves next to a black man, the black man can jump over the red man if there is a space behind the red. The red is removed from the board as the black goes deeper into enemy territory. More than one man may be captured at a time.

If a man reaches the back line on the enemy's side, it is *crowned* and becomes a *king.* A second checker is placed on top of the king to distinguish it from the other men on the board. A king can move backward or forward one square at a time, except when it jumps over one or more men.

Checkers requires careful planning of moves that will

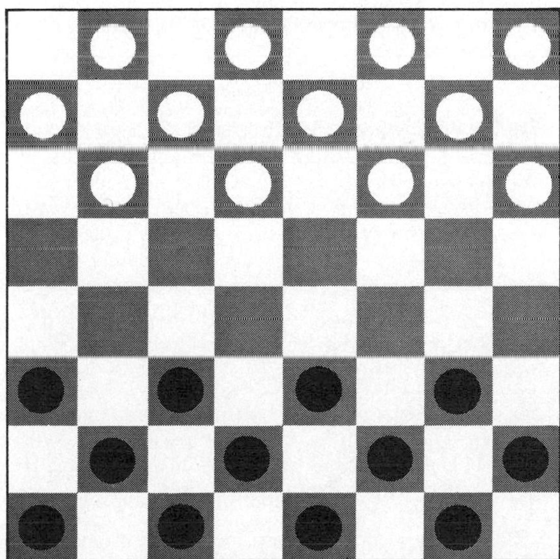

Setting Up the Checkerboard, players on opposite sides place 12 men on the first three rows of black squares. A black square must be on the lower left in setting up the board.

put the opponent on the defensive. There are no international rules governing checkers, as there are in chess. Each nation has its own set of rules. LILLIAN FRANKEL

CHECKING ACCOUNT. See BANK (Providing a Means of Payment); CHECK.

CHECKS AND BALANCES are limitations on the power of any branch of government, with each branch having some control over the actions of the others. The United States system of government is based on a set of checks and balances, designed to prevent one person or branch of government from becoming too powerful.

The Constitution of the United States divides the powers of the federal government among the President, the Congress, and the federal courts. Each branch has some powers that offset those of the other two. For example, the President can veto bills passed by Congress. But the veto power is balanced by Congress's power to pass bills over a veto. The President influences the federal courts by appointing judges, and such appointments require congressional approval. But the federal courts can restrain both the President and the Congress with their power to declare presidential orders or legislative acts unconstitutional.

The system of checks and balances also works between the two houses of Congress. Before a bill becomes law, both the Senate and the House of Representatives must approve it in identical form. If the Senate and House pass different versions, a conference committee of senators and representatives tries to work out the differences. This system ensures that both houses of Congress will have a voice in making laws.

Many countries have a democratic government without a system of checks and balances or separation of the powers of government. In Australia, Canada, and Great Britain, for example, executive power rests with the prime minister and Cabinet, who are members of Parliament, the legislative body. In addition, the courts in certain of these countries, including Great Britain and Switzerland, cannot declare an act of the nation's Parliament invalid. KENNETH JANDA

See also GOVERNMENT (Separation of Powers); UNITED STATES, GOVERNMENT OF THE (Separation of Powers).

CHEERLEADING is a colorful American sports tradition in which persons called *cheerleaders* direct spectators in organized cheering during athletic events. School cheerleading programs generally begin about sixth grade and continue through college. Some professional sports teams also have cheerleaders. Professional cheerleaders and some college cheerleaders are paid for their work. Cheerleading began at the University of Minnesota in 1898 and became nationally popular by 1920.

Cheerleaders most often perform at football and basketball games. They lead yells and chants with rhythmic body motions to generate enthusiasm and entertain spectators. They also may dance and perform acrobatic stunts. The International Cheerleading Foundation conducts cheerleading training camps in nearly every state. RANDY L. NEIL

CHEESE is a healthful, tasty food made from milk. For thousands of years, cheese has been one of the most important foods of people throughout the world. Cheese can be eaten alone or it can be served on crackers, in sandwiches, in salads, and in cooked foods.

There are hundreds of kinds of cheeses, and they differ in taste, texture, and appearance. Many cheeses spread as easily as butter, but others are hard and crumbly. Some cheeses taste sweet, and others have a sharp or spicy taste.

Cheese keeps better than milk, and it has much of milk's food value, including proteins, minerals, and vitamins. Cheese contains these nutrients of milk in concentrated form. For example, 8 ounces (227 grams) of American cheese provide as much protein and calcium as six 8-ounce (237-milliliter) glasses of milk. Cheese, like milk, supplies important amounts of vitamin A and riboflavin.

The United States leads the world in cheese production. It makes about $2\frac{1}{2}$ million short tons (2.2 million metric tons) annually. Russia and France also rank high in cheese production. Almost every state of the United States makes cheese. Wisconsin ranks first, followed by Minnesota and New York. The U.S. Department of Agriculture grades much cheese produced in the United States as AA, A, B, or C. In addition, some states have their own standards for grading cheese. Most cheese made in Canada comes from the provinces of Ontario and Quebec. The Canadian government has its own standards for cheese produced in that country.

Most cheese comes from cow's milk. People in Europe and Asia frequently make cheese from the milk of buffaloes, goats, and sheep. But cheese can be made from the milk of any animal. Herders in Lapland use reindeer milk in making cheese. In Tibet, yaks supply milk for cheese. Cheese is also made from the milk of camels, donkeys, horses, and zebras.

Kinds of Cheese

There are more than 400 kinds of cheese. They have over 2,000 names because some cheeses are known by two or more names. For example, Swiss cheese is also called Emmentaler. Cheddar cheese is widely known as American cheese in the United States. Many cheeses take their names from the country or region where they

Association of Chicagoland McDonald's Restaurants

Cheerleaders encourage enthusiasm at many sports events by leading spectators in organized cheering. Cheerleaders often perform elaborate gymnastic stunts as part of their routines.

were first produced. Swiss cheese originally came from Switzerland, and Roquefort cheese is made only near the town of Roquefort, France. Farmers in Monterey County, California, developed the cheese called Monterey Jack cheese.

Such cheeses as cheddar and Swiss are enjoyed in many parts of the world. But other cheeses are rarely eaten outside a certain area. For example, farmers in the Alps eat a local cheese called schottengseid. Some nomadic tribes in North Africa make touareg cheese.

Almost all cheeses belong to one of four main groups: (1) soft, (2) semisoft, (3) hard, and (4) very hard, or grating. The amount of moisture in the cheese determines its classification. The more moisture the cheese contains, the softer it is.

Soft Cheese. The two most popular kinds of soft cheese are cottage cheese and cream cheese. Some soft cheeses, including Brie and Camembert, develop a crust. Such cheeses become firmer and develop a sharper taste with age.

Semisoft Cheese includes such varieties as blue, brick, Limburger, Monterey Jack, mozzarella, Munster, Port du Salut, Roquefort, and Stilton. Blue, Roquefort, and Stilton cheese have streaks of blue mold running through them. The mold, which is added during the cheese-making process, gives these cheeses a special flavor. Blue and Stilton are made with cow's milk, but Roquefort is made only from sheep's milk.

Hard Cheese. Cheddar, Edam, Gruyère, and Swiss are popular varieties of hard cheese. Gruyère and Swiss cheese have holes called *eyes*. Cheese makers form the

eyes by adding bacteria that produce bubbles of carbon dioxide gas in the cheese. When the cheese is sliced, the bubbles become holes.

Very Hard, or Grating, Cheese includes Asiago, Parmesan, Romano, and sapsago. People usually grind such cheeses and sprinkle them over such foods as soups, vegetables, and pizza.

How Cheese Is Made

Almost all the cheese produced in the United States is made in large factories. The process used involves four basic steps: (1) processing the milk; (2) separating the curd; (3) ripening; and (4) packaging. Slight differences in the cheese-making process result in the production of several hundred varieties of cheese.

Processing the Milk. Cheese makers first inspect the milk for quality and then remove any solid substances by a process called *clarification*. The milk flows into a pasteurizer that kills any harmful bacteria. Pumps force the pasteurized milk into large metal tanks or vats that hold from 8,000 to 35,000 pounds (3,600 to 15,900 kilograms). About 11,000 pounds (4,990 kilograms) of milk are needed to make 1,000 pounds (450 kilograms) of cheese.

Separating the Curd. After the milk has been processed, it is treated to form a soft, custardlike substance called *curd*. The curd contains a liquid called *whey*, which must be expelled before cheese can be made. Cheese makers form the curd by first heating the milk

Some Kinds of Cheese

The four main groups of cheese are (1) soft, (2) semisoft, (3) hard, and (4) very hard or grating. The amount of moisture in a cheese determines its classification. The more moisture the cheese has, the softer it is. The drawings below show some popular cheeses in the four groups.

WORLD BOOK illustrations by James Teason

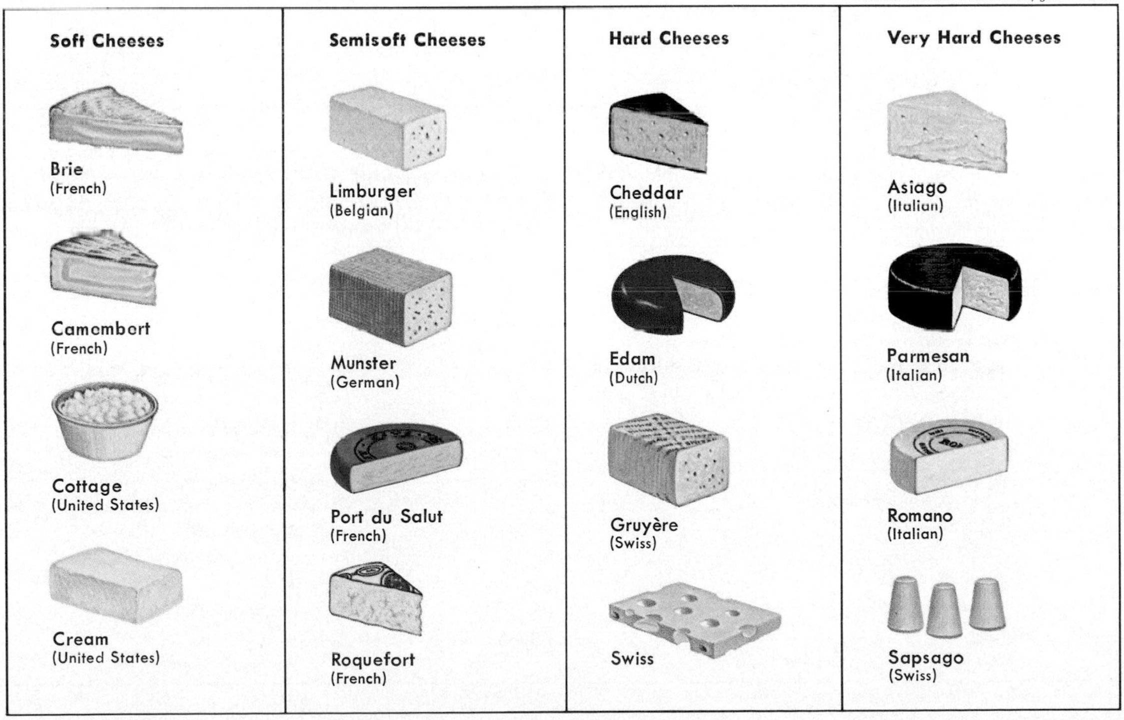

Soft Cheeses	Semisoft Cheeses	Hard Cheeses	Very Hard Cheeses
Brie (French)	Limburger (Belgian)	Cheddar (English)	Asiago (Italian)
Camembert (French)	Munster (German)	Edam (Dutch)	Parmesan (Italian)
Cottage (United States)	Port du Salut (French)	Gruyère (Swiss)	Romano (Italian)
Cream (United States)	Roquefort (French)	Swiss	Sapsago (Swiss)

How Cheese Is Made

Cheese makers manufacture cheese from milk. They treat the milk to form a custardlike substance called *curd.* The curd contains a liquid called *whey,* which must be removed before cheese can be made. Slight differences in the cheese-making process provide the many kinds of cheese.

Forming the Curd. The milk is heated and liquid called a *starter culture* is added, *above.* The starter culture sours the milk. Various enzymes are then added to thicken the milk and form the curd.

Draining the Whey. The curd is cut into small cubes, releasing some of the whey. The curd and whey are stirred and heated, forcing more whey from the curd. The liquid is then drained off, *above.*

Miles Laboratories, Inc.

Stacking the Curd. To make cheddar cheese, the curd is cut into slabs and then stacked. The slabs are chopped and put into molds. For other cheeses, the curd itself is chopped and packed in the molds.

to 86° F. (30° C) to 96° F. (36° C). Then they add a liquid called a *starter culture* to the milk. This liquid contains bacteria that form acids and turn milk sour. Vegetable dye may be added with the starter culture to give the cheese a certain color. During the souring process, mechanical paddles stir the starter culture and dye evenly through the milk.

After 15 to 90 minutes, workers add *rennet,* a substance that contains enzymes from the lining of a calf's stomach. The rennet thickens the milk. Cheese makers may also promote this action, called *curdling,* by adding other enzymes, including pepsin from the stomachs of hogs and rennins from bacteria. The paddles blend the enzymes into the milk, which is then left undisturbed for about 30 minutes so curd will form.

Special knives cut the curd into thousands of small cubes, and the whey oozes from them. The paddles stir the curd and whey, and the temperature in the vat is raised to between 102° F. (39° C) and 130° F. (54° C). The motion and heat force more whey from the curd. The whey is then drained off or the curd is lifted from the vat.

The curd then goes through one of three processes, depending on the kind of cheese being made. To make cottage cheese, which comes from skim milk, workers rinse the curd with water and mix it with cream and salt. For most other cheeses, the curd rests undisturbed and the particles stick together and form a solid mass. It is then broken up into small pieces and salted lightly.

The curd for cheddar cheese goes through a special step after being formed into a solid mass. Workers cut the solid curd into large slabs, stack them in the vat,

Leading Cheese-Producing States and Provinces

Wisconsin	822,300 short tons (746,000 metric tons)
Minnesota	283,700 short tons (257,400 metric tons)
New York	179,000 short tons (162,400 metric tons)
California	124,200 short tons (112,700 metric tons)
Iowa	103,200 short tons (93,600 metric tons)
Ontario	79,700 short tons (87,900 metric tons)

Sources: U.S. Department of Agriculture; Statistics Canada. Figures are for 1982.

Leading Cheese-Producing Countries

United States	2,438,000 short tons (2,212,000 metric tons)
Russia	1,666,000 short tons (1,511,000 metric tons)
France	1,306,000 short tons (1,185,000 metric tons)
West Germany	902,000 short tons (818,000 metric tons)
Italy	661,000 short tons (600,000 metric tons)
Netherlands	516,000 short tons (468,000 metric tons)

Source: *Production Yearbook, 1981,* FAO. Figures are for 1981.

and turn them every 10 minutes. This process, called *cheddaring*, may also be done mechanically in large towers, rotating cylinders, or steel boxes. The slabs of curd pass through a mill, which chops them into small pieces. Salt is then added to the chopped curd.

The salted curd for any kind of cheese is packed by machines into metal hoops or molds. These containers are lined with cheesecloth. The hoops hold as much as 2,000 pounds (910 kilograms) of curd. They are put into presses that keep the cheese under great pressure overnight.

The next day, workers remove the cheese from the metal hoops. The cheese is then left to dry for a period of three or four days. A crust, called the *rind*, forms on the cheese as it dries. Rindless cheeses are not dried. Instead, these cheeses are sealed into plastic film immediately after they are taken out of the metal hoops.

Ripening, also called *aging* or *curing*, helps give cheese its flavor and texture. Cheese is aged in storage rooms or warehouses that have a controlled temperature and humidity. Aging times vary for different cheeses. Brick cheese and some other types need only two months to age, but Parmesan requires about a year. The longer the curing time, the sharper the flavor of the cheese.

Packaging. After being aged, cheese is packaged in a wide variety of shapes and sizes. Some cheeses are sliced at the factory and sealed in foil or plastic. Others are sold whole—in large blocks, wedges, balls called *rounds*, or short cylinders called *wheels*.

Process Cheese

Much of the cheese produced in the United States is made into *process cheese*, a blend of natural cheeses. Process cheese and products called *process cheese foods* and *process cheese spreads* account for about 40 per cent of the cheese eaten by Americans. Process cheese keeps better than natural cheeses, and melts more evenly when used in cooking. Some process cheese is made from two or more kinds of cheese. Other process cheese is a mixture of batches of the same kind of cheese that differ in taste and texture. The cheeses are ground up and then blended with the aid of heat and chemicals called *emulsifiers*. Process cheese made from only one variety of cheese is named for that cheese. For example, process cheddar cheese is made only from cheddar. In the United States, all cheeses used in process cheese made from two or more kinds of cheese must be identified on the label.

Process cheese foods and process cheese spreads are made like process cheese. But cream, milk, skim milk, or whey are added to make them more moist. Fruit, meat, spices, or vegetables may also be added for extra flavor. *Cold-pack cheese* is a blend of natural cheeses. Its manufacturing process involves no heat. Much cold-pack cheese includes meat or wine as flavoring.

History

The first cheese was probably made more than 4,000 years ago by nomadic tribes in Asia. Through the years, knowledge of cheese-making spread to Europe.

Cheese-making began in the American Colonies in 1611. That year, settlers in Jamestown, in the Virginia Colony, imported cows from England. In 1851, an American dairyman named Jesse Williams established the nation's first cheese factory, near Rome, N.Y.

In 1917, J. L. Kraft, an American businessman, patented a method for making process cheese. His company also developed a method for wrapping individual slices of cheese mechanically.

During the 1970's, food experts discovered valuable uses for whey. Previously, some of the liquid had been dried and fed to farm animals, but most of it was thrown away. Scientists developed methods to remove such valuable food elements as proteins and *lactose* (milk sugar) from whey. Today, manufacturers add these nutritious substances to baby food, bread, ice cream, and other foods. Whey can also be made into alcohol. Liquor companies have used such alcohol in making whiskey and a sweet wine. ROBERT T. MARSHALL

See also CASEIN; NETHERLANDS (picture: The Famous Alkmaar Cheese Market).

CHEETAH is a large cat chiefly found on the grassy plains of Africa. It is the fastest animal for running short distances. Cheetahs can run at a top speed of about 70 miles (110 kilometers) per hour. But they can maintain this speed for only a few hundred yards or meters. The cheetah is sometimes called the *hunting leopard*.

E. R. Degginger

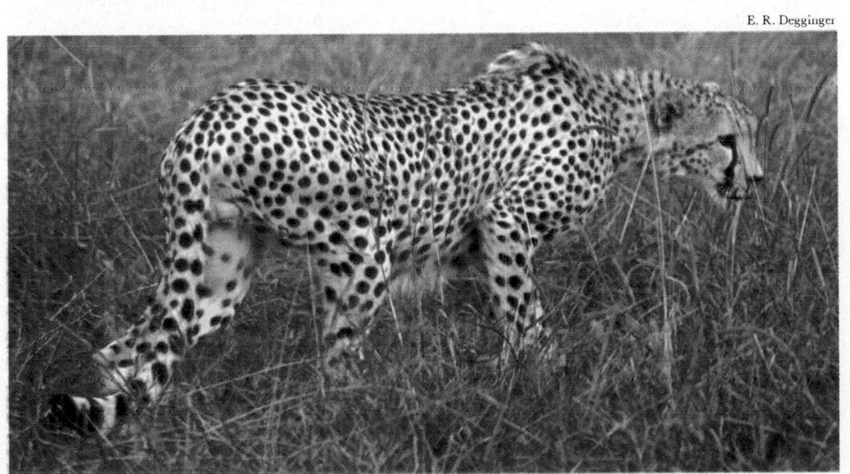

The Cheetah hunts by prowling quietly through grass or brush until it nears its prey. Then it swiftly rushes to the kill. A cheetah can run as fast as 70 miles (110 kilometers) per hour for short distances. It is the only meat-eating mammal that can overtake an antelope or gazelle.

The cheetah has a slender body and extremely long legs. An adult cheetah stands about 3 feet (0.9 meter) high, and weighs slightly more than 100 pounds (45 kilograms). Its head and body are about 4 feet (1.2 meters) long, and its tail measures about 2 feet (0.6 meter). The cheetah has a brownish-yellow coat with black spots, except for the throat and underparts, which are white. Unlike other cats, the cheetah cannot completely *sheathe* (retract) its claws.

Most adult cheetahs live alone. Observations of wild cheetahs indicate that adults may claim a territory as their own and keep other cheetahs out. Male and female cheetahs meet only briefly to mate. After a pregnancy period of about 3 months, the female gives birth to two to four cubs. More than half of all cheetah cubs are killed by hyenas, leopards, and lions. Those that survive remain with their mother for about 15 months. During this time, they learn to hunt.

Cheetahs usually hunt by day. They prefer small prey, particularly young antelope. The cheetah uses its great speed to run down its prey after stalking close to it. Cheetahs may have their dead prey taken from them by hyenas, leopards, and lions.

Cheetahs once inhabited grassy plains throughout Africa and across the Middle East into central Asia and India. Since the early 1900's, their numbers have declined rapidly. This decline has occurred chiefly because cheetahs have been hunted for their pelts and because plains lands have been changed into farming and manufacturing areas. Today, substantial numbers of cheetahs remain only in central and eastern Africa.

Scientific Classification. The cheetah, or hunting leopard, belongs to the cat family, Felidae. Its scientific name is *Acinonyx jubatus*. C. Richard Taylor

CHEEVER, JOHN (1912-1982), was an American short-story writer and novelist. Cheever's typical characters are the descendants of genteel old American families, or the inhabitants of comfortable, upper middle-class suburbia. He wrote about these people in a style that is both lyrical and lightly ironic.

In his fiction, Cheever balanced the claims of individual freedom and desire against society's values of emotional restraint and good manners. He often created characters who attempt to disrupt their seemingly tranquil lives to pursue some kind of personal satisfaction. Their attempts usually end partly in defeat and partly in success.

In his related novels *The Wapshot Chronicle* (1957) and *The Wapshot Scandal* (1964), Cheever wrote about the modern-day descendants of an old New England seafaring family. The novels reveal how the family's tradition of strong individualism and eccentricity conflicts with the restrictions of an increasingly impersonal American society. Two later novels explore darker themes. *Bullet Park* (1969) tells a story of drug addiction and insanity in a typical suburban setting. *Falconer* (1977) is a story about a college professor who kills his brother, is imprisoned, and escapes.

Susan Cowley
John Cheever

Cheever won the 1979 Pulitzer Prize for fiction for *The Stories of John Cheever* (1978). The book is a collection of six previously published volumes of his stories. Cheever was born in Quincy, Mass. Marcus Klein

CHEKHOV, *CHEHK awf,* **ANTON,** *ahn TAWN* (1860-1904), was a Russian playwright and short-story writer. Chekhov's works show the stagnant, helpless quality of Russian society, especially the middle classes, at the end of the 1800's. Most of his characters are decent, sensitive people. They dream of improving their lives, but most of them fail, victims of their own sense of helplessness and uselessness. Scholars believe Chekhov probably was criticizing the backwardness he saw in social and political life in Russia under the czars. But Chekhov never directly stated this attitude.

Perhaps Chekhov's most famous works are four plays he wrote late in his life—*The Sea Gull* (1896), *Uncle Vanya* (1899), *The Three Sisters* (1901), and *The Cherry Orchard* (1904). These plays have been called gloomy and pessimistic. But they actually blend poetic atmosphere with sympathetic treatment of characters who are trapped in unfulfilling lives and cannot help themselves.

Anton Pavlovich Chekhov was born in Taganrog. In 1879, Chekhov moved to Moscow, where he studied medicine. During this time, Chekhov wrote short, humorous stories and sketches for popular newspapers and comic sheets to help support his needy family. Chekhov graduated from medical school and became a doctor. However, he practiced medicine only occasionally, devoting himself instead to a writing career. In 1890, Chekhov visited Sakhalin Island in the Pacific Ocean to study the Russian state prisons there. His book *Sakhalin Island* (1893-1894) describes the terrible conditions under which the convicts lived. In 1901, Chekhov married Olga Knipper, an actress who played leading roles in several of his plays staged by the famous Moscow Art Theater. William E. Harkins

See also Short Story.

Additional Resources

Chekhov, Anton. *Letters of Anton Chekhov*. Ed. by Avrahm Yarmolinsky. Viking, 1973.
Hingley, Ronald. *A New Life of Anton Chekhov*. Knopf, 1976.
Simmons, Ernest J. *Chekhov: A Biography*. Little, Brown, 1962.
Valency, Maurice. *The Breaking String: The Plays of Anton Chekhov*. Oxford, 1966. A comprehensive study of the major plays and the man.

CHEMICAL is any of the many substances that make up the world's materials. Many chemicals are naturally occurring substances called *elements*. They include hydrogen, nitrogen, and sulfur. Various elements can be combined to make a large number of chemicals. Ammonia and sulfuric acid are examples of such artificially produced chemicals. See also Chemistry; Element, Chemical.

CHEMICAL-BIOLOGICAL-RADIOLOGICAL WARFARE (CBR) is war waged with chemicals, biological agents, or radioactive materials. Development of CBR weapons, and defenses against these weapons, are usually considered together in military training and strategy. These weapons can be designed to kill large numbers of people, temporarily disable them, or destroy their food supplies. The weapons are usually effective without destroying property.

Chemical agents affect the nervous system, breathing centers, skin, eyes, nose, or throat. Chemical agents include gases, liquids, sprays, and powders. They can be sprayed from airplanes, dropped as bombs, or fired by artillery in explosive shells.

Some chemical agents, called *nerve agents* or *poison gas*, can cause death. These agents may be colorless, odorless, and tasteless. They can cause death rapidly if the victim inhales them or if they are splashed on bare skin. Chemical agents have not been widely used in warfare since World War I ended in 1918.

Other chemical agents are not fatal, but they make their victims unable to fight. Blister agents cause huge blisters on the skin. A blister agent called *mustard gas* caused many casualties on both sides during World War I. Other chemical agents can cause temporary blindness or mental confusion.

Gas masks, other protective coverings for the body, and injections of antidotes are used as defenses against chemical agents. See GAS MASK.

Chemical agents also have nonmilitary uses. Riot control agents, including *tear gas*, may be used to control rioting crowds. These agents affect the eyes, nose, and throat. They cause blinding tears and often violent coughing. But the effects of the gas disappear within a few minutes after the victim reaches fresh air. Other chemicals are used to kill harmful insects.

Biological warfare is the military use of harmful microorganisms as weapons against people, animals, or crops. It is sometimes called *germ warfare*. A small number of these microorganisms could kill millions of persons if effectively distributed. Biological agents could also be used to make enemy soldiers too sick to fight, or to ruin an enemy's food supply. A biological agent that seriously damaged the enemy country's crops might be a decisive factor in a war.

Biological weapons have not played a part in modern warfare. But military strategists must assume that the enemy possesses such weapons. Therefore, much research is devoted to defenses against biological weapons.

In 1969, President Richard M. Nixon stated that the United States would not conduct biological warfare against another nation even if that nation used such warfare against the United States. Nixon ordered U.S. stocks of biological weapons destroyed. An international treaty banning biological weapons went into effect in 1975. It bars the production, possession, and use of such weapons. The treaty was ratified by Russia, the United States, and more than 40 other nations.

Radiological agents give off invisible radiation that can damage a person's internal organs and even cause death. Radiation from nuclear *fallout* could be a major factor in any war involving nuclear weapons. Radiological warfare is dangerous for all sides in a war. A nuclear weapon used against an enemy would create fallout that might be carried by winds back to the country or troops that used the weapon. Radioactivity might also make an area temporarily unfit for human life.

As in biological warfare, much research is devoted to defenses against radiological agents. These defenses include shelters to protect a person against radioactivity. Drugs that act as antidotes once radioactive agents are in the body are also under study. See FALLOUT SHELTER.

History. Radiological warfare is a recent development in war. Such warfare became possible with the development of atomic weapons during the 1940's. But chemical and biological warfare have long histories. The Spartans used pitch and sulfur in a form of chemical warfare during the Peloponnesian War in the 400's B.C. During ancient and medieval times, soldiers sometimes threw bodies of plague victims over the walls of besieged cities, or into water wells. During the French and Indian Wars (1689-1763), blankets used by smallpox victims were given to Indians in the hope they would carry the disease.

Germany introduced the use of gas in war during World War I. In April, 1915, the Germans used gas against Allied forces at Ypres, Belgium. Before the end of the war, gases of many types were used by all armies. Nearly 30 per cent of all American casualties in the war were caused by gas. Gas warfare proved so destructive that most nations have agreed to avoid its use during wars.

HAROLD C. KINNE, JR.

Additional Resources

GOODWIN, PETER. *Nuclear War: The Facts on Our Survival.* W. H. Smith, 1981.

HERSH, SEYMOUR M. *Chemical and Biological Warfare: America's Hidden Arsenal.* MacGibbon, 1969.

SEAGRAVE, STERLING. *Yellow Rain: A Journey Through the Terror of Chemical Warfare.* M. Evans, 1981.

U. S. CONGRESS OFFICE OF TECHNOLOGY ASSESSMENT. *The Effects of Nuclear War.* Allanheld, Osmun, 1980.

CHEMICAL BOND. See CHEMISTRY (Chemical Bonds); MINERAL (Chemical Bonds; with diagram).

CHEMICAL BURNS. See BURNS AND SCALDS.

CHEMICAL CHANGE. See CHEMISTRY.

CHEMICAL COMPOUND. See CHEMISTRY (Basic Chemistry).

CHEMICAL ELEMENT. See ELEMENT, CHEMICAL.

CHEMICAL ENGINEERING. See ENGINEERING (Main Branches of Engineering).

CHEMICAL EQUATION. See CHEMISTRY (Chemical Equations).

CHEMICAL EQUILIBRIUM. See EQUILIBRIUM, CHEMICAL.

CHEMICAL EVOLUTION. See LIFE (Modern Theories).

CHEMICAL INDUSTRY is made up of the many industries that use chemistry in the manufacture of a wide variety of products. These products include fuels that power cars and other vehicles, drugs that physicians use to treat diseases, and paints that brighten our homes. Plastics, detergents, synthetic fibers, and synthetic rubber are some other important products of the chemical industry.

For more information, see the WORLD BOOK articles on such specific products as DRUG; FIBER; PETROCHEMICALS; PLASTICS; and SYNTHETICS. See also CHEMISTRY (History); CHEMURGY; HAZARDOUS WASTES.

CHEMICAL MACE. See MACE.

CHEMICAL REACTION. See CHEMISTRY (Chemical Reactions).

CHEMICAL SOCIETY, AMERICAN. See AMERICAN CHEMICAL SOCIETY.

CHEMICAL WARFARE. See CHEMICAL-BIOLOGICAL-RADIOLOGICAL WARFARE.

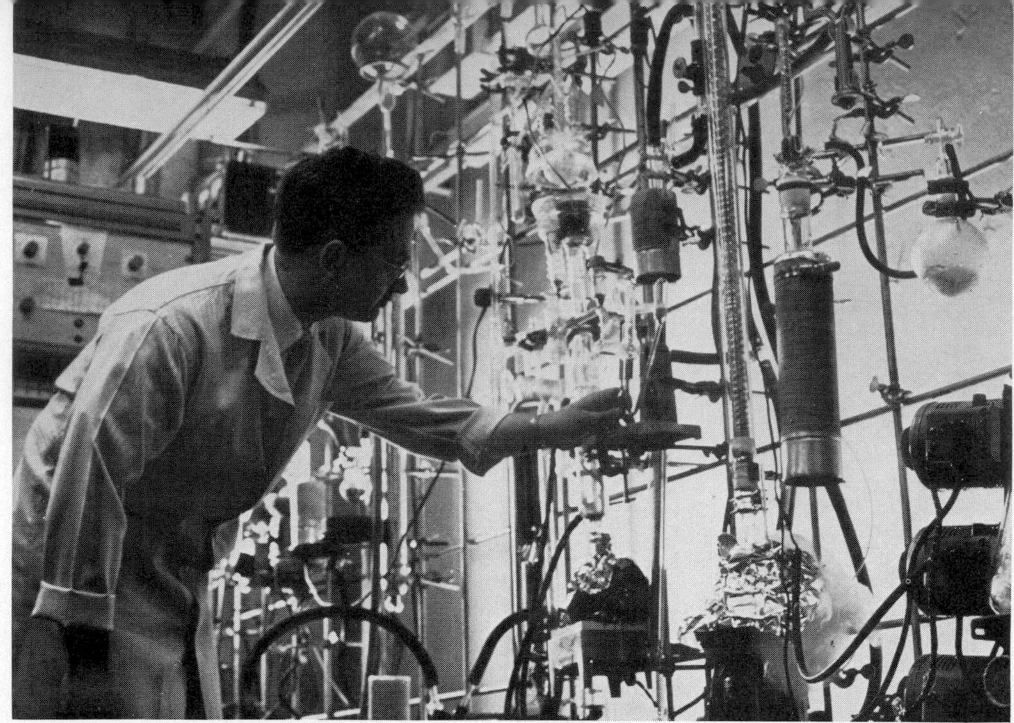

Art d'Arazien

Control of Chemical Changes is one of the chemist's main jobs. This chemist is spot-checking a complicated process taking place amid a network of tubes, flasks, hoses, and wires.

Chemistry

CHEMISTRY is the study of substances. The chemist wants to know what substances are made of, how they act, and how they change. The chemist also tries to find out why chemical changes take place and how they can be controlled. The knowledge of chemical changes has led to the invention of synthetic fibers, plastics, drugs, and many other useful substances. With the knowledge of chemistry, scientists have developed nuclear energy, powerful rocket fuels, and chemical devices that produce electricity.

Chemical changes occur everywhere. Iron rusts and becomes a brownish-red substance. Coal burns and changes into ashes and gases. The food we eat undergoes many chemical changes in our bodies. Chemical changes in batteries produce electricity, and chemical changes in gasoline supply power for automobiles. During a thunderstorm, each flash of lightning causes a chemical change in the air. When this change takes place, the nitrogen and oxygen in the air combine. They form a substance that dissolves in the raindrops and falls to earth. Plants then use this substance as fertilizer, and it undergoes even more chemical changes.

To learn what happens in chemical changes, it is necessary to understand some of the principal ideas of chemistry. Everything in the world is made up of one or more of the basic substances called *chemical elements*. Carbon, iron, oxygen, and mercury are familiar elements. Elements consist of tiny bits of matter called *atoms*. Each element has its own kind of atom which differs from the atoms of all other elements.

Atoms can join together to form larger chemical units called *molecules*. For example, oxygen atoms usually combine in groups of two to form oxygen molecules. When atoms of two or more different elements combine, they form a substance called a *chemical compound*. Water is a compound made up of two elements—hydrogen and oxygen. A molecule of water consists of two atoms of hydrogen and one of oxygen.

A chemical change takes place whenever elements unite to form a compound. Because of this chemical change, a compound has *properties* (characteristics) that are different from the elements that make it up. The properties of common salt, a compound, are different from the properties of sodium and chlorine, the elements that make it up. Sodium is a soft, silvery-white metal that can be cut with a knife. Chlorine is a poisonous, yellow-green gas. When sodium and chlorine combine chemically, they form salt—a grainy, white substance used to season food.

Chemists use special terms and symbols to name substances. Chemical formulas show the elements that make up substances. Chemical equations show how chemical changes take place. Chemists also develop theories that explain why substances act the way they do. The work of chemists often takes them into the fields of physics, biology, astronomy, and the other natural sciences. Their main purpose is to study nature so they will understand more about the world around them.

Paul R. Frey, the contributor of this article, is Professor Emeritus of Chemistry at Colorado State University and author of College Chemistry. *Aaron J. Ihde, the critical reviewer, is Professor Emeritus of Chemistry and of the History of Science at the University of Wisconsin at Madison. He is the author of* The Development of Modern Chemistry.

Chemistry / BRANCHES OF CHEMISTRY

Chemistry is divided into many branches that are not clearly separated. These branches developed as chemists began to specialize in various problems. Some chemists studied particular groups of substances, such as organic compounds. Others developed chemical techniques such as methods of analyzing any substance. Still others worked to discover ways of using many kinds of substances and chemical methods in medicine, industry, and other fields.

Specialists in different branches of chemistry often study the same substances or use the same techniques. But they do so with different purposes. For example, the analytical chemist looks for simple ways to analyze substances, including organic compounds. An organic chemist might analyze a natural organic compound as the first step in making the compound artificially. A specialist in biochemistry might analyze the same compound to see if it is useful as a drug.

The chart below describes 24 important branches and sub-branches of chemistry. Many of these branches are closely related. The branches at the top of the chart are those that study kinds of substances. The other branches deal with particular uses of substances and with methods that can be applied to any substance.

Inorganic Chemistry
The study of compounds that do not contain carbon

Colloid Chemistry—the study of organic and inorganic materials consisting of particles of one substance evenly distributed through another substance

Geochemistry—the study of organic and inorganic substances in the earth and the chemical changes they undergo

Polymer Chemistry—the study of organic and inorganic compounds made up of chainlike molecules containing a large number of atoms

Synthetic Chemistry—the production of complex compounds from simple compounds, such as the manufacture of organic substances from inorganic substances

Organic Chemistry
The study of compounds that contain carbon

Analytical Chemistry
The determination of the composition of any substance

Analytical Instrumentation—the use of instruments, mainly in quantitative analysis

Qualitative Analysis—the determination of the kinds of compounds in any substance

Quantitative Analysis—the measurement of the amounts of compounds in any substance

Radiochemistry—the study of chemical processes by using radioactive materials

Applied Chemistry
The use of chemistry in industry, medicine, and other fields

Agricultural Chemistry—the study of chemical processes in soil and crops; the development of fertilizers, weedkillers, and insecticides

Industrial Chemistry—the production of raw materials and the development of industrial chemical products

Water and Waste Chemistry—the use of chemistry in problems of water supply and distribution and in waste disposal

Biochemistry
The study of chemical processes in living things

Biogeochemistry—the study of the chemical relationships among living things and their geological surroundings

Chemotherapy or Medicinal Chemistry—the preparation of drugs for treating disease

Molecular Biophysics—the use of mathematics to explain the role of molecules in living things

Pathological Chemistry—the study of the chemical effects of disease on the body

Physical Chemistry
The use of mathematics to explain chemical processes and their relationship to energy

Chemical Thermodynamics—the study of the exchange of energy between a substance and its surroundings

Electrochemistry—the study of the effect of electricity on substances

Nuclear Chemistry—the use of chemical techniques in studying nuclear reactions

Photochemistry—the study of the effect of light on substances

Radiation Chemistry—the study of the chemical effects of radiation on substances

Structural Chemistry—the study of the way atoms link together to form molecules

Surface Chemistry—the study of chemical processes that take place at the surface of liquids and tiny solid particles

The Alchemist's Workshop was the forerunner of the modern chemistry laboratory. Here the alchemist searched for magic substances that would bring riches and unending life.

Bettmann Archive

Chemistry / HISTORY

Early Times. Long before chemistry became a science, people knew how to use various substances to make many things they needed. By the 2000's B.C., craftworkers of Egypt and Mesopotamia knew how to make weapons, tools, and ornaments from such metals as copper, gold, and silver. They made bronze by melting copper and tin together, and they prepared special substances to make glass beads and figures. Craftworkers also learned how to make perfume and wine. People could make these products because they could produce and control chemical changes. But they did not understand why these changes took place.

The first theories about chemistry and the nature of matter came from the philosophers of China, India, and Greece. These thinkers tried to explain that all things are made up of basic substances. Unlike craftworkers, philosophers had little interest in applying their knowledge to everyday uses. They formed their theories by observing the world around them. The philosophers saw, for example, that wood burned and produced fire. They supposed that fire was a basic substance, and that wood changed into fire when it burned.

Several ancient civilizations developed theories about the basic substances of nature. The *Shu Ching*, a Chinese book written several hundred years before Christ, claimed everything was made of earth, fire, water, metal, and wood. Empedocles of Greece believed there were four chief "roots" of matter—earth, fire, water, and air.

Democritus, a leading Greek scholar, taught that substances were made of atoms. According to this theory, atoms were hard bits of matter so tiny that they were invisible. This idea, proposed about 2,300 years ago, is based on the same principle as today's atomic theory of matter.

Alchemy was one of the earliest forms of chemistry. This ancient practice combined science, religion, philosophy, and magic. Alchemy developed as people applied theories about nature to metalworking, medicine, and other crafts. The alchemists worked to find a substance called the *philosopher's stone* that would change lead, iron, and other metals into gold. They also tried to produce the *elixir of life*, a substance that would provide long or unending life and health.

FAMOUS CHEMISTS

Democritus of Greece taught 2,300 years ago that all things were made of atoms.

Culver

Fisher Scientific Company

Roger Bacon, an English monk, saw the need for careful experimentation in alchemy.

Philippus Paracelsus promoted the use of chemistry in medicine during the 1500's.

Culver

Culver

Robert Boyle attacked the ancient theories of alchemy and became the first real chemist.

Alchemy began during the 300 years after the birth of Christ. Until the A.D. 1600's, alchemy was the main source of chemical knowledge. Alchemists discovered many ways of producing chemical changes in natural substances. They improved the methods of taking metals from ore, and they learned how to make and use various acids. Alchemists also designed laboratory equipment including balances for weighing chemicals, and crucibles for melting metals.

The development of alchemy took place chiefly in Alexandria, an Egyptian city that was a center of learning and religion. Alchemy also was studied in China and Greece. It spread to Arabia after the Arabs conquered Egypt in A.D. 642. Arabian alchemists developed a theory that different metals could be formed by combining mercury and sulfur in various proportions. Later, this theory was widely accepted by alchemists in other countries. Arabs and Moors invaded and conquered most of Spain during the 700's. But Spanish scholars did not translate Arabic alchemy books into Latin until the 1100's. These translations introduced alchemy to the rest of Europe and to England.

The English philosopher and alchemist Roger Bacon laid the foundation for the experimental method of chemical research. Bacon, unlike the early alchemists, planned his experiments and carefully interpreted his laboratory work.

Chemistry in Medicine. During the 1500's, some alchemists and physicians began to apply their knowledge of chemistry to the treatment of disease. Since ancient times, people had known how to prepare and use various drugs. But they did so without understanding how the drugs worked (see MEDICINE [History]). The medical chemistry of the 1500's and 1600's is called *iatrochemistry* (from the Greek word *iatros*, meaning *physician*). Iatrochemists were the first to study the chemical effects of medicines on the body.

A Swiss physician, Philippus Paracelsus, pioneered in iatrochemistry. Paracelsus accepted the belief that air, earth, fire, and water were the four basic substances. He believed they took the form of mercury, sulfur, and salt, which he called the *three principles*.

The iatrochemists did not fully understand how their medicines affected the body. But their work promoted an interest in the chemistry of the body. As scientists learned more about medicine, they gradually lost interest in the impractical theories of alchemy.

Chemistry Becomes a Science. During the 1600's, physicians continued to do much of the work in chemistry. They studied bile, blood, saliva, and urine. They also experimented with medicines made from sulfur, mercury, and other minerals. New theories were developed by several experimenters.

Jan Baptista van Helmont, a Belgian chemist and physician, thought air and water were the only elements. In one experiment, Van Helmont measured the growth of a tree that he fed only with water. This experiment led him to believe that water was the basic element of all plants. Van Helmont invented the word *gas* and studied the gases released by burning charcoal and fermenting wine. He also believed that food was digested by acids in the body.

Robert Boyle of Ireland has often been considered the last important alchemist and also the first real chemist. Boyle taught that theories must be supported by careful experiments. He accepted some of Van Helmont's ideas, and enlarged the study of gases, especially of air. Boyle believed that matter was made up of atoms. By his experiments, he showed that air, earth, fire, and water were not elements. Boyle's book, *The Sceptical Chymist* (1661), marked the final break between chemistry and alchemy. Alchemy continued to be practiced until the 1700's. But it became mostly a collection of magic that had little to do with chemistry.

The Discovery of Oxygen. After chemistry separated from alchemy, it took chemists about a hundred years to develop the basic theories of modern chemistry. During this period, chemists discovered chlorine, cobalt, manganese, and other elements. They also continued the study of gases begun by Van Helmont and Boyle. The study of gases led to the discovery of oxygen. And the role of oxygen in chemical reactions became the key to modern chemistry.

The early gas experiments of the 1700's were based on a theory advanced by Georg Stahl, a German chemist and physician. Stahl taught that a substance called *phlogiston* escaped when a material burned, or when iron became rusty. Important chemists who accepted the phlogiston theory included Carl Wilhelm Scheele, Joseph Priestley, and Henry Cavendish.

Scheele, a Swedish experimenter, thought that the heat produced by chemical reactions consisted of two substances. One substance, he said, was phlogiston. The other he called *fire air*. Although Scheele's theory was

Antoine Lavoisier founded modern chemistry by explaining how oxygen forms compounds.
Culver

Culver
Sir Humphry Davy discovered several elements and invented a safety lamp for miners.

Historical Picture Service
Jöns J. Berzelius calculated atomic weights and began the use of modern chemical symbols.

Dmitri Mendeleev discovered that an element's properties depend on its atomic weight.
Bettmann Archive

not correct, he set up an experiment and produced "fire air." This new gas made the flame of a candle burn brightly. The gas was oxygen.

Priestley, an Englishman, worked at about the same time as Scheele and developed similar theories. He, too, produced oxygen. Priestley called the gas *dephlogisticated air* (air without phlogiston).

Cavendish, another Englishman, studied the gas produced when he treated metals with acid. He found that the gas was explosive when mixed with ordinary air, and so he called it *inflammable air*. This gas was hydrogen, but Cavendish thought it was the phlogiston present in metals.

The Beginning of Modern Chemistry. Soon after Scheele, Priestley, and Cavendish proposed their theories on phlogiston, a brilliant French chemist offered an opposite theory. Antoine Lavoisier denied that phlogiston was released when a material burned or iron rusted. Instead, he said, the material or the iron united with a substance already present in the air. This substance was the same as fire air or dephlogisticated air. Lavoisier named it *oxygen*. He showed that oxygen combined with such metals as iron and mercury to form compounds. By 1800, almost all chemists had accepted Lavoisier's ideas.

During the 1800's, chemists discovered about half of the more than 100 known elements. They improved on early theories and proposed many new ones. For example, Sir Humphry Davy of England discovered sodium and potassium by sending electricity through compounds containing the two elements. He developed a theory explaining the effect of electric current on chemical compounds.

Soon, many chemists began to specialize in certain types of problems. As a result, chemistry gradually became separated into three main branches: (1) *inorganic chemistry*, or the study of compounds that do not contain carbon; (2) *organic chemistry*, or the study of compounds that contain carbon; and (3) *physical chemistry*, or the study of heat, electricity, and other forms of energy in chemical processes.

Development of Inorganic Chemistry. In 1808, the English chemist John Dalton published an atomic theory he had developed in 1803. Dalton suggested that each element was made of a certain kind of atom. The atoms of each element, he said, were different from those of all other elements, especially in weight. Dalton even calculated the weights of atoms of several elements. Dalton's ideas were sound, but his weights were not accurate. He often made incorrect assumptions or failed to analyze substances properly.

By 1826, Jöns J. Berzelius had calculated a fairly accurate list of atomic weights. Berzelius, a Swedish chemist, based his work on Dalton's atomic theory and on the *law of combining volumes* developed by the French chemist Joseph Louis Gay-Lussac. The law of combining volumes applied to elements in the form of gas. It said that elements combine in definite proportions by volume to form compounds. For example, one volume of oxygen combines with two volumes of hydrogen to form water. By experimenting with various gases and carefully analyzing many purified compounds, Berzelius measured atomic weights and wrote formulas showing the composition of compounds. He introduced the use of chemical symbols such as O for oxygen and Mg for magnesium.

Berzelius and other chemists who calculated atomic weights did not always agree on their results. They could not build a satisfactory theory that would show which weights were correct. Such a theory lay hidden in the forgotten work of an Italian physicist, Amedeo Avogadro. As early as 1811, Avogadro had pointed out the difference between atoms and *molecules* (combinations of atoms). He showed that equal volumes of two gases contain the same number of molecules when the temperature and pressure are also equal. When two volumes of gas combine chemically, the individual atoms join to form molecules. The volume of the resulting compound depends on the proportions in which the atoms combine.

Avogadro's work went unnoticed for almost 50 years. Then, in 1860, the Italian chemist Stanislao Cannizzaro showed how Avogadro's theory applied to the measurement of atomic weights. The theory proved the accuracy of the weights calculated by Berzelius.

After Cannizzaro revived Avogadro's ideas, scientists calculated atomic weights with increased accuracy. Their work led to the discovery of a principle called the *periodic law*. Dmitri Mendeleev of Russia and Julius Lothar Meyer of Germany independently proposed this law in 1869. According to the periodic law, the properties of an element depend on its atomic weight. Mendeleev and Meyer recognized this principle when they listed the elements in order of increasing atomic weight.

FAMOUS CHEMISTS

Friedrich Wöhler was the first chemist to make an organic compound in the laboratory.

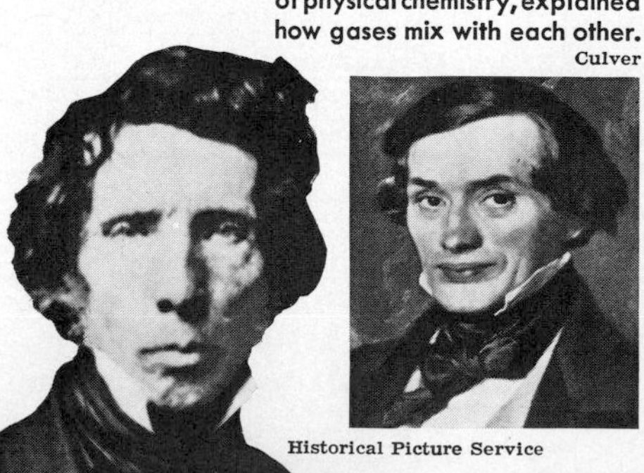

Thomas Graham, a founder of physical chemistry, explained how gases mix with each other.

Culver

Historical Picture Service

Antoine Henri Becquerel discovered that uranium gives off rays similar to X rays.

Culver

Glenn T. Seaborg was one of the discoverers of artificial elements heavier than uranium.

United Press Int.

Melvin Calvin explained how plants make food by the process of photosynthesis.

University of California

They saw that elements with similar properties appeared at regular intervals. So they arranged the elements with all similar elements in groups. Such an arrangement of the elements is called a *periodic table* or *periodic chart*. See ELEMENT, CHEMICAL (Periodic Table of the Elements).

Development of Organic Chemistry. From the time of the alchemists, experimenters had recognized and used various substances found only in plants and animals. During the 1800's, chemists learned that all these *organic* substances contain carbon and follow the same chemical laws as compounds found in minerals. The work of such men as Lavoisier, Dalton, Gay-Lussac, and Berzelius helped later chemists determine the composition of many carbon compounds.

An organic substance was produced in a laboratory for the first time in 1828. Friedrich Wöhler, a German chemist, made urea by combining mineral substances. He thus showed that living things were not the only source of organic compounds.

Justus von Liebig, another German chemist, discovered the composition of many organic compounds. Liebig became known for applying organic chemistry to the growing and preparing of food.

During the 1850's and 1860's, organic chemists developed the *valence theory*. This theory explained how atoms combined to form compounds. The idea of valence was especially important in studying organic substances. The German chemist Friedrich Kekulé von Stradonitz used the valence theory to explain how atoms of carbon and hydrogen combine to form a molecule of benzene. Kekulé's work with benzene led to an understanding of many similar organic compounds. By the end of the 1800's, the study of organic substances was a main branch of chemistry.

Development of Physical Chemistry. During the 1800's, physicists as well as chemists developed new chemical theories. Many of these new ideas dealt with the relationship between chemical reactions and such forms of energy as heat and electricity.

Thomas Graham, a Scottish chemist, was one of the founders of physical chemistry. Graham conducted research on gases and solutions. In 1833, he formulated *Graham's law of diffusion*, which explains how two gases mix with one another. He also did pioneering work with colloids. A *colloid* consists of tiny particles of one material evenly distributed in another.

In the 1870's, the American physicist Josiah Willard Gibbs developed the *phase rule*. This rule concerns the three *phases* (temporary forms) of matter—solid, liquid, and gas. For example, water (a liquid) can be boiled to form steam (a gas), or it can be frozen to form ice (a solid).

The phase rule helped Jacobus van't Hoff study how crystals are formed in various solutions. Van't Hoff, a Dutch chemist, also investigated the heat produced by chemical reactions. His theories on the arrangement of atoms in molecules led to the development of *stereochemistry*. Stereochemists are specialists in the three-dimensional structure of molecules.

Other important physical chemists of the late 1800's included Svante A. Arrhenius of Sweden and Wilhelm Ostwald of Germany. These men suggested that electricity is carried through solutions by ions. An *ion* is an electrically charged atom or group of atoms.

The Discovery of Radioactivity in the 1890's led to important advances in chemical theory during the 1900's. A radioactive element is one that gives off atomic particles and high energy rays. Antoine Henri Becquerel, a French physicist, discovered radioactivity in uranium ore in 1896. Becquerel's work led to the discovery of radium in 1898 by Marie Curie and her husband Pierre.

In 1911, the British physicist Ernest Rutherford proposed a new theory of atomic structure. According to Rutherford's theory, the atom has a positively charged nucleus surrounded by negatively charged electrons. Other physicists developed this idea further and discovered that the nucleus consists of particles which they named *protons* and *neutrons* (see ATOM [Development of the Atomic Theory]). In 1919, Rutherford changed nitrogen to oxygen by sending rays from radium through nitrogen. This was the first time that one chemical element was artificially transformed into another.

Chemists used the new information about atoms to improve their ideas about valence. In 1916, Gilbert N. Lewis of the United States proposed an atomic structure to explain the action of electrons in *chemical bonds* (forces that hold atoms together). This theory was developed further by another American chemist, Irving Langmuir, and by Walther Kossel of Germany.

In 1934, Frédéric and Irène Joliot-Curie discovered that artificial radioactivity could be produced by bombarding various elements with alpha particles. During the late 1930's, scientists learned how to produce energy by splitting the nucleus of the uranium atom. This discovery led to the birth of the atomic age in the 1940's, with the first controlled nuclear reaction. Beginning in 1940, chemists and physicists also began to produce elements not found in natural substances. These artificially created elements were made by bombarding uranium and other radioactive elements with particles such as neutrons. Glenn T. Seaborg was one of the leading United States experimenters in this field. See TRANSURANIUM ELEMENTS; ISOTOPE (Artificial Radioisotopes).

Chemistry Today. During the 1950's and 1960's, scientists took important steps in *biochemistry*, the study of the role of chemicals in living things. Melvin Calvin, an American chemist, solved many long-standing mysteries of *photosynthesis* (the process by which plants make food). In England, John C. Kendrew and Max F. Perutz analyzed the structure of complicated organic compounds found in the blood. Biochemists also learned how chemicals such as *deoxyribonucleic acid* (DNA) and *ribonucleic acid* (RNA) affect heredity (see HEREDITY; NUCLEIC ACID).

In 1962 and 1963, inorganic chemists succeeded in producing compounds of krypton, radon, and xenon. These three elements, together with argon, helium, and neon, form a chemical group called the *noble gases*. It had long been considered impossible for any noble gas to form a compound.

During the 1960's and 1970's, United States chemists developed special devices and techniques for exploring space. A variety of automatic devices were designed to analyze the soil on the moon and to search for chemical signs of life on Mars. See SPACE TRAVEL (Space Probes).

Loyola University of Chicago (WORLD BOOK photo)

A Chemistry Laboratory in a school provides the proper facilities to conduct experiments. Students work with a wide variety of chemicals at specially equipped lab tables.

Chemistry / TOOLS OF THE CHEMIST

Chemists do most of their work in a laboratory. There, they perform experiments that show them how nature behaves. In these experiments, chemists handle many substances and use various kinds of equipment. Individuals working in a chemistry laboratory may be students handling chemicals for the first time. Or they may be professional chemists doing advanced research. Whatever the job, they follow rules of safety.

Chemists often must work with dangerous chemicals. For example, certain acids can cause serious injury if spilled or splashed on the body. To guard against accidents, chemists treat all chemicals with the proper care. They usually wear an apron or a lab coat to protect themselves against accidental spilling or splashing. When handling especially dangerous chemicals, they may wear rubber gloves. Chemists also wear safety glasses to protect their eyes when working in the laboratory. Professional laboratory workers are trained to give emergency treatment in case an accident with chemicals causes an injury.

Chemistry Laboratories vary greatly, depending on the kind of work being performed. For example, the laboratory of a paint manufacturer contains materials and equipment different from those found in the laboratory of a food processor.

In a laboratory used for high school or beginning college chemistry, students perform a wide variety of experiments. The students work at *lab tables.* Each table may be about the size of a desk, with room for two students to work at the same time. Or the table may resemble a long counter, with space for as many as 10 students. The top of the lab table is made of a material such as soapstone that resists *corrosion* (wearing away) by chemicals. Students may keep notebooks, lab manuals, and various kinds of chemical apparatus in drawers in the lab table.

One or more sinks may be built into the top of a desk-shaped lab table, or at one or both ends of a long lab table. The sinks are used for disposing of liquid chemicals and for cleaning apparatus. Special outlets on top of the table provide each student with water, gas for laboratory burners, and perhaps electricity. Distilled water is kept in large bottles.

Certain tables in a laboratory may have ventilating hoods above them. A *hood* is a metal covering somewhat like a large, upside-down funnel. Experimenters use tables with hoods when working with substances that give off poisonous or irritating fumes. A fan in the ventilating system draws polluted air up through the hood. Pipes carry the air to the outside of the building.

Laboratory safety equipment includes fire extinguishers, a first-aid kit, and a chart showing how to give emergency treatment. These items are kept in places that are easy to see and easy to reach. The laboratory also may have an alarm for use if an accident sends poisonous fumes through the room.

Chemical Apparatus. The chemist uses test tubes of various sizes to hold small amounts of liquid and solid substances. When not in use, the tubes stand in racks made of wood, metal, or plastic. Glass beakers and flasks are used for larger amounts of liquid and solid substances. To grind a solid material into a fine powder, the chemist places the material into a strong bowl called a *mortar*. A small club-shaped tool called a *pestle* is used to grind the substance.

In many experiments, chemicals must be heated. Several types of laboratory burners may be used. The common Bunsen burner is connected to a gas outlet on the lab table (see BUNSEN BURNER). Another type of burner has its own small tank of compressed gas. To produce extremely high temperatures, a special electric furnace may be used.

When heating a substance in a test tube, the chemist clamps the tube in a metal holder. The chemist holds the tube over a burner or attaches the clamp to a metal stand, with the tube over a burner. Metal *tripods* (three-legged stands) and ring stands are used to heat beakers and flasks. The chemist first places a small, square wire screen on the stand, and then sets the beaker or the flask on top of the screen. The wire screen distributes the heat of the flame over the bottom of the container so that the contents reach an even temperature.

Bowls and dishes used in the laboratory are made of porcelain and platinum. These materials resist heat and corrosion better than glass does. Dishes shaped like deep saucers are used for evaporating liquids and heating solids. Small cup-shaped *crucibles* hold metals to be melted. The temperature of the heated material is controlled by adjusting a cover on the crucible to let in more or less air.

The chemist weighs solid substances on a special scale called an *analytical balance*. This balance is so sensitive that it can weigh a person's name written on paper with a pencil. A glass case encloses the balance to protect it from dust and to keep air currents from affecting measurements. The chemist works the balance by means of controls outside the case. See BALANCE.

To measure small amounts of liquids accurately, the chemist may use a pipette or a burette. A *pipette* is a glass tube open at both ends. Some pipettes widen at the middle to form a bulb. The chemist sucks some liquid up into the pipette, and traps the liquid in the tube by covering the top opening with one finger. By uncovering the opening, the chemist releases small amounts of liquid. The amount of liquid released can be measured by noting how far the level of the liquid falls in the pipette. Markings on the side of the tube measure the volume of the liquid in milliliters. A *burette* holds larger quantities than a pipette. It is somewhat like a long test tube, and has a *stopcock* (valve) at its lower end. The chemist pours the liquid into the top of the burette, and then withdraws measured amounts by opening the stopcock. The burette is marked off in milliliters.

Filter paper is used to separate solids from liquids. The chemist shapes the paper into a cone, places it in a glass funnel, and then pours the mixture containing the solid into the funnel. Liquids pass through the filter paper, but solids do not. A device called a *centrifuge* separates solids from liquids, or one liquid from another liquid. The centrifuge whirls test tubes around. The heavy substances go to the bottom of the tubes and the light substances stay at the top.

Equipment for a Chemistry Laboratory

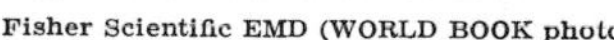
Fisher Scientific EMD (WORLD BOOK photo)

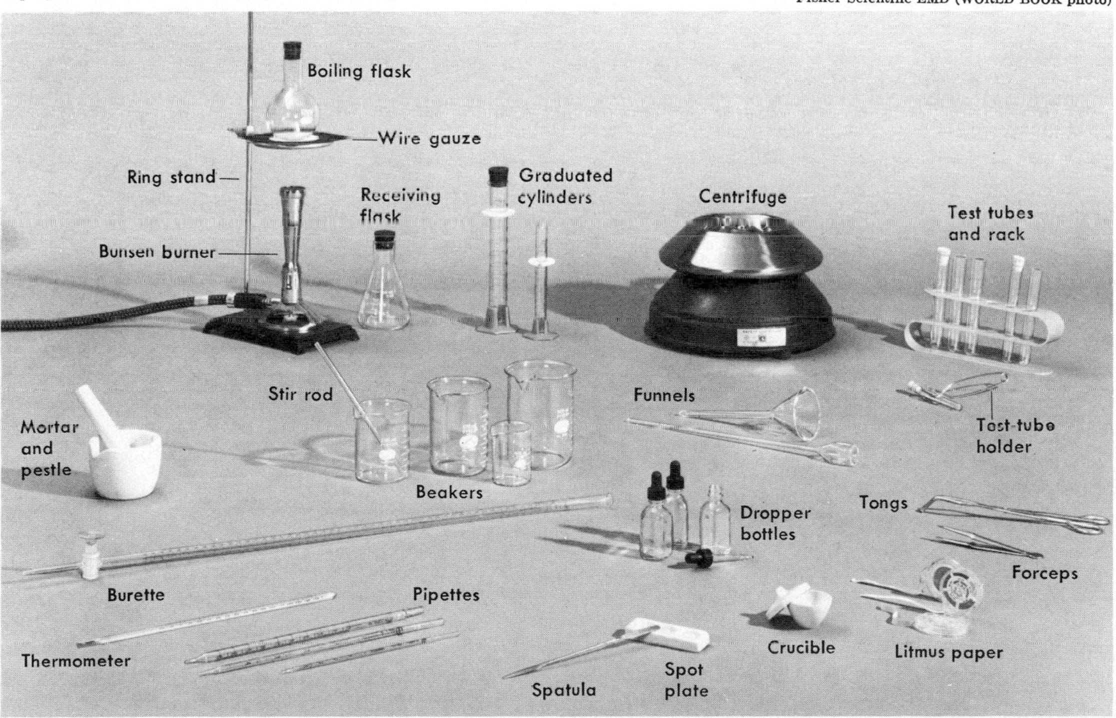

Laboratory Experiments help students understand ideas introduced in classroom lectures and textbooks. Such experiments also enable young people to develop the necessary skills to conduct chemical research.

Loyola University of Chicago (WORLD BOOK photo)

Chemistry / THE CHEMIST'S EDUCATION

Most chemists have certain personal qualifications that help in their work. First of all, chemists are curious. They want to understand what substances are, and why substances act the way they do. But chemists are not satisfied with just learning theories. They also like to build equipment and to perform experiments to test the theories. They have the patience to work a long time—perhaps several years—to solve a single problem.

The chemist's education begins in high school and college, and never really ends. A professional chemist must continue reading and studying to keep up with advances in the various fields of chemistry.

High-School Courses in science and mathematics help prepare a student for a career as a chemist. Many colleges allow high-school graduates to major in chemistry only if they have taken chemistry, physics, and three years of mathematics. Four years of English also are desirable because chemists need to know how to speak and write clearly when reporting on their work.

College Chemistry Programs usually last four years and include five or six main chemistry courses. Most courses require a year to complete. Among these courses are general chemistry, analytical chemistry, inorganic chemistry, organic chemistry, and physical chemistry.

General chemistry, a first-year course, varies in different colleges. It usually resembles a high school chemistry course. But a college course emphasizes theory, includes more details about chemical reactions, and calls for more laboratory work than a high school course.

Analytical chemistry is usually studied during the second and third years. It has two divisions—qualitative analysis and quantitative analysis. In *qualitative analysis*, students learn how to determine what kinds of elements and compounds are combined in any given sample. In *quantitative analysis*, they learn how to measure the amount of an element or a compound that is present in a particular sample.

Inorganic chemistry, taken any time after the first year, deals with compounds that do not contain carbon. It emphasizes the study of the structure and chemical reactions of such compounds.

Organic chemistry, often studied in the second and third years, deals with the element carbon and its compounds. Students learn the structure of complex organic molecules. They also study what happens when organic compounds combine chemically with other substances.

Physical chemistry, taken during the third or fourth year, relates chemistry to physics and mathematics.

During these last two years, students also may study one or more of the following courses: qualitative organic analysis, biochemistry, quantum chemistry, valence theory, structural inorganic chemistry, chemical literature, and the history of chemistry.

After completing their studies, students receive a Bachelor of Science (B.S.) degree. They may then take graduate courses leading to a Master of Science (M.S.) degree or a Doctor of Philosophy (Ph.D.) degree. During graduate work, the students specialize in some branch of chemistry. In most colleges, they can earn a doctorate without getting a master's degree first. It usually takes one year to earn a master's degree, and three or four years for a doctorate. The doctoral program is designed chiefly to help students develop their research skills.

A Science Project encourages young students to apply their knowledge of the basic principles of chemistry.

WORLD BOOK photo

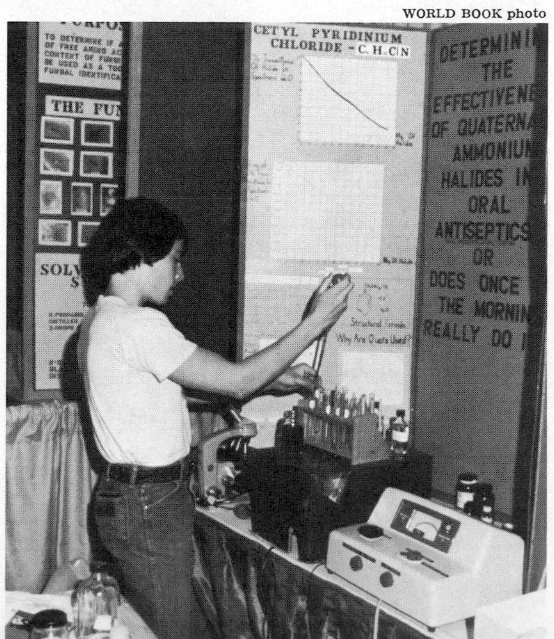

Chemistry / CAREERS

Chemists hold a wide variety of jobs in education, government, and industry. Careers in chemistry may be divided into six areas with the following job titles: (1) research chemist, (2) chemistry teacher, (3) consultant, (4) chemical sales representative, (5) chemistry literature specialist, and (6) laboratory technician. Some chemists work in more than one of these areas. Some also become administrators, such as high school principals or department heads of chemical companies.

Research Chemists conduct basic or applied research. They work in basic research to learn more about nature. In industry, basic research programs aim at a better understanding of the chemical substances produced by a company. For example, a chemist working for a plastics firm might study how molecules of plastics stick together. Universities also sponsor basic research programs, but with less practical aims than in industrial research programs. Chemists who conduct applied research programs try to develop new products and improve old ones. For example, a biochemist employed by a drug company might try to develop a new medicine for the treatment of skin diseases. See RESEARCH (Kinds of Research).

Chemistry Teachers help others learn about chemistry. These teachers work in high schools, colleges, and technical institutes.

Consultants advise, direct, and train people in all phases of chemistry. Many college teachers serve as part-time consultants to industrial firms. Some chemists work for companies that sell consulting services to industry. Others operate their own consulting businesses or work for the government.

Chemical Sales Representatives sell chemical products. They help customers select the best products to meet their needs. Sales representatives may also demonstrate how to use the products. They receive special training from their companies so that they fully understand the nature and various uses of the products.

Chemistry Literature Specialists are librarians or technical writers. Chemical librarians help research chemists locate information in books, documents, and other reading materials. Chemical writers may prepare reports on experiments or compose training manuals for chemical companies.

Laboratory Technicians conduct routine chemical analyses and help research chemists perform experiments. These technicians may also test new products or supervise a group of skilled workers.

Educational Requirements for a career in chemistry vary from job to job. Most positions of research chemist, college teacher, or consultant, require a doctor's degree. Most high school chemistry teachers must have bachelor's degrees, and some school systems hire only those with master's degrees. A bachelor's degree is required for most jobs as chemical sales representatives. Chemists need at least a bachelor's degree to become literature specialists. Some positions as literature specialists are open only to applicants with doctor's degrees. Applicants for positions as laboratory technicians should have one or two years of high school chemistry or a diploma from a junior college.

WORLD BOOK photo

As a Researcher, a chemist may make chemical analyses with such instruments as a gas chromatograph, *above*.

Loyola University of Chicago (WORLD BOOK photo)

As a Teacher, a chemist seeks to promote an active interest in chemistry and a solid understanding of this science.

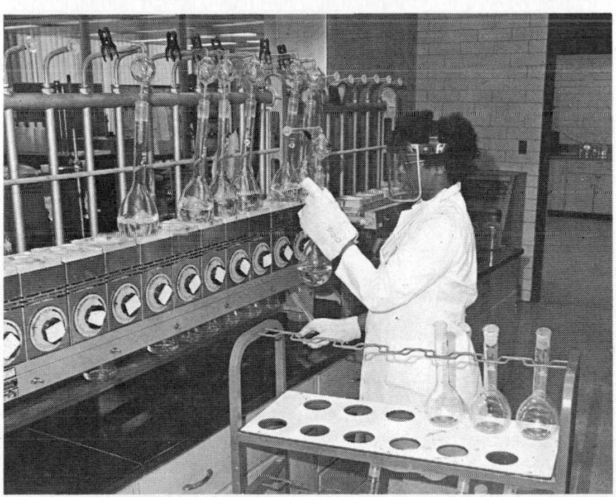

Bureau of Water Operations, City of Chicago (WORLD BOOK photo)

As a Laboratory Technician, a chemist may test a city's drinking water for harmful industrial pollutants.

Chemistry / BASIC CHEMISTRY

The world contains many thousands of different materials. Most of these materials are mixtures of two or more substances. For example, the cement used in making concrete is a mixture of lime, silica, and alumina. Each of these three substances is a combination of simpler substances. Lime is a combination of calcium and oxygen; silica is a combination of silicon and oxygen; and alumina is a combination of aluminum and oxygen. Calcium, silicon, aluminum, and oxygen cannot be broken down into other substances. They are basic substances called *elements* that combine in various ways to form all the world's materials. Combinations of elements, such as lime, silica, and alumina, are called *compounds*.

The fundamental ideas of chemistry deal with the nature of elements, and the ways in which elements combine to form compounds.

Kinds of Substances

Every substance has certain properties that distinguish it from every other substance. For example, hydrogen sulfide gas has a characteristic odor like that of rotten eggs. When a glowing ember is placed into a container of oxygen, the ember bursts into flame. Scientists divide the characteristics of substances into physical properties and chemical properties.

Physical properties can be recognized without changing a substance chemically. They include such characteristics as color, odor, taste, and density. *Density* is the mass per each unit of volume of a substance. The density of water, for example, is about 62 pounds per cubic foot (1 gram per cubic centimeter).

Chemical properties depend on the ways in which a substance reacts with other substances. Iron reacts slowly with water and forms rust. But sodium reacts so violently with water that an explosion can take place. Sulfuric acid acts on iron to form iron sulfate. But sulfuric acid does not affect platinum or gold.

The knowledge of physical and chemical properties helps scientists analyze substances and classify them into three main groups: (1) elements, (2) compounds, and (3) mixtures.

Elements, such as hydrogen, carbon, and uranium, are the simplest substances. Everything in the world is either an element or a combination of elements. Elements themselves are not combinations of any other substances. Each element is made up of tiny particles of matter called *atoms*. The atoms of one element differ from those of all other elements. Atoms themselves are made up of even tinier particles of matter.

The atoms of all elements contain the same kinds of particles. Protons and neutrons make up the *nucleus* (central core) of the atom. *Protons* are tiny, positively charged bits of matter. *Neutrons* are uncharged particles about the same weight as protons. Negatively charged *electrons* revolve around the nucleus. It takes about 1,840 electrons to equal the weight of one proton.

Atoms of different elements contain different numbers of particles. A hydrogen atom, for example, contains 1 proton and 1 electron. Uranium has 92 protons, 146 neutrons, and 92 electrons. See ATOM.

Chemists use a symbol consisting of one or two letters to stand for each element. For example, the symbol for hydrogen is H, and the symbol for helium is He. Some chemical symbols come from words of other languages. The symbol for iron, for example, is Fe. This symbol comes from *ferrum*, the Latin word for iron. See ELEMENT, CHEMICAL.

Compounds, such as water, salt, and carbon dioxide, are formed when different elements combine. For example, 2 atoms of hydrogen join with 1 atom of oxygen to form a molecule of water. A *molecule* is the smallest part of a substance that has the chemical properties of the substance.

Chemical formulas show the molecular composition of compounds. The formula for water is H_2O. The H_2 stands for 2 atoms of hydrogen, and the O stands for 1 atom of oxygen. Sulfuric acid has the formula H_2SO_4. Its molecule contains 2 atoms of hydrogen (H_2), 1 atom of sulfur (S), and 4 atoms of oxygen (O_4).

Chemists also use marks such as parentheses () and a *center dot* in writing formulas for certain compounds. For example, calcium nitrate is written $Ca(NO_3)_2 \cdot 4H_2O$. Ca means 1 calcium atom. The (NO_3) stands for the nitrate radical, composed of 1 nitrogen atom and 3 oxygen atoms. A *radical* is a group of atoms that act as a single unit in forming compounds. The 2 following the parentheses shows that the calcium nitrate molecule contains 2 nitrate radicals. The $4H_2O$ after the center dot means that 4 water molecules are contained in the calcium nitrate molecule. Compounds that contain molecules of water are called *hydrates*.

Mixtures contain varying amounts of substances that are not chemically united. Mixtures may be in the form of *solutions* or *suspensions*.

Solutions are combinations of one or more substances dissolved in one or more other substances. The dissolved substance spreads uniformly throughout a solution. For example, sugar dissolves in a cup of coffee and sweetens the entire beverage. The sweetened coffee is a solution formed by a solid dissolved in a liquid. One liquid also may dissolve in another liquid, as when alcohol dissolves in water. "Carbonated" soda pop is a solution of carbon dioxide gas dissolved in a liquid.

Suspensions are combinations in which one substance is uniformly distributed through another without dissolving in it. Suspensions of tiny particles give gems and colored glass their colors. Solid particles also may be suspended in a liquid, such as hot chocolate; and in a gas, such as smoke.

How Compounds Are Formed

Atomic Structure. To understand how elements combine to form compounds, it is necessary to understand the structure of atoms. Atoms consist mainly of electrically charged particles—electrons and protons. Each electron has a negative charge. Each proton has a positive charge. Neutrons, which are also present in atoms, have no charge.

Normally, an atom contains as many electrons as protons. The negative charges and the positive charges balance each other, and the atom is *neutral* (uncharged).

If the balance between electrons and protons is upset, the atom becomes an electrically charged unit called an *ion*. An atom becomes a positive ion if it loses one or more electrons. For example, when a hydrogen atom loses its single electron, it becomes a positive hydrogen ion (written H^+). An atom becomes a negative ion when it gains electrons. A negative chlorine ion (written Cl^-) is a chlorine atom that has gained one additional electron.

Electrons revolve at various distances from the nucleus of an atom. The paths of the electrons form a series of shells with the nucleus at the center. Each succeeding shell is farther from the nucleus than the one before it. Scientists have found that each shell can contain no more than a certain number of electrons. The first shell can hold no more than 2 electrons. The second can hold no more than 8; the third, no more than 18, and so on.

Most interactions among atoms take place in the outermost shell of each atom. The number of electrons in this shell determines the manner in which an atom combines with other atoms to form compounds. When atoms combine, they gain, lose, or share electrons in such a way that their outer shells become chemically "complete." The first shell is complete when it contains 2 electrons. Hydrogen, which has only 1 electron, can combine with another element by gaining 1 electron to fill its shell. Helium, an element that has a complete shell of 2 electrons, does not unite readily with other elements.

All shells beyond the first shell are chemically complete when they contain 8 electrons, even though they may be able to hold many more. For example, the third shell can contain as many as 18 electrons. But argon's third and last shell is chemically complete with 8 electrons, and so argon does not combine readily with any other element. The number of electrons in each shell of each of the elements is shown in the *Periodic Table of the Elements* in the WORLD BOOK article ELEMENT, CHEMICAL.

Valence is a property related to the electrons in an atom's outer shell. The valence of an element is the number of electrons the element gains or loses when it forms compounds with other elements. Electrons in the outermost shell are called *valence electrons*.

Potassium has four shells of 2, 8, 8, and 1 electrons. When potassium combines with other elements, it usually loses 1 electron and becomes a positive ion with a complete 8-electron outer shell. Because it loses 1 electron and becomes positive, potassium has a valence of +1. The plus sign represents the positive charge of the ion after the electron has been lost. Other elements that have +1 valence include hydrogen, lithium, and sodium.

On the other hand, fluorine and chlorine have 7 valence electrons. When these elements combine with other atoms, they each gain 1 electron to complete their outer shells. Such elements have a valence of −1. The minus sign shows that the atoms become negative ions by gaining one electron.

Elements with 1, 2, and 3 valence electrons usually lose these electrons during chemical combinations. Such elements have valences of +1, +2, and +3. Elements with 5, 6, and 7 valence electrons usually gain enough electrons to make a complete shell of 8 electrons. These elements have valences of −3, −2, and −1.

Carbon, and other elements with 4 valence electrons, can either lose 4 electrons or gain 4 electrons. Such elements have two valences (+4 and −4). Many other elements have more than one valence, depending on the properties of the atoms with which these elements combine.

Chemical Bonds are forces that hold atoms together. These forces arise from the interaction of valence electrons. The two principal types of chemical bonds are ionic bonds and covalent bonds.

In an *ionic bond*, valence electrons are transferred from one atom to one or more other atoms. The atom that loses electrons becomes a positive ion. The atoms that gain electrons become negative ions. An electrical force holds the oppositely charged ions together. The bond between sodium and chlorine in sodium chloride ($NaCl$) is an ionic bond. In this compound, sodium (valence +1) becomes a positive ion, and chlorine (valence −1) becomes a negative ion. Chlorine also combines with calcium to form calcium chloride ($CaCl_2$). Calcium (valence +2) has 2 valence electrons, and so it must combine with 2 chlorine atoms. Each of the 2 chlorine atoms gets one of the 2 calcium valence electrons to complete its own outer shell.

TWO EXAMPLES OF ELECTRON SHELLS

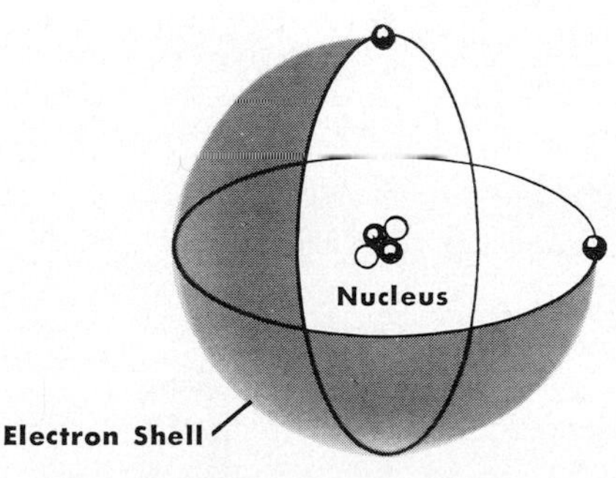

A Helium Atom contains two electrons. The paths of the electrons (shaded area) form a shell around the nucleus. A portion of the shell has been cut away to emphasize its ball-like shape.

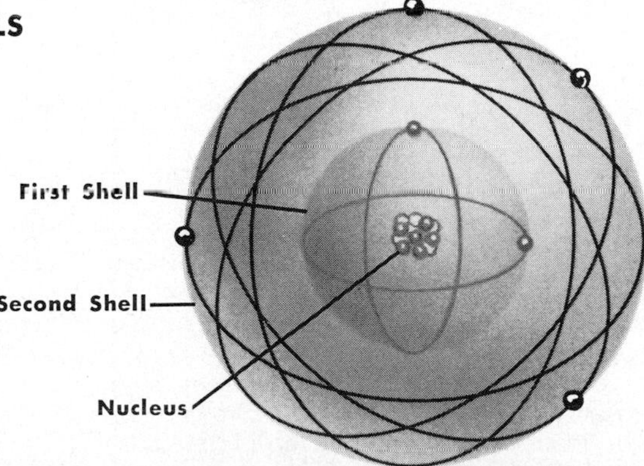

A Carbon Atom has six electrons that form two shells. The first shell has two electrons, like the shell of a helium atom. The second shell surrounds the first and contains four electrons.

A WORLD BOOK SCIENCE PROJECT

A SIMPLE CHEMICAL EXPERIMENT

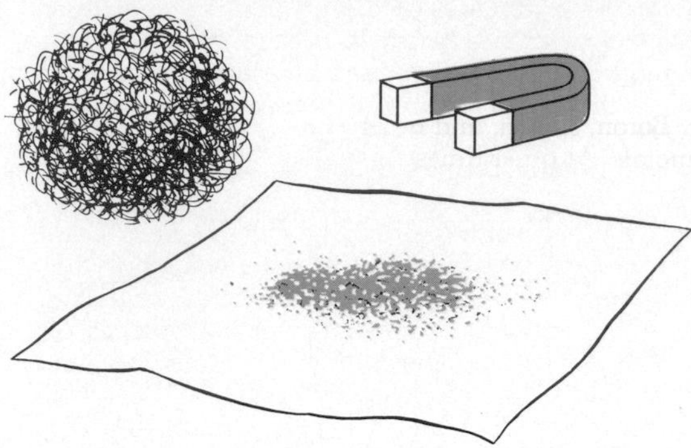

This experiment shows that iron and oxygen can combine in different ways to form two compounds. One compound is a reddish, nonmagnetic powder, and the other is a blue-black magnetic powder.

MATERIALS

Steel wool rusts slowly in water, but quickly in a solution containing hypochlorous acid. You can make such a solution by mixing bleach and vinegar. The hypochlorous acid (HClO) in the solution reacts with the iron (Fe) in steel wool to form hydrated ferric oxide ($Fe_2O_3 \cdot H_2O$). By heating this oxide, you can change it to magnetic oxide of iron (Fe_3O_4).

WORLD BOOK illustration by Raymond Perlman

PROCEDURE

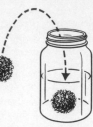

Place the ball of steel wool into one of the jars and add enough water to cover the ball. You see no change in the steel wool because water affects iron slowly.

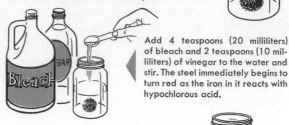

Add 4 teaspoons (20 milliliters) of bleach and 2 teaspoons (10 milliliters) of vinegar to the water and stir. The steel immediately begins to turn red as the iron in it reacts with hypochlorous acid.

In about 5 minutes, the liquid is full of red powder. This powder is hydrated ferric oxide (rust). Remove the steel wool from the jar and wait for the powder to settle.

After the powder has settled, carefully pour off the clear solution. The powder and some liquid will remain at the bottom of the jar.

Wash the powder by filling the jar with water and stirring. Once again, allow the powder to settle and pour off most of the water.

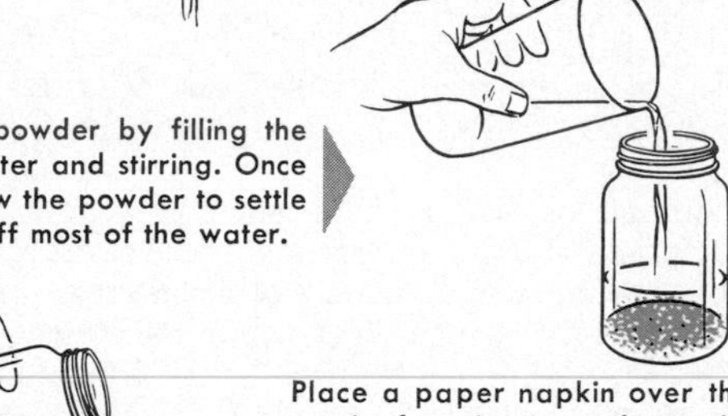

Place a paper napkin over the mouth of another jar and pour the mixture of powder and liquid into the napkin. Wait for all the liquid to filter through the paper.

Spread out the napkin and allow the powder to dry. Then test it by touching a magnet to it. Hydrated ferric oxide is not magnetic.

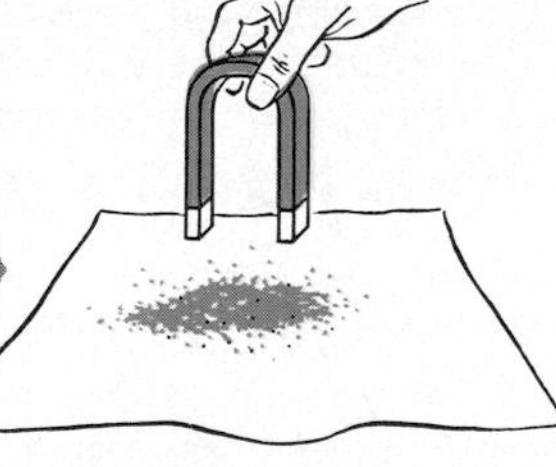

Place the powder on an old spoon and heat it in the flame of a candle. The red powder slowly turns blue-black as it changes to magnetic oxide of iron.

After the color of the powder has changed completely, test it again for magnetism. The blue-black grains will cling to the magnet.

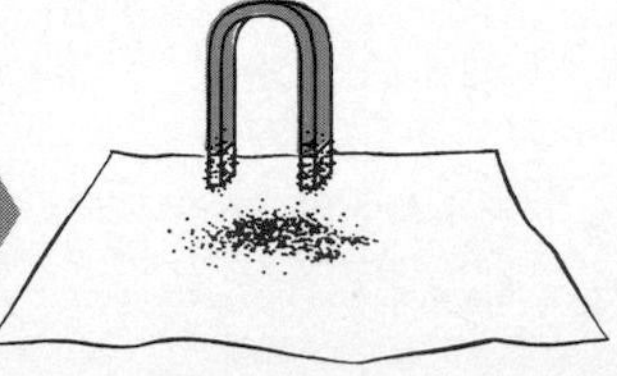

A *covalent bond* occurs when the atoms of two or more elements share pairs of valence electrons. A shared pair consists of one electron from each of two atoms. Shared electrons complete the outer shells of both atoms. For example, 2 hydrogen atoms and 1 oxygen atom are held together by covalent bonds in a molecule of water, as shown in the following diagram:

```
   ..
H : O : H
   ..
```

The dots in the diagram represent valence electrons, showing 6 for oxygen and 1 for each of the 2 hydrogen atoms. Dots placed between the element symbols stand for shared electrons. One electron of a shared pair belongs to a hydrogen atom, and the other belongs to the oxygen atom. Each shared pair makes up a complete 2-electron shell for a hydrogen atom. At the same time, the shared pairs complete an 8-electron shell for the oxygen atom.

Structural Formulas show the arrangement of atoms in a molecule and also the chemical bonds that hold the atoms together. The above diagram of the water molecule is one kind of structural formula. In another kind, the symbols for elements are connected by short lines that represent chemical bonds. Each line stands for a covalent bond formed by a pair of shared electrons. Using this method, chemists write the structural formula for water H—O—H. The formula shows that each hydrogen atom is connected to the oxygen atom by a covalent bond. The structural formula for carbon dioxide is O═C═O. The two lines on each side of the carbon atom represent double covalent bonds. The lines show that each oxygen atom shares 2 pairs of electrons with the carbon atom.

Many organic compounds have the same kind and number of atoms. These compounds differ only in structure. For example, butyl alcohol and diethyl ether both contain 4 carbon atoms, 10 hydrogen atoms, and 1 oxygen atom. These two compounds have the same molecular formula—$C_4H_{10}O$. Their structural formulas show how they differ:

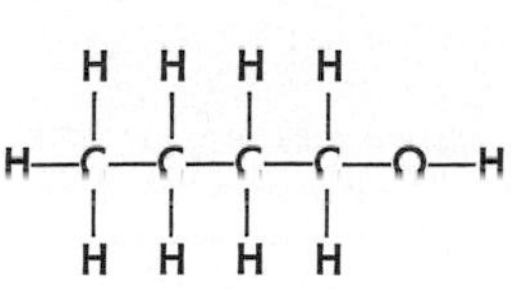

```
    H  H  H  H                 H  H     H  H
    |  |  |  |                 |  |     |  |
 H—C—C—C—C—O—H              H—C—C—O—C—C—H
    |  |  |  |                 |  |     |  |
    H  H  H  H                 H  H     H  H

  Butyl Alcohol                Diethyl Ether
```

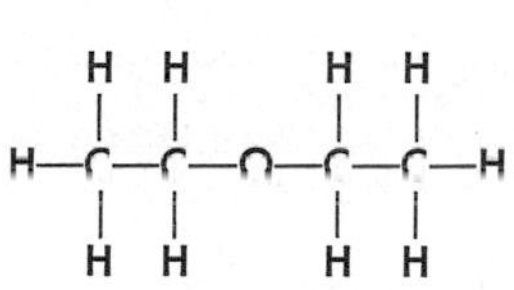

Chemists write shortened forms of structural formulas in several ways. For example, the structural formula for water may be written HOH. Diethyl ether has the formulas $CH_3CH_2OCH_2CH_3$ and $C_2H_5OC_2H_5$ which list the groups of atoms as they appear from left to right in the above illustrations.

The Language of Chemistry

Chemical Groups. Chemists have several ways of classifying substances. Chemical groups and names, as well as chemical formulas, help chemists recognize the composition and properties of a wide variety of substances.

The broadest chemical classification divides the 103 elements into two groups—metals and nonmetals. A *metal*, such as sodium or potassium, generally loses its valence electrons when it becomes part of a compound. A *nonmetal*, such as sulfur or chlorine, generally gains electrons when it forms a compound. However, the distinction between metals and nonmetals is not always clear. Boron, silicon, and other elements sometimes act like metals. At other times these elements act like nonmetals.

Chemists divide inorganic compounds into four major groups: (1) oxides, (2) acids, (3) bases, and (4) salts.

Oxides are combinations of oxygen with metals or nonmetals. Calcium oxide (CaO) is a metallic oxide. Sulfur dioxide (SO_2) is a nonmetallic oxide.

Acids, such as sulfuric acid (H_2SO_4) and carbonic acid (H_2CO_3), are combinations of a nonmetal with hydrogen. When any acid dissolves in water, it always releases positive hydrogen ions.

Bases, such as sodium hydroxide (NaOH) and calcium hydroxide [$Ca(OH)_2$], are combinations of a metal with the hydroxyl radical (OH). Bases are the chemical opposites of acids. Acids release hydrogen ions when dissolved. On the other hand, bases "accept" hydrogen ions by combining them with the hydroxyl radical. When a base is dissolved in water, it releases its hydroxyl radical, which is a negative ion (OH^-). If positive hydrogen ions (H^+) are also present in the solution, they combine with the hydroxyl ions to form molecules of water (HOH).

Salts are combinations of a metal with a nonmetal. The reaction of an acid with a base produces a salt and water. For example, hydrochloric acid (HCl) reacts with lithium hydroxide (LiOH) to form the salt lithium chloride (LiCl) and water (HOH).

Inorganic Compounds. The names of inorganic compounds consist of the names of elements combined with special prefixes and suffixes. Here are some examples: carbon monoxide (CO), iodine disulfide (I_2S_2), arsenic tribromide ($AsBr_3$), and carbon tetrachloride (CCl_4). The prefixes *mono-*, *di-*, *tri-*, and *tetra-* show that *one*, *two*, *three*, or *four* atoms of an element are contained in a compound. The suffix *-ide* ordinarily indicates that a compound consists of two elements, or of one element and one radical. Compounds of two elements are called *binary compounds*.

In the names of bases, the *-ide* ending combines with the word *hydroxyl* (the name for the OH radical) to form the term *hydroxide*. Examples are sodium hydroxide (NaOH) and potassium hydroxide (KOH).

The suffixes *-ic* and *-ous*, when added to the name of a metal, distinguish between two valences of the metal. For example, in ferr*ic* chloride ($FeCl_3$), iron has a valence of +3, and in ferr*ous* chloride ($FeCl_2$), iron has a valence of +2. In such names, *-ic* represents the higher valence, and *-ous* represents the lower valence.

To show that a binary compound is an acid, the prefix *hydro-* and the suffix *-ic* are added to the name of the nonmetal. Thus, hydrogen chloride (HCl) is also called *hydro*chlor*ic* acid, and hydrogen sulfide (H_2S) is also called *hydro*sulfur*ic* acid.

Some acids contain oxygen and occur in at least two similar forms, one having more oxygen than the other. The prefix *hydro-* is not used for these acids. The acid that contains more oxygen ends in *-ic*, and the one that contains less oxygen ends in *-ous*. Examples are chlor*ic* acid ($HClO_3$) and chlor*ous* acid ($HClO_2$).

When oxygen acids react with bases, they form salts that contain oxygen. These salts are named by adding *-ate* or *-ite* to the name of the nonmetal, depending on whether the salt has more or less oxygen. For example, sodium chlor*ate* ($NaClO_3$) contains more oxygen than sodium chlor*ite* ($NaClO_2$).

Chemists use the prefix *per-* to name compounds that contain more oxygen than compounds with *-ic* and *-ate* endings. For example, *per*chlor*ic* acid is $HClO_4$, and sodium *per*chlor*ate* is $NaClO_4$. Similarly, chemists use the prefix *hypo-* to name compounds that contain less oxygen than *-ous* and *-ite* compounds. *Hypo*chlor*ous* acid is HClO, and sodium *hypo*chlor*ite* is NaClO.

Organic Compounds have much more complicated chemical names than inorganic compounds. Most organic names consist of special terms that represent various groups of atoms rather than individual elements. A thorough knowledge of organic chemistry is necessary to understand the system of organic names. The following examples show how names indicate the composition and structure of various compounds.

Hydrocarbons include thousands of compounds that contain only the elements hydrogen and carbon. These compounds are divided into several groups called *series*, such as the *methane* series, the *ethylene* series, and the *acetylene* series. Each series includes a number of compounds that contain a particular grouping of hydrogen and carbon atoms. For example, the first four members of the methane series are methane (CH_4), ethane (C_2H_6), propane (C_3H_8), and butane (C_4H_{10}). Each member of this series contains one more carbon atom and two more hydrogen atoms than the compound that precedes it.

Hydrocarbon derivatives are substances that result from the reaction of hydrocarbons with other compounds. Examples of hydrocarbon derivatives include alcohols, aldehydes, and acids.

An *alcohol* is formed when a hydroxyl radical takes the place of a hydrogen atom in a hydrocarbon. The suffix *-ol* indicates an alcohol, as in *methanol* (CH_3OH), a derivative of methane (CH_4). This compound is also called *methyl alcohol* or *wood alcohol*.

An *aldehyde*, indicated by the suffix *-al*, results from the combination of an alcohol with oxygen. For example, methanal (HCHO) and water (HOH) are formed when methanol combines with oxygen. Another name for methanal is *formaldehyde*.

An *acid* is produced when oxygen is added to an aldehyde. For example, when methanal gains an oxygen atom, it becomes *methanoic acid* (HCOOH), more commonly known as *formic acid*.

Chemical Reactions

A chemical reaction is any process that causes a chemical change in one or more substances. Chemists describe chemical reactions in terms of the combination or separation of atoms and groups of atoms. Countless numbers of atoms take part in all chemical reactions that occur in nature or in the laboratory. A chemical description of a reaction shows the fewest possible number of atoms that may take part in the reaction.

Chemical Equations tell the changes that take place in chemical reactions. In writing chemical equations, chemists use element symbols, chemical formulas, numbers, and special signs. For example, the symbol C stands for 1 carbon atom; 2C stands for 2 carbon atoms; 3C stands for 3 carbon atoms, and so on. Some elements, such as oxygen, do not occur as single atoms, but as molecules consisting of two atoms. The formula for the oxygen molecule is O_2. In chemical equations, O_2 means 1 oxygen molecule (2 atoms); $2O_2$ means 2 oxygen molecules (4 atoms); $3O_2$ means 3 oxygen molecules (6 atoms); and so on. Similarly, a number placed in front of the formula for a compound tells how many molecules of that compound take part in a reaction. For example, CO_2 is the formula for carbon dioxide. $3CO_2$ stands for 3 carbon dioxide molecules (3 carbon atoms and 6 oxygen atoms).

The following equation shows the reaction in which carbon and oxygen combine to form carbon dioxide.

$$C + O_2 \longrightarrow CO_2$$

The equation may be read: "1 atom of carbon *reacts with* 1 two-atom molecule of oxygen *and produces* 1 molecule of carbon dioxide." Carbon and oxygen are called the *reactants*. Carbon dioxide is called the *product*.

Every chemical equation must be *balanced*. That is, the products must contain the same kind and number of atoms as the reactants. In the example above, the product and the reactants both consist of 1 atom of carbon and 2 atoms of oxygen.

Here is the reaction in which hydrogen and oxygen combine to form water:

$$2H_2 + O_2 \longrightarrow 2H_2O$$

In this reaction, 2 two-atom molecules of hydrogen react with 1 two-atom molecule of oxygen and produce 2 molecules of water. The product and the reactants both contain 4 atoms of hydrogen and 2 atoms of oxygen.

Kinds of Chemical Reactions. Four main kinds of chemical reactions are: (1) combination, (2) decomposition, (3) replacement, and (4) double decomposition.

Combination takes place when two or more substances unite to form a compound. The formation of carbon dioxide and water in the above examples illustrate combination. Combination is also called *synthesis*.

Decomposition means the breaking down of a substance into two or more parts. When sugar is heated, it decomposes into carbon and water:

$$C_{12}H_{22}O_{11} + \text{heat} \longrightarrow 12C + 11H_2O$$

Replacement, also called *substitution*, occurs when a compound loses some elements but gains others in their place. A replacement reaction between barium (Ba) and sulfuric acid (H_2SO_4) produces barium sulfate ($BaSO_4$) and hydrogen (H_2):

$$Ba + H_2SO_4 \longrightarrow BaSO_4 + H_2\uparrow$$

In this reaction, an atom of barium combines with the sulfate radical (SO_4), replacing a two-atom molecule of hydrogen. The upward arrow indicates that the hydrogen escapes as a gas.

Double decomposition, or *double replacement*, involves two compounds that exchange atoms or groups of atoms. This kind of reaction takes place when a water softener is added to hard water. Water containing calcium sulfate ($CaSO_4$) can be softened by adding sodium carbonate (Na_2CO_3), which is also called *washing soda*. The resulting chemical reaction softens the water by removing calcium from the solution. Here is the equation for the reaction:

$$Na_2CO_3 + CaSO_4 \longrightarrow Na_2SO_4 + CaCO_3 \downarrow$$

In this reaction, the sodium (Na_2) and the calcium (Ca) switch places. The sodium combines with the sulfate radical (SO_4), forming sodium sulfate (Na_2SO_4) which dissolves in the water. The calcium combines with the carbonate radical (CO_3), forming calcium carbonate ($CaCO_3$). Calcium carbonate dissolves only slightly in water, and so it forms a white powder that settles to the bottom of the solution. Such a powder is called a *precipitate*, and is shown in the equation by a downward arrow.

Chemical Weights. Chemists usually have to know the exact weights of the reactants and products involved in a chemical reaction. For example, chemical makers must know exactly how much nitrogen and hydrogen they must combine to produce a certain amount of ammonia. For a large operation, they might measure the chemical weights in tons. In laboratory experiments, chemical weights are usually measured in units called *grams*. See GRAM.

Whether chemists measure weights in tons or grams, they base their calculations on the atomic weights of the elements. The *atomic weight* of an element shows how much one atom of the element weighs when it is compared with atoms of other elements. For example, the atomic weight of hydrogen is 1.00797, and the atomic weight of nitrogen is 14.0067. This means that one atom of nitrogen weighs almost 14 times as much as one atom of hydrogen.

Chemists add the atomic weights of elements to determine the *molecular weight* of a compound. For example, one molecule of ammonia (NH_3) contains 1 atom of nitrogen and 3 atoms of hydrogen. The total weight of these atoms is the molecular weight of ammonia: 1 nitrogen atom = 14.0067; 3 hydrogen atoms (3 × 1.00797) = 3.0239 (rounded off to four decimal places). Therefore, the molecular weight of ammonia is 14.0067 + 3.0239 = 17.0306.

To calculate the weights of reactants and products in a chemical reaction, chemists first write the chemical equation for such a reaction. Here is the equation for the production of ammonia from nitrogen and hydrogen:

$$N_2 + 3H_2 \longrightarrow 2NH_3$$

The next step is to determine the atomic and molecular weights indicated by the equation. This is done as follows:

$$N_2 = 2 \times 14.0067 = 28.0134$$
$$3H_2 = 3 \times 2 \times 1.00797 = 6.0478$$
$$2NH_3 = 2 \times 17.0306 = 34.0612$$

In any chemical equation, the total weight of the reactants must equal the total weight of the products. In the equation above, for example, the total weight of the two reactants is 28.0134 + 6.0478 = 34.0612—the same as the weight of the product. It does not matter what weight units are used to weigh the reactants. The same set of numbers could be used either with grams or with tons.

PAUL R. FREY

Critically reviewed by AARON J. IHDE

Chemistry / STUDY AIDS

Related Articles. Each chemical element has a separate article in WORLD BOOK. For a list, see ELEMENT, CHEMICAL. See also the following articles:

AMERICAN CHEMISTS

Adams, Roger
Babcock, Stephen M.
Baekeland, Leo H.
Bloch, Konrad E.
Calvin, Melvin
Conant, James B.
Harkins, William D.
Julian, Percy L.
Langmuir, Irving
Lewis, Gilbert N.
Libby, Willard F.
McCollum, Elmer V.
Mulliken, Robert S.
Pauling, Linus C.
Seaborg, Glenn T.
Silliman, Benjamin
Stanley, Wendell M.
Tatum, Edward L.
Urey, Harold C.
Wald, George
Woodward, Robert B.

BRITISH CHEMISTS

Black, Joseph
Boyle, Robert
Bragg, Sir William H.
Cavendish, Henry
Chain, Ernst B.
Crookes, Sir William
Dalton, John
Davy, Sir Humphry
Faraday, Michael
Hodgkin, Dorothy C.
Priestley, Joseph
Ramsay, Sir William
Robinson, Sir Robert
Sanger, Frederick
Smithson, James
Soddy, Frederick

FRENCH CHEMISTS

Berthelot, Marcelin
Chardonnet, Hilaire
Courtois, Bernard
Curie (family)
Gay-Lussac, Joseph L.
Lavoisier, Antoine L.
Pasteur, Louis
Proust, Joseph L.

GERMAN CHEMISTS

Bodenstein, Max
Bosch, Carl
Böttger, Johann F.
Bunsen, Robert W.
Fischer, Emil
Hahn, Otto
Kekulé von Stradonitz, Friedrich August
Krebs, Sir Hans A.
Kuhn, Richard
Liebig, Baron von
Meyer, Julius L.
Nernst, Walther Hermann
Ostwald, Wilhelm
Strassmann, Fritz
Wallach, Otto
Wieland, Heinrich O.
Wöhler, Friedrich

SWEDISH CHEMISTS

Berzelius, Jöns J.
Nobel, Alfred B.
Scheele, Carl W.
Svedberg, Theodor

OTHER CHEMISTS

Andrada e Silva, José B. de
Cannizzaro, Stanislao
Debye, Peter J. W.
Geber
Hevesy, Georg von
Mendeleev, Dmitri I.
Mueller, Paul

CHEMISTRY

Oparin, Alexander I.
Semenov, Nikolai
Van't Hoff, Jacobus H.
Weizmann, Chaim
Welsbach, Baron von

Branches of Chemistry

Analytical Chemistry
Biochemistry
Chemotherapy
Chemurgy
Electrochemistry
Geochemistry
Photochemistry
Physical Chemistry
Radiochemistry

Groups of Compounds

Acid
Alcohol
Aldehyde
Alkali
Alkaloid
Amine
Anhydride
Base
Bromide
Carbide
Carbohydrate
Carbonate
Caustic
Chloride
Cyanide
Electrolyte
Ester
Glycol
Hydrate
Hydrocarbon
Hydroxide
Nitrate
Nitrite
Oxide
Phosphate
Saccharides
Salt, Chemical
Silicone
Soda
Sulfate
Sulfide

Organic Compounds

Acetic Acid
Acetone
Acetylene
Amino Acid
Aniline
Benzene
Benzine
Carbon Disulfide
Carbon Tetrachloride
Cellulose
Chloral Hydrate
Citric Acid
Cream of Tartar
Dextrose
Ethane
Ether
Ethylene
Fluorocarbon
Formaldehyde
Formic Acid
Furfural
Glucose
Glycerol
Glycogen
Guncotton
Lactic Acid
Lake (chemical)
Maltose
Methane
Methanol
Nitroglycerin
Octane
Oxalic Acid
Prussic Acid
Resorcinol
Saccharin
Salicylic Acid
Starch
Stearic Acid
Stearin
Steroid
Sucrose
Tannic Acid
Tartaric Acid
Tetraethyl Lead
Toluene
Urea

Inorganic Compounds

Alum
Ammonia
Aqua Regia
Bicarbonate of Soda
Bichloride of Mercury
Borax
Borazon
Boric Acid
Calcium Carbonate
Carbon Dioxide
Carbon Monoxide
Epsom Salt
Glauber's Salt
Heavy Water
Hydrazine
Hydrochloric Acid
Hydrofluoric Acid
Hydrogen Bromide
Hydrogen Iodide
Hydrogen Peroxide
Hydrogen Sulfide
Hypochlorous Acid
Lime
Litharge
Lye
Nitric Acid
Nitrous Oxide
Phosphoric Acid
Potash
Saltpeter
Silica Gel
Silver Nitrate
Sulfur Dioxide
Sulfuric Acid
Water (The Chemistry of Water)

Terms

Allotropy
Alloy
Boiling Point
Bond (chemical)
Colloid
Compound
Damp
Density
Electromotive Series
Emulsion
Halogen
Homolog
Isomers
Isotope
Melting Point
Mole
Molecule
Monomer
Oxidation Potential
pH
Physical Change
Polymer
Pressure
Radical
Reagent
Saturation
Solution
Solvent
Suspension
Valence
Viscosity

Processes and Tests

Absorption and Adsorption
Calcination
Catalysis
Chromatography
Combustion
Condensation
Corrosion
Crystal
Decomposition
Diffusion
Distillation
Electrolysis
Equilibrium, Chemical
Evaporation
Fermentation
Flame Test
Flotation Process
Fluoridation
Haber Process
Homogenization
Hydrogenation
Hydrolysis
Ion
Litmus
Neutralization
Oxidation
Pasteurization
Phenolphthalein
Polymerization
Reduction
Spontaneous Combustion
Sublimation
Transmutation of Elements

Other Related Articles

Alchemy
American Chemical Society
Atom
Balance
Bunsen Burner
Centrifuge
Chemical-Biological-Radiological Warfare
Coal Tar
Deuterium
Drug (How Drugs Are Produced and Sold)
Electron
Energy
Fluid
Flux
Freezing Point
Gas
Heat (Sources of Heat)
Liquid Air
Liquid Crystal
Mass
Matter
Metal
Neutron
Nobel Prizes
Noble Gas
Nutrition
Ozone
Petroleum
Physics
Proton
Radioactivity
Rare Earth
Reagent
Steam
Transuranium Element
Tritium
Vapor

Outline

I. Branches of Chemistry
II. History
III. Tools of the Chemist
A. Chemistry Laboratories
B. Chemical Apparatus

IV. The Chemist's Education
- A. High-School Courses
- B. College Chemistry Programs

V. Careers
- A. Research Chemists
- B. Chemistry Teachers
- C. Consultants
- D. Chemical Salesmen
- E. Chemistry Literature Specialists
- F. Laboratory Technicians
- G. Educational Requirements

VI. Basic Chemistry
- A. Kinds of Substances
  - 1. Elements
  - 2. Compounds
  - 3. Mixtures
- B. How Compounds Are Formed
  - 1. Atomic Structure
  - 2. Valence
  - 3. Chemical Bonds
  - 4. Structural Formulas
- C. The Language of Chemistry
  - 1. Chemical Groups
  - 2. Inorganic Compounds
  - 3. Organic Compounds
- D. Chemical Reactions
  - 1. Chemical Equations
  - 2. Kinds of Chemical Reactions
  - 3. Chemical Weights

Questions

What is a pipette? A crucible?

In what kind of chemical bond do atoms share pairs of electrons?

Who is considered the last important alchemist as well as the first chemist?

What is the valence of calcium in the compound calcium chloride ($CaCl_2$)?

What metallic element and what poisonous gas combine chemically to form a common seasoning?

How did the iatrochemists affect the study of alchemy?

What is the general name for compounds consisting of a metal combined with the hydroxyl radical?

What element was once called *fire air*? Who gave the element its present name?

How do atoms become negative ions? How do they become positive ions?

What kind of chemical reaction takes place when sugar breaks down into carbon and water?

Additional Resources

AYLESWORTH, THOMAS G. *The Alchemists: Magic into Science.* Addison-Wesley, 1973. For younger readers.

GARDNER, ROBERT. *Kitchen Chemistry: Science Experiments to Do at Home.* Messner, 1982. For younger readers.

HAWLEY, GESSNER G. *The Condensed Chemical Dictionary.* 10th ed. Van Nostrand, 1981.

SMITH, RICHARD FURNALD. *Chemistry for the Million.* Scribner, 1972.

TAYLOR, L. B., JR. *Chemistry Careers.* Watts, 1978.

WIDOM, JOANNE M., and EDELSTEIN, S. J. *Chemistry: An Introduction to General, Organic, and Biological Chemistry.* Freeman, 1981.

CHEMNITZ. See KARL-MARX-STADT.

CHEMOSTERILANT. See INSECTICIDE.

CHEMOTHERAPY, *KEE moh THEHR uh pee,* is the treatment of disease with drugs that have a toxic effect on the cause of the illness. Chemotherapy is used in both human and veterinary medicine. Some chemotherapeutic drugs produce toxic effects on bacteria, viruses, or other organisms that cause infectious diseases. Other chemotherapeutic compounds attack cancer cells.

Chemotherapeutic drugs produce their effects through an enormous variety of biochemical actions. These drugs show *selective toxicity*—that is, they are more toxic to infectious organisms or cancer cells than they are to healthy body tissues. However, many chemotherapeutic agents do produce undesirable side effects and therefore are prescribed with great caution by physicians and veterinarians. EUGENE M. JOHNSON, JR.

See also ANTIBIOTIC; CANCER (Drug Therapy); DRUG (The Drug Revolution); EHRLICH, PAUL.

CHEMURGY, *KEHM ur jee,* is the use of farm and forest products as sources of raw materials for chemical manufacturing. The term was invented by William Jay Hale (1876-1955), the American organic chemist who is often called *the father of chemurgy.* Hale discovered many ways of using farm products in the manufacture of chemicals.

Chemurgy includes three major fields of work: (1) finding new uses for plants already under cultivation, (2) finding uses for waste products, and (3) developing new kinds of plants for industrial uses.

George Washington Carver won fame for his discovery of more than 300 uses for different parts of the peanut plant, and for similar work with the sweet potato and the pecan. Cellulose is also a farm product for which many new uses have been found. Milk produces over 50 million pounds (23 million kilograms) of by-products a year, besides its use as a food. Casein is the best-known milk by-product. WALTER J. MOORE

Related Articles in WORLD BOOK include:

Carver, George Washington	Furfural
Casein	Lignin
Cellulose	Plastics

CH'EN JUNG, *chuhn rawng* (mid-1200's), was one of the greatest painters of Chinese dragons. He imagined the dragon as a personification of the power of running water and of a storm. He began his paintings in a fit of excitement, splattering ink and spitting out water, or smearing his inky cap over the paper. He later touched up his work, and the blotches became dramatic compositions of writhing dragons, half seen among clouds or rocks. ALEXANDER C. SOPER

CHENILLE, *shuh NEEL,* is a fuzzy yarn made of cotton, silk, wool, or rayon. The word *chenille* means *caterpillar* in French. Chenille yarn is used to weave rugs, to knit fabrics, and to make fringes and tassels. Bedspreads made of cotton are often decorated with patterns of colored chenille. In adddition, bathrobes are sometimes made of chenille. KENNETH R. FOX

CHENNAULT, *shuh NAWLT,* **CLAIRE LEE** (1890-1958), led the *Flying Tigers,* a small group of volunteer American aviators who supported China in its war against Japan before the U.S. entered World War II in 1941. Chennault took command of the U.S. Fourteenth Air Force in China in 1943. He retired in 1945 as a major general and became head of a Chinese airline.

Brown Brothers

Claire Lee Chennault

Chennault was born in Commerce, Tex., but he grew up in Louisiana. He served as principal of a Texas high school until World War I (1914-1918), when he joined the United States Army Air Service. Chennault became an expert in precision flying as a member of an exhibition team of air corps pilots. In 1937, Chennault became air adviser to Chiang Kai-shek, the leader of China's Nationalist government. ALFRED GOLDBERG

See also FLYING TIGERS.

CHEOPS. See KHUFU.

CHEQUE. See CHECK.

CHERBOURG, *SHAIR boorg* (pop. 32,536), is an industrial city and seaport on the northern coast of France. For location, see FRANCE (political map).

Cherbourg's harbor, formed by an artificial barrier called a *breakwater*, provides a protective dock for transatlantic ships. Cherbourg's attractions include a park filled with exotic plant life and a medieval chapel near the city. The city has both a commercial port and a naval port. Its major industries include fishing, shipping, textile production, and the manufacture of nuclear submarines and telephone equipment.

In the 1700's, King Louis XVI of France began the construction of the breakwater that forms Cherbourg's harbor. In 1940, during World War II, German armed forces captured the city and used it as a military base. Allied armies freed Cherbourg in 1944. MARK KESSELMAN

CHERIMOYA, *CHER uh MOY uh*, is a small tropical tree that bears an edible fruit. It grows wild in Peru, and is cultivated in California and Florida. The oval leaves grow 3 to 6 inches (8 to 15 centimeters) long. The tree bears yellow flowers. The egg-shaped or heart-shaped fruit weighs 1 pound (0.5 kilogram) or more. Its white pulp tastes like a mixture of pineapple and banana. The tree grows at high elevations in the tropics where the climate is relatively cool.

J. Horace McFarland
Cherimoya Fruit

Scientific Classification. The cherimoya tree belongs to the family Annonaceae. Its scientific name is *Annona cherimola*. JULIAN C. CRANE

CHERNENKO, *chehr NYEHN koh*, **KONSTANTIN USTINOVICH** (1911-1985), served as general secretary, or head, of the Communist Party of the Soviet Union from February 1984 until his death in March 1985. He succeeded Yuri V. Andropov, who died. The post of general secretary is the most powerful in the Soviet Union. In April 1984, Chernenko was also named president of the Soviet Union—officially, chairman of the Presidium of the Supreme Soviet.

In 1978, Chernenko was elected a full member of the Politburo, the Communist Party's main policymaking body. Leonid I. Brezhnev, then the top government and party leader, strongly supported his nomination. In 1976, Chernenko had become a member of the Secretariat of the Central Committee. The Secretariat directs the everyday work of the Soviet Communist Party.

Chernenko was born in Bolshaya Tes, a town near Krasnoyarsk, in Siberia. He joined the Communist Party at the age of 20. In 1948, he became head of the propaganda department of the Communist Party of the Moldavian Soviet Socialist Republic. While working in Moldavia, he began a close association with Brezhnev, who was then the top party official in the republic. Beginning in 1956, Chernenko worked under Brezhnev in Moscow. Brezhnev became head of the Soviet Communist Party in 1964. Chernenko was then promoted to increasingly higher positions in the party. He worked closely with Brezhnev at several major party and government conferences. Brezhnev died in 1982. Many people believed Chernenko would be chosen to succeed Brezhnev as Communist Party head. But Andropov was selected as party head before Chernenko. JOHN A. ARMSTRONG

Sovfoto
Konstantin Chernenko

CHEROKEE INDIANS, *CHEHR uh kee*, live in various parts of the United States. Some Cherokee make their homes on a reservation in North Carolina, but most of the tribe's approximately 100,000 members live in Oklahoma. Many others have migrated elsewhere. In the early 1800's, the Cherokee were one of the most prosperous and progressive tribes in the country.

The early Cherokee farmed and hunted in the southern Appalachian Mountains. During the 1750's and 1760's, they fought the colonists who moved into their territory. During the Revolutionary War in America (1775-1783), the Cherokee sided with the British against the colonists.

About 1800, the Cherokee began to adopt the economic and political structure of the white settlers. For example, some Cherokee owned large plantations and kept slaves. Others had small-scale farms. The tribe also established a republican form of government called the *Cherokee Nation*. In 1821, a Cherokee named Sequoya introduced a system of writing for the Cherokee language (see SEQUOYA).

During the early 1800's, white settlers demanded that the government move all Indians in the Southeastern United States to areas west of the Mississippi River. In 1835, some members of the tribe agreed to move west in a treaty they signed with the government. But most Cherokee, led by Chief John Ross, opposed the treaty. During the winter of 1838-1839, U.S. troops forced from 13,000 to 17,000 Cherokee to move to the Indian Territory, in what is now Oklahoma. Thousands of Cherokee died on the way. Their forced march became known as the *Trail of Tears*. About 1,000 Cherokee escaped removal and remained in the Great Smoky Mountains of western North Carolina. They eventually bought land there and the government let them stay. These Indians became known as the *Eastern Band of Cherokee*.

The Cherokee who went west re-established the Cherokee Nation and set up their own schools and churches. But in the late 1800's, Congress abolished the tribal

Detail of *The Cherokee Trail of Tears, 1838* (1939), an oil mural on canvas by Elizabeth Janes; Oklahoma Historical Society

The Cherokee Indians were forced to move from the Southeast to the Oklahoma area as whites took over their land. Many Indians died on the journey, which took place during the winter of 1838-1839. The trip became known as the *Trail of Tears.*

government and opened much of the Cherokee's land for resettlement by whites. Raymond D. Fogelson

See also Five Civilized Tribes; Indian Territory; Jackson, Andrew (The Indian Issue); North Carolina (picture: Skills of the Past); Ross, John; United States, History of the (picture: Eastern Indians).

Additional Resources

Collier, Peter. *When Shall They Rest? The Cherokees' Long Struggle with America.* Holt, 1973. For younger readers.

Jahoda, Gloria. *The Trail of Tears.* Holt, 1975.

Wardell, Morris L. *A Political History of the Cherokee Nation, 1838-1907.* Univ. of Oklahoma Press, 1980. Reprint of 1938 ed.

Woodward, Grace S. *The Cherokees.* Univ. of Oklahoma Press, 1979. Reprint of 1963 ed.

CHERRY is a small round fruit that grows on a tree. The fruit is usually red. But the sweet Bing cherry is nearly black, and some other varieties are flesh-colored. When the cherry tree blooms, it produces lovely clusters of small white and pink blossoms.

Cherry trees grow both wild and cultivated in almost all countries in the Temperate Zone. There are three basic kinds of cultivated cherry trees: (1) sweet cherry; (2) sour cherry; and (3) the Duke. The two most important kinds in the United States are the *sweet cherry* and the *sour cherry.* The *Duke* is a hybrid that results from a cross between the sweet cherry and the sour cherry. Hundreds of varieties have been developed from these three basic types.

Sweet Cherry Trees are tall and stout. The trunk sometimes grows 1 foot (30 centimeters) or more thick. The fruit may be black, yellow, or red, and has a sweet taste when ripe. Sweet cherry trees do not grow well in an extreme climate. Both winter cold and summer heat harm the trees. Most sweet cherries are raised along the eastern shore of Lake Michigan, in the Hudson Valley of New York, and on the Pacific Coast. A sweet cherry tree can produce fruit only after it receives pollen from a different variety of cherry tree. For this reason, fruit-growers plant several varieties of sweet cherry trees. Bees then transfer pollen from one variety to another.

Sour Cherry Trees are smaller than sweet cherry trees. They grow well in both cold and warm climates. Sour cherries are raised in such states as Michigan, New York, Pennsylvania, Oregon, and Wisconsin. The trees can produce fruit after the flowers receive pollen either from the same tree or from another tree of the same variety.

Both sweet and sour cherry trees are grown by grafting buds to seedling rootstocks (see Grafting). The trees are transplanted from the nursery when they are one year old. Sweet cherry trees are planted from 25 to 35 feet (7.6 to 10.7 meters) apart. Sour cherry trees are planted from 18 to 24 feet (5.5 to 7.3 meters) apart. Grass can be planted between the trees and mowed to enrich the soil, or a nitrogen fertilizer can be used. Fruit-growers usually prune sweet cherry trees as soon as they are transplanted. All the twigs are removed, leaving only the main stem and two main branches. Sour cherry trees are not pruned so heavily at first.

Visual Education Service

Wild American Cherries, also called *chokecherries,* have a purple-black color and a sour taste, *top.* Clusters of the tiny fragrant flowers decorate the trees in spring, *bottom.*

Cherry Growers and Industries Foundation

Pale Yellow Royal Ann Cherries, *above left,* and deep red Bings, *above right,* are two popular varieties of sweet cherries.

Leading Cherry-Growing States and Provinces

Michigan	87,400 short tons (79,300 metric tons)
Washington	56,300 short tons (51,100 metric tons)
Oregon	38,700 short tons (35,100 metric tons)
California	31,300 short tons (28,400 metric tons)
New York	14,300 short tons (13,000 metric tons)
Ontario	11,000 short tons (10,000 metric tons)
Utah	10,700 short tons (9,700 metric tons)
British Columbia	8,900 short tons (8,100 metric tons)
Wisconsin	6,000 short tons (5,400 metric tons)
Pennsylvania	3,800 short tons (3,400 metric tons)

Sources: U.S. Department of Agriculture; Statistics Canada. Figures are based on a 4-year average, 1978-1981.

Plant Diseases. The most serious plant diseases that attack cherry trees are *brown rot* and *leaf spot*. Several insects such as black aphids and tent caterpillars also harm the trees. Sometimes the trees are sprayed several times a year for protection.

Several kinds of cherry trees are native to America. Some of them are important to horticulture. *Prunus mahaleb*, which comes from Europe and Asia, is often used as a rootstock for sweet and sour cherry buds. Some kinds of cherry trees are decorative. Japanese cherry trees are noted for their delicate beauty.

Scientific Classification. Cherries belong to the rose family, *Rosaceae*. Sweet cherries are genus *Prunus*, species *P. avium;* sour cherries, *P. cerasus*. REID M. BROOKS

Related Articles in WORLD BOOK include:

Acerola
Bitters
Blight
Cherry Laurel
Maraschino Cherries
Tree (Familiar Broadleaf and Needleleaf Trees [picture])
Washington, D.C. (The National Mall)

CHERRY CREEK DAM lies on Cherry Creek, 6 miles (10 kilometers) southeast of Denver. The dam is an earth-fill type, 140 feet (43 meters) high and 14,300 feet (4,359 meters) long. Its reservoir can hold 185,000 acre-feet (228,200,000 cubic meters) of water. The dam helps protect the Denver area from Cherry Creek's seasonal flash floods. These floods originate in the foothills of the Rocky Mountains. T. W. MERMEL

CHERRY LAUREL is a shrub of eastern Europe and the Orient that is closely related to the cherry. It is not a true laurel. The common, or English, cherry laurel is a popular shrub in Europe, and in California and the southern United States. The cherry laurel's small, shiny, evergreen leaves have finely toothed edges. The small, fragrant white flowers grow in clusters. The fruits are dark purple and have a bad taste. The leaves and the round stones of the fruit are poisonous.

Grant Heilman

Cherry Laurel

Scientific Classification. The common cherry laurel belongs to the rose family, Rosaceae. It is *Prunus laurocerasus*. J. J. LEVISON

CHERRY POINT MARINE CORPS AIR STATION, N.C., is the largest air base of the United States Marine Corps. It provides major overhaul facilities for high-performance aircraft. It is the headquarters for Marine Corps Air Bases, Eastern Area, and for a marine aircraft wing. The base was established in 1942. Located 19 miles (31 kilometers) from New Bern, it covers about 12,000 acres (4,860 hectares) of former forest and swampland. Its name comes from a post office that served lumber camps in the area until 1935. JOHN A. OUDINE

CHERUBINI, *KAY roo BEE nee,* **LUIGI,** *loo EE jee* (1760-1842), was an Italian-born composer. He settled in Paris in 1788, and played an important role in Parisian musical life until his death. Cherubini composed about 30 operas and 11 masses. The operas are noted for their dramatic music, forceful use of ensembles, and rich orchestration. Cherubini's operas include *Lodoïska* (1791), *Elisa* (1794), *Médée* (1797), and *Les Deux Journées* (1800).

After 1800, Cherubini concentrated on composing religious music and on teaching. One of his finest works is *Requiem in C minor* (1816), which commemorated King Louis XVI. He taught at the Paris Conservatory from its founding in 1795, and served as director from 1822 to 1841. Maria Luigi Carlo Zenobio Salvatore Cherubini was born in Florence. MILOŠ VELIMIROVIĆ

CHERVIL. See CICELY.

CHESAPEAKE, a ship. See WAR OF 1812 (Impressment of Seamen).

CHESAPEAKE AND OHIO CANAL was a waterway planned to connect the Potomac and Ohio rivers. Construction began in 1828, with generous financial backing from towns along the Potomac River and Chesapeake Bay that hoped to establish a trade route to Ohio River settlements. The waterway began above the falls of the Potomac River at Georgetown, D.C. When construction was halted by the business depression of 1837, the canal extended only about 100 miles (160 kilometers) westward. Halfhearted building continued until 1850. The canal was used until 1924 as far as Cumberland, Md., where building ended. It cost $11 million. The canal was 184 miles (296 kilometers) long, 60 feet (18 meters) wide, and averaged 6 feet (1.8 meters) deep. W. Turrentine Jackson

CHESAPEAKE AND OHIO CANAL NATIONAL HISTORICAL PARK lies between Washington, D.C., and Cumberland, Md. A small section is in West Virginia. It was established in 1961. It includes one of the oldest U.S. lock canals for mule-drawn boats. Completed in 1850, the canal was used until 1924. For the area of the park, see National Park System (table: National Historical Parks).

CHESAPEAKE BAY is a long, narrow arm of the Atlantic Ocean that runs north from the coast of Virginia, and divides Maryland into two parts. It is 200 miles (320 kilometers) long and from 4 to 40 miles (6 to 64 kilometers) wide. The Indians called this bay the *Great Salt Water*.

The channel at the entrance to Chesapeake Bay is 12 miles (19 kilometers) wide. Seagoing ships can sail almost the entire length of the bay. The shore is cut by smaller bays and by the wide mouths of several rivers. Rivers emptying into the bay include the James, York, Rappahannock, Potomac, and Susquehanna. Important bay ports include Baltimore, Md., and Norfolk and Portsmouth, Va. The U.S. Naval Academy is at Annapolis on the western shore. Bostwick H. Ketchum

See also Maryland (physical map).

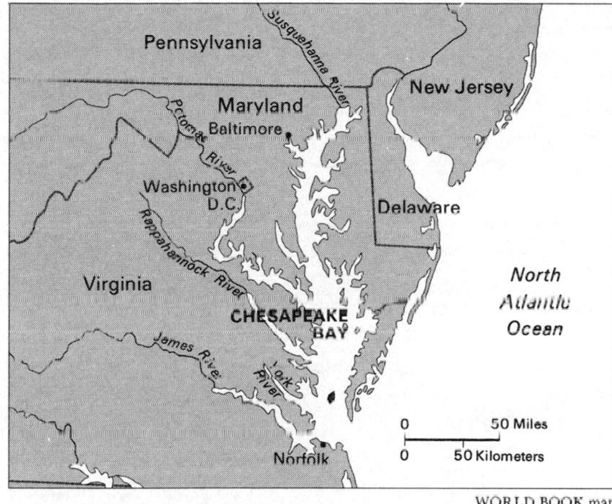

WORLD BOOK map

Location of Chesapeake Bay

CHESAPEAKE BAY BRIDGE-TUNNEL stretches across the mouth of the Chesapeake Bay. The total length of the facility—including bridges, tunnels, and causeways—is 23 miles (37 kilometers). The bridge-tunnel carries automobile and truck traffic between the Delmarva Peninsula and Norfolk, Va. Ocean-going ships can use the main channels of the bay without interference. The bridge-tunnel consists of a series of causeways connecting two separate tunnels that run under the main channels in the bay. The Thimble Shoal tunnel and the Chesapeake Channel tunnel are each about 1 mile (1.6 kilometers) long. Two bridges near the northern shore keep channels open for small vessels. Completed in 1964, the bridge-tunnel cost $200 million. Chesapeake Bay Bridge and Tunnel Commission

CHESAPEAKE BAY RETRIEVER is a hunting dog. Many owners claim that it is the best of all duck retrievers, especially in cold, rough waters. It has a thick, oily coat that sheds water. The Chesapeake has unusual endurance and has fine working qualities in water and in the field. Males stand 23 to 26 inches (58 to 66 centimeters) high at the shoulder, and weigh 55 to 75 pounds (25 to 34 kilograms). Most Chesapeakes range from brown to a light straw in color. See also Dog (picture: Sporting Dogs). Maxwell Riddle

WORLD BOOK photo

The Chesapeake Bay Retriever Is a Strong Swimmer.

CHESNUTT, CHARLES WADDELL (1858-1932), is generally considered to have been the first major black American writer of fiction. His first book, *The Conjure Woman and Other Tales* (1899), is written in the style of folk tales and tells about slavery in the South. Chesnutt's other fiction describes racial difficulties of black Americans, especially those who have both black and white ancestry. He featured these themes in *The Wife of His Youth and Other Stories of the Color Line* (1899). The same themes dominate his three novels, *The House Behind the Cedars* (1900), *The Marrow of Tradition* (1901), and *The Colonel's Dream* (1905).

Chesnutt was born in Cleveland, Ohio. His family moved to Fayetteville, N.C., when he was 8 years old. He attended school until he was 13 and later studied with tutors or taught himself. Chesnutt left the South during his 20's. He worked as a court stenographer in Cleveland and passed examinations that permitted him to become a lawyer. In 1928, Chesnutt received the Spingarn medal, partly for his "pioneer work as a literary artist depicting the life and struggles of Americans of Negro descent." Darwin T. Turner

CHESS

Chuck Jones

Chess is a game for all ages. Bobby Fischer, *above*, became U.S. chess champion at 14 and won the world chess championship at 29.

CHESS is a game of skill played by two persons, using a set of pieces, or *men*, on a board marked with squares. Chess requires imagination and the ability to think of most moves before playing them. The moves in chess have often been compared with those made by two opposing generals on a battlefield. Chess resembles war in that it consists of attack and defense, and has as its object making the king surrender.

The Board and the Pieces. The chessboard is divided into sixty-four squares, in eight rows of eight squares each. The squares are colored alternately light and dark. The board is the same as that used for checkers, but chess uses all the squares, instead of only half of them. The board must be placed so that each player has a light-colored square at his right hand.

Each player receives a set of sixteen men. One set is light in color, for the *white* side. The other is dark in color, for the *black* side. Eight men in each set are of the lowest grade, and are named *pawns*. The other eight are of various grades, and are called *pieces*. The pieces in each set consist of a *king*, a *queen*, two *bishops*, two *knights*, and two *rooks*, or *castles*.

The Position of the Pieces. Each player first arranges all his men on the two rows of squares nearest to him. The pieces stand on the *first rank* (nearest row). The pawns stand on the row immediately in front of the pieces. The king and queen occupy the central squares of the first row, with king facing king and queen facing queen, across the board. The queen, in the beginning, always stands on a square of her own color. The two bishops occupy the squares on either side of the king and queen. The rooks stand on the corner squares. The knights stand between the bishop and the rook. See diagram below (right).

The men standing beside the king are called the *king's men*. Those standing beside the queen are called the *queen's men*. Thus the bishop beside the king is the *king's bishop*. The pawns are named for the pieces in front of which they stand, such as the *king's pawn*, or the *queen's rook's pawn*. In describing the placing of the chessmen, letters may be used to indicate their names. *K* stands for King; *KB* for King's Bishop; *KKt* for King's Knight; *KR* for King's Rook; *Q* for Queen; *QB* for Queen's Bishop; *QKt* for Queen's Knight; *QR* for Queen's Rook; and *P* for Pawns.

The Moves of the Pieces. A capture is made in chess when a man takes the place of an opponent's man. The player making the successful move then removes the captured man from the board.

THE CHESSBOARD AND PIECES

There are three kinds of rows on a chessboard, as shown on the board below. The board at the right shows the position of the chessmen at the start of a game.

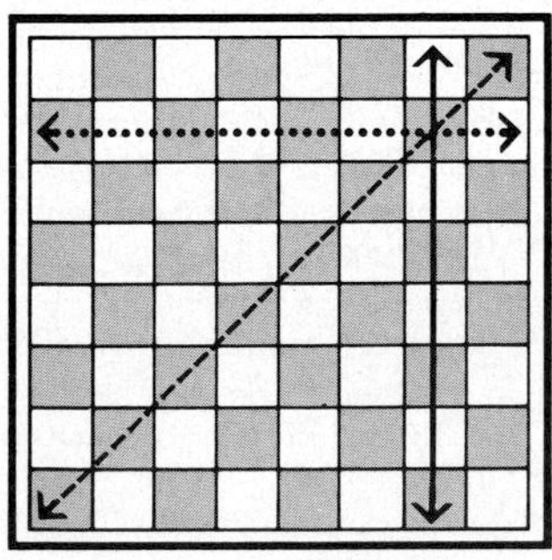

Rank ....

Any row of squares from left to right.

File ———

Any row of eight squares between players.

Diagonal ------

Any row of squares slantwise across the board.

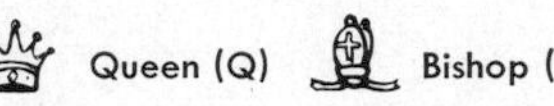

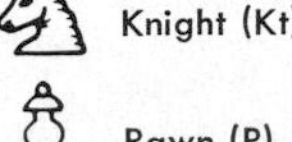

King (K) Rook (R) Knight (Kt)

Queen (Q) Bishop (B) Pawn (P)

Black

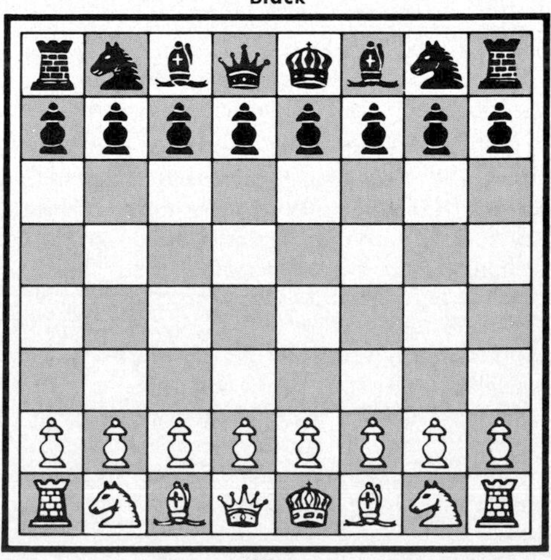

White

The *pawn* moves straight forward, one square at a time, except on the first move, when it is allowed to move either one or two squares in the same direction. When the pawn captures a man, the pawn always moves diagonally, right or left, to the position of the captured man. A pawn never moves backward or sidewise. A piece, or another pawn directly in front of it, stops a pawn's progress. Upon reaching the eighth row, a pawn is entitled to promotion. It can and must then be exchanged for any piece of its own color except a king. It is possible, therefore, for a player to have on the board two or more queens, rooks, bishops, or knights, but never more than one king. The process of promoting is known as *queening* a pawn, but the player, instead of choosing a queen, may take any one of the other pieces.

When the pawn plays forward two squares at the first move, the opponent is given the benefit of the *en passant* (*in passing*) rule. This special rule applies when the pawn making this play passes by an opposing pawn on an adjoining file, which has reached the fifth rank, counting from the opponent's side of the board. The opponent's pawn, thus passed, is entitled to capture that pawn in passing, in the same manner as if the player's pawn had moved only one square instead of two.

The *rook*, or *castle*, can move for any distance in a straight line. But the move must be forward, backward, or sidewise, and not diagonal. The *bishop* moves any distance, either forward or backward, but only diagonally, and thus always on squares of the same color. Neither the rook nor the bishop may pass over a man of either color blocking its path.

The *queen* is the most powerful piece on the board. She can move any distance in any straight line. She may move forward, backward, sidewise, or diagonally, as far as her path is clear. One of her own men may stop her progress, but she may capture an opponent exposed to direct approach. Skillful use of the queen and her supporting pieces should be mastered early in the study of the game.

The *king* is as free in his actions as the queen, but he cannot move more than *one* square at a time. When he is in the middle of the board, he commands the eight squares surrounding the central square on which he stands, and no more.

Besides his ordinary moves, the king, as a special privilege, also has a peculiar move. It is called *castling*, because the rook (castle) takes part in it. The move permits a player to move his king two squares, either to the right or the left, if the squares between king and either rook are clear. The castling move is completed by moving either rook to the side of the king opposite that from which it is taken. Castling may be done only once during the game by each player. It is *not* permissible if the king is in check, or if any square over which the king must pass in castling is under attack by an opposing piece. Also, once the king has been moved to another square, castling cannot take place. Likewise, if either rook has been moved, it can no longer take part in the castling move.

The *knight*, unlike the other pieces, can make an L-shaped movement. He moves two squares in a straight line and one to the side. The knight may move in any direction. He may also leap around any man on a square between the one on which he stands and the one he intends to occupy. The knight always moves to a square of a different color *not next* to the square from which the move starts. The knight thus commands eight squares from a central square. See diagram above.

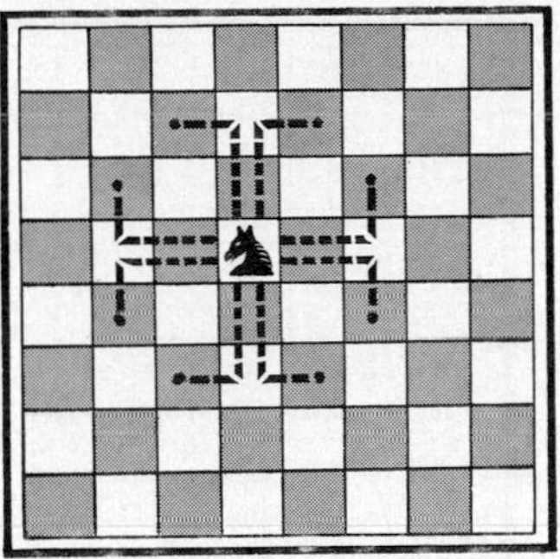

How the Knight Can Be Moved. The dotted lines show all the possible directions in which a knight can be moved.

How the Pieces Compare in Value. The pawns may each be said to have the value of *one*. The pieces have values of about *three* for a bishop or a knight, *five* for a rook, and *nine* for a queen. The knight and the bishop are usually known as *minor pieces*. The value of a piece also depends upon its ability to move. Thus a bishop is usually stronger than a knight, because he can reach distant points faster. But the knight is stronger in game endings in which the pawns are blocked, and his player's pawns cannot be attacked by a bishop.

Attack and Defense. If a man can capture an opposing man on the next move, the opposing man is said to be *attacked*. If a man can recapture an opposing man trying to capture the first man, he is said to be *defended*.

Check and Checkmate. The definite aim in chess is to force the *surrender* of the opposing king. When a piece or pawn attacks him, he is said to be *in check*. The player who attacks a king usually gives notice by saying "check," but this is not compulsory. Then the other player, in order to safeguard his king, must abandon all other plans. If necessary, he must sacrifice any of or all his own men. The king can be rescued in several ways. A player may remove him to a nearby square not commanded by any man belonging to his opponent; he may screen the king with one of his own men; or he may capture the attacking man. When the king can no longer be defended after being checked by an opponent, he is *checkmated*. The game ends right there. The king is never captured. His player simply *resigns* (surrenders).

Sometimes neither player is able to checkmate the other. Then the result is said to be a *drawn* game. Or a player may not be in check, but cannot move without exposing his king to a check. Such a condition is called *stalemate*, and the game is considered drawn.

Notation. *English notation* is the system most often used for recording games in the United States. In this system, each square on the board has a name and two numbers. The squares in each file are named for the piece which occupies the first square in that file at the start of the game. For example, the squares in the center files are called the *king's squares* and the

BLACK

QR1 / QR8	QKt1 / QKt8	QB1 / QB8	Q1 / Q8	K1 / K8	KB1 / KB8	KKt1 / KKt8	KR1 / KR8
QR2 / QR7	QKt2 / QKt7	QB2 / QB7	Q2 / Q7	K2 / K7	KB2 / KB7	KKt2 / KKt7	KR2 / KR7
QR3 / QR6	QKt3 / QKt6	QB3 / QB6	Q3 / Q6	K3 / K6	KB3 / KB6	KKt3 / KKt6	KR3 / KR6
QR4 / QR5	QKt4 / QKt5	QB4 / QB5	Q4 / Q5	K4 / K5	KB4 / KB5	KKt4 / KKt5	KR4 / KR5
QR5 / QR4	QKt5 / QKt4	QB5 / QB4	Q5 / Q4	K5 / K4	KB5 / KB4	KKt5 / KKt4	KR5 / KR4
QR6 / QR3	QKt6 / QKt3	QB6 / QB3	Q6 / Q3	K6 / K3	KB6 / KB3	KKt6 / KKt3	KR6 / KR3
QR7 / QR2	QKt7 / QKt2	QB7 / QB2	Q7 / Q2	K7 / K2	KB7 / KB2	KKt7 / KKt2	KR7 / KR2
QR8 / QR1	QKt8 / QKt1	QB8 / QB1	Q8 / Q1	K8 / K1	KB8 / KB1	KKt8 / KKt1	KR8 / KR1

WHITE

Each Square of the Chessboard Has Two Names. The "White" player uses the names which are shown printed right side up. The "Black" player uses the names printed upside down. The letters are symbols for the names of chess pieces.

queen's squares. But each player counts from his or her own side of the board. So row number 1 for one player is number 8 for the other. Other signs include *x* for *takes;* — for *moves to;* and *ch* for *check*.

The Fool's Mate. A short game in which checkmate is given after the first few opening moves is called the *fool's mate*. The moves are as follows:

WHITE	BLACK
1. P—KB4	1. P—**K3**
2. P—KKt4	2. Q—**KR5** (mate)

History. Chess was first played in Asia. The term *chess* comes from the Persian word *shah*, meaning *king*. Some scholars think chess was invented in India, and then spread to Persia (Iran) in the A.D. 500's. They point out the likeness between modern chess and an Indian game called *chaturanga*, still played in India and Iran under the name *shatranj*. The Arabs learned the game when they conquered Persia in the 600's. They brought chess with them to Spain, and from there it spread throughout Europe.

The modern era of chess dates from the 1500's, when the moves of the game took their present form. Philidor of France, who played in the 1700's, is regarded by some as the first world champion. An American, Paul Morphy once held the unofficial title of world champion. The first international tournament took place in London in 1851, but the official title *World Champion* was not used until 1866 when William Steinitz of Austria defeated Adolf Anderssen of Germany.

Some chess masters have demonstrated their skill by playing several games at once while blindfolded, memorizing the plays. Harry Nelson Pillsbury, the United States champion from 1897 to 1906, regularly played 12 to 16 games at once while blindfolded. Perhaps the greatest master of blindfold chess was Belgian-born George Koltanowski. In 1951, he played 50 opponents blindfolded and one at a time, under a time limit of 10 seconds a move. He won 43 games, drew 5, and lost 2.

Many chess champions have become skilled players at an early age. Samuel Reshevsky was a chess master at the age of 8. He came to the United States from Poland in 1920. He held the U.S. championship three times, and the International Chess Federation named him a grand master. Bobby Fischer of New York City won the U.S. chess title in 1958 at the age of 14.

In 1972, Fischer became the first American to win the official world chess championship. The International Chess Federation took away Fischer's title in 1975 after he refused to play challenger Anatoly Karpov of Russia under rules set by the federation. Karpov became the world champion by default. See FISCHER, BOBBY.

HERMANN HELMS

World Chess Champions

1866-1894	William Steinitz, Austria
1894-1921	Emanuel Lasker, Germany
1921-1927	José R. Capablanca, Cuba
1927-1935	Alexander A. Alekhine, Russia
1935-1937	Max Euwe, The Netherlands
1937-1946	Alexander A. Alekhine, Russia
1948-1956	Mikhail Botvinnik, Russia
1957-1958	Vassily Smyslov, Russia
1958-1960	Mikhail Botvinnik, Russia
1960-1961	Mikhail Tal, Russia
1961-1963	Mikhail Botvinnik, Russia
1963-1969	Tigran Petrosian, Russia
1969-1972	Boris Spassky, Russia
1972-1975	Bobby Fischer, United States
1975-	Anatoly Karpov, Russia

United States Chess Champions

1857-1871	Paul Morphy
1871-1876	George Mackenzie
1876-1880	James Mason
1880-1889	George Mackenzie
1889-1890	S. Lipschütz
1890-	Jackson Showalter
1890-1891	Max Judd
1891-1892	Jackson Showalter
1892-1894	S. Lipschütz
1894-	Jackson Showalter
1894-1895	Albert Hodges
1895-1897	Jackson Showalter
1897-1906	Harry Pillsbury
1906-1909	Open (Pillsbury died in 1906)
1909-1936	Frank Marshall*
1936-1944	Samuel Reshevsky
1944-1946	Arnold Denker
1946-1948	Samuel Reshevsky
1948-1951	Herman Steiner
1951-1954	Larry Evans
1954-1958	Arthur Bisguier
1958-1962	Bobby Fischer
1962-1963	Larry Evans
1963-1968	Bobby Fischer
1968-1969	Larry Evans
1969-1972	Samuel Reshevsky
1972-1973	Robert Byrne
1973-1974	John Grefe and Lubomir Kavalek (tie)
1974-1978	Walter Browne
1978-1980	Lubomir Kavalek
1980-1981	Walter Browne, Larry Christiansen, and Larry Evans (tie)
1981-1983	Walter Browne and Yasser Seirawan (tie)
1983-	Walter Browne, Larry Christiansen, and Roman Dzindzichashvili (tie)

*Until 1936, the United States had a series of unofficial champions. Since that time, tournaments have been held periodically to determine the U.S. champion. The U.S. Chess Federation selects the players that take part in the tournaments.
Source: U.S. Chess Federation.

Additional Resources

GOLOMBEK, HARRY. *Chess: A History*. Putnam, 1976.
PANDOLFINI, BRUCE. *Let's Play Chess! A Step-by-Step Guide for Beginners*. Simon & Schuster, 1980. Suitable for younger readers.
SCHONBERG, HAROLD C. *Grandmasters of Chess*. Rev. ed. Norton, 1981.
SUNNUCKS, ANNE, comp. *The Encyclopaedia of Chess*. 2nd ed. St. Martin's, 1977.

CHEST, or THORAX, *THOH racks*, is the part of the body between the base of the neck and the abdomen. Its sides are formed by the ribs, which are attached to the breastbone in front and to the spine in back. The *diaphragm*, a strong, dome-shaped muscle, forms the base of the chest.

A thick, vertical partition called the *mediastinum* or *mediastinal septum*, extends down the center of the thorax. Enclosed within this partition are the heart, the large blood vessels, the esophagus, the lower part of the windpipe, and various glands and nerves. The lungs and their coverings are suspended on either side of the mediastinum.

Only mammals, birds, and crocodiles have a separate chest and abdomen. WILLIAM V. MAYER

See also DIAPHRAGM; HEART; HUMAN BODY (Trans-Vision color picture); LUNG; RESPIRATION.

CHESTER is an English town located on the River Dee, south of Liverpool (see GREAT BRITAIN [political map]). It is the chief town in the district of Chester, which has a population of 116,157. A fort in Roman times, Chester gradually became important as a trading center. The town held a famous cheese market every year. Chester was the last town in England to fall to William the Conqueror, in 1070. It was a Royalist fortress during the English Civil War. The walls of the city are still intact. JOHN W. WEBB

CHESTERFIELD, EARL OF (1694-1773), was an English aristocrat, wit, and political figure. He became known for his worldly, sensible letters to his son.

Brown Bros.
Lord Chesterfield

Chesterfield was born Philip Dormer Stanhope in London. About 1732, while ambassador at The Hague, the capital of The Netherlands, he fathered an illegitimate son, Philip. When the boy was 5 years old, the earl began writing him letters. The correspondence continued for 30 years. The more than 400 letters that survive were intended to educate Philip in the art of being a gentleman—to give him polished manners, a classical education, and a realistic view of mankind. With sophistication, frankness, and affection, Chesterfield described men as selfish and women as frail creatures to be controlled.

The earl wanted his son to become a diplomat. But Philip, who turned out to be shy and socially crude, was a failure as a diplomat. He married secretly and died young, and his widow sold the earl's letters. Their publication in 1774, soon after the earl's death, made Chesterfield famous. THOMAS H. FUJIMURA

CHESTERFIELD ISLANDS form a group of small, low coral islands in the western Pacific Ocean. They lie on the Chesterfield Reefs in the Coral Sea, 300 to 400 miles (480 to 640 kilometers) northwest of the island of New Caledonia (see PACIFIC ISLANDS [map]). The Chesterfield islands cover 250 acres (101 hectares) and are uninhabited. Some islets have guano deposits. The islands are part of the French overseas department of New Caledonia.

CHESTERTON, G. K. (1874-1936), was an English author known for his essays on almost every popular subject of his time. Chesterton also wrote biographies, fiction, and poetry. He played a major part in the literary life of London for almost 40 years.

Chesterton's essays, though known for their wit and vigor, have lost the popularity they had during his lifetime. His detective stories, novels, and literary criticism now rank as his most widely read works. Chesterton's best-known stories include a series of mysteries featuring Father Brown, a Roman Catholic priest, as the detective. In his novel *The Napoleon of Notting Hill* (1904), Chesterton created a fantasy in which an eccentric rules the London of the future. Chesterton also wrote a fantasy called *The Man Who Was Thursday* (1908), which centers on spies and detectives.

Critics consider Chesterton's biographies his finest works. These writings include studies of Robert Browning, Charles Dickens, and other English authors.

Chesterton's full name was Gilbert Keith Chesterton. He was born in London. AVROM FLEISHMAN

CHESTNUT is a tree with spreading branches that grows in parts of North America, Asia, Africa, and Europe. The American chestnut is a medium-sized tree, but it may grow about 100 feet (30 meters) high.

American chestnuts once grew from central Maine, along the Appalachian Mountains, and westward to Arkansas. But a fungus disease called *chestnut blight* has killed most of the chestnuts in North America. The disease probably entered the United States in the 1800's

A Branch of An American Chestnut bears toothed, glossy green leaves and a prickly bur. The bur has nuts inside it. The inset, *below,* shows the shape of the nuts.

U. S. Forest Service

U.S. Forest Service

The Spreading Chestnut Tree makes an excellent shade tree for lawns. The trunk has unusually rough bark.

from Japan. The *chinquapin*, a small relative, grows in regions once occupied by the American chestnut.

Early Americans found the chestnut tree valuable for its long-lasting wood, the *tannin* (a substance used to tan leather) it supplied, and the nuts it produced. Chestnut wood was widely used for railroad ties, telephone and telegraph poles, fence posts, lumber, furniture, and woodwork. The wood is so durable that dead trees are still harvested for lumber and pulpwood.

Scientific Classification. The chestnut and chinquapin are in the beech family, *Fagaceae*. The American chestnut is genus *Castanea*, species *C. dentata*. T. EWALD MAKI

See also TREE (Familiar Broadleaf and Needleleaf Trees [picture]).

CHETNIKS. See YUGOSLAVIA (World War II).

CHEVALIER, *shuh VAL yay* or *shuh va LYAY*, **MAURICE,** *maw REES* (1888-1972), was a popular French actor, dancer, and singer. His trademarks were a flat straw hat, a heavy French accent, and a protruding lower lip. Chevalier starred in many motion pictures and television programs.

Born near Paris, Chevalier started out to be an electrician. He made his debut as a dancer in 1906, and soon starred in the Folies Bergère. His autobiography is *I Remember It Well* (1970). NARDI REEDER CAMPION

CHEVROLET, *SHEHV roh LAY*, **LOUIS** (1878-1941), helped organize the Chevrolet Motor Company in 1911, and designed its first automobile. He was also a leading figure in automobile racing, and was elected to the automobile racing Hall of Fame in 1952.

Chevrolet sold his interest in the motor company in 1915. He then began building racing cars. His *Monroe*, with his brother Gaston driving, won the Indianapolis 500-mile race in 1920. His *Frontenac* won the race in 1921. Chevrolet and his brother Arthur organized the Chevrolet Brothers Aircraft Company in 1929, but it failed. Born near Bern, Switzerland, Chevrolet moved to the United States in 1900. SMITH HEMPSTONE OLIVER

CHEVRON, *SHEHV ruhn*, consists of two lines joined together at one end to form an angle. Chevrons on the sleeves of military or other types of uniforms indicate the rank of the wearer. In architecture, the word describes the angles formed by roof rafters. Chevrons in heraldry represent the rafters of a house, and signify the accomplishment of a memorable and important work. A chevron often served to symbolize that the bearer had founded a family. THOMAS E. GRIESS

CHEWING GUM is a confection that is chewed but not swallowed. People in most countries chew gum because they like the taste. Many people find that gum chewing also relieves the boredom of monotonous tasks. In addition, medical studies have shown that the act of chewing anything aids concentration and reduces tension. The most popular flavors of gum include spearmint, peppermint, fruit, and cinnamon.

How Gum Is Made. The main ingredient of chewing gum is an insoluble, rubberlike gum base. At one time, a rubbery substance called *chicle* was the principal base for chewing gum. Chicle is obtained by boiling down the *latex* (milky juice) of the sapodilla tree, which grows in Mexico and Central America. Various kinds of trees in Indonesia, Malaya, and South America also contain substances suitable for gum base.

During the mid-1900's, manufacturers began to make synthetic gum bases that resemble chicle. These gum bases consist of synthetic rubber, waxes, a plastic substance called *vinyl resin*, and other types of plastics. Sometimes synthetic gum bases are mixed with chicle and other natural gums.

Gum manufacturers add softeners, sweeteners, and flavorings to the gum base. Softeners, which are made from refined vegetable oils, soften and blend the ingredients of the gum base. Softeners also help the gum retain the right amount of moisture. Most chewing gum is sweetened with corn syrup and sugar. Sugarless gum is sweetened with mannitol and sorbitol, substances that are found in certain fruits, plants, and trees. A stick of gum that contains sugar has about 10 calories. A stick of sugarless gum has 6 or 7 calories. Various flavorings, including peppermint and spearmint oils, juices of many fruits, and cinnamon and other spices, are added to the gum. Gum will not hurt the body if a person accidentally swallows it.

During the manufacturing process, the gum base is softened, heated, and purified. All the ingredients of the gum are then slowly blended in mixing machines. Other machines push a thick ribbon of finished gum out of the mixers and flatten it into a thin sheet. After cooling, the gum hardens and is cut into individual sticks or pellets. Machines wrap the sticks of gum. Gum pellets are candy-coated before being packaged.

History. The ancient Greeks chewed gum that they made from the sap of the mastic tree. More than 1,000 years ago, the Mayan Indians of Mexico chewed chicle. Later, Indians in New England taught the white settlers to chew gum obtained from the hardened sap of the spruce tree. During the 1850's, people chewed paraffin wax, but if often crumbled or stuck to the teeth.

In 1860, Antonio López de Santa Anna, the Mexican general who had led the attack against the Alamo in 1836, brought chicle to the United States. He hoped to sell it as a type of rubber. Santa Anna gave some chicle to a New York City druggist named Thomas

How Chewing Gum Is Made

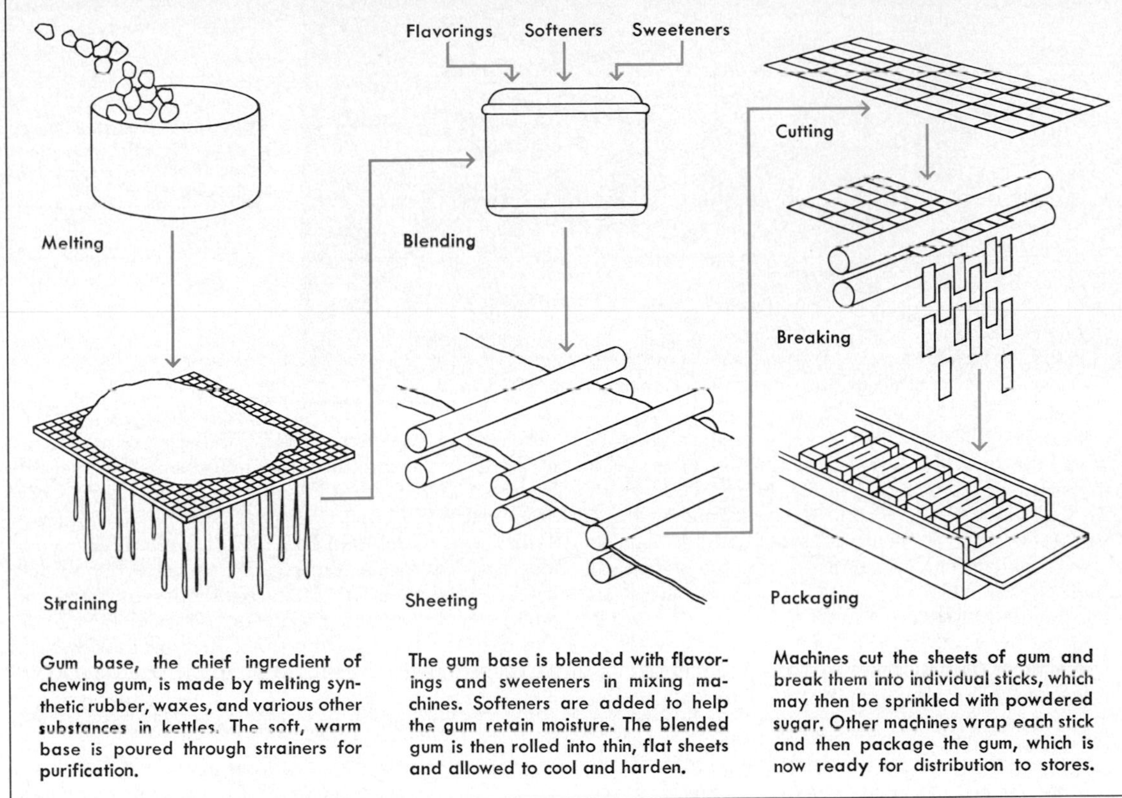

Gum base, the chief ingredient of chewing gum, is made by melting synthetic rubber, waxes, and various other substances in kettles. The soft, warm base is poured through strainers for purification.

The gum base is blended with flavorings and sweeteners in mixing machines. Softeners are added to help the gum retain moisture. The blended gum is then rolled into thin, flat sheets and allowed to cool and harden.

Machines cut the sheets of gum and break them into individual sticks, which may then be sprinkled with powdered sugar. Other machines wrap each stick and then package the gum, which is now ready for distribution to stores.

WORLD BOOK diagram by Dick Fickle

Adams. Adams tried to make the chicle into a type of rubber, but it would not harden. When Adams boiled the chicle, he discovered that it made an excellent chewing gum. He began to manufacture it, and soon other companies started to produce various flavors of chicle gum. Bubble gum was first produced in 1928.

In the mid-1900's, chewing gum companies began to manufacture sugarless gum. Many dentists recommend sugarless gum because they believe sugar can contribute to tooth decay. Today, chewing gum is produced by more than 500 companies in over 90 countries. The United States ranks as the major gum producer. Other gum-producing countries include Canada, Egypt, England, Iraq, and Turkey. DAVID SLOANE

See also BUBBLE GUM; CHICLE; LATEX; SAPODILLA.

CHEWINK. See TOWHEE.

CHEYENNE, *SHY ehn* or *shy AN* (pop. 47,283), one of the most historic towns of the Old West, is the capital and second largest city of Wyoming. Only Casper is larger. Cheyenne serves as the trade center of a large agricultural area and as a major defense center of the United States. It lies near the southeast corner of Wyoming. For location, see WYOMING (political map).

Description. Cheyenne, the county seat of Laramie County, covers about 15 square miles (39 square kilometers). Cheyenne's annual Frontier Days celebration, which began in 1897, is one of the nation's most famous rodeos. The State Capitol, completed in 1888, also attracts many tourists. The Wyoming State Museum exhibits historical items of the Old West.

Just outside Cheyenne lies Warren Air Force Base, the site of the control center of one of the world's largest intercontinental ballistic missile networks. The base is the headquarters of a missile unit that controls about 200 missiles. These missiles are spread out over 8,000 square miles (21,000 square kilometers) in the surrounding region of Wyoming, Colorado, and Nebraska.

Nearly a third of Cheyenne's people work for the federal, state, or local government. Oil refining and cattle and sheep ranching also contribute to the economy of the city.

History. Major General Grenville M. Dodge, the chief engineer of the Union Pacific Railroad, founded Cheyenne in 1867. He chose the site as a terminal for the railroad, which was being built westward from Omaha, Neb. Dodge named the city after the Cheyenne Indians, who lived in the area.

Shortly after Dodge founded Cheyenne, thousands of people rushed there ahead of the railroad. Cheyenne became a boom town known for lawlessness. Outlaws controlled the town for a short time until vigilante groups restored order.

During the late 1860's, cattlemen drove their animals north via trails from Texas to rangelands in Wyoming. Cheyenne served as a railroad shipping point and, by the early 1880's, was the center of a large cattle-ranching area. The city became the state capital in 1890.

Fort D. A. Russell was built nearby at the same time as Cheyenne. It protected the railroad construction

Cheyenne Frontier Days is a six-day celebration that attracts thousands of spectators to the city.

Severin, Black Star

crews from Indian attacks. In 1930, the post was renamed Fort Francis E. Warren in honor of Wyoming's first governor. It became Warren Air Force Base in 1947. In 1963, the base became the headquarters of the 90th Strategic Missile Wing, control center of ballistic missile installations. Cheyenne has a mayor-council form of government. JAMES M. FLINCHUM, JR.

For the monthly weather in Cheyenne, see WYOMING (Climate). See also WYOMING (pictures).

CHEYENNE INDIANS are a group of American Indians separated geographically into two groups, the Northern Cheyenne and the Southern Cheyenne. About 3,000 Northern Cheyenne live on a reservation in Montana, and about 4,000 Southern Cheyenne live in Oklahoma. Many Cheyenne also live and work in cities.

All the Cheyenne once fished and hunted in the region around Lake Superior. After the mid-1700's, they moved to the Great Plains, where they lived in tepees and hunted buffalo. In the early 1830's, the Cheyenne divided into the Northern and Southern groups. Troops of the Colorado militia massacred about 300 peaceful Southern Cheyenne and Arapaho at Sand Creek, Colorado, in 1864. The surviving Indians moved to a reservation in Oklahoma in 1869. The Northern Cheyenne fought to keep their hunting lands when white settlers tried to take them. In 1876, Northern Cheyenne and Sioux forces defeated Lieutenant Colonel George A. Custer in the Battle of the Little Bighorn in Montana. The government gave the Northern Cheyenne a reservation in Montana in 1884. JOHN WOODENLEGS, SR.

See also BLACK KETTLE; INDIAN WARS (Death on the Plains).

CHIANG CH'ING. See JIANG QING.

CHIANG CHING-KUO, *jyahng jihng GWOH* (1910-), became the leader of the Nationalist Chinese government on Taiwan in 1975. He succeeded his father, Chiang Kai-shek, who died that year. Chiang Ching-kuo served as prime minister of the government

Photo by Stanley J. Morrow, 1878; Smithsonian Institution, Washington, D.C.

The Cheyenne Indians lived in tepees and hunted buffaloes on the Great Plains. They staked out and dressed the buffalo hides and hung the meat on racks to dry in the sun, *left.*

from 1972 to 1978, when he became Taiwan's president.

Chiang was born in Chekiang Province and attended several Chinese schools. He went to Russia in 1925. There, he graduated from Sun Yat-sen University in 1927 and from a military academy in 1930. Chiang returned to China in 1937 and held a series of government positions of increasing importance. After the Chinese Communists conquered China in 1949, the Nationalists moved their government to the island of Taiwan. Chiang took charge of the Nationalist secret police and directed youth and veterans' organizations. He served as minister of defense from 1965 to 1969, and as deputy prime minister from 1969 to 1972. RALPH N. CLOUGH

CHIANG KAI-SHEK, *jyahng ky SHEHK* (1887-1975), was the political and military leader of the Nationalist Chinese government on Taiwan from 1949 until his death in 1975. He took command of the Kuomintang Party in the 1920's. This was the Nationalist Party that had overthrown the Manchu dynasty and proclaimed a republic in 1912. Chiang was the decisive power in China from the mid-1920's until 1949, when Communists took control. He then fled to Taiwan and established his government there.

Chiang was born in the province of Chekiang. He received a military education in China and in Tokyo, Japan. In Tokyo he met Sun Yat-sen, the Chinese revolutionary leader, and joined Sun's revolutionary organization. Sun sent Chiang to Russia in 1923. When Chiang returned to China, Sun appointed him president of the Whampoa Military Academy. Sun died in 1925, and the next year Chiang took command of the Nationalist Army. See SUN YAT-SEN.

Nationalist Victory. In 1926, Nationalist forces, aided by Communist organizers, left Canton on a campaign against warlords in the north. The warlords were defeated and the Nationalists became the strongest force in China. Russian advisers tried but failed to seize political power at Hankow and Shanghai. The Russians were expelled from China. In 1927, Chiang established a capital at Nan-ching. That same year, he married Soong Mei-ling (see CHIANG SOONG MEI-LING). He later became a Christian. The National Government of China was created in 1928.

From 1928 to 1937, Chiang improved economic and political institutions in China. But political consolidations proved difficult. The Japanese military and Chinese Communists continually sabotaged Chiang's regime.

The Japanese attack on China in 1937 made it necessary for the Nationalists to form a united front with the Communists. Chiang assumed full military power in this union as generalissimo. After the Japanese captured Nan-ching later that year, he made the city of Ch'ung-ch'ing his wartime capital. Chiang led China to victory in 1945.

Wide World

Chiang Kai-shek

Wide World

Madame Chiang Kai-shek

Communist Triumph. Near the end of World War II, when Japanese surrender became inevitable, the Communists again began to battle Chiang. He issued a new constitution and called for a popular election. In 1948, he was elected president of China. Li Tsung-jen became vice-president. But these popular measures failed to ensure political stability. The Communists were winning the civil war. Chiang's resignation and Li's assumption of the presidency did not save the situation. By the end of 1949, the Communists had driven Chiang and his Nationalist armies from the Chinese mainland to the island of Taiwan, which lies off the coast of China in the China Sea. See CHINA (Civil War).

On Taiwan, Chiang took full military and civil authority. He established Taipei as the capital of his government. Chiang was re-elected president in 1954, 1960, 1966, and 1972. IMMANUEL C. Y. HSU

Additional Resources

BERKOV, ROBERT. *Strong Man of China: The Story of Chiang Kai-Shek.* Books for Libraries, 1970. Reprint of 1938 ed.

CROZIER, BRAIN, and CHOU, ERIC. *The Man Who Lost China: The First Full Biography of Chiang Kai-Shek.* Scribner, 1976.

MORWOOD, WILLIAM. *Duel for the Middle Kingdom: The Struggle between Chiang Kai-Shek and Mao Tse-Tung for Control of China.* Everest House, 1980.

PAYNE, P. S. R. *Chiang Kai-Shek.* Weybright & Talley, 1969.

CHIANG SOONG MEI-LING, *jyahng sung may LIHNG*, or MAYLING (1897?-), the wife of Chiang Kai-shek, is a Chinese social leader. She was the third daughter of Charles Jones Soong. She was born in Shanghai, and graduated from Wellesley College in Massachusetts. In 1927, she married Chiang Kai-shek and supported him through difficult crises of his career (see CHIANG KAI-SHEK). She joined him in captivity during the Sian mutiny in 1936, just before China's war with Japan.

In 1943, she served as her husband's interpreter at the Cairo Conference, when he met with U.S. President Franklin D. Roosevelt and British Prime Minister Winston Churchill. During World War II and the Communist conquest of mainland China, she pleaded the Nationalist cause in the United States. IMMANUEL C. Y. HSU

CHIBCHA INDIANS, *CHIB chuh*, lived on the high plains of the central Colombian Andes. Our only sources of information about them are archaeology and Spanish records. The Spanish conquered the Chibcha in the 1500's. The Chibcha culture changed quickly, and their language became extinct in the 1700's.

The Chibcha were once classified as a highly advanced civilization, as great as those of the Aztec, Inca, and Maya. They worked gold, drilled emeralds, made pottery and basketry, and wove textiles. But their craftwork was not as highly developed as that of other Indian cultures in Colombia. They did some farming in lowlands and on terraced hillsides. Research shows they had only small villages. CLIFFORD EVANS

See also EL DORADO.

Tom Kinney

The Skyscrapers of Downtown Chicago form a magnificent backdrop for the city's beautiful lakefront. The world's tallest building, the 110-story Sears Tower, rises at the left.

CHICAGO

CHICAGO is a huge city in northeastern Illinois that ranks as the leading industrial and transportation center of the United States. According to the 1980 census, it was the second largest city in the United States, after New York City. But in 1982, U.S. Bureau of the Census estimates reported that Los Angeles had passed Chicago in population, making Chicago the nation's third largest city. About 3 million people live in this energetic city along the southwest shore of Lake Michigan. The Chicago area produces more steel, cookies and candy, radios and TV sets, and paint and machine tools than does any other area of the country. Trucks and railroad cars carry more goods in and out of Chicago than in and out of any other U.S. city.

The American poet Carl Sandburg called Chicago the "City of the Big Shoulders." And the city does do things in a big way. For example, Chicago has the world's tallest building, largest grain market, biggest post office building, and busiest airport.

Chicago also has one of the world's most beautiful lakefronts. Most of it is public parkland, with broad beaches and lawns stretching far along the shoreline. In addition, the city has an excellent symphony orchestra and fascinating museums of art, history, and science. Chicago surprises many of its almost 8 million annual visitors who learn that the city, built for business and industry, has a tradition of beauty and culture.

Throughout its history, Chicago has been known for providing good jobs. Young men from Germany and Ireland came to Chicago to dig a shipping canal soon after Chicago became a city in 1837. During the next 100 years, thousands of European families came to work in Chicago's factories, steel mills, and shipping businesses. By the late 1800's, Chicago had become an industrial and commercial giant.

In 1871, the Great Chicago Fire destroyed much of the city. But Chicagoans rebuilt their city with a daring that made it a center of world architecture. During the 1920's, Chicago gained a reputation for crime and violence that it has never lived down. Yet this was also a creative period in the arts, and the booming industries continued to attract new residents.

Since the 1940's, most newcomers to Chicago have been blacks and whites from poor areas of the South and Spanish-speaking families from Mexico and Puerto Rico. Many of them lack the skills needed for today's jobs. About 650,000 Chicagoans, nearly a fifth of the population, receive welfare aid. Chicago's many other problems include a high crime rate, an inadequate mass transportation system, and air pollution.

Lois Wille, the contributor of this article, is Associate Editorial Page Editor of the Chicago Tribune. *She is the author of* Forever Open, Clear and Free, *a history of the Chicago lakefront.*

Facts in Brief

Population: *City*—3,005,072. *Metropolitan Area*—6,060,387. *Consolidated Metropolitan Area*—7,937,326 (7,171,408 in Illinois, 642,781 in Indiana, and 123,137 in Wisconsin).

Area: 228 sq. mi. (591 km²). *Metropolitan Area*—1,911 sq. mi. (4,949 km²). *Consolidated Metropolitan Area*—5,694 sq. mi. (14,747 km²), consisting of 4,491 sq. mi. (11,632 km²) in Illinois, 925 sq. mi. (2,396 km²) in Indiana, and 278 sq. mi. (720 km²) in Wisconsin.

Climate: *Average Temperature*—January, 25° F. (−4° C); July, 75° F. (24° C). *Average Annual Precipitation* (rainfall, melted snow, and other forms of moisture)—33 in. (84 cm). For the monthly weather in Chicago, see ILLINOIS (Climate).

Government: Mayor-council. *Terms*—4 years for the mayor and the 50 council members.

Founded: 1803. Incorporated as a city in 1837.

WORLD BOOK photo

Elevated Trains, which run on tracks above the streets, carry thousands of workers to and from their jobs in downtown Chicago.

CHICAGO/*The City*

Chicago extends about 25 miles (40 kilometers) along the southwest shore of Lake Michigan in northeastern Illinois. It covers 228 square miles (591 square kilometers). The city lies on a plain 595 feet (181 meters) above sea level.

The Chicago River flows westward from Lake Michigan near the center of the city. It is famous as *the river that flows backward.* The river flowed into the lake until 1900. That year, engineers reversed the flow to prevent sewage in the river from polluting the lake, which provides Chicago's water supply. About 1 mile (1.6 kilometers) inland from the lake, the river splits into two branches. One branch flows northwest through Chicago. The other flows south into the Chicago Sanitary and Ship Canal, which cuts southwest through the city.

Chicago has four main sections. They are (1) Downtown Chicago, (2) the North Side, (3) the West Side, and (4) the South Side.

Downtown Chicago is known for its spectacular skyscrapers; huge department stores; fashionable shops; and beautiful "front yard," Grant Park. Every workday, about 310,000 persons stream into the downtown area to work in its offices and stores. About 70,000 others visit the area to shop or conduct other personal business. Thousands of people also live downtown in luxurious high-rise apartment buildings.

The main downtown area extends about 10 blocks south of the Chicago River's main stem. The river's south branch borders it on the west, and the lake borders it on the east. Within this area, elevated trains run along a rectangular "loop" of tracks 5 blocks wide and 7 blocks long. These tracks give the main downtown area its nickname, the *Loop*. The trains travel between the Loop and suburbs on the edge of the city.

The heart of the Loop is the intersection of State and Madison streets. These two streets form the base lines of Chicago's street-numbering system. Madison, which runs east and west, divides the north and south numbers. State, a north-south street, divides the east and west numbers. State Street is also one of the world's great shopping areas.

Three blocks west of State Street is LaSalle Street, Chicago's financial district. Along the street stand eight major banks, the Midwest Stock Exchange, and the Chicago Board of Trade, the world's largest grain market. The City Hall-County Building also faces LaSalle Street.

Wacker Drive, a double-deck boulevard, follows the inside curve of the Chicago River and its south branch. Local traffic uses the upper, street-level deck, and express traffic uses the lower level. The drive connects with 17 of the 19 downtown bridges that cross the river. The Merchandise Mart, one of the world's largest commercial buildings, stands across the river from Wacker Drive. It has over 4 million square feet (370,000 square meters) of floor space. East of the Mart rises Marina City, two circular, 60-story apartment buildings.

A stunning group of modern office buildings, set in airy plazas, lines South Wacker Drive and the riverfront. The most impressive is the 110-story, smoky-gray Sears Tower, the world's tallest building. It rises 1,454 feet (443 meters).

Two blocks east of State Street in the main downtown area is Michigan Avenue. Fashionable shops, hotels, and tall office buildings line its west side. Grant Park covers about 300 acres (120 hectares) between Michigan Avenue and the lake. Its attractions include Bucking-

WORLD BOOK map

Chicago Is Located in Northeastern Illinois.

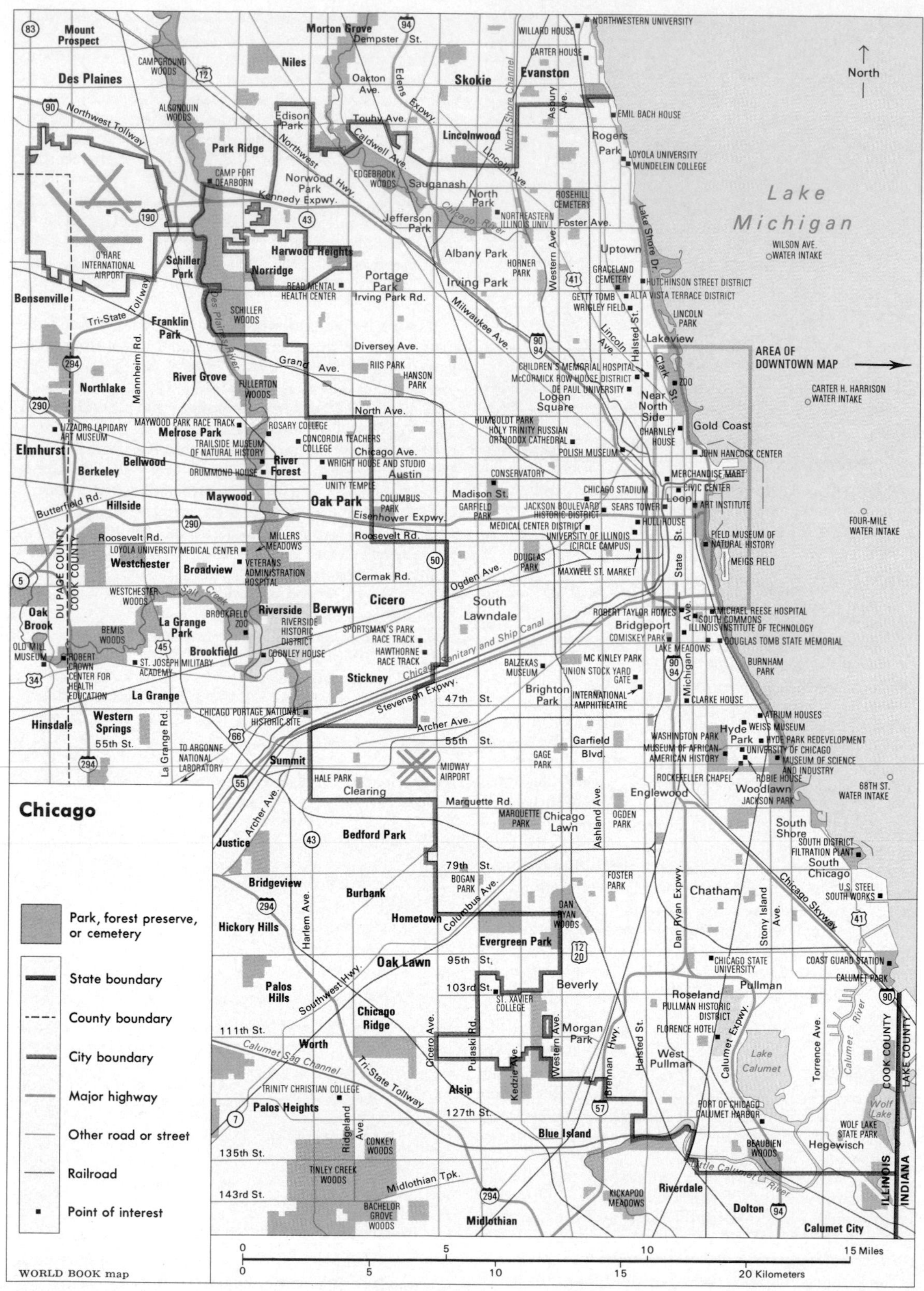
Chicago
Park, forest preserve, or cemetery
State boundary
County boundary
City boundary
Major highway
Other road or street
Railroad
Point of interest
WORLD BOOK map
0
5
10
15 Miles
0
5
10
15
20 Kilometers
North
Lake Michigan
AREA OF DOWNTOWN MAP
Mount Prospect
Des Plaines
Morton Grove
Niles
Skokie
Evanston
Park Ridge
Lincolnwood
Rogers Park
Edison Park
Norwood Park
Sauganash
North Park
Jefferson Park
Albany Park
Uptown
Harwood Heights
Norridge
Portage Park
Irving Park
Schiller Park
Bensenville
Franklin Park
River Grove
Northlake
Lakeview
Logan Square
Near North Side
Gold Coast
Melrose Park
Elmhurst
Berkeley
Bellwood
River Forest
Oak Park
Austin
Loop
Hillside
Maywood
Westchester
Broadview
Cicero
Berwyn
Riverside
South Lawndale
Bridgeport
Oak Brook
La Grange Park
Brookfield
La Grange
Stickney
Brighton Park
Hinsdale
Western Springs
Summit
Clearing
Garfield Blvd.
Hyde Park
Woodlawn
Englewood
Chicago Lawn
South Shore
South Chicago
Justice
Bedford Park
Bridgeview
Burbank
Hickory Hills
Hometown
Evergreen Park
Chatham
Oak Lawn
Palos Hills
Beverly
Pullman
Roseland
Chicago Ridge
Worth
Morgan Park
West Pullman
Palos Heights
Alsip
Blue Island
Hegewisch
Riverdale
Dolton
Midlothian
Calumet City
Lake Calumet
Wolf Lake
ILLINOIS
INDIANA
COOK COUNTY
LAKE COUNTY
DU PAGE COUNTY
COOK COUNTY
Dempster St.
Oakton Ave.
Edens Expwy.
Touhy Ave.
Caldwell Ave.
Northwest Hwy.
Northwest Tollway
Kennedy Expwy.
Lincoln Ave.
North Shore Channel
Asbury Ave.
Chicago River
Foster Ave.
Western Ave.
Lake Shore Dr.
Irving Park Rd.
Milwaukee Ave.
Tri-State Tollway
Des Plaines River
Mannheim Rd.
Diversey Ave.
Grand Ave.
Halsted St.
Clark St.
North Ave.
Chicago Ave.
Madison St.
Butterfield Rd.
Eisenhower Expwy.
Roosevelt Rd.
State St.
Cermak Rd.
Ogden Ave.
Salt Creek
Chicago Sanitary and Ship Canal
Stevenson Expwy.
47th St.
Archer Ave.
55th St.
Michigan Ave.
La Grange Rd.
Marquette Rd.
Ashland Ave.
79th St.
Columbus Ave.
Harlem Ave.
Dan Ryan Expwy.
Stony Island Ave.
Chicago Skyway
95th St.
103rd St.
Southwest Hwy.
111th St.
Cicero Ave.
Pulaski Rd.
Kedzie Ave.
Calumet Sag Channel
Tri-State Tollway
127th St.
Brennan Hwy.
Calumet Expwy.
Torrence Ave.
Calumet River
Ridgeland Ave.
135th St.
143rd St.
Midlothian Tpk.
Little Calumet River
83
94
12
90
190
43
41
294
290
5
34
45
50
66
55
7
57
20
CAMPGROUND WOODS
ALGONQUIN WOODS
CAMP FORT DEARBORN
EDGEBROOK WOODS
O'HARE INTERNATIONAL AIRPORT
READ MENTAL HEALTH CENTER
SCHILLER WOODS
FULLERTON WOODS
WILLARD HOUSE
NORTHWESTERN UNIVERSITY
CARTER HOUSE
EMIL BACH HOUSE
LOYOLA UNIVERSITY
MUNDELEIN COLLEGE
NORTHEASTERN ILLINOIS UNIV.
ROSEHILL CEMETERY
HORNER PARK
GRACELAND CEMETERY
HUTCHINSON STREET DISTRICT
GETTY TOMB
ALTA VISTA TERRACE DISTRICT
WRIGLEY FIELD
LINCOLN PARK
WILSON AVE. WATER INTAKE
RIIS PARK
HANSON PARK
CHILDREN'S MEMORIAL HOSPITAL
McCORMICK ROW HOUSE DISTRICT
DE PAUL UNIVERSITY
ZOO
CARTER H. HARRISON WATER INTAKE
MAYWOOD PARK RACE TRACK
LIZZADRO LAPIDARY ART MUSEUM
ROSARY COLLEGE
CONCORDIA TEACHERS COLLEGE
TRAILSIDE MUSEUM OF NATURAL HISTORY
HUMBOLDT PARK
HOLY TRINITY RUSSIAN ORTHODOX CATHEDRAL
POLISH MUSEUM
CHARNLEY HOUSE
JOHN HANCOCK CENTER
WRIGHT HOUSE AND STUDIO
DRUMMOND HOUSE
UNITY TEMPLE
CONSERVATORY
MERCHANDISE MART
CIVIC CENTER
CHICAGO STADIUM
COLUMBUS PARK
GARFIELD PARK
JACKSON BOULEVARD HISTORIC DISTRICT
SEARS TOWER
ART INSTITUTE
MEDICAL CENTER DISTRICT
HULL HOUSE
UNIVERSITY OF ILLINOIS (CIRCLE CAMPUS)
FIELD MUSEUM OF NATURAL HISTORY
FOUR-MILE WATER INTAKE
MILLERS MEADOWS
LOYOLA UNIVERSITY MEDICAL CENTER
VETERANS ADMINISTRATION HOSPITAL
DOUGLAS PARK
MAXWELL ST. MARKET
MEIGS FIELD
WESTCHESTER WOODS
BROOKFIELD ZOO
RIVERSIDE HISTORIC DISTRICT
SPORTSMAN'S PARK RACE TRACK
HAWTHORNE RACE TRACK
ROBERT TAYLOR HOMES
MICHAEL REESE HOSPITAL
SOUTH COMMONS
ILLINOIS INSTITUTE OF TECHNOLOGY
COMISKEY PARK
DOUGLAS TOMB STATE MEMORIAL
LAKE MEADOWS
BEMIS WOODS
OLD MILL MUSEUM
ROBERT CROWN CENTER FOR HEALTH EDUCATION
ST. JOSEPH MILITARY ACADEMY
COONLEY HOUSE
BALZEKAS MUSEUM
MC KINLEY PARK
UNION STOCK YARD GATE
INTERNATIONAL AMPHITHEATRE
CLARKE HOUSE
BURNHAM PARK
CHICAGO PORTAGE NATIONAL HISTORIC SITE
TO ARGONNE NATIONAL LABORATORY
ATRIUM HOUSES
WEISS MUSEUM
HYDE PARK REDEVELOPMENT
WASHINGTON PARK
MUSEUM OF AFRICAN-AMERICAN HISTORY
UNIVERSITY OF CHICAGO
MUSEUM OF SCIENCE AND INDUSTRY
GAGE PARK
HALE PARK
MIDWAY AIRPORT
ROCKEFELLER CHAPEL
ROBIE HOUSE
JACKSON PARK
68TH ST. WATER INTAKE
MARQUETTE PARK
OGDEN PARK
SOUTH DISTRICT FILTRATION PLANT
BOGAN PARK
FOSTER PARK
U.S. STEEL SOUTH WORKS
DAN RYAN WOODS
CHICAGO STATE UNIVERSITY
COAST GUARD STATION
CALUMET PARK
ST. XAVIER COLLEGE
PULLMAN HISTORIC DISTRICT
FLORENCE HOTEL
TRINITY CHRISTIAN COLLEGE
PORT OF CHICAGO CALUMET HARBOR
WOLF LAKE STATE PARK
CONKEY WOODS
BEAUBIEN WOODS
TINLEY CREEK WOODS
KICKAPOO MEADOWS
BACHELOR GROVE WOODS

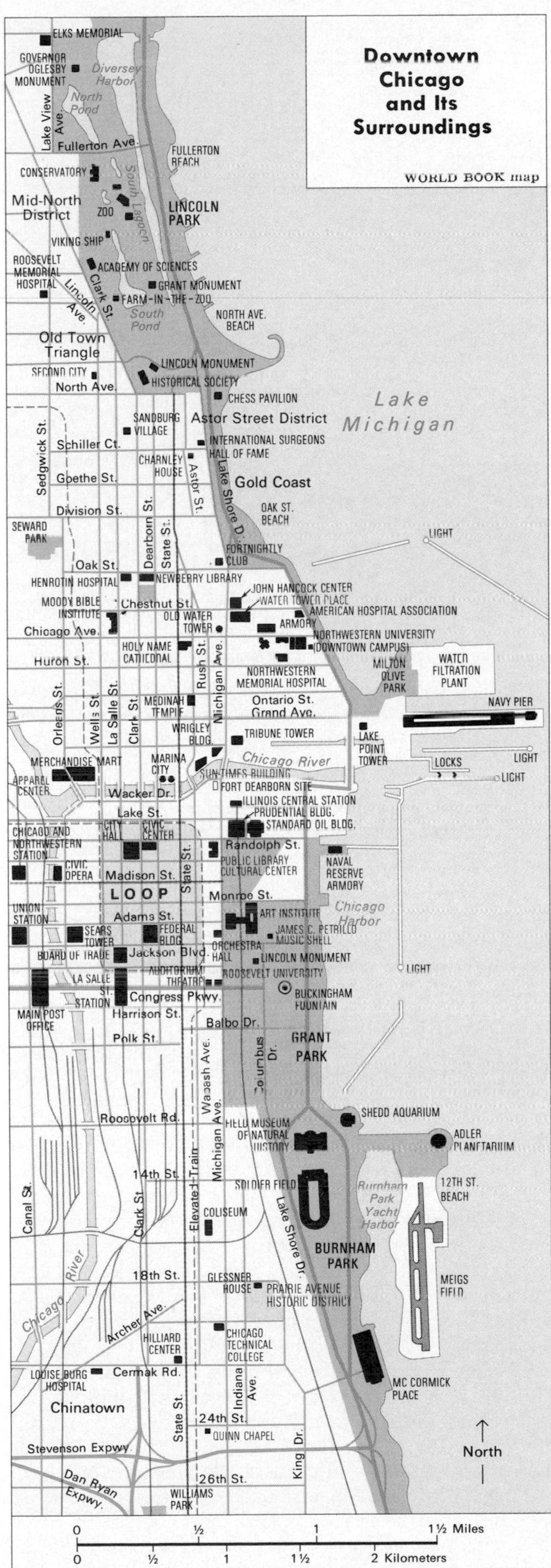

ham Memorial Fountain, the John G. Shedd Aquarium, the Field Museum of Natural History, and the world-famous Art Institute of Chicago.

Beautiful Lake Shore Drive runs along the lakefront on Grant Park's east side. It extends from the downtown area far into the North and South sides. Many strikingly modern high-rise apartment buildings have been built along the drive.

North of the Chicago River, Michigan Avenue forms the core of the northern downtown area. This area stretches about 14 blocks to Oak Street. It has been named the *Magnificent Mile* because of its many elegant stores, hotels, restaurants, and office buildings.

Chicagoans' favorite landmark, the Old Water Tower, stands at Michigan and Chicago avenues. The little tower was one of the few structures in the area to survive the Great Chicago Fire. The 100-story John Hancock Center rises one block north of the tower. "Big John," as Chicagoans call the building, houses a department store, offices, and over 700 apartments.

The North Side is almost entirely residential. It stretches from the downtown area north about 9 miles (14.5 kilometers) and northwest about 13 miles (21 kilometers). Over $1\frac{1}{3}$ million persons live in this section.

The area just north of downtown is called the Near North Side. One famous Near North neighborhood is the Gold Coast, a luxurious residential area that begins at Oak Street. It extends about 10 blocks north along Lake Shore Drive and a few blocks west. The area is a blend of graceful old apartment buildings, Victorian mansions, and expensive skyscraper apartments.

Just west of the Gold Coast stands Carl Sandburg Village, a high-rise apartment complex. It has about 6,000 residents, most of them young people who work downtown. Old Town lies west of Sandburg Village. This neighborhood has many gift shops, nightclubs, fine restaurants, and charming old homes that have been modernized. Southwest of Old Town stands the bleak, crime-ridden Cabrini-Green Homes project. This group of high-rise apartment buildings houses about 15,000 poor people, nearly all of them black.

Lincoln Park, Chicago's largest and most popular park, begins north of the Gold Coast and marks the end of the Near North Side. The park stretches along almost two-thirds of the North Side lakefront and covers about 1,185 acres (480 hectares). The park includes beaches, lagoons, and an attractive zoo. North of Old Town, a long line of luxury apartment buildings overlooks Lincoln Park and extends along the lakeshore.

The rest of the North Side consists largely of middle-class white neighborhoods. Most people in these neighborhoods live in three- to six-unit brick apartment buildings or single-family brick bungalows. More expensive homes can be found in such neighborhoods as Edgebrook and Sauganash on the Far Northwest Side.

The North Side also has many pockets of poverty, in addition to the Cabrini-Green project. Most of the more than 50,000 blacks on the North Side live in old, poorly maintained areas just northwest of the Loop. But a growing number of upper-income black people are moving into new high-rise apartments near the downtown area. About 140,000 Spanish-speaking people also re-

Dan Morrill

The Gold Coast on Chicago's Near North Side is a luxurious residential area. These expensive high-rise apartment buildings along Lake Michigan overlook popular Oak Street Beach.

side on the North Side. The majority live in run-down neighborhoods scattered throughout much of the area.

To many Chicagoans, the most famous North Side street is Milwaukee Avenue, which was once an old Indian trail. It runs diagonally across the North Side and into the northwest suburbs. From the 1860's until the 1940's, many thousands of families from Poland settled along Milwaukee Avenue. As their fortunes improved, they moved to better homes on the Northwest Side. Many of the Polish food stores, bakeries, and restaurants remain and are popular with Chicagoans.

Chicago-O'Hare International Airport, the world's busiest airport, lies in the far northwest corner of the city. The John F. Kennedy Expressway cuts through the North Side and links O'Hare Airport with the Near Northwest Side, just northwest of the Loop.

The West Side lies west of the Loop between Grand Avenue on the north and the Chicago Sanitary and Ship Canal on the south. About 510,000 Chicagoans live on the West Side. Nearly 60 per cent of the residents are blacks, and about 9 per cent are Mexican Americans. Almost all the rest are white.

One of the city's chief industrial districts lies along the canal. It has many factories, rail yards, truck-loading docks, and warehouses. Most of the rest of the West Side consists of residential neighborhoods. Abandoned, decaying buildings scar many of these areas, and high crime rates and unemployment plague the residents. Nearly all the housing is over 50 years old. Much of it consists of overcrowded apartment buildings neglected by landlords who long ago moved to better areas.

The West Side also has areas of old but well-kept houses and small apartment buildings. Blacks, Mexican Americans, and people of East European descent occupy such an area in South Lawndale, which borders suburban Cicero. Austin, an attractive neighborhood that borders suburban Oak Park, has many families of Irish and Italian descent, as well as many blacks.

The Dwight D. Eisenhower Expressway cuts through the West Side between the Loop and the western suburbs. Just west of downtown, it tunnels through the Chicago Post Office, the world's largest post office building. It has about 22,000 employees and handles over 4 billion pieces of mail yearly. West of the post office, the expressway passes the University of Illinois at Chicago Circle and the West Side Medical Center. The center's seven hospitals and three medical schools make it the world's largest concentration of medical facilities.

The South Side is Chicago's biggest section in area and population. It stretches about 16 miles (26 kilometers) south of downtown and the West Side and covers more than half the city's area. Over $1\frac{1}{2}$ million persons live on the South Side. It includes industrial areas, an international port, spacious parks, pleasant residential communities, and poverty-stricken neighborhoods.

About half the South Siders are blacks. Many of the others are children or grandchildren of German, Irish, or East European immigrants. Most blacks and whites live in separate communities.

But the South Side has a few successfully integrated communities. Three of them—Lake Meadows, Prairie Shores, and South Commons—lie close to downtown on the Near South Side. These privately financed developments consist chiefly of handsome high-rise apartment buildings. They attract many people who work downtown or at three nearby institutions: the Illinois Institute of Technology, Mercy Hospital, and Michael Reese Hospital and Medical Center. Hyde Park, another integrated community, lies farther south along the lake. It is the site of the University of Chicago.

Chicago's biggest public housing project, the Robert Taylor Homes, covers about 15 blocks along South State Street and the Dan Ryan Expressway. Its 25,000 residents, almost all blacks, live in 28 crowded buildings, where assault and robbery are constant threats.

The South Side's largest park is Burnham Park. It stretches south from Grant Park and covers 598 acres (242 hectares) along the lakefront. McCormick Place, a giant convention and exhibition center, stands in the north end of Burnham Park. The park's southern edge borders Jackson Park, which covers 543 acres (220 hectares) along the lake. About 12 blocks west, Washington Park occupies 368 acres (149 hectares).

The Chicago Skyway, an elevated toll road, crosses the industrial Far Southeast Side. The skyway runs from the Dan Ryan Expressway, the South Side's major north-south route, to the Indiana border. On the way, it passes steel mills, oil refineries, warehouses, grain elevators, and huge stockpiles of iron ore and limestone. Near the Indiana border, the skyway soars 125 feet (38 meters) above the Calumet River. Cargo ships follow the river inland from Lake Michigan to terminals along Lake Calumet, Chicago's largest harbor.

The Far Southwest Side is one of Chicago's newest and most pleasant communities. It has block after block of neat, single-family homes and only scattered industrial districts. Nearly all the residents are white.

Two well-known Near Southwest Side neighborhoods are Chinatown and Bridgeport. Chinatown has a small residential section and a long line of restaurants, food stores, and gift shops. Bridgeport is a neat community of small bungalows. Large numbers of city employees and four Chicago mayors have lived there.

The famous Union Stock Yards, which closed in 1971, lie southwest of Bridgeport. The huge stockyards once supplied meat to much of the nation.

Metropolitan Area. The Chicago metropolitan area consists of three Illinois counties. The area has over 6 million persons. About $5\frac{1}{4}$ million live in Cook County. Cook County includes all of Chicago proper. It ranks as the second largest U.S. county in population, after Los Angeles County. The other counties of the Chicago metropolitan area are McHenry to the north and DuPage to the west. The consolidated metropolitan area, or *Greater Chicago*, includes the Chicago metropolitan area; Grundy, Kane, Kendall, Lake, and Will counties in Illinois; Lake and Porter counties in Indiana; and Kenosha County in Wisconsin.

The Chicago metropolitan area has changed dramatically since the 1940's. The suburban population has grown rapidly while that of Chicago proper has fallen. Many factories and offices have been built in the suburbs. Today, Chicago's suburbs have most of the people and about half the jobs in the metropolitan area.

Northwest Cook County has had the greatest growth. It has so many shopping centers, restaurants, and recreational facilities that many residents rarely visit downtown Chicago. Arlington Heights, the center of this area, has grown from 5,700 persons in 1940 to over 66,000 today. The nearby towns of Des Plaines, Mount Prospect, and Schaumburg consisted mostly of vegetable farms in 1960. Today, they have more than 50,000 residents each.

The old, elegant towns of Winnetka, Kenilworth, and Wilmette lie along the lake north of the city limits. Some Chicago suburbs have a large number of both black and white residents. One is Park Forest, south of the city. This attractive, well-planned community was built in the late 1940's. The newer Park Forest South is also integrated. A few towns in the far south metropolitan area have mostly black residents.

Charles Lieberman

Chicago's Far Northwest Side has some of the city's most beautiful and spacious neighborhoods. In the Sauganash area, *above,* large, lovely homes line the winding, tree-lined streets.

Charles Lieberman

The West Side of Chicago has many decaying neighborhoods like this one, with old, neglected housing. Other West Side areas, especially those bordering the suburbs, are old but well kept.

Robert H. Glaze, Artstreet

Rows of Single-Family Brick Bungalows can be found in many Chicago neighborhoods. About 24 per cent of the city's families live in single-family houses. The rest live in apartments.

Chicago has always been known as a city where industrious people could find good jobs. By the 1860's, when Chicago was only 30 years old, its reputation was spreading throughout the poor farmlands and slums of Europe. Many thousands of European families moved to the booming prairie town, where they settled in separate sections. By the end of the 1800's, the city consisted of many small communities that duplicated the language and customs of such countries as Germany, Italy, Poland, and Ireland.

Most of the old European ethnic communities have faded away. But they have left a rich heritage. Many Chicagoans enjoy visiting the city's numerous ethnic restaurants, food stores, and gift shops. They also take pride in the impressive churches and charming blocks of homes constructed by the hard-working European immigrants who built the city.

Today, almost 85 per cent of all Chicagoans were born in the United States. About half of the people are white, and about two-fifths are black. Protestants make up the largest religious group—about half the people. About 40 per cent of the people are Roman Catholics, and about 5 per cent are Jewish.

Ethnic Groups. Blacks make up Chicago's largest ethnic group, with about 1,197,000 persons. Most of them live in neighborhoods that are nearly all black. These communities range from the attractive, tree-lined streets of Avalon Park and South Shore on the South Side to the crumbling slums of the Near West and Near Northwest sides. As in other U.S. cities, blacks in Chicago have generally suffered from poverty, a lack of education, and discrimination in jobs and housing. But Chicago also has many successful black business people. In fact, Chicago has over 8,700 businesses owned by blacks, more than any other city in the United States.

Chicago's fastest-growing ethnic group consists of Spanish-speaking people, or *Latinos*. The city has about 422,000 Latinos, about $1\frac{1}{2}$ times as many as in 1970. About 61 per cent are Mexican American, 26 per cent Puerto Rican, and 3 per cent Cuban. The rest trace their ancestry to other Latin-American countries. Latinos generally face the same problems of poverty and discrimination as the city's blacks.

Other large ethnic groups include Poles, Germans, Irish, and Italians. Chicago's Polish immigrants became known for budgeting their money and building homes—chiefly on the Northwest Side—as soon as they had saved enough. They founded some of the city's most pleasant neighborhoods. Thousands of German and Scandinavian immigrants started farms outside the city. They founded a number of today's prosperous suburbs. People of Irish descent have long been a major force in Chicago politics. Many government officials, judges, and police officers are of Irish descent. Chicago also has many people of other ethnic backgrounds, including Asian Indian, Chinese, English, Filipino, Greek, Russian, Swedish, and Ukrainian.

Housing. About 24 per cent of all Chicago families live in single-family houses, and about 35 per cent live in buildings with two, three, or four apartments. The rest live in large apartment buildings. Some areas, especially along the lakefront, have many high-rise apartment buildings. But most neighborhoods have a mixture of houses—chiefly bungalows—and small apartment buildings.

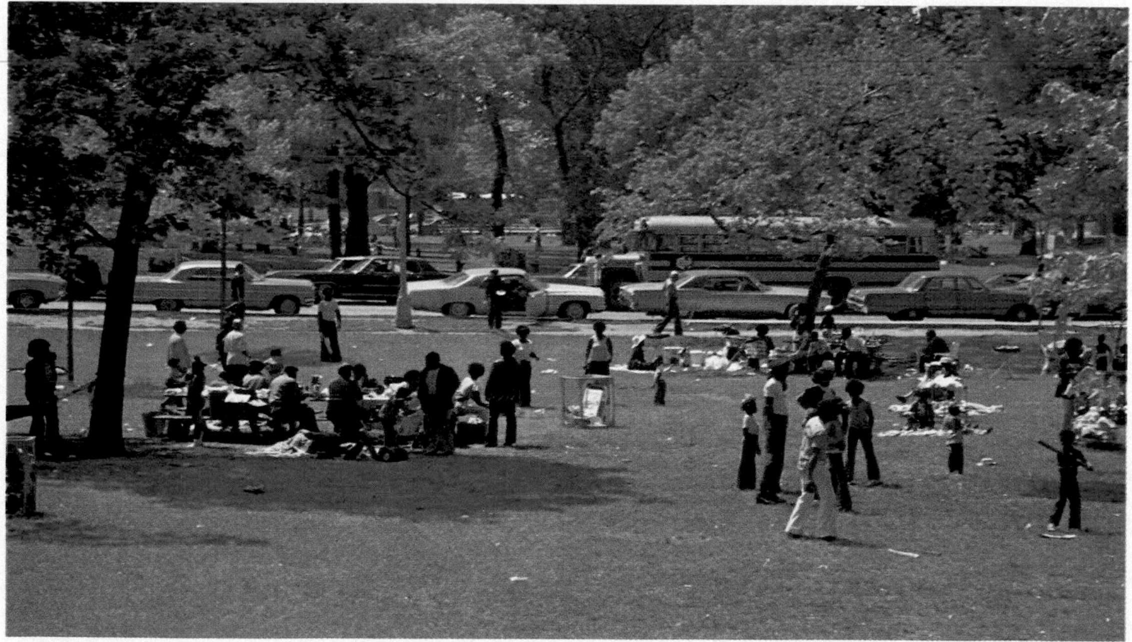

WORLD BOOK photo

Jackson Park, along Lake Michigan on the South Side, attracts many family picnickers. Chicago's 3,000 acres (1,200 hectares) of lakefront parkland become a huge playground in summer.

Although Chicago has many pleasant residential areas, housing is one of its worst problems. About two-thirds of the city's 1,200,000 housing units are over 35 years old. In low-income neighborhoods, numerous buildings have been overcrowded and poorly maintained for many years. Many other buildings are unusable and have been abandoned by their owners. The Chicago Housing Authority, a city agency, maintains 30,000 apartments for low-income families. Most of these dwellings are in crowded, crime-plagued, high-rise projects.

Education. Chicago has the third largest public school system in the United States, with about 600 schools and 510,000 students. Only New York City and Los Angeles have larger systems. The Board of Education governs the public school system. The mayor appoints its 11 members to five-year terms. About 146,000 Chicago students attend Catholic schools, and about 35,000 go to other private schools.

Chicago's largest institution of higher education is the Chicago Circle campus of the University of Illinois, with about 20,000 students. Two other state universities—Chicago State and Northeastern Illinois—are also in the city. Well-known private schools include the University of Chicago, Roosevelt University, and three Catholic institutions—DePaul University, Loyola University of Chicago, and Mundelein College. Northwestern University in suburban Evanston has a downtown Chicago campus, where several of its graduate professional schools are located. Chicago has six medical schools and ranks as one of the world's leading centers of medical education and research.

Other educational institutions in Chicago include the Illinois Institute of Technology, the School of the Art Institute of Chicago, and several business and law schools. The seven Community Colleges of Chicago, which are public junior colleges, have about 47,000 students.

Sports and Recreation. Chicagoans enthusiastically support spectator sports, and professional teams represent Chicago in all major U.S. sports. The Chicago Cubs of the National League play baseball in Wrigley Field on the North Side. Another baseball team, the Chicago White Sox of the American League, plays in Comiskey Park on the South Side.

The Chicago Black Hawks of the National Hockey League and the Chicago Bulls of the National Basketball Association play in the Chicago Stadium on the West Side. Soldier Field, on the lakefront south of Grant Park, is the home of the Chicago Bears of the National Football League.

Chicago has more than 400 parks. They total about 7,000 acres (2,833 hectares). The lakefront parkland, which covers about 3,000 acres (1,200 hectares), becomes a huge playground in warm weather. In addition to beaches, this parkland has bicycle paths, golf courses, soccer fields, softball diamonds, and tennis courts. It also has several harbors for the thousands of boats that cruise up and down the shoreline in summer.

The Cook County Forest Preserves dot Chicago's outskirts and suburban areas. The various preserves cover about 64,000 acres (25,900 hectares) of woodland. They have picnic grounds, golf courses, bridle paths, swimming pools, nature museums, and toboggan runs.

WORLD BOOK photo

The State Street Mall in downtown Chicago is in a district that includes some of the city's best-known department stores. The tree-lined mall stretches for nine blocks.

Social Problems. The chief social problems in Chicago, as in most other large U.S. cities, involve poverty and racial discrimination. The Chicago area has one of the lowest unemployment rates in the nation. Yet almost 20 per cent of all Chicagoans receive public welfare aid.

Chicago's blacks and Latinos carry most of the burden of poverty. For example, more than a fifth of all Chicago black families have an annual income of less than $4,000. In some black communities, about 15 per cent of the adults able to work do not have jobs. Many of these people have no job skills.

Family breakdown also contributes to poverty in the city. About 475,000 Chicagoans who receive welfare aid are women and children with no other means of support. On the poverty-stricken Near West Side, about 40 per cent of the children have no father in the home. In some areas, most babies are born to unmarried women.

Crime and inadequate health care also trouble poor neighborhoods. In parts of the South and West sides, a resident is 30 times more likely to be a victim of a violent crime—such as murder or robbery—than is a resident of the prosperous Far Northwest and Far Southwest sides. The infant death rate in poor neighborhoods is more than twice the rate in middle-class areas.

Cultural Life and Places to Visit

Chicago ranks among the greatest cultural centers of the United States. Its cultural life and many other features help attract about 5 million tourists every year. Nearly 3 million more persons visit Chicago annually for business meetings, conventions, and trade shows.

The Arts. The world-famous Chicago Symphony Orchestra performs in Orchestra Hall on Michigan Avenue for about 30 weeks beginning each September. In summer, the orchestra plays outdoors at Ravinia Park in north suburban Highland Park. From late June to the end of August, the Grant Park Symphony Orchestra presents free concerts in the outdoor band shell in Grant Park.

The Lyric Opera Company of Chicago has an annual fall season in the Civic Opera House on Wacker Drive. The company brings the world's leading opera singers to Chicago. Visiting dance companies, orchestras, and concert stars also perform in the Opera House and in the Auditorium Theatre on Michigan Avenue. This theater was designed during the 1880's by the noted architects Louis Sullivan and Dankmar Adler.

Several downtown and suburban theaters present popular Broadway plays. Some downtown and suburban theaters often stage new plays, plays for children, and experimental works as well as standard dramas and musicals. Old Town on the Near North Side is the home of Second City, a nationally known nightclub-theater. New Town, on the Mid-North Side, has a number of folk music clubs and experimental theater groups.

Architecture. Chicago has dominated American architecture since the late 1800's. New styles and new construction techniques have first appeared in Chicago and then spread to other cities. Designers and engineers from around the world visit Chicago to study its spectacular buildings.

The city's tradition of architectural pioneering began after the Great Chicago Fire of 1871 destroyed much of the city. Outstanding architects, including William Le Baron Jenney, Daniel H. Burnham, and Louis Sullivan, helped to rebuild Chicago. Their work produced a famous style of architecture that is known as the *Chicago School.*

The great development of the Chicago School was the skyscraper. Architects stripped away the heavy walls of stone and brick that had supported tall buildings. Instead, they designed structures with steel skeletons, which allowed buildings to soar to great heights and yet look light and graceful.

In 1884, Jenney designed the world's first skyscraper, the 10-story Home Insurance Building, in downtown Chicago. But this building and some other masterpieces of the Chicago School have been demolished. Many other examples of this type of architecture still stand, however. One of these structures is the Reliance Building, designed by Burnham and John W. Root, at State and Washington streets. Another is Jenney's Sears, Roebuck and Company store at State and Van Buren. A third Chicago School masterpiece is the Carson Pirie Scott and Company Building, designed by Sullivan. It curves gracefully around a corner at State and Madison streets. All three of these Loop structures were built in the 1890's.

The German architect Ludwig Mies van der Rohe, master of the glass-and-steel style, began a second generation of the Chicago School during the 1940's. His Chicago masterpieces include buildings at the Illinois Institute of Technology and apartments on Lake Shore Drive near Chicago Avenue. Other Chicago structures that reflect the influence of Mies include the Chicago Civic Center, the John Hancock Center, and McCormick Place.

Frank Lloyd Wright, who developed the *prairie school* of architecture, moved to Chicago in the 1880's. He created houses and other buildings that were long, low, and fluid—like the sweep of the Midwestern prairie. Many of Wright's works are in west suburban Oak Park, where his own home and studio still stand. His best-known design in the city is Robie House. This house was built in 1909 and is located in the University of Chicago area.

Museums. Several of Chicago's finest museums stand in Grant Park. On the park's south end, the Field Museum of Natural History exhibits mounted animals, life-sized displays of prehistoric people, and dinosaur skeletons. Across from the Field Museum, the John G. Shedd Aquarium has about 4,600 fish and other water animals. Nearby, the Adler Planetarium depicts the movements of heavenly bodies in its domed theater. The Art Institute of Chicago, located on Grant Park's north end, is famous for its collection of French impressionist art. The museum also has fine galleries of primitive art and Oriental art.

The huge Museum of Science and Industry, one of

Chicago Park District

At the Band Shell in Grant Park, Chicagoans enjoy free outdoor concerts in summer. The lakefront park is also the setting of beautiful Buckingham Fountain and outstanding museums.

Larry Reynolds, Bruce Coleman Inc.

The Art Institute of Chicago ranks as one of the world's greatest museums. It attracts more than a million visitors a year, including many tour groups of schoolchildren. These children are viewing part of the institute's outstanding collection of French impressionist art.

Chicago's best-known institutions, stands in Jackson Park. Its displays include an operating coal mine, a World War II German submarine, and many exhibits that explain the mysteries of chemistry and physics.

The Chicago Academy of Sciences and the Chicago Historical Society, two museums in Lincoln Park, trace the Chicago area's history from the Ice Age to modern times. On the South Side, the Du Sable Museum of African-American History is named after Chicago's first settler, Jean Baptiste Point du Sable, a black man.

Libraries. The Chicago Public Library, with about $4\frac{3}{4}$ million volumes, is the nation's second largest public library, after New York City's. The library has about 75 branches. The Great Chicago Fire destroyed the main library in the downtown area in 1871. But it was restarted the following year when the British people donated 8,000 books to the city.

Many private libraries in Chicago specialize in particular subjects, such as history or science. On the Near North Side is Newberry Library, one of the nation's leading historical research libraries. The John Crerar Library at the Illinois Institute of Technology has fine collections on science and technology. The Art Institute houses the Burnham Library of Architecture and the Ryerson Art Library. The Municipal Reference Library in City Hall, the Chicago Academy of Sciences, and the Chicago Historical Society have fine materials on Chicago history.

Places to Visit. Following are descriptions of a few of the Chicago area's many interesting places to visit. Other places of interest are discussed and pictured earlier in this article.

Brookfield Zoo, in west suburban Brookfield, covers

WORLD BOOK photo

The Museum of Science and Industry in Jackson Park has more than 3 million visitors yearly. Its many displays include this World War II British Spitfire suspended from the ceiling.

about 200 acres (81 hectares) and exhibits animals in natural settings. The zoo's Seven Seas Panorama has a porpoise show, and the children's zoo features baby animals.

Buckingham Memorial Fountain, in Grant Park, is the world's largest lighted fountain. It operates daily from May 30 through September 30. The fountain contains about $1\frac{1}{2}$ million gallons (5.7 million liters) of water and shoots its central spout about 135 feet (41 meters) in the air. Colorful lights illuminate the fountain each evening.

Chicago Board of Trade, at LaSalle and Jackson streets, is the world's largest commodity exchange. In its hectic main hall, hundreds of brokers buy and sell grains and various other farm products for future delivery. Visitors may watch from a gallery.

Dearborn Street Plazas, along downtown Dearborn Street, display magnificent works of art. A five-story sculpture by the Spanish artist Pablo Picasso stands in Richard J. Daley Plaza. Some people think the work is a likeness of the artist's pet Afghan hound. Others think the gigantic sculpture resembles a woman's head. Alexander Calder, an American artist, designed the tall, red metal sculpture in the Federal Building Plaza. It looks like a drooping flower. The Russian-born artist Marc Chagall created a huge outdoor design of ceramic tiles for the First National Bank Plaza.

Sears Tower, 110 stories high on Wacker Drive, is the world's tallest building. A public observation deck on the 103rd floor gives a spectacular view of Chicago and the Lake Michigan shoreline.

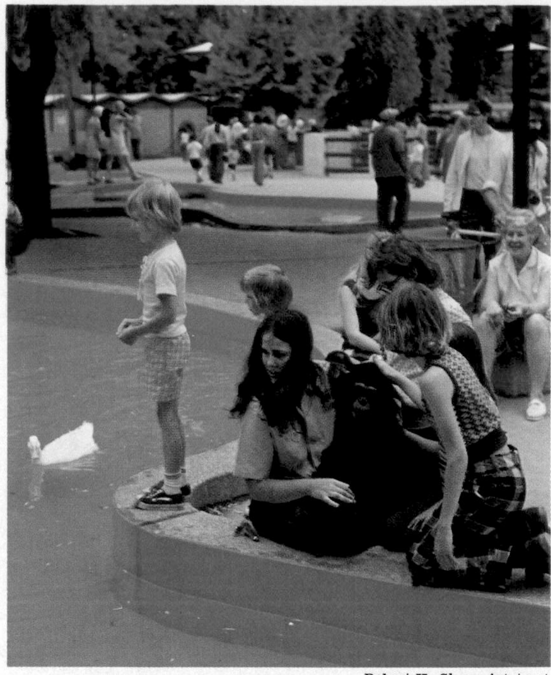

Robert H. Glaze, Artstreet

Lincoln Park is Chicago's largest and most popular park. Its attractions include beaches, lagoons, sports fields, two museums, a conservatory, a main zoo, and a special children's zoo, *above.*

Gerald Brimacombe, Black Star

The Magnificent Mile extends along Michigan Avenue north of the main downtown area. The elegant shops, hotels, restaurants, and office buildings that line the avenue have made it a popular place to visit for Chicagoans and tourists alike.

WORLD BOOK photo

The Chicago Picasso stands in Richard J. Daley Plaza. The Spanish artist Pablo Picasso designed the five-story steel sculpture.

Chicago ranks as the chief center of industry and transportation in the United States. It also serves as the financial capital of the Midwest. The value of all goods and services produced yearly in the Chicago metropolitan area totals about $70 billion. Only about 20 countries in the world annually produce goods and services worth more.

Nearly 3 million persons work in the Chicago metropolitan area. The number of jobs has grown rapidly since the mid-1900's. But the growth has been in Chicago's suburbs, not in the city itself. In 1950, for example, about 80 per cent of all the jobs in the metropolitan area were in the city. Today, only about 50 per cent are in Chicago. The large expanses of open land, the relatively low property taxes, and the ever-increasing population have attracted businesses and industries to the suburbs. Many of these firms moved to the suburbs from Chicago. Many other companies came from outside Illinois to build headquarters, branch offices, or research plants.

Chicago's superb location has always helped attract businesses. Chicago is the only place in North America where the Great Lakes connect with the huge Mississippi River system. The city also lies in the heart of a rich farming and mining region. In addition, it lies in the heart of a great population center. About a third of the people of the United States live within 500 miles (800 kilometers) of Chicago.

Industry. The Chicago metropolitan area has about 14,000 industrial plants. They employ almost 1 million persons, nearly a third of all the workers in the area. The Chicago metropolitan area leads the nation in three manufacturing industries. These industries are the manufacture of (1) metals, chiefly iron and steel; (2) electrical equipment and supplies; and (3) machinery. Altogether, these three industries employ nearly 400,000 workers.

The Chicago area also has the nation's largest construction industry, with almost 140,000 employees. In addition, the area is an important center of printing and publishing and of food production. About 89,000 persons work in printing and publishing, and about 69,000 in food production.

The Chicago area is one of the nation's chief industrial research centers. Its industries operate about 1,200 research laboratories. Chicago has been a leader in atomic research ever since the Italian physicist Enrico Fermi produced the world's first nuclear chain reaction at the University of Chicago in 1942. The U.S. Atomic Energy Commission (AEC) operates the Argonne National Laboratory in suburban Lemont. The laboratory has pioneered in the development of nuclear reactors for electric power production. Nearly a third of the Chicago area's electric power comes from nuclear power plants. No other area in the United States uses as much nuclear power as the Chicago area. The Fermi National Accelerator Laboratory, which houses one of the largest particle accelerators in the world, is located near suburban Batavia (see FERMI NATIONAL ACCELERATOR LABORATORY).

LTV Steel Company

Steel Plants, such as this one on the city's Far Southeast Side, help make Chicago the nation's chief industrial center. The Chicago area produces more iron and steel than does any other area of the country. It is also the nation's leading producer of electrical equipment and machinery.

Chicago was once the world's leading meat-packing center. The poet Carl Sandburg called the city the "Hog Butcher for the World." The city's famous Union Stock Yards processed about 18 million head of livestock yearly. But the yards began to decline in the 1950's with the growth of regional livestock centers, and the Union Stock Yards closed in 1971.

Trade. Chicago is one of the busiest ports in the United States. The city became a seaport in 1959 upon the opening of the St. Lawrence Seaway. This inland waterway links the Great Lakes and the Atlantic Ocean. Cargo ships sail to and from Chicago through the seaway and four of the Great Lakes—Ontario, Erie, Huron, and Michigan. The city's port facilities employ about 29,000 persons and handle about 43 million short tons (39 million metric tons) of manufactured goods, raw materials, and produce every year.

The city has 18 terminals that receive cargo ships and barges. Two terminals are at Navy Pier in the downtown Chicago Harbor. The rest are along the Calumet River, Lake Calumet, and Calumet Harbor, at the mouth of the Calumet River. Six of the Calumet terminals have gigantic grain elevators that bulge with wheat and other grains every spring. Ice closes the St. Lawrence Seaway in winter. But early in April, after the ice has thawed, ships from dozens of countries arrive at the Calumet terminals to pick up Midwest grain and carry it to ports throughout the world.

Chicago is a busy port for river barges as well as for ocean-going ships. The barges use the Chicago Sanitary and Ship Canal, which connects with the Mississippi River system. This system links Chicago with the Gulf of Mexico and with ports as far east as Pittsburgh, Pa., and as far west as Omaha, Nebr.

Chicago Mercantile Exchange

The Chicago Mercantile Exchange is the world's busiest market for perishable commodities. Traders shout their bids and offering prices for such products as eggs, hogs, and cattle.

Edward Simonek

Dozens of Truck Trailers, carried piggyback by railroad flatcars, await pickup at a terminal south of downtown Chicago. The city is the leading transportation center of the United States.

The Chicago area also ranks as one of the nation's leading wholesale and retail trading centers. More than 11,000 wholesale companies and about 28,500 retail firms operate in Chicago. Sears, Roebuck and Company, the world's largest retail firm, has its headquarters in Chicago.

Finance. Chicago is the financial capital of the Midwest. The city's Midwest Stock Exchange ranks as the third largest securities market in the United States behind the New York and American stock exchanges. The Seventh Federal Reserve District Bank has its headquarters in Chicago. Four Chicago banks are among the nation's 50 biggest commercial banking firms. At the Chicago Board of Trade, traders make contracts for about 90 per cent of the nation's future grain deliveries. The Chicago Mercantile Exchange is the world's busiest market for future deliveries of such farm products as eggs, cattle, and hogs.

Transportation. Chicago is the nation's biggest transportation center. In no other area of the country do the railroad yards or trucking firms handle as much freight. Chicago's railroad yards handle about 23 million short tons (21 million metric tons) of goods yearly. The 17 major railroads that serve the city operate over about half the nation's railway system. About 2,000 trucking companies operate out of Chicago. They transport about 27 million short tons (24 million metric tons) of freight a year.

Three airports serve the city. Chicago-O'Hare International Airport, in the northwest corner of the city, is the world's busiest airport. Every year, about 550,000 commercial flights land and take off at O'Hare, and about 38 million passengers pass through the airport. Cargo planes using O'Hare carry about 659,000 short tons (597,900 metric tons) of freight yearly.

Chicago Midway Airport, on the South Side, is heavily used by small private planes owned by business firms. Midway once ranked as the world's busiest airport. But its runways are too short for large jet airplanes, and so few commercial flights now land there. Chicago's third airport, Meigs Field, has been built on an artificially created peninsula that juts into Lake Michigan just south of Grant Park. Meigs Field is used mostly by private planes and by small commuter aircraft that fly to nearby cities.

About two-thirds of all Chicago area jobholders drive to work. Three major expressways, heavily used by commuters from the suburbs, stretch through the city from an interchange near the downtown area. The John F. Kennedy Expressway extends northwest, the Dwight D. Eisenhower Expressway runs west, and the Dan Ryan Expressway stretches south. In addition, Edens Expressway extends from the Kennedy Expressway through the north suburbs, and the Adlai E. Stevenson Expressway runs southwest from the Dan Ryan.

The publicly owned Chicago Transit Authority (CTA) operates a system of bus lines and elevated and subway trains in the city. About 450,000 persons use this system daily to get to work. In 1974, Chicago area residents voted to establish a Regional Transit Authority (RTA) to operate a public transportation system for the area. The CTA became part of the new RTA, as did the six commuter railroads that serve the city. These railroad lines between the city and the suburbs carry over 100,000 passengers each workday. Both the CTA and the commuter railroads faced financial difficulties that the RTA was designed to eliminate. However, the RTA has also faced financial difficulties.

Communications. Chicago has two general daily newspapers. They are the *Chicago Sun-Times* and the *Chicago Tribune*. Both of these newspapers are published in the morning and afternoon. The two newspapers have a combined daily circulation of about 1½ million copies. Another daily newspaper, the *Chicago Daily Defender*, is directed chiefly at the city's black readers. This paper has a circulation of more than 20,000 copies. Chicago also has about 30 foreign-language newspapers and about 100 neighborhood and suburban papers.

Several national magazines are published in Chicago. Other national magazines and nationally circulated newspapers have branch offices in the city. Chicago also ranks as a leading center of the advertising and book-publishing industries.

The city has seven commercial television stations and a nonprofit station associated with the national Corporation for Public Broadcasting. Chicago also has more than 40 radio stations, including several that feature foreign-language broadcasts.

Chicago's government is headed by a mayor and a City Council, which consists of an alderman from each of the city's 50 wards. The voters elect the mayor and the aldermen, as well as a city treasurer and a city clerk, to four-year terms. The mayor appoints the other top officials, including a deputy mayor, city department heads, police commissioner, and fire commissioner.

Unlike most other large U.S. cities, Chicago has a weak-mayor, strong-council form of government. In theory, the mayor of Chicago thus has less power than do the mayors of most other large cities. Chicago's mayor must obtain the City Council's approval on many important decisions and appointments. On many other matters, including the levying of taxes, the mayor must have the approval of the state legislature. In addition, some services provided by city governments in other cities are provided by the state and county governments in Chicago. The state, for example, administers most of Chicago's welfare services. Several other important government functions are administered by separate government units, such as the Chicago Park District and the Metropolitan Sanitary District.

In spite of the weak-mayor system, Chicago had the most powerful mayor of any major U.S. city during the third quarter of the 1900's. Richard J. Daley was named head of the Central Committee of the Cook County Democratic Organization in 1953 and was elected mayor of Chicago in 1955. He held both jobs until his death in 1976.

Chicago is strongly Democratic, and much of Daley's power came from his role as Democratic county chief. Under his leadership, the county Democratic organization became probably the strongest urban political organization in the nation. As its leader, Daley had the chief voice in deciding who ran on the Democratic ticket. As a result, he determined who held many important state, county, and city offices. In addition, most of Chicago's aldermen were Democrats who loyally followed Daley's leadership. All these factors gave Daley extraordinary power—and earned him the title "last of the big-city bosses."

Chicago has an annual budget of more than $1 billion. Real estate taxes provide about a fourth of the city's income. Other taxes include a motor vehicle tax, parking tax, and sales tax. Additional sources of income include grants by the state and federal governments.

Symbols of Chicago. The city's flag was adopted in 1939. The stars signify the building of Fort Dearborn, the Great Chicago Fire, and the city's two world's fairs. The blue stripes stand for the Chicago River and its two branches. *Urbs in Horto,* the Latin motto on Chicago's seal, means *City in a Garden.*

Chicago in Flames, View from Randolph Street Bridge No. 1 (1871-72), a color lithograph by an unknown artist; Chicago Historical Society

The Great Chicago Fire of 1871 forced thousands of panic-stricken people to flee before the racing flames. The fire killed at least 300 persons and destroyed about $200 million in property.

American Indians lived in the Chicago area more than 5,000 years ago. During the 1600's, when the first white people arrived, Potawatomi Indians lived near the little river they called the *Checagou*. The name *Chicago* comes from this Indian word. The Potawatomi hunted buffalo, deer, and other wildlife. They raised such crops as corn, squash, and pumpkins. They also traded with nearby tribes by traveling the many trails that fanned out from the mouth of the Chicago River.

The river itself was part of another well-traveled route through the area. The Potawatomi paddled canoes down the river to a muddy *portage* (overland route) that led to the Des Plaines River. They then carried their canoes over the portage and followed the Des Plaines to the Illinois River. The Illinois connected with the mighty Mississippi River. The Potawatomi were peaceful and prosperous. When the first whites arrived, the friendly Potawatomi greeted them warmly.

Exploration and Early Settlement. The first white people to reach the Chicago area were probably the French-Canadian explorer Louis Jolliet and a French Jesuit priest named Jacques Marquette. They arrived at the portage in 1673 on their way north to Canada. During the next 25 years, French fur traders and missionaries frequently used the portage. But then the Fox Indians to the south closed the route to the portage to white men. As a result, little is known about life in the Chicago area from about 1700 to the 1770's.

In the 1770's, a prosperous Negro fur trader from New Orleans moved up the Mississippi to the Chicago area. He was Jean Baptiste Point du Sable, who established a trading post on the north bank of the Chicago River mouth. His business prospered and became the center of a permanent Chicago settlement.

Indian Troubles. In the late 1700's, a series of wars broke out in the northern United States between Indians and U.S. troops. As part of the agreement that ended the fighting, the Indians gave a tract of land at the mouth of the Chicago River to the United States. In 1803, the government built a small military post called Fort Dearborn on the river's south bank.

By 1812, a small settlement of farmers and traders had grown up near Fort Dearborn. But soon after the War of 1812 began between Britain and the United States, the American government ordered the fort abandoned. Officials thought the little outpost would be too difficult to defend.

On Aug. 15, 1812, about 100 soldiers and settlers left the fort and headed southeast for Fort Wayne in Indiana. They had traveled only a short distance when more than 500 Indians attacked. The Indians killed about half the group, captured the others, and burned Fort Dearborn. The Chicago area remained unsettled after the massacre until 1816, when American soldiers rebuilt the fort.

Birth of the City. In 1816, several survivors of the massacre who were released by the Indians returned to Chicago. Other settlers also moved to the area, and a new community grew up around rebuilt Fort Dearborn. When Illinois became a state in 1818, the Chicago settlement was included within its boundaries. By 1833, Chicago had grown to more than 150 persons—large enough to be incorporated as a village.

In 1834 and 1835, U.S. government agents forced the Potawatomi and neighboring tribes to sell their land. In payment, the Indians received a small sum of money and territory west of the Mississippi. More than 3,000 Indians left their homeland for reservations in Kansas. After their departure, the village of Chicago boomed. It grew to about 4,000 persons by 1837. On March 4, 1837, Chicago was incorporated as a city.

Growth as a City. In 1848, a shipping canal was completed through the old Indian portage. Chicago was thus linked with the Mississippi River system. Transportation soon became the city's major industry. But the canal played only a secondary role.

Chicago's most spectacular achievement between 1848 and 1856 was the growth of its railroads. The city's first railroad, the Galena and Chicago Union, began operation in 1848. By 1856, Chicago had become the hub of 10 main railroad lines with about 3,000 miles (4,800 kilometers) of track. Nearly 100 trains arrived or departed daily. The city had become the world's busiest rail center. It had also become the biggest city in Illinois, with a population of over 100,000.

Chicago boomed during the American Civil War (1861-1865). Cattle from the West streamed into Chicago's stockyards, and the huge Union Stock Yards were completed in 1865. The grain trade thrived, making the Chicago Board of Trade the nation's chief grain market. The city's manufacturing industries also grew rapidly.

After the war, immigrants from Germany, Poland, and other European countries poured into Chicago. Crowded neighborhoods of factory workers living in small wooden cottages sprouted around the city. And Chicago continued to prosper. By 1870, it was the world's largest grain, livestock, and lumber market. Its population had grown to nearly 300,000.

As the world's lumber capital, Chicago was fittingly built almost entirely of wood. Houses, churches, stores, grain elevators, factories, and even streets were nearly all made of wood.

The Great Chicago Fire. The summer of 1871 was unusually dry in Chicago. Only about a fourth the normal amount of rain fell between July and October. With all its wooden buildings, Chicago was like kindling. Then on the evening of Oct. 8, 1871, a fire started on the Southwest Side of the city.

Historians believe the fire started in a barn owned by Mrs. Patrick O'Leary. According to legend, a cow kicked over a lighted lantern in the barn. Fanned by strong winds, the flames raced north and east through the city. They leaped across the river and chased panic-stricken families fleeing north toward Lincoln Park. Hundreds of other families fled into the chill waters of the lake. The fire raged for over 24 hours. It wiped out the downtown area and most North Side homes. It killed at least 300 persons, left 90,000 homeless, and destroyed about $200 million worth of property.

A City Reborn. Chicago rose from the ruins of the fire and became one of the world's great cities. The opportunity to rebuild Chicago attracted many of the nation's finest architects, such as William Le Baron Jenney, Louis Sullivan, Daniel H. Burnham, John W. Root, and the German-born Dankmar Adler. The world's first metal-frame skyscraper, the 10-story Home Insurance Building, was erected in Chicago. The structure, designed by Jenney, was completed in 1885. Chicago became the nation's architectural capital.

Chicago's industry skyrocketed along with its buildings. More and more workers, many of them immigrants, crowded into the city. Many lived in hurriedly constructed, barrackslike housing. Much of it quickly turned into slums. Working conditions were also miserable. The factory workers protested, and a wave of strikes erupted. In 1886, eight policemen and two other persons were killed when police tried to break up a strikers' meeting at Haymarket Square, a produce center west of downtown (see HAYMARKET RIOT).

In 1889, Hull House, one of the first settlement houses in the United States, opened in Chicago. Jane Addams and Ellen Starr founded it to help immigrant workers adjust to life in the city. See HULL HOUSE.

By 1890, Chicago had become the second largest city in the United States. Only New York City had more people. More than a million persons lived in Chicago. Nearly 80 per cent of them were European immigrants or the children of immigrants.

In 1893, the World's Columbian Exposition opened in Jackson Park. This elaborate fair observed the 400th anniversary of Christopher Columbus' arrival in the New World. But Chicago also staged the fair to draw attention to the city's accomplishments. The fair's chief architect was Daniel H. Burnham, who later laid out several of Chicago's major streets. But Burnham's dream of a lakefront dotted with specially built recreational islands has been only partly realized.

Chicagoans bragged so much about the Columbian Exposition that Charles A. Dana, a New York City

Chicago Historical Society

The World's Columbian Exposition was held in Chicago in 1893 to honor Columbus' arrival in America. Visitors marveled at the fair's pools, fountains, and gleaming white buildings.

newspaper editor, nicknamed Chicago the *Windy City*. The howling gusts that blow across the city from Lake Michigan have helped make the nickname last. Chicago also received the nickname *Second City* because it ranked second to New York City in population and other areas.

Tragedy and Racial Conflict. The years of civic pride that began with the Columbian Exposition were marred by tragedy. In 1903, a fire in the Iroquois Theater took 575 lives. In 1915, the tour boat *Eastland* sank in the Chicago River, and 812 persons drowned.

During World War I (1914-1918), Chicago's industries expanded to meet wartime needs. Thousands of blacks from the South moved to Chicago to work in its war industries. Prevented from living in most sections of the city, they crowded into an old run-down area on the South Side. On July 27, 1919, a black youth swimming off the 27th Street beach drifted south—beyond the limits of the black ghetto. When he tried to swim ashore, whites stoned him. The boy swam back out and drowned. The incident started the biggest race riot in Chicago history. It raged for four days and left 23 blacks and 15 whites dead. More than 500 other persons were injured, and about 1,000 homes were burned.

The Roaring Twenties were years of crime and creativity in Chicago. During the 1920's, the city's industries prospered, and people spent money wildly.

The 18th Amendment to the U.S. Constitution, which went into effect in 1920, prohibited the manufacture and sale of alcoholic beverages. But many people drank illegally in clubs called *speakeasies*. Gangsters in Chicago took over the illegal distribution of liquor, a practice called *bootlegging*. Various gangs fought for control of bootlegging, gambling, and other illegal activities. Gangland murders became common. The violence reached its peak in the St. Valentine's Day Massacre of 1929. Four gangsters, disguised as policemen, shot down seven members of a rival gang. The gangster era gave Chicago a reputation for crime and violence that it has never completely lived down.

But the Roaring Twenties were also creative years in Chicago. Many talented writers worked in the city. They included the poets Carl Sandburg and Edgar Lee Masters, the novelists Theodore Dreiser and Upton Sinclair, the short-story writer Sherwood Anderson, and the founder of *Poetry* magazine, Harriet Monroe. Jazz musicians, led by the great trumpeter Louis Armstrong, moved up the Mississippi River from New Orleans. The jazz clarinetist Benny Goodman, who played in Hull House as a child, formed his first band in Chicago. The city also had a thriving movie industry.

Ending a Century of Progress. The Great Depression of the 1930's brought business failure and unemployment to Chicago. In spite of these problems, the city opened the Century of Progress Exposition in 1933. Chicago staged the gigantic fair to celebrate the 100th anniversary of its incorporation as a village. The exposition, held on the lakefront, featured outstanding exhibits of science and industry. It brought enormous business to the city during the depths of the depression.

The Mid-1900's. During World War II (1939-1945), Chicago became the site of one of the most important events in world history. On Dec. 2, 1942, the first nuclear chain reaction was set off at the University of Chicago. It led to the development of the atomic bomb and of nuclear energy for peaceful uses.

Many giant public construction projects were started in Chicago after the war, and the civic building boom continued into the 1960's. New projects included four expressways, two huge water filtration plants, the McCormick Place convention and exposition center, O'Hare Airport, and the Chicago Civic Center. Huge slum areas were cleared and replaced with middle-income apartment complexes.

A building boom also took place in the downtown area and along the North Side lakefront. The John Hancock Center, the First National Bank Building, and many apartment buildings were erected. Work also began on Sears Tower and the Standard Oil Building.

During the 1950's and 1960's, Chicago thus remained economically strong. But jobs for unskilled workers had begun to disappear. At the same time, increasing numbers of poor people, both blacks and whites, moved to Chicago from the South. Mounting social problems began to plague Chicago, and the city failed to deal with them successfully. Tens of thousands of poor newcomers needed welfare aid to survive. Urban renewal programs demolished slums, but much of the land remained vacant. Public housing for the poor was badly planned. Huge, crowded high-rise buildings packed closely together bred crime. The city's neighborhoods became more and more racially segregated. Black neighborhoods expanded, and whites moved to the suburbs.

In April, 1968, riots broke out on the West Side following the assassination of the black civil rights leader Martin Luther King, Jr. Eleven persons were killed, and damage was estimated at $10 million. In August, 1968, several bloody clashes occurred between young demonstrators and police during the Democratic National Convention. Many of the demonstrators were protesting the nation's role in the Vietnam War.

Recent Developments. Today, Chicago remains a prosperous industrial giant. But problems continue to trouble the city. About a fifth of Chicago's people receive welfare aid. The crime rate is high, especially in poor neighborhoods. There is a shortage of decent housing for low-income families, and the mass transportation system has become inadequate. In addition, the public school system has failed to provide satisfactory education for many of the city's children.

An era in Chicago politics ended in 1976, when Mayor Richard J. Daley died. Daley, a Democrat, had been mayor since 1955. He won six four-year terms to the office, more than any other Chicago mayor. For details on Daley's role as mayor, see the *Government* section of this article. In 1979, Jane M. Byrne, a former city official and protégé of Daley, became Chicago's first woman mayor. Byrne received 82 per cent of the votes cast—the highest percentage ever in a Chicago mayoral election. In the 1983 Democratic mayoral primary election, Byrne was defeated by Harold Washington, a black and a member of the United States House of Representatives. Washington won the 1983 general election and became Chicago's first black mayor. LOIS WILLE

Related Articles in World Book include:

Biographies

Alinsky, Saul David
Burnham, Daniel H.
Byrne, Jane M.
Capone, Al
Daley, Richard J.
Du Sable, Jean Baptiste P.
Field (family)
Jolliet, Louis
Marquette, Jacques
Palmer, Potter
Sandburg, Carl
Thompson, William H.
Washington, Harold

Buildings and Institutions

Art Institute of Chicago
Field Museum of Natural History
Hull House
Merchandise Mart
Museum of Science and Industry

History

Fort Dearborn
Haymarket Riot
Jazz (Other Stars of the 1920's)

Other Related Articles

Architecture (Early Modern Architecture in America)
Chicago Sanitary and Ship Canal
Illinois (pictures)
Saint-Gaudens, Augustus (picture)
Skyscraper (with picture)
Subway (picture)
Taft, Lorado (picture)
Water (illustration: How Chicago Treats Its Water)

Outline

I. The City
- A. Downtown Chicago
- B. The North Side
- C. The West Side
- D. The South Side
- E. Metropolitan Area

II. People
- A. Ethnic Groups
- B. Housing
- C. Education
- D. Sports and Recreation
- E. Social Problems

III. Cultural Life and Places to Visit
- A. The Arts
- B. Architecture
- C. Museums
- D. Libraries
- E. Places to Visit

IV. Economy
- A. Industry
- B. Trade
- C. Finance
- D. Transportation
- E. Communications

V. Government

VI. History

Questions

What are some of Chicago's major problems?

Why is Chicago called the *Windy City*?

How does Chicago rank in population among U.S. cities?

What is unusual about the flow of the Chicago River?

What was the great development of the Chicago school of architecture?

Where did the Great Chicago Fire start?

What important event in world history took place at the University of Chicago in 1942?

About how many Chicagoans receive welfare aid?

In what three manufacturing industries does Chicago lead the nation?

What is the Loop? The Gold Coast? The Magnificent Mile? Old Town?

Additional Resources

Bach, Ira J. *Chicago's Famous Buildings: A Photographic Guide to the City's Architectural Landmarks and Other Notable Buildings.* 3rd ed. Univ. of Chicago Press, 1980.

Cutler, Irving. *Chicago: Metropolis of the Mid-Continent.* 3rd ed. Kendall-Hunt, 1982. The history and future of the city.

Fodor's Chicago. McKay. Published annually.

CHICAGO, ART INSTITUTE OF. See Art Institute of Chicago.

CHICAGO, UNIVERSITY OF, is a leading educational and research institution on Chicago's South Side. Its campus lies on both sides of the Midway Plaisance. This wide street served as one of the main avenues of the World's Columbian Exposition of 1893. Unlike most American universities, Chicago began as a full university. It provided facilities for research and graduate study as well as undergraduate education. The university became famous for its experiments to improve higher education in the United States. It is also known as the birthplace of nuclear energy.

Educational Program. The University of Chicago is coeducational. The university's undergraduate school is called the College. Its students divide their study about equally between specialized courses and general education in broad fields of knowledge. Graduate divisions provide advanced instruction in the biological sciences, humanities, physical sciences, and social sciences. Graduate schools of business, divinity, education, law, library, medicine, and social service administration offer professional training. The university also maintains an extension division for adult education. Students at the University of Chicago may qualify for B.A., B.S., M.A., M.S., and Ph.D. degrees and for professional degrees.

Research Program. The university ranks as a leading research center in the physical, biological, and social sciences. It played an important part in developing the atomic bomb during World War II. Experiments there resulted in the first artificially produced nuclear chain reaction on Dec. 2, 1942. Enrico Fermi, then professor of physics at the university, and a team of scientists conducted this research. After the war, the university established the Enrico Fermi Institute for research in high energy physics. The university also operates the Argonne National Laboratory near Lemont, Ill., for the U.S. Department of Energy, and the Yerkes Observatory in Williams Bay, Wis.

The university's medical school, biological science laboratories, hospitals, and clinics have made it an important center for research in the fields of biochemistry, cardiology, endocrinology, genetics, pathology, radiology, and virology. Scientists in the university's institutes and laboratories conduct research on cancer and related problems.

In 1892, Chicago became the first university to establish a department of sociology. Many outstanding American sociologists have taught at the university. Two of them—Albion W. Small and George E. Vincent—wrote the first textbook on sociology in 1894. Sophonisba Breckinridge, a pioneer teacher of social work, taught at the university for 38 years and helped establish the School of Social Service Administration. Leading American economists who have taught at the university include Thorstein Veblen and Milton Friedman. Veblen's book *The Theory of the Leisure Class* (1899) has become required reading for almost every student of economics. Friedman's theories in two of his books, *Capitalism and Freedom* (1962) and *A Monetary History of the United States, 1867-1960* (1963),

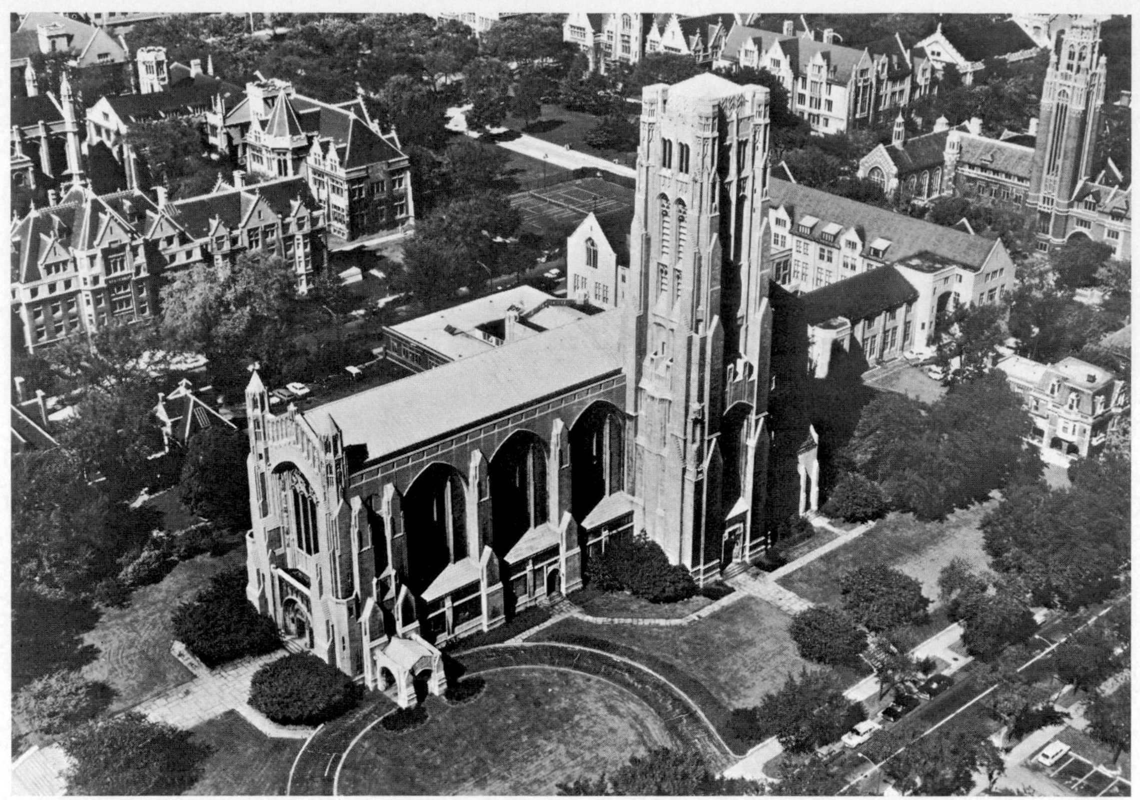

University of Chicago

The Rockefeller Memorial Chapel is a center of religious life at the University of Chicago. John D. Rockefeller donated about $2 million for the chapel, which was completed in 1928.

have sparked widespread debate among economists.

Campus laboratory schools conduct precollegiate education at nursery, elementary, and high school levels. The American philosopher John Dewey established the laboratory schools in 1896. The Oriental Institute, founded by James H. Breasted in 1919, conducts research in the Middle East.

History. The University of Chicago was incorporated in 1890 and opened for classes on Oct. 1, 1892. Endowments to the university included $35 million contributed by John D. Rockefeller during his lifetime.

William Rainey Harper, the university's first president, planned it as a model university. His first faculty included nine former presidents of colleges and seminaries. Harper introduced the quarter system, which divides the calendar year into four academic sessions. He insisted that women receive equal educational and teaching opportunities at the university. Harper established an extension division as one of the main divisions of the university and developed the first practical correspondence course in the United States. In 1892, he started the University of Chicago Press, which has become one of the nation's largest academic publishers. It publishes about 200 new books each year. For the enrollment of the University of Chicago, see UNIVERSITIES AND COLLEGES (table).

D. J. R. BRUCKNER

Related Articles in WORLD BOOK include:

Argonne National Laboratory	Breckinridge, Sophonisba
Breasted, James Henry	Friedman, Milton
Hutchins, Robert Maynard	Harper, William Rainey
Rockefeller	Veblen, Thorstein
	Yerkes Observatory

CHICAGO BOARD OF TRADE. See CHICAGO (Places to Visit).

CHICAGO DRAINAGE CANAL. See CHICAGO SANITARY AND SHIP CANAL.

CHICAGO NATURAL HISTORY MUSEUM. See FIELD MUSEUM OF NATURAL HISTORY.

CHICAGO RIVER. See CHICAGO (The City).

CHICAGO SANITARY AND SHIP CANAL connects Lake Michigan with the Des Plaines River by way of the Chicago River. The canal, sometimes called the Chicago Drainage Canal, carries Chicago's treated sewage into the Des Plaines River, near Lockport, Ill. The Des Plaines River flows southwest and helps form the Illinois River. The Mississippi River receives the Illinois River and carries its waters on to the Gulf of Mexico. Before completion of the canal in 1900, Chicago sewage was dumped into Lake Michigan. This caused pollution of water used in the city water system.

The natural course of the Chicago River is eastward, through downtown Chicago into Lake Michigan. Engineers made the river flow westward through the Drainage Canal. The river is now an outlet instead of an inlet of Lake Michigan. It was the first river in the world to flow away from its mouth.

Chicago's sewage is treated in plants of The Metropolitan Sanitary District of Greater Chicago, then turned into the channel. The Chicago Sanitary and Ship Canal is 30 miles (48 kilometers) long, 202 feet (62 meters) wide, and 24 feet (7.3 meters) deep. The rate of flow is controlled by sluice gates at Chicago Harbor and at the O'Brien Lock in the Calumet River, and by pumps at Wilmette Harbor.

In 1924, the Great Lakes border states protested that the canal had lowered the level of the lakes and endangered shipping. Six years later, the Supreme Court of the United States ordered a reduction in the amount of water removed from the lake. By 1939, this amount was set at 1,500 cubic feet (42 cubic meters) of water a second, in addition to domestic pumpage. In 1967, the Supreme Court ruled that no more than 3,200 cubic feet (91 cubic meters) of water a second could be removed from the lake.

The canal was built between 1892 and 1900. It forms a link in the Illinois Waterway, a part of the Lakes-to-Gulf Waterway. DON R. BROWN

See also CANAL.

CHICAGO STATE UNIVERSITY. See UNIVERSITIES AND COLLEGES (table).

CHICANOS. See MEXICAN AMERICANS.

CHICHAGOF ISLAND, *CHIHCH uh GAWF,* Alaska, is a mountainous and heavily forested island. Chichagof Island lies about 75 miles (121 kilometers) southwest of Juneau.

The island is about 75 miles (121 kilometers) long and 50 miles (80 kilometers) wide. Salmon and halibut fishing, fish canning, lumbering, and gold mining are the main industries on the island. Deposits of nickel and tungsten also occur. The largest settlements on Chichagof Island are Hoonah, Pelican, and Tenakee Springs. The island was named for Admiral Vasili Chichagof, a Russian explorer. NEAL M. BOWERS

CHICHÉN ITZÁ. See MAYA (Government).

CHICHESTER, *CHIHCH ihs tur,* **SIR FRANCIS** (1901-1972), an English adventurer, made long-distance boat and airplane voyages. In August 1966, he sailed alone from England to Australia in his 53-foot (16-meter) yacht, *Gipsy Moth IV.* He returned to England in May 1967, passing through the dangerous seas around Cape Horn.

Chichester's other long-distance journeys included one of the first solo flights from England to Australia, in 1929; and the first east-west flight across the Tasman Sea between New Zealand and Australia, in 1931. He won the first solo sailing race across the Atlantic in 1960.

Chichester was born in Shirwell, England. At the age of 18, he went to New Zealand. He stayed there 10 years, working as a sheep farmer, coal miner, and gold prospector.

CHICKADEE is a small bird of North America, related to the titmouse. It grows about 5 inches (13 centimeters) long. Its tail grows longer in comparison to its body than the tails of most birds. It has a short bill. The chickadee is quick and active, but not timid. It can hang upside down on a small twig to get insects.

Seven kinds of chickadees live in North America, and other species inhabit Europe and Asia. The familiar *black-capped chickadee* is olive-gray and white, with a black head and throat. The *boreal chickadee* of the north woods has a brown cap, and the *chestnut-backed chickadee* of the Pacific Coast has a brown back. The *mountain chickadee* has a black cap, but has a white line over each eye. Most chickadees have light-gray underparts with rust-colored sides. The birds usually call their own name, *chick-a-dee,* and repeat *dee-dee-dee* several times. Sometimes they sing two or three clear whistles over and over.

Charles J. Ott, NAS

The Boreal Chickadee lives in the north woods of Canada and Alaska.

Farmers consider chickadees valuable because they eat moths, caterpillars, beetles, and other insects. The birds also eat weed seeds.

Scientific Classification. Chickadees belong to the titmouse family, Paridae. The black-capped chickadee is *Parus atricapillus.* The boreal chickadee is *P. hudsonicus.* The chestnut-backed chickadee is *P. rufescens.* ARTHUR A. ALLEN

See also BIRD (picture: Birds' Eggs); TITMOUSE.

CHICKAMAUGA, BATTLE OF. See CIVIL WAR (Chickamauga; table: Major Battles).

CHICKAMAUGA AND CHATTANOOGA NATIONAL MILITARY PARK. See NATIONAL PARK SYSTEM (table: National Military Parks).

CHICKASAW INDIANS are a tribe that originally lived in the Southern United States. Their territory included northern Mississippi, northwestern Alabama, and western Tennessee and Kentucky. In the 1830's, the United States government relocated the tribe in what is now Oklahoma.

The Chickasaw lived in several villages of small, one-room log cabins. Each village was headed by a chief. The people supported themselves by farming, fishing, hunting, and trading with neighboring tribes.

The Spanish explorer Hernando de Soto was the first white person to come into contact with the Chickasaw. He and his group spent the winter of 1540-1541 in one of their villages while searching for gold. Before leaving, De Soto demanded that some of the Chickasaw join him to help carry supplies. The Indians became angry and attacked the expedition, killing about 12 men.

The Chickasaw were fierce warriors. They helped Great Britain fight France and Spain for control of what is now the Southeastern United States. They also supported the British during the Revolutionary War (1775-1783). During the Civil War (1861-1865), the tribe fought for the Confederacy.

In 1837, the government moved the Chickasaw west to the Indian Territory to make room for additional white settlement in the South. The forced march of the Indians to their new territories became known as the *Trail of Tears* because thousands of Indians died on the way. In 1907, the Chickasaw territory became part of the new state of Oklahoma.

Today, about 6,500 people of Chickasaw descent make their homes in Oklahoma. A tribal government elected by the Chickasaw helps provide for the general welfare of the tribe. ARRELL MORGAN GIBSON

See also FIVE CIVILIZED TRIBES; INDIAN TERRITORY.

chicken

Barred Plymouth Rocks

New Hampshires

J. Mechling

White Leghorns

Black Minorcas

CHICKEN is a bird raised for meat and eggs. Roosters pecking and scratching in search of food and hens clucking over fluffy yellow chicks are a common barnyard sight in almost every country. The early morning crowing of roosters has served the farmer as an alarm clock for thousands of years.

Chickens are the only birds that have *combs*. A comb is a piece of red flesh on the top of a chicken's head. Although chickens have wings, many have bodies so heavy that they can fly only a few yards or meters at a time. Otherwise, chickens are much like other birds.

The United States ranks third in the production of chickens, after China and Russia. About 95 of every 100 farm birds raised in the United States are chickens. Many farms raise only chickens. Thousands of birds may live in wire cages. Sometimes the cages are piled one on top of another. Often the chickens do not touch the ground from the time they are hatched until they are killed for their meat. Machines supply them with food.

Chickens in the United States may also be raised in

John W. West, the contributor of this article, is Associate Dean of Agriculture at California State Polytechnic College in San Luis Obispo.

White Plymouth Rocks

Silver-Gray Dorkings

Rhode Island Reds

Important Breeds of chickens, shown on these two pages, are raised for both eggs and meat. Altogether, poultry farmers have developed more than 50 standard breeds of chickens.

Buff Orpingtons

White Wyandottes

small flocks on farms that specialize in other crops. Young people raise chickens as part of their activities in 4-H Clubs and in the Future Farmers of America. Some people make chicken-raising a hobby and display their prize birds at shows and fairs. In some countries outside the United States, cockfighting is considered a sport (see COCKFIGHTING).

Industries use by-products made from chicken eggs in making such products as soap, paint, and leather. Drug companies make medicines from eggs and certain parts of chickens. Ground eggshells provide good fertilizer.

Chickens are not very intelligent. Scientists have been able to train some to perform simple tricks, such as picking up every fifth kernel of corn from a line of corn kernels. But when chickens are separated from food by a fence open at one end, most of them are not intelligent enough to walk around the fence to reach the food.

Kinds of Chickens

More than 50 *standard breeds* of chickens have been developed. Chickens of each standard breed have about the same body size and shape. The American Poultry Association sets these standards. Many farmers in the United States raise chickens that have been produced by cross-breeding two or more standard breeds of chickens. These chickens are called *crossbreds*. Breeders mate chickens of different breeds to develop birds that have more meat, lay more eggs, or are better in some other way.

Poultry farmers group the standard breeds into 12 main classes, most of them named after the regions where the breeds originated. Chickens raised for eggs and meat make up the four most important classes. These are American, Mediterranean, English, and Asiatic. Breeds of chickens in the other eight classes have little importance in the United States. They are raised mainly for show purposes because of their unusual sizes, shapes, and colors. These classes are Continental, French, Game, Hamburg, Oriental, Ornamental Bantam, Polish, and Miscellaneous.

Standard-bred chickens are divided into more than 180 *varieties*. Poultry farmers identify the varieties of chickens within a breed by the colors of their feathers and by the types of their combs. Chickens have seven kinds of combs: *single*, *rose*, *pea*, *strawberry*, *V-shaped*, *cushion*, and *buttercup*.

American Class chickens were developed in the United States and Canada. The five leading breeds are *Plymouth Rock*, *New Hampshire*, *Wyandotte*, *Rhode Island Red*, and *Rhode Island White*. The other breeds of American class chickens are *Buckeye*, *Chantecler*, *Delaware*, *Dominique*, *Holland*, *Java*, *Jersey Giant*, and *Lamona*.

American class chickens have yellow skin, nonfeath-

Chicken Terms

Brood is a group of baby chickens.
Chick is a baby chicken.
Cockerel is a male chicken less than a year old.
Flock is a group of chickens.
Hen is an adult female chicken.
Pullet is a female chicken less than a year old.
Rooster, or **cock,** is an adult male chicken.

ered shanks (lower legs), and red ear lobes. All chickens in this class lay brown-shelled eggs except Lamonas, which lay white-shelled eggs. Plymouth Rocks were developed in the 1860's and Wyandottes in the late 1800's. Rhode Island Reds and Rhode Island Whites were developed in the early 1900's and New Hampshires in the early 1930's.

Mediterranean Class chickens include the best egg-laying breed, the *Leghorn*. A White Leghorn hen may lay as many as 300 eggs a year. Two other Mediterranean breeds raised in the United States are *Minorca* and *Ancona*. Minorcas have won many contests for laying the largest eggs of all breeds. Other breeds of the Mediterranean class are *Blue Andalusian*, *Spanish*, and *Buttercup*.

Mediterranean class chickens have nonfeathered shanks and white ear lobes. They lay white-shelled eggs. Leghorns and Anconas have yellow skin and the other breeds have white skin. Leghorns and Anconas originated in Italy, and Minorcas on Minorca Island off the east coast of Spain. The Blue Andalusian and Spanish breeds were developed in Spain, and the Buttercup was developed in Sicily. The Mediterranean class chickens were brought to the United States in the early 1800's.

English Class chickens are raised mainly for their meat. Only the *Australorp* and *Orpington* breeds are widely raised in the United States, because these breeds are also fair egg layers. The other breeds of the English class are *Cornish*, *Dorking*, *Sussex*, and *Redcap*.

English class chickens grow to a large size and have nonfeathered shanks and red ear lobes. All have white skin except the Cornish breed, which has yellow skin. Dorkings and Redcaps lay white-shelled eggs and the other breeds lay brown-shelled eggs. Most chickens have four toes on each foot, but Dorkings have five on each foot.

The English class developed largely from chickens brought to England by the Romans about A.D. 43. The Australorp breed, however, was developed from Orpingtons taken to Australia.

Asiatic Class chickens are large, sturdy birds raised mainly for show purposes. In the 1800's, United States poultrymen mated them with American and English class chickens to improve the vigor of these breeds.

PARTS OF A CHICKEN

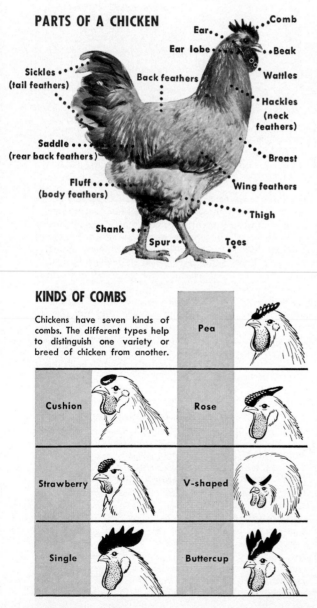

KINDS OF COMBS

Chickens have seven kinds of combs. The different types help to distinguish one variety or breed of chicken from another.

Pea

Cushion

Rose

Strawberry

V-shaped

Single

Buttercup

IMPORTANT BREEDS OF CHICKENS

Breeds	Comb	Standard Weight Cock (lbs.)	Cock (kg)	Hen (lbs.)	Hen (kg)
AMERICAN CLASS					
Buckeye	Pea	9	4.1	6½	2.9
Chantecler	Cushion	8½	3.9	6½	2.9
Delaware	Single	8½	3.9	6½	2.9
Dominique	Rose	7	3.2	5	2.3
Holland	Single	8½	3.9	6½	2.9
Java	Single	9½	4.3	7½	3.4
Jersey Giant	Single	13	5.9	10	4.5
Lamona	Single	8	3.6	6½	2.9
New Hampshire	Single	8½	3.9	6½	2.9
Plymouth Rock	Single	9½	4.3	7½	3.4
Rhode Island Red	Single or Rose	8½	3.9	6½	2.9
Rhode Island White	Rose	8½	3.9	6½	2.9
Wyandotte	Rose	8½	3.9	6½	2.9
ASIATIC CLASS					
Brahma	Pea	11½	5.2	9	4.1
Cochin	Single	11	5.0	8½	3.9
Langshan	Single	9½	4.3	7½	3.4
ENGLISH CLASS					
Australorp	Single	8½	3.9	6½	2.9
Cornish	Pea	10½	4.8	8	3.6
Dorking	Single or Rose	8¼	3.7	6½	2.9
Orpington	Single	10	4.5	8	3.6
Redcap	Rose	7½	3.4	6	2.7
Sussex	Single	9	4.1	7	3.2
MEDITERRANEAN CLASS					
Ancona	Single or Rose	6	2.7	4½	2.0
Blue Andalusian	Single	7	3.2	5½	2.5
Buttercup	Buttercup	6½	2.9	5	2.3
Leghorn	Single or Rose	6	2.7	4½	2.0
Minorca	Single or Rose	8½	3.9	7	3.2
Spanish	Single	8	3.6	6½	2.9

Agricultural Extension Service, Ohio State University

An Electric Brooder warms chicks as they feed in a brooder house. Chicks live in such houses until they are about 2 months old.

Progressive Farmer

Egg-Laying Hens raised in modern laying houses live in wire cages with sloping floors. The eggs roll to the front of each cage.

Asiatic class breeds are *Brahma*, *Cochin*, and *Langshan*. These chickens have feathered shanks and red ear lobes. All lay brown-shelled eggs, and have yellow skin except the Black Langshan, which has white skin. Brahmas, Cochins, and Langshans originated in China, and were brought to the United States in the 1800's.

Other Classes. The eight other classes of standard-breed chickens include Ornamental chickens and Game chickens. These classes are Continental, French, Game, Hamburg, Oriental, Ornamental Bantam, Polish, and Miscellaneous. Ornamental chickens are noted for their unusual colors and feather arrangements. Some have extremely long or strangely shaped tail feathers. Others may have crests of feathers on their heads or clusters of feathers covering their legs and feet. Game chickens are noted for their strength and vigor. Some Ornamental and Game chickens weigh less than $1\frac{1}{2}$ pounds (0.7 kilogram). These small chickens are called *bantams* (see BANTAM). In the United States, Ornamental and Game chickens are raised mainly by *fanciers* (people who keep chickens as a hobby).

Crossbreds. In the 1950's, *Rock Cornish* chickens became popular in the United States. These chickens are developed by mating Cornish chickens with White Plymouth Rocks. Although large when fully grown, a Rock Cornish chicken is usually butchered when only 6 weeks old. The chicken then weighs about $1\frac{1}{4}$ pounds (0.6 kilogram) and supplies about enough meat for one serving.

Chicken Farming

About 10 per cent of the farmers in the United States raise chickens. Some farmers specialize in raising *pullets* (young hens) that they sell to farmers who sell eggs commercially. Other farmers raise only meat-producing chickens.

Hatcheries. Farmers buy almost all of the chickens they raise from breeder hatcheries or commercial hatch-

Leading Broiler-Raising States

Arkansas	673,136,000 broilers
Georgia	626,551,000 broilers
Alabama	515,729,000 broilers
North Carolina	419,740,000 broilers
Mississippi	316,304,000 broilers
Maryland	260,477,000 broilers
Texas	212,600,000 broilers
Delaware	181,862,000 broilers
California	171,622,000 broilers
Virginia	144,041,000 broilers

Source: U.S. Department of Agriculture. Figures are for 1983.

Leading Egg-Producing States

California	8,173,000,000 eggs
Pennsylvania	4,716,000,000 eggs
Georgia	4,671,000,000 eggs
Indiana	4,619,000,000 eggs
Arkansas	3,768,000,000 eggs
North Carolina	3,149,000,000 eggs
Texas	3,089,000,000 eggs
Ohio	2,980,000,000 eggs
Florida	2,959,000,000 eggs
Alabama	2,813,000,000 eggs

Source: U.S. Department of Agriculture. Figures are for 1983.

ORNAMENTAL AND GAME CHICKENS

Chickens of the Ornamental and Game breeds have become noted for their distinctive colors, sizes, and shapes. They are raised mainly by *fanciers*, people who keep chickens as a hobby.

Mille Fleur Booted Bantam Rooster

Black-Tailed Japanese Bantam Rooster

White-Crested Black Polish Rooster

Grant Heilman

Old English Black-Breasted Red Game Rooster

eries. Chicken hatcheries produce about $4\frac{1}{2}$ billion baby chicks a year. *Breeder hatcheries* hatch chicks from eggs laid by their own chickens. *Commercial hatcheries* may get their eggs from several different farms.

Hens hatch their eggs by *brooding* (sitting on them to keep them warm). Hatcheries use *incubators* (egg-hatching machines) usually heated by electricity. The eggs must be kept at a temperature of $99\frac{1}{2}°$ to 100° F. (37.5° to 37.8° C). Chicken eggs take 21 days to hatch. Some hatcheries can hatch as many as a million eggs at one time. See INCUBATOR.

Egg-Laying Chickens. Female chickens do not have to be mated to lay eggs, but only fertilized eggs can hatch into chicks. Pullets begin laying eggs when they are about 5 months old. Hens usually lay more than 240 eggs a year. But, after about 14 months of laying eggs, the egg production of most hens declines. The hens are then sold for meat. There are more than 292 million egg-laying chickens in the United States. They lay about 69 billion eggs each year. About 437 million of these eggs are consumed on farms. The remaining $68\frac{1}{2}$ billion eggs are sent to market. Many eggs are dried and powdered and sold to bakeries and other food processors. See EGG.

Most commercial egg farms buy pullets from farms that specialize in raising them. The pullets they buy from the farms are usually old enough to be able to lay eggs. Before they are sold to the commercial egg producing farms, the pullets have been injected with

Golden Sebright Bantam Rooster

Shostal

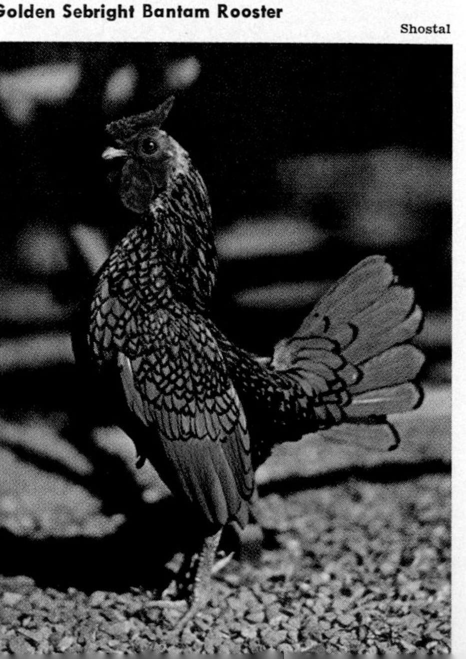

vaccines that develop resistance to certain diseases. The pullets are also treated to prevent parasites. Their combs, beaks, and wattles are trimmed before they are shipped to the egg farm.

Once at the egg farm, the pullets are placed in laying houses that are specially equipped to handle laying chickens. The chickens are fed a special diet to improve egg laying.

Meat Chickens. Farmers in the United States raise more than $4\frac{1}{5}$ billion meat chickens a year. The age of a chicken, not its size, determines how it should be cooked. Most of the meat chickens are sold as *broilers* and *fryers*. These are young male and female chickens that are usually 9 to 12 weeks old. Scientific feeding has made it possible to raise chickens weighing more than 4 pounds (1.8 kilograms) at this age. Some farmers raise five crops of broilers a year.

Chickens kept until they are 4 to 6 months old are sold as *roasters*. Most roasters are males. Farmers usually keep female chickens of this age as egg layers. Old, tough chickens are sold for *stewing*. Most stewing chickens are hens past the egg-laying age. *Capons* are male chickens that have had their reproductive organs removed by an operation. Capons produce more meat than other chickens do.

Chickens raised for meat are sold to consumers dressed and drawn. A *dressed* chicken has been killed, bled, and plucked. A *drawn* chicken has had its head, shanks, and feet cut off, and its internal organs removed. Some drawn chickens are quick-frozen. Others are cut up and the parts are packaged and sold separately.

Backyard Chicken Raising. Many families in farm areas keep small flocks of chickens in their backyards to provide fresh eggs and meat. A flock of 6 to 10 White Leghorns lays enough eggs to supply a family of five for a year. New Hampshires, Plymouth Rocks, and Rhode Island Reds provide both eggs and meat.

Backyard flocks need a light, dry shed, or *chicken coop*, in which to sleep and nest. The coop should provide about 4 square feet (0.4 square meter) of floor space for each chicken. A concrete floor prevents rats from invading the chicken coop.

Food. Farmers generally put the food in feeders where it will always be available. The feeders are small narrow troughs. A supply of clean water should also be available to the chickens at all times. Chicken feed includes corn, soybean-oil meal, fish meal, bone meal, milk, meat scraps, salt and other minerals, and vitamins. Medicines called *antibiotics* are often added to feed to make the chickens grow faster and to protect them against disease.

Chickens require several kinds of minerals, such as calcium and phosphorus. Fish meal and bone meal, ground oyster shells, or ground limestone provide most of these minerals. Fish meal, green grass, and alfalfa meal supply vitamins. Commercial feed companies make special mashes or mixtures that contain most of the vitamins and minerals that chickens need. See ANTIBIOTIC; NUTRITION.

Diseases. One of the worst diseases that attacks chickens is *pullorum*, a type of diarrhea that can kill most of a brood within a few weeks after the chicks are hatched. *Fowl paralysis*, *fowl pox*, and diseases of the breathing organs, such as *gapes*, also affect chickens. *Coccidiosis* is a type of plague that kills many chickens. *Newcastle disease* is a virus disease that is serious among young chickens. Worm parasites often cause stunted growth or death. Insects such as mites and lice attack chickens. Rats, weasels, and hawks also kill chickens.

History

Scientists believe that chickens are descended from a type of wild fowl that lives in the jungles of southeast Asia. People began taming and raising these wild jungle chickens 3,000 to 5,000 years ago. Ancient records show that the Chinese began raising chickens about 1400 B.C. Chicken raising gradually spread throughout the world, as people moved to new areas.

Spanish explorers brought the first chickens to North and South America in the 1500's. English colonists also brought chickens with them when they sailed to the United States. Settlers at Jamestown raised small flocks as early as 1607. As the pioneers moved west, chicken raising spread across the country.

Farms that raise only chickens appeared in the United States in the early 1900's. The number of these farms increased rapidly after the discovery of the value of vitamins in chicken feed about 1925. With the new feeds, farmers could raise chickens indoors in winter and so could raise chickens and maintain egg production throughout the year.

Scientific care and feeding have greatly increased the number of eggs chickens lay. In 1940, the average hen in the United States laid about 100 eggs a year. By 1983, yearly egg production had risen to about 247 eggs per hen. The average American consumes about 265 eggs and about 53 pounds (24 kilograms) of chicken meat annually.

Scientific Classification. Chickens belong to the partridge, quail, and pheasant family, Phasianidae. All varieties of chickens descend from the jungle fowl, which is genus *Gallus*, species *G. gallus*. JOHN W. WEST

Related Articles in WORLD BOOK include:

Cockfighting
Egg
Embryo (picture)
Feather
Gizzard
Incubator
Jungle Fowl
Nutrition (picture)
Poultry

Outline

I. Kinds of Chickens
A. American Class
B. Mediterranean Class
C. English Class
D. Asiatic Class
E. Other Classes
F. Crossbreds

II. Chicken Farming
A. Hatcheries
B. Egg-Laying Chickens
C. Meat Chickens
D. Backyard Chicken Raising
E. Food
F. Diseases

III. History

Questions

How do chickens differ from other birds?
Who brought the first chicken to America? When?
What breed of chickens lays the most eggs? What breed lays the largest eggs?
Where do farmers obtain most of the chickens they raise?
From what type of bird did the chicken originate?
What are chickens used for besides meat and eggs?
At what age are most meat chickens sold?
What determines how a chicken should be cooked?
What are dressed and drawn chickens?

CHICKEN HAWK. See HAWK.

CHICKEN POX, also called *varicella,* is a common, generally mild, contagious disease of children. The attack may be so mild that it is not recognized. However, newborn infants may die from the disease. Chicken pox also may kill children receiving radiation or drug treatment for leukemia or other forms of cancer. Such treatment weakens the body's ability to fight infection.

The first symptom of the disease is a kind of skin rash. Fever, headache, and a general feeling of discomfort often accompany the rash. Some patients also develop a sore throat. Red blotches appear first on the skin of the back or chest. They change into pimples after a few hours, and then into blisters that enlarge and may become filled with a milky liquid. The blisters dry up in a few days, and are covered with *scabs* (dried tissue). The skin disorders appear in groups. New blotches form while old ones change to blisters and dry up.

The *incubation period* (time between exposure to the disease and the appearance of symptoms) ranges from 14 to 21 days. Chicken pox is caused by the *varicella zoster virus,* which is one of the herpes viruses. This same virus causes shingles (see SHINGLES). A child who has had chicken pox usually does not get it again. Adults may get the disease if they did not have it as a child. In some patients, secondary infections follow the chicken pox. An uncommon but serious complication is *Reye's syndrome* (see REYE'S SYNDROME).

Treatment of chicken pox consists of keeping the patient in good general condition. The patient should be prevented from scratching the skin, so that no danger of infection or scars results. In 1984, a vaccine that prevents chicken pox became available. HUGH C. DILLON, JR.

See also DISEASE (table: Some Communicable Diseases; graph: Main Contagious Diseases).

CHICLE, *CHIHK uhl,* is a gumlike substance obtained from the latex of certain tropical trees. It is an important ingredient in much chewing gum. United States industries import about 5 million pounds (2.3 million kilograms) of chicle yearly.

Most chicle comes from the latex of *sapodilla,* or *sapota,* trees which grow in Belize, Guatemala, and Mexico. The finest chicle comes from Guatemala.

Workers collect the latex during the rainy season. They *tap* the trees by making V-shaped cuts in the bark. The latex flows from the cuts and collects in a container at the tree's base. Some trees die as a result of the tapping. Others die unless they are untapped for at least five years.

Wm. Wrigley Jr. Company

A Worker Taps a Tree to obtain latex for making chicle.

The milklike latex is boiled until it becomes thick and sticky. It is then *kneaded* (squeezed) to press out the water. Chicle is marketed in 20- to 30-pound (9- to 14-kilogram) lumps. It can be shaped or molded more easily than rubber because it is extremely plastic. CHARLES L. MANTELL

See also CHEWING GUM (How Gum Is Made); SAPODILLA; LATEX.

CHICOPEE, *CHIHK uh PEE,* Mass. (pop. 55,112), is an industrial city on the Connecticut River, 5 miles (8 kilometers) north of Springfield (see MASSACHUSETTS [political map]). The falls on the Chicopee River led to industrial development in the early 1800's. Factories in the city make tires and tubes, electronic products, firearms, lawnmowers, athletic equipment, and cheesecloth.

Chicopee is the home of the College of Our Lady of the Elms. Westover Air Force Base is near the city.

Chicopee was settled in 1641 and became a city in 1890. Chicopee has a mayor-council form of government. WILLIAM J. REID

CHICORY, *CHIHK uhr ee,* is a small plant whose root is sometimes mixed with coffee, or used as a coffee substitute. It grows wild in Europe, Asia, and North America. Chicory is cultivated in the United States and southern Canada.

The chicory plant has spreading branches, coarse leaves, and bright blue, pink, or white flowers. The root of the plant is long, fleshy, and milky. Chicory is also called *succory.*

Pure-food laws in the United States forbid the mixing of ground chicory root with coffee unless the label is plainly marked. Chicory can be discovered in coffee by putting a spoonful of the mixture into a glass of cold water. The coffee will float on the surface. But the chicory will separate from the coffee and color the water. Some persons prefer coffee that is flavored with chicory.

Scientific Classification. Chicory belongs to the composite family, Compositae. The plant is classified as genus *Cichorium,* species *C. intybus.* HAROLD NORMAN MOLDENKE

CHIEF, INDIAN. See INDIAN, AMERICAN (Government).

CHIEF EXECUTIVE. See PRESIDENT OF THE UNITED STATES.

CHIEF JUSTICE is the presiding judge of a court that has several judges, such as the Supreme Court of the United States. The chief justice presides over the court and assigns tasks to the members of the court. Although a chief justice has only one vote, the position presents an opportunity for leadership. The President nominates the chief justice of the United States, and the Senate confirms the nomination. In many state courts, the judge who has served the longest time on the bench is designated as chief justice. In some states, the office is rotated. ERWIN N. GRISWOLD

See also SUPREME COURT OF THE UNITED STATES.

CHIEF OF STAFF. See GENERAL STAFF; JOINT CHIEFS OF STAFF.

CHIFFON, *shih FAHN,* is a soft, sheer, plain weave fabric made of silk, nylon, or rayon. Clothing manufacturers use it for making veils, trimmings, and party dresses. Chiffon is made 39 or 42 inches (99 to 107 centimeters) wide. *Chiffon* is a French word which means *rag.* The term is also used to describe lightweight, sheer fabric, such as chiffon velvet. CHRISTINE W. JARVIS

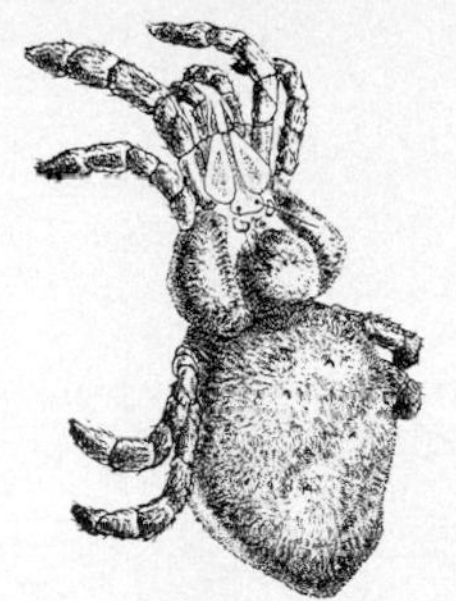

Monsanto Magazine

Larvae of Chiggers attack farmers in the Middle West and South at harvest time.

CHIGGER, or JIGGER, is the common name of two kinds of pests that attack human beings. One is the chigoe flea, and the other is the larva of a harvest mite. Only the latter lives in the United States.

The harvest mite is a tiny red creature with a body divided into two parts. It creeps into skin pores and hair follicles to feed, and causes a rash and instant itching. The female chigoe digs into the flesh and lays eggs that cause a sore. Mites usually attack small animals.

The harvest mite is merely a nuisance in North America and Europe. But in Oriental countries and many Pacific islands, it is a serious danger because it carries a typhuslike disease called Japanese river fever, or *tsutsugamushi*. The parasitic larvae of the harvest mite usually get the disease from infected rodents. The mite keeps the disease during its nymphal and adult stages, and gives it to the larvae of the next generation, which pass it on to human beings. Harvest mites are common in the Middle West and the South.

Scientific Classification. The chigoe flea belongs to the jigger and sticktight family, *Tungidae*. It is genus *Tunga*, species *T. penetrans*. Harvest mites (North American chiggers) make up the family *Trombidiidae*. They are genus *Trombicula*, species *T. alfreddugesi*. CARL D. DUNCAN

See also CHIGOE; MITE.

CHIGOE, *CHIG oh*, is a flea that lives in tropical America and, by introduction, in Africa and India. It is sometimes called *jigger*, or *chigger*, though it differs from the creatures called by those names in the United States. The female chigoe flea burrows into the skin of a human being, dog, or pig. It usually attacks humans between the fingers or toes, or on the bottoms of the feet. The chigoe makes a bad wound that may become infected.

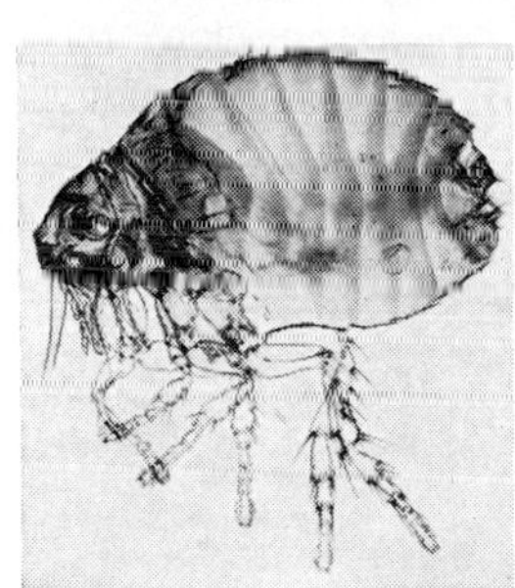

Roy M. Allen

A Chigoe is about 1/25 inch (1 millimeter) long.

Scientific Classification. The chigoe flea is a member of the jigger and sticktight family, *Tungidae*. It is classified as genus *Tunga*, species *T. penetrans*. FRANK B. GOLLEY

See also CHIGGER; FLEA.

CHIHLI, GULF OF. See YELLOW SEA.

CHIHUAHUA, *chee WAH wah* (pop. 365,760), is a chief city in northern Mexico and capital of Chihuahua state. It is about 780 miles (1,260 kilometers) northwest of Mexico City, in the center of a rich cattle and silver-mining region. For location, see MEXICO (political map). The city was founded in 1709.

Chihuahua has a mild climate. Nearby are large cattle ranches and plants for smelting silver, gold, lead, and zinc. The city has won fame as a breeding center for tiny dogs called Chihuahuas. JOHN A. CROW

CHIHUAHUA, *chee WAH wah*, is the largest state in Mexico. It has a population of 2,062,499 and covers 95,403 square miles (247,092 square kilometers). It borders Texas and New Mexico in the United States (see MEXICO [political map]). Most of it lies on a hot, dry plateau. Irrigation projects have made it a major producer of wheat, potatoes, and cotton. Ranchers raise cattle, sheep, and goats. Mines in the north and west produce gold, silver, copper, and other minerals. Forests on the mountain slopes provide lumber. Chihuahua became a state when Mexico became a republic in 1824. The city of Chihuahua is the state capital. See also CHIHUAHUA (city). CHARLES C. CUMBERLAND

CHIHUAHUA, *chee WAH wah*, is the smallest breed of dogs. Chihuahuas, classed as toy dogs, weigh from 1 to 6 pounds (0.5 to 2.7 kilograms). They have slender bodies and are quick in movement. Chihuahuas may be almost any color, and appear in two varieties, long-haired and short-haired. They used to be called "pillow dogs," because their owners let them sleep inside pillows for warmth. Chihuahuas are a pure American breed that comes from Mexico. Some experts believe they originated more than 500 years ago. JOSEPHINE Z. RINE

See also DOG (color picture: Toy Dogs); MULTIPLE BIRTH (picture).

A Chihuahua stands only 5 inches (13 centimeters) high. A straw hat holds two full-grown chihuahuas, *below*.

Walter Chandoha

CHILBLAIN, *CHILL BLAYN*, is a condition in which the skin stings, itches, burns, and sometimes turns red. It affects particularly the skin of the feet. The principal cause is exposure to cold, or to cold and wet. The feet become sensitive to cold after one attack, and easily suffer further attacks.

Chilblain usually may be prevented by protecting the feet with warm shoes and heavy stockings during cold, wet weather. Regular exercise and massage help to improve the circulation in the area affected by chilblain. J. F. A. MCMANUS

See also FROSTBITE; IMMERSION FOOT.

Phoebe Dunn

Billy Barnes

Daniel D. Miller, Tom Stack & Assoc.

Children of Different Ages vary widely in their social development. A toddler may be content to play alone, *top left*. By the early school years, many youngsters prefer to play in a group, *right*. Being part of "the gang" is extremely important to most preteen-agers, *bottom left*.

CHILD

CHILD is a person between about 18 months and 13 years of age. Childhood is one of the major stages in a person's development. At 18 months of age, children have just begun to outgrow baby clothes, though many must still wear diapers. By the age of 13, most boys and girls have nearly doubled in height and quadrupled in weight. They have also begun to develop sexually. They are thus starting to look more and more like young adults. But growing up involves far more than physical growth and development. It also involves significant changes in a child's behavior, thought processes, emotions, and attitudes. These psychological changes largely determine the kind of adult that a child will become.

Strictly speaking, a child is anyone who is not yet an adult. According to this definition, childhood extends from birth until sometime past the age of 20—the age at which most people reach their full adult physical growth. However, childhood is usually considered to be a much shorter period. In most developed countries, it is regarded as one of three stages that people pass through from birth to adulthood. The other stages are infancy and adolescence. Infancy extends from birth to about 18 months of age. Adolescence begins at about age 13 and lasts to adulthood. Childhood is the period between infancy and adolescence. In some developing countries, people are considered to be adults after they reach the age of 12 or 13, and adolescence is not regarded as a distinct stage of development.

Jerome Kagan, the contributor of this article, is Professor of Psychology at Harvard University and coauthor of Child Development and Personality.

Parents play a vital role in their children's development. One of the chief concerns of parents is to help their children develop normally. The word *normal* has two meanings as applied to child development. One meaning concerns the absence of physical and mental disorders that are considered abnormal in every society. These disorders include epilepsy, schizophrenia, and spastic paralysis. Relatively few children are born with or develop such disorders, and so the vast majority of children are normal according to this definition.

The second meaning of *normal* concerns the degree to which a child possesses certain skills or traits that the child's particular society values. Children are regarded as normal in this sense of the word if they compare favorably with the majority of children in developing a valued trait or skill. In every society, normal development includes learning to communicate, to get along with other people, and to act intelligently and responsibly. These skills and traits are essential to group living, and so all parents are expected to help their children develop them.

Other skills and traits are valued only by particular societies. In developed countries, for example, children are expected to learn how to read and write. A child who fails to acquire these skills may be considered abnormal. In developing countries, on the other hand, many children never attend school. Instead, they may be assigned farm or household chores. These children are regarded as normal if they acquire the necessary farm or household skills. They are not considered abnormal if they cannot read and write. In some societies, particularly those in the West, such personality traits as competitiveness and independence are encouraged. In other societies, these traits are considered abnormal and so are discouraged.

The role of parents thus varies according to the skills and personality traits that children are expected to develop. The role of parents also varies according to the needs of children at different stages of their development and according to the different needs of individual children.

This article discusses the stages of childhood, individual differences among children, and special problems of childhood. It also describes how parents can best promote their children's development. For similar information about infancy and adolescence, see the articles ADOLESCENT and BABY.

The Stages of Childhood

A child's psychological growth depends on the child's environment. Environment consists of everything with which a child comes in regular or frequent contact, including other people. The majority of children receive the environmental help they need for normal psychological development.

However, psychological growth is also affected by physical factors. For example, advances in learning ability are influenced by the development of the nervous system. Children do not develop physically at the same rate. As a result, their readiness for psychological growth also varies. A child who develops at a somewhat slower rate than average is not necessarily abnormal.

Childhood can be divided into four stages based on periods of major psychological change. These stages are (1) the toddler stage, (2) the preschool years, (3) the early school years, and (4) the preteen-age years.

The Toddler Stage lasts from about 18 months to 3 years of age. A child's physical growth is generally slower during this second 18 months after birth than it was during the first 18 months.

By 18 months of age, most children can feed themselves, walk and run a short distance, stack some blocks, and say a few meaningful words. A toddler is expected to improve all these skills. But the development of language skills—especially the building of sentences—is a major challenge. Most 2-year-olds use one or two words for an entire thought. Parents cannot always be sure what the words mean. For example, a child who says "milk" or "milk gone" may mean anything from "I want some milk" to "I just spilled my milk." By 3 years of age, however, most children can link several words together to form a fairly complete sentence. They can speak about 900 words—an enormous increase over the average 10- to 20-word vocabulary at 18 months of age.

Toddlers also vastly improve their powers of imitation and imagination. Some kinds of imitation are fun and attract attention, such as imitating the sounds that animals make. Most toddlers have an active imagination and love to pretend. They may pretend that a cup of water is a cup of tea or that a tricycle is an automobile or an airplane.

A toddler's social relationships develop slowly. Until children are about 2 years old, they tend to be shy around other youngsters. Children usually overcome this shyness after a few minutes, though they may still consider another child more as an object than as a person. By 3 years of age, children start to realize that they have things in common with other children. They then begin to regard them as equals.

Toddlers form their strongest attachments to their parents or substitute parents. In most cases, the mother is especially looked to for help, comfort, and companionship. The majority of children in Western societies have fewer contacts with the father, though they respect and imitate him. Above all, toddlers want to feel assured that they have their parents' acceptance and approval. As a result, they are sensitive to any sign of rejection or disapproval.

The Preschool Years extend from about 3 to 5 years of age. This period helps prepare children for the degree of independence and responsibility they will be given during the next stage of childhood, the early school years. Preschoolers are highly active and constantly exploring the world around them. At the same time, they are beginning to learn that there are certain standards of behavior—things they should and should not do.

By about 3 or 4 years of age, the majority of children have become increasingly aware of themselves and of other people. They are not only more conscious of their own actions, but they have also begun to realize that other people have feelings like their own. Children

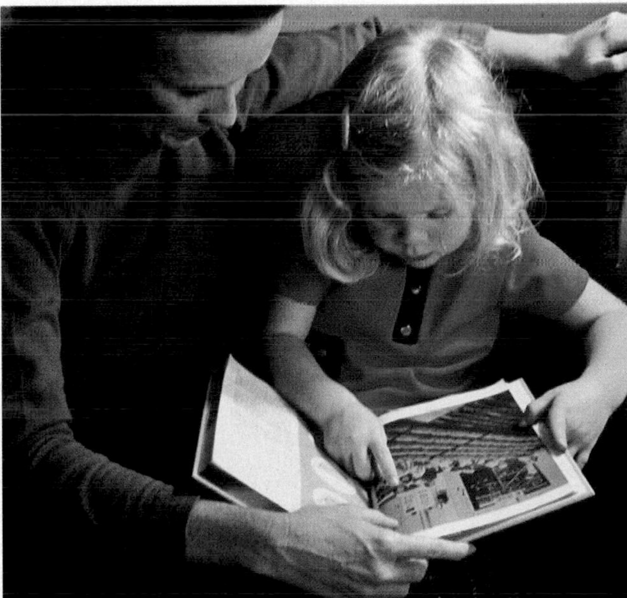

WORLD BOOK photo

Developing Language Skills is a major challenge for children during the toddler stage. Many parents use stories and pictures to help toddlers increase their vocabulary and build sentences.

WORLD BOOK photo by Milt & Joan Mann

Playing Make-Believe can help children learn adult roles. These youngsters may be pretending that they are parents preparing to take their children for a ride in the family automobile.

then start to govern some of their actions according to the pleasure or displeasure that they give another person.

One of the first standards that all children are expected to learn is control of the bowels and bladder—a process called *toilet training*. However, the age when such control becomes possible varies greatly among children. In addition, the age when a child is expected to develop the control varies greatly among societies. Most children, however, have started to develop it by their third year.

Other standards of behavior besides toilet training are also taught to children in every society. These standards include obedience, truthfulness, respect for property, and various *sex role* standards—that is, the roles that people are expected to play as males or females. As in the case of toilet training, the age when children are expected to learn each standard varies among societies. Most children, however, are capable of such learning by about 3 or 4 years of age.

Most parents use rewards and punishments to teach their children standards of behavior. They reward children for desired actions and punish them for undesired ones. A word of praise or a hug is usually a sufficient reward. Punishment usually consists of a strong "no" or a light slap. Gradually, a child learns that some actions are good and some are bad. In most cases, however, it is the parents who must decide the goodness or badness of an action.

Preschoolers also learn standards of behavior through a more or less unconscious process called *identification*. The process often begins during the toddler stage, but it becomes fully developed during the preschool years. Children *identify* with another person if they feel that they have the same physical and psychological characteristics as that person. Most children identify with one or more members of their family, especially their parents.

The majority of 3- and 4-year-olds do not know they have a choice in their actions. If something they do displeases their parents, they feel anxious, ashamed, or sorry. But they do not blame themselves for the action. By about 5 years of age, however, most children start to realize that they can choose one action rather than another. Children then begin to feel guilt, as well as shame, if they behave wrongly.

The Early School Years, which last from about age 5 to 8, mark a major turning point in a child's psychological development. Children continue to improve their physical skills during this stage. But the period is distinguished mainly by important advances in a child's mental, emotional, and social development.

In most societies, children have been taught basic standards of social behavior by their fifth year. They are also learning to judge whether particular actions are right or wrong. A child can thus be given more independence. However, adults channel this independence along definite lines. In the United States and most other developed countries, children must start school at about 5 or 6 years of age.

Every schoolchild is expected to learn to solve problems, a skill that improves with practice. A 5-year-old may try to solve a problem by choosing the first solution that comes to mind. But a 6- or 7-year-old thinks about other possible solutions and recognizes why one is better than another. Children this age also begin to see how things are alike and how they differ. Finally, children gain confidence in their mental powers and start to enjoy solving problems correctly.

By the age of 7 or 8, most children begin to *rationalize* their beliefs—that is, to find reasons for holding them. They may thus decide that the standards of behavior they have learned are good standards to hold. Children this age also increasingly compare themselves with other youngsters. Such comparisons contribute to a child's *self-image*—that is, the opinion one has of oneself. The self-image formed during childhood can influence a person's behavior throughout life.

Children begin to form a self-image during the preschool years as they identify with their parents or other family members. A child's self-image is favorable or unfavorable, depending on the attitudes and emotions of the persons with whom the child identifies. For example, children who see mainly negative qualities in their parents will likely view themselves in a negative light. Children form a more favorable self-image if they have a better impression of their parents. When children compare themselves with other children, they reinforce or alter their basic self-image.

The Preteen-Age Years extend from about age 8 to 13. This stage is also known as *preadolescence*. During preadolescence, the rate of physical growth, which had been declining since infancy, increases sharply. The preteen-ager begins to grow heavier and taller and to develop the sexual characteristics of an adult. Most girls, for example, have their first menstrual period by

Jim Collins

Learning to Concentrate is one of the major achievements of children during the early school years. Typical third-graders, *left,* take great pride in doing their work accurately.

age 12 or 13. Most boys develop hair on their body and face, and their voice deepens. The entire stage during which a person matures sexually is called *puberty*. Some children reach sexual maturity before age 13. But the majority do not become sexually mature until the early teen-age years (see SEX [Puberty]).

During the preteen-age years, a child's circle of friends and acquaintances, or *peer group*, plays an increasingly important role in the child's development. Preteens begin to look chiefly to their peer group, rather than to their parents, for acceptance and approval. They judge themselves according to peer group standards, and so their self-image continues to develop. A child's behavior may also change noticeably under peer group pressure.

During late preadolescence, children may begin to worry if a new standard of behavior conflicts with an earlier one. They often relieve such anxieties by talking them over with their friends. Nevertheless, older preadolescents feel a growing need to keep their beliefs consistent. They may therefore revise or reject a conflicting standard. Children this age also begin to reason that a "wrong" action may be permitted under some circumstances.

Individual Differences Among Children

Two main forces—heredity and environment—account for the individual differences among children. Heredity is the process by which children inherit physical and mental traits from their parents. Environment consists of all the things in a child's surroundings that affect the child's development of the inherited traits.

Individual differences among children are caused by heredity and environment acting together, not separately. In general, heredity limits what the environment can do in influencing a child's development. For example, every child inherits a tendency to grow to a certain height. Not even the best environmental conditions will enable a child to grow much taller than this height. But children need the right conditions, including proper nourishment and exercise, to grow as tall as their heredity allows. Heredity and environment together thus determine the physical differences among children. The two forces together also account for individual differences in intelligence.

Physical Differences. Children differ greatly in their physical appearance and rate of growth. For example, the normal weight for 9-year-old boys in the United States ranges from 56 to 81 pounds (25 to 37 kilograms). Their normal height may be 50 to 56 inches (130 to 140 centimeters). The normal ranges for 9-year-old girls are slightly lower. But most girls grow rapidly at about 9 to 12 years of age. Girls are normally heavier and taller than boys during these years. At about age 12, however, most boys start to grow rapidly, and the girls' growth rate declines. By age 14, most boys are again heavier and taller than most girls their age. Some children begin this rapid growth a year or two earlier or later than the majority. Children are not necessarily abnormal if their height and weight vary somewhat from the normal ranges for their age.

Differences in Intelligence among children are usually measured by *IQ* (intelligence quotient) tests. These tests are designed to indicate a child's general mental ability in relation to other children of the same age. Each child's performance on the tests is rated by an IQ score. On most such tests, about two-thirds of all children score from 84 to 116. About a sixth score below 84, and a sixth score above 116.

The IQ scores of persons related by blood generally differ less than do the scores of unrelated persons. Some experts therefore conclude that general mental ability is largely inherited and is only slightly affected by environment. Other experts, however, believe that environment has a strong influence on a person's intelligence. Their view is supported by studies of *culturally deprived* children. Children are considered culturally deprived if their home life lacks the kinds of experiences that will help them profit from formal schooling. Many such children have an IQ score below 80. But in a number of cases, culturally deprived children have dramatically improved their score after receiving special training and encouragement in foster homes or in school.

Some experts question the usefulness of IQ tests on the grounds that they do not measure basic mental skills. These experts point out that intelligence involves a variety of separate powers, such as memory, logic, evaluation, and originality. A child may have little ability in some of these areas but exceptional talent in

Average Height and Weight for Children

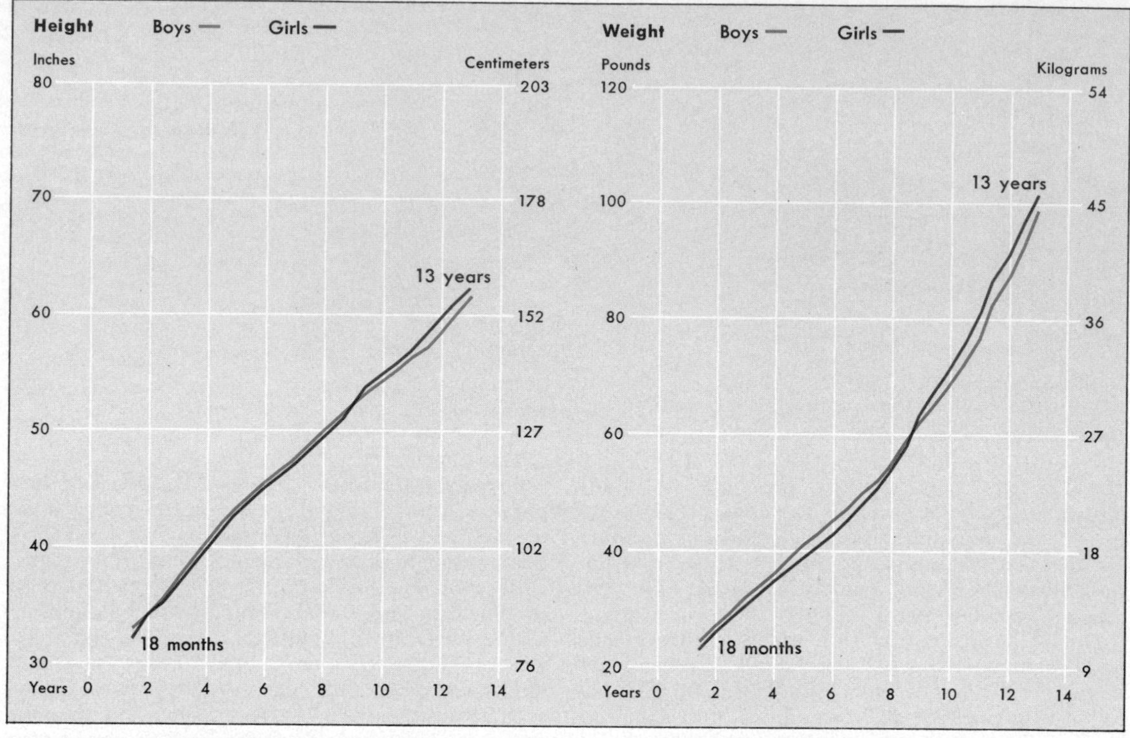

Source: National Center for Health Statistics, U.S. Public Health Service.

one or more other areas. The critics therefore believe that children should be tested and evaluated for each mental skill separately. For more information on intelligence and IQ tests, see the articles INTELLIGENCE and INTELLIGENCE QUOTIENT.

Special Problems of Childhood

Some children develop patterns of behavior that are a problem to themselves and to the people around them. Under certain conditions, such behavior may be a symptom of a deeper psychological or physical disorder. A child who is psychologically disturbed may benefit from professional counseling.

A child's behavior is a symptom of a psychological disorder if it (1) differs widely from normal behavior, (2) has undesirable consequences or side effects, and (3) distresses the child. All three conditions must be present before behavior becomes a symptom. For example, a child who shows exceptional ability in school differs greatly from most other schoolchildren. But the child's behavior is not considered a symptom because it does not usually have undesirable consequences or cause psychological distress.

A number of childhood problems may be symptoms of deeper physical or psychological disorders. Two of the most common such problems are (1) unrealistic fears and (2) aggressive and antisocial behavior.

Unrealistic Fears. All children are afraid on occasion. Fear is thus a normal emotion. Fears are unrealistic if they occur regularly in the absence of real danger. In some cases, such fears may be directly related to a frightening past experience. For example, a child who has a fear of all animals may have developed the fear after being attacked by an animal. In other cases, unrealistic fears may be only indirectly related to a past event. For instance, a child who feels extreme guilt over an action may expect severe punishment. The child may then develop an abnormal fear of death, accidents, or illness.

Aggressive and Antisocial Behavior. Psychologists define *aggression* as angry, hostile behavior that is intended to hurt or upset others. Such behavior in young children can result from *frustration.* Children may feel frustrated if their demands are not met or if their feelings of worthiness and self-respect are threatened. If a child's anger becomes intense, it may erupt into a tantrum—a common form of aggression in young children.

Children can learn to control aggression if they are taught at an early age that some of their demands will not be met. A child who develops such a *frustration tolerance* is less likely to have severe or frequent tantrums. But children may have great difficulty developing the necessary tolerance if their parents are overly strict or overly permissive. If parents are too strict, a child may feel increasingly frustrated in trying to meet their high goals. If they are too permissive, the child may react aggressively to any frustration. In addition, parents encourage aggression if they are frequently angry and hostile themselves.

Most children learn to control aggression by the preteen-age years. They may do so partly by channeling their energies into hobbies, sports, schoolwork, and other activities. Some children, however, do not learn to deal with aggression effectively. Instead, they may relieve feelings of frustration and hostility by antisocial behavior, such as bullying other children, stealing, or destroying property. Such behavior worsens if the peer group encourages it.

Other Special Problems may also be symptoms of psychological or physical disorders. These problems include (1) *hyperactivity* (extreme restlessness); (2) poor performance in school; (3) extreme shyness; and (4) bed-wetting.

Hyperactivity. Most hyperactive children cannot concentrate on anything for more than a few minutes at a time. Scientists do not know the exact cause of the disturbance. There is evidence that some cases may be caused by an allergy to certain chemical additives in food, especially particular food colorings and dyes.

Poor Performance in School is frequently caused by a child's failure to learn to read. Failure in reading may be due to a physical or psychological problem, such as poor eyesight, poor hearing, or extreme shyness. The reading ability of most hyperactive or mentally retarded children is severely limited (see MENTAL RETARDATION). In many cases, however, reading problems can be avoided if parents prepare their children for learning to read. Parents should thus make a practice of reading stories and poems to their children during the toddler and preschool years. Parents should also acquaint their children with books and other reading materials and help them build a vocabulary. Schoolchildren who lack such preparation may fall behind their classmates in learning to read. Children also need a motive for learning to read. Parents help provide such a motive if they show that they value learning.

Extreme Shyness. In some cases, children become overly shy if they are dominated by older brothers and sisters. Shyness may also begin as an inherited tendency. However, the precise causes of extreme shyness are not well understood.

Bed-Wetting. A habit of bed-wetting after about 5 years of age is a physical or psychological symptom. Parents should not punish or threaten a child who has the problem. In every case, a physician or psychologist should be consulted.

The Role of Parents

Mothers and fathers can best promote the development of their children in three major ways. They can do so by (1) understanding a child's basic needs, (2) motivating the child's behavior, and (3) serving as models of appropriate behavior.

Understanding a Child's Basic Needs. All children have certain basic physical and psychological needs. Both sets of needs must be met if a child is to develop normally. Poor physical health may harm a child's psychological development, and psychological problems may affect a child physically.

Basic Physical Needs. Children need regular, nourishing meals, proper clothing, and a clean, comfortable home. They also require a reasonable amount of play and exercise and enough space to play in. In addition, children who learn good health habits and standard safety practices reduce the risk of diseases and accidents.

Improved health care has greatly increased the life expectancy of children in many countries during the 1900's. For example, such diseases as diphtheria and whooping cough formerly killed thousands of children every year. But the development of immunization programs has sharply reduced the death rate from these diseases. Most children receive their first immunizations before 18 months of age. A child should be reimmunized for diphtheria, polio, tetanus, and whooping cough at about 4 to 6 years of age. For detailed information on the physical needs of children, see HEALTH; NUTRITION; and SAFETY.

Basic Psychological Needs are determined by the skills and personality traits that a child is expected to develop. Some skills and traits are encouraged in every society. All children therefore have certain basic psychological needs. Toddlers, for example, need to develop self-confidence, and so they must feel loved, wanted, and respected. Toddlers should also have enough variety in their routine to help them develop language skills. Preschoolers especially need close contact with adults they like and admire. Such contacts help promote normal emotional development.

Children are expected to behave more responsibly after they reach school age. They must therefore be convinced that required standards of behavior do not change from day to day. Preteens have a strong need to feel as successful as other children their age. Success often means measuring up to the sex role valued by society. The preteen thus requires freedom to develop the appropriate masculine or feminine qualities (see SEX [Sex Roles]).

Motivating the Child's Behavior. Parents *motivate* a child when they encourage the child to adopt a certain type of behavior. Rewarding good behavior is one means of motivation. Persistent misbehavior should be punished. But punishments should be just. Children will understandably be upset if they are punished for behavior that they continually see in their parents. Parents should try to motivate children without making them think they are being manipulated. Instead, children should be made to feel that they were personally responsible for improvements in their behavior.

Rewards and punishments work in cases that are not complicated by other factors. Children whose parents regularly encourage schoolwork are more likely to succeed in school than are children who lack such encouragement. A child who is taught to control aggression is less likely to become a bully than is a child who is not taught such control. Motivation is not always effective, however, because other factors also influence a child's behavior. For example, children cannot be motivated to learn to read if they believe they lack the ability. Parents may also be unable to motivate a child who feels resentful or hostile toward them.

Serving as Models of Appropriate Behavior. Children model themselves largely on their parents. They do so mainly through identification. Children identify with a parent when they believe they have the qualities and feelings that are characteristic of that parent. The things parents do and say—and the way they do and say them—therefore strongly influence a child's behavior. However, parents must consistently behave like the type of person they want their child to become.

A parent's actions also affect the self-image that children form through identification. Children who see mainly positive qualities in their parents will likely learn to see themselves in a positive way. Children who observe chiefly negative qualities in their parents will have difficulty seeing positive qualities in themselves. Children may modify their self-image, however, as they become increasingly influenced by peer group standards during the preteen-age years.

Isolated events, even dramatic ones, do not necessarily have a permanent effect on a child's behavior. Children interpret such events according to their established attitudes and previous training. For example, children who know they are loved can accept the divorce of their parents or a parent's early death. But if children feel unloved, they may interpret such events as a sign of rejection or punishment.

In the same way, all children are not influenced alike by toys and games, reading matter, and television programs. As in the case of a dramatic change in family relations, the effect of an activity or experience depends on how the child interprets it. Each child's interpretation, in turn, depends on the child's standards of behavior. For instance, violent behavior on television may heighten the aggressive tendencies of a child who considers such behavior permissible. Children are less likely to be influenced by TV violence if they have learned that violent behavior is wrong (see TELEVISION [Effects on Learning]). In the end, the day-to-day behavior of parents themselves has a more powerful influence on their children than do isolated events and experiences.

JEROME KAGAN

Related Articles in WORLD BOOK include:

CHILD TRAINING

See LEARNING with its list of *Related Articles*. See also the following:

Day-Care Center
Early Childhood Education
Education
Etiquette
Habit
Health
Juvenile Delinquency
Kindergarten
Library (Services for Children)
Lisping
Literature for Children
Nursery School
Parent Education
Pediatrics
Physical Education (In Elementary Schools)
Reading
School
Sex (Boys and Girls)
Sex Education
Special Education
Storytelling
Stuttering

RECREATION

Doll
Game
Hobby
Play
Recreation
Toy

OTHER RELATED ARTICLES

Adolescent
Adoption
Child Abuse
Child Labor
Child Welfare
Childhood Education International, Association for
Children's Bureau
Cultural Deprivation
Divorce (Child Custody Arrangements)
Family
Foster Parent
Growth
Heredity
Homosexuality
Hyperactive Child
Minor
Orphanage
Parent
UNICEF

Outline

I. The Stages of Childhood
A. The Toddler Stage
B. The Preschool Years
C. The Early School Years
D. The Preteen-Age Years

II. Individual Differences Among Children
A. Physical Differences
B. Differences in Intelligence

III. Special Problems of Childhood
A. Unrealistic Fears
B. Aggressive and Antisocial Behavior
C. Other Special Problems

IV. The Role of Parents
A. Understanding a Child's Basic Needs
B. Motivating the Child's Behavior
C. Serving as Models of Appropriate Behavior

Questions

Why can most children be given more independence by about 5 years of age?

In what ways do all children differ? What two main forces account for these differences?

What are the two meanings of the word *normal* as applied to child development?

How do most parents use rewards and punishments to teach their children standards of behavior during the preschool years?

What determines a child's basic psychological needs?

What is frequently the cause of poor performance in school?

How can young children learn to control aggression?

Why are children strongly influenced by their parents' behavior?

How do friends and acquaintances influence a child's behavior during the preteen-age years?

Why does the role of parents vary from one society to another?

Additional Resources

DEMAUSE, LLOYD, ed. *The History of Childhood*. Psychohistory Press, 1974. Essays on child development and parent-child relationships throughout history.

FLAVELL, JOHN H. *The Developmental Psychology of Jean Piaget*. Van Nostrand, 1963.

GORDON, THOMAS. *P.E.T., Parent Effectiveness Training: The Tested New Way to Raise Responsible Children*. McKay, 1970.

ILG, FRANCES, and others, eds. *Child Behavior*. Rev. ed. Harper, 1981.

KAGAN, JEROME. *Understanding Children: Behavior, Motives, and Thought*. Harcourt, 1971. *The Growth of the Child: Reflections on Human Development*. Norton, 1978.

MONTESSORI, MARIA. *The Absorbent Mind*. Holt, 1967. *The Child in the Family*. Avon, 1970.

MURPHY, LOIS B., and MORIARTY, A. E. *Vulnerability, Coping and Growth: From Infancy to Adolescence*. Yale, 1976.

MUSSEN, PAUL H., CONGER, J. J., and KAGAN, JEROME. *Child Development and Personality*. 5th ed. Harper, 1979.

PIAGET, JEAN, and INHELDER, BARBEL. *The Psychology of the Child*. Basic Books, 1969.

SEGAL, JULIUS, and YAHRAES, H. C. *A Child's Journey: Forces That Shape the Lives of Our Young*. McGraw, 1978.

SHARP, EVELYN. *Thinking Is Child's Play*. Avon, 1969.

SPOCK, BENJAMIN M. *Raising Children in a Difficult Time: A Philosophy of Parental Leadership and High Ideals*. Norton, 1974.

CHILD, LYDIA MARIA (1802-1880), was an American abolitionist, author, and editor. She became known for her book *An Appeal in Favor of That Class of Americans Called Africans* (1833), which condemned slavery.

Lydia M. Francis was born in Medford, Mass. In 1826, she founded *Juvenile Miscellany*, the nation's first magazine for children. In 1828, she married David Child, a Boston lawyer and abolitionist. She became involved in abolitionism in 1831, when she met the famous abolitionist William Lloyd Garrison.

Dictionary of American Portraits

Lydia Maria Child

From 1841 to 1843,

Child served as editor of the *National Anti-Slavery Standard*, the weekly publication of the American Anti-Slavery Society. She wrote a series of letters supporting John Brown, the noted abolitionist, after he led his historic raid at Harpers Ferry, Va., in 1859. Child also edited *Incidents in the Life of a Slave Girl* (1861), the recollections of a former slave named Harriet Jacobs. In addition, Child wrote several books on Indians, one of her earliest interests. NANCY SPELMAN WOLOCH

CHILD ABUSE is a term that refers to the mistreatment of children by their parents or guardians. Child abuse includes such acts as beating children so badly that physical harm results, inflicting them with burns, and starving them. Many cases are never reported. However, some authorities estimate that nearly 2 million children are abused each year in the United States.

Many studies have been made to determine the causes of child abuse. These studies show that people who abuse children have severe emotional problems, and that most of them were injured or neglected by their own parents. Many parents and guardians who commit child abuse have permanently or temporarily lost contact with reality. They abuse a child because they see the youngster not as a helpless dependent, but as a threatening symbol. The child may represent to the adult a hated brother or sister.

Some parents and guardians abuse children because the youngsters fail to meet the demands of adults. Others are too immature to care about the harm to the child. Some studies link child abuse with unemployment. A lack or loss of income often creates tension, and some parents react by beating their children.

Many abused children suffer a permanent injury, such as brain damage, paralysis, or physical deformity. Some even die. Many develop emotional problems.

Little was done toward stopping child abuse until the 1800's. In the late 1800's and early 1900's, citizens set up agencies from time to time to deal with child abuse. During the 1950's, more and more people became aware of the problem. All 50 states soon passed laws requiring physicians to report suspected cases of abuse to a government authority. In 1974, the U.S. Congress set up the National Center on Child Abuse and Neglect. The center studies the causes and prevention of child abuse and helps support programs that deal with the problem. Today, state welfare departments have experts who investigate such cases and counsel families of abused children. In extreme cases, a juvenile court may be asked to place a child in a foster home or other child-care facility. An organization called Parents Anonymous works to rehabilitate child abusers through group participation. G. LEWIS PENNER

Additional Resources

HELFER, RAY E., and KEMPE, C. H., eds. *The Battered Child*. 2nd ed. Univ. of Chicago Press, 1974.

HYDE, MARGARET O. *Cry Softly: The Story of Child Abuse*. Westminster, 1980. For younger readers.

KEMPE, RUTH S. *Child Abuse*. Harvard, 1978.

POLANSKY, NORMAN A., and others. *Damaged Parents: An Anatomy of Child Neglect*. Univ. of Chicago Press, 1981.

CHILD-CARE CENTER. See DAY-CARE CENTER; NURSERY SCHOOL.

CHILD LABOR is the use of children to work in factories or other places of employment. The regulation of child labor was an important social problem during the 1700's and 1800's. Businesses in Great Britain, the United States, and other countries hired young children to work for low wages. Many children were under 10 years old, and some were only 5 or 6. Children often worked in mines, or with dangerous machines in factories. Some toiled as long as 16 hours a day. A few children were even chained to their machines.

Social reformers condemned child labor practices for ruining the health and spirit of children. Perhaps the most famous of these reformers was Charles Dickens, an English novelist. He exposed the evils of child labor to his large reading audience in the novel *Oliver Twist*.

Gradually, countries passed laws to correct the abuses of child labor. Children still work today. But in Canada, Great Britain, the United States, and many other countries, most working children are teen-agers who hold part-time jobs. Their working conditions are carefully regulated by law. However, in Asia and other parts of the world, millions of boys and girls still hold full-time jobs. In some countries, children under 15 form a large part of the total working force, and there is little or no control over their working conditions.

Abuses of Child Labor. Since ancient times, children have worked to help support their families, especially on farms. But child labor created no major social problems until the factory system of labor began.

The Industrial Revolution in England began in the 1700's and lasted until the mid-1800's. During this period, businesses hired many children. Children worked for lower wages than adults, and were not so likely as adults to cause labor troubles. Factory owners wanted to use their small, nimble fingers for tending machines. Children worked for low pay in dirty, poorly lighted factories, mills, and mines. They often performed jobs that really required adult strength. Many children worked to help support their unemployed parents. Orphans were pressed into labor. Similar conditions were common in the United States and Canada at this time.

Child workers were often deprived of the chance to attend school. Uneducated, the only work they were capable of doing was unskilled labor. Thus, they had little chance to better themselves.

Early Child Labor Laws. In 1802, the British Parliament passed the first law regulating child labor. The law prohibited the employment of *pauper children* (children dependent on charity) under 9 years of age. Pauper children under 14 could not work at night, and their workday was limited to 12 hours. In 1819, the law was extended to include all children. No real provision for enforcing these laws was made until 1833. Germany was the second country to pass national child labor laws. It did so in 1839.

In 1836, Massachusetts passed the first state child labor law in the United States. The law prohibited the employment of children under 15 in any factory unless the children had attended school for at least three months during the preceding year. But by 1860, only a few states had outlawed factory employment of children under 10 or 12 years of age.

U.S. Federal Laws. The first federal child labor law was passed by the U.S. Congress in 1916. It set standards for the hiring of children by industries involved in interstate or foreign commerce. The standards included

The George Eastman House Collection, Rochester, N.Y.

Child Labor in Factories is now regulated by both state and federal laws. But in the 1700's and 1800's, many children worked 16 hours a day in textile factories. The American photographer Lewis W. Hine took this picture, *Carolina Cotton Mill,* in 1908.

a 16-year minimum age for work in mines and quarries, a 14-year minimum age for other types of work, an 8-hour day, and a 48-hour week. It prohibited night work for children under 16. However, in 1918, the Supreme Court of the United States declared the law unconstitutional. This ruling was reversed in 1941, in the case of the *United States v. Darby.*

A law passed by Congress in 1919 taxed the profits of companies that did not obey the standards of the 1916 law. In 1922, this law was also ruled unconstitutional. In 1924, Congress passed a constitutional amendment to authorize federal laws for regulating the labor of persons under 18. But this amendment failed to receive the required approval of three-fourths of all the states.

The Fair Labor Standards Act of 1938 helped to promote child labor reform. The law included basic standards for the employment of minors. Later upheld by the Supreme Court, this law declared that boys and girls 16 and over may be employed in any occupations except those declared hazardous by the U.S. secretary of labor. The minimum age for hazardous occupations was set at 18. Children 14 and 15 years old were permitted to work in only a limited number of occupations outside of school hours. This law firmly established the constitutional legality of child labor laws.

U.S. State Laws. All 50 states, the District of Columbia, and Puerto Rico now have child labor laws that regulate the employment of children. Most state laws set a minimum age for general employment, a higher minimum age for hazardous work, and limitations on the daily and weekly hours of work. Federal and state child labor laws vary widely. When both federal and state laws apply, the higher standard must be observed.

The states work with the U.S. Department of Labor's Employment Standards Administration in employment certificate programs. In most states, school officials issue these certificates to persons from 14 to 17 years of age. The use of certificates guards against employment that might damage the health and welfare of young persons. The certificates also protect employers from unknowingly violating federal and state child labor law requirements. They furnish employers with reliable proof of the ages of the boys and girls they employ.

In the United States today, about 5 million children between the ages of 14 and 18 work sometime during the year.

Canadian Laws. The provinces of Canada have child labor laws that regulate employment in mines, factories, and shops. The first of these laws came in 1873, when Nova Scotia set 10 as the minimum age for mine workers. The law limited boys under 12 years old to 60 hours of work a week below ground. In time, the minimum age was raised and the hours of work lowered. In most of the provinces today, a higher minimum age is fixed for work in mines than in other places of work.

Most of the provinces have laws regulating child labor in factories. The standards vary, but all set minimum ages for employment and limit the hours boys and girls can work. The minimum age for employment in factories varies from 14 to 16. School attendance laws restrict the employment during school hours of children who are still required to attend school. WILLIAM E. AMOS

See also COAL (picture: A Pennsylvania Mine of the Late 1800's); INDUSTRIAL REVOLUTION (pictures).

Additional Resources

CHALLIS, JAMES, and ELLIMAN, D. *Child Workers Today.* Quartermaine, 1979. An international survey of contemporary conditions.

HOLLAND, RUTH. *Mill Child.* Crowell, 1970. Emphasis on reformers of child labor movement.

TRATTNER, WALTER I. *Crusade for the Children: A History of the National Child Labor Committee and Child Labor Reform in America.* Discusses early efforts to eliminate child labor in Great Britain and the U.S. Quadrangle, 1970.

CHILD PROTECTION AND TOY SAFETY ACT. See TOY (History).

CHILD WELFARE is a program of financial, medical, psychological, and social services provided to parents and children. Child welfare agencies administer these services. In the United States, such agencies receive financial support through federal and state tax funds and through contributions from individuals. Each agency must be licensed annually by the department of public welfare in its state.

Since the early 1960's, the federal government has taken on much responsibility for the welfare of children. Amendments to the Social Security Act made more children eligible for benefits under the Aid to Families with Dependent Children (AFDC) program. Other federal acts created programs that provide food for low-income families, food stamps, and school lunches. The Head Start program helps prepare children of poor families for school. The Department of Health and Human Services operates most of the government's child welfare programs. Several other federal agencies also participate in this field.

Child welfare agencies provide adoption services, health care, and professional homemakers who go to homes to help during periods of stress. Day care for children whose parents both have jobs has also become an important service. Child welfare agencies also investigate cases of suspected child abuse or neglect. The agencies may place the children involved in such cases in temporary or permanent foster homes. EDWARD ZIGLER

See also AID TO FAMILIES WITH DEPENDENT CHILDREN; CHILD ABUSE; DAY-CARE CENTER.

CHILDBIRTH is the process by which a woman gives birth to a baby. A pregnant woman carries a baby within her body inside a hollow, muscular organ called the *uterus*. After about nine months, the baby passes out of the uterus and through the *vagina*, or *birth canal*. Childbirth is painful, but the severeness of the pain varies among women.

The Birth Process is called *labor*. It consists of a series of actions that begin when the muscles of the uterus start to tighten and relax in a rhythmic pattern. As labor progresses, these muscle contractions become stronger and occur more frequently, causing the *cervix* (mouth of the uterus) to open. After the cervix has opened to a diameter of about 4 inches (10 centimeters), the woman begins to "push" with her abdominal muscles in time with the contractions. This action forces the baby through the cervix and out of the mother's body through the vagina. The *amniotic sac*, a membrane containing water that envelops the baby, breaks before or during labor. The water flows out through the vagina.

Most babies are born headfirst. But in some deliveries, called *breech births*, the feet or buttocks come out first. After the baby has passed out of the mother's body, the *umbilical cord* is cut and clamped, and the infant starts to breathe. The umbilical cord is a tubelike structure that connects the baby to the *placenta*, an organ attached to the wall of the uterus. Food and oxygen from the mother's blood pass through the placenta to the baby during pregnancy. After the baby is born, the muscles of the uterus continue to contract until the placenta separates from the uterus and is expelled through the vagina. The discharged placenta is called the *afterbirth*.

The period of labor varies greatly in length among women. It averages 13 to 14 hours for women having their first babies and lasts 7 to 8 hours thereafter.

A woman may have to undergo an operation called a *Caesarean section* to deliver a baby. The surgeon removes the baby and the placenta through an incision made in the abdomen and uterus. Caesarean sections are performed for many reasons, but chiefly because the baby cannot pass through the birth canal. The woman's pelvis may be too small, or the baby may be too large.

Methods of Childbirth. Most women deliver their babies in hospitals, which have specially equipped labor and delivery rooms. During childbirth, a woman may receive medication to relieve her labor pains. In some cases, a physician will administer a drug to *induce* (bring on) labor. Before delivery, the physician may widen the woman's vaginal opening by making a small incision called an *episiotomy*.

In many cases, physicians use an electronic *fetal monitor* to record the baby's heartbeat during labor. A signal from this machine warns if the baby is in danger. If so, a Caesarean section may be necessary.

During the 1960's and the 1970's, many hospitals developed educational programs to prepare women for childbirth. A number of these programs instruct both the mother and the father on pregnancy, childbirth, and infant care. In addition, such programs as *natural childbirth* and the *Lamaze method* became increasingly popular. They teach various relaxation exercises and breathing techniques to help lessen the discomfort of labor, thus reducing the need for painkilling drugs. Such drugs are passed on to the baby through the placenta, and so some women choose to avoid them. Some women also prefer not to use the drugs so they can be alert throughout labor and function effectively during the "pushing" state.

The *Leboyer method* of delivery was introduced in the United States in the mid-1970's. This method emphasizes making birth as gentle as possible for the baby. For example, it calls for a quiet, dimly lit room rather than the standard bustling, brightly lighted delivery room. Other hospitals developed *birthing rooms* as an alternative to the regular labor and delivery rooms. Most birthing rooms resemble a home bedroom. They are designed to make the delivery more relaxed and informal, while still having the hospital's facilities at hand if complications occur. LOIS KAZMIER HALSTEAD

See also MIDWIFE; PREMATURE BIRTH; REPRODUCTION (pictures: Birth of a Baby).

CHILDHOOD EDUCATION INTERNATIONAL, ASSOCIATION FOR, is an organization that works for the education and welfare of children. The members are parents, teachers, and persons who work with children, such as librarians, doctors, and social workers.

The association seeks to promote good practices in schools and to raise the quality of teaching. It operates an information service on matters of education and child development, holds an annual study conference, and publishes bulletins. Its journal, *Childhood Education*, is published six times a year. Founded in 1892, the organization has about 25,000 members in about 400 branches in the United States and several other countries. It has headquarters at 3615 Wisconsin Avenue NW, Washington, D.C. 20016. Critically reviewed by the ASSOCIATION FOR CHILDHOOD EDUCATION INTERNATIONAL

CHILDREN. See CHILD.

CHILDREN'S BUREAU is a division of the United States Department of Health and Human Services (HHS). The bureau develops and coordinates federal programs for children and issues publications about child care.

The Children's Bureau was established in 1912. It conducted pioneering research into the relationship between the health of pregnant women and that of their babies. From 1921 to 1929, the bureau administered a federal program that worked to reduce infant deaths in the United States. This program was the first to use government funds for a public health service.

Today, the bureau is a part of the Administration for Children, Youth, and Families in HHS's Office of Human Development Services. It administers federal programs in such areas as adoption, foster-child care, juvenile delinquency, and services for runaway youths. The bureau includes the National Center for Child Abuse and Neglect. EDWARD ZIGLER

See also LATHROP, JULIA C.; WALD, LILLIAN D.

CHILDREN'S CRUSADE. See CRUSADES.

CHILDREN'S LITERATURE. See LITERATURE FOR CHILDREN.

CHILDREN'S THEATER. See THEATER (Children's Theater).

The Andes—Margaret Durrance, Rapho Guillumette

Facts in Brief

Capital: Santiago.

Official Language: Spanish.

Official Name: República de Chile (Republic of Chile).

Form of Government: Military rule.

Area: 292,135 sq. mi. (756,626 km²). *Greatest Distances*—north-south, 2,650 mi. (4,265 km); east-west, 225 mi. (362 km). *Coastline*—3,317 mi. (5,338 km).

Elevation: *Highest*—Ojos del Salado (22,572 ft., or 6,880 m); *Lowest*—sea level.

Population: *Estimated 1985 Population*—12,168,000; distribution, 83 per cent urban, 17 per cent rural; density, 41 persons per sq. mi. (16 persons per km²). *1970 Census*—9,311,237. *Estimated 1990 Population*—13,238,000.

Chief Products: *Agriculture*—barley, beans, cattle, corn, flax, fruits, hemp, lentils, milk, oats, peas, pigs, potatoes, rice, rye, sheep, sunflowers, tobacco, wheat, wines. *Manufacturing and Processing*—bakery goods, beef, blankets, canned food, cement, clothing, drugs, flour, glassware and pottery, household appliances, leather goods, paper and paper containers, rubber goods, shoes, soaps, stoves, textiles, tires. *Mining*—coal, copper, gold, iodine, iron ore, lead, nitrates, petroleum, silver, zinc. *Forest Products*—pinewood, pulp.

National Anthem: "Cancion Nacional de Chile" ("National Anthem of Chile").

National Holiday: Independence Day, September 18.

Money: *Basic Unit*—peso; 100 centésimos equal 1 peso. For the value of the peso in dollars, see MONEY (table: Exchange Rates).

Tierra del Fuego—Paul Almasy

Santiago—Margaret Durrance, Rapho Guillumette

CHILE, *CHIHL ee*, or *CHEE lay*, is the southernmost country of South America. It clings to the Pacific Ocean side of the Andes Mountains and covers about half the continent's western coast. This narrow, mountainous country is more than 10 times as long as it is wide. Indians gave Chile its name. They called the region *chilli*, meaning *place where the land ends*.

Chile has huge deposits of minerals that account for most of its wealth. Copper, iron ore, and nitrates rank as the country's most important mineral products. Chile is one of the world's largest producers of copper. Large numbers of manufacturing plants and factories make Chile one of the leading industrial nations of Latin America.

About four-fifths of the Chilean people live in cities and towns, and the rest live on farms and ranches. The farms and ranches raise cattle, fruit, wheat, vegetables, and other agricultural products. But Chile does not produce enough food for its growing population. This shortage causes a serious economic problem. Chile must use the money it earns from mineral exports to pay for food imports. The country cannot afford all the machines and spare parts that it needs for industrial expansion.

A few Chilean families have great wealth, but about half the people are poor. The rest belong to a large and growing middle class. About 40 per cent of Chile's families live as comfortably as do city people in Western Europe. But many city laborers, farmers, and miners earn barely enough for their simplest needs. Many poor rural families live in one-room houses that have no electricity or running water. Most poor city people live in tiny shacks in rundown neighborhoods. Few Chileans can afford automobiles, but many in the cities have radios and a growing number have television sets.

A higher percentage of Chileans receive an education than do the people of most other Latin-American countries. Nevertheless, most adults in Chile have gone to school for only a few years. About 90 per cent of the people 15 years old and older can read and write.

The natural beauty of Chile attracts many tourists. Sparkling lakes and the snow-capped peaks of the Andes provide good sports areas. In winter, the mountain slopes attract skiers from all parts of the world. Fishing enthusiasts cast for trout in the lakes and streams. Santiago, the capital and largest city of Chile, offers excellent theater and ballet. Viña del Mar, near Valparaíso, is one of the most fashionable seaside resorts in South America.

This article was contributed by Kalman H. Silvert, former Professor of Politics at New York University and author of Chile: Yesterday and Today *and* Conflict Society: Reaction and Revolution in Latin America.

Chile / GOVERNMENT

Chile's Flag. The white star is for unity, red for the blood of heroes, white for the snow of the Andes, and blue for the sky.

WORLD BOOK map

Chile is over 10 times as long as it is wide. It is only about one-tenth as large as the U.S., not including Alaska and Hawaii.

The Chilean Coat of Arms bears the motto, "by right or by might," in Spanish.

National Government. Throughout most of the 1900's, Chile had freely elected civilian governments headed by a president and a Congress. But in 1973, Chilean military leaders overthrew the civilian government. A military leader became president. The military leaders abolished the Congress and outlawed all political party activities. They established a four-member military *junta* (council) to rule the country.

The leader of the junta serves as president of Chile and holds most of the policy-making authority. The three other junta members and an 18-member Cabinet appointed by the president help the president to carry out the operations of the government.

Local Government. In 1973, the junta divided Chile into 13 military districts for purposes of local government. A governor heads each district. Chile also has 25 provinces. The governor of each military district and the chief official of each province are selected by the president and generally carry out policies determined by the national government.

Courts. The Supreme Court, Chile's highest court, has 13 members. It supervises a national court system that includes 15 courts of appeal. Judges of the Supreme Court and courts of appeal are appointed by the president of Chile from lists submitted by the Supreme Court.

Armed Forces. Men between the ages of 20 and 45 must serve at least one year in the Chilean army, navy or air force. The armed forces have a total membership of about 92,000.

WORLD BOOK photo

The Presidential Palace, in Santiago, occupies an entire city block. It houses the offices of Chile's president.

MAP INDEX

Cities and Towns

City	Population	Key
Ancud	17,617	J 4
Andacollo	9,238	D 2
Angol	30,827	G 4
Antofagasta	162,656	B 2
Arica	117,288	A 2
Buin*	22,308	D 6
Bulnes	9,004	F 5
Calama	60,086	A 2
Cañete	13,244	G 4
Carahue	4,884	H 4
Castro	14,175	G 1
Cauquenes	25,087	F 5
Chañaral	14,385	C 2
Chiguayante	33,257	F 4
Chillán	117,074	F 5
Chuquicamata	20,920	A 2
Coihaique	21,947	H 2
Colina*	13,503	C 6
Collipulli	9,411	G 4
Concepción	200,602	F 1
Constitución	17,558	E 5
Copiapó	62,729	C 2
Coquimbo	68,549	D 2
Coronel	47,826	F 4
Curacautín	10,505	H 5
Curanilahue	16,614	G 4
Curicó	50,580	E 5
El Belloto	14,231	C 5
El Monte*	9,541	D 6
Graneros	11,360	D 6
Illapel	14,509	B 5
Iquique	103,395	A 2
La Calera	33,011	C 5
La Laja	17,733	G 4
La Ligua*	12,916	C 5
La Serena	82,910	D 2
La Unión	22,352	I 4
Lautaro	13,921	H 5
Lebu	19,431	G 4
Limache	20,074	C 5
Linares	53,916	E 5
Llaillay	13,298	C 6
Loncoche	10,634	H 5
Los Andes	33,341	C 6
Los Ángeles	71,853	G 5
Lota	60,895	G 4
María Elena	6,852	A 2
Melipilla	36,855	D 5
Molina	13,058	E 5
Mulchén	17,411	G 5
Nueva Imperial	11,537	H 4
Osorno	90,743	I 4
Ovalle	49,273	D 2
Parral	21,134	F 5
Pedro de Valdivia	5,406	B 2
Peñaflor	26,394	D 6
Penco	27,484	F 4
Pitrufquén	11,401	H 4
Potrerillos	7,495	C 2
Puerto Aisén	9,795	H 2
Puerto Montt	84,491	G 2
Puerto Natales	13,611	J 2
Puerto Varas	13,808	J 4
Punta Arenas	78,247	J 2
Quillota	49,994	C 5
Quilpué	59,585	C 5
Quintero	15,803	C 5
Rancagua	130,940	D 6
Rengo	13,627	D 6
Río Bueno	12,696	I 4
San Antonio	63,294	D 5
San Carlos	24,150	F 5
San Felipe	36,860	C 6
San Fernando	37,436	D 6
San Javier	16,993	E 5
San Pedro*	19,388	F 1
Santa Cruz	11,292	D 5
Santiago	3,899,495	E 2
Schwager	15,719	F 4
Sewell	9,800	D 6
Talagante	24,888	D 6
Talca	129,926	E 5
Talcahuano	187,507	E 1
Taltal	9,851	B 2
Temuco	157,258	H 5
Tocopilla	25,820	A 2
Tomé	38,649	F 4
Traiguén	13,583	G 4
Valdivia	110,486	F 1
Vallenar	40,500	C 2
Valparaíso	266,354	D 2
Victoria	21,062	G 5
Villa Alemana*	47,467	C 5
Villarrica	17,615	H 5
Viña del Mar	277,068	C 5

Source: 1980 official estimates.
*Does not appear on map; key shows general location.

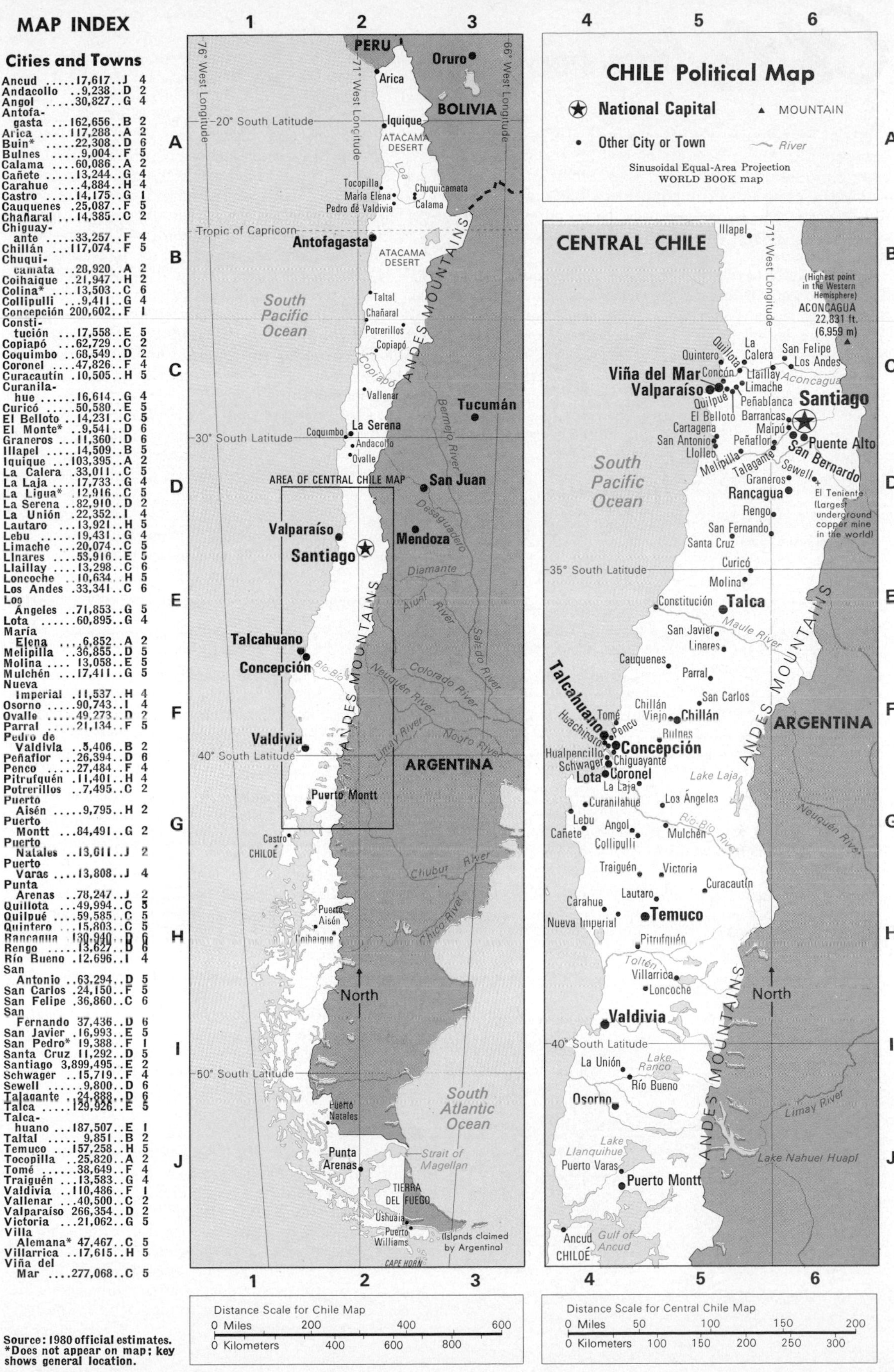

Chile / THE PEOPLE

About 90 per cent of Chile's people live in a valley between the Andes Mountains on the east and the coastal mountains on the west. This thickly populated valley makes up less than a fourth of Chile's land. The rest of the people live in the other three-fourths of the country—on rocky islands, in desert lands, and in mountain forests.

About a third of the Chileans have mixed Indian and Spanish ancestry. Most of the others are descended from Spanish or other European settlers and immigrants. Araucanian Indians make up about 2 per cent of the population.

Food. Chileans eat their main meal in the early afternoon. Most well-to-do families prefer French-style cooking. Their dinner consists of soup, meat or seafood with vegetables, and dessert and coffee. Conger eel, shrimp, swordfish, and tuna are popular among well-to-do and middle-class Chileans. Beans and bread make up the chief foods of most Chilean workers. These people also eat vegetables; such fruits as grapes, lemons, oranges, and plums; and small amounts of cheese, meat, milk, and seafood. Most Chileans drink wine with their meals. Coffee and tea are also popular.

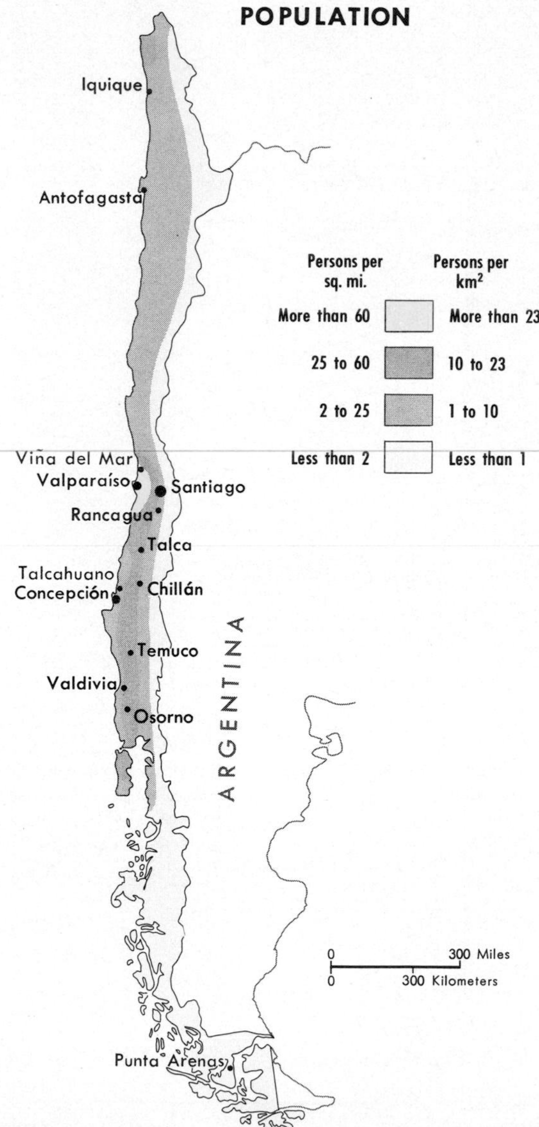

Chileans like thick soups of corn or rice mixed with vegetables and pieces of chicken or other meat. A popular soup called *cazuela de ave* is made of chicken, potatoes, corn, rice, onions, and spicy peppers. *Pastel de choclo*, a baked corn cake, combines grated corn with beaten eggs, minced meat, onions, olives, and raisins.

Clothing. Most Chilean farmworkers wear rough work clothes and sandals called *alpargatas*, which have soles made of rope or rubber. In the cities, most of the people dress much as city people do in the United States, Canada, and Europe.

Chile's cowboy-farmers are called *huasos*. They wear big, flat-topped, brown or black hats; short capes called *mantas;* scarves; leggings with leather fringes; and high-heeled boots. Araucanian Indian women wear bright-colored shawls, woolen headbands, and silver necklaces.

At town festivals, many Chileans dress in colorful Spanish-type costumes. The women wear lace head coverings called *mantillas* and large shell combs.

Shelter. Tenant farmers called *inquilinos* live in one-room houses grouped near the edges of large estates. Most of these houses are made of adobe and have dirt floors and thatched or red-tiled roofs. Most estate owners have large Spanish-style houses with several courtyards. Many owners of large estates live in a city and leave their land in the charge of a manager. The owners themselves run most of the smaller estates.

Most poor city laborers, called *rotos* (tattered ones), live in rough shacks grouped into shantytowns. Some of these shantytowns stand near the centers of cities, but most are on the outskirts. The shantytowns grow so rapidly that they are called *poblaciones callampas* (toadstool towns).

Chile's cities have many handsome steel and glass apartment buildings, hotels, and office buildings. A group of public buildings in Santiago forms one of Latin America's finest city government centers. Some of Santiago's industrial workers live in modern housing developments built by the government. Several mining companies provide modern houses for their workers.

Religion. Chilean law provides freedom of worship and forbids any religious group from taking an official part in the government. Most Chileans are Roman Catholics. Jews and Protestants make up about 5 per cent of the population. Some Araucanian Indians still follow their ancient tribal religion.

Education. Compared to the people of most other Latin-American countries, Chileans are well educated. Almost 90 per cent of Chile's people can read and write. In 1928, the government established a system of free elementary schools. The law requires all children from 7 to 15 years old to attend school. But some country areas have no schools, and the children of some poor city families do not go to school. Few Chileans attend school beyond the elementary grades. Only about 30 per cent of Chile's children go to high school, and less than 1 per cent graduate.

Shostal

Araucanian Indians live on forest reservations in south-central Chile. They still practice ancient crafts, such as weaving blankets on hand looms.

Luis Gonzales

Folk Dancers perform the lively *cueca* to the gay music of guitars. The cueca is Chile's national dance.

Europa Press News Service

The University of Chile in Santiago is the nation's largest educational center. It is supported by the government.

Fishermen who sail the stormy waters of the Chilean archipelago bring their catches to the market of Puerto Montt.

Ewing Krainin

Well-to-Do Chileans spend their vacations at such fashionable Pacific coast resorts as Viña del Mar, near Valparaíso.

Europa Press News Service

United Nations

A Crab Fisherman pulls his catch from the Pacific waters off Chile's coast. Fish and many other kinds of seafood are popular throughout the country.

George Pickow, Three Lions

Brightly Dressed Huasos, Chile's cowboy-farmers, often stage rodeos to display their skill and daring as horsemen.

Soccer is Chile's most popular sport. The players shown below are competing in a game at National Stadium in Santiago.

Europa Press News Service

Chile has almost 8,000 elementary schools but only about 800 high schools and trade schools. Most of the high schools are private institutions. The largest of Chile's eight universities, the government-supported University of Chile in Santiago, has more than 22,500 students. The Catholic University of Chile, also in Santiago, is one of the outstanding Roman Catholic universities in Latin America.

Arts. Chile has made notable contributions in music and literature. The *cueca* is a lively folk dance in which couples swing large handkerchiefs. The guitar is the favorite musical instrument.

The first famous literary work about Chile was a poem called *La Araucana.* It was written by Alonso de Ercilla y Zúñiga, a Spanish army captain stationed in Chile. This poem, published in the late 1500's, describes the struggles of the Araucanian Indians against the Spanish conquerors of Chile.

Claudio Arrau of Chile is one of the world's finest concert pianists. Two Chilean poets have won Nobel prizes for literature. Gabriela Mistral received the prize in 1945, and Pablo Neruda was awarded it in 1971.

Recreation. Soccer is Chile's main sport, as it is in most Latin-American countries. Thousands of Chileans watch professional teams play in large stadiums in Santiago and Valparaíso. Many towns hold celebrations after local soccer matches. People fish for record-size marlin and swordfish in the Pacific Ocean and big trout in the inland lakes. Well-to-do Chileans enjoy horse racing, skiing in the Andes, tennis, and yachting. The most fashionable seaside resorts are in Concón, Viña del Mar, and Zapallar. Cartagena and San Antonio also have resorts.

Health and Welfare. Chile has an unusually high number of cases of tuberculosis, pneumonia, and serious stomach diseases. Physicians blame these illnesses on poor diet, impure water, and unsanitary housing.

More than three-fourths of the Chilean people receive free medical care from the government. Since 1943, many hospitals, public health centers, and water purification systems have been built—some with aid from the United States. Large Chilean cities have ample government and private medical services. But the country's rural areas have a shortage of doctors, nurses, and hospitals.

The University of Chile operates two important medical training institutions—the Inter-American Center of Biostatistics and a radioisotope laboratory. Both receive financial assistance from the Pan American Health Organization. In the biostatistics center, students learn how to gather facts about the condition of people's health. At the laboratory, physicians learn to treat diseases with radioisotopes.

In 1924, Chile established one of the first social security systems in the Western Hemisphere. This system includes separate insurance and welfare organizations called *cajas* for government employees, factory workers, and other laborers. The cajas provide many services in addition to insurance. For example, they make loans, operate restaurants, and sell low-cost food and clothing.

In 1925, Chile started Latin America's first school of social work. Many Latin-American countries have copied Chile's welfare programs and send their social workers to train at this school in Santiago.

Chile/CLIMATE

Chile's mountains, valleys, and islands give the country a variety of climates. But temperatures are generally moderate. Even the desert is not extremely hot. Pacific breezes from the cold Peru Current cool most of the land. Rainfall increases from north to south.

As in all countries south of the equator, the seasons in Chile are the opposite of those in the United States and Canada. Chile's summer comes from December through February, and winter lasts from June through August. Temperatures in the Northern Desert region range from a low of 74° F. (23° C) to a high of 92° F. (33° C). The Central Valley region has a climate similar to that of southern California. Days are warm and nights are cool, with mild, rainy winters and dry summers. In Santiago, the winter low rarely reaches the freezing point and the summer high rarely goes above 84° F. (29° C). The Archipelago region is cold, windy, and rainy all year. Some areas there have 200 inches (510 centimeters) of rain a year. Temperatures in the Archipelago range from 24° to 59° F. (−4° to 15° C).

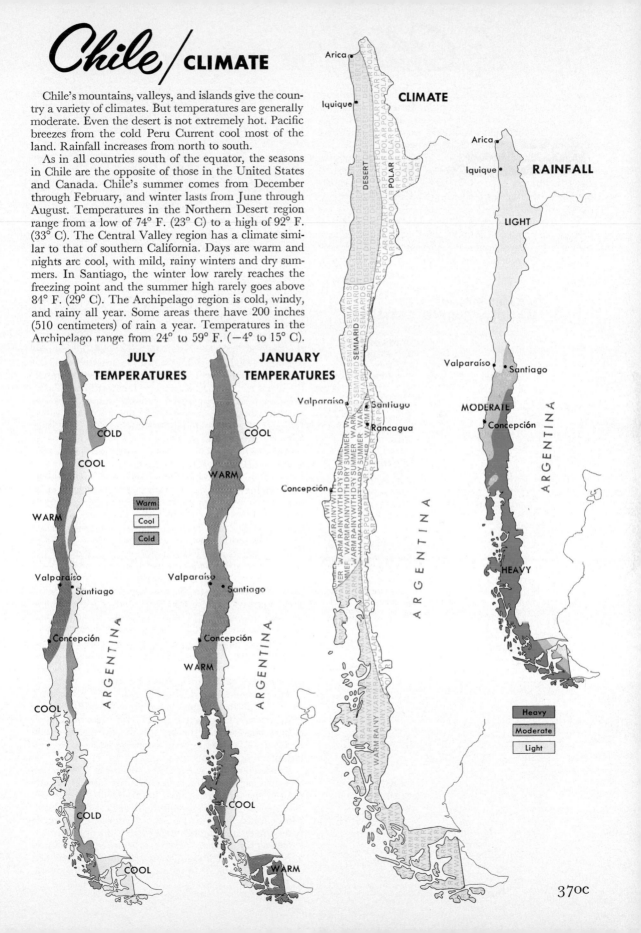

JULY TEMPERATURES
COLD
COOL
WARM
Warm
Cool
Cold
Valparaíso
Santiago
Concepción
ARGENTINA
COOL
COLD
COOL

JANUARY TEMPERATURES
COOL
WARM
Valparaíso
Santiago
Concepción
WARM
ARGENTINA
COOL
WARM

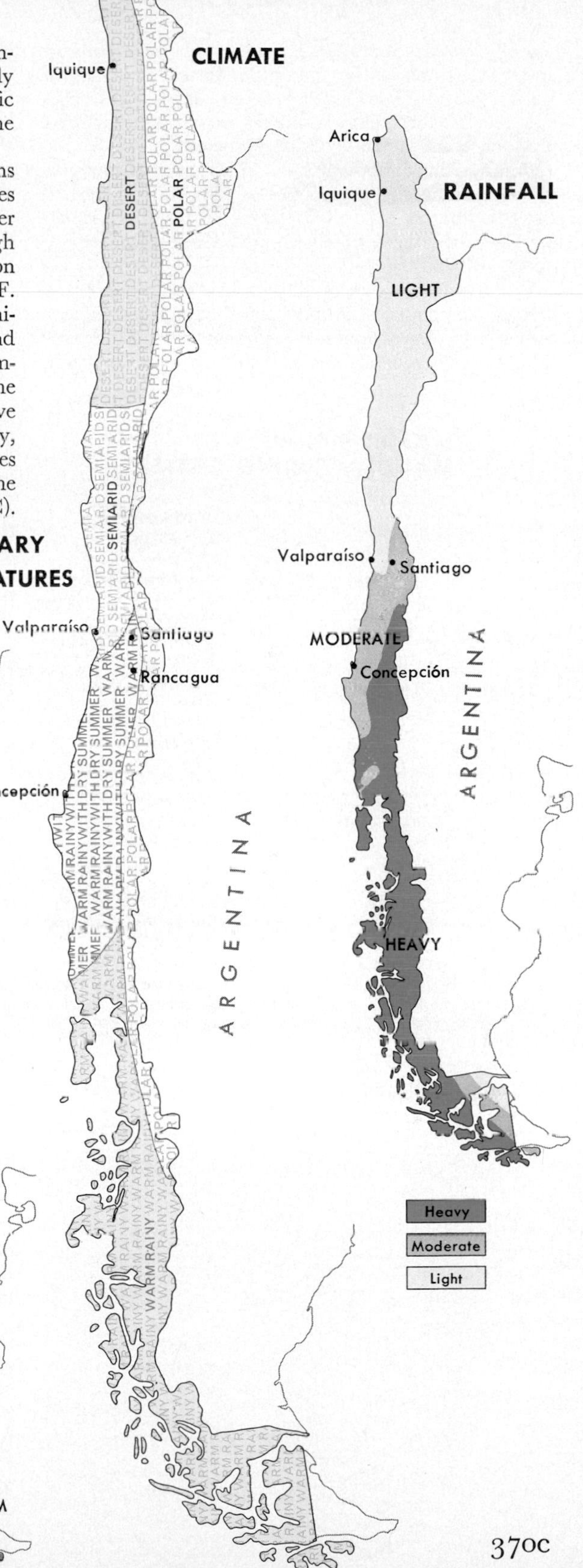

Chile / THE ECONOMY

Chile exports more copper than any other country and ranks among the leading industrial nations of Latin America. But Chile's economy has failed to provide enough food and reasonably priced manufactured products to meet the needs of the people.

Mining. The export value of Chile's mineral products makes mining the nation's most important industry. Copper, iron ore, and nitrates account for about three-fourths of the value of all exports. The mines employ about 100,000 men.

Chile ranks as one of the world's leading copper-producing countries. Almost all the nation's copper comes from three mines—Chuquicamata and Portrerillos in northern Chile and El Teniente in central Chile near Santiago. Chuquicamata produces more copper than any other mine in the world, and El Teniente is the largest underground copper mine anywhere. United States copper companies owned the three mines until 1967, when the Chilean government purchased partial control. In 1971, Chile placed the mines under complete government ownership.

Iron ore is Chile's second most important export. Most of the high-grade ore comes from the area around La Serena in north-central Chile. Other large iron-ore deposits lie in the Andes east of Antofagasta. The government owns and operates the iron mines.

Chile provides the world's entire supply of natural sodium nitrate. This mineral is used as a fertilizer and in making explosives. Chile also produces most of the world's crude iodine, which is taken from sodium nitrate. Almost all the nitrate comes from a narrow strip 450 miles (724 kilometers) long in the Atacama Desert.

Most Chilean coal is dug from undersea mines in the Gulf of Arauco, about 300 miles (480 kilometers) south of Valparaíso. Chile's industries use most of the coal. Petroleum comes from government-owned wells on the island of Tierra del Fuego and the nearby mainland.

Small mining operations produce, in order of importance, manganese, lead and zinc, gold, and silver. Deposits of such materials as limestone and gypsum fully meet the needs of Chile's construction industry.

Manufacturing. Chile is one of the leading manufacturing countries of Latin America. Most of its factories produce goods for home use, such as clothing, food products, and home appliances. One of the most modern steel plants in the Western Hemisphere operates at Huachipato near Concepción. Concepción, Santiago, and Valparaíso are Chile's leading manufacturing centers. Manufacturing employs more than a fifth of Chile's workers and accounts for about a fourth of the country's total economic production.

Major food products, in order of importance, include flour; canned fish, fruits, and vegetables; condensed and powdered milk; and bakery goods. Chile produces such textile products as blankets; clothing; and cotton, rayon, and woolen cloth. Other products, in order of importance, include paper and paper containers, heaters and stoves, household appliances, cleaning powders and soaps, glassware and pottery, cement, shoes and other leather goods, tires, and medicines.

Agriculture employs about a third of Chile's work force. But farm production accounts for only about a tenth of the total production of Chile's economy. Agriculture lags behind the rest of the economy largely because of wasteful land management and old-fashioned farming methods.

From the 1500's, when Chile became a Spanish colony, to the mid-1960's, a few wealthy families owned most of the farm and ranch lands. Their large estates were called *fundos*. Tenant farmers worked on the land. Most Chilean farmers who did not work on these estates barely made a living on their small plots of land.

During the 1960's, the government began a land reform program. It bought many large estates, divided the land, and sold it to tenant farmers. Rural coopera-

MAJOR MINING AND MANUFACTURING CENTERS

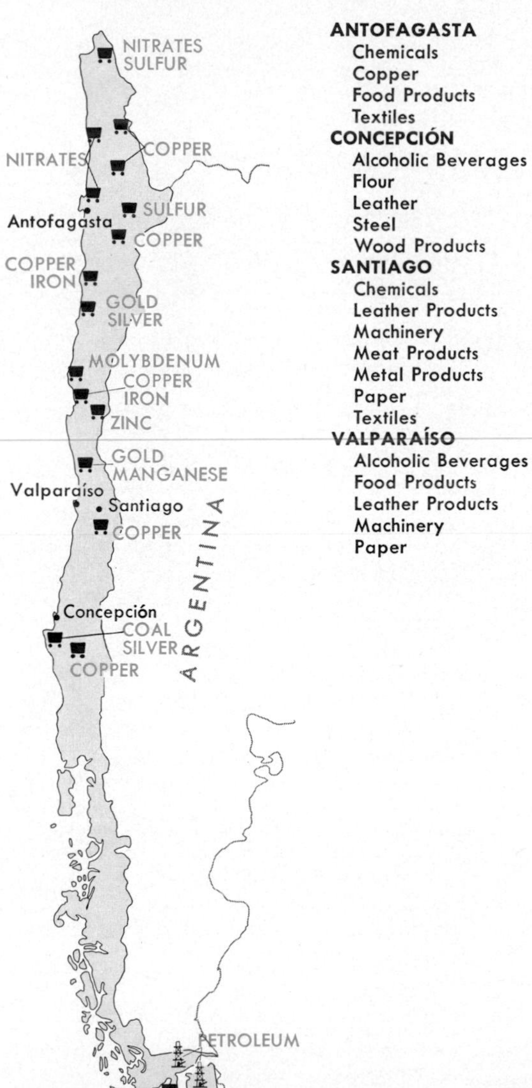

Three Lions

Sheep Raising is a major agricultural industry in Chile. The highest quality wool comes from sheep that graze in the southern province of Magallanes.

tives, training programs, and government credit helped the new farm owners. In the 1970's, the government speeded up the land reform program.

Cattle and wheat together account for almost a third of all Chilean agricultural production. In addition to cattle, the livestock industry produces hogs and sheep. Grains other than wheat are, in order of importance, oats, corn, rice, barley, and rye. Other important crops include beans, peas, and potatoes. Chile also produces flaxseed, hemp, sunflowers, and tobacco.

Chile's fruits and wines supply its entire home market and also provide some exports. The fruits include apples, cherries, grapes, lemons, oranges, peaches, and pears.

Foreign Trade. Chile exports more than it imports. But more money goes out than comes in because the country makes large payments on foreign debts. Chile's main exports, in order of importance, are copper, iron ore, nitrates, and manganese ore. Chemical products, farming and mining tools, food, industrial machinery and equipment, and transportation equipment make up the major imports.

European countries trade extensively with Chile. Beginning in the early 1960's, Chile's trade increased with Argentina and other South American countries. Chile is a member of an economic union called the Latin American Integration Association.

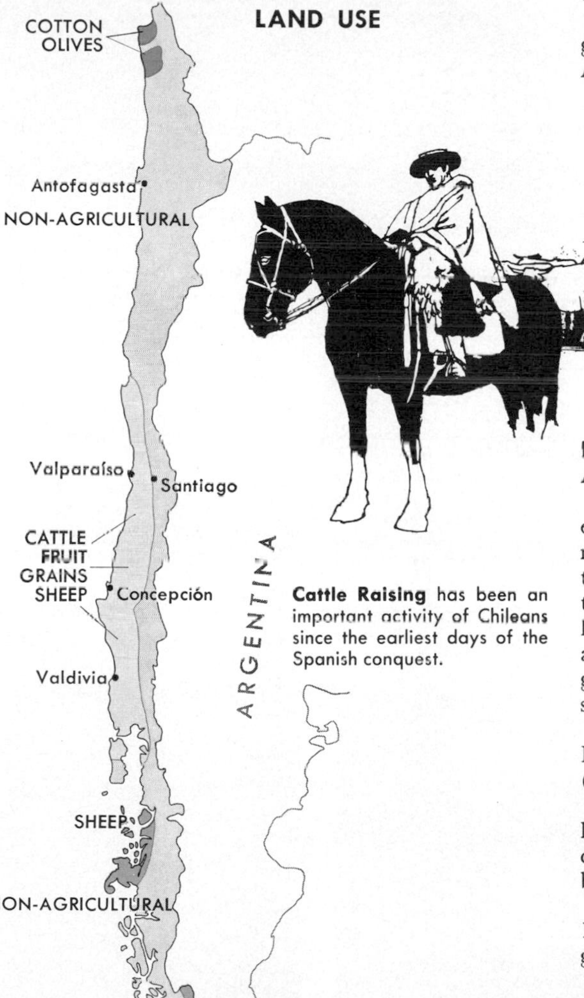

by Donald M. Taka for WORLD BOOK

Cattle Raising has been an important activity of Chileans since the earliest days of the Spanish conquest.

Transportation and Communication. Most travelers enter and leave Chile by air. Airlines, highways, and railroads provide transportation in northern and central Chile. Southern Chile depends largely on air transport and coastal shipping. Most Chilean cities have paved streets, but dirt roads connect many cities and towns, especially in the south-central region. The government operates Chile's telephone and telegraph systems.

Railroads link Chile with Argentina, Bolivia, and Peru. The railroad system covers about 5,000 miles (8,000 kilometers). The government operates most of it.

Chile has about 30,000 miles (48,000 kilometers) of highways. The chief ones link Santiago with Concepción and Valparaíso. The Pan American Highway runs between Peru and Puerto Montt, Chile.

In spite of its long coastline, Chile has only about 135 cargo ships. Most of them are too old to provide good service.

Chile has about 60 daily newspapers, about 135 radio stations, and 5 television stations. The government operates one of the TV stations, and four universities operate the others.

Chile / NATURAL RESOURCES

Chile has vast natural resources of minerals, rich land, forests, and power sources.

Minerals account for most of the country's wealth. The Chilean Andes probably have the largest copper deposits in the world. The Atacama Desert has large quantities of nitrates and iodine. Chile's iron ore and coal deposits rank among the largest in Latin America. Other minerals include gold, manganese, molybdenum, and silver. Important chemicals include borax, phosphates, potash, and salt. Chile also has large supplies of limestone, gypsum, and other materials used in constructing roads and buildings. Petroleum deposits lie at the southern end of the country.

Land suitable for farming amounts to about $2\frac{1}{2}$ acres (1 hectare) for each Chilean. Few countries in the Western Hemisphere have that much farmland in relation to their populations. The Central Valley is Chile's best farming region. It has rich soil, snow-fed streams, winter rains, and summer sunshine. Chile's southern region provides over 15 million acres (6 million hectares) of fine grasslands, used chiefly for grazing sheep.

Forests cover a fifth of the country. They supply wood for Chile's pulp and paper industry. Much pine is cut for export, mostly to Argentina. Even so, Chile uses only a small part of its forests.

Water Power. Many short, swift rivers provide the factories with most of their electricity. Much additional water power from the rivers awaits development by government hydroelectric projects.

Fisheries. The Pacific waters off Chile's long coast teem with food fish and many kinds of shellfish. Since the mid-1960's, commercial fishing has become an important industry in Chile. Much of the annual catch is used in the production of fishmeal and fish oil.

Leo Matiz, Pix from Publix

Nitrate Workers blast natural sodium nitrate from the Atacama Desert. The nitrate is used as fertilizer and in making explosives. Crude iodine also comes from sodium nitrate. Until the 1920's, when Germany began exporting man-made nitrate, Chile provided the world's entire supply of the mineral.

Rapho Guillumette

The Copper-Mining Town of Sewell clings to an Andean mountainside southeast of Santiago. It is the site of El Teniente, the largest underground copper mine in the world.

Huachipato Steel Mill is one of the most efficient steel plants in the Western Hemisphere. It was built in the late 1940's with the help of U.S. engineers.

United Nations

Hydroelectric Plant at Los Molles converts water power from the Andes into electricity. Power is generated by water rushing down through a 4,000-foot (1,200-meter) pipeline.

United Nations

Chile / LAND REGIONS

Long, narrow Chile stretches along more than half the Pacific coastline of South America. The country is 2,650 miles (4,265 kilometers) long, but only about 225 miles (362 kilometers) wide at its widest point. The Andes tower between Chile and eastern South America. The Chilean Andes include 22,572-foot (6,880-meter) *Ojos del Salado* (Salt Springs Peak), the second highest mountain in the Western Hemisphere. A lower coastal range of mountains, 1,000 to 7,000 feet (300 to 2,100 meters) high, rises steeply along Chile's Pacific coastline.

Many lakes lie among the snow-capped Andes. More than 30 short rivers cut across Chile from the Andes to the Pacific. The rivers provide water for irrigation and serve as sources of hydroelectric power. Waterfalls make the rivers useless for transportation.

The Northern Desert extends about 1,100 miles (1,770 kilometers) from the Peruvian border to the Aconcagua River, north of Valparaíso. This region covers a third of Chile. Over one million persons, some of them miners, live there. The Atacama Desert, one of the world's driest areas, covers most of the region's northern 700 miles (1,100 kilometers). Its hills contain Chile's greatest wealth, large deposits of copper, nitrates, borax, and sulfur. Fruits and barley grow in irrigated valleys from the Copiapó River to the Aconcagua 400 miles (640 kilometers) south. The Andes are rich in gold, silver, copper, nickel, lead, and manganese.

The Central Valley, fertile and beautiful, spreads 600 miles (970 kilometers) south from the Aconcagua River to Puerto Montt. About 85 of every 100 persons in Chile live in this valley, north of the Bío-Bío River. Here are Santiago, the capital; Concepción, an industrial center; and Valparaíso, Chile's main port and fishing center. Orchards, pasture land, and irrigated fields of grain cover the area. Mines produce, in order of importance, copper, manganese, molybdenum, gold, silver, and cobalt.

South of the Bío-Bío River, the region is heavily forested. Where the forests have been cut down, farmers raise, in order of importance, wheat, potatoes, oats, hay, barley, and apples. Chile's Lake District, in the mountains, occupies the eastern portion of the region.

The Archipelago extends south about 1,000 miles (1,600 kilometers), from Puerto Montt to Cape Horn. More than 250,000 Chileans live in the Archipelago. This cold, rainy region has towering mountains, dense forests, and many windswept islands. One of Chile's greatest sheep-raising areas is located at the southeastern tip of the mainland and on the island of Tierra del Fuego. The sheep-raising center, Punta Arenas, is on the mainland side of the Strait of Magellan. The stormy strait separates Tierra del Fuego from the mainland.

Islands. Chile owns Easter Island, 2,400 miles (3,860 kilometers) west of the mainland, and the Juan Fernández Islands, 400 miles (640 kilometers) westward. See Easter Island; Juan Fernández.

Physical Features Index

Specially created for **World Book Encyclopedia** by Rand McNally and World Book editors

Chile / HISTORY

Pedro de Valdivia led a Spanish force into Chile from Peru in 1540. He founded the city of Santiago, now the capital of Chile.

by Tom Dunnington for WORLD BOOK, adapted from sketch by Fr. Pedro Subercaseaux

Spain ruled Chile for about 300 years. A few Spaniards with titles of nobility held power, and the people had no voice in the government. Ever since Chile won independence in 1818, the nation has progressed toward democratic government. It won its rich copper and nitrate lands in a war with Peru and Bolivia that ended in 1883. Since then, good times or bad times in Chile have depended largely on the rise and fall of the world demand for copper and nitrates.

Spanish Conquest. Before white men arrived in what is now Chile, Araucanian Indians lived in the region. During the 1400's, the Inca Indians pushed south from Peru and conquered northern Chile. But they never defeated the Araucanians in central and southern Chile.

The Spaniards defeated the Incas in 1532 and seized their gold and other riches. In 1535, Diego de Almagro, one of the Spanish conquerors of Peru, invaded Chile. He found no gold there and returned to Peru. Another Spaniard, Pedro de Valdivia, led a group of settlers to Chile in 1540. In 1541, Valdivia founded Santiago, which became Chile's capital. For 300 years, the Araucanians continued to fight settlers south of the Bío Bío River. In 1883, the Indians agreed to live peacefully on reservations given them by the Chilean government.

From the 1500's to the early 1800's, the viceroy of Peru governed Chile under the rule of Spain. Spain paid little attention to Chile because it produced no gold or silver. But the Spaniards who colonized Chile became prosperous by raising cattle and wheat. They sold most of their products in Peru.

The Spanish colonists held most of the land under grants from their king. They considered the Indians who lived on the land part of the property and forced the Indians to work for them. In 1791, Spain freed the Indians. The Spaniards brought more than 10,000 Negro slaves to Chile from Peru to work on the land.

The first move to end Spain's rule came in 1810, when a *junta* (council) composed largely of landowners declared Chile independent. Spanish forces from Peru regained control of Chile in 1814.

Independence. Bernardo O'Higgins, a soldier, won permanent independence for Chile. His Irish father had been a viceroy of Peru, and his mother was born in Chile of Spanish parents. In 1817, O'Higgins and José de San Martín, an Argentine general, led an army from Argentina across the Andes Mountains. They defeated the Spanish at Chacabuco, and then won final victory at the Maipo River on April 5, 1818. O'Higgins became dictator of Chile.

O'Higgins wrote Chile's first constitution. He made enemies of Chile's wealthy landowners because he taxed them to build schools and roads. O'Higgins also took away the landowners' Spanish titles and tried to break up their big estates. The landowners rebelled in 1823 and forced O'Higgins to resign.

Years of Development. Between 1823 and 1891, Chileans laid the foundation for much of their nation's present political and economic life. A constitution adopted in 1833 stayed in effect until 1925. It formed the basis of the next—and present—constitution. Political parties were formed and the tradition of civilian control over the military was established. In 1823, Chile became the first country in the Western Hemisphere to abolish slavery completely. In 1883, the nation won possession of its mineral-rich northern lands.

A series of weak governments ruled Chile from 1823 to 1830. Diego Portales, a wealthy trader, seized power in 1830 and ruled as dictator until he was assassinated in 1837. Portales supervised the preparation of the 1833 constitution. It gave Chile a strong president elected by a congress and it granted many powers to the Roman Catholic Church. The constitution limited voting to men 25 and older who owned property and could read and write.

Portales led one of Chile's first political parties, the Conservative Party. The Liberal Party opposed the Conservatives. Wealthy landowners made up both parties. The farmers and workers had no party and most could not vote anyway. In the 1860's, some Liberals broke from their party and formed the Radical Party.

In 1836, Chile declared war on Peru and Bolivia to

Oil painting by José Gil de Castro; Collection of Luis Alvarez Urquieta (Organization of American States, Washington, D.C.)

by Tom Dunnington for WORLD BOOK, adapted from painting by Fr. Pedro Subercaseaux

Bernardo O'Higgins, *left,* was the hero of Chilean independence. A famous picture, *The Embrace at Maipú,* shows O'Higgins with his wounded arm in a sling as he greets Argentine General José de San Martín after their 1818 defeat of the Spanish forces at the Maipo River.

prevent them from forming a confederation. Portales believed such a confederation would hurt Chile's economy. Chile won the war in 1839. In 1866, Chile joined forces with Peru and Bolivia to fight off an attempt by Spain to regain its former colonies. The three nations defeated Spain in 1869. In 1879, Chile turned against Peru and Bolivia in the War of the Pacific. Chile won this war in 1883. The Chileans took the provinces of Tacna, Arica, and Tarapacá from Peru and the province of Atacama from Bolivia. Chile returned Tacna to Peru in 1929 but kept the other provinces with their valuable deposits of nitrates and copper (see TACNA-ARICA DISPUTE).

Chile also carried on a boundary dispute with Argentina during the 1800's. The two countries reached agreement in 1902. They built a huge statue of Christ to symbolize the peace (see CHRIST OF THE ANDES).

Era of Change. Income from Atacama's copper and nitrates enriched Chile's treasury. But the new wealth also brought violence and change to the nation.

In 1891, President José Manuel Balmaceda tried to use some of the money for public works that would improve living conditions. Congress opposed him, and civil war broke out. More than 10,000 Chileans died in the fighting. Balmaceda's forces were defeated, and he killed himself.

Congress then voted to limit the power of the president and to increase its own power. After 1891, Congress could depose members of the Cabinet and reject the president's budget. Congress controlled the government from 1891 to 1925. During this period, Chile built many warships but spent little to improve public services. Factories were built and the cities grew. The first trade unions were formed, and the number of political parties increased.

During World War I (1914-1918), Chile remained neutral. The nation's industries expanded because of the wartime demand for nitrates used in making explosives. Industrial growth led to an enlarged middle class of clerks, professional men, and shopkeepers.

A few Chileans made fortunes during the war, but most of the people still worked hard for low wages. After the war, unemployment spread and many people went hungry. Riots and strikes created a state of rebellion during the presidential election campaign of 1920. A large number of middle-class people became members of the Radical Party. The Radicals joined forces with the factory workers and miners who formed the Communist and Socialist-Labor parties. These three parties supported one candidate, Arturo Alessandri Palma. He received the largest number of votes, but not a majority. Congress declared Alessandri president.

Years of Progress. Since 1920, Chile's middle class and laborers have had a strong influence on govern-

IMPORTANT DATES IN CHILE

1535 Spanish soldiers invaded Chile from Peru.

1541 Pedro de Valdivia founded Santiago.

1810 (September 18) Chile proclaimed its independence.

1814 Spain regained Chile.

1818 Chile won independence in the Battle of the Maipo River.

1822 Bernardo O'Higgins wrote the first constitution.

1823 Chile abolished slavery.

1833 Diego Portales had Chile's second constitution written.

1891 Congress seized power.

1925 A new constitution restored power to the president and established free schools.

1925-1931 Carlos Ibáñez del Campo ruled Chile as dictator.

1939 The Chilean government's development corporation launched its industrialization program.

1948 President Gabriel González Videla led an expedition to Antarctica and claimed part of it for Chile.

1949 Women won the right to vote in national elections.

1960 An earthquake and tidal wave killed more than 5,700 Chileans and caused over $600 million in damage.

1969 Congress lowered the voting age to 18.

1970 Salvador Allende Gossens, the first Marxist to be freely elected to head a nation in the Western Hemisphere, became president.

1973 Military leaders overthrew Allende's government and took control of Chile.

ment policy. They have helped shape Chile's economy around industrial development.

In 1925, during Alessandri's presidency, the 1833 constitution was rewritten. The new constitution restored power to the president and provided that presidents be elected directly by the people. All men 21 or older could vote if they could read and write. It established free schools and made public welfare a government responsibility.

Alessandri had political enemies who fought him bitterly. In 1924 and again in 1925, they forced him to go into temporary exile in Italy. Military officers, led by Carlos Ibáñez del Campo, seized the government in 1925. Ibáñez ruled as dictator from 1925 to 1931. But he failed to solve economic problems caused by a worldwide depression. Riots similar to those in 1920 sent Ibáñez into temporary exile in Argentina. Alessandri was elected president again in 1932. During his term, Chile had a slow economic recovery. In 1934, Chilean women won the right to vote in local elections.

The Radical Party, combined with left wing parties, won the 1938 election, and Pedro Aguirre Cerda became president. Aguirre Cerda set up a government corporation to supervise Chile's industrial expansion. This corporation, the Corporación de Fomento de la Producción (CORFO), has built irrigation and electric power projects, operated mines, and opened factories.

In 1943, during World War II, Chile broke relations with Germany and Japan. President Juan Antonio Ríos, a member of the Radical Party, based Chile's major aid to the Allies on copper, nitrates, and other war supplies. Ríos died in office in 1946.

In the 1946 election, Gabriel González Videla won the largest number of votes, but not a majority. Congress named him president. González personally led an expedition to Antarctica in 1948. He claimed a large area of Antarctica for Chile and named it O'Higgins Land. In 1949, Chilean women won the right to vote in national elections. In 1952, the voters gave Carlos Ibáñez, the former dictator, more votes than any other candidate, but not a majority. Congress declared him president. Ibáñez did not rule as a dictator, as he had before.

In the 1958 election, Jorge Alessandri Rodríguez, a son of Arturo Alessandri Palma, received the most votes, but not a majority. Congress named him president. Alessandri could not slow down inflation, and an earthquake and tidal wave in 1960 further upset the economy. In 1961, the government launched an economic development program and built new housing for workers.

Recent Developments. Eduardo Frei Montalva, the leader of the Christian Democratic Party, became president in 1964 after winning a majority of votes. Under Frei's leadership, Chili began a program of industrial expansion, land reform, and school construction.

In the 1970 presidential election, Chile's political parties divided into three groups that centered around the Conservative and Liberal parties on the right; the Christian Democrats in the center; and the Communist, Marxist, Radical, and Socialist parties on the left. The leftist candidate, Salvador Allende Gossens, won the most votes—a little more than a third of the total—and Congress named him president. Allende became the first Marxist to be elected democratically to head any country in the Western Hemisphere.

Under Allende's leadership, the government took control of a number of industries and stepped up land reform. These actions caused many investors to send their money to other countries. Many middle- and upper-class Chileans opposed Allende, but many lower-class farmers and workers supported him. Demonstrations both in favor of and against the government occurred during the early 1970's. Inflation and other economic problems led to widespread strikes.

In September 1973, after months of unrest, military leaders overthrew the government. They reported that Allende had committed suicide after refusing to resign from office. The military leaders formed a junta, headed by General Augusto Pinochet Ugarte, to rule Chile. Fighting then erupted between supporters and opponents of the junta. The junta arrested many of its opponents, restricted freedom of the press, and banned political parties. Pinochet's government returned most state-owned companies to private ownership. In the early 1980's, some demonstrations and riots against the government took place. KALMAN H. SILVERT

Related Articles in WORLD BOOK include:

BIOGRAPHIES

Allende Gossens, Salvador
Mistral, Gabriela
Neruda, Pablo
O'Higgins (family)

CITIES

Santiago
Valparaíso
Viña del Mar

OTHER RELATED ARTICLES

Andes Mountains
Atacama Desert
Cape Horn
Cerro Tololo Inter-American Observatory
Christ of the Andes
Easter Island
Juan Fernández
Latin America
Ojos del Salado
Patagonia
San Martín, José de
South America
Tierra del Fuego

Outline

I. Government

II. The People
- A. Food
- B. Clothing
- C. Shelter
- D. Religion
- E. Education
- F. Arts
- G. Recreation
- H. Health and Welfare

III. Climate

IV. The Economy
- A. Mining
- B. Manufacturing
- C. Agriculture
- D. Foreign Trade
- E. Transportation and Communication

V. Natural Resources
- A. Minerals
- B. Land
- C. Forests
- D. Water Power
- E. Fisheries

VI. Land Regions
- A. The Northern Desert
- B. The Central Valley
- C. The Archipelago
- D. Islands

VII. History

Questions

Where do most of Chile's people live?
How did Chile get its name?
Who were the original inhabitants of Chile?
What changes resulted from the constitution of 1925?
Where are Chile's chief copper and nitrate deposits?
What part did Chile take in World Wars I and II?
What is an *inquilino?* A *roto?* A *fundo?* A *caja?*
Who was Diego Portales?

Reading and Study Guide

See *Chile* in the RESEARCH GUIDE/INDEX, Volume 22, for a *Reading and Study Guide.*

Additional Resources

ALEXANDER, ROBERT J. *The Tragedy of Chile.* Greenwood, 1978. Studies the effects of authoritarian rule in modern Chile.

BIANCHI, LOIS. *Chile in Pictures.* Sterling, 1977. Covers the land, history, government, people, and economy. For younger readers.

BOWEN, J. DAVID. *The Land and People of Chile.* Rev. ed. Lippincott, 1976. For younger readers.

GALDAMES, LUIS. *A History of Chile.* Ed. by Isaac J. Cox. Russell & Russell, 1964. A standard history, originally pub. in 1906.

LOVEMAN, BRIAN. *Struggle in the Countryside: Politics and Rural Labor in Chile, 1919-1973.* Indiana Univ. Press, 1976.

CHILE SALTPETER. See SALTPETER.

CHILI CON CARNE, *CHIL ee kun KAHR nee,* is a Mexican dish that consists of minced red peppers and meat. Cooks often add kidney beans to this highly seasoned dish. The Spanish word *chili* means *red pepper. Con carne* means *with meat.*

CHILKAT INDIANS. See INDIAN, AMERICAN (Table of Tribes).

CHILL, WIND. See WIND CHILL.

CHILLICOTHE, *CHIL uh KAHTH ee,* Ohio (pop. 23,420), is an industrial city and trading center for a fertile farming region. The city lies on the Scioto River in south-central Ohio, 45 miles (72 kilometers) south of Columbus (see OHIO [political map]). Chief industries in the city include the manufacture of paper, aluminum kitchen utensils, shoes, floor tile, and railroad springs. Chillicothe served as the first state capital (1803-1810), and was the capital again from 1812 to 1816. It has a mayor-council government. The city is the seat of Ross County. See also MOUND CITY GROUP NATIONAL MONUMENT. JAMES H. RODABAUGH

CHILLS AND FEVER. See FEVER; MALARIA.

CHIMAERA. See FISH (Sharks, Rays, and Chimaeras; picture: The Chief Kinds of Fish).

CHIMBORAZO, *CHIM boh RAH zoh,* is a volcanic mountain in the Andes of Ecuador, about 120 miles (193 kilometers) from the Pacific Coast. For location, see ECUADOR (map). Snow-covered Mount Chimborazo rises 20,561 feet (6,267 meters) above sea level. It is the highest of about 30 Andes peaks that form an "avenue of volcanoes." MARGUERITE UTTLEY

CHIMERA, *ky MEER uh,* was a fire-breathing monster in Greek mythology. It had the head of a lion and the tail of a dragon. Its body was shaggy like that of a goat. For many years the Chimera laid waste the lands of Lycia and Caria. The king of Lycia ordered Bellerophon to destroy the monster. The goddess Athena gave Bellerophon a golden bridle with which he could tame the winged horse Pegasus. Then Bellerophon flew over the Chimera and killed it. The word *chimerical* is used to describe anything wild or fantastic. In art and architecture, a chimera is a representation of a fantastic, imaginary monster. PADRAIC COLUM

See also GARGOYLE; PEGASUS.

CHIMES, also called *tubular bells,* are a percussion instrument that consists of 18 to 20 brass or steel tubes hung on a frame. The tubes have a range of $1\frac{1}{2}$ octaves. The tubes are arranged with low notes on the left and high notes on the right. The player strikes the tubes with one or two mallets of pressed leather. The chimes produce deep, ringing sounds. The player can sustain the sounds by operating a *sustaining pedal* with the foot. Chimes made of stone were used in the Far East as early as 2300 B.C. In 1885, John Hampton of Coventry, England, developed the kind of chimes used today in bands, orchestras, and other musical groups. JOHN H. BECK

See also MUSIC (picture: Percussion Instruments).

CHIMNEY ROCK. See NORTH CAROLINA (Places to Visit).

CHIMNEY SWEEP is a worker who climbs up chimneys to clean out the soot. A brush on a long handle is also sometimes called a chimney sweep. In earlier times, many chimney sweeps worked in Europe and in North America. A few of them still work at the trade.

CHIMNEY SWIFT. See SWIFT.

CHIMPANZEE is an African ape. Chimpanzees are one of the four kinds of apes, along with gibbons, gorillas, and orang-utans. The chimpanzee ranks as one of the most intelligent animals and resembles human beings more closely than does any other animal.

Chimpanzees have many characteristics that make them especially interesting and valuable to human beings. The chimpanzee's playfulness and curiosity make it a popular animal at zoos. Young chimpanzees can be tamed and trained easily, and they make excellent circus performers. Scientists use chimpanzees in medical and psychological research because the animals have many similarities to human beings.

Most zoologists classify chimpanzees into two species. The first species is known simply as the chimpanzee. It lives throughout much of Central Africa, from Lake Victoria in the east to Sierra Leone in the west. Scientists divide this species into three subspecies—the common, or masked, chimpanzee; the tschego; and the eastern, or long-haired, chimpanzee. The second species, the pygmy chimpanzee, lives only in Zaire, south of the Congo River and west of the Lualaba River. This article discusses primarily the first species.

The Body of a Chimpanzee. Chimpanzees range in height from $3\frac{1}{4}$ feet (1 meter) to $5\frac{1}{2}$ feet (1.7 meters). An adult male chimpanzee weighs about 110 pounds (50 kilograms). An adult female weighs about 90 pounds (41 kilograms). Pygmy chimpanzees are somewhat smaller and lighter.

The chimpanzee's body is covered with long, black hair. Like the other apes, the chimpanzee does not have a tail. It has large ears, and its arms are longer than its legs. The chimpanzee's long hands are well adapted for grasping and holding onto objects. In addition, the big toes of the chimpanzee face sideways like thumbs, enabling the animal to grasp branches with its feet while climbing.

Baldness is common among both male and female chimpanzees. The bald area in males forms a triangle on the forehead. The bald patch in female chimpanzees extends from the forehead to the crown of the head.

The Life of a Chimpanzee. Chimpanzees live in forests, including tropical rain forests; and in forested, grassy plains. They move about in search of food and usually range over an area of 10 to 20 square miles (26 to 52 square kilometers). Chimpanzees travel in groups that vary in number and change members frequently. There are four chief types of groups: (1) bands of adult males and females, (2) all-male bands, (3) bands of mothers and their infants, and (4) mixed bands of both

Richard Wrangham, Anthro-Photo

Chimpanzees live together in groups. The chimpanzees shown in the background are grooming each other. They pick through each other's hair to remove any dirt, burs, or insects. Adult chimpanzees spend about an hour a day grooming.

sexes and all ages. Sometimes a male chimpanzee may travel alone.

Chimpanzees live both in trees and on the ground. They spend from 50 to 75 per cent of each day in the trees. They sleep in tree nests made of branches, leaves, and twigs. The animals make new nests each night rather than return to former nests. They build the nests at least 15 feet (4.6 meters) above the ground. When resting during the day, chimpanzees lie along a limb and grasp overhead branches, or they may sprawl out on the ground.

Chimpanzees usually walk on all fours, supporting the upper part of their bodies with their knuckles. They seldom stand erect to walk or run, except when excited or to see over tall grass. The males occasionally show off their strength by walking upright, waving branches, and screaming loudly.

The chimpanzee's chief foods include fruits, leaves, palm nuts, seeds, and stems. They also eat ants, bird eggs, fish, and termites. They occasionally kill and eat baboons, wild hogs called *bush pigs*, and red-tail monkeys.

Chimpanzees in the wild mate chiefly from August to November, but those in captivity mate more frequently throughout the year. Most female chimpanzees bear their first young at the age of 11 or 12 years. The pregnancy period lasts about 230 days. In most cases, the female gives birth to a single baby, though twins do occur. Female chimpanzees generally give birth once every three or four years.

The females raise their young almost entirely by themselves. The infants ride under the mother's body, supported by her arm, until they are about 5 months old. Then they ride on the mother's back. Young chimpanzees often chase one another playfully through the trees. Chimpanzees leave their mothers at about 6 years of age.

Chimpanzees seldom fight among themselves or become aggressive. The adults spend about an hour each day in a friendly, social activity called *grooming*. During this period, two or more chimpanzees sit and pick through each other's hair. They remove any dirt, insects, leaves, or burs that they might find.

Chimpanzees express themselves vocally by means of barks, grunts, and screams. When they find a large food supply, the animals jump through the trees, hoot loudly, and beat on tree trunks. This activity alerts all other chimpanzees within hearing distance. They also communicate with body postures, facial expressions, and hand gestures. Chimpanzees may greet each other by

The Skeleton of a Chimpanzee

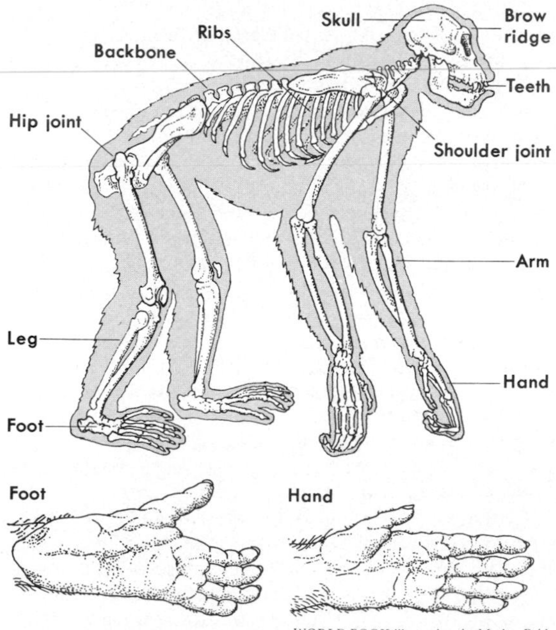

WORLD BOOK illustrations by Marion Pahl

A Chimpanzee's Hands and Feet are well adapted for grasping branches and other objects. The hands have long, muscular fingers. The big toes of the feet face sideways like thumbs, which helps the chimpanzee grasp branches while climbing.

touching various parts of the other's body or by embracing. Their facial expressions cover a wide variety of emotions, including excitement, fear, and rage.

Chimpanzees make and use tools more than any other animal except human beings. For example, they strip the leaves from stems and use the stems as tools to catch termites. They also use leaves to make "sponges" for soaking up water to drink.

Biologists believe chimpanzees live from 30 to 38 years in their natural surroundings. They generally live from 40 to 60 years in zoos and research centers.

Research on Chimpanzees. Chimpanzees and human beings share many physical and social traits. For example, human and chimpanzee *polypeptides* (compounds that make up proteins) are 99 per cent identical. In addition, human beings and chimpanzees both have similar abilities to solve certain problems.

Because of the chimpanzee's many similarities to human beings, scientists frequently use these apes in medical and psychological research. Chimpanzees have been subjects in studies on alcoholism and many other diseases. Scientists also use chimpanzees in studying the effects of various drugs and medical problems associated with organ transplants.

Psychologists use chimpanzees in the study of certain kinds of behavior, such as communication, intelligence, and learning. In one experiment, chimpanzees were shown an object and then given two objects to feel. By feeling, the chimpanzees learned to identify the object that was identical to the one they had seen. Scientists once believed that only human beings had this ability.

During the early and mid-1900's, scientists tried to teach human speech to chimpanzees. These attempts failed because chimpanzees do not have the physical ability to make most of the sounds used in human speech. Beginning in the 1960's, scientists attempted to teach sign language and other types of language to chimpanzees. Researchers wanted to find out if chimpanzees could learn language similar to that used by people. The scientists succeeded in teaching chimpanzees the *American Sign Language*, a set of hand gestures used primarily by the deaf in North America.

During the mid-1960's, scientists at the University of Nevada in Reno taught more than 160 signs of the American Sign Language to a chimpanzee named Washoe. Washoe learned the names of objects and actions. In the opinion of some researchers, she also combined signs in meaningful ways. During the 1970's, many other chimpanzees were taught sign language. At the Yerkes Primate Research Center in Atlanta, Ga., a chimpanzee named Lana learned to use various symbols on a computer keyboard to ask for food, companionship, and music.

In spite of such accomplishments in teaching chimpanzees to use sign language or symbols, some researchers questioned whether the apes had learned to use language the way people do. These researchers acknowledged that chimpanzees had learned to use "words" (either hand signs or symbols) in appropriate situations. But they doubted that the chimpanzees understood what the signs or symbols represented.

In 1980, researchers at the Yerkes Primate Research Center presented evidence that chimpanzees can understand what symbols really mean. Two chimpanzees, named Sherman and Austin, were shown various symbols. The two apes previously had learned to associate each of these symbols with a certain food or tool. After viewing each symbol, the chimpanzees classified it by pressing a "food" or a "tool" symbol on a keyboard. Sherman and Austin consistently put each symbol into the correct category the first time they were shown it. Their responses indicated that they understood what the symbols represented, much as people understand what words represent.

The great demand for chimpanzees for research and other purposes has created a serious threat to the animals. Human beings hunt chimpanzees for export to research institutions, circuses, and zoos. In some areas, people hunt chimpanzees for food and for use as household pets. In addition, people have destroyed many of the forests and grassy plains where the animals once lived. Some African countries have established game preserves in order to protect chimpanzees. Conservationists have also proposed the development of captive breeding programs to stop the threat to wild chimpanzee populations.

Scientific Classification. Chimpanzees belong to the anthropoid ape family, Pongidae. They make up the genus *Pan*. The chimpanzee is *P. troglodytes*, and the pygmy chimpanzee is *P. paniscus*. DUANE M. RUMBAUGH

See also APE; GOODALL, JANE; CULTURE (The Culture of Animals).

Additional Resources

BREWER, STELLA. *The Chimps of Mt. Asserik*. Knopf, 1978. Discusses chimpanzee behavior and habitat.

LAWICK-GOODALL, JANE VAN. *My Friends, the Wild Chimpanzees*. National Geographic Society, 1967. *In the Shadow of Man*. Houghton, 1971. Author is entered in *World Book* under the name Goodall, Jane.

TEMERLIN, MAURICE K. *Lucy: Growing Up Human, a Chimpanzee Daughter in a Psychotherapist's Family*. Science & Behavior, 1975.

TERRACE, HERBERT S. *Nim: A Chimpanzee Who Learned Sign Language*. Knopf, 1979.

YERKES, ROBERT M. *Chimpanzees: A Laboratory Colony*. Yale, 1943.

CH'IN DYNASTY, *chin*, was a Chinese *dynasty* (family of rulers) that governed from 221 B.C. to 206 B.C. The dynasty began after Shih Huang Ti, ruler of the state of Ch'in in northwestern China, conquered rival northern and central states. He later extended his rule to southeastern China. The dynasty had complete control over the areas it ruled. Earlier, local Chinese chiefs had much control over their regions.

Shih Huang Ti ruled his empire with an iron hand. He made former local rulers move to his huge new capital at Hsien-yang and appointed local administrators who were responsible to him. He banned most books in an attempt to silence critics, to promote obedience, and to blot out knowledge about the past. He ordered large numbers of laborers to complete the Great Wall of China to keep invaders out. But Shih Huang Ti gave his country a lasting ideal—national unity. The name *China* came from the name of his dynasty.

Shih Huang Ti died in 210 B.C., and his son proved to be a weak ruler. Rebellions began in 209 B.C., and the Ch'in dynasty soon collapsed. The Han dynasty then gained control of China. EUGENE BOARDMAN

See also GREAT WALL OF CHINA; SHIH HUANG TI.

WORLD BOOK photo by Robert Borja

Scenic Limestone Hills near the city of Kuei-lin in southern China are among the most unusual features of China's vast and varied countryside. Only Russia and Canada have more land than China.

CHINA

CHINA is a huge country in eastern Asia. It is the world's largest country in population and the third largest country in area. About a fifth of all the people in the world live in China. The country covers more than a fifth of Asia. Only Russia and Canada have more territory. China's vast land area includes some of the driest deserts and highest mountains in the world, as well as some of the richest farmland.

The Chinese call their country Chung-kuo, which means *Middle Country*. This name may have come into being because the ancient Chinese thought of their country as both the geographical center of the world and the only truly cultured civilization. The name *China* was given to the country by foreigners. The word may have come from *Ch'in*, which was the name of an early Chinese *dynasty* (series of rulers from the same family).

Most of the Chinese people live crowded together in the eastern third of the country. This region has most of China's major cities and nearly all the land suitable for farming. Agriculture has always been the chief economic activity in China. About 72 per cent of the people live in rural villages, and about three-fourths of all workers are farmers. Although only a small percentage of the people live in urban areas, China has several of the largest cities in the world. They include Shanghai and Peking, the nation's capital.

China has the world's oldest living civilization. Its written history goes back about 3,500 years. The Chinese people take great pride in their nation, its long history, and its influence on other countries. The Chi-

The seven contributors of this article are all members of the staff of the Center for Chinese Studies at the University of Michigan. The contributors are Robert F. Dernberger, Professor of Economics; Norma Diamond, Professor of Anthropology; Richard Edwards, Professor of Chinese Art; Albert Feuerwerker, Professor of History; Donald J. Munro, Professor of Philosophy; Rhoads Murphey, Professor of Geography; and William Pang-yu Ting, Assistant Professor of Political Science.

Facts in Brief

Capital: Peking.

Official Language: Chinese (Northern dialect).

Form of Government: Communist dictatorship.

Area: 3,678,470 sq. mi. (9,527,200 km²). *Greatest Distances*—north-south, 2,500 mi. (4,023 km); east-west, 3,000 mi. (4,828 km). *Coastline*—4,019 mi. (6,468 km), including 458 mi. (737 km) for Hai-nan Island.

Elevation: *Highest*—Mount Everest, 29,028 ft. (8,848 m); *Lowest*—Turfan Depression, 505 ft. (154 m) below sea level.

Population: *Estimated 1985 Population*—1,047,800,000; distribution, 72 per cent rural, 28 per cent urban; density, 285 persons per sq. mi. (110 per km²). *1982 Census*—1,008,175,288. *Estimated 1990 Population*—1,117,700,000.

Chief Products: *Agriculture*—rice, wheat, cotton, corn, tea, tobacco, sorghum, hogs, barley, millet, peanuts, potatoes, sheep, soybeans, sweet potatoes. *Manufacturing*—iron and steel, machinery, textiles, chemicals. *Mining*—coal, iron ore, petroleum, tungsten, antimony, tin, lead, manganese, and salt.

National Anthem: "March of the Volunteers."

Money: *Basic Unit*—yuan. For its price in U.S. dollars, see MONEY (table: Exchange Rates). See also YUAN.

Björn Klingwall

China's Many Large Cities include Shanghai, *above.* China has more people than any other country.

Shostal

Farming is the leading economic activity in China. About three-fourths of all Chinese workers are farmers.

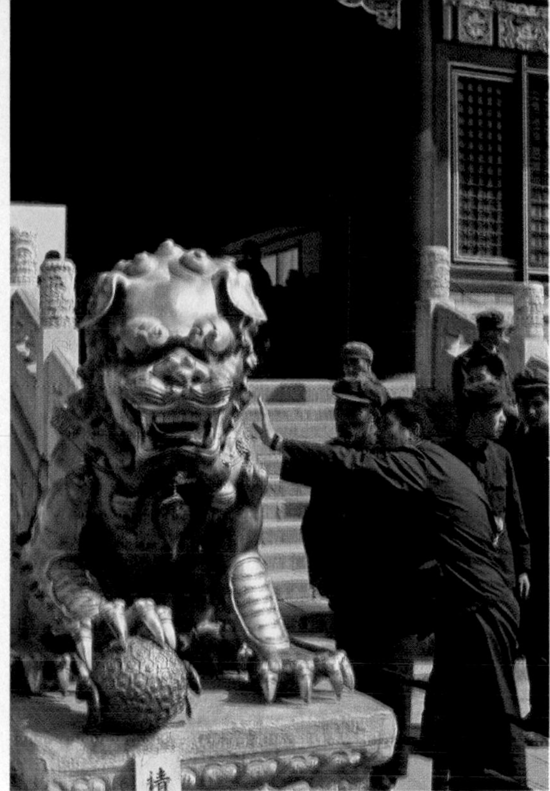

Henry Weaver, Lensman

China's Artistic Heritage goes back many centuries. This superb sculpture stands outside the old imperial palace in Peking.

nese were the first people to develop the compass, gunpowder, paper, porcelain, and silk cloth. Over the centuries, Japan, Korea, Vietnam, and other Asian lands have borrowed from Chinese art, language, literature, religion, and technology.

In early times, the Chinese people were divided into many small states. In 221 B.C., the Ch'in dynasty established an empire with a strong central government. This empire lasted in some form for more than 2,000 years. During those years, Chinese society survived wars, rebellions, and the rise and fall of numerous dynasties. The Chinese developed an increasingly powerful and efficient system of government, built great cities, and created magnificent works of literature and art. From time to time, nomadic invaders conquered all or part of China. However, these invaders had little effect on Chinese civilization.

During the 1800's, the Chinese empire began to weaken. In 1911, revolutionaries overthrew the empire. The next year, China became a republic. But the *Kuomintang* (Nationalist Party), which ruled the republic, never established an effective government. In 1949, the Chinese Communist Party, led by Mao Zedong, defeated the Nationalists and set up China's present government. The Communists gave the nation the official name *Chung-hua Jen-min Kung-ho-kuo* (People's Republic of China). The Nationalists fled to the island of Taiwan, where they reestablished their own government. This article discusses only the People's Republic of China. For information about the Republic of China, which is ruled by the Nationalists on Taiwan, see the article TAIWAN.

China has gone through many major changes under the Communists. All important industries have been placed under state ownership and direction. The government also controls trade and finance. Agricultural land is owned and farmed by large groups of peasants rather than by individual families as in the past. The Communists have dramatically increased industrial production and have expanded and improved education and medical care. The supply of food for China's people is generally sufficient though not plentiful. Nevertheless, China remains a poor country by world standards. The Communist Party and the government are making major efforts to overcome that poverty and modernize China by the year 2000.

WORLD BOOK map

China lies in eastern Asia. It covers more than a fifth of Asia and borders 11 other countries and the North Pacific Ocean.

1
2
3
4
5
6
7
8
A
B
C
D
E
F
G
H
I
J
K
RUSSIA
(U.S.S.R.)
Karaganda
Dzhezkazgan
Semipalatinsk
Irtysh
Barnaul
Biysk
Ob
Novokuznetsk
Abakan
Abaza
Bratsk Reservoir
Cheremkhovo
Angarsk
Irkutsk
Yenisey
Zyryanovsk
Lake Zaysan
Balkhash
Lake Balkhash
Ili
Uvs Lake
Hovsgol Lake
Har Us Lake
Hyargas Lake
Hovd
Selenge
Suhbaatar
Moron
Uliastay
Ulan Bator
Tsetserleg
Altay
MONGOLIA
Dzhambul
Chimkent
Frunze
Alma-Ata
Rybach'ye
Issyk-Kul Lake
Namangan
Kokand
Andizhan
Osh
Fergana
A-le-t'ai
Chuguchak
Karamai
Ma-na-ssu Lake
Po-le
Wu-su
K'uei-t'un
Ma-na-ssu
Kuldja
Ch'ang-chi
Urumchi
Ch'i-t'ai
Turfan
Ha-mi
Dalandzadgad
Karashahr
A-k'o-su
Kashgar
A-t'u-shih
Tarim
Po-ssu-t'eng Lake
K'u-erh-le
Yarkand
Sinkiang
Lop Nor Lake
AFGHANISTAN
Kargahalik
Ch'er-erh-ch'en
Charkhlik
Khotan
A-ya-k'o-k'u-mu Lake
PAKISTAN
An-hsi
Yu-men
Chia-yu-kuan
Chiu-ch'uan
Inner Mongolia
Lin-ho
Teng-k'ou
Wu-hai
Wu-ta
Shih-tsui-shan
Leng-hu
Chang-yeh
Yin-ch'uan
Wu-chung
Ta-ch'ai-tan
Wu-wei
Chung-wei
Ningsia
Srinagar
Indus
Te-ling-ha
T'ien-chun
Men-yuan
Koko Nor Lake
Ta-t'ung
Ko-erh-mu
Tu-lan
Hsi-ning
Kansu
Yung-teng
K'a-shun Lake
Tsinghai
Kung-ho
Lan-chou
Ku-yuan
Jih-t'u
Lahore
Chia-man-t'e-k'a-mu Lake
Huang Ho
Lin-hsia
P'ing-liang
Jullundur
Sutlej
Shih-ch'uan-ho
Ko-chih
T'ung-jen
Ludhiana
Kai-tse
Ma-ch'in
CHINA
T'ien-shui
Pao-chi
Chandigarh
Tibet
Ch'i-lin Lake
Yangtze
Ang-la-jen Lake
An-to
Yu-shu
Wu-tu
Ganges
T'ang-ku-la-yu-mu Lake
Pan-ko
A-pa
Han-chung
Delhi
Meerut
Ang-tse Lake
Chia-jen Lake
Salween
Szechwan
New Delhi
Moradabad
Na-ch'u
Kan-tzu
Chung-pa
Na-mu Lake
Ma-erh-k'ang
Mien-yang
Bareilly
Ch'ang-tu
Kuan-hsien
Nan-ch'ung
Agra
Ch'eng-tu
Te-yang
La-tzu
Jih-k'a-tse
Lhasa
Mekong
Sui-ning
NEPAL
Lucknow
Tse-tang
Lin-chih
Pa-t'ang
Ya-an
Gwalior
Jumna
Chiang-tzu
Yang-cho-yung Lake
K'ang-ting
Ch'ung-ch'ing
Jhansi
Kanpur
Kathmandu
Le-shan
Gorakhpur
Thimphu
Nei-chiang
Tzu-kung
Allahabad
Ya-lung
I-pin
Lu-chou
BHUTAN
Ganges
Chao-chueh
Banaras
Patna
Siliguri
Brahmaputra
Ledo
Hsi-ch'ang
Tsun-i
Tropic of Cancer
Chung-tien
Chao-t'ung
Pi-chieh
Gaya
Bhagalpur
Gauhati
Irrawaddy
Kweichow
INDIA
Li-chiang
Kuei-yang
BANGLADESH
Myitkyina
Pi-chiang
Tu-k'ou
An-shun
Tung-ch'uan
Tu-yun
Asansol
Imphal
Hsia-kuan
Ch'u-ching
Bilaspur
Jamshedpur
Chindwin
Pao-shan
Hsing-i
Dacca
K'un-ming
Nagpur
Howrah
Calcutta
Yunnan
I-liang
Nan-tan
Lu-hsi
Raipur
Lin-ts'ang
T'ung-hai
20° North Latitude
Chien-shui
Pai-se
Chittagong
Lashio
Wen-shan
T'ien-tung
Ko-chiu
Ching-hsi
Mahanadi
BURMA
Ssu-mao
Godavari
Cuttack
Lan-ts'ang
Mandalay
Red
P'ing-hsiang
Ching-hung
Pakokku
Keng Tung
Warangal
Phongsali
VIETNAM
Hanoi
Haiphong
Bay of Bengal
Irrawaddy
Salween
Guntur
Vijayawada
Rajahmundry
Vishakhapatnam
Luang Prabang
North
Prome
Toungoo
Chiang Mai
LAOS
THAILAND
Vinh
Vientiane
Mekong
Pegu
85° East Longitude
100°
50°
70°
85°
35°
0
250
500
750
1,000
1,250
1,500
1,750
2,000
2,250
2,500
2,750

9
10
11
12
13
14
15
16
A
B
C
D
E
F
G
H
I
J
K
China
Political Map
International boundary
Regional boundary
Road
Railroad
Canal
Great Wall of China
National capital
Regional capital
Other city or town
WORLD BOOK map
RUSSIA (U.S.S.R.)
Inner Mongolia
Heilungkiang
Kirin
Liaoning
Hopeh
Shansi
Shensi
Honan
Shantung
Kiangsu
Anhwei
Hupeh
Chekiang
Hunan
Kiangsi
Fukien
Kwangtung
Kwangsi
NORTH KOREA
SOUTH KOREA
JAPAN
TAIWAN
PHILIPPINES
Luzon
HONG KONG (Great Britain)
MACAO (Portugal)
Peking
Tientsin
Shanghai
Shen-yang
Harbin
Ch'ang-ch'un
Port Arthur-Dairen
Wu-han
Nan-ching
Canton
Sian
Cheng-chou
Tsinan
T'ai-yuan
Fu-chou
Ch'ang-sha
Hang-chou
Taipei
Pyongyang
Seoul
Tokyo
Yokohama
Nagoya
Osaka
Kyoto
Kobe
Vladivostok
Khabarovsk
Blagoveshchensk
Sapporo
Hokkaido
Honshu
Shikoku
Kyushu
Sakhalin
Kuril Islands
Ryukyu Islands
Hai-nan Island
Lake Baikal
Sea of Japan
Yellow Sea
East China Sea
South China Sea
Philippine Sea
North Pacific Ocean
Korea Bay
Po Gulf
Formosa Strait
Gulf of Tonkin
Tropic of Cancer
20° North Latitude
115° East Longitude
North
2,000
2,250
2,500
2,750
3,000 Miles
3,000
3,250
3,500
3,750
4,000
4,250
4,500 Kilometers

China Map Index

Provinces

Map Key		Name	Population	Area In sq. mi.	Area In km²	Capital
G	11	Anhwei	49,665,724	54,016	139,900	Ho-fei
H	12	Chekiang	38,884,603	39,305	101,800	Hang-chou
I	11	Fukien	25,931,106	47,529	123,100	Fu-chou
B	12	Heilungkiang	32,665,546	179,000	463,600	Harbin
G	10	Honan	74,422,739	64,480	167,000	Cheng-chou
E	10	Hopeh	53,005,875	78,260	202,700	Shih-chia-chuang
I	9	Hunan	54,008,851	81,275	210,500	Ch'ang-sha
G	10	Hupeh	47,804,150	72,394	187,500	Wu-han
E	7	Kansu	19,569,261	141,500	366,500	Lan-chou
I	10	Kiangsi	33,184,827	63,630	164,800	Nan-ch'ang
G	11	Kiangsu	60,521,114	39,460	102,200	Nan-ching
C	12	Kirin	22,560,053	72,200	187,000	Ch'ang-ch'un
J	10	Kwangtung	59,299,220	89,340	231,400	Canton
I	8	Kweichow	28,552,997	67,180	174,000	Kuei-yang
D	11	Liaoning	35,721,693	58,300	151,000	Shen-yang
F	10	Shansi	25,291,389	60,657	157,100	T'ai-yuan
F	11	Shantung	74,419,054	59,189	153,300	Tsinan
F	9	Shensi	28,904,423	75,599	195,800	Sian
G	7	Szechwan	99,713,310	219,700	569,000	Ch'eng-tu
F	6	Tsinghai	3,895,706	278,400	721,000	Hsi-ning
I	7	Yunnan	32,553,817	168,420	436,200	K'un-ming

Autonomous Regions

Map Key		Name	Population	Area In sq. mi.	Area In km²	Capital
D	10	Inner Mongolia	19,274,279	454,600	1,177,500	Hu-ho-hao-t'e
J	9	Kwangsi	36,420,960	85,100	220,400	Nan-ning
E	8	Ningsia	3,895,578	25,640	66,400	Yin-ch'uan
D	4	Sinkiang	13,081,681	635,833	1,646,800	Urumchi
G	4	Tibet	1,892,393	471,662	1,221,600	Lhasa

Special Municipalities

Map Key		Name	Population	Area In sq. mi.	Area In km²
E	10	Peking	9,230,687	6,873	17,800
G	12	Shanghai	11,859,748	2,240	5,800
E	11	Tientsin	7,764,141	4,250	11,000

Population*

Year	Population
1982	1,008,175,288
1975	830,491,000
1970	759,620,000
1965	695,000,000
1960	635,950,000
1955	582,340,000
1953	582,603,417
1950	532,870,000
1945	453,615,000
1912	353,260,000
1851	431,896,000
1776	268,238,000
1578	60,693,000
1491	53,281,000
1391	56,875,000
742	51,500,000
140	49,150,000
A.D. 2	57,671,000

Cities and Towns

Amoy ....100,000-300,000. .I 11
An-ch'ing .....100,000-300,000. .H 11
An-shan ......300,000-1,000,000. .D 12
An-shun .... 50,000-100,000. .I 8
An-yang ......100,000-300,000. .F 10
Canton .... 1,840,000. .J 10
Chan-chiang ....100,000-300,000. .J 9
Chang-chou ....100,000-300,000. .I 11
Ch'ang-chou ....100,000-300,000. .G 12
Ch'ang-ch'un ....1,000,000. .C 12
Ch'ang-sha ....300,000-1,000,000. .H 10
Ch'ang-te ....100,000-300,000. .H 9
Chao-tung ..... 50,000-100,000. .C 12
Ch'ao-yang ....100,000-300,000. .D 11
Chefoo ......100,000-300,000. .E 12
Chen-chiang ....100,000-300,000. .G 11
Cheng-chou ....300,000-1,000,000. .F 10
Ch'eng-te ..... 50,000-100,000. .E 11
Ch'eng-tu ....1,107,000. .H 8
Chia-hsing ..... 50,000-100,000. .G 12
Chia-mu-ssu ....100,000-300,000. .B 13
Chi-an ....100,000-300,000. .I 10
Chiang-men ....100,000-300,000. .J 10
Chiao-tso .....100,000-300,000. .F 10
Ch'i-ch'i-ha-erh ....300,000-1,000,000. .C 12
Ch'ih-feng ..... 50,000-100,000. .D 11
Chi-hsi ....300,000-1,000,000. .C 13
Chin-chou ....300,000-1,000,000. .D 11
Ch'ing-chiang ....100,000-300,000. .G 11
Ching-te-chen ....100,000-300,000. .H 11
Chin-hsi .... 50,000-100,000. .E 11
Ch'in-huang-tao ....100,000-300,000. .E 11
Chi-ning ......100,000-300,000. .F 11
Chi-ning .... 50,000-100,000. .E 10
Chiu-chiang ....100,000-300,000. .H 11
Ch'uan-chou ....100,000-300,000. .I 11
Chu-chou .....100,000-300,000. .H 10
Ch'ung-ch'ing ....2,121,000. .H 8
Dairen, see Port Arthur-Dairen
Foochow, see Fu-chou
Fo-shan ......100,000-300,000. .J 10
Fu-chou (Foochow) ....300,000-1,000,000. .I 12
Fu-hsien ...... 50,000-100,000. .E 12
Fu-hsin ....300,000-1,000,000. .D 12
Fu-shun ......300,000-1,000,000. .D 12
Fu-yang .... 50,000-100,000. .G 10
Hai-k'ou ......100,000-300,000. .K 9
Hailar .... 50,000-100,000. .B 11
Ha-mi .... 50,000-100,000. .D 6
Han-chung .... 50,000-100,000. .G 8
Hang-chou ...300,000-1,000,000. .H 12
Han-tan ......300,000-1,000,000. .F 10
Harbin .... 1,552,000. .C 12
Heng-yang ...300,000-1,000,000. .I 10
Ho-fei ....300,000-1,000,000. .G 11
Ho-kang .....100,000-300,000. .B 13
Ho-pi ....100,000-300,000. .F 10
Hsiang-fan ....100,000-300,000. .G 10
Hsiang-t'an ....300,000-1,000,000. .H 10
Hsien-yang .... 50,000-100,000. .G 9
Hsing-t'ai ....100,000-300,000. .F 10
Hsin-hsiang ....100,000-300,000. .F 10
Hsi-ning ......100,000-300,000. .F 7
Hsin-wen ...... 50,000-100,000. .F 11
Hsin-yang ....100,000-300,000. .G 10
Hsuan-hua ...100,000-300,000. .E 10
Hsu-ch'ang ....100,000-300,000. .G 10
Huai-nan .....300,000-1,000,000. .G 11
Huang-shih ...100,000-300,000. .H 10
Hu-ho-hao-t'e .300,000-1,000,000. .E 9
Hu-lan .... 50,000-100,000. .C 12
Hun-chiang .... 50,000-100,000. .D 12
I-ch'ang ......100,000-300,000. .H 9
I-ch'un .... 50,000-100,000. .B 13
I-pin ....100,000-300,000. .H 8
I-tu .... 50,000-100,000. .F 11
I-yang ....100,000-300,000. .H 10
K'ai-feng .....300,000-1,000,000. .F 10
Kalgan ....100,000-300,000. .F 10
Kan-chou .....100,000-300,000. .I 10
Karamai ...... 50,000-100,000. .C 4
Kashgar ...... 50,000-100,000. .D 2
Kirin ....300,000-1,000,000. .C 12
Ko-chiu .... 50,000-100,000. .J 7
K'o-erh-ch'in-yu-I-ch'ien-ch'i .... 50,000-100,000. .C 11
Kuei-lin ......100,000-300,000. .I 9
Kuei-yang ....300,000-1,000,000. .I 8
Kuldja .... 50,000-100,000. .C 3
K'un-ming ....300,000-1,000,000. .I 7
Lan-chou .....300,000-1,000,000. .F 8
Le-shan .... 50,000-100,000. .H 8
Lhasa .... 50,000-100,000. .H 4
Liao-yang ....100,000-300,000. .D 12
Liao-yuan ....100,000-300,000. .D 12
Lien-yun-kang 100,000-300,000. .F 11
Lin-hsia .... 50,000-100,000. .F 7
Liu-chou .....300,000-1,000,000. .J 9
Lo-yang ......300,000-1,000,000. .F 10
Lu-chou ......100,000-300,000. .H 8
Ma-an-shan ...100,000-300,000. .G 11
Mao-ming ....100,000-300,000. .J 9
Mien-yang ..... 50,000-100,000. .G 8
Mukden, see Shen-yang
Mu-tan-chiang 300,000-1,000,000. .C 13
Nan-ch'a ...... 50,000-100,000. .B 13
Nan-ch'ang ...300,000-1,000,000. .H 11
Nan-ching (Nanking) ....1,419,000. .G 11
Nan-ch'ung ...100,000-300,000. .H 8
Nanking, see Nan-ching
Nan-ning .....300,000-1,000,000. .J 9
Nan-t'ung ....100,000-300,000. .G 12
Nan-yang ....100,000-300,000. .G 10
Nei-chiang ...100,000-300,000. .H 8
Nen-chiang .... 50,000-100,000. .B 12
Ning-po ......100,000-300,000. .H 12
Pai-ch'eng ....100,000-300,000. .C 12
Pao-chi ......100,000-300,000. .G 8
Pao-ting ......300,000-1,000,000. .E 10
Pao-t'ou ......300,000-1,000,000. .E 9
Pei-an .... 50,000-100,000. .B 12
Pei-hai .... 50,000-100,000. .J 9
Peking .... 9,230,687. .E 10
Peng-pu ......300,000-1,000,000. .G 11
Pen-hsi ......300,000-1,000,000. .D 12
P'ing-hsiang ..100,000-300,000. .I 10
P'ing-ting-shan 100,000-300,000. .G 10
Port Arthur-Dairen ....1,508,000. .E 12
Shanghai ....11,859,748. .G 12
Shao-hsing ...100,000-300,000. .H 12
Shao-kuan ...100,000-300,000. .I 10
Shao-yang ....100,000-300,000. .I 9
Sha-shih .....100,000-300,000. .H 10
Shen-yang (Mukden) ....2,411,000. .D 12
Shih-chia-chuang300,000-1,000,000. .E 10
Shuang-ya-shan100,000-300,000. .B 13
Sian ...... 1,310,000. .G 9
Soochow, see Su-chou
Ssu-p'ing .....100,000-300,000. .D 12
Su-chou (Soochow) ....300,000-1,000,000. .G 12
Suchow ......300,000-1,000,000. .G 11
Sui-hua .... 50,000-100,000. .C 12
Sui-ning .... 50,000-100,000. .H 8
Swatow ......300,000-1,000,000. .J 11
T'ai-chou .....100,000-300,000. .G 11
T'ai-yuan .....300,000-1,000,000. .F 10
T'ang-shan ...300,000-1,000,000. .E 11
Tan-tung .....100,000-300,000. .E 12
T'ao-an .... 50,000-100,000. .C 12
Ta-t'ung ......300,000-1,000,000. .E 10
Te-chou .... 50,000-100,000. .F 10
Te-yang .... 50,000-100,000. .H 8
T'ieh-ling ...... 50,000-100,000. .D 12
T'ien-shui ..... 50,000-100,000. .G 8
Tientsin ....7,764,141. .E 11
Ts'ang-chou ..100,000-300,000. .E 11
Tsinan .... 1,000,000. .F 11
Tsingtao ....1,121,000. .F 11
Tsun-i ....100,000-300,000. .I 8
Tu-k'ou ......100,000-300,000. .I 7
T'ung-ch'uan .. 50,000-100,000. .F 9
T'ung-hua ....100,000-300,000. .D 12
T'ung-liao ..... 50,000-100,000. .D 12
T'ung-ling ..... 50,000-100,000. .G 11
T'un-hsi .... 50,000-100,000. .H 11
Tu-yun .... 50,000-100,000. .I 8
Tzu-kung .....300,000-1,000,000. .H 8
Tzu-po .... 50,000-100,000. .F 11
Urumchi .....300,000-1,000,000. .C 4
Wan-hsien ....100,000-300,000. .H 9
Wei-fang .....100,000-300,000. .F 11
Wen-chou (Yungkia) ....100,000-300,000. .H 12
Wu-chou .....100,000-300,000. .J 9
Wu-han ... 2,146,000. .H 10
Wu-hsi ....300,000-1,000,000. .G 12
Wu-hu ....300,000-1,000,000. .G 11
Yang-chou ....100,000-300,000. .G 11
Yang-ch'uan ..100,000-300,000. .F 10
Yen-chi .... 50,000-100,000. .D 13
Yin-ch'uan ....100,000-300,000. .E 8
Ying-k'ou .....100,000-300,000. .E 12
Yu-men .... 50,000-100,000. .E 6
Yungkia, see Wen-chou
Yu-tz'u .... 50,000-100,000. .F 10

*Estimates, except 1953 and 1982 censuses.

Sources: Total China populations from United Nations and John D. Durand, "The Population Statistics of China, A.D. 2-1953" from "Population Studies," March 1960; province areas from Cartographical Publishing House, Peking; populations of provinces, autonomous regions, and special municipalities from 1982 census; 1957 estimates for other large cities from State Statistical Bureau, Peking; population ranges for other places from "Atlas of the Provinces of the People's Republic of China," Map Publishing House, Peking, 1977.

China's Capitol is the Great Hall of the People in Peking. The National People's Congress and other governmental bodies meet in its huge chambers.

New China Pictures

The Chinese government is dominated by three organizations. They are the Chinese Communist Party, the military, and a branch of the government known as the State Council. Almost all the leaders in the military and the State Council also hold high positions in the Communist Party. Thus, the party strictly controls the political system. All persons who hold a middle- or lower-level position in the party or the government are called *cadres*. China's constitution, adopted in 1982, calls for the people to concentrate on modernizing agriculture, industry, the military, and science and technology.

The Communist Party. China has the largest Communist Party in the world. About 35 million Chinese belong to the party. However, they make up only about 4 per cent of the country's total population. China also has a number of minor political parties, but they have little or no power.

The Communist Party has four main decision-making bodies. These are the National Party Congress, the Central Committee, the *Politburo* (Political Bureau), and the Secretariat. The National Party Congress has about 2,000 representatives, selected by party members throughout the nation. The Central Committee consists of about 200 leading party members. The members are elected by the National Party Congress. The Politburo has about 25 members, who are top party leaders elected by the Central Committee. The Politburo includes a standing committee of 5 or 6 of the most important Communist Party leaders. The Secretariat has about 10 members, elected by the Central Committee.

China's Flag was adopted in 1949. The large star and four small stars stand for the Communist Party and its members.

The State Emblem of China is framed by wheat and rice, the nation's leading agricultural products.

The Communist Party's constitution states that the National Party Congress and the Central Committee are the most important bodies of the party. However, the congress actually has little real power. In general, it automatically approves policies set by the Central Committee and the Politburo. The Politburo also establishes policy guidelines for the party. The Secretariat is responsible for day-to-day decisions and supervision of party actions.

In theory, the highest post in the Communist Party is that of general secretary. In practice, however, Deng Xiaoping is the most powerful person in the party and in the country. Deng's posts include the chairmanship of

New China Pictures

The National People's Congress performs legislative duties and transmits national government policies to lower levels of government. The Communist Party completely controls the congress.

the Military Affairs Council of both the party and the government and the chairmanship of the Central Advisory Commission to the Communist Party. This commission provides advice and recommendations about party policies to the Central Committee.

National Government. China's constitution establishes the National People's Congress as the highest government authority. According to the Chinese electoral law, members of the National People's Congress are elected at the provincial level by provincial people's congresses, which themselves are indirectly elected by lower level congresses. The Communist Party has an important influence on the selection of candidates for these and all other elections in China.

The members of the National People's Congress serve five-year terms. The congress carries out various legislative duties. But in practice, it has no real power. Its chief function is to transmit policies of the national government and of the party to lower levels of government. A standing committee handles the work of the congress when it is not in session.

The State Council carries on the day-to-day affairs of the government. The council is led by the premier, China's head of government. The premier is nominated by the Central Committee of the Communist Party and approved by the president, who is chiefly a ceremonial official. The premier is assisted by 2 vice premiers and about 40 ministers. The ministers head government departments, including the defense ministry and the ministries responsible for economic planning.

Political Divisions. China has 29 major political divisions. They consist of 21 provinces; 5 *autonomous* (self-governing) regions; and 3 special municipalities. The autonomous regions are Inner Mongolia, Kwangsi, Ningsia, Sinkiang, and Tibet. These regions have many people who belong to non-Chinese ethnic groups. Although the regions are called autonomous, they are actually governed much like the rest of the nation. Local governments in these regions do have some powers to safeguard the culture and interests of the minority peoples. The special municipalities—Peking, Shanghai, and Tientsin—are huge metropolitan areas administered by the national government. Each consists of an urban center and a rural area.

China has three levels of local government. The 29 major political units are divided into about 2,100 counties. These counties are subdivided into more than 50,000 townships and towns. Each local government unit has a people's congress and an executive body patterned after the State Council.

Courts in China do not function as a completely independent branch of government as they do in the United States and many other Western nations. Instead, the courts base their decisions largely on the policies of the Communist Party.

The highest court in China is the Supreme People's Court. It hears cases that involve national security or violations by high officials. In addition, this court supervises people's courts in the provinces and counties. The Supreme People's Procuratorate sees that the national constitution and the State Council's regulations are observed.

The Armed Forces of China are jointly commanded by the Military Affairs Council of the Communist Party and the Military Affairs Council of the government. China has an army, navy, and air force, which together make up the People's Liberation Army (PLA). The PLA has more than 4 million members—about $3\frac{1}{2}$ million in the army, 300,000 in the navy, and 400,000 in the air force. Over 5 million men and women serve in China's *militia* (citizens' army). Men may be drafted for military service after they reach the age of 18. The period of service is three years in the army, four years in the air force, and five years in the navy.

The armed forces have held enormous political power in the People's Republic of China since its birth in 1949. On the average, military officers make up about a third of the members on the Communist Party's Central Committee. Besides its military duties, the PLA helps carry out party policies and programs among the people.

CHINA/*People*

Population. About a fifth of the world's people live in China. In 1982, China took its first census since 1953. This census reported a population of 1,008,175,288. By 1985, the population had grown to an estimated 1,047,800,000.

Nearly 12 million persons live in Shanghai. Shanghai ranks as the world's largest city in terms of population. However, the city includes a large rural area, as well as an urban area. Peking, the capital, has over 9 million residents. China has at least 13 other cities with a population of 1 million or more. However, about 72 per cent of China's people live in rural villages and small towns. Most live in densely populated areas in eastern China. Western China makes up half the land area of the country, but has less than 10 per cent of the population.

China's government is concerned about the nation's high birth rate and seeks to limit population growth.

Steve Vidler, De Wys, Inc.

The Han Ethnic Group makes up about 94 per cent of China's people. These Han people are buying bread in Sian.

China Population Density and Major Ethnic Groups

About 94 per cent of the Chinese people belong to the Han ethnic group and live crowded together in eastern China. The rest of the population consists of about 50 minority groups. They live chiefly in the border areas and in western China.

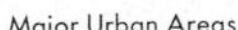

Major Urban Areas

- ● More than 5 million inhabitants
- • 2 million to 5 million inhabitants
- ○ 1 million to 2 million inhabitants

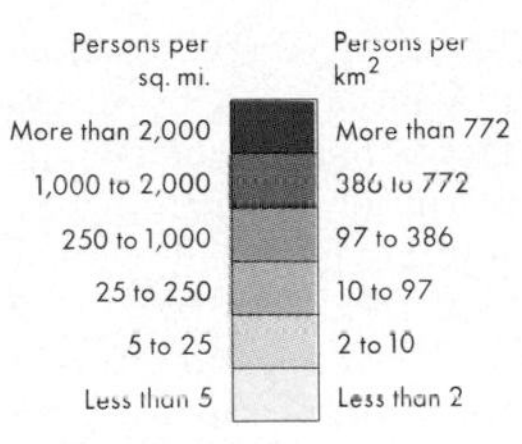

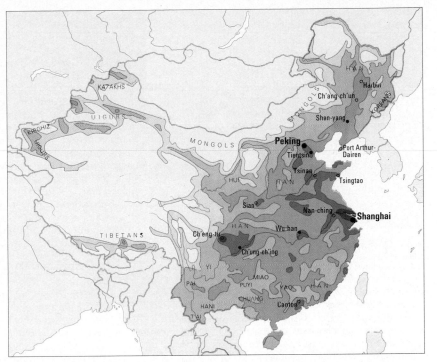

WORLD BOOK map

By law, men may not marry until they are 22 years old, and women until they are 20. People are encouraged to postpone marriage until they are in their late 20's and to have no more than one child.

Nationalities. About 94 per cent of the Chinese people belong to the *Han* nationality, which has been the largest nationality in China for centuries. The rest of the population consists of about 50 minority groups, including Kazakhs, Mongols, Tibetans, and Uigurs. Almost all the peoples of China belong to the Asian geographical race (see Races, Human). The nationalities are distinguished chiefly by language and culture.

Most of China's minority peoples live in the border regions and the far western parts of the country. Some groups, such as the Mongols in the north and the Kazakhs in the northwest, herd sheep and goats. These people move from place to place during the year to feed their herds on fresh pastures. The Uigurs raise livestock and grow a wide variety of crops on oases in the deserts of northwestern China. The Tibetan people

Henry Herr Gill

Bicycles are a common means of transportation in China's cities. Millions of people live in the cities of eastern China, where the overcrowding has created a severe housing shortage.

Photri

Colorful Folk Dances are part of the cultural heritage of China's minority peoples, such as the Mongols, *above*. Many Mongols still follow their old way of life as nomadic herders.

practice simple forms of agriculture in China's southwestern highlands.

Languages. The Han people speak Chinese. Spoken Chinese has many dialects, which differ enough in pronunciation to be considered separate languages. To bring about better communication among the people of China, the government has made the Northern Chinese dialect the official language. Many non-Chinese call the official language Mandarin, but the Chinese prefer the term *p'u-t'ung hua* (common language). Northern Chinese is spoken by about 70 per cent of the nation's people, and it is now taught in all Chinese schools. Other varieties of Chinese include Min, Wu, and Yueh (Cantonese), each of which has many local dialects. For more information, see CHINESE LANGUAGE.

Although each dialect of Chinese has its own pronunciation, all speakers of Chinese write the language in the same way. The Chinese writing system uses *characters* instead of an alphabet. Each character is a symbol that represents a complete word or syllable.

Scholars have developed several systems of writing the Chinese language in the Roman alphabet. The spellings of most of the Chinese personal names and all the place names in this article are based on the Wade-Giles system. This system was developed during the 1800's by two English scholars, Sir Thomas Wade and Herbert A. Giles. In 1979, China began using the Pinyin system in all news reports sent abroad and in all communications with other nations. Many Chinese names are spelled somewhat differently in the two systems. For example, the name of the man who led the country's Communist revolution is spelled Mao Zedong in the Pinyin system and Mao Tse-tung in the Wade-Giles system. This article uses Pinyin spellings for Mao and other Communist leaders.

The minority peoples of China speak many languages, including Korean, Mongolian, and Uigur. Each group uses its own language in its schools and publications. Most members of China's minority groups learn Chinese as a second language.

CHINA/Way of Life

Family Life has always been extremely important in Chinese culture. Before 1949, some Chinese lived in large family units. As many as 100 or more relatives lived together under the rule of the oldest male. The ideal was "five generations under one roof." However, those who lived this way were mainly the families of rich rural landowners, wealthy merchants, and government officials. Among the common people, most households consisted of only parents and children, but some also included grandparents and uncles. Today, the Chinese live in these smaller types of family units.

In the past, only men were expected to work outside the home. But today, almost all adults have a job. In many families, a grandparent looks after the house and children during the day. More and more children attend nursery school and kindergarten so that mothers can be free to work.

Relationships within Chinese families have become less formal and more democratic. Parents no longer expect their children to show unquestioning obedience. In the past, a father could legally kill his children if they disobeyed him. Young people today generally choose their own marriage partners on the basis of shared interests and mutual attraction. However, parents still play a role in arranging some marriages, especially in rural areas. Any couple would at least consult their parents about such a major decision.

Chinese families traditionally valued sons far more than daughters. A husband could divorce his wife if she failed to give birth to sons. In some cases, daughters were killed at birth because girls were considered useless. Today, girls as well as boys are valued. This change came about partly because the Communist government strongly supports the idea that women should contribute to the family income and participate in social and political activities. Women do many kinds of work outside the home. Many young husbands share in the shopping, housecleaning, cooking, and caring for the children to show that they believe the sexes are equal. However, equality between the sexes is more widely accepted in the cities than in the countryside.

Björn Klingwall

Family Life has been an important part of Chinese culture throughout the country's history. This playground in a Shanghai neighborhood is a favorite spot for family outings.

K. Scholz, Shostal

Typical Chinese Farmhouses are built of mud or clay bricks and have a tile or straw roof. The peasants farm the land co-operatively. But most families have a small plot for their own use.

Rural Life. Traditionally, most Chinese lived in villages of 100 to 200 households. Many families owned their land, though in numerous cases it was not large enough to support them. Many other families owned no land. The members of these families worked as tenants or laborers for big landowners and rich peasants. The tenant farmers had to pay extremely high rents—from 30 to 60 per cent of the harvest. In some cases, peasant families were so poor that they became beggars or bandits, or even sold their children as servants or slaves to rich families.

Under the Communist system, peasants belong to agricultural *collectives* (groups). The collectives are organized on three levels. The highest level is the *commune*, which administers economic activities for 20 or more villages. Larger projects, such as the building of dams and roads, are usually planned and carried out by the central or provincial government.

Communes are divided into smaller units called *production brigades*. A production brigade may consist of one large village or several small ones. Within a brigade, neighborhoods or villages of 20 to 30 families make up units called *production teams*.

Brigades and production teams own land, tools, work animals, and small workshops in common. Individuals who produce more goods than the amount owed the government may sell the surplus on the open market. Each family owns its house and a plot on which it can grow vegetables and raise chickens or a pig for its own use.

The standard of living in rural China has risen slowly but steadily. However, it is higher in some areas than in others because some areas have better farmland and weather than other regions. The average income in rural areas is low, but most families have enough to eat and money to buy clothing. Some families also have a few luxuries. Such luxuries include bicycles, radios, sewing machines, and watches.

Most rural families live in two- or three-room houses. Older houses are made of mud bricks and have a tile or straw roof. Newer houses are made of clay bricks or stone and have a tile roof. Some of the more prosperous villages are constructing apartment buildings. The people contribute the labor, and the brigade or team pays for the building materials. Except in remote areas, most houses have electricity.

Rural people work many hours a day, especially at planting and harvesting time. They must go to team and brigade meetings to help decide how to divide the work and profits. They also attend political meetings and night classes, where they learn how to read and write or how to use scientific farming methods. Even so, the people have time for recreation. Many brigades own a television set and show motion pictures once a week. They also have a small library and equipment for such

K. Scholz, Shostal

Bridge Construction, *left,* and other public-improvement projects help provide better living and economic conditions in rural China. Such projects are usually planned and carried out by the central or provincial government.

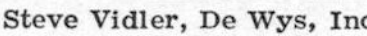

Steve Vidler, De Wys, Inc.

WORLD BOOK photo by Robert Borja

The Housing in China's Cities is a mixture of new and old, as shown by these two photographs taken in the city of Kuei-lin. Some city residents live in modern apartment complexes, *left.* Others live in older neighborhoods where the houses resemble those in rural areas, *right.*

sports as basketball and table tennis. Some brigades have a small choral group, orchestra, or theater group.

City Life. Many city residents live in older neighborhoods where the houses resemble those in the countryside. Many other city dwellers live in big apartment complexes. City governments construct some apartment buildings, and large factories build others.

Families are assigned an apartment by the factory or other unit for which they work. Most apartments have plumbing and heating, but many have less space than rural houses have. China's cities are overcrowded, and new housing is in great demand. In some cases, two families must share an apartment.

Each city neighborhood or apartment complex has an elected residents' committee. The committee supervises various neighborhood facilities and programs, such as day-care centers, evening classes, and after-school activities for children. When fights, petty crimes, or acts of juvenile delinquency occur in the neighborhoods, committee members talk with the people involved and try to help them solve the problem. These neighborhood organizations seek to keep crime from being a serious problem in spite of the overcrowding in China's cities.

People in the cities are better paid than most people in the countryside. Factory workers earn about $30 to $40 a month, and highly skilled people can make $60 to $70 monthly. Most households have at least two wage earners. Rents are only a few dollars a month, and a family of five needs no more than $30 a month for food. Medical care, child care, and recreational activity cost little. As a result, most city people gener-

Steve Vidler, De Wys, Inc.

Small Food Shops like this one are common in the cities of China. Most cities also have at least one government-owned department store as well as many small specialty shops.

Milt and Joan Mann

Dining in a Restaurant is a popular activity in China just as it is in Western countries. People in different parts of China eat different foods, but grain is the basic food in all areas.

© Cheng Zhishan, New China Pictures

Ancient Chinese Exercises called *tai chi chuan* are performed by many Chinese first thing every morning. Tai chi chuan emphasizes relaxation, balance, and proper techniques of breathing.

ally have some spare money. Many families have saved this money because the consumer goods they would like to buy have not been available.

For many years, the Chinese government has tried to eliminate the gap between living standards in the city and in the countryside. However, city people still have an easier life and more cultural advantages. Like rural people, city residents attend classes and meetings. On their days off, they enjoy browsing in stores; dining at a restaurant; or going to a park, museum, theater, or sporting event.

Food. Grain is the main food in China. Most working adults eat more than 1 pound (0.5 kilogram) of grain a day. Rice is the favorite grain among people in the south. In the north, people prefer wheat, which they make into bread and noodles. Northerners also eat corn, *kaoliang* (sorghum), and millet. The Chinese vary their diet with many kinds of vegetables, especially cabbage, cucumbers, eggplant, radishes, tomatoes, and turnips. Every area has its fruit specialties, such as bananas and oranges in the south and apples and peaches in the north.

Meat makes up only a small part of the Chinese diet. Many families eat meat only on special occasions. Pork is the favorite meat, but it is rationed so that everyone gets a share. The people also like such high-protein foods as eggs, fish, and poultry, which are becoming increasingly available. Soybeans provide an additional source of protein. Tea has long been the favorite beverage in China.

Clothing. Most Chinese make their own clothes, chiefly of cotton or synthetic materials. The government rations cotton cloth, which is in short supply. However, fabrics made of synthetic fibers are becoming increasingly available as China's petroleum and chemical industries develop.

The Chinese dress for comfort and practicality rather than for style. Some women, especially in the cities, wear skirts or dresses. But throughout China, both men and women generally wear Western-style shirts and loose-fitting trousers. They dress in dull blues, greens, or dark colors. Only children and young women wear bright colors and patterns. Men wear their hair short. Women also wear their hair in short simple styles. Most girls and young women wear their hair in braids.

Government officials and technicians may buy better-quality clothing at special stores. Such clothing includes high-collared suits, which are worn for formal occasions. But most of the time, it is difficult to tell from a person's clothing whether that person is an ordinary worker, a government official, or a technician. In earlier times, however, the kinds of clothes that people wore indicated their place in Chinese society. For example, scholars traditionally dressed in long blue gowns. Women of the upper classes wore elaborate hairdos, long fingernails, and colorful robes. In contrast, peasants wore patched and faded jackets and trousers.

Health Care in China combines traditional Chinese medicine and modern Western medicine. Traditional

New China Pictures

Sporting Events, such as softball, *above,* are favorite pastimes in China. Other popular sports in the country include baseball, basketball, soccer, and volleyball.

medicine is based on the use of herbs, attention to diet, and *acupuncture*. Acupuncture is a technique in which thin needles are inserted into the body at certain points to relieve pain or treat disease (see ACUPUNCTURE). From Western medicine, the Chinese have adopted many drugs and surgical methods.

All Chinese cities and towns and most communes have hospitals. Medical teams from the hospitals visit the villages periodically. Villages also have small clinics staffed by part-time medical workers called *barefoot doctors*. The term indicates that these workers share the simple life of the peasants they serve. It does not mean that they are actually barefoot. Barefoot doctors, many of whom are women, receive a year or two of training at a nearby hospital. They can treat simple illnesses, assist at childbirth, prepare medicines made of herbs, and issue prescriptions.

Barefoot doctors organize public health programs in their communities. They check the purity of drinking water, vaccinate people against diseases, and make sure that garbage is disposed of. They also supervise the extermination of harmful insects and rodents. In addition, the barefoot doctors encourage people to practice birth control, and they give advice on infant care and nutrition. All these programs have made the people much healthier than they were in the 1950's. The Chinese have almost wiped out cholera, typhoid, and other terrible diseases that once killed millions of them each year.

Religion is discouraged by the Communist government of China. However, it played an important part in traditional Chinese life. Confucianism, Taoism, and Buddhism were the major religions throughout most of China's history. The religious beliefs of many Chinese included elements of all three religions.

Confucianism is based on the ideas of Confucius, a Chinese philosopher who was born about 550 B.C. It stresses the importance of moral standards and of a well-ordered society in which parents rule their children, men rule women, and the educated rule the common people. In addition, Confucianism strongly emphasizes deep respect for one's ancestors and for the past. See CONFUCIANISM.

Björn Klingwall

Chinese Physicians practice a combination of traditional Chinese medicine and modern Western medicine. The doctors pictured above are examining patients in a clinic in Shanghai.

Taoism is also a native Chinese religion. It teaches that a person should withdraw from everyday life and live in harmony with nature. Taoism began during the 300's B.C. and is based largely on a book called the *Tao Te Ching* (*The Classic of the Way and the Virtue*). Taoism came to include many elements of Chinese folk religion and so became a religion with many protective gods. See TAOISM.

Buddhism reached China from India before A.D. 100 and became well established throughout the country during the 300's. Under the influence of Confucianism and Taoism, Chinese varieties of Buddhism developed. They taught strict moral standards and the ideas of rebirth and life after death. The Chinese Buddhists worshiped many gods and appealed to them for help in times of troubles. See BUDDHISM.

The Chinese government regards religion as superstition. It encourages the people to study science and political writings to solve their problems. The Communists especially oppose Confucianism because it emphasizes the past and justifies inequality in society. They have tried to remove all Confucian influences from family life, education, and politics. The Communists have also turned Taoist and Buddhist temples into museums, schools, and meeting halls.

Among China's minority peoples, about 25 million persons are Muslims. The government permits them to follow their religion, but it does not encourage them to do so. Christian missionaries worked in China for many years. A few churches remain open in the larger cities, but no one knows how many Chinese still believe in Christianity.

Education. The Chinese have always prized education and respected scholars. Before the Communists came to power in 1949, there were two major reasons for this high regard for education. (1) The Confucians believed that people could perfect themselves through study. The Confucians made no sharp distinction between academic education and moral education. They believed that the function of all study was to build character. (2) The ability to read and write and a knowledge of Confucian sacred writings paved the way to financial security and social position. Candidates for government jobs had to pass an examination based on the Confucian works.

Education continues to play a central role in Chinese society. The Communists regard it as a key to reaching their political, social, and economic goals. Since their rule began, they have conducted adult education programs in an effort to teach all Chinese to read and write. Government officials claim that more than 90 per cent of Chinese adults can now read and write. China's formal education system stresses scientific and technical training. This training is intended to give students the skills needed to modernize China's economy and improve the standard of living.

Moral education also remains important in China, but it teaches morality as defined in a Communist sense. The Chinese say that students should be both politically committed to Communist ideas and tech-

Foreign Language Classes are an important part of every Chinese student's education. These youngsters are learning English, the most widely studied foreign language in China.

WORLD BOOK photo by Robert Borja

nically skilled. Courses combine the teaching of academic facts and political values. For example, a geography text might provide information not only about China's physical features but also about the desirability of having patriotic feelings toward the land. Special courses teach the ideas of such Communist thinkers as Karl Marx, V. I. Lenin, and Mao Zedong. Most classrooms have posters describing the deeds of model citizens as moral examples for the students.

An important issue in Chinese education involves the conflict between basic Communist principles and the desire to modernize China's economy rapidly. Rapid modernization requires high-quality education with special opportunities and facilities for talented students. However, a Communist principle stresses equality in education. Supporters of this principle would like to increase the educational opportunities of peasants and workers at the expense of more privileged groups, such as scientists and government officials. Since 1949, the Communists have alternately stressed equality in education and high-quality education for modernization. At present, supporters of rapid modernization control the educational system.

Students who show outstanding ability on nationwide examinations go to *key schools,* which have the best faculties and facilities. The key schools exist at the elementary, secondary, and college levels.

Elementary and Secondary Schools. The Chinese have made great progress in providing elementary school education for their children. The law does not require children to go to school. However, about 95 per cent of Chinese children attend elementary school. Youngsters enter elementary school at the age of 6 or 7 and stay for 5 years. They study the Chinese language, mathematics, music, natural science, painting, physical education, and political education. In the third grade, they also begin to study English, Russian, or some other foreign language.

After completing elementary school, many Chinese students enter secondary schools called *middle schools.* The Ministry of Education in Peking selects the courses and textbooks for all middle schools throughout China. The middle school courses include many of the subjects studied in elementary school plus history, hygiene, literature, and physiology. China has about 123,000 middle schools. More than 58 million students attend these schools, nearly four times the number enrolled in 1966.

Rural areas of China lag behind the cities in educational progress. For example, the goal for 1985 is for most city students to attend middle school for five years. But the most the government expects for rural students by 1985 is that they attend middle school for three years.

Higher Education. Young people who wish to attend an institution of higher learning must pass an entrance examination. Some students who pass the examination enter a university. The chief university subjects include languages, mathematics, and natural sciences. Others who pass the examination enter a technical college. Each technical college specializes in one particular field, such as agriculture, forestry, medicine, mining, or teacher training. Many technical schools are administered by the government ministry specifically concerned with the subject that is taught. This system enables government leaders to plan the number of graduates who will have the special skills needed to run China's farms and factories.

China has about 675 institutions of higher learning, including both universities and technical colleges. Altogether, they have about 1,144,000 students, and enrollments are gradually increasing. Nevertheless, only a small percentage of the students who wish to attend college can do so because of a shortage of faculties and facilities. Unsuccessful candidates can continue their education at "workers' universities" run by factories. These schools offer short-term courses. Youths who dropped out of middle school can resume their studies at spare-time schools or through television and correspondence courses.

Detail of a painting on clay tile (A.D. 1-99) by an unknown Chinese artist; Museum of Fine Arts, Boston, Denman Waldo Ross Collection

Paintings on the Tiles of Tombs during the Han dynasty were done in a graceful, lively style. This tomb tile shows two officials of the Chinese emperor's court.

China's visual arts date from at least the 4000's B.C. Many extraordinary ancient works have been discovered, chiefly in tombs. Chinese visual arts in general reached their highest development during four dynasties. These dynasties were the Han (202 B.C. to A.D. 220); the T'ang (618-907); the Sung (960-1279); and the Ming (1368-1644). The masterpieces of these dynasties include not only paintings and sculptures but also such objects as pottery, ivory and jade carvings, furniture, and lacquer ware. See BRONZE; FURNITURE (China); IVORY; JADE; LACQUER WARE; PORCELAIN.

In present-day China, artists receive support from the government or work as amateurs in addition to their regular jobs. The Communists teach that the arts originate from the people—that is, the farmers, workers, and soldiers. The Communists also stress that all art should express the aims of their new society. As a result, much Chinese art today deals with events from the Communist revolution or from the daily life of workers and peasants. In addition, the Communists promote the preservation of folk dances and other traditional arts of China's minority peoples.

Literature. China has one of the oldest and greatest literatures in the world. The first significant work of Chinese literature was a collection of poems called the *Classic of Songs*. Some of these poems probably date from the 1100's B.C. For more information on China's rich literary heritage, see CHINESE LITERATURE.

Painting has been an established art in China since at least the 300's B.C. Most early paintings were of people, but landscapes became the chief subject of Chinese painting by the A.D. 900's. During the Sung dynasty, many artists painted landscapes called *shan-shui* (mountain-water), which showed towering mountains and vast expanses of water. In these paintings, the artist tried to suggest a harmony between nature and the human spirit.

Chinese painting was closely linked with the arts of poetry and *calligraphy* (fine handwriting). The Chinese traditionally considered calligraphy a branch of painting. During the 1200's, it became popular for painters to combine shan-shui with written inscriptions that formed part of the overall design. In many cases, these inscriptions consisted of a poem along with a description of the circumstances under which the painting was created.

Buddhist Temple Amid Clearing Mountain Peaks (A.D. 967), an ink painting on silk attributed to Li Ch'eng; Nelson Gallery-Akins Museum, Kansas City, Mo., Nelson Fund

Landscapes became the chief subject of Chinese painting by the A.D. 900's. The work above is a fine example of the *shan-shui* (mountain-water) style developed during the Sung dynasty.

Chinese artists used the same brush for painting and calligraphy. It consisted of a wooden or bamboo handle with bristles of animal hair arranged to form an extremely fine point. The artist could paint many kinds of lines by adjusting the angle of the brush and the pressure on it. Chinese artists painted chiefly with black ink made of pine soot and glue. They sometimes used vegetable or mineral pigments to add color to their paintings. Chinese painters created many works on silk scrolls, which could be rolled up for storage and safekeeping. Other paintings were done on plaster walls and on paper. See PAINTING (Chinese Painting).

Sculpture and Pottery. The earliest Chinese sculptures were small figures placed in tombs. From the Shang dynasty (1766?-1122 B.C.) through the Chou dynasty (1122-256 B.C.), sculptors created chiefly bronze and jade works. Shang and Chou artists used bronze to make elaborate sacrificial vessels used in ceremonies for the dead. These works were cast in molds, and most had complicated designs based on animal forms.

In 1974, thousands of clay figures of people and horses were discovered in burial pits near the tomb of China's first emperor. These figures, which are the earliest known life-sized Chinese sculptures, date from the 200's B.C.

Buddhism reached China from India during the Han period. Sculptors then began to turn their skills to the service of this new religion. Temples were built in or near cities. In rural areas, cliffsides were hollowed out to form elaborate chapels. Sculptors decorated the chapels with figures of Buddha and his attendants. Some sculptures were carved from local stone. Others were molded of clay and painted. Still other sculptures were cast of bronze and coated with gold. As artistic expressions of religious faith, these works rival the finest sculptures in the monasteries and cathedrals of Europe. See SCULPTURE (China).

Ink painting on silk (1279-1368) by an unknown Chinese artist; National Museum, Taipei, Taiwan (Wan-go H. C. Weng)

Fine Handwriting called *calligraphy* forms an essential part of many Chinese paintings. Artists of the Yuan period often combined calligraphy with paintings of bamboo, as on the fan above.

The Chinese have made pottery since prehistoric times. They began to use the potter's wheel before 2000 B.C. and produced glazed pottery as early as the 1300's B.C. During the T'ang dynasty, the Chinese developed the world's first porcelain. Porcelain dishes and vases produced during the T'ang, Sung, Ming, and early Ch'ing periods are among the greatest treasures of Chinese art.

Bronze vessel (1100's B.C.) by an unknown Chinese artist; Freer Gallery of Art, Smithsonian Institution, Washington, D.C.

Jade disk (400-200 B.C.) by an unknown Chinese artist; Nelson Gallery-Akins Museum, Kansas City, Mo., Nelson Fund

Chinese Ceremonial Art included works created in bronze and jade. Bronze vessels like the one above were used in ceremonies for the dead during the Shang dynasty. The elaborately carved jade disk on the right, called a *pi*, was used as a symbol of heaven in religious ceremonies. It dates from the Chou dynasty.

Gilded bronze statue by an unknown Chinese sculptor; Asian Art Museum of San Francisco, Avery Brundage Collection

Steve Vidler, De Wys, Inc.

Chinese Sculpture was greatly influenced by Buddhism. One of the oldest Chinese Buddhist sculptures is a seated Buddha, *left,* which dates from A.D. 338. Sculptors also created huge figures of Buddha and his attendants for cliffside chapels, such as the Feng-hsien cave in Honan province, *right.*

Architecture. Traditionally, most of the public buildings in China were constructed of wood on a stone foundation. The most outstanding feature of Chinese architecture was a large tile roof with extending edges that curved gracefully upward. These roofs were supported by wooden columns connected to the ceiling beams by wooden brackets. Walls did not support the roof but merely provided privacy. Most buildings had only one story, but the Chinese also built many-storied towers called *pagodas* (see PAGODA). Chinese architects no longer use the traditional styles, and new buildings in Chinese cities look much like those in Western cities.

Music. Chinese music sounds much different from Western music because it uses a different scale. The scales most commonly used in Western music have eight tones, but the Chinese scale has five tones. Melody is the most important element in Chinese music. Instruments and voices follow the same melodic line instead of blending in harmony.

Chinese musical instruments also differ from those played by Western musicians. Chinese instruments include the *ch'in*, a seven-stringed instrument, and the *sheng*, a mouth organ made of seven bamboo pipes. The Chinese also have a lutelike instrument called the *p'i-p'a* and two kinds of flutes, the *hsiao* and the *ti.* Today, Chinese musicians also play Western instruments and perform the music of many of the great European composers.

Theater. Formal Chinese drama began during the Yuan dynasty (1279-1368). Since the 1800's, the most popular form has been *Peking opera.* This type of drama

Unglazed clay jar (about 1200 B.C.); Freer Gallery of Art, Smithsonian Institution, Washington, D.C.

White Pottery made during the Shang dynasty had a polished surface with carved designs. The jar above is a fine example of this pottery.

Multicolor Ceramics were developed in the T'ang era. Potters combined different color glazes to form patterns like the one on the vase below.

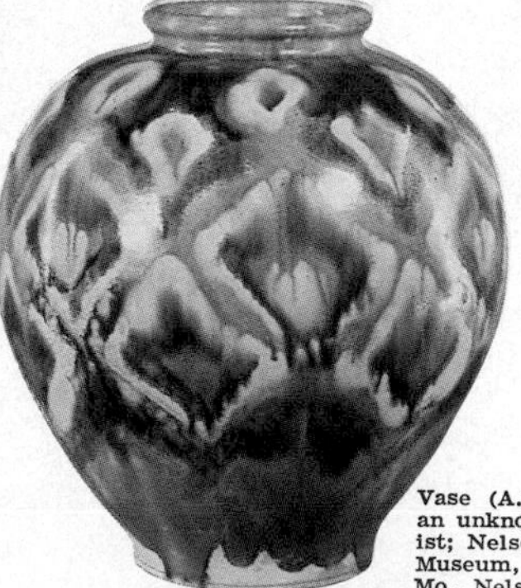

Vase (A.D. 618-907) by an unknown Chinese artist; Nelson Gallery-Akins Museum, Kansas City, Mo., Nelson Fund

Bowl (late 1400's); Freer Gallery of Art, Smithsonian Institution, Washington, D.C.

Fine White Porcelain was produced during the Ming dynasty. Like much Ming porcelain, the bowl above is decorated with a blue underglaze.

WORLD BOOK photo by Robert Borja

Chinese Musicians play both Western and Chinese instruments. In the group shown above, the girl on the left is playing a cello, and her friends are playing traditional Chinese instruments.

combines spoken dialogue and songs with dance and symbolic gestures. Peking opera features colorful and elaborate costumes. The plays are based on traditional Chinese stories, history, and folklore. During the 1950's, the Chinese began to develop a dance form called *revolutionary ballet*. Revolutionary ballet uses Western ballet forms to present stories about the struggle that led to Communist rule in China.

Steve Vidler, De Wys, Inc.

Peking Opera, the most popular form of drama in China, combines dialogue and songs with dance and symbolic gestures. The plays are based on stories from Chinese history and folklore.

CHINA / *The Land*

China is the world's third largest country. Only Russia and Canada are larger. China's land is as varied as it is vast. It ranges from subarctic regions in the north to tropical lowlands in the south and from fertile plains in the east to deserts in the west.

Several regions of China have traditionally been known by certain names. Northeastern China is called *Manchuria*. *Sinkiang* covers the far northwest, and *Tibet* covers the far southwest. *Inner Mongolia* lies in the north. The eastern third of China, south of Manchuria and Inner Mongolia, is commonly called *China Proper*. It has always had most of China's people.

China can be divided into eight major land regions. They are (1) the Tibetan Highlands, (2) the Sinkiang-Mongolian Uplands, (3) the Mongolian Border Uplands, (4) the Eastern Highlands, (5) the Eastern Lowlands, (6) the Central Uplands, (7) the Szechwan Basin, and (8) the Southern Uplands.

The Tibetan Highlands lie in southwestern China. The region consists of a vast plateau bordered by towering mountains—the Himalaya on the south, the Pamirs on the west, and the Kunlun on the north. The world's highest mountain, Mount Everest, rises 29,028 feet (8,848 meters) above sea level in the Himalaya in southern Tibet. Two of the world's longest rivers, the Huang Ho and Yangtze, begin in the highlands and flow eastward across China to the sea.

Tibet suffers from both drought and extreme cold. Most of the region is a wasteland of rock, gravel, snow, and ice. A few areas provide limited grazing for hardy yaks—woolly oxen that furnish food, clothing, and transportation for the Tibetans. Crops can be grown only in a few lower-lying areas. See TIBET.

The Sinkiang-Mongolian Uplands occupy the vast desert areas of northwestern China. The region has plentiful mineral resources. However, it is thinly populated because of its remoteness and harsh climate.

The eastern part of the Sinkiang-Mongolian Uplands consists of the Ordos Desert and a portion of the Gobi Desert. The western part of the region is divided into two areas by the Tien Shan range, which has peaks more than 20,000 feet (6,096 meters) above sea level. South of the mountains lies one of the world's driest deserts, the Takla Makan. The Turfan Depression, an oasis near the northern edge of the Takla Makan, is the lowest point in China. It lies 505 feet (154 meters) below sea level. To the north of the Tien Shan, the Dzungarian Basin stretches northward to the Altai Mountains along the Mongolian border.

The Mongolian Border Uplands lie between the Gobi Desert and the Eastern Lowlands. The Greater Khingan Mountains form the northern part of the region. The terrain there is rugged, and little agriculture is practiced. The southern part of the region is thickly covered with *loess*, a fertile, yellowish soil deposited by the wind. Loess consists of tiny mineral particles and is easily worn away. The Huang Ho and its tributaries have carved out hills and steep-sided valleys in this soft soil. The name *Huang Ho* means *Yellow River* and comes from the large amounts of loess carried by the river.

The Eastern Highlands consist of the Shantung Peninsula and eastern Manchuria. The Shantung Peninsula

The Sinkiang-Mongolian Uplands are a vast area of deserts and rugged mountains in northwestern China. This photograph shows the edge of the Gobi Desert in the eastern part of the region.

Jean DeLord, De Wys, Inc.

is a hilly region with excellent harbors and rich deposits of coal. The hills of eastern Manchuria have China's best forests, and timber is a major product of the region. The highest hills are the Ch'ang Pai Mountains (Long White Mountains) along the Korean border. To the north, the Amur River forms the border with Russia. Just south of the river are the Lesser Khingan Hills.

The Eastern Lowlands lie between the Mongolian Border Uplands and the Eastern Highlands and extend south to the Southern Uplands. From north to south, the region consists of the Manchurian Plain, the North China Plain, and the valley of the Yangtze River. The Eastern Lowlands have China's best farmland and many of the country's largest cities.

The Manchurian Plain has fertile soils and large deposits of coal and iron ore. Most of Manchuria's people live on the southern part of the plain near the Liao River. To the south lies the wide, flat North China Plain in the valley of the Huang Ho. Wheat is the main crop in this highly productive agricultural area. Major flooding of the Huang Ho occurs about every 5 years, with disastrous floods at least every 25 years. These frequent and destructive floods have earned the river the nickname "China's Sorrow."

The Yangtze Valley has the best combination of level land, fertile soil, and sufficient rainfall anywhere in China. In the so-called Fertile Triangle between Nan-ching, Shanghai, and Hang-chou, the rural population exceeds 5,000 persons per square mile (1,900 per square kilometer). The Yangtze River and its many tributaries have long formed China's most important trade route.

Photri

The Eastern Lowlands have China's most productive farmland. These farmers are planting rice seedlings in a flooded field in the Yangtze Valley, which forms the southern part of the Eastern Lowlands. Wheat is the main crop in northern parts of the region.

The Central Uplands are an area of hills and mountains between the Eastern Lowlands and the Tibetan Highlands. The Tsinling Mountains are the chief physical feature of the region. Peaks in the range rise more than 12,000 feet (3,658 meters) above sea level near the city of Sian. The Tsinling cross the region from east to west. They form a natural barricade against seasonal winds that carry rain from the south and dust from the north. For this reason, the Tsinling Mountains are China's most significant geographic boundary. To the north of the mountains are dry wheat-growing areas. To the south lie warm, humid areas where rice is the major crop.

The Szechwan Basin lies south of the Central Uplands. It is a region of hills and valleys surrounded by high mountains. A mild climate and a long growing season make the Szechwan Basin one of China's main agricultural regions. Most crops are grown on *terraced fields*—that is, on level strips of land cut out of the hillsides. The name *Szechwan* means *Four Rivers* and refers to the four streams that flow into the Yangtze in the region. The rivers have carved out deep gorges in the

Physical Features

Altai Mountains ...B 3
Amur River ....A 6
Ch'ang Pai Mountains ....B 7
Dzungarian Basin ..B 2
Gobi (Desert) .....C 4
Grand Canal ......D 6
Greater Khingan Range ....A 6
Hai-nan Island ....E 5
Himalaya (Mountains) .....E 2
Hsi Chiang (West River) ....E 5
Huang Ho (Yellow River) ...D 5
Koko Nor Lake ....C 3
Kunlun Mountains .C 2
Lesser Khingan Range ....A 6
Liao River ....B 6
Loess Hills ....C 5
Manchurian Plain ..B 6
Mekong River .....D 3
Mount Everest .....E 2
Mount Godwin Austen ....C 1
Mount Kailas ......D 1
Mount Makalu .....D 2
Namcha Barwa (Mountain) ......D 3
Nan Ling Mountains ....E 5
Nan Mountains ....C 3
North China Plain ....D 6
Ordos Desert ....C 5
Pamirs (Mountains) .....C 1
P'o-yang Lake ....D 6
Shantung Peninsula ....C 6
Sheng-li Peak ......B 2
Szechwan Basin ....D 4
Ta-hsueh Mountains ....D 4
Takla Makan Desert ....C 2
Tarim Basin ....C 2
Tibet, Plateau of ..D 2
Tien Shan (Mountains) ....B 1
Tsaidam Basin .....C 3
Tsinling Mountains ....D 5
Tung-t'ing Lake ...E 5
Turfan Depression ..B 3
Yangtze River .....D 6
Yellow Sea ....C 6
Yunnan Plateau ....E 4

Shostal

The Central Uplands include dry wheat-growing areas like this one near the city of Sian. To the south of this area, the Tsinling Mountains cross the Central Uplands from west to east.

red sandstone of the region and so made land travel difficult. Ships can travel on the Yangtze into western Szechwan, but only small craft can navigate the river's swift-flowing tributaries.

The Southern Uplands cover southeastern China, including the island of Hai-nan. The Southern Uplands are a region of green hills and mountains. The only level area is the delta of the Hsi Chiang (West River). The Hsi Chiang and its tributaries form the main transportation route for southern China. Canton (Kuang-chou), southern China's only major city, lies near the mouth of the Hsi Chiang. Deep, rich soils and a tropical climate help make the delta area an extremely productive agricultural region.

The rest of the Southern Uplands is so hilly and mountainous that little land can be cultivated, even by terracing. The central part of the region, near the city of Kuei-lin, is one of the most beautiful areas in China. It has many isolated limestone hills that rise 100 to 600 feet (30 to 182 meters) almost straight up.

Henry Herr Gill

The Southern Uplands are a region of green hills and mountains. This picture shows part of the city of Kuei-lin and the Li River, one of the many important waterways in the central part of the region.

China has an extremely wide range of climates because it is such a large country and has such a variety of natural features. The most severe climatic conditions occur in the Takla Makan and Gobi deserts. Daytime temperatures in these deserts may exceed 100° F. (38° C) in summer, but nighttime lows may fall to −30° F. (−34° C) in winter. Both Tibet and northern Manchuria have long, bitterly cold winters. In contrast, coastal areas of southeastern China have a tropical climate.

Seasonal winds called *monsoons* greatly affect China's climate. In winter, monsoons carry cold, dry air from central Asia across China toward the sea. These high winds often create dust storms in the north. From late spring to early fall, the monsoons blow from the opposite direction and spread warm, moist air inland from the sea. Because of the monsoons, more rain falls in summer than in winter throughout China. Most parts of the country actually receive more than 80 per cent of their rainfall between May and October.

Summers tend to be hot and humid in the eastern half of China Proper and in southern Manchuria. In fact, summer temperatures average about 80° F. (27° C) throughout much of China. However, northern China has longer and much colder winters than the south has. In January, daily low temperatures average about −13° F. (−25° C) in northern Manchuria and about 20° F. (−7° C) throughout much of northern China Proper. In contrast, Canton has an average January temperature of 57° F. (14° C). Southern China and the Yangtze Valley west of Wu-han are shielded from the cold winter winds by mountains. The Szechwan Basin is especially well protected, and frost rarely occurs there.

The amount of precipitation varies greatly from region to region in China. The deserts of Sinkiang and Inner Mongolia receive less than 4 inches (10 centimeters) of rain yearly. More than 40 inches (100 centimeters) of rain falls each year in many parts of southern China Proper. Some areas of southeastern China receive up to 80 inches (200 centimeters) annually. In northern China the amount of precipitation varies widely from year to year. However, most areas receive less than 40 inches (100 centimeters) yearly. For example, annual precipitation averages about 25 inches (63 centimeters) in Peking and 28 inches (70 centimeters) in Shen-yang (Mukden). Snowfalls occur only in the north. But even there, they are infrequent and usually light.

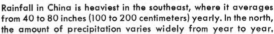

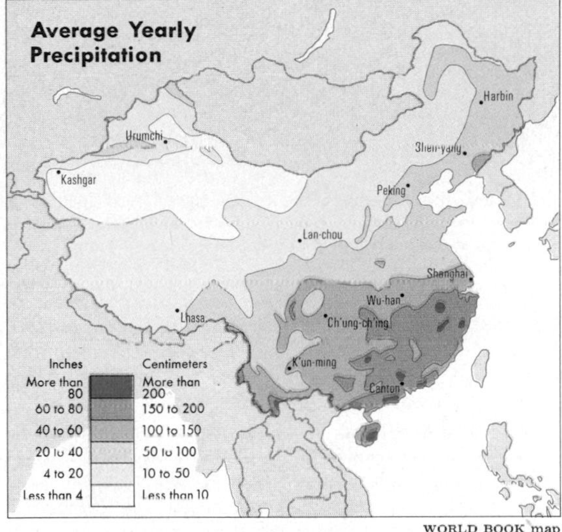

WORLD BOOK map

Rainfall in China is heaviest in the southeast, where it averages from 40 to 80 inches (100 to 200 centimeters) yearly. In the north, the amount of precipitation varies widely from year to year.

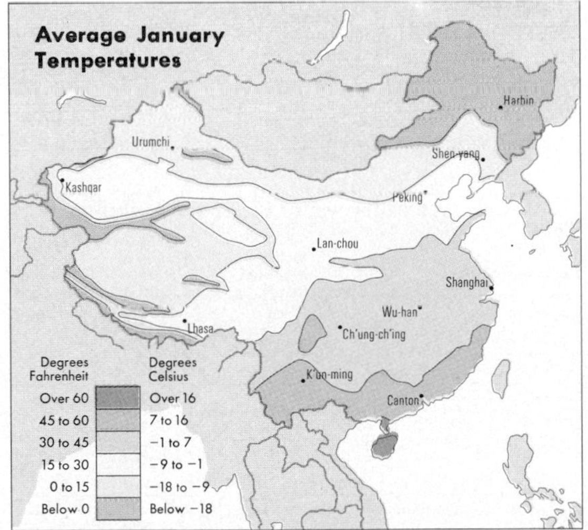

WORLD BOOK map

Northern and western China have far colder winters than the south. January temperatures average below 0°F. (−18°C) in Manchuria and Tibet but over 60°F. (16°C) on the south coast.

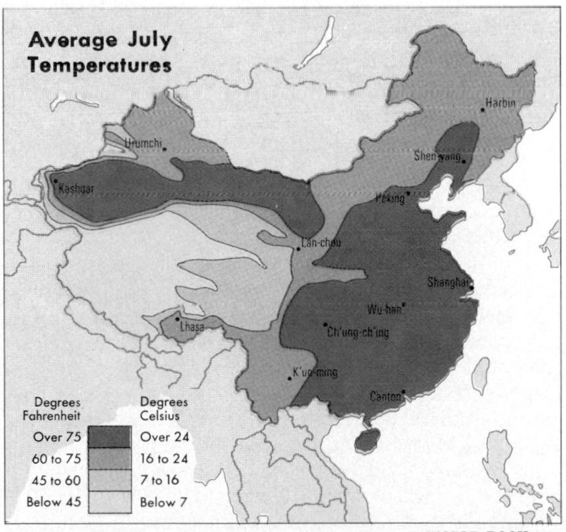

WORLD BOOK map

Temperatures in July average above 75°F. (24°C) throughout China Proper and in southern Manchuria. Daytime temperatures may exceed 100°F. (38°C) in the deserts of northwestern China.

Emil Schulthess, Black Star

Chinese Agriculture produces nearly all the food needed to feed the nation's people. These women are picking tea, which is one of the main crops grown in southern China.

China has one of the world's largest economies in terms of its *gross national product* (GNP). The GNP is the value of all goods and services produced in a country yearly. China ranks among the world's 10 leading countries in GNP. However, China ranks below more than 100 other countries in *per capita* (per person) GNP, which is determined by dividing the GNP by the nation's population. Economists consider China a developing country because it has such a low per capita GNP and because only about 10 per cent of all workers are employed in industry.

The national government has tremendous control over China's economy. It owns and operates all important industrial plants and directly controls most nonagricultural employment and wages. The government also controls and operates the banking system, all long-distance transportation, and foreign trade. It rations food, clothing, and other necessities and sets the prices of most goods and services. The government receives most of its income from the profits of state-owned businesses. Government planners have used these profits to invest heavily in the development of China's manufacturing industries.

The Communist government has achieved an impressive record of economic growth. The Communists have provided widespread employment opportunities, job security, and a more even distribution of income among the people. The prospects for China's economy to continue growing remain favorable. The country has enough mineral and fuel resources to become one of the world's developed nations. Another extremely important resource is China's hard-working and skillful people.

China's government makes plans for the country's economy that cover five-year periods. These five-year plans determine how much money the government will invest in each type of industry and agriculture. The plans help determine the quantity of goods each worker is expected to produce.

Agriculture is the backbone of China's economy. About three-fourths of all workers are farmers. In southern China, rice and tea are the major crops. Wheat is the chief crop in the north, followed by corn and *kaoliang* (sorghum). China produces more cotton, rice, tobacco, and vegetables than any other country. In addition, it is a leading producer of apples, corn, oats, sugar cane, tea, and wheat. Chinese farmers also raise a wide variety of other crops, including millet, peanuts, and soybeans. Farmers on Hai-nan Island grow tropical crops, such as bananas, coconuts, and coffee.

Only about 13 per cent of China's land area can be cultivated. Thus, farmers have extremely little cropland to support themselves and the rest of the huge population. However, they manage to provide almost enough food for all the people. Only small supplies must be imported. This accomplishment is made possible partly by the long growing season in southern China. Farmers there can grow two or more crops on the same land each year. Chinese farmers must do most

China's Gross National Product

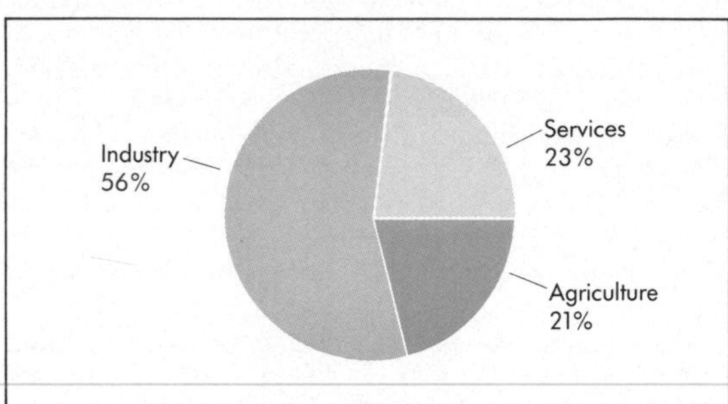

The gross national product (GNP) is the total value of goods and services produced by a country in a year. The GNP measures a nation's total economic performance and can also be used to compare the economic output and growth of countries. China's GNP was $468,000,000,000 in 1979.

Production and Workers by Economic Activities

Economic Activities	Per Cent of GDP Produced	Employed Workers Number of Persons	Employed Workers Per Cent of Total
Manufacturing & Mining	56	44,367,000	11
Trade & Finance	23	13,376,000	3
Agriculture, Forestry, & Fishing	21	307,960,000	76
Community Services	(*)	11,310,000	3
Construction	(†)	8,903,000	2
Government	(*)	4,680,000	1
Other Services	(*)	7,272,000	2
Transportation, Communication, & Utilities	(*)	7,834,000	2
Total	100	405,702,000	100

*Included in Trade & Finance.
†Included in Manufacturing & Mining.
Sources: *China Under the Four Modernizations*, Joint Economic Committee, U.S. Congress, August 1982; National Foreign Assessment Center, CIA.

of their work by hand with simple tools. They make extensive use of irrigation and organic fertilizers and practice soil conservation.

During the 1950's, the Communists *collectivized* China's agriculture. They organized the peasants into groups to farm the land cooperatively. The basic unit in the collectivized system is the production team, which on the average consists of about 30 households. Each production team pays an agricultural tax and agrees to sell a certain portion of its output to the state. However, the team decides what crops to grow and how to use its workers. It also decides how to distribute the output that remains after the tax has been paid and the required sale to the state has been made.

Collectivization has expanded China's farm output by increasing both the size of the labor force and the amount of cultivated land. However, unfavorable terrain and climate have limited the annual rate of growth in productivity to 2 to 3 per cent since the 1950's. Faster growth will require the introduction of higher-yielding seeds, increased use of machinery, expanded irrigation, and wider use of chemical fertilizers.

Livestock production has increased significantly in China since the 1950's. In rural areas, many families raise chickens and ducks, and nearly every household has a pig. Pigs provide both meat and fertilizer. The Chinese use so much pig manure to fertilize the soil that the pig is called the "Chinese fertilizer factory." China has over 250 million hogs, more than a third of the world's total. China also has large numbers of cattle, goats, horses, and sheep.

Manufacturing in China is concentrated in and around large cities near the coast. A shortage of modern transportation has hampered attempts to build factories in other areas. Shanghai is China's biggest industrial center. Peking and Tientsin also have many large manufacturing plants. In Manchuria, the Chinese have developed a major center of heavy industry in the Shen-yang area, with smaller centers at An-shan, Ch'ang-ch'un, Fu-shun, and Pen-ch'i.

After the Communists came to power, they began to rebuild China's factories in an effort to make the nation an industrial power. They concentrated on the development of heavy industries, such as the produc-

Henry Weaver, Lensman

Raising Hogs is a major agricultural activity in China. Hogs are the main source of meat for the Chinese, and Chinese farmers use huge quantities of hog manure to fertilize the soil.

China Land Use

This map shows the major uses of land in China. Nearly all of China's cropland is in the eastern half of the country. Extremely dry conditions in western China make much of the land there unproductive.

WORLD BOOK map

tion of metals and machinery. Since 1949, China's industrial production has grown at an average annual rate of more than 12 per cent. Today, China has one of the world's largest steel industries. It produces about 40 million short tons (36 million metric tons) of steel annually. The machine-building industry provides metalworking tools and other machines for new factories. Other major manufactured products include fertilizer and other chemicals, irrigation equipment, locomotives, military equipment, ships, tractors, and trucks.

China's consumer goods industries have not grown as quickly as heavy industries. The largest consumer goods industries are the textile industry and the food-processing industry. As the standard of living in China improves, demand is growing for such consumer goods as bicycles, radios, sewing machines, and watches. As a result, the Chinese are increasing their production of these items.

The continuation of China's rapid pace of industrial development faces some major obstacles. The greatest problem is China's outdated technology and a shortage of highly trained engineers and technicians. To help solve this problem, China's leaders have made contracts with foreign companies to modernize the country's factories and to build new ones. They have also begun to improve and expand scientific and technical education in China and to send students abroad for training. Waste and inefficiency in industry are also problems. Steps to combat these problems include greater government control over factories and the introduction of wage and bonus systems that give workers more pay for more production.

Mining. China is one of the world's largest producers of coal. Coal deposits occur in many parts of China, but the best fields are in the north.

During the early 1950's, more than 90 per cent of China's energy came from coal. Since that time, however, the Chinese have discovered and rapidly made use of large deposits of petroleum. Today, oil provides about 20 per cent of China's energy, and natural gas supplies about 10 per cent. China's largest oil field is at Ta-ch'ing in northern Manchuria. Other major Chinese oil fields include those at Sheng-li on the Shantung Peninsula; at Takang, near Tientsin; and at Karamai in Sinkiang.

The Chinese have greatly increased the mining of iron ore to meet the needs of their growing iron and steel industry. Today, China is a leading producer of iron ore. Most of the country's iron ore comes from large, low-grade deposits in the northeastern provinces. Some mines in central and northern China yield rich iron ore.

China outranks all other countries in the production of tungsten, and it is a leading producer of antimony, gold, and tin. China also mines bauxite, lead, manganese, salt, uranium, and zinc.

Fishing Industry. China has one of the world's largest fishing industries. The Chinese catch about 4½ million short tons (4.1 million metric tons) of fish and shellfish annually. About one-fourth of the catch comes from freshwater fisheries, and the rest comes from the sea. Fish farming is growing in importance in China. Fish farmers raise fish in ponds both for food and for use in fertilizer.

Trade is vital to China's economic development. During the 1950's, the Chinese imported from Russia most of the machinery needed to build their industries. However, friendly relations between China and Russia broke down in the early 1960's. The Chinese then began to follow a policy of economic self-reliance and sought to limit imports. But China's present leaders have largely abandoned the principle of self-reliance. They are importing the machinery and other technology needed to modernize China's economy. In addition, the Chinese are even seeking foreign loans to finance these imports.

China's chief imports are metals and machinery. Other leading imports include grain, cotton, and fertilizers. The country's main exports consist of textiles, tea, and such foods as fruits, grain, pork, and vegetables. During the 1970's, the Chinese began to export large quantities of petroleum. They hope to export more and more petroleum to help pay for their imports. Japan is China's largest trading partner, followed by Hong Kong, West Germany, and France.

Transportation. The Chinese rely mainly on simple, traditional means for transportation over short distances. The people carry heavy loads fastened to their back or hanging from poles carried across their shoulders. Carts and wagons are pulled either by people or by donkeys, horses, or mules. Boats are pulled along canals and rivers by animals on the bank.

Railroads make up by far the most important part of China's modern transportation system. The country has about 33,000 miles (53,000 kilometers) of railroad tracks. Rail lines link all the major cities and manufacturing centers. The railroads transport over 60 per cent of the freight hauled by modern means. They also carry much of China's passenger traffic.

China has about 500,000 miles (800,000 kilometers) of highways, of which only about an eighth are paved.

Björn Klingwall

The Production of Machinery plays a vital role in the development of China's economy. This factory manufactures tractors, which will help modernize agriculture in China.

Henry Weaver, Lensman

Dockworkers load agricultural products onto barges and small boats, which transport the goods over China's inland waterways. For most transportation over short distances, the Chinese use simple, traditional means. For example, they carry heavy loads on their back or hanging from a pole that rests across the shoulders.

Highway traffic in China consists chiefly of trucks and buses. China has very few automobiles.

About one-fourth of China's more than 100,000 miles (160,000 kilometers) of inland waterways can be used by passenger steamers and freighters. The Grand Canal, which is the world's longest artificially created waterway, extends more than 1,000 miles (1,600 kilometers) from Hang-chou in the south to Peking in the north. For location, see CHINA (terrain map).

China's major ports include Canton, Dairen, Shanghai, and Tsingtao. The chief airports are at Peking, Shanghai, and Canton. The Civil Aviation Administration of China (CAAC) operates flights that link over 70 cities within the country. The CAAC and several foreign airlines fly planes between China and a number of cities in Asia and Europe. The CAAC also has flights to San Francisco.

Communication in China comes under strict government control. China's rulers decide what people read in newspapers and magazines, what they hear on radio, and what they see on television.

The government and the Chinese Communist Party publish hundreds of daily newspapers and many weeklies. China's leading newspaper is *Jen Min Jih Pao* (People's Daily) of Peking, the official paper of the Communist Party. In addition to printed newspapers, China has countless mimeographed and handwritten newssheets. So-called big-character posters were formerly a means of communication and personal expression in China. People expressed opinions on the posters and hung them on walls in cities. In the late 1970's, many people began using posters to complain about the political system in the country. In 1980, the Chinese government outlawed the practice of hanging posters on the walls.

China has about 260 radio stations and about 120 television stations. Many Chinese families own a radio. Radio programs are also broadcast over loudspeakers in many public areas. Few Chinese families can afford a television set, and so most sets are owned by groups. The Chinese use their telephone and telegraph systems mainly for official purposes or in emergencies. The people depend chiefly on the postal system for personal communication.

Steve Vidler, De Wys, Inc.

Wall Posters served as a means of communication in China for many years. People used the posters to express their opinions. They hung them on walls in parks and other public areas. In 1980, the Chinese government outlawed such posters after people began using posters to criticize the country's political system.

WORLD BOOK photo by Robert Borja

The Great Wall of China was constructed by the ancient Chinese to keep out invaders from central Asia. It extends about 4,000 miles (6,400 kilometers) across northern China.

The oldest written records of Chinese history date from the Shang dynasty (1766?-1122 B.C.). These records consist of inscriptions inside bronze vessels and notations scratched on thousands of turtle shells and animal bones. About 100 B.C., a Chinese historian named Ssu-ma Ch'ien wrote the first major history of China. Through the centuries, the Chinese have always appreciated the importance of history and so have kept detailed records of the events of their times.

Beginnings of Chinese Civilization

People have lived in what is now China since long before the beginning of written history. A type of prehistoric human being called *Peking man* lived about 375,000 years ago in what is now northern China. By about 10,000 B.C., a number of New Stone Age cultures had developed in this area. From two of these cultures—the Yang-shao and the Lung-shan—a distinctly Chinese civilization gradually emerged.

The Yang-shao culture reached the peak of its development about 3000 B.C. The culture extended from the central valley of the Huang Ho to the present-day province of Kansu. In time, the Yang-shao culture was displaced by the Lung-shan, which spread over most of China Proper. The Lung-shan people lived in walled communities, cultivated millet and rice, and raised cattle and sheep.

China's first dynasty, the Shang dynasty, arose from the Lung-shan culture during the 1700's B.C. The Shang kingdom was centered in the Huang Ho Valley. It became a highly developed society governed by a hereditary class of aristocrats. The dynasty's outstanding accomplishments included the creation of magnificent bronze vessels, the development of horse-drawn war chariots, and the establishment of a Chinese system of writing.

In 1122 B.C., the Chou people of western China overthrew the Shang and established their own dynasty. The Chou dynasty ruled China until 256 B.C. From its beginning, the dynasty directly controlled only part of northern China. In the east, the Chou gave authority to certain followers, who became lords of semi-independent states. As time passed, these lords grew increasingly independent of the royal court and so weakened its power. Battles over the years between the Chou rulers and non-Chinese invaders further weakened the dynasty. In 771 B.C., the Chou were forced to abandon their capital, near what is now Sian, and move eastward to Loyang.

During the later Chou period, the rulers of the eastern states fought one another for the control of all China. The fighting reached a peak between 403 and 221 B.C. Efforts to find a way to restore order to Chinese society

IMPORTANT DATES IN CHINA

1766?-1122 B.C. China's first dynasty, the Shang, ruled the nation.

1122 B.C. The Chou people of western China overthrew the Shang and set up a new dynasty that ruled until 256 B.C.

221-206 B.C. The Ch'in dynasty established China's first strong central government.

202 B.C.-A.D. 220 China became a powerful empire under the Han dynasty. Chinese culture flourished.

581-618 The Sui dynasty reunified China after almost 400 years of division.

618-907 The T'ang dynasty ruled China during a period of prosperity and great cultural accomplishment.

960-1279 The Sung dynasty ruled the empire and made Neo-Confucianism the official state philosophy.

1275-1292 Marco Polo visited China.

1279 The Mongols gained control of all China.

1368-1644 The Ming dynasty governed China.

1644-1912 The Manchus ruled China as the Ch'ing dynasty.

1842 The Treaty of Nan-ching gave Hong Kong to Great Britain and opened five Chinese ports to British trade.

1851-1864 Millions of Chinese died in bloody warfare during the Taiping Rebellion.

1900 Secret societies attacked and killed Westerners and Chinese Christians during the Boxer Rebellion.

1912 The Republic of China was established.

1928 The Nationalists, led by Chiang Kai-shek, united China under one government.

1931 The Japanese seized Manchuria.

1934-1935 Mao Zedong led the Chinese Communists on their Long March to Shensi.

1937-1945 War with Japan shattered China.

1949 The Chinese Communists defeated the Nationalists and established the People's Republic of China.

1953 China began its First Five-Year Plan for economic development.

1958 The Communists launched the Great Leap Forward, which severely weakened China's economy.

1962 Chinese troops fought a border war with India.

1963 Friendly relations between China and Russia ended.

1966-1969 The Cultural Revolution disrupted education, the government, and daily life in China.

1971 China was admitted to the United Nations (UN).

1972 U.S. President Richard M. Nixon visited China.

1976 Communist Party Chairman Mao Zedong and Premier Zhou Enlai died.

1979 China and the United States established normal diplomatic relations.

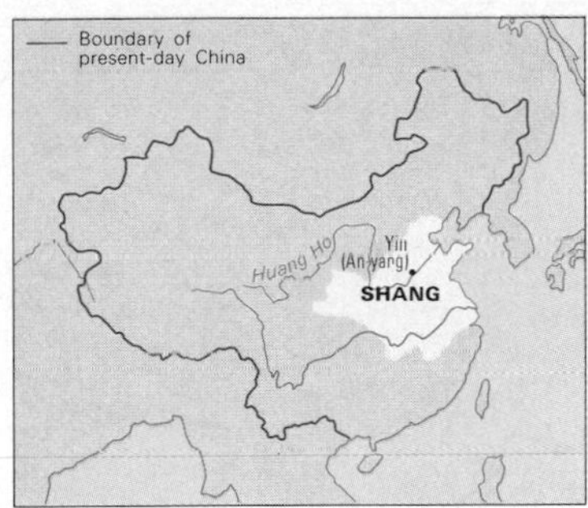

China's First Dynasty, the Shang, arose in the Huang Ho Valley during the 1700's B.C. It ruled China until 1122 B.C.

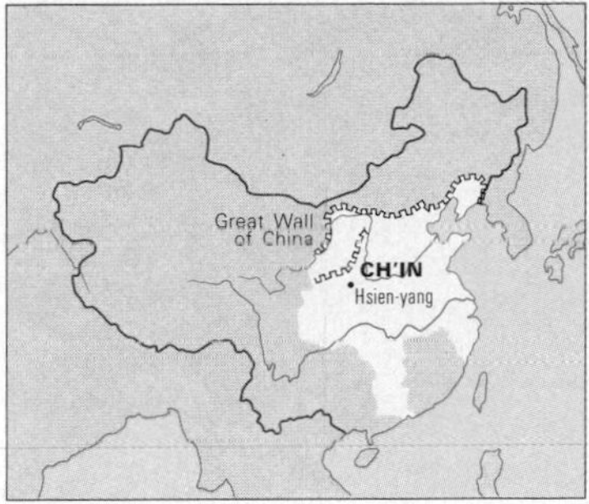

The Ch'in Dynasty, in 221 B.C., established China's first empire controlled by a strong central government.

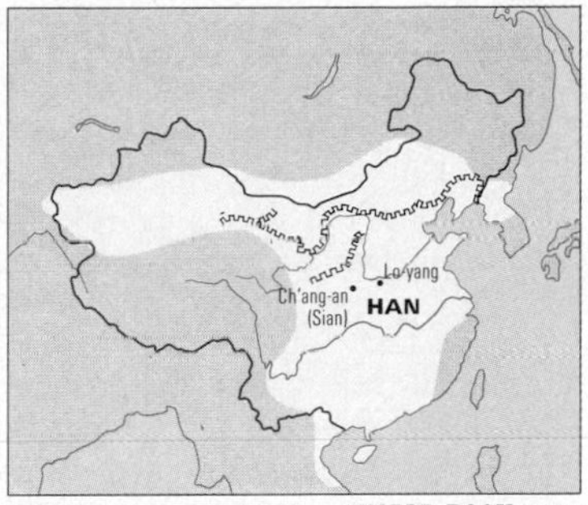

WORLD BOOK maps

The Han Dynasty gained control of China in 202 B.C. Han rulers expanded the Chinese empire into central Asia.

helped produce a flowering of Chinese thought during this period. The great philosopher Confucius proposed new moral standards to replace the magical and religious standards of his time. This development in Chinese thought compared in many ways to the shift from religion to philosophy that occurred among the people of Greece at about the same time.

In 221 B.C., the Ch'in state defeated all its rivals and established China's first empire controlled by a strong central government. The Ch'in believed in a philosophy called *Legalism*, and their victory resulted partly from following Legalistic ideas. Legalism emphasized the importance of authority, efficient administration, and strict laws. A combination of Legalistic administrative practices and Confucian moral values helped the Chinese empire endure for more than 2,000 years.

The Age of Empire

The Early Empire. The Ch'in dynasty lasted only until 206 B.C. However, it brought great changes that influenced the entire age of empire in China. The first Ch'in emperor, Shih Huang Ti, abolished the local states and set up a strong central government. His government standardized weights and measures, the currency, and the Chinese writing system. To keep out invaders, Shih Huang Ti ordered the construction of the Great Wall of China. Laborers built the wall by joining shorter walls constructed during the Chou dynasty. The Great Wall stretches about 4,000 miles (6,400 kilometers) from near the coast to the province of Kansu in north-central China.

Shih Huang Ti taxed the Chinese people heavily to support his military campaigns and his vast building projects. These taxes and the harsh enforcement of laws led to civil war soon after his death in 210 B.C. The Ch'in dynasty quickly collapsed. The Han dynasty then gained control of China. It ruled from 202 B.C. to A.D. 220.

During the Han period, Confucianism became the philosophical basis of government. Aristocrats held most of the important state offices. However, a person's qualifications began to play a role in the selection and placement of officials. Chinese influence spread into neighboring countries, and overland trade routes linked China with Europe for the first time.

In A.D. 8, a Han official named Wang Mang seized the throne and set up the Hsin dynasty. However, the Han dynasty regained control of China by A.D. 25. Art, education, and science thrived during this later Han period. Writers produced histories and dictionaries. They also collected classics of literature from earlier times. In A.D. 105, the Chinese invented paper. During the late Han period, Buddhism was introduced into China from India.

Political struggles at the royal court and administrative dishonesty plagued the last century of Han rule. In addition, powerful regional officials began to ignore the central government. Large-scale rebellion finally broke out, and the Han fell in 220. China then split into three competing kingdoms. Soon afterward, nomadic groups invaded northern China. A series of short-lived non-Chinese dynasties ruled all or part of the north from 304 to 581. In the south, the so-called Six Dynasties followed one another from 317 to 589. During these centuries of division, Buddhism spread across China and influenced all aspects of life.

The brief Sui dynasty (581-618) reunified China. By 605, the Grand Canal linked the Yangtze Valley with northern China. The canal made the grain and other products of the south more easily available to support the political and military needs of the north.

The T'ang Dynasty replaced the Sui in 618 and ruled China for nearly 300 years. The T'ang period was an age of prosperity and great cultural accomplishment. The T'ang capital at Ch'ang-an (now Sian) had more than a million persons, making it the largest city in the world. It attracted diplomats, traders, poets, and scholars from throughout Asia and the Mediterranean area. Some of China's greatest poets, including Li Po and Tu Fu, wrote during the T'ang period. Buddhism remained an enormous cultural influence, but followers adapted it to Chinese ways. Distinctly Chinese schools of Buddhism developed, including *Ch'an* (Zen) and *Ching-t'u* (Pure Land). During the 800's, however, a revival of Confucianism began.

In 755, a rebellion led by a northern general named An Lu-shan touched off a gradual decline in T'ang power. From 875 to 884, another great rebellion further weakened the T'ang empire, which finally ended in 907. During the period that followed, a succession of

"Five Dynasties and Ten Kingdoms" struggled for control of the shattered empire. In 960, the Sung dynasty reunified China.

The Sung Dynasty brought two major changes that affected the Chinese empire throughout the rest of its existence. First, the Sung rulers firmly established a system of civil service examinations that had begun during the T'ang period. They thus completed the shift of social and political power from aristocratic families to officials selected on the basis of talent. The second significant change was the development of *Neo-Confucianism*, which combined the moral standards of traditional Confucianism with elements of Buddhism and Taoism. The philosopher Chu Hsi was largely responsible for this new Confucianism. The Sung dynasty established Neo-Confucianism as the official state philosophy, and all later Chinese dynasties continued to support it.

During the Sung period, the introduction of early-ripening rice made it possible to grow two or three crops a year in the south. The increased rice production helped support the population, which for the first time exceeded 100 million. Chinese inventions during this period included gunpowder, the magnetic compass, and movable type for printing. Literature, philosophy, and history flourished as more and more people learned how to read and write. In the fine arts, the great Sung achievements were hard-glazed porcelains and magnificent landscape paintings.

The Sung dynasty never had great military strength. In 1126, it lost northern China to invaders from Manchuria. The Sung then moved their capital from K'ai-feng to Hang-chou on the wealthy lower Yangtze Delta, and the dynasty became known as the Southern Sung.

Mongol Rule. During the 1200's, Mongol warriors swept into China from the north. The Mongol leader Kublai Khan established the Yuan dynasty. It controlled China from 1279 to 1368, the first time that all China had come under foreign rule. During the Yuan period, Europeans became aware of China through the reports of travelers and traders. The most enthusiastic reports came from Marco Polo, a trader from Venice. After traveling widely in China from 1275 to 1292, Polo returned home with glowing accounts of the highly civilized country he called *Cathay*.

The Mongols ruled China harshly. During the mid-1300's, rebellions drove the Mongols out of China and led to the establishment of the Ming dynasty.

The Ming Dynasty ruled from 1368 to 1644, a period of stability, prosperity, and revived Chinese influence in eastern Asia. Literature and art flourished again. In reaction to Mongol rule, the Ming emperors looked down on all things foreign. When European traders visited China during the 1500's and 1600's, the Ming rulers treated them as inferiors. In addition, the Chinese considered the Europeans' trade activities to be smuggling and piracy. The low opinion the Chinese had of European traders hampered Roman Catholic missionaries who began to reach China about 1600.

The Early Rule of the Manchus. In 1644, the Manchu people of Manchuria invaded China and established the Ch'ing dynasty. The Manchus ruled China until 1912. Like the Mongols, the Manchus were foreigners. But unlike the Mongols, the Manchus had adopted many elements of Chinese culture before they gained control of the empire. The Manchus strongly supported Neo-Confucianism and modeled their political system after that of the Ming.

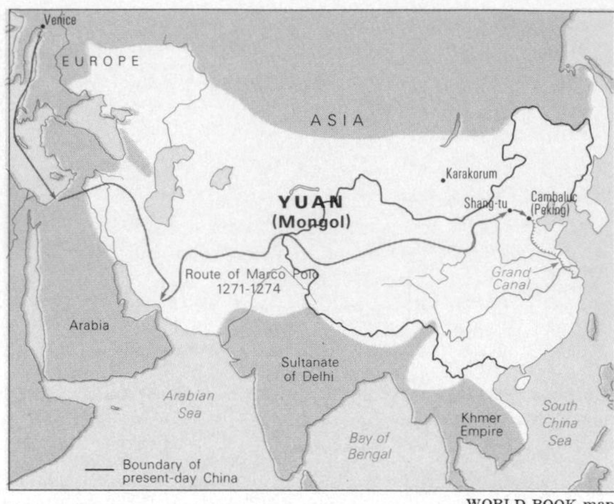

WORLD BOOK map

The Yuan (Mongol) Dynasty ruled China from 1279 to 1368. During this period, China was part of the vast Mongol Empire. Marco Polo, a trader from Venice, visited China during the Yuan period and carried home reports of a highly civilized country.

From 1661 to 1799, the Ch'ing empire enjoyed stability and prosperity. Chinese influence extended into Mongolia, Tibet, and central Asia. Commerce and the output of agriculture and the handicraft industry increased remarkably. China's population expanded rapidly. It rose from about 150 million in 1700 to more than 400 million by 1850.

By the late 1700's, the standard of living in China began to decline as the population grew faster than agricultural production. After the 1760's, political dishonesty plagued the Ch'ing administration. In 1796, the worsening economic and political conditions touched off a rebellion, which was led by anti-Manchu secret societies. The rebellion lasted until 1804 and greatly weakened the Ch'ing dynasty.

Clash with the Western Powers. European merchants had little effect on China before the 1800's. The Chinese government restricted foreign trade to the port of Canton and severely limited contact between foreigners and Chinese. China exported large quantities of tea and silk to the West but purchased few goods in return. To balance their trade, European merchants began to bring opium to China during the early 1800's. The Chinese had outlawed the importation of opium, and so the Europeans were smuggling the drug.

Opium smuggling created much local disorder in China, and the large outflow of silver to pay for the opium seriously disturbed the economy. In March 1839, Chinese officials tried to stop the illegal trade by seizing 20,000 chests of opium from British merchants in Canton. The Opium War then broke out between China and Great Britain. Britain easily won the war, which ended with the Treaty of Nan-ching in 1842.

The Treaty of Nan-ching was the first of what the Chinese called the *unequal treaties*. It gave the Chinese island of Hong Kong to Great Britain and opened five Chinese ports to British residence and trade. The Treaty of Nan-ching also granted British officials the right to deal on equal terms with Chinese officials and to try criminal cases involving British citizens. China signed similar treaties with France and the United States in 1844 and with several other European nations by 1851. These treaties stated that any rights granted to one foreign power must also be given to the other nations. The Western nations thus acquired a common interest in maintaining their special privileges in China.

From 1858 to 1860, China and the foreign powers signed more treaties. These treaties opened additional ports to trade, permitted foreign shipping on the Yangtze, and allowed missionaries to live and own property in the interior of China. The treaties also called for the Western nations to establish permanent diplomatic offices in Peking. Great Britain added the Kowloon Peninsula to its Hong Kong colony, and Russia received all Chinese territory north of the Amur River and east of the Ussuri River.

The Taiping Rebellion. A series of uprisings during the mid-1800's posed a serious threat to the survival of the Ch'ing dynasty. The most important uprising was the Taiping Rebellion. It lasted from 1851 to 1864 and caused the loss of millions of lives. The Taipings were a semireligious group that combined Christian beliefs with ancient Chinese ideas for perfecting society. They challenged both the Ch'ing dynasty and Confucianism with a program to divide the land equally among the people. After 14 years of bloody civil war, local Chinese officials organized new armies, which defeated the Taipings. The Ch'ing received some military aid from the foreign powers. These nations wanted the dynasty to survive so that the terms of the unequal treaties could remain in effect.

The Fall of the Manchus. A disastrous war with Japan in 1894 and 1895 forced the Chinese to recognize Japan's control over Korea. China also had to give the Japanese the island of Taiwan, which China had controlled since 1683. France, Germany, Great Britain, and Russia then forced the crumbling Chinese empire to grant them more trading rights and territory. The division of China into a number of European colonies appeared likely. But the Chinese people had begun to develop strong feelings of belonging together as a nation. This growth of nationalism helped prevent the division of the country. In addition, the United States wanted China to remain independent. In 1899, the United States persuaded the other Western powers to accept the *Open-Door Policy*, which guaranteed the rights of all nations to trade with China on an equal basis.

By the 1890's, some Chinese violently opposed the spread of Western and Christian influences in China. Chinese rebels formed secret societies to fight these influences. The best-known society was called the *Boxers* by Westerners because its members practiced Chinese ceremonial exercises that resembled shadowboxing. In the Boxer Rebellion of 1900, the Boxers and other secret societies attacked and killed Westerners and Chinese Christians. Even the Manchu court supported this campaign of terror. A rescue force from eight nations crushed the rebellion.

In the years following the Boxer Rebellion, the Manchus set out to reform the Chinese government and economy. They abolished the Confucian civil service examinations, established modern schools, and sent students abroad to study. They also organized and equipped a Western-style army. In addition, the Ch'ing court reorganized the central government, promised to adopt a constitution, and permitted the provinces to elect their own legislatures.

The Manchu reforms came too late to save the dynasty. A movement to set up a republic had been growing since the Japanese defeat of China in 1895. In 1905, several revolutionary republican organizations combined to form the United League. They chose as their leader Sun Yat-sen, a Western-educated physician.

From 1905 to 1911, the rebels staged a series of unsuccessful armed attacks against the Manchus. Finally, on Oct. 10, 1911, army troops loosely associated with the United League revolted at Wu-ch'ang. By the year's end, all the southern and central provinces had declared their independence from Manchu rule.

Modern China

The Early Republic. In December 1911, the leaders of the revolution met in Nan-ching to establish the Re-

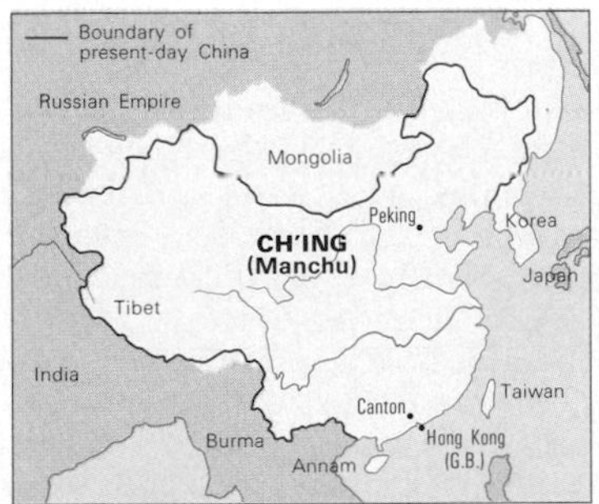

The Ch'ing Dynasty, an empire established by the Manchu people of Manchuria, ruled China from 1644 to 1912.

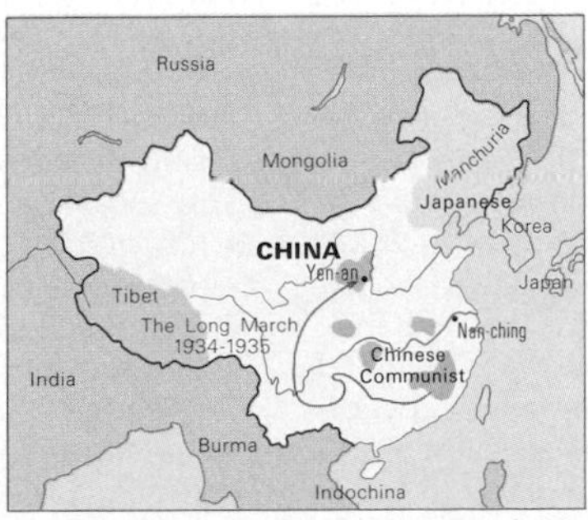

In 1934, the Nationalists forced the Communists to flee their bases in southern China and begin their famous Long March.

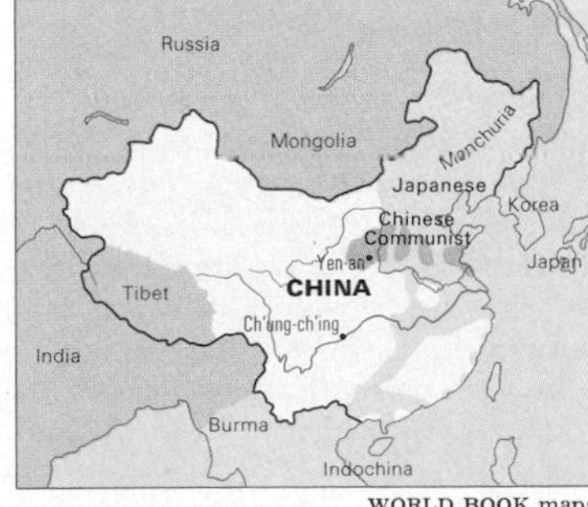

WORLD BOOK maps

Japanese Expansion into China reached its greatest extent in 1944, when the Japanese controlled much of eastern China.

Photoworld

Troops from Eight Nations crushed the Boxer Rebellion of 1900—an anti-Western campaign waged by Chinese secret societies. Victorious foreign troops paraded in Peking, *above.*

public of China. They named Sun Yat-sen temporary president of the republic. The desperate Manchus then called upon a retired military official named Yuan Shih-k'ai to try to defeat the republicans. However, Yuan secretly arranged a settlement with Sun and his followers. The last Manchu emperor, a 6-year-old boy, gave up the throne on Feb. 12, 1912. On March 10, Yuan became president in place of Sun, who had agreed to step down.

Yuan quickly moved to expand his personal power and ignored the wishes of the republicans. In 1913, the former revolutionaries established the *Kuomintang* (Nationalist Party) and organized a revolt against Yuan. The revolt failed, and the Nationalist leaders fled to Japan. Yuan's presidency became a dictatorship, and he took steps to establish himself as emperor. But even Yuan's own followers opposed the reestablishment of the empire. A rebellion by military leaders in the provinces forced him to abandon his plans.

The Warlord Period. Yuan Shih-k'ai died in 1916, and the power of the central government quickly crumbled. Presidents continued to hold office in Peking, but the real power in northern China lay in the hands of *warlords* (local military leaders). With the support of southern warlords, Sun Yat-sen set up a rival government in Canton in 1917. By 1922, the republic had failed hopelessly and civil war was widespread.

Meanwhile, great changes were occurring in Chinese culture and society. For example, a magazine called *New Youth* attacked Confucianism and presented a wide range of new philosophies and social theories. On May 4, 1919, students in Peking demonstrated against the Versailles Peace Conference. The conference permitted Japan to keep control of the German holdings it had seized in China during World War I (1914-1918). The student demonstrations helped spread the ideas presented by *New Youth* and other journals. This revolution in thought became known as the *May Fourth Movement.* It contributed greatly to the growth of Chinese nationalism and so strengthened the drive for political revolution.

In 1919, Sun began to reorganize the Nationalist Party and to recruit supporters from among students. At almost the same time, the first Communist student groups appeared in Peking and Shanghai. In 1923, Russia sent advisers to China to help the Nationalists. The Russians also persuaded the Chinese Communists to join the Nationalist Party and help it carry out the revolution. The party began to develop its own army and to organize workers and peasants to prepare for an attack on the northern warlords.

Sun Yat-sen died in 1925, and leadership of the Nationalist Party gradually passed to its military commander, Chiang Kai-shek. In 1926, the Nationalists began a campaign to defeat the northern warlords and soon won some major victories. In 1927, Chiang and his troops turned against the Communists and destroyed the Communist-backed labor unions in Shanghai. Most Communist leaders fled to the hills in the province of Kiangsi in southern China. In 1928, the Nationalists captured Peking and united China under one government for the first time since 1916.

Nationalist Rule. The Nationalist government was a one-party dictatorship that never gained full control of China. Communist opposition and Japanese aggression severely limited the Nationalist government's power and accomplishments.

By 1931, the Communists had established 15 rural bases and set up a rival government in southern and central China. In 1934, Chiang Kai-shek's armies forced the Communists to evacuate their bases and begin their famous *Long March.* By the end of 1935, the Communists had marched more than 6,000 miles (9,700 kilometers) over a winding route to the province of Shensi in northern China. Of the approximately 100,000 Communists who began the march, only a few thousand survived to reach Shensi. During the Long March, Mao Zedong became the leader of the Chinese Communist Party.

While Chiang was fighting the Communists, the Japanese were seizing more and more Chinese territory. In 1931, the Japanese occupied Manchuria and made it a puppet state called *Manchukuo.* They then extended their military influence into Inner Mongolia and other parts of northern China. Chiang agreed to a series of Japanese demands because he felt unprepared to fight the Japanese until he had defeated the Communists.

Many students and intellectuals opposed Chiang's giving in to Japan. They organized demonstrations and anti-Japanese associations. Dissatisfaction with Chiang's policies spread to Manchurian troops who were blockading the Communist-held areas in the northwest. In 1936, the Manchurian forces kidnapped

Chiang in Sian. He was released only after agreeing to end the civil war and form a united front with the Communists against the Japanese.

War with Japan. The Japanese army launched a major attack against China in 1937. The Chinese resisted courageously, but Japanese armies controlled most of eastern China by the end of 1938. The Nationalist forces withdrew to the province of Szechwan, where they made Ch'ung-ch'ing the wartime capital.

China joined the Allies in World War II on Dec. 8, 1941, one day after the Japanese attacked the United States at Pearl Harbor, Hawaii. The Allies provided China with aid, but constant warfare against the Japanese exhausted China's resources and strength. The cost of the war caused severe inflation, which demoralized the Chinese people and weakened support for the Nationalists.

For the Communists, the war against Japan provided an opportunity for political and military expansion. In northern China, they gained control of large areas that the Japanese army had overrun but lacked the forces to defend. The Communists enlarged their army and organized the people to provide food and shelter for their soldiers. They also began a social revolution in the countryside, which included redistributing land to the peasants in Communist-controlled areas. When the war against Japan ended in August 1945, the Communists held an area in northern China with a population of about 100 million. In addition, they claimed to have an army of more than 900,000 soldiers.

Civil War. In 1946, the United States sent General George C. Marshall to China to attempt to arrange a political settlement between the Nationalists and the Communists. However, neither the Nationalists nor the Communists believed that they could achieve their goals by coming to terms with the other side. In mid-1946, full-scale fighting began.

The superior military tactics of the Communists and the social revolution they conducted in the countryside gradually turned the tide against the Nationalists. After capturing Tientsin and Peking in January 1949, Mao Zedong's armies crossed the Yangtze River and drove the Nationalists toward southern China. On Oct. 1, 1949, Mao proclaimed the establishment in Peking of the People's Republic of China. In December of that year, Chiang Kai-shek and his followers fled to the island of Taiwan.

Eastfoto

Chinese Communists, led by Mao Zedong, defeated the Natonalist government in a war from 1946 to 1949. Mao is shown here on horseback, moving with his soldiers across Shensi in 1947.

The Beginning of Communist Rule took place under the direction of Mao Zedong, the chairman of the Communist Party. Premier Zhou Enlai directed all government departments and ministries. Military and economic aid from Russia helped support the new government. From 1949 to 1952, the new government firmly established its control over China and promoted the recovery of the nation's economy. It seized farmland from landlords and redistributed the land among the peasants. This process of land redistribution was a bloody one. Estimates of the number of landlords killed range from 50,000 to several million.

In 1953, China began its First Five-Year Plan for economic development. From 1953 to 1957, industry grew at the rapid rate of about 15 per cent a year. By 1957, the Communists had brought all important industries under government control. Also, peasants were forced or persuaded to combine their landholdings into agricultural cooperatives. But agricultural production increased much more slowly than industrial output.

The Great Leap Forward was the name given to China's Second Five-Year Plan. Launched in 1958, the Great Leap Forward was a campaign to accelerate dramatically China's economic development. It was based on Mao's firm belief that human willpower and effort could overcome all obstacles. Thus, the government tried to speed development by greatly increasing the number of workers and their hours while ignoring China's lack of capital and modern technology. The government combined the agricultural cooperatives into huge communes to improve the efficiency of farmworkers. In industry, laborers worked extra shifts. Machinery was operated continuously, without being stopped even for maintenance.

The Great Leap Forward shattered China's economy. From 1959 to 1961, China experienced economic depression, food shortages, and a decline in industrial output. By 1962, the economy began to recover. However, the Chinese had not solved the problem of achieving economic growth while maintaining revolutionary values. Disagreement over this issue began to produce a major split within the Communist Party between *radicals* and *moderates*. The radicals called for China to strive for a classless society in which everyone would work selflessly for the common good. The moderates stressed the importance of economic development. They believed that the policies of the radicals were unrealistic and hampered the modernization of China.

Break with Russia. Friendly relations between China and Russia ended in the early 1960's. China had criticized the Russians as early as 1956 for their policy of "peaceful coexistence" with the West. Unlike the Russians, the Chinese at that time believed that war with the West was inevitable. They also accused Russia of betraying the aims of Communism. In 1960, Russia stopped its technical assistance to China. In 1962, the Russians refused to support China in its border war with India. Russia signed a nuclear test ban treaty with the United States and Great Britain in 1963. The Chinese then broke with the Russians, whom they accused of joining an anti-Chinese plot.

The Cultural Revolution. In 1966, Mao Zedong gave his support to the radicals in the Communist Party. Mao thus began what he called the *Cultural Revolution.* The radicals accused many top party and government officials of failing to follow Communist principles and removed them from their positions. Students and other young people formed semimilitary organizations called the *Red Guards.* They demonstrated in the major cities against those whom they called counterrevolutionaries and anti-Maoists. The universities were closed from 1966 to 1970, and the entire educational system was disrupted. Radicals seized control of many provincial and city governments. Violence frequently broke out as competing radical groups struggled for power.

Mao's attempt to put China back on a revolutionary path wrecked the government and economy so severely that he had to call out the army in 1967 to restore order. In 1969, the Communist Party, the government, and the educational system gradually began to resume their normal activities. But the conflict between radicals and moderates within the party continued.

Improved Relations with the West. During the early 1970's, Canada and several other Western nations established diplomatic relations with the People's Republic of China. The United States continued to recognize the Nationalist government on Taiwan. But in 1971, the United States ended its long-standing opposition to United Nations (UN) membership for the People's Republic. Instead, it favored UN membership for both the People's Republic and Taiwan. In October 1971, the UN voted to admit the People's Republic in place of Taiwan.

In 1972, U.S. President Richard M. Nixon traveled

Eastfoto

The Red Guards demonstrated in China's cities during the Cultural Revolution (1966-1969). The Cultural Revolution was Mao Zedong's attempt to return China to a revolutionary course.

Dirck Halstead, Black Star

Chinese Leader Deng Xiaoping visited the United States in 1979. At a White House ceremony, *above,* he and President Jimmy Carter signed agreements on trade and other matters.

to China and met with Premier Zhou Enlai and Communist Party chairman Mao Zedong. During Nixon's visit, the United States and China signed the Shanghai Communiqué, which looked forward to the establishment of normal relations. The two nations opened diplomatic offices in each other's country in 1973.

China After Mao. Both Zhou Enlai and Mao Zedong died in 1976. A power struggle then developed between a group of moderates led by Hua Guofeng and a radical group led by Mao's widow, Jiang Qing. Hua's group won the struggle, and he succeeded Zhou as premier and Mao as chairman of the Communist Party. Hua's group arrested and imprisoned Jiang Qing and three of her followers—the so-called Gang of Four (see JIANG QING for further details).

In 1977, Deng Xiaoping, a moderate, became vice-premier and vice-chairman of the Communist Party. On Jan. 1, 1979, China and the United States established normal diplomatic relations. By 1980, Hua had lost most of his power and Deng had become China's most powerful leader. Hua resigned as premier in 1980 and as Communist Party chairman in 1981. Deng used his influence to help Zhao Ziyang become premier and Hu Yaobang become Communist Party chairman (now general secretary). Both Zhao and Hu are moderates. Deng resigned as vice-premier in 1980, and in 1982 his post of Communist Party vice-chairman was abolished. But Deng remains China's most powerful leader (see DENG XIAOPING).

Many other changes have taken place in China since Mao's death. The moderates have sought to reduce the peoples' admiration of Mao. Many people admire Mao so much that they believe China should continue to follow all his policies. The moderates praised Mao's leadership, but denounced the idea that all his policies should be followed. The moderates have greatly increased trade and cultural contact with foreign countries. They set out to modernize China's economy with technical help from abroad.

ROBERT F. DERNBERGER, NORMA DIAMOND, RICHARD EDWARDS, ALBERT FEUERWERKER, DONALD J. MUNRO, RHOADS MURPHEY, and WILLIAM PANG-YU TING

CHINA/Study Aids

Related Articles in World Book include:

BIOGRAPHIES

Ch'en Jung
Chiang Ching-kuo
Chiang Kai-shek
Chiang Soong Mei-ling
Chuang Tzu
Confucius
Deng Xiaoping
Genghis Khan
Hsun-tzu
Hu Yaobang
Hua Guofeng
Hui-tsung
Jiang Qing
Ku K'ai-chih
Kublai Khan
Lao Tzu
Lee, Tsung Dao
Li Po
Li Xiannian
Li Yuan
Lin Biao
Lin Yutang
Liu Pang
Liu Shaoji
Ma Yuan
Mao Zedong
Mencius
Pu-Yi
Shih Huang Ti
Soong Ching-ling
Sun Yat-sen
Wang Wei
Wu, Chien-Shiung
Wu Tao-tzu
Yang, Chen Ning
Zhao Ziyang
Zhou Enlai

CITIES

Amoy
Canton
Ch'ung-ch'ing
Fu-chou
Hang-chou
Harbin
Lan-chou
Lhasa
Nan-ching
Ning-po
Peking
Port Arthur
Shanghai
Shen-yang
Su-chou
Tientsin
Wen-chou
Wuhan

HISTORY

Boxer Rebellion
Burma Road
Cathay
Chennault, Claire L.
Ch'in Dynasty
Chinese-Japanese Wars
Chou Dynasty
Cold War
Flying Tigers
Great Wall of China
Han Dynasty
Indochina
Korean War
Ming Dynasty
Mongol Empire
Open-Door Policy
Polo, Marco
Shang Dynasty
Stilwell, Joseph W.
Sui Dynasty
Sung Dynasty
T'ang Dynasty
Trans-Siberian Railroad
Treaty Port
World War II

PHYSICAL FEATURES

Amur River
China Sea
Gobi
Himalaya
Hsi Chiang
Huang Ho
Mekong River
Mount Everest
Mount Makalu
Ta-ch'en Islands
Takla Makan Desert
Tien Shan
Yalu River
Yangtze River
Yellow Sea

REGIONS

Manchuria
Sinkiang
Tibet
Turkestan

RELIGIONS

Buddhism
Christianity
Confucianism
Islam
Taoism

OTHER RELATED ARTICLES

Architecture (Chinese Architecture)
Army (The Chinese Army)
Asia (Way of Life in East Asia)
Book (History; pictures)
Bronze (pictures)
Calendar (The Chinese)
Chinese Language
Chinese Literature
Clothing (picture: Traditional Costumes)
Dancing (Oriental Dancing)
Drama (China)
Enamel (picture)
Fan
Flag (picture: Historical Flags)
Food
Houseboat
Invention (China)
Jade
Jinrikisha
Junk
Kite
Lacquer
Lacquer Ware
Macao
Mah Jongg
Mandarin
Money (How Money Developed; pictures)
Monsoon
Music (Asian Music)
Opium
Pagoda
Painting (Chinese Painting)
Palanquin
Paper (History)
Peking Man
Porcelain
Printing (History)
Races, Human
Sampan
Sculpture (China)
Silk
Soybean

Outline

I. Government
A. The Communist Party
B. National Government
C. Political Divisions
D. Courts
E. The Armed Forces

II. People
A. Population
B. Nationalities
C. Languages

III. Way of Life
A. Family Life
B. Rural Life
C. City Life
D. Food
E. Clothing
F. Health Care
G. Religion
H. Education

IV. The Arts
A. Literature
B. Painting
C. Sculpture and Pottery
D. Architecture
E. Music
F. Theater

V. The Land
A. The Tibetan Highlands
B. The Sinkiang-Mongolian Uplands
C. The Mongolian Border Uplands
D. The Eastern Highlands
E. The Eastern Lowlands
F. The Central Uplands
G. The Szechwan Basin
H. The Southern Uplands

VI. Climate

VII. Economy
A. Agriculture
B. Manufacturing
C. Mining
D. Fishing Industry
E. Trade
F. Transportation
G. Communication

VIII. History

Questions

How has family life in China changed since the Communists came to power?

What three groups dominate China's government?

When was the People's Republic of China established?

Why did the Chinese have a high regard for education in the past? Why do the Communists prize it today?

How does the government control China's economy?

Which dynasty established China's first empire controlled by a strong central government?

How does China rank among the countries of the world in population? In area?

Reading and Study Guide

See *China* in the RESEARCH GUIDE/INDEX, Volume 22, for a *Reading and Study Guide*.

Additional Resources

Level I

RAU, MARGARET. *The People of New China.* Simon & Schuster, 1978. Focus is on contemporary life.

ROBERSON, JOHN R. *China: From Manchu to Mao (1699-1976).* Atheneum, 1980.

Level II

BUTTERFIELD, FOX. *China: Alive in the Bitter Sea.* Times Books, 1982. Discusses contemporary Chinese people and society.

GERNET, JACQUES. *A History of Chinese Civilization.* Cambridge, 1982. From earliest times to the present.

HINTON, HAROLD C., ed. *The People's Republic of China: A Handbook.* Westview, 1979.

KAPLAN, FREDRIC M., and DE KEIJZER, ARNE. *The China Guidebook.* 3rd ed. Houghton, 1982.

ROZMAN, GILBERT. *The Modernization of China.* Macmillan, 1981. Focuses on the economic, political, and social development from the 1700's to the present.

CHINA, porcelain ware. See PORCELAIN.

CHINA SEA is the name of two seas of the Pacific Ocean along the east coast of Asia. Both seas were the

WORLD BOOK map

Location of the China Sea

scenes of important naval battles during World War II.

The *East China Sea* (area 482,300 square miles, or 1,249,200 square kilometers) extends north from Taiwan to Japan and Korea. Shanghai, China, and Nagasaki, Japan, have been the main ports of the sea.

The *South China Sea* (area 1,300,000 square miles, or 3,370,000 square kilometers) is connected to the East China Sea by Formosa Strait. The South China Sea includes the Gulf of Tonkin and Gulf of Thailand on the west and Manila Bay on the east. Violent tropical storms called *typhoons* sweep over the sea. The Mekong and Menam rivers empty into the South China Sea, and the seaports of Canton, Hong Kong, Singapore, and Manila lie along its coasts. BOSTWICK H. KETCHUM

CHINA SYNDROME. See NUCLEAR ENERGY (Hazards and Safeguards).

CHINA-WOOD OIL. See TUNG OIL.

CHINA'S SORROW. See HUANG HO.

CHINATOWN. See NEW YORK CITY (Manhattan); SAN FRANCISCO (Downtown San Francisco); VANCOUVER (The City); CALIFORNIA (picture).

CHINAWARE. See PORCELAIN.

CHINCH BUG is a small, dark insect, usually with whitish wings. Chinch bugs destroy more corn, wheat, and other small grains than any other pest. They live throughout the United States, Canada, Central America, and the West Indies. The full-grown bug is about $\frac{1}{6}$ inch (4 millimeters) long. It spends the winter in old grass and rubbish. Early in spring, the female lays about 500 eggs on the roots and stems of grain. After the bugs hatch, they feed on grain and grasses. At first, the chinch bugs are red, but they change color later.

Chinch bugs feed on wheat in spring and on corn after harvesttime. After the young hatch, chinch bugs stay together in large broods until all the food in the area has been eaten. They separate when the young become fully grown. By the middle of summer the

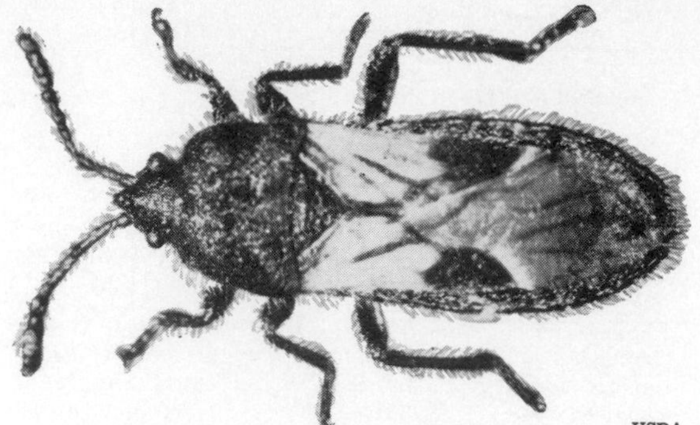

USDA

The Chinch Bug Is One of the Worst Grain Pests.

young are fully developed and lay eggs. Their eggs hatch in late July or early August. This second batch of young chinch bugs destroys still more grain. Chinch bugs reproduce rapidly during dry seasons.

Chinch bugs can be destroyed just before they move from the small grain fields to the corn fields. Farmers spray an insecticide called *lindane* on the small grain stubble or on a strip of land surrounding the field. Sometimes enough of these bugs escape so that they threaten the corn crop. Then the farmer must spray the base of the corn plants with lindane.

Scientific Classification. Chinch bugs belong to the order *Hemiptera* and the chinch bug family, *Lygaeidae.* They are genus *Blissus*, species *B. leucopterus.* H. H. ROSS

CHINCHILLA is a small animal prized for its soft, thick fur. It is a *rodent*, a small mammal with teeth specially suited for gnawing. Chinchillas grow about half as big as rabbits and have bushy tails like squirrels. Their thick, shiny, blue-gray fur is 1 inch (2.5 centimeters) or more deep. The pelts can be made into soft, luxurious coats. A pelt measures 14 by 4 inches (36 by 10 centimeters), and from 120 to 150 pelts are needed to make a full length coat. A pelt may cost as much as $60, but the average price is about $17.

Chinchillas are native to the snow-capped Andes Mountains, living in the high valleys from Peru and northern Bolivia to southern Chile. By the 1940's, hunters had nearly exterminated the animal in its natural surroundings. Today, most chinchilla pelts come from animals raised commercially on ranches in Canada, Europe, South Africa, South America, the United States, and Zimbabwe. By the 1970's, the number of wild chinchillas was increasing in Chile, where the animal is protected by law.

The chinchilla is clean and odorless. It eats roots and

The Chinchilla's Fur Is Made Into Expensive Coats.

Cache Valley Chinchilla Corp.

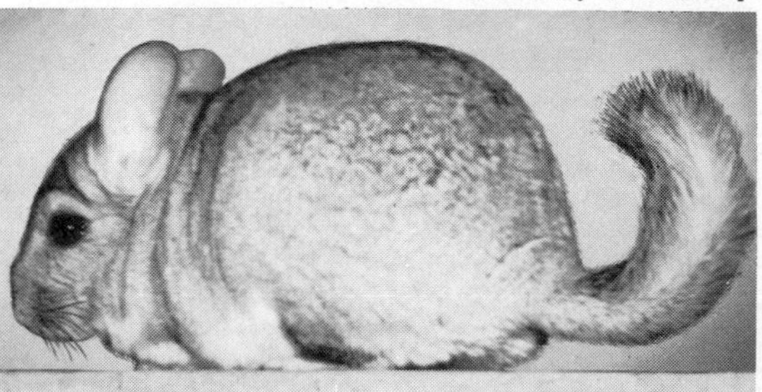

grasses. In captivity, its diet consists of grains, barks, scientifically prepared pellets, and alfalfa, bean, oat, and timothy hay. Chinchillas should be fed at regular intervals, preferably in the early evening. They sleep in the day and become active at night. Chinchillas thrive on fresh air but must be protected from drafts.

Chinchillas are kept in pens. The rack of pens used on most chinchilla ranches is 2 by 6 and 8 feet (0.6 by 1.8 and 2.4 meters) high, and houses 32 adult animals. Most breeders place a nest box in the pen. Chinchilla breeders once mated one female with one male (pair mating). But many ranches now use *polygamous breeding*, mating one male with as many as seven females. Chinchillas begin breeding at about 9 months of age, and the female usually has two litters a year. The average litter has two babies, but a litter may have seven. The babies weigh about 1¼ ounces (35 grams) each and are born with their eyes open, fully furred, and with all their 20 teeth. The young chinchillas are taken from the mother when they are 45 to 60 days old, and they reach maturity in 12 to 18 months. Fully grown, they weigh from 18 to 35 ounces (510 to 992 grams) and are about 12 inches (30 centimeters) long.

The Chincha and Inca Indians ate chinchillas and used their fur for clothing. The Spaniards who came to South America in the 1500's named the animal after the Chinchas. They introduced chinchilla fur into Europe, and the demand for the fur became so great that the chinchilla was almost wiped out.

In 1923, an American mining engineer, M. F. Chapman, trapped 11 chinchillas in Chile and took them to California. In the late 1970's, there were about 3,000 chinchilla ranches in the United States and Canada.

Scientific Classification. Chinchillas belong to the chinchilla family, *Chinchilladae*. The three domesticated kinds are genus *Chinchilla*, species *C. brevicaudata; C. costina;* and *C. langigera*. Critically reviewed by the EMPRESS CHINCHILLA BREEDERS COOPERATIVE

See also ANIMAL (color picture: Animals of the Mountains); FUR (Kinds of Fur; How Fur Is Obtained).

CHINCHONA. See CINCHONA.

CHINESE CABBAGE, or CELERY CABBAGE, is a plant which is closely related to the mustard and cabbage. It is one of the oldest food crops of China, and is now grown in the United States. The plant has wide, thick leaves which form a long, cylindrical head. Chinese cabbage should be grown in the fall. About 75 days before the first frost, seeds should be planted about 1 foot (30 centimeters) apart in rows 2 feet (61 centimeters) apart. The plant should get plenty of water. Chinese cabbage is high in vitamins A and C.

Scientific Classification. The Chinese cabbage is in the mustard family, *Cruciferae*. It is classified as genus *Brassica*, species *B. pekinensis*. ARTHUR J. PRATT

Chinese Cabbage

W. Atlee Burpee Co.

CHINESE CALENDAR. See CALENDAR (The Chinese Calendar).

CHINESE EXCLUSION ACT. See ORIENTAL EXCLUSION ACTS.

CHINESE GORDON. See GORDON, CHARLES GEORGE.

CHINESE-JAPANESE WARS refers to two wars between China and Japan. They were the war of 1894-1895 and the war of 1937-1945. The first of these wars was fought over Korea (Choson), which had been a tributary state of China for many hundreds of years. A rebellion broke out in Korea in 1894, and China sent troops there to end it. Japan also sent troops to protect its large interests in Korea. The rebellion was crushed, but Japan refused to withdraw its troops. Fighting broke out between the Japanese and Chinese in July 1894. Japanese forces destroyed the Chinese Navy and took several Chinese cities. The war ended on April 17, 1895, with the Treaty of Shimonoseki, which not only granted independence to Korea but gave Japan the island of Taiwan and the Liaotung peninsula. The Chinese also agreed to pay Japan about $150 million and allow the Japanese to operate factories in China. But Russia, Germany, and France forced Japan to return Liaotung, at an additional cost to China.

The first Chinese-Japanese War weakened China and opened the way to greater foreign imperialism there. It sowed the seed of the Russo-Japanese War of 1904-1905, which the Japanese won. In 1910, Korea was annexed by Japan and given the Japanese name *Chosen*.

After World War I, Japan began to extend its influence in China. The Chinese could not prevent Japanese forces from taking Manchuria in 1931 and Jehol Province in 1933. Japan set up a puppet state called "Manchukuo." But China had developed unity and strength by the time Japan attacked again in 1937. An undeclared war was fought until 1941, when China declared war on Japan, Germany, and Italy. During the first stage of the war, Japan captured much Chinese territory, though Chinese armies fought bitterly. The Chinese forces of Generalissimo Chiang Kai-shek and the Communists stopped fighting each other long enough to fight the Japanese. The Japanese seized important coastal cities and the most advanced industrial regions. But the Chinese moved their capital and industries westward. The Chinese guerrillas fought behind Japanese lines.

In the second stage of the war, neither side made important territorial gains. After Japan attacked the United States and Great Britain in 1941, the war became part of World War II. The second Chinese-Japanese war ended with the surrender of Japan to the Allies in September 1945. IMMANUEL C. Y. HSU

See also CHINA (History); JAPAN (History); KOREA (History).

CHINESE LANGUAGE is one of the world's oldest languages. About 95 per cent of the people of China speak Chinese. Approximately 75 per cent of the people of Singapore speak Chinese, and almost all the people of Hong Kong and Taiwan speak it. In addition, Chinese is the most common language of the Chinese communities of such cities as New York City and San Francisco, and Vancouver, Canada.

Chinese is written the same way throughout China. However, the language consists of hundreds of dialects that vary from one area of the country to another. These dialects differ so greatly that a person who lives in one area may not be able to converse with someone from another area. The pronunciation of many words depends on the dialect being spoken.

Chinese belongs to the Sino-Tibetan family of languages. This family includes Burmese, Thai, and Tibetan. See LANGUAGE (Other Language Families).

Written Chinese has no alphabet. Instead, it consists of about 50,000 *characters*. A person who knows about 5,000 of the most frequently used characters can read a Chinese newspaper or modern novel. Scholars who read ancient Chinese literature and documents must learn many more characters.

The earliest Chinese writing was made up of *pictographs*. These characters resembled the objects they represented. For example, the character for *fish* was 魚 , and the one for *moon* was 月 .

Modern Chinese has two main groups of characters, *simple ideographs* and *compound ideographs*. Ideographs represent ideas rather than objects. A simple ideograph consists of only one character. Examples include the characters for *up* (上) and *down* (下). A compound ideograph consists of two or more characters. The character 吠 (to bark) is a compound ideograph formed by the characters 口 (mouth) and 狗 (dog).

The Chinese also developed a technique called *character borrowing*. It involves "borrowing" the character of one word to represent another word that has a similar pronunciation. For example, 然 means *burn*, but it also is used to represent *yes*. The character is pronounced *rahn* for both meanings.

The meaning of a character that stands for more than one word may be difficult to determine. To make the meaning of such a character clear, the Chinese developed *phonetic compounds*. A phonetic compound is a character that has an additional character or marking to help the reader determine the word it represents.

Spoken Chinese. The common dialect of Chinese is *Northern Mandarin* or *Northern Chinese*. The Chinese call the dialect *p'u-t'ung hua*, which means *standard language*. Northern Chinese is the official language of China and is taught in all the nation's schools. About 600 million persons speak it. They live throughout northern China and in several southwestern provinces. Other major dialects include *Cantonese*, *Hsiang*, *Kan-Hakka*, *Min*, and *Wu*. They are spoken in many areas of China and in the Chinese communities of various cities in other countries.

Chinese dialects differ in the use of *tones*. A tone is the pitch used in saying a particular word. Northern Chinese has four tones—*high-level* (high and unwavering), *rising*, *low-dipping* (falling and rising), and *falling*. Some other dialects have as many as nine tones. The use of tone is an important means of separating words of different meanings but similar pronunciation. For example, *ma* means *mother* in a high-level tone, *horse* in

Kinds of Chinese Characters

Pictographs are ancient characters that resembled the objects they represented. The pictograph on the far left stands for *man*. The second character is the modern symbol.

Ancient character from *Chinese Calligraphy*, 3rd ed., by Chiang Yee, 1973, Harvard Univ. Press.

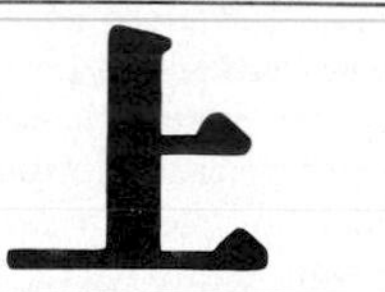

Simple Ideographs are characters that represent ideas rather than objects. The character on the left is a simple ideograph that stands for the concept of *up*.

Compound Ideographs have two or more characters that represent ideas. The word *trust*, shown on the left, is a compound ideograph. It consists of the character for *man* and the one for *word*.

Character Borrowing involves using the same character to represent words with similar pronunciations. The words for *inside* and *village* are both pronounced *li* and are represented by the symbol at the left.

Phonetic Compounds consist of two elements. One gives the character's meaning and the other its pronunciation. The character on the left means *nephew*. The right-hand element indicates the meaning, and the left-hand one shows the pronunciation, *sheng*.

Detail of *The Fishermen* (1352), an ink painting on paper by Yuan Wu Chen; the Freer Gallery of Art, Washington, D.C.

Examples of Chinese Writing appear in many ancient Chinese paintings. The painting above includes a poem.

a low-dipping tone, *scold* in a falling tone, and *hemp* in a rising tone. Each of these words has a different character when written in Northern Chinese.

Chinese is spoken with no tenses. For example, the sentence *Ta shi xuezhe* could mean *He* is *a scholar* or *He* was *a scholar*, depending on how it is used.

Many language experts consider Chinese to be *monosyllabic*—that is, almost all the words have only one syllable. Even words of more than one syllable can be broken down into single-syllable words. For example, *xuezhe* (scholar) consists of two single-syllable words—*xue* (learn) and *zhe* (one who).

Development. The earliest known examples of Chinese are inscriptions carved in bones and shells during the Shang dynasty (1500-1027 B.C.). This early language had a simple structure. It was the basis of a later language called *classical*, or *literary*, *Chinese*.

The dialects of present-day Chinese developed from classical Chinese. Northern Chinese began to be used during the A.D. 1300's. This dialect became China's official language because it was spoken in Peking, the capital. However, written Northern Chinese was not widely used until the Literary Revolution, a cultural movement that began in 1917.

Through the years, the government has promoted the use of Northern Chinese through the nation's educational program. In 1919, for example, Chinese schools began to use a system of *phonetic signs* to teach standard pronunciation. This method involved books that taught the pronunciation in Northern Chinese of Chinese characters. In 1949, Chinese educators began to simplify characters to make them easier to learn and write.

In the mid-1950's, the government introduced *Pinyin*, a system of writing Chinese using the Roman alphabet. This alphabet consists of the 26 letters used to write English and many other languages. In 1978, the government directed that Chinese names and words used in English and other foreign language publications be written in Pinyin. Pinyin replaced the *Wade-Giles system* and other writing systems that use the Roman alphabet. Two British diplomats, Thomas Wade and Herbert Giles, developed this system during the late 1800's and early 1900's. DAVID R. KNECHTGES

See also CHINA (Languages).

Additional Resources

CHANG, RAYMOND and MARGARET S. *Speaking of Chinese*. Norton, 1978. Discusses history of the Chinese language. Wade-Giles and Pinyin systems are also discussed.

PEKING LANGUAGE INSTITUTE. *Chinese for Beginners*. China Books & Periodicals, 1976. An excellent guide to learning spoken Chinese.

CHINESE LITERATURE is one of the oldest and greatest of the world's literatures. Chinese writers have produced important works for almost 3,000 years.

During most of China's history, the Chinese did not consider literature a separate art form. They expected all cultured people to write in a graceful, elegant style, regardless of the topic. Many masterpieces of Chinese literature deal with subjects that some Western writers regard as nonliterary. These topics include history, philosophy, politics, religion, and science.

Until the 1900's, government service was the occupation of greatest prestige in China. For more than 1,000 years, people gained a government position primarily by passing an examination that tested their ability to compose both poetry and prose. Almost all of China's greatest writers before the 1900's were government officials. Most of them received their appointments because of their skill with words.

Many works of Chinese literature teach a moral lesson or express a political philosophy. These themes appear especially in the writings of Confucians. Confucianism is a philosophy founded by Confucius, who lived from about 551 to 479 B.C. It was the dominant Chinese philosophy until the 1900's. Many other writers were Buddhists or Taoists, rather than Confucians. Buddhism was a major Chinese religion, and Taoism was both an important religion and a philosophy. The Buddhists and Taoists were less interested than the Confucians in morality and politics. But they used literature to express religious and philosophical ideas.

During the 1900's, Chinese literature has made a sharp break with the past. This break resulted partly from the influence of Western culture on Chinese writers. But the rise of the Communist Party to power in China made an even greater impact. Ever since the Chinese Communists took control in 1949, they have required Chinese writers to stress Communist ideals.

Early Chinese Literature

Beginnings. The first significant work of Chinese literature was a collection of 300 poems called the *Classic of Songs*. The earliest of these poems probably date back to the 1100's B.C. Some of the poems may have originated as songs about farming, love, and war. Others were used in such ceremonies as weddings and religious sacrifices. The earliest prose in Chinese literature was a collection of historical writings called the *Classic of Documents*. It consists largely of speeches supposedly made by the earliest Chinese rulers. However, the speeches were probably fiction written during the Chou dynasty (about 1027 to 256 B.C.).

The *Classic of Songs* and the *Classic of Documents*, along with several other books, formed the basis of Confucianism. The Confucians considered these books to be models of literary excellence. They also honored them as works of moral wisdom because the books emphasized Confucian ideals of duty, moderation, proper conduct, and public service.

Taoism probably began during the 300's B.C., partly as a reaction against Confucianism. Unlike the Confucians, the Taoists believed people should avoid social obligations and live simply and close to nature. Taoist ideas strongly influenced poets who wrote about the beauties of nature. Taoism produced two literary masterpieces. The first, *The Classic of the Way and the Virtue*, was probably written by Lao Tzu, the founder of Taoism. Most of the other work, the *Chuang Tzu*, is credited to Chuang Tzu, a philosopher.

An important collection of poems called the *Elegies of Ch'u* appeared during the 300's B.C. Most of them were probably written by a poet named Ch'ü Yüan. Many of the poems describe flights to imaginary regions inhabited by mythical creatures, gods, and spirits.

Poetry. Perhaps the four greatest Chinese poets lived during the T'ang dynasty (A.D. 618-907). They were, in the order of their birth, Wang Wei, Li Po, Tu Fu, and Po Chü-i.

Leisure Enough to Spare (1360), an ink painting on paper by Yao T'ing-mei; the Cleveland Museum of Art, John L. Severance Fund

Traditional Chinese Poetry was closely associated with painting. A poet painted this scroll and wrote the poem at the left. The poem describes the beauties of nature and the pleasures of solitude.

Wang Wei wrote four-line poems that describe scenes from nature. His works, which emphasize quiet and contemplation, show the influence of Buddhism.

Li Po wrote imaginative poems about his dreams and fantasies and his love of wine. Unlike most poets of his time, he wrote in the style of old Chinese ballads.

Tu Fu is considered China's greatest poet by many critics. He surpassed all other T'ang poets in range of style and subject matter. In some of his early poems, Tu Fu expressed disappointment at failing an examination for government service. A bloody rebellion from 755 to 757 inspired him to write poems condemning the absurdity he saw in war. In his late poems, Tu Fu emphasized clever use of language, developing a style that influenced Chinese poets for centuries.

Po Chü-i wrote satiric poems in ballad style. The poems protested against various government policies and programs of his day.

Drama and Fiction developed as important forms of Chinese literature during the 1200's. Chinese plays resemble European opera, combining singing and dancing with dialogue. The two most famous Chinese plays are *The Western Chamber*, written by Wang Shih-fu, and *Injustice to Tou O*, written by Kuan Han-Ch'ing. Both plays were written in the 1200's. T'ang Hsien-tsu ranks as the greatest Chinese playwright. His most notable play was *Peony Pavilion* (about 1600).

Lo Kuan-chung, who died about 1400, rewrote traditional historical tales into long, complicated stories that resemble novels by Western authors. Lo wrote *Romance of the Three Kingdoms*, which describes the struggle for power among three rival states during the A.D. 100's and 200's. Lo and a writer named Shih Nai-en wrote *Water Margin*, also known as *All Men Are Brothers*. It tells about an outlaw gang that may actually have existed in the A.D. 1100's.

A great comic novel called *The Journey to the West* appeared in the 1500's. The novel, attributed to Wu Ch'eng-en, describes a pilgrimage of a Buddhist monk to India in the A.D. 600's. An unknown writer of the 1500's wrote *Golden Lotus*, a famous novel about moral corruption. *Dream of the Red Chamber*, perhaps the greatest Chinese novel, was written by Ts'ao Hsüeh-ch'in in the 1700's. It describes the decline of a prominent aristocratic family.

Modern Chinese Literature

Until the 1800's, China was almost isolated from the West. Many European missionaries and traders traveled to China during the 1800's, and the Chinese were gradually exposed to Western culture. By the early 1900's, the works of most Chinese authors showed some influence of Western literature. The most important Chinese author of the early 1900's was Lu Hsün, who wrote satiric short stories of social criticism.

The Chinese Communists, led by Mao Zedong, came to power in 1949 after a long civil war. The Communists demanded that all literature serve the new state. They ordered writers to create works that could be easily understood by the peasants, soldiers, and workers. The heroes of literary works had to represent the working class. Some older writers in China attacked the new literature, which they considered dull. The government prohibited these writers from publishing their works.

Today, the most widely read writings in China are the poems and sayings of Mao Zedong. But writers who live outside China produce the most significant Chinese literature. Their works are published in Taiwan and Hong Kong. Many of these writers live in the United States, and their works reflect knowledge of both traditional Chinese literature and Western literature. The chief authors of this group include Yang Mu, Pai Hsien-yung, and Yü Kuang-chung. DAVID R. KNECHTGES

Related Articles in WORLD BOOK include:

Chinese Language	Confucius	Li Po
Chuang Tzu	Drama (Asian Drama)	Lin Yutang
Confucianism	Lao Tzu	Taoism

Additional Resources

BIRCH, CYRIL, and KEENE, DONALD, eds. *Anthology of Chinese Literature*. 2 vols. Grove, 1965-1972.

HSIA, CHIH-TSING. *The Classic Chinese Novel: A Critical Introduction*. Columbia Univ. Press, 1968.

HSU, KAI-YU, and WANG, TING, eds. *Literature of the People's Republic of China*. Indiana Univ. Press, 1979.

LIU, JAMES J. *Chinese Theories of Literature*. Univ. of Chicago Press, 1975. An interpretation of Chinese literature for Westerners.

LIU, WU-CHI. *An Introduction to Chinese Literature*. Indiana Univ. Press, 1966.

CH'ING DYNASTY. See MANCHUS; CHINA (History).

CHINOOK, *shih NOOK*, is a warm dry wind that blows down the slopes of the Rocky Mountains in winter and early spring. It was named by early settlers who thought that it came from the country of the Chinook Indians along the Columbia River. Chinooks blow in the northwestern United States and in southwestern Canada. They usually blow from the west.

A chinook gets warmer as it moves down the mountain slope. Its temperature increases by about 1 degree

Fahrenheit for every 180 feet (1 degree Celsius for every 99 meters) of descent. For example, a chinook that descends 5,500 feet (1,680 meters) is about 30° F. (17° C) warmer when it reaches the foot of the mountain. The wind takes up moisture by evaporation. It often melts snow as it spreads out at the mountain base, exposing grass so that cattle can graze. Similar winds that blow in other parts of the world are called *foehns* (see FOEHN).

Wet chinook is the name used by residents along the Pacific Coast in Washington and Oregon for warm, moist winds from the southwest. VANCE E. MOYER

CHINOOK INDIANS are a people of the Pacific Northwest. Most of them live in Oregon and Washington. They once lived in fishing villages at the mouth of the Columbia River in what is now Washington. The Chinook belong to a larger group of Indians called *Chinookans*. The Chinookans include other peoples who lived along the Columbia and Willamette rivers and spoke dialects similar to the Chinook language. The Chinookans have intermarried with members of other Indian groups or with non-Indians. They now make a living by farming, ranching, and other activities.

In traditional Chinook society, people were divided into three groups. The chief and his family belonged to the wealthy, ruling class. The common people had fewer possessions of their own. Slaves, captured in raids or acquired by trading with other Indian groups, formed the lowest group and were considered as property. The Chinooks made their living by trading, by fishing, and by gathering berries, nuts, and roots.

European explorers encountered Chinooks in 1792 when the whites reached the mouth of the Columbia River. During the 1800's, both whites and other Indians in the region learned a simplified form of the Chinook language to make trading easier. The Chinooks became known for their skill in dealing with explorers and settlers. A series of epidemics in the 1800's destroyed most Chinookan societies. During the early 1900's, the remaining Chinookans moved to reservations and small towns in Oregon and Washington. MICHAEL SILVERSTEIN

CHINOOK SALMON. See SALMON (Kinds).

CHIPEWYAN INDIANS. See MANITOBA (Indian Days); INDIAN, AMERICAN (Table of Tribes).

CHIPMUNK is a small, striped animal that lives in *burrows* (tunnels) in Asia and North America. Chipmunks often leave their homes to look for food. They hop along on strong hind legs, searching for seeds and nuts. They store food in their tunnels. They eat by holding a piece of food in their small, slender front feet and nibbling at it with their sharp front teeth. Chipmunks sleep through much of the winter, but they may awaken on warm winter days and eat some of their food.

Woodrow Goodpaster, National Audubon Society

The Chipmunk gathers nuts, dried fruits, and seeds to store in its burrow. It lives on them during the long winter months.

Chipmunks are rodents, and are in the same family as woodchucks and squirrels. Most American chipmunks are about 8 inches (20 centimeters) long including the tail. They have light-colored stripes on the face, back, and sides. The stripes are bordered by black. The rest of the back, legs, and tail are reddish-brown. The underside of a chipmunk is light gray or white.

Most female chipmunks bear from two to eight young twice a year. Chipmunks may live 2 or 3 years, if they do not become the victims of the hawks and flesh-eating animals that prey on them.

Scientific Classification. Chipmunks belong to the squirrel family, *Sciuridae*. In America, the eastern chipmunk is genus *Tamias*, species *T. striatus*. The western chipmunk is genus *Eutamias*. There are more than a dozen species in this genus. DANIEL BRANT

See also RODENT; SQUIRREL.

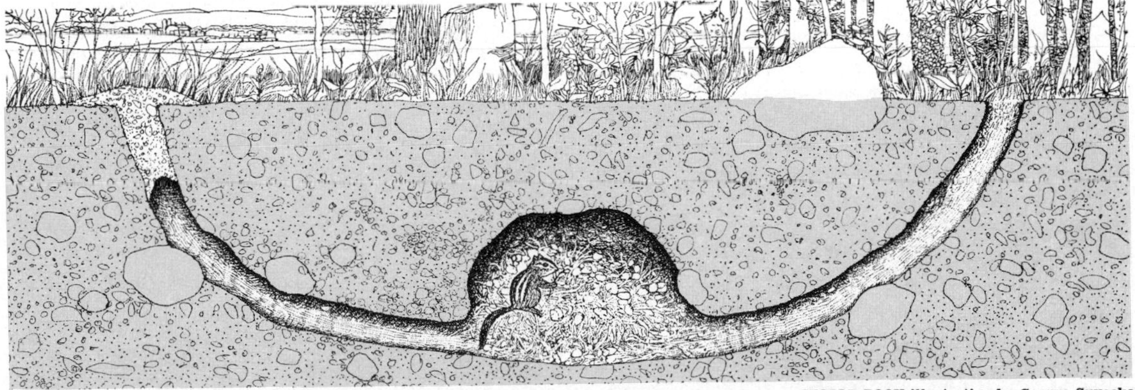

WORLD BOOK illustration by George Suyeoka

The Chipmunk Begins Its Underground Nest by digging a hole, *left*. It carves a tunnel, and may make another small opening, *right*. The chipmunk then builds a nesting area, pushes the dirt out, and may plug the first entrance to its nest.

CHIPPENDALE, THOMAS (1718-1779), became the most famous English cabinetmaker of his time. He developed his own style, but he also borrowed freely from Gothic, Chinese, and French designs. Chippendale carved richly and masterfully in low relief. His furniture featured the cabriole leg with a claw and ball ending, and the pierced, ribband-back chair. He used mahogany almost exclusively for his furniture (see FURNITURE [Chippendale Furniture; picture]).

Chippendale was born in Otley, near Bradford. His father was a cabinetmaker and wood carver. His family moved to London about 1727. In 1753, Chippendale established his famous furniture factory at Martin's Lane. He published a collection of designs, *The Gentleman and Cabinet Maker's Director*, in 1754. OTTO V. HULA

CHIPPEWA INDIANS, *CHIP uh wah*, form one of the largest tribal groups in North America. They once lived in the forest country around the shores of Lake Superior. The American poet Henry Wadsworth Longfellow based many of the customs in his poem *Hiawatha* on the Chippewa. The Chippewa are also called the Anishinabe, Ojibwa, Ojibway, Ojibwe, or Otchipwe.

The Chippewa were skilled in fishing. They gathered in summer around the falls of Sault Ste. Marie to spear sturgeon. They also hunted in the forests and gathered wild plants, especially the wild rice of the lake country. They used much of the plentiful birchbark in the northern forests. They covered their wigwams with strips of the bark and made beautiful bark canoes, boxes, dishes, and baskets.

Many Chippewa belonged to a secret religious organization called the *midewiwin*. Members of this organization tried to gain long life by using herbs and magic. The priests kept records by scratching symbols on birchbark.

The Chippewa lived in isolated areas, and so they had few battles with white people. But they often fought the Sioux and the Fox tribes, especially over possession of wild-rice fields. During the 1800's, the Chippewa ceded their tribal lands to the federal governments of Canada and the United States, and these governments established federal reservations for the tribe.

Today, from 75,000 to 250,000 Chippewa live chiefly in Michigan, Minnesota, Wisconsin, and Ontario. About half the Chippewa, including many of the poorest ones, live on federal reservations. Chippewa are employed in a wide range of occupations, including agriculture, the arts, and such professions as education, law, and medicine. Many make a living by hunting, trapping, lumbering, or working as guides. Chippewa Indians harvest almost all the wild rice that is eaten in the United States. GERALD VIZENOR

CHIRICAHUA NATIONAL MONUMENT, *CHIR ih KAH wuh*, is in southeastern Arizona. It has weirdly magnificent pinnacles and columns, eroded in volcanic rocks high in a forested range. Erosion during countless centuries formed the strange landscape. Located within Coronado National Forest, this monument was established in 1924. For its area, see NATIONAL PARK SYSTEM (table: National Monuments). C. LANGDON WHITE

CHIRICO, *KEY rih koh*, **GIORGIO DE** (1888-1978), was an Italian painter. He did his most significant work between 1910 and 1920. Most of Chirico's paintings during this period show a vast city square in bright afternoon light. The square is empty except for a statue and one or two lonely human figures. Chirico created a puzzling or even menacing atmosphere by combining the emptiness of the square with irregular perspectives, brilliant light, and long shadows. His scenes resemble the paintings of the surrealists during the 1920's, but he was not considered a surrealist.

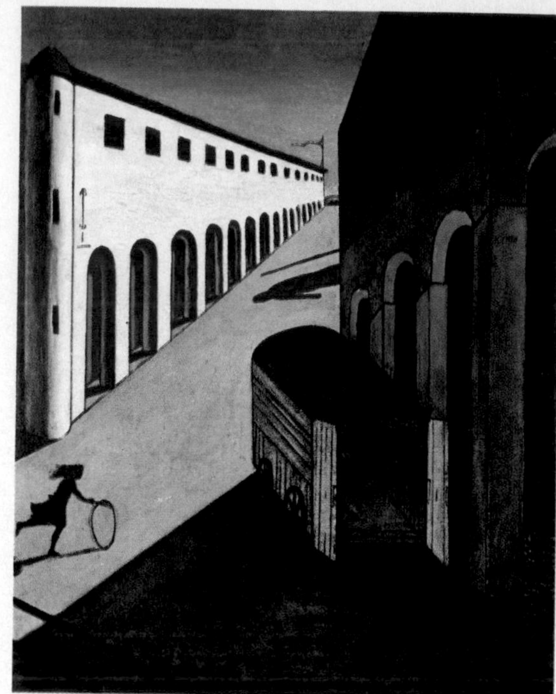

Mystery and Melancholy of a Street (1914), an oil painting on canvas; private collection (WORLD BOOK photo by Henry Beville)

Chirico's Major Paintings express hidden danger by combining shadows, isolated figures, and exaggerated perspective.

Chirico was born in Vólos, Greece. He studied art in Munich, Germany, for two years before moving to Italy in 1909. In 1917, Chirico helped found an Italian painting movement called the *Scuola Metafisica* (Metaphysical School). Artists in the movement painted fantastic scenes similar to Chirico's works. Chirico led the movement until it broke up in 1919. In the 1920's, he began painting in a more traditional style and disclaimed his earlier work. WILLARD E. MISFELDT

See also PAINTING (Surrealism).

CHIROMANCY. See PALMISTRY.

CHIROPRACTIC, *KY ruh PRAK tihk*, is a method of treating illness, especially through manual manipulation of the patient's spine. Chiropractors believe that mislocated vertebrae may interfere with proper nerve function. According to chiropractic, this condition may cause or contribute to some diseases and lowers the body's resistance to others. In making diagnoses, chiropractors often use X rays along with standard physical and laboratory examinations.

Several studies have shown that chiropractic can relieve pain and structural disorders in the joints and muscles. Most chiropractors confine their treatment to these problems, but some treat a wide range of illnesses. Most physicians do not believe spinal manipulation is an effective treatment for such conditions as cancer, advanced infections, and kidney disease. The laws of all the states of the United States and of all the provinces of Canada prohibit chiropractors from performing major surgery or prescribing drugs.

The word *chiropractic* comes from Greek words that mean *done by the hands*. Ancient Greek and Roman physicians may have used the technique. The principles of modern chiropractic were established in 1895 by Daniel David Palmer of Iowa. Palmer later opened the first school for training chiropractors.

The United States has nine chiropractic colleges that are recognized by the Council on Chiropractic Education (CCE). Chiropractic colleges offer a four-year program that leads to the degree of Doctor of Chiropractic (D.C.). To qualify for admission, an applicant must have completed at least two years of college. The program includes courses in many areas of science, plus clinical experience in chiropractic methods of diagnosis and treatment. Many countries, including the United States and Canada, require graduates to pass an examination prior to obtaining a license to practice chiropractic. Additional information on chiropractic may be obtained from the American Chiropractic Association, which has headquarters at 1916 Wilson Boulevard, Arlington, VA 22201. RICHARD C. SCHAFER

CHIROPRACTOR. See CHIROPRACTIC.

CHISANBOP, *CHIHZ uhn bahp* or *JEE suhn bahp*, is a method of calculation based on the use of the fingers. The word *Chisanbop* is a trademark. It comes from a Korean word meaning *finger calculation method*. The method can be used to add, subtract, multiply, and divide.

Chisanbop is based on the decimal system. In Chisanbop, each of the 10 fingers represents a certain value. The right thumb equals 5, and the other fingers of the right hand each equal 1. The left thumb equals 50, and the other fingers on the left hand each equal 10. Suppose you want to add 10 to 12. First press down one left-hand finger to represent 10. Then press down another left-hand finger and two right-hand fingers to stand for 12. By adding the values of each finger pressed down, you get the answer—22.

Sung Jin Pai, a Korean mathematician, developed Chisanbop in the late 1940's and taught it to his son, Hang Young Pai. Hang Young Pai improved the method and began to teach Chisanbop in the United States in 1976. Today, Chisanbop is also taught in Australia, Canada, England, Japan, and Mexico. Chisanbop can be learned by children as young as kindergartners because it is simple to use. The method can also be used to teach blind people mathematics because sight is not needed to learn it. HANG YOUNG PAI

CHISHOLM, *CHIHZ uhm*, **SHIRLEY** (1924-), became the first black woman to serve in the United States Congress. Chisholm, a New York Democrat, was a member of the U.S. House of Representatives from 1969 to 1983. She served in the New York Assembly from 1964 to 1968. She campaigned for, but did not win, the 1972 Democratic presidential nomination.

Chisholm has worked for the reform of U.S. political parties and legislatures to meet the needs of more citizens. She was a severe critic of the seniority system in Congress and protested her 1969 assignment to the House Agriculture Committee. She won reassignment to a committee on which she felt she could be of greater service to the people of her Brooklyn inner-city district.

Mount Holyoke College

Shirley Chisholm

Shirley Anita St. Hill Chisholm was born in Brooklyn. She graduated from Brooklyn College and earned a master's degree at Columbia University. She taught nursery school and directed day-care centers in New York City. From 1959 to 1964, she was an educational consultant for the city's Bureau of Child Welfare. She has written an autobiography, *Unbought and Unbossed* (1970). CHARLES V. HAMILTON

CHISHOLM TRAIL, *CHIHZ uhm*, was a famous route that Texas cattle ranchers used in driving their herds north to the railroads in Kansas. In 1866, Jesse Chisholm, a halfbreed Cherokee Indian trader, drove a wagon through Indian Territory (now Oklahoma) to his trading post near Wichita, Kans. Cattle drivers who followed Chisholm's wagon ruts to Abilene, Kans., gave the trail his name. The trail extended south to Mexico.

The Chisholm Trail and its users are celebrated in

How Chisanbop Works

In Chisanbop, each finger represents a certain value, as shown below on the left. To add 10 and 12, a person presses down the fingers indicated in the drawing on the right. The dark gray finger represents 10, and the light gray fingers together total 12.

WORLD BOOK illustration by Robert Keys

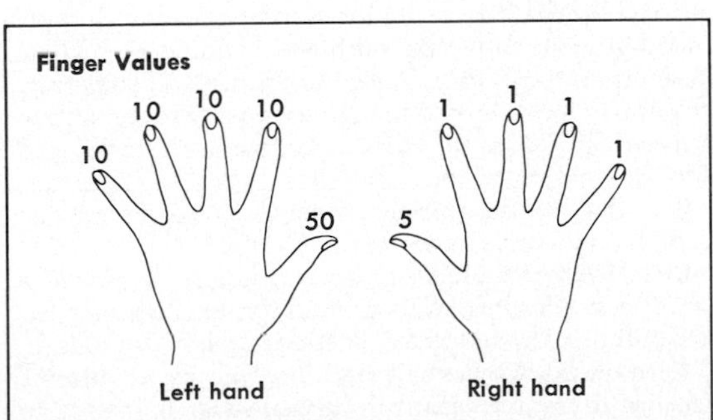

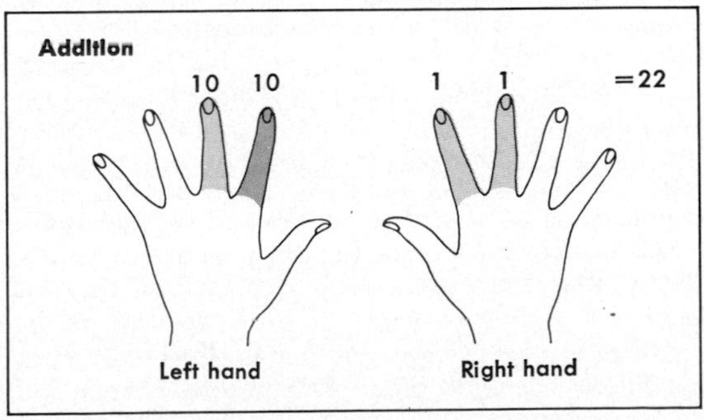

frontier lore and cowboy songs. Ranchers began a series of "long drives" in 1868, and moved about 1½ million cattle over the trail in three years. They liked the route because it had no settlements, hills, or wooded areas. As the railroads moved west across the plains, settlers soon followed, and the route of the trail shifted westward. Ellsworth, 60 miles (97 kilometers) west of Abilene on the Kansas Pacific Railroad, and later Newton, farther south on the Atchison, Topeka, and Santa Fe Railroad, became terminal points for cattle drives between 1872 and 1875. For the location of these towns, see KANSAS (political map). Saloons and gambling halls lined the streets of these "cow towns." The cattle drives ended and the trail fell into disuse as the railroads pushed across the plains and farmers built fences on their homesteads. W. TURRENTINE JACKSON

See also WESTERN FRONTIER LIFE (The Cattle Boom).

CHITAL. See DEER (Asian and European Deer).

CHITON. See CLOTHING (Ancient Times; picture); GREECE, ANCIENT (Family Life); TUNIC.

CHITON, *KY tuhn,* is a sea animal with a tough protective shell. The shell of most chitons consists of eight overlapping pieces bound together by leathery flesh. There are 800 living species of chitons. They live in shallow waters in most parts of the world. Some chitons are less than 1 inch (2.5 centimeters) long, but *Steller's chiton* may grow to a length of about 12 inches (30 centimeters). Chitons have a large, flat muscular organ called a *foot,* which they use to cling to rocks by means of suction. Some chitons eat only plant life. Other chitons eat small sea animals.

Jeff Foott, Bruce Coleman Inc.

A Chiton has a shell that consists of eight overlapping pieces. The animal clings to rocks with its muscular foot.

Scientific Classification. Chitons belong to the phylum *Mollusca.* They make up many families of the class *Amphineura.* R. TUCKER ABBOTT

See also MOLLUSK (Chitons); SHELL (Chitons).

CHIVALRY. See ETIQUETTE; KNIGHTS AND KNIGHTHOOD.

CHIVE is a green vegetable that is closely related to the onion. The chive plant grows wild in Europe and Asia, and is cultivated in most parts of the United States. The root of the chive plant is a small, egg-shaped bulb from which grow long, thin, tubelike leaves. The plant bears showy lavender flowers.

People chop the leaves of the chive plant and use them to flavor food. For example, chive leaves may be used in salads, soups, omelets, and cheeses. Chives contain a fairly large amount of vitamin C. The plants are often potted and grown indoors.

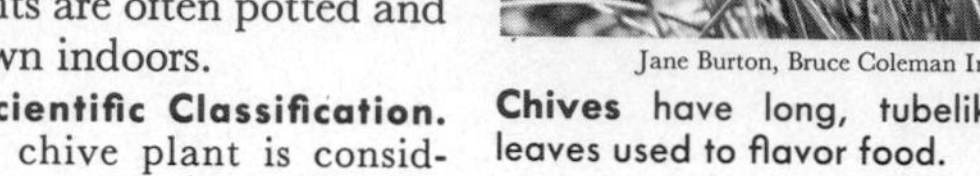

Jane Burton, Bruce Coleman Inc.

Chives have long, tubelike leaves used to flavor food.

Scientific Classification. The chive plant is considered a member of either the amaryllis family, Amaryllidaceae, or the lily family, Liliaceae. The scientific name of the chive plant is *Allium schoenoprasum.* S. H. WITTWER

CHLORAL HYDRATE is a drug that was once widely used to induce sleep. But it has been used less often since the introduction of barbiturates into medical practice. Chloral hydrate has a disagreeable taste, and is usually taken in a flavored mixture. Addiction to chloral hydrate is rare. Large doses of it can cause nausea and vomiting. Overdoses can cause coma and death.

Chloral hydrate occurs as clear, colorless crystals. It dissolves in alcohol, ether, water, and olive oil, and melts at about 52° C (126° F.). Chloral hydrate is a chlorinated derivative of ethyl alcohol. Its chemical formula is $CCl_3CH(OH)_2$. SOLOMON GARB

CHLORDANE is a chemical that was once widely used to control various insect pests. It is a dark, heavy liquid that dissolves in organic solvents. However, it does not dissolve in water. In 1978, the United States Environmental Protection Agency (EPA) suspended most uses of chlordane because of evidence that the chemical could cause cancer. After 1980, the use of chlordane was limited chiefly to termite control. Chlordane's chemical formula is $C_{10}H_6Cl_8$. W. V. MILLER

CHLORIDE is one of a group of chemical compounds that contain chlorine and a metal. A chloride may be formed when hydrochloric acid reacts with any one of many metals.

Chemically, chlorides are classed as salts. Sodium chloride (NaCl), or common table salt, is formed when hydrochloric acid reacts with sodium. Like many other chlorides, however, sodium chloride is plentiful in nature. Silver chloride consists of one atom of silver and one of chlorine. It is used in photography. Zinc chloride is used in preservative and embalming fluids, in medical products, and as a flux in electroplating and soldering. Calcium chloride is used to melt ice on city streets and to reduce dust. Other chlorides include iron chloride, lead chloride, and mercurous chloride.

See also BICHLORIDE OF MERCURY; HYDROCHLORIC ACID; SALT; SALT, CHEMICAL.

CHLORINE, *KLAWR een,* is a poisonous, yellow-green gas. It has a strong, suffocating odor, and irritates the eyes and throat. But it combines with the metal sodium to form ordinary table salt (sodium chloride). Chlorine also has many important industrial uses. It is used to purify water, to kill bacteria in waste material, and to make weed and insect killers.

Chlorine is used in processing certain foods and in the manufacture of various drugs, dyes, metals, and plastics. The paper pulp and textile industries use it as a bleach. Chlorine is also utilized in producing many kinds of industrial chemicals. These chemicals include ethylene dichloride used in premium gasoline and fluorocarbons used as refrigerants and aerosol propellants. See FLUOROCARBON.

Chlorine Compounds. Chlorine is never found in nature as an individual element. But its compounds, such as sodium chloride, are widespread. For example, sodium chloride can be found in oceans, in salt lakes, and in beds of salt rock.

Chlorine combines with metals to form such salts as magnesium chloride and potassium chloride. It reacts violently with hydrogen in sunlight to form hydrogen chloride. Hydrogen chloride in solution with water produces hydrochloric acid, which is used in dyeing processes and in cleaning metal. Chlorine dissolved in water produces both hydrochloric and hypochlorous acid. The solution is used as a bleach and disinfectant. Chlorine also replaces bromine and iodine from their salts.

Manufacturers make chlorine by passing electricity through melted sodium chloride or a water solution of sodium chloride (see ELECTROLYSIS). Chlorine can also be placed under pressure and made into a liquid. Liquid chlorine is usually shipped in steel tanks for safety. Chemists make chlorine in laboratories by treating hydrochloric acid with manganese dioxide, or by mixing sulfuric acid with bleaching powder.

Discovery of Chlorine. Carl Wilhelm Scheele, a Swedish chemist, discovered chlorine in 1774 by treating *muriatic acid* (hydrochloric acid) with manganese dioxide. A few years later, Antoine Lavoisier, a French chemist, concluded that all acids contain oxygen. Chlorine was called *oxymuriatic acid gas*, because chemists believed it also contained oxygen. In 1810, Sir Humphry Davy determined that chlorine was an element. He named it *chloros*, a Greek word meaning *greenish-yellow*.

Properties. Chlorine has the chemical symbol Cl. The gas is about $2\frac{1}{2}$ times heavier than air. It belongs to the halogen family of chemical elements. Chlorine melts at $-100.98°$ C and boils at $-34.6°$ C. The density of chlorine is 0.00295 grams per cubic centimeter at 20° C. The element's atomic number is 17, and its atomic weight is 35.453. OTTO THEODOR BENFEY

Related Articles in WORLD BOOK include:

Bleach
Davy, Sir Humphry
Fumigation
Halogen
Hydrochloric Acid
Salt (Uses of Salt)
Scheele, Carl Wilhelm
Sewage
Water (Purifying and Treating Water)

Uses of Chlorine and Chlorine Compounds

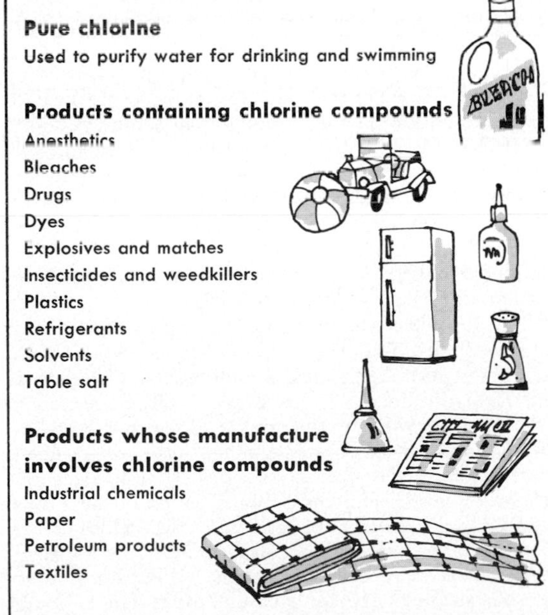

Pure chlorine
Used to purify water for drinking and swimming
Products containing chlorine compounds
Anesthetics
Bleaches
Drugs
Dyes
Explosives and matches
Insecticides and weedkillers
Plastics
Refrigerants
Solvents
Table salt
Products whose manufacture involves chlorine compounds
Industrial chemicals
Paper
Petroleum products
Textiles

CHLOROFORM, *KLAWR uh fawrm* (chemical formula, $CHCl_3$), is a heavy, colorless liquid used in the manufacture of *fluorocarbons*. Fluorocarbons are an important group of chemical compounds used as cooling agents in home air conditioners and refrigerators and as propellants in some aerosol sprays. Chloroform also serves as an industrial solvent and is used in the manufacture of antibiotics, dyes, and pesticides.

Chloroform has powerful anesthetic properties, and physicians once commonly used it to deaden pain and to produce general anesthesia. But chloroform can damage the heart, liver, and kidneys when used as an anesthetic. For this reason, other less toxic anesthetics have largely replaced chloroform.

Until 1976, chloroform was an ingredient in some cough medicines, liniments, and toothpastes. That year, the U.S. Food and Drug Administration (FDA) banned the use of chloroform in drugs and cosmetics. The FDA took this action after tests showed that chloroform could cause cancer in laboratory animals. Chloroform is an unwanted by-product formed in drinking water when chlorine is added at treatment plants to kill disease-causing bacteria. In 1979, the Environmental Protection Agency (EPA) issued regulations to limit the amount of chloroform in drinking water.

Chloroform was discovered in 1831 by three chemists, each working independently of the others. They were Eugene Soubeiran of France, Justus von Liebig of Germany, and Samuel Guthrie of the United States. Sir James Simpson of Edinburgh publicly demonstrated chloroform as an anesthetic in 1847. Queen Victoria helped win acceptance for the new drug. AUSTIN SMITH

See also ANESTHESIA.

CHLOROMYCETIN, *KLAWR uh my SEE tihn*, is the trade-name used by the Parke-Davis Company for the disease-fighting drug, chloramphenicol. It is made from living mold and also is produced by a synthetic process. Chloromycetin attacks germs called *rickettsiae*. It has been effective in treating such diseases as Rocky Mountain spotted fever, virus pneumonia, and various types of typhus. Chloromycetin is especially useful in the treatment of typhoid fever and some bacterial dysenteries. KENNETH B. RAPER

See also ANTIBIOTIC.

CHLOROPHYLL, *KLAWR uh fihl*, is the green coloring matter found in certain cells of higher plants. It is contained within these cells in round, flattened bodies called *chloroplasts*. Chlorophyll is also found in *algae* (simple plants) and some *bacteria* (tiny, one-celled organisms). Most plant cells do not produce chlorophyll unless the plant is exposed to light. This is why plants kept away from light are white or yellow rather than green. See BLANCHING.

By means of chlorophyll, living plant cells can change light energy into chemical energy. Plant cells take carbon dioxide from the air and water from the soil. The cells change carbon dioxide and water into sugars or other simple organic compounds. The plant can do this only with the aid of chlorophyll and light. Chlorophyll uses light energy to form the sugar molecule in the following way. When a molecule of chlorophyll located in a chloroplast absorbs light, the molecule becomes activated and loses an electron. After it has lost an electron, it has a positive charge. The molecule can then remove electrons from other substances, including water. This loss of electrons makes the water molecule unstable, and it decomposes to release oxygen. This oxygen is the basis of all higher plant and animal life. When water decomposes, hydrogen is also produced. Plants use this hydrogen to convert carbon dioxide into sugar. This process of manufacture of simple sugars by plants is called *photosynthesis*.

Chlorophyll occurs in several forms. The most common are *chlorophyll a* ($C_{55}H_{72}O_5N_4Mg$) and *chlorophyll b* ($C_{55}H_{70}O_6N_4Mg$). When dried, chlorophyll looks like a blue or green-black powder. ARTHUR W. GALSTON

See also CHLOROPLAST; LEAF (Photosynthesis); PHOTOSYNTHESIS.

CHLOROPLAST, *KLAWR uh plast,* is a small body that occurs within the cells of green plants. It contains the green pigment, *chlorophyll*. Chloroplasts serve as the site of the process of photosynthesis. Some plant cells contain only one chloroplast, others contain many. Chloroplasts may have various shapes, but most of them resemble disks. Chloroplasts are not attached to the cell wall, but float in the cell's jellylike cytoplasm. Most chloroplasts measure about $\frac{1}{100}$ inch (0.25 millimeter) across. GEORGE B. CUMMINS

See also CHLOROPHYLL; PHOTOSYNTHESIS.

CHLORPROMAZINE, *klawr PROH muh zeen,* is a drug used to reduce tension in mentally ill persons. It also helps control nausea, vomiting, and continuous hiccuping. The drug may also produce drowsiness and lower the patient's blood pressure. It was developed in France in the 1950's. Chlorpromazine's trade name is *Thorazine*. R. WILL BURNETT

CHOCOLATE is a food made from the seeds of a tropical tree called the *cacao*. The word *cacao* apparently comes from two Maya Indian words meaning *bitter juice*. The word *chocolate* came from two Maya words meaning *sour water*.

The Cacao Tree produces the seeds, or cacao beans, from which all chocolate and chocolate products are made. These trees flourish in a warm, moist climate. They live within an area about 20° latitude north and south of the equator. Most of the world's cacao beans come from West Africa, where Ghana, the Ivory Coast, and Nigeria are the largest producers. Brazil is the largest cacao bean producer in the Western Hemisphere.

The cultivated cacao tree grows about 25 feet (7.6 meters) high. It produces leaves, flowers, and fruit in all seasons of the year. The flowers are small. They grow singly and in clusters on the main stem of the branches and on the trunk. The ripe fruit, or pod, may be red, yellow, golden, pale green, or a combination of these colors. The pod resembles a long cantaloupe and contains 20 to 40 almond-shaped seeds. When these seeds are fermented and dried, they become the commercial cacao bean.

Because of a mistake in spelling, probably made by English importers many years ago, these beans became known as *cocoa beans* in English-speaking countries. This causes many people to think the beans come from the coconut palm tree instead of the cacao tree.

Harvesting the Cacao Beans. Workers cut the pods from the trees with knives attached to long poles, or with machetes. They gather the pods into heaps, cut them open, and scoop out the beans. The beans are then placed in piles, covered with banana leaves, and allowed to ferment. After fermentation, the beans are dried in the sun or in artificial heat to prevent molding. Then workers place them in bags for shipment.

Manufacturing Chocolate. Chocolate manufacturers receive many types of beans. They blend them so they yield the flavor and color desired in the final product. The first steps in processing the seeds include cleaning, roasting, hulling, blending, and grinding them. Cacao seeds with the shells removed are called *nibs*. The nibs are quite dry, even though they contain about 54 per cent *cocoa butter*, the natural fat of the cacao bean. In the grinding process, the nibs are ground fine, and the cocoa butter is released. The mixture of cocoa butter and finely ground nibs forms a free-flowing substance known as *chocolate liquor*.

Chocolate Products are all manufactured from the chocolate liquor. They include baking chocolate, cocoa, milk chocolate, and sweet and semisweet chocolate.

Baking Chocolate is the commercial form of chocolate liquor. Manufacturers cool and solidify the chocolate liquor into cakes. The bitter, unsweetened baking chocolate is used in many baked products.

Cocoa. In making cocoa powder, huge hydraulic presses force some of the cocoa butter out of the heated chocolate liquor. The mass remaining in the hydraulic presses is in the form of large, hard cakes. Manufacturers change this remainder into its final usable form by grinding it into fine reddish-brown powder. People can prepare a hot beverage from the cocoa powder by adding sugar, hot milk, and sometimes vanilla. Confectioners, bakers, ice cream manufacturers, and other food producers use cocoa in their products.

Milk Chocolate probably ranks as the most popular of all chocolate products. Chocolate liquor, whole milk solids, and granulated sugar are the basic ingredients in this form of chocolate. Extra cocoa butter, obtained from cocoa powder production, is added to the chocolate liquor. First the ingredients are mixed well. Then the mixture passes through a series of large, steel roll refiners. The shearing and rubbing action of these rolls reduces the mass to a smooth paste. Machines called *conches* then process the chocolate for 72 hours. In these machines, a large cylindrical stone rolling on a stone bed pushes the chocolate back and forth. This rubbing action smooths off any rough edges on the chocolate particles, helps develop the desired flavor, and finishes blending the entire mass. Milk chocolate is sold in the form of bars of solid chocolate, and as the coating on some candies.

Sweet Chocolate and *Semisweet Chocolate* are processed in the same way as milk chocolate. But manufacturers do not add milk solids to the mixture in making these products. Manufacturers sell large amounts of both sweet and semisweet chocolate to confectioners for making chocolate-covered candies. Increasingly large amounts of semisweet chocolate are used to make home-made cookies, candy, cakes, and other items.

Food Value of Chocolate. Chocolate serves as both a confection and a food. It possesses a pleasing and widely popular flavor, and also ranks high in food value. Chocolate contains a high concentration of energy-producing compounds. Many persons whose work requires physical endurance, including soldiers, explorers, and athletes, rely on chocolate as a source of quick energy for carrying out their tasks. Chocolate also contains small amounts of *caffeine* and *theobromine*. Both of these alkaloids have a mild stimulating effect (see ALKALOID).

History. Historians do not know how long the Maya Indians of Central America and the Aztec Indians of Mexico had cultivated cacao beans. But they cultivated the beans before Columbus arrived in America. Botanists believe that the cacao tree originated in the Amazon-Orinoco river basin in South America. It is in this area and the upper Amazon tributaries that present-day botanists and geneticists are searching for original types of cacao which may have resistance to the diseases that plague this tree in cultivation.

The cacao bean played an important role in the traditions, religion, and legends of the Aztecs. They believed that one of their prophets had brought the seeds from paradise and sown them in his garden. The Aztecs thought that by eating the fruit, the prophet acquired universal wisdom and knowledge. The Aztecs used the cacao beans as money. They also ground the beans to make a rich beverage.

In 1528, Hernando Cortés, the conqueror of Mexico, took some cacao beans to Spain. In about 1606, cacao beans were introduced into Italy. Shortly after, people in Austria and France began to use the beans. Eventually, their popularity spread to England. By 1707, cocoa had become a fashionable beverage in London.

Workers in a Cacao Orchard break open the fruit and scoop out the tiny beans, which are used in making chocolate.

The Nestlé Co.

Leading Cacao Bean Growing Countries

Cacao bean production in 1979

Brazil	692,300,000 lbs. (314,000,000 kg)
Ivory Coast	687,800,000 lbs. (312,000,000 kg)
Ghana	584,200,000 lbs. (265,000,000 kg)
Nigeria	306,400,000 lbs. (139,000,000 kg)
Cameroon	235,900,000 lbs. (107,000,000 kg)
Ecuador	187,400,000 lbs. (85,000,000 kg)
Mexico	79,400,000 lbs. (36,000,000 kg)
Dominican Republic	72,800,000 lbs. (33,000,000 kg)
Colombia	70,500,000 lbs. (32,000,000 kg)
Papua New Guinea	66,100,000 lbs. (30,000,000 kg)

Source: *Foreign Agriculture Circular*, "Cocoa," February 1980, U.S. Department of Agriculture.

Today, chocolate is popular in most of the world. Countries in which large amounts of chocolate are eaten include Belgium, Germany, Great Britain, Norway, Switzerland, and the United States. ERNEST P. IMLE

CHOCTAW INDIANS, *CHAHK taw*, are a tribe that originally lived in what is now Alabama and Mississippi. They hunted and raised corn and other crops. One of their chief religious ceremonies was a harvest celebration called the Green Corn Dance. According to one legend, the Choctaw were created at a sacred mound called Nanih Waiya, near Noxapater, Miss.

In 1540, the Spanish explorer Hernando de Soto led the first European expedition through Choctaw territory. Fighting broke out after the Choctaw refused to supply the Spaniards with a guide and transportation. Several Spaniards and many Indians were killed.

In 1830, the United States government passed the Indian Removal Act. This act called for eastern Indians to be moved west to make room for more white settlers. The government then forced the Choctaw to sign the Treaty of Dancing Rabbit Creek. The treaty exchanged the tribe's eastern land for an area in the Indian Territory, in what is now Oklahoma. About 14,000 Choctaw moved there in several groups during the early 1830's. About a fourth of the Indians died on the journey, which they called the *Trail of Tears*. About 5,000 Choctaw remained in Mississippi.

The Choctaw who moved to the Indian Territory established their own government and school system. During the Civil War (1861-1865), the Choctaw fought for the Confederacy. After the South lost the war, the Indians were forced to give up much of their land. The tribal government was dissolved by 1907, when Oklahoma became a state. In the 1970's, Congress again recognized the tribe's right to elect its own chief.

Today, about 11,000 Choctaw live in Oklahoma, and about 4,000 live in Mississippi as a separate tribe. Many Choctaw are farmers or foresters. CLARA SUE KIDWELL

See also FIVE CIVILIZED TRIBES; INDIAN TERRITORY.

CHOKE. See CARBURETOR.

CHOKEDAMP. See DAMP.

CHOLERA, *KAHL uhr uh,* is an infectious intestinal disease common in India and other Asiatic countries. It is caused by a bacterium called *Vibrio cholerae,* and is very contagious. The microorganism usually is transmitted in food and water contaminated by persons who have the disease. Flies also help spread the germs.

Cholera bacteria settle in the intestines. There they produce an intense inflammation that soon results in a general body poisoning. The patient suffers diarrhea and vomiting, which results in the loss of body fluid. The loss of fluid becomes so extensive that even the tissue and blood fluids are reduced. After three to five days, the dehydration and changes in body chemistry result in shock, and the patient may die.

Cholera patients must be kept in strict isolation. All the utensils they use are boiled. Waste materials are either burned or treated with strong chemical disinfectants. Doctors begin to replace the lost body fluids and chemicals promptly by means of injections.

Strict sanitary measures are necessary to prevent cholera. During an epidemic, spread of the disease can be checked by sterilizing all water, pasteurizing milk, and cooking all foods. Control of flies and other insects is also important. Cholera is subject to a strict international quarantine. Cholera vaccine provides some immunity. Persons going to Asia usually receive two injections of vaccine, with periodic stimulating injections to maintain the partial protection. PAUL S. RHOADS

CHOLESTEROL, *kuh LEHS tuh rohl,* is a fatty substance found in all animal tissues. The human body manufactures most of its own cholesterol, but some enters the body in food. Butter, eggs, fatty meats, and the meat of such organs as the brain and liver contain much cholesterol.

Cholesterol makes up an important part of the membranes of each cell in the human body. In addition, the liver uses cholesterol to make *bile acids,* which aid digestion. The body also uses cholesterol in the production of certain hormones, including the sex hormones. Hormones are chemical substances that influence many body activities.

All the body's cells can manufacture cholesterol, but most cholesterol is produced by the cells of the liver. Special carrier molecules called *lipoproteins* transport cholesterol from the liver through the bloodstream to cells throughout the body. Three types of lipoproteins—high-density lipoprotein (HDL), low-density lipoprotein (LDL), and very low-density lipoprotein (VLDL)—transport cholesterol. Cholesterol in the blood thus can be identified as HDL-cholesterol, LDL-cholesterol, or VLDL-cholesterol, depending on which lipoprotein is carrying it.

Although the body needs cholesterol, high levels of LDL- and VLDL-cholesterol have been linked to certain diseases, particularly *arteriosclerosis* (hardening of the arteries). Arteriosclerosis develops when fatty deposits that contain cholesterol collect on the inner walls of the blood vessels. These deposits narrow the blood vessels. Blood clots can easily block such narrowed vessels. A clot that blocks an artery of the heart can cause a heart attack.

Because of the problems associated with high levels of cholesterol in the blood, many physicians and nutritionists recommend a diet low in cholesterol. They also urge moderate intake of foods that are high in saturated fats, because such fats increase the body's production of cholesterol. In 1984, researchers in the United States announced the results of a 10-year study of cholesterol and heart disease. The study showed that lowering cholesterol levels in the blood significantly reduced heart attacks in middle-aged men with high cholesterol levels. However, some experts question the value of low cholesterol diets for people with normal or low cholesterol levels. D. RALPH STRENGTH

See also ARTERIOSCLEROSIS; LIPID.

CHOLLA. See CACTUS (Kinds of Cactuses).

CHOLON. See HO CHI MINH CITY.

CHOMSKY, *CHAHM skee,* **NOAM,** *nohm* (1928-), an American linguist, originated *transformational grammar.* Transformational grammar is a system for describing precisely the rules that determine all the sentences that can possibly be formed in any language.

Chomsky claims that every human being knows the general principles of language at birth. He thinks these principles exist in every language and make up a universal grammar. Chomsky developed this theory because he disagreed with the idea that children learn to speak merely by imitating others. Learning by imitation, in his view, does not explain how people form sentences that they have never used before. He believes that the hearing of spoken language merely triggers the language ability that a child has from birth.

Avram Noam Chomsky was born in Philadelphia. He graduated from the University of Pennsylvania in 1949 and earned a Ph.D. degree there in 1955. Chomsky joined the faculty of the Massachusetts Institute of Technology in 1955. His books include *Syntactic Structures* (1957), *Aspects of the Theory of Syntax* (1965), and *Language and Mind* (1968). He has also written numerous articles on United States foreign policy. JOHN LYONS

CHOPIN, *SHOH pan* or *shaw PAN,* **FRÉDÉRIC FRANÇOIS,** *FREHD uh rihk frahn SWAH* (1810?-1849), a Polish-born composer, ranks as one of the masters of piano composition. Chopin wrote *chamber music* (music for small groups of instruments), a few songs, and several pieces for piano and orchestra. But his fame rests almost entirely on his more than 200 compositions for solo piano.

His Life. Chopin was born in Zelazowa-Wola, near Warsaw. A child prodigy, Chopin played the piano in public when he was only eight. He began to compose soon afterward. He studied at the Warsaw Conservatory from 1826 to 1829 before leaving Poland in 1830. He settled in Paris in 1831, and, except for some travel, lived there the rest of his life.

In 1837, Chopin began a famous love affair with George Sand, a French woman novelist. He traveled with her to the Mediterranean island of Majorca during the winter of 1838-1839. Bad weather there weakened his already failing health. His affair with George Sand ended with a quarrel in 1847. He was then seriously ill with tuberculosis. He died on Oct. 17, 1849.

Portrait by Eugène Delacroix, The Louvre, Paris (Art Reference Bureau)
Frédéric Chopin

His Works. Chopin was a master of small musical forms. His works for solo piano include three sonatas, four ballades, four large-scale scherzos, about 40 mazurkas in a Polish $\frac{3}{4}$ dance rhythm, and about 15 polonaises in a stately Polish dance rhythm. His other solo pieces include more than 25 études, 18 waltzes, a barcarole, a berceuse, a bolero, a fantasia, a tarantella, and several rondos. The fantasia is perhaps his greatest single work. His études are valuable for their music and for use in teaching piano.

Chopin is unique among composers because his music has always been as highly esteemed by musicians as by the public. He was a creator of melody, and some of his pieces now seem as familiar as folk music.

Chopin did much to influence piano composition. He had a keen appreciation for the capability of the piano to produce beautiful music. He designed his compositions to display the resources of the instrument to full effect. His best works were written in patterns that he worked out or perfected himself. Chopin also influenced the whole future of music by including Slavic folk harmonies and rhythms in his work.

Some biographers and critics say Chopin's music expresses Polish patriotism. The Slavic harmonies and rhythms in his mazurkas and polonaises show his ties with Poland. However, the rest of his music is at least as French or international in style as it is Polish. It is probably safe to say Chopin was first of all a creative musician, not a nationalist. Herbert Weinstock

Additional Resources

Abraham, Gerald. *Chopin's Musical Style.* Greenwood, 1980. Reprint of 1939 ed.

Atwood, William G. *The Lioness and the Little One: The Liaison of George Sand and Frédéric Chopin.* Columbia Univ. Press, 1980.

Marek, George R., and Gordon-Smith, Maria. *Chopin.* Harper, 1978.

Weinstock, Herbert. *Chopin: The Man and His Music.* Da Capo, 1981. Reprint of 1949 ed.

CHOPIN, *SHOH pan,* **KATE** (1851-1904), was an American novelist and short story writer. She was the first American female novelist to write frankly about women's feelings toward their roles as wives and mothers.

Chopin's best-known novel, *The Awakening* (1899), deals with a woman who is dissatisfied with her passionless husband. The woman gradually gives in to her strong desires for other men and commits adultery. The novel focuses on the restrictions that social and religious institutions of the late 1800's placed on women, and the consequences women suffered when they rebelled. Chopin's realistic treatment of the subject of adultery shocked many readers, and her novel was severely criticized.

Kate O'Flaherty Chopin was born in St. Louis. For many years, she lived in or near New Orleans. She wrote more than 100 short stories, many of which were published in the collections *The Bayou Folk* (1894) and *A Night in Acadie* (1897). These stories provide a colorful picture of life in the Cajun and Creole communities of central Louisiana. Eugene K. Garber

CHOPSTICKS are utensils used in many Asian countries to eat and serve food. Most of the food in those countries is served in small pieces, which can be easily handled with a pair of chopsticks. The Chinese name for chopsticks, *kuai-*, is a pun on *kuai,* a word that means both *quick* and *piece.* The English word may come from pidgin English, a dialect used by early traders in China. *Chop* means *quick* in pidgin English.

Chopsticks are slim, tapered sticks about 10 inches (25 centimeters) long. Most are made of wood or bamboo, but some are ivory or silver. A person using chopsticks holds them parallel to each other. The top stick, which moves up and down, is held by the thumb and the index and middle fingers, like a pencil. The bottom stick rests at the base of the thumb and is braced against the top of the fourth finger. The ends of the chopsticks thus hold the food securely. Many non-Asians use chopsticks when eating Oriental food. Norma Diamond

CHORAL MUSIC. See Classical Music (Choral Music).

CHORALE, *kuh RAL,* is the music for a hymn. The term particularly refers to hymns of the German Protestant churches. Chorales developed during the early 1500's. The earliest chorales had a single-part melody and words that were sung by a congregation in unison without accompaniment. Gradually, chorales became more elaborate. Composers added harmony and counterpoint as well as instrumental accompaniment. Many composers used chorales in larger works, such as cantatas, oratorios, and passion music.

Martin Luther, the founder of Protestantism in Germany, considered chorales important because they gave a congregation additional opportunities to participate in church services. Luther wrote or adapted a large number of chorales, including the famous "A Mighty Fortress Is Our God." Ellen Pfeifer

See also Hymn.

CHORDATE, *KAWR dayt,* is the name of a large *phylum* (group) of land, marine, and freshwater animals. Chordates include lancelets, amphibians, fish, reptiles, birds, and mammals. At some time during their life cycle, all chordates have a *notochord* (a stiff tubular cord that runs down the back of the body). In vertebrates, the notochord is surrounded or replaced by a bony structure called a *vertebral column.* Chordates also have a hollow nerve tube that runs above the notochord. Chordates are segmented in some way, and they have left and right sides that are alike. Chordates also have gill slits, but in many cases these appear only during the undeveloped stage. See also Vertebrate.

CHOREA, *kaw REE uh,* formerly called *St. Vitus's dance,* is a condition closely associated with rheumatic fever. It occurs most commonly in children between the ages of 7 and 15 years. Doctors do not know exactly what causes chorea. It often occurs with rheumatic fever, and some physicians believe chorea may be caused by the germs of that disease (see Rheumatic Fever). These germs may be in the patient's body for weeks or months before symptoms of chorea develop.

Chorea develops gradually. The patient becomes inattentive, nervous and irritable, and cries easily. The patient has difficulty writing, often stumbles, and falls easily. Uncoordinated movements of the face, limbs, and body soon develop. These movements are completely without purpose. They become worse when the patient is excited, but disappear during sleep. The symptoms may last from two to four months or more, but the patient eventually recovers. Doctors treat chorea with sedatives. Patients must remain in bed, have a nutritious diet, and avoid fatigue. Doctors try to prevent chorea by treating infections promptly.

The word *chorea* comes from a Greek word meaning *dance*. The disease probably was named for the muscular twitchings of the limbs and body that resemble a grotesque dance. The name *St. Vitus's dance* comes from a form of hysteria that was widespread in Europe during the 1500's. Persons with this condition sought cures at shrines of St. Vitus. JOHN A. BIGLER

CHOREOGRAPHY. See BALLET (Choreography).

CHORUS. See DRAMA (Greek Drama); OPERA (The Singers).

CHOSON. See KOREA (The Yi Dynasty).

CHOU DYNASTY, *joh*, was a Chinese *dynasty* (family of rulers) that governed from about 1122 B.C. to 256 B.C. It was China's longest-ruling dynasty.

The dynasty began when the Chou—tribes of western China—conquered the ruling Shang dynasty. Chou rulers set up a society with three classes—aristocrats, commoners, and slaves. The commoners, like those in medieval Europe, farmed their own land and that of the aristocrats. The Chou rulers divided the kingdom into many states. A local chief headed each state, but the chiefs enforced the central government's rules.

A weak Chou ruler was overthrown by his enemies in 771 B.C. The dynasty then moved its capital east from Hao (near what is now Sian) to Lo-yang. The move marked the beginning of the *Eastern Chou period*. During this period, cities grew, a merchant class developed, and the use of money replaced *barter* (trade). The famous philosophers Confucius and Lao Tzu developed their ideas during this time (see CONFUCIUS; LAO TZU).

The Chou central government gradually lost power to its large states, and the dynasty finally ended in 256 B.C. Seven large states controlled China until 221 B.C., when the Ch'in dynasty took over. EUGENE BOARDMAN

CHOU EN-LAI. See ZHOU ENLAI.

CHOUART, MÉDARD. See GROSEILLIERS, SIEUR DES.

CHOUTEAU, *shoo TOH*, is the name of a family that played an important part in settling the American Middle West and in developing the fur trade.

René Auguste Chouteau (1749-1829) was one of the founders of St. Louis. He and Pierre Laclède Liguest visited the site in 1763. A year later, they returned to build a trading post. St. Louis soon became a thriving town. After the United States purchased Louisiana in 1803, Chouteau served the new government as a territorial judge, an Indian commissioner, and a colonel of the militia. In 1808, St. Louis was incorporated as a town. Chouteau became the first president of its board of trustees. He was born in New Orleans.

Jean Pierre Chouteau (1758-1849), the brother of René Auguste, shared with him a monopoly of trade with the Osage Indians in Missouri from 1794 to 1802. His popularity with them became so great that, when Spain granted this trade to a rival company, Jean Pierre persuaded 3,000 Osage Indians to move with him to Oklahoma. There he built a trading post which later became Salina, Okla. He became U.S. Indian agent to the Osage tribes and remained a dominant influence with them for many years.

In 1809, Chouteau and other business people formed the St. Louis Missouri Fur Company to exploit the western fur trade. He was one of the first to settle Oklahoma, and the state celebrates his birthday as "Oklahoma Historical Day." He was born in New Orleans.

Pierre Chouteau, Jr. (1789-1865), often called *Cadet*, was a son of Jean Pierre. He acquired great wealth from the fur business and became one of the most powerful financiers of his day. After heading the western department of the American Fur Company for John Jacob Astor, he bought out Astor and created a fur-trading monopoly. His company pioneered in the use of steamboats in the fur trade. It was the first fur-trading company to take a steamboat up the Missouri River to Montana. When the fur trade declined, Chouteau moved to New York and invested in iron and steel works. He served as a member of the Missouri State Constitutional Convention in 1820. Pierre, S. Dak., and Chouteau, Mont., were both named for him. Chouteau was born in St. Louis, Mo.

François Chouteau (1797-1836), also a son of Jean Pierre, helped his brother, Pierre, Jr., acquire the independent fur posts for the American Fur Company. He founded Kansas City, Mo., by establishing a trading post on the present site of the city in 1821. He was born in St. Louis. HOWARD R. LAMAR

CHOW CHOW, commonly called *chow*, is a dog bred in China. It has erect ears and a bushy tail that curls over its back. Its long hair is black, blue-gray, red, or cream, and the same color all over, although the color may be lighter underneath and on its legs. It has a square head, small ears, "three-cornered" eyes, and small straight hind legs. Chows are strong, active, and intelligent. JOSEPHINE Z. RINE

See also DOG (picture: Some Breeds of Dogs).

CHRÉTIEN DE TROYES, *kray TYAN du TRAWH*, was a French poet who wrote from about 1160 to about 1190. He introduced the tales of King Arthur and the Knights of the Round Table into French literature. Chrétien wrote long verse romances of love and adventure. They show the character of medieval chivalry, the splendor of festivals and tournaments, and the importance of courtly love during the late 1100's. Chrétien's romances were very popular, and were imitated for more than 100 years. His *Perceval*, also called *The Tale of the Grail*, is the earliest known literary version of the legend of the Holy Grail. His other romances include *Cligès*, *Erec and Enide*, *Lancelot*, and *Yvain*.

Little is known of Chrétien's life. He probably wrote at the courts of Champagne and Flanders in northern France. RICHARD O'GORMAN

CHRIST, JESUS. See JESUS CHRIST.

CHRIST OF THE ANDES is a bronze statue of Christ on the Argentina-Chile border in the Andes Mountains. It was dedicated on March 13, 1904, as a symbol of perpetual peace between Argentina and Chile.

The two nations jointly erected the statue to commemorate the settlement of a boundary dispute. The statue stands on the summit of Uspallata Pass, 12,674 feet (3,863 meters) above sea level, between Mendoza, Argentina, and Santiago, Chile. It is molded from the metal of old Argentine cannons, and was created by the Argentine sculptor Mateo Alonzo. The figure of Christ, 26 feet (7.9 meters) high, stands on a granite hemisphere. The left hand holds a large cross, and the right hand is raised in blessing. An inscription in Spanish at the base of the statue reads: "Sooner shall these mountains crumble into dust than Argentines and Chileans break the peace sworn at the feet of Christ the Redeemer." Arthur P. Whitaker

Burton Holmes, Ewing Galloway

Christ of the Andes

CHRISTCHURCH (pop. 289,392) is the third largest city of New Zealand. Only Auckland and Wellington are larger. Christchurch is a major industrial center. It lies on the South Island near the east coast. For location, see New Zealand (map). Tunnels that run through the nearby Port Hills link the city with Lyttelton, the South Island's chief port.

The Avon River winds through Christchurch. The city has many large parks and gardens, and a Gothic-style Anglican cathedral stands in the central square.

The chief products of Christchurch include clothing, electrical goods, fertilizers, leather, and processed meat and wool. An international airport and major railroads serve the area. The Canterbury Association, an Anglican church group that came from Great Britain, founded Christchurch in 1850. Gordon R. Lewthwaite

CHRISTENING. See Baptism.

CHRISTIAN. See Christianity.

CHRISTIAN is the name of several Danish kings. Christian I ruled from 1448 to 1481. For Christian III, see Denmark (A Great Power).

Christian IX (1818-1906) became king in 1863. He was often called the *father of the royal families of Europe.* His children or grandchildren ruled in England, Russia, Greece, and Norway. During Christian's reign, the Danish government established many reforms. A law made elementary education compulsory and established rural schools for adults. Denmark became the *dairy of Europe* and developed many industries.

Christian X (1870-1947), son of Frederik VIII, succeeded his father in 1912. He supported constitutional reforms that brought greater democracy to Denmark. His governments also passed many social reforms, such as old-age pensions. In World War II, when Germany occupied Denmark, he refused to become a puppet king and symbolized Danish resistance. Raymond E. Lindgren

CHRISTIAN, CHARLIE (1919-1942), was the first great electric guitarist and an influential figure in the development of jazz. Christian revolutionized guitar playing by utilizing the instrument's full potential for sound, melody, and rhythmic expression. His creativity established the guitar as a solo instrument in jazz. Christian specialized in playing improvised melodies in a lively single-string style—that is, playing one note at a time instead of chords.

Charles Christian was born in Dallas. He grew up in Oklahoma City, Okla., where a talent scout named John Hammond discovered him in 1939. From 1939 to 1941, Christian played with clarinetist Benny Goodman's band and sextet. During those years, he also performed with other jazz musicians, including trumpeter Dizzy Gillespie and pianist Thelonious Monk, at Minton's Play House in Harlem in New York City. Together, they developed a form of modern jazz called *bebop*. Christian died of tuberculosis. Burt Korall

See also Jazz (picture: Benny Goodman).

CHRISTIAN ATHLETES, FELLOWSHIP OF. See Fellowship of Christian Athletes.

CHRISTIAN CHURCH (DISCIPLES OF CHRIST). See Disciples of Christ.

CHRISTIAN ENDEAVOR is an international youth organization of the evangelical Protestant churches. It strives to unite its members for Christian growth and service. Its motto is "For Christ and the Church." Francis E. Clark began the movement in 1881 in Portland, Me. The movement spread rapidly in the United States, and, in 1885, the United Society of Christian Endeavor was founded. In 1927, its name was changed to the International Society of Christian Endeavor to include Canada and Mexico.

The World's Christian Endeavor Union was formed in 1895. Today, the movement has thousands of societies in local churches. It has over 3 million members in about 75 nations and island groups. Its headquarters are at 1221 E. Broad Street, Columbus, Ohio 43216.

Critically reviewed by Christian Endeavor

CHRISTIAN ERA is the period from the birth of Christ to the present. In the A.D. 500's, the monk Dionysius Exiguus introduced the present custom of reckoning time by counting the years from the birth of Christ, which he miscalculated four to six years later than the actual date. This method was in use in Christian countries by about 1400. See also New Testament (The Birth of Jesus); B.C.; A.D. Howard R. Burkle

CHRISTIAN REFORMED CHURCH was founded in 1857 in the United States by a group of Dutch people. They broke away from the Dutch Reformed Church (now the Reformed Church in America) but continued to follow the teachings of John Calvin. The Christian Reformed Church adopted its present name in 1904.

CHRISTIAN SCIENTISTS are members of a religious movement that stresses spiritual healing. Mary Baker Eddy, a New England woman, founded the Christian Science movement in the 1800's. The religion has deep roots in Protestant Christianity. It is "designed to commemorate the word and works of our Master, which should reinstate primitive Christianity and its lost element of healing." See Eddy, Mary Baker.

The central institution of Christian Science is The First Church of Christ, Scientist, in Boston. Called *The Mother Church,* it was founded in 1879 by Mrs. Eddy and a group of followers. About two-thirds of the 3,000 churches and societies that exist around the world are in the United States.

Beliefs. Mrs. Eddy's principal book, *Science and Health with Key to the Scriptures* (1875), contains the full statement of Christian Science beliefs. Church members study this book and the Bible every day. *Lesson-sermons* compiled from these two books are the chief feature of Sunday worship at all churches.

Christian Science is based on the teaching that God is wholly good and all-powerful, and that people are created by Him. In this teaching, everything eternal, spiritual, and wholly good is called *reality*. Whatever is unlike God—such as sin, evil, grief, sickness, or injustice—has no foundation in reality. Mankind imperfectly understands reality, but through prayer and by learning more about God, people can begin to see and experience the true reality.

Christian Scientists view healing as an awakening to this reality. To understand truth means not to ignore evil and sickness, but to wipe them out through prayer and spiritual understanding. They teach that this message is essentially the message of Jesus. No church *dogma* (belief) or penalty enforces reliance on prayer for healing, but it is a natural part of their way of life.

Organization. The Church of Christ, Scientist, took its final form in 1892. There is no clergy in the Christian Science church. Services are conducted by members elected to serve as *readers*. The church is administered by the Board of The Mother Church in Boston. Local churches govern themselves democratically. There are about 4,800 *practitioners*, who devote their full time professionally to healing.

The church maintains reading rooms in many cities and provides printed materials about the religion in many public places. A publishing society in Boston supervises the publications printing Christian Science teachings. The monthly *The Christian Science Journal* provides a directory of local churches and practitioners. The weekly *Christian Science Sentinel* and monthly *The Herald of Christian Science* contain accounts of Christian Science healing. *The Christian Science Quarterly* contains citations from the Bible and the religion's textbook for Sunday services and daily study. In 1908, Mrs. Eddy founded *The Christian Science Monitor*. This world-famous daily newspaper is published in Boston.

Critically reviewed by the Christian Scientists

Additional Resources

Beasley, Norman. *The Cross and the Crown: The History of Christian Science*. Duell, 1952.

Gottschalk, Stephen. *The Emergence of Christian Science in American Religious Life*. Univ. of California Press, 1973.

John, DeWitt, and Canham, E. D. *The Christian Science Way of Life*. Christian Science Publishing Society, 1962.

Orcutt, William D. *Mary Baker Eddy and Her Books*. Christian Science Publishing Society, 1950.

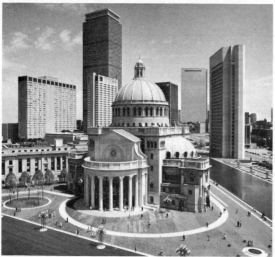

The First Church of Christ, Scientist

The First Church of Christ, Scientist, is the central institution, or *Mother Church,* of Christian Science. The domed structure stands in the Christian Science Center in Boston. The church's administration building, *right,* rises 28 stories above the center.

CHRISTIAN SOCIALISM. See Kingsley, Charles.

CHRISTIANIA. See Oslo.

CHRISTIANITY is the religion founded upon the life and teachings of Jesus Christ. It has spread throughout the world, and is the prevailing religion in the Western Hemisphere. There are about a billion Christians. They make up the largest religious group in the world. Christianity has influenced government, thought, and art for almost 2,000 years.

Origin of Christianity

Jesus Christ founded the Christian faith. He began His career in Palestine, instructing and preaching to people about the Kingdom of God. He traveled around the country with a group of followers called *disciples*. He chose 12 disciples, called *apostles*, to preach His doctrine. Like the Old Testament prophets, Jesus insisted upon justice toward people and humility toward God. He also preached mercy and brotherhood, and told of the love of God for all creatures.

The Jewish religious leaders of Jesus' time did not approve of His claim that He was the *Messiah*, or the promised deliverer of the Jews. (The name *Christ* comes from a Greek word for *Messiah*.) They considered this action to be blasphemy. The Roman authorities felt that Jesus' claim to be King of the Jews amounted to treason. They feared that He meant to lead an uprising against Roman rule in Palestine. As a result, He was tried, condemned to death, and crucified.

After the death of Jesus, His followers scattered in fear. However, they soon reassembled. One after another, beginning on the first Easter morning, reported that they had met Jesus alive. This rising from the dead is called the *Resurrection*, and forms one of the basic doctrines of the Christian faith. Christians believe Jesus remained on earth for 40 days after His Resurrection, and then ascended into Heaven.

The Cross is the symbol of Christianity. Jesus Christ, the founder of Christianity, died on a cross in ancient Palestine.

Beginning of the Church. The Christian movement received a new incentive at Pentecost, 50 days after Easter, when the disciples reported a strange and powerful inspiration. They said the Holy Spirit had entered into them. They spoke of unusual deeds they had performed, such as speaking many languages. Some Christians believe the church began at this time.

The first believers in Christ were Jews by birth and training, and, at first, they were considered a sect of Judaism. But gradually they came to think of themselves as belonging to an independent religion. The followers of Christ first received the name *Christians* at Antioch, Syria (now in Turkey), where one of the first Christian communities outside of Palestine grew up.

Spread of Christianity

The Early Church. Christianity spread rapidly, due to the work of St. Paul and the apostles. The Romans persecuted the Christians for many years. But Emperor Constantine granted them freedom of religion through the Edict of Milan in A.D. 313. Christianity became the official religion of the Roman Empire in the late 300's. Missionaries carried the faith throughout the world.

In instructing and preaching, church leaders used the writings of early theologians and writers called *Church Fathers*. They included St. Ignatius, St. Basil, St. Jerome, and St. Augustine. The church taught the Old Testament and used early religious writings, especially those that became books of the New Testament. These include the *Epistles* (letters) of St. Paul, which helped unify the scattered Christian communities.

The Middle Ages. The church strongly affected political and intellectual life during medieval times. It developed great economic and political power, and held much territory. This expansion led to constant struggles between the church and temporal rulers. Christianity bound almost all Europe together in a single faith. When the Muslims invaded the Holy Land, European nations joined forces to fight them in the Crusades.

The church also preserved learning during the Dark Ages through its monasteries. Monasticism began to develop as early as the A.D. 300's. But monasteries did not become an important force until the early 1200's, when the Dominican and Franciscan orders were founded in Europe. Monks were often the only educated people. They wrote chronicles and kept libraries of handwritten manuscripts. See CRUSADES; MONASTICISM.

Division of the Church

Heresies and Schisms. Even in the early years of the church, *heresies* (beliefs opposed to official doctrine) developed. The more important heresies included Arianism, Nestorianism, the Iconoclastic heresy, and the Albigensian heresy. See HERESY.

But Christianity remained practically one great community for almost a thousand years. In the 800's, however, a *schism* (division) began to separate the church at Rome and the church at Constantinople (now Istanbul). In 1054, rivalries between the two groups resulted in a separation between the Eastern Orthodox Churches and the Roman Catholic Church.

Another schism, the Great Schism of the West, began in the late 1300's. This schism led to rival popes, and seriously divided the church for almost 40 years.

The Protestant Reformation. In the 1500's, large groups of Christians, who came to be called *Protestants*, broke away from the Roman Catholic Church. The movement, called the Protestant Reformation, was a protest over religious matters and against the worldly power of the church. Protestants have since divided into many sects and denominations. Roman Catholics began the Counter Reformation to reunite the church.

Christianity Today

The three great divisions of Christianity today are the Protestant denominations, the Roman Catholic Church, and the Eastern Orthodox Churches. In the 1800's, some Christian groups began what is called the *ecumenical movement*, to seek ways to unite. Protestant and Orthodox groups have founded such organizations as the World Council of Churches. Today, Christian groups often combine to fight common enemies, such as totalitarianism. HOWARD R. BURKLE

Related Articles in WORLD BOOK include:

Apostles' Creed	New Testament
Bible	Protestantism
Eastern Orthodox Churches	Religion
	Roman Catholic Church
Jesus Christ	Scholasticism
Lord's Prayer	Ten Commandments

See also *Christianity* in the RESEARCH GUIDE/INDEX, Volume 22, for a *Reading and Study Guide*.

Additional Resources

BAINTON, ROLAND. *The Church of Our Fathers*. Scribner, 1941. For younger readers.

BARRACLOUGH, GEOFFREY, ed. *The Christian World: A Social and Cultural History*. Abrams, 1981.

CLEBSCH, WILLIAM A. *Christianity in European History*. Oxford, 1979.

LITTELL, FRANKLIN H. *The Macmillan Atlas History of Christianity*. Macmillan, 1976.

LIVINGSTONE, ELIZABETH A., ed. *The Concise Oxford Dictionary of the Christian Church*. Oxford, 1978.

The Pelican History of the Christian Church. 5 vols. Penguin, 1960-1968.

SMART, NINIAN. *In Search of Christianity: The Diverse Vitality of Christian Life*. Harper, 1979.

WALKER, WILLISTON. *History of the Christian Church*. 3rd ed. Scribner, 1970.

CHRISTIE, DAME AGATHA (1890-1976), was an English writer of detective stories. Her stories are noted for their clever plots. Dame Agatha introduced the Belgian private investigator Hercule Poirot in her first detective novel, *The Mysterious Affair at Styles* (1920). Poirot is also featured in her first famous detective novel, *The Murder of Roger Ackroyd* (1926), and in many later novels. Miss Jane Marple, an elderly spinster, appears in many stories, including *Murder at the Vicarage* (1930) and *Nemesis* (1971). Tommy and Tuppence Beresford, a married couple, are the amateur detectives in several novels, including *N or M?* (1941) and *By the Pricking of My Thumbs* (1968).

Dame Agatha wrote 83 books of detective and mystery fiction—67 novels and 16 collections of short stories. She also wrote 16 plays. Her best known plays include the suspense dramas *The Mousetrap* (1952) and *Witness for the Prosecution* (1953). Dame Agatha wrote six novels under the name Mary Westmacott and *An Autobiography* (published in 1977, after her death). She was born Agatha Mary Clarissa Miller in Torquay (now part of Torbay), Devon. She was made Dame Commander in the Order of the British Empire in 1971. PHILIP DURHAM

WORLD BOOK photo by Dan Miller

A Nativity Scene, also called a *crèche,* shows figures of Mary and Joseph praying over the Christ child. The Wise Men, shepherds, and various animals surround the Holy Family.

CHRISTMAS

CHRISTMAS is a Christian holiday that celebrates the birth of Jesus Christ. No one knows the exact date of Christ's birth, but most Christians observe Christmas on December 25. On this day, many go to church, where they take part in special religious services. During the Christmas season, they also exchange gifts and decorate their homes with holly, mistletoe, and Christmas trees. The word *Christmas* comes from *Cristes maesse,* an early English phrase that means *Mass of Christ.*

The story of Christmas comes chiefly from the Gospels of Saint Luke and Saint Matthew in the New Testament. According to Luke, an angel appeared to shepherds outside the town of Bethlehem and told them of Jesus' birth. Matthew tells how the Wise Men, called *Magi,* followed a bright star that led them to Jesus.

The first mention of the celebration of Christmas occurred in A.D. 336 in an early Roman calendar, which indicates December 25 as the day of observance. This celebration was probably influenced by *pagan* (unchristian) festivals held at that time. The ancient Romans held year-end celebrations to honor Saturn, their harvest god; and Mithras, the god of light. Various peoples in northern Europe held festivals in mid-December to celebrate the end of the harvest season. As part of all these celebrations, the people prepared special foods, decorated their homes with greenery, and joined in singing and gift giving. These customs gradually became part of the Christmas celebration.

In the late 300's, Christianity became the official religion of the Roman Empire. By 1100, Christmas had become the most important religious festival in Europe, and Saint Nicholas was a symbol of gift giving in many European countries. During the 1400's and 1500's, many artists painted scenes of the *Nativity,* the birth of Jesus. Examples of these works appear in the articles BOTTICELLI, SANDRO and PAINTING (The Renaissance).

The popularity of Christmas grew until the Reformation, a religious movement of the 1500's. This movement gave birth to Protestantism. During the Reformation, many Christians began to consider Christmas a pagan celebration because it included nonreligious customs. During the 1600's, because of these feelings, Christmas was outlawed in England and in parts of the English colonies in America. However, people continued to exchange Christmas gifts and soon started to follow the other old customs again.

In the 1800's, two more Christmas customs became popular—decorating Christmas trees and sending Christmas cards to relatives and friends. Many well-known Christmas carols, including "Silent Night" and "Hark! The Herald Angels Sing," were composed during this period. In the United States and other countries, Santa Claus replaced Saint Nicholas as the symbol of gift giving.

The celebration of Christmas became increasingly important to many kinds of businesses during the 1900's. Today, companies manufacture Christmas ornaments, lights, and other decorations throughout the year. Other

Robert J. Myers, the contributor of this article, is coeditor of American Christmas *and the author of* Celebrations: The Complete Book of American Holidays.

firms grow Christmas trees, holly, and mistletoe. Many stores and other businesses hire extra workers during the Christmas season to handle the increase in sales.

The word *Xmas* is sometimes used instead of Christmas. This tradition began in the early Christian church. In Greek, *X* is the first letter of Christ's name. It was frequently used as a holy symbol.

Christmas Around the World

Christmas is the happiest and busiest time of the year for millions of Christians throughout the world. People of different countries celebrate the holiday in various ways, depending on national and local customs.

In the United States and Canada, people decorate their homes with Christmas trees, wreaths, and many kinds of ornaments. City streets sparkle with colored lights, and the sound of bells and carols fills the air.

During the weeks before Christmas, children write letters to Santa Claus and tell him what presents they would like to receive. Many department stores hire people to wear a Santa Claus costume and listen to children's requests. People share holiday greetings by sending Christmas cards to relatives and friends. Many companies give presents to their employees.

A Christmas tree is the main attraction in most homes. Relatives and friends may join in trimming the tree with lights, tinsel, and colorful ornaments. Presents are placed under the tree. Many young children believe the presents are brought by Santa Claus, who arrives on Christmas Eve in a sleigh pulled by reindeer. Some youngsters hang up stockings so Santa can fill them with candy, fruit, and other small gifts. Families open their presents on Christmas Eve or Christmas morning.

In many parts of the United States and Canada, groups of carolers walk from house to house and sing Christmas songs. Some people give the singers money or small gifts or invite them in for a warm drink.

Many people attend church services on Christmas Eve or Christmas morning. Churches are decorated with evergreen branches, red poinsettias, and scenes of the Nativity. Churchgoers listen to readings from the Bible and join in singing Christmas carols.

"Merry Christmas" Around the World

Country	Greeting
China	**Sheng Dan Kuai Le**
Denmark	**Glaedelig Jul**
Finland	**Hauskaa Joulua**
France	**Joyeux Noël**
Germany and Austria	**Fröhliche Weihnachten**
Greece	**Kala Christougenna**
Hungary	**Kellemes Karácsonyi Ünnepeket**
Italy	**Buon Natale**
Japan	**Meri Kurisumasu**
The Netherlands	**Zalig Kerstfeest**
Norway	**Gledelig Jul**
Poland	**Wesolych Swiat**
Portugal and Brazil	**Boas Festas**
Russia	**S Rozhdestvom Kristovym**
Spain, Mexico, and other Spanish-speaking countries	**Feliz Navidad**
Sweden	**God Jul**
United States, Canada, and other English-speaking countries	**Merry Christmas**

A traditional Christmas dinner includes stuffed turkey, mashed potatoes, cranberry sauce, and a variety of other dishes. Some families have ham or roast goose instead of turkey. Favorite desserts include mince pie or pumpkin pie, plum pudding, and fruitcake. Eggnog is a popular Christmas beverage in many homes.

In some parts of the United States and Canada, various ethnic groups observe Christmas customs of their ancestors. For example, Spanish traditions are popular in the Southwestern United States. Many families in the province of Quebec follow French customs. Some black Americans combine Christmas with *Kwanzaa*, an Afro-American holiday. Kwanzaa lasts seven days, from December 26 through January 1. Each day, families light a candle symbolizing one of seven principles, including creativity, faith, and unity. See KWANZAA.

In the British Isles. Many Christmas customs that are popular in the United States and Canada originated in

Owen Franken, Stock, Boston

The Christmas Parade in many U.S. communities includes hundreds of colorful floats. The highlight of the parade is the float featuring Santa Claus in his sleigh pulled by reindeer.

Ted Spiegel, Black Star

Outdoor Decorations brighten many public buildings during the Christmas season. This picture shows strings of lights on the British Columbia Parliament buildings in Victoria, Canada.

© Susan McCartney

Christmas Carolers provide holiday entertainment in many public places. An English choir, dressed in clothing of the 1800's, sings carols near Tower Bridge in London, *above.*

the British Isles. They include sending Christmas cards and hanging a sprig of mistletoe in a room or hallway. According to tradition, a person may kiss anyone standing under the mistletoe. On Christmas Eve, children hang up stockings for *Father Christmas*, the British version of Santa Claus, to fill with presents. On the afternoon of Christmas Day, most British families watch their monarch give a special Christmas message on television. In England, dinner on Christmas Day features roast turkey and dessert of mince pie and plum pudding.

During the days before Christmas, children or groups of adults go from house to house singing Christmas carols. Children ask for money for themselves, but adults usually ask for money for charity. This tradition began many years ago, when visitors sang carols in return for a drink from the *wassail bowl*. The bowl contained hot punch made from ale, apples, eggs, sugar, and spices. The word *wassail* comes from *Was haile*, an old Saxon greeting that means *Be healthy*. Today, English people at large parties still drink punch, but it is usually made from wine and other alcoholic beverages, fruit, and spices.

In Ireland, people put a lighted candle in their window on Christmas Eve as a sign of welcome to passing travelers. In Wales, people have caroling contests during the weeks before Christmas. Roast turkey is the main course for dinner. People in Scotland also have roast turkey and exchange small gifts. Some Scottish families decorate a Christmas tree and sing carols, but most hold their main celebrations on New Year's Day.

In France, children put their shoes in front of the fireplace so *Père Noël* (Father Christmas) can fill them with gifts. Many families attend midnight Mass and then have a festive supper called *Le réveillon*. Large numbers of French families also decorate their homes with small Nativity scenes. In these scenes, clay figures called *santons* (little saints) portray the story of Jesus' birth. Some people put additional santons in their Nativity scenes every year. They buy these figures at special holiday fairs that are held before Christmas.

In Germany, children receive candy and other sweets on December 6 from Saint Nicholas, a Christian bishop who died in the A.D. 300's. Saint Nicholas also collects children's lists telling what gifts they wish to receive from the *Christkindl* (Christ child). The Christkindl does not appear in person. Instead he sends *Weihnachtsmann* (Christmas Man), the German version of Father Christmas, who delivers the presents on Christmas Eve.

Most German families have a Christmas tree that they decorate with lights, tinsel, and ornaments. Spicy cakes called *lebkuchen* are made in various shapes and used as decorations.

In Spain, people dance and sing in the streets after midnight Mass on Christmas Eve. Most Spanish homes and churches display a miniature Nativity scene called a *Nacimiento*. During the evening of January 5, children

© Gaston Malherbe from Louis Mercier

Christmas Fairs in France feature a variety of holiday gifts and decorations. The most popular are handmade clay figures called *santons* (little saints), such as those shown above. The French use santons in Nativity scenes.

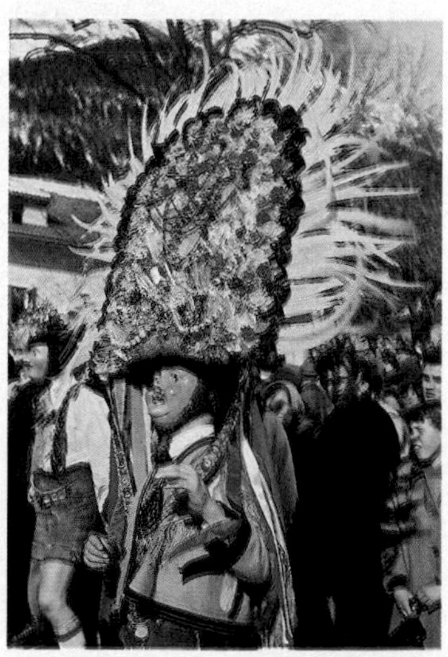

Betty Crowell, Atoz Images

Mummers act out Christmas plays in parades and festivals. These Austrian mummers wear masks to frighten evil spirits.

Netherlands Information Service

Saint Nicholas, accompanied by his servant *Swarte Piet* (Black Pete) and other attendants, arrives in The Netherlands by boat from Spain, *above.* According to legend, Saint Nicholas brings gifts to children on the eve of December 6.

Fred Ward, Black Star

On St. Lucia Day, December 13, Swedish girls carry lighted candles and bring coffee and buns to their families.

put their shoes on a balcony or near a window. The next day is Epiphany, the last day of the Christmas season. It celebrates the visit of the Magi to the infant Jesus. According to legend, the Wise Men arrive during the night before Epiphany and fill the children's shoes with small gifts. See EPIPHANY.

In The Netherlands, Belgium, and Luxembourg, according to legend, Saint Nicholas gives presents to children on the eve of December 6. Wearing a red robe, he arrives on a boat from Spain and rides down the streets on a white horse. His servant, *Swarte Piet* (Black Pete), accompanies him. Saint Nicholas goes down the chimney of each house and leaves gifts in shoes that the children have put by the fireplace.

In Italy, most homes and churches have a *presepio* (Nativity scene). On Christmas Eve, the family prays while the mother places a figure of the *Bambino* (Christ child) in the manger. Many Italians serve eels for dinner on Christmas Eve. They also bake a Christmas bread called *panettone*, which contains raisins and candied fruit. Italian children receive gifts from *La Befana*, a kindly old witch, on the eve of Epiphany.

In Poland, people attend *Pasterka* (Shepherd's Mass) at midnight on Christmas Eve. Many Polish families follow the Christmas tradition of breaking an *oplatek*, a thin wafer made of wheat flour and water. Nativity scenes are stamped on the oplatek. The head of the family holds the wafer, and each person breaks off a small piece and eats it. The Christmas meal features fish, sauerkraut, potato pancakes, and beet soup.

In Denmark, Norway, and Sweden, Christmas dinner includes rice pudding, called *julgröt*, which has a single almond in it. According to tradition, whoever gets the almond will have good luck throughout the new year.

Santa Claus is a familiar figure in the Scandinavian countries. But many children there believe that a lively elf brings them gifts from Santa on Christmas Eve. The Danes and Norwegians call this elf *Julenissen*, and the Swedes refer to him as *Jultomten*.

The Christmas season in Sweden begins on St. Lucia Day, December 13. In the morning of this day, the oldest daughter in the home dresses in white and wears a wreath with seven lighted candles on her head. She serves the other members of the family coffee and buns in bed.

A popular Christmas custom in Norway is *ringe in Julen* (ringing in Christmas). Throughout the country, people ring church bells at 5 P.M. on Christmas Eve. In Denmark, people decorate their Christmas tree with

Fritz Prenzel

Christmas Comes in Summer in Australia and New Zealand. Many people there go to the beach on Christmas Day. These children are chatting with Santa Claus in downtown Sydney, Australia.

A Mexican Tradition at Christmastime is breaking the *piñata.* A piñata is a paper or clay figure filled with candy and small gifts. It is hung from the ceiling, and the children take turns trying to break it with a stick while blindfolded. The piñata can be raised and lowered, which makes the task more difficult.

© Michael A. Vaccaro from Louis Mercier

small paper cones filled with candy. Children are not allowed to see the tree until Christmas Eve.

In Australia and New Zealand, December comes during the summer. Many people celebrate Christmas by going on a picnic or to the beach. Schoolchildren have a six-week summer vacation at Christmastime. Caroling takes place in many cities and towns. Popular Christmas foods include turkey and plum pudding. Both Father Christmas and Santa Claus are popular symbols of gift giving in Australia and New Zealand.

In Latin America. The nine days before Christmas have special importance in Mexico. These days are called *posadas,* which means *inns* or *lodgings.* On each day, Mexicans reenact Mary and Joseph's search for lodgings on the first Christmas Eve. Two children carrying figures of Mary and Joseph lead a procession of people to a particular house. The people knock on the door and ask for lodgings. They are refused at first but finally are admitted.

After each posada ceremony, Mexicans feast and celebrate. Children enjoy trying to break the *piñata,* a brightly decorated paper or clay figure containing candy and small gifts. The piñata may be shaped like an animal, an elf, a star, or some other object. It is hung from the ceiling, and the children take turns trying to hit it with a stick while blindfolded. When someone breaks the piñata, the gifts and candy fall to the floor, and the children scramble for them.

In Venezuela, people have a late supper after returning from midnight Mass on Christmas Eve. Most of these meals include *hallacas,* which are corn-meal pies stuffed with chicken, pork, beef, and spices. A favorite Christmas dish in Argentina is *niños envueltos* (wrapped children). It consists of rolled beef slices filled with seasoned mincemeat.

Children in some Latin-American countries, including Brazil, Colombia, and parts of Mexico, receive gifts on Christmas Day. In Argentina, Venezuela, Puerto Rico, and most areas of Mexico, the Wise Men leave the presents on the eve of Epiphany.

In Asia. Relatively small numbers of Christians live in the countries of Asia, and so Christmas is not widely celebrated there. In areas where Christmas is observed, people follow such Western customs as attending religious services, giving presents, singing carols, and decorating Christmas trees.

Leon V. Kofod

Japanese Children sing carols while reenacting the Nativity during a Christmas play. Many Japanese also follow such Western customs as giving gifts and decorating Christmas trees.

Victor Englebert

A Procession of Priests concludes Epiphany services of the Coptic Orthodox Church in Ethiopia. Epiphany, observed in January, celebrates the Wise Men's visit to the Christ child.

WORLD BOOK photo

An Advent Calendar and Wreath help keep track of the four weeks before Christmas. A flap on the calendar is lifted each day, and a candle on the wreath is lit every Sunday.

The Japanese celebrate Christmas by exchanging gifts and presenting religious plays. Evergreen branches decorate city streets, and most department stores display a huge Christmas tree. People dressed as Santa Claus mingle with the crowds of shoppers.

In the Philippines, people attend *Misas de Gallo* (Masses of the Cock), which are celebrated early each morning on the nine days before Christmas. On Christmas Eve, Filipinos parade through the streets carrying colorful star-shaped lanterns called *paroles*. These lanterns are also displayed in the windows of most homes.

On Christmas Eve, Christians from throughout the world gather for midnight Mass in Bethlehem, the town in present-day Jordan where Jesus was born. They kneel to kiss the silver star that is set in the ground at the spot where Jesus' birth is believed to have taken place.

In Africa, as in Asia, the celebration of Christmas is not widespread because most of the countries have a small Christian population. Missionaries brought Christmas customs to Africa and so people in the Christian communities generally follow Western traditions. However, Africans sing carols and hymns in their own languages. In Ethiopia, members of the Coptic Orthodox Church celebrate Christmas on January 7. They hold religious services and later feast and dance.

The Celebration of Christmas

Religious Practices. For most Christians, the Christmas season begins on the Sunday nearest November 30. This date is the feast day of Saint Andrew, one of the 12 apostles of Christ. The nearest Sunday is the first day of *Advent*, a four-week period during which Christians prepare for Christmas. The word *advent* means *a coming* and refers to the coming of Jesus on Christmas Day.

Many Christians have an Advent wreath in their homes during the holiday season. Most of these wreaths are made of evergreen or holly branches and may lie on a table or hang on a door. Four candles, one for each Sunday of Advent, are placed among the branches. On the first Sunday, the family lights one candle and joins in prayer. They repeat this ceremony on each Sunday of Advent, lighting one additional candle each time. Three of the candles are dark purple, and the fourth is pink or light purple. It remains unlit until the third Sunday, when people celebrate the beginning of the second half of Advent. A large red candle, which symbolizes Jesus, is added to the wreath on Christmas Day.

In many countries, people use special Advent calendars or Advent candles to keep track of the 24 days before Christmas. An Advent calendar has a colorful Christmas scene, and each date is printed on a flap. One flap is lifted daily to uncover a holiday picture or a Biblical verse. On an Advent candle, the dates appear in a row down the side. Each evening, the candle is lit and then burned down to the next date. By Christmas Day, the entire candle has melted.

During the Christmas season, many churches display a *crèche* (Nativity scene). It shows figures of Mary and Joseph praying over the infant Jesus in the stable. Figures of the Magi, angels, shepherds, and various animals surround the Holy Family.

For many Christians, the Christmas season reaches a climax at midnight Mass or other religious services on Christmas Eve. Churches are decorated with candles, lights, evergreen branches, and bright red poinsettias. People sing Christmas carols and listen to readings from the Gospels of Saint Luke and Saint Matthew. Priests and ministers speak to the congregations about the coming of Christ and the need for peace and understanding among all people. Most churches also hold services on Christmas Day.

WORLD BOOK photo by Dan Miller

Church Services on Christmas Morning are a highlight of the holiday season for millions of Christians. Many churches also hold midnight services on Christmas Eve.

WORLD BOOK photo by Dan Miller

A Visit with Santa is a Christmas treat for children throughout the world. In many department stores, youngsters wait in line to tell Santa what presents they would like for Christmas.

The Christmas season ends on Epiphany, January 6. In Western Christian churches, Epiphany celebrates the coming of the Wise Men to the Christ child. Among Eastern Christians, this day celebrates Christ's baptism. Epiphany falls on the 12th day after Christmas. The song "The Twelve Days of Christmas" refers to the 12 days between Christmas and Epiphany.

Gift Giving. The custom of giving gifts to relatives and friends on a special day in winter probably began in ancient Rome and northern Europe. In these regions, people gave each other small presents as part of their year-end celebrations.

By 1100, Saint Nicholas had become a popular symbol of gift giving in many European countries. According to legend, he brought presents to children on the eve of his feast day, December 6. Nonreligious figures replaced Saint Nicholas in certain countries soon after the Reformation, and December 25 became the day for giving gifts.

Today, Santa Claus brings presents to children in many countries, including the United States, Canada, and Australia. A number of other countries have their own versions of Santa Claus, such as Father Christmas in the British Isles, Père Noël in France, and Weihnachtsmann in Germany.

Saint Nicholas still brings presents in some countries, including The Netherlands, Austria, Belgium, and parts of Germany. Children fill shoes with straw and carrots for his horse and place them in front of the fireplace. By morning, the straw and carrots have been replaced by presents. Youngsters in many Spanish-speaking nations have a similar custom. However, they leave the food for the camels of the Wise Men and put the shoes outside a window on the eve of Epiphany. The Magi place small gifts in the shoes during the night. The custom of hanging stockings by the fireplace probably developed from those traditions.

In some areas of northern Germany, Saint Nicholas' assistant, *Knecht Ruprecht* (Servant Rupert), gives presents to good children. He gives whipping rods to the parents of bad ones. In Sweden, many children receive presents from the elf Jultomten, called Julenissen in Denmark and Norway.

In Italy, La Befana brings presents on the eve of Epiphany. According to legend, the Wise Men asked the kindly old witch to accompany them to see the infant Jesus. She refused, saying she was too busy and had to clean her house, and so she missed the wondrous sight. Each year, La Befana goes from house to house, leaving gifts and looking for the Christ child.

In Australia, the British Isles, New Zealand, and parts of Canada, people exchange presents on Christmas Day and on *Boxing Day*, the day after Christmas. This custom may have originated in ancient Rome, where apprentice workers received money gifts in small boxes from their employer's customers.

Christmas Feasting. The year-end festivities of ancient European peoples included huge feasts, many of which lasted for several days. The preparation of special foods later became an important part of the Christmas celebration throughout the world.

At the first Christmas feasts, people roasted boars, pigs, and peacocks over large open fires. Today, roast turkey is the most popular main course in the United States, Canada, Australia, and New Zealand. In the British Isles, people serve roast goose. Fish is the feature

WORLD BOOK photo by Dan Miller

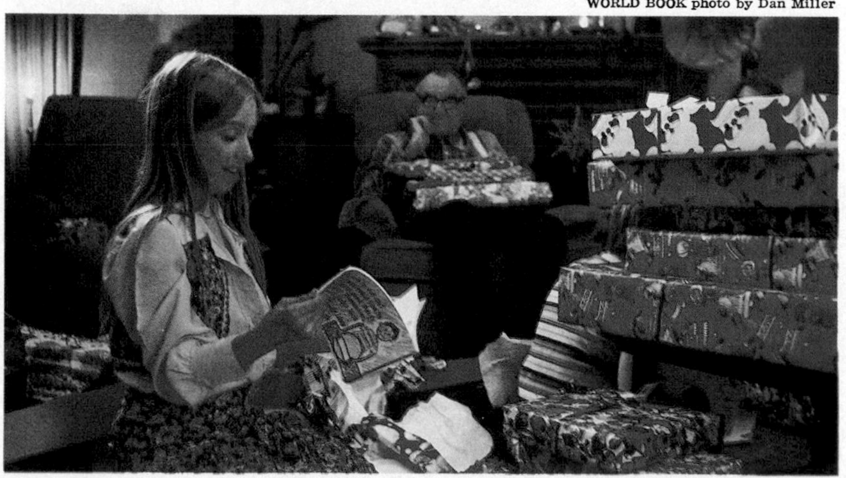

Opening Christmas Gifts is one of the most exciting parts of the holiday celebration. Most people use colorful paper and shiny ribbons to wrap the presents they give.

of Christmas dinner in a number of countries. For example, Austrians eat baked carp and Norwegians dine on *lutefisk* (dried cod). Vegetables, relishes, hot breads, and a variety of other dishes accompany the main course of the Christmas feast everywhere.

Popular beverages served especially at Christmastime include eggnog in the United States and hot, spicy wassail in England. Many people in Sweden drink *glögg*, a hot punch made with spices, sweet liquors, raisins, and nuts.

Favorite Christmas desserts in the United States include fruitcake, mince pie, and pumpkin pie. Plum pudding is traditional in Canada and the British Isles. The French serve a Christmas cake called *bûche de Noël*, which looks like a miniature log. Italians finish their meal with *torrone*, a candy made of egg whites, honey, and nuts. Fruit-filled breads called *stollen* are favorites in Germany. In Mexico and other Latin-American countries, Christmas dinner includes thin, round pastries called *buñuelos*, which are usually eaten with cinnamon and sugar.

Christmas Decorations. The traditional colors of Christmas are green and red. Green represents the continuance of life through the winter and the Christian belief in eternal life through Christ. Red symbolizes the blood that Jesus shed at His Crucifixion. Christmas decorations that feature these colors include the Christmas tree, the Christmas wreath, holly, and mistletoe.

The Christmas Tree probably developed in medieval Germany from the "Paradise Tree," a type of evergreen. This tree, decorated with red apples, was used in a popular Christmas play about Adam and Eve. By 1605, many German families decorated their homes with evergreens for Christmas. They trimmed the trees with fruits, nuts, lighted candles, and paper roses. Later decorations included painted eggshells and various cookies and candies.

The first Christmas trees in the United States were used in the early 1800's by German settlers in Pennsylvania. During the mid-1800's, the custom of trimming Christmas trees spread rapidly throughout the world. Today, some form of Christmas tree is part of every Christmas celebration. Decorations include tinsel, bright ornaments, and candy canes. A star is mounted on top of many Christmas trees and other Christmas displays. It represents the star that led the Wise Men to the stable in Bethlehem where Jesus was born.

WORLD BOOK photo by Dan Miller

A Traditional Christmas Dinner in the United States and Canada includes stuffed turkey, mashed potatoes, and various relishes. Fruitcake and mince pie are favorite desserts.

The Christmas Wreath, like the evergreens used as Christmas trees, symbolizes the strength of life overcoming the forces of winter. In ancient Rome, people used decorative wreaths as a sign of victory and celebration. The custom of hanging a wreath on the front door of the home probably came from this practice.

Holly is an evergreen tree with glossy leaves and bright red berries. It is used in making Christmas wreaths and other decorations. Early Christians decorated their homes and churches with this tree at Christmastime.

Robert H. Glaze, Artstreet

Strings of Colored Lights brighten millions of homes at Christmastime. Other outdoor decorations include candles, stars, evergreen wreaths, and figures of Santa Claus and carolers.

They called it the *holy tree*, and the word *holly* may have come from this name. The pointed leaves supposedly resemble the crown of thorns that Jesus wore when He was crucified. The red berries symbolize the drops of blood He shed.

Mistletoe is an evergreen plant with dark leaves and shiny white berries. Ancient Celtic priests considered the plant sacred and gave people sprigs of it to use as charms. The custom of decorating homes with mistletoe probably came from its use as a ceremonial plant by early Europeans. In many countries, a person standing under a sprig of mistletoe may be kissed.

Christmas Carols. The word *carol* came from a Greek dance called a *choraulein*, which was accompanied by flute music. The dance later spread throughout Europe and became especially popular with the French, who replaced the flute music with singing. People originally performed carols on several occasions during the year. By the 1600's, carols involved singing only, and Christmas had become the main holiday for these joyful songs.

Most of the carols sung today were originally hymns composed in the 1800's. They include "O Little Town of Bethlehem" and "Hark! The Herald Angels Sing." The words of the famous carol "Silent Night" were written on Christmas Eve in 1818 by Joseph Mohr, an Austrian priest. Franz Gruber, the organist of Mohr's church, composed the music that same night, and the carol was sung at midnight Mass. "O Holy Night," another famous carol, was introduced at midnight Mass in 1847. Adolphe Adam, a French composer, wrote the music. Popular nonreligious carols include "Jingle Bells" and "White Christmas."

Christmas Cards. The first Christmas card was created in 1843 by John Calcott Horsley, an English illustrator. It resembled a postcard and showed a large family enjoying a Christmas celebration. The message on the card read, "Merry Christmas and a Happy New Year to You." About 1,000 of the cards were sold. By 1860, the custom of exchanging Christmas cards had spread throughout Great Britain. The first Christmas cards manufactured in the United States were made in 1875 by Louis Prang, a German-born Boston printer.

WORLD BOOK photo

Christmas Cards are one of the favorite traditional ways of sending holiday greetings to friends and relatives. Billions of the cards are delivered to all parts of the world every year.

Other Customs. In some countries, especially Great Britain, France, and the Scandinavian nations, many families burn a *Yule log* at Christmastime. The log is a large piece of a tree trunk, and people keep an unburned part of it to light the next year's log. Early Europeans believed the unburned wood had magic powers. Today, some people think they will have bad luck if the Yule log fire goes out.

Large numbers of people enjoy reading Christmas stories and poems during the holiday season. For example, *A Christmas Carol* (1843) by the English novelist Charles Dickens ranks as one of the most famous tales ever written. The poem "A Visit from St. Nicholas" (1823), popularly known by its first line, " 'Twas the Night Before Christmas," is read aloud in many homes on Christmas Eve. Clement Moore, an American scholar, supposedly wrote this poem as a Christmas present for his children. Several musical productions

Hallmark Historical Collection

The First Christmas Card, *left,* was created in 1843 by John Calcott Horsley, an English illustrator. It featured a drawing of a family enjoying Christmas together. Smaller drawings on the card showed people helping the needy. About 1,000 copies of Horsley's card were sold.

are also Christmas traditions. They include *The Nutcracker*, a ballet by Peter Ilich Tchaikovsky of Russia, and *Amahl and the Night Visitors*, an opera by Gian Carlo Menotti of Italy. ROBERT J. MYERS

Related Articles in WORLD BOOK include:

Advent	Moore, Clement C.
Boxing Day	Moses, Grandma (picture)
Carol	New Testament (The Birth of Jesus)
Dickens, Charles (The First Phase)	Nicholas, Saint
Holly	Santa Claus
Jesus Christ	Santa Claus (Ind.)
Mistletoe	Yule

Outline

I. Christmas Around the World
- A. In the United States and Canada
- B. In the British Isles
- C. In France
- D. In Germany
- E. In Spain
- F. In The Netherlands, Belgium, and Luxembourg
- G. In Italy
- H. In Poland
- I. In Denmark, Norway, and Sweden
- J. In Australia and New Zealand
- K. In Latin America
- L. In Asia
- M. In Africa

II. The Celebration of Christmas
- A. Religious Practices
- B. Gift Giving
- C. Christmas Feasting
- D. Christmas Decorations
- E. Christmas Carols
- F. Christmas Cards
- G. Other Customs

Questions

What is the legend of *La Befana?*

Why are the colors green and red associated with Christmas?

What does the Mexican tradition of *posadas* represent?

How did the Christmas tree probably develop?

What is a *Yule log?* An *Advent wreath?* An *Advent calendar?*

What are some special foods that Scandinavians serve at Christmastime?

What does the word *Christmas* mean?

What is *Epiphany?* When does it occur?

Why was the celebration of Christmas outlawed during the 1600's in England and in parts of the English colonies in America?

When was the first Christmas card created?

Additional Resources

Level I

ASSOCIATION FOR CHILDHOOD EDUCATION INTERNATIONAL. *Told Under the Christmas Tree.* Macmillan, 1962.

BARTH, EDNA, comp. *A Christmas Feast: Poems, Sayings, Greetings, and Wishes.* Houghton, 1979.

FOLEY, DANIEL J. *Christmas the World Over.* Chilton, 1975.

'Round the World Christmas Program Series. Titles in this series begin *Christmas in . . .* , such as *Christmas in Austria,* 1982. Pub. by World Book, Inc., each book focuses on the customs of a single country.

SAWYER, RUTH. *Joy to the World: Christmas Legends.* Little, Brown, 1966.

Level II

DEL RE, GERARD and PATRICIA. *The Christmas Almanack.* Doubleday, 1979.

MYERS, ROBERT J. *Celebrations: The Complete Book of American Holidays.* Doubleday, 1972.

STEVENS, PATRICIA B. *Merry Christmas! A History of the Holiday.* Macmillan, 1979.

TIME-LIFE BOOKS. *The Glory and Pageantry of Christmas.* Hammond, 1974.

WERNECKE, HERBERT H., ed. *Celebrating Christmas Around the World.* Westminster, 1980.

CHRISTMAS DISEASE. See HEMOPHILIA.

CHRISTMAS ISLAND (pop. 674) is one of the largest islands formed by coral in the Pacific Ocean. It lies 1,334 miles (2,147 kilometers) south of Honolulu. The island has a coastline of 80 miles (130 kilometers), and covers about 140 square miles (363 square kilometers). It is low, dry, and sandy. The British used the island as a nuclear test site from 1957 until late 1962. In 1962, the U.S. held nuclear tests there.

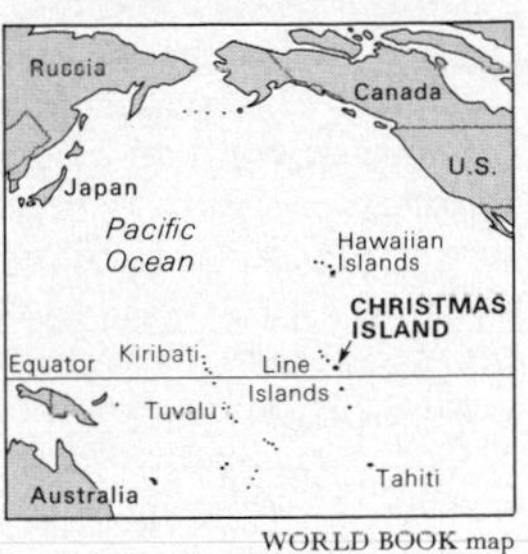

WORLD BOOK map

Christmas Island

On Christmas Day, 1777, the British explorer James Cook became the first European to reach the island. The island was annexed by Great Britain in 1888, and became part of the Gilbert and Ellice Islands colony in 1919. American forces built an airfield on Christmas Island during World War II (1939-1945). In 1979, Christmas Island became part of the independent nation of Kiribati (see KIRIBATI). EDWIN H. BRYAN, JR.

See also LINE ISLANDS; PACIFIC ISLANDS (map).

CHRISTMAS ISLAND is an island in the Indian Ocean south of Java. It covers 52 square miles (135 square kilometers) and has a population of about 3,200. The island is governed as part of Australia.

CHRISTMAS TREE. See CHRISTMAS (Christmas Decorations).

CHRISTMAS TREE. See PETROLEUM (Completing the Well).

CHRISTOPHE, *krees TAWF,* **HENRI,** *ahn REE* (1767-1820), was a black king of northern Haiti. He helped to free his country from slavery and from French rule. When slavery ended, he forced his people to continue working. But they resisted his severity and the compulsory labor laws. Although the country was prosperous, the people rebelled in 1820. Ill and unable to fight, he killed himself with a silver bullet.

Christophe was born a slave on the English island of Grenada. In the Haitian revolt of 1791, he fought the French so ably that the black liberator Toussaint L'Ouverture made him a general. Christophe also served under Jean Jacques Dessalines, another patriot leader. In 1807, he became president of northern Haiti, and king in 1811. His life inspired Eugene O'Neill's play, *The Emperor Jones.* DONALD E. WORCESTER

CHRISTOPHER, SAINT, is the patron saint of ferry workers and travelers. Little is known of his life, but he is believed to have been martyred about A.D. 250. Legend says he was a ferryman who carried people across a bridgeless river. One day, he carried over a child who seemed to grow heavier at each step. When they reached the shore, he remarked that one would think he had been carrying the burden of the world. To this the Christ child replied: "Thou hast borne upon thy back the world and Him who created it." It is believed that those who seek his protection will not be harmed. For this reason, many people carry St. Christopher medals. Eastern Orthodox Churches celebrate St. Christopher's day on May 9. Since the 1969 revision of the Roman Catholic ritual, St. Christopher's feast no longer appears in the Roman Catholic liturgy. But he is still venerated as a saint. FULTON J. SHEEN

CHROMATOGRAPHY, *KROH muh TAHG ruh fee*, is a method of separating the substances that make up a mixture. This separation is achieved by passing the mixture through an *adsorbent* material (see ABSORPTION AND ADSORPTION). Except in the case of gases, the mixture is placed in solution before being exposed to the adsorbent material. The adsorbent material attracts the substances to different extents, causing them to separate from one another.

Chromatography is used to measure low concentrations of substances, such as pollutants in air and water. Chemists use this method to separate and identify the products of chemical reactions that form more than one compound. It can also be used to collect quantities of pure substances for various purposes.

There are several chromatographic methods, including *liquid column*, *thin layer*, and *gas chromatography*.

Liquid Column Chromatography uses a column of adsorbent material in a tube. A sample of a mixture is placed at one end of the column. Then a fluid called an *eluant* is poured through the column. The individual substances in the mixture differ in their tendency to be adsorbed, and so they move through the column at varying rates. Each substance is collected as it emerges from the column or is removed from the adsorbent material.

Thin Layer Chromatography uses a thin film of adsorbent material on a flat plate made of glass, metal, or plastic. A sample of the mixture being studied is applied near one edge of the plate. This edge is brought into contact with the eluant, which moves upward through the adsorbent material. The substances in the mixture separate on the plate.

Gas Chromatography is used in analyzing gases and substances that are easily converted into gases when heated. In most cases, helium is used as the eluant to move the gaseous mixture through a column of adsorbent material. KENNETH SCHUG

CHROME. See CHROMIUM.

CHROME, *krohm*, is a name given to a number of substances which are used as pigments in paints. *Chrome yellow* is a compound of chromic acid and lead. *Chrome green*, a compound of chromium and oxygen, is used in a number of green paints which are not poisonous. *Chrome red* is a compound of chromium and lead. Chrome colors are clear and bright. THOMAS MUNRO

CHROMIC ACID is the common name for chromium trioxide, an important industrial compound. Its chemical formula is CrO_3. Most chromic acid is made by adding sulfuric acid to potassium dichromate. These substances react with each other, producing bright red crystals of chromic acid. The crystals readily absorb water and react with other substances. Chromic acid is poisonous and can cause serious burns.

Chromic acid is used in chromium plating, which provides a shiny protective finish for automobile bumpers and similar metal products. It is also used in the production of fungicides, fire-retardant chemicals, and industrial *catalysts* (see CATALYSIS). Researchers use solutions of chromic acid in preparing compounds needed for certain laboratory experiments. KENNETH SCHUG

CHROMITE. See CHROMIUM.

CHROMIUM, a chemical element, is a hard, brittle, gray metal. It is sometimes called *chrome*. Chromium resists corrosion, and becomes bright and shiny when polished. For these reasons, chromium is widely used to *plate* (coat) other metals, giving them a durable, shiny finish. Chromium is used to plate automobile bumpers, door handles, and trim.

Chromium hardens steel. Chromium-steel *alloys* (mixtures) are used to make armor plate for ships and tanks, safes, ball bearings, and the cutting edges of high-speed machine tools. Alloys that contain more than 10 per cent of chromium are called *stainless steels*. Stainless steel does not rust easily. It is commonly used to make eating utensils and kitchen equipment.

Chromium combines with other elements to form colored compounds. The word *chromium* comes from the Greek word *chroma*, meaning *color*. Chromium compounds color rubies red and emeralds green. Many chromium compounds are important in industry. Potassium dichromate ($K_2Cr_2O_7$) is used in tanning leather. Lead chromate ($PbCrO_4$) is a paint pigment called *chrome yellow*. Chromium compounds are used in the textile industry as *mordants* (substances that fix dyes permanently to fabrics), and in the aircraft industry to *anodize* aluminum (coat the metal with a thick, protective oxide film).

Chromium does not occur in nature as an uncombined metal. It is almost always found combined with iron and oxygen in a mineral called *chromite*. Chromite is mined chiefly in Albania, Russia, South Africa, Turkey, and Zimbabwe.

Chromium has the chemical symbol Cr. Its atomic number is 24 and its atomic weight is 51.996. Chromium melts at 1857° C (±20° C) and boils at 2672° C. Louis Nicolas Vauquelin, a French chemist, discovered the element chromium in 1797. ALAN DAVISON

See also STAINLESS STEEL.

CHROMOSOME, *KROH muh sohm*, is a threadlike structure found in the nucleus of each plant and animal cell. It can be seen through a microscope as a particle only when the cell is ready to divide into two cells. Before division begins, the chromosomes are duplicated. During division, each duplicate chromosome forms into a pair of rods. The new cells that are formed re-

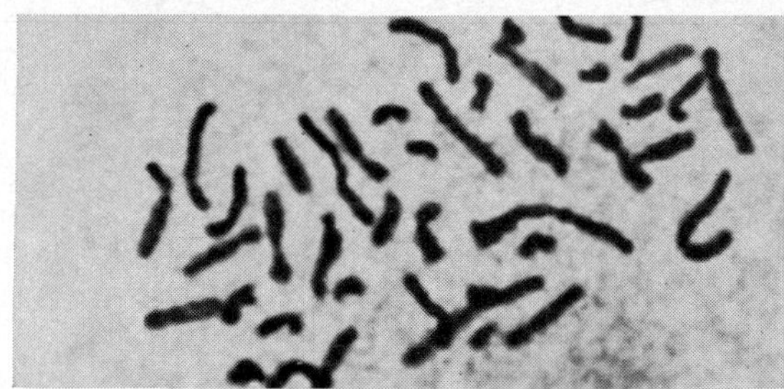

American Genetic Assn.

Human Chromosomes can be seen when stained and magnified. This is possible only when the cell is almost ready to divide.

ceive one rod from each pair. The new cells then have a set of chromosomes exactly like those of the original cell. Each *species* (kind of organism) has a characteristic number of chromosomes in each body cell. Human beings typically have 46 chromosomes (23 pairs) in most of their cells. Chromosomes are made up largely of *DNA* (deoxyribonucleic acid) and proteins. DNA is the coded information for every living thing's *heredity* (the passing of characteristics from parents to offspring).

Chromosomes consist of large numbers of DNA units called *genes*. J. HERBERT TAYLOR

For a more detailed discussion of chromosomes, see CELL; HEREDITY (The Physical Basis of Heredity). See also GENETICS; NUCLEIC ACID.

CHROMOSPHERE. See SUN (Regions of the Sun).

CHRONICLES, BOOKS OF, are two historical books in the Old Testament, or Hebrew Bible. Beginning with Adam, they trace the *genealogies* (family histories) of the tribes of Israel, particularly Judah and Levi. A major part of Chronicles is devoted to the history of the kingdom of Judah. Much of the material resembles that in the Books of Kings, but the Chronicles include additional details. Originally, Chronicles formed a single book with Ezra and Nehemiah. ROBERT GORDIS

CHRONOMETER, *kruh NAHM uh tuhr*, is an instrument that keeps time with extreme accuracy. Clockmakers developed the chronometer for use on ships, because navigators needed a precise clock in order to determine their position at sea. Astronomers and other scientists who require accurate time measurements have also used chronometers.

The *marine chronometer* consists of an accurate clock that has been specially mounted to eliminate the effect of a ship's motion. It is usually set to *Greenwich mean time*, an international time standard. To find a ship's position, a navigator notes the time and measures the positions of certain stars. The navigator compares these positions with tables that show the stars' positions at Greenwich mean time, and then calculates the ship's position.

Elgin National Watch Co.

The Marine Chronometer is used by ships' officers to tell location at sea from the time. It has more than 1,000 parts.

The first reliable chronometer was developed in 1735 by John Harrison, an English clockmaker. In 1776, Pierre LeRoy, a French watchmaker, constructed a chronometer that became the model for the modern chronometer. During the 1800's, improved metals that resisted expansion led to better clockworks and more accurate chronometers. Today, many ships rely chiefly on radar and other electronic systems for navigation. Radio time signals and electric and atomic clocks have replaced mechanical chronometers in most other applications. LAURENCE W. FREDRICK

See also ATOMIC CLOCK; CLOCK (picture: Marine Chronometers); WATCH.

CHRYSALIS, *KRISS uh liss*, is the third, or *pupal*, stage in the life cycle of the butterfly. When the caterpillar (butterfly larva) is mature, it sheds its skin and develops the hard-shell covering of the chrysalis. The chrysalis hangs from a silk pad by a spike, or by this and a loop of silk around the body. It has no cocoon (see COCOON). The body of the butterfly develops under the hard shell of the chrysalis. Finally, the covering breaks open and the butterfly emerges. ALEXANDER B. KLOTS

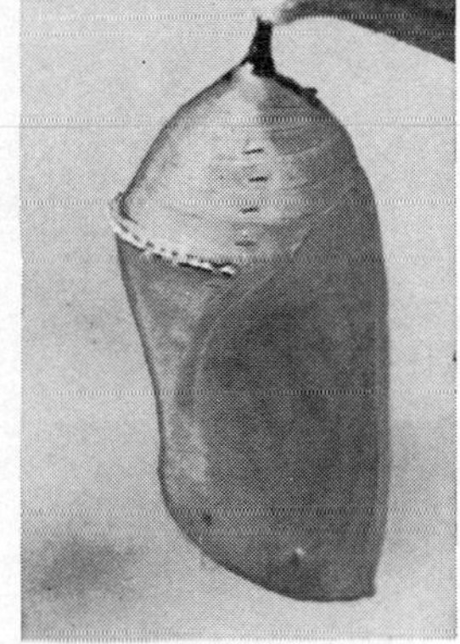

L. W. Brownell

A Chrysalis hangs from the branch of a tree. Inside, a caterpillar changes into the form of a butterfly.

See also BUTTERFLY; CATERPILLAR; METAMORPHOSIS; PUPA.

CHRYSANTHEMUM, *krihs AN thuh muhm*, is a group of strong-scented shrubby herbs that grow in many temperate regions. Gardeners cultivate the plants for their beautiful and abundant blossoms, which usually appear in autumn. Chrysanthemum comes from two Greek words meaning *golden flower*.

Many independent flowers make up each daisy-like blossom. By careful *disbudding* (removing buds), flowers 8 inches (20 centimeters) across may be developed. Most blossoms are grown as clusters. Some are trained to trail from hanging baskets. Colors range from white or yellow to pink or red.

Chrysanthemums are easy to grow. They thrive in fertile, drained soil and full sunlight. Chrysanthemums grow from cuttings or root divisions. Most are perennial. In northern climates a covering of *mulch* (straw, leaves, or loose materials) may be needed in winter.

Cultivated chrysanthemums are "short-day plants." They flower during the reduced daylight hours of au-

Chicago Park District

A Globe-Shaped Flower

J. C. Allen

A Small-Flower Variety

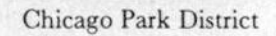

Chicago Park District

A Shaggy-Appearing Chrysanthemum

N.Y. Bot. Garden

Two Types of Petals

Chicago Park District

A Bloom with Narrow Petals

tumn. Covering the plants in late afternoon will stimulate them to flower earlier in the season. Florists have learned to produce chrysanthemum flowers throughout the year by regulating the light in the greenhouse.

The chrysanthemum has been called the *flower of the East*. People in Asian countries have cultivated chrysanthemums for over 2,000 years. In China during the 400's, T'ao Yüan Ming became a famous breeder of these plants. After his death, his native city was named Chühsien (*City of Chrysanthemums*). Chrysanthemums also flourished in Japan. In 797, the *Mikado* (ruler of Japan) made this flower his personal emblem. He decreed that it could be used only by royalty. In October, the Japanese celebrate the Feast of the Chrysanthemums.

Scientific Classification. Chrysanthemums belong to the composite family, Compositae. They make up the genus *Chrysanthemum*. ROBERT W. SCHERY

See also FLOWER (picture: Garden Perennials).

CHRYSLER, *KRYS luhr,* **WALTER PERCY** (1875-1940), an American automobile manufacturer, was a founder and the first president of the Chrysler Corporation. The company makes Chrysler, Dodge, Imperial, and Plymouth cars. Chrysler served as president of the company from 1925 to 1935, and as chairman of the board of directors from 1935 to his death. While he was president, the company built the Chrysler Building in New York City, one of the country's largest.

Chrysler was born in Wamego, Kans. His great interest in automobiles began in 1908 when he bought his first car. He became works manager for the Buick Motor Company in 1912, and four years later became president of the company. Next, he became a vice-president of General Motors Corporation, and retired as a millionaire at 45. In 1920, Chrysler returned to business as manager of the Willys-Overland Corporation. In 1924, while president of the Maxwell Motor Corporation, he and his associates produced the six-cylinder Chrysler automobile. V. E. CANGELOSI and R. E. WESTMEYER

CHRYSLER CORPORATION, *KRYS luhr,* is one of the largest manufacturers of automobiles in the world. It makes Chrysler, Dodge, Imperial, and Plymouth passenger cars, Dodge trucks, and automobile parts and accessories. The company also produces chemical and plastics products, industrial and marine engines, and outboard motors.

Chrysler Corporation introduced the high-compression engine and torsion bar suspension to the automobile industry. Other engineering features introduced by the company include the alternator, full-time power steering, and unitized body construction. The company manufactured the modified Redstone missile that helped launch the first United States satellite.

Walter P. Chrysler organized the company in 1925. It started with four manufacturing plants. It now has about 50 plants in the United States and 12 in Canada. The company also has manufacturing interests in seven other countries. During the late 1970's, Chrysler faced increasingly serious financial problems. In 1980, the U.S. government helped the corporation avoid bankruptcy by guaranteeing $1\frac{1}{2}$ billion in private loans.

The company's main offices are in Detroit. For sales, assets, and number of employees, see MANUFACTURING (table: 50 Leading U.S. Manufacturers).

Critically reviewed by the CHRYSLER CORPORATION

CHRYSOSTOM, *KRIHS uh stuhm* or *krih SAHS tuhm,* **SAINT JOHN** (345?-407?), was one of the most beloved and celebrated of the fathers of the early Christian church. He was born at Antioch, Syria (now in Turkey). His talent in preaching earned him the title Chrysostom, which means *golden-mouthed*. In 398, he went to Constantinople as patriarch. There his zeal for charity gained him the title John the Almoner. The Emperor banished him to the shores of the Black Sea for his preaching against worldliness. He made the journey bareheaded in the burning sun, and died on the way. His feast day is January 27. His *Homilies* are among the best of ancient Christian writings. FULTON J. SHEEN

CHRYSOTILE. See ASBESTOS (Types of Asbestos).

CHUANG TZU was a Chinese philosopher of the 300's B.C. He ranks with Lao Tzu as the most important figure in the development of the philosophy called *Taoism*. Chuang Tzu probably wrote parts of a book called the *Chuang Tzu*, which was named after him. The book's wit and imaginative style make it one of the greatest works of Chinese literature. The *Chuang Tzu* also helped shape the branch of Buddhism called *Zen*.

The *Chuang Tzu* teaches the mystical doctrine that all things come together in an indefinable harmony called the *Tao* (Way). The book urges that people live spontaneously, calmly accepting inevitable changes—even death. One passage asks: "How do I know hating death is not like having strayed from home when a child and not knowing the way back?" N. SIVIN

See TAOISM; LAO TZU.

CHUB is the name given to several small fishes. The *creek chub*, also called the *horned dace*, may be found in small rivers and lakes of the middle and eastern United States and Canada. It may reach a length of 1 foot (30 centimeters) when fully grown, but is usually smaller. It is blue on top and silver underneath. During the mating season, several females lay eggs in a nest made by a male. The male chub then covers the eggs with small

Treat Davidson, Photo Researchers

The Chub sometimes grows to a length of 1 foot (30 centimeters). Small chubs are used as bait by fishermen.

stones until they hatch. Chubs feed on small insects and at times on very small fish. The *silver chub*, *flatheaded chub*, *hornyhead chub*, and *shortjaw chub* are a few of the other chubs found in North America. See also FISH (picture: Fish of Temperate Fresh Waters).

Scientific Classification. The creek chub belongs to the family *Cyprinidae*. It is genus *Semotilus*, species *S. atromaculatus*. CARL L. HUBBS

CHUCK WAGON was a mess wagon or rolling kitchen which provided food for cowhands trailing herds north from Texas or for round-up crews on western ranches. The term comes from the slang expression *chuck*, meaning *food* or *grub*. Two teams of horses usually pulled the chuck wagon, loaded with food, utensils, and bedding. It led the way from camp to camp. Some chuck wagons were farm wagons fitted with shelving and boxes. Others were specially built. A cook could quickly get a meal for 40 cowhands. WALKER D. WYMAN

CHUCKWALLA is a large, harmless lizard found in desert areas of the southwestern United States. The chuckwalla is about $1\frac{1}{4}$ feet (38 centimeters) long and rusty-brown in color. It eats tender leaves and flowers. When an enemy tries to pull it out of a hole, the chuckwalla fills its lungs with air. This makes it difficult to pull out.

Scientific Classification. The chuckwalla belongs to the family *Iguanidae*. It is classified as genus *Sauromalus*, species *S. ater*. CLIFFORD H. POPE

CHUKAR. See PARTRIDGE (with picture).

CH'UNG-CH'ING (pop. 2,121,000), also spelled *Chungking*, served as the capital of the Republic of China from 1937 to 1946. The Nationalist government of China moved to Ch'ung-ch'ing when Japanese forces overran Nan-ching, the capital, in 1937. But the Nationalists moved the government back to Nan-ching in 1946 at the end of World War II.

Ch'ung-ch'ing covers an area of 116 square miles (300 square kilometers), and is a center of political and industrial activity in western China. The city is an inland port 1,600 miles (2,570 kilometers) up the Yangtze River in Szechwan Province. Ch'ung-ch'ing's products include iron and steel, leather, medicine, paint oils, and silk. See also CHINA (political map).

Ch'ung-ch'ing was the most heavily bombed city in China during World War II. Bombs destroyed many of the old streets, which go up hillsides in stairsteps.

Gray-walled, ancient Ch'ung-ch'ing has a history of more than 4,000 years. It became part of China in 220 B.C., when the Emperor Shih Huang Ti brought the territory under his rule. It was one of China's treaty ports until 1943, when the United States gave up its special privileges. THEODORE H. E. CHEN

See also TREATY PORT.

CHUNGKING. See CH'UNG-CH'ING.

CHURCH comes from a Greek word meaning *the Lord's house*. The word has many meanings. It may mean the world community of Christians. *Church* may refer to any denomination or group professing the same Christian creed, as the Methodist Church. It may also signify a national religious body, such as the Church of England. It may refer to the formal institutions of a religion or to the ecclesiastical organization, power, and authority of a religious body. In early Christianity, *church* often meant the worship of God by a group of Christians, such as the Church in Antioch, Syria.

Church is also a building used for public Christian worship. Early Christians met secretly outdoors, in catacombs, or in private houses. The earliest-known Christian sanctuary, a private house in Dura, eastern Syria, dates from about A.D. 200. After the Roman Emperor Constantine stopped the persecution of Christians in the A.D. 300's, Christians began building churches. They combined the architecture of private homes and that of the ancient Roman *basilicas* (see BASILICA). Constantine built a number of splendid churches, including Old St. Peter's in Rome.

Many Christian churches are large and richly

E. P. Haddon, U.S. Fish & Wildlife Service

The Chuckwalla, one of the largest of American lizards, was at one time used for food by Indians in the Southwest.

decorated. Their builders believed that a church could present an image of heaven for its worshipers. Churches reflect the architecture of the period and region in which they are built. For example, the Cathedral of Notre Dame, Paris, is an outstanding example of Gothic architecture in the Middle Ages. Churches today often reflect a combination of traditional architecture and new building styles (see ARCHITECTURE [pictures]; CATHEDRAL). Church plans also reflect the differences in Christian worship. The Roman Catholic Church stresses the altar as the focus of worship. Protestant churches emphasize the congregation, and are built so that everyone can see the minister. OTTO G. VON SIMSON

See also RELIGION (table); CHRISTIANITY.

CHURCH, FREDERICK EDWIN (1826-1900), was an American painter known for his huge, dramatic landscapes. Church traveled widely searching for subjects. He painted New York's Catskill Mountains, the Andes Mountains of South America, the wilderness of Ecuador, the lush vegetation of Jamaica, and icebergs near Labrador. Many of Church's paintings feature the vivid use of light, such as brilliant rainbows and fiery sunsets. Church carefully studied and sketched his subjects, using the sketches to paint large composite scenes in his studio. Church's most famous paintings include *Heart of the Andes* (1859) and *Icebergs* (1861).

Church was born in Hartford, Conn. At the age of 18, he studied with the famous American landscape artist Thomas Cole. Early in his career, Church became a leading member of the first school of American landscape painting, called the Hudson River School. His early works, like those of other members of the school, were panoramic, detailed scenes of nature. Church's *Niagara Falls* (1857) is an example. SARAH BURNS

See HUDSON RIVER SCHOOL.

CHURCH AND STATE is a term that refers to the relations between churches and governments. These relations have been an issue at least since the time of Christ.

In Early Times. The Old Testament implies that such a problem may have existed in early times. In ancient Greece and Rome, closely related bodies handled both religious and governmental affairs, so that controversy between them did not arise. The problems first became serious in the later days of the Roman Empire, after Christianity became the state religion about A.D. 380. The position of the Christian church then became an urgent question. Historians believe that Pope Gelasius I, who reigned from 492 to 496, first formulated a doctrine of equality and coordination between the church and the civil government. But it was not until the Concordat of Worms in 1122 that the powers of the two bodies were strictly defined.

The Middle Ages brought a struggle between the Roman Catholic Church and various European rulers. At the height of papal supremacy, Boniface VIII, pope from 1294 to 1303, issued a *bull* (papal decree) called *Unam Sanctam*. This controversial bull declared that the pope should have a voice in civil, as well as religious, affairs. The bull is often called *the Doctrine of the Two Swords*. The doctrine angered King Philip IV of France. He forced the next pope, Clement V, to move the papal court to Avignon, France, in 1309. This temporary exile of the popes is often called *the seventy years' captivity*. This exile helped cause the Great Schism of the West (see POPE [The Troubles of the Papacy]). But, by the end of the 1400's, the church and many of the governments had established an uneasy peace.

The Reformation of the 1500's radically changed the church-state situation. There were now several Christian churches, not just one. The conflict over spiritual authority led to religious wars in many countries (see PEASANTS' WAR). Lutheranism made the prince of a country the head of the church (see LUTHERANS). The idea then spread that the ruler of the country should determine the religion of his subjects. If the king and parliament shared ruling power, they would both decide. Their disagreement in England in the 1600's resulted in civil war (see ENGLAND [The Civil War]). But, with minor exceptions, the principle continued until the American and French revolutions.

After the 1700's, many democratic nations maintained the separation of church and state. This principle of religious freedom is embodied in Amendment 1 of the United States Constitution, and in many other constitutions. It declares that churches are private associations subject to the law of the country, but essentially free to teach what they wish.

The 1900's. A new phase in church-state relationship began with the totalitarian dictatorships of the 1900's. These governments denied freedom of religion, and subjected churches, and often religious leaders, to interference and persecution.

Related Articles in WORLD BOOK include:

- Constitution of the United States (Article VI; Amendment 1)
- Education (How Should Education Be Financed?)
- Freedom of Religion
- Pope
- Reformation
- Roman Catholic Church
- Totalitarianism

CHURCH MUSIC. See HYMN; CLASSICAL MUSIC (Choral Music).

CHURCH OF CHRIST. See CHURCHES OF CHRIST.

CHURCH OF CHRIST, SCIENTIST. See CHRISTIAN SCIENTISTS.

CHURCH OF ENGLAND, also called the ESTABLISHED CHURCH, is established by law as the national church of the English people. It is also the mother church of the Anglican Communion, an international organization of 23 self-governing churches. About half the people of England belong to the Church of England.

Doctrines. The Church of England claims to teach and uphold the doctrines of the apostles and to be a branch of the one universal Church of Christ. Its doctrines are stated in the Book of Common Prayer. They include the Apostles' and Nicene creeds, the historic sacraments, and the apostolic ministry of bishops, priests, and deacons. The church includes both Roman Catholic and Protestant teachings.

Organization. England is divided into two religious provinces, Canterbury and York, each governed by an archbishop. The archbishop of Canterbury also bears the title "Primate of All England." The provinces are divided into dioceses under the authority of bishops. The church owns buildings, land, and other property. Its chief support comes from endowments. Parliament has authority over it in all civil matters.

History. The first certain historical note about the Church of England dates from A.D. 314, when three British bishops attended the Council of Arles. St. Augustine came as a missionary to the Angles in 597. From 664 until the reign of Henry VIII, England recognized the pope's spiritual authority. Henry quarreled with the pope and declared that, as bishop of Rome, the pope had no more authority in England than any other foreign bishop. In 1534, the Act of Supremacy made the king head of the national church.

Severe religious struggles divided the church for many years. Some members wished to follow the Lutheran reforms of Germany. A movement toward Calvinism developed after the first Book of Common Prayer was issued in 1549. This led to the second Prayer Book in 1552.

Under Elizabeth I in 1558, the Church of England became independent. The third Prayer Book was adopted in 1559, and the Thirty-Nine Articles were put in their present form in 1571 (see THIRTY-NINE ARTICLES).

The Anglican Communion today includes the Church of Wales, the Church of Ireland, the Episcopal Church in Scotland, the Anglican Church of Canada, and the Episcopal Church in the U.S. WALTER H. STOWE

Related Articles in WORLD BOOK include:

Anglicans	Oxford Movement
Augustine of Canterbury, Saint	Puritans (History)
Cranmer, Thomas	Reformation
England (Religion)	Ridley, Nicholas
Episcopal Church	Test Act
Hampton Court Conference	Toleration Act
Henry (VIII)	

Additional Resources

The Book of Common Prayer. Oxford, 1976. Official liturgies of the various rites of the church.

NEILL, STEPHEN. *Anglicanism*. 4th ed. Oxford, 1978.

PULLAN, LEIGHTON. *The History of the Book of Common Prayer*. West, 1981. Reprint of 1901 ed.

WATSON, EDWARD W. *The Church of England*. 3rd ed. Greenwood, 1981. Reprint of 1961 ed.

CHURCH OF GOD IN CHRIST, THE, is a Christian denomination that bases its faith on the doctrines of the apostles as received on Pentecost (Acts 2: 4). Bishop C. H. Mason and others founded the church in 1895. They began preaching that there could be no salvation without holiness. The Baptist Church expelled them because of this teaching. Members believe that the church name was revealed to the bishop in 1897 from a reference in I Thessalonians 2: 14. In 1907, a church meeting in Memphis, Tenn., formed the First General Assembly of the Church of God in Christ. The church supports seven schools. CHARLES HARRISON MASON

CHURCH OF IRELAND. See CHURCH OF ENGLAND; IRELAND (Religion).

CHURCH OF JESUS CHRIST OF LATTER-DAY SAINTS. See MORMONS.

CHURCH OF THE BRETHREN. See BRETHREN, CHURCH OF THE.

CHURCH OF THE NAZARENE is a Protestant denomination that follows the teachings of early Methodism. The church was established in 1908 in Pilot Point, Tex., by a merger of three independent Holiness groups. The church has about 5,000 congregations and maintains missions in all parts of the world.

The Church of the Nazarene supports a theological seminary and 11 colleges. The central Nazarene Publishing House produces religious books and periodicals, including the official church newspaper, *Herald of Holiness*. The church also sponsors radio programs principally in English and Spanish, called *Showers of Blessing* and *La Hora Nazarena*. International headquarters are at 6401 The Paseo, Kansas City, Mo. 64131.

Critically reviewed by the CHURCH OF THE NAZARENE

CHURCH OF WALES. See CHURCH OF ENGLAND (History).

CHURCH SCHOOL. See PAROCHIAL SCHOOL; RELIGIOUS EDUCATION.

CHURCHES OF CHRIST are a group of religious congregations that accept the New Testament as their sole rule of faith and practice. They maintain that it sets forth faith, repentance, confession, and baptism as the conditions of salvation. Members believe that the first Church of Christ was established on Pentecost after the Resurrection and Ascension of Jesus Christ. They claim that the church spread throughout the Roman world but later declined until the 1800's. Then Thomas Campbell, his son Alexander, and their associates restored it. Thomas Campbell was an Irish-born Presbyterian clergyman who settled in Pennsylvania in 1807.

The Churches of Christ regard Christ as the founder, head, and Saviour of the church. They regard the Campbells as restorers of the primitive church. They contend that the word of God is the seed of the kingdom. When it is faithfully preached and obeyed, without addition or subtraction, it will produce true Christians, or a church of Christ. The churches consider the entire Bible to be inspired by God, but believe that the Old Testament was binding only in earlier times.

There are about 18,500 independent Churches of Christ, with about 2,400,000 members. A group of elders presides over each church, and a group of deacons serves each. Most of the churches are in the Southern and Southwestern United States, with the largest number in Texas and Tennessee. The churches conduct extensive evangelical programs. They support about 300 workers in more than 80 countries. They also operate 5 senior colleges, 14 junior colleges, 2 graduate schools of religion, 18 schools of preaching, and several orphanages and old-age homes. The churches publish 10 religious papers. B. C. GOODPASTURE

See also DISCIPLES OF CHRIST.

CHURCHES OF CHRIST, NATIONAL COUNCIL OF. See NATIONAL COUNCIL OF CHURCHES.

CHURCHES OF GOD consist of about 15 religious groups in the United States that use the same name—Church of God—but differ in faith and practice. Most of these groups trace their origins to the Pentecostal, Holiness, or Adventist movements.

The largest of the churches, the Church of God with headquarters in Cleveland, Tenn., was founded in 1886. It became one of the first Pentecostal Churches (see PENTECOSTAL CHURCHES). Another major group, the Church of God with headquarters in Anderson, Ind., was established about 1880. This group developed into one of the largest Holiness churches. The Holiness Movement stresses sanctification and the literal interpretation of the Bible. The Church of God (Abrahamic Faith), which is one of the oldest Churches of God, is an outgrowth of the Adventist Movement (see ADVENTISTS). JOHN THOMAS NICHOL

CHURCHILL, JENNIE JEROME. See CHURCHILL, SIR WINSTON L. S. (Boyhood and Education; picture).

CHURCHILL, JOHN. See MARLBOROUGH, DUKE OF.

Karsh, Ottawa

SIR WINSTON CHURCHILL

PRIME MINISTER OF GREAT BRITAIN 1940-1945 • 1951-1955

Winston S. Churchill

CHURCHILL, SIR WINSTON LEONARD SPENCER (1874-1965), became one of the greatest statesmen in world history. Churchill reached the height of his fame as the heroic prime minister of Great Britain during World War II. He offered his people only "blood, toil, tears, and sweat" as they struggled to keep their freedom. Churchill also was a noted speaker, author, painter, soldier, and war reporter.

Early in World War II, Britain stood alone against Nazi Germany. The British refused to give in despite the huge odds against them. Churchill's personal courage, the magic of his words, and his faith in victory inspired the British to "their finest hour." The mere sight of this stocky, determined man—a cigar in his mouth and two fingers raised high in a "V for victory" salute—cheered the people. He seemed to be John Bull, the symbol of the English people, come to life.

Churchill not only made history, he also wrote it. As a historian, war reporter, and biographer, he showed a matchless command of the English language. In 1953, he won the Nobel prize for literature. Yet as a schoolboy, he had been the worst student in his class. Churchill spoke as he wrote—clearly, vividly, majestically. Yet he had stuttered as a boy.

The vigor of Churchill's body equaled that of his mind. His tremendous physical endurance allowed him to live a long, eventful life. In youth, his boundless energy found release on the battlefield. Churchill loved the rough and ready life of a soldier, but he also had great sensitivity. He expressed this side of his nature beautifully in his paintings.

Churchill entered the service of his country in 1895 as an army lieutenant under Queen Victoria. He ended his career in 1964 as a member of the House of Commons under Queen Elizabeth II, the great-great-granddaughter of Queen Victoria. Few men ever served their country so long or so well.

Early Life

Boyhood and Education. Winston Churchill was born on Nov. 30, 1874, in Blenheim Palace in Oxford-

Carol L. Thompson, the contributor of this article, is the editor of Current History *magazine.*

shire, England. He was the elder of the two sons of Lord Randolph Churchill (1849-1895) and Lady Churchill (1854-1921), an American girl whose maiden name was Jennie Jerome. Lord Randolph was the third son of the seventh Duke of Marlborough. The first Duke of Marlborough had been one of England's greatest military commanders. Winston's mother was famous for her beauty. Her father, Leonard Jerome, made and lost several fortunes in business.

Young Winston, a chunky lad with a mop of red hair, had an unhappy boyhood. He talked with a stutter and lisp, and did poorly in his schoolwork. His stubbornness and high spirits annoyed everyone. In addition, his parents had little time for him.

Winston stood in fear and wonder of his father. Lord Randolph, a leader in the Conservative party, showed little affection for Winston. Winston's mother charmed everyone with her beauty and wit. As Lord Randolph's wife, she had many duties. Little time was left for Winston. Churchill later wrote of his mother: "She shone for me like the Evening Star. I loved her dearly—but at a distance."

When Winston was 6 years old, his brother, John, was born. The difference in their ages prevented any real companionship. At the age of 12, Winston entered Harrow School, a leading English secondary school. Winston entered as the lowest boy in the lowest class, and in that unhappy position he stayed. At Harrow, however, his love of the English language began to grow. There, he said later, he "got into my bones the essential structure of the ordinary English sentence . . ."

Lord Randolph noticed that Winston spent many hours playing with toy soldiers. He decided that soldiering was the only career for a boy of limited intelligence. In 1893, at the age of 18, Winston entered the Royal Military College at Sandhurst. He had failed the entrance examinations twice before passing them. But he soon led his class in tactics and fortifications, the most important subjects. He was graduated eighth in a class of 150. In 1895, Churchill was appointed a second lieutenant in the 4th Hussars, a proud cavalry regiment.

Soldier and Reporter. Twenty-year-old Lieutenant Churchill ached for adventure. For a soldier, adventure meant fighting. But the only fighting at the moment was in Cuba, where the people had revolted against their Spanish rulers. Churchill was on leave from the army, and used his family's influence to go to Cuba as an observer with the Spanish. While there, he wrote five colorful articles on the revolt for a London newspaper. Churchill returned to London with a love for Havana cigars that lasted the rest of his life.

In 1896, Churchill's regiment was sent to Bangalore, in southern India. There he acquired a fondness for polo, and read many books he had neglected in school. The works of Edward Gibbon and Thomas B. Macaulay interested him the most.

In 1897, Churchill learned that fighting had broken out in northwestern India between British forces and

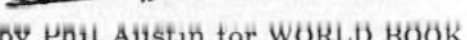

By Phil Austin for WORLD BOOK

Churchill's Birthplace was Blenheim Palace. Winston, *right,* grew up there with his younger brother, John. Their mother was an American heiress.

Hulton Picture Library from Publix

IMPORTANT DATES IN CHURCHILL'S LIFE

1874 (Nov. 30) Born in Oxfordshire, England.
1895 Graduated from Royal Military College.
1901 Entered House of Commons.
1908 (Sept. 12) Married Clementine Hozier.
1911 Appointed first lord of the admiralty.
1915 Resigned from the admiralty.
1939 Appointed first lord of the admiralty.
1940 Became prime minister of Great Britain.
1945 Became leader of the opposition.
1951 Became prime minister of Great Britain.
1953 Knighted. Won Nobel prize for literature.
1955 Retired as prime minister.
1963 Made honorary citizen of the United States.
1964 Retired from House of Commons.

As a War Correspondent, Churchill, *far right,* was captured during the Boer War in South Africa. He escaped and crossed 300 miles (480 kilometers) of enemy territory to safety.

Camera Press, Pix from Publix

Pushtun warriors. He obtained a leave from his regiment, and persuaded two newspapers to hire him as a reporter. Churchill joined the advance guard of the Malakand Field Force and took part in bloody hand-to-hand fighting. After returning to Bangalore, Churchill wrote about the campaign in his first book, *The Story of the Malakand Field Force* (1898).

Churchill's adventurous spirit made him restless again. A British force was being built up in Egypt to invade the Sudan. Churchill got himself transferred to the force, and again obtained a newspaper assignment. In 1898, he took part in the last great cavalry charge of the British army, in the Battle of Omdurman. Churchill returned to England and wrote a book about the Sudanese campaign, *The River War* (1899).

In 1899, while working on his book, Churchill resigned from the army and ran for Parliament as a Conservative from Oldham. But he did not impress the voters of Oldham, most of whom were laborers and belonged to the Liberal party. He lost his first election.

The Boer War in South Africa began in October 1899. A London newspaper hired Churchill to report the war between the Boers (Dutch settlers) and the British. Soon after Churchill arrived in South Africa, the Boers ambushed an armored train on which he was riding. He was captured and imprisoned, but made a daring escape. He scaled the prison wall one night, and slipped by the sentries. Then, traveling on freight trains, he crossed 300 miles (480 kilometers) of enemy territory to safety. He became a famous hero overnight.

Early Political Career

First Public Offices. In 1900, Churchill returned to England and to politics. Oldham gave him a hero's welcome, and the voters elected him to Parliament.

In January 1901, Churchill took his seat in the House of Commons for the first time. He soon began to criticize many Conservative policies openly and sharply. In 1904, Churchill broke with his party completely. He dramatically crossed the floor of Commons, amid the howls of Conservatives and the cheers of Liberals, to sit with the Liberals. In the next election, in 1906, Churchill ran as a Liberal and won.

With enormous energy, Churchill moved through three government positions during the next few years. He served as undersecretary of state for the colonies (1906-1908), president of the board of trade (1908-1910), and home secretary (1910-1911). His appointment to the board of trade was his first cabinet position.

Churchill's Family. In the spring of 1908, Churchill met Clementine Hozier (1885-1977), the daughter of a retired army officer. Clementine and Churchill were married on Sept. 12, 1908. Years later, Churchill wrote that he "lived happily ever afterwards." He also wrote: "My most brilliant achievement was my ability to persuade my wife to marry me." Churchill became a devoted parent to his four children: Diana (1909-1963), Randolph (1911-1968), Sarah (1914-1982), and Mary (1922-). Another daughter, Marigold, died in 1921 at the age of 3.

World War I. In 1911, Prime Minister Herbert H. Asquith appointed Churchill first lord of the admiralty. The build-up of German military and naval forces had convinced Asquith that the admiralty needed a strong leader. Churchill was one of the few people in England who realized that war with Germany would probably come. He reorganized the navy, developed antisubmarine tactics, and modernized the fleet. He also created the navy's first air service. When Britain entered World War I, on Aug. 4, 1914, the fleet was ready.

In 1915, Churchill urged an attack on the Dardanelles and the Gallipoli Peninsula, both controlled by Turkey (see GALLIPOLI PENINSULA). If successful, the attack would have opened a route to the Black Sea. Aid could then have been sent to Russia, Britain's ally. But the campaign failed disastrously, and Churchill was blamed. He resigned from the admiralty, although he kept his seat in Parliament. Churchill regarded himself as a political failure. "I am finished," he told a friend. In November 1915, Churchill joined the British army in France. He served briefly as a major in the 2nd Grenadier Guards. Then he was promoted to lieutenant colonel and given command of a battalion of the 6th Royal Scots Fusiliers.

David Lloyd George became prime minister in December 1916. He appointed Churchill minister of munitions in July 1917. While in the admiralty, Churchill had promoted the development of the tank. Now he began large-scale tank production. Churchill visited the battlefields frequently. He watched every important engagement in France, often from the air.

Between Wars

World War I ended in November 1918. The next January, Churchill became secretary of state for war and for air. As war secretary, he supervised the *demobilization* (release of men) of the British army. In 1921, Lloyd George named him colonial secretary.

Three days before the 1922 election campaign began, Churchill had to have his appendix removed. He was able to campaign only briefly, and lost the election. He said he found himself "without office, without a seat, without a party, and without an appendix."

In 1924, Churchill was returned to Parliament from

Churchill and His Bride, Clementine Hozier, were married in 1908, soon after they met. Churchill wrote that his "most brilliant achievement" was persuading his wife to marry him.

Hulton Picture Library from Publix

Epping after he rejoined the Conservative party. He was later named chancellor of the exchequer under Prime Minister Stanley Baldwin. Churchill's father had held this office almost 40 years earlier. The Conservatives lost the 1929 election, and Churchill left office. He did not hold a cabinet position again until 1939. He kept his seat in Parliament throughout this period.

During the years between World Wars I and II, Churchill spent much of his spare time painting and writing. He did not begin painting until in his 40's, and surprised critics with his talent. He liked to use bold, brilliant colors. Many of Churchill's paintings have hung in the Royal Academy of Arts.

Painting provided relaxation and pleasure, but Churchill considered writing his chief occupation after politics. In his four-volume *World Crisis* (1923-1929), he brilliantly recorded the history of World War I. In *Marlborough, His Life and Times* (1933-1938), he wrote a monumental six-volume study of his ancestor.

In speaking and in writing after 1932, Churchill tried to rouse his nation and the world to the danger of Nazi Germany. The build-up of the German armed forces alarmed him, and he pleaded for a powerful British air force. But he was called a warmonger.

Wartime Prime Minister

World War II Begins. German troops marched into Poland on Sept. 1, 1939. The war that Churchill had so clearly foreseen had begun. On September 3, Great Britain and France declared war on Germany. Prime Minister Neville Chamberlain at once named Churchill first lord of the admiralty, the same post he had held in World War I. The British fleet was notified with a simple message: "Winston is back."

In April, 1940, Germany attacked Denmark and Norway. Britain quickly sent troops to Norway, but they had to retreat because they lacked air support. In the parliamentary debate that followed, Chamberlain's government fell. On May 10, King George VI asked Churchill to form a new government. That same day, Germany invaded Belgium, Luxembourg, and The Netherlands.

At the age of 66, Churchill became prime minister of Great Britain. He wrote later: "I felt as if I were walking with destiny, and that all my past life had been but a preparation for this hour and for this trial."

Rarely, if ever, had a national leader taken over in such a desperate hour. Said Churchill: "I have nothing to offer but blood, toil, tears, and sweat."

The months that followed brought a full measure of blood, toil, tears, and sweat. Belgium surrendered to Germany on May 28, and the defeat of France appeared likely at any moment. On June 4, Churchill told Commons that even though all of Europe might fall, ". . . we

Wide World

During the Battle of Britain, German planes bombed the House of Commons. The next morning, on May 11, 1941, Prime Minister Churchill had tears in his eyes as he inspected the damage to his beloved Commons.

United Press Int.

Churchill's Famous Victory Salute became an inspiring symbol of faith in eventual victory during World War II. He first used this simple gesture—two fingers raised high in a V—early in the war.

United Press Int.

The Big Three Led the Allies during World War II. Churchill, U.S. President Franklin D. Roosevelt, *left*, and Russian Premier Joseph Stalin met in Iran in 1943.

Speaking to the U.S. Congress in 1943, Churchill told of British military victories in Africa. He made several visits to Washington, D.C., during the war.

Wide World

shall not flag or fail. We shall go on to the end . . . we shall fight in the seas and oceans . . . we shall fight on the beaches, we shall fight on the landing-grounds, we shall fight in the fields and in the streets, we shall fight in the hills; we shall never surrender . . ." On June 22, France surrendered to Germany.

The Battle of Britain. Britain now stood alone. A German invasion seemed certain. In a speech to Commons on the day after France asked Germany for an armistice, Churchill declared: "Let us therefore brace ourselves to our duties, and so bear ourselves that, if the British Empire and its Commonwealth last for a thousand years, men will say, 'This was their finest hour.' "

The Germans had to defeat the Royal Air Force (RAF) before they could invade across the English Channel. In July, the German *Luftwaffe* (air force) began to bomb British airfields and ports. In September, the Luftwaffe began nightly raids on London. The RAF, badly outnumbered, fought bravely and finally defeated the Luftwaffe. Churchill expressed the nation's gratitude to its airmen: "Never in the field of human conflict was so much owed by so many to so few."

While the battle raged, Churchill turned up everywhere. He defied air-raid alarms and went into the streets as the bombs fell. He toured RAF headquarters, inspected coastal defenses, and visited victims of the air raids. Everywhere he went he held up two fingers in a "V for victory" salute. To the people of all the Allied nations, this simple gesture became an inspiring symbol of faith in eventual victory.

Churchill had a strong grasp of military reality. He had denied the pleas of the French for RAF planes, knowing that Britain needed them for its own defense. He decided that the French fleet at Oran in Algeria had to be destroyed. Otherwise, French warships might be surrendered and used to strengthen the German navy. He boldly sent the only fully equipped armored division in England to Egypt. Churchill reasoned that, if a German invasion of England could not be prevented, one armored division could not save the country. But that division could fight the Germans in Egypt.

Meetings with Roosevelt. In August, 1941, Churchill and President Franklin D. Roosevelt met on a cruiser off the coast of Newfoundland. They drew up the Atlantic Charter, which set forth the common postwar aims of the United States and Britain. Churchill and Roosevelt exchanged more than 1,700 messages and met nine times before Roosevelt's death in 1945.

The United States entered the war after Japan attacked Pearl Harbor on Dec. 7, 1941. Later that month, Churchill and Roosevelt conferred in Washington, D.C. On December 26, Churchill addressed Congress. He stirred all Americans with his faith ". . . that in the days to come the British and American peoples will . . . walk together side by side in majesty, in justice, and in peace."

Relations between Churchill and Roosevelt always remained friendly even though differences arose between them. Churchill gloried in the British Empire, but Roosevelt was suspicious of British colonial policies. Churchill distrusted Russia, but Roosevelt did not.

In August, 1942, Churchill journeyed to Moscow to meet with Premier Joseph Stalin of Russia. Russia had entered the war in June, 1941, after being invaded by Germany. Almost immediately, Stalin had demanded that the British open a second fighting front in western Europe to relieve the strain on Russia. Churchill explained to Stalin that it would be disastrous to open a second front in 1942 because the Allies were unprepared.

In January, 1943, Churchill and Roosevelt met in Casablanca, Morocco. They announced that the Allies would accept only *unconditional* (complete) surrender from Germany, Italy, and Japan. After returning to England, Churchill fell ill with pneumonia. But he recovered with incredible vigor.

Wide World

Churchill Warned the World about Russia's iron curtain in a 1946 speech at Fulton, Mo. With him was U.S. President Harry S. Truman, *left.*

Wide World

A Farewell to His Queen, Elizabeth II, took place at a party held on Churchill's retirement.

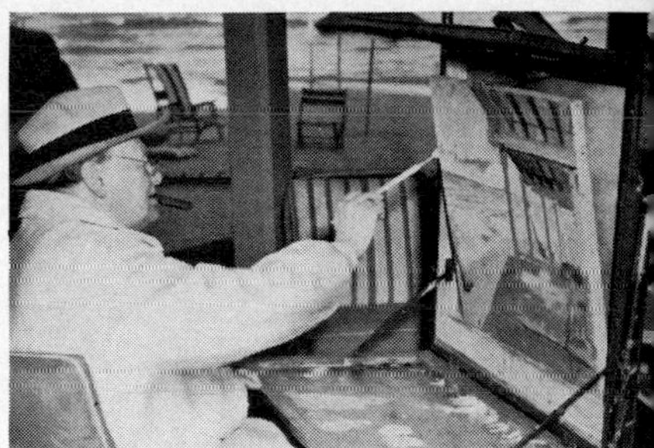

United Press Int.

An Accomplished Artist, Churchill won fame as a painter with several exhibitions of his works.

The Big Three. The first meeting of Churchill, Stalin, and Roosevelt took place in Teheran, Iran, in November, 1943. The Big Three, as they were called, set the British-American invasion of France for the following spring. On his way home from Teheran, the 69-year-old Churchill was again struck down by pneumonia. Again he recovered rapidly.

In February, 1945, the Big Three met in Yalta in Russia. The end of the war in Europe was in sight. The three leaders agreed on plans to occupy defeated Germany. Churchill distrusted Stalin. He feared Russia might keep the territories in eastern Europe that its troops occupied. Roosevelt, a close friend of Churchill's as well as an ally, died two months after the conference, and Harry S. Truman became President.

Germany surrendered on May 7, 1945, almost five years to the day after Churchill became prime minister. In July, Churchill met with Truman and Stalin in Potsdam, Germany, to discuss the administration of Germany. But Churchill's presence at the meeting was cut short. He had lost his post as prime minister.

An election had been held in Britain. The Conservatives suffered an overwhelming defeat by the Labour party. The Labour party's promise of sweeping socialistic reforms appealed to the voters. In addition, the people were voting against the Conservative party. Many blamed the Conservatives, who had been in office before the war, for failing to prepare Britain for World War II. The defeat hurt Churchill deeply. Clement R. Attlee succeeded him as prime minister.

Postwar Leader

Leader of the Opposition. Churchill took his place as leader of the opposition in the House of Commons. He urged Parliament to plan for national defense, and warned the western world against the dangers of communism. On March 5, 1946, speaking at Fulton, Mo., Churchill declared: "Beware . . . time may be short . . . From Stettin in the Baltic to Trieste in the Adriatic, an Iron Curtain has descended across the continent." Many persons in the United States and Britain called the speech warmongering.

Politics, lecturing, painting, and writing kept Churchill busy. But these activities did not completely satisfy his great energy. He found much to do around Chartwell Manor, his country estate in Kent. He took pride in his cattle and his race horses. In 1948, the first volume of Churchill's *Second World War* was published. The sixth and last volume of these magnificent memoirs appeared in 1953.

Return to Power. The Conservatives returned to power in 1951. Churchill, now almost 77 years old, again became prime minister. As usual, he concentrated most of his energy on foreign affairs. He worked especially hard to encourage British-American unity. He visited Washington in 1952, 1953, and 1954.

In April, 1953, Churchill was knighted by Queen Elizabeth. The queen made him a knight of the Order of the Garter, Britain's highest order of knighthood. Churchill had been offered this honor in 1945. He had refused it because of his party's defeat in the election. He had also refused an earldom and a dukedom. As an earl or a duke, he could not have served in Commons. In June, 1953, Sir Winston suffered a severe stroke that paralyzed his left side. He made a remarkable recovery.

Late in 1953, Sir Winston won the Nobel prize for literature. He was honored for ". . . his mastery of historical and biographical presentation and for his brilliant oratory. . ."

On Nov. 30, 1954, Churchill celebrated his 80th birthday. Members of all political parties gathered to honor him. Gifts and congratulations poured in from all corners of the world. The show of affection and respect touched Churchill deeply. His eyes bright with tears, he denied having inspired Britain during World War II. "It was the nation and the race dwelling all round the globe that had the lion's heart," he said. "I had the luck to be called on to give the roar."

For some time it had been rumored that Churchill would retire because of his advanced age. But he showed no intention of doing so, and seemed to enjoy keeping people guessing. However, the years and two world wars had taken a toll. In April, 1955, Churchill retired.

End of an Era. Churchill went back to his painting and writing. He worked on his four-volume *History of the English-Speaking Peoples* (1956-1958). He had begun this study 20 years earlier. He still took his seat in Commons, his body now bent with age. Here, where his voice once rang eloquently, he now sat silently.

In 1963, Congress made Churchill an honorary U.S. citizen. The action reflected the American people's affection for the man who had done so much for the cause of freedom. Churchill's remarkable career ended in

1964. He did not run in the general election that year. Churchill had served in Parliament from 1901 to 1922, then from 1924 until his retirement 40 years later.

Churchill suffered a stroke on Jan. 15, 1965. He died nine days later, at the age of 90. He was buried in St. Martin's Churchyard in Oxfordshire, near his birthplace, Blenheim Palace. CAROL L. THOMPSON

Related Articles in WORLD BOOK include:

Atlantic Charter	Roosevelt, Franklin D.
Caricature (picture)	Teheran Conference
Cold War	World War I
Great Britain (History)	World War II
Potsdam Conference	Yalta Conference

Outline

I. Early Life
- A. Boyhood and Education
- B. Soldier and Reporter

II. Early Political Career
- A. First Public Offices
- B. Churchill's Family
- C. World War I

III. Between Wars

IV. Wartime Prime Minister
- A. World War II Begins
- B. The Battle of Britain
- C. Meetings with Roosevelt
- D. The Big Three

V. Postwar Leader
- A. Leader of the Opposition
- B. Return to Power
- C. End of an Era

Questions

What was the nationality of Churchill's mother?

How did Churchill join the Liberal party in 1904?

How did the U.S. Congress honor Churchill in 1963?

Why did Churchill's father decide that Winston should become a soldier?

In what field did Churchill win a Nobel prize?

How did Churchill become a hero in the Boer War?

How did Churchill feel about becoming prime minister of Great Britain in 1940?

Who were the Big Three?

What did Churchill mean when he held up two fingers in a "V"?

To whom did Churchill refer when he said: "This was their finest hour"?

Reading and Study Guide

See *Churchill, Sir Winston,* in the RESEARCH GUIDE/INDEX, Volume 22, for a *Reading and Study Guide.*

Additional Resources

CHURCHILL, RANDOLPH S., and GILBERT, MARTIN. *Winston S. Churchill.* 5 vols. 1966- . Covers years 1874 to 1939.

JAMES, ROBERT RHODES. *Churchill: A Study in Failure, 1900-1939.* Weidenfeld, 1970. A criticism of Churchill's political career during these years.

LASH, JOSEPH P. *Roosevelt and Churchill, 1939-1941: The Partnership That Saved the West.* Norton, 1976.

MORGAN, TED. *Churchill: Young Man in a Hurry.* Simon & Schuster, 1982.

PELLING, HENRY. *Winston Churchill.* Dutton, 1974.

TAYLOR, A. J. P., and others. *Churchill Revised: A Critical Assessment.* Dial, 1969.

CHURCHILL DOWNS. See KENTUCKY (pictures); KENTUCKY DERBY; LOUISVILLE (History).

CHURCHILL RIVER is in Saskatchewan and Manitoba in western Canada (see CANADA [terrain map]). Almost 1,000 miles (1,600 kilometers) long, the river flows east from Lac la Loche in northwestern Saskatchewan and empties into Hudson Bay. The river's mouth is almost entirely surrounded by land. This gives the town of Churchill, Man., the best natural harbor on Hudson Bay. The river was named for John Churchill, third governor of the Hudson's Bay Company and later Duke of Marlborough. W. L. MORTON

United Press Int.

Churchill's Grave is in St. Martin's Churchyard in Oxfordshire, near his birthplace, Blenheim Palace.

CHURCHILL RIVER flows through Newfoundland in eastern Canada (see CANADA [terrain map]). The chief river on the Labrador Peninsula, it flows east for about 600 miles (970 kilometers), and empties into Lake Melville, a part of Hamilton Inlet on the Atlantic Ocean. The river originates as the Ashuanipi River at Ashuanipi Lake on the Quebec border. Churchill Falls (formerly Grand Falls) are about 220 miles (354 kilometers) from the mouth of the river. The river was called the Hamilton River until 1965, when it was renamed to honor Sir Winston Churchill. A giant project to develop the river's hydroelectric potential was completed in 1974 at Churchill Falls. The power plant there has a capacity of more than 5 million kilowatts of electricity and is one of the largest power projects in the Western Hemisphere. FRED W. ROWE

CHURN is a container in which cream or milk is stirred or beaten. Rapid stirring in a churn causes the fat particles to separate from the liquid. They are then worked into a solid mass called butter (see BUTTER).

Two main types of churns are used—continuous churns and conventional churns. Continuous churns keep a steady flow of butter moving through the various steps of the butter-making process. They can turn cream into butter in three minutes or less. They produce over 75 per cent of the butter made in the United States.

Conventional churns have large stainless steel drums with paddles inside to stir the cream. These churns can make as much as 8,500 pounds (3,860 kilograms) of butter in about 45 minutes.

Critically reviewed by NATIONAL DAIRY COUNCIL

CHURUBUSCO, BATTLE OF. See MEXICAN WAR.

CHYLE. See LYMPHATIC SYSTEM (Absorption of Fats).

CHYME. See DIGESTIVE SYSTEM.